OPERATING GRANTS
for
NONPROFIT ORGANIZATIONS

10th Edition

Schoolhouse Partners LLC
West Lafayette, Indiana

Why 'Partners'? Partners work together as a team, with each person contributing different skills and expressing his or her individual interests and opinions to the unity and efficiency of the group in order to achieve common goals. Our aim is to make worthwhile resources available to you so that you and your institution or organization can and will achieve those goals.

Table of Contents

Introduction

For over three decades the GRANTS Database and its print directories, including the annual *Operating Grants for Nonprofit Organizations*, have provided the grant seeking community with funding sources to enrich or improve the lives of community residents. Funding in support of operating costs is one of the most difficult grants to find. Expenses may include overhead, salary support, administration, utilities, and other ongoing costs of an organization that are not related to a specific project. Since operating costs do not fund a specific goal or objective, the struggle to locate and fund ongoing expenses is fierce. This directory is a tool that can greatly assist with this difficult task.

With local funding sources declining and funding amounts diminishing, the struggle to fund community-based projects is immense. For decades the GRANTS Database has provided those seeking funding for community and economic development projects, health care and humanities, research, and performing arts programs with up-to-date information.

Operating Grants for Nonprofit Organizations

Operating Grants for Nonprofit Organizations, now in its ninth edition, features more than 1,900 current funding programs that support some or all general operating expenses of nonprofits and other institutions. Listings in the main section of *Operating Grants* contain annotations describing each program's overall focuses and goals, program requirements explaining eligibility, funding amounts, deadlines for Application, restrictions, *Catalog of Federal Domestic Assistance* program number (for U.S. government programs only), samples of previously awarded grants, sponsor name and address, contact information, and the sponsor's Internet Web address. Grantseekers with access to the Internet can use the addresses to locate further information about the organizations and their application procedures. Internet addresses are also provided, when available, within listings. Some of the grant programs listed in the main section have geographic restrictions for applicants.

The following people have devoted a great deal of patience, hard work and thought to keep this project and the database an informative service for the user. It is especially important to mention the GrantSelect team members – Louis S. Schafer, Ed.S., and Anita Schafer – for their diligent research, editorial work, development and assignment of index terms, and production – as well as all Schoolhouse Partners team of editors, who contribute to the grants editorial effort on a daily basis.

Inclusion in the book indicates that each funder gives some form of operating support, has an active funding program that accepts unsolicited inquiries, and gives monetary awards. Funders' interests span a wide range of areas, including the arts, humanities, child development, social and human services, youth programs, economic development, education, environmental programs, health care, religious programs, community development, and more.

Using *Operating Grants* for Grantseeking

By using this edition of *Operating Grants for Nonprofit Organizations*, grantseekers can match the needs of their particular programs with those sponsors offering funding in the grantseekers' area of interest. The information listed here is meant to eliminate the costs incurred by both grantseekers and grantmakers when inappropriate proposals are submitted for a sponsor's funding program. However, because the GRANTS Database is updated on a daily basis, with program listings continually added, deleted, and revised, grantseekers using this edition of may also search the GRANTS database online through *GrantSelect* (www.grantselect.com).

All new and revised information within *Operating Grants for Nonprofit Organizations* has been taken from: (1) the sponsor's updated of previously published program statements included in earlier editions of GRANTS publications; (2) questionnaires sent to sponsors whose programs were not listed in previous editions; or (3) other materials published by the sponsor and furnished to Schoolhouse Partners. Updated information for U.S. government programs includes new and revised program information published in the *Federal Register*; the latest edition of the *Catalog of Federal Domestic Assistance*; the *NIH Guide*, published weekly by the National Institutes of Health; and the *NSF E-Bulletin*, a monthly publication of the National Science Foundation. Included in this edition are identifying document numbers from the NIH and NSF publications. Located at the ends of the program descriptions in certain entries, the numbers indicated the ongoing NIH program number (PA) or the request for applications number (RFA). For programs of the National Science Foundation, the *NSF Bulletin* number appears. This information will help users identify the programs when seeking additional information from program staff.

While Schoolhouse Partners has made every effort to verify that all information is both accurate and current within the confines of format and scope, the publisher does not assume and hereby disclaims any liability to any party for loss or damages caused by errors or omissions in this *Operating Grants for Nonprofit Organizations*, whether such errors or missions result from accident, negligence, or any other cause. Anyone having questions regarding the content, format, or any other aspect of the *Operating Grants for Nonprofit Organizations*, GrantSelect, or the GRANTS Database should contact the Editors, GRANTS, Schoolhouse Partners or editor@schoolhousepartners.net.

How to Use This Directory

Operating Grants for Nonprofit Organizations is designed to allow the user quick and easy access to information regarding funding programs in a researcher's specific area of interest. This *Funding Sources* is composed of a main section, Grant Programs, which lists grant programs in alphabetical order, and three indexes: the Subject Index, the Grants by Program Type Index, and the Geographic Index.

GRANT PROGRAMS

Each listing in this section consists of the following elements: an annotation describing each program's focus and goals, requirements explaining eligibility, funding amounts, application and renewal dates, sponsor information, contact information, and Internet address.

GRANT TITLE ———— **Paul G. Allen Family Foundation Grants**   **4298** ——— ACCESSION NUMBER

The single foundation, created through the consolidation of Allen's six previous foundations (The Allen Foundation for the Arts, The Paul G. Allen Charitable Foundation, The Paul G. Allen Foundation for Medical Research, The Paul G. Allen Forest Protection Foundation, The Allen Foundation for Music, and The Paul G. Allen Virtual Education Foundation), will continue to focus on the Allen family's philanthropic interests in the areas of arts and culture, youth engagement, community development and social change, and scientific and technological innovation. The Arts and Culture Program fosters creativity and promotes critical thinking by helping strong arts organizations become sustainable and supporting projects that feature innovative and diverse artistic forms. ——— GRANT DESCRIPTION
The Youth Engagement Program improves the way young people learn by supporting organizations that use innovative teaching strategies and provide opportunities for children to address issues relevant to their lives. The Community Development and Social Change Program promotes individual and community development by supporting initiatives and organizations that provide access to resources and opportunities. The Scientific and Technological Innovation Program advances promising scientific and technology research that has the potential to enhance understanding and stewardship of the world in which we live. Organizations may only receive one grant per year. Organizations must not have any delinquent final reports due to any of the Paul G. Allen Foundations for previous grants. Grantseekers are encouraged to apply through the online application process, where basic organizational and project information will be requested. Guidelines are available online.

REQUIREMENTS ———— *Requirements* 501(c)3 tax-exempt organizations, status from the Internal Revenue government entities, and IRS-recognized tribes are eligible. Eligible organizations must be located in, or serving populations of, the Pacific Northwest, which includes Alaska, Idaho, Montana, Oregon, and Washington.

RESTRICTIONS ———— *Restrictions* In general, the foundation will not consider requests for general fund drives, annual appeals, or federated campaigns; special events or sponsorships; direct grants, scholarships, or loans for the benefit of specific individuals; projects of organizations whose policies or practices discriminate on the basis of race, ethnic origin, sex, creed, or sexual orientation; contributions to sectarian or religious organizations whose principle activity is for the benefit of their own members or adherents; loans or debt retirement; projects that will benefit the students of a single school; general operating support for ongoing activities; or projects not aligned with the foundation's specified program areas. 509(a) private foundations are ineligible.

APPLICATION/ DUE DATE ———— *Date(s) Application Is Due* Mar 31; Sep 30.

Contact Grants Administrator, (206) 342-2030; fax: (206) 342-3030; ——— CONTACT
email: info@pgafamilyfoundation.org

INTERNET ADDRESS ———— *Internet* http://www.pgafamilyfoundation.org

Sponsor Paul G. Allen Family Foundation ——— SPONSOR INFORMATION
505 Fifth Ave S, Ste 900
Seattle, WA 98104

vi

SUBJECT INDEX

The most effective way to access specific funding programs is through the Subject Index. This index lists the subject terms with applicable grants program titles – and their accession numbers – alphabetically under each term. Terms were assigned to target the specific area of research designated in the description of each program. Cross-references are used to link subjects and assist the user in finding specific grant information.

Following are general guidelines that can make your search of this index more successful. First, check under the specific topic of interest rather than a more general term. For instance, if you are interested in chemical engineering, look under "Chemical Engineering" rather than "Engineering." Items indexed under "Engineering" indicate funding in broad areas of engineering.

Use general headings when you want grants covering broader areas or if you can't find a specific topic. For example, many grants list funding for humanities research, health programs, or science and technology. To find these grants use such headings as "Humanities," "Medical Programs," "Science," or "Technology." For additional grant information on more specific humanities research opportunities, such as in American History or Cultural Anthropology, also check under the topics "United States History" and "Anthropology, Cultural."

Grants concerning study of a particular country are listed under the name of the country. Grants concerning the history, literature, art and language of a country are listed under the name of the country also, e.g., "Chinese Art" and "Chinese Language/Literature."

SUBJECT TERM —————————— **Education**
A.L. Mailman Family Foundation Grants, 5
AAAS Science & Technology Policy Fellowships - Health, Education & Human Services, 22
AARP Andrus Foundation Grants, 104
Abbott Laboratories Fund Grants, 125
ACIE Host University Edmund S. Muskie/Freedom Support Act Graduate Fellowships, 156
ACT Awards, 189
Akonadi Foundation Anti-Racism Grants, 351 ——————————**PROGRAM TITLE**
Akron Community Foundation Grants, 352
Albert and Margaret Alkek Foundation Grants, 370
Albuquerque Community Foundation Grants, 379
Alcoa Foundation Grants, 380
Alcon Foundation Grants Program, 382

GEOGRAPHIC INDEX

This index lists programs that have state, regional, or international geographic focus. The Geographic Index is arranged by state, followed by Canadian programs, then by international programs by country, and lists grant program titles and their corresponding accession numbers.

COUNTRY——————————————— **United States**

   Alabama ——————————————————————————————— STATE
   3M Fndn Grants, 2
   Alabama Humanities Fndn Grants Program, 368
   Arkema Inc. Fndn Science Teachers Program, 705
   CDC Injury Control Research Centers Grants, 1198
PROGRAM TITLE————— DOE Experimental Program to Stimulate Competitive Research (EPSCoR), 1653
   Hill Crest Fndn Grants, 2293
   Linn-Henley Charitable Trust Grants, 2777
   NOAA Community-Based Restoration Program (CRP) Grants, 3843
   Southern Company's Longleaf Pine Reforestation Fund, 4726

PROGRAM TYPE INDEX

This index is broken into 44 categories according to the type of program funded:

- Adult Basic Education
- Adult/Family Literacy Training
- Awards/Prizes
- Basic Research
- Building Construction and/or Renovation
- Capital Campaigns
- Centers: Research/Demonstration/Service
- Citizenship Instruction
- Community Development
- Consulting/Visiting Personnel
- Cultural Outreach
- Curriculum Development/Teacher Training
- Demonstration Grants
- Development (Institutional/Departmental)
- Dissertation/Thesis Research Support
- Educational Programs
- Emergency Programs
- Endowments
- Environmental Programs
- Exchange Programs
- Exhibitions, Collections, Performances, Video/Film Production
- Faculty/Professional Development
- Fellowships
- General Operating Support
- Graduate Assistantships
- Grants to Individuals
- International Exchange Programs
- International Grants
- Job Training/Adult Vocational Programs
- Land Acquisition
- Matching/Challenge Funds
- Materials/Equipment Acquisition (Computers, Books, Tapes, etc.)
- Preservation/Restoration
- Professorships
- Publishing/Editing/Translating
- Religious Programs
- Scholarships
- Seed Grants
- Service Delivery Programs
- Symposia, Conferences, Workshops, Seminars
- Technical Assistance
- Training Programs/Internships
- Travel Grants
- Vocational Education

Government and Organization Acronyms

AAAAI	American Academy of Allergy Asthma and Immunology
AAAS	American Association for the Advancement of Science
AACAP	American Academy of Child and Adolescent Psychiatry
AACN	American Association of Critical Care Nurses
AACR	American Association of Cancer Research
AAFCS	American Association of Family and Consumer Sciences
AAF	American Architectural Foundation
AAFP	American Academy of Family Physicians Foundation
AAFPRS	American Academy of Facial Plastic and Reconstructive Surgery
AAP	American Academy of Pediatrics
AAR	American Academy in Rome
AAS	American Antiquarian Society
AASL	American Association of School Libraries
AAUW	American Association of University Women
ABA	American Bar Association
ACC	Asian Cultural Council
ACF	Administration on Children, Youth and Families
ACLS	American Council of Learned Societies
ACM	Association for Computing Machinery
ACE	American Council on Education
ACMP	Amateur Chamber Music Players
ACS	American Cancer Society
ADA	American Diabetes Association
ADHF	American Digestive Health Foundation
AF	Arthritis Foundation
AFAR	American Federation for Aging Research
AFOSR	Air Force Office of Scientific Research
AFUD	American Foundation for Urologic Disease
AFUW	Australian Federation of University Women
AGS	American Geriatrics Society
AHA	American Heart Association
AHAF	American Health Assistance Foundation
AFHMR	Alberta Heritage Foundation for Medical Research
AHRQ	Agency for Healthcare Research and Quality
AICR	American Institute for Cancer Research
AIIS	American Institute for Indian Studies
AJA	American Jewish Archives
AJL	American Jewish Libraries
ALA	American Library Association
ALISE	Association for Library and Information Science Education
AMNH	American Museum of Natural History
AMS	American Musicological Society
ANL	Argonne National Library
ANS	American Numismatic Society
AOA	American Osteopathic Association
AOCS	American Oil Chemists' Society
APA	American Psychological Association
APAP	Association of Performing Arts Presenters
APEAL	Asian Pacific Partners for Empowerment and Leadership
APS	Arizona Public Service
APSA	American Political Science Association
ARIT	American Research Institute in Turkey
ARO	Army Research Office
ASA	American Statistical Association
ASCSA	American School of Classical Studies at Athens
ASECS	American Society for Eighteenth-Century Studies
ASF	American-Scandinavian Foundation
ASHA	American Speech-Language-Hearing Association
ASHRAE	American Society of Heating, Refrigerating, and Air Conditioning Engineers
ASME	American Society of Mechanical Engineers
ASNS	American Society for Nutritional Sciences
ASPRS	American Society of Photogrammetry and Remote Sensing
ASTA	American String Teachers Association
ATA	Alberta Teachers Association
AWHONN	Association of Women's Health, Obstetric, and Neonatal Nurses
AWU	Associated Western Universities
AWWA	American Water Works Association
BA	British Academy
BBF	Barbara Bush Foundation
BCBS	Blue Cross Blue Shield
BCBSM	Blue Cross Blue Shield of Michigan
BCBSNC	Blue Cross Blue Shield of North Carolina
BWF	Burroughs Wellcome Fund
CBIE	Canadian Bureau for International Education
CCF	Catholic Community Foundation
CCF	Common Council Foundation
CCFF	Canadian Cystic Fibrosis Foundation
CCFF	Christopher Columbus Fellowship Foundation
CDC	Centers for Disease Control and Prevention
CDECD	Connecticut Department of Economic and Community Development
CDI	Children's Discovery Institute
CEC	Council for Exceptional Children
CEF	Chemical Educational Foundation
CES	Council for European Studies
CF	The Commonwealth Fund
CFF	Cystic Fibrosis Foundation
CFFVR	Community Foundation for the Fox Valley Region
CFKF	Classic for Kids Foundation

CFNCR	Community Foundation for the National Capital Region
CFPC	College of Family Physicians of Canada
CFUW	Canadian Federation of University Women
CHCF	California Health Care Foundation
CHEA	Canadian Home Economics Association
CICF	Central Indiana Community Foundation
CIES	Council for International Exchange of Scholars
CIUS	Canadian Institute of Ukrainian Studies
CLA	Canadian Lung Association
CLF	Canadian Liver Foundation
CMS	Centers for Medicare and Medicaid Services
CNCS	Corporation for National and Community Service
CRI	Cancer Research Institute
CTCNet	Community Technology Centers Network
DAAD	Deutscher Akademische Austauschdienst (German Academic Exchange Service)
DHHS	Department of Health and Human Services
DOA	Department of Agriculture
DOC	Department of Commerce
DOD	Department of Defense
DOE	Department of Energy
DOI	Department of the Interior
DOJ	Department of Justice
DOL	Department of Labor
DOS	Department of State
DOT	Department of Transportation
EFA	Epilepsy Foundation of America
EIF	Entertainment Industry Foundation
EPA	Environmental Protection Agency
ESF	European Science Foundation
ETS	Educational Testing Service
FCAR	Formation de Chercheurs et L'Aide a la Recherche
FCD	Foundation for Child Development
FDA	Food and Drug Administration
FIC	Fogarty International Center
GAAC	German American Academic Council
GCA	Garden Club of America
GEF	Green Education Foundation
GNOF	Greater New Orleans Foundation
HAF	Humboldt Area Foundation
HBF	Herb Block Foundation
HHS	Health and Human Services
HHMI	Howard Hughes Medical Institute
HRSA	Health Resources and Services Administration
HUD	Department of Housing and Urban Development
ICC	Indiana Campus Compact
IIE	Institute of International Education
IRA	International Reading Association
IRC	International Rescue Committee
IREX	International Research and Exchanges Board
IUCP	Indiana University Center on Philanthropy
IYI	Indiana Youth Institute
JDF	Juvenile Diabetes Foundation International
JMO	John M. Olin Foundation
JSPS	Japan Society for the Promotion of Science
KFC	Kidney Foundation of Canada
LISC	Local Initiatives Support Corporation
LSA	Leukemia Society of America
MFRI	Military Family Research Institute
MHRC	Manitoba Health Research Council
MLA	Medical Library Association
MLB	Major League Baseball
MMA	Metropolitan Museum of Art
MMS	Massachusetts Medical Society
MSSC	Multiple Sclerosis Society of Canada
NAA	Newspaper Association of America
NAACP	National Association for the Advancement of Colored People
NAGC	National Association for Gifted Children
NAPNAP	National Association of Pediatric Nurse Associates and Practitioners
NARSAD	National Alliance for Research on Schizophrenia and Depression
NASA	National Aeronautics and Space Administration
NASE	National Association for the Self-Employed
NASM	National Air and Space Museum
NATO	North Atlantic Treaty Organization
NCCAM	National Center for Complementary and Alternative Medicine
NCFL	National Center for Family Literacy
NCI	National Cancer Institute
NCIC	National Cancer Institute of Canada
NCRR	National Center for Research Resources
NCSS	National Council for the Social Studies
NEA	National Education Association
NEH	National Endowment for the Humanities
NEI	National Eye Institute
NFID	National Foundation for Infectious Diseases
NFL	National Football League
NFWF	National Fish and Wildlife Foundation
NGA	National Gardening Association
NHGRI	National Human Genome Research Institute
NHLBI	National Heart, Lung and Blood Institute
NHSCA	New Hampshire State Council on the Arts
NIA	National Institute on Aging
NIAF	National Italian American Foundation
NIAAA	National Institute on Alcohol Abuse and Alcoholism

NIAF	National Italian American Foundation
NIAID	National Institute of Allergy and Infectious Diseases
NIAMS	National Institute of Arthritis and Musculoskeletal Skin Diseases
NICHD	National Institute of Child Health and Human Development
NIDA	National Institute on Drug Abuse
NIDCD	National Institute on Deafness and Other Communication Disorders
NIDCR	National Institute of Dental and Craniofacial Research
NIDDK	National Institute of Diabetes, and Digestive and Kidney Diseases
NIDRR	National Institute on Disability and Rehabilitation Research
NIEHS	National Institute of Environmental Health Sciences
NIGMS	National Institute of General Medical Sciences
NIH	National Institutes of Health
NIJ	National Institute of Justice
NIMH	National Institute of Mental Health
NINDS	National Institute of Neurological Disorders and Strokes
NINR	National Institute of Nursing Research
NIOSH	National Institute for Occupational Safety and Health
NIST	National Institute of Standards and Technology
NJSCA	New Jersey State Council on the Arts
NKF	National Kidney Foundation
NL	Newberry Library
NLM	National Library of Medicine
NMF	National Medical Fellowships, Inc.
NMSS	National Multiple Sclerosis Society
NNEDVF	National Network to End Domestic Violence Fund
NOAA	National Oceanic and Atmospheric Administration
NRA	National Rifle Association
NRC	National Research Council
NSERC	Natural Sciences and Engineering Research Council of Canada
NSF	National Science Foundation
NSTA	National Science Teachers Association
NYCH	New York Council for the Humanities
NYCT	New York Community Trust
NYFA	New York Foundation for the Arts
NYSCA	New York State Council on the Arts
OAH	Organization of American Historians
ODKF	Outrigger Duke Kahanamoku Foundation
OJJDP	Office of Juvenile Justice and Delinquency Prevention
ONF	Oncology Nursing Foundation
ONR	Office of Naval Research

OREF	Orthopaedic Research and Education Foundation
ORISE	Oak Ridge Institute for Science and Education
OSF	Open Society Foundation
PAS	Percussive Arts Society
PCA	Pennsylvania Council on the Arts
PDF	Peace Development Fund
PDF	Parkinson's Disease Foundation
PhRMA	Pharmaceutical Research and Manufacturers of American Foundation
PHSC	The Photographic Historical Society of Canada
PSEG	Public Service Enterprise Group
RCF	Richland County Foundation
RCPSC	Royal College of Physicians and Surgeons of Canada
RSC	Royal Society of Canada
RWJF	Robert Wood Johnson Foundation
SAMHSA	Substance Abuse and Mental Health Services Administration
SLA	Special Libraries Association
SME	Society of Manufacturing Engineers
SOCFOC	Sisters of Charity Foundation of Cleveland
SORP	Society of Biological Psychiatry
SSHRC	Social Sciences and Humanities Research Council of Canada
SSRC	Social Science Research Council
STTI	Sigma Theta Tau International
SVP	Social Venture Partners
SWE	Society of Women Engineers
TAC	Tennessee Arts Commission
TOMF	Tucson Osteopathic Medical Foundation
TRCF	Three Rivers Community Fund
TSYSF	Teemu Selanne Youth Sports Foundation
UPS	United Parcel Service
USHMM	United States Holocaust Memorial Museum Research Institute
USIA	United States Information Agency
USAID	United States Agency for International Development
USDA	United States Department of Agriculture
USFA	United States Fencing Association
USGA	United States Golf Association
USIP	United States Institute of Peace
USTA	United States Tennis Association
UUA	Unitarian Universalist Association
WAWH	Western Association of Woman Historians
WHO	Women Helping Others

How To Write A Winning Grant
by Louis S. Schafer, Ed.S.

A number of foundations and grant funders set aside large sums of money in support of a variety of programs. A successful grant proposal is one that is well-prepared, thoughtfully planned, and concisely packaged. In order to secure funding, a grant writer must submit a proposal written according to the specifications of the prospective funder. This involves profiling the organization, outlining the demographics of the target population, describing a significant need or opportunity, and proposing a program that meets the need or takes advantage of that opportunity.

Yet, grant writing involves a lot more than simply sitting down at a computer and composing a narrative. The process also includes a number of important considerations: strategic planning, research, preparing the proposal, building an evaluation plan, and follow-up. Because of the intense competition for funding, giving organizations publish specific deadlines, restrictions, and requirements about formatting, content and how to submit the proposal. These stipulations function as a type of preliminary screening device to be used when you have completed the writing process. Grants that do not follow the funder's specific directions usually do not make it into the boardroom, which is where they will be considered by top decision makers for final approval.

A well-designed funding request breaks down the proposed program into measurable evaluation goals that will be accomplished according to a specified schedule. Furthermore, a sound request should provide a detailed budget, outlining how the funds will be used. Typically, all of this vital information must be provided within two to ten pages, not including attachments.

Success in grant writing continues to gain importance in the economy of the nonprofit world. Expectations for knowing how to write grants and secure approval crosses all fields and ranks, and has become a unique skill in most areas. In fact, to some, grants represent the very lifeblood of an ongoing program and, without them, a great many of those programs would cease to exist.

Thus, each of the twelve steps highlighted below represents a cross-section of what experts, program officers, foundation staff, and others with grant writing experience have to say on gaining advantage in the highly competitive environment of the grant writer. By following these steps, nearly any grant can become a winning proposal.

Step 1: Know What Ingredients to Include
Grant writing must combine skillful and formulaic writing with customized language that leads the funder organization to conclude that the proposal will fulfill their philanthropic mission, and that the nonprofit organization has the capacity to actually accomplish what it is proposing. Whether a grant proposal is two pages or twenty pages long, it should contain an executive summary, a profile of the organization, the objectives of the proposal stated in terms of the beneficiaries or clients, specific steps that are attached to a time line by which the proposal will be achieved, a detailed program budget, a clearly described plan by which the organization will evaluate the proposal, and a plan of sustainability. In addition, the proposal should be prefaced by a carefully written cover letter. It can often also contain attachments such as the 501(c)3 designation letter and letters of endorsement from key constituents.

Step 2: Essential Tools of the Trade
You should begin by gathering together a number of grant writing tools that are essential to you as a writer. For example, if you are writing from a novice perspective, it makes sense to learn and understand the meanings of the vocabulary being used in grant guidelines or to access a glossary of common terms. Some sponsor guidelines will even provide just such a glossary unique to the particular sponsor.

If you have never written a grant proposal before do some research on the topic before you begin. The old adage "learning by doing" certainly can apply to the best means for an individual to learn how to write a grant proposal. Yet, numerous how to listings and guidelines offer insights to novice grant writers, and even those with experience. Much like texts on how-to write resumes, a wide variety of articles exist on the subject of writing grant proposals. You should always keep a few of these close at hand.

Finally, most novice or experienced grant writers working in a new area seek out copies of proposals that have been successful with a particular sponsor. Some federal agencies like the U.S. Department of Education may make winning proposals available or provide grant workshop participants with a copy of a successful proposal to aid new writers in understanding how the agency means or expects its proposals to be prepared for successful results.

Step 3: Proposal Uniqueness

Educators, program creators, and service providers generally seek funding from a variety of organizations that provide open competitions for funds to support projects complimentary to the organization's mission.

Before beginning the writing process, take some time to contact the right person within the funding organization office. It is best to do this by telephone, followed up by an email. Tell them a little about your project, and ask them if it sounds like something they might consider for funding. Be direct, concise, and forthcoming, and listen closely to their responses.

Never write from a "boiler-plate, one-size-fits-all" perspective. In fact, project development, application completion, and application submissions should concisely follow the unique guidelines provided by the funding organization. The funding organization will know if you have sent them a mass-mailing, and will likely reciprocate with a standard form letter without much rejection explanation.

Step 4: Write for the Reader

Any proposal should offer a concise plan to fill a need or solve a problem, and your reader will evaluate your plan according to how well your written presentation answers questions about what you are proposing, how you plan to do it, when you plan to do it, and how much it is going to cost.

Don't assume that the funder knows much about your subject area. Most grant readers and evaluators are generalists. They will probably know something about topics like Shakespeare, water pollution, and HIV/AIDS, but you should not assume that they are familiar with "Troilus and Cressida," taconite disposal methods or Kaposi's sarcoma. If your topic is complex, you might add an informative article or suggest some background reading.

Therefore, to present the information well, you should begin by ascertaining - not assuming - the level of knowledge that your audience possesses and take the positions of all your readers into account. You might also provide, for those outside of your specific area of expertise, an executive summary written in non-technical language, or you might include your own glossary of terms that explains technical language use in the body of the proposal. Don't take for granted that everyone who reads your proposal understands your jargon.

The most basic composition of a proposal, as with any other written document, is simple; it needs a beginning (the introduction), a middle (the body of material to be presented) and an end (the conclusion or recommendation).

Step 5: Research Your Perspective Funders

Research prospective grant funders using one of Schoolhouse Partners' nine directories, or by utilizing our online database known as *GrantSelect*. Thoroughly search for requests for proposals from grant funders that might match your proposed project. Both the hard copy and online versions of the database provide a wealth of information concerning how-to, when-to, who-to, and so on. Search there using vital keywords, such as "education," "elementary and secondary education" or "children and youth."

After you identify several potential funders, follow the funders' specifications for a first approach, which should be by an initial telephone contact, email, letter or the submission of a full request. Your goal is to pre-qualify your request and to learn the name of a person to whom you can direct your final grant proposal. This is essential, so that your submission does not get lost in the shuffle.

Step 6: Profiling Your Organization

Grant writers should begin by profiling their organization using demographic information. In a couple short paragraphs explain exactly what it is you or your organization does, as well as why the grantor can trust you or your organization to handle the project and money appropriately. If the proposal is in support of an individual, you may focus on that person's stellar credit history and budgeting skills. If it is for an organization, you will want to add information showing a track record of successfully achieving goals and a governing body that is more than capable or carrying out the project being outlined.

Ideally you want to portray a pattern of growth and change over time (e.g. graduated high school and sought a college education to improve myself or the non-profit started as a small two-person operation and has now grown to more than 20 volunteers). It is always best to show people helping people to accomplish something that they could not accomplish without the funding organization's assistance.

Step 7: The Problem or Needs Statement

This is the main part, or body, of your proposal. You want to convince the grantor that your project is vital, that your group can accomplish it, that it can be done within the budget parameters, and that no one else is meeting that need. Unless you are applying to a government agency or targeted foundation, you should assume that the reader does not know very much about your organization, the issue, or the problems at hand.

Describe the problem or need in both factual and human interest terms, if possible. Providing sound data demonstrates that your organization is expert in the field. If there are no good data on your issue, consider doing your own research study, even if it is simple and short-term.

Outline your issue in as local a context as possible. If you want to educate people in your county about HIV/AIDS, tell the funder about the epidemic in your county — not in the United States as a whole.

Always describe a problem or need that is about the same size as your solution or target audience. Do not, under any circumstances, draw a dark picture of nuclear war, teen suicide and lethal air pollution if you are planning a modest neighborhood arts program for children. Make sure that the problem and solution are of similar scope and size.

List a precise estimate of how many individuals will be impacted by the funding, their socio-economic and ethnic information, and measurable statistics about their current situation and/or academics. In the first few lines of this section, identify the issue, opportunity or problem in terms of measurable evaluative benefits to your target group. This forms the executive summary section, which should be only one or two paragraphs in length.

Step 8: Overview of How You Will Solve the Problem

Next, you should offer some detail of precisely how you will take advantage of an opportunity or solve a serious problem for your target audience. Perhaps, if you are an educator, your school has a large problem with truancy, which you think you could combat by hiring a social worker to work with the families of students with histories of habitual truancy. After researching other schools that have had success using a similar approach, you decide to fund the salary of an additional social worker for one year through a grant.

Then, if your truancy rate shows improvement, you will request that the district fund the position permanently, which will pay for itself in state funds based on daily attendance rates. This plan provides the objectives section of your grant proposal, which should be a detailed single paragraph in length.

Step 9: Evaluation Plan

By now, you should have begun formulating exactly how you will evaluate your success. If you are attempting to reduce truancy at your school, state precisely what percentage of reduction you believe will occur; if you are sending a group a ten-year-olds to baseball camp, list the number that will be impacted and what they will gain from the experience; and if you plan to install a security system within a library, discuss the amount of savings that will occur from theft prevention measures. Don't hesitate to detail the evaluation of three or four goals that you have established.

Explain exactly what your organization plans to do about the problem. What are your overall goals and how will you measure reduction or eradication of the problem? You might say: "The goals of this project are to increase the understanding among Indianapolis middle school students about the impact of smoking on their health, and to reduce the number of students who smoke by at least ten percent"

Step 10: Timelines and Budgets

Next, take the time to break your plan down into specific steps that are tied to a specific, well-designed timeline. Each step should become one sentence in the methods section of your grant request, and should have measurable goals or outcomes aligned with it. The entire section should be one to two paragraphs. Follow this with both a narrative and detailed budget.

Don't support the budget need by outlining a problem as the *absence* of equipment. "We don't have enough beds in our battered women's shelter" is not the problem itself. The problem is increased levels of domestic violence and, therefore, more shelter beds is a solution.

Instead, the budget should be written in narrative format, with a specific explanation for each expenditure. For example: "We will hire one school social worker at an annual salary of $36,000 including benefits," then list the benefit costs. Format the same budget information as a chart using Excel or some other type of spreadsheet. This budget detail should be attached to the body of your grant proposal, and should be in the format requested by the funder.

Here the funder will further want to know if other organizations have committed funds to the project or have been asked to do so. Few funders want to be the sole support of any project. (This may not be true if the project cost is very small — less than $5,000, for example — or if a corporation is seeking public visibility by sponsoring the project.) Funders generally expect you to ask for support from more than one source. So make sure you identify and outline other funding sources. In this section, you can also describe the in-kind contributions (goods or services instead of cash) that people are giving to the project.

Step 11: Sustainability and Finishing Touches

Now ask yourself, if you continue this project in the future, how will it be supported? Most funders don't want to support the same set of projects forever. Many funders see their niche as funding innovation: supporting new approaches to old problems or finding solutions to new problems.

What the funder really wants to see is that you have a long-term vision and funding plan for the project, that the project is "sustainable," especially if it is a new activity. "We plan to offer free books to children by organizing a regular donation and distribution campaign."

Prior to forwarding your final submission, take the time to revise your grant proposal so that you can insert language that resonates with the funder. Make sure that you have followed the exact directions that the funder specified in its guidelines, and never, ever miss the deadline. The final section of the proposal should explain how you will communicate information about the program to your funder.

Have any participating agencies or constituents write a letter of support to your contact at the funding organization. Have the proposal reviewed by someone who has not read it before. Then revise it for spelling, punctuation, grammar and clarity. Always use 12-point font with 1-inch margins. Do not fold the proposal before forwarding.

Step 12: Forwarding the Proposal
Step away from the proposal for a few hours. Then come back and reread everything you have written to ensure there are no typos, everything is clear and concise, and that you have said everything that you had hoped to say. Make certain that: your sentence structure matches the intended message; that, if you wanted to create and keep momentum for an idea, you have utilized longer sentences; and, if there is a specific point you wanted to make, it is highlighted.

Now, read the request for proposal and make sure you understand exactly what the grantor wanted you to include. Some may require a list of your board members, a copy of your financial statement from the previous year, a cover letter from your CEO, a copy of your IRS tax free letter, or other information. Make sure you include all of these as attachments.

Reread the proposal guidelines to see how many copies you should forward. Some may require 3 or 5 copies. Also pay attention to the deadline. Check if it is postmark or delivery deadline and make sure that you get it there in time.

Conclusion
Writing and submitting grants can be both agonizing and fulfilling, but by following the above steps you will greatly enhance your chances of success..

Among the country's largest grantmakers, about one proposal in three is typically funded. You may find that you can get project money but not the operating money you need to keep your basic activities going. You may be surprised by funders' generosity, but you may also be surprised by their periodic changes in focus, especially if those changes leave you on the outside looking in.

But remember that the U.S. has an extraordinary fundraising climate. People from other countries envy the major corporations and large family foundations that form the backbone of many of our innovative social and cultural programs. Most funders have board and staff people who are thoughtful, careful, curious, well-educated about community issues and willing to help you. If you have a good project that has been carefully planned to meet some real needs, you will find people willing to talk with you and advise you on what you might do to move closer to success.

1st Source Foundation Grants 1

Established in 1952 in Indiana and administered by the 1st Source Bank, the Foundation supports community foundations, youth clubs and organizations involved with television, education, health, and human services. The Foundation provides support to organizations working in the following areas: social welfare and human services; education; culture and the arts; and community, civic and neighborhood involvement. Giving is primarily centered in Indiana, and the major type of funding given is for general operating support. Since there are no specific applications forms required or deadlines with which to adhere, applicants should send a letter of request detailing the project and the amount of funding needed. Most recent awards have ranged from $500 to $60,000.

Requirements: Any 501(c)3 serving the residents of Indiana communities where 1st Source Banks are located are eligible to apply.

Geographic Focus: Indiana

Amount of Grant: 500 - 60,000 USD

Samples: Kelly Cares Foundation, South Bend, Indiana, $10,000 - general operating support; Elevate Ventures, Elkart, Indiana, $60,000 - general operating support; Culver Academies, Culver, Indiana, $7,500 - general operating support.

Contact: Terry Gerber, Director; (574) 235-2790 or (574) 235-2254

Internet: https://www.1stsource.com/about-us/community-involvement

Sponsor: 1st Source Foundation

100 N Michigan Street, P.O. Box 1602

South Bend, IN 46601-1630

2COBS Private Charitable Foundation Grants 2

The Foundation, established in Colorado in 2005, supports a variety of causes, which include: health care; cancer services; community services; and local community foundations. Although giving is centered around the Durango, Colorado, region, it is not uncommon for support to be offered to 501(c)3 programs across the country. There are no specific application formats or deadlines with which to adhere, and applicants should send a letter of request outlining the program need and overall budget.

Geographic Focus: All States

Amount of Grant: 250 - 1,000 USD

Contact: Christopher J. O'Brien; (970) 247-7828 or (970) 385-1740

Sponsor: 2COBS Private Charitable Foundation

10 Town Plaza, Suite 100

Durango, CO 81301-6910

4-C's Foundation Grants 3

Established in Tennessee in 2004 by a donation from TAP Publishing, the 4-c's Foundation limits its grants to the Crossville, Tennessee region. Currently the Foundation supports organizations involved with education via funding for general operations and awards scholarships to graduates of Cumberland County High School and Stone Memorial High School.

Geographic Focus: Tennessee

Contact: Fran Young, President; (931) 484-8674

Sponsor: 4-C's Foundation

294 Cleveland Street

Crossville, TN 38555-4854

4:19 Foundation Grants 4

The 4:19 Foundation, established in Connecticut in 2002, offers general operating support to Lutheran faith-based organizations that provide services to poor and underprivileged communities as part of their mission's ministry work. Giving is primarily in the State of Maryland. There are no specific guidelines, application forms, or deadlines with which to adhere. Potential applicants should first contact the foundation in writing, outlining the need and overall operating budget.

Requirements: Protestant agencies and churches in Maryland are eligible to apply.

Restrictions: No grants are given to individuals

Geographic Focus: Maryland

Samples: St. Matthew Lutheran Church, Bel Air, Maryland, $12,000 - proclaiming the Gospel; Hartford Christian School, Dublin, Maryland, $6,000 - Christian education; John Carroll School, Bel Air, Maryland, $5,000 - Christian education.

Contact: Blaise Sedney, President; (410) 893-0185

Sponsor: 4:19 Foundation

105 Colvard Court

Forest Hill, MD 21050-1531

5 51 5 Foundation Grants 5

The 5 51 5 Foundation, established in New York in 2007, offers funding in the way of general operating support of K-12 education, higher education, and community education programs. Its primary geographic focus is Maryland, Massachusetts, New Hampshire, and New York. There are no specific application guidelines or deadlines with which to adhere, and applicants should begin by contacting the Foundation directly.

Requirements: 501(c)3 organizations and educational facilities that either serve or are located in Maryland, Massachusetts, New Hampshire, and New York are eligible to apply.

Geographic Focus: Maryland, Massachusetts, New Hampshire, New York

Amount of Grant: 10,000 - 3,000,000 USD

Samples: Spence School, New York, New York, $100,000—for general operating purposes; John Hopkins Medicine, Baltimore, Maryland, $32,448—for general operating purposes; Dartmouth College, Hanover, New Hampshire, $3,000,000—for general operating purposes.

Contact: Richard Gold, Secretary; (203) 618-4623; fax (203) 302-3123

Sponsor: 5 51 5 Foundation

755 Fifth Avenue, Apt. 12B

New York, NY 10021

20th Century Trends Institute Grants 6

Classified as a private operating foundation in 1991 in both New York and Vermont, the 20th Century Trends Institute evolved into a private foundation in 2002. Currently, the Foundation offers funding to secondary education and higher education throughout Connecticut and New York. Support comes primarily in the form of general operations funding. There are no specific guidelines, application forms, or deadlines with which to adhere, and potential applicants should contact the office in writing, explaining their need and overall operating budget.

Geographic Focus: Connecticut, New York

Samples: New York University, New York, New York, $6,000 - general operating fund; Choate Rosemary Hall, Wallingford, Connecticut, $20,500 - general operating fund; Darien High School, Darien, Connecticut, $1,000 - general fund.

Contact: Ward Frank Cleary, Vice President; (203) 324-6777, ext. 208; fax (203) 324-9621; cleary@curtisbb.com

Sponsor: 20th Century Trends Institute

666 Summer Street

Stamford, CT 06901-1401

41 Washington Street Foundation Grants 7

The Foundation, established in 2003 in Michigan, offers grant support primarily in Grand Rapids and Holland, Michigan. Its primary fields of interest include: Christian agencies and churches; Pre-K through 12th grade education; higher education; and community service programs. Support is given in the form of capital campaigns, general operating funds, and program grants. There are no application forms or deadlines with which to adhere, and applicants should approach the Foundation initially in writing.

Requirements: The Foundation offers grants to 501(c)3 organizations serving the Grand Rapids and Holland, Michigan, regions.

Geographic Focus: Michigan

Amount of Grant: Up to 100,000 USD

Samples: West Michigan Christian, Muskegon, Michigan, $7,000 - for educational support; Muskegon Rescue Mission, Muskegon, Michigan, $101,000 - for a homeless shelter; Covenant Life Church, Grand Haven, Michigan, $5,000 - for religious purposes.

Contact: James P. Hovinga, Director; (616) 850-1330; fax (616) 850-7640

Sponsor: 41 Washington Street Foundation

914 S. Harbor Drive

Grand Haven, MI 49417-1745

80 / 20 Fund Grants 8

The 80-20 Fund supports and promotes various public charities and private operating foundations which are qualifying 501(c)3 organizations by annually making direct qualifying grants to such organizations. Giving is primarily in the Boston, Massachusetts, region. There are no specific applications, guidelines, or deadlines with which to adhere. Applicants an initial approach in writing, along with a copy of their IRS determination letter.

Restrictions: No grants to individuals.
Geographic Focus: Massachusetts
Samples: Graham Weston Gift Fund, Boston, Massachusetts, $300,000—to establish a donor advised fund.
Contact: James E. Irwine, Treasurer; (210) 223-0875 or (210) 775-2370
Sponsor: 80 / 20 Fund
112 E Pecan Street, #555
San Antonio, TX 78205

153 Fishes Charitable Foundation Grants 9

The 153 Fishes Charitable Foundation, established in Alabama in 2006, is primarily interested in the support of Christian churches and agencies in Alabama and Georgia. Its primary field of interest is housing development for the needy. Potential applicants should approach the foundation with a written application, describing the organization, the reason for the request, and the charitable purpose of the grant being solicited. Completed application letters should be received by June 1 each year.

Restrictions: No grants are made available to individuals.
Geographic Focus: Alabama, Georgia
Date(s) Application is Due: Jun 1
Amount of Grant: Up to 10,000 USD
Contact: Denney E. Barrow, President; (205) 995-9061
Sponsor: 153 Fishes Charitable Foundation
12 Montagel Way
Shoal Creek, AL 35242-5944

1675 Foundation Grants 10

The foundation is a private family foundation dedicated to improving the quality of life for individuals and families through the support of non-profit organizations working in the areas of health, human services, education, the environment, and history. Priority is given to organizations serving Chester County, southeastern Pennsylvania, the Greater Boston area, and other geographic areas of interest to the Trustees. Grants are made for operating support, special projects, endowment, and capital. Grants range from $2,000 to $50,000 and are made twice a year at the discretion of the Trustees. Requests should be in writing and mailed to the executive director.

Requirements: 501(c)3 nonprofit organizations and public charities under IRS Code 509(a) are eligible.
Restrictions: The foundation does not make grants to individuals, nor are they made for political purposes.
Geographic Focus: Massachusetts, Pennsylvania
Date(s) Application is Due: Mar 1; Oct 1
Amount of Grant: 2,000 - 50,000 USD
Contact: Marge Brennan, Grants Manager; (610) 896-3868; fax (610) 896-3869; mbrennan@1675foundation.org
Internet: http://www.1675foundation.org/guidelines.htm
Sponsor: 1675 Foundation
16 East Lancaster Avenue, Suite 102
Ardmore, PA 19003-2228

1912 Charitable Foundation Grants 11

The Foundation, established in West Virginia in 1996, has as its priority to support both higher education and Protestant churches/agencies. The primary type of funding is in the form of general operations money, and the average grant ranging from $1,000 to $15,000. There are no specific deadlines, guidelines, or applications with which to adhere. Initial approach should be by letter.

Requirements: 501(c)3 organizations serving the residents of West Virginia are able to apply.
Restrictions: No grants are given to individuals.
Geographic Focus: West Virginia
Samples: Wade Center, Bluefield, West Virginia, $5,000—general operations; The Children's Home, Prnceton, West Virginia, $1,500—general operations.
Contact: Diana S. Coulthard, Secretary; (304) 325-7151; fax (304) 327-9663
Sponsor: 1912 Charitable Foundation
211 Federal Street, P.O. Box 950
Bluefield, WV 24701-0950

1988 Irrevocable Cochrane Memorial Trust Grants 12

The Trust, established in Minnesota in 1989 and placed under the supervision of the U.S. Bank, gives support primarily to organizations in the Washington, DC, area and throughout Maryland. Funding is primarily given to support Roman Catholic churches, schools, and their agencies. Fields of interest include: the environment, preservation of natural resources, community foundations, higher education, human services, and secondary schools. Applicants should forward a letter offering a detailed project description and the amount of funding requested. There are no deadlines.

Requirements: 501(c)3 organizations serving the residents of Washington, DC, and the State of Maryland are eligible to apply.
Geographic Focus: District of Columbia, Maryland
Amount of Grant: Up to 75,000 USD
Samples: American Chestnut Land Trust, Prince Frederick, Maryland, $50,000 - operating costs; Bethlehem House, Washington, DC, $40,000 - general operations; Catholic Campaign for Human Development, Washington, D.C. - annual support.
Contact: John L. Jerry, (651) 466-8708 or (651) 466-8724
Sponsor: 1988 Irrevocable Cochrane Memorial Trust
101 East 5th Street, P.O. Box 64713
Saint Paul, MN 55164-0713

A.C. Ratshesky Foundation Grants 13

The foundation gives priority consideration to programs in education and training, and arts and culture. Support for programs that serve disadvantaged Jewish populations is also of special interest. Preference is given to small and medium-sized organizations. The foundation makes grants for operating support, start-up support/seed money, programs, and organizational capacity building or technical assistance. Contact office for application forms.

Requirements: Boston area nonprofits may apply.
Restrictions: Grants are not awarded to individuals or for continuing support, annual campaigns, general endowments, deficit financing, land acquisition, scientific or other research, publications, conferences, or loans.
Geographic Focus: Massachusetts
Date(s) Application is Due: Feb 1; Jul 1; Oct 1
Amount of Grant: 5,000 - 10,000 USD
Samples: Cambridge School Volunteers Inc., Cambridge, MA, $5,000—to train and deploy supportive adults to move low-income Cambridge public school students toward school success and access to higher education; Centro Presente, Inc., Somerville, MA, $5,000—to support an award-winning arts education and leadership development program for 60 Latino immigrant youth in Cambridge and Somerville; Charlestown Working Theater, Inc., Charlestown, MA, $5,000—to provide programming in acting, music, and visual arts for 350 children and youth in Charlestown.
Contact: Yasmin Shah, Program Officer; (617) 391-3094 or (617) 426-7080; fax (617) 426-7087; yshah@gmafoundations.com
Internet: http://ratsheskyfoundation.grantsmanagement08.com/?page_id=5
Sponsor: A.C. Ratshesky Foundation
77 Summer Street, 8th Floor
Boston, MA 02110-1006

A.V. Hunter Trust Grants 14

The purpose of the foundation's grant program is to support Colorado nonprofits that give direct aid, comfort, support, or assistance to children or aged persons or indigent adults. Types of support include program support and general operating support.

Requirements: Applications are considered from charitable 501(c)3 nonprofit Colorado-based organizations or projects or endeavors located in Colorado. The trust will consider only one request from an organization during any 12-month period.
Restrictions: The Foundation does not fund: new programs in their first three years of operation; grants or loans to individuals; developmental, pass-through or start-ups; research projects; publications, films or other media projects; capital campaigns or capital acquisitions, including construction and renovations; grants for education or scholarship aid; grants to cover deficits or retirement of debt; purchase of tickets for fundraising benefits, special events or sponsorships; endowments; recruiting and training; or gathering and disseminating information.
Geographic Focus: Colorado
Date(s) Application is Due: Mar 1; Jun 1; Aug 1
Amount of Grant: 10,000 - 20,000 USD
Contact: Barbara L. Howie, Executive Director; (303) 399-5450; fax (303) 399-5499; barbarahowie@avhuntertrust.org
Internet: http://avhuntertrust.org
Sponsor: A.V. Hunter Trust
650 South Cherry Street, Suite 535

Glendale, CO 80246

Aaron Copland Fund for Music Performing Ensembles　　　**15**

The program's objective is to support organizations whose performances encourage and improve public knowledge and appreciation of serious contemporary American music. Funds are available for general operating support or project support to professional performing ensembles with a history of substantial commitment to contemporary American music and with plans to continue that commitment. Guidelines are available online.

Requirements: Applicants must meet the following requirements: nonprofit tax-exempt status; performance history of at least two years at the time of application; at least 20 percent of the ensemble's programming (in terms of duration) for the preceding two seasons consists of contemporary American music; and demonstrated commitment to contemporary American music.

Restrictions: Individuals, student ensembles, festivals, and presenters without a core ensemble are not eligible. Grants will not be made for the purpose of commissioning composers.

Geographic Focus: All States

Date(s) Application is Due: Jun 30

Amount of Grant: 1,000 - 20,000 USD

Contact: James M. Kendrick, Secretary; (212) 461-6956; fax (212) 810-4567; recording@coplandfund.org

Internet: http://www.coplandfund.org/ensembles.html

Sponsor: American Music Center

322 8th Avenue, Suite 1401

New York, NY 10001

Aaron Copland Fund for Music Supplemental Grants　　　**16**

The Program's objective is to support non-profit organizations that have a history of substantial commitment to contemporary American music. Applications may be submitted by non-profit organizations that have a history of substantial commitment to contemporary American music but whose needs are not addressed by the Fund's programs of support for performing organizations and recording projects, such as presenters and music service organizations. Applicants may request either general operating support or support for special projects. Applicants should be aware that support in one year does not imply continuation of that support. Special projects relating to a broad spectrum of American music will be viewed more favorably than those relating to a single work or to a single composer.

Requirements: Organizations must have been in existence for at least two years at the time of application. Presenters, or organizations that are otherwise involved with performances, must have presented two full seasons prior to the season for which support is requested.

Restrictions: Projects that are part of the curriculum of an educational institution are not eligible for support.

Geographic Focus: All States

Date(s) Application is Due: Sep 30

Contact: Jessica Rauch, Grants Manager; (212) 461-6956 or (212) 366-5260, ext. 29; fax (212) 810-4567; grantsmanager@coplandfund.org

Internet: https://grants.coplandfund.org/supplemental-program

Sponsor: Aaron Copland Fund for Music

254 West 31st Street, 15th Floor

New York, NY 10001

Aaron Copland Fund Supplemental Program Grants　　　**17**

The program's objective is to support nonprofit organizations that have a history of substantial commitment to contemporary American music. Applicants may request either general operating support or support for special projects. Special projects relating to contemporary American music generally will be viewed more favorably than those relating to an individual work or to an individual composer.

Requirements: Nonprofit organizations with a history of substantial commitment to contemporary American music that have been in existence for at least two years at the time of application are eligible.

Restrictions: No grants are made to individuals.

Geographic Focus: All States

Date(s) Application is Due: Sep 15

Amount of Grant: 1,000 - 20,000 USD

Contact: James M. Kendrick, Secretary; (212) 461-6956; fax (212) 810-4567; recording@coplandfund.org

Internet: http://www.coplandfund.org/supplemental.html

Sponsor: American Music Center

322 8th Avenue, Suite 1401

New York, NY 10001

Abbot and Dorothy H. Stevens Foundation Grants　　　**18**

The Abbot and Dorothy H. Stevens Foundation funds Massachusetts non-profits with a emphasis on the greater Lawrence/Merrimack Valley area. Giving primarily for the arts, education, conservation, and health and human services. Fields of interest include: arts; children/youth, services; crime/violence prevention, domestic violence; education; elderly; environment, natural resources; health care; health organizations, association; historic preservation/historical societies; humanities; human services; immigrants; medical school/education; museums. Types of support include: building/renovation; capital campaigns; continuing support; endowments; equipment; general/operating support; management development/capacity building; matching/challenge support; program-related investments/loans; program development; technical assistance.

Requirements: Massachusetts 501(c)3 tax-exempt organizations serving the greater Lawrence and Merrimack Valley are eligible. There is no deadline date when applying for funding, nor is there a application form required. The Foundation will however accept the Associated Grantmakers Common Proposal Form. Applicants should submit a copy of their IRS Determination Letter and one copy of their proposal when applying for funding. The board meets and reviews proposals monthly except for the months of July and August.

Restrictions: Grants do not support national organizations, state or federal agencies, individuals, annual campaigns, deficit financing, exchange programs, internships, professorships, scholarships, or fellowships.

Geographic Focus: Massachusetts

Amount of Grant: 1,000 - 20,000 USD

Samples: Boston Childrens Museum, Boston, MA, $15,000; Boston Symphony Orchestra, Boston, MA, $10,000; Boston Ballet, Boston, MA, $5,000.

Contact: Josh Miner, Executive Director; (978) 688-7211; fax (978) 686-1620; grantprocess@stevensfoundation.com

Sponsor: Abbot and Dorothy H. Suitevens Foundation

P.O. Box 111

North Andover, MA 01845-7211

Abbott Fund Access to Health Care Grants　　　**19**

Abbott's Access to Health Care programs seek innovative solutions to improve and expand access to health care services for disadvantaged populations. Specific areas of focus include cardiovascular health, diabetes, nutrition, maternal and child health and neonatal care. Many Abbott Fund programs are engaged in closing gaps in ethnic and minority communities, promoting health and nutrition education for families, training health workers, and improving delivery of health services. Complete and submit the Abbott Fund online grant application, posted when available. It should include your organization's Federal Tax ID. At times when the Abbott Fund is accepting unsolicited grant applications, it will acknowledge receipt of an online application via email. The Fund will notify an applicant of its decision on a funding request within six to eight weeks.

Requirements: Grants are made to tax-exempt organizations supporting access to health care.

Restrictions: The Abbott Fund does not accept unsolicited grant applications for projects outside the United States. Contributions will not be made to individuals; for-profit entities; purely social organizations; political parties or candidates; sectarian religious organizations; advertising; symposia, conferences, and meetings; ticket purchases; memberships; business-related purposes; volunteer efforts of non-Abbott employees; or marketing sponsorships.

Geographic Focus: Arizona, California, Illinois, Kansas, Massachusetts, Michigan, New Jersey, New York, North Carolina, Ohio, Puerto Rico, Texas, Utah, Virginia

Amount of Grant: 20,000 - 100,000 USD

Contact: Cindy Schwab, Vice President; (847) 937-7075; fax (847) 935-5051; cindy.schwab@abbott.com

Internet: http://www.abbottfund.org/tags/access

Sponsor: Abbott Fund

100 Abbott Park Road, Department 379, Building 6D

Abbott Park, IL 60064-3500

Abbott Fund Community Grants　　　**20**

The Abbott Fund Community Grant program is active in communities around the world where Abbott has a significant presence. It pursues local partnerships and creative programs that address unmet needs of a community. Emphasis is placed on improving access to health care and promoting science education. The program also supports major civic, arts and other cultural institution programming, primarily in the Chicago metropolitan area where Abbott is headquartered. Complete and submit the Abbott Fund online grant application, posted when available. It should include your organization's Federal Tax ID. At times when the Abbott Fund is accepting unsolicited grant applications, it will acknowledge receipt of an online application via email. The Fund will notify an applicant of its decision on a funding request within six to eight weeks.

Requirements: Grants are made to tax-exempt organizations supporting company operating areas in Arizona, California, Illinois, Kansas, Massachusetts, Michigan, New Jersey, New York, North Carolina, Ohio, Puerto Rico, Texas, and Virginia, and Utah. It also supports the communities of: Abingdon, England; Brockville, Canada; Campoverde, Italy; Clonmel, Ireland; Cootehill, Ireland; Delkenheim, Germany; Kanata, Canada; Katsuyama, Japan; Ludwigshafen, Germany; Queenborough, England; Rio de Janeiro, Brazil; Sligo, Ireland; and Zwolle, the Netherlands.

Restrictions: Contributions will not be made to individuals; for-profit entities; purely social organizations; political parties or candidates; sectarian religious organizations; advertising; symposia, conferences, and meetings; ticket purchases; memberships; business-related purposes; volunteer efforts of non-Abbott employees; or marketing sponsorships.

Geographic Focus: Arizona, California, Illinois, Kansas, Massachusetts, Michigan, New Jersey, New York, North Carolina, Ohio, Puerto Rico, Texas, Utah, Virginia, Brazil, Canada, Germany, Great Britain, Ireland, Italy, Japan, Netherlands

Amount of Grant: 10,000 - 100,000 USD

Contact: Cindy Schwab, Vice President; (847) 937-7075; fax (847) 935-5051; cindy.schwab@abbott.com

Internet: http://www.abbottfund.org/tags/community/1

Sponsor: Abbott Fund

100 Abbott Park Road, Department 379, Building 6D
Abbott Park, IL 60064-3500

Abbott Fund Global AIDS Care Grants 21

Abbott has been a significant contributor to the fight against HIV/AIDS for more than two decades. Since 2000, Abbott and the Abbott Fund have invested $225 million in grants and product donations targeted to resource poor countries most impacted by HIV/AIDS. The focus of these efforts includes expanding access to care, testing and treatment; strengthening HIV/AIDS health care systems; preventing mother-to-child transmission; and supporting children and families affected by HIV/AIDS. In addition, Abbott and the Abbott Fund have helped pioneer innovative model programs to combat the disease. For example, we helped build the Baylor International Pediatric AIDS Initiative's first pediatric outpatient clinic in Romania in 2001 that has served an average of 600 patients per year. The clinic has reduced pediatric HIV mortality rates by more than 90 percent. Today Baylor has replicated the Romania model in additional clinics throughout Africa and now serves nearly 60,000 children and young people with HIV – including those at two clinics built by and supported by the Abbott Fund in Malawi and Tanzania.

Requirements: Grants are made to tax-exempt organizations supporting global HIV/AIDS programs.

Restrictions: Contributions will not be made to individuals; for-profit entities; purely social organizations; political parties or candidates; sectarian religious organizations; advertising; symposia, conferences, and meetings; ticket purchases; memberships; business-related purposes; volunteer efforts of non-Abbott employees; or marketing sponsorships.

Geographic Focus: Arizona, California, Illinois, Kansas, Massachusetts, Michigan, New Jersey, New York, North Carolina, Ohio, Puerto Rico, Texas, Utah, Virginia

Amount of Grant: 10,000 - 100,000 USD

Contact: Cindy Schwab; (847) 937-7075; cindy.schwab@abbott.com

Internet: http://www.abbottfund.org/project/20/30/Helping-Children-and-Young-People-Living-with-HIV-AIDS

Sponsor: Abbott Fund

100 Abbott Park Road, Department 379, Building 6D
Abbott Park, IL 60064-3500

Abby's Legendary Pizza Foundation Grants 22

As a company, Abby's Legendary Pizza Foundation contributes to many community-based events and programs. Non-profits such as the Children's Miracle Network, the American Cancer Society, the Alzheimer's Association, and many others benefit from the Foundation's partnership as a business that cares about local people and causes. Typically, the Foundation provides support for: athletics, sports, and amateur leagues; child development; and higher education. The Foundation also supports most local high schools in its hometown communities throughout the states of Oregon and Washington. There are no identified annual deadlines for application submission, and interested parties should contact their local Abby's Legendary Pizza. Most recently, awards have ranged from $25 to $5,200.

Requirements: 501(c)3 non-profits either located in, or serving the residents of, Abby's Legendary Pizza communities should apply.

Geographic Focus: Oregon, Washington

Amount of Grant: 25 - 5,200 USD

Samples: Pilot Rock Little League, Pilot Rock, Oregon, $708 - general operations; University of Oregon Duck Athletic Fund, Eugene, Oregon, $5,200 - educational programming support; Umpqua United Soccer Club, Roseburg, Oregon, $3,800 - support of local athletics.

Contact: B, Mills Sinclair, Trustee; (541) 689-0019

Internet: http://abbys.com/fundraising/

Sponsor: Abby's Legendary Pizza Foundation

1960 River Road
Eugene, OR 97404-2502

Abel and Sophia Sheng Charitable Foundation Grants 23

Established in New Jersey in 2006, the Abel and Sophia Sheng Charitable Foundation awards grants to nonprofit organizations in its areas of interest, including: fine arts, secondary education, higher education, museums, hospitals, and general charitable giving. The primary type of funding is general operating support. There are no application forms or deadlines, and interested applicants should begin by contacting the office directly in writing with a general description of their program and overall budgetary needs.

Geographic Focus: Massachusetts, New York, Rhode Island

Contact: Abel Sheng, (201) 784-0238 or (201) 567-5991; fax (201) 567-8862

Sponsor: Abel and Sophia Sheng Charitable Foundation

52 Rio Vista Drive, P.O. Box 1042
Alpine, NJ 07620-1042

Abelard Foundation East Grants 24

The Abelard Foundation is a family foundation, with offices on both the east and west coasts, which has been making grants in support of progressive social change since 1958. The foundation is committed to social change activities that expand and protect civil liberties and civil and human rights; increase opportunities for the poor, the disenfranchised, and people of color; and enhance and expand community involvement in, and control over, economic and environmental decisions affecting members of the community. Grants support activities such as community and grassroots organizing, action research, and advocacy. Seed grants, project, and/or general support grants are awarded for new projects or organizations addressing issues that traditional philanthropic sources might avoid. By supporting model efforts that can be duplicated elsewhere and that offer the potential for broader impact, the foundation encourages grantees to use these funds as leverage in gaining additional support. The foundation accepts proposals on a year-around basis. The average grant size is $10,000.

Requirements: Eligible applicants must represent or be associated with a nonprofit, 501(c)3 tax-exempt organization. The foundation gives priority to projects that are in their first years of development and have budgets less than $300,000. Nonprofit organizations offering services east of the Mississippi are eligible. The foundation is not able to respond to phone inquiries. Inquiries should be made by mail or email.

Restrictions: The foundation does not support social service programs offering ongoing or direct delivery of service; medical, educational, or cultural institutions; capital expenditure, construction, or renovation programs; programs undertaken at government initiative; or scholarship funds or other aid to individuals.

Geographic Focus: Alabama, Arkansas, Connecticut, Delaware, District of Columbia, Florida, Georgia, Illinois, Indiana, Kentucky, Louisiana, Maine, Maryland, Massachusetts, Michigan, Minnesota, Mississippi, Missouri, New Hampshire, New Jersey, New York, North Carolina, Ohio, Pennsylvania, Rhode Island, South Carolina, Tennessee, Vermont, Virginia, West Virginia, Wisconsin

Date(s) Application is Due: Mar 15; Sep 15

Amount of Grant: Up to 10,000 USD

Samples: Alabama Coalition for Immigrant Justice, Birmingham, Alabama, $10,000 - to advance just policies, encourage grassroots leadership and participation, build alliances, and amplify the voices of immigrants in Alabama; Chicago Workers Collaborative, Chicago, Illinois, $10,000 - to promote full employment and equality for the lowest wage-earners in the Chicago region; Tunica Teens in Action, Tunica, Mississippi, $10,000 - organizing in the rural, mid-south Mississippi Delta, particularly around education.

Contact: Susan B. Collins; (212) 819-8200; eastabel@aol.com

Internet: http://foundationcenter.org/grantmaker/abelardeast/index.html

Sponsor: Abelard Foundation East

P.O. Box 148
Lincoln, MA 01773

Abelard Foundation West Grants   **25**

The Abelard Foundation West is committed to grassroots social change activities that expand and protect civil liberties and civil and human rights; increase opportunities for the poor, the disenfranchised, and people of color; and enhance and expand community involvement in, and control over, economic and environmental decisions affecting members of the community. Grants support activities such as community and grassroots organizing, action research, and advocacy. Seed grants, project, and/or general support grants are awarded for new projects or organizations addressing issues that traditional philanthropic sources might avoid. By supporting model efforts that can be duplicated elsewhere and that offer the potential for broader impact, the foundation encourages grantees to use funds as leverage in gaining additional support. Applicants located in the Northern Rockies, the Great Basin, the Northwest, the Southwest, or California should contact the office listed at the website. Deadlines for Letters of Inquiry are January 15th and June 15th (LOIs must be received by these dates) for Spring and Fall grant making meetings. Decisions usually take at least 4-6 months from the date of submittal.

Requirements: 501(c)3 organizations located in the Northern Rockies, the Great Basin, the Northwest, the Southwest, and California are eligible.

Restrictions: The foundation does not support social service programs offering ongoing or direct delivery of service; medical, educational, or cultural institutions; capital expenditure, construction, or renovation programs; programs undertaken at government initiative; or scholarship funds or other aid to individuals.

Geographic Focus: Arizona, California, Colorado, Idaho, Kansas, Montana, Nebraska, Nevada, North Dakota, Oklahoma, Oregon, South Dakota, Utah, Washington, Wyoming

Date(s) Application is Due: Jan 15; Jun 15

Amount of Grant: 6,000 - 12,000 USD

Samples: Arab Resource and Organizing Center, San Francisco, California, $10,000 - support civil rights and community empowerment for Arab Americans and Arab Immigrants; Community to Community Development, Bellingham, Washington, $10,000 - support community organizing and civic engagement among immigrant communities in northwestern Washington; Midwest Center for Equality and Democracy, Kansas City, Missouri, $9,000 - to advance equality, civil rights, and worker rights in Kansas City.

Contact: Patricia St. Onge, President; (510) 834-2995; fax (510) 834-2998; info@commoncounsel.org

Internet: http://www.commoncounsel.org/Abelard%20Foundation%20West

Sponsor: Abelard Foundation West

678 13th Street, Suite 100

Oakland, CA 94612

Abeles Foundation Grants   **26**

Established in New Mexico in 2002, the Abeles Foundation is an organization that provides general operating support in the areas of elementary and secondary education, public foundations, higher education, and the performing arts in the Albuquerque and Santa Fe areas. The Foundation makes gifts to organizations based on their interactions within the community. There is no formal application required or specified annual deadlines. Applicants should contact the Foundation directly. Awards range up to about $1,200.

Restrictions: No grants are made to individuals and applicant's organization must be a qualified 501(c)3 organization.

Geographic Focus: New Mexico

Amount of Grant: Up to 1,200 USD

Samples: Alameda County Food Bank, Oakland, California, $300 - general operations; Amy Biehl Foundation, Newport Beach, California, $500 - general operations; Camperships for Nebagamon, East Troy, Wisconsin, $200 - general operations.

Contact: Richard A. Abeles; (505) 988-1115; fax (505) 984-2040; rick@abeles.net

Sponsor: Abeles Foundation

3730 Old Santa Fe Trail

Santa Fe, NM 87505-4573

Abel Foundation Grants   **27**

The Abel Foundation awards grants to eligible Nebraska nonprofit organizations in its areas of interest, which include: environmental programs and natural resource conservation; health care; higher education; Protestant religion and churches; arts and culture; and social services. Types of support include building construction and/or renovation, capital campaigns, general operating support, and program grants. Contact the office for application forms. Application deadlines are March 31, July 15, and October 31 each year. Applications qualifying for review will be considered within one to three months of receipt.

Requirements: Nebraska nonprofit organizations are eligible. Preference is given to requests from Lincoln, Nebraska, and the state's southeastern region.

Restrictions: The Foundation does not accept applications from organizations: that have had requests approved or declined in the past 12 months; or that are currently received payments for a multi-year grant.

Geographic Focus: Nebraska

Date(s) Application is Due: Mar 31; Jul 15; Oct 31

Amount of Grant: 50 - 40,000 USD

Contact: J. Ross McCown, Vice President; (402) 434-1212; fax (402) 434-1799; rossm@nebcoinc.com or nebcoinfo@nebcoinc.com

Internet: http://www.abelfoundation.org/grant.htm

Sponsor: Abel Foundation

1815 Y Street, P.O. Box 80268

Lincoln, NE 68501-0268

Abell-Hanger Foundation Grants   **28**

The foundation makes grants to nonprofit Texas organizations, other than private foundations, that are involved in such undertakings for the public and society benefit, including: arts, cultural, and humanities; education; health; human services; and religion. Types of support include general operating support, continuing support, annual campaigns, capital campaigns, building construction/renovation, equipment acquisition, endowment funds, program development, seed funds, scholarship funds, research grants, and matching funds. Block scholarship grants are made only to institutions of higher education located in Texas. Recipient colleges and universities are free to administer the grants. Education grants are limited generally to institutions of higher education, including religious institutions (Baptist, Christian, Lutheran, Methodist, and Presbyterian). Applicants must seek funding for the same proposal from various sources because sole sponsorship of programs is rarely undertaken. Grant requests are considered and awarded throughout each year. The trustees prefer to consider only one request per applicant each fiscal year. Unsuccessful proposals may not be resubmitted for at least 12 months. Applicant organizations that have never received funding from the foundation should request a pre-proposal questionnaire; the trustees will review the request to determine whether it warrants a complete proposal.

Requirements: Applicant organizations must be located in Texas and be 501(c)3 tax-exempt. National organizations with significant operations in, or providing material benefits to the citizens of, Texas will be considered based on the degree of operations/benefits within the state.

Restrictions: The foundation does not fund grants, scholarships, or fellowships for individuals.

Geographic Focus: Texas

Date(s) Application is Due: Feb 28; May 31; Aug 31; Nov 15

Amount of Grant: 10,000 - 500,000 USD

Samples: American Fallen Warrior Memorial Foundation, Midland, Texas, $5,000 - for the Texas Permian Basin Honor Flight (2014); Midland Community Theater, Midland, Texas, $45,000 - for general operating support and an outreach program (2014); Midland ISD Educational Foundation, Midland, Texas, $500,000 - for recruitment and retention of ISD teachers (2014).

Contact: David L. Smith, Executive Director; (432) 684-6655; fax (432) 684-4474; ahf@abell-hanger.org

Internet: http://www.abell-hanger.org/GrantCriteria.htm

Sponsor: Abell-Hanger Foundation

P.O. Box 430

Midland, TX 79702-0430

Abell Foundation Arts and Culture Grants   **29**

In recognition of the overall economic health of a city, the Foundation seeks funding opportunities to strengthen existing cultural arts organizations and to support emerging arts groups that are providing programming in underserved neighborhoods. The Foundation looks for initiatives that help keep artists working and living in the metropolitan area; increase organizations' capacity to expand audiences; attract more cultural visitors; and stabilize and revitalize neighborhoods. The Foundation also supports pilot projects that seek to determine the outcomes of cultural arts curricula on overall student academic achievement while at the same time reinforcing the State's mandate to integrate the cultural arts into the K-12 educational programming.

Requirements: 501(c)3 organizations serving Maryland communities, especially in the Baltimore area, may apply. The foundation prefers grantees that show strong fiscal management, their project's benefit to the community, ability to achieve goals, unique work, and other sources of financial support.

Restrictions: The Foundation does not fund educational programs at higher education institutions, medical facilities, individual scholarships, fellowships,

annual operating expenses, sponsorships, deficit financing, endowments, travel or memberships.
Geographic Focus: Maryland
Date(s) Application is Due: Jan 1; Mar 1; May 1; Aug 1; Sep 1; Nov 1
Amount of Grant: 5,000 - 50,000 USD
Samples: Baltimore Office of Promotion and the Arts, Baltimore, Maryland, $25,000 - support of Free Fall Baltimore, an initiative designed to provide 30 low-budget arts and cultural organizations with the opportunity to offer free events (2014).
Contact: Holly Russell, Grants Manager; (410) 547-1300; fax (410) 539-6579; hollyd@abell.org or abell@abell.org
Internet: http://www.abell.org/arts-culture
Sponsor: Abell Foundation
111 S Calvert Street, Suite 2300
Baltimore, MD 21202-6174

Abell Foundation Community Development Grants   30
The Foundation recognizes the need to enhance the livability of neighborhoods and create desirable housing and commercial areas as a means to retain and attract both residents and jobs. By encouraging investment in redevelopment projects and housing renovations, leveraging of public and private capital, community planning and maximizing reuse of historic structures, the Foundation focuses on those initiatives that foster improvement of downtown and neighborhoods. It further seeks to promote cost-efficient delivery of municipal services, maximize Baltimore's use of competitive funding sources and increase the tax base. The Foundation also encourages efforts to tie the health of the City to the region and state, through the support of housing mobility, regional planning and growth management.
Requirements: 501(c)3 organizations serving Maryland communities, especially in the Baltimore area, may apply. The foundation prefers grantees that show strong fiscal management, their project's benefit to the community, ability to achieve goals, unique work, and other sources of financial support.
Restrictions: The Foundation does not fund educational programs at higher education institutions, medical facilities, individual scholarships, fellowships, annual operating expenses, sponsorships, deficit financing, endowments, travel or memberships.
Geographic Focus: Maryland
Date(s) Application is Due: Jan 1; Mar 1; May 1; Aug 1; Sep 1; Nov 1
Amount of Grant: 5,000 - 300,000 USD
Samples: 1000 Friends of Maryland, Baltimore, Maryland, $200,000 - two-year funding for continued support of the Sustainable Growth for Maryland campaign (2014); Civic Works, Baltimore, Maryland, $299,211 - wo-year funding for continued support of the Real Food Farm in Clifton Park (2014); Enoch Pratt Free Library, Baltimore, Maryland, $175,000 - renovation costs of the Job and Career Center at the Pratt Central Library (2014).
Contact: Tracey M. Barbour-Gillett, Program Officer; (410) 547-1300; fax (410) 539-6579; tbarbour@abell.org or abell@abell.org
Internet: http://www.abell.org/community-development
Sponsor: Abell Foundation
111 S Calvert Street, Suite 2300
Baltimore, MD 21202-6174

Abell Foundation Conservation and Environment Grants   31
The Abell Foundation supports organizations that are working to protect and preserve Maryland's natural resources. Partnering with the public and private sectors, the Foundation places special emphasis on those initiatives supporting ecosystem-wide conservation programs, including forests, wetlands, agricultural lands, watersheds and air and water quality. The Foundation also focuses attention on local projects reinforcing Maryland's Smart Growth, Rural Legacy and Green Print initiatives. Areas of interest include: environmental justice in under-served communities; advocacy for healthy air and clean water; enforcement and legal compliance initiatives; preservation of farmland and creation of effective buffer zones; preservation of park lands for recreational and educational purposes; sustainable and safe use of resources; and watershed and habitat protection.
Requirements: 501(c)3 organizations serving Maryland communities, especially in the Baltimore area, may apply. The foundation prefers grantees that show strong fiscal management, their project's benefit to the community, ability to achieve goals, unique work, and other sources of financial support.
Restrictions: Grants are not given to individuals, or for sponsorships, deficit financing, operating budgets, annual sustaining funds, travel, or loans. The foundation currently does not fund housing projects, hospitals, or medical research.
Geographic Focus: Maryland

Date(s) Application is Due: Jan 1; Mar 1; May 1; Aug 1; Sep 1; Nov 1
Amount of Grant: 5,000 - 100,000 USD
Samples: 1000 Friends of Maryland, Baltimore, Maryland, $90,000 - two-year funding for continued support of staffing and expenses related to the Partners for Open Space campaign (2014); Chesapeake Climate Action Network, Tacoma Park, Maryland, $25,000 - continued staffing support and expansion of the Maryland Healthy Communities campaign (2014).
Contact: Lynn Heller, Program Officer; (410) 547-1300; fax (410) 539-6579; lheller@abell.org or abell@abell.org
Internet: http://www.abell.org/conservation-environment
Sponsor: Abell Foundation
111 S Calvert Street, Suite 2300
Baltimore, MD 21202-6174

Abell Foundation Criminal Justice and Addictions Grants   32
The Foundation seeks to increase access to substance abuse treatment and supportive services such as housing and job training for the uninsured and drug addicted individuals residing in Baltimore City. The Foundation works to increase the impact and effectiveness of treatment services through cutting edge research and support of innovative service models designed to reach under-served populations. The Foundation supports programs and initiatives that increase public safety and reduce recidivism with a special focus on initiatives that address the barriers facing the returning ex-offender. Areas of interest include: substance abuse treatment, prevention, and research; supportive housing; prisoner reentry; criminal justice system reform; and juvenile justice. A particular emphasis is placed on initiatives that provide transitional housing and the necessary wraparound services to support a successful return to the community.
Requirements: 501(c)3 organizations serving Maryland communities, especially in the Baltimore area, may apply. The foundation prefers grantees that show strong fiscal management, their project's benefit to the community, ability to achieve goals, unique work, and other sources of financial support.
Restrictions: The Foundation does not fund educational programs at higher education institutions, medical facilities, individual scholarships, fellowships, annual operating expenses, sponsorships, deficit financing, endowments, travel or memberships.
Geographic Focus: Maryland
Date(s) Application is Due: Jan 1; Mar 1; May 1; Aug 1; Sep 1; Nov 1
Amount of Grant: 5,000 - 50,000 USD
Samples: Maryland Community Health Initiatives, Baltimore, Maryland, $35,000 - purchase of equipment and facility improvements of the Penn North Recovery Community Center (2014).
Contact: Amanda Owens, Program Officer; (410) 547-1300; fax (410) 539-6579; aowens@abell.org or abell@abell.org
Internet: http://www.abell.org/criminal-justice-addictions
Sponsor: Abell Foundation
111 S Calvert Street, Suite 2300
Baltimore, MD 21202-6174

Abell Foundation Health and Human Services Grants   33
Through grants awarded in this area, the Foundation seeks to address societal issues associated with family disintegration, family planning, child support, teenage parenting, domestic violence, children's health and well-being, child abuse and neglect, hunger, food self-sufficiency and homelessness. The Foundation also supports advocacy programs for better health care and social services for children and youth as well as for a comprehensive system of universal health care. Of particular concern is the support of efforts to combat childhood lead paint poisoning and mental health disorders. Furthermore, the Foundation continues to provide opportunities for low-income families to live in quality housing in good neighborhoods in the region. While the Foundation's primary focus is on the development of permanent housing, it also will consider emergency and transitional housing.
Requirements: 501(c)3 organizations serving Maryland communities, especially in the Baltimore area, may apply. The foundation prefers grantees that show strong fiscal management, their project's benefit to the community, ability to achieve goals, unique work, and other sources of financial support.
Restrictions: The Foundation does not fund educational programs at higher education institutions, medical facilities, individual scholarships, fellowships, annual operating expenses, sponsorships, deficit financing, endowments, travel or memberships.
Geographic Focus: Maryland
Date(s) Application is Due: Jan 1; Mar 1; May 1; Aug 1; Sep 1; Nov 1
Amount of Grant: 5,000 - 50,000 USD
Samples: Benefits Data Trust, Baltimore, Maryland, $50,000 - support of the Maryland Benefits Center's initiative to provide comprehensive benefits

access for low?income seniors in Baltimore City (2014); Johns Hopkins University School of Medicine, Baltimore, Maryland, $150,000 - support of the Preconception Women's Health and Pediatrics initiative for low?income women in Baltimore City (2014); Samaritan Community, Baltimore, Maryland, $25,000 - continued support of the Food Pantry and Emergency Assistance programs (2014).
Contact: Theresa Staudenmaier, Program Officer; (410) 547-1300; fax (410) 539-6679; staudenmaier@abell.org or abell@abell.org
Internet: http://www.abell.org/health-human-services
Sponsor: Abell Foundation
111 S Calvert Street, Suite 2300
Baltimore, MD 21202-6174

Abernethy Family Foundation Grants   34
The Abernethy Family Foundation was established in 2000 in Florida with a mission of supporting elementary and secondary education programs, curriculum development, agricultural programs, and health care within St. Lucie and Indian River counties, Florida. General operating funding is its primary type of support. There are no deadlines with which to adhere, and applicant organizations should begin by requesting an application form directly from the Foundation.
Restrictions: Giving is restricted to eligible organizations within St. Lucie and Indian River counties, Florida.
Geographic Focus: Florida
Contact: Bruce R. Abernethy, Jr; (772) 489-4901; babernethy@bruceapa.com
Sponsor: Abernethy Family Foundation
500 Virginia Avenue, Suite 202
Fort Pierce, FL 34982-5882

Able To Serve Grants   35
Able to Serve Inc. is a public charity, providing services and opportunities for persons with mental and physical disabilities. Able primarily serves Wake and Johnston counties in North Carolina with some services extended to surrounding counties when resources are available. There are currently four programs that cover the services Able fund within the local community; Local Ministry Network, Community Partnerships, Van Transportation Services, and Computer Learning/Donations.
Requirements: Able to Serve provides each service and program at no charge to the individual or family receiving services within the Wake and Johnston counties of North Carolina.
Geographic Focus: North Carolina
Contact: Carlton S. McDaniel; (919) 779-5545; carlton@abletoserve.com
Internet: www.abletoserve.com
Sponsor: Able To Serve
P.O. Box 334
Garner, NC 27529-0334

Able Trust Vocational Rehabilitation Grants for Agencies   36
The trust supports individuals and non-profit vocational rehabilitation programs throughout Florida with fund-raising, grant making and public awareness of disability issues. The program provides grant funds to Florida not-for-profit agencies and Floridians with disabilities for a wide array of projects leading to the employment of individuals with disabilities. To be considered for funding a proposal must address the employment of individuals with disabilities and priority is given to those projects with direct employment placement outcomes during the grant time period. Grants to organizations are typically around $45,000. Historically grants have been made between $5,000 and $200,000. The amount is relative to the scale, scope and complexity of the proposed employment project.
Requirements: Agency applicants must be a 501(c)3 organization serving the disability community in Florida and interested in providing employment services for individuals with disabilities. Any employment program that will provide direct placement in competitive employment, the transition from school-to-work, transition from sheltered/work enclave settings to community-based employment, job skills training such as resume and interview assistance, computer skills, office skills and etiquette, transportation training to access work, and other research, public awareness and promotion that focuses on creating employment opportunities for individuals with disabilities. There are no deadlines. Guidelines, helpful tips and application forms can be found at the sponsor's website.
Restrictions: Grants funds may not be used to purchase: vehicles, property, building improvements, capital campaigns, endowments, fellowships, scholarships, travel grants, tuition where state and federal aid is available, lobbying, medical items, incurred debt, and program expenses prior to grant approval.
Geographic Focus: Florida

Amount of Grant: 5,000 - 200,000 USD
Contact: Guenevere Crum, Senior Vice President; (850) 224-4493; fax (850) 224-4496; guenevere@abletrust.org or info@abletrust.org
Internet: http://www.abletrust.org/grant/booklet.shtml
Sponsor: Able Trust
3320 Thomasville Road, Suite 200
Tallahassee, FL 32308

Abundance Foundation International Grants   37
The Abundance Foundation makes grants to organizations aligned with its mission to improve global health through education, economic empowerment and health systems strengthening. It is focused on programs that unlock the potential of local communities particularly in Africa, Central America and Haiti. Its grantee partners train, support and empower local leaders to create new capabilities that result in lasting improvement in quality of life. In addition to direct grant funding that allows for upscaling of successful existing programs, the Foundation raise awareness about local leaders whose vision and heroism are creating positive change in their communities.
Geographic Focus: All States, Haiti
Contact: Stephen Kahn, President; (510) 841-4123; fax (510) 841-4093; info@abundancefound.org
Internet: http://www.abundancefound.org/grants/
Sponsor: Abundance Foundation
127 University Avenue
Berkeley, CA 94710-1616

A Charitable Foundation Grants   38
Founded in 1997 in Nevada and funded by the Tactical Investment Management Corporation, A Charitable Foundation offers support primarily in California, Hawaii, and New York, as well as Brazil. Its major fields of interest include: educational research; the environment; food banks; human services; and international development. Types of support include annual campaigns, building and renovation projects, emergency assistance, basic research, and grants to individuals. Applications should include a detailed description of the project, purpose of the research (if applicable), and a detailed budget. There are no annual deadlines, and grants typically range from $2000 to $35,000.
Geographic Focus: California, Hawaii, New York, Brazil
Amount of Grant: 250 - 30,000 USD
Samples: Self-Realization Fellowship, Los Angeles, California, $35,000 - support of a fellowship program; Wailua United Church of Christm Wailua, Hawaii, $18,000 - for public charity work; Hawaii Food Bank, Honolulu, Hawaii, $10,000 - public charities.
Contact: David S. Druz, President; (702) 248-8184; ddruz@aol.com
Sponsor: A Charitable Foundation
2657 Windmill Parkway, Suite 220
Henderson, NV 89014

Achelis Foundation Grants   39
Elisabeth Achelis was born in Brooklyn Heights in 1880. She used her inheritance from her father Fritz Achelis, who was President of the American Hard Rubber Company, to establish the Achelis Foundation in 1940 to aid and contribute to charitable, benevolent, educational and religious uses and purposes for the moral, ethical, physical, mental and intellectual well-being and progress of mankind; to aid and contribute to methods for the peaceful settlement of international differences; to aid and contribute to the furtherance of the objects and purposes of any charitable, benevolent, educational or religious institution or agency; and to establish and maintain charitable, benevolent and educational institutions and agencies. The Achelis Foundation shares trustees, staff, office space, and even a website with the Bodman Foundation which has a similar mission and geographic area of concentration (both foundations give in New York City, while the Bodman Foundation also gives in New Jersey). Funding is concentrated in six program areas: arts and culture; education; employment; health; public policy; and youth and families. Most recent awards have ranged from $10,000 to $200,000, though typical awards average $20,000 to $50,000.
Requirements: 501(c)3 organizations based in New York City that fall within the foundation's areas of interest are welcome to submit an inquiry or proposal letter by regular mail (initial inquiries by email or fax are not accepted, nor are CDs, DVDs, computer discs, or video tapes). An initial inquiry to the foundation should include only the following items: a proposal letter that briefly summarizes the history of the project, need, objectives, time period, key staff, project budget, and evaluation plan; the applicant's latest annual report and complete set of audited financial statements; and the applicant's IRS 501(c)3 tax-exemption letter. Applications may be submitted at any time during

the year. Each request is reviewed by staff and will usually receive a written response within thirty days. Those requests deemed consistent with the interests and resources of the foundation will be evaluated further and more information will be requested. Foundation staff may request a site visit, conference call, or meeting. All grants are reviewed and approved by the Trustees at one of their three board meetings in May, September, or December.

Restrictions: The foundation generally does not make grants for the following purposes or program areas: nonprofit organizations outside of New York; annual appeals, dinner functions, and fundraising events; endowments and capital campaigns; loans and deficit financing; direct grants to individuals; individual day-care and after-school programs; housing; organizations or projects based outside the U.S; films or video projects; small art, dance, music, and theater groups; individual K-12 schools (except charter schools); national health and mental health organizations; and government agencies or nonprofit organizations significantly funded or reimbursed by government agencies. Limited resources prevent the foundations from funding the same organization on an ongoing annual basis.

Geographic Focus: New York

Amount of Grant: 10,000 - 200,000 USD

Samples: American Ballet Theatre, New York, New York, $25,000 - general operating support (2014); East Harlem School at Exodus House, New York, New York, $25,000 - general operating support (2014; International Center for the Disabled, New York, New York, $25,000 - to support the ReadyNow program (2014).

Contact: John B. Krieger, Executive Director; (212) 644-0322; fax (212) 759-6510; main@achelis-bodman-fnds.org

Internet: http://www.achelis-bodman-fnds.org/guidelines.html

Sponsor: Achelis Foundation

767 Third Avenue, 4th Floor

New York, NY 10017-2023

Ackerman Foundation Grants   40

The Ackerman Foundation was established as a charitable trust in 1992 by James F. Ackerman, a local entrepreneur and philanthropist. As an Indianapolis based organization, grants are made predominately to central Indiana organizations as well as a few national medical research institutions. Specifically, the foundation focuses on Indiana cultural institutions and organizations benefiting health and human services, community development, and education. Grant requests will be considered for both operating fund purposes and as capital campaigns. The foundation does not have grant application forms. To be considered for assistance, an organization should write a brief one or two page letter describing its proposal. The Trustees of the foundation meet semi-annually on the business day that falls on or closest to June 15 and December 15.

Requirements: Established under the laws of the State of Indiana, the foundation considers grant proposals from eligible organizations which are tax exempt under the United States Internal Revenue Service Code section 501(c)3.

Restrictions: The foundation does not make grants to individuals.

Geographic Focus: All States

Date(s) Application is Due: May 15; Nov 15

Amount of Grant: 500 - 100,000 USD

Samples: Conner Prairie Museum, Fishers, Indiana, $5,000 - general operating support; Brebeuf Jesuit Prep School, Indianapolis, Indiana, $10,000 - general operating support; Providence Cristo Rey High School, Indianapolis, Indiana, $25,000 - general operating support.

Contact: John F. Ackerman, Grants Director; (317) 663-0205; fax (317) 663-0215; jdisbro@cardinalep.com

Internet: http://ackermanfoundation.com/

Sponsor: Ackerman Foundation of Indiana

280 E. 96th Street, Suite 350

Indianapolis, IN 46240-3858

Actuarial Foundation Advancing Student Achievement Grants   41

The foundation considers proposals for funding of mentoring programs that involve actuaries in supporting the teaching and learning of mathematics at all levels. Grants may be awarded to U.S. and Canadian local groups that can provide the support necessary to develop a network of mathematics mentors in the public and private school systems. Such groups include actuarial clubs and other education-oriented organizations. The programs can also encourage interest in mathematics applications in business and societal issues by students and teachers. Applicants will be given wide latitude in designing and organizing programs to best utilize local community resources. Preference is given to innovative programs that do not merely replicate existing grant programs. Grants support direct project overhead expenses.

Requirements: U.S. and Canadian local groups or organizations are eligible. Collaboration among school systems, local actuarial clubs, corporations, and other stakeholders in education is encouraged.

Geographic Focus: All States, Canada

Amount of Grant: Up to 25,000 USD

Contact: Administrator; (847) 706-3535; fax (847) 706-3599; ASA@ActFdn.org

Internet: http://www.actuarialfoundation.org/grant/index.html

Sponsor: Actuarial Foundation

475 N Martingale Road, Suite 600

Schaumburg, IL 60173-2226

Adams-Mastrovich Family Foundation Grants   42

Mary Adams Balmat established the Adams-Mastrovich Family Foundation in 1957. Born in 1898 in Lead, South Dakota, she married William Emory Adams II in 1927. He was a prominent businessman in Deadwood, South Dakota, as well as its mayor for six terms during the 1920s. The couple maintained residences in both South Dakota and California. Their home in Deadwood now belongs to the local Historic Preservation Commission. Over the years Mary shared her resources with education, the performing arts, institutions of higher learning, Roman Catholic parishes, hospitals, museums and libraries, as well as programs for battered women and an organization serving delinquent teenage boys. The Foundation continues to support these same organizations today, primarily throughout South Dakota and Los Angeles County, California. Types of funding include: building and renovation, ongoing operating support, equipment purchase, program development, and support of scholarship funds. Applications must be submitted through our online grant application form, with the annual submission deadline August 1. The Board meets in September for final decision-making.

Requirements: 501(c)3 organizations located in, or serving residents of, South Dakota or Los Angeles County, California, are eligible to apply. Grants to religious organizations and their affiliates are made only to organizations that are a part of or affiliated with the Roman Catholic Church.

Restrictions: The foundation will not consider funding requests for the following: political campaigns or lobbying activities; fundraising campaigns; endowment campaigns; individuals; travel for groups or individuals; conferences, seminars, workshops, or symposia; or benefits or fundraisers. No capital requests will be considered unless solicited by the Foundation's advisory board.

Geographic Focus: California, South Dakota

Date(s) Application is Due: Aug 1

Amount of Grant: Up to 100,000 USD

Samples: American Indian Healing Center, Whittier, California, $5,000 - support for healthy eating program; Catholic Education Foundation, Los Angeles, California, $5,000 - tuition awards program; Custer County Historical Society, Broken Bow, Nebraska, $5,000 - preservation and display of historic items.

Contact: Halsey H. Halls, Vice President; (612) 667-9084 or (612) 316-4112

Sponsor: Adams-Mastrovich Family Foundation

P.O. Box 53456, MAC S4101-22G

Phoenix, AZ 85072-3456

Adams and Reese Corporate Giving Grants   43

At Adams and Reese, the Corporation takes pride in giving back to its communities and believes success is directly related to the prosperity and the quality of life within the communities it serves. Its corporate philanthropy program, HUGS (Hope, Understanding, Giving, and Support) was founded in 1988 by Partner, Mark Surprenant. Since its inception, the firm has devoted financial resources and thousands of volunteer hours to offer assistance to those in need. A fundamental commitment to volunteerism is the deep-rooted characteristic of the corporation. Primary activities include grants in support of health, youth development, and human services. Fields of interest are: general charitable giving, operating support, health care organizations, legal services, social services, and youth programs.

Requirements: Regions of grant application eligibility include: Birmingham and Mobile, Alabama; Jacksonville, Sarasota, St. Petersburg, Tallahassee, and Tampa, Florida; Baton Rouge and New Orleans, Louisiana; Jackson, Mississippi; Columbia, South Carolina; Chattanooga, Memphis, and Nashville, Tennessee; Houston, Texas; and Washington, DC.

Geographic Focus: Alabama, District of Columbia, Florida, Louisiana, Mississippi, South Carolina, Tennessee, Texas

Contact: Mark Surprenant, Liaison Partner; (504) 581-3234; fax (504) 566-0210; Mark.Surprenant@arlaw.com

Internet: http://www.adamsandreese.com/community/

Sponsor: Adams and Reese Corporation

701 Poydras Street, Suite 4500

New Orleans, LA 70139-7755

Adams County Community Foundation of Indiana Grants   **44**

The Adams County Community Foundation and supporting organization, John and Kay Boch, award numerous grants annually. Areas of primary interest include: children and youth; community and economic development; education; and parks and recreation. Money awarded from the various funds helps to enrich and enhance the quality of life throughout Adams County, Indiana. Grants awarded annually help both businesses and the communities in which it serves. Quarterly deadlines are the second Thursday of January, April, July, and October.

Requirements: Applicants must support businesses, educational programs, or residents of Adams County, Indiana.

Geographic Focus: Indiana

Date(s) Application is Due: Jan 14; Apr 14; Jul 14; Oct 13

Amount of Grant: 200 - 2,000 USD

Contact: Coni Mayer, Executive Director; (260) 724-3939; fax (260) 724-2299; accfoundation@earthlink.net

Internet: http://www.adamscountyfoundation.org/default.aspx

Sponsor: Adams County Community Foundation

102 N. Second Street

Decatur, IN 46733

Adams County Community Foundation of Pennsylvania Grants   **45**

The Adams County Community Foundation was established in October of 2007 as a Pennsylvania corporation to succeed the Adams County Foundation which for 22 years had operated as a trust-based community foundation. The Foundation is a public charity that the IRS has determined to be a 501(c)3 organization. The purpose of this foundation is to inspire people and communities to build and distribute charitable funds for good, for Adams County, forever. After one year of operation, the foundation had acquired nine funds established by individual people or families, members of the Foundation's Board of Directors, groups of business people, a local charity and by a visionary patriot from the 1700s. The Foundation's assets are managed by a professional investment company hired by the Board of Directors and overseen by the Foundation's Investment & Finance Committee. From these funds, distribution of grants is made to qualified, local charities who demonstrate that they are meeting community needs. With a 16 member Board of Directors, Adams County Community Foundation serves as a good steward of the monies of our donors and demonstrates accountability, transparency, confidentiality, compassion, inclusiveness and excellence in its work. The foundation gives to organizations that assist, promote and improve the moral, mental, social and physical well-being of area residents. Fields of interest include: arts; Christian agencies and churches; community and economic development; education; and health organizations.

Requirements: Applicants must serve residents living in Adams County, Pennsylvania.

Geographic Focus: Pennsylvania

Contact: Barbara Ernico, (717) 337-0060 or (717) 337-3353; fax (717) 337-1080; info@adamscountycf.org

Internet: http://www.adamscountycf.org/receive.html

Sponsor: Adams County Community Foundation of Pennsylvania

101 W Middle Street, P.O. Box 4565

Gettysburg, PA 17325-2109

Adams Family Foundation I Grants   **46**

The Foundation, founded in 1993, offers support primarily in Tennessee and the southeastern portion of the United States. Its major fields of interest include: the arts, children and youth services, Christian agencies and churches, elementary and secondary education programs, and human services. The primary type of funding is general operating support. There are no specific deadlines with which to adhere, and applicants should forward a request by letter outlining the project and a detailed budgetary need. Most grants are in the neighborhood of $500 to $10,000, though occasionally reach as high as $100,000.

Requirements: Any 501(c)3 that is located in, or offers support to, Tennessee or the southeastern portion of the United States is eligible to apply.

Geographic Focus: Tennessee

Amount of Grant: Up to 100,000 USD

Samples: Adams Memorial Public Library, Woodbury, Tennessee, $41,000 - general operating fund; Middle Tennessee Christian School, Murfreesboro, Tennessee, $10,000 - general operating fund; Special Kids, Murfreesboro, Tennessee, $6,000 - general operating fund.

Contact: Robert G. Adams; (615) 890-2020 or (615) 896-0374;

Sponsor: Adams Family Foundation I

2217 Battleground Drive

Murfreesboro, TN 37129-6006

Adams Family Foundation II Grants   **47**

The Adams Family Foundation, established in 1993 by the founder of the Murfreesboro-based National HealthCare L.P. and National Health Investors, is primarily interested in supporting: boys and girls clubs; Boy Scouts of America; children and youth services; Christian agencies and churches; human service organizations; and secondary education. Funding is typically in the form of general operating support. Grants are usually in the $250 to $100,000 range, although occasionally somewhat higher. There are no particular deadlines, and applicants should approach the Foundation initially by letter describing their program and specifying an amount needed.

Requirements: 501(c)3 organizations serving the residents of the general Murfreesboro, Tennessee, region are eligible.

Geographic Focus: Tennessee

Amount of Grant: 250 - 200,000 USD

Contact: W. Andrew Adams, Trustee; (615) 848-2638 or (615) 848-0171

Sponsor: Adams Family Foundation II

801 Mooreland Lane

Murfreesboro, TN 37128-4634

Adams Family Foundation of Minnesota Grants   **48**

The Adams Family Foundation, established in Minnesota in 2000, is most interested in supporting youth development, local libraries, and environmental awareness. Additionally, its fields of interest include higher education and the arts. The primary type of support in for general operations. Although there are no specific deadlines or applications with which to adhere, applicants should submit a detailed description of the proposed program, purposes of the organization, and budgetary needs. Awards generally range from $500 to $3,000.

Requirements: Nonprofit organizations within the northern and west central Minnesota regions may apply.

Geographic Focus: Minnesota

Amount of Grant: 500 - 3,000 USD

Samples: Center for the Arts, Fergus Falls, Minnesota, $3,080 - support for local arts; Kaddatz Galary, Fergus Falls, Minnesota, $1,607 - general operations / support for the arts; Otter Tail County Historical Society, Fergus Falls, Minnesota, $3,000 - general operations and history.

Contact: Virginia S. Adams, President; (218) 736-4842; adams@prtel.com

Sponsor: Adams Family Foundation

504 South Oak Street

Fergus Falls, MN 56537-2614

Adams Family Foundation of Ohio Grants   **49**

The Adams Family Foundation was established in Muskingum County, Ohio, with the intent of providing financial awards to local organizations that have the mission of supporting the residents of Muskingum County. Its primary areas of interest include community services, human services, family, and religious organizations. Grants are typically given for general operating support. There are no specific application materials or annual deadlines identified, and interested parties should contact the Foundation directly by way of a brief letter outlining the need and budgetary requirements.

Requirements: 501(c)3 organizations serving the residents of Muskingum County, Ohio, are eligible to apply.

Geographic Focus: Ohio

Contact: Robert Gregory Adams, Presiident; (740) 826-4154

Sponsor: Adams Family Foundation

165 W. Main Street

New Concord, OH 43762

Adams Family Foundation of Tennessee Grants   **50**

The Adams Family Foundation, established in Tennessee in 2006, provides grants to individuals for family services, cemetery and burial needs, and for the prevention of domestic violence in the Paris, Tennessee, region. Its primary fields of interest have been identified as: agriculture and food; education; and youth development programs. There are no application forms or deadlines with which to adhere, and those in need should forward a letter of request directly to the Foundation office. Most recently, awards have ranged from $1,000 to $2,000.

Geographic Focus: Tennessee

Amount of Grant: 1,000 - 2,000 USD

Contact: David E. Sullivan, Director; (731) 642-2940 or (731) 642-2752

Sponsor: Adams Family Foundation

1101 East Wood Street, P.O. Box 909

Paris, TN 38242-0909

Adams Foundation Grants 51

Established in 1955, the Adams Foundations was initially funded through a donation by Rolland L. Adams, who became owner of the Bethlehem Globe newspaper in 1929. The newspaper won a Pulitzer Prize for editorial writing in 1972. Abarta, which operates the Foundation, was founded by members of the Adams, Bitzer, Roehr and Taylor families - names which form the acronym of the company title. Grants are currently awarded in both Pittsburgh, Pennsylvania, and Ithaca, New York, along with the surrounding areas of these two communities. It supports food banks and civic centers, as well as organizations involved with arts and culture, education, mental health, and arthritis treatments. Funding comes in the form of general operating support. Applicants should submit letters of application detailing the project need and funding requested. Though there are no specified annual deadlines, the board meets each February and August. Most recent grant awards have ranged from $3,500 to $125,500.

Requirements: Any 501(c)3 organization serving the residents of Pittsburgh, Pennsylvania, and Ithaca, New York, are eligible to apply.
Geographic Focus: New York, Pennsylvania
Amount of Grant: 3,500 - 150,000 USD
Samples: Pittsburgh Ballet Theater, Pittsburgh, Pennsylvania, $125,000 - operating support for educational art program; Arthritis Foundation of Western Pennsylvania, Pittsburgh, Pennsylvania, $27,500 - operating support for public health programs; Donald Staylor Scholarship Fund, Cornell University, Ithaca, New York - education endowment.
Contact: Shelley M. Taylor, President; (412) 963-1087 or (412) 963-3163
Sponsor: Adams Foundation
1000 Gamma Drive, 5th Floor
Pittsburgh, PA 15238-2929

Adam Smith Institute Grants 52

The Institute is the United Kingdom's leading innovator of free-market economic and social policies. Politically independent and non-profit, the Institute promotes its ideas through grants, reports, briefings, events, media appearances, and its website and blog. Giving is primarily in London, England, and goes to general operating costs for museums. There are no specific deadlines or application forms with which to adhere.
Geographic Focus: All States, United Kingdom
Contact: Grants Manager; (301) 770-3750
Internet: http://www.adamsmith.org/
Sponsor: Adam Smith Institute
6163 Executive Boulevard
Rockville, MD 20852-3901

Adelaide Christian Home For Children Grants 53

The Adelaide Christian Home For Children provides support to evangelical Christian organizations serving children and youth, with priority given to local California ministries. Its primary fields of interest include: Christian agencies and churches; education; human services; religion; and youth development. Target populations are children, the economically disadvantaged; and single parents. Interested parties should be aware that there is a formal application. Though there are no specified annual deadlines, the board does meet in both January and September to decide funding awards.
Geographic Focus: California
Amount of Grant: Up to 120,000 USD
Samples: Agape Pregnancy Center, San Clemente, California, $10,000 - general operating support for programs serving women facing a crisis pregnancy situation; Christian Missions in Many Lands, Spring Lake, New Jersey, $119,000 - financial assistance to church workers and missionaries; Verdugo Pines Bible Camp, Wrightwood, California, $30,000 - camp and conference center for young people and adults.
Contact: Sherry Parsons, Director; (949) 361-1346
Sponsor: Adelaide Christian Home For Children
122 Avenida Del Mar
San Clemente, CA 92672

Adler-Clark Electric Community Commitment Foundation Grants 54

Established in Wisconsin in 2004, the Adler-Clark Electric Community Commitment Foundation offers grants in Clark County, Wisconsin. It supports athletics and amateur leagues, fire prevention and control, education, food banks, food services, health care, human services, public libraries, and recreation programs. Types of support include: equipment purchase; general operations; and program development. A formal application is required, and the annual deadline has been identified as December 1. Funding amounts range from $500 to $3,000.
Geographic Focus: Wisconsin
Date(s) Application is Due: Dec 1
Amount of Grant: 500 - 3,000 USD
Samples: Clark County Sheriff's Department, Neillsville, Wisconsin, $2,000 - K-9 unit materials; Willard Historical Society, Willard, Wisconsin, $1,875 - Settlers Park landscaping edging; Colby Hornet Athletic Boosters, Colby, Wisconsin, $2,250 - New uniforms and basketballs.
Contact: Timothy E. Stewart, Trustee; (715) 267-6188 or (800) 272-6188
Internet: http://www.cecoop.com/home
Sponsor: Adler-Clark Electric Community Commitment Foundation
P.O. Box 190
Greenwood, WI 54437-9419

Adolph Coors Foundation Grants 55

The Coors Foundation supports organizations that promote the western values of self-reliance, personal responsibility, and integrity. The foundation believes these values foster an environment where entrepreneurial spirits flourish and help Coloradans reach their full potential. High priority is placed on programs that help youth to prosper, that encourage economic opportunities for adults, and that advance public policies that uphold traditional American values. Traditional areas of support include one-on-one mentoring programs, job training, and a variety of self-help initiatives. The foundation also has an interest in bringing integrative medicine into the medical mainstream. In each of its giving areas, the foundation seeks evidenced-based results. Civic and cultural programs attracting the Foundation's attention are typically those that enhance our culture and heritage, that demonstrate our creativity as a people and that are likely to be of economic benefit to and broadly used by the communities they serve. Past grants have supported boys and girls clubs and inner-city health programs. Types of support include building funds, general operating budgets, seed money, and special projects. The foundation has moved to an online screening and application system which is accessible from the foundation website. Application deadlines are March 1, July 1, and November 1.

Requirements: All applicants must be classified as 501(c)3 organizations by the Internal Revenue Service and must operate within the United States.
Restrictions: The foundation does not provide support for the following expenses or entities: organizations primarily supported by tax-derived funds; conduit organizations that pass funds to non-exempt organizations; organizations with two consecutive years of operating loss; K-12 schools or the ancillary programs and projects of those schools; individuals; research projects; production of films or other media-related projects; historic renovation; churches or church projects; museums or museum projects; animals or animal-related projects; preschools, day-care centers, nursing homes, extended-care facilities, or respite care; deficit funding or retirement of debt; special events, meetings, or seminars; purchase of computer equipment; adaptive sports programs; and national health organizations. Organizations applying for start-up funding must have been in operation for at least one full year.
Geographic Focus: All States
Date(s) Application is Due: Mar 1; Jul 1; Nov 1
Samples: A Christian Ministry in the National Parks, Denver, Colorado, $20,000 - general operating support; Accion New Mexico, Albuquerque, New Mexico, $10,000 - general operating support; Cato Institute, Washington, D.C., $150,000 - general operating support.
Contact: Jeanne Bistranin; (303) 388-1636; fax (303) 388-1684
Internet: http://www.coorsfoundation.org/Process/index.html
Sponsor: Adolph Coors Foundation
4100 E Mississippi Avenue, Suite 1850
Denver, CO 80246

Advance Auto Parts Corporate Giving Grants 56

The Advance Auto Parts Corporate Giving program was founded on the belief that good business is more than just selling merchandise. Since the company was founded in 1932, it has been guided by the following principles, known as the Advance Values: inspire and build the self-confidence and success of every Team Member; serve customers better than anyone else and help them succeed; and grow the business and profitability with integrity. While the corporation understands that there are a variety of worthy causes in every community, to maximize its giving and make the greatest possible impact, Advance has chosen to focus its charitable efforts on serving those in need through support of the following four impact areas: health – improving the health and well-being of others; education – helping people reach their potential by providing educational opportunities; at-risk children and families

– helping children and families to assure their critical needs are met through comprehensive, community-based programs; and disaster relief – providing timely support to those impacted by disasters such as earthquakes, hurricanes, floods and other natural disasters.

Geographic Focus: All States
Contact: Grants Manager; (540) 362-4911; fax (540) 561-1448
Internet: http://corp.advanceautoparts.com/english/about/public.asp
Sponsor: Advance Auto Parts Corporate Giving
5008 Airport Road
Roanoke, VA 24012

Advent Software Corporate Giving Grants 57

Advent Software makes charitable contributions to nonprofit organizations to nonprofit organizations involved with education and low-performing K-12 schools. The primary field of interest is elementary and secondary education, and comes in the form of general operation funds. Advent Software will also leverage Community Involvement to support Advent's business strategy, streamline program operations, and support employees and the company.

Geographic Focus: California, Massachusetts, New York, China, Denmark, India, Netherlands, Norway, Singapore, Sweden, Switzerland, United Kingdom
Contact: Director; (415) 543-7696; fax (415) 543-5070; nfo@advent.com
Internet: http://www.advent.com/about/community-involvement
Sponsor: Advent Software Corporation
600 Townsend Street
San Francisco, CA 94103

AEC Trust Grants 58

The AEC Trust is a private foundation established in 1980 as a philanthropic, grantmaking organization. The trust awards grants to eligible nonprofits in Colorado, Florida, Georgia, and Massachusetts in its areas of interest, including: AIDS, arts and culture, community development, elementary education, the environment, health care, higher education, social services, museums, and women. Types of support include building construction/renovation, capital campaigns, challenge/matching grants, equipment acquisition, general operating support, land acquisition, project support, and publications. Request guidelines in writing. There are two annual deadlines: April 1 and September 1.

Requirements: 501(c)3 nonprofit organizations in the communities of Boulder, Colorado, Gainesville, Florida, Atlanta, Georgia, and Amherst, Massachusetts, are eligible.

Restrictions: Grants do not support individuals, international organizations, political organizations, religious organizations, school districts, special events/benefit dinners, state and local government agencies, United Way agencies, national public charities, endowments, sponsorships, or annual fund campaigns.

Geographic Focus: Colorado, Florida, Georgia, Massachusetts
Date(s) Application is Due: Apr 1; Sep 1
Amount of Grant: 5,000 - 50,000 USD
Samples: Center for Human Development, Amherst, Massachusetts, $50,000 - Family Outreach Amherst Project; Conservation Trust for Florida, Micanopy, Florida, $50,000 - Land Conservation and Landowner Education; Feminist Women's Health Center, Atlanta, Georgia, $5,000 - Lifting Latino Voices Initiative.
Contact: Edith Dee Cofrin, Chairperson; (800) 839-1754 or (401) 881-3409; requests@foundationsource.com
Internet: https://online.foundationsource.com/public/home/aec
Sponsor: AEC Trust
501 Silverside Road, Suite 123
Wilmington, DE 19809-1377

AED New Voices Fellowship Program 59

The program seeks to strengthen small nonprofit organizations by supporting resident fellows who can bring a new voice to an organization and its field of work. Applications are reviewed under one of the following categories: foreign policy, peace and security; HIV/AIDS; international economic policy international human rights; migrant and refugee rights; racial justice and civil rights; and women's and reproductive rights. Awards include support for fellow's salary, fringe benefits, and to purchase a computer. Preference is given to nonprofits with budgets between $100,000 and $2 million. Applications are prepared jointly by an organization and its proposed fellow.

Requirements: 501(c)3 nonprofit organizations that reflect diverse educational, cultural, and experiential backgrounds are eligible. Potential fellows should have completed an undergraduate or graduate degree or have comparable education, skills, and relevant experience.

Restrictions: Groups with budgets of more than $5 million are not eligible.

Geographic Focus: All States

Date(s) Application is Due: Jan 10
Amount of Grant: 100,000 USD
Contact: Officer; (202) 884-8607; fax (202) 884-8400; newvoice@aed.org
Internet: http://www.aed.org/newvoices
Sponsor: Academy for Educational Development
1825 Connecticut Avenue NW, Suite 744
Washington, D.C. 20009-5721

AEGON Transamerica Foundation Arts and Culture Grants 60

The AEGON Transamerica Foundation will consider favorably grants to established organizations with reputations for excellence and cost-effectiveness. The Foundation's Arts and Culture Grants program is interested in supporting programs that foster creativity in the areas of music and the performing arts, including venues for artistic expression; all of which contribute to the quality of life, sustainability and growth of our communities. Types of support include continuing support, matching funds, operating budgets, employee-related scholarships, and special projects. Contributions are normally made on a year-to-year basis with no assurance of renewal of support. In certain cases, pledges may be considered for periods not exceeding three years.

Requirements: Nonprofit organizations within the Foundation's focus areas and mission, and that are designated for a community where there is a significant employee presence are eligible. Requests can be directed to the attention of the AEGON Transamerica Foundation at one of the following locations: Louisville, Kentucky; Atlanta, Georgia; Baltimore, Maryland; Bedford, Texas; Cedar Rapids, Iowa; Exton, Pennsylvania; Harrison, New York; Little Rock, Arkansas; Los Angeles, California; Plano, Texas; and St. Petersburg, Florida.

Restrictions: Individuals, as well as the following types of organizations or programs are not eligible to receive grants from the Foundation: athletes or athletic organizations; conferences, seminars or trips; courtesy or goodwill advertising; fellowships; fraternal organizations; K-12 school fundraisers or events; political parties, campaigns or candidates; religious or denominational organizations except for specific programs broadly promoted and available to anyone and free from religious orientation; or social organizations.

Geographic Focus: Arkansas, California, Florida, Georgia, Iowa, Kentucky, Maryland, New York, Pennsylvania, Texas
Amount of Grant: 1,000 - 50,000 USD
Contact: David Blankenship, Foundation President; (319) 398-8895 or (319) 355-8511; fax (319) 398-8030; david.blankenship@transamerica.com or shaegontransfound@aegonusa.com
Internet: http://www.transamerica.com/about_us/aegon_transamerica_foundation.asp
Sponsor: AEGON Transamerica Foundation
4333 Edgewood Road, NE
Cedar Rapids, IA 52499-0010

AEGON Transamerica Foundation Civic and Community Grants 61

The AEGON Transamerica Foundation will consider favorably grants to established organizations with reputations for excellence and cost-effectiveness. The Foundation's Civic and Community Grants provides funding for programs that strive to promote community development, encourage civic leadership, enhance workforce and business development opportunities, and empower people and strengthen communities. Types of support include continuing support, matching funds, operating budgets, employee-related scholarships, and special projects. Contributions are normally made on a year-to-year basis with no assurance of renewal of support. In certain cases, pledges may be considered for periods not exceeding three years.

Requirements: Nonprofit organizations within the Foundation's focus areas and mission, and that are designated for a community where there is a significant employee presence are eligible. Requests can be directed to the attention of the AEGON Transamerica Foundation at one of the following locations: Louisville, Kentucky; Atlanta, Georgia; Baltimore, Maryland; Bedford, Texas; Cedar Rapids, Iowa; Exton, Pennsylvania; Harrison, New York; Little Rock, Arkansas; Los Angeles, California; Plano, Texas; and St. Petersburg, Florida.

Restrictions: Individuals, as well as the following types of organizations or programs are not eligible to receive grants from the Foundation: athletes or athletic organizations; conferences, seminars or trips; courtesy or goodwill advertising; fellowships; fraternal organizations; K-12 school fundraisers or events; political parties, campaigns or candidates; religious or denominational organizations except for specific programs broadly promoted and available to anyone and free from religious orientation; or social organizations.

Geographic Focus: Arkansas, California, Florida, Georgia, Iowa, Kentucky, Maryland, New York, Pennsylvania, Texas
Amount of Grant: 1,000 - 50,000 USD

Contact: David Blankenship, Foundation President; (319) 398-8895 or (319) 355-8511; fax (319) 398-8030; david.blankenship@transamerica.com or shaegontransfound@aegonusa.com
Internet: http://www.transamerica.com/about_us/aegon_transamerica_foundation.asp
Sponsor: AEGON Transamerica Foundation
4333 Edgewood Road, NE
Cedar Rapids, IA 52499-0010

AEGON Transamerica Foundation Health and Welfare Grants   62
The AEGON Transamerica Foundation will consider favorably grants to established organizations with reputations for excellence and cost-effectiveness. The Foundation's Health and Welfare Grants initiative is interested in supporting programs committed to improving the condition of the human body through nutrition, housing for the homeless, disease prevention and other support services. Types of support include continuing support, matching funds, operating budgets, employee-related scholarships, and special projects. Contributions are normally made on a year-to-year basis with no assurance of renewal of support. In certain cases, pledges may be considered for periods not exceeding three years.
Requirements: Nonprofit organizations within the Foundation's focus areas and mission, and that are designated for a community where there is a significant employee presence are eligible. Requests can be directed to the attention of the AEGON Transamerica Foundation at one of the following locations: Louisville, Kentucky; Atlanta, Georgia; Baltimore, Maryland; Bedford, Texas; Cedar Rapids, Iowa; Exton, Pennsylvania; Harrison, New York; Little Rock, Arkansas; Los Angeles, California; Plano, Texas; and St. Petersburg, Florida.
Restrictions: Individuals, as well as the following types of organizations or programs are not eligible to receive grants from the Foundation: athletes or athletic organizations; conferences, seminars or trips; courtesy or goodwill advertising; fellowships; fraternal organizations; K-12 school fundraisers or events; political parties, campaigns or candidates; religious or denominational organizations except for specific programs broadly promoted and available to anyone and free from religious orientation; or social organizations.
Geographic Focus: Arkansas, California, Florida, Georgia, Iowa, Kentucky, Maryland, New York, Pennsylvania, Texas
Amount of Grant: 1,000 - 50,000 USD
Contact: David Blankenship, Foundation President; (319) 398-8895 or (319) 355-8511; fax (319) 398-8030; david.blankenship@transamerica.com or shaegontransfound@aegonusa.com
Internet: http://www.transamerica.com/about_us/aegon_transamerica_foundation.asp
Sponsor: AEGON Transamerica Foundation
4333 Edgewood Road, NE
Cedar Rapids, IA 52499-0010

AFG Industries Grants   63
The corporation awards general operating grants to nonprofits in its headquarters area in the categories of arts and humanities, civic and public affairs, education at all levels, health care, and social services. There are no application deadlines. Submit a brief letter of inquiry.
Requirements: Tennessee nonprofits are eligible.
Geographic Focus: Tennessee
Amount of Grant: 100,000 - 250,000 USD
Contact: Human Resources; (800) 251-0441 or (423) 229-7200; fax (423) 229-7459
Internet: http://www.afgglass.com
Sponsor: AFG Industries
P.O. Box 929
Kingsport, TN 37662

African American Fund of New Jersey Grants   64
Since 1980 the African American Fund of New Jersey (AAFNJ) has touched the lives of more than three million people who live in New Jersey urban areas. The fund concentrates on providing significant funding to New Jersey's African-American communities to promote and enhance human-services delivery and community empowerment. Primary funding consideration is given to proposals which fall in the areas of pre-school through high-school educational initiatives, technology initiatives, environmental and health-related initiatives, community issues, and building wealth. Programs that emphasize positive family values, traditions, social customs, and family practices that have contributed to the survival of the African-American family are encouraged. Types of support include general operating grants, program

development grants, and technical assistance. Proposals must demonstrate the intention to commit the necessary financial and human resources to a program that is well coordinated with related human services within the respective communities. Annual deadline dates may vary; prospective applicants should contact program staff or visit the AAFNJ website for exact dates, guidelines, and application forms.
Requirements: Any 501(c)3 agency, community-based organization, or school operating in the state of New Jersey may submit a proposal to AAFNJ for funding consideration. AAFNJ also accepts applications from organizations that are closely aligned with theirs.
Geographic Focus: New Jersey
Date(s) Application is Due: Sep 1
Amount of Grant: 500 - 5,000 USD
Samples: Actor's Shakespeare Co., Jersey City, New Jersey; Community Empowerment Organization, Pleasantville, New Jersey; South Jersey Interfaith Coalition for Literacy, Cherry Hill, New Jersey.
Contact: Sondra Clark; (973) 676-5283; fax (973) 672-5030; sclark@aafnj.org
Internet: http://www.aafnj.org/index.php/grants/grants
Sponsor: African American Fund of New Jersey
132 South Harrison Street
East Orange, NJ 07018

African American Heritage Grants   65
Grants are awarded to assist organizations in the preservation and promotion of historic African American properties and sites in Indiana. Awards are made on a four-to-one matching basis, funding 80% of the total project cost up to $2,500, whichever is less.
Requirements: Civic groups, schools, libraries, historical societies, and other nonprofit agencies are eligible to apply for grants for organizational assistance, studies assisting in or leading to the preservation of a historic African American place, and programs promoting the preservation, interpretation, and/or visitation of a historic African American place. Contact the regional community preservation specialist that serves your community (see website for list of regional offices or contact the state headquarters office) for guidelines and forms.
Restrictions: Properties must be located in Indiana.
Geographic Focus: Indiana
Amount of Grant: 500 - 2,500 USD
Samples: Historic Eleutherian College Inc. - $2,500 to pay for a comprehensive master restoration and conservation plan for the c.1850 former African American college, which is now a National Historic Landmark.
Contact: Carla Jones, Receptionist, State Headquarters; (317) 639-4534; fax (317) 639-6734; info@historiclandmarks.org
Internet: http://www.historiclandmarks.org/help/grants.html
Sponsor: Historic Landmarks Foundation of Indiana
340 W Michigan Street
Indianapolis, IN 46202

A Friends' Foundation Trust Grants   66
The Foundation, founded as the Hubbard Foundation in 1959 by philanthropist Frank M. Hubbard, primarily serves central Florida with its support of health research and health care, education at all levels, children and youth activities, the arts, and religious agencies. Grants typically range from $5,000 to $35,000, though some higher amounts are given. There are no specific application formats or deadlines with which to adhere, and applicants should send a letter of request to the Foundation address listed.
Requirements: Applicants must be 501(c)3 organizations serving the residents of central Florida.
Geographic Focus: Florida
Amount of Grant: 5,000 - 35,000 USD
Samples: Fisher House Foundation, Rockville, Maryland, $5,000 - general operations; Bok Tower Gardens, Lake Wales, Florida, $22,500 - general operations; Adult Literacy League, Orlando, Florida, $2,000 - general operations.
Contact: L. Evans Hubbard, (407) 876-3122; ehubbard@cfl.rr.com
Sponsor: A Friends' Foundation Trust
9000 Hubbard Place
Orlando, FL 32819

Agnes Gund Foundation Grants   67
The foundation awards general operating grants in its areas of interest, including health organizations, higher education, and performing arts (dance, music). There are no application deadlines or forms. Submit a letter of inquiry.
Requirements: Although there are no funding restrictions there is a focus on New York City.

Restrictions: Applicants must be a tax-exempt organization.
Geographic Focus: New York
Amount of Grant: 5,000 - 100,000 USD
Samples: Museum of Modern Art (New York, NY)—for general operating support, $1 million; Cleveland Museum of Art (OH)—for general operating support, $200,000; Virginia Museum of Fine Arts (Richmond, VA)—for general operating support, $100,000; Creative Capital Foundation (New York, NY)—for general operating support, $75,000.
Contact: Program Director; (330) 385-3400
Sponsor: Agnes Gund Foundation
517 Broadway, 3rd Floor
East Liverpool, OH 43920

Air Products and Chemicals Grants   68

The foundation supports nonprofit organizations in company-operating areas in the fields of precollege and higher education; fitness, health, and welfare; community and economic development, arts and culture; and the environment and safety. Types of support include capital grants, employee matching gifts, general operating support, multiyear-continuing grants, project grants, seed grants, fellowships, employee-related scholarships, and donated equipment. There are no application forms; requests must be in writing. Guidelines are available online.
Requirements: 501(c)3 nonprofits in company-operating areas are eligible.
Restrictions: Grants are not made to/for individuals, sectarian or denominational organizations, political candidates or activities, veterans organizations, organizations receiving United Way support, labor groups, elementary or secondary schools, capital campaigns of national organizations, hospital operating expenses, national health organizations, or goodwill advertising.
Geographic Focus: All States
Contact: Kassie Hilgert, Program Manager; hilgerk@airproducts.com
Internet: http://www.airproducts.com/Responsibility/SocialResponsibility
Sponsor: Air Products and Chemicals Corporation
7201 Hamilton Boulevard
Allentown, PA 18195-1501

Akonadi Foundation Anti-Racism Grants   69

The foundation's mission is to work with others to eliminate racism, with a particular focus on structural and institutional racism. Grants have supported programmatic approaches including research, policy work, advocacy, litigation, organizing, media, arts, diversity training, education, and other tools in their anti-racism work. The foundation awards general operating grants and project grants. Grants are made to organizations in the San Francisco Bay area and to national organizations with national reach. Letters of interest will be accepted year round. Full proposals should only be submitted upon request.
Geographic Focus: California
Date(s) Application is Due: Feb 18
Amount of Grant: 10,000 - 50,000 USD
Samples: Asian Pacific Environmental Network (Oakland, CA)—to involve Asian-Pacific Islanders in grassroots organizing to fight environmental racism, $20,000; Ctr for Third World Organizing (Oakland, CA)—for general support, $30,000; Leadership Excellence (Oakland, CA)—for leadership development for black youths and for critical analysis of racism, $25,000; Poverty and Race Research Action Council (Washington DC)—to support a civil-rights teaching curriculum, institutes on civil rights, and teacher workshops, $25,000.
Contact: Grants Administrator; (510) 663-3867; info@akonadi.org
Internet: http://www.akonadi.org/application_guidelines.html
Sponsor: Akonadi Foundation
469 9th Street, Suite 210
Oakland, CA 94607

Alabama Power Foundation Grants   70

The foundation's mission is to improve the lives and circumstances of Alabama residents and to strengthen the communities in which they live. It supports programs that will improve education (by supporting innovative programs and assisting teachers in their crucial responsibilities), strengthen communities, promote arts and culture or restore and enhance the environment. The project must meet several of the guidelines to be considered. The majority of grants are made to support targeted efforts with specific objectives. The foundation also provides general operating assistance to organizations, capital grants for endowment and building, and scholarship funds. Applications should be sent to the local Alabama Power Company office for review and recommendation to the foundation. The amount of the request determines the review frequency.
Requirements: Applications are accepted from Alabama nonprofit organizations whose programs fall within foundation guidelines.

Restrictions: Grants are not made to individuals, for sectarian religious purposes, or for political activities.
Geographic Focus: Alabama
Date(s) Application is Due: Feb 1; May 1; Aug 1; Nov 1
Amount of Grant: 1,000 - 100,000 USD
Contact: William Johnson, President; (205) 257-2508; fax (205) 257-1860
Internet: http://www.alabamapower.com/foundation/grantsandinitiatives.asp
Sponsor: Alabama Power Foundation
600 N 18th Street, P.O. Box 2641
Birmingham, AL 35291-0011

Alabama State Council on the Arts Community Operating Support   71
Grants

The Community Arts Program supports projects which may include, but are not limited to community festivals, after-school programs, performances, workshops, or exhibitions. Projects that increase the capacity of an arts organization or groups of artists are also eligible. Established Local Arts Councils and Arts Centers with a successful track record of diverse programs and services in the community and region may qualify for an Operating Support grant. Successful applicants should have support and cooperation from local governmental entities. This category provides support and stability to large arts organizations with far-reaching cultural impact, year round operations and strong community service and educational outreach. Interested applicants are strongly encouraged to seek counsel from a program manager prior to submitting an application. The Council must approve an organization's eligibility for this category. Note that a letter of intent to apply must be submitted one year in advance. The annual deadline for final applications is June 1.
Requirements: To be eligible for operating support, an organization must meet all these requirements: be incorporated and recognized as having non-profit tax exempt status by the Internal Revenue Service for at least three years prior to application, or have been an agency of a city or county government for that length of time; have an actual three-year average cash income of at least $600,000; have a full-time administrative staff responsible for the overall functions of the organization; and have an annual audit conducted by an independent Certified Public Accountant.
Geographic Focus: Alabama
Date(s) Application is Due: Jun 1
Contact: Deb Boykin, Community Arts Program Manager; (334) 242-4076, ext. 243; fax (334) 240-3269; deb.boykin@arts.alabama.gov or staff@arts.alabama.gov
Internet: http://www.arts.state.al.us/programs/community_arts/operate_support.aspx
Sponsor: Alabama State Council on the Arts
201 Monroe Street, Suite 110
Montgomery, AL 36130-1800

Alabama State Council on the Arts Performing Arts Operating   72
Support Grants

The Performing Arts grant program supports projects and activities which are presented to ensure that high quality performances of music, dance and theater are available to Alabama audiences and to support Alabama's performing arts organizations and artists. Eligible projects and activities may include producing, commissioning, planning processes and touring. Operating Support grants are awarded to organizations that demonstrate a consistent track record of high artistic achievement, public service, and managerial competency. Eligible organizations are expected to also have a well-developed and sustainable educational outreach program. Grant funds are discretionary and may be used in the day- to- day institutional activities of the organization in order to encourage originality and maintain a high level of artistic excellence in production.
Requirements: New operating support applicants must submit a one year notification (in writing) of intent to apply. The deadline for this notification is June 1 of previous fiscal year. New applicants must have sustained threshold budget level (verified by independent audit) for two years before letter of intent. Applicants must prove a three-year average cash income of at least $650,000.
Geographic Focus: Alabama
Contact: Yvette Jones-Smedley, Performing Arts Program Manager; (334) 242-4076, ext. 226; fax (334) 240-3269; yvette.jones-smedley@arts.alabama.gov or staff@arts.alabama.gov
Internet: http://www.arts.state.al.us/programs/performing_arts/operate_support_grant.aspx
Sponsor: Alabama State Council on the Arts
201 Monroe Street, Suite 110
Montgomery, AL 36130-1800

Alabama State Council on the Arts Visual Arts Operating Support Grants 73

The goal of the Alabama State Council on the Arts Visual Arts program is to nurture excellence, professionalism, multiculturalism, audience access, and educational impact in the disciplines of painting, sculpture, crafts, print-making, design, photography, filmmaking, and media that have origins and/or impact in Alabama. Operating Support grants provide support and stability to large arts organizations with far-reaching cultural impact. Funding is provided for general program development and to stimulate private and additional public funding. Eligible groups are expected to be well established with ongoing fundraising efforts. They must show a high level of professionalism, both artistically and administratively, and must engage in strong community service and educational outreach. The annual deadline for application submission is June 1.
Requirements: Operating Support grants are available to major presenters, museums, art centers, local art councils, and professional arts producing institutions. To be eligible for Operating Support, an organization must have a three-year average cash income of at least $800,000. New organizations seeking Operating Support funding must submit a one year notification in writing of their intent to seek Operating Support funding.
Geographic Focus: Alabama
Contact: Elliot A. Knight, Visual Arts Program Manager; (334) 242-4076, ext. 250; fax (334) 240-3269; elliot.knight@arts.alabama.gov or staff@arts.alabama.gov
Internet: http://www.arts.state.al.us/programs/visual_arts/operate_support.aspx
Sponsor: Alabama State Council on the Arts
201 Monroe Street, Suite 110
Montgomery, AL 36130-1800

Aladdin Industries Foundation Grants 74

The foundation awards grants, primarily in Tennessee, in its areas of interest, including arts and culture, youth services, health and human services, education, business, drug abuse, and the elderly. Types of support include general operating support, seed grants, and employee-related scholarships. Proposals are reviewed quarterly.
Requirements: Most grants are awarded in Tennessee. Proposals are reviewed quarterly.
Geographic Focus: Tennessee
Contact: L.B. Jenkins, Secretary & Treasurer; (615) 748-3360
Sponsor: Aladdin Industries Foundation
703 Murfreesboro Road
Nashville, TN 37210-4521

Alaska State Council on the Arts Operating Support Grants 75

Alaska State Council on the Arts Operating Support Grants assist with a portion of an organization's ongoing artistic and administrative functions. These may include, but are not limited to, salaries, travel, promotion, and production costs of an entire program or a majority of the organization's yearly activities. The council funds applications in all areas of the arts: dance, visual arts, literature, music, theater, media arts, and traditional Native arts. Applications that promote and develop the cultural heritage of Alaska and the creation of new works by Alaskan artists are encouraged.
Requirements: The council awards funds only to Alaskan nonprofit organizations, schools, or government agencies. Eligible organizations must: be involved in producing, presenting, or undertaking a series of events or ongoing arts programs; provide proof of 501(c)3 status; be at least three years from the date of incorporation; and have a cash budget of at least $50,000. A maximum award amount is not set; however, applicants must provide matching funds, and grants will not exceed 50 percent of the total cash expenses.
Geographic Focus: Alaska
Date(s) Application is Due: Mar 1
Contact: Andrea Noble-Pelant, Visual and Literary Arts Program Director; (907) 269-6605 or (907) 269-6610; fax (907) 269-6601; andrea.noble@alaska.gov
Internet: https://www.eed.state.ak.us/aksca/grants2.html#osla
Sponsor: Alaska State Council on the Arts
161 Klevin Street, Suite 102
Anchorage, AK 99508-1506

Alberta Law Foundation Grants 76

The objectives of the foundation are to conduct research into and recommend reform of law and the administration of justice; establish, maintain, and operate law libraries; contribute to the legal education and knowledge of the people of Alberta and provide programs and facilities for those purposes; provide assistance to native people's legal programs, student legal aid programs, and programs of like nature; and contribute to the costs incurred by the Legal Aid Society of Alberta to administer a plan to provide legal aid. To be considered for funding, programs or projects must fall within these objectives. Operating grants and project grants are awarded. The application process begins with a discussing the program or project idea with the executive director. This will be followed by an exchange of drafts during the development of the application.
Restrictions: Grants will not be made to an individual or for the support of a commercial venture. Funds are not available for bursaries, fellowships, sabbatical leave support, endowments, building funds, etc.
Geographic Focus: All States, Canada
Contact: David Aucoin, Executive Director; (403) 264-4701; fax (403) 294-9238; contact@albertalawfoundation.org
Internet: http://www.albertalawfoundation.org/Apply/general.html
Sponsor: Alberta Law Foundation
407 8th Avenue SW, Suite 300
Calgary, AB T2P 1E5 Canada

Albert and Bessie Mae Kronkosky Charitable Foundation Grants 77

The charitable foundation supports efforts to improve the quality of life in San Antonio-area counties for the elderly and those with disabilities; programs encouraging character and leadership development of youth; efforts to free children from abuse and neglect; cultural activities and broadening public participation in museums and libraries; improvement of public parks, zoos, and wildlife sanctuaries; prevention of cruelty to animals; and assistance for victims of public disasters in Texas. The foundation also supports a computer resources program that is designed to build the capacity of nonprofit organizations. Eligible organizations may submit proposals for computer resources for administrative purposes, such as office administration, program evaluation, donor management, and client tracking. Letters of inquiry may be submitted at any time. The distribution committee will meet bi-monthly in January, March, May, July, September and November.
Requirements: Nonprofits in Texas counties Bandera, Bexar, Comal, and Kendall, are eligible to receive grant support.
Restrictions: Grants do not support economic development, annual fund and fundraising event sponsorships, political or lobbying activities, or religious organizations for sectarian purposes.
Geographic Focus: Texas
Amount of Grant: 550 - 1,000,000 USD
Samples: Operations grant of $132,450 to enable St. Paul Lutheran Child Development Center to continue is parenting education program; operations grant of $57,300 to St. Peter the Apostle Catholic Church to continue its parenting education program.
Contact: Grants Administrator; (888) 309-9001 or (210) 475-9000; fax (210) 354-2204; kronfndn@kronkosky.org
Internet: http://www.kronkosky.org
Sponsor: Albert and Bessie Mae Kronkosky Charitable Foundation
112 E Pecan Street, Suite 830
San Antonio, TX 78205

Alberto Culver Corporate Contributions Grants 78

The company prefers to make small donations to a large number of organizations rather than substantial contributions to a few institutions. Major areas of support are civic and community programs, health and welfare, education, culture and art, and youth activities. Special consideration is given to proposals that benefit a large number of people; directly or indirectly assist women's groups or other purchasers or potential customers of Alberto-Culver products; are involved in programs that rehabilitate, train, teach skills or employ the underprivileged, handicapped or minorities; have received support from Alberto-Culver in the past; and received matching grants for donations. Grants are awarded for one year and may be renewed.
Requirements: Only 501(c)3 organizations are eligible. Requests should be in writing on organization letterhead and should state amount requested, and whether the donation will be used for operating funds, capital expansion, supplies or special projects. The objectives and programs of the organization should be clearly defined.
Restrictions: Grants are not awarded to support United Way affiliates, religious groups, preschools, K-12 schools, tax-supported colleges, projects that duplicate other efforts, and multiyear commitments.
Geographic Focus: All States
Contact: V. James Marino, Director; (708) 450-3000; fax (708) 450-3435
Internet: http://www.alberto.com
Sponsor: Alberto Culver
2525 Armitage Avenue
Melrose Park, IL 60160

Albert Pick Jr. Fund Grants 79

The fund contributes to organizations in the following categories: culture, education, health and human services, civic and community organizations. The fund will consider assistance to new and creative programs within these areas and to operating support. Support will be given to requests from organizations that conduct their programs in Chicago, IL, only. The fund functions on a calendar year; applications are considered four times a year based on dates of board meetings. The fund prefers that prospective grantees call or write for guidelines prior to sending their proposals.

Requirements: Only Illinois organizations may apply.

Restrictions: Funds will not be provided for reduction or liquidation of debts, religious purposes, endowments, long-term commitments, building programs, individuals, political purposes, or advertising/program books.

Geographic Focus: Illinois

Date(s) Application is Due: Jan 21; Apr 1; Jul 1; Oct 1

Amount of Grant: 3,000 USD

Samples: Children First Fund/CPS Foundation (Gale Academy Links to Literacy Program) $6900; Art Resources in Teaching (Chicago, IL)—for general operating support, $7500; Chicago Academy of Sciences/Peggy Notebaert Nature Museum (Chicago, IL)—for general operating support, $10,000; Chicago Opera Theater (Chicago, IL)—for general operating support, $10,000.

Contact: Cleopatra Alexander, Executive Director; (312) 236-1192; cleopatra@albertpickjrfund.org

Internet: http://www.albertpickjrfund.org

Sponsor: Albert Pick Jr. Fund

30 N Michigan Avenue, Suite 1002

Chicago, IL 60602

Albertson's Charitable Giving Grants 80

Albertson's Inc invests in its operating communities and makes corporate contributions to support nonprofits. Areas of charitable giving include health and hunger relief—food banks, churches, and other community-based relief groups; health and nutrition—medical services, flu shots, health screening for diseases such as diabetes and heart disease; and education and development of youth—academic excellence or nurturing efforts. Submit requests in writing and include information about the organization's goals, accomplishments, evaluation plans, leadership, and finances. Requests are accepted throughout the year.

Requirements: Tax-exempt organizations in Arizona, Arkansas, California, Colorado, Delaware, Florida, Georgia, Idaho, Illinois, Indiana, Iowa, Kansas, Louisiana, Maine, Maryland, Massachusetts, Michigan, Minnesota, Mississippi, Missouri, Montana, Nebraska, Nevada, New Hampshire, New Jersey, New Mexico, North Dakota, Oklahoma, Oregon, Pennsylvania, South Dakota, Tennessee, Texas, Utah, Vermont, Washington, Wisconsin, and Wyoming are eligible. Applicants must pass an online eligibility test. Preference will be given to requests that offer volunteerism opportunities.

Restrictions: Contributions cannot be made to churches or religious organizations for purposes of religious advocacy.

Geographic Focus: Arizona, Arkansas, California, Colorado, Delaware, Florida, Georgia, Idaho, Illinois, Indiana, Iowa, Kansas, Louisiana, Maine, Maryland, Massachusetts, Michigan, Minnesota, Mississippi, Missouri, Montana, Nebraska, Nevada, New Hampshire, New Jersey, New Mexico, North Dakota, Oklahoma, Oregon, Pennsylvania, South Dakota, Tennessee, Texas, Utah, Vermont, Washington, Wisconsin, Wyoming

Contact: Community Relations Manager; (877) 932-7948 or (208) 395-6200; fax (208) 395-4382; albertsonscustomercare@albertsons.com

Internet: http://www.albertsons.com/abs_inthecommunity

Sponsor: Albertson's

250 E Parkcenter Boulevard

Boise, ID 83706

Albert W. Cherne Foundation Grants 81

The foundation awards grants to nonprofit organizations, primarily in Minnesota, for general operating support, continuing support, and annual campaigns in its areas of interest, which include adult basic education and literacy, children and youth services, services for the disabled, and human services.

Requirements: Grants support nonprofit organizations primarily in the five-county metropolitan area of Minneapolis and Saint Paul, MN.

Restrictions: Grants do not support veterans, fraternal, or labor organizations; religious purposes; conduit organizations; civil rights/social action groups; mental health counseling; specific-disease organizations; housing programs; individuals; capital improvements; or endowment funds.

Geographic Focus: Minnesota

Amount of Grant: 1,000 - 55,000 USD

Samples: Planned Parenthood of Minnesota (Saint Paul, MN)—to support a high-risk youth program, $5000; Loring Nicollet-Bethlehem Community Ctrs (Minneapolis, MN)—to support adult education and literacy programs, $12,000; YMCA, Greater Lake County Family (Waukegan, IL)—for a dining hall, $75,000.

Contact: Sara Ribbens, President; (952) 944-4378; fax (952) 944-3070; sararibbens@awchernefoundation.org

Sponsor: Albert W. Cherne Foundation

P.O. Box 975

Minneapolis, MN 55440

Albert W. Rice Charitable Foundation Grants 82

The Albert W. Rice Charitable Foundation was established in 1959 to support and promote quality educational, human-services, and health-care programming for underserved populations. In the area of education, the foundation supports academic access, enrichment, and remedial programming for children, youth, adults, and senior citizens that focuses on preparing individuals to achieve while in school and beyond. In the area of health care, the foundation supports programming that improves access to primary care for traditionally underserved individuals, health education initiatives and programming that impact at-risk populations, and medical research. In the area of human services the foundation tries to meet evolving needs of communities. Currently the foundation's focus is on (but is not limited to) youth development, violence prevention, employment, life-skills attainment, and food programs. Grant requests for general operating support are strongly encouraged. Program support and occasional capital support will also be considered. Special consideration is given to charitable organizations that serve the people of Worcester, Massachusetts, and its surrounding communities. The majority of grants from the Rice Foundation are one year in duration; on occasion, multi-year support is awarded. Applicants must apply online at the grant website. Applicants are strongly encouraged to do the following before applying: review the downloadable state application procedures for additional helpful information and clarifications; review the downloadable online-application guidelines at the grant website; review the foundation's funding history (link is available from the grant website); review the online application questions in advance; and review the list of required attachments. These will generally include: a list of board members, financial statements (audited, reviewed, or compiled by independent auditor); an organization summary; a list of other funding sources; an IRS Determination letter; and other required documents. All attachments must be uploaded in the online application as PDF, Word, or Excel files. The application deadline for the Albert W. Rice Charitable Foundation is 11:59 p.m. on July 1. Applicants will be notified of grant decisions before September 30.

Requirements: Applicants must have 501(c)3 tax-exempt status.

Restrictions: The foundation does not support requests from individuals, organizations attempting to influence policy through direct lobbying, or any political campaigns.

Geographic Focus: Massachusetts

Date(s) Application is Due: Jul 1

Samples: Big Brothers, Big Sisters of Central Massacusetts Metrowest, Worcester, Massachusetts, $30,000, program development; Youth Opportunities Upheld, Worcester, Massachusetts, $20,000, Dynamic Youth Academy; Legal Assistance Corporation of Central Massachusetts, Worcester, Massachusetts, $20,000.

Contact: Michealle Larkins; (866) 778-6859; michealle.larkins@baml.com

Internet: https://www.bankofamerica.com/philanthropic/fn_search.action

Sponsor: Albert W. Rice Charitable Foundation

225 Franklin Street, 4th Floor, MA1-225-04-02

Boston, MA 02110

Albuquerque Community Foundation Grants 83

The foundation seeks to improve the quality of life in the greater Albuquerque, New Mexico, area by providing support for projects and organizations that serve the community in arts and culture, education, environmental and historic preservation, children and youth, and health and human services. Through its grant program, the foundation supports projects that are innovative, meet the needs of underserved segments of the community, encourage matching funds or additional gifts, promote cooperation among agencies, empower the disadvantaged and disabled, and enhance the effectiveness of local charitable organizations. Types of support include continuing support, general operating support, program development, publication, seed grants, scholarships funds and scholarships to individuals, and technical assistance.

Requirements: IRS 501(c)3 organizations based in Albuquerque, NM, are eligible. Proposals are reviewed on the basis of the following priorities: impact, innovation, leverage, management, and nonduplication.

Restrictions: Grants are generally not made to or for individuals, political or religious purposes, debt retirement, payment of interest or taxes, annual campaigns, endowments, emergency funding, to influence legislation or elections, scholarships, awards, or to private foundations and other grantmaking organizations.

Geographic Focus: New Mexico

Date(s) Application is Due: Apr 16; Aug 15

Amount of Grant: Up to 10,000 USD

Contact: R. Randall Royster, Executive Director; (505) 883-6240; fax (505) 883-3629; rroyster@albuquerquefoundation.org

Internet: http://www.albuquerquefoundation.org/grants/grant-home.htm

Sponsor: Albuquerque Community Foundation

P.O. Box 36960

Albuquerque, NM 87176-6960

Alcatel-Lucent Technologies Foundation Grants 84

The Alcatel-Lucent Foundation is the philanthropic arm of Alcatel-Lucent and it leads the company's charitable activities. With a focus on volunteerism, the Foundation's mission is to support the commitment of Alcatel-Lucent to social responsibility by serving and enhancing the communities where its employees and customers live and work. To accomplish its mission, the Foundation manages grants and employee volunteerism on a global level. It receives its income from the corporation - Alcatel-Lucent - whose name it bears. However, legally the Foundation is an independent, charitable, non-profit and private entity and is governed by its own board of trustees that is separate from the corporate board of directors. Global Foundation grants are dedicated to the main focus areas of the Foundation and are managed by the Foundation.

Requirements: Giving is on an international basis.

Geographic Focus: All States, All Countries

Amount of Grant: 500 - 5,000 USD

Contact: Bishalakhi Ghosh, Executive Director; +91-99-58418547 or +91-22-66798700; fax +91-22-26598542; bishalakhi.ghosh@alcatel-lucent.com

Internet: http://www.alcatel-lucent.com/wps/portal/foundation

Sponsor: Alcatel-Lucent Technologies Foundation

600 Mountain Avenue, Room 6F4

Murray Hill, NJ 07974-2008

Alcoa Foundation Grants 85

General priorities of the foundation include safe and healthy children and families—ensuring that children and their families have the tools, the knowledge and the services to remain healthy and safe at home, in the community and in the workplace; conservation and sustainability—educating young leaders on conservation issues, protecting forests, promoting sound public policy research, and understanding the linkages between business and the environment; skills today for tomorrow—providing individuals with critical skills and services to be economically connected, workplace-ready, and productive in a changing economy; business and community partnerships—strengthening the nonprofit sector and developing meaningful partnerships among nonprofits, the private sector, and local government; and global education in science, engineering, technology and business—broadening student participation in areas central to Alcoa to prepare a diverse cross-section of our communities for a global workplace. Types of support include capital grants, building funds, challenge grants, matching gifts, general support, research grants, scholarships, and seed money. Initial contact should be a letter of inquiry.

Requirements: The foundation awards grants to nonprofit public charities in communities where Alcoa has a presence. Local Alcoans work within their communities to evaluate organizations and make recommendations for funding to Alcoa Foundation. Nonprofit organizations that serve localized communities should find the Alcoa facility nearest to them and write a one-page letter describing their mission, nature of request, connection to the areas of excellence and offering contact information. If interested, the Alcoa location contact will notify the requesting organization and invite them to submit more information. Areas of operation include western Pennsylvania; Davenport, Iowa; Evansville, Indiana; Massena, New York; New Jersey; Cleveland, Ohio; Knoxville, Tennessee; and Rockdale, Texas.

Restrictions: The foundation does not make gifts to local projects other than those near Alcoa plant or office locations; endowment funds, deficit reduction, or operating reserves; hospital capital campaign programs unless the hospital presents a comprehensive area analysis that justifies, on a regional rather than an individual institutional basis, the need for the capital improvement;

individuals, except for the scholarship program for children of Alcoa employees; tickets and other promotional activities; trips, tours, or student exchange programs; or documentaries and videos.

Geographic Focus: All States

Amount of Grant: 1,000 - 50,000 USD

Contact: Meg McDonald, President and Treasurer; (412) 553-2348; fax (412) 553-4498; alcoa.foundation@alcoa.com

Internet: http://www.alcoa.com/global/en/community/foundation.asp

Sponsor: Alcoa Foundation

201 Isabella Street

Pittsburgh, PA 15212-5858

Alcon Foundation Grants 86

The foundation supports organizations in the fields of health care, leadership programs, research, education and community responsibility. Programs that advance the education and skill levels of eye care professionals are given special consideration. General operating grants to organizations and institutions improving education and research in the areas of specialization of Alcon Laboratories—ophthalmology and vision care. Grants are also awarded to community activities that benefit company employees. Applications may be submitted at any time.

Requirements: Grants are not made for building programs.

Restrictions: Non 501(c)3organizations, individuals and scholarship programs, religious, veterans or fraternal organizations, political causes, capital campaigns, matching gifts, trips, tournaments and tours, and endowments are not supported.

Geographic Focus: All States

Amount of Grant: 100 - 50,000 USD

Samples: National Sjogrens Syndrome Assoc (Phoenix, AZ)—for general operating support, $2500.

Contact: Mary Dulle, Chair; (817) 293-0450; Mary.Dulle@Alconlabs.com

Internet: http://www.alconlabs.com/corporate-responsibility/alcon-foundation.asp

Sponsor: Alcon Foundation

6201 S Freeway

Fort Worth, TX 76134

Alexander & Baldwin Foundation Mainland Grants 87

The foundation awards grants to eligible U.S. nonprofit organizations in its areas of interest, including health and human services, education, the community, culture and arts, the maritime arena and the environment. Grant preferences are given to organizations and projects that address significant community needs, have the active support of A&B employees, are preventive in nature, and have demonstrated support of the community. Start-up, general operating and special project needs, as well as major and minor capital requests are considered. Although the majority of grants range between $1,000 and $5,000, the Foundation considers request upward of $20,000.

Requirements: The foundation gives funding to community-based projects and organizations that qualify with 501(c)3 status.

Restrictions: Grants are not awarded to support United Way agencies for operating support, individuals, events, travel expenses, or scholarships.

Geographic Focus: All States

Date(s) Application is Due: Jan 1; Feb 1; Mar 1; Apr 1; May 1; Jun 1; Jul 1; Aug 1; Sep 1; Oct 1; Nov 1; Dec 1

Amount of Grant: 1,000 - 5,000 USD

Contact: Paul L. Merwin, (707) 421-8121; fax (707) 421-1835; plmifm@aol.com

Internet: http://www.alexanderbaldwinfoundation.org/appguide.htm

Sponsor: Alexander and Baldwin Foundation

555 12th Street

Oakland, CA 94607

Alexander and Baldwin Foundation Hawaiian and Pacific Island Grants 88

The Alexander and Baldwin Foundation awards grants to eligible Hawaii nonprofit organizations in its areas of interest, including health and human services, education, the community, culture and arts, the maritime arena and the environment. Grant preferences are given to organizations and projects that address significant community needs, have the active support of A&B employees, are preventive in nature, and have demonstrated support of the community. Start-up, general operating and special project needs, as well as major and minor capital requests are considered. Deadlines listed are for organizations in Hawaii and the Pacific Islands. Although the majority of grants range between $1,000 and $5,000, the Foundation considers request upward of $20,000.

Requirements: The foundation gives funding to community-based projects and organizations that qualify with 501(c)3 status.

Restrictions: Grants are not awarded to support United Way agencies for operating support, individuals, events, travel expenses, or scholarships.
Geographic Focus: Hawaii
Date(s) Application is Due: Feb 1; Apr 1; Jun 1; Aug 1; Oct 1; Dec 1
Amount of Grant: 1,000 - 5,000 USD
Contact: Linda M. Howe, (808) 525-6642; fax (808) 525-6677; lhowe@abinc. com or giving@abinc.com
Internet: http://alexanderbaldwin.com/corporate-responsibility/commitment/
Sponsor: Alexander and Baldwin Foundation
P.O. Box 3440
Honolulu, HI 96801-3440

Alexander Eastman Foundation Grants 89

The purposes of the Alexander Eastman Foundation are served through grant support to organizations awarded in response to proposals and special initiative commitments planned collaboratively by the Foundation with local service providers. Grants are awarded to support the capital, special projects and operations needs of qualifying organizations. In considering proposals, priority is given to funding activity which serves the Foundation's priority interests. The Alexander Eastman Foundation supports: Education - provide information and community education to improve the health and well-being of residents of the greater Derry area; address goals for healthy individuals and families through a long-term commitment to prevention, health promotion and education of consumers and providers; foster individual responsibility, independence, self-care and healthy life-style choices; Family Systems - strengthen families as the critical unit for community health and well-being; recognize the changing nature of families and provide resources and assistance to reduce stress on families and improve family function; Access - expand access to quality health care and prevention services for people with financial need. Applications are available at the Foundations website.
Requirements: Nonprofit organizations serving Derry, Londonderry, Windham, Chester, Hampstead, and Sandown, NH, are eligible.
Restrictions: Grants are made neither to individuals nor to qualifying organizations to support the cost of services to particular individuals, except through the Alexander Eastman Scholarship Program.
Geographic Focus: New Hampshire
Date(s) Application is Due: Apr 1; Oct 1
Contact: Amy Lockwood, Director of Grants; (888) 228-1821, ext. 80; alockwood@alexandereastman.org
Internet: http://www.alexandereastman.org/02grants.html
Sponsor: Alexander Eastman Foundation
26 South Main Street, PMB 250
Concord, NH 03301

Alexander H. Bright Charitable Trust Grants 90

The trust operates in Massachusetts and awards general operating grants to nonprofit organizations in its areas of interest, including wildlife and environmental conservation, children and youth, education, and social services. There are no application forms. The board meets in March, June, September, and December.
Requirements: Northeast U.S. nonprofits are eligible. Preference is given to requests from Massachusetts.
Geographic Focus: Connecticut, Maine, Massachusetts, New Hampshire, Rhode Island, Vermont
Amount of Grant: 100 - 75,000 USD
Contact: Grants Administrator; (617) 227-2676 or (617) 624-0800
Sponsor: Alexander H. Bright Charitable Trust
88 Broad Street
Boston, MA 02110

Alex Stern Family Foundation Grants 91

The Alex Stern Family Foundation awards grants to North Dakota and Minnesota nonprofits in its areas of interest, which include: arts and culture; child welfare; the elderly; alcohol abuse; community affairs; family and social services; education; minorities; hospices; and cancer research. Types of support include: general operating support; continuing support; annual campaigns; building construction and renovation; equipment acquisition; emergency funds; program development; scholarship funds; research; and matching funds. The annual deadlines for submission are March 31 and August 31. Applications are reviewed in June and November. Most recent awards have ranged from $1,000 up to $75,000.
Requirements: Moorhead, Minnesota, and Fargo, North Dakota, nonprofit organizations are eligible to apply.

Restrictions: Grants are not awarded to individuals or for endowments.
Geographic Focus: Minnesota, North Dakota
Date(s) Application is Due: Mar 31; Aug 31
Amount of Grant: 1,000 - 75,000 USD
Samples: Dakota Medical Foundation, Fargo, North Dakota, $75,000 - capital campaign; Blue Stem Performing Center, Noorhead, Minnesota, $20,000 - general operating support; Jamestown College, Jamestown, North Dakota, $7,500 - scholarship funding.
Contact: Donald L. Scott, Executive Director; (701) 237-0170; fax (701) 271-0408; donlscott@yahoo.com
Sponsor: Alex Suitern Family Foundation
4141 28th Avenue South
Fargo, ND 58104-8468

Alfred and Tillie Shemanski Testamentary Trust Grants 92

Alfred Shemanski was an immigrant from Poland with little formal education. He understood the struggles of being a stranger in a strange land and became a champion for both Jewish and secular education. His successes never blinded him to the plight of those less fortunate. Mr. Shemanski exercised philanthropy in the purest definition of the word — love of mankind. The Alfred & Tillie Shemanski Trust was established in 1974 to: improve the capacity of and cooperation among Jewish congregations in the City of Seattle, Washington; support interfaith tolerance and understanding; provide scholarship assistance, primarily to the University of Washington and Seattle University; and support and promote quality educational, human-services, and health-care programming for economically disadvantaged individuals and families. Grant requests for general operating support, start-up funding, and prizes or awards are encouraged. Grants from the Shemanski Trust are one year in duration. Application materials are available for download at the grant website. Applicants are strongly encouraged to review the state application guidelines for additional helpful information and clarifications before applying. Applicants are also encouraged to review the trust's funding history (link is available from the grant website). The application deadline for the Shemanski Trust is October 15. Applicants will be notified of grant decisions before November 30.
Requirements: Applicants must serve residents of the Seattle and Puget Sound area.
Restrictions: Requests for fundraising events or sponsorship opportunities will not be considered. The trust does not support requests from individuals, organizations attempting to influence policy through direct lobbying, or any political campaigns.
Geographic Focus: Washington
Date(s) Application is Due: Oct 15
Samples: Seattle University, Seattle, Washington, $45,000, for Schemanski Scholarship Fund; College Success Foundation, Issaquah, Washington, $10,000, scholarship funds; Temple De Hirsch Sinai, Seattle, Washington, $35,000, education initiative; Mockingbird Society, Seattle, Washington, $10,000, Mockingbird Network (foster-youth-led program)(2010).
Contact: Nancy Atkinson; (800) 848-7177; nancy.l.atkinson@baml.com
Internet: https://www.bankofamerica.com/philanthropic/fn_search.action
Sponsor: Alfred and Tillie Shemanski Testamentary Trust
800 5th Avenue, WA1-501-33-23
Seattle, WA 98104

Alfred Bersted Foundation Grants 93

The Alfred Bersted Foundation was established in 1972 to support and promote quality educational, human services, and health care programming for underserved populations. The Foundation specifically serves the people of DeKalb, DuPage, Kane, and McHenry counties in Illinois. Application materials are available for download at the grant website. Applicants are strongly encouraged to review the state application guidelines for additional helpful information and clarifications before applying. Applicants are also encouraged to review the foundation's funding history (link is available from the grant website). The foundation has a rolling application deadline. In general, applicants will be notified of grant decisions three to four months after proposal submission. The annual deadlines for application submission are April 15 and September 15, with decisions being made by June 30 and November 30, respectively.
Requirements: Applicant organizations must have 501(c)3 tax-exempt status and a physical presence in one of the following counties: DeKalb, DuPage, Kane, or McHenry.
Restrictions: The Alfred Bersted Foundation does not make grants to degree-conferring institutions of higher education, religious houses of worship, or organizations testing for public safety. In general, grant requests for endowment campaigns will not be considered.
Geographic Focus: Illinois

Date(s) Application is Due: Apr 15; Sep 15
Contact: Debra L. Grand, Senior Vice President; (312) 828-2055; ilgrantmaking@ustrust.com
Internet: https://www.bankofamerica.com/philanthropic/fn_search.action
Sponsor: Alfred Bersted Foundation
231 South LaSalle Street, IL1-231-13-32
Chicago, IL 60604

Alfred C. and Ersa S. Arbogast Foundation Grants 94

The Alfred C. and Ersa S. Arbogast Foundation, established in Indiana, supports organizations and programs throughout the State of Indiana, as well as a few throughout the United States. The Foundation's primary fields of interest include: animal/wildlife preservation and protection; human service programs; and United Ways and federated programs. The major type of support being offered is general operations funding. There are no particular deadlines or application formats with which to adhere, and applicants should submit the following: copy of IRS determination letter; and a detailed description of the project, with the amount of funding requested.
Requirements: 501(c)3 organizations located in, or supporting the residents of, Indiana can apply, as well as non-profits whose goals are aligned with the Arbogast Foundation's.
Geographic Focus: All States
Samples: Truck of Love, Rock Hill, South Carolina, $2,500 - general operations; Colorado Music Festival, Lafayette, Colorado, $1,500 - general operations funding; Goshen Community Chorale, Goshen, Indiana, $1,000, - general operating funds.
Contact: Michelle Kindler; (260) 428-5009 or (574) 267-9187
Sponsor: Alfred C. and Ersa S. Arbogast Foundation
114 E. Market Street, P.O. 1387
Warsaw, IN 46580

Alfred E. Chase Charitable Foundation Grants 95

The Alfred E. Chase Charitable Foundation was established in 1956 to support and promote quality educational, human-services, and health-care programming for underserved populations. Special consideration is given to charitable organizations that serve the people of the city of Lynn and the North Shore of Massachusetts. The foundation is a generous supporter of the Associated Grant Makers (AGM) Summer Fund which provides operating support for summer camps serving low-income urban youth from Boston, Cambridge, Chelsea, and Somerville. Excluding the grant to the AGM Summer Fund, the typical grant range is $10,000 to $30,000. In the area of education the foundation supports academic access, enrichment, and remedial programming for children, youth, adults, and senior citizens that focuses on preparing individuals to achieve while in school and beyond. In the area of human services the foundation supports organizations meeting the basic needs of all individuals to include but not limited to youth development, violence prevention, employment, life skills attainment, and food programs. In the area of health care, the foundation supports programming that improves access to primary care for traditionally underserved individuals, as well as supporting health education initiatives and programs that impact at-risk populations. Grant requests for general operating support are strongly encouraged. Program support will also be considered. Small, program-related capital expenses may be included in general operating or program requests. The majority of grants from the Chase Charitable Foundation are one year in duration. On occasion, multi-year support is awarded. Applicants must apply online at the grant website. Applicants are strongly encouraged to do the following before applying: review the downloadable Massachusetts state application procedures for additional helpful information and clarifications; review the downloadable online-application guidelines at the grant website; review the foundation's funding history (link is available from the grant website); review the online application questions in advance; and review the list of required attachments. These will generally include: a list of board members, financial statements (audited, reviewed, or compiled by independent auditor); an organization summary; a list of other funding sources; an IRS Determination letter; and other required documents. All attachments must be uploaded in the online application as PDF, Word, or Excel files. The application deadline is 11:59 p.m. on April 1. Applicants will be notified of grant decisions before June 30.
Requirements: Applicants must have 501(c)3 tax-exempt status.
Restrictions: The foundation does not support requests from individuals, organizations attempting to influence policy through direct lobbying, or any political campaigns.
Geographic Focus: Massachusetts
Date(s) Application is Due: Apr 1

Amount of Grant: 10,000 - 30,000 USD
Samples: Uphams Corner Community Center, Dorchester, Massachusetts, $15,000; Massachusetts Advocates for Children, Boston, Massachusetts, $20,000; Union Social Action Foundation, Cambridge, Massachusetts, $15,000.
Contact: Miki C. Akimoto; (866) 778-6859; miki.akimoto@baml.com
Internet: https://www.bankofamerica.com/philanthropic/fn_search.action
Sponsor: Alfred E. Chase Charitable Foundation
225 Franklin Street, 4th Floor, MA1-225-04-02
Boston, MA 02110

Alfred I. DuPont Foundation Grants 96

Grants are awarded primarily to elderly adults requiring health, economic, or educational assistance. Support is also given for higher education and medical research. All grants to the elderly are made to individuals in the southeastern United States. General operating support and grants to individuals are awarded. An application form is required. Applications are accepted at any time and are dealt with promptly.
Requirements: Nonprofit organizations in the southeastern U.S. are eligible. Preference is given to those in Florida.
Geographic Focus: Florida
Amount of Grant: 1,000 - 35,000 USD
Contact: Rosemary Cusimano Wills, Secretary; (904) 232-4123
Sponsor: Alfred I. DuPont Foundation
4600 Touchton Road E, Building 200, Suite 120
Jacksonville, FL 32246

Alfred P. Sloan Foundation Civic Initiatives Grants 97

The goal of the Program is to make a contribution to the Foundation's home area, New York City. There are two directions to the Program: to respond to special opportunities in New York City; and to fund high-leverage projects in New York City that are related to other parts of our program. Interested readers should refer to the descriptions of other program areas in the Foundation website. Grant requests can be made at any time for support of activities related to Foundation program areas and interests. The Foundation is generally limited to supporting tax-exempt organizations.
Requirements: Concise, well-organized proposals are preferred. In no case should the body of the proposal exceed 20 double-spaced pages.
Restrictions: The Foundation's activities do not normally extend to religion, the creative or performing arts, elementary or secondary education, medical research or health care, the humanities or to activities outside the United States. Grants are not made for endowments or for buildings or equipment.
Geographic Focus: New York
Contact: Paula J. Olsiewski, Program Director; (212) 649-1658 or (212) 649-1649; fax (212) 757-5117; olsiewski@sloan.org
Internet: http://www.sloan.org/major-program-areas/select-national-issues/civic-initiatives/
Sponsor: Alfred P. Sloan Foundation
630 Fifth Avenue, Suite 2200
New York, NY 10111-0242

A Little Hope Grants 98

A Little Hope is a not-for-profit publicly supported charitable foundation, recognized by the IRS under 501(c)3, which grants funds to organizations that provide bereavement support services and grief counseling to children and teens who have experienced the death of a parent, sibling or loved one. Strong preference is given to applicants who demonstrate a commitment to the use of community trained volunteers, whose programs demonstrate multicultural competence in addressing children and adolescent's bereavement needs, and whose programs are likely to be replicable in other communities. Grant applications are by invitation only and are processed during the last quarter of each year. To be considered, email (no telephone calls): the name of your program, your website address, the name of your executive director, and the name of the program director, including their credentials. No other information is needed or will be processed. Do not send letters of inquiry or any other materials unless they have been requested by A Little Hope. No other organizations are authorized to solicit RFP's or information on our behalf.
Geographic Focus: All States
Contact: Tanhya Vancho, Vice President and Secretary; (516) 639-6727; granting@alittlehope.org
Internet: http://www.alittlehope.org/granting/applicants.aspx
Sponsor: A Little Hope
810 Seventh Avenue, 37th Floor
New York, NY 10019

Allegheny Foundation Grants 99

The foundation awards general operating grants, seed grants, and grants for projects and programs to nonprofit organizations in western Pennsylvania in the areas of education, historic preservation, and civic development. There are no application forms or deadlines. The foundation generally considers grants at an annual meeting held in November; however, requests may be submitted at any time and will be reviewed as soon as possible.

Requirements: Initial inquiries should be in letter form signed by the organization's president, or authorized representative, and have the approval of the board of directors. The letter should include a concise description of the specific program for which funds are requested. Additional information must include a budget for the program and for the organization, the latest audited financial statement, an annual report, and a board of director's list. A copy of the organization's 501(c)3 letter is required. Only Pennsylvania residents may apply.

Restrictions: Grants are not made to individuals.

Geographic Focus: Pennsylvania

Amount of Grant: 1,000 - 100,000 USD

Samples: Allegheny Institute for Public Policy—$100,000; The Extra Mile Education Foundation, Inc.—$100,000; Beginning with Books, Inc.— $25,000; Historical Society of Carnegie Pennsylvania—$10,000.

Contact: Matthew Groll, Executive Director; (412) 392-2900

Internet: http://www.scaife.com/alleghen.html

Sponsor: Allegheny Foundation

1 Oxford Center, 301 Grant Street, Suite 3900

Pittsburgh, PA 15219-6401

Allegheny Technologies Charitable Trust 100

The corporation awards one-year renewable grants to nonprofit organizations to enhance the quality of life for people in company operating locations. Areas of interest include arts and culture, civic and public affairs, education, health, and social services. Types of support include capital grants, general operating grants, program development grants, and employee matching gifts. Applicants should submit a letter of inquiry that describes the organization, purpose of grants, and funds sought. No particular form or information is required. Potential applicants are requested to provide proof of exempt public charity status. There are no deadlines.

Requirements: 501(c)3 organizations in company-operating areas are eligible.

Restrictions: Contributions are made only to public charities. Individuals and private foundations are excluded.

Geographic Focus: Pennsylvania

Amount of Grant: 1,000 - 35,000 USD

Contact: Jon D. Walton, Jr., Trustee; (412) 394-2800; fax (412) 394-3034

Internet: http://www.alleghenytechnologies.com

Sponsor: Allegheny Technologies

1000 Six PPG Place

Pittsburgh, PA 15222

Allen Hilles Fund Grants 101

The fund awards grants to support education, women's issues, economic development in disadvantaged communities, activities of the Religious Society of Friends, and organizations with annual budgets of less than $2 million. Types of support include project grants, seed money, and operating support for small organizations.

Requirements: Philadelphia-area and Wilmington, Delaware, nonprofit organizations are eligible.

Restrictions: Funding requests for endowments, scholarships, capital expenditures, political purposes, or agency promotion (i.e., marketing, development, publication of annual reports, or fundraising events) are denied.

Geographic Focus: Delaware, Pennsylvania

Date(s) Application is Due: Feb 1; May 1; Oct 1

Amount of Grant: 3,000 - 10,000 USD

Samples: Fellowship Farm (Pottstown, PA)—to support the Peace and Unity summer camp, $3000; Fair Hill Burial Ground Corporation (Philadelphia, PA)— to support children's educational programming, $2000; Women's Law Project (Philadelphia, PA)—for operating support, $3000; Simpson United Memorial United Methodist Church (Philadelphia, PA)—to support an after-school program, $3000.

Contact: Judith L. Bardes, Manager; (610) 828-8145; fax (610) 834-8175; hilles@grants-info.org or judy1@aol.com

Internet: http://www.grants-info.org/hilles

Sponsor: Allen Hilles Fund

P.O. Box 540

Plymouth Meeting, PA 19462

Alletta Morris McBean Charitable Trust Grants 102

The foundation awards grants in the areas of historic preservation and land preservation/conservation to organizations located in and around Newport, RI. Grant requests are considered two times each year when the trustees meet. Types of programs to receive support include capital construction; environmental programs; exhibitions, collections, and performances; general operations; seed funds; materials/equipment acquisition; preservation/ restoration; matching/challenge grants; and capital campaigns.

Requirements: Rhode Island tax-exempt organizations in Newport and Aquidneck Island are eligible.

Geographic Focus: Rhode Island

Date(s) Application is Due: Feb 28; Jul 31

Amount of Grant: 50,000 - 100,000 USD

Samples: Foundation for Newport (RI)—for general operating support, $70,000; Preservation Society of Newport County (RI)—$500,000.

Contact: Charlene Kleiner, (650) 558-8480; fax (650) 558-8481; McBeanproperties@worldnet.att.net

Sponsor: Alletta Morris McBean Charitable Trust

400 S El Camino Real, Suite 777

San Mateo, CA 94402-1724

Alliant Energy Corporation Contributions 103

As a complement to its Foundation, the Alliant Energy Corporation also makes charitable contributions to local, county, and regional nonprofit organizations directly. Support is given primarily in areas of company operations in Illinois, Iowa, Minnesota, and Wisconsin; giving also to national organizations. The Corporation's primary areas of interest include: breast cancer; community development; diabetes; economic development; employment; energy resources; the environment; financial services; housing development; human services; job training and retraining; and sustainable development. Types of support include: fundraising; general operations; outreach; program development; scholarship funds; sponsorships; technical assistance; and volunteer development. A formal application is required, although there are no identified annual deadlines.

Geographic Focus: Illinois, Iowa, Minnesota, Wisconsin

Contact: Jo Ann Healy, Contributions Manager; (608) 458-5718; fax (608) 458-0134; joannhealy@alliantenergy.com

Internet: http://www.alliantenergy.com/CommunityInvolvement/ CommunityOutreach/RequestSponsorshipsAdvertising/index.htm

Sponsor: Alliant Energy Corporation

4902 N. Biltmore Lane, Suite 1000

Madison, WI 53718-2148

Allstate Corporate Hometown Commitment Grants 104

Allstate takes a special interest in the greater Chicagoland community, the company's hometown for more than 75 years. The corporation is particularly invested in this community because it recognizes that a thriving hometown is critical to Allstate's success. The company recruits local talent, relies on local infrastructure, and depends on the city's vibrancy to ensure that its associates have a rich quality of life. By supporting organizations that build strong Chicagoland communities, the company contributes to the city's position as a center of global culture, education and business.

Requirements: The Allstate Corporation makes grants to Chicago area nonprofit, tax-exempt groups under Section 501(c)3 of the Internal Revenue Code.

Geographic Focus: Illinois, Indiana

Contact: Executive Director; (847) 402-5000 or (847) 402-5502; fax (847) 326-7517; allfound@allstate.com

Internet: http://www.allstate.com/social-responsibility/corporate/corporate-giving.aspx

Sponsor: Allstate Corporation

2775 Sanders Road, Suite F4

Northbrook, IL 60062

Alpha/Omega Charitable Foundation Grants 105

Established in the State of Florida in 1994, the Alpha/Omega Charitable Foundation is interested in supporting: animal and wildlife preservation/ protection; overall animal welfare; environmental land resources; higher education; and human services. Its primary geographic focus is in Florida and Connecticut. Since no application form is required, applicants should submit a detailed description of their project, a budget narrative and budget detail, a brief history and mission of the organization, and any attached descriptive literature available at the time of submission. The annual deadline is September 30, and funded projects range from $5,000 to $30,000.

Geographic Focus: Connecticut, Florida

Date(s) Application is Due: Sep 30
Amount of Grant: 5,000 - 30,000 USD
Samples: Coral Spring Harbor Laboratories, Coral Spring Harbor, New York, $25,000 - general operations; Green Vale School, Old Brookville, New York, $25,000 - general educational programs; Adopt A Dog, Greenwich, Connecticut, $15,000 - general operations.
Contact: Larry B. Alexander, Vice President; (203) 622-9360
Sponsor: Alpha/Omega Charitable Foundation
31 Brookside Drive
Greenwich, CT 06830-6422

Alpha Natural Resources Corporate Giving   106

The Alpha Natural Resources Corporate Giving program makes contributions to nonprofit organizations involved with helping children and families, improving education, strengthening arts and culture programs, and providing social services to those in need of health care and emergency fuel. Its primary fields of interest include: aging centers and services; the arts; children's services; primary education; secondary education; the environment; family services; food services; health care; higher education; housing and shelter; human services; substance abuse prevention; and youth development. Types of support given include: annual campaigns, product donations; employee volunteer services; scholarships; general operating support; and matching funds.
Requirements: Applicants must be 501(c)3 organizations located in, or serving the residents of, areas in which Alpha Natural Resources operates. These include selected regions of Kentucky, Illinois, Pennsylvania, Virginia, and West Virginia.
Geographic Focus: Illinois, Kentucky, Pennsylvania, Virginia, West Virginia
Amount of Grant: Up to 20,000 USD
Contact: Corporate Giving Administrator; (276) 619-4410
Internet: Alpha Natural Resources Corporate Giving
Sponsor: Alpha Natural Resources
1 Alpha Place, P.O. Box 16429
Bristol, VA 24209

Alpine Winter Foundation Grants   107

Established in California in 1963, the Alpine Winter Foundation's primary purpose is to support alpine safety, health programs, and education within the Tahoe-Donner, California, region. Applications should be in the form of a written request, and should include the specific purpose and history of the requesting organization. There are no specific deadlines with which to adhere.
Requirements: Giving is limited to organizations described in Section 170(b)(1)(a) and Section 501(c)3(a) that promote alpine safety, heath, and education within the Tahoe-Donner area of California,
Geographic Focus: California
Amount of Grant: Up to 40,000 USD
Contact: Mary S. Tilden, President; (415) 221-7762
Sponsor: Alpine Winter Foundation
3863 Jackson Street, P.O. Box 591659
San Francisco, CA 94118-1610

Altman Foundation Arts and Culture Grants   108

The Foundation mission is to support programs and institutions that enrich the quality of life in New York City, with a particular focus on initiatives that help individuals, families and communities benefit from the services and opportunities that will enable them to achieve their full potential. The Foundation has had a longstanding interest in the arts, reflecting not only Benjamin Altman's personal commitment, but also the Foundation's recognition of the value of the arts in enriching the lives of New Yorkers and the city as a whole. In this program area, the Foundation seeks: to promote positive youth development through arts and cultural programming; to promote the acquisition of pre-professional arts skills among under-served youth; and to promote access to the arts for under-served populations.
Requirements: IRS 501(c)3 organizations in New York are eligible.
Restrictions: Grants are not awarded to individuals. As a general rule, the foundation does not consider requests for bricks and mortar funds or the purchase of capital equipment.
Geographic Focus: New York
Amount of Grant: 10,000 - 100,000 USD
Samples: Brooklyn Botanic Garden Corporation—to help support the Garden Apprentice Program for middle and high school youth, $40,000; Figure Skating in Harlem—to help support the after-school skating and health program, $25,000; Rocking the Boat—to help support the Job Skills Program, $50,000.

Contact: Karen L. Rosa, Vice President and Executive Director; (212) 682-0970; krosa@altman.org
Internet: http://www.altmanfoundation.org/guide.html
Sponsor: Altman Foundation
521 Fifth Avenue, 35th Floor
New York, NY 10175

Altman Foundation Strengthening Communities Grants   109

The Foundation mission is to support programs and institutions that enrich the quality of life in New York City, with a particular focus on initiatives that help individuals, families and communities benefit from the services and opportunities that will enable them to achieve their full potential. The Foundation has an historic interest in ensuring that individuals and families living in the city have access to the services and resources they need to pursue and sustain successful lives. The Foundation has chosen to focus on efforts that: build and preserve economic security and independence among lowincome individuals and families; and promote and sustain the availability of, and equitable access to, essential community resources needed to support stable, healthy communities.
Requirements: IRS 501(c)3 organizations in New York are eligible.
Restrictions: Grants are not awarded to individuals. As a general rule, the foundation does not consider requests for bricks and mortar funds or the purchase of capital equipment.
Geographic Focus: New York
Amount of Grant: 10,000 - 100,000 USD
Contact: Karen L. Rosa, Vice President and Executive Director; (212) 682-0970; krosa@altman.org
Internet: http://www.altmanfoundation.org/guide.html
Sponsor: Altman Foundation
521 Fifth Avenue, 35th Floor
New York, NY 10175

Altria Group Arts and Culture Grants   110

For more than 50 years, Altria Group has been a strong supporter of both the visual and performing arts. The Group champions organizations that inspire and reflect the qualities it values in its business operations – creativity, diversity, excellence and innovation. Altria supports arts and cultural initiatives in Richmond, Virginia, Washington, D.C., and other communities where its companies operate. The Group's arts and culture grants are focused on: innovative programs to develop new audiences and increase access to the arts; major sponsorships that bring thought-provoking, world-class cultural experiences to our communities; and arts education programs that enhance the overall performance and development of middle school students, primarily in the public schools of Greater Richmond, Virginia.
Requirements: Unsolicited applications are generally not accepted. The company utilizes an invitation process for giving, which is the result of a letter of inquiry.
Geographic Focus: District of Columbia, Virginia
Date(s) Application is Due: Jan 30
Amount of Grant: 15,000 - 1,000,000 USD
Contact: Grants Administrator; (804) 274-2200
Internet: http://www.altria.com/en/cms/Responsibility/investing-in-communities/programs/arts-and-culture/default.aspx
Sponsor: Altria Group
6601 West Broad Street
Richmond, VA 23230-1723

Altria Group Education Grants   111

Quality education is the bedrock of our children's success and our country's continued progress. Yet, recent studies have shown that American students are lagging their international peers in important measures of performance and success. The Group supports organizations working to improve educational outcomes for underserved youth, while also addressing the demand for a diverse, highly skilled workforce. Altria and its companies focus their education contributions in four areas: middle-and high-school enrichment programs for urban public schools, particularly those that contribute to everyday student success, math and science excellence, and access to and preparation for higher education; technical education at community colleges and universities, including agricultural studies programs at select land-grant institutions; strengthening management skills among school leaders; and higher education and scholarship support. The Group's contributions are primarily focused in Central Virginia, with some donations in other geographies where Altria's companies operate. Altria also supports major national scholarship organizations and colleges and universities where we recruit future employees.

Requirements: Unsolicited applications are generally not accepted. The company utilizes an invitation process for giving, which is the result of a letter of inquiry.
Geographic Focus: All States
Amount of Grant: 1,000 - 75,000 USD
Contact: Program Manager; (804) 274-2200
Internet: http://www.altria.com/en/cms/Responsibility/investing-in-communities/programs/education/default.aspx
Sponsor: Altria Group
6601 West Broad Street
Richmond, VA 23230-1723

Altria Group Positive Youth Development Grants 112

Philip Morris USA has had a focus on positive youth development since the creation of its Youth Smoking Prevention department in 1998. Today that program has evolved to Underage Tobacco Prevention, and Altria's tobacco operating companies invest in a range of programs to support its goals of helping reduce underage tobacco use. As part of these efforts, the Group's tobacco operating companies have become a leading funder of positive youth development in the U.S. These investments focus on organizations and programs that emphasize kids' strengths, promote positive behaviors, connect youth with caring adults and enhance community-based resources for kids. These programs are designed to help kids develop the confidence and skills they need to avoid risky behaviors, such as underage tobacco use. The Group's tobacco companies also support adolescent tobacco cessation programs. Its tobacco operating companies' funding supports organizations that: provide evidence-based programs for kids like mentoring, life skills education and substance abuse prevention curricula; help national youth-serving organizations reach more young people, improve program quality and better measure their impact; help community leaders align youth programs and policies; and conduct research on effective positive youth development programs.
Requirements: Unsolicited applications are generally not accepted. The company utilizes an invitation process for giving, which is the result of a letter of inquiry.
Geographic Focus: All States
Date(s) Application is Due: Feb 20
Amount of Grant: 10,000 - 75,000 USD
Contact: Grants Administrator; (804) 274-2200
Internet: http://www.altria.com/en/cms/Responsibility/investing-in-communities/programs/positive_youth_development/default.aspx
Sponsor: Altria Group
6601 West Broad Street
Richmond, VA 23230-1723

Alvin and Fanny Blaustein Thalheimer Foundation Grants 113

The foundation makes grants that strengthen the lives of individuals, families, and communities in the Baltimore region. Program areas include economic opportunity—technical and business entrepreneurship training, and asset-building strategies; health and human services—improve quality of service, and advocacy and policy initiatives; arts and culture—strengthening education and outreach programs that link arts institutions with communities and schools; and strengthening Jewish communities—renewal and development of communities in Eastern Europe and the Former Soviet Union; and addressing threats of anti-Semitism. Guidelines are available online.
Requirements: Only Maryland organizations are eligible to apply.
Restrictions: Grants are not made to individuals.
Geographic Focus: Maryland
Samples: Bon Secours of Maryland Foundation, $135,000 over three years for Our Money Place, a financial service center for the low-income communities of West Baltimore; Caroline Center, $40,000 over two years for occupational training programs designed to help economically disadvantaged women become self- sufficient; CASA of Maryland, $70,000 over two years for the Financial Empowerment Program at the Baltimore Worker's Rights Center; Center for Fathers, Families, and Workforce Development, $50,000 over two years.
Contact: Betsy Ringel, Executive Director; (410) 347-7103; fax (410) 347-7210; info@blaufund.org
Internet: http://www.blaufund.org/foundations/alvinandfanny_f.html
Sponsor: Alvin and Fanny Blaustein Thalheimer Foundation
10 E Baltimore Street, Suite 1111
Baltimore, MD 21202

AMA Foundation Fund for Better Health Grants 114

The philosophy of the AMA Foundation Fund for Better Health begins with the idea that local communities and organizations have great knowledge and insight into their community's health care issues. Based on this thought, the AMA Foundation, with support from the AMA Alliance, created the Fund for Better Health. Through this program, the AMA Foundation provides seed grants for grassroots, public health projects in communities throughout America. Over the years, the fund has provided over 200 grants totaling nearly $300,000 to projects that address healthy lifestyles, domestic violence prevention, substance abuse prevention, health literacy, patient safety and care for the uninsured. A maximum of $5,000 will be distributed to each grant recipient. The number of grant recipients will be determined by the AMA Foundation after all applications have been received. Typically, the number of grants awarded does not exceed twenty.
Requirements: Organizations are eligible to apply for grants which further the charitable and educational purposes of the AMA Foundation. Grants made in 2009 support programs addressing the issue of healthy lifestyles in the areas of nutrition and physical fitness, alcohol, substance abuse and smoking prevention (and cessation), and violence prevention. The three types of organizations eligible to apply are organizations with annual operating budgets of $1 million or less; new organizations begun in the last 5 years; or established organizations starting a new service or expanding a current service to an underserved population.
Restrictions: None of the funds awarded are to pay for staff salary or overhead expenses.
Geographic Focus: All States
Date(s) Application is Due: Jul 15
Amount of Grant: Up to 5,000 USD
Contact: Dina Lindenberg, Program Officer; (312) 464-4193; fax (312) 464-5973; dina.lindenberg@ama-assn.org or amafoundation@ama-assn.org
Internet: http://www.ama-assn.org/ama/pub/about-ama/ama-foundation/our-programs/public-health/fund-better-health.shtml
Sponsor: American Medical Association Foundation
515 N State Street
Chicago, IL 60654

Amelia Sillman Rockwell and Carlos Perry Rockwell Charities Grants 115

The Amelia Sillman Rockwell and Carlos Perry Rockwell Charities Fund was established in 1962 to support and promote quality educational, human-services, and health-care programming for underserved populations. Special consideration is given to charitable organizations that serve children or the elderly. Grant requests for general operating support are strongly encouraged. Program support will also be considered. Small, program-related capital expenses may be included in general operating or program requests. The majority of grants from the Rockwell Charities Fund are one year in duration; on occasion, multi-year support is awarded. Applicants must apply online at the grant website. Applicants are strongly encouraged to do the following before applying: review the downloadable state application procedures for additional helpful information and clarifications; review the downloadable online-application guidelines at the grant website; review the foundation's funding history (link is available from the grant website); review the online application questions in advance; and review the list of required attachments. These will generally include: a list of board members, financial statements (audited, reviewed, or compiled by independent auditor); an organization summary; a list of other funding sources; an IRS Determination letter; and other required documents. All attachments must be uploaded in the online application as PDF, Word, or Excel files. The application deadline for the Rockwell Charities Fund is 11:59 p.m. on February 1. Applicants will be notified of grant decisions before May 31.
Requirements: Applicants must have 501(c)3 tax-exempt status.
Restrictions: The trust does not support requests from individuals, organizations attempting to influence policy through direct lobbying, or any political campaigns.
Geographic Focus: Massachusetts
Date(s) Application is Due: Feb 1
Samples: Elizabeth Stone House, Jamaica Plains, Massachusetts, $10,000, general operating support; First Congregational Church, South Windsor, Connecticut, $1,000, for favored charity of Rockwell; Rogerson Communities, Boston, Massachusetts, $10,000, Adult Day Health Programs.
Contact: Miki C. Akimoto; (866) 778-6859; miki.akimoto@baml.com
Internet: https://www.bankofamerica.com/philanthropic/fn_search.action
Sponsor: Amelia Sillman Rockwell and Carlos Perry Rockwell Charities Fund
225 Franklin Street, 4th Floor, MA1-225-04-02
Boston, MA 02110

Ameren Corporation Community Grants 116

The corporation awards grants in Ameren Illinois and Ameren Missouri service areas to programs in arts and culture, civic affairs, public safety, housing, higher education, services for youth and the elderly, and the environment. Types of support include annual campaigns, building construction and renovation, capital campaigns, challenge/matching grants, conferences and seminars, equipment acquisition, federated giving, general operating support, multi-year support, project development, seed money, and sponsorships. Applicants should provide the following information on the nonprofit's letterhead: organization's mission and how the project addresses its mission; program description and expected outcomes; fundraising goal and current funding status; the organization's budget and audited financial statements; tax status determination letter; roster of governing board and executive staff; and specific amount requested. Nonprofits in the Saint Louis, Missouri, metropolitan area should send applications to Ameren Corporate Contributions at the office listed. Nonprofits in the Springfield, Illinois, metropolitan area should send applications to Ameren Public Affairs, 607 E Adams Street, C1301, Springfield, Illinois 62739.

Requirements: Illinois and Missouri tax-exempt organizations in Ameren service areas are eligible.

Restrictions: Grants do not support individuals or political, religious, fraternal, veteran, social, or similar groups. Ameren cannot donate electric or natural gas service.

Geographic Focus: Illinois, Missouri

Amount of Grant: 5,000 - 75,000 USD

Contact: Otie Cowan, Community Relations Manager; (314) 554-4740; fax (314) 554-2888; ocowan@ameren.com

Internet: http://www.ameren.com/CommunityMembers/CharitableTrust/Pages/Corporationcharitabletrust.aspx

Sponsor: Ameren Corporation

P.O. Box 66149, MC 100

Saint Louis, MO 63166-6149

American Chemical Society Green Chemistry Grants 117

The American Chemical Society Green Chemistry Institute sponsors a green chemistry grant program by promoting funding, increasing opportunities, and developing information on the benefits of green chemistry. Its efforts span the spectrum from theory and basic research through application and commercialization of science and technology. The program also sponsors a number of research fellowships and scientific exchanges through its grants programs.

Geographic Focus: All States

Contact: Gayle Peterman, Finance and Grants Manager; (202) 872-6092 or (202) 872-4481; fax (202) 872-6319; g_peterman@acs.org

Internet: http://portal.acs.org/portal/acs/corg/content?_nfpb=true&_pageLabel=PP_TRANSITIONMAIN&node_id=1456&use_sec=false&sec_url_var=region1&__uuid=c14e3223-89d3-4263-8072-51ccffe52007

Sponsor: American Chemical Society

1155 Sixteenth Street, NW

Washington, D.C. 20036-4801

American Eagle Outfitters Foundation Grants 118

The foundation directs financial and volunteer contributions toward projects that try to improve the quality of life in American Eagle communities. The foundation supports Jumpstart, Big Brothers Big Sisters, The Student Conservation Association (SCA) and community initiatives. Supporting and mentoring preschool children, volunteering with kids, high school and college students with conservation service internships and volunteer opportunities are all supported. Applicants and programs must fall within the scope of the foundation's mission statement; creatively involve AE business unit and/or employees in projects; provide regular reports of financial and program activities; direct at least 70 percent of the money raised toward beneficiaries; be willing to provide documentation to AE verifying financial donations; be in a community where AE operates business; significantly affect the surrounding community; and be inclusive in policies and practices involving all genders, races, ages, ethnic origin, sexual orientation, or creed. Funding guidelines and procedures are available online. Requests are considered at quarterly meetings.

Requirements: 501(c)3 public charities are eligible.

Restrictions: The foundation will not contribute to: fashion shows or other requests for clothing donations except for occasions where the company may provide disaster-related support to communities resulting from acts of nature (i.e., floods, tornadoes, hurricanes, fires, etc.); organizations that discriminate based on race, creed, color, sex, age, national origin, veteran status, or physical or mental disabilities; individual religious organizations; political organizations, campaigns, or candidates for political office; lobbying groups; medical or health-related causes; veteran or fraternal organizations; individuals; goodwill advertising in journals or program books; capital campaigns such as building grants; organizations that spend more than 30 percent of their total budget on fundraising efforts; or programs in communities without AE stores.

Geographic Focus: All States

Amount of Grant: 1,000 - 25,000 USD

Contact: Foundation Administrator; (877) 409-9587

Internet: http://www.ae.com/web/corp/foundation.htm

Sponsor: American Eagle Outfitters Foundation

150 Thorn Hill Drive

Warrendale, PA 15086

American Express Charitable Fund Grants 119

The American Express Charitable Fund supports community foundations and organizations involved with arts and culture, education, hunger, housing development, disaster relief, public safety, human services, community development, and civic affairs. The grantmaker has identified the following major areas of interest: employee matching gifts - fund matches contributions made by employees of American Express to nonprofit organizations on a one-for-one basis from $25 to $8,000 per employee, per year; and Global Volunteer Action Fund (GVAF) - fund awards grants of up to $1,000 to nonprofit organizations with which employees or teams of employees of American Express volunteer. Aside from these, applications are accepted from community organizations and municipal agencies for general operating support.

Requirements: Giving is primarily on a national basis in areas of company operations, with emphasis on: the State of Arizona; Los Angeles and San Francisco, California; Washington, DC; southern Florida; Atlanta, Georgia; Chicago, Illinois; Boston, Massachusetts; Greensboro, North Carolina; New York, New York; Philadelphia, Pennsylvania; Dallas and Houston, Texas; and Salt Lake City, Utah.

Restrictions: No support is available for discriminatory organizations, religious organizations not of direct benefit to the entire community, or political organizations. No grants are offered to individuals (except for employee-related scholarships), or for fundraising, goodwill advertising, souvenir journals, dinner programs, travel, books, magazines, articles in professional journals, endowments or capital campaigns, traveling exhibitions, or sports sponsorships.

Geographic Focus: Arizona, California, District of Columbia, Florida, Georgia, Illinois, Massachusetts, New York, North Carolina, Pennsylvania, Texas, Utah

Amount of Grant: Up to 25,000 USD

Samples: Ballet Arizona, Phoenix, Arizona, $25,000 - general operating support; United Arts Council of Greater Greensboro, Greensboro, North Carolina, $17,000 - general operating fund; Broward Partnership for the Homeless, Ft. Lauderdale, Florida, $16,200 - general operating support.

Contact: Mary Ellen Craig, Director; (212) 640-5660

Internet: http://about.americanexpress.com/csr/e-driven.aspx

Sponsor: American Express Charitable Fund

200 Vesey Street, 48th Floor

New York, NY 10285-1000

American Express Foundation Community Service Grants 120

Whether it is feeding the hungry, mentoring students, building homes for the homeless or cleaning up the environment, tens of thousands of American Express employees serve their communities through volunteerism and personal financial contributions, and the Foundation views this activity as an extension of the service ethic that lies at the heart of its business. It encourages good citizenship by supporting organizations that cultivate meaningful opportunities for civic engagement by employees and members of the community. The Foundation also serves its communities by supporting immediate and long-term relief and recovery efforts to help victims of natural disasters. Funding also goes to support preparedness programs that allow relief agencies to be better equipped in responding to emergencies as they occur.

Requirements: Eligible organizations must: certify tax-exempt status under Section 501(c)3 and 509(a)1, 2 or 3 of the U.S. Internal Revenue Code. Organizations outside the U.S. must be able to document not-for-profit status.

Restrictions: The program does not fund: individual needs, including scholarships, sponsorships and other forms of financial aid; fund-raising activities, such as galas, benefits, dinners and sporting events; goodwill advertising, souvenir journals or dinner programs; travel for individuals or groups; sectarian activities of religious organizations; political causes, candidates, organizations or campaigns; or books, magazines or articles in professional journals.

Geographic Focus: All States, All Countries

Samples: Association for Persons with Special Needs, Singapore - volunteers were engaged in the development of the center and as mentors to its clients;

Feeding America, Chicago, Illinois - funds the expansion of its Store Donation Program which recovers perishable products that do not meet retailers' marketing standards.
Contact: Timothy McClimon; (212) 640-5661; fax (212) 693-1033
Internet: http://about.americanexpress.com/csr/comm_serv.aspx
Sponsor: American Express Foundation
200 Vesey Street, 48th Floor
New York, NY 10285-4804

American Express Foundation Historic Preservation Grants   **121**
The funding supports organizations and projects that preserve or rediscover important cultural works and major historic sites in order to provide ongoing access and enjoyment for current and future audiences. The types of programs supported include a broad range of arts and culture: from historic landmarks and public spaces to dance, theater, music, film and the visual arts. The Foundation emphasizes preserving works that represent a range of diverse cultures. Supported programs must embrace preservation and enable ongoing public access and exposure through one or more of the following: ensuring public engagement with a restored work of art or historic site; producing or presenting a new interpretation of a work that is in danger of being lost; or preserving significant cultural traditions.
Requirements: Eligible organizations must: certify tax-exempt status under Section 501(c)3 and 509(a)1, 2 or 3 of the U.S. Internal Revenue Code. Organizations outside the U.S. must be able to document not-for-profit status.
Restrictions: The program does not fund: individual needs, including scholarships, sponsorships and other forms of financial aid; fund-raising activities, such as galas, benefits, dinners and sporting events; goodwill advertising, souvenir journals or dinner programs; travel for individuals or groups; sectarian activities of religious organizations; political causes, candidates, organizations or campaigns; or books, magazines or articles in professional journals.
Geographic Focus: All States, All Countries
Amount of Grant: Up to 100,000,000 USD
Samples: Asociacion Civil Responde, Buenos Aires, Argentina - funded the historic preservation and adaptive reuse of Villa Dominguito; Fund for Boston Neighborhoods, Boston, Massachusetts - the restoration of historic artworks within America's first town meeting hall, Faneuil Hall.
Contact: Timothy McClimon; (212) 640-5661; fax (212) 693-1033
Internet: http://about.americanexpress.com/csr/hpc.aspx
Sponsor: American Express Foundation
200 Vesey Street, 48th Floor
New York, NY 10285-4804

American Foodservice Charitable Trust Grants   **122**
American Foodservice Charitable Trust provides funding in the following areas of interest: Christian agencies & churches; community/economic development; higher education; hospitals (general) and; youth development. The types of support available are: general/operating support; program development; scholarship funds. Giving is primarily available in the areas of: King of Prussia, Pennsylvania; Thomasville, Georgia; and Fort Worth, Texas.
Requirements: Qualifying IRA 501(c)3 nonprofit organizations are eligible to apply. There's no application form nor is there a deadline date to adhere to when submitting a proposal to the Foundation.
Restrictions: No grants to individuals.
Geographic Focus: Georgia, Pennsylvania, Texas
Amount of Grant: 200 - 8,000 USD
Samples: Catholic Social Services, West Chester, PA, $200—social services grant; American Red Cross, Philadelphia, PA, $1,000—disaster relief grant; Police Atheletic League, Philadelphia, PA, $2,000—youth program grant.
Contact: Richard S. Downs, Trustee; (610) 933-9792
Sponsor: American Foodservice Charitable Trust
860 First Avenue, Suite 9A
King of Prussia, PA 19406-1404

American Foundation Grants   **123**
The foundation is a public charity that helps individuals, families, and corporations create foundations that give financial support to their favorite charities. The foundation's primary focus is helping charities become more efficient and successful by supporting efforts in the following areas: governance and organization (structure)—efforts made to create, strengthen, and reinforce the mission statement of an organization; human resources—staff recruitment for competence and expertise; and operations—access to high technology and leading-edge equipment and procedures. The foundation favors organizations with the following characteristics: competent management, clearly defined missions, organizational ethos, a multiplying and continuing impact, providing needed service, and fiscally responsible. Application and guidelines are available online.
Requirements: 501(c)3, 509(a)1, and 509(a)2 public charities are eligible.
Restrictions: Funding will not be considered for the following requests: organizations without tax-exempt 501(c)3, 509(a)1 or 509(a)2 public charity status; general endowment funds; direct aid to individuals; or governmental or quasi-governmental entities or activities other than colleges or universities.
Geographic Focus: All States
Contact: Grants Administrator; (602) 955-4770; fax (602) 955-4707; grantinfo@americanfoundation.org
Internet: http://www.americanfoundation.org
Sponsor: American Foundation
4518 N 32nd Street
Phoenix, AZ 85018

American Woodmark Foundation Grants   **124**
The American Woodmark Foundation, formed in 1995 in Virginia, is the major vehicle by which American Woodmark Corporation makes its charitable donations. Currently, the Foundation supports organizations involved with education at all levels, domestic violence, housing, and public safety. Types of support include: annual campaigns; building construction and renovation; capital campaigns; continuing support; curriculum development; equipment purchase; and general operating support. The Foundation will forward a formal application upon request. Though there are no specified deadlines, the Board meets four times each year, in January, April, July, and October.
Requirements: Applicants must: have tax-exempt status under Section 501(c)3; be classified as public charities; and be located in a community where American Woodmark Corporation has a facility. This includes company operations in: Kingman, Arizona; Jackson and Toccoa, Georgia; Grant County, Indiana; Monticello and Hazard, Kentucky; Cumberland, Maryland; Tahlequah, Oklahoma; Humboldt, Tennessee; Winchester-Frederick County, Clarke County and Orange; Virginia; and Moorefield, West Virginia.
Geographic Focus: Arizona, Georgia, Indiana, Kentucky, Maryland, Oklahoma, Tennessee, Virginia, West Virginia
Amount of Grant: 500 - 4,000 USD
Samples: Wayne County Historical Society, Monticello, Kentucky, $1,800 - lifts for handicap visitors; North Georgia Technical College, Clarksville, Georgia, $1,000 - scholarships fund; Eastern West Virginia Community and Technical College, Moorefield, West Virginia, $3,550 - operation funds.
Contact: Brenda DuPont, Director; (540) 665-9129
Internet: http://www.americanwoodmark.com/about.asp?iAreaID=1&iSectionID=7
Sponsor: American Woodmark Foundation
3102 Shawnee Drive
Winchester, VA 22601-4208

Amerigroup Foundation Grants   **125**
Helping to create healthy communities is the cornerstone of the Amerigroup Foundation's mission. The objective is to serve as a national resource that fosters an environment where there is a continuum of education, access and care, all of which improve the health and well-being of the financially vulnerable and uninsured Americans. The Foundation primarily provides grants in the form of general support, but program development and sponsorships are also available to qualified non-profit organizations. Most recently, grants have ranged from $250 to $35,000.
Requirements: 501(c)3 non-profits are eligible to apply from the following states: Arizona, California, Colorado, Connecticut, Florida, Georgia, Indiana, Kansas, Kentucky, Louisiana, Maine, Maryland, Massachusetts, Missouri, Nevada, New Hampshire, New Jersey, New Mexico, New York, Ohio, South Carolina, Tennessee, Texas, Virginia, Washington, West Virginia, and Wisconsin.
Restrictions: Funding is unavailable for: projects or organizations that offer a direct benefit to the trustees of the Foundation or to employees or directors of Amerigroup; projects or organizations that might in any way pose a conflict with Amerigroup's mission, goals, programs, products or employees; projects or organizations that do not benefit a broad cross section of the community; individuals; political parties, candidates or lobbying activities; benefits, raffles, souvenir programs, trips, tours or similar events; for-profit entities, including start-up businesses.
Geographic Focus: Arizona, California, Colorado, Connecticut, Florida, Georgia, Indiana, Kansas, Kentucky, Louisiana, Maine, Maryland, Massachusetts, Missouri, Nevada, New Hampshire, New Jersey, New Mexico, New York, Ohio, South Carolina, Tennessee, Texas, Virginia, Washington, West Virginia, Wisconsin
Amount of Grant: 250 - 35,000 USD

Samples: College of William and Mary, Williamsburg, Virginia, $35,000 - general operations; Nature Discovery Center, Bellaire, Texas, $10,000 - general operations; Snohomish County Human Services, Everett, Washington, $30,000 - general operations.
Contact: Manager; (757) 490-6900 or (757) 962-6468; fax (757) 222-2360
Internet: http://www.realsolutions.com/company/pages/Foundation.aspx
Sponsor: Amerigroup Foundation
4425 Corporation Lane
Virginia Beach, VA 23462-3103

AMERIND Community Service Project Grants 126

AMERIND Risk Management Corporation's Community Service program seeks to advance the community aspect of AMERIND's vision to Protect Tribal Families First. Funding limitations for small community service projects include: housing fairs will receive a standard $500 per event; youth activities, including graffiti paint-outs, community clean-up, meth awareness will range from $100 (less than 100 participants) to $250 (more than 100 participants); and health fairs will receive a standard $250. The AMERIND Outreach Committee meets once every month to discuss funding requests received by organizations.
Requirements: Requests for AMERIND contributions must meet of the following criteria; the project must address a demonstrated need in a Native American community in which AMERIND has a presence; the project must provide an opportunity for Native Americans to make learning about fire safety and home safety fun; or the project must support a project or program involving fire safety and/or home safety, business related or other related area to expand, improve and protect the lifestyles of Native Americans and their families.
Restrictions: Powwows and rodeos are considered advertising and are not funded. AMERIND does not contribute to: individual requests; trip expenses; organizations that charge a fee or dues; lobbying organizations; or political organizations.
Geographic Focus: All States
Contact: Mike Jennings, Chief Financial Officer; (505) 404-5000 or (800) 352-3496; fax (505) 404-5001; outreach@amerind-corp.org
Internet: http://www.amerind-corp.org/index.php/about-amerind/community-outreach/community-service-projects
Sponsor: AMERIND Risk Management Corporation
502 Cedar Drive
Santa Ana Pueblo, NM 87004

AmerUs Group Charitable Foundation 127

The foundation awards general support grants to nonprofits in the metropolitan areas of Des Moines, Indianapolis, Topeka, Boston, and Long Island; in the areas of arts and culture, civic and community, education, health and human services, United Way, and new initiatives. Guidelines and application are available online.
Requirements: Nonprofit organizations in metro Des Moines, Indianapolis, Topeka, and Boston, and Long Island, New York, are eligible to apply.
Restrictions: Grants do not support athletic organizations, conferences, goodwill advertising, endowments, fellowships, festival participation, fraternal organizations, hospital or health care facilities, individual K-12 schools, political parties, religious groups for religious programs, social organizations, and trade or professional associations.
Geographic Focus: Indiana, Iowa, Massachusetts, New York
Date(s) Application is Due: Feb 9; May 4; Aug 3
Amount of Grant: Up to 150,000 USD
Samples: American Institute of Business (Des Moines, IA)—$5000; Children and Families of Iowa (Des Moines, IA)—$18,000,; Iowa National Heritage Foundation (IA)—$2500; Young Women's Resource Ctr (IA)—$2500.
Contact: D'Arcy Reinhard, (515) 557-3917
Internet: http://www.avivausa.com
Sponsor: Aviva World
699 Walnut Street, Suite 2000
Des Moines, IA 50309

Ametek Foundation Grants 128

Corporate contributions are made through the foundation to nonprofit organizations in company-operating areas. The foundation supports programs and projects in the categories of health, education, and social services, with education being the largest area of support. Under the category of health, grants are awarded to hospitals, health care facilities, and for medical research. Support for education is given to colleges and universities and technical schools, as well as scholarship funds. Welfare funding supports philanthropic organizations, including the United Way. Arts groups, museums, and civic

groups also receive support. Types of support include general operating support, annual campaigns, building construction/renovation, equipment acquisition, endowment funds, scholarship funds, research, technical assistance, and matching funds. Annual application deadline dates may vary; contact the office for specific dates. The board meets in November and May to consider requests.
Requirements: IRS 501(c)3 organizations are eligible.
Restrictions: Grants are not made to individuals or to political, fraternal, or veterans organizations.
Geographic Focus: All States
Date(s) Application is Due: Feb 28; Sep 1
Amount of Grant: 1,000 - 25,000 USD
Samples: Rochester City School District (Rochester, NY)—grant recipient, $116, 231; Gnaden Huetten Memorial Hospital (Lehighton, PA)—grant recipient, $1000; Abilities, Inc of Florida (Clearwater, FL)—grant recipient, $15,000.
Contact: Kathryn Londra, (610) 647-2121; fax (610) 296-3412
Sponsor: Ametek Foundation
37 N Valley Road, Building 4, P.O. Box 1764
Paoli, PA 19301-0801

Amgen Foundation Grants 129

Amgen seeks to: advance science education, improve quality of care and access for patients, and support resources that create sound communities where Amgen staff members live and work. Requests must be received at least 90 days in advance of the desired contribution date. Guidelines are available online.
Requirements: 501(c)3 tax-exempt organizations located in Amgen communities are eligible. Eligible grantees may include public elementary and secondary schools, as well as public colleges and universities, public libraries and public hospitals.
Restrictions: In general, Amgen does not consider requests for the following: support to individuals, fundraising or sports-related events, corporate sponsorship requests, religious organizations unless the program is secular in nature and benefits a broad range of the community, political organization or lobbying activity, labor unions, fraternal, service or veterans' organizations, private foundations, or organizations that are discriminatory.
Geographic Focus: All States
Samples: California State U (Camarillo, CA)—for scientific equipment, $950,000; Institute for Systems Biology (Seattle, WA)—for the endowment and operations, $3 million; International Federation of the Red Cross and Red Crescent Societies (Geneva)—for relief efforts in South Asia and Africa, $1 million.
Contact: Contact; (805) 447-4056 or (805) 447-1000; fax (805) 447-1010
Internet: http://wwwext.amgen.com/citizenship/apply_for_grant.html
Sponsor: Amgen Foundation
1 Amgen Center Drive, MS 38-3-B
Thousand Oaks, CA 91320-1799

AMI Semiconductors Corporate Grants 130

The company makes grants to nonprofit organizations in support of the performing arts, economic development, business education, health cost containment, and social services for senior citizens. Types of support include conferences and seminars, general operating support, matching grants, multiyear grants, professorships, research, and scholarships. There are no application deadlines. Submit a letter of inquiry that includes a description of the organization and program, amount of funds requested, purpose of the request, recently audited financial statement, and proof of tax-exempt status. Contact office for grant availability.
Restrictions: The company does not support political or lobbying groups.
Geographic Focus: All States
Amount of Grant: 1,000 - 2,500 USD
Contact: Tamera Drake, (208) 234-6890; tamera_Drake@amis.com
Internet: http://www.amis.com/about
Sponsor: AMI Semiconductors
2300 Buckskin Road
Pocatello, ID 83201

Amon G. Carter Foundation Grants 131

The foundation awards grants that support benevolent, charitable, and educational purposes with emphasis on the arts and humanities. Other areas supported include education, health and medical services, human and social services, programs benefiting the youth and elderly, civic and community endeavors that enhance quality of life, religion, and visual and performing arts. Types of support include general operating support, continuing support, annual campaigns, capital campaigns, building construction/renovation, equipment acquisition, endowment funds, emergency funds, program development, professorships, seed money, research, and matching funds. The foundation's primary focus is directed to the Fort Worth/Tarrant County area of Texas, although the directors occasionally award a grant outside the Texas area. Proposals must be in writing, briefly giving background information on the requesting organization, specifically stating the purpose of the request and the amount being requested. A current copy of the organization's IRS determination letter must be furnished. Applications are accepted at any time for consideration during the April, September, and December board meetings.

Restrictions: Grants, loans, or scholarships are not made to individuals. Online applications are not accepted.

Geographic Focus: All States

Amount of Grant: 1,000 - 250,000 USD

Contact: Terry Woodfin, Program Contact; (817) 332-2783; fax (817) 332-2787; terry@agcf.org

Internet: http://www.agcf.org

Sponsor: Amon G. Carter Foundation

P.O. Box 1036

Fort Worth, TX 76101-1036

Amway Corporation Contributions 132

The Amway Corporation gives primarily in areas of company operations, including: Buena Park and Lakeview, California; Norcross, Georgia; Honolulu, Hawaii; Arlington, Texas; and Kent, Washington, with emphasis on the greater Grand Rapids, Michigan, area, and in Africa, Asia, Australia, Europe, and Latin America. Its primary area of interests include: at-risk children and families; the arts; children services; developmentally disables; disaster preparedness; health care; and nutrition. Major types of support offered are general operations and in-kind gifts. A formal application is required, and the annual deadlines are January 1 and November 1. Final notification is within sixty days of the deadline.

Restrictions: No support for fraternal organizations or school athletic teams, bands, or choirs, political, legislative, or lobbying organizations. No grants to individuals, or for travel, scholarships, religious projects, sports or fundraising events, movie, film, or television documentaries, general awareness campaigns, marketing sponsorships, cause-related marketing, or advertising projects; no in-kind gifts for conferences or conventions, personal use, distribution at an expo, fair, or event, family reunions, or sports fundraising events.

Geographic Focus: All States

Date(s) Application is Due: Jan 1; Nov 1

Contact: Giving Manager; (616) 787-7000; contributions@amway.com

Internet: http://www.amway.com/about-amway/campaigns-and-sponsorships

Sponsor: Amway Corporation

5101 Spaulding Plaza, SE

Ada, MI 49355-0001

Andersen Corporate Foundation 133

The Foundation contributes to: organizations that enhance self-sufficiency for people living in poverty, senior citizens, and people with disabilities; organizations that promote safe and healthy environments, as well as organizations that seek to improve health through prevention and education programs, primarily for young people, senior citizens, and people in vulnerable situations; organizations that offer intellectual and social opportunities with a focus primarily on young people, senior citizens, and people with disabilities; and support that builds, promotes, and preserves communities. Complete guidelines are available online.

Requirements: All grant recipients must meet these giving guidelines: the organization's programs and services are consistent with Andersen Corporate Foundation's mission and values; the organization's purpose and programs fit within Andersen Corporate Foundation's defined program focus areas; the organization can demonstrate sound fiscal management and effective delivery of services; nonprofit corporation is registered under section 501(c)3 of the IRS Code in the United States or for Canadian Charities with the Canadian Revenue Agency.

Restrictions: The Foundation avoids making grants in organizations that are in competition with each other to provide the same service to the community. The Foundation does not support endowments or make grants to individuals. Funding is not granted to national research organizations.

Geographic Focus: Iowa, Minnesota, Virginia, Wisconsin, Canada

Date(s) Application is Due: Apr 15; Jul 15; Oct 15; Dec 15

Contact: Program Director; (888) 439-9508 or (651) 439-1557; fax (651) 439-9480; andersencorpfdn@srinc.biz

Internet: https://www.srinc.biz/bp/index.html

Sponsor: Andersen Corporate Foundation

342 5th Avenue N

Bayport, MN 55003

Anderson Foundation Grants 134

Established in Ohio in 1949, the Anderson Family Foundation Trust gives grants in the greater Toledo, Ohio, region, including Maumee and Columbus. Giving also to organizations located within the areas of the Anderson plants in the following states: Champaign, Illinois; Delphi, Lafayette, and Dunkirk, Indiana; and Albion, Potterville, Webberville, and White Pigeon, Michigan. The Foundation's primary fields of interest include: agriculture; arts; children and youth services; education; the environment; government and public administration; higher education; human services; religion; secondary school education; and federated giving programs. Types of support include: annual campaigns; building and renovation programs; capital campaigns; conferences and seminars; emergency funds; general operating support; matching/challenge grants; program development; publications; research; scholarship funds; and seed money. Specific application forms are not required, and board decisions are made on the 3rd Monday of the month in March, June, September, and December. Grant amounts range up to $100,000 on occasion, though most average between $5,000 and $10,000.

Requirements: Nonprofit 501(c)3 agencies in Ohio, Illinois, Indiana, and Michigan serving areas of company operation are eligible to apply.

Restrictions: No support is available for private foundations, public high schools, or elementary schools. No grants are given to individuals, or for endowment funds, travel, or building or operating funds for churches or elementary schools.

Geographic Focus: Illinois, Indiana, Michigan, Ohio

Date(s) Application is Due: Feb 28; May 30; Aug 30; Nov 30

Amount of Grant: Up to 100,000 USD

Samples: Chance for Change Foundation, Toledo, Ohio, $5,000 - human services; DeKalb County Fair Association, DeKalb, Indiana, $5,000 - agriculture ($5,000); Camp Tecumseh, Brookston, Indiana, $5,000 - human services.

Contact: Fredi Heywood, Chairman; (419) 243-1706 or (419) 893-5050; fax (419) 242-5549; fredi@toledocf.org

Sponsor: Anderson Foundation

480 W. Dussel Drive, P.O. Box 119

Maumee, OH 43537-0119

Andre Agassi Charitable Foundation Grants 135

The foundation awards grants to at-risk youth programs targeting education and recreation in the Las Vegas area. There are no application forms or deadlines. Submitted requests will be considered for funding in the following calendar year. Detailed guidelines are available online.

Requirements: Nevada 501(c)3 nonprofits serving the Las Vegas metropolitan area are eligible.

Restrictions: Grants do not support organizations or projects outside the Las Vegas community, organizations that discriminate, individuals, advertising, religious or sectarian organizations for religious purposes, or political organizations and programs designed to influence legislation or elect candidates to public office.

Geographic Focus: Nevada

Samples: Las Vegas Philharmonic, Las Vegas, NV, $10,000—art program for underprivileged youths; Boys and Girls Club of Nevada, Las Vegas, NV, $334,403—after school program; Center for Independent Living, Las Vegas., NV, $5,000—residential treatment for adolescents.

Contact: Julie Pippenger, Chief Operating Officer; (702) 227-5700; fax (702) 866-2928; info@agassi.net

Internet: http://www.agassifoundation.org

Sponsor: Andre Agassi Charitable Foundation

3960 Howard Hughes Parkway, Suite 750

Las Vegas, NV 89169

Andrew Family Foundation Grants 136

The Andrew Family Foundation is a private, philanthropic organization that will consider proposals from public, non-profit organizations under IRS Section 501(c)3 to support projects and organizations that foster individual growth and enhance communities through education, humanitarian efforts, and the arts. Funding primarily in the Illinois with a special interest in the Cook County region. The types of support available include: annual campaigns; building/renovation; capital campaigns; general/operating support; scholarship funds. There is no deadline date when applying for funding. Qualified grant proposals will be reviewed by the Andrew Family Foundation Grant Making Committee prior to quarterly board meetings. The committee will make a recommendation to the Board of Directors of the Foundation.

Requirements: 501(c)3 tax-exempt organizations are eligible to apply for funding. To begin the application process, take the Eligibility Quiz to confirm that you qualify for a grant from the foundation. Upon successful completion of the Eligibility Quiz, you will be invited to complete an online Letter of Inquiry. The Board will review your Letter of Inquiry and may invite you to submit a Full Application for review. Generally, the Board meets in February, May, August and November of each year.

Restrictions: The foundation does not provide funds: to individuals; taxable corporations; religious programs; political organizations; and other private foundations.

Geographic Focus: Illinois

Contact: Connor Humphrey; (708) 460-1288 or (602) 828-8471; fax (602) 385-3267; aff@inlignwealth.com or Connor.Humphrey@GenSpring.com

Internet: https://online.foundationsource.com/andrew/board2.htm

Sponsor: Andrew Family Foundation

14628 John Humphrey Drive

Orland Park, IL 60462

Anheuser-Busch Foundation Grants — 137

Support is provided almost exclusively to causes that are located in communities in which the company has manufacturing facilities. Contributions are made for education, health, social services, minorities and youth, cultural enrichment, and environmental protection programs. Types of support include capital grants, employee matching gifts, equipment and material acquisition, general operating support, and donated products. Full proposals are accepted throughout the year.

Requirements: 501(c)3 tax-exempt organizations in corporation operation areas can apply, which includes California, Colorado, Florida, Georgia, Hawaii, Kentucky, Massachusetts, Missouri, New Hampshire, New Jersey, New York, Ohio, Oklahoma, Texas, and Virginia.

Restrictions: Grants are not made to individuals; political, social, fraternal, religious, or athletic organizations; or hospitals for operating funds.

Geographic Focus: California, Colorado, Florida, Georgia, Hawaii, Kentucky, Massachusetts, Missouri, New Hampshire, New Jersey, New York, Ohio, Oklahoma, Texas, Virginia

Amount of Grant: 25,000 - 100,000 USD

Contact: Assistant Manager; (314) 577-2453; fax (314) 557-3251

Internet: http://anheuser-busch.com/index.php/our-responsibility/community-our-neighborhoods/

Sponsor: Anheuser-Busch Foundation

One Busch Place

Saint Louis, MO 63118-1852

Animal Welfare Trust Grants — 138

Animal Welfare Trust's grant program seeks to assist organizations whose work can help alleviate animal suffering and/or raise public consciousness toward giving animals the respect they so need and deserve. Although general organizational funding will be considered, preference will be given to well-defined projects with clear goals and objectives. Capital projects will not be considered. Areas of priority include farm animal welfare, vegetarianism and humane education. Grants will generally be made in the $2,500 to $20,000 range, although requests outside either end of this range will be considered. Grant requests can be for a single or multi-year period, depending on the nature of the project. Animal Welfare Trust anticipates giving out 10 to 15 grants per year.

Requirements: Grants will be made largely to organizations classified as public charities under section 501(c)3 of the IRS code. Under certain circumstances grants will be considered outside the boundaries of public charities, including organizations outside the United States that can meet appropriate legal standards.

Geographic Focus: All States

Amount of Grant: 5,000 - 75,000 USD

Contact: Brad Goldberg, President and Director; (914) 381-6177; fax (914) 381-6176; email@animalwelfaretrust.org

Internet: http://fdncenter.org/grantmaker/awt/prog.html

Sponsor: Animal Welfare Trust

141 Halstead Avenue, Suite 301, P.O. Box 737

Mamaroneck, NY 10543

ANLAF International Fund for Sexual Minorities Grants — 139

Astraea's primary purpose is to advance the economic, political, educational, and cultural well-being of lesbians. Astraea raises and distributes funds to organizations, individuals, and projects that promote a feminist perspective advancing the social, political, economic, educational, and cultural well-being of lesbians and all women and girls. Programs and policies will be supported that actively work to eliminate those forms of oppression based on sexual orientation, class, race, age, physical and mental ability, religious affiliation, and all other factors that affect lesbians and gay men in the United States and internationally. Organizations may apply for general support or project support. Deadlines are the beginning of June and the beginning of November; contact program staff for exact dates.

Requirements: Groups must be based in Latin America, the Caribbean, Asia, the Pacific, Eastern Europe, the former Soviet Republics, the Middle East, and Africa.

Restrictions: Astraea Foundation generally does not fund government agencies or organizations with budgets above $500,000.

Geographic Focus: All States

Date(s) Application is Due: Mar 15; Oct 15

Amount of Grant: Up to 10,000 USD

Samples: Audre Lorde Project (Brooklyn, NY)—for the LBTST Women of Color Organizing Initiative, $4000; Triangle Project (Cape Town, Africa)—for expansion of services to the lesbian/gay/bisexual/transsexual communities in rural areas of the Western Cape, $4000.

Contact: Namita Chad, Grants Administrator; (212) 529-8021; fax (212) 982-3321; namita@astraeafoundation.org or grants@astraeafoundation.org

Internet: http://www.astraea.org/PHP/Grants/Main.php4

Sponsor: Astraea Lesbian Foundation for Justice

116 E 16th Street, 7th Floor

New York, NY 10003

Anne J. Caudal Foundation Grants — 140

The Anne J. Caudal Foundation was established in 2007 to benefit disabled veterans of any time or of any branch of the United States armed forces and to perpetuate the recognition or memory of their accomplishments or sacrifice in time of war or otherwise. Special consideration is given to organizations that serve disabled veterans in New Jersey. Grant requests for general operating support are strongly encouraged. Program support will also be considered. Small, program-related capital expenses may be included in general operating or program requests. The majority of grants from the Caudal Foundation are one year in duration. On occasion, multi-year support is awarded. Application materials are available for download from the grant website. The application deadline for the Anne J. Caudal Foundation is July 1. Applicants are encouraged to review the state application guidelines for additional helpful information and clarification before applying. Applicants are also encouraged to view the foundation's funding history (link is available at the grant website). Applicants will be notified of grant decisions before August 15.

Requirements: Applicants must have 501(c)3 tax-exempt status.

Restrictions: The foundation does not support requests from individuals, organizations attempting to influence policy through direct lobbying, or any political campaigns.

Geographic Focus: All States

Date(s) Application is Due: Jul 1

Samples: United States Wounded Soldiers Foundation, Dallas, Texas, $12,500; Our Military Kids, McLean, Virginia, $12,500; Jewish Family Service of New Jersey, Wayne, New Jersey, $12,500.

Contact: Maryann Clemente; (646) 855-0786; maryann.clemente@baml.com

Internet: https://www.bankofamerica.com/philanthropic/fn_search.action

Sponsor: Anne J. Caudal Foundation

One Bryant Park, NY1-100-28-05

New York, NY 10036

Anne Thorne Weaver Family Foundation Grants — 141

Established in Nebraska in 1993, the Anne Thorne Weaver Family Foundation offers grants in its primary fields of interest, which include: the arts; community development; economic development; higher education; and human services. Support is offered throughout the States of Nebraska and Iowa, although giving is centered primarily around the Omaha metropolitan area. Funds are primarily offered to fund general operations. An application form is required, and can be secured through the Foundation office. Initially, applicants should send a query letter with a detailed description of the project and budgetary needs. There are no identified annual deadlines. Typical amounts range between $50 and $5,000, with amounts occasionally reaching as much as $75,000.

Requirements: Any 501(c)3 supporting residents of Nebraska are eligible.

Geographic Focus: Iowa, Nebraska

Amount of Grant: 50 - 5,000 USD

Samples: Omaha Performing Arts, Omaha, Nebraska, $5,000 - annual fund drive for general operations; Pets for Vets, Wilmington, North Carolina, $5,000 - annual fund drive for general operations; Art Museum of Nebraska, Kearney, Nebraska, $75,000 - annual fund drive for general operations.

Contact: Anne Thorne Weaver, President; (402) 391-1511 or (402) 551-1919

Sponsor: Anne Thorne Weaver Family Foundation

1301 S. 75th Street, No. 200

Omaha, NE 68124

GRANT PROGRAMS | 27

Annie Lee Robbins Charitable Foundation Grants 142

Annie Lee Robbins was born and raised in Corsicana, Texas. She loved children and animals, loved to read and was active in Kinsole Hose, a Corsicana women's social club. Miss Robbins created the Annie Lee Robbins Charitable Foundation to benefit the citizens of Navarro County. Her greatest wish was that a senior citizens meeting place be established in the Corsicana community. Her dream became a reality in 2000, when the Senior Activity Center was completed. Its primary fields of interest include: the arts; culture and humanities; education; and human services. The Foundation is currently managed by the Bank of America Philanthropic Solutions. The annual deadline for applications is March 1, with award notifications by June 30.

Requirements: If there are not any qualified 501(c)3 organizations as such in Navarro County, then distributions can be made to qualified 501(c)3 organizations in the State of Texas.

Geographic Focus: Texas

Date(s) Application is Due: Mar 1

Contact: Jenae Guillory, Philanthropic Relationship Manager; (214) 209-1965 or (214) 209-1370; tx.philanthropic@ustrust.com

Internet: https://www.bankofamerica.com/philanthropic/grantmaking.go

Sponsor: Annie Lee Robbins Charitable Foundation

901 Main Street, 19th Floor

Dallas, TX 75202-3714

Ann Jackson Family Foundation Grants 143

The foundation awards grants to eligible nonprofit organizations in its areas of interest, including secondary education, healthcare, child welfare, animal welfare, and the disabled. Types of support include building construction/renovation, capital campaigns, and general operating grants. Most grants are awarded to nonprofits in Santa Barbara, California. There are no application forms or deadlines. Contact the foundation for document attachments required.

Geographic Focus: California

Amount of Grant: 5,000 - 50,000 USD

Samples: All Saints By the Sea Episcopal Church, Santa Barbara, CA, $14,000—general purposes grant; Bowl Foundation of Santa Barbara, Santa Barbara, CA, $20,000—building project grant; Dunn School, Los Olivos, CA, $50,000—faculty housing grant.

Contact: Palmer Jackson, President; (805) 969-2258

Sponsor: Ann Jackson Family Foundation

P.O. Box 5580

Santa Barbara, CA 93150-5580

Ann L. and Carol Green Rhodes Charitable Trust Grants 144

Ann Rhodes and her mother Carol Green Rhodes were both very supportive of the local arts throughout their lives. Their Charitable Trust was established in 2010 to honor their love of theater and the local community. Ann was also an animal-lover who fed the wild animals that came into her backyard each night. The Trust supports charitable organizations focused on the arts, museums open to the public, theaters and other performing arts organizations, organizations whose primary purpose is to support the arts, organizations providing human services; and occasional support for animal-related charitable organizations. Ann Rhodes requested that preference be given to organizations that she supported in her lifetime. Applicants must apply online at the grant website. Applicants are strongly encouraged to do the following before applying: review the downloadable state application procedures for additional helpful information and clarifications; review the downloadable online-application guidelines at the grant website; review the trust's funding history (link is available from the grant website); review the online application questions in advance; and review the list of required attachments. These will generally include: a list of board members, financial statements (audited, reviewed, or compiled by independent auditor); an organization summary; a list of other funding sources; an IRS Determination letter; and other required documents. All attachments must be uploaded in the online application as PDF, Word, or Excel files. This trust has bi-annual application deadlines of March 31 and September 30. Grant awards are typically between $3,000 and $25,000.

Requirements: Applicants must have 501(c)3 tax-exempt status and serve residents of Tarrant County, Texas..

Restrictions: The Trust does not support requests from individuals, organizations attempting to influence policy through direct lobbying, or any political campaigns.

Geographic Focus: Texas

Date(s) Application is Due: Mar 31; Sep 30

Amount of Grant: 3,000 - 25,000 USD

Samples: Casa Manana Musicals, Fort Worth, Texas, $75,000, general operating support; Imagination Celebration of Fort Worth, Fort Worth, Texas, $10,000, to fund arts education programming for youth; Amphibian Productions, Fort Worth, Texas, $45,500, to underwrite production of Wittenberg.

Contact: Mark J. Smith, Philanthropic Relationship Manager; (817) 390-6028; tx.philanthropic@ustrust.com

Internet: https://www.bankofamerica.com/philanthropic/fn_search.action

Sponsor: Ann L. and Carol Green Rhodes Charitable Trust

500 West 7th Street, 15th Floor

Fort Worth, TX 76102-4700

Ann Peppers Foundation Grants 145

The foundation awards grants to eligible California nonprofit organizations in its areas of interest, including arts and cultural programs, disabled, elderly, health care, private education, and social services. Types of support include capital grants, general operating grants on a temporary basis, matching grants, scholarships, and research grants. Grants are initiated by the foundation manager. There are no application deadlines; the board meets quarterly to consider requests.

Requirements: Southern California 501(c)3 nonprofits, colleges, and universities are eligible. Preference is given to requests from Los Angeles County.

Geographic Focus: California

Amount of Grant: 2,000 - 50,000 USD

Samples: Boys Republic (Chino Hills, CA)—for kitchen renovation at residential facility, $5,000; Pepperdine University (Malibu, CA)—for scholarships, $25,000; Huntington Medical Research Institute (Pasadena, CA)—to purchase imaging technology for preclinical breast cancer, $5,000; Marymount College (Rancho Palos Verdes, CA)—for scholarships, $10,000.

Contact: Jack Alexander, Secretary; (626) 449-0793

Sponsor: Ann Peppers Foundation

625 S Fair Oaks Avenue

South Pasadena, CA 91030

Anschutz Family Foundation Grants 146

The foundation makes grants in Colorado's rural and urban communities, to assist the elderly, the young, and the economically disadvantaged. Support is given to programs and projects that strengthen families and enable individuals to become productive and responsible citizens of society. Religious organizations, including Christian, Lutheran, Presbyterian, Roman Catholic, and the Salvation Army, also are eligible for funding. Types of support include special projects, general operating budgets, continuing support, seed money, emergency funds, technical assistance, and publications.

Requirements: Nonprofit organizations in Colorado may apply.

Restrictions: Grants are not awarded to individuals, programs outside of Colorado, graduate and post-graduate research, religious organizations for religious purposes, special events, promotions or conferences, candidates for political office, endowments, debt reduction, multi-year grants, and capital campaigns.

Geographic Focus: Colorado

Date(s) Application is Due: Jan 15; Aug 1

Amount of Grant: 2,500 - 10,000 USD

Samples: The Center for Hearing, Speech, and Language (Denver, CO)—to support Kidscreen, a vision, hearing, speech and language developmental screening service for low-income families, $5,000; The Learning Source for Adults and Families (Denver, CO)—general operating support for neighborhood literacy programs for adults and families, $7,500; Seniors Resource Center (Denver, CO)—for general operating support for programs that maximize seniors' independence and dignity, $5000; Women's Resource Center (Durango, CO)—To support the resource and referral program, $5,000.

Contact: Sue Anschutz-Rodgers, President & Executive Director; (303) 293-2338; fax (303) 299-1235; info@anschutzfamilyfoundation.org

Internet: http://www.anschutzfamilyfoundation.org/info.htm

Sponsor: Anschutz Family Foundation

555 17th Street, Suite 2400

Denver, CO 80202

Anthony R. Abraham Foundation Grants 147

For more than 30 years, the Anthony R. Abraham Foundation mission has been to help non-profit organizations worldwide. The foundations strives to: provide programs and services to help people around the world become self-productive and give back to their communities; ensure that no child is denied medical treatment due to a lack of insurance; provide education that breaks barriers; guarantee that research into the cure of catastrophic diseases continues; help raise the quality of life. It's been a privilege for the Foundation to be able to help ease poverty, raise hospitals, build orphanages

and further medical research and the Foundation looks forward to doing even more. Some of the organizations helped include: Domestic organizations -St. Jude Children's Research Hospital; Camillus House; Miami Rescue Mission; Habitat for Humanity of Greater Miami; America's Second Harvest; Miami Children's Hospital; Jackson Memorial Hospital; Florida Heart Research Institute; Big Brothers/Big Sisters; Alonzo Mourning Charities; Honey Shine Mentoring Program; Cancer Link; The Miami Lighthouse for the Blind; Overtown Youth Center. International organizations: Brothers of the Good Shepherd; School for the Blind, Lebanon; Rene Moawad Foundation; Haitian Foundation; Children's International Network; Doctors without Borders; Little Sisters of Nazareth; Maronite Order of the Holy Family.
Requirements: Non-profit 501(c)3 organization requesting funding should fill out a funds-request form and submit it at the Foundation's website. The Foundation will contact you, if your organization qualifies under the Foundation's guidelines and the law.
Restrictions: Grants are not made to individuals.
Geographic Focus: All States
Amount of Grant: 100 - 50,000 USD
Contact: Anthony R. Abraham, Chairman; (305) 665-2222
Internet: http://www.abrahamfoundation.com/about
Sponsor: Anthony R. Abraham Foundation
1320 S Dixie Highway, Suite 241
Coral Gables, FL 33146-2937

Antone & Edene Vidinha Charitable Trust Grants 148
The trust provides partial support to programs and projects of tax-exempt, public charities in Hawaii to improve the quality of life in the state, particularly the island of Kauai. Grants of one year's duration are awarded in categories of interest to the trust, including: churches on Kauai; hospitals; health organizations which benefit the people of Kauai; educational scholarships to colleges and universities in the State of Hawaii for deserving students from the Island of Kauai. Types of support include building/renovation; equipment; general/operating support; program development; scholarship funds. Grants average from $2,000 - $80,000.
Requirements: 501(c)3 nonprofit organizations in Hawaii are eligible to apply.The Trust places a special emphasis on the island of Kauai. Contact Paula Boyce to acquire the cover sheet/application forms and any additional guidelines required to begin the application process. Proposals must be submitted by December 1st.
Restrictions: No grants to/for: individuals; endowments; multi-year pledges.
Geographic Focus: Hawaii
Date(s) Application is Due: Dec 1
Amount of Grant: 2,000 - 80,000 USD
Samples: Lihue Missionary Church, Lihue, HI, $19,800—equipment acquisition/program support grant; University of Hawaii Foundation, Honolulu, HI, $80,000—scholarship funds; Christ Memorial Episcopal Church, Kilauea, HI, $30,000—parish hall restoration.
Contact: Paula Boyce, c/o Bank of Hawaii; (808) 538-4944; fax (808) 538-4647; pboyce@boh.com
Internet: http://www.hawaiicommunityfoundation.org/index.php?id=290
Sponsor: Antone and Edene Vidinha Charitable Trust
Bank of Hawai'i, Foundation Administration Department 758
Honolulu, HI 96802-3170

Appalachian Community Fund General Grants 149
The Appalachian Community Fund (ACF) makes grants on a yearly basis from the General Fund program, which is supported by a combination of unrestricted funds and monies from the Alexander Fund of the New York Community Trust. ACF's General Fund is an annual board-directed program focusing on organizing for social change and is monies organizations may use for general support as well as for programs and projects. Organizations may apply for funding in one of two categories: Emerging Group/Seed Grant—up to $5,000 for groups in earlier stages of development; and Movement Building Group—up to $10,000 for more established groups.
Requirements: Nonprofit organizations in select Appalachian counties - including Kentucky, West Virginia, Virginia, and Tennessee - are eligible to apply.
Restrictions: ACF does not fund: profit-making organizations; electoral lobbying for initiatives or public office; individual efforts; major capital projects; or social services organizations (unless they demonstrate some analysis and strategies to challenge the systems that lead to the problem).
Geographic Focus: Kentucky, Tennessee, Virginia, West Virginia
Date(s) Application is Due: Nov 22
Amount of Grant: Up to 10,000 USD
Contact: Margo Miller, Executive Director; (865) 523-5783; fax (865) 523-1896; margo@appalachiancommunityfund.org or info@appalachiancommunityfund.org

Internet: http://www.appafund.org/html/generalfund.html
Sponsor: Appalachian Community Fund
530 South Gay Street, Suite 1120
Knoxville, TN 37902

Appalachian Regional Commission Export and Trade Development 150
Grants
Expanding export trade opportunities is an important strategy for increasing economic and employment success in the Appalachian Region. In 1995, ARC established the ARC Export Trade Advisory Council (ETAC) to advise the Commission on developing trade policy issues and to serve as an advocate for the Region within the global businesses community. Council members include trade directors and other officials from the 13 Appalachian states, international trade experts from the U.S. Commercial Service, representatives from the Development District Association of Appalachia, and members of the ARC federal staff. Through the council's Appalachia USA initiative, created in 2005, ETAC members plan and administer a variety of activities focused on promoting export opportunities for businesses across the Region. ETAC helps establish and sustain export trade partnerships and information-sharing opportunities, and focuses special attention on helping small to medium-sized Appalachian businesses become more successful in international commerce. Projects include support for conferences and events stressing trade economics and best practices, and for research on issues affecting the Region's ability to engage, compete, and succeed in the global economy of the 21st century.
Requirements: States, and through states, public bodies and private nonprofit organizations are eligible to apply.
Restrictions: Generally, ARC grants are limited to 50% of project costs.
Geographic Focus: Alabama, Georgia, Kentucky, Maryland, Mississippi, New York, North Carolina, Ohio, Pennsylvania, South Carolina, Tennessee, Virginia, West Virginia
Contact: Jill Wilmoth, Budget and Program Specialist; (202) 884-7668 or (202) 884-7700; fax (202) 884-7691; jwilmoth@arc.gov
Internet: http://www.arc.gov/export
Sponsor: Appalachian Regional Commission
1666 Connecticut Avenue NW, Suite 700
Washington, D.C. 20009-1068

Ar-Hale Family Foundation Grants 151
Established in Ohio in 1990, the Ar-Hale Family Foundation (formerly the Ar-Hale Foundation) is dedicated to supporting philanthropic and religious initiatives that personally impact the lives of families and children. Support is given primarily to communities where American Trim does business and in the communities where American Trim shareholders reside. The Foundation's major fields of interest include the support of: athletics and sports (primarily baseball); Catholic agencies and churches; Christian agencies and churches; K-12 education; family services; health care programs and access; higher education; human services; performing arts; and YMCAs and YWCAs. Many types of funding is offered, including: annual campaigns; building and renovation support; capital campaigns; consulting services; continuing support; curriculum development; emergency funds; endowments; fellowships; film, video, and radio production; general operating support; management development; capacity building; challenge support; program development; scholarships to individuals; seed money; and technical assistance. There are no annual deadlines, and most recent awards have ranged from $250 to $20,000.
Requirements: Non-profit organizations located in, or serving the residents, the following areas may apply: Louisville, Kentucky; Allen, Auglaize, and Shelby counties in Ohio; the cities of Dayton and Lima, Ohio; Shawnee, Oklahoma; and Erie, Pennsylvania.
Restrictions: No support is offered for political organizations.
Geographic Focus: Kentucky, Ohio, Oklahoma, Pennsylvania
Amount of Grant: 250 - 20,000 USD
Contact: Arlene F. Hawk, President; (419) 331-1040; dprueter@cox.net
Sponsor: Ar-Hale Family Foundation
P.O. Box 210
Lima, OH 45802-0210

Aragona Family Foundation Grants 152
Giving primarily in Austin, Texas, the Aragona Family Foundation provides general operating support grants in the following areas of interest: animals/wildlife, preservation/protection; cancer; children/youth, services; community/economic development; education; food banks; hospitals (general); philanthropy/voluntarism; protestant agencies & churches. Grants range from $2,000 - $100,000.

Requirements: Qualifying 501(c)3 organizations are eligible to apply for funding. There is no: application form required; deadline date to adhere to.
Geographic Focus: Texas
Amount of Grant: 2,000 - 100,000 USD
Samples: St. Stephens Episcopal School, Austin, TX, $100,000—to further the organizations charitable mission; Harvard University, Cambridge, MA, $533,300—to further the organizations charitable mission.
Contact: Joseph C. Aragona, President; (512) 328-2178
Sponsor: Aragona Family Foundation
3311 Westlake Drive
Austin, TX 78746-1901

Aratani Foundation Grants   153
The foundation awards grants to nonprofits in its areas of interest, including education, health care, museums, recreation, and religion. Preference is given to Japanese-American cultural organizations. Types of support include annual campaigns, building construction/renovation, capital campaigns, conferences and seminars, continuing support, curriculum development, endowments, exchange programs, fellowships, general operating support, program development, scholarship funds, and seed grants.
Requirements: The Foundation gives primarily in the state of California but funding is also available in the states of: New York; District of Columbia; Washington; Florida; Rhode Island; Oregon. Application forms are not required, but application outlines are available. Contact the Foundation directly for additional guidelines. Applications maybe submitted in English and Japanese. There are no application deadline dates.
Restrictions: Grants are not made to individuals.
Geographic Focus: California, District of Columbia, Florida, New York, Oregon, Rhode Island, Washington
Amount of Grant: 1,000 - 150,000 USD
Samples: Asian Pacific American Legal Center of South California, Los Angeles, CA, $50,000; Asian Pacific American Institute for Congressional Studies, Washington, DC, $10,000; Buddhist Churches of America, San Francisco, CA, $200,000.
Contact: George Aratani, President; (310) 530-9900
Sponsor: Aratani Foundation
23505 Crenshaw Boulevard, North 230
Hollywood, CA 90505

Arbor Day Foundation Grants   154
The mission of the National Tree Trust continues through the Arbor Day Foundation, a nonprofit, environmental education organization with a mission of inspiring people to plant, nurture, and celebrate trees. The Program provides appropriate support and resources to urban and community forestry and conservation nonprofit organizations working to engage the members of their community in urban and community forestry. The programs of the Foundation are Seeds—technology, general office equipment and supplies, rent for office space, salaries and wages, general printing and postage, and professional contract services; Roots—education, involvement of underserved communities, tree planting and maintenance, community nursery, and service learning; and Branches—community outreach. Guidelines are available online.
Requirements: Eligible organizations will include qualified 501(c)3 nonprofits that have been in existence for two years, and are either an urban and community forestry organization or a conservation-focused organization working on urban and community forestry projects.
Geographic Focus: All States
Contact: Mark Derowitsch, Public Relations Manager; (888) 448-7337; mderowitsch@arborday.org
Internet: http://www.arborday.org/programs/
Sponsor: Arbor Day Foundation
100 Arbor Avenue
Nebraska City, NE 68410

Arcadia Foundation Grants   155
The foundation awards grants to Pennsylvania nonprofit organizations to improve the quality of life. Areas of interest include hospitals and hospital building funds, health agencies and services, nursing, hospices, early childhood, adult and higher education, libraries, child development and welfare agencies, youth organizations, and social service and general welfare agencies, including care of the handicapped, aged, and hungry. Also supported are family services, environment and conservation, wildlife and animal welfare, religious organizations, historical preservation, and music organizations. Types of support include general operating support, continuing support, annual campaigns, capital campaigns, building construction/renovation, equipment acquisition, endowment funds, program development, scholarship funds, and research. Applications are accepted between September 1 and November 1.
Requirements: Eastern Pennsylvania organizations whose addresses have zip codes of 18000-19000 are eligible. Application form not required. The initial approach should be a letter or proposal—not exceeding two pages.
Restrictions: Grants are not awarded to support individuals, deficit financing, land acquisition, fellowships, demonstration projects, publications, or conferences.
Geographic Focus: Pennsylvania
Date(s) Application is Due: Nov 1
Samples: Thomas Jefferson U (Philadelphia, PA)—for a new medical education building, $1 million.
Contact: Marilyn Lee Steinbright, President; (610) 275-8460
Sponsor: Arcadia Foundation
105 E Logan Street
Norristown, PA 19401

Arca Foundation Grants   156
The Arca Foundation believes that access to knowledge, vigorous public education and citizen engagement are essential to democracy. However, there exist structures and private interests that serve to limit the transparency of our government, stifle public debate on critical issues, and foster an environment where government is not effectively serving the interests of its citizens. In order to promote greater social equity and justice at home and abroad, the foundation supports organizations and projects that work to advance transparent, accountable, and just policies. They support strategic initiatives that work to directly affect policies by: Developing and advocating for innovative ideas; Promoting transparency and access to information; Fostering greater public debate on critical issues; Educating key stakeholders; Engaging citizens in strategic organizing and advocacy that builds power and drives change.
Requirements: Domestically, in the current sociopolitical climate, the foundation is concerned about the promotion of a more equitable, accountable, and transparent economic recovery. They are considering proposals that work to advance more just policies on this and other critical issues. Internationally, the foundation has a long history of working to promote greater dialogue between the U.S. and Cuba. They are considering proposals that advance policies that further normalized US-Cuban relations, as well as proposals that work to foster more just policies on a range of international issues. The Arca Foundation has two deadlines annually, on March 1 and September 1 of every year, for consideration in June and December respectively. When deadline dates fall on a weekend, the deadline is effective on the next weekday. The foundation will not respond to letters of inquiry, but will accept complete proposals submitted according to the application guidelines on regular grant deadlines.
Restrictions: The foundation does not fund organizations that provide direct social services, scholarship funds or scholarly research, capital projects or endowments, individuals, or government programs. Proposals received via fax or email will not be considered. Late proposals will not be considered, and extensions are not available for any reason.
Geographic Focus: All States
Date(s) Application is Due: Mar 1; Sep 1
Amount of Grant: 50,000 USD
Contact: Emily Casteel, Program Associate; (202) 822-9193; fax (202) 785-1446; grants@arcafoundation.org
Internet: http://www.arcafoundation.org/howtoapply.htm
Sponsor: Arca Foundation
1308 19th Street NW
Washington, D.C. 20036

ARCO Foundation Education Grants   157
The foundation will concentrate its aid to education in support of the following: precollege programs to improve the quality of teaching and learning in urban public education; programs aimed at decreasing attrition rates among low-income and minority students; programs to motivate low-income and minority students to succeed in college, especially in mathematics-based careers of engineering, science, and business; support for laboratory renovation and scientific equipment in academic disciplines of interest at major research universities; programs to retain the most talented young faculty in academic careers in selected disciplines; selected liberal arts programs at colleges and universities of interest; state associations of private colleges in the states where the company has interests; academic programs relevant to energy interests at regional universities and colleges; and national education associations and organizations that seek to improve education in public high schools and at higher academic levels. Grants are awarded for operating budgets, seed

money, equipment, land acquisition, matching funds, employee matching gifts, employee related scholarships, special projects, and technical assistance. Applications are accepted at any time; annual report should be obtained prior to submitting a formal proposal.

Requirements: The foundation is a regional organization funding nonprofit organizations in states where ARCO has facilities and personnel, including Alaska, Arizona, California, Colorado, Nevada, Texas, and Washington. Requests from those states and those nearby should be addressed to the local community affairs managers.

Restrictions: The foundation discourages applications from the following: programs not focused on promoting self-sufficiency and economic development of minority populations; historic preservation or urban development projects not tied to neighborhood economic revitalization; proposals from religious organizations; or funding requests from federal, state, county, and municipal agencies, including school districts. The foundation does not generally consider support of hospital building or endowment campaigns, medical equipment, medical research programs, single-issue health organizations, or health services not directed at low-income people.

Geographic Focus: Alaska, Arizona, California, Colorado, Nevada, Texas, Washington

Amount of Grant: 1,500 - 360,000 USD

Samples: U of Montana (Butte, MT)—to help retain and graduate minority students pursuing engineering degrees, $16,500; U of California (Davis, CA)—to help retain and graduate minority students pursuing engineering degrees, $47,000.

Contact: Virginia Victorin; (213) 486-3342; fax (213) 486-0113

Internet: http://www.ntlf.com/html/grants/5977.htm

Sponsor: ARCO Foundation

151 South Flower Street

Los Angeles, CA 90071

Arcus Foundation Fund Grants 158

The Arcus Foundation is a private grantmaking foundation that supports organizations around the world working in two areas - lesbian, gay, bisexual, and transgender (LGBT) human rights; and conservation of the world's great apes. In the former area, the Foundation supports organizations that are working to achieve social justice that is inclusive of sexual orientation, gender identity and race. In the latter area, it supports organizations seeking to ensure respect and survival of great apes and their natural habitat. Specifically, the Arcus Fund supports efforts within Michigan to improve the quality of life for the gay, lesbian, bisexual and transgender (GLBT) community. Areas of special interest include social equity, public awareness and understanding, health and safety, and scientific inquiry. Types of support include: annual campaigns; building/renovation; capital campaigns; conferences and seminars; consulting services; continuing support; curriculum development; employee matching gifts; endowments; general operating support; matching/challenge support; program development; program evaluation; program-related investments/loans; publication; and technical assistance.

Requirements: Nonprofit organizations are eligible.

Restrictions: No grants to are given to individuals, or for religious or political activities, medical research or film/video production.

Geographic Focus: Michigan

Amount of Grant: 1,000 - 50,000 USD

Contact: Myron Cobbs, Program Assistant; (269) 373-4373, ext. 110; fax (269) 373-0277; myron@arcusfoundation.org or info@arcusfoundation.org

Internet: http://www.arcusfoundation.org/pages_2/home.cfm

Sponsor: Arcus Foundation

402 East Michigan Avenue

Kalamazoo, MI 49007

Arie and Ida Crown Memorial Grants 159

The program supports programs that offer opportunities to the disadvantaged, strengthens the bond of families, and improves the quality of people's lives. As a general rule, the Foundation funds organizations that serve the greater Chicago area as well as organizations that serve the broader Jewish community. Most grants are awarded to organizations within the city of Chicago. Organizations are supported in the areas of arts and culture (concentrating on educational and enrichment programs for youth), civic affairs, education, health (stressing access to services, hospice and health promotion), and human service (focusing on programs which offer assistance for children and families).

Requirements: Nonprofit organizations in Chicago and Cook County, IL, may apply for grant support.

Restrictions: Grants are not made to support individuals, conference expenses, film projects, government programs (50 percent government funded), or research projects.

Geographic Focus: Illinois

Date(s) Application is Due: Jan 31; Jul 31

Amount of Grant: 1,000 - 200,000 USD

Contact: Susan Crown, President; (312) 236-6300; fax (312) 984-1499; AICM@crown-Chicago.com

Internet: http://www.crownmemorial.org/

Sponsor: Arie and Ida Crown Memorial

222 N LaSalle Street, Suite 2000

Chicago, IL 60601

Arizona Commission on the Arts Community Investment Grants 160

Community Investment Grants (CIG) provide funding support for arts organizations that demonstrate exceptional alignment with the criteria of the CIG program. Organizations may use CIG funds for general operating expenses (frequently the most difficult type of grant to obtain) as well as leverage for other public and private funding. CIG eligibility levels are based on organizational adjusted annual income. The annual deadline for application submission is March 19. Depending upon organizational size, awards can range from $5,000 to $1,250,000.

Requirements: Community Investment grant awards are available to nonprofit arts organizations of all sizes, local arts agencies and tribal cultural organizations whose primary mission is to produce, present, teach or serve the arts. CIG awards must be matched with cash (at least 1:1) by the organization. An applicant must be incorporated as an Arizona nonprofit organization with tax-exempt status or be a unit of government. Eligible organizations include Arizona arts organizations, local arts agencies and tribal cultural organizations.

Restrictions: Matching grants do not assist communities that have a percent for art ordinance in place.

Geographic Focus: Arizona

Date(s) Application is Due: Mar 19

Amount of Grant: 5,000 - 1,250,000 USD

Contact: Kristen Pierce; (602) 771-6517 or (602) 771-6501; fax (602) 256-0282; kpierce@azarts.gov or info@azarts.gov

Internet: http://www.arizonaarts.org/artists/aguide/index.htm

Sponsor: Arizona Commission on the Arts

417 West Roosevelt Street

Phoenix, AZ 85003-6501

Arizona Commission on the Arts Tribal Museum Assessment Grants 161

The program is designed for tribal museums that have or intend to hire a professional, full-time managing director. Applicants are eligible to apply for up to 50 percent of the managing director's salary.

Requirements: Arizona 501(c)3 tax-exempt organizations, schools, and units of tribal government may apply.

Geographic Focus: Arizona

Date(s) Application is Due: Feb 10

Contact: Shelley Cohn, Executive Director; (602) 255-5882; fax (602) 256-0282; scohn@ArizonaArts.org or info@arizonaarts.org

Internet: http://www.arizonaarts.org/guide/gos_tribal.htm

Sponsor: Arizona Commission on the Arts

417 West Roosevelt Street

Phoenix, AZ 85003-6501

Arizona Community Foundation Grants 162

The foundation focuses on areas that bring together donor interests with community needs, best practices and respected research to influence long-term systemic change. The foundation's goal is to improve conditions, circumstances and opportunities for people across Arizona and beyond. The foundation focus areas include: arts in the schools; arts in the communities; children, youth and families; campaign for working families; community development; communities for all ages; capacity building; alliance of Arizona nonprofits; strategic partnerships; Hispanics in partnership; and the tapestry community fund. Types of support include general operating support, continuing support, building construction/renovation, equipment acquisition, emergency funds, program development, publication, seed money, scholarship funds, research, technical assistance, and matching funds. For a complete list of criteria, visit the website.

Requirements: Arizona 501(c)3 organizations are eligible as well as public schools, Native American tribes and their component agencies, and selected public programs.

Restrictions: Grants will not be made to individuals; for deficit financing; endowment funds; employee matching gifts; basic research; conferences and seminars; religious organizations for religious purposes; direct lobbying or influencing of elections; tax-supported governmental functions or programs;

fund-raising campaigns and expenses; telephone and/or mail solicitation, capital campaigns; or support of veteran, fraternal, and labor organizations.
Geographic Focus: Arizona
Date(s) Application is Due: Apr 1; Oct 1
Contact: Alice McKinney, Grants Administrator; (602) 381-1400 or (800) 222-8221; fax (602) 381-1575; amckinney@azfoundation.org
Internet: http://www.azfoundation.org/File/static/grant_seekers/initiatives.shtml
Sponsor: Arizona Community Foundation
2201 E Camelback Road, Suite 202
Phoenix, AZ 85016

Arizona Diamondbacks Charities Grants   163

The major-league baseball franchise awards grants in Arizona to support as wide as possible a variety of charitable causes. Priority will to be given to organizations that fall under the foundation's focus areas of health care for the indigent, homelessness and youth education. Types of support include general support, project grants, donated equipment, employee matching gifts, corporate sponsorships, and speakers. Organizations wishing to apply for a grant can fax a request to the community affairs department.
Requirements: Applicants must be 501(c)3 Arizona-based organizations committed to spending grant proceeds in Arizona.
Geographic Focus: Arizona
Samples: Arizona's Children (Phoenix, AZ)—for a program to provide behavioral health services to children and their families; Golden Gate Community Ctr (Phoenix, AZ)—to help replace evaporative coolers in the center's gymnasium; Make Way for Books (Tucson, AZ)—to promote early literacy in low-income area preschools.
Contact: Program Contact; (602) 462-6500; fax (602) 462-6575
Internet: http://arizona.diamondbacks.mlb.com/ari/community/foundation.jsp
Sponsor: Arizona Diamondbacks
P.O. Box 2095
Phoenix, AZ 85001

Arizona Foundation for Legal Services and Education Grants   164

The foundation awards general support grants to nonprofit organizations providing legal aid to the poor in Arizona. Application guidelines are available online in the Fall. Initial contact should be letter of inquiry; telephone calls also are welcome.
Requirements: Arizona nonprofits are eligible.
Geographic Focus: Arizona
Amount of Grant: 2,000 - 200,000 USD
Samples: Advocates For The Disabled (AZ)—$22,000; Florence Immigrant and Refugee Rights Project (AZ)—$105,000; The Justice Project (AZ)—$6000; William E. Morris Institute for Justice (AZ)—$85,000.
Contact: Lara Slifko, (602) 252-4804; fax (602) 271-4930; Lara.Slifko@azflse.org
Internet: http://www.azflse.org/AZFLSE/legalservices/ioltagrants.cfm
Sponsor: Arizona Foundation for Legal Services and Education
111 W Monroe, Suite 1800
Phoenix, AZ 85003-1742

Arizona Public Service Corporate Giving Grants   165

Grants are awarded to support Arizona nonprofit organizations in the areas of health and human services, community development, arts and culture, education, and environment. The foundation awards support for project grants, capital building funds, research, employee matching gifts, in-kind services, conferences and seminars, and operating support. Applications are accepted on an ongoing basis.
Requirements: Arizona 501(c)3 nonprofits are eligible.
Restrictions: APS Corporate Giving does not fund individual request, charter or private schools, religious, political fraternal, legislative or lobbying efforts to organizations, travel-related or hotel expenses, private or family foundation, private non-profit organizations, salaries and/or debt reduction.
Geographic Focus: Arizona
Samples: Hospice of the Valley (Phoenix, AZ)—for operating support, $10,000; Arizona Bridge to Independent Living (Phoenix, AZ)—for program support, $3000; Arizona Wolf Trap—to sponsor a series of field trips for children to visit performing arts centers.
Contact: Cindy Slick; (602) 250-4707; fax (602) 250-2113; Cindy.Slick@aps.com
Internet: http://www.aps.com/main/community/dev/default.html
Sponsor: Arizona Public Service Corporation
P.O. Box 53999, MS 8010
Phoenix, AZ 85072-3999

Arizona Republic Foundation Grants   166

The foundation awards grants in Arizona, with emphasis on the Phoenix metropolitan area, in its focus areas, including arts and culture, children, hunger, homelessness, the elderly, neighborhoods, victims of domestic violence, literacy, and community-based education programs. Support is given for general support, operating expenses, project grants, in-kind services, and donated products. Contact office for deadlines and availability.
Requirements: Arizona nonprofits may apply.
Geographic Focus: Arizona
Samples: Aunt Rita's Foundation (Phoenix, AZ)—AIDS assistance program; East Valley Child Crisis Center (Phoenix, AZ); Valley Citizen's League (Phoenix, AZ); Kids Voting Arizona (Phoenix, AZ).
Contact: Gene D'Adamo, Vice President; (602) 444-8202
Internet: http://www.azcentral.com/arizonarepublic/relations/initiatives.html
Sponsor: Arizona Republic Foundation
200 E Van Buren
Phoenix, AZ 85004

Arizona Republic Newspaper Corporate Contributions Grants   167

The corporation awards grants in Arizona, primarily in the Phoenix metropolitan area, for programs in its areas of interest, including child abuse prevention, domestic violence prevention, education and literacy, arts, drowning prevention, community leadership, regional community building, diversity and cultural awareness. Initiatives focus on the basic needs of individuals, with children as a primary focus. Priority is given to agencies that serve low-income and under-served families and children. Application materials and proposal guidelines are available from the office. Annual deadline dates may vary; contact program staff for exact dates.
Requirements: Arizona nonprofits may apply.
Geographic Focus: Arizona
Amount of Grant: 10,000 - 20,000 USD
Samples: Downtown Neighborhood Learning Ctr (Phoenix, AZ)—for general support, $15,000; Area Agency on Aging (Phoenix, AZ)—to support an elderly abuse prevention program, $20,000.
Contact: Laura McBride; (602) 444-8071; fax (602) 444-8242
Internet: http://www.azcentral.com/arizonarepublic/relations
Sponsor: Arizona Republic Newspaper
200 E Van Buren
Phoenix, AZ 85004

Arkansas Arts Council General Operating Support   168

The Arkansas Arts Council General Operating Support grants help fund administrative operating expenses of established nonprofit local arts agencies or single discipline organizations with a budget equal to or greater than $50,000. Funding may be spent only for non-programmatic, administrative expenses. These can include, but are not limited to, administrative staff salaries, general marketing and fundraising costs, facility rental, utilities, maintenance of the facility, staff travel, or other expenses associated with the general operation of the organization. Grant review criteria for the organization is based on the organization's history and program description, community interaction and accessibility, its educational outreach, and long ranging planning and evaluation. Applicants may request a percentage of the adjusted operating total income of their last completed fiscal year, with the amount based on their budget size. The deadline is January 25, with a letter of intent due by December 7. The application and detailed financial guidelines are available at the website.
Requirements: An organization is eligible for general operating support (GOS) if it received a GOS for the current year as a 501(c)3 arts organization with a total operating budget equal to or greater than $50,000, or it has been approved as a newly eligible GOS applicant after filing a letter of intent by a certain date. It may also be eligible if it meets the following criteria: employs a full-time executive director if its annual budget total ranges from $150,000 to $999,999; or employs at least a part time paid executive director, with its annual budget ranging from $50,000 to $149,999. Applicants may also be eligible if they have an independent audit of their current fiscal year on file with the Council, with a budget of $500,000 or more, or have an IRS tax form 990 on file with a budget of less than $500,000. GOS requests for administrative support must be matched two to one by the applicant's expenditures on artistic programming. The cash must be from sources other than the Arkansas Arts Council, the Mid-America Arts Alliance, or the National Endowment for the Arts. Other portions of the proposal not involved in the specific Arts Council request and its match may be funded by government sources.
Restrictions: Funding may not be used for artistic or technical staff, or for contracted administrative or artistic costs.

Geographic Focus: Arkansas
Date(s) Application is Due: Jan 25
Contact: Jess Anthony, Grant Programs Manager; (501) 324-9768; fax (501) 324-9207; jess@arkansasheritage.org
Internet: http://www.arkansasarts.org/grants/gos.aspx
Sponsor: Arkansas Arts Council
323 Center Street, Suite 1500
Little Rock, AR 72201-2606

Arkell Hall Foundation Grants   169

The primary mission of the foundation is the operation and maintenance of a home for elderly women. Funds that may become available above the needs of the home may be distributed annually to tax-exempt organizations providing services in the target community—Western Montgomery County, NY—with preference given to those active in service to senior citizens, education (higher education, medical education, adult basic education and literacy), religion (Christian, Christian Reformed Church, Lutheran, Methodist, Roman Catholic, the Salvation Army, and United Methodist), and health care. Types of support include capital, challenge, endowment, general support, matching, and seed money grants. Grants are made on a single-year basis and are awarded annually in October or November. It is recommended that requests be submitted between July 1 and September 15. Initial review of requests is performed upon receipt. Results are forwarded to the applicant within one month.
Requirements: IRS 501(c)3 organizations directly impacting the Western Montgomery County, NY, community are eligible.
Restrictions: Requests that do not include written proof of 501(c)3 status will not be considered. Projects or organizations with large service areas, such as national or regional, will not qualify for funding, nor will projects in which the target community is not the primary area of focus.
Geographic Focus: New York
Date(s) Application is Due: Oct 1
Amount of Grant: 1,000 - 50,000 USD
Samples: Cornell University, College of Human Ecology (Ithaca, NY)—for general support, $20,000; College of Saint Rose (Albany, NY)—to support scholarships for single mothers, $3000.
Contact: Joseph Santangelo; (518) 673-5417; fax (518) 673-5493
Sponsor: Arkell Hall Foundation
68 Front Street, P.O. Box 240
Canajoharie, NY 13317-0240

Arlington Community Foundation Grants   170

The foundation awards grants in Arlington to educators and nonprofit organizations for innovative projects that supplement and enrich the learning environment for preschool to adult students. The focus is curriculum enrichment, the arts (musical, dramatic, visual), pursuit of higher education, vocational education, after school and summer programs, life-long learning, environmental issues, parent involvement, and community involvement. The community enhancement grants support arts and humanities, children & families, community improvement, health, housing/homeless & hunger, legal, social services, and senior enrichment. The purpose of the Prompt Response Fund is to enable nonprofit groups in Arlington respond quickly to unanticipated opportunities or unexpected, urgent community needs. Deadlines may vary. Guidelines and applications are available online.
Requirements: Organizations and individuals with projects designed to meet educational needs of Arlington residents are encouraged to apply.
Restrictions: The foundation does not make grants for endowments, capital campaigns, religious purposes, individual debts, or political lobbying.
Geographic Focus: Virginia
Contact: Wanda L. Pierce; (703) 243-4785; fax (703) 243-4796; info@arlcf.org
Internet: http://www.arlcf.org/grants.html
Sponsor: Arlington Community Foundation
2525 Wilson Boulevard
Arlington, VA 22201

Armstrong McDonald Foundation Animal Welfare Grants   171

The Armstrong McDonald Foundation was incorporated in the State of Nebraska in 1986. The mission of the Foundation is to continue the philanthropic ideals and goals of James M. McDonald, Sr. through prudent and impartial review of all qualifying grant requests received annually to insure that awards are made to soundly conceived and operated non-profit organizations. For its Animal Welfare funding, the Foundation will consider only requests for assistance with endangered species reproduction research; for training of guide dogs for the visually impaired; and for training of dogs to be companions for the physically

challenged or for mobility restricted seniors. The Foundation provides a formal downloadable application which is to be completed by all applicants approved for submission of a grant request. All required application materials need to be postmarked or received by email on or before September 30.
Requirements: The Armstrong McDonald Foundation will only accept unsolicited grant requests from those IRS approved non-profits listed on the Pre-Approved for Grant Submission List. Please note that this list will be updated annually in December with additions and/or deletions. All other IRS approved non-profits desiring to submit a grant request to this foundation must meet the following three qualifications: be incorporated in either the State of Arizona or Nebraska; have a physical office located in their state of incorporation; and spend any awarded grant funds within their state of incorporation.
Restrictions: Grants do not support advocacy organizations, individuals, international organizations, political organizations, or state and local government agencies. The foundation does not fund capital campaigns, salaries/stipends, and multi-year projects. Organization must have received a grant from the foundation within the last five years unless it is located within the states of Arizona or Nebraska. No organization east of the Mississippi is eligible for a grant.
Geographic Focus: All States
Date(s) Application is Due: Sep 30
Amount of Grant: 1,000 - 80,000 USD
Contact: Laurie L. Bouchard, President; (520) 878-9627; fax (520) 797-3866; info@ArmstrongMcDonaldFoundation.org
Internet: http://www.armstrongmcdonaldfoundation.org/cat.html
Sponsor: Armstrong McDonald Foundation
P.O. Box 70110
Tucson, AZ 85737-0110

Arronson Foundation Grants   172

The foundation supports nonprofit organizations in the areas of religion, including churches (Baptist, Christian, Jewish, Roman Catholic, and Salvation Army) and religious education, higher education, health care, hospices, Jewish welfare, international ministries/missions, and youth. The foundation awards grants primarily in New York, NY; Philadelphia, PA; and Israel. Types of support include endowment funds, general operating support grants, research, scholarships, and seed money grants. Applicants should submit a brief letter of inquiry and include information on the organization and its work. There are no application deadlines.
Requirements: Nonprofit organizations in Pennsylvania, with emphasis on the Philadelphia area, are eligible to apply.
Geographic Focus: Pennsylvania
Amount of Grant: 200 - 25,000 USD
Contact: Joseph Kohn; (215) 238-1700 or (215) 238-1968; jkohn@kohnswift.com
Sponsor: Arronson Foundation
1 S Broad Street, Suite 2100
Philadelphia, PA 19107

Arthur and Rochelle Belfer Foundation Grants   173

The foundation awards grants to nonprofit organizations of the Jewish faith, with a focus on New York. Grants are targeted toward programs supporting the elderly and women; education/higher education; institutions such as seminaries, synagogues, and temples; hospitals; Jewish welfare; and medical centers. Types of support include general support grants and fellowships. There are no application deadlines. Applicants should send a brief letter of inquiry describing the program.
Restrictions: Grants are not made to individuals.
Geographic Focus: New York
Amount of Grant: 1,000 - 100,000 USD
Samples: Joan S. Brugge, PhD, chair, Department of Cell Biology, arvard Medical School—for breast cancer studies; Dana-Farber Cancer Institute (Boston, MA)—for general support, $1 million; Anti-Defamation League of B'nai B'rith (New York, NY)—for operating support, $22,000; American Friends of Israel Museum (New York, NY)—for operating support, $5000.
Contact: Robert Belfer, President; (212) 508-6020
Sponsor: Arthur and Rochelle Belfer Foundation
767 Fifth Avenue, 46th Floor
New York, NY 10153-0002

Arthur E. and Josephine Campbell Beyer Foundation Grants   174

Established in Indiana, giving is centered in the Noble County region. The Foundation's primary fields of interest include: higher education; human services; and recreation. Grants are offered in the form of scholarship funding and general operations. Since there are no application forms required, applicants should submit personal contact information in writing, along with a detailed description of the project, the primary contact person, and budgetary needs. The annual deadline for submission is May 31. Amounts range from $1,000 to $6,000.

Geographic Focus: All States
Date(s) Application is Due: May 31
Amount of Grant: 1,000 - 6,000 USD
Samples: Life and Family Services, Kendallville, Indiana, $6,000 - for purchase of baby store supplies; Noble House, Albion, Indiana, $5,500 - for general operating expenses and transportation; Kendallville Day Care, Kendallville, Indiana, $5,000 - scholarship funding.
Contact: Jenny King, Vice President and Trust Officer; (260) 461-6458; fax (260) 461-6678; jennifer.i.king@wellsfargo.com
Sponsor: Arthur E. and Josephine Campbell Beyer Foundation
1919 Douglas Street
Omaha, NE 68102-1310

Arthur F. and Alice E. Adams Charitable Foundation Grants   175

Established in Florida in 1987, the Arthur F. and Alice E. Adams Charitable Foundation is managed by a board of governors with the Wells Fargo Philanthropic Services acting as corporate governor. The Foundation offers support in the arts, education, and human services. Primary fields of interest include: performing arts centers, opera, and medical research. Grants range from $5,000 to $250,000, with giving in the areas around Miami, New York City, and Memphis. The annual deadline is February 15, though board members meet in both May and November. Applicants should forward a letter describing their need and budget.

Requirements: 501(c)3 organizations located in, or serving the residents of, the following areas are eligible to apply: Miami, Florida; New York, New York; and Memphis, Tennessee.
Restrictions: No grants are awarded to individuals.
Geographic Focus: Florida, New York, Tennessee
Date(s) Application is Due: Feb 15
Amount of Grant: 5,000 - 250,000 USD
Samples: Circuit Playhouse on the Square, Memphis, Tennessee, $125,000 - capital campaign; Preservation League of New York, Albany, New York, $50,000 - general operating support; Florida International University Foundation, Miami, Florida, $50,000 - ongoing support.
Contact: Peter Thompson, Vice President; (336) 747-8186 or (908) 598-3582; fax (855) 224-4572; grantadministration@wellsfargo.com
Sponsor: Arthur F. and Alice E. Adams Charitable Foundation
1525 W. W.T. Harris Boulevard, D1114-044
Charlotte, NC 28288-5709

Arthur F. and Arnold M. Frankel Foundation Grants   176

Established in New York in 1990, the Arthur F. and Arnold M. Frankel Foundation offers financial support in both New York City and throughout the State of California. The Foundation's primary fields of interest include: the arts; health care and health care access; and human service programs. A specific application form is required, and can be secured by contacting the Foundation office. Most recent grant awards have ranged from $1,000 to as much as $155,000. There have been no annual deadlines identified.

Geographic Focus: California, New York
Amount of Grant: 1,000 - 155,000 USD
Samples: Fractured Atlas, New York, New York, $154,700 - general support for area arts program; Center For Independent Doctors, Sharon, Massachusetts, $74,290 - general operating support; Mehadi Foundation, Burbank, California, $107,000 - general operating support for helping veterans heal.
Contact: Jedd H. Wider; (212) 362-2703; fax jwider@morganlewis.com
Sponsor: Arthur F. and Arnold M. Frankel Foundation
101 Park Avenue
New York, NY 10178-6000

Artist Trust GAP Grants   177

The mission of the trust is to support individual artists working in all disciplines in order to enrich community life throughout the state of Washington. Grants for Artist Projects (GAP) provide support for artist-generated projects, which can include but are not limited to the development, completion, or presentation of new work. Projects created in all disciplines are eligible. A multidisciplinary panel of artists and arts professionals from around Washington State select GAP recipients. Applications/guidelines are available online only to Artist Trust members. Non-members may visit Artist Trust's office to pick up guidelines or request paper guidelines by sending a self-addressed, stamped, business-sized envelope to Artist Trust Office: Attn: GAP, 1835 12th Avenue, Seattle, WA, 98122-2437.

Requirements: The applicant must be a practicing artist and submit only one application per year; be 18 years of age or older by the application deadline; and be a resident of the state of Washington at the time of application and when the award is granted. Applications must be made in the name of an individual artist.
Restrictions: The applicant must not be a graduate or undergraduate matriculated student enrolled in any degree program. Applications made in the name of collectives, companies, bands, groups, and ensembles will not be accepted.
Geographic Focus: Washington
Date(s) Application is Due: Jun 25
Amount of Grant: 1,500 USD
Samples: Heather Dew, Oaksen, Seattle, WA, $1,500— to go towards production costs for a location shooting of interviews throughout the State for the feature documentary, It's About Time; Jason Skipper, Tacoma, WA, $1,500—to help defray the cost of living during, while Jason works on his short story; Alma Garcia, Seattle, WA, $1,500— to fund childcare, allowing the author to transform a short story collection into a novel.
Contact: Monica Miller, Director of Programs; (206) 467-8734, ext. 10; fax (206) 467-9633; info@artisttrust.org
Internet: http://www.artisttrust.org/grants
Sponsor: Artist Trust
1835 12th Avenue
Seattle, WA 98122-2437

Arts and Science Council Grants   178

The council administers a number of grant programs, allocating funds to affiliate organizations, schools, artists, and arts, science, history, and heritage organizations based on a competitive application process. Types of grants offered are fellowships, basic operating grants, Community Cultural Connections grants, education grants, Grassroots Grants Program, and the Regional Artist Project Grants Program. Application forms are available on the Web site.

Requirements: Artists and organizations in North Carolina's Mecklenburg County, and the City of Charlotte are eligible.
Geographic Focus: North Carolina
Amount of Grant: Up to 13,000,000 USD
Contact: Cathy Switalski, Grants Officer; (704) 372-9667, ext. 246; fax (704) 372-8210; cathy.switalski@artsandscience.org
Internet: http://www.artsandscience.org/index.asp?fuseaction=GrantsServices.GrantPrograms
Sponsor: Arts and Science Council - Charlotte/Mecklenburg
227 W Trade Street, Suite 250
Charlotte, NC 28202

Arts Council of Winston-Salem and Forsyth County Organizational   179
Support Grants

The council awards a variety of grants to area organizations and individuals. The Organizational Support Grant is an evaluative program that rewards organizations demonstrating artistic and organizational excellence with financial support for operating and administrative costs. To apply for an Grant, whether a new applicant or current Funded Partner, applicants must attend one of two mandatory information sessions scheduled each year.

Requirements: Only members of The Arts Council of Winston-Salem and Forsyth County with an individual 501(c)3 IRS designation are eligible to apply.
Geographic Focus: North Carolina
Date(s) Application is Due: May 2
Contact: Chris Koenig, Director of Partner & Grant Programs; (336) 722-2585, ext. 121; fax (336) 761-8286; ckoenig@intothearts.org
Internet: http://www.intothearts.org/grants/available.asp
Sponsor: Arts Council of Winston-Salem and Forsyth County
226 North Marshall Street
Winston-Salem, NC 27101

ArvinMeritor Foundation Health Grants   180

The foundation provides grants primarily in company-operating locations in the areas of education and training, civic and health, youth organizations, and arts and culture. In the area of Health, the foundation supports programs designed to promote health research, treatment, education, and awareness; and reduce the cost of illness. Types of support include general operating budgets, building funds, continuing support, equipment, and projects. The committee foundation meets every six to eight weeks to review grant requests. Contact program staff for current guidelines.

Requirements: Nonprofit 501(c)3 organizations should submit a one- to two-page letter outlining the purpose and needs of the program, its budget, duration, goals, leadership, and amount requested.

Restrictions: Ineligibility applies to individuals; organizations that limit participation or services based on race, gender, religion, color, creed, age, or national origin; projects without ties to a community that is home to an ArvinMeritor facility; organizations that pose any conflict with the goals and mission of ArvinMeritor, its employees, communities, or products; operating expenses for United Way local agencies, except through the foundation's support of annual United Way campaigns; sponsorships of fund raising activities by individuals (i.e., walk-a-thons); requests for loans or debt retirement; religious or sectarian programs for religious purposes; labor, political, or veterans organizations; fraternal, athletic, or social clubs; or seminars, conferences, trips, and tours.
Geographic Focus: All States
Contact: Jerry Rush; (248) 435-7907; jerry.rush@arvinmeritor.com
Internet: http://www.arvinmeritor.com/community/community.asp
Sponsor: ArvinMeritor Foundation
2135 W Maple Road
Troy, MI 48084

ArvinMeritor Foundation Human Services Grants   181
The foundation provides grants primarily in company-operating locations in the areas of education and training, civic and health, youth organizations, and arts and culture. In the area of Human Services, the foundation supports programs designed to provide emergency help and critical support toward promoting self-sufficiency. Types of support include general operating budgets, building funds, continuing support, equipment, and projects. The committee foundation meets every six to eight weeks to review grant requests. Contact program staff for current guidelines.
Requirements: Nonprofit 501(c)3 organizations should submit a one- to two-page letter outlining the purpose and needs of the program, its budget, duration, goals, leadership, and amount requested.
Restrictions: Ineligibility applies to individuals; organizations that limit participation or services based on race, gender, religion, color, creed, age, or national origin; projects without ties to a community that is home to an ArvinMeritor facility; organizations that pose any conflict with the goals and mission of ArvinMeritor, its employees, communities, or products; operating expenses for United Way local agencies, except through the foundation's support of annual United Way campaigns; sponsorships of fund raising activities by individuals (i.e., walk-a-thons); requests for loans or debt retirement; religious or sectarian programs for religious purposes; labor, political, or veterans organizations; fraternal, athletic, or social clubs; or seminars, conferences, trips, and tours.
Geographic Focus: All States
Contact: Jerry Rush, Senior Director; (248) 435-7907; fax (248) 245-1031; jerry.rush@arvinmeritor.com
Internet: http://www.arvinmeritor.com/community/community.asp
Sponsor: ArvinMeritor Foundation
2135 W Maple Road
Troy, MI 48084

Aspen Community Foundation Grants   182
The Aspen Community Foundation awards grants to 501(c)3 nonprofits that serve the residents of Pitkin, Garfield, and west Eagle Counties of Colorado in its areas of interest, including: health and human services (particularly with respect to children and families); education programs that develop thoughtful, self-sufficient citizens who contribute to their communities; and strengthening community to promote positive community integration, inter-ethnic understanding, citizen responsibility, volunteerism, and the capacity of communities to solve problems. Types of support include technical assistance, capital grants, general operating support, continuing support, program development, seed grants, and matching funds. Organizations applying for projects that have not previously received funds from the foundation should review their proposals with the program director in advance of submission.
Requirements: The foundation supports 501(c)3 organizations that enhance the quality of life in Pitkin, Garfield, and west Eagle counties of Colorado.
Restrictions: The foundation does not consider grants for projects that have been completed or that will be held prior to the allocations decisions; deficits, retirement of debt, or endowments; religious purposes; political campaigns or organizations that publicly take political positions; medical research; organizations primarily supported by tax-derived funding; or conduit organizations. The foundation does not give priority to applications for hospital equipment; conferences; sports/recreational groups; civic, environmental, or media projects; or arts and culture groups.
Geographic Focus: Colorado

Amount of Grant: 1,000 - 100,000 USD
Contact: Tamara Tormohlen, Executive Director; (970) 925-9300; fax (970) 920-2892; info@aspencommunityfoundation.org
Internet: http://www.aspencommunityfoundation.org/grant-making/apply-for-a-grant-through-acfs-competitive-cycle/
Sponsor: Aspen Community Foundation
110 East Hallam Street, Suite 126
Aspen, CO 81611

AT&T Arts and Culture Grants   183
The program supports innovative artistic projects by nationally and internationally recognized arts and cultural institutions. The foundation actively collaborates with local AT&T regional offices both to identify and develop proposals that reflect the central interests of AT&T and the AT&T Foundation. These interests include assisting in the creation, production, and presentation of new artistic work; bringing the work of women and artists of diverse cultures to a wider public; and mobilizing new technologies to promote artistic innovation and to increase access to the arts. Guidelines and application are available online.
Requirements: To qualify for consideration, organizations must have been professionally managed for at least five years and must compensate both artistic and managerial personnel.
Restrictions: Grants generally do not support student or amateur groups; arts education programs; individual artists; artistic training or scholarships; film and media productions; competitions; arts programs designed primarily for rehabilitation or therapy; public radio and television stations for unrestricted purposes, equipment acquisition, or program underwriting; science museums or science/technology exhibitions, except through the AT&T:NEAT (New Experiments in Art & Technology) initiative; and the purchase of equipment.
Geographic Focus: All States
Samples: Arena State (Washington, DC), Children's Theatre Co (Minneapolis, MN), Goodman Theatre (Chicago, IL), Lincoln Ctr Theater (New York, NY), Magic Theatre (San Francisco, CA), and Wilma Theater (Philadelphia, PA)—to support the production of new plays at these theaters and provide related support for the artists and playwrights, $3425,000.
Contact: Program Contact; (212) 387-4801; fax (212) 387-4882
Internet: http://www.att.com/foundation/guidelines.html#arts
Sponsor: AT&T Foundation
32 Avenue of the Americas, 24th Floor
New York, NY 10013

Athwin Foundation Grants   184
Established in 1956, the Athwin Foundation serves the Minneapolis, St. Paul, Bloomington, Minnesota, Wisconsin area. Primary areas of interest include: arts and culture, church related projects, education, and social services. Providing support in the form of: capital campaigns, general/operating support and, program development. Contact the Foundation by submitting a Letter of Inquiry, if they are interested in your project, a formal request will be made & then a proposal maybe submitted.
Requirements: IRS 501(c)3 non-profit organizations are eligible to apply. The foundation prefers applicants to use the Minnesota Common Grant Application Form that can be obtained by calling the Minnesota Council on foundations (612) 338-1989 or by visiting their web site.
Restrictions: Grants do not support: individuals, scholarships, fellowships, or loans.
Geographic Focus: Minnesota, Wisconsin
Date(s) Application is Due: Mar 1
Amount of Grant: 2,000 - 100,000 USD
Samples: Foundation of Childrens Hospitals and Clinics of Minnesota, Roseville, MN, $100,000— for general operating support; Neighborhood Involvement Program, Minneapolis, MN, $15,000—for general operating support; Jungle Theater, Minneapolis, MN, $2,000—for general operating support.
Contact: Bruce Bean, Trustee; (952) 915-6165
Sponsor: Athwin Foundation
5200 Wilson Road, Suite 307
Minneapolis, MN 55424-1344

Atkinson Foundation Community Grants   185
Community grants are awarded to agencies located within San Mateo County, CA, or serving residents of the county, with primary emphasis on the North County and Coastside areas. International grants are awarded to nonprofits in Latin America. The goals of the program are to provide opportunities for people to reach their highest potential and to improve the quality of their lives; and to foster the efforts of individuals and families to become socially,

economically, and physically self-sufficient. Program priorities are to support nonprofit agencies that serve children, youth, and families; the elderly and the ill; immigrants; the disadvantaged, needy, and homeless; the mentally and physically disabled; and those suffering from drug, alcohol, or physical abuse. Priority also will be given to programs that provide basic human social, physical, and economic services; secondary, vocational, and higher education; adult literacy and basic skills; planning and health education; respite and child care; rehabilitation and job training; counseling; and community enrichment, including environmental conservation. Types of support include general operating support, continuing support, program development, seed grants, scholarship funds, and technical assistance. It is suggested that organizations contact the foundation by phone prior to submission of a grant request to ascertain whether or not the request is within current guidelines.

Requirements: International grants are awarded to organizations working in the Caribbean, Central America, and Mexico; domestic grants are awarded in San Mateo County, CA. 501(c)3 tax-exempt organizations are eligible but those serving residents of San Mateo County, CA, are given preference.

Restrictions: The fund does not make grants to organizations without proof of tax-exempt status; grants to organizations chartered outside the United States; grants, scholarships, or loans to individuals; grants designed to influence legislation; grants for doctoral study or research; grants for travel to conferences or events; grants for media presentations; donations to annual campaigns or special fund-raising events; sponsorship of sports groups; or grants to national or statewide umbrella organizations.

Geographic Focus: California, Antigua & Barbuda, Bahamas, Barbados, Belize, Costa Rica, Cuba, Dominica, Dominican Republic, El Salvador, Grenada, Guatemala, Haiti, Honduras, Jamaica, Mexico, Nicaragua

Date(s) Application is Due: Feb 1; May 1; Aug 1; Nov 1

Amount of Grant: 5,000 - 15,000 USD

Contact: Elizabeth Curtis; (650) 357-1101; atkinfdn@aol.com

Internet: http://www.atkinsonfdn.org/guidelines.html

Sponsor: Atkinson Foundation

1720 South Amphlett Boulevard, Suite 100

San Mateo, CA 94402-2710

Atlanta Foundation Grants   186

Grants are awarded to assist Georgia charitable and educational institutions to improve the quality of life in Fulton and DeKalb Counties. Primary areas of interest include education, cultural programs, housing, and other charitable giving. Additional areas of support include adult basic education and literacy training; higher education; health care organizations; recreation; and youth, family, and human services. The board meets in August to consider requests.

Requirements: Nonprofit organizations in Georgia's DeKalb and Fulton Counties may apply for grant support.

Restrictions: Grants are not awarded to individuals or for scholarships, fellowships, or loans.

Geographic Focus: Georgia

Date(s) Application is Due: Mar 1; Sep 1

Amount of Grant: 2,500 - 50,000 USD

Contact: Trustee; grantinquiriesga@wachovia.com

Internet: http://www.wachovia.com/corp_inst/charitable_services/0,,4269_3296,00.html

Sponsor: Atlanta Foundation

3414 Peachtree Road, 5th Floor, MC GA8023

Atlanta, GA 30326

Atlanta Women's Foundation Grants   187

The foundation awards grants to southern nonprofits to encourage projects that empower women and girls. The foundation supports efforts to promote economic justice, end all forms of violence, and develop alternatives to homelessness and other effects of poverty. Types of support include start-up and operating costs, conferences, fund-raising efforts that show a significant return, films, and small equipment.

Requirements: Southern nonprofits serving one or more of the following counties: Barrow, Bartow, Butts, Carroll, Cherokee, Clayton, Cobb, Coweta, DeKalb, Douglas, Fayette, Forsyth, Fulton, Gwinnett, Hall, Henry, Newton, Paulding, Pickens, Rockdale, Spalding, and/or Walton are eligible.

Restrictions: Grants are not awarded for endowments, debt reduction, religious groups, building funds, or large equipment (e.g., vehicles).

Geographic Focus: Georgia

Amount of Grant: 5,000 - 25,000 USD

Samples: Alternate Life Paths (Atlanta, GA)—for support services and emergency, transitional, and group housing for homeless girls, $15,000; Flint

Circuit Council on Family Violence (McDonough, GA)—to provide mental-health services, shelter, and job-placement and relocation assistance to women experiencing domestic violence, $15,000; Fulton County Juvenile Justice Fund (Atlanta, GA)—for an emergency safe house for girls and teenagers who are victims of sexual exploitation, $20,000; International Women's House (Decatur, GA)—to provide emergency housing and mental-health services to refugee and immigrant battered women, $10,000.

Contact: DiShonda Hughes, Program Contact; (404) 577-5000, ext. 104; fax (404) 589-0000; dhughes@atlantawomen.org or info@atlantawomen.org

Internet: http://awf.techbridge.org/grants/grants.asp

Sponsor: Atlanta Women's Foundation

50 Hurt Plaza, Suite 401

Atlanta, GA 30303

Atran Foundation Grants   188

The foundation supports Jewish nonprofits with a focus on New York and Israel in the areas of higher education, Jewish education, religious education, community services, Jewish welfare, temples, international ministries and missions, temples, medical centers, and women's affairs. Types of support include conferences and seminars, endowment funds, general support, matching funds, multiyear/continuing support, project support, research, scholarships, and seed money grants. The foundation requires that proposals be in writing. Proposals should include the nature of the project, its objectives and significance, time estimate, and budget.

Requirements: 501(c)3 tax-exempt Jewish organizations are eligible.

Restrictions: Grants are not made to individuals.

Geographic Focus: All States

Date(s) Application is Due: Sep 30

Amount of Grant: 250 - 100,000 USD

Samples: Yivo Institute for Jewish Research (New York, NY)—for project support, $90,000; Brandeis University (Waltham, MA)—for operating support, $28,000; Folksbiene Yiddish Theater (New York, NY)—for operating support, $15,000.

Contact: Diane Fischer, President; (212) 505-9677

Sponsor: Atran Foundation

23-25 E 21st Street, 3rd Floor

New York, NY 10010

Auburn Foundation Grants   189

The purpose of the Foundation is to stimulate giving and cooperative leadership among the citizens of Auburn; help improve the lives of all community residents, especially those who are most vulnerable; and enrich the cultural environment and community life. Of special interest are projects that bring together all ages and sections of the town, or that contribute to healthy, active living.

Requirements: Any nonprofit organization that serves residents of Auburn is invited to apply.

Restrictions: Grants will not be awarded to for-profit businesses or expenses already incurred by the applicant.

Geographic Focus: Massachusetts

Date(s) Application is Due: Apr 15

Amount of Grant: 5,000 USD

Samples: Bancroft School (Worcester, MA)—for general support, $45,000; New England Science Ctr, Rutland House (Worcester, MA)—for repairs, $20,000; Tower Hill Botanic Garden (Boylston, MA)—for general support, $30,000.

Contact: Lois Smith, Senior Program Officer; (508) 755-0980, ext. 107; lsmith@greaterworcester.org

Internet: http://www.greaterworcester.org/grants/Auburn.htm

Sponsor: Auburn Foundation

370 Main Street, Suite 650

Worcester, MA 01608-1738

Audrey and Sydney Irmas Charitable Foundation Grants   190

The foundation awards grants to eligible nonprofit organizations in its areas of interest, including arts and culture, higher education, homeless and urban issues, hospitals, and Jewish welfare. Grants support long-term, nonrenewable pledges and general operating grants. Most grants are made to Los Angeles County, CA, nonprofits.

Requirements: 501(c)3 nonprofit organizations are eligible.

Geographic Focus: California

Amount of Grant: 1,000 - 75,000 USD

Contact: Robert Irmas; (818) 382-3313; fax (818) 382-3315; robirm@aol.com

Sponsor: Audrey and Sydney Irmas Charitable Foundation

16830 Ventura Boulevard, Suite 364

Encino, CA 91436-2797

Avon Foundation Speak Out Against Domestic Violence Grants 191

The Foundation is committed to helping end the cycle of domestic violence with the launch of the Speak Out Against Domestic Violence program in 2004. Since launching the program, more than $4 million has been awarded to domestic violence organizations across the US. Speak Out supports awareness, education, direct services and prevention programs.

Requirements: To be considered for funding, you must complete an application and submit it by May 1.

Restrictions: Proposals must come from from non-profit organizations (501(c)3 organizations) and agencies that assist children who have been exposed to domestic violence.

Geographic Focus: All States

Amount of Grant: 10,000 - 50,000 USD

Contact: Christine Jaworsky, (866) 505-2866 or (212) 282-5519; info@ avonfoundation.org

Internet: http://www.avoncompany.com/women/speakout/index.html

Sponsor: Avon Foundation

505 Eighth Avenue, Suite 1601

New York, NY 10018-6505

Avon Products Foundation Grants 192

The foundation's two-fold focus is to support education, community and social services, and arts organizations and programs that provide economic opportunities for women and girls; and to support breast cancer and other women's health organizations and programs. The foundation awards grants in cities and regions with a large concentration of representatives and business operations, with the majority of funds going to US-based institutions. National, international, and New York metropolitan area programs are administered through the foundation's headquarters in New York. For regional funding support, refer to the Avon Foundation website.

Requirements: Applying organizations must be tax-exempt; national and municipal organizations are eligible. Request the guidelines brochure prior to submitting a formal proposal.

Restrictions: Grants do not support individuals; memberships; lobbying organizations; political activities and organizations; religious, veteran, or fraternal organizations; fundraising events; and journal advertisements.

Geographic Focus: All States

Amount of Grant: Up to 23,000,000 USD

Contact: Grants Administrator; (866) 505-2866; info@avonfoundation.org

Internet: http://www.avoncompany.com/women/avonfoundation

Sponsor: Avon Products Foundation

1345 Avenue of the Americas

New York, NY 10105

AWDF Main Grants 193

AWDF's grant-making ensures resources reach the hundreds of African women's organizations that are working in diverse ways to improve the lives of women and African society at large. The AWDF Main Grants program is pan-African and supports local, national, sub-regional and regional organizations in Africa working towards women's empowerment. AWDF will give grants for projects related to any of its thematic areas, applicants are expected to build in reasonable core costs into their project proposals. Grants can be given to support the capacity and institutional strengthening of organizations including grants for strategic planning, governance systems and fundraising/communication strategies. Typically, grants in this category range from $1,000 to $25,000.

Geographic Focus: All States, All Countries

Amount of Grant: 1,000 - 25,000 USD

Contact: Bisi Adeleye-Fayemi, Executive Director/President; 233 (0) 302 521257 or 233 (0) 302 923626; grants@awdf.org or awdf@awdf.org

Internet: http://www.awdf.org/the-process/main-grants

Sponsor: African Women's Development Fund

PMB CT 89 Cantonments

Accra, Ghana

AWDF Small Grants 194

AWDF's grant-making ensures resources reach the hundreds of African women's organizations that are working in diverse ways to improve the lives of women and African society at large. The AWDF Small Grants Program (SGP), currently operates in some selected countries in Africa, namely Ghana, Uganda, Sierra Leone, Liberia and Nigeria. The objective of this program is to support small, community/rural based grassroots women's groups, which are most likely not to have access to any financial support or meet the eligibility criteria for AWDF'S main funding programme. Beneficiaries should, however, be running projects which fall within AWDF's six thematic areas. The SGP also supports emerging or emergency issues, such as community disasters, activities that require a rapid response, and others. The grants range from $1,000 to $5,000. The AWDF makes grants in three cycles, March, August and November. Applications can be sent in at any time.

Geographic Focus: All States, All Countries

Amount of Grant: 1,000 - 5,000 USD

Contact: Bisi Adeleye-Fayemi, Executive Director/President; 233 (0) 302 521257 or 233 (0) 302 923626; grants@awdf.org or awdf@awdf.org

Internet: http://www.awdf.org/the-process/small-grants

Sponsor: African Women's Development Fund

PMB CT 89 Cantonments

Accra, Ghana

AWDF Solidarity Fund Grants 195

AWDF's grant-making ensures resources reach the hundreds of African women's organizations that are working in diverse ways to improve the lives of women and African society at large. The Solidarity Fund has been established to create an additional source of funding for current or potential AWDF grantees, to enable them engage in activities which promote learning and the sharing of experiences on a local, national and international level. To this end, the Solidarity Fund will support African women to participate in exchange visits, conferences, seminars and workshops, thereby providing valuable opportunities for networking and information, all of which are vital to the strengthening of the African women's movement. Organizations can apply for grants ranging from $1,000 to $5,000. Applications to the Solidarity Fund can be sent in at any time, and must be received at least three months before the identified activity.

Geographic Focus: All States, All Countries

Amount of Grant: 1,000 - 5,000 USD

Contact: Bisi Adeleye-Fayemi, Executive Director/President; 233 (0) 302 521257 or 233 (0) 302 923626; grants@awdf.org or awdf@awdf.org

Internet: http://www.awdf.org/the-process/solidarity-fund

Sponsor: African Women's Development Fund

PMB CT 89 Cantonments

Accra, Ghana

Ayres Foundation Grants 196

Incorporated in Indiana in 1944, the Ayres Foundation was established with donations from Theodore B. Griffith, his wife, and their company, L.S. Ayres. Though giving was initially centered around Indianapolis and central Indiana, it has spread throughout the state. Giving is primarily intended to support community services, education, and to strengthen cultural programs. The Foundation's fields of interest include: the arts; community and economic development; higher education; and secondary education programs. Population groups most often supported have been: people with disabilities; economically disadvantaged; mentally challenged; and physically disabled individuals. Types of support offered include: annual campaigns; building and renovation projects; capital campaigns; general operating funds; equipment purchase and rental; program development; and seed money. There is no application form specified, and annual deadlines are April 15 and October 15. Final notification of awards is given approximately eight weeks after each deadline. Grant amounts typically range from $200 to $25,000.

Requirements: Nonprofit 501(c)3 organizations located in, or serving the residents of, Indiana are eligible to apply.

Geographic Focus: Indiana

Date(s) Application is Due: Apr 15; Oct 15

Amount of Grant: 200 - 25,000 USD

Contact: John E.D. Peacock; (317) 443-1868; ayresfoundationinc@gmail.com

Sponsor: Ayres Foundation

545 West 93rd Street

Indianapolis, IN 46260-1415

Azadoutioun Foundation Grants 197

The foundation provides general operating and project support for programs and activities in its areas of interest, including adult basic education and literacy, reading, the environment, human services, and international economic development. Types of support include general operating support and program development. Application forms are not required; initial approach should be by letter. Letters of application are accepted at any time. Grants to support Ammenia's attempt to educate it's citizens in the fields of agriculture and ecology. The foundation operates a farm to assist in educating individuals in the field of agriculture to enable them to operate farms for the benefit of citizens.

Restrictions: Grants are not made to individuals.

Geographic Focus: All States
Amount of Grant: 5,000 - 50,000 USD
Contact: Laurie LeBlanc, (978) 374-5504; lleblanc9498C@aol.com
Sponsor: Azadoutioun Foundation
160 2nd Street
Cambridge, MA 02142

Babcock Charitable Trust Grants   198

The Babcock Charitable Trust was established in Pennsylvania in 1957, by way of a donation from Fred C. and Mary A. Babcock. The Trust's primary purpose has always been to support both education and health care throughout the states of Pennsylvania and Florida, although they occasionally give outside of this primary region. With that in mind, the Trust's specified fields of interest include: children and youth services; education; health care programs; higher education; and religion. Application forms are not required, and there are no specific deadlines. Applicants should provide, in written form, a brief overview or history of their organization, a mission statement, a detailed description of the project proposed, and an amount of funding requested. The amount of funding ranges up to $25,000.
Geographic Focus: Florida, Maryland, Massachusetts, New York, Pennsylvania, Wisconsin
Amount of Grant: Up to 25,000 USD
Contact: Courtney B. Borntraeger, Treasurer; (412) 351-3515
Sponsor: Babcock Charitable Trust
1105 N. Market Street, Suite1300
Wilmington, DE 19801

Back Home Again Foundation Grants   199

Based in Indianapolis, Indiana, the Back Home Again Foundation offers funding in the areas of: animal welfare; the arts; children's services and programs; food services; health organizations; higher education; human services; museums; performing arts; and recreational programming. Since there are no specific application forms or deadlines with which to adhere, applicants should contact the office directly with a description of their program or project, and a detailed budget. Grants range from $1,500 to $30,000.
Geographic Focus: Indiana
Amount of Grant: 1,500 - 30,000 USD
Contact: Randolph H. Deer, Secretary; (317) 844-2886
Sponsor: Back Home Again Foundation
5846 West 73rd Street
Indianapolis, IN 46268

Bacon Family Foundation Grants   200

The foundation awards grants to Colorado nonprofit organizations in its areas of interest, including arts and culture, community development, disabilities, economic development, education, food distribution, environment, health care, historic preservation, homelessness, housing, literacy, recreation/parks, religion, social services, and youth. Types of support include capital campaigns, challenge/matching grants, equipment acquisition, general operating support, project grants, and seed grants. A letter should outline the project or program in brief but sufficient detail for the Foundation to initially evaluate the proposal. There are no application deadlines. The Bacon Family Foundation meets quarterly to consider applications.
Requirements: Colorado nonprofit organizations are eligible. Preference will be given to requests from western Colorado.
Restrictions: No grants are made to individuals.
Geographic Focus: Colorado
Contact: Linda Simpson, (970) 243-3767; lsimpson@wc-cf.org
Internet: http://www.wc-cf.org/bacon.htm
Sponsor: Bacon Family Foundation
P.O. Box 4570
Grand Junction, CO 81502-4570

Bailey-Fischer and Porter Grants   201

The company awards general support grants in its headquarters area in support of education at all levels, the arts, and civic and public affairs. There are no application deadlines. Applicants should submit a brief letter of inquiry.
Requirements: Philadelphia nonprofits are eligible.
Geographic Focus: Pennsylvania
Contact: Maria Novak, (215) 674-6000; fax (215) 674-7183
Sponsor: Bailey-Fischer and Porter
125 E County Line Road
Warminster, PA 18974

Ball Brothers Foundation General Grants   202

Founded in the name of Edmund B. Ball and his brothers, the Foundation seeks to build and sustain a high quality of life in Indiana by awarding grants to nonprofit organizations in broad subject areas, including elementary, secondary, higher, and adult basic education and literacy skills; cultural activities; community betterment; the environment; and health and human services. Usually, Muncie and Delaware Counties receive a higher priority for funding than requests from across the state. Types of support include general operations, annual campaigns, capital campaigns, building construction/renovation, program development, conferences and seminars, professorships, publication, curriculum development, research, fellowships, matching funds, seed grants, and technical assistance. Preference will be given to catalytic grants that will stimulate others to participate in problem solving or in matching fund programs and to innovative approaches for addressing either traditional or emerging community needs. Applications are reviewed by the board of directors in January, May, and September of each calendar year. Proposals are encouraged to be submitted from February to May. Grant seekers may send a preliminary proposal, complete proposal, or ask for a personal visit to discuss a potential grant request.
Requirements: Indiana 501(c)3 nonprofits and organizations are eligible.
Restrictions: The Foundation will not support: direct assistance to individuals or scholarships; applications coming from outside of Indiana; booster organizations; on-going salary requests of staff personnel to support an organization; services that the community-at-large should normally underwrite (i.e. roads, bus transportation, etc.); capital building projects; research projects (except for philanthropic studies); or unsolicited proposals (all requests must begin with a preliminary proposal).
Geographic Focus: Indiana
Date(s) Application is Due: Apr 1; Sep 1
Amount of Grant: Up to 100,000 USD
Contact: Donna Munchel, Executive Assistant; (765) 741-5500; fax (765) 741-5518; donna.munchel@ballfdn.org or info@ballfdn.org
Internet: http://www.ballfdn.org
Sponsor: Ball Brothers Foundation
222 South Mulberry Street
Muncie, IN 47305

Ball Brothers Foundation Rapid Grants   203

Ball Brothers Foundation offers funding opportunities for a limited number of Ball Rapid Grants that are designed to provide funding to organizations requiring immediate funding for the following types of needs: to continue or complete a project; to provide professional development; to buy equipment or materials for a project; for travel to meet representatives to advance ideas for a current or future project; to formulate a project idea; to carry out a mandated law or event; or for seed money to begin a new project. Generally requests up to $5,000 are considered. Ball Rapid Grants do not fall within the normal granting period. Requests may be submitted at any time between February 1 and November 30; decisions will be made within four business days and awards sent within 7 to 10 business days.
Requirements: Ball Brothers Foundation is restricted by its charter to grants to nonprofit institutions and organizations within Indiana.
Restrictions: The Foundation will not support: direct assistance to individuals or scholarships; applications coming from outside of Indiana; booster organizations; on-going salary requests of staff personnel to support an organization; services that the community-at-large should normally underwrite (i.e. roads, bus transportation, etc.0; capital building projects; research projects (except for philanthropic studies); or unsolicited proposals (all requests must begin with a preliminary proposal).
Geographic Focus: Indiana
Date(s) Application is Due: Nov 30
Amount of Grant: Up to 5,000 USD
Contact: Donna Munchel, Executive Assistant; (765) 741-5500; fax (765) 741-5518; donna.munchel@ballfdn.org or info@ballfdn.org
Internet: http://www.ballfdn.org/index/staff/generalinfo.asp
Sponsor: Ball Brothers Foundation
222 South Mulberry Street
Muncie, IN 47305

BancorpSouth Foundation Grants   204

The BancorpSouth Foundation supports organizations involved with orchestras, secondary and higher education, legal aid, housing, youth development, and human services. Support is available in the form of general/operating grants in areas of operation, that include Arkansas, Mississippi and Tennessee. Applications for funding are accepted on a rolling basis and reviewed quarterly.

Requirements: Arkansas, Mississippi and Tennessee 501(c)3 non-profit organizations are eligible to apply. There is no application deadline nor is there an application form required when applying for funding. Applicants should include a detailed description of project and amount of funding requested in the proposal.
Restrictions: No grants to individuals.
Geographic Focus: Arkansas, Mississippi, Tennessee
Amount of Grant: 5,000 - 15,000 USD
Contact: Nash Allen, Grants Manager; (662) 680-2000
Sponsor: BancorpSouth Foundation
P.O. Box 789
Tupelo, MS 38802-0789

Banfi Vintners Foundation Grants 205
The foundation awards general operating grants to nonprofits in its areas of interest, including higher education, civic and public affairs, arts and humanities, wildlife protection, health (hospitals and disease research/prevention), religion, science, social services, and international. Grants are made nationwide, with preference given to requests from Massachusetts and the New York, NY, area.
Geographic Focus: Massachusetts, New York
Amount of Grant: 100 - 465,000 USD
Samples: Colgate U (Hamilton, NY)—for operating support, $75,000; Friends for Long Island's Heritage (Syosset, NY—for operating support, $25,000; Huntington Hospital Assoc (Huntington, NY)—for operating support, $25,000; Cornell U (Ithaca, NY)—for operating support, $465,000.
Contact: Philip Calderone, Executive Director; (516) 626-9200
Sponsor: Banfi Vintners Foundation
1111 Cedar Swamp Road
Glen Head, NY 11545

BankAtlantic Foundation Grants 206
The Foundation was created in 1994 as a 501(c)3 corporate foundation. Since then, the BA Foundation and BankAtlantic have awarded more than $10 million to charitable organizations throughout the state of Florida. The Foundation supports four key areas: community and economic development; human services; education; and the arts. The Foundation considers requests for specific projects, as well as for general operations. The majority of the grants made by the Foundation fall within the $1000 to $3000 range.
Requirements: Giving is limited to Florida. Funding consideration will be given to programs where BankAtlantic has a business presence. The Foundation will fund an organization one time per calendar year, up to three consecutive years. After three consecutive years of support, an organization may reapply after a one-year non-funding period.
Restrictions: No support is offered for hospitals, K-12 schools, national health-related organizations, political or lobbying organizations, religious, veteran, or fraternal organizations, school athletic teams, cheerleading squads, bands, or choirs. No grants are given to individuals, or for capital or building campaigns, courtesy or goodwill advertising to benefit publications, endowments, fund raising events, ticket purchases, travel, medical research, social functions, or sporting events.
Geographic Focus: Florida
Date(s) Application is Due: Mar 30; Oct 31
Amount of Grant: 1,000 - 3,000 USD
Contact: Marcia Barry-Smith; (954) 940-5058; fax (954) 940-5030
Internet: https://www.bankatlantic.com/bafoundation/
Sponsor: BankAtlantic Foundation
2100 West Cypress Creek Road
Fort Lauderdale, FL 33309-1823

Bank of America Charitable Foundation Volunteer Grants 207
Bank of America employees volunteer thousands of hours globally in our neighborhoods each year. In fact, more than 3,000 charitable organizations benefit from the Foundation's employees' dedication each year. To honor those who give their time and service to causes important to them, the Bank of America Charitable Foundation awards grants, which are up to $500 per employee for each calendar year and are made in the name of the employee, to eligible charitable organizations. An unrestricted grant is made to any eligible nonprofit organization for which an employee or retiree has committed substantial volunteer hours within a calendar year. For 50 hours of volunteer time within a calendar year, Bank of America Charitable Foundation will give a $250 grant; for 100 hours of volunteer time within a calendar year, the grant is $500. Employee hour registration must be completed by January 31 after the year in which the hours were volunteered. Organizations must verify hours by May 15 after the year in which the hours were volunteered.

Requirements: Charitable organizations in the United States must be tax-exempt under section 501(c)3 of the Internal Revenue Code and not be classified as a private foundation. Charitable Organizations located in England or Wales must be registered with the Charity Commission. Charitable organizations outside of the United States, England or Wales must be qualified as eligible for donations from CAFAmerica. Employees must complete an application and have the recipient organization verify the hours.
Geographic Focus: All States, District of Columbia, Guam, Marshall Islands, Northern Mariana Islands, Puerto Rico, U.S. Virgin Islands, American Samoa, Canada, United Kingdom
Date(s) Application is Due: Jan 31
Amount of Grant: 250 - 500 USD
Contact: Anne M. Finucane, Foundation Chairperson/Chief Marketing Officer; (617) 434-9410 or (800) 218-9946; anne.m.finucane@bankofamerica.com
Internet: http://www.bankofamerica.com/foundation/index.cfm?template=fd_volunteergrants
Sponsor: Bank of America Charitable Foundation
100 North Tryon Street
Charlotte, NC 28255

Barbara Delano Foundation Grants 208
The foundation awards grants internationally in its fields of interest, including environmental conservation and wildlife preservation. Types of support include annual campaigns, building construction/renovation, equipment acquisition, challenge/matching grants, and general operating support. The board meets in the spring and fall.
Requirements: BDF only accepts proposals for programs outside the United States, primarily in developing countries. BDF only supports research directly related to the implementation of a conservation program.
Geographic Focus: All States
Date(s) Application is Due: Sep 1; Oct 15
Amount of Grant: 1,000 - 80,000 USD
Samples: Environmental Investigation Agency (Washington, DC)— for the Tigers in Crisis Campaign, $80,000; Cheetah Conservation Fund (Cincinatti, OH)—for rhino fencing, $5000; Environmental Investigation Agency (Washington, DC)—for Tigers in Crisis Campaign, $70,000.
Contact: Stephanie Carnow, Program Assistant; (415) 834-1758; fax (415) 834-1759; bdfoundation@usa.net
Internet: http://www.bdfoundation.org
Sponsor: Barbara Delano Foundation
450 Pacific Avenue, 2nd Floor
San Francisco, CA 94133-4640

Barbara Meyer Elsner Foundation Grants 209
Established in Wisconsin in 1991, the Barbara Meyer Elsner Foundation offer grant funding in its primary fields of interest, which include: animals and wildlife; and the arts. Its support comes in the form of general operations funding. There are no annual deadlines or specified application forms, so potential applicants should begin the process by contacting the Foundation either via telephone or in writing. Typically, grants range from $50 to $1,000, though occasionally higher amounts are given.
Requirements: All 501(c)3 organization in, or serving the residents of, Wisconsin are eligible to apply.
Geographic Focus: Wisconsin
Amount of Grant: Up to 50,000 USD
Samples: Milwaukee Art Museum, Milwaukee, Wisconsin, $4,000 - general operations; Franklin Lloyd Wright Fund, Madison, Wisconsin, $50,200 - general operations; Wild Spaces, Milwaukee, Wisconsin, $1,500 - general operations.
Contact: Barbara Elsner, Secretary-Treasurer; (414) 961-2496
Sponsor: Barbara Meyer Elsner Foundation
2420 N. Terrace Avenue
Milwaukee, WI 53211-4511

Barker Foundation Grants 210
The foundation offers funding to New Hampshire non-profit organizations in the areas of: children/youth services; education; health organizations, association; hospitals (general); and human services. Giving primarily for health associations, social services and youth. Grants are awarded in the following types: Annual campaigns building/renovation; capital campaigns; continuing support; equipment; general/operating support and; program development.
Requirements: New Hampshire nonprofit organizations are eligible for funding. The Foundation accepts written requests only. No formal application form

is required. Send a 1 page concept paper and request for guidelines to the Foundation with a SASE for response.

Restrictions: Grants are not made to individuals.

Geographic Focus: New Hampshire

Amount of Grant: 2,000 - 13,000 USD

Samples: Boys and Girls Club of Greater Nashua, Nashua, NH, $10,000; Senior Activity Center, Nashua, NH, $2,000; Nashua Soup Kitchen and Shelter, Nashua, NH, $13,000.

Contact: Allan Barker, Treasurer

Sponsor: Barker Foundation

P.O. Box 328

Nashua, NH 03061-0328

Barker Welfare Foundation Grants 211

The mission of the foundation is to make grants to qualified charitable organizations whose initiatives improve the quality of life, with an emphasis on strengthening youth and families and to reflect the philosophy of Catherine B. Hickox, the Founder. Consideration will be given to applications from institutions and agencies operating in the fields of health, welfare, education and literacy, cultural activities, and civic affairs, primarily serving the metropolitan area of New York, NY, and Michigan City, IN. The foundation board meets twice per year to consider requests.

Requirements: In advance of submitting a request, a brief letter or telephone call is suggested to determine if the organization seeking to apply for a grant falls within the current general policy of the Foundation. Before the Foundation sends out its application form, a brief 2-3 page letter describing the organization, the purpose and amount requested should be sent. A copy of the first page of the most recent 990 filed with the IRS and a current budget for the whole organization and a budget for program/project (if requesting program/ project support) including income and expense should be sent with the letter of inquiry. Grants are made to tax-exempt organizations which have received a ruling by the Internal Revenue Service that they are organizations described in Section 501(c)3 and classified in Section 509(a)(1),(2), or (3) of the Internal Revenue Code (publicly supported organizations and their affiliates).

Restrictions: Appeals for the following will be declined: organizations not located in nor directly serving the defined areas; national health; welfare; or education agencies; institutions or funds; scholarships; fellowships; loans; student aid; appeals from individuals; medical and scientific research; private elementary and secondary schools; colleges; universities; professional schools; trade organizations; films; program advertising; conferences; seminars; benefits and fund raising costs; start-up organizations; emergency funds; and deficit financing; lobbying-related or legislative activities; endowment funds; and intermediary organizations.

Geographic Focus: Indiana, New York

Date(s) Application is Due: Feb 1; Aug 1

Amount of Grant: 7,500 - 15,000 USD

Contact: Sarane Ross, President; (516) 759-5592; BarkerSMD@aol.com

Internet: http://www.barkerwelfare.org

Sponsor: Barker Welfare Foundation

P.O. Box 2

Glen Head, NY 11545

Barrasso Usdin Kupperman Freeman and Sarver Corporate Grants 212

Barrasso Usdin Kupperman Freeman and Sarver are dedicated to giving back to the community of New Orleans. Through its partnerships the Corporation makes charitable contributions to educational institutions and nonprofit organizations involved with arts and culture, health care, and youth development. Primary fields of interest include: the arts; education; health care; legal services; and youth development. Types of support are employee volunteer programs, general operations funding, pro bono services, program development, and contributions to scholarship funds. There are no no specified application materials or deadlines, and interested groups should contact the corporate giving office.

Requirements: Limited to schools and 501(c)3 organizations either in, or serving, the New Orleans region.

Geographic Focus: Louisiana

Contact: Corporate Giving Manager; (504) 589-9700 or (504) 589-9734; fax (504) 589-9701

Internet: http://www.barrassousdin.com/community.php

Sponsor: Barrasso Usdin Kupperman Freeman and Sarver LLC

909 Poydras Street, 24th Floor

New Orleans, LA 70112-4053

Barr Fund Grants 213

The fund awards grants to Illinois nonprofits in its areas of interest, including services for children and youth, orchestras, higher education, mental health/ crisis services, Jewish temples and organizations, and social services. Grants are awarded for general operating support. There are no application forms or deadlines. Submit a letter of request.

Requirements: Illinois nonprofits are eligible.

Restrictions: Individuals are not eligible.

Geographic Focus: Illinois

Amount of Grant: 100 - 75,000 USD

Contact: Donald Lubin, President; (312) 782-4710; fax (312) 876-8000

Sponsor: Barr Fund

230 West Monroe Street, Suite 330

Chicago, IL 60606-4701

Batchelor Foundation Grants 214

The foundation supports food banks and organizations involved with arts and culture, education, the environment, animals and wildlife, health, human services, and economically disadvantaged people. Special emphasis is directed toward programs designed to engage in medical research and provide care for childhood diseases; and promote study, preservation, and public awareness of the natural environment. Funding is available in the form of: capital campaigns; continuing support; endowments; general/operating support; and program development grants. There are no application forms. Initial approach should be a letter that details the grant proposal.

Requirements: Florida area nonprofits are eligible.

Restrictions: Individuals are not eligible.

Geographic Focus: Florida

Amount of Grant: 1,000 - 1,000,000 USD

Samples: Community Partnership for Homeless, Miami, FL, $1,056,600—for general operating support and endowment; Fairchild Tropical Botanic Garden, Coral Gables, FL, $540,000— For general operating support; University of Miami, Miami, FL, $525,000— for general operating support.

Contact: Anne Batchelor-Robjohns, Co-C.E.O; (305) 416-9066 or (305) 534-5004; jbatchelor@bellsouth.net

Sponsor: Batchelor Foundation

111 NE 1st Street, Suite 820

Miami, FL 33132

Batts Foundation Grants 215

Established in 1988, the Batts Foundation supports organizations involved with arts and culture, K-12 and higher education, disease, and human services. Types of support include: annual campaigns, building and renovation; capital campaigns; continuing support; operating support; endowments; matching grants; program development; and scholarship funding. Grants will be awarded primarily in the western Michigan area, particularly the communities of Huron, Zeeland, and Grand Rapids. There are no application forms or deadlines with which to adhere, and applicants should begin by submitting a one page letter summarizing the project.

Requirements: Michigan nonprofit organizations are eligible.

Restrictions: Individuals are ineligible.

Geographic Focus: Michigan

Amount of Grant: 250 - 25,000 USD

Contact: Robert Batts, Director; (616) 956-3053; jsand@battsgroup.com

Sponsor: Batts Foundation

3855 Sparks Drive SE, Suite 222

Grand Rapids, MI 49546-2427

Baughman Foundation Grants 216

The foundation awards grants to eligible nonprofit organizations in its areas of interest, including civic affairs, community development, higher education, and youth programs. Types of support include building construction/renovation, endowment funds, operating budgets, and special projects. Giving is primarily in southwest Kansas, the Oklahoma panhandle, and southeast Colorado. The board meets monthly; application deadlines are the first Wednesday of each month. Please contact the Foundation for guidelines.

Requirements: Grants are only available to charitable organizations as defined under IRS Code Section 501(c)3.

Geographic Focus: Colorado, Kansas, Oklahoma

Contact: Carol Feather-Francis, President; (620) 624-1371

Sponsor: Baughman Foundation

112 West 3rd Street, P.O. Box 1356

Liberal, KS 67905-1356

Baxter International Corporate Giving Grants 217

As a complement to its Foundation, the Baxter Corporation makes charitable contributions to nonprofit organizations directly. Primary fields of interest include: disaster preparedness and services; elementary and secondary education; employment services; the environment; health care and health care rights; health organizations; hemophilia; immunology; kidney diseases; mathematics; patients' rights; science; teacher training and education; and youth services. Types of support include: conferences and seminars; curriculum development; donated products; employee volunteer services; general operating support; in-kind and matching gifts; and sponsorships. Support is given primarily in areas of company operations.

Geographic Focus: All States, All Countries
Amount of Grant: Up to 500,000 USD
Contact: Department Chair; (224) 948-2000
Internet: http://www.sustainability.baxter.com/community-support/
Sponsor: Baxter International Corporation
1 Baxter Parkway
Deerfield, IL 60015-4625

Baxter International Foundation Grants 218

The Baxter International Foundation's grant program is focused on increasing access to healthcare worldwide. The foundation funds initiatives that improve the access, quality and cost-effectiveness of healthcare. Grants awarded most recently fulfilled local needs to increase access to dental care, mental health, and other healthcare services for children, the uninsured, veterans, and the elderly. Funding often comes in the form of salary support and general operations. Focusing on these priorities, the foundation's primary concern is on communities where Baxter has a corporate presence. In Illinois, grants are restricted to Lake, McHenry and Cook counties. The foundation also funds programs throughout the U.S., Asia, Australia, Canada, Europe, Latin America and Mexico.

Requirements: U.S. nonprofits in Lake, McHenry and Cook counties of Illinois are eligible to apply. Internationally, the following regions are eligible to apply: U.S., Asia, Australia, Canada, Europe, Latin America, and Mexico.

Restrictions: In general, The Baxter International Foundation does not make grants to: capital and endowment campaigns (includes requests for infrastructure of any kind, equipment, vehicles, etc.); disease or condition-specific organizations or programs; educational grants/continuing professional education scholarships; educational institutions, except in instances where a grant would help achieve other goals, such as increasing community-based direct health services or the skills and availability of community health-care providers, in areas where there are Baxter facilities; general operating support or maintenance of effort; hospitals; individuals, including scholarships for individuals; lobbying and political organizations; magazines, professional journals, documentary, film, video, radio or website productions; medical missions; organizations seeking travel support for individuals or groups, medical missions or conferences; organizations soliciting contributions for advertising space, tickets to dinners, benefits, social and fund-raising events, sponsorships and promotional materials; organizations with a limited constituency, such as fraternal, veterans or religious organizations; research.

Geographic Focus: All States, Illinois, All Countries
Date(s) Application is Due: Jan 21; Apr 13; Jul 13; Sep 29
Amount of Grant: Up to 100,000 USD
Samples: Access OC, Laguna Hills, California, $49,400 - to support the hiring of a case manager for a new case management program to work with referred patients in Orange County so they can reduce co-morbidities and obtain needed specialty surgeries at their outpatient surgery center; BraveHearts, Harvard, Illinois, $40,000 - to support the salary of a new Volunteer Coordinator needed for all 3 programs within the organization; Kenosha Community Health Center, Kenosha, Wisconsin, $100,000 - upport the hiring of two case managers to be located at the local non-profit agency.
Contact: Foundation Contact; (847) 948-4605; fdninfo@baxter.com
Internet: http://www.baxter.com/about_baxter/sustainability/international_foundation/grants_program.html
Sponsor: Baxter International Foundation
One Baxter Parkway
Deerfield, IL 60015-4633

Bay and Paul Foundations Arts and Humanities Education Grants 219

The Bay and Paul Foundations' overall mission is to foster and accelerate initiatives that prepare agents of change working to strengthen our social compact and develop authentic solutions to the challenges of this pivotal century. The Foundation welcome applications related to arts programming integral to the curriculum and culture of the learning environment. Though often school-based, it favors initiatives that engage the broader community to help youth and adults acquire powerful expressive literacies and cross-cultural intelligences. Successful applicants embrace the arts not as an adjunct or enrichment offering but as central to learning, growth, achievement, and an evolving sense of personal and collective identity. The Foundation no longer accepts unsolicited proposals; all full proposals will be by invitation only and are considered stage two of a two-part process. Applicants may submit an online funding inquiry (OFI) related to one or more of its current program areas. Annual funding cycles for OFI's are from January 19 through February 19 and July 19 through August 19.

Requirements: Nonprofits in Connecticut, Massachusetts, Maine, New Hampshire, New Jersey, New York, Rhode Island, and Vermont are eligible.

Restrictions: Grants do not support requests for endowments, building campaigns, building construction or maintenance, sectarian religious programs, books or studies, individual scholarships or fellowships, loans, travel, film, television or video productions, programs consisting primarily of conferences, for annual fund appeals, or to other than publicly recognized charities. First time grants for K-12 arts-in-education programs and K-12 science and math programs are currently geographically restricted to the New York City metropolitan area.

Geographic Focus: Connecticut, Maine, Massachusetts, New Hampshire, New Jersey, New York, Rhode Island, Vermont
Date(s) Application is Due: Feb 19; Aug 19
Amount of Grant: 3,000 - 10,000 USD
Contact: Danielle Reda; (212) 663-1115; fax (212) 932-0316; info@bayandpaul.org
Internet: http://bayandpaulfoundations.org/areas-of-focus/arts-humanities-education/index.html
Sponsor: Bay and Paul Foundations
17 West 94th Street, 1st Floor
New York, NY 10025

Bearemy's Kennel Pals Grants 220

The program provides direct support for animals in domestic pet programs including animal welfare organizations, pet rescue and rehabilitation organizations, and therapeutic and humane education pet programs. Grants will be a one-time contribution and generally range from $1,000 to $10,000, but the average grant tends to be $4,000. Programs that will be funded include: (1) Individual Project grants generally for one-time purchases or to fulfill a short-term need. Examples include equipment purchases or spay/neuter events, etc; (2) Organization Program grants - start-up or operational costs for ongoing programs. Examples include spay/neuter programs, humane education initiatives, and service dog training programs.

Requirements: While the geographic focus of the program is broad (United States and Canada), priority is given to organizations located near Build-A-Bear Workshop stores. United States applicants must be a tax-exempt organization under Section 501(c)3 of the IRS Code, and not a private foundation, within the meaning of Code Sections 509(a)(1) or 509(a)(2), or a state college or university within the meaning of Code Section 511(a)(2)(B) (a Public Charity). In addition, grant recipients must certify that they are not a supporting organization within the meaning of Code Section 509(a)(3). Canadian applicants must be a registered Canadian charity.

Restrictions: Grant types not funded: (1) Capital Campaigns; (2) Construction or new facility expenses; (3) Fundraising or Event Sponsorships; (4) Political Activities; (5) Religious organizations for religious purposes.

Geographic Focus: All States, Canada
Date(s) Application is Due: Mar 31; Jun 30; Sep 31; Dec 31
Amount of Grant: 1,000 - 10,000 USD
Contact: Maxine Clark; (314) 423-8000, ext. 5366; giving@buildabear.com
Internet: http://www.buildabear.com/aboutus/community/bearhugs.aspx
Sponsor: Build-A-Bear Workshop Bear Hugs Foundation
1954 Innerbelt Business Center Drive
Saint Louis, MO 63114

Beattie-McCay Sancuary Grants 221

The Foundation is focused on animal welfare, with funding going toward general operations and to individuals involved in helping animals. Giving is primarily in the Los Angeles metropolitan area of California. Though an application form is required, the Foundation requires an initial letter of inquiry. There are no deadlines.

Geographic Focus: California
Contact: Peggy McCay, President; (323) 650-8588
Sponsor: Beattie-McCay Sancuary
2714 Carmar Drive
Los Angeles, CA 90046-1009

Bedford Community Health Foundation Grants 222

The foundation awards grants to nonprofit health associations. Types of support include general operating support, equipment acquisition, and scholarships to individuals. Application forms are not required. Grants may be submitted throughout the year, however the Board of Trustees will only review grants at the May and November meetings. Applicants should call the executive director to discuss the proposal and to arrange a meeting.

Requirements: Nonprofits serving Bedford and Bedford County are eligible.

Restrictions: Individuals are not eligible.

Geographic Focus: Virginia

Date(s) Application is Due: Apr 1; Oct 1

Amount of Grant: 250 - 50,000 USD

Contact: Contact; (540) 586-5292; fax (540) 587-5819; bchf@bchf.org

Internet: http://www.bchf.org

Sponsor: Bedford Community Health Foundation

P.O. Box 1104

Bedford, VA 24523

Beerman Foundation Grants 223

The foundation awards general support grants to nonprofits in Ohio in its areas of interest, including Christian and Jewish religion, higher education, community services, Holocaust, Israel, Jewish education, Jewish welfare, museums, religious higher education, social issues, temples, and youth groups such as YMCA/YWCA. Applicants should submit a brief letter of inquiry describing the program and organization. Specify charitable function and purpose of funds sought. There are no application deadlines.

Requirements: Nonprofit organizations in Ohio are eligible.

Geographic Focus: Ohio

Contact: Timothy D. Albro; (937) 222-1285, ext. 104; talbro@beermanrealty.com

Internet: http://www.beermanrealty.com/beerman_foundation.asp

Sponsor: Beerman Foundation

11 West Monument Building, 8th Floor

Dayton, OH 45402

Beim Foundation Grants 224

The foundation awards grants to eligible nonprofit organizations in its areas of interest, including arts and culture, environmental conservation, education, and social services. Types of support include program grants, general operating grants, capital campaigns, building construction/renovation, land acquisition, equipment acquisition, and seed grants. High priority is given to the following types of projects: capital drives and equipment purchases; innovative start-up programs that require a moderate amount of grant money; intergenerational projects that involve community service; cooperative projects that involve several agencies or volunteers; on-going programs that have proven themselves unique and essential; matching funds drives. Low priority is given to the following types of projects: medical research, debt retirement, national fundraising programs, and requests from public schools and governmental agencies due to the lack of good financial data. Deadlines are February 3 for education, and human services; and July 3 for arts, arts small capital equipment, and environment. Guidelines are available online.

Requirements: 501(c)3 tax-exempt organizations located within Minnesota, as well as the city of Denver, CO; counties of Park and Gallatin in Montana; county of Santa Fe in New Mexico; and county of Cumberland in Maine are eligible.

Restrictions: The foundation does not fund individuals; private foundations; political organizations or campaigns; religious organizations, including schools, except for secular human service activities; memberships, subscriptions, tickets for benefits, conferences, fundraising events, or annual campaigns; organizations that have as a substantial part of their purpose the influencing of legislation; endowment; multi-year commitments; or international efforts.

Geographic Focus: Colorado, Maine, Minnesota, New Mexico

Date(s) Application is Due: Jan 17; Jul 18

Amount of Grant: 2,000 - 10,000 USD

Contact: Administrator; (612) 605-8192; contact@beimfoundation.org

Internet: http://www.beimfoundation.org/guide.html

Sponsor: Beim Foundation

3109 W 50th Street, Suite 120

Minneapolis, MN 55410-2102

Beldon Fund Grants 225

The fund focuses project and general support grants in two programs: human health and the environment, and key states. Human health and the environment—the fund seeks proposals that engage new constituencies in exposing the connection between toxic chemicals and human health and in promoting public policies that prevent or eliminate environmental risks to people's health. The program focuses grant making in three areas: new advocates, human exposure to toxic chemicals, and environmental justice. Key states—the fund believes that states hold the key to bringing about rapid, real change on environmental issues and policy in the United States. By strengthening public support for environmental protection in several of these key states, the fund hopes to transform the nation's approach to environmental protection. The fund is currently accepting proposals from Florida, Michigan, Minnesota, Wisconsin, and North Carolina for this program. Proposals do not need to be tied to any particular issue or set of issues, but targeted issues must be those that will build active public support for the environment. From time to time, the fund will add and remove states from this program. Types of support include special projects, seed money, general operating budgets, and technical assistance. One-year and multiyear grants are awarded. Due date applies to the letter of intent; full proposals are by invitation. By supporting effective, nonprofit advocacy organizations, the Beldon Fund seeks to build a national consensus to achieve and sustain a healthy planet. The Fund plans to invest its entire principal and earnings by 2009 to attain this goal.

Requirements: 501(c)3 tax-exempt organizations are eligible.

Restrictions: Grants do not support international efforts, academic or university efforts, school-based environmental education, land acquisition, wildlife or habitat preservation, film or video production, deficit reduction, endowments, capital campaigns, acquisitions of museums, service delivery, scholarshp, publications, or arts/culture.

Geographic Focus: Florida, Michigan, Minnesota, North Carolina, Wisconsin

Date(s) Application is Due: Feb 28; Jun 13

Amount of Grant: 5,000 - 100,000 USD

Contact: Holeri Faruolo, Grants Manager; (800) 591-9595 or (212) 616-5600; fax (212) 616-5656; info@beldon.org

Internet: http://www.beldon.org

Sponsor: Beldon Fund

99 Madison Avenue, 8th Floor

New York, NY 10016

Belk Foundation Grants 226

The Foundation makes grants to a wide variety of community-based nonprofit organizations and institutions whose missions and actions support the advancement of Christian causes and the up-building of mankind. The Foundation supports local and regional organizations by: assisting secondary schools, colleges and universities and their programs; assisting religious institutions and organizations and their programs; supporting area arts and other cultural organizations and their programs; supporting community-based human services organizations and their programs; and aiding hospitals and health care organizations and their programs.

Requirements: 501(c)3 nonprofits in communities in the 14 states where Belk stores are located. Preference is given to organizations in North Carolina.

Restrictions: Grants are not awarded to: individuals, including students; public, government or quasi-governmental programs, agencies or organizations (excluding certain public secondary schools, colleges and universities); or international programs and/or organizations. Additionally, the Foundation does not provide door prizes, gift certificates, merchandise or other giveaways.

Geographic Focus: Alabama, Arkansas, Florida, Georgia, Kentucky, Louisiana, Maryland, Mississippi, North Carolina, South Carolina, Tennessee, Texas, Virginia, West Virginia

Date(s) Application is Due: Apr 15; Oct 15

Contact: Susan C. Blount; (704) 426-8396; susan_blount@belk.com

Internet: http://www.belk.com/AST/Misc/Belk_Stores/About_Us/Belk_Community/Belk_Foundation.jsp

Sponsor: Belk Foundation

2801 W Tyvola Road

Charlotte, NC 28217-4500

Belo Foundation Grants 227

The foundation supports primarily Dallas-Fort Worth area nonprofits. The company's giving focuses on two main areas: enhancing urban parks and open spaces, and journalism education that promotes an informed citizenry. Past grant winners include local groups that commissioned art works for downtown public places, schools, universities, and children's agencies. Belo provides funds for capital and endowment campaigns, scholarship funds, operating budgets, and building construction and renovation.

Requirements: The foundation supports charitable organizations focusing on its areas of interest in the cities where Belo has companies.

Geographic Focus: All States

Samples: YMCA of Metropolitan Dallas (Dallas, TX)—for capital support of its campaign to build eight new facilities and to expand and improve 15 existing branches, $75,000; Bacone College (Muskogee, OK)—for its capital campaign, $10,000.
Contact: Amy Meadows; (214) 977-6661; fax (214) 977-6620
Internet: http://www.belo.com/about/foundation.x2
Sponsor: Belo Foundation
P.O. Box 655237
Dallas, TX 75625-5237

Belvedere Community Foundation Grants 228

The mission of the Belvedere Community Foundation is to: preserve and enhance the quality of life in Belvedere, California; form an endowment fund with contributions from all of its citizens; and provide grants to support projects and volunteers working to enhance the quality of life throughout the community. Grants are targeted at supporting: preservation and enhancement to historically important structures, as well as the natural beauty of the community; positive community interaction; educational opportunities, particularly those focused on stewardship of natural resources and awareness of cultural heritage; healthy living, particularly as it pertains to the benefits of an active lifestyle; funds for emergency preparedness and public safety; seed funding for new community based projects or to aid projects launched by other locally based, non profits aligned with the goals of the Foundation; and crisis funding to existing community based programs in times of urgent need. The Foundation has two online grant cycles per year, with deadlines on March 1 and September 1. Grant requests should be submitted by the beginning of the relevant grant cycle and all applicants will receive a response within 60 days.
Requirements: Any 501(c)3 organization supporting the residents of Belvedere, California, are eligible to apply.
Geographic Focus: California
Date(s) Application is Due: Mar 1; Sep 1
Amount of Grant: Up to 10,000 USD
Contact: Juli Tantum; (415) 435-3695; info@belvederecommunityfoundation.com
Internet: http://belvederecommunityfoundation.com/grants.htm
Sponsor: Belvedere Community Foundation
P.O. Box 484
Belvedere, CA 94920

Bemis Company Foundation Grants 229

Funding is concentrated on those institutions, programs and organizations that encourage the development of educational, social welfare and health, cultural and civic institutions. Programs such as the Bemis Scholarship Program are designed to benefit employees. Additionally, funds are directed to organizations reflecting employees' volunteerism wherever possible, and employee matching programs such as FoodShare and the Educational and Nonprofit Gift Matching Plans are designed to enhance employees' personal donations.
Requirements: Grant proposals need not follow a specific format, but all proposals should cover the following points: name of organization and amount requested, brief description of the objectives for which the grant is sought, details regarding how the objectives are to be met, budget-including information about existing and other sources of income, and officers and Board members. Grant applications should also include a statement that the organization has tax-exempt status under Section 501(c)3 of the Internal Revenue Code and that contributions to it are tax deductible.
Restrictions: All initial inquiries should be made by mail, not by telephone or personal visit. Bemis does not make grants to individuals or organizations for religious or political purposes, either for lobbying efforts or campaigns. Bemis generally does not make grants for educational capital funds programs, endowment purposes, or for trips or tours. No grants will be made for more than three years.
Geographic Focus: All States
Contact: Grant Administrator; BemisFoundation@bemis.com
Internet: http://www.bemis.com/citizenship
Sponsor: Bemis Company Foundation
222 South Ninth Street, Suite 440
Minneapolis, MN 55402-3373

Ben & Jerry's Foundation Grants 230

The foundation funds grassroots projects that typically are initiated and run by young people, that demonstrate long-term viability, and that empower those who traditionally have been disenfranchised in society. A variety of youth-led efforts will be funded, including ones that support minority or at-risk youths in leadership skills. Additional grantmaking areas include children and families and the environment. Each quarter, the foundation also funds a small number of material grants. The foundation accepts and reviews letters of intent throughout the year. Formal proposals will be invited, and the deadlines are listed. Small awards of under $1000 require only a letter. A letter of interest cover page is available on the Web site.
Requirements: Grants are distributed to organizations with IRS 501(c)3 status or who have a sponsoring agency with this status. Generally, the foundation funds projects with budgets less than $250,000. For all correspondence, use recycled paper, and print on both sides. Avoid plastic covers, sheet protectors, and glossy photos.
Restrictions: The foundation does not fund discretionary or emergency requests, colleges or universities, individuals or scholarship programs, research projects, capital campaigns, state agencies, religious programs, international or foreign-based programs, or social service programs.
Geographic Focus: All States
Amount of Grant: 1,001 - 15,000 USD
Samples: People Escaping Poverty Project (Moorhead, MN)—for general and program support, $10,000; Sunshine Project (Austin, TX)—for a national grassroots coalition that brings together arms-control, biotechnology, health, and social-justice organizations in order to monitor U.S. biodefense research, $10,000; Swell Cinema (San Francisco, CA)—to produce a collection of 10 short films designed to increase voter participation in the 2004 elections, $10,000; Tennesseans for Fair Taxation (Knoxville, TN)—to strengthen its Workshop Facilitator Network, which trains members and volunteers to advocate a revamped tax structure in Tennessee that would ensure adequate revenue for the benefit of all state residents, $10,000.
Contact: Contact; (802) 846-1500; fax (802) 846-1556; info@benjerry.com
Internet: http://www.benjerry.com/foundation/index.html
Sponsor: Ben and Jerry's Foundation
30 Community Drive
South Burlington, VT 05403-6828

Bender Foundation Grants 231

The foundation supports projects for higher education, health agencies, Jewish welfare funds and organizations, Christian youth organizations, and social welfare. Emphasis is support for programs to assist the elderly and aging, children and parenting, and environmental programs. Grants are awarded for challenge/matching grants, endowments, general operations, and scholarships.
Requirements: Grants are made to organizations and institutions in Maryland and Washington, DC. An applicant should initially send a brief letter of intent. Full proposals are by invitation.
Restrictions: Grants are not made to individuals.
Geographic Focus: District of Columbia, Maryland
Date(s) Application is Due: Nov 30
Amount of Grant: 100 - 100,000 USD
Samples: Jewish Community Center of Greater Washington (Rockville, MD)—for fitness center, $87,500; Discovery Creek Childrens Museum (Washington, DC)—general support, $50,000; Anti-Defamation League of Bnai Brith(Washington, DC)—for Concert Against Hate, $25,000.
Contact: Julie Bender Silver, President; (202) 828-9000; fax (202) 785-9347
Sponsor: Bender Foundation
1120 Connecticut Avenue NW, Suite 1200
Washington, D.C. 20036

Beneficia Foundation Grants 232

Incorporated in Pennsylvania in 1953, the foundation awards grants in support of the arts and environmental conservation, with an emphasis on tropical and marine ecosystems, natural resource conservation, animals and wildlife, and the arts. The foundation favors programs that are innovative, catalytic, address unmet needs, strive for self-sustainability, and have limited alternative sources of funding. Project grants and general operating grants are awarded. Full proposals are by invitation only. Interested applicants should send a pre-proposal concept in writing to the Foundation office. The Board meets in May to consider concept proposals, and the annual deadline for full proposal submissions is January 15.
Requirements: Nonprofit 501(c)3 tax-exempt organizations are eligible.
Restrictions: Individuals are not eligible to apply.
Geographic Focus: All States
Date(s) Application is Due: Jan 15
Amount of Grant: 10,000 - 100,000 USD
Samples: Bat Conservation International, Austin, Texas, $100,000 - unrestricted general operations; Enchantment Theater, Glenside, Pennsylvania, $75,000 - unrestricted; Ocean Conservancy, Washington, DC, $80,000 - general operations.
Contact: Feodor U. Pitcairn, Executive Director; (215) 887-6700
Sponsor: Beneficia Foundation
1 Pitcairn Place, Suite 3000
Jenkintown, PA 19046

Bennett Family Foundation of Texas Grants 233

The Bennett Family Foundation of Texas was established by Daniel A. Bennett, founder of Sunbelt Sportswear, in San Antonio, Texas, in 1993. Giving is concentrated in the State of Texas, though some giving has occurred in Maryland, New York, California, New Jersey, North Carolina, and Florida. The Foundation's primary interest areas include: environmental programs, the arts, medical research, and community development. Most recently, grant amounts have ranged from $500 to $25,000. Applicants should submit an outline of the purpose, a copy of their IRS determination letter, and an overall budget. The annual deadline is October 30.

Requirements: Copy of the 501(c)3 IRS determination letter from the applicant organizations.

Restrictions: No grants are given to individuals

Geographic Focus: Texas

Date(s) Application is Due: Oct 30

Amount of Grant: 500 - 25,000 USD

Samples: College of Notre Dame, Baltimore, Maryland, $5,000 - general operating fund; Tree Foundation, Sarasota, Florida, $25,000 - general operating fund; Our Lady of the Lake University, San Antonio, Texas, $5,000 - general operating fund.

Contact: Daniel A. Bennett, President; (210) 824-3224 or (210) 804-0100

Sponsor: Bennett Family Foundation

3011 Nacogdoches Road, Building 2

San Antonio, TX 78217

Berks County Community Foundation Grants 234

The foundation supports a broad range of community projects in this Pennsylvania county, including the arts and culture, economic development, education, the environment, and health and human services. Types of support include general operating grants, capital campaigns, demonstration grants, seed grants, and program grants. Although applicants do not have to be located in Berks County, they must provide programs and services within the county.

Requirements: Tax exempt or public benefit organizations, individuals, associations and private or public agencies are eligible to apply. The grant must be used for charitable purposes only. Organizations are eligible to apply to more than one grant program in the same year.

Geographic Focus: Pennsylvania

Contact: Richard Mappin; (610) 685-2223; fax (610) 685-2240; info@bccf.org

Internet: http://www.bccf.org/pages/grants.html

Sponsor: Berks County Community Foundation

501 Washington Street, Suite 801, P.O. Box 212

Reading, PA 19603-0212

Bernard and Audre Rapoport Foundation Education Grants 235

Bernard and Audre Rapoport Foundation is interested in the broad area of education but with a special concern for early learning up to and through the elementary years. Other areas of interest include adult education and training initiatives, and programs that enhance the capabilities of teachers and other professionals in public schools. The primary focus of the Foundation is on programs that benefit children and youth in Waco and McLennan County, Texas. Proposals that fall outside of this geographical focus are considered as long as they offer imaginative, and when possible, long-range solutions to the problems of the most needy members of society, and ideally solutions that can be replicated in other communities.

Requirements: Program seeking funding must be a catalyst for change and promote both individual competence and social capacity.

Restrictions: Bernard and Audre Rapoport Foundation only supports organizations that are nonprofit 501(c)3 tax-exempt.

Geographic Focus: All States

Date(s) Application is Due: Jun 15; Aug 15

Amount of Grant: 4,000 - 250,000 USD

Contact: Carole Jones, Foundation Coordinator; (254) 741-0510; fax (254) 741-0092; carole@rapoportfdn.org

Internet: http://www.rapoport-fdn.org/

Sponsor: Bernard and Audre Rapoport Foundation

5400 Bosque Boulevard, Suite 245

Waco, TX 76710

Bernard and Audre Rapoport Foundation Health Grants 236

Bernard and Audre Rapoport Foundation seeks to improve the quality and delivery of healthcare services to all citizens, especially to women, children, and those who do not have access to conventional medical resources. Community-based outreach initiatives such as immunization programs are of interest to the Foundation. The primary focus of the Foundation is on programs that benefit children and youth in Waco and McLennan County, Texas. Proposals that fall outside of this geographical focus are considered as long as they offer imaginative, and when possible, long-range solutions to the problems of the most needy members of society, and ideally solutions that can be replicated in other communities.

Requirements: Program seeking funding must be a catalyst for change and promote both individual competence and social capacity.

Restrictions: Bernard and Audre Rapoport Foundation only supports organizations that are nonprofit 501(c)3 tax-exempt.

Geographic Focus: All States

Date(s) Application is Due: Jun 15; Aug 15

Amount of Grant: 4,000 - 250,000 USD

Contact: Carole Jones, Foundation Coordinator; (254) 741-0510; fax (254) 741-0092; carole@rapoportfdn.org

Internet: http://www.rapoport-fdn.org/

Sponsor: Bernard and Audre Rapoport Foundation

5400 Bosque Boulevard, Suite 245

Waco, TX 76710

Bernard F. Reynolds Charitable Trust Grants 237

The independent foundation, eastablished in New York in 1999, is interested in supporting human rights programs and agencies, both in the U.S. and internationally. The brainchild of Bernard F. Reynolds, chief executive officer of ASI Solutions, the charitable group hopes to battle hunger, homelessness, and displacement of the world's most vulnerable population. There are no specific applications required or deadlines with which to adhere. Applicants should contact the charitable trust via written proposal.

Geographic Focus: All States

Amount of Grant: Up to 140,000 USD

Samples: Save the Children, Westport, Connecticut, $2,000—general support; Cold Spring Harbor Labs, Cold Spring Harbor, New York, $5,200—for general support; Ramallah Center for Human Rights Studies, Palestine, Israel, $160,000—for general support.

Contact: Bernard F. Reynolds, (631) 367-9513

Sponsor: Bernard F. Reynolds Charitable Trust

6 Merry Meeting Lane

Lloyd Harbor, NY 11743-1609

Bernard Osher Foundation Local Arts and Educational Grants 238

The purpose of the Bernard Osher Foundation is to improve the quality of life in San Francisco, Alameda, and the State of Maine. Grantees over the years have included performing arts groups, literary programs, colleges and universities, environmental groups, and social service groups. Organizations that have not previously received funding from the Foundation are considered new grant seekers. Such organizations may submit an unsolicited letter of inquiry that is no longer than two pages. Such letters may be sent by mail or email, and should contain; a brief institutional description, including when the organization was established, its location, and the total size of its annual operating budget; an overview of the proposed project or activity for which you are seeking support, including the timing of the work; and a list of foundations and corporations providing support to the organization or project and the amount of their contributions. Longstanding grantees can model their renewal request on previous submissions and all proposals should include the following: contact information (name, title, address, email, telephone number) for the person who can answer questions about the report/proposal; a brief company description highlighting any significant changes that have occurred during the last year; a description of the work to be funded, a program/project budget, if applicable; and any other materials you feel are relevant; a copy of the organization's latest financial statement; a copy of the organization's IRS status letter confirming non-profit status; a list the organization's board of directors; and a list of foundations and corporations providing support to the organization or project and the amount of their contributions. There are no application deadlines.

Requirements: Maine and California 501(c)3 organizations are eligible to apply with preference given to those serving Alameda and San Francisco Counties.

Restrictions: Individuals are ineligible.

Geographic Focus: California, Maine

Contact: Jeanie Hirokane, Corporate Secretary and Executive Administrator; (415) 861-5587; fax (415) 677-5868; jhirokane@osherfoundation.org

Internet: http://www.osherfoundation.org/index.php?culture

Sponsor: Bernard Osher Foundation

One Ferry Building, Suite 255

San Francisco, CA 94111

Berrien Community Foundation Grants 239

The community foundation awards grants to nonprofits in Berrien County, Michigan, that address community needs. The Foundation is very interested in providing start-up funding for programs that address our focus areas of nurturing children, building community spirit/arts and culture and youth leadership and development. Higher priority is given to requests that demonstrate community-based collaborative solutions likely to stay in place after Foundation funding concludes. Low priority is given to requests for bricks and mortar, operational funds on a repetitive basis, annual fund drives, equipment, and ongoing programs where alternative funding is not planned to carry a program/project forward following a Foundation grant. Low priority is also given to advertising and capital campaigns and grants to cover deficits or other previously incurred obligations. Applicants must first call the Foundation's program director to discuss the proposed program/project.

Requirements: Grant applications will only be accepted from nonprofit 501(c)3 and grass roots organizations serving Berrien County residents.

Restrictions: Grants are not made for sectarian religious purposes, national fundraising efforts, political organizations or campaigns. Grants are not made to individuals, and form letters/emails are neither reviewed nor acknowledged.

Geographic Focus: Michigan

Date(s) Application is Due: Sep 1

Amount of Grant: Up to 10,000 USD

Contact: Anne McCausland, Program Director; (269) 983-3304, ext. 2; AnneMcCausland@BerrienCommunity.org

Internet: http://www.berriencommunity.org

Sponsor: Berrien Community Foundation

2900 South State Street, Suite 2 East

Saint Joseph, MI 49085

Besser Foundation Grants 240

The foundation limits its giving to nonprofits in the Alpena, MI area. Areas of interest include education, social services, civic affairs, arts and culture, religion, and international. Types of support include scholarship funds, matching funds, operating budgets, and continuing support. The board meets quarterly to consider requests.

Requirements: Only nonprofits in Michigan may apply.

Restrictions: Unless specifically requested by a Trustee, the Foundation will not consider grant requests from organizations outside of Alpena; nor for endowment funds, to defray meeting or conference expenses, or to pay for travel of individuals or groups. We will not relieve organizations or the public of their responsibilities, nor make grants to individuals for any purpose.

Geographic Focus: Michigan

Samples: Jesse Besser Museum, Alpena, MI, $220,00; Alpena Community College, Alpena, MI, $100,000; Child and Family Services of Northeast Michigan, Alpena, MI, $40,000.

Contact: J. Richard Wilson, President; (989) 354-4722; fax (517) 354-8099; besserfoundation@verizon.net

Sponsor: Besser Foundation

123 North Second Avenue, Suite 3

Alpena, MI 49707-2801

Bethesda Foundation Grants 241

The foundation awards grants to nonprofits in Hornell, NY, in its areas of interest, including education, hospitals, health care, substance abuse services, nutrition, AIDS research, and social services. Types of support include general operating support, equipment acquisition, program development, and scholarship funds. Application forms must be obtained from the office. The board meets in March, June, September, and December.

Requirements: Nonprofit organizations in Hornell, NY, are eligible.

Geographic Focus: New York

Amount of Grant: 1,000 - 24,000 USD

Contact: Grants Administrator; (513) 745-1616; fax (513) 745-1623; bethesdafoundation@trihealth.com

Internet: http://www.bethesdafoundation.com

Sponsor: Bethesda Foundation

10506 Montgomery Road, Suite 304

Cincinnati, OH 45242

Better Way Foundation Grants 242

Formerly Alpha Omega Foundation, the Better Way Foundation was established in Florida in 1994. Giving is centered geographically in California, Indiana, Minnesota, Washington, and Tanzania. For the most part, the Foundation supports programs designed to provide holistic and cost-effective development opportunities to young children and families. Special emphasis is directed toward programs designed to improve early childhood outcomes. Its primary fields of interest include: Catholic agencies and churches; early childhood education; family services; health care; higher education; human services; and nutrition. Types of funding support includes: capital campaigns; general operating support; program development; research; and scholarship funding. Application forms are not required, and there are no annual deadlines. Funding amounts range up to $200,000.

Requirements: Unsolicited full proposals are not accepted. Organizations interested in presenting an idea for funding must submit a brief letter of inquiry.

Geographic Focus: California, Indiana, Minnesota, Washington, Tanzania

Amount of Grant: Up to 200,000 USD

Contact: Matthew Rauenhorst, (952) 656-4597 or (952) 656-4806; info@betterwayfoundation.org

Sponsor: Better Way Foundation

10350 Bren Road West

Minnetonka, MN 55343-9014

Bible Students Aid Foundation Grants 243

Established in Kentucky in 1987, the Bible Students Aid Foundation offers funding in Kentucky, Indiana, and Ohio. The Foundation's primary fields of interest include: education; and Christian agencies and churches. Specifically, grants are given to support Bible students in need of financial assistance with expenses for education, utilities, groceries, prescriptions, and rent and mortgage payments. Funding comes in the form of either operating expenses or grants to individuals. There are no specific deadlines or applications forms, and applicants should contact the Foundation directly to offer a full description of their need and finances required.

Geographic Focus: Indiana, Kentucky, Ohio

Amount of Grant: 2,000 - 15,000 USD

Contact: Ted Snawder, Vice-President; (502) 625-2282

Sponsor: Bible Students Aid Foundation

P.O. Box 34290

Louisville, KY 40232-4290

Bierhaus Foundation Grants 244

Established in 1950 in Indiana, the Bierhaus Foundation offer funding in its areas of interest, including: education; health organizations; human services, and Protestant agencies and churches. With a geographic focus throughout the State of Indiana, funding is most often offered in the form of ongoing operations. Typically, grants range from $4,000 to $40,000. Applicants should begin the process by contacting the Foundation office by either letter or telephone, offering a detailed description of the project and amount of money being sought. There are no specific deadlines.

Requirements: 501(c)3 organizations either in, or serving the residents of, Indiana can apply.

Geographic Focus: Indiana

Amount of Grant: 4,000 - 40,000 USD

Samples: Vincennes University, Vincennes, Indiana, $28,805 - general operating support; Aurthur Foundation, Bruceville, Indiana, $5,000 - general operating support; Wabash Valley Christian Academy, Vincennes, Indiana, $4,000 - general operating support.

Contact: Jayne Young, President; (812) 882-0990

Sponsor: Bierhaus Foundation

P.O. Box 538

Vincennes, IN 47591

Bildner Family Foundation Grants 245

The foundation awards grants to nonprofit organizations in its areas of interest, including arts and performing arts, health care and health organizations, Jewish and social service delivery. Types of support include continuing support, general operating support, and program support. The majority of grants are awarded in New Jersey and New York. There are no application forms or deadlines.

Restrictions: The foundation does not support private foundations or individuals.

Geographic Focus: New Jersey, New York

Amount of Grant: 2,000 - 300,000 USD

Samples: Dartmouth College, $6 million for residence hall construction; Rutgers, (New Brunswick, NJ)—for general support, $162,197; Bergen Community College (Paramus, NJ)—to develop the Center for the Study of International Understanding, $225,000.

Contact: Allen Bildner, President

Sponsor: Bildner Family Foundation

293 Eisenhower Parkway, Suite 150

Livingston, NJ 07039

Bill & Melinda Gates Foundation Agricultural Development Grants 246

The Agricultural Development Program supports projects that enable small farmers in developing countries to break the cycle of hunger and poverty, to sell what they grow or raise, increase their incomes, and make their farms more productive and sustainable. Previously funded initiatives include projects that employ a collaborative and comprehensive approach to agricultural development; provide small farmers with the supplies and support they need to succeed; address the needs of women farmers; help small farmers profit from their crops; use science and technology to develop crops that can thrive; gather and analyze data to improve decision-making; encourage greater investment and involvement in agricultural development; and encourage policy and advocacy efforts that accelerate progress against the world's most acute poverty. Additional information on each agricultural development initiative can be found on the website. New proposals are considered, as well as expansion of existing initiatives currently funded by the Foundation.

Requirements: Proposals should aim to help the world's poorest people lift themselves out of hunger and poverty. The Foundation seeks proposals that: are able to produce measurable results; use preventive approaches; promise significant and long-lasting change; leverage support from other sources; and accelerate or are in accordance with work the Foundation already supports.

Restrictions: The majority of funding is made to organizations that are independently identified by Foundation staff. Unsolicited proposals are not accepted. Proposals must be made through 501(c)3 or other tax-exempt organizations. The Foundation is unable to make grants directly to individuals. The Foundation will not fund projects addressing health problems in developed countries; political campaigns and legislative lobbying efforts; building or capital campaigns; or projects that exclusively serve religious purposes.

Geographic Focus: All Countries

Contact: Sam Dryden, Director, Agricultural Development; (206) 709-3400 or (206) 709-3140; info@gatesfoundation.org

Internet: http://www.gatesfoundation.org/agriculturaldevelopment/Pages/default.aspx

Sponsor: Bill and Melinda Gates Foundation

P.O. Box 23350

Seattle, WA 98102

Bill & Melinda Gates Foundation Emergency Response Grants 247

The Foundation supports effective relief agencies and local organizations that respond quickly to people's most pressing needs in challenging conditions. The Foundation is interested in proposals that deliver food and clean water; improve sanitation; provide medical attention and shelter; prevent or minimize outbreaks of disease; and support livelihoods through cash-for-work programs. The Foundation currently supports people affected by the global food crisis; people in Sri Lanka and Pakistan displaced by political unrest and violence; victims of the earthquake in Haiti; communities affected by Typhoon Ketsana in the Philippines and Vietnam; and a consortium of leading humanitarian aid organizations.

Requirements: Relief agencies must have extensive experience and local relationships and be able to deliver help within days, when needs are most crucial. The Foundation also funds organizational capacity-building and explores learning opportunities to reinforce emergency response capabilities.

Restrictions: The majority of funding is made to organizations that are independently identified by Foundation staff. Unsolicited proposals are not accepted. Proposals must be made through 501(c)3 or other tax-exempt organizations. The Foundation is unable to make grants directly to individuals. The Gates Foundation will not fund:projects addressing health problems in developed countries; political campaigns and legislative lobbying efforts; building or capital campaigns; or projects that exclusively serve religious purposes.

Geographic Focus: All Countries

Contact: Coordinator; (206) 709-3140; info@gatesfoundation.org

Internet: http://www.gatesfoundation.org/topics/Pages/emergency-response.aspx

Sponsor: Bill and Melinda Gates Foundation

P.O. Box 23350

Seattle, WA 98102

Bill & Melinda Gates Foundation Financial Services for the Poor 248

Grants

The Gates Foundation seeks to deliver reliable access to a range of safe, affordable financial tools and services to help the world's poorest households build better, healthier lives. The Foundation currently supports distribution channels, saving products, financial systems, and complementary financial systems. To ensure these services benefit the poorest populations will require new models and innovative approaches. New proposals are considered, as well as expansion of existing initiatives currently funded under the Gates Foundation.

Requirements: New technologies and innovative partnerships make it possible to create a "next-generation" banking system. The Foundation seeks to partner with banks, governments, mobile phone companies, retail store chains, and others to make financial services and technology accessible to billions of people throughout the world. The Foundation seeks proposals that are able to produce measurable results; use preventive approaches; promise significant and long-lasting change; leverage support from other sources; and accelerate or are in accordance with work the Foundation already supports.

Restrictions: The majority of funding is made to organizations that are independently identified by Foundation staff. Unsolicited proposals are not accepted. Proposals must be made through 501(c)3 or other tax-exempt organizations. The Foundation is unable to make grants directly to individuals. The Foundation will not fund projects addressing health problems in developed countries; political campaigns and legislative lobbying efforts; building or capital campaigns; or projects that exclusively serve religious purposes.

Geographic Focus: All States, All Countries

Contact: Rodger Vorhies, Director, Financial Services for the Poor; (206) 709-3140; info@gatesfoundation.org

Internet: http://www.gatesfoundation.org/financialservicesforthepoor/Pages/default.aspx

Sponsor: Bill and Melinda Gates Foundation

P.O. Box 23350

Seattle, WA 98102

Bill & Melinda Gates Foundation Library Grants 249

The Foundation supports proposals that seek to improve the quality and availability of library resources, particularly information technology. The Foundation seeks proposals that make information technology more accessible and affordable; provide quality computer hardware and Internet services; provide free access to the Internet and technological training; and work towards narrowing the technological gap. For most people in developing and transitioning countries, quality Internet access is not available or affordable. Worldwide, approximately 5 billion people - nearly 90 percent of the world's population - do not have Internet access. Grants are offered to libraries in the United States and on a global basis. Detailed information is available at the Foundation website.

Requirements: Support is only given to libraries located within the United States, Chile, Mexico, Botswana, Lithuania, Latvia, Romania, Ukraine, Poland, Bulgaria, and Vietnam. The Gates Foundation seeks proposals that are able to produce measurable results; use preventive approaches; promise significant and long-lasting change; leverage support from other sources; and accelerate or are in accordance with work the Foundation already supports.

Restrictions: The majority of funding is made to organizations that are independently identified by Foundation staff. Unsolicited proposals are not accepted. Proposals must be made through 501(c)3 or other tax-exempt organizations. The Foundation is unable to make grants directly to individuals. The Foundation will not fund projects addressing health problems in developed countries; political campaigns and legislative lobbying efforts; building or capital campaigns; or projects that exclusively serve religious purposes.

Geographic Focus: All States, Botswana, Bulgaria, Chile, Latvia, Lithuania, Mexico, Poland, Romania, Ukraine, Vietnam

Contact: Deborah Jacobs, Director, Global Libraries; (206) 709-3140; info@gatesfoundation.org

Internet: http://www.gatesfoundation.org/libraries/Pages/default.aspx

Sponsor: Bill and Melinda Gates Foundation

P.O. Box 23350

Seattle, WA 98102

Bill & Melinda Gates Foundation Water, Sanitation and Hygiene 250

Grants

Poor sanitation causes severe diarrhea, which kills 1.5 million children each year. Smart investments in sanitation can reduce disease, increase family incomes, keep girls in school, help preserve the environment, and enhance human dignity. The Foundation is looking to work with partners in an effort to expand affordable access to sanitation. Detailed information is available at the Foundation website.

Requirements: The Gates Foundation seeks proposals that are able to produce measurable results; use preventive approaches; promise significant and long-lasting change; leverage support from other sources; and accelerate or are in accordance with the foundation already supports.

Restrictions: The majority of funding is made to organizations that are independently identified by Foundation staff. Unsolicited proposals are not accepted. Proposals must be made through 501(c)3 or other tax-exempt organizations. The Foundation is unable to make grants directly to individuals.

The Gates Foundation will not fund projects addressing health problems in developed countries; political campaigns and legislative lobbying efforts; building or capital campaigns; or projects that exclusively serve religious purposes.

Geographic Focus: All States, All Countries
Contact: Kellie Sloan, Interim Director of Water, Sanitation, and Hygiene; (206) 709-3140; info@gatesfoundation.org
Internet: http://www.gatesfoundation.org/watersanitationhygiene/Pages/home.aspx
Sponsor: Bill and Melinda Gates Foundation
P.O. Box 23350
Seattle, WA 98102

Bindley Family Foundation Grants 251

Established in 1997 in Indiana, the Bindley Family Foundation gives primarily in the Indianapolis metropolitan area. Its primary fields of interest include children, education, and health service organizations. There are no specific application forms or deadlines, and applicants should begin by contacting the foundation to offer an overview of their program, project, and budgetary needs. Funding generally is offered in the form of operating support or scholarship endowments. Grants typically range from $2,000 to $15,000, though a small number are significantly higher.

Geographic Focus: Illinois, Indiana
Amount of Grant: 2,000 - 50,000 USD
Samples: Brebeuf Preparatory School, Indianapolis, Indiana, $48,213 - for operating support and scholarships; School on Wheels, Indianapolis, Indiana, $10,000 - operating support; Northwestern University, Evanston, Illinois, $7,500 - for operating expenses.
Contact: James F. Bindley, Executive Director; (317) 704-4770
Sponsor: Bindley Family Foundation
8909 Purdue Road, Suite 500
Indianapolis, IN 46268-3150

Blade Foundation Grants 252

The foundation awards general operating grants to cultural, educational, and social service organizations in Ohio. Scholarships also are awarded to children of employees of Toledo Blade with at least three years of employment. There are no application deadlines for grants.

Requirements: Ohio nonprofits and individuals are eligible.
Geographic Focus: Ohio
Contact: Dave Huey, (419) 724-6417
Sponsor: Blade Foundation
541 N Superior Street
Toledo, OH 43660

Blanche and Irving Laurie Foundation Grants 253

The Blanche and Irving Laurie Foundation was established in 1983 by New Brunswick philanthropist Irving Laurie. The foundation makes charitable gifts to institutions and nonprofits in broad areas of interest, including the arts, especially theater and music; education; health care; social services; and needs and concerns of the Jewish community. Capital grants, operating support grants, grants for programs/projects, and scholarships are awarded. Applicants should submit seven copies of a written proposal containing the following items: copies of the most recent annual report, audited financial statement, and 990; a detailed description of the project and amount of funding requested; and a copy of the current year's organization budget and/or project budget. The foundation's board meets quarterly to evaluate proposals. Final notification occurs within three to four months from submission. Typically, awards range from $3,000 to $150,000.

Requirements: Nonprofit organizations in New Jersey are eligible to apply, as well as others from around the United States.
Restrictions: Giving is primarily concentrated in New Jersey. The foundation does not support medical research.
Geographic Focus: All States
Amount of Grant: 3,000 - 150,000 USD
Samples: American Repository Ballet, New Brunswick, New Jersey, $10,000 - support of the Dance Power program (2014); Brandis University, Waltham, Massachusetts, $50,000 - in support of the theater department (2014); La Jolla Playhouse, La Jolla, California, $20,000 - production support (2014).
Contact: Gene R. Korf; (973) 993-1583 or (908) 371-1777
Sponsor: Blanche and Irving Laurie Foundation
P.O. Box 53
Roseland, NJ 07068-5788

Blanche and Julian Robertson Family Foundation Grants 254

The Blanche and Julian Robertson Family Foundation is totally committed to the goal of improving the quality of life in Salisbury and Rowan County. The general direction of the Foundation's interest is: programs which address social problems and nurture positive social relationships; efforts aimed at enriching lives through exposure to the cultural arts; neighborhood revitalization programs, especially when such programs encourage development of transitional housing and enable first-time homeowners to purchase homes; programs that improve opportunities for youth at risk and families in crisis; efforts to improve broad-based educational, recreational, and athletic opportunities; efforts which address health and the environment. The Foundation is also interested in programs and projects that demonstrate the attributes of leverage (where a grant will attract matching gifts or other funding), as well as innovation, thoroughness, passion, and commitment. Contact the office for application and guidelines.

Requirements: North Carolina nonprofits serving Salisbury and Rowan County are eligible to apply.
Restrictions: The Foundation does not make grants outside Salisbury and Rowan County.
Geographic Focus: North Carolina
Date(s) Application is Due: Mar 30
Contact: David Setzer; (704) 637-0511; bjrfoundation@aol.com
Sponsor: Blanche and Julian Robertson Family Foundation
141 East Council Street, P.O. Box 4242
Salisbury, NC 28145-4242

Blandin Foundation Expand Opportunity Grants 255

The Blandin Foundation's vision for its work is to be the premier partner for building healthy rural communities, grounded in strong economies, where burdens and benefits are widely shared. This vision drives the Foundation's priorities, including areas of focus for grant-making. Expand Opportunity Grants is an evolving area of work in which the Blandin Foundation seeks to blend educational attainment, economic opportunity and broader inclusion in rural Minnesota communities, so all residents have greater opportunities to prosper. Emphasis is on work that moves beyond traditional approaches and that increases impact through a synergistic approach. Roughly 75% of Foundation grants will be made in this focus area. Priority will be given to projects that demonstrate: a strategy involving inter-relationships between economy, education and inclusivity; and clear outcomes such as expanded enterprises and entrepreneurship, increased educational or economic success for populations that have faced historical barriers, and expanded relationships between educational systems, employers and parents.

Requirements: Grants will be made to organizations with a nonprofit 501(c)3 tax exempt status. Units of government may also apply for a grant, but only if the purpose of the grant request goes beyond the normal limits of expected government services and taxpayer responsibility. Grant proposals greater than $50,000 should be received by: March 15 for review in June, September 15 for review in December, and December 15 for review in March. Quick Response grants (less than $50,000), BCLP Quick Start grants and Itasca County Area community donations may be submitted at any time.
Restrictions: The Blandin Foundation does not make grants directly to individuals, except in the case of its Educational Awards Program. Funding does not support: grants outside the state of Minnesota; religious activities; medical research; publications, films or videos; travel grants for individuals or groups; camping and athletic programs; ordinary government services; grants to individuals; grants solely intended to influence legislation.
Geographic Focus: Minnesota
Date(s) Application is Due: Mar 15; Sep 15; Dec 15
Amount of Grant: Up to 250,000 USD
Contact: Wade Fauth, Grants Director; (218) 327-8706 or (218) 326-0523; fax (218) 327-1949; bfinfo@blandinfoundation.org
Internet: http://www.blandinfoundation.org/grants/grants-detail.php?intResourceID=5
Sponsor: Blandin Foundation
100 North Pokegama Avenue
Grand Rapids, MN 55744

Blandin Foundation Itasca County Area Vitality Grants 256

The Blandin Foundation's vision for its work is to be the premier partner for building healthy rural communities, grounded in strong economies, where burdens and benefits are widely shared. This vision drives the Foundation's priorities, including areas of focus for grant-making. Itasca County Area Vitality Grants carry on the legacy and commitments of businessman and Blandin Foundation founder Charles K. Blandin to his adopted hometown of Grand Rapids, Minnesota, and surrounding communities. These are grants

available only for cultural and social services activities that directly benefit the communities of Itasca County and the neighboring communities of Blackduck, Northome, Hill City and Remer, Minnesota. Low priority is placed on large capital grants, recreation and community amenities. Priority will be given to projects that demonstrate: clear articulation of strategies and outcomes that will strengthen the local community, with particular consideration given to proposals that build the capacity of distressed populations to live in greater dignity; cost-effective service delivery strategies, including collaboration with organizations addressing similar issues; and community support and sustainability evidenced by significant matching contributions.
Requirements: Grants will be made to organizations with a nonprofit 501(c)3 tax exempt status. Units of government may also apply for a grant, but only if the purpose of the grant request goes beyond the normal limits of expected government services and taxpayer responsibility. Grant proposals greater than $50,000 should be received by: March 15 for review in June, September 15 for review in December, and December 15 for review in March. Quick Response grants (less than $50,000), BCLP Quick Start grants and Itasca County Area community donations may be submitted at any time.
Restrictions: The Blandin Foundation does not make grants directly to individuals, except in the case of its Educational Awards Program. Funding does not support: grants outside the state of Minnesota; religious activities; medical research; publications, films or videos; travel grants for individuals or groups; camping and athletic programs; ordinary government services; grants to individuals; grants solely intended to influence legislation.
Geographic Focus: Minnesota
Date(s) Application is Due: Mar 15; Sep 15; Dec 15
Amount of Grant: Up to 250,000 USD
Contact: Wade Fauth, Grants Director; (218) 327-8706 or (218) 326-0523; fax (218) 327-1949; bfinfo@blandinfoundation.org
Internet: http://www.blandinfoundation.org/grants/grants-detail.php?intResourceID=5
Sponsor: Blandin Foundation
100 North Pokegama Avenue
Grand Rapids, MN 55744

Blandin Foundation Rural Community Leadership Grants   257
The Blandin Foundation has had a quarter-century commitment to developing and sustaining the capacity of rural residents to build healthy communities. Its primary investment in this focus area has been, and will continue to be, through its Blandin Community Leadership programs. In addition, a small number of grants will be made to support leadership development efforts that complement those of the Foundation. Priority will be given to projects that demonstrate rural leaders acting collaboratively on community strengthening efforts.
Requirements: Grants will be made to organizations with a nonprofit 501(c)3 tax exempt status. Units of government may also apply for a grant, but only if the purpose of the grant request goes beyond the normal limits of expected government services and taxpayer responsibility. Grant proposals greater than $50,000 should be received by: March 15 for review in June, September 15 for review in December, and December 15 for review in March. Quick Response grants (less than $50,000), BCLP Quick Start grants and Itasca County Area community donations may be submitted at any time.
Restrictions: The Blandin Foundation does not make grants directly to individuals, except in the case of its Educational Awards Program. Funding does not support: grants outside the state of Minnesota; religious activities; medical research; publications, films or videos; travel grants for individuals or groups; camping and athletic programs; ordinary government services; grants to individuals; grants solely intended to influence legislation.
Geographic Focus: Minnesota
Date(s) Application is Due: Mar 15; Sep 15; Dec 15
Amount of Grant: Up to 250,000 USD
Contact: Wade Fauth, Grants Director; (218) 327-8706 or (218) 326-0523; fax (218) 327-1949; bfinfo@blandinfoundation.org
Internet: http://www.blandinfoundation.org/html/scholarships.cfm
Sponsor: Blandin Foundation
100 North Pokegama Avenue
Grand Rapids, MN 55744

Blowitz-Ridgeway Foundation Grants   258
The foundation supports nonprofit agencies that provide medical, psychiatric, and psychological care to economically disadvantaged children and adolescents. Program and capital grants are awarded, primarily in Illinois, in support of medical, psychiatric, psychological, and/or residential care; and research programs in medicine, psychology, social science, and education. The foundation supports operating budgets, and applicants may request commitments that extend beyond one year, but requests for annual funding will not be considered. Applications are accepted throughout the year and are reviewed in the order in which they are received. Guidelines and applications are available online.
Requirements: 501(c)3 nonprofit organizations that offer services to people who lack resources to provide for themselves may apply.
Restrictions: Grants will not be awarded to government agencies or to organizations that subsist mainly on third-party funding and have demonstrated no ability or expended little effort to attract private funding. Grants will not be made for religious or political purposes or for the production or writing of audio-visual materials.
Geographic Focus: Illinois
Amount of Grant: 5,000 - 30,000 USD
Samples: Elizabeth Ann Seton Program, $5,000 in general operating support of programs for pregnant and parenting mothers; The Enterprising Kitchen, $15,000 for programs improving self-sufficiency and employability of low-income women; Faith in Action of McHenry County, $7,000 to recruit volunteers; Gospel Rescue Mission, $10,000 for children's social and recreational activities; Guardian Angel Community Services, $5,000 for the Groundwork Domestic Violence Program.
Contact: Serena Moy; (847) 330-1020; serena@blowitzridgeway.org
Internet: http://www.blowitzridgeway.org/information/information1.html
Sponsor: Blowitz-Ridgeway Foundation
1701 E Woodfield Road, Suite 201
Schaumburg, IL 60173

Blue Mountain Community Foundation Grants   259
The Foundation administers charitable funds to benefit people of the Blue Mountain Area. Most of the money for discretionary grants is designated by donors for use by agencies serving Walla Walla County. The Foundation's grant making policies are generally directed toward the fields of social and community services, the arts and humanities, education and health. In reviewing grant applications, careful consideration will be given to: potential impact of the program/project on the community and the number of people who will benefit; local volunteer involvement and support; commitment of the organization's Board of Directors; degree to which the applicant works with or complements the services of other community organizations; organization's fiscal responsibility and management skills; possibility of using the grant as seed money for matching funds from other sources; ability of the organization to obtain additional funding and to provide ongoing funding after the term of the grant.
Requirements: Nonprofit organizations serving the Walla Walla Valley, from Dayton to Milton-Freewater are encouraged to submit proposals.
Restrictions: Grants usually will not be made for the following: programs outside the Blue Mountain Area, operating expenses, annual fund drives, field trips, travel to or in support of conferences. No grants will be made for sectarian religious purposes nor to influence legislation or elections.
Geographic Focus: Oregon, Washington
Date(s) Application is Due: Jul 1
Amount of Grant: 125 - 4,000 USD
Contact: Lawson F. Knight, Executive Director; (509) 529-4371; fax (509) 529-5284; BMCF@bluemountainfoundation.org
Internet: http://www.bluemountainfoundation.org/grant-making-programs.php
Sponsor: Blue Mountain Community Foundation
8 South Second, Suite 168, P.O. Box 603
Walla Walla, WA 99362-0015

Blum-Kovler Foundation Grants   260
The Blum-Kovler Foundation was established in 1985 after Everett Kovler retired from his position as President of James Beam Distilling Company. The foundation awards general operating grants to eligible nonprofit organizations in its areas of interest, including social services, Jewish welfare funds, higher education, health services and medical research, and cultural programs. The foundation also supports youth- and child-welfare agencies and public-interest and civic-affairs groups. Grants are awarded primarily in the Chicago metropolitan area and in the Washington, D.C. area. There are no application forms. Applicants should submit a one to two page written proposal with a copy of their IRS determination letter by mid-November to considered for the current year. Typical grant awarded is between $1,000-$5,000.
Requirements: Illinois and District of Columbia nonprofits are eligible.
Geographic Focus: District of Columbia, Illinois
Amount of Grant: 1,000 - 1,000,000 USD
Samples: Camp of Dreams, Chicago, Illinois, $3,000; Community Foundation for the National Capital Region, Washington, D.C., $1,316,527; Compassion and Choices, Denver, Colorado, $1,000.

Contact: Hymen Bregar, Secretary; (312) 664-5050
Peter Kovler, Chairperson and Vice President; (312) 664-5050
Sponsor: Blum-Kovler Foundation
875 N Michigan Avenue, Suite 3400
Chicago, IL 60611-1958

Blumenthal Foundation Grants   261
In 1924 Mr. I.D. Blumenthal was a traveling salesman in need of repair to his car's radiator. A local tinsmith in Charlotte, North Carolina, repaired the radiator with a "magic powder". Impressed with the product, I.D. teamed with the tinsmith and Solder Seal became the first product of the Radiator Specialty Company. The Blumenthal Foundation was founded in 1953 and was endowed with the success of the Radiator Specialty Company. The foundation focuses the majority of its grants on programs and projects that have an impact on Charlotte, and the state of North Carolina. The philanthropic efforts of the Foundation are focused in nine areas of grant making: arts, science and culture; civic and community; education; environment; foundation affiliates; health; Jewish institutions and philanthropies; religious and interfaith; and social sciences. The foundation believes that basic operational funding for non-profits is just as important, if not more so, than support for special programs or projects; consequently, grants are provided for seed money, annual operating costs, capital campaigns, conferences and seminars, special projects, and endowments. Interested organizations may click the Grant Guidelines link at the website for detailed submission instructions. Applications must be mailed. There are no deadlines, and requests are accepted on an ongoing basis. The Board of Trustees meets quarterly to consider grant applications.
Requirements: 501(c)3 organizations and institutions that serve the city of Charlotte and the State of North Carolina in the foundation's areas of interest are eligible to apply.
Restrictions: Grants are not made to individuals for any purpose.
Geographic Focus: North Carolina
Samples: Arts & Science Council, Charlotte, North Carolina, $20,000 - support of the Annual Fund Drive; Charlotte Symphony, Charlotte, North Carolina, $20,000 - designed to offset the Symphony's operating shortfall as it works to rebuild its fiscal base; Toe River Health District, Spruce Pine, North Carolina, $2,500 - to purchase a Point of Care computer system to aid in providing healthcare to residents of Avery, Mitchell and Yancey counties.
Contact: Philip Blumenthal, Director; (704) 688-2305; fax (704) 688-2301; foundation@gunk.com
Internet: http://www.blumenthalfoundation.org/BFGrantListings.htm
Sponsor: Blumenthal Foundation
P.O. Box 34689
Charlotte, NC 28234-4689

BMW of North America Charitable Contributions   262
BMW of North America funds charitable programs that benefit society in the areas of education, road-traffic safety, and the environment. The corporation supports education at all levels and specifically focuses on the following: intercultural learning for K-12 students and their teachers; automotive technology, mechanics, and career and repair programs in high schools, technical schools, and community colleges; and research in the areas of safety design, ergonomics, and new materials. In the area of road traffic safety, the corporation supports driver-education programs geared at teenagers and new drivers; basic auto-maintenance programs for women; consumer education on general road-safety issues; and programs to promote the safety of children and young people on the road. In the area of the environment, BMW is committed to sustainable development and focuses grant making on the following: conservation/preservation of natural resources, in particular park lands and waterways; research and promotion of alternative fuels; and environmental education for K-12 students. In general, grants are awarded for specific projects rather than for general operating support, although some operating and capital grants are given consideration. Interested organizations may download application instructions and guidelines at the grant website. Organizations wishing to be considered for a grant must submit an application; telephone solicitations will not considered.
Requirements: 501(c)3 charities or 501(c)9 organizations are eligible to apply.
Restrictions: The corporate giving program does not support non-tax-exempt organizations; individuals; religious organizations for religious purposes; political candidates or lobbying organizations; organizations with a limited constituency, such as fraternal, labor, or veterans groups; travel by groups or individuals; national or local chapters of disease-specific organizations; national conferences, sports events, and other one-time, short-term events; sponsorships or advertising; anti-business groups; team sponsorships or athletic scholarships; or organizations outside the United States or its territories.

Geographic Focus: All States
Contact: Grants Coordinator; (201) 307-4000; fax (201) 307 3607
Internet: http://www.bmwgroupna.com/philanthropy.htm
Sponsor: BMW of North America
300 Chestnut Ridge Road
Woodcliff Lake, NJ 07677-7731

Bodman Foundation Grants   263
The Bodman Foundation was established by George M. Bodman and his wife Louise Clarke Bodman in 1945. George was born in Toledo, Ohio, in 1882 and died in 1950. Mrs. Bodman was born in Chicago in 1893 and died in 1955. The Bodmans lived for much of their lives in Red Bank, New Jersey, and in New York City, where George Bodman was a senior partner at the investment banking firm of Cyrus J. Lawrence and Sons. The Bodmans were generous supporters of numerous cultural, civic, and service organizations. During World War I Mr. Bodman headed the Intelligence Service of the War Trade Board. During World War II, he served as executive assistant to the Red Cross Commissioner for Great Britain and was regional director in charge of American Red Cross Club operations in England, Scotland, and Ireland. The Bodman Foundation's Certificate of Incorporation states that its funds are to be used for the aid, support or benefit of religious, educational, charitable, and benevolent objects and purposes for the moral, ethical and physical well-being and progress of mankind." The Bodman Foundation shares trustees, staff, office space, and even a website with the Achelis Foundation which has a similar mission and geographic area of concentration (both foundations give in New York City, while the Bodman Foundation also gives in New Jersey). Funding is concentrated in six program areas: arts and culture, education, employment, health, public policy, and youth and families. Most recently, awards have ranged from $15,000 to $200,000.
Requirements: 501(c)3 organizations based in New York City that fall within the foundation's areas of interest are welcome to submit an inquiry or proposal letter by regular mail (initial inquiries by email or fax are not accepted, nor are CDs, DVDs, computer discs, or video tapes). An initial inquiry to the foundation should include only the following items: a proposal letter that briefly summarizes the history of the project, need, objectives, time period, key staff, project budget, and evaluation plan; the applicant's latest annual report and complete set of audited financial statements; and the applicant's IRS 501(c)3 tax-exemption letter. Applications may be submitted at any time during the year. Each request is reviewed by staff and will usually receive a written response within thirty days. Those requests deemed consistent with the interests and resources of the foundation will be evaluated further and more information will be requested. Foundation staff may request a site visit, conference call, or meeting. All grants are reviewed and approved by the Trustees at one of their three board meetings in May, September, or December.
Restrictions: The foundation generally does not make grants for the following purposes or program areas: nonprofit organizations outside of New York; annual appeals, dinner functions, and fundraising events; endowments and capital campaigns; loans and deficit financing; direct grants to individuals; individual day-care and after-school programs; housing; organizations or projects based outside the U.S; films or video projects; small art, dance, music, and theater groups; individual K-12 schools (except charter schools); national health and mental health organizations; and government agencies or nonprofit organizations significantly funded or reimbursed by government agencies. Limited resources prevent the foundations from funding the same organization on an ongoing annual basis.
Geographic Focus: New Jersey, New York
Amount of Grant: 15,000 - 200,000 USD
Contact: John B. Krieger, Executive Director; (212) 644-0322; fax (212) 759-6510; main@achelis-bodman-fnds.org
Internet: http://www.achelis-bodman-fnds.org/guidelines.html
Sponsor: Bodman Foundation
767 Third Avenue, 4th Floor
New York, NY 10017-2023

Boeckmann Charitable Foundation Grants   264
The foundation awards grants to nonprofits in support of education—colleges and universities, parochial secondary education, religious education, and campus crusades; community, family, and youth services; national and international ministries and missions; religious welfare; religious broadcasting; and temples. Grants support general operations. Applicants should submit a brief letter of inquiry describing the program and the organization. There are no application deadlines.
Requirements: Christian, Evangelical, and Presbyterian nonprofits in California are eligible.

Geographic Focus: California

Amount of Grant: Up to 17,000,000 USD

Samples: Church on Way (Van Nuys, CA)—operating support, $300,200; Hispanic Christian Communications Network (Los Angeles, CA)—operating support, $10,000; Valley Interfaith Council (Chatsworth, CA)—operating support, $2000.

Contact: Herbert Boeckmann II, Chief Executive Officer; (818) 787-3800

Sponsor: Boeckmann Charitable Foundation

15505 Roscoe Boulevard

North Hills, CA 91343

Boeing Company Contributions Grants　　　　265

The Boeing U.S. contributions program welcomes applications in five focus areas: education; health and human services; arts and culture; civic; and the environment. Primary fields of interest include: arts; elementary and secondary education; the environment; family services; prevention of domestic violence; health care; public affairs; public safety; substance abuse programs; and general human services. The largest single block of charitable contributions goes toward supporting programs and projects related to education. Boeing also looks for innovative initiatives that promote the economic well-being of the community and neighborhood revitalization. Boeing invests in programs that promote participation in arts and cultural activities and experiences, programs that increase public understanding of and engagement in the processes and issues that affect communities and programs that protect and conserve the natural environment. Boeing accepts applications for cash grants, in-kind donations, and services.

Requirements: To apply for support you must be a U.S. based IRS 501(c)3 qualified charitable or educational organization or an accredited K-12 educational institution. U.S. grant guidelines and applications are available online.

Restrictions: Grants do not support: an individual person or families; adoption services; political candidates or organizations; religious activities, in whole or in part, for the purpose of further religious doctrine; memorials and endowments; travel expenses; nonprofit and school sponsored walk-a-thons, athletic events and athletic group sponsorships other than Special Olympics; door prizes or raffles; U.S. hospitals and medical research; school-affiliated orchestras, bands, choirs, trips, athletic teams, drama groups, yearbooks and class parties; general operating expenses for programs within the United States; organizations that do not follow our application procedures; follow-on applications from past grantees that have not met our reporting requirements or satisfactorily completed the terms of past grants; fundraising events, annual funds, galas and other special-event fundraising activities; advertising, t-shirts, giveaways and promotional items; documentary films, books, etc; debt reduction; dissertations and student research projects; loans, scholarships, fellowships and grants to individuals; for-profit businesses; gifts, honoraria, gratuities; capital improvements to rental properties.

Geographic Focus: Alabama, Arizona, California, Colorado, District of Columbia, Florida, Georgia, Hawaii, Illinois, Kansas, Maryland, Missouri, Nevada, New Mexico, Ohio, Oklahoma, Oregon, Pennsylvania, South Carolina, Texas, Utah, Washington, Australia, Canada

Contact: Antoinette Bailey, (312) 544-2000; fax (312) 544 - 2082

Internet: http://www.boeing.com/companyoffices/aboutus/community/charitable.htm

Sponsor: Boeing Company Contributions

100 North Riverside

Chicago, IL 60606-1596

Boettcher Foundation Grants　　　　266

Grant support is given to promote the general well-being of humanity. Grants are awarded for arts and culture, community and social service, education and healthcare. Organizations seeking support from the Foundation should send a preliminary letter, describing the organization that wishes to submit a proposal and the project for which funding is being requested. The letter should be signed by the head of the applicant agency and should include a statement related to the priority of the project within the organization's overall plans. Letters of inquiry should be mailed or emailed.

Requirements: Capital grants are made in the form of challenges, conditional on an applicant agency's ability to raise the balance of the funds needed for a project. Although no absolute guidelines have been established, 50 to 75 percent of the goal should already be in hand before the grant request will be considered.

Restrictions: The Foundation does not accept proposals, or provide grants, for the following giving interests: operations; gymnasiums/athletic fields; housing; purchase of tables or tickets for dinner/events; individuals; large urban hospitals; out-of-state projects; media presentations; small business start-ups; open space/parks; conferences, seminars, workshops; organizations that primarily serve animals; debt reduction; pilot programs; endowments; religious groups or organizations for their religious purposes; scholarships; travel.

Geographic Focus: Colorado

Samples: Children's Hospital (Denver, CO)—for its fund-raising campaign to build a new hospital, $5 million; Colorado College (Colorado Springs, CO)—to renovate Palmer Hall, a classroom building, $400,000; Johnson and Wales U (Denver, CO)—for renovations and restoration at its Park Hill Campus, $100,000.

Contact: Grants Administrator; (800) 323-9640 or (303) 534-1937; grants@boettcherfoundation.org

Internet: http://www.boettcherfoundation.org/grants/index.html

Sponsor: Boettcher Foundation

600 Seventeenth Street, Suite 2210 South

Denver, CO 80202-5422

Bohemian Foundation Pharos Fund Grants　　　　267

The foundation awards grants to improve the quality of life in Fort Collins in its areas of interest, including youth, building the capacity of organizations working together, and citizen involvement. In the area of youth, the foundation makes grants that support youth at all social, economic, and developmental stages to achieve their greatest potential; support youth development in the areas of education and training; strengthen and align systems that affect learning and life-long opportunities; and support youth within the context of their families, communities, and the policy environment. In the area of building the capacity of organizations working together, the foundation makes grants that facilitate collaboration among community service entities to improve their effectiveness; strengthen the effectiveness of organizations working together to discover solutions to community concerns and issues; and support the development of relationships among organizations. In the area of citizen involvement, the foundation makes grants to support programs that demonstrate the need of greater public awareness; support programs that utilize existing research or information and make it more accessible to the public; and support programs, projects, or events that raise consciousness about community issues. Types of support include general operating grants, capital grants, equipment purchase, program support, and technical assistance. One request per grant cycle is permitted. Complete guidelines are available online.

Requirements: Grants are available to nonprofit, 501(c)3 organizations (other than private foundations) in Fort Collins, Colorado.

Restrictions: The program will not fund requests with the following criteria: multi-year requests; multi-program requests; fundraising events; tuition-based private schools; political campaigns or specific legislative issues; activities that have a specific religious purpose; non-501(c)3 organizations; private foundations, including private operating foundations; individual team requests; discriminatory programs; programs serving individuals; debt reduction.

Geographic Focus: Colorado

Date(s) Application is Due: Feb 1; Sep 15

Amount of Grant: Up to 30,000 USD

Contact: Grants Administrator; (970) 482-4642; fax (970) 482-6139; info@bohemianfoundation.org

Internet: http://www.bohemianfoundation.org

Sponsor: Bohemian Foundation

103 West Mountain Avenue

Fort Collins, CO 80524

Boise Cascade Corporation Contributions Grants　　　　268

The corporate contributions program makes grants to charitable organizations and programs in communities where Boise Cascade operates. Areas of interest include education, environment, and culture. General operating grants, capital grants, and grants for programs/projects are awarded. Requests must be made in writing and sent to the location nearest the requesting organization.

Requirements: U.S. 501(c)3 nonprofit organizations in company-operating areas may apply.

Restrictions: The corporation will not support areas where the corporation has minimal or no operations; individuals, private foundations, or international organizations; trips, athletic teams, scholarships, or sports vehicle sponsorships; or religious, fraternal, social, labor, or veterans organizations.

Geographic Focus: All States

Contact: Corporate Contributions, Contribution Program Manager; (208) 384-6161; fax (208) 384-7189; bcweb@bc.com

Internet: http://www.bc.com/corporate/community.jsp

Sponsor: Boise Cascade Corporation

P.O. Box 50

Boise, ID 83728-0001

Bonfils-Stanton Foundation Grants 269

Colorado nonprofit organizations are eligible to apply, and funds must be used within the state for the benefit of Colorado citizens. The focus of the foundation is to advance excellence in the areas of arts and culture, community service, and science and medicine. Types of support include operating grants, capital campaigns, and capacity-building grants. Proposals will be reviewed at quarterly meetings. Guidelines and forms are available online.

Requirements: Colorado 501(c)3 organizations are eligible.

Restrictions: Areas generally not eligible for funding include loans, grants, or scholarships to individuals; events, media productions, seminars, conferences, or travel expenses related to meetings; activities or initiatives that have a religious purpose or objective; endowment funding, fellowships, endowed chairs; funding to retire operating debt; requests from organizations outside the State of Colorado or that are not for the benefit of Colorado citizens.

Geographic Focus: Colorado

Date(s) Application is Due: Jan 31; Apr 30; Jul 31; Oct 31

Samples: ArtReach (CO)—for a Web-based ticket reservation system; Capitol Hill Community Services (CO)—to fund meal sites for the homeless; Kids in Need of Dentistry (CO)—to develop a comprehensive technology plan.

Contact: Susan France, Vice President of Programs; (303) 825-3774; fax (303) 825-0802; susan@bonfils-stanton.org

Internet: http://www.bonfils-stantonfoundation.org

Sponsor: Bonfils-Stanton Foundation

1601 Arapahoe Street, Suite 500

Denver, CO 80202

Booth Ferris Foundation Grants 270

The foundation awards grants in the fields of education (K-12, private higher education, theological education, smaller colleges, secondary schools, and adult basic education) and civic and urban programs for social services, environmental conservation, and cultural activities. Types of support include project, capital, and capacity- building grants. Grants are awarded nationwide, with a focus on the metropolitan New York area. There are no application forms or deadline dates. Awards are decided on a quarterly basis.

Requirements: Organizations must be classified by the IRS as public charities and tax-exempt under section 501(c)3 of the Internal Revenue Code of 1986.

Restrictions: A minimum of three years must elapse between grant awards. No grants are made to individuals, private foundations or for loans. Grants are not made to organizations whose primary work is conducted outside of the US, to individuals, to federated campaigns, or to work with specific diseases or disabilities. Proposals from educational institutions for scholarships, fellowships and for unrestricted endowment are discouraged, as are proposals for individual research efforts at such institutions. Proposals from social services and cultural institutions from outside the metropolitan New York area will not be considered.

Geographic Focus: New York

Amount of Grant: 50,000 - 400,000 USD

Samples: Harlem RBI (New York, NY)—for organizational development, $150,000; Bowdoin College (Brunswick, ME)—to construct an academic building, $150,000.

Contact: Booth Ferris Foundation, (212) 464-2487; (212) 464-2487

Internet: http://fdncenter.org/grantmaker/boothferris

Sponsor: Booth Ferris Foundation

NY1-N040, 345 Park Avenue, 4th Floor

New York, NY 10154

Borkee-Hagley Foundation Grants 271

The foundation awards grants in a wide range of interests, including social services to children and families, religious organizations, and environmental programs. Delaware nonprofits receive preference. The board meets in December to consider requests.

Requirements: Delaware nonprofits are eligible to apply.

Restrictions: No support for specific churches or synagogues. Grants are not made to individuals.

Geographic Focus: Delaware

Date(s) Application is Due: Nov 1

Amount of Grant: 1,000 - 25,000 USD

Samples: Artistic Productions Inc (Hockessin, DE)—$1000; Delaware Hospice (Wilmington, DE)—$13,000; Better Life Outreach Ministries (Newport, DE)—$5000; Children and Families First (Wilmington, DE)—$13,000.

Contact: Henry H. Silliman Jr., President; (302) 652-8616

Sponsor: Borkee-Hagley Foundation

P.O. Box 4590

Wilmington, DE 19807-4590

Boston Foundation Grants 272

The Boston Foundation has a particular concern for low income and disenfranchised communities and residents and supports organizations and programs whose work helps advance the Foundation's high priorities in a variety of subject areas: Arts and Culture; Civic Engagement; Community Safety, Economic Development; Education/Out-of-School Time, Health and Human Services; Housing and Community Economic Development; the Nonprofit Sector, Urban Environment and Workforce Development. The Foundation generally makes the following types of grants: Project or program support for community-based efforts that improve the quality of life in the community, test new models, and promote collaborative and innovative ventures; advocacy and public policy research that is linked to specific action; support for planning to enable organizations and residents to assess community needs, respond to new challenges and opportunities, and provide for the inclusion of new populations; organizational support to develop and build the capacity of nonprofit organizations - support that helps organizations keep pace with the changing requirements and demands of their communities and broader environments; small grants awarded on a rolling basis for one-time organizational development needs through the Vision Fund. In addition, on a very limited basis, the Foundation will consider development grants and strategic alliances.

Requirements: Grants are made only to tax-exempt organizations in Massachusetts.

Restrictions: The committee does not consider more than one proposal from the same organization within a 12-month period. Discretionary grants are generally not made to the following applicants: city or state government agencies or departments; individuals; medical research; endowments; equipment; replacement of lost/expired government funding or gap funding to cover the full cost of providing services; scholarships and fellowships; video and film production; construction and renovation projects and capital campaigns; programs with religious content; travel; summer camps and lobbying. Activities that are generally lower priorities for the Foundation are conferences, lectures, one-time events, programs benefiting only a small number of participants or routine service delivery and/or operating expenses.

Geographic Focus: Massachusetts

Date(s) Application is Due: Jan 5; Jul 1

Samples: Raw Art Works in Lynn, MA, $75,000 - for arts-based youth development programs to young people in Lynn; Boston Private Industry Council, Boston, MA, $200,000 - to administer the Accuplacer assessment to all program participants to determine the need for remedial writing support, and provide college transition coaching to 75 participating students headed to Bunker Hill and Roxbury Community College;

Contact: Corey Davis, Grants Manager; (617) 338-1700; fax (617) 338-1604; info@tbf.org

Internet: http://www.tbf.org

Sponsor: Boston Foundation

75 Arlington Street, 10th Floor

Boston, MA 02116

Boston Foundation Initiative to Strengthen Arts & Cultural Service 273 Organizations

The program supports Boston-area nonprofits with missions and programs that are substantially focused on serving and enhancing the capacity of individual artists and/or arts and cultural organizations. Organizations may submit proposals in either of two categories: externally focused activities that enhance or expand service delivery to artists and/or cultural organizations; or internally focused work or activities that build a service organization's own management and service capacity. Proposals that blend the two approaches are also welcomed. Evaluation criteria include management excellence, capacity to serve, and impact on and service to artists and/or small, community-based arts organizations within the greater Boston area. The listed application deadline is for letters of inquiry; full proposals are by invitation.

Requirements: 501(c)3 nonprofit agencies that provide services to artists and/or cultural nonprofits within the greater Boston service area are eligible.

Geographic Focus: Massachusetts

Date(s) Application is Due: Oct 14

Samples: American Composers Forum, Boston Area Chapter, (MA)—to implement a strategic plan, $7000; Cultural Access Consortium (MA)—to work with five theater companies to develop and implement access strategies, $20,000; StageSource (MA)—to enhance current and launch new professional development and job resource programs for theater artists, $15,000; The Art Connection (MA)—to frame works of art, facilitating donations from and placements to less affluent artists and nonprofit agencies, $10,000.

Contact: Ann McQueen, (617) 338-1700; mcg@tbf.org

Internet: http://www.tbf.org/current/current-L2.asp?id=3177

Sponsor: Boston Foundation
75 Arlington Street, 10th Floor
Boston, MA 02116

Boston Globe Foundation Grants 274

The foundation concentrates on three focus areas: strengthen the reading, writing, and critical thinking of young people, while fostering their inherent love of learning; strengthen the roads that link people to culture; and strengthen the civic fabric of the city. The foundation also sponsors the Neighbor to Neighbor Initiative, which funds exceptional Dorchester focused nonprofits.
Requirements: Massachusetts nonprofit organizations in the greater Boston area are eligible.
Restrictions: The Foundation will only review one proposal per year from any organization.
Geographic Focus: Massachusetts
Amount of Grant: 5,000 - 15,000 USD
Contact: Leah P. Bailey, Director; (617) 929-2895; fax (617) 929-2041; foundation@globe.com
Internet: http://bostonglobe.com
Sponsor: Boston Globe Foundation
P.O. Box 55819
Boston, MA 02205-55819

Boston Women's Fund Grants 275

The fund gives grants to support community-based projects in the greater Boston, MA, area run by and for women/girls organized for social and economic change. Also funded are direct service projects that have an organizing component. Types of support include challenge/matching grants, general operating grants, grants in aid, project grants, seed money grants, and technical assistance. Groups just getting started are encouraged to apply, particularly those including women/girls who are most vulnerable and have the least access to other resources—minority women, low-income women, girls, disabled women, lesbians, and older women. To apply, send a letter of intent to the foundation by September ninth. Letter of intent is available on the website.
Requirements: Applicant must be a Boston-area group with an organizational budget of less than $150,000 per year.
Geographic Focus: Massachusetts
Date(s) Application is Due: Oct 1
Amount of Grant: Up to 15,000 USD
Contact: Catherine Joseph, Program Director; (617) 725-0035, ext. 3002; fax (617) 725-0277; Catherine@bostonwomensfund.org
Internet: http://www.bostonwomensfund.org/grantinfo.html
Sponsor: Boston Women's Fund
14 Beacon Street, Suite 805
Boston, MA 02108

Boulder County Arts Alliance Neodata Endowment Grants 276

Boulder County Arts Alliance Neodata Endowment awards grants to eligible Boulder County nonprofit organizations in its area of interest, including arts and performing arts. Types of support include general operating support, equipment support, unrestricted fellowships, organizational projects, and grants for individual artists. The Alliance offers grants twice per year, with deadlines being the end of February and end of August. The minimum amount awarded is $1,000. Awards generally do not exceed $1,500.
Requirements: Colorado 501(c)3 nonprofit organizations serving the Boulder area are eligible.
Geographic Focus: Colorado
Date(s) Application is Due: Feb 28; Aug 29
Amount of Grant: 500 - 1,500 USD
Contact: John Farmer; (303) 447-2422; info@bouldercountyarts.org
Internet: http://www.bouldercountyarts.org/grants_neodata
Sponsor: Boulder County Arts Alliance
2590 Walnut Street, Suite 9
Boulder, CO 80302

Boyle Foundation Grants 277

The Boyle Foundation was established in Massachusetts in 1990, and works diligently to support its primary fields of interest, including: animal welfare and wildlife; education; and health care. Most often, funding comes in the form of general operating support. An application form is required, though interested parties should begin by forwarding a letter of interest to the office. That letter should include a brief history of organization and description of its mission, along with a detailed description of the project and the amount of funding

requested. Most recently, grant awards have ranged from as little as $750 to a maximum of $9,500. There are no specified annual deadlines for submission.
Requirements: Applicants must either be located in, or support the residents of, the State of Massachusetts.
Geographic Focus: Massachusetts
Amount of Grant: 750 - 9,500 USD
Contact: Brian E. Boyle, (508) 349-7955
Sponsor: Boyle Foundation
P.O. Box 786
Truro, MA 02666-0786

Brainerd Foundation Grants 278

The foundation is dedicated to protecting the environmental quality of the Pacific Northwest, including Washington, Oregon, Idaho, Montana, Alaska, and British Columbia. Program grants are made in the following areas: endangered ecosystems—conservation biology, conservation assessment, and mining reform and roadless areas; and communications and capacity building—organizational development, and allied voices. Program grants are awarded to cover costs associated with activities such as public education and grassroots outreach, media strategies, litigation, scientific and economic studies, computer networking, and building organizational capacity. Opportunity Fund grants are awarded to organizations for support such as outreach, litigation, applied research, and other unexpected needs. Additional types of support include general operating support, continuing support, equipment acquisition, conferences and seminars, seed money, research, technical assistance, and employee matching gifts. Applications are available online.
Requirements: Nonprofit organizations in the Pacific Northwest are eligible.
Restrictions: The foundation does not favor proposals for school education programs, land acquisition, endowments, capital campaigns, projects sponsored by government agencies, basic research, fellowships, or books or videos that are not part of a broader strategy.
Geographic Focus: Alaska, Idaho, Montana, Oregon, Washington, Canada
Amount of Grant: 250 - 25,000 USD
Contact: Ann Krumboltz, Executive Director; (206) 448-0676; fax (206) 448-7222; annk@brainerd.org
Internet: http://www.brainerd.org/grants/intro.php
Sponsor: Brainerd Foundation
1601 Second Avenue, Suite 610
Seattle, WA 98101-1541

Brett Family Foundation Grants 279

The foundation awards grants in two focus areas: Boulder County nonprofits that provide direct services and support for underserved and frequently marginalized populations; and organizations throughout the state of Colorado advocating for social, economic, gender, and racial justice. The foundation accepts proposals in two general grant cycles: March and September. The March cycle will be devoted entirely to Social Justice grants (primarily community organizing and advocacy organizations), while the September cycle will be dedicated to Direct Services in Boulder County.
Requirements: 501(c)3 nonprofit organizations serving the communities of Boulder County are eligible.
Geographic Focus: Colorado
Date(s) Application is Due: Mar 1; Sep 1
Contact: Brian Hiatt, (303) 442-1200; bhiatt@brettfoundation.org
Internet: http://www.brettfoundation.org
Sponsor: Brett Family Foundation
1123 Spruce Street
Boulder, CO 80302

Brico Fund Grants 280

The mission of the fund is to effect systemic change—to change attitudes, policies and societal patterns. Grants are made to secure full participation in society for women and girls; restore and sustain the earth's natural systems; promote a just and equitable society; and nourish the creative spirit. Types of support include general operating, program, and rarely, capital and endowment grants. Applicants should complete the fund's preliminary application form and a two-page letter of intent, describing the organization's intended project or program.
Requirements: The fund supports organizations with projects and programs within the Greater Milwaukee community. Some funding is done statewide or nationally for programs of broader scope.
Restrictions: Grants do not support conferences and meetings, disease-specific programs, educational institutions, individuals, media projects, medical institutions, religions, or organizations with a focus on animals.

Geographic Focus: Wisconsin
Date(s) Application is Due: Jan 15; Jul 15
Amount of Grant: 1,000 - 500,000 USD
Samples: 1000 Friends (WI)—for the opening of a Milwaukee office to explore transportation and smart growth issues, $30,000; Fondy Market—to support building of the market, $50,000; Growing Power—for operating support, $115,000; Midtown Neighborhood Assoc—to support an urban tree house and education program, $35,000.
Contact: Melissa Nimke, Grants Administrator; (414) 272-2747; fax (414) 272-2036; mbn@bricofund.org or bricofund@bricofund.org
Internet: http://www.bricofund.org
Sponsor: Brico Fund
205 E Wisconsin Avenue, Suite 200
Milwaukee, WI 53202

Bright Family Foundation Grants 281

Established in 1986, the foundation primarily serves the Stanislaus County area of California. Areas of interest include: religion; education; medical services; medical school/education; internships; human services; children/youth services; arts & culture. The Board meets once a year in December to review proposals. Deadline date for applications is November 1.
Requirements: Stanislaus County, CA, IRS 501(c)3 tax-exempt organizations within a 20 mile radius of Modesto, CA, are eligible to apply.
Geographic Focus: California
Date(s) Application is Due: Nov 1
Amount of Grant: 5,000 - 50,000 USD
Samples: Beggs High School, Beggs, OK, $32,000—scholarship program; UCSF School of Medicine, San Francisco, CA, $45,000; Modesto Symphony Orchestra, Modesto, CA, $20,000.
Contact: Calvin Bright, President; (209) 526-8242
Sponsor: Bright Family Foundation
1620 North Carpenter Road, Building B
Modesto, CA 95351-1155

Brinson Foundation Grants 282

The foundation supports education, public health, and scientific research programs that engage, inform, and inspire committed citizens to confront the challenges that face humanity. Grantmaking priorities are education—awareness and outreach, democracy and citizenship, economically disadvantaged, and libraries and literacy; public health—awareness and outreach, and economically disadvantaged; and scientific research—astrophysics, cosmology, geophysics, medical research (i.e., Alzheimer's disease, cancer, Lou Gehrig's Disease (ALS), and stroke). Types of support include general operating grants and project grants. The foundation does not accept unsolicited grant applications. Grantseekers are asked to review the foundation's mission, vision, beliefs, priorities (accessed from the Who We Are link), and guidelines. If a grantseeker believes the request would match one or more of the foundation's grantmaking priorities, they can make an inquiry by completing the online Grantseeker Information Form. The completed form should be emailed to the office. Further application is by invitation.
Requirements: The foundation will consider inviting grant applications from organizations: whose request matches one or more of the Foundation's grantmaking priorities; located in the United States of America that are exempt from tax under Section 501(c)3 of the Internal Revenue Code and are defined as charitable organizations as described in Section 509(a)1, 2 or 3 or 170(b)1A; located outside the United States of America provided they produce a written legal opinion stating that they are a charitable equivalency to a qualifying U.S. organization and/or a written affidavit containing sufficient information for the Foundation to make a reasonable judgment that the organization is charitable. The Foundation's education and public health grants are generally made to organizations that serve individuals and communities in the greater Chicago area. It also considers leading U.S.-based programs that reach broader populations across the U.S. and internationally or have the potential to have a meaningful impact on best practices at the national or international level. The Foundation's physical science research grants are made to leading organizations across the United States. In this priority area, the location of the program is less critical than the match with the Foundation's grantmaking priorities.
Restrictions: The Foundation will not consider grant inquiries from organizations that: discriminate on the basis of race, gender, religion, ethnicity or sexual orientation. The Foundation will not consider grant inquiries that request funding for: activities that attempt to influence public elections; voter registration; political activity; lobbying efforts; promotion of a specific religious faith; medical research involving human cloning. The Foundation discourages grant inquiries requesting funds for: capital improvements; endowments; fundraising events.
Geographic Focus: All States
Samples: Adler Planetarium and Astronomy Museum, Chicago, Illinois, $80,000 - for cosmology and astrophysics research; Lincoln Park Zoo, Chicago, Illinois, $55,000 - for general support; Institute for Humane Studies, Arlington, Virginia, $20,000 - summer seminars for college students.
Contact: Cheryl A. Heads, Grants Manager; (312) 799-4500; fax (312) 799-4310; mail@brinsonfoundation.org
Internet: http://www.brinsonfoundation.org/grant_seekers/grantseekers.shtml
Sponsor: Brinson Foundation
737 N Michigan Avenue, Suite 1850
Chicago, IL 60611

Bristol-Myers Squibb Foundation Health Disparities Grants 283

One mission of the Bristol-Myers Squibb Foundation is to reduce health disparities by strengthening community-based health care worker capacity, integrating medical care and community-based supportive services, and mobilizing communities to fight disease. To this end, this Foundation attempts to address health disparities in four strategic disease areas representing major public health burdens and in four highly affected geographies: hepatitis in Asia, HIV/AIDS in Africa, serious mental illness in the U.S., and cancer in Europe. Additional areas of concern include: metabolic diseases; infectious diseases; rheumatoid arthritis; cardiovascular diseases; substance abuse; women's health issues; and overall health care giving.
Requirements: Nonprofit organizations in communities where Bristol-Myers Squibb maintains a facility should submit their requests for company contributions directly to that location. Contact persons are listed at the company website.
Restrictions: The foundation does not support individuals; conferences, special events, or videos; political, fraternal, social, or veterans organizations; religious or sectarian activities, unless they benefit the entire community; organizations funded through federated campaigns; endowments; or courtesy advertising.
Geographic Focus: Connecticut, Indiana, Massachusetts, New Jersey, New York
Contact: John Damonti; (212) 546-4000 or (800) 332-2056; fax (212) 546-9574
Internet: http://www.bms.com/foundation/reducing_health_disparities/Pages/default.aspx
Sponsor: Bristol-Myers Squibb Foundation
345 Park Avenue, Suite 4364
New York, NY 10154

British Columbia Arts Council Arts & Cultural Service Organization 284 Operating Assistance

British Columbia Arts Council Operating Assistance contributes to the support of service organizations that provide quality services to an established membership base and demonstrate ongoing local, provincial and/or national activity with provincial impact. The Council's approach is to consider three dimensions of artistic work: idea - the intention or artistic impetus behind the work; practice - the effectiveness of how the work is put into practice and the impact it has on those experiencing it; and development - the contribution the work makes to the development of the artist, the art form and the arts more widely. The annual deadline for applications is September 23.
Requirements: An eligible applicant must: be registered as a non-profit society in good standing in the Province of British Columbia and have operated as a service organization for two fiscal years prior to application; have received at least two Professional Project Assistance awards from the British Columbia Arts Council; provide public programming and have done so in the immediately preceding two years; compensate artists by paying fees at industry standards and adhere to international intellectual property rights standards; have professional artistic/curatorial and administrative leadership; and demonstrate need for financial assistance as defined by Council policy.
Restrictions: Operating assistance is not available for: start-up costs; seed money; capital expenditures (construction, renovation, or purchase of property or equipment); feasibility studies; budget deficits; or for-profit entities.
Geographic Focus: Canada
Date(s) Application is Due: Sep 23
Contact: Monique Lacerte-Roth, Program Coordinator; (250) 356-5488 or (250) 356-1718; fax (250) 387-4099; monique.lacerteroth@gov.bc.ca
Internet: https://www.bcartscouncil.ca/guidelines/organizations/community/arts_cultural_orgs_operating_assistance.html
Sponsor: British Columbia Arts Council
P.O. Box 9819, Station Provincial Government
Victoria, BC V8W 9W3 Canada

British Columbia Arts Council Community Arts Councils Local Government Matching Grants 285

This program assists British Columbia arts councils that have received financial assistance from municipal or regional governments in the previous fiscal year. Community Arts Councils that received financial assistance from municipal or regional governments in their most recently completed fiscal year are eligible for 100% matching funding to a maximum of $4,000 for use in the forecast funding year. Funds received from local governments are to be for general operating purposes, as opposed to special projects, in order to qualify for matching funds.

Requirements: British Columbia community arts councils who have received financial assistance from municipal or regional governments in the previous fiscal year are eligible to apply.

Restrictions: In-kind contributions are not eligible for matching funds. Funds received from a local government in the current year cannot be applied to the Local Government Matching request, but will be considered in the following year's request.

Geographic Focus: Canada
Date(s) Application is Due: Sep 30
Amount of Grant: Up to 4,000 CAD
Contact: Monique Lacerte-Roth, Community Arts Coordinator; (250) 356-5488 or (250) 356-1718; fax (250) 387-4099; monique.lacerteroth@gov.bc.ca
Internet: https://www.bcartscouncil.ca/guidelines/organizations/community/operating_assistance.html
Sponsor: British Columbia Arts Council
P.O. Box 9819, Station Provincial Government
Victoria, BC V8W 9W3 Canada

British Columbia Arts Council Early Career Development Internships 286

The British Columbia Arts Council Early Career Development internship program provide arts and cultural organizations from across British Columbia with the opportunity to host emerging practitioners in paid internships of up to one year. Both the intern to be hosted and a designated mentor within the organization must be identified within the application and both must provide a statement regarding their interest and participation. The application deadline is June 16.

Requirements: Individuals and organizations may apply to this program through separate components. Applicants to this program must be working within the arts disciplines funded by the BC Arts Council, including: community-based arts practice; museums, archival and curatorial practice; literary (creative writing, publishing); dance (performance, choreography); media arts (film, video, audio/sound art, new media); theater (acting, directing, technical, design, musical theater); music (performance, composition); or visual arts, craft, and curatorial practice.

Geographic Focus: Canada
Date(s) Application is Due: Jun 16
Contact: Lori Dunn, Performing Arts Internship Officer; (250) 237-1538 or (250) 356-1718; fax (250) 387-4099; lori.dunn@gov.bc.ca
Internet: https://www.bcartscouncil.ca/guidelines/artists/youth/early_career_development.html
Sponsor: British Columbia Arts Council
P.O. Box 9819, Station Provincial Government
Victoria, BC V8W 9W3 Canada

British Columbia Arts Council Media Arts Organizations Operating Assistance 287

British Columbia Arts Council Media Arts Organizations Operating Assistance contributes to the support of professional, not-for-profit media arts organizations that sustain an annual artistic program encompassing production, distribution, collections and dissemination activities. Media arts are defined as works in film, video, audio/sound art and new media. New media includes new information and communications technologies used for artistic expression. The annual deadline for application submission postmarks is September 30.

Requirements: An eligible applicant must: be registered as a non-profit society in good standing in the Province of British Columbia and have operated as an arts festival organization for two fiscal years prior to application; in the case of new applicants, have received at least two Professional Project Assistance awards from the British Columbia Arts Council; provide public programming and have done so during the immediately preceding two years; compensate artists by paying fees at industry standards and adhere to international intellectual property rights standards; have professional artistic/curatorial and administrative leadership; and demonstrate the need for financial assistance as defined by Council policy. Additional specific eligibility requirements are outlined at the website.

Restrictions: Operating assistance is not available for: start-up costs; seed money; capital expenditures (construction, renovation, or purchase of property or equipment); feasibility studies; budget deficits; or for-profit entities.

Geographic Focus: Canada
Date(s) Application is Due: Sep 30
Contact: Sherry Ewings, Media Arts Officer; (250) 356-0081 or (250) 356-1718; fax (250) 387-4099; sherry.ewings@gov.bc.ca
Internet: https://www.bcartscouncil.ca/guidelines/organizations/mediaarts/operating_assistance.html
Sponsor: British Columbia Arts Council
P.O. Box 9819, Station Provincial Government
Victoria, BC V8W 9W3 Canada

British Columbia Arts Council Operating Assistance for Community Arts Councils 288

British Columbia Arts Council Operating Assistance for Community Arts Councils support the operations of community arts councils throughout British Columbia. Awards may cover up to 50 percent of the overall operating budget of an arts council. Support levels are determined by the population served and the applicant community's distance from major urban centers. Applications are evaluated on the amount requested, the justification for expenditures, the level of the organization's activity, and its financial need. Arts councils should contact the office for guidelines and eligibility criteria.

Requirements: Applicants must be registered nonprofit societies in British Columbia. Arts councils seeking Basic Assistance for the first time should be aware that admission to this program occurs every five years, following the federal census. In other years, eligible arts councils that are not receiving Community Arts Council Assistance may apply for a Community Arts Development Project Assistance award.

Restrictions: Awards are not available for capital expenditures. Awards will not be made retroactively.

Geographic Focus: Canada
Date(s) Application is Due: Sep 30
Contact: Monique Lacerte-Roth, Community Arts Coordinator; (250) 356-5488 or (250) 356-1718; fax (250) 387-4099; monique.lacerteroth@gov.bc.ca
Internet: https://www.bcartscouncil.ca/guidelines/organizations/community/operating_assistance.html
Sponsor: British Columbia Arts Council
P.O. Box 9819, Station Provincial Government
Victoria, BC V8W 9W3 Canada

British Columbia Arts Council Operating Assistance for Performing Arts Organization 289

The mission of the Council is to engage all British Columbians in a healthy arts and cultural community that is recognized for excellence. In the area of performing arts, the Council understands that operating assistance contributes to the support of organizations that sustain an annual artistic program encompassing creation, development, production, and public presentation. The Council's approach is to consider three dimensions of artistic work: idea - the intention or artistic impetus behind the work; practice - the effectiveness of how the work is put into practice and the impact it has on those experiencing it; and development - the contribution the work makes to the development of the artist, the art form and the arts more widely. Applicants are urged to contact their Program Officer prior to submission. The annual submission deadline for completed applications is March 15.

Requirements: An eligible applicant must: be registered as a non-profit society in good standing in the Province of British Columbia and have operated as a performing arts organization for two fiscal years prior to application; in the case of new applicants, have received at least two Professional Project Assistance awards from the British Columbia Arts Council; provide public programming and have done so in the immediately preceding two years; compensate artists by paying fees at industry standards and adhere to international intellectual property rights standards; have professional artistic/curatorial and administrative leadership; and demonstrate need for financial assistance, as defined by Council policy.

Restrictions: Operating assistance is not available for: start-up costs; seed money; capital expenditures (construction, renovation, or purchase of property or equipment); feasibility studies; budget deficits; or for-profit entities.

Geographic Focus: Canada
Date(s) Application is Due: Mar 15
Contact: Lori Dunn; (250) 387-1538 or (250) 356-1718; lori.dunn@gov.bc.ca
Internet: https://www.bcartscouncil.ca/guidelines/organizations/performing arts/operating_assist.htm
Sponsor: British Columbia Arts Council
P.O. Box 9819, Station Provincial Government
Victoria, BC V8W 9W3 Canada

British Columbia Arts Council Operating Assistance for Visual Arts Organizations   **290**

Funds are available from the British Columbia Arts Council to professional, non-profit visual arts organizations that engage people in the recognition, understanding, and development of human and natural history and the visual arts, including the diverse cultures of first peoples and the world. Awards under this program are intended to support the public programming of established organizations with stable curatorial and administrative leadership. The annual deadline for submission of applications is September 30.

Requirements: Eligible applicants must: be registered as a non-profit society in the Province of British Columbia, or be a public museum operated by a municipality with a community-based board of management that sets policy for the museum's public programs and services; have received at least two Project Assistance awards from the British Columbia Arts Council in the previous three years and have completed at least two full years of operation; provide year-round public programming, and have done so during the immediately preceding two years; compensate artists by paying fees to professional artists at industry standard; employ competent curatorial and administrative leadership; provide an audited or independently prepared financial statement for the most recently completed fiscal year; demonstrate a diversified revenue base; if the applying organization has members, be able to demonstrate a range of membership that is representative of its constituency; and demonstrate financial need for assistance.

Restrictions: Awards under this program are not available for: start-up costs, seed money, capital expenditures (construction, renovation, or purchase of property or equipment), feasibility studies, budget deficits, or for-profit entities. Awards under this program are not available for archives-only organizations, single theme or specialty museums or industrial or heritage sites, organizations dedicated to a temporary exhibition or those which quality for operating assistance under other programs.

Geographic Focus: Canada
Date(s) Application is Due: Sep 30
Contact: Sue Donaldson; (250) 356-1729 or (250) 356-1718; fax (250) 387-4099; sue.donaldson@gov.bc.ca
Internet: https://www.bcartscouncil.ca/guidelines/organizations/visualartists/operating_assistance.html
Sponsor: British Columbia Arts Council
P.O. Box 9819, Station Provincial Government
Victoria, BC V8W 9W3 Canada

British Columbia Arts Council Professional Arts Festival Operating Assistance   **291**

British Columbia Arts Council Operating Assistance contributes to the support of established arts festivals organizations that produce a major annual festival, present and feature professional artists, have a clear unifying theme or vision, and have stable artistic and administrative leadership. All applicants, especially new applicants, are urged to discuss their request with Council staff prior to submission. The annual deadline for application submissions is September 30.

Requirements: An eligible applicant must: be registered as a non-profit society in good standing in the Province of British Columbia and have operated as an arts festival organization for two fiscal years prior to application; in the case of new applicants, have received at least two Professional Project Assistance awards from the British Columbia Arts Council; provide public programming and have done so during the immediately preceding two years; compensate artists by paying fees at industry standards and adhere to international intellectual property rights standards; have professional artistic/curatorial and administrative leadership; and demonstrate the need for financial assistance as defined by Council policy.

Restrictions: Operating assistance is not available for: start-up costs; seed money; capital expenditures (construction, renovation, or purchase of property or equipment); feasibility studies; budget deficits; or for-profit entities.

Geographic Focus: Canada
Date(s) Application is Due: Sep 30
Contact: Monique Lacerte-Roth, Community Arts Officer; (250) 356-5488 or (250) 356-1718; fax (250) 387-4099; monique.lacerteroth@gov.bc.ca
Internet: https://www.bcartscouncil.ca/guidelines/organizations/festivals/prof_arts_operating_assistance.html
Sponsor: British Columbia Arts Council
P.O. Box 9819, Station Provincial Government
Victoria, BC V8W 9W3 Canada

British Columbia Arts Council Professional Arts Periodicals Operating Assistance   **292**

Applications for British Columbia Arts Council Professional Arts Periodicals operating assistance awards are available once each fiscal year. Assistance is available to non-profit organizations that publish arts periodicals devoted primarily (at least 75%) to the first publication of any form of artistic expression or social, cultural, or intellectual commentary or inquiry. Awards under this program are intended to support the artistic development of established periodicals with regular publication and stable artistic and administrative leadership. The annual deadline for application submission postmarks is March 15.

Requirements: An eligible applicant must: be registered as a non-profit society in good standing in the Province of British Columbia and have operated for two fiscal years prior to application; in the case of new applicants, have received at least two Professional Project Assistance awards from the British Columbia Arts Council; provide public programming and have done so during the immediately preceding two years; compensate artists by paying fees at industry standards and adhere to international intellectual property rights standards; have professional artistic/curatorial and administrative leadership; and demonstrate the need for financial assistance as defined by Council policy. Additional specific eligibility requirements are outlined at the website.

Restrictions: Operating assistance is not available for: start-up costs; seed money; capital expenditures (construction, renovation, or purchase of property or equipment); feasibility studies; budget deficits; or for-profit entities. Furthermore, awards are not available for periodicals that: primarily offer news reporting or cover current events; advocate for political organizations or causes; are academic or scholarly journals; promote commercial enterprise; or are in-house newsletters or magazines that publish material of interest to their memberships.

Geographic Focus: Canada
Date(s) Application is Due: Mar 15
Contact: Sue Donaldson, Literary Officer; (250) 356-1729 or (250) 356-1718; fax (250) 387-4099; sue.donaldson@gov.bc.ca
Internet: https://www.bcartscouncil.ca/guidelines/organizations/publishers/arts_periodicals_oper_assist.html
Sponsor: British Columbia Arts Council
P.O. Box 9819, Station Provincial Government
Victoria, BC V8W 9W3 Canada

British Columbia Arts Council Professional Arts Training Organization Operating Assistance   **293**

British Columbia Arts Council Operating Assistance contributes to the support of organizations that sustain annual programs of professional arts training. Eligible activities may include specialized training for professional artists and cultural workers or specialized training for those who are committed to pursuing professional careers in the arts. All applicants, especially new applicants, are urged to discuss their request with Council staff prior to submission. The annual deadline for application submission postmarks is March 30.

Requirements: An eligible applicant must: be registered as a non-profit society in good standing in the Province of British Columbia and have operated for two fiscal years prior to application; in the case of new applicants, have received at least two Professional Project Assistance awards from the British Columbia Arts Council; provide public programming and have done so during the immediately preceding two years; compensate artists by paying fees at industry standards and adhere to international intellectual property rights standards; have professional artistic/curatorial and administrative leadership; and demonstrate the need for financial assistance as defined by Council policy. Additional specific eligibility requirements are outlined at the website.

Restrictions: Operating assistance is not available for: start-up costs; seed money; capital expenditures (construction, renovation, or purchase of property or equipment); feasibility studies; budget deficits; or for-profit entities.

Geographic Focus: Canada
Date(s) Application is Due: Mar 15
Contact: Walter Quan; (250) 356-1728 or (250) 356-1718; walter.quan@gov.bc.ca
Internet: https://www.bcartscouncil.ca/guidelines/special_programs/training/professional_arts_training_orgs_oper_assist.html
Sponsor: British Columbia Arts Council
P.O. Box 9819, Station Provincial Government
Victoria, BC V8W 9W3 Canada

British Columbia Arts Council Project Assistance for Performing Artists   **294**

British Columbia Arts Council Professional Project Assistance for Performing Artists supports initiatives in the development, creation, production and/or live performance of classical, experimental, original and traditional art forms from all world cultures. Grants are intended to contribute to the successful realization of a single event or activity. The maximum contribution to a project in this program is 50% of the total budget of the project. Receipt of funding does not guarantee assistance in subsequent years. All applicants, especially

new applicants, are urged to discuss their request with Council staff prior to submission. The annual deadline for application submission is April 15.
Requirements: An eligible applicant must: be based in British Columbia and offer performances or programming in British Columbia; engage competent artistic/ curatorial and project management leadership as demonstrated in previous achievements, collaborations, partnerships, relationships, etc; and compensate artists and other professional practitioners by paying fees at industry standards and adhere to international intellectual property rights standards. In addition to the general eligibility criteria listed above, a professional performing arts organization must: be a professional performing arts organization registered and in good standing as a non-profit society in the Province of British Columbia for at least one year; demonstrate the need for financial assistance, as defined by Council policy; provide financial statements for the most recently completed fiscal year; not currently receive operating assistance from the British Columbia Arts Council; and have operated and offered public programming for a minimum of one year as a non-profit society.
Restrictions: General exclusions for Professional Project Assistance include: operating costs; project phases that have begun prior to the application deadline; touring expenses; project/budget deficits; capital expenditures (construction, renovation, or purchase of property or equipment); fundraising; start-up costs or seed money; feasibility studies; for-profit entities; international travel costs of foreign artists visiting British Columbia; travel to international symposia; conferences or competitions; projects that are secondary to other purposes (e.g. fundraising events, conventions, or family, religious or community celebrations or anniversaries); subsistence to artists or curators; the cost of producing recordings; and the creation or preparation of work for competitions.
Geographic Focus: Canada
Date(s) Application is Due: Apr 15
Contact: Lori Dunn, Performing Arts Coordinator; (250) 387-1538 or (250) 356-1718; fax (250) 387-4099; lori.dunn@gov.bc.ca
Internet: https://www.bcartscouncil.ca/guidelines/artists/performingarts/project_assistance.html
Sponsor: British Columbia Arts Council
P.O. Box 9819, Station Provincial Government
Victoria, BC V8W 9W3 Canada

British Columbia Arts Council Public Museums Operating Assistance   295
Operating Assistance contributes to the support of public program activities at professional, non-profit public museums that sustain an annual artistic and curatorial program encompassing creation, development, presentation, collections and dissemination activities. The annual deadline for application submission postmarks is September 30.
Requirements: An eligible applicant must: be registered as a non-profit society in good standing in the Province of British Columbia and have operated as a public museum for two fiscal years prior to application; in the case of new applicants, have received at least two Professional Project Assistance awards from the British Columbia Arts Council; provide public programming and have done so during the immediately preceding two years; compensate artists by paying fees at industry standards and adhere to international intellectual property rights standards; have professional artistic/curatorial and administrative leadership; and demonstrate the need for financial assistance as defined by Council policy. Additional specific eligibility requirements are outlined at the website.
Restrictions: Operating assistance is not available for: start-up costs; seed money; capital expenditures (construction, renovation, or purchase of property or equipment); feasibility studies; budget deficits; or for-profit entities.
Geographic Focus: Canada
Date(s) Application is Due: Sep 30
Contact: Sue Donaldson, Museums and Visual Arts Officer; (250) 356-1729 or (250) 356-1718; fax (250) 387-4099; sue.donaldson@gov.bc.ca
Internet: https://www.bcartscouncil.ca/guidelines/organizations/museums/public_museums_operating_assistance.html
Sponsor: British Columbia Arts Council
P.O. Box 9819, Station Provincial Government
Victoria, BC V8W 9W3 Canada

Broms Family Foundation Grants   296
The major purpose of the Foundation is its support of Jewish organizations and federated giving programs. The primary fields of interest include cancer, diabetes, education, girls clubs, and Jewish agencies and temples.
Requirements: An application form is required. Applicants should submit the following: listing of board of directors, trustees, officers and other key people and their affiliations; and a copy of current year's organizational budget and/or project budget.

Restrictions: Giving primarily in Minnesota and New York. No grants to individuals.
Geographic Focus: Minnesota, New York
Contact: Richard Broms, President; (952) 829-7850
Sponsor: Broms Family Foundation
6600 City West Parkway, Suite 100
Eden Prairie, MN 55344

Brookdale Foundation Relatives as Parents Grants   297
The Brookdale Foundation Relatives as Parents Grants (RAPP) awards seed grants to community-based organizations to develop services for grandparents and other relatives acting as surrogate parents, in addition to state agencies planning to offer such services. Currently RAPP provides extensive services, primarily to relative caregivers caring for children outside the foster care system, in 44 states, the District of Columbia, and Puerto Rico. As part of their program, they conduct the National Orientation and Training Conference and provide technical assistance through site bulletins, a listserv, annual newsletter, conference calls and webchats to facilitate opportunities for networking and information exchange. Programs and funding vary by state. Additional information is available at the website. Examples of previously funded programs are also available at the website.
Geographic Focus: All States, District of Columbia, Puerto Rico
Contact: Valerie Hall, Grant Coordinator; (212) 308-7355; fax (212) 750-0132; vah@brookdalefoundation.org
Internet: http://www.brookdalefoundation.org/RAPP/rapp.html
Sponsor: Brookdale Foundation
950 Third Avenue, 19th Floor
New York, NY 10022-3668

Brooklyn Benevolent Society Grants   298
The society awards general support grants to nonprofits of the Christian and Roman Catholic faiths, including the Salvation Army. Youth organizations such as YMCA/YWCA and child welfare groups, community service organizations, religion (divinity schools, parochial schools, missions, religious welfare) and religious organizations, and welfare groups. Grant making is focused in the New York, NY, area. Send a brief letter of inquiry describing the program and organization descriptions.
Requirements: Nonprofit organizations of the Christian and Roman Catholic faiths in New York are eligible.
Geographic Focus: New York
Samples: Fordham U (New York, NY)—for general support, $10,000; Our Lady of Perpetual Help High School (Brooklyn, NY)—for general support, $7500; Salvation Army Wayside Home and School for Girls (NY)—for general support, $6000.
Contact: Grants Administrator; (718) 624-0176
Sponsor: Brooklyn Benevolent Society
57 Willoughby Street
Brooklyn, NY 11201

Brooklyn Community Foundation Caring Neighbors Grants   299
The Caring Neighbors Fund assists vulnerable Brooklyn families and individuals with immediate need for a social safety net and seeks to provide access to health and mental health services. Its goals are to: offer paths out of poverty by supporting the work of emergency food providers and human services agencies; provide access to care for unaddressed physical or mental health needs in accessible community settings; ensure that homeless individuals and families can access safe temporary shelter and support services. The Foundation typically has two grant cycles annually, Letter of Inquiry are accepted then. Contact the Foundation directly for current grant cycles. Organizations invited to submit a complete proposal should expect a final decision from the Foundation within eight to twelve weeks of receipt.
Requirements: Organizations applying for a grant from the Brooklyn Community Foundation must be classified as tax-exempt under Section 501(c)3 of the Internal Revenue Code and as public charities under Section 509(a) of that Code. Fiscally sponsored organizations may also apply. Your organization need not be based in Brooklyn; however grants from the Brooklyn Community Foundation must directly benefit Brooklyn neighborhoods and/or Brooklyn residents. Applying for funding is a two part process: 1st step—begins with a Letter of Inquiry (LOI). This is the opportunity for an organization to provide the Foundation with an overview of the group and its proposed activities, project or program; 2nd step—applicants who have been selected to proceed to the next stage will receive an email from the Foundation's staff indicating that the organization has been approved to submit a complete proposal which

best describes in detail the activities, program or project. If selected, your organization will have 30 days to submit a complete a proposal online.
Restrictions: The Foundation does not: fund individuals; support for-profit organizations; purchase tickets for dinners, golf outings or similar fundraising events; make contributions to candidates for elective office or for partisan political purposes; provide funding for religious purposes.
Geographic Focus: New York
Samples: New York Asian Women's Center, $10,000; St. John's Bread & Life, $250,000; Brooklyn Bureau of Community Service, $25,000.
Contact: Diane John, (718) 722-5952 or (718) 722-2300; fax (718) 722-5757; info@BrooklynCommunityFoundation.org
Internet: http://www.brooklyncommunityfoundation.org/grants/caring-neighbors
Sponsor: Brooklyn Community Foundation
45 Main Street, Suite 409
Brooklyn, NY 11201

Brooklyn Community Foundation Community Arts for All Grants   300
The Arts for All Fund makes the arts a fun and essential component of life in Brooklyn, New York. Its goals are to: serve Brooklynites with diverse interests by supporting the outreach efforts of local arts and cultural organizations integrate the arts into schools and after-school programs; promote collaborations that employ the arts to address pressing community issues. Types of support available include: program, capacity building, capital, and operating support. The Foundation typically has two grant cycles annually, Letter of Inquiry are accepted then. Contact the Foundation directly for current grant cycles. Organizations invited to submit a complete proposal should expect a final decision from the Foundation within eight to twelve weeks of receipt.
Requirements: Organizations applying for a grant from the Brooklyn Community Foundation must be classified as tax-exempt under Section 501(c)3 of the Internal Revenue Code and as public charities under Section 509(a) of that Code. Fiscally sponsored organizations may also apply. Your organization need not be based in Brooklyn; however grants from the Brooklyn Community Foundation must directly benefit Brooklyn neighborhoods and/or Brooklyn residents. Applying for funding is a two part process: Ist step—begins with a Letter of Inquiry (LOI). This is the opportunity for an organization to provide the Foundation with an overview of the group and its proposed activities, project or program; 2nd step—applicants who have been selected to proceed to the next stage will receive an email from the Foundation's staff indicating that the organization has been approved to submit a complete proposal which best describes in detail the activities, program or project. If selected, your organization will have 30 days to submit a complete a proposal online.
Restrictions: The Foundation does not: fund individuals; support for-profit organizations; purchase tickets for dinners, golf outings or similar fundraising events; make contributions to candidates for elective office or for partisan political purposes; provide funding for religious purposes.
Geographic Focus: New York
Samples: Bedford Stuyvesant Restoration Corp., Brooklyn, NY, $25,000—education, arts & culture, project support; Arts of St. Anna's, Brooklyn, NY, $10,000—arts & culture education, theater, project support; Asian American Women Artist Alliance, Brooklyn, NY, $500—arts & culture education, arts/culture, project support.
Contact: Diane John, (718) 722-5952 or (718) 722-2300; fax (718) 722-5757; info@BrooklynCommunityFoundation.org
Internet: http://www.brooklyncommunityfoundation.org/grants/arts-for-all
Sponsor: Brooklyn Community Foundation
45 Main Street, Suite 409
Brooklyn, NY 11201

Brooklyn Community Foundation Community Development Grants   301
The Community Development Fund supports efforts to provide affordable housing and neighborhood stability. It encourages thoughtful planning initiatives, quality urban design and sensitivity to the historic character of Brooklyn, New York neighborhoods. It also promotes family and individual economic health through support services and effective job training programs. The Fund's goals are to: strengthen and preserve access to affordable housing in Brooklyn neighborhoods; raise individual and family income by providing Brooklyn residents access to quality job training, career placement and financial support services; build the local economy by supporting neighborhood entrepreneurs and local efforts to improve our retail corridors. Types of support available include: program, capacity building, capital, and operating support. The Foundation typically has two grant cycles annually, Letter of Inquiry are accepted then. Contact the Foundation directly for current grant cycles.

Organizations invited to submit a complete proposal should expect a final decision from the Foundation within eight to twelve weeks of receipt.
Requirements: Organizations applying for a grant from the Brooklyn Community Foundation must be classified as tax-exempt under Section 501(c)3 of the Internal Revenue Code and as public charities under Section 509(a) of that Code. Fiscally sponsored organizations may also apply. Your organization need not be based in Brooklyn; however grants from the Brooklyn Community Foundation must directly benefit Brooklyn neighborhoods and/or Brooklyn residents. Applying for funding is a two part process: Ist step—begins with a Letter of Inquiry (LOI). This is the opportunity for an organization to provide the Foundation with an overview of the group and its proposed activities, project or program; 2nd step—applicants who have been selected to proceed to the next stage will receive an email from the Foundation's staff indicating that the organization has been approved to submit a complete proposal which best describes in detail the activities, program or project. If selected, your organization will have 30 days to submit a complete a proposal online.
Restrictions: The Foundation does not: fund individuals; support for-profit organizations; purchase tickets for dinners, golf outings or similar fundraising events; make contributions to candidates for elective office or for partisan political purposes; provide funding for religious purposes.
Geographic Focus: New York
Samples: Bedford Stuyvesant Restoration Corp., Brooklyn, NY, $10,000—project support; Brand New Day, Inc., Elizabeth, NJ, $20,000—neighborhood renewal, community development, general operating support grant; Bridge Street Development, Corp., $600—neighborhood renewal, housing, sponsorship grant.
Contact: Diane John, (718) 722-5952 or (718) 722-2300; fax (718) 722-5757; info@BrooklynCommunityFoundation.org
Internet: http://www.brooklyncommunityfoundation.org/grants/community-development
Sponsor: Brooklyn Community Foundation
45 Main Street, Suite 409
Brooklyn, NY 11201

**Brooklyn Community Foundation Education & Youth Achievement   302
  Grants**
The Education and Youth Achievement Fund promotes access to quality education and academic success for all children and adults in the Brooklyn area of New York. It also supports programs that help young people make smart life choices and nurture their social and emotional well-being. Its goals are to: combine tutoring, academic support networks, and enrichment activities to advance student achievement; encourage action-oriented, youth-led community projects that promote collaboration, leadership development, and critical thinking; build bridges between youth and trusted, responsible adult role models through effective mentoring programs. Types of support available include: program, capacity building, capital, and operating support. The Foundation typically has two grant cycles annually, Letter of Inquiry are accepted then. Contact the Foundation directly for current grant cycles. Organizations invited to submit a complete proposal should expect a final decision from the Foundation within eight to twelve weeks of receipt.
Requirements: Organizations applying for a grant from the Brooklyn Community Foundation must be classified as tax-exempt under Section 501(c)3 of the Internal Revenue Code and as public charities under Section 509(a) of that Code. Fiscally sponsored organizations may also apply. Your organization need not be based in Brooklyn; however grants from the Brooklyn Community Foundation must directly benefit Brooklyn neighborhoods and/or Brooklyn residents. Applying for funding is a two part process: Ist step—begins with a Letter of Inquiry (LOI). This is the opportunity for an organization to provide the Foundation with an overview of the group and its proposed activities, project or program; 2nd step—applicants who have been selected to proceed to the next stage will receive an email from the Foundation's staff indicating that the organization has been approved to submit a complete proposal which best describes in detail the activities, program or project. If selected, your organization will have 30 days to submit a complete a proposal online.
Restrictions: The Foundation does not: fund individuals; support for-profit organizations; purchase tickets for dinners, golf outings or similar fundraising events; make contributions to candidates for elective office or for partisan political purposes; provide funding for religious purposes.
Geographic Focus: New York
Samples: Shoot Hoops Not Guns Basketball, Association, Inc., Brooklyn, NY, $500—community quality of life, youth, program support grant; United Community Centers, Inc., Brooklyn, NY, $30,000—neighborhood renewal, youth, project support grant; Refuge Inc., Staten Island, NY, $450—quality of life, youth, project support grant.

Contact: Diane John, (718) 722-5952 or (718) 722-2300; fax (718) 722-5757; info@BrooklynCommunityFoundation.org
Internet: http://www.brooklyncommunityfoundation.org/grants/education-youth
Sponsor: Brooklyn Community Foundation
45 Main Street, Suite 409
Brooklyn, NY 11201

Brooklyn Community Foundation Green Communities Grants 303
The Green Communities Fund fosters the development of green spaces, jobs, and neighborhoods. Its goals are to: encourage the protection and creation of open space, parks and community gardens; seek new ways to introduce and encourage environmental awareness in all neighborhoods through grassroots programming; train job seekers for green careers and connect them to employment opportunities. Types of support available include: program, capacity building, capital, and operating support. The Foundation typically has two grant cycles annually, Letter of Inquiry are accepted then. Contact the Foundation directly for current grant cycles. Organizations invited to submit a complete proposal should expect a final decision from the Foundation within eight to twelve weeks of receipt.
Requirements: Organizations applying for a grant from the Brooklyn Community Foundation must be classified as tax-exempt under Section 501(c)3 of the Internal Revenue Code and as public charities under Section 509(a) of that Code. Fiscally sponsored organizations may also apply. Your organization need not be based in Brooklyn; however grants from the Brooklyn Community Foundation must directly benefit Brooklyn neighborhoods and/or Brooklyn residents. Applying for funding is a two part process: 1st step—begins with a Letter of Inquiry (LOI). This is the opportunity for an organization to provide the Foundation with an overview of the group and its proposed activities, project or program; 2nd step—applicants who have been selected to proceed to the next stage will receive an email from the Foundation's staff indicating that the organization has been approved to submit a complete proposal which best describes in detail the activities, program or project. If selected, your organization will have 30 days to submit a complete a proposal online.
Restrictions: The Foundation does not: fund individuals; support for-profit organizations; purchase tickets for dinners, golf outings or similar fundraising events; make contributions to candidates for elective office or for partisan political purposes; provide funding for religious purposes.
Geographic Focus: New York
Contact: Diane John, (718) 722-5952 or (718) 722-2300; fax (718) 722-5757; info@BrooklynCommunityFoundation.org
Internet: http://www.brooklyncommunityfoundation.org/grants/green-communities
Sponsor: Brooklyn Community Foundation
45 Main Street, Suite 409
Brooklyn, NY 11201

Brown Foundation Grants 304
The Brown Foundation distributes funds for public charitable purposes, principally for support, encouragement and assistance to education, community service and the arts. The Foundation's current emphasis is in the field of public education at the primary and secondary levels with focus on supporting non-traditional and innovative approaches designed to improve public education primarily within the State of Texas. The visual and performing arts remain an area of interest. The Foundation also focuses on community service projects which serve the needs of children and families. The Foundation is interested in funding projects which fulfill one or more of the following criteria: addressing root causes of a concern rather than treating symptoms; serving as a catalyst to stimulate collaborative efforts by several sectors of the community; resulting in a long-lasting impact on the situation beyond the value of the grant itself; reflecting and encouraging sound financial planning and solid management practices in administration of the project. Proposals should be submitted a minimum of 4 months before funds are required.
Requirements: 501(c)3 tax-exempt organizations, public charities, and units of government are eligible.
Restrictions: Grants are not made to individuals. Only one application within a twelve month period will be considered. No proposal from an organization previously funded by the Foundation will be considered unless a full and timely report of expenditure of the previous grant has been submitted. The Foundation does not expect to support: grants to religious organizations for religious purposes; testimonial dinners, fundraising events or marketing events; grants intended directly or indirectly to support candidates for political office or to influence legislation; grants to other private foundations; grants to cover past operating deficits or debt retirements.
Geographic Focus: Texas

Contact: Nancy Pittman, Executive Director; (713) 523-6867; fax (713) 523-2917; bfi@brownfoundation.org or mbasurto@brownfoundation.org
Internet: http://www.brownfoundation.org/Guidelines.asp
Sponsor: Brown Foundation
P.O. Box 130646
Houston, TX 77219-0646

Brunswick Foundation Dollars for Doers Grants 305
Established in 1957, the Brunswick Foundation is a 501(c)3 charitable organization that enhances the interests of its employees and the communities in which they live and work, as well as supporting causes and projects that complement the business interests of Brunswick Corporation. The Dollars for Doers program recognizes the volunteer efforts of Brunswick employees by issuing grants to 501(c)3 organizations. The foundation awards grants to nonprofit organizations for which an individual employee or group of employees has completed volunteer work, such as serving on a Board of Directors or participating in a fundraising event.
Requirements: IRS 501(c)3 organizations in Alabama, Arizona, Connecticut, Florida, Georgia, Illinois, Indiana, Kentucky, Louisiana, Maryland, Michigan, Minnesota, Mississippi, Nebraska, North Carolina, Oklahoma, Oregon, South Carolina, Tennessee, Texas, Washington, and Wisconsin are eligible.
Restrictions: Grants are not made to religious organizations for religious purposes; for any form of political activity; to veterans groups, fraternal orders, or labor groups; for loans of any kind; or for trips, tours, dinners, tickets, or advertising.
Geographic Focus: Alabama, Arizona, Connecticut, Florida, Georgia, Illinois, Indiana, Kentucky, Louisiana, Maryland, Michigan, Minnesota, Mississippi, Nebraska, North Carolina, Oklahoma, Oregon, South Carolina, Tennessee, Texas, Washington, Wisconsin
Contact: B. Russell Lockridge; (847) 735-4467; fax (847) 735-4765
Internet: http://www.brunswick.com/company/community/brunswickfoundation.php
Sponsor: Brunswick Foundation
1 North Field Court
Lake Forest, IL 60045-4811

Brunswick Foundation Grants 306
The Brunswick Foundation Grant Program awards direct donations to 501(c)3 organizations that enhance marine, fitness, bowling or billiards activities and related industry interests, or any other Brunswick business interest. The foundation also supports programs where Brunswick Corporation employees volunteer and efforts to provide a higher education for children of employees. Types of support include employee-matching gifts, general operating budgets, building construction and renovation, capital campaigns, special projects, research, and continuing support. Requests for guidelines must be in writing, or applicants may submit a letter describing the purpose of the organization and the request.
Requirements: IRS 501(c)3 organizations in Alabama, Arizona, Connecticut, Florida, Georgia, Illinois, Indiana, Kentucky, Louisiana, Maryland, Michigan, Minnesota, Mississippi, Nebraska, North Carolina, Oklahoma, Oregon, South Carolina, Tennessee, Texas, Washington, and Wisconsin are eligible.
Restrictions: Grants are not made to religious organizations for religious purposes; for any form of political activity; to veterans groups, fraternal orders, or labor groups; for loans of any kind; or for trips, tours, dinners, tickets, or advertising.
Geographic Focus: Alabama, Arizona, Connecticut, Florida, Georgia, Illinois, Indiana, Kentucky, Louisiana, Maryland, Michigan, Minnesota, Mississippi, Nebraska, North Carolina, Oklahoma, Oregon, South Carolina, Tennessee, Texas, Washington, Wisconsin
Date(s) Application is Due: Mar 22
Amount of Grant: 500 - 2,000 USD
Contact: B. Russell Lockridge; (847) 735-4467; fax (847) 735-4765
Internet: http://www.brunswickcorp.com
Sponsor: Brunswick Foundation
1 North Field Court
Lake Forest, IL 60045-4811

Build-A-Bear Workshop Foundation Grants 307
The foundation is committed to improving communities and impacting lives through meaningful philanthropic programs that help children and families, animals and the environment. Grants range between $1,000 and $10,000 with the average grant being $2,500. Application and guidelines are available online.
Requirements: Priority is given to 501(c)3 tax-exempt organizations.
Restrictions: The foundation does not awards grants to support: capital campaigns; fundraising sponsorships or events; political activities; religious organizations for religious purposes.
Geographic Focus: All States

Amount of Grant: 1,000 - 10,000 USD
Contact: Maxine Clark; (314) 423-8000, ext. 5366; giving@buildabear.com
Internet: http://www.buildabear.com/aboutus/community/babwfoundation.aspx
Sponsor: Build-A-Bear Workshop Bear Hugs Foundation
1954 Innerbelt Business Center Drive
Saint Louis, MO 63114

Bullitt Foundation Grants   308

The foundation functions to protect and restore the environment of the Pacific Northwest, including Washington, Oregon, Idaho, western Montana, coastal rainforests in Alaska, and British Columbia, Canada. Program priorities include aquatic ecosystems; terrestrial ecosystems; conservation and stewardship in agriculture; energy and climate change; growth management and transportation; toxic and radioactive substances; training, organizational development, and unique opportunities (including education and public outreach). Areas of interest include air pollution, climate change, endangered species, energy conservation, environmental education and justice, human health, transportation, and tribal communities. The foundation supports challenge/matching, general operating, project/program, seed money, demonstration, and development grants, as well as requests for conferences/seminars and technical assistance support. Grants will be awarded for one year with possible renewal.
Requirements: Nonprofit organizations in the Pacific Northwest, including Washington, Oregon, Idaho, western Montana, coastal rainforests in Alaska, and British Columbia, Canada are eligible.
Geographic Focus: Alaska, Idaho, Montana, Oregon, Washington, Canada
Date(s) Application is Due: May 1; Nov 1
Contact: Program Officer; (206) 343-0807; fax (206) 343-0822; info@bullitt.org
Internet: http://www.bullitt.org
Sponsor: Bullitt Foundation
1212 Minor Avenue
Seattle, WA 98101-2825

Bunbury Company Grants   309

The company seeks to assist organizations primarily in Mercer County, but also in Burlington, Camden, Hunterdon, Mercer, Middlesex, Monmouth, Ocean, and Somerset with programs in the following areas: educational programs that provide opportunities for intellectual, societal or cultural growth to youth and families; environmental programs that help conserve threatened farmland, habitat or waterways and regional planning efforts that help advance these goals; community building and social service programs that empower the undeserved; cultural programs that promote local artistic initiatives. The Foundation is particularly interested in programs that are local and have the ability to positively impact the quality of life within their community. The Foundation provides basic needs support for: general operating support; building funds; challenge or matching funds; and funds for special programs.
Requirements: An applicant must have tax-exempt status under Section 501(c)3 of the Internal Revenue Service Code and be a publicly supported charity under Section 509. Nonprofit organizations additionally must be registered with the State of New Jersey as a charity unless they are schools that file their cirricula with the Department of Education and are exempted from the provisions of the New Jersey Charitable Registration and Investigation Act.
Restrictions: The Foundation will not provide support for the following: endowment campaigns; sporting activities, outings or events; fraternal or religious organizations, including schools with religious affiliation; individual fellowships or scholarships; summer camps or day care facilities, unless part of a comprehensive after care program; organizations with multiple chapters if outside Mercer County; specific cultural performances; publications or surveys.
Geographic Focus: New Jersey
Date(s) Application is Due: Mar 1; May 3; Aug 2; Nov 7
Amount of Grant: 15,000 USD
Contact: Manager; (609) 333-8800; fax (609) 333-8900; BunburyCo@aol.com
Internet: http://www.bunburycompany.org/grant-guidelines.html
Sponsor: Bunbury Company
2 Railroad Place
Hopewell, NJ 08525

Burlington Northern Santa Fe Foundation Grants   310

The foundation is focused on the communities where the company operates and areas where its railways pass. The foundation supports education, including scholarships for Native Americans and scholarships for children of employees in conjunction with the National Merit Scholarships program; the arts, including museums, performing arts, and libraries; and civic and public affairs. Support goes to the Nature Conservancy and for local fire departments and law enforcement.

Types of support include general operating support, continuing support, annual campaigns, capital campaigns, and program development. Health and human services funding concentrates on the United Way. Awards are made for a single year and for continuing support. The company also matches employee funds given to public and private colleges and universities, cultural organizations, and hospitals in the United States. Requests for applications should describe the purpose for the grant. Requests are reviewed every six weeks.
Requirements: Any 501(c)3 organization located in Schaumburg, IL, and communities where the corporation operates, including 28 states and two Canadian provinces, are eligible to apply.
Geographic Focus: All States
Samples: Texas Christian University, Fort Worth, TX, $600,000 - for Career Services Center and Neeley Schools Next Generation Leadership Program; Hastings Rural Fire District, Glenvil, NE, $20,000 - for replacement of rescue truck and grass firefighting rig; Foss Waterway Seaport, Tacoma, WA, $50,000 - for restoration and development of waterfront cultural center and maritime museum.
Contact: Deanna Dugas, Manager Corporate Contributions; (817) 867-6407; fax (817) 352-7924; Deanna.dugas@bnsf.com
Sponsor: Burlington Northern Santa Fe Foundation
2650 Lou Menk Drive, 2nd Floor, P.O. Box 961057
Fort Worth, TX 76131-2830

Burton D. Morgan Foundation Adult Entrepreneurship Grants   311

The Foundation is interested in supporting organizations that assist innovative entrepreneurs with launching their ventures and building sustainability. The Foundation believes that innovative entrepreneurship draws upon creativity, involves an element of risk, and creates value. Support is awarded to charitable organizations that provide the following kinds of entrepreneurship-related services: information, incubation, networking, continuing education, access to capital, risk management, and business planning. The Foundation is particularly interested in building entrepreneurial networks that foster a stronger entrepreneurial culture in Northeast Ohio.
Requirements: Grants are made to organizations recognized as tax-exempt under the Internal Revenue Service code section 501(c)3 which are not private foundations. The Foundation's geographic preferences complement its program and project focus by targeting: entrepreneurship-related programs in Summit County, Ohio, and surrounding counties, known collectively as the Northeast Ohio region; and Hudson, Ohio-based nonprofit organizations.
Restrictions: The Foundation does not usually make multi-year grants and does not ordinarily consider grants to annual fund drives, to units of government, or to organizations and institutions which are primarily tax supported, including state universities. The Foundation no longer makes grants to arts, mental health, and social service organizations and programs.
Geographic Focus: Ohio
Date(s) Application is Due: Mar 1; Jun 1; Oct 1
Contact: Deborah D. Hoover, President; (330) 665-1630 or (330) 655-1660; dhoover@bdmorganfdn.org
Internet: http://www.bdmorganfdn.org/Adult_entrepreneurship.php
Sponsor: Burton D. Morgan Foundation
22 Aurora Street
Hudson, OH 44236

Burton D. Morgan Foundation Collegiate Entrepreneurship Grants   312

The Burton D. Morgan Foundation supports entrepreneurship programs and activities on college and university campuses primarily in Northeast Ohio. Morgan believed that entrepreneurship should have a home on college campuses, but separate from schools of management. Accordingly, he encouraged the Foundation to establish campus entrepreneurship centers that combine a variety of disciplines and programs. The Foundation has since expanded its emphasis on cross-campus entrepreneurship programs at the collegiate level through its collaboration with the Ewing Marion Kauffman Foundation.
Requirements: Grants are made to organizations recognized as tax-exempt under the Internal Revenue Service code section 501(c)3 which are not private foundations. The Foundation's geographic preferences complement its program and project focus by targeting: entrepreneurship-related programs in Summit County, Ohio, and surrounding counties, known collectively as the Northeast Ohio region; and Hudson, Ohio-based nonprofit organizations.
Restrictions: The Foundation does not usually make multi-year grants and does not ordinarily consider grants to annual fund drives, to units of government, or to organizations and institutions which are primarily tax supported, including state universities. The Foundation no longer makes grants to arts, mental health, and social service organizations and programs.
Geographic Focus: Ohio

Date(s) Application is Due: Mar 1; Jun 1; Oct 1
Contact: Deborah D. Hoover, President; (330) 665-1630 or (330) 655-1660; dhoover@bdmorganfdn.org
Internet: http://www.bdmorganfdn.org/Collegiate_entrepreneurship.php
Sponsor: Burton D. Morgan Foundation
22 Aurora Street
Hudson, OH 44236

Burton D. Morgan Foundation Youth Entrepreneurship Grants   **313**
The Burton D. Morgan Foundation supports youth education programs for elementary, middle, and high school students with a focus on the free enterprise system, financial literacy and entrepreneurship. The Foundation values programs that inspire students to become financially independent and fiscally responsible and to envision a future that includes the highest educational attainment possible. To achieve these goals, teachers must receive the necessary training to incorporate entrepreneurial thinking and economic concepts into coursework and extracurricular activities. While not every student will become an entrepreneur, every student will benefit from learning about entrepreneurship and, thereby, be better equipped to chart their own futures. The Foundation also believes that Northeast Ohio youth entrepreneurship programs will benefit from networking and collaborating and that students will be best served by the creation of educational pathways from one educational level to another.
Requirements: Grants are made to organizations recognized as tax-exempt under the Internal Revenue Service code section 501(c)3 which are not private foundations. The Foundation's geographic preferences complement its program and project focus by targeting: entrepreneurship-related programs in Summit County, Ohio, and surrounding counties, known collectively as the Northeast Ohio region; and Hudson, Ohio-based nonprofit organizations.
Restrictions: The Foundation does not usually make multi-year grants and does not ordinarily consider grants to annual fund drives, to units of government, or to organizations and institutions which are primarily tax supported, including state universities. The Foundation no longer makes grants to arts, mental health, and social service organizations and programs.
Geographic Focus: Ohio
Date(s) Application is Due: Mar 1; Jun 1; Oct 1
Contact: Deborah D. Hoover, President; (330) 665-1630 or (330) 655-1660; dhoover@bdmorganfdn.org
Internet: http://www.bdmorganfdn.org/youth_entrepreneurship.php
Sponsor: Burton D. Morgan Foundation
22 Aurora Street
Hudson, OH 44236

Burton G. Bettingen Grants   **314**
The fields of activity of the corporation are education at all levels, mental health, crime and abuse victims and public protection programs, religion (Christian, Roman Catholic, and Salvation Army), environment, and welfare. Top funding priority is children and youth. The current focus is on child prostitutes, runaways, and abandoned children. Nonprofits servicing the economically disadvantaged also may apply. The corporation provides broad types of support, including operating, capital, research, challenge/matching grants, and endowments. A letter of inquiry stating the applicant's background, goals and objectives, and the specific need for funding is welcome. Unsolicited submissions are considered but receive low priority.
Requirements: IRS 501(c)3 organizations are eligible. Giving primarily, but not limited to, Southern California.
Restrictions: The corporation does not award grants to individuals; for general fundraising events, dinners, or mass mailings; or to grantmaking organizations.
Geographic Focus: California
Amount of Grant: 5,000 - 200,000 USD
Contact: Patricia Brown; (323) 938-8478; burtonbet@aol.com
Sponsor: Burton G. Bettingen Corporation
134 S Mansfield Avenue
Los Angeles, CA 90036-3019

Bush Foundation Arts & Humanities Grants: Short-Term   **315**
Organizational Support
These grants are approved for one or more years and are intended to support particular activities for a finite period. Successful applicants typically propose activities that are part of a plan to achieve long-term organizational goals. Applicants should determine their own priorities when applying - the purposes of successful proposals are broad; however, the foundation typically approves only 10 to 15 requests each year.

Requirements: To be eligible for consideration, your organization must: Operate year-round programs based in Minnesota, North Dakota or South Dakota; Create or present performing, visual, humanities or media and/or literary arts; Have at least a three-year programming history in Minnesota or the Dakotas; Have had an average annual operating expense of more than $100,000 during the three most recently completed fiscal years; And, pay artists a reasonable salary or fee.
Restrictions: Funds are not available for sponsorship or presentation of one-time productions, events such as festivals or programs that operate only in the summer.
Geographic Focus: Minnesota, North Dakota, South Dakota, Wisconsin
Date(s) Application is Due: Mar 1; Jul 1; Nov 1
Contact: Program Officer; (651) 227-0891; info@bushfoundation.org
Internet: http://www.bushfoundation.org/grants/arts_humanities.asp#Short_Term_Support
Sponsor: Bush Foundation
332 Minnesota Street, Suite East 900
St. Paul, MN 55101-1315

Bush Foundation Ecological Health Grants   **316**
As part of the foundation's goal to improve the ecological health of their region, it seeks to help people and organizations develop ways to treat ecological health as an interdependent system, rather than as isolated problems to be solved. Through these efforts, the foundation hopes to help restore, preserve, and protect our resources in order to sustain the interdependent health of humans, animals, and ecosystems. This condition of interdependence is captured in the term 'ecological health.' Guidelines are available at the Bush Foundation website.
Requirements: The Foundation will make grants to benefit ecological health work in the three-state Bush region of Minnesota, North Dakota and South Dakota. Proposals that incorporate ecological health in other program areas (e.g., arts and culture) are encouraged. The preference is for initiatives that have a direct and practical bearing on humans and their communities. Specifically, the foundation will support work that: Promotes clean and renewable energy in order to improve ecological health; Protects and improves human health by reducing exposure to environmental toxins; Improves water quality by reducing pollutants in surface and ground water; Promotes decisions on land use that protect and preserve ecological health; Or, encourages farming and ranching practices that benefit the environment and the health of communities.
Restrictions: The Foundation does not make grants to environmental education programs, animal welfare organizations, humane societies, nature centers, outdoor recreation programs or day care centers. Single-issue environmental requests are unlikely to receive support.
Geographic Focus: Minnesota, North Dakota, South Dakota
Samples: Examples of desired results: A better informed public (community) that understands the link between human health and ecological health; Increased working relationships among environmental, health, and child development professionals; Improved quality of ground and surface water achieved through behavior change, policy change, and civic action.
Contact: Kelly Kleppe, Grants Manager; (651) 379-2222; kkleppe@bushfoundation.org
Internet: http://www.bushfoundation.org/grants/ecological_health.asp
Sponsor: Bush Foundation
332 Minnesota Street, Suite East 900
St. Paul, MN 55101-1315

Bush Foundation Health & Human Services Grants   **317**
The foundation responds to a broad range of human services proposals. Proposals are reviewed on a case-by-case basis; applicant organizations take the lead in identifying promising solutions to the challenges faced by people who use their programs. In recent years, most grant dollars given to human services organizations have been for programs serving children, youth, and families. The foundation also considers program proposals that will improve the quality, accessibility, and efficiency of health care services in the region.
Requirements: The foundation is most interested in proposals that: (1) Promote opportunities for individuals and communities to become fully contributing members of society by supporting organizational projects that remove barriers to effective education, economic security and good health; (2) Improve the abilities of immigrant and refugee organizations, groups and individuals to obtain basic needs and rights, promote refugee and immigrant civic engagement and enhance their contribution to economic and cultural life; (3) The foundation will also consider proposals for comprehensive capital campaigns for building purchases, major building renovations and new construction to improve physical facilities. To be eligible for consideration, your organization must be a 501(c)3 nonprofit, tax-exempt organization, located in Minnesota, North Dakota or South Dakota, and able to demonstrate that you can take the lead

in identifying promising solutions to challenges faced by people who use your programs. The two-step application process begins with a letter of inquiry. Guidelines for writing the letter of inquiry are on the information sheet which is available by contacting the sponsor or by download at the website.
Restrictions: The foundation does not make grants to: Individuals; Government agencies (except in special cases dictated by foundation priorities); Projects not benefiting the three-state region of Minnesota, North Dakota and South Dakota; Or, projects outside the United States. Download the Grant Restrictions file from the website for more details.
Geographic Focus: Minnesota, North Dakota, South Dakota
Date(s) Application is Due: Mar 1; Jul 1; Nov 1
Contact: Program Officer; (651) 227-0891; grants@bushfoundation.org
Internet: http://www.bushfoundation.org/grants/human_services.asp
Sponsor: Bush Foundation
332 Minnesota Street, Suite East 900
St. Paul, MN 55101-1315

Bush Foundation Regional Arts Development Program II Grants   318
This program is an investment in the vitality, creative potential and long-term sustainability of mid-size arts and humanities organizations throughout Minnesota, North Dakota and South Dakota as a strategy towards the foundation's goal — to maintain a diverse, vibrant and sustainable environment for the arts and humanities. Grants through this program are long-term (10 years) and non-prescriptive in the use of grant funds.
Requirements: This program is open to organizations that meet all of the following criteria: Are based in Minnesota, North Dakota or South Dakota; Create, present or serve the performing, visual, media or literary arts or humanities; Have at least a five-year programming history; Have an annual operating budget larger than $250,000 but no greater than $5 million during the three most recently completed fiscal years; Pay artists a reasonable salary or fee; Produce, present or develop year-round arts programs for the public, rather than sponsor one-time events; Have filed a final report on all previous Foundation grants, with the exception of capital grants; Have 501(c)3 tax-exempt status. The two-step application process begins with a preliminary proposal. The Foundation will consider preliminary proposals one time per year.
Restrictions: This program is not open to organizations that exist as a government agency, local arts council, public education institution, library or public broadcasting entity, such as a nonprofit radio or television station.
Geographic Focus: Minnesota, North Dakota, South Dakota
Date(s) Application is Due: Mar 1; Jul 1
Amount of Grant: Up to 100,000 USD
Contact: Program Officer; (651) 227-0891; info@bushfoundation.org
Internet: http://www.bushfoundation.org/grants/arts_humanities.asp#RADP
Sponsor: Bush Foundation
332 Minnesota Street, Suite East 900
St. Paul, MN 55101-1315

Bushrod H. Campbell and Adah F. Hall Charity Fund Grants   319
Grants are awarded to organizations in the Boston area devoted to basic needs for the elderly, projects relating to medicine and medical research, health care, hospitals, the blind and deaf, and certain discretionary projects. Grants are also awarded countrywide for projects addressing population control. Types of support include capital grants, general operating grants, program grants, and research grants.
Requirements: Tax-exempt organizations located within Boston and neighboring communities and U.S. tax-exempt organizations devoted to population control are eligible.
Restrictions: Grants are not awarded to individuals.
Geographic Focus: Massachusetts
Date(s) Application is Due: Jan 15; Apr 15; Aug 15; Oct 15
Amount of Grant: 3,000 - 7,500 USD
Contact: Brenda Taylor; (617) 239-0556; fax (617) 227-4420
Sponsor: Bushrod H. Campbell and Adah F. Hall Charity Fund
111 Huntington Avenue at Prudential Center
Boston, MA 02199-7613

Butler Manufacturing Company Foundation Grants   320
The foundation's purpose is to provide sustained financial assistance to worthy charitable, educational, and health and welfare programs in the United States and to enhance the quality of life in those communities where employees of Butler Manufacturing Company reside. The focus of the support includes youth programs, minority development, job training for the disadvantaged, neighborhoods, and support of nonresidential building programs using the company's products; scholarships for children of employees, and grants to colleges

and universities serving locations where employees reside; and the community's principal arts organizations. Types of support include capital grants, general operating grants, employee matching gifts, program development grants, and scholarships to children of employees. Applications are considered quarterly.
Requirements: Applicants must be nonprofit institutions meeting the human needs of society in the greater Kansas City area and other communities where employees reside.
Geographic Focus: Missouri
Amount of Grant: 500 - 50,000 USD
Samples: Missouri Repertory Theatre (MO)—for project support, $5000; Kansas City Neighborhood Alliance (MO)—for operating support, $5000.
Contact: Foundation Administrator; (816) 968-3208; fax (816) 968-3211; blfay@butlermfg.org
Internet: http://www.butlermfg.org/faq/index.asp#Ans10
Sponsor: Butler Manufacturing Company Foundation
P.O. Box 419917
Kansas City, MO 64141-0917

Bydale Foundation Grants   321
The foundation emphasizes international understanding, public policy research, environmental quality, cultural programs, the law and civil rights, social services, higher education, and economics. Funding includes support for: conference/seminars, continuing support, general operating support, matching/challenging support, program development, publication, research, and seed money. An application form is not required. Submit an initial approach in the form of a letter or proposal.
Requirements: U.S. 501(c)3 nonprofits are eligible.
Geographic Focus: All States
Date(s) Application is Due: Nov 1
Samples: Clean Water Fund (Washington, DC)—$5000; Greenhouse Crisis Foundation (Washington, DC)—$20,000; Greenpeace USA (Washington, DC)—$2500.
Contact: Milton Solomon; (914) 428-3232; fax (914) 428-1660
Sponsor: Bydale Foundation
11 Martine Avenue
White Plains, NY 10606

Byron W. and Alice L. Lockwood Foundation Grants   322
The foundation awards grants to Washington nonprofit organizations in its areas of interest, including arts, biomedical research, higher education, hospitals and health care organizations, housing and homelessness, museums, religion and religious welfare programs, and social services. Types of support include capital improvements, continuing support, general operating grants, professorships, projects grants, and research grants. There are no application forms; submit a letter of request.
Requirements: Washington nonprofit organizations are eligible. Grants are awarded primarily in Washington's Seattle and Puget Sound areas.
Geographic Focus: All States
Date(s) Application is Due: Oct 31
Amount of Grant: 900 - 56,000 USD
Samples: Seattle's Union Gospel Mission (Seattle) for capital improvements at the men's shelter, $50,000; Youth Suicide Prevention Plan for Washington State,.
Contact: Lee Kraft, Executive Director; (206) 230-8489
Sponsor: Byron W. and Alice L. Lockwood Foundation
P.O. Box 4
Mercer, WA 98040

C.F. Adams Charitable Trust Grants   323
Charles Francis Adams created the C. F. Adams Charitable Trust in 1987. He was a direct descendant of John Adams, the second President of the United States, and John Quincy Adams, the sixth President. He was an avid sailor, dedicated civic leader and respected businessman. The primary objectives of the C.F. Adams Charitable Trust are to: encourage Downeast Maine communities to work together to preserve their local cultural heritage, improve their quality of life, adapt to a changing environment, and achieve a sustainable economy; promote innovative broad-based efforts to engage families in meeting the mental health needs of children in Massachusetts and to emphasize the extraordinary therapeutic benefits of the arts; and expand public awareness of the Adams family legacy and to preserve its unique heritage. Types of support include: general operating support; income development; management development; capacity building; and program development. Applicants should begin by forwarding a brief letter containing a detailed description of the project and the amount of funding requested. Recent grants have ranged

from $750 to $75,000. The Trust currently commits up to $400,000 per year in Massachusetts to children's mental health and arts therapy programs that fall within the priorities outlined above.

Requirements: Giving is primarily in eastern Massachusetts and down east Maine.

Restrictions: No grants are given to individuals.

Geographic Focus: Maine, Massachusetts

Amount of Grant: 750 - 75,000 EUR

Samples: Adolescent Consultation Services, Cambridge, Massachusetts, $30,000 - Massachusetts Alliance of Juvenile Court Clinics; Hand In Hand Mano En Mano, Milbridge, Maine, $22,000 - operating support; Quoddy Tides Foundation, Eastport, Maine, $30,000 - operating support.

Contact: James H, Lowell, Trustee; (617) 422-0064; info@cfadamstrust.org

Internet: http://www.cfadamstrust.org/index.html

Sponsor: C.F. Adams Charitable Trust

141 Tremont Street, Suite 200

Boston, 02111-1209

C.W. Titus Foundation Grants 324

The foundation awards grants to eligible nonprofit organizations in Missouri and Oklahoma for programs in its areas of interest, including arts and culture, healthcare and health organizations, and social services. Types of support include building construction/renovation, general operating support, and materials/equipment acquisition. There are no application forms or deadlines.

Requirements: Missouri and Oklahoma nonprofit organizations are eligible.

Geographic Focus: Missouri, Oklahoma

Amount of Grant: 1,000 - 10,000 USD

Samples: Southwest Missouri State U Foundation (Springfield, MO)—to construct and equip a new master-control facility for the university's Ozarks Public Television station, $1 million.

Contact: Grants Administrator

Sponsor: C.W. Titus Foundation

950 Philtower Building, Suite 950

Tulsa, OK 74103-4123

Cabot Corporation Foundation Grants 325

The goal of Cabot Corporation Foundation is to support community outreach objectives, with priority given to science and technology, education, and community and civic improvement efforts in the communities where the company has major facilities or operations. Types of support include capital grants, challenge grants, employee matching gifts, fellowships, general support, professorships, project support, research, scholarships, and seed money. The board meets in January, April, July, and October to consider requests. Applications must be received at least 30 days before a board meeting.

Requirements: The Foundation supports only nonprofit 501(c)3 tax-exempt organizations in areas of company operation. Modest support is available for international organizations that qualify under U.S. tax regulations.

Restrictions: Contributions are not made to individuals; fraternal, political, athletic or veterans organizations; religious institutions; capital and endowment campaigns; sponsorships of local groups/individuals to participate in regional, national, or international competitions, conferences or events; advertising sponsorships; or Tickets or tables at fundraising events.

Geographic Focus: Georgia, Illinois, Louisiana, Massachusetts, New Mexico, Pennsylvania, Texas, West Virginia, Belgium, Canada, China, Switzerland, United Kingdom

Amount of Grant: 2,000 - 75,000 USD

Contact: Cynthia L. Gullotti, Program Manager; (617) 345-0100; fax (617) 342-6312; Cynthia_Gullotti@cabot-corp.com or cabot.corporation.foundation@cabotcorp.com

Internet: http://www.cabot-corp.com/About-Cabot/Corporate-Giving

Sponsor: Cabot Corporation Foundation

Two Seaport Lane, Suite 1300

Boston, MA 02210-2019

Caddock Foundation Grants 326

The foundation supports nonprofit national and international Evangelical Christian religious organizations including churches and religious institutions, community groups, hospitals, international missions and ministries, religious centers and facilities, and youth organizations. Types of support include conferences/seminars, fellowships, and general operating support. Application must be made in writing and include a description of the organization and its objectives and the purpose of the grant. There are no application deadlines.

Restrictions: Grants are made to Evangelical Christian organizations. Grants are not made to individuals.

Geographic Focus: All States

Amount of Grant: 1,800 - 390,000 USD

Samples: Set Free Prison Ministries (Riverside CA)—for operating support, $152,000; Grace Evangelical Society (Roanoke, TX)—for operating support, $40,000.

Contact: Richard E. Caddock, Jr., Treasurer; (951) 683-5361

Sponsor: Caddock Foundation

1717 Chicago Avenue

Riverside, CA 92507

Caesar Puff Foundation Grants 327

The Caesar Puff Foundation was established in Pennsylvania by a donation from Virginia A. Campana, and serves non-profit organizations in Ohio, Pennsylvania, and West Virginia. The Foundation's primary fields of interest include: animal welfare, Christian agencies and churches, food banks, higher education, public libraries, media/communications programs, and residential/custodial care units (including hospices). There are no specific application forms or deadlines, and applicants should contact the Foundation officer before sending a full application.

Restrictions: No grant support is offered to individuals.

Geographic Focus: Ohio, Pennsylvania, West Virginia

Date(s) Application is Due: Mar 14

Amount of Grant: 4,000 - 100,000 USD

Samples: Rostraver Public Library, Belle Vernon, Pennsylvania, $90,692; Family Hospice and Palliative Care, Pittsburgh, Pennsylvania, $4,000; Franciscan University of Steubenville, Steubenville, Steubenville, Ohio, $4,000.

Contact: Beverly Suchenek, (313) 222-6297

Sponsor: Caesar Puff Foundation

P.O. Box 75000, MC 3302

Detroit, MI 48275-3302

Caesars Foundation Grants 328

Founded as Harrah's Foundation in Nevada in 2002, giving is in the area of company operations. The foundation supports programs designed to help older individuals live longer, healthier, and more fulfilling lives; promote a safe and clean environment; and improve the quality of life in communities where Caesars operates. Fields of interest include: aging centers and services; Alzheimer's disease; developmentally disabled services; the environment; food distribution programs; food services; health care; patient services; higher education; hospitals; human services; mental health services; public affairs; public safety; nutrition; and youth services. Types of support being offered include: building and renovation; capital campaigns; continuing support; general operating support; program development; research; scholarship funding; and sponsorships. There are no specific deadlines or application forms. Caesars Foundation Trustees meet on a quarterly basis, typically around the second week of each quarter. Check with your nearest Caesars Entertainment property for deadlines. The foundation generally funds programs and projects of $10,000 or more.

Requirements: Eligible organizations are 501(c)3 nonprofits operating programs in the communities where Caesars employees and their families live and work. Applying organizations must also: demonstrate diversity by providing services and volunteer opportunities to all without regard to race, ethnicity, gender, religion, sexual orientation, identity or disability; illustrate strong leadership that will significantly strengthen communities in which Caesars operates; show sound administrative and financial condition; provide opportunities for Caesars staff involvement as volunteers and/or opportunity to serve on Board of Directors; and, provide branding opportunities and openly support Caesars Foundation in a public forum.

Restrictions: The Foundation is not designed to react to last-minute requests or event sponsorships—plan the timing of your proposal accordingly. Caesars Foundation does not accept requests for in-kind contributions.

Geographic Focus: Arizona, California, Illinois, Indiana, Iowa, Louisiana, Mississippi, Missouri, Nevada, New Jersey, North Carolina, Pennsylvania

Amount of Grant: 10,000 USD

Samples: Atlantic Cape Community College Foundation, Atlantic City, New Jersey, $75,000 - general operating support; Calumet College of St. Joseph, Whiting, Indiana, $60,000 - construction of new student center building; University of Chicago Medical Center, Chicago, Illinois, $50,000 - research and development.

Contact: Gwen Migita, Community Affairs; (702) 880-4728 or (702) 407-6358; fax (702) 407-6520; caesarsfoundation@caesars.com

Internet: http://www.caesarsfoundation.com/

Sponsor: Caesars Foundation

1 Caesars Palace Drive

Las Vegas, NV 89109-8969

Caleb C. and Julia W. Dula Educational and Charitable Foundation Grants 329

Grants are given in the areas of the arts and humanities (particularly museums and libraries), child welfare, the aged, community funds and appeals, health care, religion, and historical preservation. Most groups receiving foundation grants have an established reputation in their particular field. There are no set requirements. Applicants should submit a letter that describes the organization, project, and amount requested.

Requirements: Grants are given to support projects of tax-exempt organizations.

Restrictions: Support is not available to individuals.

Geographic Focus: All States

Date(s) Application is Due: Apr 1; Oct 1

Amount of Grant: 5,000 - 50,000 USD

Contact: James F. Mauze, (314) 726-2800; jfmauze@msn.com

Sponsor: Caleb C. & Julia W. Dula Educational and Charitable Foundation

112 S Hanley Road

Saint Louis, MO 63105

California Arts Council Creating Public Value Grants 330

The California Arts Council's (CAC) Creating Public Value Program (CPV) is designed to promote a framework for thinking about the intrinsic and instrumental benefits of the arts; and to recognize that the resources artists, arts organizations, and others bring to a community play a key role in making a positive contribution to the individual and collective lives of all Californians. Through CPV, the CAC will partner with small California arts organizations in rural and underserved communities to support new or expanded projects to highlight the fact that the arts are of benefit to all Californians and are worthy of state and federal investment. CPV proposals must utilize the tools of the program identified as The Three Rs: relationships (building new or expanding existing partnerships); relevance (to audiences and community by expanding public participation); and, return on investment (through public awareness, promoting your organization's public value and social/economic impact to civic and political leaders, community supporters, audiences, and participants).

Requirements: CPV supports small arts organizations based in rural or underserved communities to implement new or expanded projects. The base of operations must be located within these communities. Applicants may apply under one of two categories: rural or underserved.

Restrictions: The Council does not fund: former grantee organizations not in compliance with CAC grant requirements (as stipulated in grant agreement); continuation of current work or previously funded CPV projects; non-arts organizations not involved in arts activities; for-profit organizations; other state agencies; programs not accessible to the public; projects with religious or sectarian purposes; organizations or activities that are part of the curricula base of schools, colleges, or universities; indirect costs of schools, colleges, or universities; trust or endowment funds; purchase of equipment, land, buildings, or construction (capital outlay or expenditures); out-of-state travel activities; hospitality or food costs; and expenses incurred before the starting or after the ending date of the grant.

Geographic Focus: California

Date(s) Application is Due: Feb 10

Amount of Grant: Up to 10,000 USD

Contact: Lucero Arellano, Arts Programs; (916) 322-6338 or (916) 322-6555; fax (916) 322-6575; larellano@cac.ca.gov

Internet: http://www.cac.ca.gov/programs/cpv.php

Sponsor: California Arts Council

1300 I Street, Suite 930

Sacramento, CA 95814

California Arts Council State-Local Partnership Grants 331

The State-Local Partnership Program fosters cultural development on the local level through a partnership between the California Arts Council and the designated local arts agency of each county. The Partnership provides grant opportunities for general operating support and technical assistance for county-designated local arts agencies. This partnership includes funding, cooperative activities, information exchange, and leadership enabling individuals, organizations, and communities to create, present, and preserve the arts of all cultures to enrich the quality of life for all Californians. The grant application and eligibility list is available online at the California Arts Council website. May 3 is the annual deadline for submitting grant applications.

Requirements: Local arts agencies in California are eligible to apply. A local arts agency is a nonprofit organization, or agency of city or county government, officially designated to provide financial support, services, and/or other programs

to a variety of arts organizations, individual artists, and the community as a whole. Matching funds, at a level of 1:1, are mandatory. The required match may be from any public or private source. In some instances, in-kind donated services for which a market value can be determined may be used for up to 50% of the required match. Applicants must: be a current grantee through the State-Local Partnership Program; be designated by resolution of their county board of supervisors to serve as the local partner; meet the legal eligibility requirements of all California Arts Council program grantees listed under Requirements; and provide a public office staffed by, at the minimum, a part-time director/professional administrator to be accessible during normal business hours.

Geographic Focus: California

Date(s) Application is Due: May 3

Contact: Rob Lautz, (916) 324-6617 or (916) 322-6555; fax (916) 322-6575; rlautz@cac.ca.gov

Internet: http://www.cac.ca.gov/programs/slp201011.php

Sponsor: California Arts Council

1300 I Street, Suite 930

Sacramento, CA 95814

California Arts Council Statewide Networks Grants 332

The Statewide Networks Program (SN) is a California Arts Council (CAC) partnership with culturally specific, multicultural, and discipline-based statewide and regional arts networks and service organizations. Its goal is to promote the public value of the arts in communities by strengthening and expanding an organization's delivery of services to its constituents through communications, professional development opportunities, networking and arts advocacy. For this purpose, SN supports new approaches or expansions to an organization's work in the areas of organizational capacity and community building through advocacy, thus fostering an environment where all California cultures are represented. SN grants will be based on a ranking system and will range between $5,000 and $20,000.

Requirements: Statewide and regional culturally specific, multicultural, and discipline-based arts networks and service organizations are eligible to apply. Applicant organizations must have at least a two-year track record of developing its field and providing services to its constituent base (individual artists and/or arts organizations). All grant recipients must provide a dollar-for-dollar (1:1) match. The cash match may be from corporate or private contributions, local or federal government, or earned income. Other State funds cannot be used as a match. A combination of cash and in-kind contributions may be used to match CAC request.

Restrictions: SN requests cannot exceed an organization's total income based on its last completed budget. The Council does dot fund: previous grantee organizations that have not completed grant requirements (progress and final reports, final invoice, etc.); continuation of current work or previously funded SN projects; for-profit organizations; non-arts service organizations; indirect costs of schools, community colleges, colleges, or universities; trust or endowment funds; programs not accessible to the public; projects with religious or sectarian purposes; organizations or activities that are part of the curricula base of schools, colleges, or universities; purchase of equipment, land, buildings, or construction (capital outlay expenditures); out of state travel activities; hospitality or food costs; or expenses incurred before the starting or after the ending date of the contract.

Geographic Focus: California

Date(s) Application is Due: Mar 16

Amount of Grant: 5,000 - 20,000 USD

Contact: Lucero Arellano, SN Program Specialist; (916) 322-6338 or (916) 322-6555; fax (916) 322-6575; larellano@cac.ca.gov

Internet: http://www.cac.ca.gov/programs/sn.php

Sponsor: California Arts Council

1300 I Street, Suite 930

Sacramento, CA 95814

California Endowment Local Opportunities Fund Grants 333

The fund will support a full spectrum of programs or activities to assist organizations in addressing the health needs of their local communities. The most common types of grants available include program grants—for specific projects or programs, including expansion of an existing project or program, pilot projects, or start-up of a new project or program; core operating support—day-to-day core operating costs for an existing program or for the general work of an organization; capacity building—to develop either the management or administrative capacity of an organization or to develop the organization's capacity to effectively implement a particular program; and planning—to develop a detailed plan and strategy for implementation of a project or program that will address a locally defined health need or health-related priority. Priority will be given to applications that address a locally defined health need or health-related priority in an underserved community; are from a grassroots, nontraditional and/or emerging organization, or that address an issue or community that traditionally does not benefit from mainstream funding resources; and utilize the talents, cultures, and assets of the local community to address the health priorities of that community.

Requirements: California nonprofit organizations are eligible. Requests for core operating support will only be considered from organizations with annual operating budgets of less than $500,000 (as determined by financial statements and the annual operating budget submitted with the application).

Geographic Focus: All States

Date(s) Application is Due: Jan 10; May 15; Sep 15

Amount of Grant: Up to 50,000 USD

Samples: Horizons Foundation (San Francisco, CA)—for organizational development and regranting assistance needed to expand programs that address disparities in health and well-being among lesbian, gay, bisexual, and transgender residents of the San Francisco Bay area, $150,000; Asian Pacific Fund (San Francisco, CA)—to strengthen community institutions and expand programs and services needed to address disparities among Asian residents of the San Francisco Bay area, $150,000; Los Angeles Brotherhood Crusade (CA)—for organizational development and regranting assistance needed to expand programs that address disparities in health and well-being among minorities in South Central Los Angeles, $150,000.

Contact: Coordinator; (800) 449-4149 or (818) 703-3311; fax (818) 703-4193

Internet: http://www.calendow.org/apply/frm_apply.htm

Sponsor: California Endowment

1000 North Alameda Street

Los Angeles, CA 90012

California Wellness Foundation Work and Health Program Grants 334

The foundation focuses its activities on specific priority areas where it has a significant, long-term commitment. Within each priority area, the foundation allocates the majority of its funds toward initiatives. Initiatives are targeted grantmaking programs with distinct objectives and are generally announced through requests for proposals. The foundation awards general grants and project grants. Under general grants, requests for core operating support for organizations that provide direct services to Californians for disease prevention or health promotion are of primary interest. Priority areas under general grants are diversity in the health professions, environmental health, healthy aging, mental health, teenage pregnancy prevention,, violence prevention, women's health, and work and health. Special projects grants are awarded to areas that fall outside the priority areas. Of particular interest are proposals to help California communities respond to cutbacks in federally funded programs. Activities commonly supported under special projects include strengthening traditional safety-net providers, educating consumers about changes in health care systems, advocating for underserved communities in health policy debates, and informing public decision making through policy analysis.

Requirements: Eligible applicants are California 501(c)3 nonprofit organizations, or organizations with a preapproved fiscal sponsor. An organization should first write a succinct letter of interest (one to two pages) that describes the organization, its leadership, the region and population(s) served, and the activities for which funding is needed, including the amount requested.

Geographic Focus: California

Amount of Grant: 5,000 - 200,000 USD

Samples: California Institute for Rural Studies (Davis, CA)—to articulate and distribute research findings on the health of farmworkers to policy makers, opinion leaders, the news media, and the public, $125,000 over three years; California State U, Stanislaus Foundation (Modesto, CA)—to provide holistic, prevention-based health-education services to Southeast Asian women and children living in Stanislaus County, $180,000 over three years; California State U, Auxiliary Services (CA)—to strengthen community organizations working to meet the health needs of residents of East Los Angeles and California's West San Gabriel Valley, $135,000 over three years; California Institute for Nursing and Healthcare (Berkeley, CA)—to develop and disseminate a plan for diversifying the nursing work force in California, $120,000 over three years.

Contact: Grants Administrator; (818) 702-1900; fax (818) 593-6614

Internet: http://www.tcwf.org/grants_program/index.htm

Sponsor: California Wellness Foundation

6320 Canoga Avenue, Suite 1700

Woodland Hills, CA 91367-7111

Callaway Foundation Grants 335

The Foundation awards grants for the benefit of projects and people in LaGrange and Troup County, Georgia. Areas of interest, include: arts and entertainment, elementary, higher, and secondary education; libraries; health and hospitals; community funds; care for the aged; community development; historic preservation; and church support. Types of support include annual campaigns, building construction/renovation, capital campaigns, continuing support, equipment acquisition, general operating support, land acquisition, and matching/challenge support. Preference is given to enduring construction projects and capital equipment. The Foundation Board meets four times per year in January, April, July, and October. Grant requests and applications are due the last day of the month preceding the meetings.

Requirements: IRS 501(c)3 nonprofit organizations in LaGrange and Troup County, Georgia are eligible to apply. Letters of request should briefly cover all aspects of the project, including complete financial planning and costs involved. Copies of budgets and current financial statements should also be included. An application form is available at the Foundation's website.

Restrictions: Grants are usually not made for loans, debt retirement, endowment or operating expenses. Requests from churches located outside Troup County, Georgia, are not considered.

Geographic Focus: Georgia

Date(s) Application is Due: Mar 31; Jun 30; Sep 30; Dec 31

Amount of Grant: 1,000 - 4,000,000 USD

Contact: H. Speer Burdette, President; (706) 884-7348; fax (706) 884-0201; hsburdette@callaway-foundation.org

Internet: http://www.callawayfoundation.org/grant_policies.php

Sponsor: Callaway Foundation

209 Broome Street, P.O. Box 790

La Grange, GA 30241

Callaway Golf Company Foundation Grants 336

The foundation strives to support initiatives in communities where Callaway Golf Company employees live and work. The geographic area of focus is primarily North San Diego County, California. The foundation offers support in the form of: matching funds, special projects, and general operating budgets. Areas of interest include but are not limited to: children and youth; biomedical research, with a special interest in the field of cancer; golf; education; boys & girls clubs of America; drug prevention; American Red Cross; housing; veterans; youth programs; food banks; social services; emergency programs; scholarship program for dependents of Callaway Golf employees; grants for training, competition and equipment needs. The foundation does not require the completion of a formal application document but requests a description of the organization and its history, the project at issue including goals and time lines, the qualifications of the leadership personnel involved in the project, and a detailed project budget. Grants are awarded semiannually. The Callaway Golf Company Foundation does not accept unsolicited requests for grants.

Requirements: IRS 501(c)3 nonprofit organizations in California are eligible.

Restrictions: The foundation will not fund applicants that illegally discriminate on the basis of gender, race, color, religion, national origin, ancestry, age, marital status, medical condition, or physical disability, either in the services they provide or in the hiring of staff; or promote political or particular religious doctrines.

Geographic Focus: California

Amount of Grant: 500 - 10,000 USD

Samples: Saint Judes Children's Research Hospital, $300; Utah Food Bank Services, $100; Purdue Foundation, $1,000.

Contact: Paul Thompson, Executive Director; (760) 930-8686; fax (760) 930-5021; cgcfoundation@callawaygolf.com

Internet: http://www.callawaygolf.com/Global/en-US/Corporate/CallawayGolfFoundation.html

Sponsor: Callaway Golf Company Foundation

2180 Rutherford Road

Carlsbad, CA 92008-7328

Cambridge Community Foundation Grants 337

Cambridge Community Foundation is dedicated to improving the quality of life for the residents of Cambridge, Massachusetts. The CCF serves Cambridge through our support of nonprofit community organizations, by making direct financial grants, providing technical assistance, and forming partnerships among organizations to coordinate services, address gaps, and highlight emerging issues. CCF primarily supports work in: early childhood services; youth service; senior services; community services; emergency outreach; arts; and the environment. See, the Foundations website http://www.cambridgecf.org/grant.html to download Proposal Summary Sheets, and additional guidelines.

Requirements: To be eligible to apply, the agency must be tax-exempt 501(c)3 under the IRS code), and the program must serve the people of Cambridge, Massachusetts.

Restrictions: Support is not provided to municipal, state, or federal agencies. Grants for individuals, scholarships, research studies, conferences, films, capital fund drives, or loans are not eligible.

Geographic Focus: Massachusetts

Date(s) Application is Due: Apr 1; Oct 1

Amount of Grant: 500 - 60,000 USD

Samples: Family First, Cambridge, MA — funding for the Family First parenting education and support programs for low-income and homeless families living in Cambridge; Big Sister Association of Greater Boston, Boston, MA — funding to support Cambridge girls who participate in Big Sister's traditional one-to-one community-based mentoring program; YNA Care Network, Inc./Hospice of Cambridge, Cambridge, MA — funding to support the patient care needs and running of the Chilton House, Cambridge's hospice, as well as bereavement support groups and counseling services to patient family members.

Contact: Robert S. Hurlbut, Jr., Executive Director; (617) 576-9966; fax (617) 876-8187; RHurlbut@CambridgeCF.org or info@cambridgecf.org

Internet: http://www.cambridgecf.org

Sponsor: Cambridge Community Foundation

99 Bishop Richard Allen Drive

Cambridge, MA 02139

Camp-Younts Foundation Grants 338

The foundation supports social services, higher and secondary education, youth organizations, Protestant religion, and hospitals and other health organizations in Florida, Georgia, North Carolina, and Virginia. Applicants should submit a letter describing the program, a copy of the 501(c)3 tax-determination letter, listing of board members, and an audited budget for the previous year.

Requirements: Nonprofit organizations in Florida, Georgia, North Carolina, and Virginia may request grant support.

Geographic Focus: Florida, Georgia, North Carolina, Virginia

Date(s) Application is Due: Sep 1

Amount of Grant: 1,000 - 55,000 USD

Samples: Virginia Baptist General Board (Richmond, VA)—for operating support, $40,000; Saint Edwards School (Bon Air, VA)—for operating support, $25,000.

Contact: Bobby Worrell, Executive Director; (757) 562-3439

Sponsor: Camp-Younts Foundation

P.O. Box 4655

Atlanta, GA 30302

Campbell Hoffman Foundation Grants 339

The mission of the Campbell Hoffman Foundation is to promote and fund efforts to increase access to comprehensive health care for underserved and uninsured populations in the Northern Virginia region. Northern Virginia is defined as the counties of Arlington, Fairfax, Loudoun and Prince William and the cities of Alexandria, Falls Church, Fairfax, Manassas and Manassas Park. A letter of Inquiry should be submitted, as the initial approach, when approaching the Foundation for funding. Upon review, if the letter of inquiry meets with Foundations criteria, the applicant will be asked to submit a proposal; guidelines will be provided to them when the proposal is requested.

Requirements: Eligible organizations include nonprofit 501(c)3 organizations, government agencies and faith-based organizations. Eligible organizations must be both located in and serve the target populations of Northern Virginia.

Restrictions: The Foundation will not provide funding for capital campaigns, endowment campaigns, special events and/or conferences (including travel to and participation in same), emergency funding, loans, capital projects (including but not limited to building, construction or renovation), land purchases, lawsuits, films, video or publications. The Foundation may choose to provide general operating support.

Geographic Focus: Virginia

Samples: Northern Virginia Family Service, $12,200—expand Dentral Resource Recruitment Program; Arlington Free Clinic, $30,000—continue integration of mental health into primary care setting; Loudoun Community Health Center, $45,000—initiate mental heatlh program; integrate w/ primary care; create community mental health provider coalition.

Contact: Lyn S. Hainge, Executive Director; (703) 749-1794; fax (703) 442-0846; lhainge@campbellhoffman.org

Internet: http://www.campbellhoffman.org/applicants/default.aspx

Sponsor: Campbell Hoffman Foundation

1420 Spring Hill Road, Suite 600

McLean, VA 22102

Campbell Soup Foundation Grants 340

Since 1953, the Campbell Soup Foundation has provided financial support to local champions that inspire positive change in communities throughout the United States where Campbell Soup Company employees live and work. The Foundation places particular emphasis on Camden, New Jersey, birthplace of Campbell's flagship soup business and world headquarters. The Campbell Soup Foundation focuses its giving on four key areas: hunger relief-supporting food bank organizations in the communities of operation; wellness-addressing the health of consumers in the communities where they live; education-leveraging the Campbell brand portfolio to support educational programs; community revitalization-enhancing the quality of life in the communities that Campbell operates in. The Foundation only considers applications that meet the following criteria: the proposal must fit one of the key focus areas; the organization must display strong and effective leadership; the proposed plan must be clear and compelling, with measurable and sustainable commitments expressed in terms of real results; the proposed activity must be sufficiently visible to leverage additional support from other funding sources. There is no formal deadline. Proposals are accepted and reviewed on a rolling basis.

Requirements: The Foundation limits grants to nonprofit organizations which are tax-exempt under Section 501(c)3 of the Internal Revenue Code. Grants are made to institutions that serve: Camden, New Jersey; Davis, California; Sacramento, California; Stockton, California; Bloomfield, Connecticut; Norwalk, Connecticut; Lakeland, Florida; Downers Grove, Illinois; Marshall, Michigan; Maxton, North Carolina; Camden, New Jersey; South Plainfield, New Jersey; Napoleon, Ohio; Wauseon, Ohio; Willard, Ohio; Denver, Pennsylvania; Downingtown, Pennsylvania; Aiken, South Carolina; Paris, Texas; Richmond, Utah; Everett, Washington; Milwaukee, Wisconsin. Organizations do not need to be located in these communities in order to qualify for funding. However, the programs to be funded must serve these communities. Proposals must be submitted electronically via email to community_relations@campbellsoup.com. Proposals should be prepared in a concise, narrative form, without extensive documentation.

Restrictions: Grants are not made to the following: organizations that are based outside the United States and its territories; individuals; organizations that limit their services to members of one religious group or whose services propagate religious faith or creed; political organizations and those having the primary purpose of influencing legislation of/or promoting a particular ideological point of view; units of government; events and sponsorships; sports related events, activities and sponsorships. Organizations may not submit the same or similar proposals more than once in a Foundation fiscal year (July 1 - June 30). Proposals submitted via regular mail will not be reviewed.

Geographic Focus: Connecticut, Florida, Illinois, Michigan, New Jersey, North Carolina, Ohio, Pennsylvania, South Carolina, Texas, Utah, Washington, Wisconsin

Contact: Grant Administrator; (856) 342-6423 or (800) 257-8443; fax (856) 541-8185; community_relations@campbellsoup.com

Internet: http://www.campbellsoupcompany.com/community_center.asp

Sponsor: Campbell Soup Foundation

1 Campbell Place

Camden, NJ 08103-1701

Cape Branch Foundation Grants 341

The foundation awards grants to New Jersey nonprofit organizations in its areas of interest, including education and secondary education, natural resource conservation, and museums. Types of support include general operating support, building construction/renovation, land acquisition, scholarship funds, and research grants. There are no application forms or deadlines. A letter should be submitted outlining purpose and amount of request.

Requirements: New Jersey nonprofit organization are eligible.

Geographic Focus: New Jersey

Amount of Grant: 1,000 - 329,268 USD

Contact: Dorothy Frank, (609) 987-0300; fax (609) 452-1024

Sponsor: Cape Branch Foundation

P.O. Box 86

Oldwick, NJ 08858

Capezio/Ballet Makers Inc Grants and Awards 342

Grants are awarded to dance organizations to create a greater awareness and appreciation of dance as an art form and support efforts which preserve the legacy of the past, recognize the accomplishments of the present and encourage new or emerging talents, trends and practices. Types of support include awards, conferences and seminars, general operating grants, program grants, scholarships, and seed money grants. The Capezio Dance Award is also made by the trustees annually to an individual, company, or organization that brings respect, stature, and distinction to dance. Contact the program office for guidelines.

Requirements: Organizations must provide evidence of nonprofit status in their letters of application.

Restrictions: Awards are not made to individuals, companies, schools, or organizations for which dance is not a major priority.

Geographic Focus: All States

Date(s) Application is Due: Apr 1

Amount of Grant: 500 - 1,000 USD

Contact: Program Director; (973) 595-9000, ext. 203; fax (973) 595-0341

Internet: http://capeziodance.com/about/foundation/index.html

Sponsor: Capezio/Ballet Makers Dance

1 Campus Road

Totowa, NJ 07512

Cargill Citizenship Fund-Corporate Giving Grants 343

Cargill's purpose is to be the global leader in nourishing people. Cargill measures their performance through engaged employees, satisfied customers, profitable growth and enriched communities. Corporate giving is one important way Cargill works to enrich the 1,000 communities where they conduct business. With 149,000 employees in 63 countries, Cargill people are working everyday to nourish the lives of those around us. The Cargill Citizenship Fund provides strategic grants to organizations serving communities where Cargill has a presence. The Fund provides direct grants for regional, national and global partnerships and provides matching grants for selected local projects supported by our businesses. Cargill seeks to build sustainable communities by focusing our human and financial resources in three areas: Nutrition and Health-support for programs and projects that address long-term solutions to hunger, increase access to health education and/or basic health care in developing and emerging countries, and improve youth nutrition and wellness; Education-support for innovative programs that improve academic achievement, develop logic and thinking skills, promote leadership development, and/or increase access to education for socio-economically disadvantaged children. Cargill also supports mutually beneficial partnerships with selected higher education institutions; Environment-support for projects that protect and improve accessibility to water resources; promote biodiversity conservation in agricultural areas; and educate children about conservation and/or proper sanitation. Application and additional guidelines are available at: http://www.cargill.com/wcm/groups/public/@ccom/documents/document/doc-giving-funding-app.pdf

Requirements: Applicants must have 501(c)3 status or the equivalent; and they must be located in communities where Cargill has a business presence. Only under special circumstances will Cargill consider general operating or capital support. Organizations requesting capital or operating support should contact the Cargill Citizenship Fund staff before applying.

Restrictions: Cargil will not fund: organizations without 501(c)3 status or the equivalent; organizations that do not serve communities where Cargill has a business presence; individuals or groups seeking support for research, planning, personal needs or travel; public service or political campaigns; lobbying, political or fraternal activities; benefit dinners or tickets to the same; fundraising campaigns, walk-a-thons, or promotions to eliminate or control; specific diseases; athletic scholarships; advertising or event sponsorships; religious groups for religious purposes; publications, audio-visual productions or special broadcasts; endowments; medical equipment.

Geographic Focus: All States, Albania, Algeria, Andorra, Angola, Armenia, Austria, Azerbaijan, Belarus, Belgium, Benin, Bosnia & Herzegovina, Botswana, Bulgaria, Burkina Faso, Burundi, Cameroon, Cape Verde, Central African Republic, Chad, Comoros, Congo, Congo, Democratic Republic of, Cote d' Ivoire (Ivory Coast), Croatia, Cyprus, Czech Republic, Denmark, Djibouti, Egypt, Equatorial Guinea, Eritrea, Estonia, Ethiopia, Finland, France, Gabon, Gambia, Georgia, Germany, Ghana, Greece, Guinea, Guinea-Bissau, Hungary, Iceland, Ireland, Italy, Kenya, Kosovo, Latvia, Lesotho, Liberia, Libya, Liechtenstein, Lithuania, Luxembourg, Macedonia, Madagascar, Malawi, Mali, Malta, Mauritania, Mauritius, Moldova, Monaco, Montenegro, Morocco, Mozambique, Namibia, Niger, Nigeria, Norway, Poland, Portugal, Romania, Russia, Rwanda, San Marino, Sao Tome & Principe, Senegal, Serbia, Seychelles, Sierra Leone, Slovakia, Slovenia, Somalia, South Africa, Spain, Sudan, Swaziland, Sweden, Switzerland, The Netherlands, Turkey, Ukraine, United Kingdom, Vatican City

Amount of Grant: 500 - 100,000 USD

Contact: Stacey Smida; (952) 742-4311; stacey_smida@cargill.com

Internet: http://www.cargill.com/wcm/groups/public/@ccom/documents/document/doc-giving-funding-app.pdf

Sponsor: Cargill Corporation

P.O. Box 5650

Minneapolis, MN 55440-5650

Cargill Foundation Eliminating Barriers Grants 344

The Foundation seeks to fulfill its mission to prepare the next generation for success in school, work and life by investing in organizations and programs that demonstrate leadership and effectiveness in educating socio-economically disadvantaged children and eliminating barriers to their educational success. The Eliminating Barriers program specifically supports services that occur before or after the school day. Generally, paid program staff or volunteers provide these services.

Requirements: Only funds programs in Minneapolis and its northern and western suburbs.

Restrictions: The Foundation generally does not consider: programs outside the Minneapolis area; individuals; athletic scholarships; religious organizations for religious purposes; membership in civic organizations or trade associations; benefit fundraising events or tickets for the same; endowments or endowment campaigns; recognition or testimonial events; fundraising campaigns for specific diseases or medical research; public service or political campaigns or political lobbying activities; or participation in conferences or travel for groups or individuals.

Geographic Focus: Minnesota

Date(s) Application is Due: Apr 17

Contact: Stacey Smida, Grants Manager; (952) 742-4311; fax (952) 742-7224; stacey_smida@cargill.com

Internet: http://www.cargill.com/worldwide/usa/cargill-foundation/index.jsp

Sponsor: Cargill Foundation

P.O. Box 5650

Minneapolis, MN 55440-5650

Carl and Eloise Pohlad Family Foundation Grants 345

The mission of the foundation is to improve the lives of economically disadvantaged children and youth and participate in projects that positively impact the quality of life in the Minneapolis/St.Paul area. The foundation awards grants to Minnesota nonprofits in its areas of interest, including arts and culture, economic development, education, environment, health care, housing, and social services. Types of support include general operating support, continuing support, capital campaigns, building construction/renovation, endowments, emergency funds, scholarship funds, and research.

Requirements: Minnesota nonprofits are eligible.

Restrictions: Individuals are not eligible. Capital request are considered only for physical plant improvements or significant technology investments. Capital requests for housing construction, endowment, program start-up or expansion or to establish operating reserves are not considered.

Geographic Focus: Minnesota

Amount of Grant: Up to 32,000,000 USD

Contact: Josette Elstad, Grants Manager; (612) 661-3910; fax (612) 661-3715; info@pohladfamilygiving.org

Internet: http://www.pohladfamilyfoundation.org/pff/pff_default.aspx

Sponsor: Carl and Eloise Pohlad Family Foundation

60 South Sixth Street, Suite 3900

Minneapolis, MN 55402

Carl C. Icahn Foundation Grants 346

The foundation awards grants to New York and New Jersey nonprofits in the areas of education, arts and culture, health care, child welfare, and Jewish temples and organizations. Types of support include general operating support, annual campaigns, building construction/renovation, and matching funds. There are no application deadlines or forms.

Requirements: New York and New Jersey nonprofits are eligible to apply.

Restrictions: No grants are provided to individuals.

Geographic Focus: New Jersey, New York

Amount of Grant: 500 - 1,600,000 USD

Samples: Randall's Island Sports Foundation, New York, NY, $1,666,000—to support program/general purposes; Wildlife Conservation Society, Pelham, NY, $10,000—to support program/general purposes; The Ladies' Village Improvement Society, East Hampton, NY, $500—to support program/general purposes.

Contact: Gail Golden-Icahn; (212) 702-4300; fax (212) 750-5815

Sponsor: Carl C. Icahn Foundation

767 5th Avenue, 47th Floor

New York, NY 10153-0023

Carl Gellert and Celia Berta Gellert Foundation Grants 347

The foundation funds religious, charitable, scientific, literary or educational purposes restricted in the nine counties of the greater San Francisco Bay Area (Alameda, Contra Costa, Marin, Napa, San Francisco, San Mateo, Santa Clara, Solano and Sonoma). No grants are made to individuals. Types of support include general operations, annual and capital campaigns, building construction/ renovation, equipment acquisition, debt reduction, program/ project development, medical research, publication, and scholarships.

Requirements: California 501(c)3 tax-exempt nonprofit organizations that are not private foundations are eligible.

Restrictions: Grants are not awarded to individuals.

Geographic Focus: California

Date(s) Application is Due: Aug 15

Amount of Grant: 1,000 - 10,000 USD

Samples: U of San Francisco, School of Business and Management (CA)—to renovate and add a new wing to the McLaren Center, home of the School of Business and Management, $500,000.

Contact: Jack Fitzpatrick, Executive Director; (415) 255-2829

Internet: http://home.earthlink.net/~cgcbg

Sponsor: Carl Gellert and Celia Berta Gellert Foundation

1169 Market Street, Suite 808

San Francisco, CA 94103

Carl J. Herzog Foundation Grants   348

The foundation awards grants, primarily in Connecticut, for research and general operating support in its areas of interest, including medical research, dermatology research, hospitals, and education. There are no application deadlines or forms.

Requirements: 501(c)3 tax-exempt organizations are eligible.

Geographic Focus: Connecticut

Amount of Grant: 1,000 - 200,000 USD

Samples: Meharry Medical College (Nashville, TN)—for scholarships for minority students, $250,000.

Contact: David Babson, (203) 629-2424

Sponsor: Carl J. Herzog Foundation

321 Railroad Avenue

Greenwich, CT 06836-0788

Carl M. Freeman Foundation FACES Grants   349

Founded in 2000 in Delaware, FACES stands for Freeman Assists Communities with Extra Support. The FACES program is designed to find and fund the smaller, overlooked projects in it's neighborhoods. The grants are limited to Montgomery County nonprofit organizations with operating budgets of $750,000 or less and Sussex County nonprofit organizations with operating budgets of $500,000 or less. Funding applications are available in five areas of interest: arts/culture; education/environment; health & human services; housing and; other-this may include anything you feel does not fit in the above categories, for example spaying cats/dogs. Additional guidelines and applications are available at: http://www.freemanfoundation.org/carl/CarlMFreemanFoundation/Grants/GrantGuidelines/ApplyForaGrant/tabid/185/Default.aspx.

Requirements: 501(c)3 tax-exempt organizations in Montgomery & Sussex County are eligible. Nonsectarian religious programs also are eligible.

Restrictions: Grants will not be distributed to: individuals; political associations or candidates; organizations that would disperse the funding to others; organizations that discriminate by race, creed, gender, sexual orientation, age, religion, disability or national origin.

Geographic Focus: Delaware, Maryland, West Virginia

Samples: Charles Town Health Right, Inc., Charles Town, WV—to help purchase needed medical and support supplies in order to meet daily medical needs; Olney Community Band, Silver Spring, MD—to support the 2009 Concert Series and help present affordable concerts to diverse crowds; Sussex Technical Adult Division, Georgetown, DE—to support the Even Start Family Literacy Program, which helps improve the literacy skills of low income and low literate families.

Contact: Trish Schechtman, Relationship Manager; (302) 436-3555; trish@freemanfoundation.org

Internet: http://www.freemanfoundation.org/carl/CarlMFreemanFoundation/Grants/FACES/tabid/204/Default.aspx

Sponsor: Carl M. Freeman Foundation

36097 Sand Cove Road

Selbyville, DE 19975

Carl M. Freeman Foundation Grants   350

The Carl M. Freeman Foundation has historically emphasized it's support in the following communities: Montgomery County, Maryland; Sussex County, Delaware; and the Eastern Panhandle of West Virginia . Funding is available for a wide variety of community organizations, having supported everything from arts organizations and hunger centers to educational and health related organizations. To simplify the application process, funding applications are available in five areas of interest: arts/culture; education/

environment; health & human services; housing and; other-this may include anything you feel does not fit in the above categories, for example spaying cats/dogs. Additional guidelines and applications are available at: http://www.freemanfoundation.org/carl/CarlMFreemanFoundation/Grants/GrantGuidelines/ApplyForaGrant/tabid/185/Default.aspx

Requirements: 501(c)3 tax-exempt organizations in Maryland, Delaware and West Virginia are eligible. Nonsectarian religious programs also are eligible.

Restrictions: Grants will not be distributed to: individuals; political associations or candidates; organizations that would disperse the funding to others; organizations that discriminate by race, creed, gender, sexual orientation, age, religion, disability or national origin.

Geographic Focus: Delaware, Maryland, West Virginia

Amount of Grant: 5,000 - 30,000 USD

Contact: Trish Schechtman, Relationship Manager; (302) 436-3555; trish@freemanfoundation.org

Internet: http://www.freemanfoundation.org/carl/CarlMFreemanFoundation/Grants/GrantGuidelines/tabid/181/Default.aspx

Sponsor: Carl M. Freeman Foundation

36097 Sand Cove Road

Selbyville, DE 19975

Carl R. Hendrickson Family Foundation Grants   351

The Carl R. Hendrickson Family Foundation was established in 1991 to support and promote quality education, human-services, and health-care programming for under-served populations. Carl R. Hendrickson was a Chicago entrepreneur who, along with his father and brothers, built the Hendrickson Trucking Company. Carl and his wife, Agnes, had one child, Virginia, who followed in her father's footsteps by leading the family business and by serving as President of the Hendrickson Foundation. Virginia died in 1995, leaving no heirs. The Hendricksons prided themselves on their entrepreneurial spirit, having been in the forefront of the trucking business by inventing the tandem truck. Reflecting the Hendrickson family's strong Christian faith, special consideration is given to charitable organizations that help individuals meet their basic needs while also addressing their spiritual needs. Preference is given to organizations or programs that approach their mission from an entrepreneurial perspective. The majority of grants from the Family Foundation are one year in duration. Application guidelines as well as a link to the downloadable application are given at the grant website. Applicants are also encouraged to review the Illinois state application guidelines and the foundation's funding history before applying. The deadline for application is July 31. Grant decisions will be made by November 1.

Requirements: Applicants must have 501(c)3 tax-exempt status. Applications must be mailed.

Restrictions: In general, grant requests for individuals, endowment campaigns or capital projects will not be considered. The foundation does not support requests from individuals, organizations attempting to influence policy through direct lobbying, or any political campaigns.

Geographic Focus: Illinois

Date(s) Application is Due: Jul 31

Contact: Debra L. Grand, Senior Vice President; (312) 828-2055; ilgrantmaking@bankofamerica.com

Internet: https://www.bankofamerica.com/philanthropic/fn_search.action

Sponsor: Carl R. Hendrickson Family Foundation

231 South LaSalle Street, IL1-231-13-32

Chicago, IL 60604

Carl W. and Carrie Mae Joslyn Trust Grants   352

Grants support activities providing services to resident children, elderly, and the disabled in El Paso County, Colorado. Areas of interest include education, medical care, rehabilitation, children and youth services, and aging centers and services. Types of support include general operating support, annual campaigns, building construction and renovation, equipment acquisition, endowment funds, and program development. Application must be in writing and must specifically describe the use of the funds. Grants are not sustaining and new applications must be submitted semiannually for renewal.

Requirements: Nonprofit organizations located in, or serving the residents of, El Paso County, Colorado, are eligible.

Restrictions: Grants are not made to individuals or for research, scholarships, fellowships, loans, or matching gifts.

Geographic Focus: Colorado

Date(s) Application is Due: Apr 30; Oct 31

Amount of Grant: 500 - 15,000 USD

Samples: Pikes Peak Hospice, Colorado Springs, Colorado, $5,000; Silver Key Senior Services, Colorado Springs, Colorado, $5,000; Saint Marys High School, Colorado Springs, Colorado, $3,000.
Contact: Susan Bradt Laabs; (719) 227-6435; fax (719) 2276448
Sponsor: Carl W. and Carrie Mae Joslyn Charitable Trust
Trust Department, P.O. Box 1699
Colorado Springs, CO 80942

Carnahan-Jackson Foundation Grants   353
The foundation's areas of interest include higher and other education, libraries, hospitals, youth, the disabled, drug abuse programs, ecology, housing, community development, dance and other performing arts groups, and churches. Types of support include general operating support, continuing support, capital campaigns, building construction/renovation, equipment acquisition, programs/projects, seed grants, curriculum development, scholarship funds, and matching funds.
Requirements: IRS 501(c)3 organizations serving western New York, particularly Chautauqua County, are eligible.
Geographic Focus: New York
Amount of Grant: 2,500 - 125,000 USD
Contact: Stephen E. Sellstrom, (716) 483-1015
Sponsor: Carnahan-Jackson Foundation
13 East 4th Street, P.O. Box 3326
Jamestown, NY 14701-3326

Carnegie Corporation of New York Grants   354
The Carnegie Corporation of New York provides research, study, and support for projects to improve government at all levels, to increase public understanding of social policy issues, to equalize opportunities for minorities and women, and to increase participation in political and civic life. Also supported are projects that promote electoral reform; education reform from early childhood through higher education; early childhood development; and urban school reform. The foundation will also fund research on the increasing availability and success of after-school and extended service programs for children and teenagers, particularly those in urban areas, that promote high academic achievement. Dissemination of best practices in teacher education will also be emphasized. There is no formal procedure for submitting a proposal. To apply under any of the corporation's grantmaking programs, applicants should submit a full proposal that describes the project's aims, duration, methods, amount of financial support required, and key personnel. The board meets four times a year, in October, February, April, and June.
Requirements: Only full proposals that have been invited for submission will be considered. After a letter of inquiry has been reviewed, applicants may be invited via email to submit a full proposal.
Restrictions: Grants are not made for construction or maintenance of facilities or endowments. The Corporation does not generally make grants to individuals except through the Carnegie Scholars Program, that supports the work of select scholars and experts conducting research in the foundation's fields of interest.
Geographic Focus: All States
Amount of Grant: Up to 4,000,000 USD
Samples: Massachusetts Institute of Technology, Cambridge, Massachusetts, $1,000,000 - international peace and security (2015); Center for Better Schools, Portsmouth, Rhode Island, $650,000 - strengthening teaching and human capital (2015); Citizen Schools, Boston, Massachusetts, $500,000 - strengthening education (2015).
Contact: Nicole Howe Buggs, Grants Manager; (212) 371-3200; fax (212) 754-4073; externalaffairs@carnegie.org
Internet: https://www.carnegie.org/grants/grantseekers/
Sponsor: Carnegie Corporation of New York
437 Madison Avenue
New York, NY 10022

Carolyn Foundation Grants   355
Priorities for funding include community and environmental grantmaking. In the community focus area needs are addressed only in the communities of interest to the foundation: Minneapolis, Minnesota and, New Haven, Connecticut. There are two community focus areas for funding: economically disadvantaged children and youth; and community and cultural vitality. The foundation works to empower economically disadvantaged children and youth by supporting their families and others to inspire, nurture, educate and guide them to achieve long-term stability and well-being. In the environmental focus area, the Carolyn Foundation environmental committee is currently most interested in funding renewable energy programs. The Foundation will consider other environmental proposals if funds allow. All proposals submitted must:

address root causes and create systemic and sustainable solutions and change; address global issues with local interventions that address local needs, as well as global needs; develop and implement solutions that can be replicated in other areas; collaborate effectively with others in the community: government, non-government, foundations and private parties. The Carolyn Foundation makes grants twice a year, in June and January. Applications must be submitted by January 15 for June grants, and July 15 for January grants. This is a postmark deadline. Grant applications will be reviewed by the Executive Director and a committee of foundation volunteers. Declinations will be sent at the time a decision is made to no longer consider a proposal, typically before the end of the review cycle. Successful applicants will be notified in June and January.
Requirements: IRS 501(c)3 nonprofit organizations in Minnesota and Connecticut may apply for the environmental grants. The Community grants program is limited to the cities of Minneapolis, Minnesota and New Haven, Connecticut. The foundation encourages use of Carolyn Foundation Application Form adapted from the Minnesota Common Grant Application Form. Applicants choosing not to use the common grant form must address the same information as required by the common grant. All proposals must use the Carolyn Foundation Cover Sheet, available at the Foundation's website. It is request that summary information and description of the project be no longer than six pages, printed on one side on 8 1/2 x 11-inch paper. Supporting documents, such as financial information, list of Officers, Directors, and Executive Staff, IRS determination letter may be in addition to the six pages. Do not send bound proposals, cassettes or VCR tapes.
Restrictions: Grants are not awarded to individuals, political organizations or candidates, veterans organizations, fraternal societies or orders, annual fund drives, umbrella organizations, or to deficits already incurred. The foundation does not generally make grants to religious organizations for religious purposes or to organizations in support of operations carried on in foreign countries.
Geographic Focus: Connecticut, Minnesota
Date(s) Application is Due: Jan 15; Jul 15
Amount of Grant: 5,000 - 50,000 USD
Samples: Clean Water Fund, Minneapolis, MN, $25,000—for development and use of safer alternatives for toxic substances; Indian Child Welfare Law Center, Minneapolis, MN, $15,000—for Indian Children's Stability Program; Hiawatha Leadership Academy, Minneapolis, MN, $20,000—for increasing salaries of the teaching staff.
Contact: Becky Erdahl, Executive Director; (612) 596-3279 or (612) 596-3266; fax (612) 339-1951; berdahl@carolynfoundation.org
Internet: http://www.carolynfoundation.org/guidelines.html
Sponsor: Carolyn Foundation
706 2nd Avenue South, Suite 760
Minneapolis, MN 55402

Carpenter Foundation Grants   356
The foundation's primary areas of interest include the arts, education, public interest, and human services. The foundation is deeply concerned with the well-being of children and families and their relationship to their neighborhoods and communities. Also of concern is the health of the web of agencies and organizations which serve them. Grants are awarded for general operating support, program development, capital campaigns, equipment acquisition, scholarship funds, seed money, matching funds, and technical support. Deadlines are generally about six weeks before the quarterly board meetings, held in January, March, June, and September.
Requirements: Tax exempt agencies in the Jackson and Josephine Counties of Oregon may submit proposals.
Restrictions: Grants are not made to individuals. The foundation rarely makes grants for historical applications, hospital construction or equipment, group or individual trips, or activities for religious purposes.
Geographic Focus: Oregon
Amount of Grant: 250 - 25,000 USD
Samples: Community Health Center (Medford, OR)—fir a program to provide discounted medications to low-income/uninsured patients, $15,000; Science Works Hands-On Museum, (Ashland, OR)—in support of a life science hands-on exhibition for local schools and students, $6,000; Southern Oregon State College (Ashland, OR)—for faculty development opportunities which improve teaching, $25,000; Oregon Water Trust, (Portland, OR)—for a community outreach and education project to locally distribute the General Elections Voter's Guide, $12,000.
Contact: Polly Williams, Program Officer; (541) 772-5732; fax (541) 773-3970; carpfdn@internetcds.com
Internet: http://www.carpenter-foundation.org
Sponsor: Carpenter Foundation
711 E Main Street, Suite 10
Medford, OR 97504

Carrie E. and Lena V. Glenn Foundation Grants 357

Established in 1971, the Glenn Foundation provides annual grants in the following areas of interest: arts; children/youth; services; Christian agencies & churches; Elementary/secondary education; Environment; and Human services.

Requirements: Federally tax-exempt institutions and not-for-profit agencies that serve Gaston County, NC. agencies or out-of-county agencies whose projects have an impact on Gaston County citizens are eligible to apply.

Restrictions: Funding is not available for: planning grants; grants to individuals; scholarships; capital campaigns; umbrella campaigns; and multi-year grants.

Geographic Focus: North Carolina

Date(s) Application is Due: Mar 1

Amount of Grant: 3,000 - 25,000 USD

Samples: Community Foundation of Gaston County, Gastonia, NC., $25,000 - for purchase and installment of This Little Light of Mine, a painting by John Biggers, recreated as mosaic time mural; Gastonia Potters House, Lowell, NC., $10,000 - for operating expenses for residential drug rehabilitation program for women; Alliance for Children and Youth, Gastonia, NC., $8,885 - for Strengthening Families program for parents and their children;

Contact: Barbara H. Voorhees, Executive Director; (704) 867-0296; fax (704) 867-4496; glennfnd@bellsouth.net

Sponsor: Carrie E. and Lena V. Glenn Foundation

1552 Union Road, Suite D

Gastonia, NC 28054

Carrie Estelle Doheny Foundation Grants 358

The foundation primarily funds local, not-for profit organizations endeavoring to advance education, medicine and religion, to improve the health and welfare of the sick, aged, incapacitated, and to aid the needy. Educational funding includes support of inner city Catholic schools, and scholarship funds for Catholic high schools and universities. Adult education programs and religious education are also supported. Medical funding is focused in two areas: research and care of the disadvantaged. Religious funding is directed to support the gospel values as expressed in the Roman Catholic faith. Health and welfare funding is directed to organizations who assist individuals to lead independent satisfying lives. Specific areas of interest include adoption and foster care service groups, programs for the disabled, health education programs, and senior programs. Aiding the needy funding includes inner city youth clubs, summer camps, and food banks. Applications are accepted anytime, an application form is required for submission and may be downloaded from the foundation web site. The board meets on the last Friday of each month, except for the month of September. Requests should be submitted approximately 6 weeks in advance to allow sufficient time for processing and for distribution to the Board members prior to the meeting. Allow 2 or 3 months for notification of the Board's decision. This is done in writing following the Board of Directors Meeting each month.

Requirements: The Foundation limits its grants to programs located within the fifty states and certified as 501(c)3 non-profit public charities by the Internal Revenue Service. The vast majority of funding is done in the Greater Los Angeles area.

Restrictions: Grant requests are not considered from individuals or from tax-supported entities. Areas also excluded from consideration include support for individuals, endowment funds, publishing books, television or radio programs, travel funds, advertisement, scholarships, or political purposes in any form.

Geographic Focus: All States

Amount of Grant: 5,000 - 150,000 USD

Samples: Boys & Girls Club of Venice, Venice, CA, $7,000—collaborative mentoring program support; YMCA of Greater Los Angeles, CA, $10,000—camperships for disadvantaged youth; South Central Lamp, Los Angeles, CA, general operating support.

Contact: Shirley Bernard, Senior Grants Administrator; (213) 488-1122; fax (213) 488-1544; doheny@dohenyfoundation.org

Internet: http://www.dohenyfoundation.org/grant/grant.htm

Sponsor: Carrie Estelle Doheny Foundation

707 Wilshire Boulevard, Suite 4960

Los Angeles, CA 90017

Carrier Corporation Contributions Grants 359

Carrier donates approximately $2 million around the world to registered nonprofit organizations. In the United States, Carrier funds only qualified 501(c)3 organizations that meet its eligibility criteria and operate in locations where the company has a significant employee base. Carrier believes in helping people in the communities where they live, work and do business. To better serve those communities and to better align its corporate contributions with mission and values, it focuses giving on the following these areas: environment and sustainability; civic & community; education; arts & culture; health & human services. All U.S. non-profits are required to complete an online grant application. Applications are accepted from March 1 through June 1 of each year, and are reviewed for funding to be paid the following year. Applicants will receive notification in the first quarter of the calendar year in which funding will occur.

Requirements: Carrier funds only qualified 501(c)3 organizations that meet eligibility criteria and operate in locations where it has a significant employee base.

Restrictions: Carrier will not fund: individuals; religious organizations; alumni groups, sororities or fraternities; booster clubs; political groups; any organization determined by Carrier to have a conflict of interest; any organization whose practices are inconsistent with the company's Code of Ethics

Geographic Focus: Alabama, Arizona, Connecticut, Georgia, Illinois, Indiana, Michigan, Nevada, New York, North Carolina, South Carolina, Tennessee, Texas

Date(s) Application is Due: Jun 1

Contact: Rajan Goel, Vice President; (860) 674-3420; fax (860) 622-0488

Internet: http://www.corp.carrier.com/vgn-ext-templating/v/index.jsp?vgnextoid=6afa80757d7e7010VgnVCM100000cb890b80RCRD

Sponsor: Carrier Corporation

One Carrier Place

Farmington, CT 06034-4015

Carylon Foundation Grants 360

The foundation awards general support grants to nonprofits of the Christian, interdenominational, Jewish, and Presbyterian faiths. Higher education institutions, health care organizations, international missions/ministries, medical centers, religious organizations, and temples receive support. Application may be made by submitting a brief letter describing the organization and program. There are no application deadlines.

Geographic Focus: All States

Amount of Grant: 50 - 50,000 USD

Samples: Rush-Presbyterian-Saint Lukes Medical Center (Chicago, IL)—for educational programs, $25,000; Holocaust Museum (Chicago, IL)—for operating support, $220,500; Weizmann Institute of Science (Palm Beach, FL)—for operating support, $10,000.

Contact: Marcie Mervis, Trustee; (312) 666-7700

Sponsor: Carylon Foundation

2500 W Arthington

Chicago, IL 60612-4108

Castle and Cooke California Corporate Giving Grants 361

Castle and Cooke Real Estate makes charitable contributions to nonprofit organizations on a case by case basis. Support is given primarily in Sierra Vista, Arizona, Bakersfield, California, and Keene's Pointe, Florida. The primary type of support is for general operating expenses. Application forms are required and are sent out annually in January. Initial approach is to contact the headquarters directly to be added to application form mailing list. The deadline for applications is the end of March.

Requirements: 501(c)3 organizations serving the residents of Sierra Vista, Arizona, Bakersfield, California, and Keene's Pointe, Florida, are eligible to apply.

Geographic Focus: Arizona, California, Florida

Date(s) Application is Due: Mar 31

Contact: Renee Massey; (661) 664-6562; rmassey@castlecooke.com

Sponsor: Castle and Cooke California

10000 Stockdale Highway, Suite 300, P.O. Box 11165

Bakersfield, CA 93389-1165

Castle Rock Foundation Grants 362

The foundation's grants are awarded to promote a better understanding of the free-enterprise system; preserve principles on which democracy was founded, ensure a limited role for government, and protect individual rights; encourage personal leadership; and uphold traditional American values. Types of support include general operating grants and special project grants.

Requirements: U.S. 501(c)3 organizations are eligible.

Restrictions: Grants requests from human service agencies, museums, organizations primarily supported by tax-derived funding, endowments, scientific or medical research, publications or media projects, churches, debt retirement, special events, or individuals will be denied.

Geographic Focus: All States

Date(s) Application is Due: Mar 15

Amount of Grant: 25,000 - 75,000 USD

Samples: College Fund/United Negro Fund, Fairfax, VA, $40,000 for scholarships; Congressional Medal of Honor Society, Mt. Pleasant, SC, $20,000 for general operating expense; Foundation for Research on economics

and the Environment, $50,000 for general operating expense; Fund for American Studies, Washington, DC, $25,000 for general operating expense.
Contact: Sally W. Rippey, Executive Director; (303) 388-1683; fax (303) 388-1684; generalinfo@castlerockfdn.org
Internet: http://www.castlerockfoundation.org
Sponsor: Castle Rock Foundation
4100 E Mississippi Avenue, Suite 1850
Denver, CO 80246

Caterpillar Foundation Grants   363
The foundation awards grants internationally to nonprofits in company-operating locations in support of arts, community development, environment, higher education, and health and human services. Youth health is a priority of small grants given under the civic and community activities program. Types of support include general operating support, capital campaigns, program development, and employee matching gifts. There are no application deadlines or required forms.
Requirements: Go to the Caterpillar Foundation website (above) for details about what to include in a proposal.
Restrictions: Grants do not support fraternal organizations, religious organizations for religious purposes, political activities, individuals, United Way organizations, ticket purchase, or advertising for fund-raising benefits.
Geographic Focus: All States
Samples: Nature Conservancy (Arlington, VA)—to initiate a project to protect the world's vanishing freshwater supplies and preserve large river systems, $12 million; Purdue U at West Lafayette (IN)—to construct a new engineering building, $5 million; Peng Cheng University, Xuzhou, China—to create the Caterpillar English Language Center.
Contact: Grants Administrator; (309) 675-4464
Internet: http://www.cat.com/cda/layout?m=39201&x=7
Sponsor: Caterpillar Foundation
100 NE Adams Street
Peoria, IL 61629-1480

Catherine Manley Gaylord Foundation Grants   364
The foundation awards grants to supplement the operating budgets of recognized public charities in the metropolitan Saint Louis, MO, area. Grants support general operations, materials and equipment, scholarships, symposiums and conferences, education and adult basic education, community development, and religious programs. Applications are accepted at any time.
Requirements: Saint Louis metro area 501(c)3 nonprofits may apply.
Geographic Focus: Missouri
Contact: Cindy Davis, Secretary; (314) 621-5757; fax (314) 621-5799
Sponsor: Catherine Manley Gaylord Foundation
1015 Locust Street, Suite 500
Saint Louis, MO 63101

Cause Populi Worthy Cause Grants   365
The main purpose of the Worthy Cause marketing grant is to enhance the visibility, online presence, community engagement and fund raising aspects of qualifying nonprofit institutions. Cause Populi, LLC will provide grants of up to $50,000 per project to qualifying non-profits. Grant applications and awards will be reviewed on a monthly basis. The grant is awarded as a matching in-kind donation to the selected non-profit institution(s), and may only be applied towards services provided by Cause Populi. Typical projects funded by the grant would include website redevelopment services, event management and promotion, marketing campaign services, social networking campaigns, etc. The grant award may be applied towards a specific project, or a group of related projects. Applicants may attach documentation describing the project in detail. The deadline for grant applications is the 21st day of each month. Applications will be reviewed upon submission, and awards will be made on a first-come, first-serve basis until the monthly award funds have been allocated. Applications received after this date may be deferred to a future award cycle.
Requirements: Donated services will be distributed under this program to qualifying organizations only, not to individuals. This donation is only available to nonprofits with 501(c)3 designation. The grant award and services may not be transferred, donated or resold.
Geographic Focus: All States, All Countries
Amount of Grant: Up to 50,000 USD
Contact: Eduardo J. Alarcon; (305) 913-4604; ealarcon@causepopuli.com
Internet: http://causepopuli.com/marketing-services-grant-for-non-profits/
Sponsor: Cause Populi
201 S. Biscayne Boulevard
Miami, FL 33131

CCA Assistance to Artist-Run Centres Grants   366
Canada Council for the Arts Assistance to Artist-Run Centres Grants provide funding to artist-run centres that provide visual artists and their audiences with an informed and professional forum for research, production, presentation, promotion and dissemination of new works in contemporary visual arts. The Grants also contribute to various services offered to visual artists, in addition to activities such as discussions, symposiums or publications on issues arising from visual arts practices. Awards begin at $20,000 with no upper limit.
Requirements: Applicants must: be incorporated, non-profit and Canadian; be directed by a board and the majority of the board members must be practicing visual artists; have a principle mandate to encourage research, production, presentation, promotion and dissemination of new works in contemporary visual arts; maintain a permanent, dedicated space that is accessible to the public; have maintained an annual program of artistic activities, accessible to the public, for a minimum of three consecutive years; and pay professional artists' fees to artists participating in programming activities with fees which meet or exceed national standards. Visual arts include drawing, painting, sculpture, photography, printmaking, installation, performance art, architecture and craft.
Restrictions: Organizations including video, film, new media, audio and interdisciplinary works in its programming must apply to for the Council's Media Arts or Inter-Arts grants.
Geographic Focus: Canada
Date(s) Application is Due: Oct 15
Contact: Jim Logan, Program Officer; (800) 263-5588 or (613) 566-4414, ext. 5266; fax (613) 566-4332; jim.logan@canadacouncil.ca
Francois Dion, Program Officer; (800) 263-5588 or (613) 566-4414, ext. 5268; fax (613) 566-4332; francios.dion@canadacouncil.ca
Internet: http://www.canadacouncil.ca/grants/visualarts/au127227986137031250.htm
Sponsor: Canada Council for the Arts
350 Albert Street, P.O. Box 1047
Ottawa, ON K1P 5V8 Canada

CCA Grants to Media Arts Organizations   367
The Canada Council for the Arts Grants to Media Arts offers funding to Canadian organizations that demonstrate a sustained commitment to research and development and the creation, presentation, dissemination, distribution or acquisition of independent Canadian media artworks. The purpose is to strengthen organizations throughout Canada to ensure the conditions necessary for the vitality and advancement of independent media arts in Canada. There are three Grant components: multi-year operating; initiatives; and emergency fund. The multi-year operating component is offered on a multi-year basis for three consecutive years to support organizations in carrying out their planned activities. It may include an amount for the acquisition of equipment. The initiatives component is for organizations receiving assistance from the multi-year operating component that wish to carry out a one-time initiative over a well-defined period that was not initially included in the three-year activity plan. The emergency fund component is intended solely for organizations that are already receiving assistance from the multi-year operating component. The award is to provide one-time non-recurring funding on an exceptional basis to organizations with an emergency. The maximum multi-year operating amount (including equipment) is $40,000 for the first year, $20,000 for the second year, and $20,000 for the third year. The maximum initiatives amount is $75,000. The maximum emergency amount is $5,000.
Requirements: All eligible organizations must: be incorporated as a non-profit organization or constituted as a non-profit cooperative under federal or provincial legislation for non-profit companies and have been active for at least two full years; have a board of directors, the majority of whose members are artists or professionals working in the field of Canadian independent media arts (or for festivals and cinematheques, an advisory committee made up of artists or professionals); support the practice of Canadian independent media arts; demonstrate a sustained commitment to research and development and the creation, presentation, dissemination, distribution or collection of Canadian independent media artworks; have an administrative structure and a management system suited to the nature of its activities; demonstrate sound financial management; pay artists' fees, distribution or dissemination rights to artists or pay fees to distributors for independent Canadian media artworks presented or acquired. Eligibility is contingent upon having received Council funding previously. See website for prior funding requirements. There are additional eligibility criteria for organizations relating to the activities performed which include: dissemination, distribution, production, national arts service, and cinematheque. See guidelines at website for requirements related to organizational activities. Aboriginal arts organizations and arts organizations of diverse cultural and regional communities of Canada are eligible.

Restrictions: Overdue final reports must be submitted and approved prior to applying. Organizations that have received a notice of exclusion from the Council are ineligible. Museums, public art galleries, libraries and educational institutions, crown corporations and municipal or governmental organizations are ineligible.
Geographic Focus: Canada
Date(s) Application is Due: Dec 1
Contact: Michele Stanley, Program Officer, Multi-Year and Emergency Fund Components; (800) 263-5588 or (613) 566-4414, ext. 5251; fax (613) 566-4409; michele.stanley@canadacouncil.ca
Internet: http://www.canadacouncil.ca/mediaarts/
Sponsor: Canada Council for the Arts
350 Albert Street, P.O. Box 1047
Ottawa, ON K1P 5V8 Canada

CCA Opera/Music Theatre Annual Funding Grants 368

Canada Council for the Arts Opera/Music Theatre Annual Funding Grants contribute to the development and presentation of traditional and alternative repertoire (including Canadian repertoire), and to the creation, production and presentation of new, original Canadian opera and music theatre works. Funding is based on the program's assessment criteria and available funds.
Requirements: Eligible applicants must: be a professional, non-profit Canadian opera/music theatre company; have a board of directors; have completed at least three full years of professional activities; produce and stage at least two productions a year and give at least two performances of each production (small music theatre companies must produce and stage at least one major production a year along with relevant public activities such as workshops, public readings or training sessions for singers and/or performers in techniques appropriate to this repertoire); receive significant support from other levels of government, the public and the private sectors; and engage professional artistic and administrative personnel. First time applicants must: have received project grants in each of the last two competitions and meet the basic eligibility criteria. The peer assessment committee's decision to award an annual grant for the first time will be based on the organization's performance against the assessment criteria, the organization's ability to demonstrate that it fulfills a distinctive role within its community, and the availability of funds. Aboriginal arts organizations and arts organizations from diverse cultural and regional communities of Canada are eligible.
Restrictions: Opera/music theatre organizations cannot request operating support from more than one Council grant. Activities involving market-driven forms of music and/or music for which an established commercial support structure exists are not eligible.
Geographic Focus: Canada
Date(s) Application is Due: Dec 1
Contact: Daniel Swift, Program Officer; (800) 263-5588 or (613) 566-4414, ext. 5248; fax (613) 566-4409; daniel.swift@canadacouncil.ca
Internet: http://www.canadacouncil.ca/grants/music/lm127227298757031250.htm
Sponsor: Canada Council for the Arts
350 Albert Street, P.O. Box 1047
Ottawa, ON K1P 5V8 Canada

CCA Operating Grants to Professional Theater Organizations 369

Canada Council for the Arts Operating Grants to Professional Theatre Organizations provide multi-year and annual funding to non-profit, professional Canadian theatre organizations. Funding contributes to the general operating expenses. Funding is based on the assessment criteria and funds available.
Requirements: Eligible applicants must: be incorporated, non-profit Canadian theatre organizations; be directed by recognized theatre professionals; operate on a full-time basis and support ongoing activities; have received at least one Council production grant in the three preceding years or have produced five preceding seasons with an average of at least two productions per year; and if not previously funded by this Grant, have had at least one production from the last two years of sustained activity assessed by the Council. Aboriginal arts organizations and arts organizations of diverse cultural and regional communities of Canada are eligible.
Geographic Focus: Canada
Date(s) Application is Due: Mar 1
Contact: Robert Allen, Program Officer; (800) 263-5588 or (613) 566-4414, ext. 4485; fax (613) 566-4410
Internet: http://www.canadacouncil.ca/grants/theatre/ho127227295916250000.htm
Sponsor: Canada Council for the Arts
350 Albert Street, P.O. Box 1047
Ottawa, ON K1P 5V8 Canada

CCA Professional Choir Program Annual Funding Grants 370

Canada Council for the Arts Professional Choir Program Annual Funding Grants assist professional Canadian choirs to develop and present choral repertoire. The program's particular emphasis is excellence in the presentation of Canadian music and encouragement to showcase Canadian artists. The goals of the Grants are: to contribute to the activities of professional Canadian choirs, from any cultural background, devoted to the development and presentation of choral music; to encourage innovative education and outreach programs that attract and serve new audiences for choral music, including young audiences; to stimulate the appreciation and enjoyment of choral music in Canada; and to encourage exemplary management and governance practices within the choral field. Funding is based on the assessment criteria and available funds.
Requirements: Eligible applicants must: be an incorporated, non-profit Canadian professional choir; have completed at least three seasons of professional activities; have a consistent core or membership of singers; have a season of activities (concerts) planned that includes a variety of self-produced programs showcasing Canadian choral music works; have a paid, professional Choral Conductor/Artistic Director; have a paid, professional administrative staff to support their artistic activities; have a board of directors; have experienced financial stability for at least the past two years and receive significant support from other levels of government, the public or the private sector; be adult choirs that have received project grants in each of the last two competitions and meet the basic eligibility criteria in order to apply for annual funding. Eligible choirs that received at least $20,000 at the last competition may be eligible for multi-year funding. All other choirs must apply for annual funding. Aboriginal arts organizations and arts organizations from diverse cultural and regional communities of Canada are eligible.
Restrictions: Choirs cannot request operating support from more than one Council grant.
Geographic Focus: Canada
Date(s) Application is Due: Jan 15
Contact: Andre Jutras, Program Officer; (800) 263-5588 or (613) 566-4414, ext. 5071; fax (613) 566-4409; andre.jutras@canadacouncil.ca
Internet: http://www.canadacouncil.ca/grants/music/dk127245411285312500.htm
Sponsor: Canada Council for the Arts
350 Albert Street, P.O. Box 1047
Ottawa, ON K1P 5V8 Canada

CCA Professional Orchestra Program Annual and Multi-Year Grants 371

Canada Council for the Arts Professional Orchestra Program Annual and Multi-Year Grants provide funding to professional Canadian orchestras for their activities. Grants contribute to the development and presentation of orchestra repertoire, with particular concern for excellence in the presentation of Canadian composition and of Canadian artists. Funding is awarded using a competitive process with award amounts based on the assessment criteria and available funds.
Requirements: Eligible organizations must: be a Canadian professional, non-profit orchestra; have a board of directors; have completed at least three year of professional activities; receive significant support from other levels of government, the public or the private sector; engage professional artistic and administrative personnel; and demonstrate a strong commitment to Canadian creation/repertoire as part of their ongoing annual programming. Applicant organizations eligible for first time annual funding must have received project grants in each of the last two competitions. If applicant organizations have received multi-year funding in the past or have received annual funding from each of the last two years, they must apply for multi-year funding, unless stipulated otherwise by the Music Section. Aboriginal arts organizations and arts organizations from diverse cultural and regional communities of Canada are eligible.
Restrictions: Applicants cannot request operating support from more than one Council grant.
Geographic Focus: Canada
Date(s) Application is Due: Feb 1
Contact: Daniel Swift, Program Officer; (800) 263-5588 or (613) 566-4414, ext. 5248; fax (613) 566-4409; daniel.swift@canadacouncil.ca
Internet: http://www.canadacouncil.ca/grants/music/be129038237771080058.htm
Sponsor: Canada Council for the Arts
350 Albert Street, P.O. Box 1047
Ottawa, ON K1P 5V8 Canada

CCHD Economic Development Grants 372

The program focus of CCHD's Economic Development Program concentrates on Economic Development Institutions (EDIs). EDIs typically are community-based organizations and businesses. They create good jobs and just workplaces, and they develop assets for low-income people that are owned by families and communities. EDIs coincide with the CCHD mission by their commitment to the development of low income people. All EDIs have structures that promote low income leadership and ownership. CCHD funds may be used for general operating expenses, including staff salaries/training, procurement of technical assistance, board development costs and other overhead costs. For business development, CCHD funds may be used as part of a financing package for start-up or expansion, including start-up costs or working capital. For real estate development, CCHD funds may be used for pre-development or continuing operating expenses.

Requirements: In order to be considered for funding by CCHD, an applicant organization must demonstrate that it is committed to both goals. Priority will be given to eligible applicants that address one or more of the following four priorities: to advance economic development models that enhance the scale of impact through replication or the transformation of an established model; to encourage collaboration that generates cooperation and solidarity among diverse groups in the interest of a more integrated and mutually understanding society; to link economic development with community organizing so that beneficiaries work together and with others on additional efforts to effect institutional change; or to facilitate the development of information systems in organizations that enhance planning, accountability and mutual learning by organizations and by CCHD.

Restrictions: Funds may not be used for capital expenditures (e.g. real estate, vehicles, equipment). Additionally, the following are ineligible for funding: Economic Development Institutions (EDIs) structured without opportunities for participatory control and ownership by low income people; EDIs structured without opportunities to develop community-held assets (e.g. sole proprietorships, simple partnerships or fee-simple housing projects are not eligible); EDIs owned or controlled by governmental agencies (federal, state or local), educational or ecclesiastical bodies; EDIs the primary focus of which is direct service (such services may complement an eligible EDI, but they cannot be the EDI's primary focus); EDIs that are not structured to stand on their own as sustainable institutions; or EDIs that intend to re-grant CCHD monies to other organizations.

Geographic Focus: All States
Date(s) Application is Due: Nov 1
Amount of Grant: Up to 50,000 USD
Contact: Ralph McCloud, Director; (202) 541-3367 or (202) 541-3210; fax (202) 541-3329; rmccloud@usccb.org or cchdgrants@usccb.org
Internet: http://www.usccb.org/about/catholic-campaign-for-human-development/grants/economic-development-grants-program/index.cfm
Sponsor: United States Conference of Catholic Bishops
3211 Fourth Street, NE
Washington, D.C. 20017-1194

CDECD Arts Catalyze Placemaking Leadership Grants 373

Arts Catalyze Placemaking (ACP) Arts Leadership grants provide funding for arts-based projects, activities and programs that engage partners and advance Connecticut cities, towns, and villages as meaningful communities in which to live, work, learn and play. Funding depends on the level of the project. ACP-2 grants range from $5,000 to $25,000. ACP-3 grants provide two options: planning grants range from $2,500 to $10,000 and fund the planning of projects, activities, or program that allow applicants to identify and design a future ACP-3 implementation project; implementation grants range from $25,001 to $100,000, and fund projects, activities, or programs designed to catalyze placemaking. Eligible expenses include the following: up to 35% of administrative expenses; artist fees; project documentation; marketing, promotional, and printing expenses; technology (hardware, software, professional services; installation, staff training, etc.); limited brick and mortar expenses; and any other costs directly related to the project, activity, or program. Additional information is available at the website, including frequently asked questions,, match requirements, webinars, and information sessions.

Requirements: Lead applicants must be one of the following qualifying entities: artist (with a fiscal sponsor); arts organization; colleges and universities; municipal department (restricted level B); or arts program of a 501(c)3 non-arts organization. All Arts Leadership (ACP-2 and ACP-3) proposals must include a Connecticut artist as an integral part of the planning and/or implementation phase of the proposed project, activity or program. Applicants must supply a one-page resume and/or bio of the artist to be engaged and a brief outline of how the artist is involved in the project, activity or program. In cases where the project artist is retained for their specific discipline expertise, applicants must also submit two to four samples of the artist's work (digital materials may include photographs, video, recordings, etc.).

Restrictions: Ineligible expenses include the following: any project, activity or program whose membership and/or participation policies do not comply with non-discrimination laws; interest expenses paid on loans or payments to reduce or eliminate deficits; activities to eliminate or reduce existing deficits; political

contributions; lobbying activities and lobbying fees; activities that have already been completed; any project, activity or program that is already funded by another COA program during the same fiscal year; religious programming, activities or paraphernalia; general brick and mortar expenses; travel and conference registration expenses (except as noted for ACP-3 Planning); hospitality expenses; and expenses not related to the project, activity or program.

Geographic Focus: Connecticut
Date(s) Application is Due: Nov 8
Amount of Grant: 5,000 - 100,000 USD
Contact: John Cusano, Southwest and Eastern Connecticut Program Manager; (860) 256-2723; fax (860) 256-2811; John.Cusano@ct.gov
Internet: http://www.ct.gov/cct/cwp/view.asp?a=3933&q=507176
Sponsor: Connecticut Department of Economic & Community Development
One Constitution Plaza, 2nd Floor
Hartford, CT 06103

CDECD Arts Catalyze Placemaking Sustaining Relevance Grants 374

Arts Catalyze Placemaking Sustaining Relevance Grants provide support to arts organizations whose on-going work is relevant to the community and supports COA's creative placemaking goals. Sustaining Relevance grants may be applied to any aspect of an organization's operations and/or expansion of those operations that directly support COA's creative placemaking goals. Sustaining funding is intended to advance Connecticut cities, towns and villages as meaningful communities in which to live, work, learn and play. Eligible expenses include but are not limited to: operating costs such as rent, telephone, postage and shipping, marketing, etc; documentation (photo, video, audio, collection of statistical information, etc.) and evaluation (hiring of evaluation consulting services) of organizational projects, activities and programs as described in the Activities, Goals and Outcomes Worksheet; materials and supplies, including printing; staff salaries (includes benefits) for existing or new staff; outside professional services hired to provide assistance in support of mission and/or organizational capacity; artist fees;office technologies including hardware, software, professional installation, staff training, etc; and travel and conference registration expenses for staff and/or volunteers to attend local, regional or national relevant industry conferences, workshops, retreats, and clinics that support the work of the organization (may not exceed 25% of the COA grant). Application deadlines vary according to grant levels and funding available. Additional information is available at the website, including frequently asked questions, budget instructions, matching and in-kind requirements, information sessions, and webinars.

Requirements: Lead applicants must be a Connecticut 501(c)3 nonprofit arts organization whose primary purpose is to create, perform, present, or otherwise promote the visual, performing, or literary arts. Organizations applying must have at least a three year history of arts programming.

Restrictions: Ineligible expenses include the following: any project, activity or program whose membership and/or participation policies that do not comply with non-discrimination laws; interest expenses paid on loans or payments to reduce or eliminate deficits; activities to eliminate or reduce existing deficits; political contributions; lobbying activities and lobbying fees; activities that have already been completed; any project, activity or program that is already funded by another COA program during the same fiscal year; religious programming, activities or paraphernalia; general brick and mortar expenses; and hospitality expenses.

Geographic Focus: Connecticut
Date(s) Application is Due: Oct 25
Contact: John Cusano, Southwest and Eastern Connecticut Program Manager; (860) 256-2723; fax (860) 256-2811; John.Cusano@ct.gov
Internet: http://www.ct.gov/cct/cwp/view.asp?a=3933&q=507176
Sponsor: Connecticut Department of Economic & Community Development
One Constitution Plaza, 2nd Floor
Hartford, CT 06103

CE and S Foundation Grants 375

The foundation is interested in supporting projects that improve people's lives. Focus areas for grant making include higher education; international cooperation; urban environmental improvement, and emergency disaster relief. Preference is given to those programs that have developed methods for measuring success. Before a grant proposal is submitted, the foundation requests that organizations first call the executive director to discuss the particulars of the project and the ways in which it fits the foundation guidelines.

Requirements: Nonprofit organizations are eligible to apply.

Restrictions: The foundation does not provide support individuals or for medical research.

Geographic Focus: All States

Amount of Grant: 500 - 100,000 USD

Samples: Bellarmine University, Louisville, a 6-year grant to fund a principled and innovative enhancement of teaching and learning, to benefit both students and faculty; Greater Louisville Project, supporting the largest city-county government consolidation in 40 years anticipating transitional needs of the new Metro government and its stewardship of the now 16th largest city in the nation; Metro Parks and Louisville Olmsted Parks Conservancy.

Contact: Bruce Maza, Executive Director; (502) 583-0546; fax (502) 583-7648; bruce@cesfoundation.com

Internet: http://www.cesfoundation.com/grantmaking.html

Sponsor: CE and S Foundation

1650 National City Tower

Louisville, KY 40202

Cemala Foundation Grants   376

The Cemala Foundation is a private family foundation established in 1986 by Martha A. and Ceasar Cone II to continue the family tradition of commitment to enhancing the quality of life of the community through grants to qualified charitable organizations. Areas of interest are: arts/culture; education; health; homelessness; human services; the state of North Carolina and; public interest. Application and additional guidelines are available at the Foundation's website.

Requirements: Grants are made only to non-profit charitable organizations which are tax exempt under Section 501(c)3 of the Internal Revenue Code or to public governmental units. Generally, grants are limited to projects which benefit the citizens of Guilford County, North Carolina. Occasionally, projects which benefit the state of North Carolina as a whole are considered.

Restrictions: The Foundation does not consider support for annual campaigns, endowments, sectarian religious activities, or requests under $1,000. Grants are not made to individuals. Grants from the Cemala Foundation are usually awarded for one year only. Only one grant application may be submitted in any twelve-month period. Organizations receiving grants are required to complete an evaluation report within twelve months after receipt of the funds.

Geographic Focus: North Carolina

Date(s) Application is Due: Mar 1; Sep 1

Amount of Grant: 3,000 - 200,000 USD

Contact: Susan S. Schwartz, Executive Director; (336) 274-3541; fax (336) 272-8153; cemala@cemala.org

Internet: http://www.cemala.org/grant/guidelines.php

Sponsor: Cemala Foundation

330 South Greene Street, Suite 101

Greensboro, NC 27401

Central Minnesota Community Foundation Grants   377

The community foundation administers charitable funds in the form of grants to nonprofit organizations for the benefit of residents of central Minnesota. The goal of the foundation is to identify and address social and cultural needs and to foster a sense of human interdependence dedicated to building self-capacity and fullness of life for all. The board of directors gives preference to applications that address themselves to developing capacity and self-help by attempting to address the causes of problems rather than dealing only with the symptoms; enhancing human dignity by providing support for those who participate actively in determining the course of their own lives; responding to new, innovative programs of organizations by addressing opportunities and dilemmas of emerging and changing needs; preserving the historic sense of voluntarism; fostering equal opportunity and enhancement of cultural heritage and diversity; supporting programs and projects that will enable charitable agencies to reduce costs and increase efficiency; and supporting community studies, programmatic research, or other types of projects intended to help citizens understand their problems and options, foster the refinement of public policy, and encourage coordination and cooperation. Applications are accepted four times each year; contact program staff for dates. Only one grant application per year will be considered from eligible applicants.

Requirements: The primary geographic focus of the foundation includes Benton, Sherburne, and Stearns Counties, but grants also are made to organizations located in rural central Minnesota counties. IRS 501(c)3 organizations are eligible, but applicants not meeting this requirement may apply through a fiscal agent.

Restrictions: The foundation will not fund individuals, endowments, medical research, capital campaigns to which the foundation can contribute no more than a tiny fraction of the total need, debt retirement or deficit financing, dollar-for-dollar replacement of government funding that has been reduced or eliminated, religious organizations for direct religious activities, political organizations or political campaigns, fraternal organizations, societies or orders, telephone solicitations, national fundraising efforts, or grants for travel.

Geographic Focus: Minnesota

Amount of Grant: Up to 31,000,000 USD

Contact: Susan Lorenz, Program Officer; (877) 253-4380 or (320) 253-4380; fax (320) 240-9215; slorenz@communitygiving.org

Internet: http://www.communitygiving.org/about_us_cm_6.php4

Sponsor: Central Minnesota Community Foundation

101 S 7th Avenue, Suite 100

Saint Cloud, MN 56301

Central New York Community Foundation Grants   378

The foundation is looking for innovative programs that address problems to be solved or opportunities to be seized in the Central New York area, specifically Onondaga and Madison Counties. Proposals are invited that suggest practical approaches to community problems; promote cooperation among agencies without duplicating services; generate community support, both professional and volunteer; demonstrate the organization's ability to secure realistic funding; strengthen an agency's effectiveness or stability; and address prevention as well as remediation. Types of support include capital grants, program development, seed money grants, and training grants. Prospective applicants are strongly encouraged to discuss the appropriateness of their grant request with staff before beginning the application process. Applications will not be accepted by fax.

Requirements: New York 501(c)3 tax-exempt organizations in Onondaga and Madison Counties are eligible.

Restrictions: The foundation generally does not make grants for annual operating budgets, except when it is seed or bridge money; endowments; sectarian purposes; loans or assistance to individuals; or medical research.

Geographic Focus: New York

Amount of Grant: 500 - 50,000 USD

Samples: Urban League of Onondaga County (Syracuse, NY)—for salary support of technicians at its computer centers in inner-city Syracuse, $15,000; Earlville Opera House (Carlville, NY)—to renovate a workshop and studio space for year-round use, $20,000; Syracuse Community Health Ctr (Syracuse, NY)—to construct an education and resource center for patients, $39,500; Interreligious Council of Central New York (Syracuse, NY)—for its Communitywide Dialog on Racism, Race Relations, and Racial Healing program, $20,000.

Contact: Kim Scott; (315) 422-9538; fax (315) 471-6031; kim@cnycf.org

Internet: http://www.cnycf.org/seekers/grants.cfm

Sponsor: Central New York Community Foundation

500 S Salina Street, Suite 428

Syracuse, NY 13202-3302

CFFVR Alcoholism and Drug Abuse Grants   379

The Community Foundation for the Fox Valley Region (CFFVR) was established as a public, nonprofit organization in 1986 to enhance the quality of life for all people of the region. Since it was founded, funds within the Foundation have awarded more than $125 million in grants to nonprofit organizations, primarily in Wisconsin's Fox Valley region. The purpose of the Alcoholism and Drug Abuse Grants program is to: supports new or existing programs and projects that address the prevention and/or treatment of alcohol and other drug abuse in the Fox Valley and surrounding area.

Requirements: Organizations serving residents of Outagamie, Calumet, Waupaca, Shawano and northern Winnebago counties are eligible to apply. The grant application form is available at the CFFVR website.

Geographic Focus: Wisconsin

Amount of Grant: 2,500 USD

Contact: Todd Sutton, Community Engagement Manager; (920) 830-1290, ext. 28; fax (920) 830-1293; lfilapek@cffoxvalley.org

Internet: https://www.cffoxvalley.org/Page.aspx?pid=652

Sponsor: Community Foundation for the Fox Valley Region

4455 West Lawrence Street, P.O. Box 563

Appleton, WI 54912-0563

CFFVR Appleton Education Foundation Grants   380

The Appleton Education Foundation (AEF) seeks to improve the well being of children, teachers and community by enhancing the quality of education within the Wisconsin, Appleton Area School District. AEF role is to fund initiatives that fall outside the school budget. Grants are available up to $500 for a single classroom or up to $1,500 for multiple classes, disciplines or schools. Grant application is available online.

Requirements: Any educator employed by the Wisconsin, Appleton Area School District or any community member in partnership with an educator is eligible to apply for a grant.

Restrictions: Generally, equipment alone does not qualify for a grant. Equipment required to complete a project or implement a program that meets the mission of the Foundation will be considered. Equipment upgrades are considered on an individual basis.
Geographic Focus: Wisconsin
Date(s) Application is Due: Apr 10; Nov 10
Contact: Julie Krause, Director; (920) 832-1517; jkrause@cffoxvalley.org
Internet: https://www.cffoxvalley.org/Page.aspx?pid=415
Sponsor: Community Foundation for the Fox Valley Region
4455 West Lawrence Street, P.O. Box 563
Appleton, WI 54912-0563

CFFVR Basic Needs Giving Partnership Grants 381
Supported by the U.S. Oil Open Fund for Basic Needs within the Community Foundation and the J.J. Keller Foundation, the partnership assists established charitable organizations with successful programs that address root causes of poverty. Available forms of support include: capacity building; general operating support; project support; project analysis & advocacy. A single organization may request up to $15,000 per year for three years, and collaborative proposals may request up to $100,000 per year for three years. Multiple years of support will be considered only if there is a compelling case for multi-year funding and the project clearly demonstrates how progression shall occur over time.
Requirements: Eligible applicants are well-established charitable organizations that are exempt from federal income taxes under the Internal Revenue Code and have been in operation for a minimum of three years. Wisconsin organizations must serve residents in Outagamie, Calumet, Waupaca, Shawano, or northern Winnebago counties.
Restrictions: Grants from the Basic Needs Giving Partnership will not support the following: technology projects; capital campaigns or building projects; organizational set-up costs; annual fund drives or endowments; lobbying for specific legislation; activities that occur before funding is awarded; organizations with past-due or incomplete grant reports.
Geographic Focus: Wisconsin
Date(s) Application is Due: Feb 15; Sep 15
Contact: Martha Hemwall, Community Engagement Officer; (920) 830-1290, ext. 26; mhemwall@cffoxvalley.org
Internet: https://www.cffoxvalley.org/Page.aspx?pid=400
Sponsor: Community Foundation for the Fox Valley Region
4455 West Lawrence Street, P.O. Box 563
Appleton, WI 54912-0563

CFFVR Bridge Grants 382
The Community Foundation for the Fox Valley Region (CFFVR) Bridge Program, is a temporary grant program that's to be used as a financial bridge through the economic downturn. Bridge grants will provide general operating support to charitable organizations which, due to the current economic decline, are in need of temporary funding to help maintain programs necessary to their core mission, and demonstrated prior financial health and high potential for future stability. These charitable organizations must serve residents in the Community Foundation service area, which includes Calumet, Outagamie, Shawano, Waupaca and northern Winnebago counties of Wisconsin. Applicants may request up to $25,000 for general operating support. Multiple organizations seeking to collaborate or merge for reasons of efficiency may be eligible for additional funding. Multiple organizations considering applying should contact Marti Hemwall at (920) 830-1290, before completing an application (available online).
Requirements: Eligible applicants are established Wisconsin, 501(c)3 charitable organizations that can provide compelling evidence of an urgent or impending financial need caused by the economic downturn and are able to demonstrate prior financial health and high potential for future stability. Charitable organizations must serve residents in the Community Foundation service area, which includes Calumet, Outagamie, Shawano, Waupaca and northern Winnebago counties.
Restrictions: Not eligible: educational institutions, government programs or entities, religious organizations, churches and funding for endowments. Programs and offices within an organization and organizations with a fiscal sponsor are not eligible to apply.
Geographic Focus: Wisconsin
Amount of Grant: 25,000 USD
Contact: Marti Hemwall, Program Director; (920) 830-1290, ext. 26; mhemwall@cffoxvalley.org
Internet: https://www.cffoxvalley.org/Page.aspx?pid=654
Sponsor: Community Foundation for the Fox Valley Region
4455 West Lawrence Street, P.O. Box 563
Appleton, WI 54912-0563

CFFVR Clintonville Area Foundation Grants 383
Clintonville Area Foundation (CAF) grants are awarded from unrestricted funds to support specific projects or new programs for which a moderate amount of grant money can make an impact on an area of need. Grants are made for a broad range of purposes to a wide variety of charitable organizations in the focus areas of health, education and community development. The Foundation is interesting in supporting: creative new activities or services—new programs, one-time projects, events, exhibits, studies or surveys; enhancement or strengthening of existing activities—projects to enhance, expand or strengthen the range, quantity and/or quality of an organization's programs and services; small capital investments—items that are directly related to program delivery or service to clients, such as a refrigerator for a food pantry or equipment to comply with ADA requirements. Grant applications are available online.
Requirements: Wisconsin 501(c)3 nonprofit organizations that serve the residents of the Clintonville area are eligible. General questions can also be directed to the CAF Grants Committee Chair or the Foundation.
Restrictions: The Clintonville Area Foundation will not generally fund the following: general operating expenses not related to the proposed project; annual fund drives or fundraising events; endowment funds; programs with a sectarian or religious purpose that promote a specific journey of faith; major capital projects such as the acquisition of land or buildings; medical research; travel for individuals or groups such as bands, sports teams or classes; activities that occur before funding is awarded; organizations with past-due or incomplete grant reports.
Geographic Focus: Wisconsin
Date(s) Application is Due: Dec 31
Contact: Jenny Goldschmidt, CAF Grants Committee Chair; (715) 823-7125, ext. 2603; clintonvillefoundation@gmail.com
Todd Sutton, Community Engagement Manager; (920) 830-1290, ext. 28; tsutton@cffoxvalley.org
Internet: https://www.cffoxvalley.org/Page.aspx?pid=415
Sponsor: Community Foundation for the Fox Valley Region
4455 West Lawrence Street, P.O. Box 563
Appleton, WI 54912-0563

CFFVR Doug and Carla Salmon Foundation Grants 384
The Doug and Carla Salmon Foundation provides need-based college scholarships to highly motivated students and financial support to local charitable organizations in the Fox Valley region of Wisconsin. Grants support capital campaigns and, the development of administrative endowments. There are no deadline dates. Mail a letter of inquiry, to begin the application process to: Doug and Carla Salmon Foundation, 660 West Ridgeview Drive, Appleton, Wisconsin 54911.
Requirements: Wisconsin 501(c)3 tax-exempt organizations serving residents of Outagamie, Calumet, Waupaca, Shawano and northern Winnebago counties are eligible to apply.
Geographic Focus: Wisconsin
Contact: Sue Detienne; (920) 424-2228; rdetienne@new.rr.com
Internet: https://www.cffoxvalley.org/Page.aspx?pid=403
Sponsor: Community Foundation for the Fox Valley Region
4455 West Lawrence Street, P.O. Box 563
Appleton, WI 54912-0563

CFFVR Environmental Stewardship Grants 385
The Environmental Stewardship Fund was established by the Community Foundation in 2006 to support the Wisconsin, Fox Valley-area charitable organizations and projects that further the conservation of nature and enhance education about and enjoyment of the natural world. Funding priority is given to projects that: strengthen the connection between the people and the land; further environmental values; have a wide impact; are visible and inspiring; match groups with similar aspirations.
Requirements: Wisconsin 501(c)3 tax-exempt organizations serving residents of Outagamie, Calumet, Waupaca, Shawano and northern Winnebago counties are eligible to apply. The grant application form is available at the CFFVR website.
Restrictions: Projects that will not be funded: major capital expenses; ongoing operating expenses unrelated to the proposed project; annual fund drives or fund-raising events; recurring events; endowment funds; conference fees; lobbying; activities that occur before funding is awarded; organizations with past-due or incomplete grant reports.
Geographic Focus: Wisconsin
Amount of Grant: 5,000 USD
Samples: Wisconsin League of Conservation Voters, $2,000—a Green Bay based organizer will educate members of Fox Valley environmental groups on such tools as working with the media and advocating with legislators to further a conservation agenda endorsed by more than 80 Wisconsin environmental and conservation

groups; Town of Greenville Pebbleidge Park, $2,250—shoreline planting will accompany a 2.5-acre prairie in this 13-acre park on Design Drive; Appleton Area School District, $3,000—Author Paul Fleischman will present three days of classroom workshops on the diversity and nature themes in his book Seedfolks.
Contact: David Horst; (920) 830-1290, ext. 24; dhorst@cffoxvalley.org
Internet: https://www.cffoxvalley.org/Page.aspx?pid=347
Sponsor: Community Foundation for the Fox Valley Region
4455 West Lawrence Street, P.O. Box 563
Appleton, WI 54912-0563

CFFVR Frank C. Shattuck Community Grants   386
The Frank C. Shattuck Community Fund supports new or supplements existing services for youth and the elderly and benefits education, the arts and health care in Winnebago and Outagamie counties of Wisconsin. Funding is available for programs, capital expenses or operating expenses of qualifying charitable organizations. Grants to projects may be either one-time payments or multi-year commitments. Application forms are available online.
Requirements: Wisconsin 501(c)3 organizations that serve residents in Outagamie or northern Winnebago counties are eligible to apply. To begin the application process, submit the following prior to the application deadline: grant application form; list of the organization's governing board members, including their professional or community affiliation; current year (board-approved) operating budget.
Restrictions: The Shattuck Fund will not typically support the following: grants for religious or political purposes; grants to support endowment funds of organizations; travel for individuals or groups such as bands, sports teams or classes; reimbursement for previously incurred expenses.
Geographic Focus: Wisconsin
Date(s) Application is Due: Mar 1; Sep 1
Contact: Shelly Leadley, Donor Relations Officer; (920) 830-1290, ext. 34; sleadley@cffoxvalley.org
Internet: https://www.cffoxvalley.org/Page.aspx?pid=339
Sponsor: Community Foundation for the Fox Valley Region
4455 West Lawrence Street, P.O. Box 563
Appleton, WI 54912-0563

CFFVR Mielke Family Foundation Grants   387
Mielke Family Foundation grants, enhance the quality of life for residents of Appleton and, Shawano, Wisconsin. Priority areas of giving are: projects that primarily serve individuals residing within either the Appleton Area School District or the Shawano School District; special events, start-up expenses of projects expected to become self-sustaining, studies to determine future courses of action or needs, enrichment programs, or actions to meet similar objectives. Application forms are available online at the Community Foundation for the Fox Valley Region website.
Requirements: Applicants must: be a nonprofit 501(c)3 or qualifying tax-exempt organization; be able to demonstrate, to the satisfaction of the Foundation, that it has the capability to complete the proposed project.
Restrictions: The Mielke Family Foundation typically will not support: transportation costs for individuals or groups such as bands, sports teams or classes; general operating expenses not related to the proposed project; deficits incurred for past activities; programs or needs that do not serve residents in the Appleton Area School District or the Shawano Area School District. The Foundation typically prefers not to engage in long-term grant commitments.
Geographic Focus: Wisconsin
Contact: Cathy Mutschler, Community Engagement Officer; (920) 830-1290, ext. 27; fax (920) 830-1293; cmutschler@cffoxvalley.org
Internet: https://www.cffoxvalley.org/Page.aspx?pid=415
Sponsor: Community Foundation for the Fox Valley Region
4455 West Lawrence Street, P.O. Box 563
Appleton, WI 54912-0563

CFFVR Myra M. and Robert L. Vandehey Foundation Grants   388
The Myra M. and Robert L. Vandehey Foundation's mission is support the charitable interests of the Myra and Robert Vandehey family. Areas of interest include: education; children and youth; health care and; family services. Funding opportunities are limited to nonprofit organizations that serve residents in the Fox Cities or Keshena areas of Wisconsin. Contact the Vice President for CFFVR prior to submitting a request to verify that the need aligns with current priorities. Unsolicited grant requests are not accepted from organizations not previously awarded support. Applications may be submitted at any time, and no application form is required.

Requirements: Wisconsin 501(c)3 nonprofit organizations that serve residents in the Fox Cities or Keshena are eligible for funding.
Restrictions: No grants to individuals.
Geographic Focus: Wisconsin
Samples: Fox Valley Technical College Foundation, Appleton, WI, $20,000—educational grant; Boys & Girls Clubs of the Fox Valley, Appleton, WI, $25,000—youth development grant; Nami Fox Valley, Inc., $10,000—mental health and crisis intervention grant.
Contact: Cathy Mutschler, Vice President Community Engagement; (920) 830-1290, ext. 29; cmutschler@cffoxvalley.org
Internet: https://www.cffoxvalley.org/Page.aspx?pid=415
Sponsor: Community Foundation for the Fox Valley Region
4455 West Lawrence Street, P.O. Box 563
Appleton, WI 54912-0563

CFFVR SAC Developmental Disabilities Grants   389
The Community Foundation for the Fox Valley Region Inc. was established as a public, nonprofit organization in 1986 to enhance the quality of life for all people of the region. Since it was founded, funds within the Foundation have awarded more than $125 million in grants to nonprofit organizations, primarily in Wisconsin's Fox Valley region. The service region includes Outagamie, Calumet, Waupaca, Shawano and northern Winnebago counties. The SAC Developmental Disabilities Fund supports projects or programs that address the recreational, social and educational needs of people with developmental disabilities and other handicapping conditions.
Requirements: Wisconsin 501(c)3 tax-exempt organizations serving residents of Outagamie, Calumet, Waupaca, Shawano and northern Winnebago counties are eligible to apply. The grant application form is available at the CFFVR website.
Geographic Focus: Wisconsin
Date(s) Application is Due: Feb 1; Aug 1
Amount of Grant: 5,000 USD
Contact: Todd Sutton, Grants Officer; (920) 830-1290, ext. 28; fax (920) 830-1293; tsutton@cffoxvalley.org
Internet: https://www.cffoxvalley.org/Page.aspx?pid=415
Sponsor: Community Foundation for the Fox Valley Region
4455 West Lawrence Street, P.O. Box 563
Appleton, WI 54912-0563

CFFVR Schmidt Family G4 Grants   390
The Schmidt Family G4 grants provide funding to improve the quality of life of those most in need in the Fox Valley, Wisconsin region, with a focus on at-risk youth and self-sufficiency for women. This goal will be accomplished by seeking to address immediate needs and to affect meaningful change in the following areas: at-risk youth—especially those with a physical or mental illness, those who have experienced abuse or those who have significant financial need; adult self-sufficiency—with a priority on issues that affect the stability and independence of women, as well as literacy, job skills training and transitional living for all. The G4 Committee prefers: not to be the sole funder for most projects it considers, unless the amount requested is small and/or a one-time request; to support specific projects or new programs for which a moderate amount of grant money can make a significant impact on an area of need and sustainability. A broad array of requests will be considered, including capital campaigns, existing programs or recurring events as long as they fall within the other listed giving guidelines. Grant awards will typically not exceed $15,000. To assist with the educational aspect of this fund, a formal application is required (available online). Prior to submitting an application, organizations are strongly encouraged to contact Cathy Mutschlerto, discuss the potential proposal and process. Complete and submit the application prior to the March 1, October 1 deadlines.
Requirements: IRS 501(c)3 nonprofit organizations, as well as government agencies are eligible to apply for funding. Organizations that are not public charities may apply through a fiscal sponsor. Organizations must serve Fox Valley residents, particularly in Outagamie, Calumet or northern Winnebago counties of Wisconsin.
Restrictions: The G4 Fund typically will not support the following: organizations that have received funding from the G4 Committee in the most recent 20 months; multi-year requests; programs with a sectarian or religious purpose that promote a specific journey of faith; travel for individuals or groups such as bands, sports teams or classes; reimbursement for previously incurred expenses; endowment funds; fund-raising events; requests from organizations with past-due or incomplete grant reports; a program or need previously declined unless the organization is invited back by the committee; programs or needs that do not serve Fox Valley residents, particularly Outagamie, Calumet or northern Winnebago counties.

Geographic Focus: Wisconsin
Date(s) Application is Due: Mar 1; Sep 1
Amount of Grant: 15,000 USD
Contact: Cathy Mutschler, VP Community Engagement; (920) 830-1290, ext. 29; cmutschler@cffoxvalley.org
Internet: https://www.cffoxvalley.org/Page.aspx?pid=340
Sponsor: Community Foundation for the Fox Valley Region
4455 West Lawrence Street, P.O. Box 563
Appleton, WI 54912-0563

CFFVR Shawano Area Community Foundation Grants   391
Shawano Area Community Foundation works to preserve and improve the quality of life in Shawano, Wisconsin and, the surrounding area, including communities having economic, educational, cultural and recreational ties with the area. Grant applications are available online.
Requirements: Wisconsin 501(c)3 non-profits in or serving surrounding area of Shawano are eligible to apply.
Geographic Focus: Wisconsin
Date(s) Application is Due: Oct 1
Amount of Grant: 5,000 USD
Samples: City of Shawano/County Library, Shawano, WI, $3,000—reading machine for visually impaired; Shawano Oral Health Fund, Shawano, WI, $1,500—program support for ssecond grade children in Shawano County; St. John's Trinity Lutheran Church, Shawano, WI, $1,000—food purchase grant.
Contact: Susan Hanson; (715) 253-2580; shawanofoundation@granitewave.com
Internet: https://www.cffoxvalley.org/Page.aspx?pid=412
Sponsor: Community Foundation for the Fox Valley Region
4455 West Lawrence Street, P.O. Box 563
Appleton, WI 54912-0563

CFFVR Wisconsin King's Daughters and Sons Grants   392
The Wisconsin Branch of the International Order of King's Daughters and Sons, in alignment with the priorities of its national parent organization, will provide grants to Fox Valley charitable organizations who provide services related to autism and literacy. Application is available online.
Requirements: Wisconsin 501(c)3 non-profit organizations in the Fox Valley region may apply. Organizations that are not public charities may apply through a fiscal sponsor.
Geographic Focus: Wisconsin
Date(s) Application is Due: Oct 15
Amount of Grant: 3,000 USD
Contact: Kathy Mutschler, Director, Donor Engagement; (920) 830-1290, ext. 27; fax (920) 830-1293; cmutschler@cffoxvalley.org
Internet: https://www.cffoxvalley.org/Page.aspx?pid=875
Sponsor: Community Foundation for the Fox Valley Region
4455 West Lawrence Street, P.O. Box 563
Appleton, WI 54912-0563

CFFVR Women's Fund for the Fox Valley Region Grants   393
The Women's Fund provides grants for programs that inspire women and girls to flourish personally, economically and professionally. Grants have been distributed to programs supporting the following areas: arts & culture; physical and mental health; economic, self-suffICency; education; parenting and child care; violence prevention. The Women's Fund believes that no project is too small or too new to be considered. Innovative approaches and projects with limited access to other funding are encouraged. Collaborative efforts are welcome. Grant applicants should address one or more of these funding priorities as they relate to women and girls: promotes economic self-sufficiency; improves safely from violence; provides opportunities to develop life skills; promotes physical and/or mental health; enhances dignity and self-worth; promotes leadership development; provides opportunities for artistic development and/or exposure to the arts; provides gender-specific solutions to problems facing women and girls; creates an environment that encourages social change. To apply submit a letter of interest by the deadline.
Requirements: To be eligible for a grant, the project must be consistent with the Women's Fund mission; benefits women and girls in the Wisconsin, Fox Valley region; organization must be a tax-exempt, not-for-profit organization under the Internal Revenue Code, section 501(c)3.
Restrictions: The Women's Fund will not fund: individuals, endowments, government agencies (however educational institutions may qualify), projects with a religious focus, and political parties, candidates or partisan activities.
Geographic Focus: Wisconsin
Date(s) Application is Due: Mar 15

Contact: Becky Boulanger, Program Director; (920) 830-1290, ext. 17; bboulanger@cffoxvalley.org or grants@womensfundfvr.org
Internet: https://www.cffoxvalley.org/Page.aspx?pid=415
Sponsor: Community Foundation for the Fox Valley Region
4455 West Lawrence Street, P.O. Box 563
Appleton, WI 54912-0563

Chahara Foundation Grants   394
The foundation awards general operating grants to Boston-area nonprofit organizations run by and for lower-income women. Grants are focused on community-based and community-driven nonprofits that serve those with the least access to funding, particularly women of color, older women, girls, lesbians, bisexual and transgendered women, and women with disabilities.
Requirements: Nonprofit organizations run by and for lower-income women in the greater Boston, MA, area are eligible.
Geographic Focus: Massachusetts
Amount of Grant: Up to 20,000 USD
Samples: Association of Haitian Women in Boston (Boston, MA)— to human rights to have representation, to have health, education, and decent housing, $20,000; Homes for Families (Boston, MA)—to educate, organize and advocate for improved public policies to address the root causes of family homelessness with holistic and community-based solutions, $20,000.
Contact: Contact; (617) 247-1580; fax (617) 247-7177; carol@chahara.org
Internet: http://www.chahara.org
Sponsor: Chahara Foundation
4 Copley Place
Boston, MA 02116-6504

Chamberlain Foundation Grants   395
The foundation awards grants to Pueblo, CO, nonprofit organizations in its areas of interest, including arts and culture, education, religion, and science. Types of support include general operating support, equipment acquisition, and program development. Submit a brief proposal that includes the purpose of the request and its relevance to the foundation; amount requested; brief history of the organization and its achievements; names, titles, and qualifications of key personnel; name of agency that conducted the last annual audit; copy of the IRS tax-exemption letter; list of other sources of financial support during the past 12 months; and names and affiliations of board members, trustees, and officers of the organization by either of the two deadlines.
Requirements: 501(c)(30 Pueblo, CO, nonprofit organizations are eligible.
Restrictions: Grants do not support individuals; conferences; political activities; religious organizations whose services are limited to members; veteran, labor, fraternal, athletic, or social clubs; national health agencies concerned with specific diseases or health issues; operating expenses for United Way-supported organizations; publications, advertising campaigns, or travel expenses.
Geographic Focus: Colorado
Amount of Grant: 1,000 - 20,000 USD
Samples: YMCA of Pueblo, Pueblo, CO, $20,000; Bessemer Historical Society, Pueblo, CO, $8,000; Animal Welfare and Protection Society, Pueblo, CO, $20,000.
Contact: David Shaw; (719) 543-8596; fax (719) 543-8599
Sponsor: Chamberlain Foundation
501 North Main Street, Suite 222
Pueblo, CO 81003

Champ-A Champion Fur Kids Grants   396
Grants for children's health and wellness are awarded twice each year. The program provides direct support for children in the areas of health and wellness such as childhood disease research foundations, child safety organizations and organizations that serve children with special needs. The goal is to provide grants to help many programs that are working hard to make the world a healthier and happier place for kids. Programs funded include: (a) Individual Project grants (generally for one-time purchases or to fulfill a short-term need, such as the purchase of materials or equipment); or, (b) Organization Program grants (start-up or operational costs for ongoing programs. Examples include funds for research, health and wellness educational programs, or financial assistance for children and families in-need.)
Requirements: United States applicants must be a tax-exempt organization under Section 501(c)3 of the IRS Code, and 'not a private foundation,' within the meaning of Code Sections 509(a)(1) or 509(a)(2), or a state college or university within the meaning of Code Section 511(a)(2)(B) (a 'Public Charity'). In addition, grant recipients must certify that they are not a supporting organization within the meaning of Code Section 509(a)(3). Canadian applicants must be a registered Canadian charity.

Restrictions: Programs that will not be funded include: (1) Annual Appeals or Capital Campaigns; (2) Construction or New Facility expenses; (3) Fundraising or Event Sponsorships; (4) Political Activities; (5) Religious organizations for religious purposes.
Geographic Focus: All States, Canada
Date(s) Application is Due: Feb 28; Aug 30; Nov 30
Amount of Grant: 1,000 - 10,000 USD
Samples: Angels with Special Needs (Columbia, SC); Building A Generation (Redlands, CA); Hearts and Noses Hospital Clown Troupe (Needham, MA); Catholic Charities of the Diocese of Santa Rosa (Santa Rosa, CA); Hole in the Wall Gang Fund (New Haven, CT); St. Patrick Center (St. Louis, MO); The Children's Hospital Foundation (Omaha, NE); Youth in Need (St. Charles, MO)
Contact: Maxine Clark; (314) 423-8000, ext. 5366; giving@buildabear.com
Internet: http://www.buildabear.com/aboutus/community/bearhugs.aspx
Sponsor: Build-A-Bear Workshop Bear Hugs Foundation
1954 Innerbelt Business Center Drive
Saint Louis, MO 63114

Chapman Charitable Foundation Grants 397
At Chapman, the ongoing business mission includes supporting the non-profit community through innovation, service and charity. The corporation accomplishes this mission through its corporate endeavors by striving to provide non-profit agencies with comprehensive coverage at the most reasonable price. Likewise, since its inception in 2000, the Chapman Charitable Foundation has donated over $6.75 million dollars to more than 470 California based Social Service Agencies. Primarily, the foundation supports organizations involved with education, forest conservation, health, human services, and religion. Particular fields of interest include: children and youth services, foster care, Christian agencies and churches, education (all levels), the environment, health care access, health care clinics and centers, hospitals, human services, and religion. Applicants should begin by contacting the Foundation with a one-page letter of inquiry. The foundation utilizes a Recommendation Committee to select potential grantees. Application forms are not required.
Geographic Focus: California
Amount of Grant: Up to 150,000 USD
Samples: AIDS Healthcare Foundation, Los Angeles, California, $10,000 - general operations; Michael Pourson Ministries, San Rafael, California, $108,000 - support programs; Pachamana Alliance, San Francisco, California, $36,000 - general operations.
Contact: Mari Perez, Grants Coordinator; (626) 405-8031; fax (626) 405-0585; mperez@chapmanins.com or info@chapmanins.com
Internet: http://www.chapmanins.com/about/foundation
Sponsor: Chapman Charitable Foundation
265 North San Gabriel Boulevard
Pasadena, CA 91107-3423

Charity Incorporated Grants 398
Grants are awarded to eligible Minnesota nonprofit organizations in support of Christian churches and organizations; elementary, secondary, and higher education; and social services for children/youth and families. Types of support include general operating grants, matching gifts, program development, and seed money grants. Submit a letter of proposal describing the organization and request, and include a copy of the IRS tax-exemption letter.
Requirements: Minnesota 501(c)3 tax-exempt organizations are eligible.
Restrictions: The foundation does not provide grants to individuals.
Geographic Focus: Minnesota
Amount of Grant: Up to 344,529 USD
Contact: Deanna Hulme, Grants Administrator; (320) 743-5466
Sponsor: Charity Incorporated
5786 118th Avenue
Clear Lake, MN 55319

Charles A. Frueauff Foundation Grants 399
The foundation considers proposals 501(c)3 organizations that support private four-year colleges and universities, social service agencies, and health-related agencies and institutions. Types of support include building construction/renovation, capital campaigns, equipment acquisition, general operating support, matching/challenge grants, annual campaigns, and emergency funds. Consideration will be given to programs that support persons leaving welfare, preparing students for employment in non-profit agencies, tutoring at-risk youth, and revitalizing neighborhoods. Applicants are requested to send via postal service a one-page letter of inquiry and include the following information: very brief agency mission and purpose; agency location; brief

purpose of request and amount requested; and email address if you wish to receive notification via email.
Requirements: Applicants must be private nonprofit corporations with 501(c)3 status.
Restrictions: The foundation funds nationwide except: Arizona, Alaska, California, Hawaii, Idaho, Iowa, Michigan, Minnesota, Montana, Nevada, New Mexico, North Dakota, Ohio, Oregon, Utah, Washington, Wisconsin, and Wyoming. K-12 schools are ineligible. Grants are not awarded to individuals, provide emergency funds, fund research, or for loans. Multi-year grants, international projects, state supported colleges or universities, primary and secondary schools, churches, or fund raising drives and special events are not supported.
Geographic Focus: Alabama, Arkansas, Colorado, Connecticut, Delaware, District of Columbia, Florida, Georgia, Illinois, Indiana, Kansas, Kentucky, Louisiana, Maine, Maryland, Massachusetts, Mississippi, Missouri, Nebraska, New Hampshire, New Jersey, New Mexico, New York, North Carolina, Oklahoma, Pennsylvania, Rhode Island, South Carolina, South Dakota, Tennessee, Texas, Vermont, Virginia, West Virginia
Date(s) Application is Due: Mar 15; Sep 15
Samples: Melmark Home (Berwyn, PA)—for classroom and office renovation, $50,000; Stetson U (Deland, FL)—to provide scholarships to students majoring in the natural sciences, $100,000.
Contact: Sue Frueauff, (501) 324-2233; fax (501) 324-2236
Internet: http://www.frueaufffoundation.com/application/default.asp
Sponsor: Charles A. Frueauff Foundation
200 South Commerce, Suite 100
Little Rock, AR 72201

Charles Delmar Foundation Grants 400
Established in 1957, the Foundation supports organizations involved with inter-American studies, higher, secondary, elementary, and other education, underprivileged youth, the disadvantaged, the aged, the homeless and housing issues, general welfare organizations, and fine and performing arts. Giving primarily in the Washington, D.C. area in the U.S., and in Europe and South America. There are no specific deadlines with which to adhere. Contact the Foundation for further application information and guidelines.
Restrictions: No grants to individuals, or for building or endowment funds, or matching gifts; no loans.
Geographic Focus: District of Columbia, Maryland, Virginia, West Virginia, Albania, Andorra, Argentina, Armenia, Austria, Azerbaijan, Belarus, Belgium, Bolivia, Bosnia & Herzegovina, Brazil, Bulgaria, Chile, Colombia, Croatia, Cyprus, Czech Republic, Denmark, Ecuador, Estonia, Finland, France, Georgia, Germany, Greece, Guyana, Hungary, Iceland, Ireland, Italy, Kosovo, Latvia, Liechtenstein, Lithuania, Luxembourg, Macedonia, Malta, Moldova, Monaco, Montenegro, Norway, Paraguay, Peru, Poland, Portugal, Romania, Russia, San Marino, Serbia, Slovakia, Slovenia, Spain, Sweden, Switzerland, The Netherlands, Turkey, Ukraine, United Kingdom, Vatican City
Amount of Grant: 500 - 10,000 USD
Samples: James River Association, Mechanicsville, VA, $4,000 - for general support; Pan American Development Foundation, Washington, DC, $5,000 - for environmental operations; College of Wooster, Wooster, OH, $9,000 - for general support;
Contact: Mareen D. Hughes, President; (703) 534-9109
Sponsor: Charles Delmar Foundation
5205 Leesburg Pike, Suite 209
Falls Church, VA 22041-3858

Charles G. Koch Charitable Foundation Grants 401
The foundation provides funding for academic and public policy research directed at solving social problems through voluntary action and free enterprise. In the area of research, the foundation primarily funds organizations working with doctorate-level investigators in disciplines such as economics, history, philosophy, political science, and organizational behavior. Types of support include general operating, scholarship funds, conferences and seminars, research, special projects, and seed money. There are no application deadlines. Submit preproposal letters (three-page limit).
Geographic Focus: All States
Amount of Grant: 25,000 - 300,000 USD
Contact: Kelly Young, Vice President; (202) 393-2354; fax (202) 393-2355; email@cgkfoundation.org
Internet: http://www.cgkfoundation.org
Sponsor: Charles G. Koch Charitable Foundation
655 15th Street NW, Suite 445
Washington, D.C. 20005-2001

Charles H. Farnsworth Trust Grants   **402**

The Charles H. Farnsworth Trust was established in 1930 to assist older adults to live in dignity and with independence. In describing the purpose of his legacy, Mr. Farnsworth made clear his interest in supporting housing, particularly in developing affordable housing options, and in providing support services to older adults. Program interests include: development of housing, especially housing with support services; services for elderly persons (i.e. health care, homemaker assistance, and nutritional support to enable the elderly to continue living in the community); and research, planning, and communication to better inform individuals, institutions, and the community at large on ways to improve the quality and quantity of housing and support services for seniors. Capital grants related to construction or renovation of housing for older adults is of particular interest. While general operating grants are provided, requests for support for new or special projects/programs are preferred. Planning grants investigating strategies for the development of supportive housing for the elderly are encouraged. Capital grants generally range between $25,000 and $250,000. General operating grants are usually no more than $10,000. Applicants must apply online at the grant website. Applicants are strongly encouraged to do the following before applying: review the downloadable state application procedures for additional helpful information and clarifications; review the downloadable online-application guidelines at the grant website; review the trust's funding history (link is available from the grant website); review the online application questions in advance; and review the list of required attachments. These will generally include: a list of board members, financial statements (audited, reviewed, or compiled by independent auditor); an organization summary; a list of other funding sources; an IRS Determination letter; and other required documents. All attachments must be uploaded in the online application as PDF, Word, or Excel files. The Farnsworth Trust has biannual deadlines of February 1 and October 15. Grant applicants for the February deadline will be notified of grant decisions by May 31 and applicants for the October deadline will be notified of grant decisions by December 31.

Restrictions: Grant opportunities are restricted to the Greater Boston area.
Geographic Focus: Massachusetts
Date(s) Application is Due: Feb 1; Oct 15
Amount of Grant: 10,000 - 250,000 USD
Contact: Michealle Larkins; (866) 778-6859; michealle.larkins@baml.com
Internet: https://www.bankofamerica.com/philanthropic/fn_search.action
Sponsor: Charles H. Farnsworth Trust
225 Franklin Street, 4th Floor, MA1-225-04-02
Boston, MA 02110

Charles H. Pearson Foundation Grants   **403**

The Charles H. Pearson Foundation Fund was established in 1922 to support and promote quality educational, human-services, and health-care programming for underserved populations. In the area of education, the fund supports academic access, enrichment, and remedial programming for children, youth, adults, and senior citizens that focuses on preparing individuals to achieve while in school and beyond. In the area of health care, the fund supports programming that improves access to primary care for traditionally underserved individuals, health education initiatives and programming that impact at-risk populations, and medical research. In the area of human services the fund tries to meet evolving needs of communities. Currently the fund's focus is on (but is not limited to) youth development, violence prevention, employment, life-skills attainment, and food programs. Grant requests for general operating support are strongly encouraged. Program support will also be considered. Small, program-related capital expenses may be included in general operating or program requests. The majority of grants from the Pearson Fund are one year in duration; on occasion, multi-year support is awarded. Applicants must apply online at the grant website. Applicants are strongly encouraged to do the following before applying: review the downloadable state application procedures for additional helpful information and clarifications; review the downloadable online-application guidelines at the grant website; review the foundation's funding history (link is available from the grant website); review the online application questions in advance; and review the list of required attachments. These will generally include: a list of board members, financial statements (audited, reviewed, or compiled by independent auditor); an organization summary; a list of other funding sources; an IRS Determination letter; and other required documents. All attachments must be uploaded in the online application as PDF, Word, or Excel files. The application deadline for the Charles H. Pearson Foundation Fund is 11:59 p.m. on July 1. Applicants will be notified of grant decisions before September 30.

Requirements: Applicants must have 501(c)3 tax-exempt status.

Restrictions: In general, capital requests are not advised. The fund does not support endowment campaigns, events such as galas or award ceremonies, and costs of fundraising events. The fund does not support requests from individuals, organizations attempting to influence policy through direct lobbying, or any political campaigns.
Geographic Focus: Massachusetts
Date(s) Application is Due: Jul 1
Samples: United Way of Massachusetts Bay, Boston, Massachusetts, $36,000,; Berklee College of Music, Boston, Massachusetts, $25,000, Berklee City Music Faculty Outreach Program to help underserved youth in the Boston Public Schools; Community Legal Services and Counseling Center, Cambridge, Massachusetts, general operating support to provide free legal services and affordable mental health services to underserved families and individuals.
Contact: Michealle Larkins; (866) 778-6859; michealle.larkins@baml.com
Internet: https://www.bankofamerica.com/philanthropic/fn_search.action
Sponsor: Charles H. Pearson Foundation Fund
225 Franklin Street, 4th Floor, MA1-225-04-02
Boston, MA 02110

Charles H. Price II Family Foundation Grants   **404**

The Charles H. Price II Family Foundation, established in Kansas City, Missouri, by a prominent American businessman and former Ambassador of the United States, offers support to educational programs and research primarily in Missouri and California (though funding is also occasionally provided outside of these two states). Grants are given for general operating support and scholarships. There are no specific applications or deadlines with which to adhere, and applicants should approach the Foundation in writing via a letter of application.
Geographic Focus: California, Missouri
Amount of Grant: 500 - 5,000 USD
Contact: Charles H. Price II, Director; (816) 360-6174 or (816) 360-6176
Sponsor: Charles H. Price II Family Foundation
1 W. Armour Boulevard, Suite 300
Kansas City, MO 64111-2004

Charles M. and Mary D. Grant Foundation Grants   **405**

The Foundation awards grants primarily in the southeast United States in its areas of interest, including community and economic development, health and human services, environment, and education. The Foundation prefers project support, but considers operating support proposals from organizations with budgets of less than $1 million. Grants are made in September. A minimum of three years must elapse between grant awards. Further information is available at the website.
Requirements: Southeast U.S. 501(c)3 tax-exempt organizations are eligible. Specific grant guidelines are available online with the application, which must be filed online.
Restrictions: No grants are made to individuals or for loans. A minimum of three years must elapse between grant awards.
Geographic Focus: Alabama, Florida, Georgia, Kentucky, Mississippi, North Carolina, South Carolina, Tennessee, Virginia, West Virginia
Date(s) Application is Due: Apr 30
Amount of Grant: 20,000 - 40,000 USD
Contact: Casey Castaneda, Program Officer; (212) 464-2487; fax (212) 464-2305; casey.b.castaneda@jpmchase.com
Internet: http://fdncenter.org/grantmaker/grant
Sponsor: Charles M. and Mary D. Grant Foundation
J.P. Morgan Private Bank, Philanthropic Services
Dallas, TX 75222-7237

Charles M. Bair Family Trust Grants   **406**

The trust awards general support grants to Montana nonprofits in its areas of interest, including museums, performing arts, arts and culture, higher education, youth, and social services. Application forms are required.
Requirements: Montana nonprofit organizations are eligible, with emphasis on Yellowstone, Meagher and Wheatland counties.
Restrictions: Funding is not provided for: churches, conventions, or associations of churches; individuals; conferences; symposiums; or for fundraising events.
Geographic Focus: Montana
Date(s) Application is Due: Jan 15; Aug 1
Amount of Grant: 2,000 - 300,000 USD
Contact: Grants Administrator, c/o U.S. Bank, Tax Department
Sponsor: Charles M. Bair Family Trust
P.O. Box 20678
Billings, MT 59115

Charles Nelson Robinson Fund Grants 407

The Charles Nelson Robinson Fund was established in 1970 to support and promote quality educational, human-services, and health-care programming for underserved populations in Hartford, Connecticut. Preference is given to organizations that provide human services programming to underserved adults. Grants from the Robinson Fund are one year in duration. Applicants must apply online at the grant website. Applicants are strongly encouraged to do the following before applying: review the downloadable state application procedures for additional helpful information and clarifications; review the downloadable online-application guidelines at the grant website; review the foundation's funding history (link is available from the grant website); review the online application questions in advance; and review the list of required attachments. These will generally include: a list of board members, financial statements (audited, reviewed, or compiled by independent auditor); an organization summary; a list of other funding sources; an IRS Determination letter; and other required documents. All attachments must be uploaded in the online application as PDF, Word, or Excel files. The Charles Nelson Robinson Fund has an annual deadline of 11:59 p.m. on February 15. Applicants will be notified of grant decisions by letter within two to three months of the proposal deadline.

Requirements: Applicant organizations must have 501(c)3 tax-exempt status and have a principal office located in the city of Hartford, Connecticut.

Restrictions: Grant requests for capital projects will not be considered. Applicants will not be awarded a grant for more than three consecutive years. The fund does not support requests from individuals, organizations attempting to influence policy through direct lobbying, or any political campaigns.

Geographic Focus: Connecticut

Date(s) Application is Due: Feb 15

Samples: Hartford Interval House, Hartford, Connecticut, $5,000, general operating support; Loaves and Fishes Ministries, Hartford, Connecticut, $4,000, general operating support; Bulkeley High School, Hartford, Connecticut, $3,000, VOAG Horse Care Program.

Contact: Carmen Britt; (860) 657-7019; carmen.britt@baml.com

Internet: https://www.bankofamerica.com/philanthropic/fn_search.action

Sponsor: Charles Nelson Robinson Fund

200 Glastonbury Boulevard, Suite # 200, CT2-545-02-05

Glastonbury, CT 06033-4056

Charles Stewart Mott Foundation Anti-Poverty Program 408

This program focuses on improving education, expanding economic opportunity, building organized communities, and special initiatives as pathways out of poverty. The overall goal is to help people vocalize and mobilize around local concerns, grow through participation in educational opportunities, and attain economic self-sufficiency by engaging more fully in the economy. Types of support include challenge/matching grants, conferences and seminars, demonstration grants, general operating grants, program grants, seed money grants, technical assistance, and training grants. The board meets in March, June, September, and December. Organizations should apply at least four months prior to the start date of the project for which they are seeking funds.

Requirements: Nonprofits and K-12 organizations are eligible to apply. A proposal may be submitted by a church-based or similar organization if the project falls clearly within program guidelines and is intended to serve as broad a segment of the population as the program of a comparable nonreligious organization.

Geographic Focus: All States

Amount of Grant: Up to 100,000,000 USD

Samples: Children's Aid Society (New York, NY)—to expand its Carrera program, a long-term, holistic approach to working with adolescents who are at high risk for teenage pregnancy, $873,782; Corp for a Skilled Workforce (Ann Arbor, MI)—to strengthen workforce development organizations in Michigan, $250,000; Pacific Institute for Community Organization (Oakland, CA)—for the Louisiana Interfaith Together project's work to engage residents of low-income communities in improving the educational outcomes of children in Louisiana, $220,000 over two years; Public/Private Ventures (Philadelphia, PA)—to assist and evaluate the Fathers at Work Initiative, which seeks to reduce poverty by increasing employment, earnings, and responsible fatherhood among young, low-income fathers, $787,047.

Contact: Office of Proposal Entry; (810) 238-5651; info@mott.org

Internet: http://www.mott.org/programs/poverty.asp

Sponsor: Charles Stewart Mott Foundation

503 S Saginaw Street, Suite 1200

Flint, MI 48502-1851

Charles Stewart Mott Foundation Grants 409

The focus of the foundation's grant making is organized in four programs: civil society; environment; Flint, Michigan; and poverty. Flexibility to investigate new opportunities is maintained through an exploratory and special projects program. The civil society program promotes and supports civil society in the United States; Central/Eastern Europe and South Africa. The environment program supports efforts to achieve a healthy global environment capable of sustaining all forms of life. The Flint program seeks to strengthen the capacity of local institutions, including schools and school districts, in the foundation's home community of Flint, Michigan, to respond to economic and social needs. The poverty program addresses issues that contribute to improved life outcomes for children, youth, and families in low-income communities. Programs in low-income communities that connect schools and communities through systemic reform, improved teaching, leadership development, networking, technical assistance, and advocacy are also applicable. In all grant making, particular interest will be given to fresh approaches to solving community problems in the defined program areas; approaches that can generate long-term support from other sources and/or can be replicated in other communities; public policy development and research and development activities to further existing programs as well as to explore new fields of interest; and approaches and activities that lead to systemic change. Although proposals may be submitted at any time, applicants are strongly encouraged to submit during the first quarter of the year for which funding is requested. Grant expenditures are determined by September 1 of each year. The review process takes up to four months from the time the proposal is received. Therefore, proposals should be submitted at least four months prior to the start of the proposed grant period. Funding for unsolicited proposals is limited. It is recommended that letters of inquiry be submitted instead of a full proposal.

Requirements: Only 501(c)3 organizations are eligible, including schools and school districts.

Restrictions: Grants are not made to/for individuals; religious activities or programs that serve, or appear to serve, specific religious groups or denominations; or local projects outside the Flint area unless the projects are part of a national demonstration or foundation-planned network of grants that have clear and significant implications for replication in other communities.

Geographic Focus: All States

Samples: Regional Foundation for Local Development Zamah, Croatia, $82,000—Civil Society Grant for general purposes; Clean Wisconsin, Wisconsin, $100,000—Environmental Grant; Direct Action and Research Training Center, Florida, $300,000—Pathways Out of Poverty Grant for general purposes.

Contact: Mary A. Gailbreath, Director; (810) 238-5651; fax (810) 766-1753; info@mott.org

Internet: http://www.mott.org/about/programs.aspx

Sponsor: Charles Stewart Mott Foundation

503 S Saginaw Street, Suite 1200

Flint, MI 48502-1851

Charles T. Beaird Foundation Grants 410

The foundation focuses its grantmaking on efforts to improve the Shreveport, LA, area. Grants are made to organizations that offer opportunity, freedom of action and choice, self-betterment and promote a climate for change to the people they serve. The foundation prefers to support those programs that are small, local, innovative, and perhaps even unpopular. The foundation awards general operating support, special program/project grants, capital expenditures, start-up costs, endowment funding, and technical assistance.

Requirements: Nonprofit organizations in, or projects that take place in, the Shreveport, LA, area are eligible. Requests from other areas, if they have the potential to be replicated in the Shreveport area, may be considered.

Geographic Focus: Louisiana

Date(s) Application is Due: Mar 1; Sep 1

Contact: Grants Administrator; (318) 221-8276; fax (318) 221-5993; BeairdP@aol.com or info@beairdfoundation.org

Internet: http://www.beairdfoundation.org

Sponsor: Charles T. Beaird Foundation

330 Marshall Street, Suite 1112

Shreveport, LA 71101

Charlotte and Joseph Gardner Foundation Grants 411

The Charlotte and Joseph Gardner Foundation was established in New York in 1981, with a primary interest in offering financial support in the New York City metro area. The Foundation's major fields of interest have always been human services, sports, and recreation. Grants are given to both individuals and nonprofit organizations. Most recently, awards have ranged from $3,600

to $12,000. A formal application is not required, and there are no specific annual deadlines for submission. Interested parties should begin by contacting the Foundation office directly.
Geographic Focus: New York
Amount of Grant: 3,600 - 12,000 USD
Samples: Friends of the High Line, New York, New York, $4,000 - general operations; Advanced Research Foundation, New York, New York, $12,000 - general operations; Youth Renewal Fund, New York, New York, $3,600 - general operations.
Contact: Danielle Gardner, President; (212) 366-4833
Sponsor: Charlotte and Joseph Gardner Foundation
230 West 41st Street, Suite 1500
New York, NY 10036

Charlotte M. Robbins Trust Grants 412
The Charlotte M. Robbins Trust, established in Massachusetts, offers grants in the Massachusetts communities of Ayer, Groton, Shirley, Littleton, and Harvard in Massachusetts. Funding is primarily dedicated to aged couples and aged women who are residents of these communities, or agencies serving the aged in these named communities. Therefore, the Foundation's major field of interest is support of the aged (primarily women), either directly or through human service programs. An application form is required, though there are no specified deadlines for submission. Support is typically given for general operating costs. Recent awards have ranged from $5,000 to $20,000. There are no formal applications or annual deadlines.
Geographic Focus: Massachusetts
Amount of Grant: 5,000 - 20,000 USD
Samples: Montachusett Home Care Corporation, Leominster, Massachusetts, $12,800 - general operating support (2014); Minuteman Senior Services, Bedford, Massachusetts, $5,000 - general operating support (2014).
Contact: Amy Sahler, Trustee; (617) 897-3209 or (888) 866-3275
Sponsor: Charlotte M. Robbins Trust
P.O. Box 1802
Providence, RI 02901-1802

Chatlos Foundation Grants 413
The Chatlos Foundation supports nonprofit organizations in the USA and around the globe. Support is provided to organizations currently exempt by the Internal Revenue Service of the United States. The Foundation's areas of interest are: Bible Colleges/Seminaries, Religious Causes, Medical Concerns, Liberal Arts Colleges and Social Concerns.
Requirements: Applicants must be U.S. tax-exempt, nonprofit organizations that provide services in the following areas: bible colleges, religious causes, medical concerns, liberal arts colleges, and social concerns. Proposals must include cover letter, specific request, tax-exemption letter, and budget. If proposal is to be considered at board level, additional information will be requested.
Restrictions: The foundation will not accept requests from individual church congregations, individuals, organizations in existence for less than two years as indicated by IRS tax-exempt letter of determination, for education below the college level, for medical research projects, or for support of the arts.
Geographic Focus: All States
Amount of Grant: 10,000 - 25,000 USD
Contact: C. J. Leff, Administrator; (407) 862-5077; cj@chatlos.org
Internet: http://www.chatlos.org/AppInfo.htm
Sponsor: Chatlos Foundation
P.O. Box 915048
Longwood, FL 32791-5048

Chautauqua Region Community Foundation Grants 414
Grants support projects serving communities in Chautauqua County in its areas of interest, including arts and culture, libraries, education, housing and shelters, children and youth, human services and general charitable giving, and government and public administration. Types of support include general operating support, continuing support, building construction/renovation, equipment acquisition, conferences and seminars, publication, seed grants, emergency funds, and undergraduate and graduate scholarships to individuals.
Requirements: Nonprofit organizations may apply for grants in support of projects serving communities in Chautauqua County, excluding the Fredonia/Dunkirk area, which is served by the Northern Chautauqua Community Foundation.
Geographic Focus: New York
Date(s) Application is Due: Jan 31; Mar 1; Nov 1
Samples: Salvation Army (NY)—to support the purchasing of infant formula and diapers, $500; James Prendergast Library Assoc (NY)—to support acquisition

of books on and for small business, $2500; Research and Planning for Human Services (NY)—to support human services coordination activities, $4000.
Contact: June Diethrick, Grants Coordinator; (716) 661-3392; fax (716) 488-0387; jdiethrick@crcfonline.org
Internet: http://www.crcfonline.org/
Sponsor: Chautauqua Region Community Foundation
418 Spring Street
Jamestown, NY 14701

Chazen Foundation Grants 415
The foundation awards grants nationwide to eligible nonprofit organizations in its areas of interest, including arts; business education; higher education; hospitals; human services; Israel; Jewish agencies, temples, and federated giving programs; museums; and music performance. Types of support include building construction/renovation, capital campaigns, general operating support, grants and scholarships to individuals, professorships, and scholarship funds. Education grants are awarded to students of the Rockland County, NY, area. There are no application deadlines.
Geographic Focus: All States
Contact: Grants Administrator; (212) 750-6600
Internet: http://www.chazenscholar.com/project.php3
Sponsor: Chazen Foundation
767 5th Avenue, 26th Floor
New York, NY 10153-2696

CHC Foundation Grants 416
The foundation awards general operating grants to southeastern Idaho nonprofit organizations in its areas of interest, including children and youth, community development, natural resource conservation and protection, and social services. Applicants should submit a letter of inquiry; the foundation will invite full proposals.
Requirements: 501(c)3 southeastern Idaho nonprofit organizations may apply.
Geographic Focus: Idaho
Date(s) Application is Due: Mar 15; Sep 1
Amount of Grant: 750 - 150,000 USD
Samples: Tautphaus Park Zoo Animal Health Care Center—for building a hospital/quarantine facility for zoo animals, $250,000.
Contact: Ralph Isom, President; (208) 522-2368
Sponsor: CHC Foundation
P.O. Box 1644
Idaho Falls, ID 83403-1644

Chemtura Corporation Contributions Grants 417
Chemtura makes charitable contributions to nonprofit organizations involved with education, health care, human services, economic development. Special emphasis is directed towards programs designed to provide educational and economic opportunities for disadvantaged people. Types of support include: building and renovation; general operating funding; and in-kind gifts. Support is given in areas of company operations in California, Connecticut, Georgia, Illinois, Indiana, and Pennsylvania, and on an international basis in areas of company operations.
Geographic Focus: Connecticut, Georgia, Illinois, Indiana, Pennsylvania
Contact: Grants Director; (215) 446-3911
Internet: http://www.chemtura.com/corporatev2/v/index.jsp?vgnextoid=5fe43 8f220d6d210VgnVCM1000000753810aRCRD&vgnextchannel=5fe438f220 d6d210VgnVCM1000000753810aRCRD&vgnextfmt=default
Sponsor: Chemtura Corporation
1818 Market Street, Suite 3700
Philadelphia, PA 19103-3640

Chesapeake Bay Trust Outreach & Community Engagement Grants 418
The Outreach and Community Awareness Grant program seeks to increase public awareness and public involvement in the restoration and protection of the Bay and its rivers. In light of the Trust's commitment to the advancement of diversity in its grant-making and environmental work, the Trust strongly encourages grant applications for projects that increase awareness and participation of communities of color in the restoration and protection of the watershed. Available funding will range between $5,000 to $20,000. All eligible projects should be a component of a clearly defined plan to engage communities, raise awareness and ultimately change citizen behaviors. The strongest proposals will show committed partnerships that provide funding, technical assistance, or other in-kind services to support the successful implementation of the project. Applications must be received via the online grants system, available at the Chesapeake Bay Trust website.

Requirements: The Trust welcomes requests from the following Maryland organizations: 501(c)3 private nonprofit organizations; faith-based organizations; community associations; service, youth, and civic groups; municipal, county, regional, state, federal public agencies; soil/water conservation districts & resource conservation and development councils; forestry boards & tributary teams; public and independent higher educational institutions.

Restrictions: The Trust does not fund the following: endowments, deficit financing, individuals, building campaigns, annual giving, research, direct mail fund raising, or venture capital; mitigation or capital construction activities such as structural erosion control measures; political lobbying; reimbursement for a project that has been completed or materials that have been purchased; projects and programs located outside of Maryland; budget items that are considered secondary to the project's central objective. These items include, but are not limited to, cash prizes, cameras and video equipment, and microscopes. Funding is generally restricted to projects on public property, property owned by non-profit organizations, community-owned property, and property with conservation easements, unless otherwise specified in a grant program. Projects should be completed within approximately one year upon receipt of the grant award.

Geographic Focus: Maryland
Amount of Grant: 5,000 - 20,000 USD
Contact: Kacey Wetzel, Grant Manager; (410) 974-2941, ext. 104; fax (410) 269-0387; kwetzel@cbtrust.org
Internet: http://www.cbtrust.org/site/c.miJPKXPCJnH/b.5457559/k.402C/Outreach_and_Community_Engagement.htm
Sponsor: Chesapeake Bay Trust
60 West Street, Suite 405
Annapolis, MD 21401

Chesapeake Corporation Foundation Grants   419
The foundation supports U.S. and international nonprofits in its areas of interest, including civic affairs, community development, cultural programs, higher education, and health. Types of support include endowments, capital grants, matching gifts, and scholarships. Grants are awarded for one year with the possibility of renewal.
Requirements: Nonprofits internationally are eligible.
Restrictions: Grants do not support athletic purposes or individuals, except for employee-related scholarships.
Geographic Focus: All States
Amount of Grant: 1,000 - 10,000 USD
Samples: David I. Clay II (Williamsburg, VA)—Chesapeake Employees' Children Scholarship, $3500 annually.
Contact: J.P. Causey Jr., (804) 697-1000; fax (804) 697-1199
Internet: http://www.cskcorp.com
Sponsor: Chesapeake Corporation Foundation
P.O. Box 2350
Richmond, VA 23218-2350

Chestnut Hill Charitable Foundation, Inc Grants   420
The foundation awards grants to nonprofit organizations in the greater Boston, MA, area in support of medical research, children and youth, and arts and education. Specifically, the foundation's interests include visual arts, museums, humanities, arts and culture, early childhood education and development, education at all levels, hospitals and medical research (cancer, heart and lungs, AIDS, and diabetes), social services, and general charitable giving. Types of support include general operating support, annual campaigns, capital campaigns, building construction/renovations, programs and projects, seed grants, curriculum development, research, and matching funds. There are no application forms; submit a letter of request.
Requirements: Nonprofit organizations in the greater Boston, MA, area may submit letters of request.
Restrictions: Grants are not awarded to support individuals or political or religious organizations.
Geographic Focus: Massachusetts
Amount of Grant: 1,000 - 15,000 USD
Samples: Leslie Berg, U of Massachusetts Medical Ctr (Worcester, MA)—for the Chestnut Hill Award for Excellence in Medical Research, administered by the Medical Foundation, in Boston, $15,000.
Contact: Kay Kilpatrick, Director Corporate Giving; (617) 630-2415
Sponsor: Chestnut Hill Charitable Foundation
27 Boylston Street
Chestnut Hill, MA 02167-1700

Chicago Board of Trade Foundation Grants   421
The foundation provides grant support to organizations in the metropolitan Chicago, IL, area in its areas of interest: arts and culture, including libraries and museums; education, including higher education, adult basic education and literacy training, and science and technology; health care, including mental health services, cancer research, and rehabilitation; child and youth development; minorities; the economically disadvantaged; wildlife; and media and communication. Grants are awarded for general operating support, continuing support, annual campaigns, capital campaigns, and endowments. An application form is not required; the initial approach should be by letter, or via the CBOT Foundation form on the Web site. The board meets during the first quarter annually to consider requests.
Requirements: Nonprofit organizations in a 75-mile radius of the metropolitan Chicago, IL, area may apply for grant support.
Restrictions: Support is not given to hospitals or foundations. Loans and program-related investments will also be denied.
Geographic Focus: Illinois
Date(s) Application is Due: Oct 1
Samples: Kent State U (Kent, OH)—to coordinate research symposia on derivative markets and instruments, $1.2 million.
Contact: Grants Administrator; (312) 435-3456; fax (312) 341-3306
Internet: http://www.cbot.com/cbot/pub/page/0,3181,948,00.html
Sponsor: Chicago Board of Trade Foundation
141 W Jackson Boulevard, Suite 600-A
Chicago, IL 60604

Chicago CityArts Program Grants   422
The CityArts Program is a triennial grant program designed to assist the not-for-profit arts and cultural community in the city of Chicago through general operating support. Since its inception in 1979, the CityArts Program has awarded over $22 million to Chicago based nonprofit organizations. The CityArts Program is divided into four categories based on an organization's adjusted income budget (total income minus government contributions/ income). The adjusted income figure determines the eligible grant requested amount. CityArts also supports social service organizations with an established arts program. All social service applicants apply in the same category regardless of income budget. CityArts applicants awarded grants in year one are eligible to receive grants for two consecutive years pending availability of funds. A modified application is required for funding in years two and three, and approval for future grants also requires a completed Final Report, proof of General Liability Insurance for each year, in addition to programming and organizational evaluations by Cultural Grants staff. Approval is contingent upon applicants meeting all prior years' reporting requirements and other related requests.
Requirements: Funding is provided for nonprofit arts organizations, cultural institutions and social service agencies that, prior to the application deadline, are: incorporated in the State of Illinois as a nonprofit corporation for at least twelve months and recognized as a 501(c)3 tax exempt organization by the U.S. Department of Treasury, Internal Revenue Service; a resident company of the City of Chicago with a Chicago street address (Post Office Boxes are not acceptable); primarily serving the residents of the city of Chicago with (51% of the organization's annual programming occurring in Chicago with the intent to reach Chicago residents); and planning activities, including public programming, for the upcoming grant year.
Geographic Focus: Illinois
Amount of Grant: 4,000 - 10,000 USD
Contact: Meg Duguid, Cultural Grants Coordinator; (312) 744-9797 or (312) 744-5000; meg.duguid@explorechicago.org
Internet: http://www.cityofchicago.org/content/city/en/depts/dca/provdrs/grants/svcs/city_arts_applicationsummary.html
Sponsor: Chicago Department of Cultural Affairs
121 N. LaSalle Street
Chicago, IL 60602

Chicago Sun Times Charity Trust Grants   423
The trust supports nonprofit organizations serving the Chicago metropolitan area by awarding grants to support projects in the areas of arts and culture and education/literacy. Grants will be awarded primarily as seed money for new ideas or approaches to problems affecting the quality of life in the community. Although applications for general operating support and capital projects are considered, the trust prefers to fund efforts that solve specific problems. Proposals are reviewed two times each year.
Requirements: IRS 501(c)3 organizations serving the Chicago, IL, metropolitan area are eligible.

Restrictions: The trust does not make grants to individuals, religious organizations for religious purposes, scholarships or fellowships, medical research or national health agency drives, or to political activities.
Geographic Focus: Illinois
Amount of Grant: Up to 5,000 USD
Contact: Patricia Dudek, Client and Community Services Supervisor; (312) 321-3000; fax (312) 321-2278; pdudek@hollingerintl.com
Sponsor: Chicago Sun Times Charity Trust
350 N Orleans Street
Chicago, IL 60654

Chicago Title and Trust Company Foundation Grants   424
The company foundation supports nonprofit organizations dedicated to improving the quality of life in Chicago. Grants are awarded to support higher education; city and neighborhood cultural organizations; and community issues, such as job training, literacy, and economic development. Types of support include program development, general operating support, annual campaigns, building construction/renovation, and matching gifts.
Requirements: Nonprofit organizations serving Chicago, IL, may apply.
Geographic Focus: Illinois
Amount of Grant: 100 - 150,000 USD
Contact: Eileen Hughes, c/o Miami Corp, Treasurer; (312) 223-2911
Sponsor: Chicago Title and Trust Company Foundation
410 N Michigan Avenue
Chicago, IL 60611

Chicago Tribune Foundation Civic Grants   425
The mission of the Chicago Tribune Foundation is to promote public knowledge and strengthen the Chicago metropolitan community by encouraging journalistic excellence, diversity and liberty; supporting diverse cultural institutions; and promoting civic efforts. Grants in the civic area support business, nonprofit or educational initiatives. Grants are accepted throughout the year, but by invitation only. Funding ranges from $2,500 to $25,00. Types of support include general operating grants, matching gifts, and program development grants. A brief summary proposal should be sent, along with a detailed list of the organization's board of directors; tax-exempt status form; audited financial statement or Form 990; organizational budget; sources of support listing which funds have been sought; and annual report or other literature on the organization's financial and strategic accomplishments.
Requirements: Grants are made to Chicago-area tax-exempt organizations.
Restrictions: The Foundation does not fund individual, capital, or international grants. If an organization previously received a Foundation grant, an updated report on that year's grant must be received before another can be considered.
Geographic Focus: Illinois
Amount of Grant: 2,500 - 5,000 USD
Contact: Jan Ellen Woelffer, Grant and Charitable Program Specialist; (312) 222-3928; fax (312) 222-3888; jwoelffer@tribune.com
Internet: http://www.chicagotribune.com/chi-foundationspage-htmlstory,0,163555.htmlstory
Sponsor: Chicago Tribune Foundation
435 North Michigan Avenue, 2nd Floor
Chicago, IL 60611-4041

Chicago Tribune Foundation Grants for Cultural Organizations   426
The Foundation grants funding cultural organizations in the Chicago metropolitan area. These organizations concentrate on educational programs in the arts for children from low-income communities or programs that foster diverse arts. Art education programs may be in-school or after-school. Grants range from $2,500 to $5,000. Proposals are due February 1 for a board meeting in June.
Requirements: Nonprofit organizations are eligible for funding. The Foundation accepts, but does not require, the Chicago area grant application form. Along with the narrative, organizations should include a detailed list of their board of directors; a copy of their tax-exempt form; audited financial statements or form 990; organizational budget from the current year; sources of support listing which funds have been committed; and annual report or other literature on the organization's financial and strategic accomplishments.
Restrictions: Funding is not available for individuals or capital campaigns.
Geographic Focus: Illinois
Date(s) Application is Due: Feb 1
Amount of Grant: 2,500 - 5,000 USD
Contact: Jan Ellen Woelffer; (312) 222-3920; jwoelffer@tribune.com
Internet: http://www.chicagotribune.com/chi-foundationspage-htmlstory,0,163555.htmlstory

Sponsor: Chicago Tribune Foundation
435 North Michigan Avenue, 2nd Floor
Chicago, IL 60611-4041

Chiles Foundation Grants   427
The foundation has a deep concern for and confidence in the future of Oregon and the Pacific Northwest. Although the foundation has made a steady commitment to the improvement of the quality of life for those who live and work in this area, it is not restricted in its grant making to the Pacific Northwest. The foundation has traditionally made grants to certain select institutions of higher education for business schools, scholarships, and athletics; supports basic research in certain select medical institutions; supports religion through divinity schools and religious education; and believes that the arts and cultural activities of a community are important and supports certain select, established institutions. Types of support include building construction/renovation, equipment acquisition, and scholarship funds. Annual deadline dates may vary; contact Foundation by a letter of Inquiry. The Foundation does not accept unsolicited proposals.
Requirements: The preferred initial method of contact is a phone call to the grants administration office to determine whether a prospective proposal is within guidelines; if so, an applicant will be invited to submit a one-page written preliminary proposal. An application form will be sent after approval of the preliminary proposal by the executive committee.
Restrictions: No support for projects involving litigation. Grants are not made to individuals, for deficit financing, mortgage retirement, or projects and conferences already completed.
Geographic Focus: California, Oregon, Germany
Amount of Grant: 1,000 - 270,000 USD
Samples: Boston Symphony Orchestra, Boston, MA, $100,000— general operating support; Stanford University, Stanford, CA, $159,000—scholarship assistance; Ludwig-Maximilians University, Munich, Germany, $180,000—support continuing clinical and experimental research.
Contact: Earle M. Chiles; (503) 222-2143; fax (503) 228-7079; cf@uswest.net
Sponsor: Chiles Foundation
111 SW Fifth Avenue, Suite 4050
Portland, OR 97204-3643

Chilkat Valley Community Foundation Grants   428
The Chilkat Valley Community Foundation uses proceeds from its growing community permanent fund to award yearly grants to worthwhile programs in the Chilkat Valley. These grants are intended to support organizations and programs in the community that serve the needs of people in such areas as health, education, human services, arts and culture, youth, environment, and community development. Applications are being accepted for the following three (3) categories: operating support; new program and special projects; and capital campaigns. Funding for projects during this grant cycle will range from $500 to $3,500. Most recent awards have ranged from $500 to $2,000. The annual deadline for application submission is September 30.
Requirements: Applications are accepted from qualified 501(c)3 nonprofit organizations, or equivalent organizations located in the state of Alaska and serving the Chilkat Valley region. Equivalent organizations may include tribes, local or state governments, schools, or Regional Educational Attendance Areas. Operating Support Grants may be awarded to sustainable organizations in amounts not to exceed 10% of the organization's secured cash annual budget. Capital Grants may be awarded as the local match to another funding source. New Program and Special Project Grants may be awarded for programs and projects that are not undertaken on an annual basis. A grant requesting $1,000 or more is a challenge grant at a ratio of 1:1 (grantees must raise $1 to receive $1). Grants of $500 to $999 do not require a match. The recipient's match must be raised within twelve months of the award notification and must be raised from at least five (5) different donors.
Geographic Focus: Alaska
Date(s) Application is Due: Sep 30
Amount of Grant: 500 - 3,000 USD
Samples: Becky's Place Haven of Hope, Haines, Alaska, $2,000 - operating support (2014); Children's Reading Foundation, Haines, Alaska, $999 - support of the Play With Purpose program (2014); Haines Animal Rescue Kennel, Haines, Alaska, $1,250 - spay and neuter assistance program (2014).
Contact: Ricardo Lopez, Program Officer; (907) 274-6707 or (907)766-6868; fax (907) 334-5780; rlopez@alaskacf.org
Internet: http://chilkatvalleycf.org/projects/
Sponsor: Chilkat Valley Community Foundation
P.O. Box 1117
Haines, AK 99827

Chingos Foundation Grants 429

Established in Florida in 1985, the Chingos Foundation awards grants to Florida nonprofit organizations for protection of endangered wildlife and natural resource conservation. Grants support program development, general operations, land acquisition, and other purposes. There are no annual application deadlines or forms. Applicants should submit a letter detailing their proposed project and amount of funding needed. The Foundation board meets once each year in November.
Requirements: Florida nonprofit organizations are eligible.
Restrictions: Grants do not support humane societies or spay/neuter clinics.
Geographic Focus: Florida
Amount of Grant: 5,000 - 20,000 USD
Samples: Audubon Center for Birds of Prey, Miami, Florida, $15,000 - general operations; Florida Odyssey of the Mind, Sewell, New Jersey, $5,000 - general operations; Nature Conservancy, Florida Chapter, Altamonte Springs, Florida, $10,000 - general operations.
Contact: William Manikas, Trustee; (561) 737-7111
Jennifer Manikas, jmanikas@bellsouth.net
Sponsor: Chingos Foundation
639 E Ocean Avenue, Suite 307
Boynton Beach, FL 33435-5016

Chinook Fund Grants 430

The fund supports progressive social change, organizing, and activism efforts in Colorado. Emphasis is placed on groups with diverse membership and leadership that represent diverse populations. Priority is given to organizations that are based in minority, low-income, or other oppressed communities; operate in a democratic manner; empower communities; have difficulty obtaining funding from traditional sources; draw parallels between local problems and global issues; and work in cooperation with other organizations. The standard grant program awards grants to new and established groups working for social change. Types of support include general operating support, special projects, technical assistance, and emergency funds. Application forms are available on the Web site.
Requirements: Applicants do not have to be tax-exempt, but the activities for which funds are sought must fit within the IRS eligibility requirements for 501(c)3 organizations.
Restrictions: Groups with annual budgets over $350,000 are not eligible for grants. Groups whose purpose is to provide direct services are generally not funded. Individuals are ineligible for funding.
Geographic Focus: Colorado
Date(s) Application is Due: Feb 21; Aug 21
Amount of Grant: 500 - 7,000 USD
Samples: Jobs with Justice (Englewood, CO)—to create a series of educational forums and hearings on the growing unemployment rate in Colorado, develop programs to better serve displaced workers, and develop strategies to create jobs, $7000; Two Spirit Society of Denver (CO)—to confront and combat issues of homophobia, racism, and cultural oppression toward the Native American, non-Native, gay, lesbian, bisexual, and transgender communities, $3000; Domestic Violence Initiative for Women with Disabilities (CO)—to provide support and intervention for disabled women who are victims/survivors of domestic violence and abuse, $3000.
Contact: Eva Benavidez Clayton, Program Coordinator; (303) 455-6905; fax (303) 477-1617; ebenavidez@chinookfund.org
Internet: http://www.chinookfund.org
Sponsor: Chinook Fund
2418 W 32nd Avenue
Denver, CO 80218

Christensen Fund Regional Grants 431

The fund (TCF) focuses its grantmaking on maintaining the biological and cultural diversity of the world by focusing on four geographic regions: the greater South West (Southwest United States and Northwest Mexico); Central Asia and Turkey; the African Rift Valley (Ethiopia); and Northern Australia and Melanesia. Grants within these programs are generally directed to organizations based within those regions or, where appropriate, to internationally based organizations working in support of people and institutions on the ground. In general, grants are one year or less; currently grants up to two years are by invitation only.
Requirements: 501(c)3 nonprofit organizations and non-USA institutions with nonprofit or equivalent status in their country of origin are eligible. Partnerships or associations with USA-based nonprofit organizations are preferred.
Restrictions: The fund does not make grants directly to individuals but rather assists individuals through institutions qualified to receive nonprofit support with which such individuals are affiliated.

Geographic Focus: All States
Amount of Grant: Up to 200,000 USD
Contact: Grants Administrator; (415) 644-1600; fax (415) 644-1601; info@ christensenfund.org
Internet: http://www.christensenfund.org/index.html
Sponsor: Christensen Fund
260 Townsend Street
San Francisco, CA 94107

Christian A. Johnson Endeavor Foundation Grants 432

The foundation contributes primarily to educational projects in the eastern United States. More specifically, it concentrates its giving on private institutions of higher learning at the baccalaureate level and on educational outreach programs of visual and performing arts organizations. Types of support include general operating support, seed money grants, building construction/renovation funds, equipment acquisition, matching funds, endowments, professorships, and scholarship funds. Applicants should first submit a brief letter of inquiry describing the project, its purposes, and potential impact on the program or service of the applicant organization. If the project falls within the foundation's support areas, a formal, more detailed proposal will be requested. Proposals requested by the foundation should be submitted during the first six months of the foundation's fiscal year, specifically between October 1 and March 30.
Restrictions: The foundation does not award grants to individuals; neighborhood or community projects; city, county, state, or federal government-affiliated agencies; institutions controlled by religious institutions; or in the areas of health care and medical research.
Geographic Focus: All States
Amount of Grant: 10,000 - 250,000 USD
Contact: Julie Kidd, President; (212) 534-6620; fax (212) 410-5909
Sponsor: Christian A. Johnson Endeavor Foundation
1060 Park Avenue, Apt 1F
New York, NY 10128

Christine and Katharina Pauly Charitable Trust Grants 433

The Christine and Katharina Pauly Charitable Trust was established in 1985 to support and promote quality educational, health, and human-services programming for underserved populations. Special consideration is given to charitable organizations that serve the needs of children or older adults. The majority of grants from the Pauly Trust are one year in duration. Applicants must apply online at the grant website. Applicants are strongly encouraged to do the following before applying: review the downloadable state application procedures for additional helpful information and clarifications; review the downloadable online-application guidelines at the grant website; review the trust's funding history (link is available from the grant website); review the online application questions in advance; and review the list of required attachments. These will generally include: a list of board members, financial statements (audited, reviewed, or compiled by independent auditor); an organization summary; a list of other funding sources; an IRS Determination letter; and other required documents. All attachments must be uploaded in the online application as PDF, Word, or Excel files. The application deadline for the Christine and Katharina Pauly Charitable Trust is 11:59 p.m. on September 1. Applicants will be notified of grant decisions by December 31. The Christine and Katharina Pauly Charitable Trust was created under the wills of Ms. Hazel Katharina Pauly and Ms. Frieda Christine Oleta Pauly.
Requirements: Applicants must have 501(c)3 tax-exempt status.
Restrictions: In general, grant requests for individuals, endowment campaigns, or capital projects will not be considered. The Fund will consider requests for general operating support only if the organization's operating budget is less than $1 million. The trust does not support requests from individuals, organizations attempting to influence policy through direct lobbying, or any political campaigns.
Geographic Focus: Missouri
Date(s) Application is Due: Sep 1
Contact: George Thorn; (312) 828-4154; ilgrantmaking@bankofamerica.com
Internet: https://www.bankofamerica.com/philanthropic/fn_search.action
Sponsor: Christine and Katharina Pauly Charitable Trust
231 South LaSalle Street, IL1-231-13-32
Chicago, IL 60604

CICF City of Noblesville Community Grant 434

The City of Noblesville Community Grants were established to support the charitable intentions of Noblesville. Other purposes of the grant include, but are not limited to, basic needs, economic stability, health and wellness, education, vitality of neighborhoods and communities, arts and culture, and environment. Priority is given to programs and projects most likely to have a positive effect on the city's residents. Proposals are accepted in February and July of each year. Applicants are strongly encouraged to view the Grantseeker's Guide posted on the website.

Requirements: The Foundation gives careful consideration to projects that; most benefit Noblesville residents; promote inclusiveness and diversity; respond to basic human needs; connect individuals and families to the community; complement other organizations to eliminate duplication of services; obtain additional funding and provide ongoing funding after the project. Organizations can apply through the online application.

Restrictions: The Foundation does not fund the following: organizations that are not tax exempt; multi-year grants; grants to individuals; projects aimed at promoting a particular religion or construction projects for religious institutions; operating, program, and construction costs at schools, universities, and private academies unless there is significant opportunity for community use or collaboration; organizations or projects that discriminate based on race, ethnicity, age, gender or sexual orientation; political campaigns or direct lobbying efforts by 501(c)3 organizations; post-event, after-the-fact situations or debt retirement; medical, scientific, or academic research; publications, films, audiovisual and media materials, programs produced for artistic purposes or produced for resale; travel for bands, sports teams, classes, and similar groups; annual appeals, galas, or membership contributions; fundraising events such as golf tournaments, walk-a-thons, and fashion shows.
Geographic Focus: Indiana
Amount of Grant: 1,000 - 10,000 USD
Contact: Liz Tate; (317) 843-2479, ext. 302; fax (317) 848-5463; lizt@cicf.org
Internet: http://www.cicf.org/how-to-apply-grantmaking
Sponsor: Central Indiana Community Foundation
615 North Alabama Street, Suite 119
Indianapolis, IN 46204-1498

CICF Howard Intermill and Marion Intermill Fenstermaker Grants   435

The Central Indiana Community Foundation Intermill Fenstermaker Grant exists to support programs for children and youth with disabilities. See the website's Grantseeker's Guide for a specific description of the Fenstermaker Grant. Proposal are accepted in the months of February and July, and the application is available on the Foundation's website.
Geographic Focus: Indiana
Amount of Grant: 1,000 - 15,000 USD
Contact: Liz Tate, Vice President for Grants; (317) 634-2423, ext. 175; fax (317) 684-0943; liz@cicf.org
Internet: http://www.cicf.org/examples-of-named-funds
Sponsor: Central Indiana Community Foundation
615 North Alabama Street, Suite 119
Indianapolis, IN 46204-1498

CICF Indianapolis Foundation Community Grants   436

CICF's mission is to inspire, support, and practice philanthropy, leadership, and service in the community. Proposed programs should align with any of the Foundation's Seven Elements of a Thriving Community: basic needs; economic stability; health and wellness; education; vitality and connectivity of neighborhoods and communities; arts and culture; and the environment. The application and grant request detail form are available online. Applications are accepted during the months of February and July.

Requirements: CICF welcomes grant applications from charitable organizations that are tax exempt under section 501(c)3 of the Internal Revenue Code, and from governmental agencies. New projects or organizations with pending 501(c)3 status may submit an application with the assistance of a fiscal sponsor. Grant inquiries and proposals will be prioritized using the following criteria: organizations that serve primarily Marion County residents; organizations with a demonstrable track record; programs serving populations disadvantaged due to income, age, ethnicity, language, education, disability, transportation or other adverse conditions; project/program ideas must be fully developed; and projects that strongly connect to existing community initiatives (e.g. the Blueprint to End Homelessness, Indianapolis Cultural Development Initiative, and Family Strengthening Coalition). Application information is available online.
Geographic Focus: Indiana
Contact: Liz Tate, Vice President for Grants; (317) 634-2423, ext. 175; fax (317) 684-0943; liz@cicf.org or program@cicf.org
Internet: http://www.cicf.org/the-indianapolis-foundation
Sponsor: Central Indiana Community Foundation
615 North Alabama Street, Suite 119
Indianapolis, IN 46204-1498

CICF John Harrison Brown and Robert Burse Grant   437

The purpose of the Central Indiana Community Foundation Brown and Burse Grant is to support academic and moral values for deserving youth in the Indianapolis area. Proposals are accepted in the months of February and July, and applications are available on the Foundation's website. Organizations are encouraged to call the Foundation before submitting their proposal to be certain it is appropriate for funding.
Geographic Focus: Indiana
Amount of Grant: 1,000 - 5,000 USD
Contact: Liz Tate; (317) 634-2423, ext. 175; fax (317) 684-0943; liz@cicf.org
Internet: http://www.cicf.org/examples-of-named-funds
Sponsor: Central Indiana Community Foundation
615 North Alabama Street, Suite 119
Indianapolis, IN 46204-1498

CICF Summer Youth Grants   438

The Central Indiana Community Foundation Summer Youth Grants provide grants, coordinates professional development opportunities, and disseminates community information to support summer programs serving Marion County youth. The program is designed to make the grant process easier for charitable organizations by using a single application form. Since 1995, SYPF-Indianapolis has awarded more the $29 million in grants to support summer youth programs.

Requirements: Applicants should carefully analyze their project in terms of needs assessment, program emphasis, start and end dates, budget development, recruiting of staff, length of program day, participating ages, safety, the program's site, and collaborations with other programs. Applicants are encouraged to call the Foundation to discuss their proposal in advance. They are also encouraged to review the application and the program guide at the Foundation's website.
Geographic Focus: Indiana
Contact: Mary Johnson, Grants Associate; (317) 634-2423, ext. 554
Internet: http://www.summeryouthprogramfund-indy.org/contact/
Sponsor: Central Indiana Community Foundation
615 North Alabama Street, Suite 119
Indianapolis, IN 46204-1498

CIGNA Foundation Grants   439

The Cigna Foundation has identified four areas for grant consideration: health and human services, education, community and civic affairs, and culture and the arts. Health and education are of primary concern and receive priority. Under education, priority is placed on public secondary education, higher education for minorities, and adult basic education/literacy. The foundation also considers requests from U.S. cultural, educational, and public policy organizations that have international components. Requests are accepted and reviewed throughout the year. Consideration will be given to requests for general operating support, program development, annual campaigns, conferences and seminars, fellowships, scholarship funds and employee-related scholarships, and matching gifts and funds.
Requirements: Organizations with 501(c)3 tax-exempt status are eligible.
Restrictions: The foundation will not consider applications for grants to individuals, organizations operating to influence legislation or litigation, political organizations, or religious activities. In general, the foundation will not consider applications from organizations receiving substantial support through the United Way or other CIGNA-supported federated funding agencies; hospitals' capital improvements; or research, prevention, and treatment of specific diseases.
Geographic Focus: All States
Amount of Grant: 5,000 - 50,000 USD
Contact: Jill Holliday; (860) 226-2094 or (866) 865-5277; jill.holliday@cigna.com
Internet: http://www.cigna.com/aboutus/cigna-foundation
Sponsor: Cigna Foundation
1601 Chestnut Street, TL06B
Philadelphia, PA 19192-1540

Cincinnati Bell Foundation Grants   440

The foundation awards grants to Ohio organizations in support of elementary and secondary school programs that improve education for disadvantaged youths, such as mentoring or tutoring programs. Grants also support social services, colleges and universities, and local civic and cultural groups that make the arts accessible to everyone. Types of support include capital grants, challenge/matching grants, organizational development grants, general operating grants, and program development grants. There are no application deadlines; grant notification is made quarterly.

Requirements: 501(c)3 nonprofit organizations in the Cincinnati Bell service area are eligible. Giving primarily in northern KY, the greater Cincinnati, OH, area, and in other cities in which the company has a significant corporate presence.
Geographic Focus: Kentucky, Ohio
Contact: Robert Horine, Public Affairs Director; (513) 397-7545
Internet: http://home.cincinnatibell.com/corporate/community
Sponsor: Cincinnati Bell Foundation
201 E Fourth Street, Room 102-560
Cincinnati, OH 45202

Cincinnati Milacron Foundation Grants   441

The Cincinnati Milacron Foundation awards grants, gifts, and loans to eligible Michigan and Ohio nonprofit organizations in its areas of interest, including the arts, community development, higher education, youth programs, and religion. Types of support include annual campaigns, building/renovations, general operations, and seed money. Grants are awarded for one year and are renewable.
Requirements: Michigan and Ohio 501(c)3 nonprofits are eligible.
Restrictions: Grants are not made to individuals.
Geographic Focus: Michigan, Ohio
Amount of Grant: 5,000 - 200,000 USD
Contact: George G. Price, (513) 487-5912; fax (513) 487-5586
Sponsor: Cincinnati Milacron Foundation
2090 Florence Avenue
Cincinnati, OH 45206-2484

Cinnabar Foundation Grants   442

The foundation awards grants to nonprofits to promote environmental and wildlife conservation and protection. Types of support include general operating support, conferences and seminars, research, and scholarships to individuals. There are no application forms.
Requirements: Idaho, Montana, and Wyoming nonprofit organizations may apply.
Geographic Focus: Idaho, Montana, Wyoming
Date(s) Application is Due: Mar 15
Amount of Grant: 1,000 - 15,000 USD
Contact: James Posewitz, (406) 449-2795; cinnabar@mt.net
Sponsor: Cinnabar Foundation
P.O. Box 5088
Helena, MT 59604

Circle K Corporation Contributions Grants   443

Circle K strives to be a good corporate citizen by improving the quality of life in the communities in which it serves. The corporation's charitable support targets two key areas: youth-at-risk and education. Other fields of interest include: boys clubs; cerebral palsy; community and economic development; food services; girls clubs; housing; and youth development. Types of support include general operating funds, in-kind support, and sponsorships. Additionally, Circle K has been a national sponsor of United Cerebral Palsy (UCP) since 1984, giving hope and encouragement to thousands of children and adults with cerebral palsy and other disabilities. Circle K also facilitates an employee volunteer group, which lends time to company-sponsored community activities.
Requirements: Giving is primarily centered in areas of company operations in Alabama, Arizona, Arkansas, California, Colorado, Florida, Georgia, Illinois, Iowa, Indiana, Kentucky, Michigan, Mississippi, Nevada, New Mexico, North Carolina, Ohio, Oklahoma, Oregon, Pennsylvania, South Carolina, Tennessee, Texas, and Washington.
Geographic Focus: Alabama, Arizona, Arkansas, California, Colorado, Florida, Georgia, Illinois, Indiana, Iowa, Kentucky, Michigan, Mississippi, Nevada, New Mexico, North Carolina, Ohio, Oklahoma, Oregon, Pennsylvania, South Carolina, Tennessee, Texas, Washington
Contact: Contributions Manager; (602) 728-8000
Internet: http://www.circlek.com/CircleK/AboutUs/CommunityService.htm
Sponsor: Circle K Corporation
P.O. Box 52085
Phoenix, AZ 85072-2085

Citigroup Foundation Grants   444

The foundation supports nonprofits worldwide in Citibank communities in the areas of financial education, educating the next generation, and building communities and entrepreneurs. Financial Education grants support efforts that help increase family stability, encourage better consumer habits, increase the individual's stake in his/her community, and deliver economic and financial education to young people. Educating the Next Generation grants support educational opportunities in low-income communities, early literacy development,

technology-based curriculum resources, career and college preparation programs, teacher training and strategies that increase student achievement, student and curriculum development for graduate and undergraduate business programs, access for minorities and women within higher education and the workplace, and access to arts through curriculum and cultural institutions. Building Communities and Entrepreneurs grants reinforce community-led efforts to revitalize low-income neighborhoods through affordable housing, economic development, welfare-to-work initiatives, community infrastructure improvements, environmentally sustainable growth to local economies, community-based health and human services programs, and disaster relief efforts. Citigroup and the Citigroup Foundation prefer to solicit proposals from prospective grantees with demonstrated successes in the areas they fund. Unsolicited proposals will be accepted, but a favorable decision is less likely. Nonprofit organizations that are encouraged to submit proposals may do so at any time during a calendar year; the earlier, the better. There are no application deadlines.
Requirements: 501(c)3 nonprofit organizations in communities served by Citibank or a Citigroup company are eligible. The Citigroup Foundation receives all U.S. grant applications through an online submission system. For information on applying for a U.S. grant, contact your closest U.S. Contributions Coordinator. For information on applying for an international grant, contact the International Contributions Coordinator. Contacts are listed at the Foundation's website (given above).
Restrictions: The foundation does not to make grants to individuals for educational or other purposes; political causes or candidates; religious, veteran, or fraternal organizations, unless they are engaged in a significant project benefiting the entire community; fundraising events, telethons, marathons, races, or benefits; or courtesy advertising.
Geographic Focus: All States
Samples: Enterprise Community Partners (Columbia, MD)—for the Green Communities program a nationwide effort to build 8500 low-coast houses that conserve energy and natural resources and provide easy access to jobs, schools, and services, $1.5 million; Junior Achievement Worldwide (Colorado Springs, CO)—to expand its classroom-based program that teaches young people in more than 25 countries about finance, the principles of the banking industry, and the challenges of operating a bank, $2.7 million over three years; American National Red Cross (Washington, DC)—for relief efforts in the wake of the tsunamis in South Asia, and for the rebuilding of affected communities, $1 million, plus $2 million to be be distributed.
Contact: Pamela P. Flaherty, President; (212) 559-9163; fax (212) 793-5944; citigroupfoundation@citigroup.com
Internet: http://www.citigroup.com/citigroup/corporate/foundation/guide.htm
Sponsor: Citigroup Foundation
850 Third Avenue, 13th Floor
New York, NY 10022-6211

City of Oakland Cultural Arts Department Grants   445

The arts program awards grants to Oakland-based individuals and nonprofit organizations. Organization Project Support grants support Oakland-based nonprofit organizations producing art activities in Oakland that culminate in a local public outcome for the benefit of the community. Individual Artist Project grants support Oakland resident individual artists producing art activities in Oakland that culminate in a local public outcome for the benefit of the community. Art in the Schools grants support quality, hands-on arts experiences in school settings to educate students about the process of creating and producing arts; support and enhance the classroom curriculum; and support arts residencies on the school site before, during, or after school hours. The January 6 application deadline is for organizations and individual artists; the January 13 deadline is for art in the schools. Guidelines are available online.
Requirements: Oakland-based individuals and nonprofit organizations are eligible.
Geographic Focus: All States
Date(s) Application is Due: Jan 6; Jan 13
Contact: Andrea Leal, (510) 238-6843; aleal@oaklandnet.com
Internet: http://oaklandculturalarts.org/main/programoverview.htm
Sponsor: City of Oakland Cultural Arts Department
1 Frank H Ogawa Plaza, 9th Floor
Oakland, CA 94612

CJ Foundation for SIDS Program Services Grants   446

The CJ Foundation for SIDS offers two types of grants to support services related to the following areas of interest: SIDS (Sudden Infant Death Syndrome), SUID (Sudden Unexpected Infant Death), and Infant Safe Sleep. Program Services Grants, which are the first type, are generally for amounts greater than $5,000 and are offered by invitation only. Program Services Mini-Grants (formerly known as Express Grants) are the second type. These are for $5,000 or less and may be applied for without invitation. The purpose of the foundation's program-services grants is to support activities that promote safe sleep for infants, educate about SIDS risk reduction, and provide grief support for parents and others who have experienced the sudden, unexpected death of an infant. The grants support the following types of activities: conferences and meetings; training and workshops; community awareness events; production, purchase, and distribution of educational, bereavement, and resource materials; support groups; peer support; counseling; support of staff and consultants who implement education initiatives or provide bereavement services; and newsletter production and distribution. Interested applicants should contact the Assistant Executive Director (see contact section) to request application materials. Submission deadline for the mini-grants is September 26 (deadlines may vary from year to year).

Requirements: The applicant must demonstrate that services relating to SIDS, SUID, and/or Infant Safe Sleep are an established part of the organization's services.

Restrictions: Projects exclusively serving perinatal and/or neonatal death will not be considered. Data collection and analysis for Fetal Infant Mortality Review (FIMR) and Child Death Review (CDR) will not be considered. The foundation does not provide grants to organizations that discriminate, in policy or practice, against people based on their age, race, color, creed or gender. In general the CJ Foundation does not support the following types of requests: loans; budget requests greater than 100% of the applicant's operating budget; grants to individuals; dues; operating deficits; book publication; capital improvements/building project; chairs or professorships; endowments; annual fund drives, direct mail solicitation, or fundraising events; purchase of advertising space; purchase of products such as t-shirts, cribs, crib sheets, and sleep slacks; activities to influence legislation or support candidates for political office; and re-granting.

Geographic Focus: All States
Date(s) Application is Due: Sep 26
Amount of Grant: 500 - 5,000 USD
Samples: Association of SIDS and Infant Mortality Programs, East Lansing, Michigan, $5,000; Baptist Memorial Healthcare Foundation and NEA Baptist Charitable Foundation, Jonesboro, Arkansas, $2,852; Council for Children & Families, Seattle, Washington, $5,000.
Contact: Wendy Jacobs, Assistant Executive Director; (866) 314-7437 or (551) 996-5111; fax (551) 996-5326; wendy@cjsids.org or info@cjsids.org
Internet: http://www.cjsids.org/grants/grants-overview.html
Sponsor: CJ Foundation for SIDS
30 Prospect Avenue
Hackensack, NJ 07601

Clara Blackford Smith and W. Aubrey Smith Charitable Foundation Grants 447

The Clara Blackford Smith & W. Aubrey Smith Charitable Foundation was established in 1978. Mrs. Smith was a well-known benefactor of health care. The foundation was established under her will to support and promote quality education, health-care, and human-services programming for underserved populations. Special consideration is given to charitable organizations that serve the people of Grayson County, Texas. The foundation makes an annual grant to Denison High School in Denison, Texas to provide college scholarship assistance for deserving graduates. The majority of grants from the Smith Charitable Foundation are one year in duration; on occasion, multi-year support is awarded. Applicants must apply online at the grant website. Applicants are strongly encouraged to do the following before applying: review the downloadable state application procedures for additional helpful information and clarifications; review the downloadable online-application guidelines at the grant website; review the foundation's funding history (link is available from the grant website); review the online application questions in advance; and review the list of required attachments. These will generally include: a list of board members; financial statements (audited, reviewed, or compiled by independent auditor); an organization summary; a list of other funding sources; an IRS Determination letter; and other required documents. All attachments must be uploaded in the online application as PDF, Word, or Excel files. The Clara Blackford Smith & W. Aubrey Smith Charitable Foundation has four deadlines annually: March 1, June 1, September 1, and December 1. Applications must be submitted by 11:59 p.m. on the deadline dates. Grant applicants are notified as follows: March deadline applicants will be notified of grant decisions by June 30; June applicants will be notified by September 30; September applicants will be notified by December 31; and December applicants will be notified by March 31 of the following year.

Requirements: Applicants must have 501(c)3 tax-exempt status.

Restrictions: The foundation does not support requests from individuals, organizations attempting to influence policy through direct lobbying, or any political campaigns.
Geographic Focus: Texas
Date(s) Application is Due: Mar 1; Jun 1; Sep 1; Dec 1
Samples: Denison Independent School District, Denison, Texas, $55,000, for Smart Boards for DISD classrooms; Loy Park Improvement Association, Denison, Texas, $36,000, installation of ceiling fans in the Major Arena; Grayson County Shelter, Denison, Texas, $50,000, general operating support.
Contact: David Ross, Senior Vice President; tx.philanthropic@baml.com
Internet: https://www.bankofamerica.com/philanthropic/fn_search.action
Sponsor: Clara Blackford Smith & W. Aubrey Smith Charitable Foundation
901 Main Street, 19th Floor, TX1-492-19-11
Dallas, TX 75202-3714

Clarcor Foundation Grants 448

Clarcor, through its foundation, seeks to improve the quality of life in the communities in which the company operates. Grants support nonprofits in the categories of health, human services, education, culture and art, and civic activities. Types of support include general operating support, annual campaigns, capital campaigns, and employee matching gifts. There are no application deadlines. The board meets in February, May, August, and November.

Requirements: Tax-exempt organizations in company-operating areas in Rockford, IL; Louisville, KY; Kearney and Gothenburg, NE; Cincinnati, OH; Oklahoma, and Lancaster, PA; are eligible.

Restrictions: Grants are not made to support individuals, endowment funds, research, scholarships, fellowships, or loans.
Geographic Focus: Illinois, Kentucky, Nebraska, North Carolina, Ohio, Oklahoma, Pennsylvania
Amount of Grant: 500 - 50,250 USD
Samples: Boys & Girls Assoc of Rockford (IL)—to support the Crime Prevention program, $3000; New American Theater (Rockford, IL)—for educational outreach, $6000; Lancaster Theological Seminary (Lancaster, PA)—to fund creation of a computerized card catalog system, $2500; Boy Scouts of America (Kearney, NE)—to support the annual campaign, $1000.
Contact: Pete Nangel, (815) 962-8867; fax (815) 962-0417
Sponsor: Clarcor Foundation
840 Crescent Centre Drive, Suite 600
Franklin, TN 37067

Clarence E. Heller Charitable Foundation Grants 449

The charitable foundation supports nonprofit organizations, with priority given to proposals from California, in its areas of interest, including environment and health—to prevent serious risk to human health from toxic substances and other environmental hazards by supporting programs in research, education, and policy development; management of resources—to protect and preserve the earth's limited resources by assisting programs that demonstrate how natural resources can be managed on a sustainable and an ecologically sound basis, and supporting initiatives for sustainable agriculture, and for promoting the long-term viability of communities and regions; music—to encourage the playing, enjoyment, and accessibility of symphonic and chamber music by providing scholarship and program assistance at selected community music organizations and schools, and by helping community-based ensembles of demonstrated quality implement artistic initiatives, diversify and increase audiences, and improve fund-raising capacity; and education—to focus on support for programs that improve the teaching skills of educators and artists in environmental and arts education. Types of support include continuing support, general operating expenses, publications, research, seed money, and special projects. The foundation's board meets typically in March, June, and October. Letters of inquiry are accepted at any time.

Requirements: 501(c)3 tax-exempt organizations are eligible.
Restrictions: Grants are not made to individuals.
Geographic Focus: California
Samples: Crossroads School, Santa Monica, CA, $50,000— to support the Elizabeth Mandell Music Institute; Brentwood Agricultural Land Trust, Brentwood, CA, $50,000—for a program to save productive agricultural lands on the urban edge and market farm products from family-scale farms; Graduate School of Education, UC Berkeley, Berkeley, CA, $10,000—for the Principal Leadership Institute Scholarship Endowment Fund.
Contact: Bruce Hirsch; (415) 989-9839; fax (415) 989-1909; info@cehcf.org
Internet: http://cehcf.org/app_info.html
Sponsor: Clarence E. Heller Charitable Foundation
44 Montgomery Street, Suite 1970
San Francisco, CA 94104

Clarence T.C. Ching Foundation Grants 450

The Clarence T. C. Ching Foundation provides funding opportunities to nonprofits primarily in Honolulu, Hawaii. The Foundation's areas of interest include education and health. Types of support available are: scholarship funds; general program support and; building/renovation. Grant applications are accepted year round with no application deadline date.

Requirements: Nonprofits in Honolulu, Hawaii are eligible for funding. When applying for a grant include the following in with your proposal: copy of IRS Determination Letter; detailed description of project and amount of funding requested; listing of additional sources and amount of support; five (5) copies of the proposal.

Restrictions: No grants to individuals.

Geographic Focus: Hawaii

Amount of Grant: 500 - 70,000 USD

Samples: Contemporary Museum, Honolulu, HI, $500—general program support; St. Francis Healthcare of Hawaii, Honolulu, HI, $70,000—general program support; St. Louis Scholarship Fund, Hawaii, Honolulu, HI, $70,000—general program support.

Contact: R. Stevens Gilley, Executive Director; (808) 521-0344

Sponsor: Clarence T.C. Ching Foundation

1001 Bishop Street, Suite 960

Honolulu, HI 96813

Clark-Winchcole Foundation Grants 451

The foundation awards grants to nonprofit organizations in the District of Columbia, with an emphasis on higher education, hospitals and health care, cultural programs, youth, the disabled, and religion. Types of support include general operating support, scholarships, and building construction/renovation. Applicants should submit a letter of inquiry that includes a description of the project, amount requested, audited financial report, budget, and proof of tax-exempt status. Further information will be requested by the foundation if interested.

Requirements: Only nonprofits in the District of Columbia are eligible to apply.

Restrictions: No support for individuals and private foundations.

Geographic Focus: District of Columbia

Amount of Grant: 5,000 - 225,000 USD

Samples: Capital Hospice, Falls Church, VA, $75,000—for Patient Care program; Wesley Theological Seminary, Washington, DC, $125,000—for urban ministry program; Wolf Trap Foundation for the Performing Arts, Vienna, VA, $225,000—for Institute for Early Learning, Opera at Wolf Trap, Fund for Artistic Initiative.

Contact: Vincent Burke, President; (301) 654-3607

Sponsor: Clark-Winchcole Foundation

3 Bethesda Metro Center, Suite 550

Bethesda, MD 20814-5358

Clark and Carolyn Adams Foundation Grants 452

Established in 1998, the Clark and Carolyn Adams Foundation offers support primarily in Florida for education, human services, and religious groups. A formal application is required, though the initial approach should be in the form of a letter offering a detailed description of the proposed project and funding requested. Most recently, grants have ranged from $1,000 to $10,000, and comes in the form of general operating support. The annual deadline is June 30.

Geographic Focus: Florida

Amount of Grant: 1,000 - 10,000 USD

Samples: Carrollwood Day Care, Tampa, Florida, $1,000 - general operating support; Crisis Center of Tampa Bay, Tampa, Florida, $10,000 - general operating support; Ransom Everglades School, Coconut Grove, Florida, $10,000 - general operating support.

Contact: John Clark Adams, Trustee; (305) 448-9022

Sponsor: Clark and Carolyn Adams Foundation

540 Biltmore Way

Coral Gables, FL 33134

Clark and Ruby Baker Foundation Grants 453

The Clark and Ruby Baker Foundation was established to address a number of charitable concerns. The Baker family cared deeply about the Methodist Church and founded the Foundation to support Methodist affiliated, higher educational institutions in rural or small towns; charitable organizations that serve infirm, deserving, and aged ministers; economically disadvantaged and deserving children; and orphans and orphanages. The Foundation also provides support to charitable organizations that extend financial aid to the sick and infirm receiving medical treatment in any hospital or clinic in the state of Georgia. Capital support may be considered for the following purposes: for construction of educational facilities at a college or university; for clinics and

hospitals; for libraries; and for any building with a charitable use. Grants from the Clark and Ruby Baker Foundation are primarily one year in duration; on occasion, multi-year support is awarded. Applicants must apply online at the grant website. Applicants are strongly encouraged to do the following before applying: review the downloadable state application procedures for additional helpful information and clarifications; review the downloadable online-application guidelines at the grant website; review the foundation's funding history (link is available from the grant website); review the online application questions in advance; and review the list of required attachments. These will generally include: a list of board members, financial statements (audited, reviewed, or compiled by independent auditor); an organization summary; a list of other funding sources; an IRS Determination letter; and other required documents. All attachments must be uploaded in the online application as PDF, Word, or Excel files. The Clark and Ruby Baker Foundation application deadline is 11:59 p.m. on June 1. Applicants will be notified of grant decisions by letter within one to two months after the deadline.

Requirements: Applicants must have 501(c)3 tax-exempt status.

Restrictions: The foundation does not support requests from individuals, organizations attempting to influence policy through direct lobbying, or any political campaigns.

Geographic Focus: Georgia

Date(s) Application is Due: Jun 1

Contact: Mark S. Drake; (404) 264-1377; mark.s.drake@ustrust.com

Internet: https://www.bankofamerica.com/philanthropic/fn_search.action

Sponsor: Clark and Ruby Baker Foundation

3414 Peachtree Road, N.E., Suite 1475, GA7-813-14-04

Atlanta, GA 30326-1113

Clark Charitable Foundation Grants 454

The foundation awards operating grants to nonprofit organizations in the District of Columbia and Maryland in its areas of interest, including arts, community funds, higher education, support also for health and hospitals, and social services.

Geographic Focus: District of Columbia, Maryland

Date(s) Application is Due: Mar 1; Sep 1

Amount of Grant: 5,000 - 50,000 USD

Contact: Courtney Clark Pastrick, Secretary; (301) 657-7166

Sponsor: Clark Charitable Foundation

7500 Old Georgetown Road, 15th Floor

Bethesda, MD 20814

Clark Charitable Trust Grants 455

The Clark Charitable Trust awards grants to nonprofit organizations in its areas of interest, including basic human needs, environmental conservation and preservation, animal welfare, music, and higher education. Types of support include general operating support, annual campaigns, capital campaigns, building construction and renovation, equipment acquisition, endowment funds, scholarship funds, and matching funds. There are no application forms or deadlines specified. Submit a letter describing the project's purpose, an audited financial statement, and amount requested. Typical funding amounts have recently ranged from $1,000 to $10,000.

Requirements: Nonprofit organization are eligible.

Geographic Focus: All States

Amount of Grant: 1,000 - 10,000 USD

Samples: Babson College, Wellesley, Massachusetts, $10,000 - general operating support; Hiwassee College, Madisonville, Tennessee, $10,000 - general operating support; Last Chance Corral, Athens, Ohio, $4,000 - general operating support.

Contact: Timothy Taylor, Trustee; (781) 259-8800

Sponsor: Clark Charitable Trust

P.O. Box 681

Lincoln, MA 01773-8800

Clark Foundation Grants 456

The foundation awards grants in New York, NY, and upstate New York for charitable and educational purposes and in support of health care, youth, cultural, environmental, and community organizations. Types of support include general operating support, continuing support, annual campaigns, capital campaigns, building construction/renovation, equipment acquisition, program development, seed money, and scholarships to Cooperstown County residents.

Requirements: Nonprofits in upstate New York and New York City are eligible.

Geographic Focus: New York

Date(s) Application is Due: Jan 1; Apr 1; Jul 15; Oct 1

Amount of Grant: 20,000 - 200,000 USD
Samples: Harlem RBI (New York, NY)—for general operating support, $100,000; Partnership with Children (New York, NY)—for general support, $150,000.
Contact: Charles Hamilton, Executive Director; (212) 977-6900
Sponsor: Clark Foundation
1 Rockefeller Plaza, 31st Floor
New York, NY 10020

Claude A. and Blanche McCubbin Abbott Charitable Trust Grants   457

The Claude A. and Blanche McCubbin Abbott Charitable Trust offers grants primarily in the states of Florida and Maryland. Its identified fields of interest include Catholic agencies and churches, as well as human services. Awards typically come in the form of general operating funds. There are no specified application forms or annual deadlines, and interested parties should begin by contacting the Trust to discuss the program and needed budget support. Grant amounts have typically ranged from $100 to $2,000.
Geographic Focus: Florida, Maryland
Amount of Grant: 100 - 2,000 USD
Samples: Children's Cancer Foundation, Baltimore, Maryland, $1,000 - for general operations; Florida Studio Theatre, Sarasota, Florida, $500 - for general operations; Foundation for Baltimore County Public Library, Baltimore, Maryland, $500 - for general operations.
Contact: Christine Wells, Trustee; (410) 788-1890
Sponsor: Claude A. and Blanche McCubbin Abbott Charitable Trust
6400 Baltimore National Pike No. 105
Catonsville, MD 21228

Claude Worthington Benedum Foundation Grants   458

Grants are made in the areas of education, health and human services, community and economic development, environment, and the arts. Grants have been awarded to support education reform, teacher education, higher education, workforce development, rural health, professional developing in healthcare, human services, affordable housing, and economic development. Grants are awarded to organizations in West Virginia and southwestern Pennsylvania. Funds are provided for general operations for projects, sometimes including building and equipment, in West Virginia, and for projects in Pittsburgh that address regional problems and needs, that establish demonstration projects with strong potential for replication in West Virginia, or make outstanding contributions to the area. Additional types of support include matching funds, consulting services, technical assistance, capital campaigns, conferences and seminars, research, and seed grants. Organizations wishing to apply should request a copy of the annual report, which includes application guidelines. Applications may be submitted at any time; the board meets for review in March, June, September, and December.
Requirements: Southwestern Pennsylvania and West Virginia nonprofit organizations may apply.
Restrictions: Support is not given for national health and welfare campaigns, medical research, religious activities, fellowships, scholarships, annual campaigns, or travel.
Geographic Focus: Pennsylvania, West Virginia
Contact: Margaret M. Martin, Grants Administrator; (800) 223-5948 or (412) 246-3636; fax (412) 288-0366; mmartin@benedum.org
Internet: http://www.benedum.org/pages.cfm?id=10
Sponsor: Claude Worthington Benedum Foundation
1400 Benedum-Trees Building, 223 Fourth Avenue
Pittsburgh, PA 15222

Clayton Baker Trust Grants   459

The trust awards grants to Maryland nonprofit organizations for programs targeting the disadvantaged, with an emphasis on the needs of children. Grants are awarded nationally in the areas of environmental protection, population control, arms control, and nuclear disarmament. Types of support include general operating support, seed grants, and special projects.
Requirements: Nonprofit organizations in Maryland are eligible to apply.
Restrictions: Grants do not support the arts, research, higher educational institutions, individuals, building construction/renovation, or endowment funding.
Geographic Focus: Maryland
Date(s) Application is Due: Apr 5; Aug 5; Dec 5
Amount of Grant: 2,000 - 100,000 USD
Contact: John Powell, Jr.; (410) 837-3555; fax (410) 837-7711
Sponsor: Clayton Baker Trust
2 East Read Street, Suite 100
Baltimore, MD 21202

Cleveland-Cliffs Foundation Grants   460

Contributions are made to nonprofit organizations to enhance the quality of life of Cleveland-Cliffs Inc employees and in recognition of a corporate responsibility toward educational, health, welfare, civic, and cultural matters within the communities where the company operates. The foundation was formed for the purpose of making contributions to groups organized and operated exclusively for religious, charitable, scientific, literary, or educational purposes and for the prevention of cruelty to children or animals. Types of support include general operating support, annual campaigns, capital campaigns, building/renovation, professorships, scholarship funds, research, and employee matching gifts. The foundation's major emphasis is on supporting education through a matching gift program and direct contributions to educational institutions. Requests for support must be in writing.
Requirements: Nonprofit organizations in the mining communities in which Cleveland-Cliffs operates, including Alabama, Michigan, Minnesota, Ohio and, West Virginia are eligible.
Geographic Focus: Alabama, Michigan, Minnesota, Ohio, West Virginia
Amount of Grant: 250 - 50,000 USD
Samples: Bell Memorial Hospital, Ishpeming, MI, $400,000; University of Saint Thomas, Minneapolis, MN, $10,000; Michigan Tech Fund, Houghton, MI, $9,550.
Contact: Dana W. Byrne, Vice President; (216) 694-5700; fax (216) 694-4880; publicrelations@cleveland-cliffs.com
Internet: http://www.cliffsnaturalresources.com/Development/Community Relations/Pages/Cleveland-CliffsFoundation.aspx
Sponsor: Cleveland-Cliffs Foundation
1100 Superior Avenue, Suite 1500
Cleveland, OH 44114-2589

Clorox Company Foundation Grants   461

The Foundation makes grants primarily in its headquarters community of Oakland, California. Clorox manufacturing plants operate small giving programs in their local communities. These programs are administered independently and serve a three- to five-mile radius of the facility. The Foundation concentrates on two focus areas: education/youth development and culture/civic programs. The Foundation may shift funding priorities from year to year.
Requirements: Must be a 501(c)3 nonprofit located in Oakland, California.
Restrictions: In general, the Foundation does not fund the following: fund-raising events; athletic events or league sponsorships; field trips, tours and travel expenses; advertising or promotional sponsorships; benefit or raffle tickets; conferences, conventions, meetings; media productions; projects of a national scope; direct assistance to individuals or individual sponsorships; religious-based activities for the purpose of furthering religious doctrine; political parties, organizations, candidates or activities; exclusive membership organizations; association or membership dues; deficits or retroactive funding; capital projects; individual school projects.
Geographic Focus: California
Date(s) Application is Due: Jan 1; Apr 1; Jul 1; Oct 1
Contact: Victoria Jones; (510) 836-3223; cloroxfndt@eastbaycf.org
Internet: http://www.thecloroxcompany.com/community/guidelines.html
Sponsor: Clorox Company Foundation
De Domenico Building, 200 Frank Ogawa Plaza
Oakland, CA 94612

Clowes Fund Grants   462

Funding is concentrated in the states of Indiana, Washington, Massachusetts, and parts of northern New England. Program interest areas and priorities vary among the different geographic areas: Washington—the arts and art education in the greater Seattle area; Indiana—social services and education in greater Indianapolis (Marion County and the seven surrounding counties), education focus is on primary and secondary schools with an emphasis on classroom instruction; Massachusetts (greater Boston area)—arts, education, and social services. In the area of social services (applicable in Indiana, Massachusetts, and northern New England) the current priority is for projects or programs that address the needs of immigrant and refugee populations, and/or workforce development. Types of support include capacity building, capital, challenge, matching operating, project/program, and seed grants. Requests for funding are limited to one request per organization per calendar year. Organizations that have no prior or recent (within the past five years) grant relationship with the fund must submit a Preliminary Proposal to be considered for funding. Guidelines and application are available online.
Requirements: Nonprofit organizations in northern New England and the metropolitan Indianapolis, IN; Boston, MA; and metropolitan Seattle, WA, areas are eligible.

Restrictions: The fund does not make grants to individuals or for publications, conferences, videos, or seminars. No grants are made to organizations in foreign countries. No grants are made for programs promoting specific religious doctrine. The fund will not accept unsolicited proposals from any organization for operating support. The fund will not accept unsolicited proposals of any sort from colleges and universities.
Geographic Focus: Connecticut, Indiana, Maine, Massachusetts, New Hampshire, Rhode Island, Vermont, Washington
Date(s) Application is Due: Jan 31; Nov 1
Amount of Grant: 10,000 - 50,000 USD
Samples: Alternatives for Community & Environment, Roxbury, Massachusetts, $15,000; Indiana Latino Institute, Indianapolis, Indiana, $10,000; Girls Incorporated of Indianapolis, Indiana, $100,000.
Contact: Elizabeth Casselman, Program Manager; (800) 943-7209 or (317) 833-0144; fax (317) 833-0145; staff@clowesfund.org
Internet: http://www.clowesfund.org/index.asp?p=3
Sponsor: Clowes Fund
320 N Meridian, Suite 316
Indianapolis, IN 46204

CMA Foundation Grants 463
The foundation seeks to improve the quality of life for central Ohio residents through the promotion of wellness, prevention of disease, and delivery of services and research. The foundation will review funding requests for matching or challenge grants, multiyear commitments, and capital expenditures on a project-by-project basis. The foundation is the leading local source of funding for health care projects benefiting the local community. Application may be made online.
Requirements: Nonprofit organizations in central Ohio, including Franklin, Delaware, Fairfield, Licking, Madison, Pickaway, and Union Counties, are eligible.
Geographic Focus: Ohio
Samples: Children's Hunger Alliance (Columbus, OH)—to promote school-breakfast programs, $30,000; Educational Council Foundation (Columbus, OH)—to train middle- and high-school educators to provide information about positive health behaviors, $50,000 maximum; Franklin County Health Dept (Columbus, OH)—to expand its anti-tobacco activities, $30,000 maximum; Mount Carmel Health Systems Foundation (Columbus, OH)—to provide education, information, and self-care skills training to people who have experienced heart failure, $90,000.
Contact: Contact; (614) 240-7410; yourthoughts@goodhealthcolumbus.org
Internet: http://www.cmaf-ohio.org/cmaf/grants.html
Sponsor: Columbus Medical Association Foundation
431 E Broad Street
Columbus, OH 43215

CNA Foundation Grants 464
The CNA Foundation concentrates its support primarily in programs designed to: meet the education needs of children, assist and support children, youth and adults in developing vocational skills. Support economically disadvantaged children and families. Requests for funding are accepted year-round. However, grants will be made only in accordance with the Foundation's budgetary guidelines. Proposals must be clear and brief. The Foundation will contact the organization if more information is needed.
Requirements: IRS 501(c)3 tax-exempt organizations are eligible.
Restrictions: Grants are not made to/for individuals; political causes, candidates, or organizations; veterans, labor, alumni, military, athletic clubs, or social clubs; sectarian organizations or denominational religious organizations; capital improvement or building projects; endowed chairs or professorships; United Way-affiliated agencies; or national groups whose local chapters have already received support.
Geographic Focus: All States
Amount of Grant: 10,000 - 250,000 USD
Samples: Chicago 2016 Exploratory Committee, Chicago, IL, $250,000; National Chamber Foundation, Washington, DC, $100,000; Starlight Starbright Childrens Foundation Midwest, Chicago, IL, $50,000.
Contact: Marlene Rotstein, Director; (312) 822-7065; marlene.rotstein@cna.com or cna_foundation@cna.com
Internet: http://www.cna.com/portal/site/cna/menuitem.7204aaf0316757e8715f09f6556631a0/?vgnextoid= b1e940fa11056010VgnVCM1000005566130aRCRD
Sponsor: CNA Foundation
333 South Wabash Avenue
Chicago, IL 60604

CNCS Foster Grandparent Projects Grants 465
The Foster Grandparent Program (FGP) began in 1965 as a national demonstration effort to show how low-income persons aged sixty or over have the maturity and experience to establish a personal relationship with children having either exceptional or special needs. Originally established under the Economic Opportunity Act of 1964 the FGP was operated first as an employment program and eventually as a stipended volunteer program under various federal offices and agencies. Currently RSVP is administered through the Corporation for National and Community Service (the Corporation)'s Senior Corps program. Dual purposes of the RSVP are to provide part-time volunteer service opportunities for income-eligible persons ages fifty-five and over and to give supportive person-to-person assistance in health, education, human-services, and related settings to help address the physical, mental, and emotional needs of special/exceptional-needs infants, children, or youth. The Corporation accepts FGP grant applications only when new funding is available or when it is necessary to replace an existing sponsor. In addition, eligible agencies or organizations may, under a Memorandum of Agreement with the Corporation, receive technical assistance and materials to aid in establishing and operating a non-federally-funded FGP project using local funds. Notices for nationwide competitions for new FGP grants are posted at www.grants.gov and at the Corporation and Senior Corps websites. (Subscription links for receiving RSS feeds on new funding opportunities are also available at the websites.) Notices for applicants to replace a sponsor are advertised locally through Corporation State Offices. (A list of the offices along with their contact information is available at the Corporation website.) Grant applications are submitted through the Corporation's eGrants system. For more information, interested applicants may download the FGP Handbook from the Senior Corps and Corporation websites or contact their Corporation State Office.
Requirements: The Corporation awards grants to public agencies, Indian tribes, and secular or faith-based private non-profit organizations in the United States that have authority to accept and the capacity to administer a Foster Grandparent project. The FGP requires a non-federal share of 10% of the total project cost. FGP projects are generally expected and required to be on-going. FGP sponsors may apply for continued funding from the Corporation.
Restrictions: The total of cost reimbursements for Foster Grandparents, including stipends, insurance, transportation, meals, physical examinations, uniforms if appropriate, and recognition must be equal to at least 80 percent of the Corporation's Federal share of the grant. (Federal and non-Federal resources, including excess non-Corporation resources, can be used to make up this sum.) Key legislative pieces regulating and enabling the FGP have been the Economic Opportunity Act of 1964, Title Six of the Older Americans Act (1969), the Domestic Volunteer Service Act (DVSA) of 1973, the National and Community Service Trust Act (1993), 45 C.F.R. § 1216 (non-displacement of contracts and employed workers), the Edward Kennedy Serve America Act, and 45 C.F.R. § 2551. FGP funding generally requires an Office of Management and Budget (OMB) audit.
Geographic Focus: All States
Amount of Grant: 250,000 USD
Contact: Wanda Carney; (202) 606-6934 or (202) 606-5000
Dr. Erwin Tan, Director of Senior Corps; (202) 606-6867
Internet: http://www.nationalservice.gov/build-your-capacity/grants/managing-senior-corps-grants
Sponsor: Corporation for National and Community Service
1201 New York Avenue, NW
Washington, D.C. 20525

CNCS Senior Companion Program Grants 466
The Senior Companions Program (SCP) was established in 1973 under Title II of the Domestic Volunteer Services Act (DVSA) to provide opportunities for older adult volunteers to assist other older adults and persons with disabilities, who, without support, might not be able to live independently. Eighteen model Senior Companion projects were funded initially. Today that number has grown to 223 projects with more than 15,000 volunteers who serve through nonprofit and public organizations (local sponsors) to help home-bound clients with chores such as light housekeeping, paying bills, buying groceries, and finding transportation to medical appointments. SCP volunteers serve from fifteen to forty hours a week and receive hourly stipends. They must be fifty-five or older and meet established income eligibility guidelines. In addition to the stipend, they receive accident, personal-liability, and excess-automobile insurance coverage; assistance with the cost of transportation; an annual physical examination; recognition; and, as feasible, meals during their assignments. Volunteers receive training in how to assist persons diagnosed with Alzheimer's disease, stroke, diabetes, mental illness, etc., as well as when

to alert doctors and family members to potential health problems. Currently SCP is administered through the Corporation for National and Community Service (the Corporation)'s Senior Corps Program. The Corporation accepts SCP grant applications only when new funding is available or when it is necessary to replace an existing sponsor. In addition, eligible agencies or organizations may, under a Memorandum of Agreement with the Corporation, receive technical assistance and materials to aid in establishing and operating a non-federally-funded SCP project using local funds. Notices for nationwide competitions for new SCP grants are posted at www.grants.gov and at the Corporation and Senior Corps websites. (Subscription links for receiving RSS feeds on new funding opportunities are also available at the websites.) Notices to apply to replace a sponsor are advertised locally through Corporation State Offices. (A list of the offices along with their contact information is available at the Corporation website.) Grant applications are submitted through the Corporation's eGrants system. For more information, interested applicants may download the SCP Handbook from the Senior Corps and Corporation websites or contact their Corporation State Office.

Requirements: The Corporation awards grants to public agencies, Indian tribes, and secular or faith-based private non-profit organizations in the United States that have authority to accept and the capacity to administer an SCP project. The SCP requires a non-federal share of 10% of the total project cost. SCP projects are generally expected and required to be on-going. SCP Sponsors may apply for continued funding from the Corporation.

Restrictions: The total of cost reimbursements for Senior Companions, including stipends, insurance, transportation, meals, physical examinations, uniforms if appropriate, and recognition must be equal to at least 80 percent of the Corporation's Federal share of the grant. (Federal and non-Federal resources, including excess non-Corporation resources, can be used to make up this sum.) Key legislative pieces enabling and regulating the SCP have been the Domestic Volunteer Service Act (DVSA) of 1973, the National and Community Service Trust Act (1993), 45 C.F.R. § 1216 (non-displacement of contracts and employed workers), the Edward Kennedy Serve America Act, and 45 C.F.R. § 2551. SCP funding generally requires an Office of Management and Budget (OMB) audit.

Geographic Focus: All States
Amount of Grant: 100,000 - 300,000 USD
Contact: Wanda Carney, ; (202) 606-6934 or (202) 606-5000
Dr. Erwin Tan, Director of Senior Corps; (202) 606-6867
Internet: http://www.nationalservice.gov/build-your-capacity/grants/managing-senior-corps-grants
Sponsor: Corporation for National and Community Service
1201 New York Avenue, NW
Washington, D.C. 20525

CNCS Senior Corps Retired and Senior Volunteer Program Grants   467
The Retired and Senior Volunteer Program (RSVP), one of the largest volunteer efforts in the nation, has matched local problems with older adults who are willing to help since 1971. Each year nearly 430,000 older adults (ages fifty-five and over) provide community service through more than 740 locally-sponsored RSVP projects. RSVP volunteers serve through nonprofit and public organizations (local sponsors) to organize neighborhood watch programs, tutor children and teenagers, renovate homes, teach English to immigrants, teach computer software applications, help people recover from natural disasters, serve as museum docents—and do whatever else their skills and interests lead them to do to meet the needs of their community. While RSVP volunteers do not receive any monetary incentive or stipend, they may be reimbursed for certain out-of-pocket costs associated with their service activities. In addition, RSVP volunteers receive accident, personal-liability, and excess-automobile insurance, as well as community recognition. Currently RSVP is administered through the Corporation for National and Community Service (the Corporation)'s Senior Corps program. The Corporation solicits applications for new Senior Corps grants (new projects or new sponsors) only when funding is available. The Corporation will notify the public when new grants are being accepted by posting Notices of Funding Availability (NOFA) or Notices of Funding Opportunity (NOFO) at the Senior Corps and Corporation websites and at www.grants.gov. (Subscription links for receiving RSS feeds on new funding opportunities are also available at these websites.) The application process for an RSVP grant begins with submission of a concept paper which will be used to select applicants who will then be invited to submit a full application. Applicants apply through the Corporation's online eGrants system, the link to which is available at the website. Use of eGrants requires setting up an account; the Corporation strongly recommends that applicants create their accounts at least three weeks prior to the submission deadline.

Concept papers and full applications must be received by the Corporation by 5:00 p.m. (eastern standard time) on the applicable deadline in order to be considered. (Exceptions may apply under special circumstances; documentation is required.) Deadline dates may vary from funding opportunity to funding opportunity; organizations are encouraged to always verify current deadline dates. For more information, interested applicants may download the RSVP Handbook from the Corporation and Senior Corps websites or contact their Corporation State Office (a list of the state offices along with their contact information is available at the Corporation website).

Requirements: Eligible applicants include public agencies (e.g. state and local agencies and other units of government), non-profit organizations (both faith-based and secular), institutions of higher education, and Indian Tribes. New applicants may propose only to establish a new RSVP project in a geographic area unserved by a current RSVP grantee. Matching is required as follows: new RSVP applicants must budget and raise ten percent of their total project budget in year one, twenty percent in year two, and thirty percent in year three and subsequent years (if the grant is renewed beyond three years). All applications must include a Dun and Bradstreet Data Universal Numbering System (DUNS) number. The DUNS number does not replace the Employer Identification Number. DUNS numbers may be obtained at no cost by calling the DUNS number request line at (866) 705-5711 or by applying online. Either way, the Corporation suggests registering at least 30 days in advance of the application due date. Key programmatic requirements to consider are as follows. At a minimum, 20 percent of a sponsor's or project's RSVP volunteers must be placed in assignments to recruit other community volunteers, thus expanding the capacity of local non-profits to meet their missions. Additionally, all RSVP volunteers must be placed in assignments that address one or more of the 16 categories of community needs identified in the Domestic Volunteer Service Act as "Programs of National Significance (PNS)." In particular the Corporation is interested in supporting the following volunteer activities: providing in-home, non-medical independent-living support to those in need of extra help, including frail seniors, veterans of recent conflicts, and their caregivers; assisting children and youth to succeed academically through provision of mentoring, tutoring, and other assistance to remain in school; and enhancing energy efficiency at home through weatherization of homes, energy audits, or connecting people to related resources and information.

Restrictions: Key legislative pieces regulating and enabling the RSVP have been the Economic Opportunity Act of 1964, Title Six of the Older Americans Act (1969), the Domestic Volunteer Service Act (DVSA) of 1973, the National and Community Service Trust Act (1993), 45 C.F.R. § 1216 (non-displacement of contracts and employed workers), the Edward Kennedy Serve America Act, and 45 C.F.R. § 2551. FGP funding generally requires an Office of Management and Budget (OMB) audit.

Geographic Focus: All States
Date(s) Application is Due: Feb 22
Amount of Grant: 60,000 - 80,000 USD
Contact: Dr. Erwin Tan; (202) 606-6867 or (800) 424-8867; PNS@cns.gov
Vielka Garibaldi, Director for Grant Review Operations; (202) 606-6886
Internet: http://www.nationalservice.gov/build-your-capacity/grants/managing-senior-corps-grants
Sponsor: Corporation for National and Community Service
1201 New York Avenue, NW
Washington, D.C. 20525

Coastal Bend Community Foundation Grants   468
The community foundation awards grants to nonprofit organizations in the Aransas, Bee, Jim Wells, Kleberg, Nueces, Refugio and San Patricio counties of Texas. Grants are usually made to provide seed money for innovative and start-up programs that will generate additional future funding or revenues. Capital projects will also receive favorable consideration. The board of directors approves grant recipients in early November after considering recommendations presented by the Grants Committee. Areas of interest include alcohol and drug abuse, libraries and literacy, arts and culture, higher and other education, adult basic education, child welfare, hospitals, community development, animal welfare, human services, and general charitable giving. Grants are awarded for general operating support, program and project development, equipment, seed money, scholarship funds, and fellowships. Application forms are not required.

Requirements: Nonprofit organizations in Texas in Aransas, Bee, Jim Wells, Kleberg, Nueces, Refugio, and San Patricio counties, may submit grant proposals.
Geographic Focus: Texas
Date(s) Application is Due: Sep 1
Amount of Grant: 250 - 50,000 USD

Contact: Jim Moloney, Executive Vice President; (361) 882-9745; fax (361) 882-2865; jmoloney@cbcfoundation.org
Internet: http://www.cbcfoundation.org/grant.html
Sponsor: Coastal Bend Community Foundation
600 Building, Suite 1716
Corpus Christi, TX 78473

Coastal Community Foundation of South Carolina Grants 469

The foundation awards grants to South Carolina nonprofit organizations in its areas of interest, including arts and culture, education, environment, health, religion, justice and equity, and social services. Types of support include general operating support, emergency funds, program development, publication, seed money, scholarship funds, and technical assistance. Deadlines vary per program; check website for exact dates.
Requirements: 501(c)3 South Carolina nonprofits located in the following coastal counties are eligible to apply: Beaufort, Berkeley, Charleston, Colleton, Dorchester, Georgetown, Hampton and Jasper.
Restrictions: Grants do not support individuals (except for designated scholarship funds), endowments, deficit financing, dinners, and rarely building funds.
Geographic Focus: South Carolina
Date(s) Application is Due: Jun 1
Amount of Grant: 500 - 10,000 USD
Samples: To each, a $15,000 annual grant for 3 years: Boys & Girls Clubs for Rural Units; Child Abuse Prevention Association; Citizens Opposed to Domestic Abuse; Colleton County Arts Council; Friends of Caroline Hospice; Hope Haven of the Lowcountry (formerly Hope Cottage); Literacy Volunteers of the Lowcountry; Lowcountry Food Bank; Second Helpings;.
Contact: George C. Stevens, President-CEO; (843) 723-3635; fax (843) 577-3671; gstevens@tcfgives.org or info@ccfgives.org
Internet: http://www.ccfgives.org
Sponsor: Coastal Community Foundation of South Carolina
90 Mary Street
Charleston, SC 29403

Cobb Family Foundation Grants 470

The foundation awards grants to Florida nonprofits in its areas of interest, including community development, higher and secondary education, libraries, Protestant religion, recreation, and zoos. Grants are awarded primarily in Dade County.
Requirements: Nonprofit organizations in Florida are eligible to apply.
Geographic Focus: Florida
Amount of Grant: Up to 525,319 USD
Contact: Charles Cobb Jr., (305) 441-1700; fax (305) 445-5674
Sponsor: Cobb Family Foundation
355 Alhambra Circle, Suite 1500
Coral Gables, FL 33134

Coca-Cola Foundation Grants 471

The foundation has established education as its philanthropic focus and set aside most of its funds to support educational initiatives that address pressing needs. To help prepare youth for life, the foundation gives in three areas: higher education—pipeline programs that connect various levels of education and help students stay in school, scholarships, and minority advancement; classroom teaching and learning—innovative K-12 projects, teacher development, and small projects that deal with classroom activities; and global education—projects that encourage international studies, global understanding, and student exchange. Grants are awarded to both public and private institutions at all levels of education: universities, colleges, and secondary and elementary schools. International educational institutions and health care organizations also receive consideration. Types of support include annual campaigns, donated equipment, employee matching gifts, operating budgets, special projects, capital campaigns, continuing support, fellowships, internships, endowment funds, matching funds, and scholarship funds. Proposals may be submitted at any time.
Requirements: The following are eligible to apply: IRS 501(c)3 non-profits; a foreign organization that has received a ruling from the IRS that it is a section 501(c)3 tax exempt organization; or a foreign organization that is the equivalent of a U.S. charity.
Restrictions: The foundation does not make grants to individuals, religious endeavors, political or fraternal organizations, or organizations without 501(c)3 status.
Geographic Focus: All States
Amount of Grant: 10,000 - 6,000,000 USD

Samples: Holyfield Foundation, Inc., Fairburn, GA, $75,000—contribution to the Giving Disadvantaged Youth a Fighting Chance scholarship program; United Way of Metropolitan Atlanta, Atlanta, GA, $15,000—support for Samaritan House, Impact Group and Atlanta Union Mission; Atlanta Children's Shelter, Inc., Atlanta, GA, $10,000—contribution to support shelter programs.
Contact: Helen Smith Price; (404) 676-2568; fax (404) 676-8804
Internet: http://www.thecoca-colacompany.com/citizenship/our_communities.html
Sponsor: Coca-Cola Foundation
P.O. Box 1734
Atlanta, GA 30301

Coeta and Donald Barker Foundation Grants 472

The foundation awards grants to California and Oregon nonprofit organizations in its areas of interest, including arts, children and youth, community development, disabled, environmental conservation, family services, federated giving, health care and health organizations, heart and circulatory research, higher education, hospitals, mental health, and secondary school education. Types of support include building construction/renovation, equipment acquisition, general operating support, program development, and scholarship funds.
Requirements: California and Oregon nonprofit organizations are eligible.
Restrictions: Grants do not support sectarian religious purposes, federal and tax-dependent organizations, individuals, or endowment funds.
Geographic Focus: California, Oregon
Date(s) Application is Due: Mar 1; Aug 1
Amount of Grant: 100 - 20,450 USD
Samples: Santa Barbara Zoological Gardens (Santa Barbara, CA), $5000.
Contact: Nancy Harris; (760) 324-2656; fax (760) 321-8662
Sponsor: Coeta and Donald Barker Foundation
P.O. Box 936
Rancho Mirage, CA 92270

Colgate-Palmolive Company Grants 473

Nonprofit organizations with IRS tax-exempt status located primarily in the U.S. tristate area of New York, New Jersey, and Connecticut and in locations of foreign subsidiaries may apply for support of programs that are directed toward youth, women, minorities, education, health and welfare, culture and arts, and civic and community activities. Priority will be given to programs that address the educational needs of youth and minorities. Types of support include program grants, scholarships, general support grants, multiyear support, and employee matching gifts. Proposals are accepted at any time and should include information on the organization, purpose of request, proof of tax-exempt status, and current operating budget.
Geographic Focus: All States
Samples: American Public Health Assoc (Washington, DC)—for program support, $1 million over five years; Boys and Girls Club of Milwaukee (Milwaukee, WI)—to implement a youth credit union run by and for members, $1000; Star Seekers 4-H Club (Bartlett, IL)—to form a sister club for residents of a learning center for disabled children, $1000.
Contact: Sally Phills, Contributions Administrator; (212) 310-2000; fax (212) 310-2873; sally_phipps@colpal.com
Internet: http://www.colgate.com/app/Colgate/US/Corp/Community Programs/HomePage.cvsp
Sponsor: Colgate-Palmolive Company
300 Park Avenue
New York, NY 10022

Colin Higgins Foundation Grants 474

The foundation supports organizations that help people respond to a variety of life challenges, with a focus on responding to the AIDS pandemic by supporting innovative programs in the areas of education, service, and advocacy for people infected, affected, and at risk for HIV; and empowering lesbian, gay, bisexual, and transgender peoples by supporting community-based organizations that combat homophobia and foster leadership. The foundation is particularly interested in organizations that have a significant impact working in underserved, rural areas with traditionally underserved constituencies. The process of applying consists of two stages: submission of a letter of inquiry, and, if requested, a full proposal.
Requirements: The foundation only considers organizations with overall budgets under $2 million, or project budgets under $500,000.
Restrictions: Grants do not support projects that had previously fallen within its funding priorities, including any organizations or programs based in urban areas (population over 1 million); film and video projects; or organizations with overall budgets of over $2 million, or project budgets over $500,000. The one

exception to the exclusion of programs in urban areas is those organizations and projects working with underserved communities (i.e., communities of color, low-income communities, transgender people, etc.). The foundation does not accept letters of inquiry from universities, schools, individuals, or corporations. It does not support political or legislative activities, endowments, or deficit budgets. Additionally, the foundation does not support capital campaigns, although it will consider requests for capital improvements, and does not award grants to organizations outside the United States.
Geographic Focus: All States
Date(s) Application is Due: Jul 1
Amount of Grant: 5,000 - 15,000 USD
Samples: Iowa Pride Network, Des Moines, IA, $10,000—general support; Out Youth, Austin, TX, $15,000—Texas Gay-Straight Alliance Network; Equality Florida, St. Petersburg, FL, $15,000—Youth Voices for Equality.
Contact: Grants Administrator; (212) 509-4975; fax (212) 509-1059; info@ colinhiggins.org
Internet: http://www.colinhiggins.org/grantmaking/index.cfm
Sponsor: Colin Higgins Foundation
55 Exchange Place, Suite 402
New York, NY 10005

Collins C. Diboll Private Foundation Grants   475
The Collins C. Diboll Private Foundation awards grants to Louisiana nonprofit organizations in the areas of higher education, human services, and youth programs. The Foundation's primary field of interest include: Catholic churches and agencies; education; higher education; human services; art museums; and protestant agencies and churches. Types of support include: building construction and renovation; capital campaigns; endowment funds; and general operating support. Typical grants range from $500 up to a maximum of $200,000. There are no identified annual deadlines for submission, though a formal application is required. Applicants should also submit a detailed description of the project and the amount of funding requested, along with a copy of an IRS determination letter.
Requirements: Louisiana nonprofit organizations are eligible.
Restrictions: Individuals are not eligible to apply.
Geographic Focus: Louisiana
Amount of Grant: 500 - 200,000 USD
Samples: Tulane University, Center for Infectious Diseases, New Orleans, Louisiana, $100,000 - for research purposes; National World War II Museum, New Orleans, Louisiana, $50,000 - in support of the China-Burma-India Display Gallary; New Orleans Botanical Garden Foundation, New Orleans, Louisiana, $125,000 - rennovations for the CT Parker Building and the City Park.
Contact: Donald W. Diboll, Chairperson; (504) 582-8103 or (504) 582-8250
Sponsor: Collins C. Diboll Private Foundation
201 Saint Charles Avenue, 50th Floor
New Orleans, LA 70170-5100

Collins Foundation Grants   476
The Collins Foundation is an independent, private foundation that was created in 1947 by Truman W. Collins, Sr., and other members of the Collins family. The Foundation exists to improve, enrich, and give greater expression to humanitarian endeavors in the state of Oregon, and to assist in improving the quality of life in the state. As a general-purpose, responsive grant maker, the Foundation serves people in urban and rural communities across Oregon through its grants to nonprofit organizations working for the common good. The Foundation's broad areas of interest include: arts and humanities; children and youth; community welfare; education; the environment; health and science; and religion. Most recent awards have ranged from as little as $3,000 to a maximum of $400,000. There are no identified annual submission deadlines for applications.
Requirements: Grants are made to 501(c)3 nonprofit agencies domiciled in Oregon. The proposed project must directly benefit the citizens of Oregon.
Restrictions: Grants are not made to individuals or to organizations sponsoring requests intended to be used by or for the benefit of an individual. Grants normally are not made to elementary, secondary, or public higher education institutions; or to individual religious congregations. Grants normally are not made for development office personnel, annual fundraising activities, endowments, operational deficits, financial emergencies, or debt retirement. The Foundation will consider only one grant request from the same organization in a twelve month period, unless an additional request is invited by the Foundation.
Geographic Focus: Oregon
Amount of Grant: 3,000 - 400,000 USD

Samples: Artists Repertory Theatre, Portland, Oregon, $150,000 - support a season of plays, and reconfigure production areas and increase staffing to accommodate resident arts organizations (2014); Children's Center of Clackamas County, Oregon City, Oregon, $25,000 - to enhance follow-up support services for children who have been abused and their non-offending family members in Clackamas County (2014); Albina Opportunities Corporation, Portland, Oregon, $100,000 - to expand advisory and loan services to underserved women- and minority-owned small businesses in low- to moderate-income areas in Portland (2014).
Contact: Cynthia G. Addams, Executive Vice President; (503) 227-7171; fax (503) 295-3794; information@collinsfoundation.org
Internet: http://www.collinsfoundation.org/submission-guidelines
Sponsor: Collins Foundation
1618 South West First Avenue, Suite 505
Portland, OR 97201

Colonel Stanley R. McNeil Foundation Grants   477
Colonel Stanley R. McNeil and his wife Merna created the Colonel Stanley R. McNeil Foundation in 1993 to support and promote quality educational, human-services, and health-care programming for underserved populations. Special consideration is given to charitable organizations that serve the needs of children. During their lifetimes, the McNeils were actively involved in their local church and community. Colonel McNeil also served on a number of boards, including Lake Bluff Children's Home and Ravenswood Hospital. Although the McNeils had no children, they were strong supporters of children's causes. The foundation is particularly interested in funding programs or organizations that focus on children's causes, start-up initiatives within the human-services or arts and culture arenas, and healthcare. To better support the capacity of nonprofit organizations, multi-year funding requests are considered. Grant requests for naming opportunities that honor the donors are strongly encouraged. Applicants must apply online at the grant website. Applicants are strongly encouraged to do the following before applying: review the downloadable state application procedures for additional helpful information and clarifications; review the downloadable online-application guidelines at the grant website; review the foundation's funding history (link is available from the grant website); review the online application questions in advance; and review the list of required attachments. These will generally include: a list of board members, financial statements (audited, reviewed, or compiled by independent auditor); an organization summary; a list of other funding sources; an IRS Determination letter; and other required documents. All attachments must be uploaded in the online application as PDF, Word, or Excel files. The Colonel Stanley R. McNeil Foundation has biannual deadlines of February 1 and June 1. Applicants for the February deadline will be notified of grant decisions by June 30, and applicants for the June deadline will be notified by November 30. Typical awards have ranged from $25,000 to $50,000.
Requirements: Illinois nonprofit organizations serving the Chicago metropolitan area are eligible.
Restrictions: Because requests for support usually exceed available resources, organizations can only apply to either the Lang Burk Fund or the Colonel Stanley McNeil Foundation in the same calendar year. Grant requests to both foundations during the same calendar year will no longer be accepted. The Foundation will consider requests for general operations only if the organization's operating budget is less than $1 million. In general, grant request for individuals, endowment campaigns or capital projects will not be considered.
Geographic Focus: Illinois
Date(s) Application is Due: Feb 1; Jun 1
Amount of Grant: 25,000 - 50,000 USD
Contact: Srilatha Lakkaraju, Philanthropic Relationship Manager; (312) 828-8166; ilgrantmaking@ustrust.com
Internet: https://www.bankofamerica.com/philanthropic/fn_search.action
Sponsor: Colonel Stanley R. McNeil Foundation
231 South LaSalle Street, IL1-231-13-32
Chicago, IL 60604

Colorado Council on the Arts Colorado Creates Grants   478
The purpose of Colorado Creates, the Council's largest grant program, is to provide critical financial support that helps nonprofit cultural organizations and communities produce and present arts and cultural activities, bring jobs to their communities, and enhance the quality of life. Colorado Creates stimulates creativity and supports art and cultural activities statewide by providing: access to grants that leverage other funds and provide a seal of excellence; support for existing arts and cultural events and venues and arts education activities; support in as many communities as possible; a more

streamlined and standardized grant application; and access to general operating support. Colorado Creates awards are given once a year on a competitive basis. Proposals are reviewed by panels based on three review criteria: artistic excellence and merit of proposed activities; community involvement and benefit from proposed activities; implementation capacity, such as effective planning, management, and budgeting of the organization and the project. The application is available at the Council website.

Requirements: Grant applicants must be Colorado nonprofit organizations, departments of Colorado public colleges or universities, or government agencies. Applicants must have been providing public arts or cultural heritage programs in Colorado for at least three years by the application deadline. If awarded a grant, a nonprofit organization will be required to prove it is in good standing with the Colorado Secretary of State's office, including being current in annual corporate reports and charitable solicitation registration. Applicants are strongly encouraged to talk with a grant counselor at least three weeks before the deadline.

Restrictions: Applicants must not apply for one year if they have received funding through Grants to Artists and Organizations or Colorado Creates for three consecutive years. Department of public colleges or universities are not eligible for general operating support, but are eligible for project support. Funding is not available for the following: capital improvements, new construction, renovation or restoration; purchase of major equipment; debt and deficit reduction; out of state activities or travel outside the state of Colorado; social activities, entertainment costs, receptions, not directly associated with a cultural event; commercial (for-profit) enterprises or activities, although applicants are encouraged to involve appropriate businesses in the planning of their project; professional training or scholarships in degree-granting institutions or work toward academic degrees; research that is directed primarily to academic purposes or scholarly projects; fundraisers, benefits or prize money unrelated to the organization's mission; and art teacher positions in schools.

Geographic Focus: Colorado
Date(s) Application is Due: Jun 21
Contact: Elaine Mariner, Director; (800) 291-2787, ext. 12 or (303) 892-3802; fax (303) 892-3848
Internet: http://www.coloarts.state.co.us/default.asp
Sponsor: Colorado Council on the Arts
1625 Broadway, Suite 2700
Denver, CO 80202

Colorado Interstate Gas Grants   **479**
Nonprofits in communities served by the company are eligible to apply for grants in the categories of education, including early child development, K-12, and higher education; civic; health and welfare; minorities; cultural programs; environmental programs, particularly those focusing on air quality; and youth groups that concentrate on improving areas where CIG employees live and work. The company also supports special event sponsorships, corporate memberships, joint projects with other organizations, and employee participation in volunteer activities.

Requirements: Colorado, Wyoming, Texas, Utah, and Kansas 501(c)3 tax-exempt organizations where the company has pipelines are eligible.
Geographic Focus: Colorado
Date(s) Application is Due: Aug 1
Amount of Grant: 200 - 20,000 USD
Contact: Richard Wheatley, Media Relations; (713) 420-6828
Internet: http://www.cigco.com
Sponsor: Colorado Interstate Gas Company
P.O. Box 1087
Colorado Springs, CO 80944

Colorado Renewables in Performance Contracting Grants   **480**
The purpose of the program is to reduce the cost of incorporating renewable energy into a performance contract to the extent that the system fits within an acceptable payback period for the entire project. Additionally, this incentive is designed to promote renewable technology after, or in conjunction with, energy efficiency upgrades. The funding for this grant will be allocated on a first come, first serve basis and is a 100% matching grant.

Requirements: Organizations that are in the process of executing a performance contract, or have completed one within the last 5 years may be eligible to receive up to $25,000 in matching grant funds from the Governor's Energy Office (GEO) to add renewable energy technology to its facility. The organization's energy service company or a professional solar installer must complete the application and submit it electronically. The application form can be downloaded at the program website.

Geographic Focus: Colorado
Amount of Grant: Up to 25,000 USD
Contact: Sean Mandel, Development Manager; (303) 866-2407; fax (303) 866-2930; Sean.mandel@state.co.us
Internet: http://www.colorado.gov/energy/resources/funding-opportunities. asp#RenewPC
Sponsor: Colorado Governor's Energy Office
1580 Logan Street, Suite 100
Denver, CO 80203

Columbia Foundation Grants   **481**
The foundation currently has three program areas: arts and culture, human rights, and sustainable communities and economies. Types of support include general operating support, program development, publication, seed money, and research. Multiyear grants are made on occasion. A complete application includes application, one-page proposal summary, proposal not to exceed five pages, budgets, funding sources, board of directors, certificate of tax-exempt status, and other descriptive materials. The board of directors generally meets twice a year to consider grant applications. Applicants should submit a one- to two-page inquiry letter with cover sheet. Proposals are invited from the foundation. The deadline is May 1 for arts and culture grants; August 1 for human rights grants; and December 1 for sustainable communities and economies grants. Annual deadlines may vary; contact program staff for exact dates.

Requirements: The foundation considers proposals only from organizations certified by the IRS as public charities. Priority will be given to applications from the San Francisco Bay, CA, area. International grants support the arts in London.
Restrictions: The foundation does not customarily provide support for operating budgets of established agencies, recurring expenses for direct services or ongoing administrative costs, individual fellowships or scholarships, or agencies wholly supported by federated campaigns or heavily subsidized by government funds.
Geographic Focus: California, United Kingdom
Date(s) Application is Due: May 1; Aug 1; Dec 1
Amount of Grant: 25,000 - 100,000 USD
Samples: Royal National Theatre (London, England)—for the world premiere of The Talking Cure, a new play about Sigmund Freud and Carl Jung by leading UK playwright Christopher Hampton, $50,000; Gender Public Advocacy Coalition (Washington, DC)—to support its work to end gender-based stereotypes, discrimination and violence at the national level, $25,000; Ctr for Food Safety (Washington, DC)—for the California Food and Agriculture Initiative, to establish and staff a California office to focus on legal issues, policy initiatives, and a statewide public-education campaign about the opportunities for California to make the transition to sustainable food systems, $40,000.
Contact: Susan Clark; (415) 561-6880; fax (415) 561-6883; info@columbia.org
Internet: http://www.columbia.org
Sponsor: Columbia Foundation
P.O. Box 29470
San Francisco, CA 94129

Columbus Foundation Central Benefits Health Care Grants   **482**
The Foundation was established in 1997 with a focus on preventative health care for indigent children and adults; the Trustees have taken a step further by focusing grantmaking for the preventative health care needs of children, prenatal through age six. Proposals for funding are accepted at anytime. Funding is limited to the central Ohio area, giving primarily in Columbus, Ohio.

Requirements: Central Ohio, tax-exempt organizations are eligible to apply.
Restrictions: Individuals are ineligible.
Geographic Focus: Ohio
Contact: Tamera Durrence, Assistant Vice President and Director of Supporting Foundations; (614) 251-4000; fax (614) 251-4009; tdurrence@ columbusfoundation.org
Internet: http://www.columbusfoundation.org/find/support/cenben_usa.aspx
Sponsor: Columbus Foundation
1234 E Broad Street
Columbus, OH 43205

Columbus Foundation Community Arts Fund Grants   **483**
The Community Arts Fund (CAF) helps provide central Ohioans with a rich diversity of art and cultural activities by providing operating support to small and medium-sized arts organizations. These organizations make contributions to the ethnic and artistic diversity of the arts and increase access to the arts at a community level. To qualify, organizations must have annual budgets of less

than $350,000 and have been in existence for at least two years. A Letter of Intent (LOI) is required as the first step in the application process. The LOI will give an opportunity to provide an overview of the organization's mission and funding request. Timely feedback will be received about whether a request is competitive to move to full proposal submission. All LOIs and full proposals must be submitted using the online grantmaking process.
Requirements: Central Ohio, tax-exempt public charities under Section 501(c)3 of the Internal Revenue Service Code may submit grant requests.
Restrictions: Individuals are ineligible. Requests for religious purposes, budget deficits, endowments, conferences, scholarly research, or projects that are normally the responsibility of a public agency are generally not funded. Funding is not available for projects when funds are available elsewhere.
Geographic Focus: Ohio
Date(s) Application is Due: Nov 5
Samples: Worthington Arts Council—$10,302; Columbus Music and Arts Academy—$5,980; Little Theatre Off Broadway, Inc.—$6,121
Contact: Sandi Smith, Grants Management Officer; (614) 251-4000; fax (614) 251-4009; ssmith@columbusfoundation.org
Internet: http://www.columbusfoundation.org/gogrants/innovative_operations/arts_culture.aspx
Sponsor: Columbus Foundation
1234 E Broad Street
Columbus, OH 43205

Columbus Foundation Competitive Grants 484
The foundation's competitive grants are made in the following fields: advancing philanthropy, arts and humanities, conservation, education, health, social services, and urban affairs. The Governing Committee approves distributions from unrestricted and field of interest funds through competitive grants. Competitive grants are the most common way nonprofit organizations request funding from the Foundation. Submit a Letter of Intent or a Full Proposal by accessing our online grant application system.
Requirements: Central Ohio, tax-exempt public charities under Section 501(c)3 of the Internal Revenue Service Code may submit grant requests.
Restrictions: Individuals are ineligible. Requests for religious purposes, budget deficits, endowments, conferences, scholarly research, or projects that are normally the responsibility of a public agency are generally not funded. Funding is not available for projects when funds are available elsewhere.
Geographic Focus: Ohio
Contact: Emily Savors, Director; (614) 251-4000; fax (614) 251-4009; esavors@columbusfoundation.org
Internet: http://www.columbusfoundation.org/gogrants/index.aspx
Sponsor: Columbus Foundation
1234 E Broad Street
Columbus, OH 43205

Columbus Foundation Major Arts Organizations Grants 485
The Foundation accepts applications from regional Arts organizations with budgets at or above $350,000 per year. Criteria for awarding grants to major art organizations include the following: financial stability; attendance; inclusiveness; artistic quality; leadership; and overall administration. A Letter of Intent (LOI) is required as the first step in the application process. The LOI will give an opportunity to provide an overview of the organization's mission and funding request. Timely feedback will be received about whether a request is competitive to move to full proposal submission. All LOIs and full proposals must be submitted using the online grantmaking process. Organizations that have never received funding must contact Sandi Smith by email or at (614) 251-4000 prior to applying for arts funding. The deadline for arts proposals is the first Friday in November.
Requirements: Central Ohio, tax-exempt public charities under Section 501(c)3 of the Internal Revenue Service Code may submit grant requests.
Restrictions: Individuals are ineligible. Requests for religious purposes, budget deficits, endowments, conferences, scholarly research, or projects that are normally the responsibility of a public agency are generally not funded. Funding is not available for projects when funds are available elsewhere.
Geographic Focus: Ohio
Date(s) Application is Due: Nov 6
Contact: Sandi Smith, Grants Management Officer; (614) 251-4000; fax (614) 251-4009; ssmith@columbusfoundation.org
Internet: http://www.columbusfoundation.org/gogrants/innovative_operations/arts_culture.aspx
Sponsor: Columbus Foundation
1234 E Broad Street
Columbus, OH 43205

Columbus Foundation Traditional Grants 486
The Traditional Grants Program creates quality opportunities and meets community need by focusing on three areas: Basic Needs funds programs and projects that provide food, shelter, and clothing. Priority will be given to programs and projects that meet current needs and simultaneously integrate services designed to support long-term stability; Disadvantaged Children funds programs and projects that meet the diverse needs of at-risk children. Priority will be given to programs and projects that are in the home, build relationships with the family, and create a support network around and for the families of disadvantaged children; Developmental Disabilities funds programs and projects that address the needs of children and adults with physical or cognitive disabilities that impair functions or behavior and that occurred before a person reaches the age of 22. (Blindness/visual impairments and deafness/hearing impairments are not considered within this category.) If you are implementing your project in a Columbus City School building, or collaborating with the district on a project, and asked to submit a full application, you must request a letter of endorsement from the Office of Development.
Requirements: Central Ohio, tax-exempt public charities under Section 501(c)3 of the Internal Revenue Service Code may submit grant requests .If you are implementing your project in a Columbus City School building, or collaborating with the district on a project, and asked to submit a full application, you must request a letter of endorsement from the Office of Development. Letter of Intent deadlines are twice a year on the first Friday in February and September. See Foundations website for further guidelines.
Restrictions: Operating support will only be considered when the applicant demonstrates continuous innovation that enhances services.
Geographic Focus: Ohio
Date(s) Application is Due: Feb 5; Sep 3
Contact: Emily Savors, Director; (614) 251-4000; fax (614) 251-4009; esavors@columbusfoundation.org
Internet: http://www.columbusfoundation.org/gogrants/targeted_needs/traditional_grants.aspx
Sponsor: Columbus Foundation
1234 E Broad Street
Columbus, OH 43205

Comer Foundation Grants 487
The foundation awards grants to U.S. nonprofits in its areas of interest, including needle-exchange programs grounded in harm-reduction practice and programs providing direct services addressing health related to drug use; education—AIDS education, job training, and career guidance for low-income groups; health, with an emphasis on AIDS; social services—temporary shelters for homeless people and organizations offering diverse child, youth, and family services; and arts, culture, and humanities—to make programs of established organizations accessible to the public at large. Types of support include operating budgets, special projects, and staff development. There are no application deadlines.
Restrictions: Individuals are ineligible for grant support.
Geographic Focus: Illinois
Date(s) Application is Due: Mar 1; Jul 1; Nov 1
Amount of Grant: 5,000 - 30,000 USD
Contact: Stephanie Comer, (415) 256-9917; fax (415) 256-9918; scomer@comer-foundation.org
Internet: http://www.comer-foundation.com/home.html
Sponsor: Comer Foundation
P.O. Box 78154
San Francisco, CA 94107

Commission on Religion in Appalachia Grants 488
The commission supports Christian and interdenominational nonprofits in U.S. Appalachian regions. Churches and ministries and nonprofits in the areas of parochial education, religious welfare, civil rights, health care, and social services (domestic violence, housing, women's affairs, and food distribution) are awarded grants. The commission strongly encourages applicants to obtain guidelines prior to submitting proposals.
Requirements: Nonprofits in the Appalachian regions of Mississippi, Alabama, Georgia, South Carolina, North Carolina, Tennessee, Kentucky, Virginia, West Virginia, Ohio, Pennsylvania, Maryland, and New York are eligible.
Geographic Focus: Mississippi
Date(s) Application is Due: Jan 31
Amount of Grant: 5,000 - 15,000 USD
Contact: Grant Administrator; (304) 720-2672; fax (304) 720-2673; corainappa@aol.com

Internet: http://www.geocities.com/appalcora/About.html
Sponsor: Commission on Religion in Appalachia
P.O. Box 11908
Charleston, WV 25339-1908

Community Foundation for Greater Buffalo Grants 489

The Community Foundation for Greater Buffalo (CFGB) is a public charity holding more than 800 different charitable funds, large and small, established by individuals, families, nonprofit agencies and businesses to benefit Western New York. Since 1919, the foundation has served the needs of it's community and the wishes of it's donors through personalized service, financial stewardship, local expertise, and community leadership. The Foundation focuse's on four main areas of interest: strengthen the region as a center for arts and culture; natural, historic, and architectural resources; reduce racial and ethnic disparities; increase economic self-sufficiency for low-income individuals and families. Special funding will also be available to support the following: AIDS research and its cure ($5,000); programs that serve the visual, speech or hearing impaired ($5,000). Preference will be given to requests that align with one or more of the four focus areas.
Requirements: Applicants must be 501(c)3 not-for-profit organizations located within the eight counties of Western New York: Allegany, Cattaraugus, Chautauqua, Erie, Genesee, Niagara, Orleans, and Wyoming.
Restrictions: The Foundation will not consider competitive funding for: endowments; religious purposes; schools not registered with the New York State Education Department; attendance at or sponsorship of fundraising events for organizations; annual events or festivals; any partisan political activity. Funds from the foundation cannot be used to support or oppose a candidate for political office. Projects and activities that have occurred. The Foundation will not, except in extraordinary cases, provide payment or reimbursement for expenses incurred prior to the funding decision being communicated to the applicant.
Geographic Focus: New York
Date(s) Application is Due: Mar 1
Amount of Grant: 1,000 - 25,000 USD
Samples: Carnegie Art Center, $4,500—to support the continued restoration of the landmark Carnegie Art Center building; Grassroots Gardens, $25,000—to support new community gardens that provide beautification, food and employment; Youth Character Development, $9,100—to aid refugee students in the transition to formal education and encourage college enrollment.
Contact: Jean McKeown, Senior Program Officer; (716) 852-2857, ext. 204; fax (716) 852-2861; jeanm@cfgb.org
Internet: http://www.cfgb.org/page17000.cfm
Sponsor: Community Foundation for Greater Buffalo
712 Main Street
Buffalo, NY 14202

Community Foundation for Greater New Haven $5,000 and Under Grants 490

The Community Foundation for Greater New Haven (CFFGNH) is a philanthropic institution that was established in 1928. The foundation's mission is to create positive and sustainable change in Connecticut's Greater New Haven region by increasing the amount of and enhancing the impact of community philanthropy. Funding through the CFFGNH $5,000 and Under Grants process are available to any organization with an operating budget of $2 million or less.
Requirements: IRS 501(c)3 nonprofit organizations are eligible to apply in the greater New Haven area, which includes: Ansonia; Bethany; Branford; Cheshire; Derby; East Haven; Guilford; Hamden; Madison; Milford; New Haven; North Branford; North Haven; Orange; Oxford; Seymour; Shelton; Wallingford; West Haven and; Woodbridge.
Restrictions: No organization shall be eligible to receive a grant under this process more often than once in any period of two calendar years. Grants are not made to support religious activities, lobbying, or travel.
Geographic Focus: Connecticut
Amount of Grant: 5,000 USD
Contact: Denise Canning, Grants Manager; (203) 777-2386 or (203) 777-7076; fax (203) 787-6584; dcanning@cfgnh.org
Internet: http://www.cfgnh.org/GrantsScholarships/TypesofGrants/tabid/199/Default.aspx
Sponsor: Community Foundation for Greater New Haven
70 Audubon Street
New Haven, CT 06510

Community Foundation for Greater New Haven Responsive New Grants 491

The Community Foundation for Greater New Haven is a philanthropic institution that was established in 1928. The foundation's mission is to create positive and sustainable change in Connecticut's Greater New Haven region by increasing the amount of and enhancing the impact of community philanthropy. The Responsive New Grants Program is generally awarded to address an agency's general operating, programmatic, capital or technical assistance needs. This funding source is open to all requests for projects and organizational support.
Requirements: IRS 501(c)3 nonprofit organizations are eligible to apply in the greater New Haven area, which includes: Ansonia; Bethany; Branford; Cheshire; Derby; East Haven; Guilford; Hamden; Madison; Milford; New Haven; North Branford; North Haven; Orange; Oxford; Seymour; Shelton; Wallingford; West Haven and; Woodbridge.
Restrictions: Grants are not made to support religious activities, lobbying, or travel.
Geographic Focus: Connecticut
Date(s) Application is Due: Mar 5
Amount of Grant: 10,000 - 185,000 USD
Samples: Arts Council of Greater New Haven, New Haven, CT, $50,000—to provide general operating support; Beth El Center Inc., Milford, CT, $25,000— general operating support for transitional shelter programs for homeless individuals and families and a soup kitchen/food pantry that feeds individuals and families from Greater New Haven and Lower Naugatuck Valley; Area Congregations Together Inc., Shelton, CT, $150,000—to establish a development program.
Contact: Denise Canning, Grants Manager; (203) 777-2386 or (203) 777-7076; fax (203) 787-6584; dcanning@cfgnh.org
Internet: http://www.cfgnh.org/GrantsScholarships/TypesofGrants/tabid/199/Default.aspx
Sponsor: Community Foundation for Greater New Haven
70 Audubon Street
New Haven, CT 06510

Community Foundation for Monterey County Grants 492

The community foundation supports nonprofits in Monterey, CA, in the areas of social services, education, environment, arts, health, historic preservation, and general charitable giving. Collaboratives are highly encouraged. The foundation awards grants through its General Endowment. Technical Assistance grants and Neighborhood Grants also are awarded. Types of support include seed money, emergency funds, general operating support, building funds, equipment acquisition, land acquisition, matching funds, projects, consulting services, and technical assistance. Information on how to apply for each type of grant can be accessed online.
Requirements: 501(c)3 tax-exempt organizations in Monterey, California, may submit applications.
Restrictions: The foundation does not support individuals, religious activities, scholarships, fellowships, travel, research, salaries and other operating expenses of schools and public agencies, annual campaigns, or special events; create or add to endowment funds; or pay off debt.
Geographic Focus: California
Date(s) Application is Due: Jan 3; May 2; Aug 1
Amount of Grant: 5,000 - 40,000 USD
Contact: Jackie Wendland, Grants Administrator; (831) 375-9712, ext. 11; fax (831) 375-4731; jackie@cfmco.org
Internet: http://www.cfmco.org/grantsOverview.php
Sponsor: Community Foundation for Monterey County
2354 Garden Road
Monterey, CA 93940

Community Foundation for Northeast Michigan Common Grants 493

Community Foundation for Northeast Michigan Common Grants are made to tax-exempt, northeast Michigan charitable agencies and organizations. The foundation looks for projects that prevent community problems, benefit the greatest number of people, help deliver new services or make existing services more efficient, enhance collaboration among organizations, promote youth development, address emerging community needs, try a new approach to a persistent problem, or encourage people to develop new skills and help themselves. Common Grant application deadlines are February 1, August 1, or November 1.
Requirements: IRS 501(c)3 nonprofit organizations, schools, churches (for non-sectarian purposes), cities, townships, and other governmental units serving the four-county area of Alcona, Alpena, Montmorency, and Presque Isle in northeast Michigan are eligible to apply. Public and parochial schools in the counties of Alcona, Alpena, and Montmorency must use the Youth Advisory Council application.

Restrictions: Grants are not given to individuals, except for awards or scholarships from designated donor funds.
Geographic Focus: Michigan
Date(s) Application is Due: Feb 1; Aug 1; Nov 1
Amount of Grant: Up to 3,500 USD
Contact: Barbara Frantz, Executive Director; (877) 354-6881 or (989) 354-6881; fax (989) 356-3319; bfrantz@cfnem.org
Internet: http://www.cfnem.org/CFNEM/Common.aspx
Sponsor: Community Foundation for Northeast Michigan
100 N. Ripley, Suite F, P.O. Box 495
Alpena, MI 49707-0495

Community Foundation for Southern Arizona Grants   494

The foundation awards grants in southern Arizona for a broad array of charitable purposes in the areas of arts and humanities, education, the environment, health, social services. Types of support include challenge/matching grants, conferences and seminars, scholarships, equipment acquisition, fellowships, general support, multiyear support, project development, publications, research, seed funding, and technical assistance. Priority is given to proposals that promote collaboration and build on the strengths of individuals and communities. Deadlines are determined on a yearly basis.
Requirements: Nonprofit and grassroots organizations in southern Arizona communities are eligible. Southern Arizona communities include all of Cochise, Santa Cruz, and Pima Counties; and the areas of Yuma, Mariposa, Pinal, Graham, and Greenlee Counties that lie south of the Gila River.
Restrictions: Funds are generally not available for ongoing operating or capital campaigns, debt retirement, endowments, individuals, individual schools, sectarian activities, or underwriting of fund-raising events.
Geographic Focus: Arizona
Amount of Grant: 1,000 - 10,000 USD
Contact: Barbara Brown, Executive Vice President; (520) 770-0800, ext. 107; fax (520) 770-1500; bbrown@CFSoAZ.org
Internet: http://www.cfsoaz.org/page17480.cfm
Sponsor: Community Foundation for Southern Arizona
2250 E Broadway Boulevard
Tucson, AZ 85719

Community Foundation for the National Capital Region Community   495
Leadership Grants

The Community Foundation for the National Capital Region has a particular interest in supporting groups in the metropolitan Washington, DC, area working in the following issue areas: violence prevention; education; community building; cross-cultural or cultural partnership building; family literacy; and healthcare and dental services for underprivileged children, youth, and families. Types of support include general operating support, program development, technical assistance, and program evaluation. Approximately 30 to 40 grants per year are awarded following a Request-for-Proposal cycle, which occurs "several times per year." Letters of inquiry (three-page maximum) must meet the listed application deadlines.
Requirements: 501(c)3 nonprofits in the metropolitan Washington region, including the District of Columbia, northern Virginia, and suburban Maryland may submit letters of inquiry. Applicants must represent a neighborhood, citywide, or regional coalition effort, with one nonprofit organization serving as project sponsor.
Geographic Focus: District of Columbia, Maryland, Virginia
Contact: Dawnn Leary, Senior Philanthropic Services Officer; (202) 973-2519 or (202) 955-5890; fax (202) 955-8084; dleary@cfncr.org or info@cfncr.org
Internet: http://thecommunityfoundation.org/what-we-do/grantmaking/
Sponsor: Community Foundation for the National Capital Region
1201 15th Street NW, Suite 420
Washington, D.C. 20005

Community Foundation of Central Illinois Grants   496

The foundation funds programs in the fields of education, arts, human services, community service, or community development, and that advance one or more of the following objectives: address and help resolve important existing or emerging community issues; support new and creative projects and organizations offering the greatest opportunity for positive and significant change; promote cooperation and collaboration among organizations; identify, enhance, and develop leadership in the community through creative and innovative activities that empower individuals; and improve the quality or scope of charitable works in our community. Application guidelines are available online.

Requirements: Nonprofit organizations within a 50-mile radius of Peoria, IL, are eligible.
Restrictions: The foundation will not fund annual campaigns, individuals, or endowments, or make grants for sectarian religious purposes.
Geographic Focus: Illinois
Date(s) Application is Due: Apr 15; Sep 15
Amount of Grant: 2,500 - 3,000 USD
Contact: Kristan Creek, Program Officer; (309) 674-8730; fax (309) 674-8754; Kristan@communityfoundationci.org
Internet: http://www.communityfoundationci.org/grant_guidelines.asp
Sponsor: Community Foundation of Central Illinois
331 Fulton Street, Suite 310
Peoria, IL 61602

Community Foundation of Collier County Capacity Building Grants   497

The Community Foundation believes that all nonprofits can benefit from the best practices developed over time in excellent organizations. The Foundation wishes to help nonprofits become successful and sustainable, long term businesses. Capacity Building Grants are given to support best practices and sustainability for a variety of nonprofit organizational needs. The Foundation's focus is on substantial projects that: encourage and facilitate collaborations; improve communications between nonprofits with similar missions; engage in public-private partnerships; facilitate the development of strategic plans, business plans, plans for marketing & communications, fund raising plans; encourage program evaluation that focuses on results for participants; fund updated technology systems; and other projects that improve the sustainability of the organization. This grant program includes a Letter of Intent, an interview and donor briefings. The Letter of Intent must be submitted by 5:00 on September 18th. The most common grant will be between $5,000-$8,000 per/applicant. The grant award from the Foundation will require a 50% match by the organization.
Requirements: 501(c)3 tax-exempt organizations serving Collier County and are not deemed as not a private foundation under Section 509(a) are eligible to apply.
Restrictions: The Foundation does not fund the following through this grant program: grants to individuals; endowments; private schools; political campaigns/lobby activities; scholarly research; annual campaigns; organizations which exclude individuals based on the Foundation statement of diversity; reimbursement of funds spent; projects that present a clear or perceived conflict of interest.
Geographic Focus: Florida
Date(s) Application is Due: Sep 18
Amount of Grant: 5,000 - 8,000 USD
Contact: Mary Barrett; (239) 649-5000; mbarrett@cfcollier.org
Internet: http://www.cfcollier.org/new_grant_program.php
Sponsor: Community Foundation of Collier County
2400 Tamiami Trail N, Suite 300
Naples, FL 34103

Community Foundation of Greater Birmingham Grants   498

The community foundation serving the greater Birmingham, AL, area awards grants in arts and culture, education, environment, health, and welfare. Types of support include capital campaigns, operating support, building/renovation, equipment, program development, publication, seed money, curriculum development, and matching funds. Grant requests are considered twice a year at distribution committee meetings. The foundation requires that grant requests be submitted in writing. There is no application form. Applicants are asked to submit a cover letter and a complete statement of the purpose of the grant, including the need for the project and population and number of people to be served, project budget, other funding sources, length of time for which foundation aid is needed, a method to evaluate the project's success, description of applicant organization including annual budget, copy of IRS determination letter, and names of the board of directors or trustees.
Requirements: IRS 501(c)3 organizations that provide services in the greater Birmingham metropolitan area (Jefferson, Shelby, St. Clair, Blount and Walker counties) are eligible.
Restrictions: Grants are not made to or for individuals, operating expenses of organizations, religious organizations for religious purposes, national fund-raising drives, conference or seminar expenses, tickets for benefits, political organizations or candidates for public office, organizations with IRS 501(h) status, budget deficits, replacement of government funding cuts, or scholarships or endowment funds.
Geographic Focus: Alabama
Date(s) Application is Due: Mar 15; Sep 15

Contact: James McCrary, Senior Program Officer; (205) 327-3812 or (205) 327-3800; fax (205) 328-6576; jmccrary@foundationbirmingham.org or guidelines@foundationbirmingham.org
Internet: http://www.foundationbirmingham.org/page30508.cfm
Sponsor: Community Foundation of Greater Birmingham
2100 First Avenue N, Suite 700
Birmingham, AL 35203-4223

Community Foundation of Greater Flint Grants   499

The community foundation is interested in funding charitable organizations that are able to demonstrate they have planned their projects with respect to the community's needs in the areas of arts and humanities, community services, education, environment and conservation, ethics, health, human and social services, and philanthropy. The foundation's current objectives for the allocation of discretionary funds give top priority to programs that: advance the health and well-being of children; and/or improve the capacity of public education. Types of support include general operating support, program development, seed money, scholarship funds, and technical assistance. Applications are available on the Web site.
Requirements: IRS 501(c)3 organizations with programs of direct relevance to the residents of Genesee County, Michigan are eligible. Types of support include general operating support.
Restrictions: Grants will not be made to individuals. In general, requests for sectarian religious purposes, budget deficits, routine operating expenses of existing organizations, litigation, endowments, and other capital fund drives or projects are not funded.
Geographic Focus: Michigan
Contact: Lynn Larkin; (810) 767-8270; fax (810) 767-0496; llarkin@cfgf.org
Internet: http://www.cfgf.org/page32610.cfm
Sponsor: Community Foundation of Greater Flint
500 South Saginaw Street
Flint, MI 48502-1206

Community Foundation of Greater Greensboro Community Grants   500

The Community Foundation of Greater Greensboro awards community grants from unrestricted and field-of-interest funds, as allocated by the Board of Directors, to support a wide range of community issues. This category of grants are one-time awards given to help nonprofits meet community needs and opportunities by building their capacity to reach their missions. Grants usually range in size from a few hundred dollars up to $10,000, and tend to average $3,000 to $5,000. The current Community Grants program will focus on capacity building for nonprofits. By definition, grants will support activities based upon what different organizations need to more effectively reach their missions. For example: one organization might request dollars for a training program for staff or the board; another organization's needs might generate a grant request for strategic planning; two or more nonprofits might request funds jointly to support a restructuring effort to strategically align services or administrative functions; and other nonprofits might seek support for evaluating a program and assessing future options. Annual deadlines for applications are March 14 and August 15.
Requirements: Applicant must be a 501(c)3 nonprofit organization located in or serving the greater Greensboro, North Carolina, area.
Restrictions: Request may not exceed $10,000 and cannot be used for expenses already incurred. Typically, multi-year grant applications are not considered in this grant program. Public schools or other public agencies will typically not receive grants through this program, although they may be involved as partners in funded efforts. Grants are not awarded to individuals.
Geographic Focus: North Carolina
Date(s) Application is Due: Mar 14; Aug 15
Amount of Grant: Up to 10,000 USD
Contact: Connie Leeper; (336) 379-9100, ext. 130; cleeper@cfgg.org
Internet: http://cfgg.org/receive/community-grants-program
Sponsor: Community Foundation of Greater Greensboro
330 S. Greene Street, Suite 100
Greensboro, NC 27401

Community Foundation of Greenville Hollingsworth Funds Program   501
Project Grants

The Hollingsworth Funds, Inc. has a competitive grant process that is administered by the Community Foundation. Consistent with the purposes established by its benefactor, John D. Hollingsworth, Jr., an astute textile executive and real estate investor. The Hollingsworth Funds will serve a broad range of charitable, educational, religious, literary and cultural purposes.

The Hollingsworth Funds has adopted initial guidelines in order to assist its evaluation of charitable organizations for funding. The Hollingsworth Funds will make grants: to health and human service agencies dedicated to improving quality of life for residents of Greenville County and particularly for those which deliver services to the poor, homeless, and illiterate; to interdenominational faith-based programs that benefit a broad cross-section of the community; to a wide variety of arts and education related initiatives including high quality preschool and after school programs; for grants for capital projects that provide a public benefit on a nondiscriminatory basis; to increase the organizational capacity of a non-profit organization; to public/private partnerships. The Hollingsworth Funds will give priority to new and innovative projects that are outside of the scope of an organization's ongoing operating budget. To submit a request for funding, a charitable organization must deliver or mail two (2) complete application packets to the Community Foundation of Greenville by 4:00 pm on September 3. All applicants will be notified of their status by December 31.
Requirements: A 501(c)3 charitable organization can submit one grant application per year for an amount not to exceed $50,000 to fund innovative projects for the benefit of charitable uses within Greenville County, South Carolina, or for the benefit of residents of Greenville County.
Restrictions: The Hollingsworth Funds will not make grants: to sponsor special fundraising events, celebration functions, dinners or annual meetings; for areas that are traditionally the primary responsibility of local, state or federal governments; for core operating expenses of public, private or parochial schools; that primarily benefit the religious activities of a church, synagogue, mosque or other house of worship; to pay off existing debts; scholarship awards or grants to individuals.
Geographic Focus: South Carolina
Date(s) Application is Due: Sep 3
Amount of Grant: Up to 50,000 USD
Contact: Debbie Cooper, Director of Donor Services; (864) 233-5925 or (864) 331-8414; fax (864) 242-9292; dcooper@cfgg.com or Cfgg@cfgg.com
Internet: http://www.cfgreenville.org/page18741.cfm
Sponsor: Community Foundation of Greenville
27 Cleveland Street, Suite 101
Greenville, SC 29601

Community Foundation of Herkimer and Oneida Counties Grants   502

The community foundation serves Oneida and Herkimer Counties, NY, and awards grants for programs that have direct relevance to needs in these areas. Preference is given to requests for support of particular programs or projects that are expected to benefit the community and to requests for capital expenditures and seed money. Additional types of support include general operating support, endowment funds, fellowships, scholarship funds, consulting services, demonstration grants, matching funds, and technical assistance. Applications from organizations not previously known to the foundation are given the same consideration as requests from those it knows well. The foundation may cut off acceptance of applications at any time if it is deemed that its current grant agenda is full. A grant request should be initiated by an application in writing on the organization's letterhead, if it has one, signed by the chairperson or president of its governing board.
Requirements: The community foundation supports only nonprofit organizations in Oneida and Herkimer Counties in New York.
Restrictions: Grants will not normally be made for endowments, ongoing operations, annual budgets or deficit financing, religious purposes, or financial assistance or scholarships to individuals.
Geographic Focus: New York
Contact: Margaret O'Shea, Director of Programs; (315) 735-8212, ext. 229; fax (315) 735-9363; moshea@foundationhoc.org
Internet: http://www.foundationhoc.org
Sponsor: Community Foundation of Herkimer and Oneida Counties
1222 State Street
Utica, NY 13502

Community Foundation of Louisville Capacity Building Grants   503

Created by visionary philanthropists who want to support their community today and beyond their own lifetimes, the Fund for Louisville allows the Community Foundation to respond to emerging needs and opportunities in the Louisville area. The Community Foundation of Louisville Capacity Building Grants program was established on the belief that strong nonprofit organizations lead to effective programs and greater impact. Capacity building is investment in activities that strengthen the ability of a nonprofit to achieve higher performance and results. Eligible organizations may apply to receive a grant award of up to

$20,000. Applications are available on July 7 each year and may be submitted online only. The annual deadline for submission is August 21 at 4:00 pm.
Requirements: Eligible organizations include those that are: headquartered in Jefferson County, Kentucky (if based outside of the county, then the organization must demonstrate that a majority of beneficiaries are located in Jefferson County, Kentucky); and classified as a 501(c)3 public charity in good standing (organizations with a pending application for 501(c)3 status may apply with proof of Form 1023 receipt from the IRS).
Geographic Focus: Kentucky
Date(s) Application is Due: Aug 21
Amount of Grant: 100 - 20,000 USD
Contact: Whitney Gentry, Grants Administrator; (502) 855-6963; fax (502) 585-4649; whitneyg@cflouisville.org
Internet: http://www.cflouisville.org/connect/fund-louisville-grants
Sponsor: Community Foundation of Louisville
325 W Main Street, Suite 1110, Waterfront Plaza, West Tower
Louisville, KY 40202

Community Foundation of Muncie and Delaware County Grants   504

The Community Foundation of Muncie and Delaware County Grants provide funding in the following areas of interest: arts and culture, human services, economic development, education, and community betterment. The Foundation focus on: new and innovative projects and programs for which there is a demonstrable need or community benefit; capital needs of community institutions and organizations; emerging needs of Muncie and Delaware County; establishment of community priorities; monitoring of community services to avoid duplication and ineffective programs; acting as a catalyst for action and community participation. Applications are encouraged for types of projects that address one or more of the following: yield substantial benefits to the community for the resources invested; promote cooperation among agencies without duplicating services; enhance or improve institutional or organizational self-sufficiency; provide "seed money" for innovative community programs; encourage matching gifts or additional funding from other donors; and reach a broad segment of the community with needed services which are presently not provided. The Board of Directors review applications on a quarterly basis in the months of February, May, August, and November.
Requirements: First-time applicants must contact the Foundation to discuss their proposal prior to submission. Organizations are required to submit 18 copies of the application packet, but must submit different items depending on the type of funding requested. See website for submission details.
Restrictions: Requests of $25,000 or more are preferred during the first cycle of each year. The Foundation does not make grants to individuals or grants for religious purposes, budget deficits, for travel, fundraising events, endowments or projects normally the responsibility of a government agency.
Geographic Focus: Indiana
Amount of Grant: Up to USD
Samples: Animal Rescue Fund, to defray the cost of a van to transport animals to the vet and pick up strays in danger, $15,000; United Way of Delaware County, support to the Technology Wrap-Around Project, a pilot project to create access to computers and the Internet to ensure that those using these services can improve their lives in education, income, and health, $40,000; Gateway Health Clinic, to increase clinic hours to reduce the waiting list of patients, $25,000.
Contact: Suzanne Kadinger, Program Officer; (765) 747-7181; fax (765) 289-7770; skadinger@cfmdin.org or info@cfmdin.org
Internet: http://www.cfmdin.org/main/grant-seekers/
Sponsor: Community Foundation of Muncie and Delaware County
201 East Jackson Street
Muncie, IN 47305

Community Foundation of South Alabama Grants   505

The Community Foundation of South Alabama is the platform for building community in Baldwin, Clarke, Conecuh, Choctaw, Escambia, Mobile, Monroe and Washington counties. The Foundation provides grant support to South Alabama nonprofit organizations in four major program areas: community and civic affairs, education, arts and recreation, and social services (health and human services). Priority consideration is given to projects that clearly provide innovative responses to community needs, are collaborative in nature when appropriate, and potentially affect broad segments of the community. Types of support include general operating support, capital campaigns, endowment funds, program development, and scholarship funds. The board of directors meets annually to consider grant requests. Application forms may be obtained from the office.

Requirements: Nonprofit organizations that have a 501(c)3, government entities and religious organizations that are located in Mobile, Baldwin, Clarke, Conecuh, Washington, Choctaw, Escambia and Monroe counties are eligible.
Restrictions: Grants generally are not provided for or to individuals, recurring requests for the same purpose for which foundation grant funds have already been awarded, research that is noncommunity-related or that does not have short-range results, films, conferences and workshops, lobbying activities, and tickets to fund-raising events.
Geographic Focus: Alabama
Amount of Grant: 2,500 - 28,000 USD
Contact: Janine Phillips, Director and Program Officer; (334) 438-5591; fax (334) 438-5592; info@communityendowment.com or program@communityendowment.com
Internet: http://communityendowment.com/grants/grants.htm
Sponsor: Community Foundation of South Alabama
212 St. Joseph Street, P.O. Box 990
Mobile, AL 36601-0990

Community Foundation of South Puget Sound Grants   506

The foundation awards grants to a variety of charitable, cultural, education, health, and welfare organizations. Grants from the unrestricted funds are considered for general operational or program support. Typical grants range from $1,000 to $7,500. Emergency grants may be considered on a case-by-case basis. Application and guidelines for grants and scholarships are available online.
Requirements: The foundation awards grants to Washington tax-exempt organizations primarily for use in Thurston, Mason, and Lewis Counties, except on instructions of the donor at the time of the gift or bequest.
Restrictions: Grants do not support religious organizations for religious purposes; individuals; annual campaigns of organizations (direct mail or special events); political or lobbying activities; organizations that discriminate based on race, creed, or ethnic group; capital campaigns for bricks and mortar or endowment funds; or for multiple year commitments.
Geographic Focus: Washington
Date(s) Application is Due: Apr 3; Oct 2
Amount of Grant: 1,000 - 7,500 USD
Samples: Rochester Organization of Families, $7,000—to help maintain ROOF's Kid's Place academic enrichment program for 50 low -income, at-risk children in the first through fifth grades; Harmony Hill, $4,500—to purchase a computer server to maintain its extensive database of clients and donors; which in turn supports their mission to improve the quality of life for those affected by cancer; Thurston Mason Project Access, $4,000—to make donated medical services available to uninsured, low-income Thurston County residents with acute, urgent conditions.
Contact: Norma Schuiteman, Executive Director; (360) 705-3340; fax (360) 705-2656; legacy@thecommunityfoundation.com
Internet: http://www.thecommunityfoundation.com/grants.php
Sponsor: Community Foundation of South Puget
111 Market Street NE, Suite 375
Olympia, WA 98501

Community Foundation of St. Joseph County ArtsEverywhere Grants   507

The ArtsEverywhere Fund seeks to raise artistic quality, strengthen volunteer and staff leadership, enhance the capacity of arts organizations and the arts community, foster and support local talent, and inspire community pride. Grants will be competitively awarded in the following categories: capacity building (matching grants of up to $5,000); program or project support (matching grants of up to $5,000); and major venture funding (matching grants of up to $50,000, potentially renewable for up to three years, for a maximum commitment of $150,000). Applicants may apply for any or all types of funding.
Requirements: St. Joseph County nonprofit or public agencies with a demonstrated, substantial (though not necessarily exclusive) commitment to the arts as part of its overall mission and appropriate participation in the ArtsEverywhere initiative are eligible to apply for grant funding. Detailed guidelines and application information for each grant category are available at the website.
Restrictions: Grants are not made to fund: operational phases of established programs; endowment campaigns; religious organizations for religious purposes; individuals directly; development or public relations activities (e.g. literature, videos, etc.); retirement of debts; camperships; annual appeals or membership contributions; travel for bands, sports teams, classes, etc; computers (unless presented as a necessary component of larger program or objective); and post-event or after-the-fact situations.
Geographic Focus: Indiana
Date(s) Application is Due: May 1; Nov 1

Amount of Grant: Up to 50,000 USD

Contact: Angela Butiste, Senior Program Officer; (574) 232-0041; fax (574) 233-1906; angela@cfsjc.org

Internet: http://www.cfsjc.org/initiatives/artseverywhere/artseverywhere_grants.html

Sponsor: Community Foundation of St. Joseph County

205 W Jefferson Boulevard, P.O. Box 837

South Bend, IN 46624

Community Foundation of St. Joseph County Indiana Arts Commission (IAC) Regional Partnership   508

The Community Foundation of St. Joseph County is one of 12 regional partners with the Indiana Arts Commission (IAC), dedicated to advancing arts and culture throughout Indiana. Indiana Arts Commission grants awarded through the Regional Arts Partnership are available to qualifying nonprofit organizations through a competitive application process. Nonprofit, tax-exempt organizations or public entities with eligible arts programming and addresses in the following counties are eligible to apply for funding from the Region 2 Partner, the Community Foundation of St. Joseph County: Elkhart, Fulton, Kosciusko, Marshall, St. Joseph, and Starke. Three separate grant categories are funded, based on the need and size of the organization. The Arts Project Support Grant funds arts and non-arts organizations to support a distinct aspect of the organization's arts activities, such as a one-time event, single production or exhibition, educational seminar, or training sessions. The Arts Organization Support I Grant funds one year of annual operating support for the ongoing artistic and administrative functions of eligible arts organizations. These organizations must have arts as primary mission, with an annual income of less than $250,000. The Arts Organization Support II Grant funds two years of operating support for the ongoing artistic and administrative functions of an organization of an operating budget of over $250,000. Detailed information about each category is posted on the website.

Restrictions: Each grant has specific guidelines for approval.

Geographic Focus: Indiana

Contact: Grants Contact; (574) 232-0041; fax (574) 233-1906

Internet: http://www.cfsjc.org/grants/iac/iac_grants.html

Sponsor: Community Foundation of St. Joseph County

205 W Jefferson Boulevard, P.O. Box 837

South Bend, IN 46624

Community Foundation of St. Joseph County Special Project Challenge Grants   509

The Special Project Challenge Grants assist public and other 501(c)3 agencies in their efforts to serve community needs. For every $1 raised by the chosen agency, the Community Foundation will match $1. The foundation encourages projects in the following areas: community development and urban affairs; health and human services; parks, recreation, and environment; and youth and education.

Requirements: In additional to the online application, all applicants must submit the following materials online: up to a two page proposal narrative; a detailed project budget; current board roster with officers identified; fiscal year income statement; proof of nonprofit status. Application materials must be submitted via email to grants@cfsjc.org in word processing format (narrative or budget) or Microsoft Excel (budget). Hard copy applications are no longer accepted.

Restrictions: Grants are not made to fund: operational phases of established programs; endowment campaigns; religious organizations for religious purposes; individuals directly; development or public relations activities (e.g. literature, videos, etc.); retirement of debts; camperships; annual appeals or membership contributions; travel for bands, sports teams, classes, etc; j) computers (unless presented as a necessary component of larger program or objective); and post-event or after-the-fact situations.

Geographic Focus: Indiana

Date(s) Application is Due: Mar 1; Oct 1

Contact: Angela Butiste, Senior Program Officer; (574) 232-0041; fax (574) 233-1906; angela@cfsjc.org

Internet: http://www.cfsjc.org/grants/sproj/special_project_grants.html

Sponsor: Community Foundation of St. Joseph County

205 W Jefferson Boulevard, P.O. Box 837

South Bend, IN 46624

Community Foundation of Switzerland County Grants   510

The Community Foundation of Switzerland County is a nonprofit organization created to make Switzerland County a better place to live for present and future generations. The Foundation gives priority to applications that focus on the basic needs of the community (food, housing, shelter, health care, clothing, personal care, and transportation). The Foundation also welcomes applications for other programs and projects that benefit Switzerland County. Organizations may request up to $5,000. Applications are reviewed monthly; there are no deadlines. The application and additional guidelines are available at the website.

Requirements: Any organization with a 501(c)3 or any organization that provides a program with charitable intent or has a fiscal agent is eligible to apply.

Geographic Focus: Indiana

Amount of Grant: Up to 5,000 USD

Contact: Pam Acton, Grant Program DIrector; (812) 427-9160; fax (812) 427-4033; pacton@cfsci.org

Internet: http://www.cfsci.org/

Sponsor: Community Foundation of Switzerland County

303 Ferry Street, P.O. Box 46

Vevay, IN 47043

Community Foundation of the Eastern Shore Technical Mini Grants   511

Twice each year, the Community Foundation of the Eastern Shore awards Technical Mini Grants through its Nonprofit Support Program to a wide range of organizations, whose programs benefit health and human services, education, arts and culture, community affairs, environmental conservation, and historic preservation. The purpose of the program is to provide grants of up to $1000 to nonprofit agencies for the purchase of equipment, attendance at training or other such resources necessary to enhance staff's capability. Grants are given to individual organizations.

Requirements: To be eligible, an organization must be a designated 501(c)3 nonprofit under the Internal Revenue Code and provide evidence of that designation. The organization must be located in Maryland, providing services for residents of the lower three counties of the Eastern Shore: Worcester, Wicomico, and Somerset.

Restrictions: The Community Foundation's Technical Mini Grants Program does not make grants for: building campaigns; operational deficits; operational support; debt retirement; sectarian religious programs; endowment funds; fundraising campaigns; program development. Governmental organizations/agencies and religious organizations are not eligible to apply.

Geographic Focus: Maryland

Date(s) Application is Due: Jan 20; Jul 20

Amount of Grant: 100 - 1,000 USD

Contact: Erica N. Joseph; (410) 742-9911; fax (410) 742-6638; joseph@cfes.org

Internet: http://www.cfes.org/non_profit_support.php

Sponsor: Community Foundation of the Eastern Shore

1324 Belmont Avenue, Suite 401

Salisbury, MD 21804

Community Foundation of the Verdugos Educational Endowment Fund Grants   512

The Educational Endowment Fund provides financial support to innovative as well as traditional educational programs and projects in public and private schools and community organizations in the Crescenta Valley, California region. The goal is to enrich educational opportunities by supporting building, equipment, instruction, guidance, coaching, practical application, classroom activities, in-service, training and/or practice programs. Grants will support: equipment purchase, replacement & modernization; improvement to facilities including athletic facilities; printed materials; fundraising events or capital campaigns; classroom materials; public/private schools and colleges; child day care/development centers; libraries; hospitals; community enrichment projects; salaries. All qualified organizations are invited to submit grant applications once a year for grants that will be awarded at the Crescenta Valley Chamber of Commerce Installation Luncheon in early January. Average grant sizes are from $500 to $3,000. The grant application is available at the Community Foundation of the Verdugos website. The application must be submitted by October 9th.

Requirements: 501(c)3 IRS nonprofit public charities in the Crescenta Valley region of California (includes La Crescenta, Montrose, Tujunga and La Canada) and, organizations located outside the Crescenta Valley but delivering educational programs in the Crescenta Valley are eligible to apply. Please indicate the number of Crescenta Valley residents who will be served by your program. An organization may apply for no more than two grants during a grant cycle. Note, the president, school principal or leader must indicate awareness of multiple requests and each application must be for different types of support.

Restrictions: Grants will not support: uniforms or clothing; travel expenses; fiscal agents; individuals and individual scholarships; endowment funds; feasibility studies or consulting fees; advertising; research; political lobbying, voter registration or political campaigns; insurance or maintenance contracts; faith-based projects.

Geographic Focus: California
Date(s) Application is Due: Oct 9
Amount of Grant: 500 - 3,000 USD
Contact: Edna Karinski, Executive Director; (818) 241-8040; fax (818) 241-8045; info@communityfoundationoftheverdugos.org
Internet: http://www.glendalecommunityfoundation.org/grants_endowment.php
Sponsor: Community Foundation of the Verdugos
330 Arden Avenue, Suite 130
Glendale, CA 91203

Community Foundation of the Verdugos Grants 513

The Community Foundation of the Verdugos welcomes grant requests from public agencies and nonprofit organizations that serve the Verdugo region including Burbank, Glendale, La Canada Flintridge, La Crescenta, Montrose, and Verdugo City of California. Grant recipients must have appropriate fiscal and program accountability. Average grant amounts range from $2,500 to $10,000. Grants are provided in the following areas of interest: arts and culture; civic; health and human services (examples include projects and services for the disabled/handicapped, general community health, or homeless services); education programs; senior services; student aid (scholarships); youth services; environment and; community. Grant application and, application guidelines are available at the Foundation's website. Grants are made three times a year. Deadline for grant applications are February 1, June 1, and September 1. Scholarship deadline is March 5. Only one proposal from an organization is permitted per grant cycle. Approval or denial of your request will be provided to you in writing.
Requirements: The Foundation funds nonprofit organizations that: have IRS nonprofit status; predominantly serve the Verdugo region of California (Glendale, La Canada Flintridge, La Crescenta, Montrose, Verdugo City) and adjacent areas; capital equipment that helps to increase your organization's long-term sustainability or services to increase impact in the Verdugo region; programs (including related overhead, supplies and administrative expenses) responsive to changing community needs and which increase impact in the Verdugo region. Requests that provide significance and impact for the Verdugo region in the areas of arts and culture, children/youth, education and literacy, health and human services, civic activities, senior services, and environmental/animal related programs.
Restrictions: The Foundation does not make grants or loans to individuals unless they are students receiving scholarships. The Foundation also does not provide funds for religious or political purposes, for budget deficits, or projects that are usually the responsibility of a public agency.
Geographic Focus: California
Date(s) Application is Due: Feb 1; Mar 5; Jun 1; Sep 1
Amount of Grant: 25,000 - 10,000 USD
Samples: San Gabriel Valley Habitat for Humanity, $10,000—toward handicapped lifts; Salvation Army Glendale Corporation, $10,000—ZONE after school program for low-income and at-risk children; College View School, $10,000—toward a new playground structure.
Contact: Edna Karinski, Executive Director; (818) 241-8040; fax (818) 241-8045; info@communityfoundationoftheverdugos.org
Internet: http://www.glendalecommunityfoundation.org/grants.php
Sponsor: Community Foundation of the Verdugos
330 Arden Avenue, Suite 130
Glendale, CA 91203

Community Memorial Foundation Grants 514

The foundation encourages public/private endeavors in Illinois by nurturing the formation of creative initiatives and innovative funding strategies. Collaborative efforts may include participation with nonprofit organizations, governments, schools, and the business sector. In general, the foundation gives preference to organizations that reach underserved segments of the population. A broad range of funding includes service delivery programs for vulnerable populations, start-up funds, building construction/renovation, project support, general operating support, and educational programs. Generally, the foundation does not consider more than one proposal from any one institution and favors funding noncapital programs.
Requirements: 501(c)3 organizations located in the Illinois communities of Argo, Bridgeview, Broadview, Brookfield, Burr Ridge, Clarendon Hills, Countryside, Darien, Downers Grove, Hickory Hills, Hinsdale, Hodgkins, Indian Head Park, Justice, La Grange, La Grange Park, Lyons, McCook, North Riverside, Oak Brook, Riverside, Stickney, Summit, Westchester, Western Springs, Westmont, Willow Springs, and Willowbrooks may apply.
Restrictions: Grants are not awarded to individuals, sectarian or religious organizations, or for purposes to influence legislation or other political activities.

Geographic Focus: Illinois
Date(s) Application is Due: Mar 31; Sep 30
Amount of Grant: Up to 250,000 USD
Samples: All Saints Episcopal Church & First Congregational Church (Western Springs, IL)—to establish a program to match volunteers with service opportunities, with a particular focus on older adults, $19,750. Parent & Community Network (Western Springs, IL)—to sponsor a conference and workshops on relevant issues to parents of children in School District 204 and feeder schools, $5,000. Boy Scouts of America-Des Plaines Valley Council (La Grange, IL)—for general operating support, $10,000 challenge grant.
Contact: Deborah Kustra, Grants Manager; (630) 654-4729; fax (630) 654-3402; info@cmfdn.org
Internet: http://www.cmfdn.org/guidelines.html
Sponsor: Community Memorial Foundation
15 Spinning Wheel Road, Suite 326
Hinsdale, IL 60521

COMPAS Grants 515

COMPAS helps support the creation of art in communities across Minnesota through its granting programs through support of arts organizations' work in schools and communities. Grant programs include 3M Award for Innovation in the Arts—honors creative approaches to arts education and outreach; American Express Audience Development Fund—helps Minnesota arts organizations outside of the seven-county metropolitan area reach new audiences; Community Art Program—through the McKnight Foundation, provides grants for neighborhood arts projects; General Fund—provides resources for established arts organizations striving to reach new audiences; Medtronic Arts Access Program—promotes cross-cultural understanding and offers increased accessibility to the arts; and School Arts Fund—supports partnerships between schools and community arts organizations. Application and guidelines are available online.
Requirements: Any group, organization, or individual is eligible to apply. All proposed activities must occur within the cities of Saint Paul and/or Minneapolis.
Restrictions: Grants do not support capital improvements, mortgage payments, property purchase, or building construction; deficit financing; administrative costs unrelated to the CAP sponsored project; fundraising events; or projects that result in lobbying for particular legislation, promoting of a particular religious belief, are discriminatory, or in any way violate federal, state or local laws.
Geographic Focus: Minnesota
Amount of Grant: Up to 15,000 USD
Contact: John Mentzos, (651) 292-3287; fax (651) 292-3258; john@compas.org
Internet: http://www.compas.org/pages/grants.html
Sponsor: COMPAS
304 Landmark Center, 75 W Fifth Street
Saint Paul, MN 55102-1414

Comprehensive Health Education Foundation Grants 516

The foundation awards grants to support programs that address health inequities. The initial grantmaking effort will focus on Clark, Pierce, and Spokane Counties in Washington State. One-year grants of up to $20,000 each will be awarded to culturally appropriate, community-led collaborations to test their best idea on how to make it easier for people who suffer from health inequities to move more and eat healthier. Health inequities are defined as differences in the incidence, prevalence, mortality, and burden of diseases that exist for specific populations in the United States. Low-income individuals and people of color within the United States generally have higher rates of poor health and injury than those who are in higher-income groups and are Caucasian.
Requirements: 501(c)3 tax-exempt organizations located in Clark, Pierce, and Spokane Counties in Washington State and units of government that are nondiscriminatory in policy and practice regarding disabilities, age, sex, sexual orientation, race, ethnic origin, or creed are eligible.
Restrictions: Support will not be provided for building or land acquisitions; equipment or furniture purchases; endowment funds; emergency funds; grants to individuals; fellowships/scholarships; research; debt retirement; fundraising activities; general fund drives; indirect overhead; or CHEF programs or products.
Geographic Focus: Washington
Contact: Kari L. Lewis, Grant Coordinator; (800) 323-2433, ext. 1899; fax (206) 824-3072; KariL@chef.org
Internet: http://www.chef.org/about/grants.php
Sponsor: Comprehensive Health Education Foundation
159 S Jackson Street, Suite 510
Seattle, WA 98104

Compton Foundation Grants 517

The foundation was founded to address community, national, and international concerns in the fields of peace and world order, population, and the environment. Other concerns of the foundation include equal educational opportunity, community welfare and social justice, and culture and the arts. The foundation makes three kinds of grants. Project grants generally are made to national organizations for projects that fall within the primary areas of peace and world order, population, and the environment. These grants may be for regional (Pacific Coastal states), national, or international activities and are usually for projects of limited duration. Project grants are considered by the board two times a year. Discretionary grants are made at the discretion, and usually at the initiation, of individual board members. Most grants in this area are made for community welfare and social justice, and culture and the arts. Renewal grants provide general support to organizations whose activities have been funded by the foundation for many years and whose work continues to be considered particularly effective by the board. Many of the foundation's grants in the area of equal educational opportunity, and some grants in peace and world order and population, are renewal grants.

Requirements: The foundation makes grants only to tax-exempt organizations and institutions.

Restrictions: Grants will not be made to individuals.

Geographic Focus: All States

Date(s) Application is Due: Mar 7; Sep 7

Amount of Grant: 5,000 - 50,000 USD

Samples: Colorado Environmental Coalition—for Colorado Instream Flow Project, $20,000; Klamath Forest Alliance—for Klamath Riverkeeper and Karuk Tribe Klamath Dams Campaign, $30,000; San Francisco Education Fund—for Peer Resources Program, $10,000.

Contact: Edith T. Eddy, Executive Director; (650) 508-1181; fax (650) 508-1191; info@comptonfoundation.org

Internet: http://www.comptonfoundation.org/application_procedures.html

Sponsor: Compton Foundation

255 Shoreline Drive, Suite 540

Redwood City, CA 94065

ConAgra Foods Foundation Community Impact Grants 518

The Community Impact Grants (CIG) program will award grants between $10,000 and $100,000 to impactful, grassroots organizations that leverage innovation and creativity to address childhood hunger and nutrition needs in communities where ConAgra Foods' employees live and work or states where 20% or more of children are food insecure. Organizations that demonstrate a strong alignment with the Foundation's giving strategies (i.e., direct service, capacity building, and advocacy) and core funding priorities have the greatest chance of receiving a grant. The CIG program is a two-step, competitive process that first requires the submission of an Letter of Inquiry (LOI) and then the subsequent completion of a full application if invited to apply for a grant. For more detailed program information and guidelines see: http://www.nourishkidstoday.org/downloads/pdf/CIGGuidelines.pdf.

Requirements: The preference of ConAgra Foods Foundation is to award Community Impact Grants to organizations located in states with a child food insecurity rate of 20% or more according to Feeding America's Child Hunger Study as well as those communities where ConAgra Foods has a significant employee presence, these states include: AR, AZ, CA, CO, DC, FL, GA, IA, ID, IL, IN, LA, MA, MI, MN, MO, MS, NC, NE, NM, OH, OR, PA, SC, TN, TX, WA, and WI.

Restrictions: ConAgra Foods Foundation does not fund: professional or amateur sports organizations and teams, or athletic events and programs; political organizations; terrorist organizations or those not compliant with the USA Patriot Act; fundraising events; emergency funding; loans, debt reduction or operating deficits; individuals; endowments; capital campaigns (unless solicited at the founder's discretion); memorial campaigns; elementary and secondary education.

Geographic Focus: Arizona, Arkansas, California, Colorado, District of Columbia, Florida, Georgia, Idaho, Illinois, Indiana, Iowa, Louisiana, Massachusetts, Michigan, Minnesota, Mississippi, Missouri, New Mexico, North Carolina, Ohio, Oregon, Pennsylvania, South Carolina, Tennessee, Texas, Washington, Wisconsin

Date(s) Application is Due: Jan 29

Amount of Grant: 10,000 - 100,000 USD

Contact: Program Contact; foundation@conagrafoods.com

Internet: http://www.nourishkidstoday.org/about-us/application-guidelines.jsp

Sponsor: ConAgra Foods Foundation

One ConAgra Drive, CC-304

Omaha, NE 68102-5001

ConAgra Foods Foundation Nourish Our Community Grants 519

The Foundation awards Nourish Our Community Grants to non-profit organizations based on recommendations from employees. While any organization that is working to address community needs is eligible for funding, preference will be given to those that seek to provide children and their families with access to food and nutrition education. Organizations must be located in the communities where ConAgra Foods employees live and work in order to be considered for a Nourish Our Community grant. Nourish Our Community grants typically range from $5,000 to $25,000, with an average grant of $10,000. The grant requests are reviewed by a committee representative of a cross-section of employees within the company. Organizations can receive funding for up to three consecutive years and then must postpone applying for support for one grant making cycle. Applications for Nourish Our Community grant requests are reviewed annually. The application process for the current fiscal year is June 1-May 31. Additional guidelines are available at: http://www.nourishkidstoday.org/about-us/application-guidelines.jsp

Requirements: Non-profit organizations based in AR, AZ, CA, CO, DC, FL, GA, IA, ID, IL, IN, LA, MA, MI, MN, MO, MS, NC, NE, NM, OH, OR, PA, SC, TN, TX, WA, and WI are eligible to apply for this grant.

Restrictions: ConAgra Foods Foundation does not fund: professional or amateur sports organizations and teams, or athletic events and programs; political organizations; terrorist organizations or those not compliant with the USA Patriot Act; fundraising events; emergency funding; loans, debt reduction or operating deficits; individuals; endowments; capital campaigns (unless solicited at the founder's discretion); memorial campaigns; elementary and secondary education.

Geographic Focus: Arizona, Arkansas, California, Colorado, Connecticut, District of Columbia, Florida, Georgia, Idaho, Illinois, Indiana, Iowa, Louisiana, Maine, Massachusetts, Michigan, Minnesota, Mississippi, Missouri, New Hampshire, New Mexico, North Carolina, Ohio, Oregon, Pennsylvania, Rhode Island, South Carolina, Tennessee, Texas, Vermont, Washington, Wisconsin

Date(s) Application is Due: May 31

Amount of Grant: 5,000 - 25,000 USD

Contact: Program Contact; foundation@conagrafoods.com

Internet: http://www.nourishkidstoday.org/about-us/application-guidelines.jsp

Sponsor: ConAgra Foods Foundation

One ConAgra Drive, CC-304

Omaha, NE 68102-5001

Connelly Foundation Grants 520

To achieve its mission to foster learning and improve the quality of life, Connelly Foundation provides grants toward costs associated with programs, direct services, general operations and capital projects to non-profit organizations and institutions working in the following fields: education; health and human services; arts and culture and civic enterprise. The Foundation supports non-profits with strong leadership, sound ideas, future viability, and attainable and well defined goals. It directs its philanthropy toward 501(c)3 organizations and institutions based in and serving Philadelphia and the counties of Bucks, Chester, Delaware, Montgomery and the City of Camden. The Foundation values the proposal process. Given its preference to review a comprehensive package as a primer for discussion, letters of inquiry or requests for pre-proposal discussions are not deemed necessary. Written proposals from nonprofit organizations are accepted and reviewed by the Connelly Foundation throughout the year, there are no deadlines.

Requirements: 501(c)3 organizations and institutions based in and serving in Philadelphia and its surrounding counties of Bucks, Chester, Delaware, and Montgomery in Pennsylvania and in the City of Camden, New Jersey are eligible to apply. There are determined parameters to the Foundation's financial support. It provides non-profit organizations only one grant within a twelve month period. As a general practice, it does not fund advocacy, annual appeals, charter schools, conferences, environmental projects, feasability or planning studies, general solicitations, historic preservation projects, national organizations, organizations focused on a single disease, public schools or research.

Restrictions: The foundation does not award grants to individuals, or political or national organizations; Nor does it respond to annual appeals or general letters of solicitation.

Geographic Focus: Pennsylvania

Contact: Emily C. Riley, Executive Vice President; (610) 834-3222; fax (610) 834-0866; info@connellyfdn.org

Sponsor: Connelly Foundation

1 Tower Bridge, Suite 1450

West Conshohocken, PA 19428

ConocoPhillips Foundation Grants 521

The foundation makes charitable grants (primarily in the communities where it has operations) in support of education, medical programs, human services, civic, cultural, youth, and other services. Contributions will be considered for organizations such as: federated organizations; educational institutions, both public and private, primarily at the college level; youth organizations; hospital and medical facilities and programs such as hospital buildings and equipment, improvement campaigns and other medical facilities; cultural organizations; civic services; and human service organizations. Applicants may download the application form from the Web site. There are no application deadlines.

Requirements: 501(c)3 tax-exempt organizations and, where appropriate 170(c) organizations, and international nonprofit organizations are eligible. Proof of the exemption must be submitted with grant applications.

Restrictions: Grants do not support religious organizations for religious purposes; war veterans and fraternal service organizations; endowment funds; national health organizations and programs; grants or loans to individuals; fund-raising events; corporate memberships or contributions to chambers of commerce, taxpayer associations and other bodies whose activities are expected to directly benefit the company; or political organizations, campaigns and candidates.

Geographic Focus: Alaska, California, Illinois, Louisiana, Montana, New Jersey, Oklahoma, Pennsylvania, Texas, Washington

Date(s) Application is Due: Aug 1

Amount of Grant: Up to 46,000,000 USD

Samples: Christian Community Service (Houston, TX)—$25,000; Jewish Day School of Metropolitan Seattle (Seattle, WA)—$25,000; YMCA of Greater Seattle (Seattle, WA)—$15,000.

Contact: Community Relations Manager

Internet: http://www.conocophillips.com/about/Contribution+Guidelines/index.htm

Sponsor: ConocoPhillips Foundation Grants

600 N Dairy Ashford

Houston, TX 77079

ConocoPhillips Grants 522

ConocoPhillips maintains a philanthropic contributions budget for nonprofit, charitable programs closely tied to its corporate goals and focused primarily in locations of strong business interests. Submit an executive summary outlining the purpose of the program or project, how it will be accomplished, expected results, a budget (noting administrative expenses such as: salaries and fees, program expenses and total income), other sources of financial support and a copy of the IRS tax determination letter that confirms 501(c)3 status. The grant must be used in the United States. Requests for grants in non-U.S. locations should be made directly to the ConocoPhillips international office doing business in that part of the world. Education and youth, civic and arts, employee volunteerism, safety and social services, and the environment are focus areas.

Requirements: Applications are accepted from areas where ConocoPhillips has a strong business presence, e.g., Texas and Oklahoma. All contributions are to be used within the United States.

Restrictions: ConocoPhillips does not award funds to individuals, sectarian or religious organization, promotional sponsorship and advertising (marketing related) or an endowment.

Geographic Focus: Alaska, California, Illinois, Louisiana, Montana, New Jersey, Oklahoma, Pennsylvania, Texas

Samples: Houston Baptist U (Houston, TX)—for the Cultural Arts Ctr capital campaign, $50,000; U of Texas (Austin, TX)—for scholarships, fellowships, and special programs in business, engineering, law, and the natural sciences, $1 million.

Contact: Program Contact; (281) 293-2685

Internet: http://www.conocophillips.com/about/Contribution+Guidelines/index.htm

Sponsor: ConocoPhillips Corporation

600 N Dairy Ashford, MA 3144

Houston, TX 77079

Conseil des arts de Montreal Touring Grants 523

The Conseil des arts de Montreal Touring Grants are mainly for professional non-profit arts organizations. Funding enables the best recent works to be presented within the following categories: circus arts, dance, music, and theatre; visual arts; media arts, film and new artistic practices; and literature. The program encourages works that reflect cultural diversity, creativity, and emerging artists. Collectives formed by professional artists working in the disciplines of circus arts, digital arts and world music can also submit an application. Cultural organizations cannot submit more than one touring project per year. In exceptional cases, service organizations may submit two different projects for the tour per year. The application, tour documents, and technical documents are available at the website.

Requirements: All organizations requesting financial assistance must be recognized as a professional organization, based in the City of Montreal, presenting artistic events on a regular basis and concerned primarily with the creation, production, and presentation of artistic activities.

Restrictions: Funding is not available for individuals.

Geographic Focus: Canada

Date(s) Application is Due: Sep 30

Contact: Michel Niquette; (514) 280-3585; mniquette.p@ville.montreal.qc.ca

Internet: http://www.artsmontreal.org/en/programs/conseil-des-arts-de-montreal-en-tournee

Sponsor: Conseil des arts de Montreal

1210 Sherbrooke Street East

Montreal, QC H2L 1L9 Canada

Constellation Energy Corporate EcoStar Grants 524

Environmental stewardship is one of Constellation Energy's core foundational values. Because of this commitment to use natural resources responsibly, prevent pollution, improve energy efficiency and enhance it's stewardship efforts, EcoStar Grants are now being offered to local communities where Constellation Energy does business. See, Constellation Energy's website for: listing of funding locations; on-line application; additional guidelines. Project should fit at least one of five environmental focus areas: Pollution Prevention; Education; Energy Efficiency; Conservation; Community Activism.

Requirements: Organization must be a 501(c)3 nonprofit with a Board.

Restrictions: Grant funds limited to maximum of 20% administration and office expenses (i.e., salaries, phone and postage)

Geographic Focus: All States

Date(s) Application is Due: Mar 16

Amount of Grant: 5,000 USD

Contact: Larry McDonnell; (401) 470-7433; media@constellation.com

Internet: http://www.constellation.com/portal/site/constellation/menuitem.999b6fed85785a2399084010016176a0

Sponsor: Constellation Energy Corporate

100 Constellation Way, Suite 1000C

Baltimore, MD 21202

Constellation Energy Corporate Grants 525

Constellation Energy provides its philanthropic resources to non-profit organizations that make an impact in these key focus areas: energy Initiatives; environment; education; economic development. Applications are accepted at various times throughout the year. Grant, Sponsorship, Banner Hanging, and In-Kind requests under $10,000 are reviewed on a rolling basis. The Corporate Contributions Committee meets bi-annually, in May and October, to review significant financial grant requests of $10,000 or more. Grant requests should be submitted by April 1 and September 1 respectively. Additional guidelines and the online applications are available at the companies website.

Requirements: The company makes charitable donations to 501(c)3 tax-exempt, nonprofit organizations.

Restrictions: Constellation Energy does not make grants to: individuals; churches or religious causes; individual schools; athletic teams or events; programs located outside Constellation Energy communities.

Geographic Focus: All States

Date(s) Application is Due: Apr 1; Sep 1

Contact: Larry McDonnell; (401) 470-7433; media@constellation.com

Internet: http://www.constellation.com/portal/site/constellation/menuitem.94939662e40191875fb60610025166a0/

Sponsor: Constellation Energy Corporate

100 Constellation Way, Suite 1000C

Baltimore, MD 21202

Consumers Energy Foundation 526

Since its creation in 1990, the Consumers Energy Foundation has touched countless lives and communities through it's grant programs, corporate giving and employee volunteers. The Foundation accepts grant applications from nonprofit organizations for innovative projects and activities creating measurable impact in five areas: Social Welfare, Michigan Growth and Environmental Enhancement, Education, Community and Civic, and Culture/Arts. The Foundation's areas of support include, operating budgets and capital funds.

Requirements: The Consumers Energy Foundation provides financial support primarily to Michigan organizations classified by the Internal Revenue Service as tax-exempt under section 501(c)3 of the Internal Revenue Code.

Restrictions: The following are ineligible for funding: individuals; individual scholarships; individual sponsorship related to fund-raising; organizations that do not qualify as charitable organizations as defined by the Internal Revenue Service; organizations that practice discrimination on the basis of sex, age, height, weight, marital status, race, religion, sexual orientation, creed, color, national origin, ancestry, disability, handicap, or veteran status; organizations whose operating activities are already supported by the United Way (except when the request is approved by the appropriate community United Way organization); political organizations and political campaigns; religious organizations when the contribution will be used for denominational or sectarian purposes; labor or veterans organizations; fraternal orders; social clubs; sports tournaments; talent or beauty contests; loans for small business; debt reduction campaigns.

Geographic Focus: Michigan

Amount of Grant: 500 - 10,000 USD

Samples: Saginaw Basin Land Conservancy, $6,000—for educational outreach efforts supporting wetlands preservation and land conservation within the Saginaw Bay Watershed; American Red Cross Mid-Michigan Chapter, $10,000—for a disaster response vehicle; Kalamazoo Department of Public Safety, $15,000—for development of a Kalamazoo Regional Police and Fire Training Center.

Contact: Carolyn Bloodworth, Secretary/Treasurer; (517) 788-0432; fax (517) 788-2281; foundation@consumersenergy.com

Internet: http://www.consumersenergy.com/welcome.htm

Sponsor: Consumers Energy

1 Energy Place, Room EP8-210

Jackson, MI 49201-2276

Conwood Charitable Trust Grants 527

The Conwood Charitable Trust was established to make a positive impact upon the communities where Conwood employees live and work by financially supporting organizations with a demonstrated ability to assist individuals in need. The elderly, underprivileged, youth, educational institutions and the arts are supported through the Conwood Charitable Trust. Funds from the Trust are donated primarily in the company's hometown of Memphis and in the surrounding Mid-South area. Additionally, contributions are made to organizations in other areas of Tennessee (Tennessee Independent Colleges and Universities Association) and in North Carolina (Independent College Fund of North Carolina).

Requirements: Eligible applicants include any 501(c)3 organization that supports the people of Tennessee.

Geographic Focus: Tennessee

Amount of Grant: 2,500 - 30,000 USD

Samples: Rhodes College, Memphis, Tennessee, $28,000; Neighborhood Christian Centers, Memphis, Tennessee, $15,000; Madonna Learning Center, Germantown, Tennessee, $5,000.

Contact: Ed Roberson, Vice-President; (901) 761-2050; fax (901) 767-1302

Internet: http://www.reynoldsamerican.com/Responsibility/Community8.aspx

Sponsor: Conwood Charitable Trust

813 Ridge Lake Boulevard

Memphis, TN 38119

Cooke Foundation Grants 528

Grants are awarded primarily for culture and the arts, social services, education, programs for youth and the elderly, humanities, health, and the environment. Organizations receiving grants must be located in Hawaii or serve the people of Hawaii. Preference will be given to requests from Ohau. Types of support include general operating support, capital campaigns, building and renovations, program development, seed money, and matching funds.

Requirements: Grant making is limited to the state of Hawaii.

Restrictions: Grants are not made to individuals, churches, or religious organizations, or for endowment funds, scholarships, or fellowships.

Geographic Focus: Hawaii

Date(s) Application is Due: Mar 2; Sep 1

Amount of Grant: 5,000 - 25,000 USD

Samples: Maui Community Arts and Cultural Ctr (HI)—to support the capital campaign to complete construction, $10,000; Honolulu Dance Theatre (HI)—for a ballet performance, $2,500; Kauai Historical Society (HI)—to support the lecture series, $2,500; Honolulu Academy of Arts (HI)—annual grant, $100,000.

Contact: Carrie Shoda-Sutherland, Senior Program Officer; (808) 566-5524 or (888) 731-3863, ext. 524; fax (808) 521-6286; csutherland@hcf-hawaii.org

Internet: http://www.cookefdn.org/

Sponsor: Cooke Foundation, Limited

1164 Bishop Street, Suite 800

Honolulu, HI 96813

Cooper-Levy Trust Grants 529

The trust provides financial support for the United Way and other nonprofit agencies providing food, shelter, basic services, and medical care to low-income families and children in Washington state. Types of support include general operating support and project support. The majority of grants will be made in the Puget Sound area. Application guidelines are available online.

Requirements: Washington 501(c)3 nonprofit organizations in Washington's King, Pierce, Spokane, Snohomish, and Yakima Counties are eligible.

Restrictions: Funds are not awarded for capital campaigns; computer or office equipment; book, video, or website production; event sponsorship; scholarships; medical research; or to individuals. Grants are not directed toward projects serving older adults or indigent adults without dependent children.

Geographic Focus: Washington

Date(s) Application is Due: May 15; Oct 15

Amount of Grant: 5,000 - 10,000 USD

Contact: Therese Ogle, Grants Consultant, c/o The Private Bank, Union Bank of California; (206) 781-3472; fax (206) 784-5987; oglefounds@aol.com

Internet: http://fdncenter.org/grantmaker/cooperlevy

Sponsor: Cooper-Levy Trust

P.O. Box 3123

Seattle, WA 98114

Cooper Foundation Grants 530

The objectives of the foundation are to fund innovative ideas that promise substantial impact in Nebraska and that encourage others to make similar or larger grants for the same purpose. All grants are made in Nebraska, with the majority in Lincoln and Lancaster County. The foundation's highest priorities are education, including projects to improve teaching and learning and parent education at pre-school and K-12 levels as well as educational solutions to human service issues; human services; the arts, especially in the area of non-traditional areas of curriculum to increase accessibility by under-served audiences; the humanities; and the environment. Types of support include seed money, technical assistance, matching funds, and programs and projects. Requests for general operating funds and capital campaigns for physical facilities receive less priority.

Requirements: Nebraska 501(c)3 organizations are eligible.

Restrictions: Grants will not be made to support individuals, endowments, private foundations, businesses, proposals devoted to health issues, or proposals of a religious nature.

Geographic Focus: Nebraska

Date(s) Application is Due: Jan 15; Apr 1; Aug 1; Oct 1

Amount of Grant: Up to 10,000 USD

Samples: Lincoln Literacy Council (NE)—to support the Refugee Women's Group, $10,000; Nebraska Statewide Arboretum—to support an exhibition in eight venues across Nebraska, $5,000; Foundation for Lincoln Public Schools (NE)—for program support, to enhance reading, math and science programs, expand opportunities for low income students and families and provide additional resources to schools and teachers, $50,000.

Contact: Grants Administrator; (402) 476-7571; fax (402) 476-2356; info@cooperfoundation.org

Internet: http://www.cooperfoundation.org

Sponsor: Cooper Foundation

870 Wells Fargo Center, 1248 O Street

Lincoln, NE 68508

Cooper Industries Foundation Grants 531

Cooper and the Cooper Industries Foundation annually donate more then $3 Million to nonprofit organizations serving the communities where their employees live and work. The Cooper Industries Foundation accepts and reviews grant requests throughout the year. There is no deadline; however, budgets are compiled annually each fall for the following year. Applicants must submit a brief letter explaining the purpose of the request with: concise description of organization and its mission; purpose and amount of request; budget information and other funding sources; evidence of 501(c)3 tax-exempt status; current listing of board members.

Requirements: Only 501(c)3 tax-exempt-status organizations are eligible. Programs must: benefit a community where Cooper is a significant employer; be endorsed by local Cooper management when applicable; not duplicate the efforts of the four Cooper-created programs; fulfill an important community need. Program objectives must coincide with that of the company.

Restrictions: The following types of organizations are generally ineligible for funding: United Way-funded organizations; national and state organizations; religious organizations; veterans organizations; political candidates, labor and lobbying organizations; hospitals; primary and secondary schools; scholarship organizations (except National Merit).

Geographic Focus: Alabama, Georgia, Illinois, Missouri, New York, North Carolina, South Carolina, Texas, Wisconsin, United Kingdom

Contact: Victoria B. Guennewig, VP Public Affairs; (713) 209-8800; fax (713) 209-8982; info@cooperindustries.com

Internet: http://www.cooperindustries.com/common/aboutCooper/corporateGiving.cfm?CFID=160327&CFTOKEN=61243618

Sponsor: Cooper Industries Foundation

P.O. Box 4446

Houston, TX 77210

Cord Foundation Grants 532

The foundation makes grants to a variety of groups in three broad areas: education, social services, and the arts. Grant recipients have included higher education institutions, research groups, youth organizations, community service agencies, religious organizations, and performing and visual arts centers. Types of support include general operating support, building construction/renovation, equipment acquisition, emergency funds, program development, scholarship funds, research, and matching funds. Grants are awarded nationwide, with preference given to requests from northern Nevada. Application forms are not required.

Requirements: Nonprofit organizations are eligible but giving is primarily in the northern Nevada area.

Restrictions: The foundation does not support general fund-raising events, memorial campaigns, deficit fundings, conferences, dinners, or mass mailings.

Geographic Focus: Nevada

Amount of Grant: 10,000 - 250,000 USD

Samples: Saint Marys Hospital Foundation, Reno, NV, $200,000— for hospice program; Reno, City of, Reno, NV, $500,000—for purchase of YMCA property; Food Bank of Northern Nevada, Sparks, NV, $200,000—for new distribution center.

Contact: William Bradley, Trustee; (775) 323-0373

Sponsor: Cord Foundation

418 Flint Street

Reno, NV 89501-2008

Corina Higginson Trust Grants 533

The Corina Higginson Trust makes grants to organizations based in or benefiting the greater Washington Metropolitan area. The Trust's goals are: to increase opportunities for individuals for the purpose of improvement and development of their capabilities; to provide relief of the poor, distressed, and underprivileged; to promote social welfare by organizations designed to accomplish any of the above purposes or to lessen neighborhood tensions; to enhance opportunities for education about the arts and about the environment; and to eliminate prejudice and discrimination; or to defend civil rights secured by law.

Requirements: 501(c)3 District of Columbia, Maryland, and Virginia nonprofit organizations are eligible.

Restrictions: Grants do not support individuals, fixed assets, religious organizations, medical or health-related programs, endowment funds to individual schools, or scholarship funds.

Geographic Focus: District of Columbia, Maryland, Virginia

Date(s) Application is Due: Mar 1; Sep 1

Amount of Grant: 5,000 - 10,000 USD

Samples: Black Student Fund, Washington, DC, $5,000; Calvary Womens Services, Washington, DC, $7,500; Posse Foundation, Washington, DC, $10,000.

Contact: Wilton C. Corkern, Jr., (301) 283-2113; fax (301) 283-2049

Internet: http://www.corinahigginsontrust.org/instructionsforloi.html

Sponsor: Corina Higginson Trust

3400 Bryan Point Road

Accokeek, MD 20607

Cornerstone Foundation of Northeastern Wisconsin Grants 534

The community foundation supports nonprofit organizations primarily in Brown County, Wisconsin. The foundations area of interest are: education, cultural programs, social service and, youth agencies. With an additional interest in supporting healthcare facilities. The foundation offers the following types of support: annual campaigns; building/renovation; capital campaigns; continuing support; debt reduction; emergency funds; endowments; equipment; general/operating support; matching/challenge support; program; development. Contact the foundation by telephone for guidelines before submitting a proposal, no application form is required.

Requirements: Nonprofits in Green Bay and northeastern Wisconsin may submit applications for grant support. The primary focus is Brown County.

Restrictions: No grants are available to: individuals, religious, or political organizations.

Geographic Focus: Wisconsin

Date(s) Application is Due: Jan 15; Sep 15

Amount of Grant: 10,000 - 400,000 USD

Samples: Green Bay Symphony Orchestra, Green Bay, WI, $10,000—for youth orchestra program; Boys and Girls Club of Green Bay, Green Bay, WI, $400,000—for capital campaign; Salvation Army of Green Bay, Green Bay, WI, $24,900—for transitional housing program; N.E.W. Community Clinic, Green Bay, WI, $50,000—for medical expense program.

Contact: Sheri Prosser; (920) 490-8290; cornerstone@cfnew.org

Sponsor: Cornerstone Foundation of Northeastern Wisconsin

111 North Washington Street, Suite 450

Green Bay, WI 54301-4208

Corning Incorporated Foundation Educational Grants 535

The grants improve education by supporting selected K-12 school districts, community colleges and four-year institutions of higher learning primarily in communities where the sponsor company has operations. Areas of involvement have included community service programs for students, curriculum enrichment, student scholarships, facility improvement, and instructional technology projects for the classroom.

Requirements: Support goes to institutions that are tax-exempt under Section 501(c)3 of the Internal Revenue Code and which are public charities as defined in Section 509(a) of the Code. All requests to the foundation for support must be made in writing. Grant seekers are advised to submit a two- to three-page letter of inquiry, signed by the senior administrative officer of the organization.

Restrictions: Grants do not support individuals; political parties, campaigns, or causes; labor or veterans' organizations; religious or fraternal groups; volunteer emergency squads; athletic activities; courtesy advertising; or fundraising events.

Geographic Focus: All States

Amount of Grant: 1,000 - 25,000 USD

Samples: Wilson College (Chambersburg, PA)—for the Learning Resources Ctr, $5000; Corning City School District (Painted Post, NY)—to support computerization and curriculum enrichment, $33,000; Junior Achievement of Elmira (Corning, NY)—for general program support, $3000.

Contact: Karen Martin, Associate Director; (607) 974-8722; fax (607) 974-4756; martinkc@corning.com

Internet: http://www.corning.com/inside_corning/foundation.asp

Sponsor: Corning Foundation

1 Riverfront Plaza, MP-BH-07

Corning, NY 14831

Coughlin-Saunders Foundation Grants 536

The foundation awards grants to nonprofit organizations in its areas of interest, including arts and arts education, higher education, religion, social services, and youth organizations. Types of support include general operating support, capital campaigns, building construction/renovation, equipment acquisition, emergency funds, program development, professorships, and scholarship funds. Proposals are preferred in January or February. Grants are made primarily for projects which benefit Alexandria, Louisiana, and the surrounding area. New Orleans and the surrounding area will be considered.

Requirements: 501(c)3 tax-exempt organizations in central Louisiana may apply.

Restrictions: Grants are not made to individuals or for fund raisers. Endowments will not be funded.

Geographic Focus: Louisiana

Amount of Grant: 100 - 40,000 USD

Contact: Ed Crump Jr., Grants Administrator; (318) 561-4070; fax (318) 487-7339; csfoundation@kricket.net

Sponsor: Coughlin-Saunders Foundation

2010 Gus Kaplan Drive

Alexandria, LA 71301

Countess Moira Charitable Foundation Grants 537

The Countess Moira Charitable Foundation was established in 2000 with its mission being "to aid the well-being of youth anywhere in the World" by supporting charitable organizations that focus on the betterment of youth. Qualified organizations may submit inquiries for operating program, endowment and capital funding needs that support the mission of the foundation. There are no deadlines; inquiries will be accepted throughout the year.

Requirements: The foundation will only consider unsolicited inquiries from organizations in the New York tri-state area, or national organizations that may also utilize funds in the broader international arena. Grants will only be made to 501(c)3 nonprofit organizations. Initial contact should be made via email (see below) before making a formal grant proposal.

Restrictions: Do not send unsolicited inquiries or grant proposals via paper mail to the foundation's mailing address as these will not be considered at all. Grants will not be given for events or fundraisers nor to individuals.

Geographic Focus: Connecticut, New Jersey, New York

Samples: Astor Services for Children and Families, Rhinebeck, NY, $25,000; Camp Exclamation Point, Richmond, VT, $5,000; Westhampton Beach Performing Arts, Westhampton Beach, NY, $1,000,000.

Contact: Carolyn Gray, President; inquiries@countessmoirafdn.org

Internet: https://sites.google.com/a/countessmoirafdn.org/countessmoirafoundation/

Sponsor: Countess Moira Charitable Foundation

P.O. Box 8078

Pelham, NY 10803

Covenant Mountain Ministries Grants   **538**

The program, established in 1995, is a non-profit foundation dedicated to spreading the gospel through the establishment of churches and assisting in the creation of new ministries. Grants are given primarily to West Virginia organizations (Christian agencies, churches, and family service offices) that give aid to abused spouses and children. Funding comes in the form of general operations support. Though there are no deadlines, an application form can be secured by contacting the Ministries directly.

Geographic Focus: West Virginia

Amount of Grant: 500 - 1,500 USD

Contact: Marilyn L. Perkins, (304) 487-1680; Marilyn@Marilynperkins.com

Sponsor: Covenant Mountain Ministries

573 Pigeon Roost Trail

Princeton, WV 24740-4246

Cowles Charitable Trust Grants   **539**

The foundation awards grants, primarily in New York, Florida, and on the East Coast, for the arts and culture, including museums and the performing arts; environment; education, including early childhood education, secondary and higher education, medical school education, adult basic education and literacy, and adult continuing education; hospitals and AIDS programs, including research; social services, including family planning, human services, and federated giving; and community funds, including leadership development, civil rights, and race relations. Types of support include general operating support, capital campaigns, annual campaigns, equipment acquisition, endowment funds, continuing support, seed money, building construction/renovation, matching funds, professorships, and program development. Application forms are required; initial approach should be by letter. The board meets in January, April, July, and October.

Requirements: Nonprofit organizations may apply for grant support. Grants are awarded primarily along the Eastern Seaboard.

Geographic Focus: Florida, New York

Date(s) Application is Due: Mar 1; Jun 1; Sep 1; Dec 1

Amount of Grant: 1,000 - 40,000 USD

Samples: Church of the Holy Comforter, Burlington, NC, $53,200; Miami Art Museum of Dade County, Miami, FL, $30,000; Allen-Stevenson School, New York, NY, $27,500.

Contact: Mary Croft, Treasurer; (732) 936-9826

Sponsor: Cowles Charitable Trust

P.O. Box 219

Rumson, NJ 07760

Crail-Johnson Foundation Grants   **540**

The Crail-Johnson Foundation (CJF) has defined itself as a children's charity, and the vast majority of grant-making is directed toward programs benefiting children, youth and families in the greater Los Angeles area. Proposals, which are not relevant to the foundation's mission and funding priorities, will not be considered. CJF provides grants for program initiatives and enhancements, general operating support and capital projects as well as selected endowments. CJF provides technical assistance to selected community-based initiatives benefiting children and families. The majority of Crail-Johnson Foundation funding supports organizations located in the greater Los Angeles area and projects that directly benefit Los Angeles area residents. National organizations providing services in Los Angeles are also considered. Occasionally, grants are made to programs and projects that are regional or national in scope, where potential benefits to children and families in Los Angeles can be clearly demonstrated. Initial contact with the Crail-Johnson Foundation should be in

the form of a letter of inquiry, letters are accepted October through December each year for the following year's grant cycle and are generally considered in the order in which they are received. Organizations selected to submit proposals will be asked to complete a Grant Application Form provided by the Foundation.

Requirements: The foundation provides financial support primarily through grants to public non-profit organizations that are exempt under Section 501(c)3 of the Internal Revenue code and are not a private foundation under Section 509(a).

Restrictions: Support is not granted for programs and projects benefiting religious purposes, university level education, research, events recognizing individuals or organizations, political causes or programs attempting to influence legislation. No grants are made directly to individuals.

Geographic Focus: California

Amount of Grant: 5,000 - 50,000 USD

Samples: Heart of Los Angeles Youth, Los Angeles, CA, $25,000—Smart Start Elementary Education Program; Mentor LA, Los Angeles, CA, $25,000—staffing and special program enrichment; Strive Foundation, Houston, TX, $20,000—expansion of academic and arts Program.

Contact: Pat Christopher, Program Officer; (310) 519-7413; fax (310) 519-7221; pat-christopher@crail-johnson.org

Internet: http://www.crail-johnson.org/grants-application.htm

Sponsor: Crail-Johnson Foundation

222 W Sixth Street, Suite 1010

San Pedro, CA 90731

Cralle Foundation Grants   **541**

The foundation awards grants in the areas of education and higher education, children and youth services, community development, human services, and museums to Kentucky nonprofits. Emphasis is given to nonprofits serving residents of Louisville. Types of support include: building and renovation; capital campaigns; continuing support; endowments; equipment; operating support; matching and challenge support; program development; scholarship funds; and seed money. Interested organizations should initially send a letter requesting an application form. Applicants should submit four copies of their application. Application deadlines are March 1 and September 1. The foundation's board meets in April and October.

Requirements: Nonprofit organizations in Kentucky are eligible.

Restrictions: No grants to individuals.

Geographic Focus: Kentucky

Date(s) Application is Due: Mar 1; Sep 1

Amount of Grant: 5,000 - 50,000 USD

Samples: Maryhurst School, Louisville, KY, $40,250 - for Seven Challenges Program; Blessings in a Backpack, Louisville, KY, $25,000 - for students at Portland Elementary; Family and Children's Place, Louisville, KY, $25,000 - for operating support.

Contact: James Crain, Jr., Executive Director; (502) 581-1148; fax (502) 581-1937; jcrain37@bellsouth.net

Sponsor: Cralle Foundation, Inc.

614 West Main Sreet, Suite 2500

Louisville, KY 40202-4252

Crane Fund Grants   **542**

The Crane Fund was established in 1914 as a private charitable trust, and it grants aid to former employees of the Crane Company (or their dependents) who by reason of age or physical disability are unable to be self-supporting and are in need of assistance. The Crane Fund is administered by a Board of Trustees and a Pension Committee, both appointed by Crane Company's Board of Directors.

Geographic Focus: All States

Amount of Grant: 1,000 - 10,000 USD

Contact: Administrator; (201) 585-0888 or (203) 363-7300; cranefund@craneco.com

Internet: http://www.craneco.com/Category/33/The-Crane-Fund.html

Sponsor: Crane Company

140 Sylvan Avenue Suite 4

Englewood Cliffs, NJ 07632

Cranston Foundation Grants   **543**

The foundation directs most of its grants to the geographic areas where Cranston Print Works Company has operations and a large number of employees, including Rhode Island, Massachusetts, Louisiana, and New York. Targeted priority areas are education, health and welfare, culture and the arts, and civic and community programs. Types of support include

general operating support, employee matching gifts, and employee-related scholarships. All requests should be made in writing and should contain details and funding requirements pertaining to the project. The February deadline is for scholarships; the August deadline is for grants.
Requirements: IRS 501(c)3 organizations serving Rhode Island, Massachusetts, Louisiana, and New York are eligible.
Geographic Focus: Massachusetts, New York, Rhode Island
Date(s) Application is Due: Feb 15; Aug 31
Amount of Grant: 200 - 5,000 USD
Contact: Trustee; (401) 943-4800
Sponsor: Cranston Foundation
1381 Cranston Street
Cranston, RI 02920

Cresap Family Foundation Grants 544
The Cresap Family Foundation was established in 2012, upon the final sale of the family's business, Premium Beers of Oklahoma, one of the largest Anheuser-Busch distributorships in the United States. Though the foundation may be newly-launched, the family's spirit of giving dates as far back as 1968 when a self-made auto dealer purchased a little Anheuser-Busch distributorship in Bartlesville, Oklahoma. The Foundation's primary fields of interest include: animal welfare; arts and humanities; education; health and wellness; and youth and families. Most recent awards have ranged from $1,000 to $50,000. A Letter of Intent summarizing the project for funding should be submitted through an online application process by the May 1 deadline. Full applications will be by invitation, and must be received by July 1.
Requirements: The Trustees invite proposals from 501(c)3 organizations. Preference will be given to organizations in Central Oklahoma and counties in Northeast Oklahoma, which include: Craig, Delaware, Mayes, Nowata, Osage, Ottawa and Washington.
Geographic Focus: Oklahoma
Date(s) Application is Due: Jul 1
Amount of Grant: 1,000 - 50,000 USD
Samples: Will Rogers Elementary School, Oklahoma City, Oklahoma, $25,000 - program development (2014); Carselowey Volunteer Fire Department, Ketchum, Oklahoma, $10,000 - equipment purchase (2014); William W. Barnes Children's Advocacy, Claremore, Oklahoma, $13,100 - health care programs (2014).
Contact: Randy Macon, Executive Director; (405) 755-5571; fax (405) 755-0938; rmacon@cfok.org
Internet: http://www.cresapfoundation.org/grants-and-giving/
Sponsor: Cresap Family Foundation
2932 NW 122nd Street, Suite D
Oklahoma City, OK 73120

Crescent Porter Hale Foundation Grants 545
The foundation places emphasis on organizations engaged in Catholic endeavors, with preference given to organizations in the San Francisco Bay area counties of Alameda, Contra Costa, Marin, San Francisco, and San Mateo. Areas of concern considered desirable for funding include organizations devoted to Catholic elementary and high school, education in the fields of art and music, agencies serving disadvantaged and at-risk youth, families and elderly. Applications for capital funds, scholarship funds, requests for special projects, as well as for general operating program support will be considered. The foundation will consider other worthwhile programs that can be demonstrated as serving broad community purposes, leading toward the improvement of the quality of life. Agencies serving disadvantaged youth, the disabled, or the elderly are of particular interest. Organizations wishing to apply should address a brief letter of intent to the foundation indicating the nature of the program and/or the specific project for which funding is sought. The board meets in April, September, and December to consider requests.
Requirements: To be eligible for consideration, organizations must meet the following criteria: be a corporate non-profit organization; qualify for tax exemption by the State in which said organization or institution is incorporated; be a organization to which contributions are deductible by donors for income tax purposes, generally of the type described in Section 501(c)3 of the Internal Revenue Code of 1954 and the corresponding Sections of the 1939 Code and prior Revenue Acts; be classified as a non-private foundation pursuant to the 1969 Tax Reform Acts; have and annual financial audit in accordance with approved accounting practices.
Restrictions: Individuals are ineligible. Healthcare-related, research, or postgraduate education programs are ineligible.
Geographic Focus: California

Amount of Grant: 5,000 - 250,000 USD
Samples: The BASIC Fund, San Francisco, San Francisco, CA, $240,000—to support scholarships for elementary school children in Bay Area schools; Stagebridge, Oakland, CA, $15,000—to support its Healthy Aging theatre program; Summer Search, San Francisco, CA, $25,000—in support of its leadership development programs for low-income high school students.
Contact: Ulla Davis, Executive Director; (415) 388-2333; fax (415) 381-4799
Internet: http://www.crescentporterhale.org/policy/policy.htm
Sponsor: Crescent Porter Hale Foundation
655 Redwood Highway, Suite 301
Mill Valley, CA 94941

Crestlea Foundation Grants 546
The foundation supports Delaware nonprofits in its areas of interest, including secondary education, higher education, natural resource conservation, health care, housing development, community development, social services, and public affairs. Types of support include annual campaigns, general operating support, capital campaigns, building construction/renovation, and equipment acquisition. There are no application forms.
Requirements: Delaware nonprofits are eligible.
Geographic Focus: Delaware
Date(s) Application is Due: Nov 1
Amount of Grant: 5,000 - 50,000 USD
Samples: Philadelphia Museum of Art (Philadelphia, PA)—for operating support, $82,500; Archmere Academy (Claymont, DE)—for capital campaign, $20,000.
Contact: Stephen Martinenza, Secretary-Treasurer; (302) 654-2477
Sponsor: Crestlea Foundation
100 W 10th Street, Suite 1109
Wilmington, DE 19801

CRH Foundation Grants 547
The foundation awards general operating grants to U.S. nonprofit organizations in its areas of interest, including health and human services. Religious organizations also are eligible. Preference is given to requests from New Jersey and New York. Applications are accepted each year between May 1 and October 31. Inquiries must be in writing.
Requirements: U.S. 501(c)3 nonprofit organizations may apply.
Geographic Focus: All States
Date(s) Application is Due: Oct 31
Amount of Grant: Up to 74,000 USD
Samples: United Jewish Community (River Edge, NJ)—$4000; New York Times Neediest Cases (New York, NY)—$1000; American Cancer Society (Atlanta, GA)—$1000.
Contact: Grants Administrator; (201) 568-9300; fax (201) 568-6374
Sponsor: CRH Foundation
175 N Woodland Street
Englewood, NJ 07631

Cricket Foundation Grants 548
The Cricket Foundation of Boston awards grants to New England nonprofit organizations in its areas of interest, including: the arts; museums; and environmental conservation and protection. Types of support include: program development; matching funds; seed grants; publication funding; general operating support; and building construction/renovation. Amounts have recently ranged from $3,000 to $10,000, though are occasionally higher. The annual deadlines for submission are identified as April 30 and October 31. There are no specified application forms, and interested parties should forward a two- to three-page proposal detailing need and budget. Telephone inquiries are welcome.
Requirements: 501(c)3 New England nonprofit organizations may apply.
Restrictions: Grants do not support endowment funds, fellowships, scholarships, or loans.
Geographic Focus: Connecticut, Maine, Massachusetts, New Hampshire, Rhode Island, Vermont
Date(s) Application is Due: Apr 30; Oct 31
Amount of Grant: 3,000 - 10,000 USD
Contact: George W. Butterworth, Attorney; (617) 570-1130 or (617) 570-1787; fax (617) 523-1231; gbutterworth@goodwinprocter.com
Sponsor: Cricket Foundation
Exchange Place, Suite 2200
Boston, MA 02109-2881

Crossroads Fund Seed Grants 549

The fund supports organizations working on issues of social and economic justice in the Chicago metropolitan area. This grants program supports new, emerging, and small community based organizations that are actively engaged in social change work. Types of support include general operating grants, start-up costs, and project development. The maximum grant in this program is $10,000.

Requirements: Community organizations rooted in the Chicago metropolitan area, including northwestern Indiana, with annual expenses under $300,000 in the last completed fiscal year are eligible. Additionally, organizations must meet the Fund's general funding criteria: Working for Social Change—organizing community members to examine and challenge the underlying causes of their problems and conditions; Cross-Issue Organizing—working with an understanding of the connectedness among the various people and issues that make up the whole community; Grassroots Leadership—involving the people who are directly affected at all levels of the organization in planning, organizing and leading, and working to continue building leadership within the grassroots community; Solid Plan—having a clear purpose to the project with well-planned goals, objectives, activities and a tool to measure outcomes and impact; a timeline and budget that reflects the proposed objectives and activities; a realistic fundraising plan.

Restrictions: The fund does not support organizations that are involved in electoral campaigns; contribute substantially to support lobbying at the federal, state, or local levels; or support private, in contrast to public, interest.

Geographic Focus: Illinois, Indiana

Amount of Grant: Up to 10,000 USD

Samples: Center for Immigrant Resources and Community Arts ($5,000): youth-focused organization that uses theater and art to organize various immigrant communities across social, economic and political issues; First Defense Legal Aid ($4,000): provides legal advice and aid in Chicago Police Department stations to low-income individuals who cannot afford attorneys; Blocks Together ($7,500) grassroots, multi-issue social justice organization on the West Side of Chicago addressing affordable housing, public education & restorative justice; Next Steps ($3,000) organizes mentally disabled and often homeless individuals for greater voice in the systems that affect them, particularly major boards, institutions and decision-making bodies addressing homelessness and mental health; Waukegan Leadership Council ($3,000): protects the welfare of immigrant and Latino residents in a city that is predominately Latino from current immigration policies of indiscriminate arrest, detainment and deportation through voter registration, education and building collaborations with non-immigrant communities of color; Young Women's Empowerment Project ($9,000): run by and for women and girls with life experiences in the sex trade and street economies who use social justice, transformative justice and harm-reduction strategies to address issues affecting them. These grants included support for a research project documenting violence against their constituency.

Contact: Jane Kimondo; (773) 227-7676; jane@crossroadsfund.org

Internet: http://www.crossroadsfund.org/seedfund.html

Sponsor: Crossroads Fund

3411 W Diversey Avenue, #20

Chicago, IL 60647

Crossroads Technical Assistance Program Grants 550

Grants support Chicago area organizations working on social and economic justice issues. The program supports the specific technical assistance needs of smaller organizations, focusing on projects that reach beyond a group's regular, ongoing work to build the organization's internal capacity. Types of support include funding for technology; training; conferences; or hiring a consultant or facilitator for evaluation, planning, or a retreat. Priority is given to organizations that have been funded by the foundation in the last 2 years.

Requirements: Community-based organizations in the Chicago metropolitan area, including northwestern Indiana, that have annual expenses under $150,000, and that have been in operation for at least three years are eligible.

Restrictions: The fund does not support organizations that are involved in electoral campaigns; contribute substantially to support lobbying at the federal, state, or local levels; or support private, in contrast to public, interest.

Geographic Focus: Illinois, Indiana

Date(s) Application is Due: Mar 1; Sep 1

Amount of Grant: Up to 3,000 USD

Contact: Inhe Choi, Program Director; (773) 227-7676; fax (773) 227-7790; inhe@crossroadsfund.org or info@crossroadsfund.org

Internet: http://www.crossroadsfund.org/techassist.html

Sponsor: Crossroads Fund

3411 W Diversey Avenue, #20

Chicago, IL 60647

Crowell Trust Grants 551

The Trustees of the Trust continue to follow the directives for grantmaking which Henry Parsons Crowell established in his original indenture. Crowell identified candidates for grants from among agencies whose purpose is: Evangelism and discipleship; international cross-cultural missions; U.S. focused missions; Christian higher education; and Christian leadership development. Types of support include matching funds, operating budgets, building funds, equipment, and scholarship funds. There are no application deadlines.

Restrictions: As a general rule grants are not made to individuals, local churches, pre-kindergarten through high school education, endowment funds, land acquisition, or building construction.

Geographic Focus: All States

Amount of Grant: 10,000 - 100,000 USD

Contact: Executive Director; (719) 272-8300; fax (719) 272-8305; grantadmin@crowelltrust.org or info@crowelltrust.org

Internet: http://www.crowelltrust.org/page.php?id=8

Sponsor: Crowell Trust

1880 Office Club Pointe, Suite 2200

Colorado Springs, CO 80920

Cuesta Foundation Grants 552

The Cuesta Foundation was formed on May 16, 1962, by Charles W. Oliphant and his sister, Allene O. Mayo, to continue the philanthropic legacy of their father, A.G. Oliphant. The mission of the Foundation is to continue the philanthropic legacy of the A.G. Oliphant Family by funding 501(c)3 charities in the communities of the foundation's trustees. The Foundation offers support for operating expenses and capital needs of qualifying organizations, with its primary fields of interest being: health; social services; and community needs. A letter of inquiry, summarizing the project for funding, should be submitted through the online application process annual deadline of March 31. Grant applications by invitation must be received no later than June 30.

Requirements: Preference will be given to 501(c)3 organizations either located in, or serving the residents of, Tulsa, Oklahoma.

Geographic Focus: Oklahoma

Date(s) Application is Due: Jun 30

Contact: Eric Oliphant, President; (405) 755-5571; fax (405) 755-0958

Internet: https://www.foundationmanagementinc.com/foundations/cuesta-foundation/

Sponsor: Cuesta Foundation

2932 NW 122nd Street, Suite D

Oklahoma City, OK 73120

Cullen Foundation Grants 553

The foundation awards grants to eligible Texas nonprofit organizations in its areas of interest, including arts and culture, education, health, and public service programs. There are no application deadlines or forms. Proposals should detail the purpose and scope of the grant; the amount requested; other sources of anticipated funding; a list of trustees, directors, and staff; financial statements and tax returns of the last two years; and anticipated project budgets. Preference is given to requests from Houston.

Requirements: Texas 501(c)3 or 170(c) nonprofit organizations are eligible.

Restrictions: The board prefers not to consider galas, testimonials, and various other types of fundraising events; organizations that in turn make grants to others; activities whose sole purpose is the promotion or support of a specific religion, denomination, or church; purchase of uniforms, equipment, or trips for school-related organizations or amateur sports teams; applications from an organization more frequently than once every 12 months, whether the previous application was approved or denied; applications from an organization that has received a multi-year grant from the foundation, until all payments of that grant have been made; or oral presentations from potential applicants.

Geographic Focus: Texas

Amount of Grant: Up to 100,000,000 USD

Samples: Reasoning Mind (Houston, TX)—Bringing the internet-based 5th grade math curriculum to Houston students, $50,000; Child Advocates, Inc. (TX)—Operating support, $20,000; The Heritage Society (Houston, TX)—for the relocation and restoration of the 1868 Pilot House, $25,000; Camp for All Foundation (Houston, TX)—Improvements to the camp's drainage system and main thoroughfare, $72,950;

Contact: Sue Alexander; (713) 651-8837; salexander@cullenfdn.org

Internet: http://www.cullenfdn.org

Sponsor: Cullen Foundation

601 Jefferson, 40th Floor

Houston, TX 77002

Cummins Foundation Grants 554

The Foundation's areas of interest include: children and youth; education; elementary and secondary schools; civil rights; women; minorities; leadership development; increasing minority economic participation. Inquiries and proposals may be submitted in writing at any time during the year. A preliminary proposal should include a brief description of the problem being addressed, specifically what the program hopes to achieve, operating plan and cost, description of key leadership and how one will be able to tell whether or not the program worked. Upon receipt of the proposal, the Foundation staff will respond regarding the possibility of funding.

Requirements: The Foundation makes virtually all its local grants in communities where Cummins and its subsidiaries have manufacturing plants or affiliate businesses. These communities are: Columbus and Seymour, Indiana and their environs; Charleston, South Carolina; Jamestown, New York; Findlay, Ohio; Cookeville, Nashville and Memphis, Tennessee; Lake Mills, Iowa; Rocky Mount, North Carolina; El Paso, Texas; Fridley, Minnesota; Stoughton, Wisconsin. International grants are also reviewed by the Foundation Board. Proposals from the non-Indiana plant communities should be submitted first to the local plant manager or business leader.

Restrictions: The Foundation does not support political causes or candidates, or sectarian religious activities. No grants are made to individuals.

Geographic Focus: Indiana, Iowa, Minnesota, New York, North Carolina, Ohio, South Carolina, Tennessee, Texas, Wisconsin, Brazil, Japan, Mexico

Amount of Grant: 2,500 - 100,000 USD

Contact: Gayle Dudley Nay, (812) 377-3114; fax (812) 377-7897; Cummins. Foundation@cummins.com

Internet: http://www.cummins.com/cmi/content.jsp?siteId=1&langId=1033& menuId=82&overviewId=5&menuIndex=0

Sponsor: Cummins Foundation

500 Jackson Street

Columbus, IN 47201

Cystic Fibrosis Canada Transplant Center Incentive Grants 555

The Transplant Center Incentive grants are intended to enhance the quality of care available to cystic fibrosis transplant candidates by providing eligible centers with supplementary funding for support of personnel directly involved in the provision of patient services; travel to the annual North American Cystic Fibrosis conference; and administrative costs associated with providing data to the Canadian Cystic Fibrosis Lung Transplant Registry. Grants are renewable on an annual basis. Applications must be received at Cystic Fibrosis Canada's office no later than 1 October. The value of Transplant Centre Incentive grants will be determined in accordance with a formula which takes account of the number of patients accepted for transplantation; transplanted; followed in the first year, in the second to fifth year, and more than 5 years post-operatively in a given centre, based on an average of three years' activity, ending 31 December of the year preceding the application.

Requirements: Any Canadian lung transplant center which currently has one or more individuals with cystic fibrosis listed for transplant may apply for a Transplant Center Incentive grant.

Restrictions: Under no circumstances will funding be provided to more than one transplant centers in the same city.

Geographic Focus: Canada

Date(s) Application is Due: Oct 1

Contact: Administrator; (416) 485-9149; info@cysticfibrosis.ca

Internet: http://www.cysticfibrosis.ca/en/treatment/TransplantCentre IncentiveGrants.php

Sponsor: Cystic Fibrosis Canada

2221 Yonge Street, Suite 601

Toronto, ON M4S 2B4 Canada

D.J. McManus Foundation Grants 556

The D.J. McManus Foundation was established in New York in 1999. Its primary fields of interest include: the arts; children and youth services; the environment and natural resource preservation; higher education; and human services. Though giving is focused in the State of New York, the Foundation does offer a few awards nationally. Support is usually given in the form of general operations. Interested parties should submit a formal application, including a detailed description of the project and the amount of funding requested. There are no annual deadlines, and awards typically range from $250 to $1,200.

Restrictions: No grants are given to individuals.

Geographic Focus: All States

Samples: Archeological Institute of America, Boston, Massachusetts, $500 - general operating support; Breakthrough Collaborative, San Francisco,

California, $1,000 - general operating support; Desmond Fish Library, Garrison, New York, $1,100 - general operating support.

Contact: Deborah M. McManus, President; (212) 874-7426; fax (212) 894-7003; dmmcmanus@aol.com

Sponsor: D.J. McManus Foundation

420 W. Broadway

New York, NY 10012-3741

D. W. McMillan Foundation Grants 557

The D.W. McMillan Foundation, established in Alabama in 1956, supports organizations involved with children and youth services, health care, health organizations, homelessness, hospitals, human services, mental health and crisis services, residential and custodial care, hospices, people with disabilities, and the economically disadvantaged population. Giving is primarily centered in the states of Alabama and Florida. There are no specific deadlines, though applicants should submit proposals well before the annual board meeting on December 1. Applicants should begin by contacting the Foundation with a letter of inquiry. Final notification of awards are given by December 31 each year.

Geographic Focus: Alabama, Florida

Date(s) Application is Due: Nov 1

Samples: Department of Human Resources, Escambia County, Alabama, $160,000 - general operations; Appleton Volunteer Fire Department, Brewster, Alabama, $5,000 - general operations; Baptist Hospital, Pensacola, Florida, $30,000 - general operations.

Contact: Ed Leigh McMillan II, Treasurer; (251) 867-4881

Sponsor: D.W. McMillan Foundation

329 Belleville Avenue

Brewton, AL 36426-2039

Dade Community Foundation Community AIDS Partnership Grants 558

The Community AIDS Partnership, is a special funding initiative established in 1990 through the National AIDS Fund and local funders to increase the availability of private funds to address gaps in the local HIV/AIDS service system, particularly in the area of prevention. The Community AIDS Partnership represents one of the major sources of private philanthropic funds for HIV prevention in Miami-Dade County. As the result of a public/private partnership with Miami-Dade County, the Foundation also awards $350,000 in county funds, which represents a significant increase in the local public sector's commitment to funding HIV prevention. Through the Community AIDS Partnership, the Foundation supports quality programs that respond to the local population risk profile and that incorporate strategies with the greatest potential to effectively address the priority populations, communities and service needs related to HIV prevention in Miami-Dade County. Grant Size: $30,000 Single Organization, $60,000 for Collaborations.

Requirements: Eligible applicants include nonprofit tax-exempt organizations, as defined by the Internal Revenue Code, which are serving the residents of Miami-Dade County. Preference will be given to or- ganizations based in Miami-Dade County or if located outside the county, are working in partnership with an organization based in Miami-Dade.

Geographic Focus: Florida

Amount of Grant: 30,000 - 60,000 USD

Samples: Camillus House, $30,000 - to support a comprehensive HIV/AIDS program that targets homeless members of racial/ethnic minority communities who are either HIV positive or are at very high risk for HIV infection due to injection drug use and/or heterosexual contact; MUJER, $30,000 - to continue the Nosotras Viviremos project which seeks to increase awareness about HIV/AIDS in migrant farmworker communities in South Miami-Dade County;

Contact: Gianne Ewing-Chow, Senior Program Officer; (305) 371-2711; fax (305) 371-5342; gianne.ewingchow@dadecommunityfoundation.org

Internet: http://www.dadecommunityfoundation.org/Site/wc/wc145.jsp

Sponsor: Dade Community Foundation

200 S Biscayne Boulevard, Suite 505

Miami, FL 33131-5330

Dade Community Foundation Grants 559

The funding for this program is made available through the Foundation's unrestricted and field of interest funds. This program is designed to honor both the donors interests and address significant community issues such as: education; health; human services; arts and culture; environment; economic development; at-risk youth; abused and neglected children; living with HIV/AIDS; homelessness; social justice; care of animals; heart disease and more.

Requirements: Eligible applicants include nonprofit tax-exempt organizations, as defined by the Internal Revenue Code, which are serving the residents of Miami-Dade County. Preference will be given to organizations based in Miami-Dade County or if located outside the county, are working in partnership with an organization based in Miami-Dade.

Restrictions: The Foundation does not provide grants to individuals, for memberships, fundraising events or memorials. Grants to government agencies are made on a very restricted basis.

Geographic Focus: Florida

Date(s) Application is Due: Nov 15

Amount of Grant: 7,500 USD

Samples: Alliance for Musical Arts Productions, $7,500 - to provide after school and summer camp services to youth from low-income households living in Opa-locka; Chai Lifeline, $6,500 - to support Smile S'more, a unique program designed to bring fun and love to children who are being treated for cancer and other life-threatening illnesses on pediatric specialty units of hospitals; Earth Learning, $10,000 - to create an EarthFest network that will form an umbrella to unite Earth Day celebrations across South Florida under one banner.

Contact: Charisse Grant, Vice President for Programs; (305) 371-2711; fax (305) 371-5342; charisse.grant@dadecommunityfoundation.org

Internet: http://www.dadecommunityfoundation.org/Site/programs/overview.jsp

Sponsor: Dade Community Foundation

200 S Biscayne Boulevard, Suite 505

Miami, FL 33131-5330

DaimlerChrysler Corporation Fund Grants 560

The fund contributes to organizations grouped under the general categories of education, health and human services, civic and community, religion, and culture and the arts. Within these categories, grants are made available for public welfare or for charitable, scientific, educational, environmental, safety, building, and affirmative action purposes. Higher education grants largely support science and engineering education and business management. A major interest of the corporation is the establishment of national certification standards for elementary and secondary teachers. Another area of concern is the encouragement of early reading skills, and a pilot project has been funded for research in this area. The fund earmarks funds for its future workforce initiatives, which support business and engineering departments, community-based job-skill training, and entry-level work preparation. Types of support include matching gifts, program grants, scholarships, annual campaigns, building construction/renovation, general support, and employee matching gifts. In considering requests, the fund evaluates each applicant organization on its own merits; considered are the programs in which it is engaged, constituencies served, operation procedures, services offered, quality of management, its accountability, finances, and fund-raising practices. Applications are accepted at any time.

Requirements: Eligible for support are nonprofit, tax-exempt educational, health, civic, and cultural organizations primarily in locations where the greatest number of employees of Chrysler and its US-based subsidiaries live and work (Alabama, Delaware, Illinois, Indiana, Michigan, Missouri, New York, Ohio, and Wisconsin). Some support is targeted for national organizations as well.

Restrictions: Grants are not awarded to support endowments, conferences, trips, direct health care delivery, multiyear pledges, capital campaigns, fund-raising activities related to sponsorships, advertising, or debt retirement.

Geographic Focus: All States

Samples: Charles H. Wright Museum of African American History (Detroit, MI)—$1 million to complete an exhibit area; Second Harvest Food Bank of Central Florida, $25,000 and food via convoy of Dodge Rams, and $50,000 to help residents affected by recent tornadoes.

Contact: Brian Glowiak; (248) 512-2502; fax (248) 512-2503; mek@dcx.com

Internet: http://www.fund.daimlerchrysler.com

Sponsor: DaimlerChrysler Corporation Fund

1000 Chrysler Drive

Auburn Hills, MI 48326-2766

Dale and Edna Walsh Foundation Grants 561

The foundation joins hands with effective charitable organizations to meet human need and promote the common good worldwide. Grants support ministries, religious activities, health, relief efforts, education, community services, and arts organizations. Guidelines are available online.

Requirements: Tax-exempt, nonprofit charities are eligible.

Restrictions: The foundation does not contribute toward normal church operation; culturally liberal activist causes or organizations that primarily seek to influence legislation or government spending; or political parties or associated political organizations.

Geographic Focus: All States

Contact: Grants Administrator; (847) 230-0056; fax (847) 901-9193; Info@dewfoundation.org

Internet: http://dewfoundation.org

Sponsor: Dale and Edna Walsh Foundation

6461 Valley Wood Drive

Reno, NV 89523

Dallas Women's Foundation Grants 562

The Foundation promotes women's philanthropy and raises money to support community programs that help women and girls realize their full potential. Priority will be given to funding programs that include elements of the following: effect long-term, positive changes to help women succeed in reaching their full potential; expanded choices and opportunities for women and girls; evaluation tools that include measurement for effectiveness with clean definition of program success; and programs specifically designed to take into consideration the gender-specific needs and differences of women and girls. The Foundation also encourages projects developed in consultation and collaboration with other agencies, and which promote coordination, cooperation and sharing among organizations. Effective use of volunteers, as well as Board diversity and involvement, are equally encouraged.

Requirements: To be eligible to receive a grant from the Foundation, applicants must meet all of the following criteria: be in receipt of a current 501(c)3 tax-exempt designation from the Internal Revenue Service (dated within the last 10 years); at least 50% of the population served must be residents of Dallas, Denton, or Collin County, with priority given to organizations serving residents of Dallas County; 75% of the clients benefiting from the grant funding must be women and/or girls.

Geographic Focus: Texas

Samples: Avance (Dallas, TX)—for equipment and operating support of this organization that promotes academic achievement among Hispanics in Dallas, $10,000; U of North Texas, Division of Equity and Diversity (Dallas, TX)—for a seminar on critical issues affecting lesbians, $15,000; Interfaith Housing Coalition (Dallas, TX)—to provide transitional housing, training, and support services to Dallas-area homeless families, $20,000; English Language Ministry (Dallas, TX)—to provide free child care and English-language instruction to non-English speaking adults, particularly women, $17,500.

Contact: Pat Alexander, (214) 965-9977; fax (214) 526-3633; palexander@dallaswomensfoundation.org

Internet: http://www.dallaswomensfoundation.org/grants/highlights.html

Sponsor: Dallas Women's Foundation

4300 MacArthur Avenue, Suite 255

Dallas, TX 75209

Dana Corporation Foundation Grants 563

The foundation gives to communities throughout the country. Social services and education are top priorities. Most education grants are awarded to colleges and universities through a matching gifts program. Other grants go to civic affairs, environmental, youth, and health organizations with the smallest percentage awarded in the areas of culture and arts. Types of support include annual campaigns, building construction/renovation, continuing support, equipment acquisition, land acquisition, operating budgets, seed grants, and capital campaigns.

Requirements: 501(c)3 organizations in communities where Dana Corporation facilities are located are eligible.

Restrictions: The foundation does not make grants to individuals or to organizations that practice discrimination, religious groups for denominational purposes, political activities, or United Way-supported organizations for operating expenses. The foundation does not purchase tickets to charitable or fund-raising events or support goodwill advertising.

Geographic Focus: All States

Amount of Grant: 1,000 - 20,000 USD

Contact: Ed McNeal, (419) 535-4500

Internet: http://www.dana.com

Sponsor: Dana Corporation Foundation

P.O. Box 1000

Toledo, OH 43697

Danellie Foundation Grants 564

The foundation's primary areas of interest include services for the financially disadvantaged, including housing and social services. The types of support offered are: building/renovation; capital campaigns; continuing support; general/operating support; program development; scholarship funds and; sponsorships. Contact foundation for application guidelines. New York/New

Jersey Area Common Application Form and New York/New Jersey Common Report Form accepted. Application form required.

Requirements: Nonprofit organizations in Southern New Jersey, (including Mercer and portions of Monmouth counties), the Greater Philadelphia, Pennsylvania area and, the Balimore, Maryland region are eligible to apply. The foundation also has an international interest in Guatemala and Haiti.

Restrictions: No support for political organizations or professional sports, libraries or museums. No grants to individuals, or for endowments or radio and television.

Geographic Focus: Maryland, New Jersey

Amount of Grant: 4,000 - 180,000 USD

Samples: University of Medicine and Dentistry, Stratford, NJ, $71,000 - for Latino health clinic; Doctors of the World USA, New York, NY, $65,000 - for medical needs in Third World countries; Aid for Friends, Philadelphia, PA, $20,000 - for needy, disabled, and the elderly homebound.

Contact: Nancy Dinsmore, (856) 810-8320; danelliefoundation@verizon.net

Sponsor: Danellie Foundation

P.O. Box 376

Marlton, NJ 08053

Daniel and Nanna Stern Family Foundation Grants 565

The Daniel and Nanna Stern Family Foundation was established in 2006, with the expressed interest in providing support primarily to programs in New York City. The Foundations major fields of interest include: the arts; education; hospitals; film and video; television; and performing arts centers. Though a formal application is required, interested applicants should begin by forwarding a letter to the Foundation office, offering a detailed description of the project, the amount of funding requested, contact information, and copies of both the IRS determination letter and most recent audit. No annual deadlines for submission have been identified. Most recent awards have ranged from $50,000 to $150,000.

Requirements: Any 501(c)3 organization located in, or serving the residents of, New York City are eligible to apply.

Geographic Focus: New York

Amount of Grant: 50,000 - 150,000 USD

Samples: Allen-Stevenson School, New York, New York, $150,500 - general operating support; Carter Burden Center for the Aging, New York, New York, $48,000 - general operating support; Film Society of Lincoln Center, New York, New York, $50,000 - general operating support for the arts.

Contact: Anne Colucci, (212) 610-9006 or (212) 610-9054

Sponsor: Daniel and Nanna Stern Family Foundation

650 Madison Avenue, 26th Floor

New York, NY 10022-1029

Daniels Fund Grants-Aging 566

Bill Daniels was a visionary business leader whose compassion for people, and unwavering ethics and integrity earned him respect throughout his life. He grew up during the Great Depression, served his nation as a decorated fighter pilot, and became a driving force in establishing the cable television industry. Mr. Daniel's passion for helping others inspired him to create the Daniels Fund to extend his legacy of generosity far beyond his lifetime. The Daniels Fund provides grants to nonprofit organizations in Colorado, New Mexico, Utah, and Wyoming that fit within its nine distinct funding areas. Mr. Daniels wanted to help seniors maintain personal dignity, remain independent, and be respected. The Daniels Fund supports organizations that share this vision and recognize the exceptional value of older adults to the community. The Fund accepts grant applications any time during the year; there are no submission deadlines.

Requirements: The Daniels Fund makes grants for specific programs or projects, general operating support, or capital campaigns. The organization applying must be classified by the Internal Revenue Service as a 501(c)3 or equivalent. Eligible nonprofit organizations must provide programs or services in Colorado, New Mexico, Utah, or Wyoming. Organizations with a nationwide impact and large institutions (such as a university or school district) should call before applying. Before starting the online application process, the sponsor strongly encourages all potential applicants to call first. The Daniels Fund is rarely the sole provider of funds for a project, and encourages applicants to develop a variety of individual, government, and private funding sources.

Restrictions: The fund generally will not support medical or scientific research; arts, cultural, and museum programs; environmental stewardship programs; historic preservation projects; candidates for political office; sponsorships, tables, or tickets for special events or fundraising events; endowments; fiscal sponsorships; or debt retirement.

Geographic Focus: Colorado, New Mexico, Utah, Wyoming

Contact: Bill Fowler, Senior Vice President, Grants Program; (303) 393-7220; fax (720) 941-4201; grantsinfo@danielsfund.org or BFowler@DanielsFund.org

Internet: http://danielsfund.org/Grants/Goals-Aging.asp

Sponsor: Daniels Fund

101 Monroe Street

Denver, CO 80206

Dan Murphy Foundation Grants 567

The foundation awards grants to eligible nonprofit organizations in its areas of interest: support of activities and charities of Roman Catholic Church Archdiocese of Los Angeles, including education, health care, and social service programs. Types of support include building construction/renovation, capital support, continuing support, general operating support, matching grants, and program development. The majority of grants are awarded to Los Angeles, CA, nonprofits. There are no application forms or deadlines.

Geographic Focus: California

Amount of Grant: 10,000 - 100,000 USD

Samples: Council of Major Superiors of Women Religious (Washington, DC)—for general operating support, $150,000; Notre Dame High School of Sherman Oaks (CA)—for a matching grant for the capital campaign, $350,000; Thomas Aquinas College (Santa Paula, CA)—for the scholarship endowment fund, $545,511.

Contact: Daniel J. Donohue, President; (213) 623-3120

Sponsor: Dan Murphy Foundation

P.O. Box 711267

Los Angeles, CA 90071

Dave Coy Foundation Grants 568

The Dave Coy Foundation, established by Dave and Nina Coy, awards grants to Texas nonprofits in the areas of children and youth, social services for the economically disadvantaged, and religion (religious organizations, religious education, and religious welfare). Types of support include: general operating support; capital campaigns; building construction and renovation; equipment acquisition; and emergency funds. Most recent awards have ranged from $10,000 to $250,000. Application forms are required, and the annual deadline for submission is June 1.

Requirements: Nonprofits in Bexar County, Texas, are eligible.

Restrictions: Grants are not made to individuals.

Geographic Focus: Texas

Date(s) Application is Due: Jun 1

Amount of Grant: 10,000 - 250,000 USD

Contact: Gregg Muenster, Senior Vice President; (210) 270-5371

Internet: http://about.bankofamerica.com/en-us/global-impact/find-grants-sponsorships.html?cm_mmc=EBZ-CorpRep-_-vanity-_-EE01LT0021_Vanity_foundation-_-Enterprise&template=fd_funding#fbid=PAAFqa53JC9

Sponsor: Dave Coy Foundation

P.O. Box121

San Antonio, TX 78291

David and Barbara B. Hirschhorn Foundation Grants 569

Seeking to improve the lives of families and children and cultivate a level playing field, the David and Barbara B. Hirschhorn Foundation supports Jewish and secular initiatives that expand educational opportunity, address human service needs, and promote intergroup tolerance and understanding. Support is primarily given within the state of Maryland, providing grants of annual campaigns, capital campaigns, endowments, general/operating support. Letters of inquiry and proposals are accepted on a rolling basis. Your application will be acknowledged by postcard within two weeks.

Requirements: 501(c)3 non-profit organizations are eligible to apply. To begin the application process submit a letter of inquiry to the Foundation, no longer then 3 pages long. The initial application should include the following: information about the programs(s) for which funding is requested; need, purpose, activities, and evaluation plan of the proposed program(s); program budget (including sources of anticipated income as well as expenditure) and timeline; dollar amount of funding requested. Information about your organization: history, mission, and key accomplishments; information on Board members and key staff; current institutional operating budget (including major sources of revenue as well as expenditures); copy of IRS tax status determination letter or information about your fiscal agent. The Foundation will also accept initial applications that conform to the Association of Baltimore Area Grantmakers [ABAG] Common Grant Application.

Restrictions: No support available for: scholarships to individuals; unsolicited proposals for academic, scientific, or medical research; direct mail, annual giving, membership campaigns, fundraising and commemorative events.
Geographic Focus: All States
Amount of Grant: 2,500 - 350,000 USD
Samples: American Committee for Shaare Zedek Medical Center in Jerusalem, Baltimore, MD, $20,000; AMIT Women, Inc. New York, NY, $10,000; Institute for Christian and Jewish Studies, Inc., Baltimore, MD, $100,000;
Contact: Betsy Ringel; (410) 347-7103; fax (410) 347-7210; info@blaufund.org
Internet: http://www.blaufund.org/foundations/davidandbarbara_f.html
Sponsor: David and Barbara B. Hirschhorn Foundation
10 E Baltimore Street, Suite 1111
Baltimore, MD 21202

David Bohnett Foundation Grants 570

The foundation's mission is to improve society through social activism. Focus areas include the promotion of the positive portrayal of lesbians and gay men in the media; voter registration activities; animal language research, animal companions, and eliminating rare animal trade; environmental conservation; the reduction and elimination of the manufacture and sale of handguns in the United States; community-based social services that benefit gays and lesbians; and the development of mass transit and non-fossil fuel transportation. Types of support include general operating support, program specific grants, seed money, and multiyear grants. Applicants should email a letter of inquiry to the program officer.
Requirements: Nonprofit organizations are eligible.
Restrictions: Grants do not support individuals, videos or other film productions, or organizations outside the United States.
Geographic Focus: All States
Date(s) Application is Due: Jan 27; Jul 28
Amount of Grant: 5,000 - 50,000 USD
Samples: Disability Rights Education and Defense Fund (Berkeley, CA)—for a project to ensure that voting booths in California are accessible to disabled people, $25,000; Proteus Fund (Amherst, MA)—for the Civil Marriage Collaborative, a group of organizations working to achieve civil marital rights and oppose efforts that limit or deny those rights to lesbian, gay, bisexual, and transgender people, $100,000; Service Members Legal Defense Network (Washington, DC)—for operating support and for legal fees to support active-duty service members who are gay or lesbian, $35,000; Bill Foundation (Beverly Hills, CA)—to find permanent, safe homes for abandoned and unwanted dogs as companion animals, $10,000.
Contact: Michael Fleming, Executive Director; (310) 277-4611; fax (310) 203-8111; mfpfleming@yahoo.com
Internet: http://www.bohnettfoundation.org/grants/grantapplication.htm
Sponsor: David Bohnett Foundation
2049 Century Park E, Suite 2151
Los Angeles, CA 90067-3123

David Geffen Foundation Grants 571

The foundation supports nonprofits in Los Angeles, California, and New York, New York, with some giving in Israel as well. The Foundation offers support in its five principal funding areas: AIDS/HIV, civil liberties, the arts, issues of concern to the Jewish community, and health care. Support is provided for general operations and special projects. There are no application deadlines. Applicants are asked to submit a letter of request.
Requirements: 501(c)3 tax-exempt organizations in Los Angeles, CA, and New York, NY, may submit a proposal letter (without folder or binder) including description of the project, objectives, constituents served, evaluation criteria; background on the organization including key staff, volunteers, and board; copy of IRS letter confirming tax-exempt status; financial information including line-item budget for the project; and copy of non-discrimination policy from the organization's hiring guidelines.
Restrictions: The Foundation does not fund individuals, or organizations based outside of the United States. The foundation generally does not support documentaries or other types of audio-publication of books or magazines.
Geographic Focus: California, New York, Israel
Samples: Natural Resources Defense Council, New York, NY, $50,000; Childrens Diabetes Foundation at Denver, Denver, CO, $25,000; Morehouse College, Atlanta, GA, $50,000.
Contact: J. Dallas Dishman, Program Director; (310) 581-5955; fax (310) 581-5949; ddishman@geffenco.com
Sponsor: David Geffen Foundation
12011 San Vicente Boulevard, Suite 606
Los Angeles, CA 90049-4926

David Robinson Foundation Grants 572

Founded by David Robinson, a former National Basketball Association center who played his entire career for the San Antonio Spurs. The foundation awards grants to Texas nonprofit organizations in its areas of interest, including agriculture, family services, single parents, social services, and spirituality. The majority of grants will be awarded in the San Antonio area.
Requirements: Texas nonprofit organizations are eligible. Contributes only to pre-selected organizations.
Geographic Focus: Texas
Amount of Grant: 200 - 500,000 USD
Contact: Grants Administrator; (210) 696-8061; fax (210) 696-7754; drfoundation@express-news.net
Sponsor: David Robinson Foundation
24165 IH-10 West, Suite 217-628
San Antonio, TX 78257

Dayton Power and Light Foundation Grants 573

The Dayton Power and Light Foundation was established in 1985 reinvest in the communities it serves and contribute to the improvement of the overall quality of life. The Foundation focuses its contributions in the following strategic contribution areas: economic development - creating an engaged, vibrant, welcoming community that is seen as a great place to live and work; arts and culture - heightening the impact of arts and local culture in our communities; health and human services - to improve the quality of life for all; and education: - improving educational access and outcomes. Direct donations are also made to civic, cultural, and health and welfare organizations that do not participate in community funds, such as United Way or community chests, but serve a real need. Requests should be made via the online application format, and should include a description of the history, structure, purpose, and program of the organization and a summary of the support needed and how it will be used. The annual deadline is October 1
Requirements: 501(c)3 organizations in the greater Dayton, Ohio, area are eligible. This includes a twenty-four county service area surrounding the city (see map at the website for specific details).
Restrictions: The foundation prefers not to support: capital campaigns; college fund-raising associations; conduit organizations; endowment or development funds; fraternal, labor, or veterans organizations; hospital operating budgets; individual members of federated campaigns; individuals; national organizations outside the DP&L service territory; religious organizations; sports leagues; or telephone or mass-mail solicitations. Grants are rarely made to tax-supported institutions.
Geographic Focus: Ohio
Date(s) Application is Due: Oct 1
Amount of Grant: 1,000 - 20,000 USD
Contact: Ginny Strausburg, Executive Director; (937) 259-7925; fax (937) 259-7923; ginny.strausburg@dplinc.com
Internet: http://www.waytogo.com/cc/cc.phtml
Sponsor: Dayton Power and Light Company Foundation
1065 Woodman Drive, P.O. Box 1247
Dayton, OH 45432

Daywood Foundation Grants 574

The Foundation distributes available funds primarily to community service organizations focusing on the arts, and health and human services. Grants are available in the following types: annual campaigns; building/renovation; capital campaigns; continuing support; debt reduction; emergency funds; equipment; general/operating support; matching/challenge support; seed money.
Requirements: Nonprofit 501(c)3 organizations situated in, and benefiting Charleston, Lewisburg, Barbour, Greenbrier and Kanawha counties Of West Virginia are eligible to apply. There is no standardized grant application form. Send proposal to: William W. Booker, 1500 Chase Tower, Charleston, WV 25301.
Restrictions: Grants do not support endowment funds, research, individuals, or individual scholarships or fellowships.
Geographic Focus: West Virginia
Date(s) Application is Due: Sep 15
Samples: Clay Center for the Arts and Sciences of West Virginia, Charleston, WV, $150,000—for endowment; University of Charleston, Charleston, WV, $125,000— for pharmacy school; West Virginia Symphony Orchestra, Charleston, WV, $100,000- for endowment.
Contact: William W. Booker, Treasurer; (304) 343-4841
Sponsor: Daywood Foundation
707 Virginia Street E, Suite 1600
Charleston, WV 25301

Deaconess Community Foundation Grants 575

The foundation awards grants to eligible Ohio nonprofit organizations in its areas of interest, including health, education, welfare, community, and social service activities. Proposals that are of greatest interest to the Foundation are those that have the strongest fit to the mission statement and that have some or all of the following characteristics: projects that have specific measurable outcomes and a tangible ability to evaluate results and measure success; projects that are supported by other funding sources; and projects that have identified potential for ongoing support beyond the life of the grant. Application information is available online.

Requirements: Only qualified non-profit organizations located in Cuyahoga County which are classified by the Internal Revenue Code as tax-exempt 501(c)3 organizations are eligible for funding consideration.

Restrictions: Grant requests for the following will not be considered: individuals, governmental agencies or any other organization that is not a tax exempt 501(c)3 organization; internal operations and capital campaigns of churches; research projects; or endowments. Grant funds may not be used to carry on propaganda or otherwise attempt to influence legislation, participate in, or intervene in, any political campaign on behalf of or in opposition to any candidate for public office, or to conduct, directly or indirectly, any voter registration drive (within the meaning of Section 4945(d)2 of the Internal Revenue Code).

Geographic Focus: Ohio

Date(s) Application is Due: Jan 15; May 15; Sep 15

Samples: Achievement Centers for Children, Highland Hills, Ohio, $20,000 - program support for Family Support Services for children with disabilities and their families; The Center For Nonprofit Excellence, Cleveland, Ohio, $75,000 - program support for Building Nonprofit Excellence in 2013 which includes Needs Assessments and BVU's Consulting Center for nonprofits with missions that are aligned with DCF.

Contact: Deborah Vesy; (216) 741-4077; dvesy@deacomfdn.org

Internet: http://www.deacomfdn.org/guidelines.html

Sponsor: Deaconess Community Foundation

7575 Northcliff Avenue, Suite 203

Brooklyn, OH 44144

Deborah Munroe Noonan Memorial Fund Grants 576

The Deborah Munroe Noonan Memorial Fund was established in 1949 by her son, Walter Noonan, to support and promote quality educational, human-services, and health-care programming for underserved populations. Grant requests for general operating support are strongly encouraged. Program support will also be considered. Small, program-related capital expenses may be included in general operating or program requests. To better support the capacity of nonprofit organizations, multi-year funding requests are strongly encouraged. Applicants must apply online at the grant website. Applicants are strongly encouraged to do the following before applying: review the downloadable state application procedures for additional helpful information and clarifications; review the downloadable online-application guidelines at the grant website; review the foundation's funding history (link is available from the grant website); review the online application questions in advance; and review the list of required attachments. These will generally include: a list of board members; financial statements (audited, reviewed, or compiled by independent auditor); an organization summary; a list of other funding sources; an IRS Determination letter; and other required documents. All attachments must be uploaded in the online application as PDF, Word, or Excel files. The application deadline for the Deborah Munroe Noonan Memorial Fund is 11:59 p.m. on July 1. Applicants will be notified of grant decisions before September 30.

Requirements: Applicants must have 501(c)3 tax-exempt status and serve the people of Greater Boston.

Restrictions: The fund does not support requests from individuals, organizations attempting to influence policy through direct lobbying, or any political campaigns.

Geographic Focus: Massachusetts

Date(s) Application is Due: Jul 1

Samples: Community Music Center of Boston, Boston, Massachusetts, $21,000, general operating support of CMCB's 100th anniversary and to support a continuum of music education programs and music therapy for children, teens, adults; Family and Childrens Services of Greater Lynn, Lynn, Massachusetts, $25,000, capacity-building for program services that promote early literacy; Brockton Neighborhood Health Center, Brockton, Massachusetts, $29,000, Certified Medical Interpreter Program.

Contact: Miki C. Akimoto; (866) 778-6859; miki.akimoto@baml.com

Internet: https://www.bankofamerica.com/philanthropic/fn_search.action

Sponsor: Deborah Munroe Noonan Memorial Fund

225 Franklin Street, 4th Floor, MA1-225-04-02

Boston, MA 02110

DeKalb County Community Foundation Grants 577

The DeKalb County Community Foundation Grants support programs for DeKalb County, Indiana citizens that address today's needs and prepare for tomorrow's challenges. Grant guidelines are intentionally broad in order to meet the community's ever-changing charitable needs. Grants are awarded for charitable programs and projects in the following areas of interest: art and culture; community development; education; environment; health and human services; and youth development. Grants are also available for the general operating expenses of organizations that address local charitable needs. Applicants are encouraged to contact the Foundation before submitting a proposal to be certain it follows the grant guidelines. They are also encouraged to attend a free one hour workshop to help them understand the Foundation's grant process and learn basic proposal writing tips. The Foundation gives priority to grant proposals for programs/projects that: will be completed within one year of receiving a grant; strengthen the grant seeking organization; directly relate to the grant seeker's mission; project a high degree of community impact; benefit many local people; and are proactive rather than reactive.

Requirements: After reviewing the grant guidelines, applicants will fill out the online proposal form. Applicants should include their contact information, financial information, a brief summary of the request, their organization's mission statement, and a detailed explanation of the benefits they'll receive from the grant. They should also include their operating expenses, total budget, and their source of funds. Applicants will then email the proposal form to the Foundation contact person or mail a printed copy to the Foundation address.

Restrictions: Grants are less likely to be awarded for: repeat funding for a program/project that has received a Foundation grant within the last two years; or a funding debt. The Foundation grants to religious organizations for charitable purposes but does not award grants for religious purposes.

Geographic Focus: Indiana

Date(s) Application is Due: Jul 1

Amount of Grant: 500 - 7,000 USD

Samples: American Red Cross of Northeast Indiana, disaster services for DeKalb County; $2,500: St. Martin's Healthcare, operating expenses for medical clinic; $7,000.

Contact: Rosie Shinkel; (260) 925-0311; rshinkel@dekalbfoundation.org

Internet: http://www.dekalbfoundation.org/g_grantmaking.php

Sponsor: DeKalb County Community Foundation

650 West North Street

Auburn, IN 46706

Delaware Division of the Arts General Operating Support Grants 578

The Delaware Division of the Arts, a branch of the Delaware Department of State, is dedicated to nurturing and supporting the arts to enhance the quality of life for all Delawareans. Together with its advisory body, the Delaware State Arts Council, the Division administers grants and programs that support arts programming, educate the public, increase awareness of the arts, and integrate the arts into all facets of Delaware life. The Division awards General Operating Support grants to Delaware arts organizations in support of their annual operating expenses to ensure that year-round participation in the arts is available to the people of Delaware. These grants are funded on a matching basis, and operate on a two-year cycle. New applicants are considered in even-numbered years. The annual deadline for applications is March 2.

Requirements: To be eligible for grants for Arts Organizations, applicants must: have the promotion, presentation, production, and/or teaching of the arts as their primary purpose as outlined in their charter, incorporation papers, bylaws, and IRS nonprofit determination letter; have a stable, functioning board of directors that meets at least quarterly; be based and chartered in Delaware as a nonprofit organization; exempt from federal income tax under Section 501(c)3 or 501(c)4 or 509(a) of the Internal Revenue Code; and be eligible to receive donations allowable as charitable contributions under Section 170(c) of the Internal Revenue Code of 1954. Only arts organizations awarded general operating support for the previous year may apply. New arts organizations must first complete the Division's Start-Up program for emerging arts organizations before applying.

Restrictions: Matching funds must be cash and may not be received from the National Endowment for the Arts.

Geographic Focus: Delaware

Date(s) Application is Due: Mar 2

Contact: Paul Weagraff, Director; (302) 577-8278; paul.weagraff@state.de.us

Internet: http://www.artsdel.org/grants/default.shtml

Sponsor: Delaware Division of the Arts

820 North French Street, Carvel State Office Building

Wilmington, DE 19801

Delaware Division of the Arts Project Support Grants for Community- 579
Based Organizations

Community-based arts organizations may apply for funding to support projects that provide increased access to high-quality arts activities throughout the stae. Arts organizations with unique and unanticipated opportunities to present the literary, performing, visual, media, or folk arts in ways that will reach new audiences may apply for funding. Arts organizations may apply for funding to enable them to take advantage of unique opportunities to present their programs at events of regional, national, or international significance outside Delaware. Applicants may request up to eighty percent of the cost of the project. New arts organizations, including those who have not yet received their IRS nonprofit status, may apply for funding to support their early programming and organizational development efforts. Arts organizations may apply for funding to help make their programs more accessible to people with disabilities. Organizations will be eligible to receive only one grant award in this category per calendar year. Applications are accepted until the annual deadline of March 2.
Requirements: To be eligible to apply applicants must: Have the promotion, presentation, production, and/or teaching of the arts as their primary purpose as outlined in their charter, incorporation papers, bylaws, and IRS nonprofit determination letter; Have a stable, functioning board of directors that meets at least quarterly; Be based and chartered in Delaware as a nonprofit organization; exempt from federal income tax under Section 501(c)3 or 501(c)4 or 509(a) of the Internal Revenue Code; and eligible to receive donations allowable as charitable contributions under Section 170(c) of the Internal Revenue Code of 1954.
Restrictions: No individual may compile or submit an application on behalf of an organization if that individual is a member or relative of a member of the Delaware State Arts Council (DSAC) or DDOA staff.
Geographic Focus: Delaware
Date(s) Application is Due: Mar 2
Amount of Grant: 2,000 - 10,000 USD
Contact: Paul Weagraff, Director; (302) 577-8278; paul.weagraff@state.de.us
Internet: http://www.artsdel.org/grants/CBOOpportunity.pdf
Sponsor: Delaware Division of the Arts
820 North French Street, Carvel State Office Building
Wilmington, DE 19801

Delaware Division of the Arts Stabilization Grants 580

Arts Stabilization grants provide nonprofit arts organizations with funding for improvements to facilities owned and operated or under long-term lease by the organization. These grants provide funding for needed maintenance, repairs, or renovations of existing facilities owned and operated by the nonprofit arts organization. They also provide funding for the repair, upgrade, or replacement of facility-related equipment, such as lighting, seating, flooring, display, and storage. Applications are evaluated on the following criteria: extent to which the project will enhance accessibility to the facility, safety, and/or delivery of services; nature of the project as it relates to the Division's funding priorities; extent to which the project fits into a broader long-range plan for facilities management and maintenance; evidence of the need for the project and Arts Stabilization funding; inclusion of at least two competitive bids for the proposed project; and extent to which the budget for the project is complete and realistic. Applications are submitted through the e-grant online process. The annual deadline for applications is March 2.
Requirements: To be eligible for funding, applicants must have the promotion, presentation, production, and/or teaching of the arts as their primary purpose as outlined in their charter, incorporation papers, bylaws, and IRS nonprofit determination letter; have a stable, functioning board of directors that meets at least quarterly; be based and chartered in Delaware as a nonprofit organization; exempt from federal income tax under Section 501(c)3 or 501(c)4 or 509(a) of the IRS code; and eligible to receive donations allowable as charitable contributions.
Restrictions: The Division will not accept applications through fiscal agents. No individual may compile or submit an application on behalf of an organization if that individual is a member or relative of a member of the Delaware State Arts Council (DSAC) or DDOA staff. Arts organizations that are members of the Arts Consortium of Delaware, Inc. (ArtCo) are not eligible to apply for Arts Stabilization Grants through the Delaware Division of the Arts. Ineligible organizations include: The Christina Cultural Arts Center; Delaware Art Museum; Delaware Symphony Orchestra; Delaware Theatre Company; Grand Opera House; OperaDelaware; Rehoboth Art League; and the Wilmington Music School. Ineligible funding also includes projects determined to be routine maintenace for upkeep; purchase of computer hardware/software; purchase of office equipment; and multiple projects submitted together or separately.
Geographic Focus: Delaware

Date(s) Application is Due: Mar 2
Contact: Paul Weagraff, Director; (302) 577-8278; paul.weagraff@state.de.us
Internet: http://www.artsdel.org/grants/ArtsStabilization.pdf
Sponsor: Delaware Division of the Arts
820 North French Street, Carvel State Office Building
Wilmington, DE 19801

Delaware Division of the Arts StartUp Support Grants 581

StartUp Support Grants are available every two years to support programming and to develop and strengthen the management capacity of emerging arts organizations. They provide resources for young arts organizations to develop and enhance the basic skills of running a 501(c)3 nonprofit so that they can operate in a sustainable manner, and provide a valuable public service to the cultural life of Delaware. The Delaware Division of the Arts StartUp program consists of modest program support, training, and consultant input. Applications are evaluated on artistic quality, availability of the arts/service to the community, and management. Eligible expenses include: artist fees; administrative costs; contractual services; facilities operations; marketing and publicity; salaries and benefits; supplies and materials; professional development; technical costs; and travel. StartUp consists of program support of up to $2,500 (depending on budget size) and a series of training classes. Classes will cover the basics of being a 501(c)3 organization: mission, vision and values; board roles and responsibilities; board development; financial management; strategic planning; program planning, budgeting and evaluation; grant writing; marketing; and fundraising. Grantees are expected to send two members of the organization board/staff to each class. They will then produce a required document and submit it to the trainer and/or consultant for critique and recommended changes. When the document is adequately revised, they will submit it to the Division. Start-Up serves as the gateway for emerging arts organizations to be eligible for the Division's General Operating Support grants. Those wishing to apply should first contact the Program Coordinator to be certain their organization is eligible. The annual deadline for electronic applications is March 2.
Requirements: Applicants must have the promotion, presentaton, productions, and/or teaching of the arts as their primary purpose as outlined in their charter, incorporation papers, bylaws, and IRS nonprofit determination letter. They must have a stable board of directors that meets at least four times a year, and be functioning as an arts program for at least two years. In addition, the organization should be based and chartered in Delaware as a nonprofit; exempt from federal income tax under Section 501(c)3 or 501(c)4 or 509(a) of the IRS Code; and eligible to receive donations allowable as charitable contributions under Section 170(c) of the Internal Revenue Code of 1954. StartUp grants are funded on a matching basis. Matching funds of one to one must be cash, and may not come from the National Endowment for the Arts. Other federal grant sources may be used as match in accordance with authorizing legislation.
Restrictions: Ineligible expenses include: activities outside Delaware; activities for which academic credit is given; awards, donations or cash prizes; bad debt; building, renovating, or remodeling of facilities; capital expenditures and non-consumables valued over $3,000; circus and athletic activities; contingency funds; expenses incurred outside of the grant period; fundraising costs (capital/endowment campaigns); investments of any type; meals/refreshments; lobbying; private entertainment; projects restricted to exclusive participation or enjoyment; projects which have sectarian or religious purposes; or scholarships or research by individuals.
Geographic Focus: Delaware
Date(s) Application is Due: Mar 2
Amount of Grant: Up to 2,500 USD
Contact: Paul Weagraff, Director; (302) 577-8278; paul.weagraff@state.de.us
Internet: http://www.artsdel.org/grants/StartUp.pdf
Sponsor: Delaware Division of the Arts
820 North French Street, Carvel State Office Building
Wilmington, DE 19801

Della B. Gardner Fund Grants 582

The Della B. Gardner Fund, maintained by the Dayton Foundation, provides grants for the care and aid of worthy aged, sick and needy persons residing within the City of Middletown, Ohio. The Fund's primary fields of interest, therefore, are health and religion, with funding coming in the form of support for general operations. Once per year, the Dayton Foundation will issue a Request for Proposal (RFP) to senior-serving organizations in the Middletown area and will award up to $12,000.
Requirements: Applicants must be 501(c)3 organizations in operation for a minimum of two years and be either located in, or serving the residents of, Middletown, Ohio. Furthermore, such organizations must: have a diversity/

inclusion policy; demonstrate systemic collaboration; and address needs that are not met fully by existing organizational or community resources.
Restrictions: The Foundation generally does not award discretionary grants for: general organizational operations and ongoing programs, operational deficits or reduced or lost funding; individuals, scholarship, travel; fundraising drives; special events; political activities; public or private schools; endowment funds; hospitals and universities for internal programs; matching grants (unless local dollars are needed to fulfill a condition for a state or federal grant); neighborhood or local jurisdiction projects; newly organized not-for-profit organizations; or publications, scientific, medical or academic research projects.
Geographic Focus: Ohio
Contact: Beth Geiger, Associate Program Officer; (937) 225-9964 or (937) 222-0410; fax (937) 222-0636; bgeiger@daytonfoundation.org
Internet: http://www.daytonfoundation.org/grntfdns.html
Sponsor: Della B. Gardner Fund
40 North Main Street, Suite 500
Dayton, OH 45423

Delmarva Power and Light Company Contributions   583
The Delmarva Power and Light Company Contributions (formerly known as the Conectiv Corporate Giving program) offers support primarily in areas of company operations in Delaware and Maryland, although giving is also to national organizations. The Company makes charitable contributions to nonprofit organizations involved with education, the environment, health care, housing, public safety, youth development, and the military. Therefore, its primary fields of interest include: disasters and emergency management; education; environment; health; heart and circulatory system diseases; housing development; public utilities; scouting programs; and youth development. Types of support offered include general operations and sponsorships. Although a formal application is required, interested parties should begin by forwarding an email detailing the program in need.
Requirements: Nonprofit organizations in both Delaware and Maryland, within the regions of company operations, are welcome to apply.
Geographic Focus: Delaware, Maryland
Contact: Matt Likovich, Media Relations Manager; (410) 860-6203; matthew.likovich@delmarva.com
Internet: http://www.delmarva.com/community-commitment
Sponsor: Delmarva Power and Light Company
401 Eagle Run Road, P.O. Box 17000
Wilmington, DE 19886-7000

Delta Air Lines Foundation Arts and Culture Grants   584
Established in 1968 as Delta's company-managed giving system, the Delta Air Lines Foundation contributes more than $1 million annually in endowed funds to deserving organizations and programs. The arts and cultural activities, whether they are fine art, theatre, music, or other creative endeavors, enhance a community's quality of life. Through the Arts and Culture program the Foundation is able to understand new perspectives and better understand the world around us. Delta supports organizations that help bring the wonder and richness of human creativity to the communities it serves. Promoting understanding and appreciation for arts and cultural diversity is a top priority. Once an application is received, applicants should allow up to three months before review.
Requirements: For proposals which meet the foundation's area of focus, priority will be given to: programs meeting compelling needs in communities where Delta has a presence; proposals that exhibit clear, reasonable goals, and measurable outcomes; distinctive projects where the foundation's involvement will leave a legacy; projects that include collaboration or cooperation with other nonprofit organizations; projects that offer opportunities for Delta employee involvement. The foundation Board of Trustees reviews and approves funding in March, June, September, and November. The deadline for receiving completed proposals is the first day of each of these months.
Restrictions: The foundation will generally not consider: individual applicant's request for support of personal needs; religious activities; political organizations or campaigns; specialized single-issue health organizations; annual or automatic renewal grants; general operating expenses; endowment campaigns; capital campaigns; multiyear commitments; fraternal organizations, professional associations, or membership groups; fundraising events such as benefits; charitable dinners, or sporting events.
Geographic Focus: All States
Date(s) Application is Due: Jun 1; Sep 1; Nov 1
Contact: Administrator; (404) 715-5487 or (404) 715-2554; fax (404) 715-3267
Internet: http://www.delta.com/about_delta/community_involvement/delta_foundation/

Sponsor: Delta Air Lines Foundation
P.O. Box 20706, Department 979
Atlanta, GA 30320-6001

Dennis and Phyllis Washington Foundation Grants   585
The foundation supports a broad spectrum of worthy causes benefiting people of all ages primarily serving the State of Montana and surrounding states where the Washington Companies are located. Priorities for funding are direct service, youth oriented programs and the advancement of educational opportunities through scholarships to units of higher education in Montana. The Foundation also focuses on the needs of economical and socially disadvantaged people, troubled or at-risk youth and individuals with special needs.
Requirements: Eligible applicants must be a charitable, nonprofit entity with tax exempt status under Section 501(c)3. Organizations applying for support must be categorized in one of the four giving areas of education, health and human services, community service and arts and culture. The Foundation places particular emphasis on those organizations and programs that provide a direct service to economically and socially disadvantaged youth and their families, at-risk or troubled youth, and individuals with special needs. Preference is given to applicants who are able to demonstrate that a majority, if not all, of Foundation funds will be used for direct services. The Foundation prefers giving to organizations with no or low administrative costs. Organizations may apply for funding only in the year in which funds will be used. The Foundation prefers that organizations show evidence of substantial financial support from their community, constituency groups or other funding sources prior to applying.
Restrictions: Applications will not be considered for the following organizations or purposes: organizations that, in policy or practice, unfairly discriminate against race, ethnic origin, sex, creed, or religion; to fund loans, debt retirement or operational deficits; to fund on-going, general operations; to individuals, unless under an approved educational scholarship program; to sectarian or religious organizations for religious purposes where the principal activity is for the benefit of their own members or adherents; to veterans or fraternal organizations, unless their programs are available to members of the community as a whole; for travel expenses or trips; to general endowment funds, private or public foundations and most capital campaigns; for operation expenses of tax-supported groups; for sponsorships including auctions, dinners, tickets, advertising, or annual fundraising events; for political action or legislative advocacy groups or influencing legislation or elections; for operational costs or curriculum development at educational institutions; the purchase of motor vehicles or other forms of transportation; to organizations acting on behalf of, but without the authority of, qualified tax exempt organizations.
Geographic Focus: Montana
Samples: Horatio Alger Assoc (Alexandria, VA)—to provide college scholarships for students from Montana who plan to attend the U of Montana, $1 million over four years.
Contact: Mike Halligan, Executive Director; (406) 523-1325
Internet: http://www.dpwfoundation.org/home.htm
Sponsor: Dennis and Phyllis Washington Foundation
P.O. Box 16630
Missoula, MT 59808-6630

Denver Foundation Technical Assistance Grants   586
All nonprofit organizations need help from time to time in order to function more effectively and efficiently. This is especially true of new or emerging nonprofit organizations or those with smaller budgets. The Denver Foundation has set aside funds specifically to provide grants for nonprofit organizations to get this kind of help, usually called technical assistance. Technical Assistance (TA) can be many things, and what is most important is that TA helps the staff and/or board of the organization learn something new and increase its capacity to lead, manage and direct the organization. Examples of Technical Assistance include: obtaining training on a specific topic, such as marketing, volunteer management, financial management or fund raising; hiring a facilitator for a board retreat; or working with a consultant to develop a fund raising plan or a strategic plan for the organization.
Requirements: To qualify for a grant an organization must be a 501(c)3 tax-exempt nonprofit organization, serve residents in seven specific Denver counties, and provide a service that falls under one of the four funding areas.
Restrictions: The Foundation will not consider requests to fund the following: requests from organizations that have received funding from the program for the three previous consecutive calendar years; organizations with fund balance deficits in their most recently completed fiscal year; organizations that discriminate on the basis of race, color, religion, gender, age, national origin; disability, marital status, sexual orientation, or military status; debt

retirement; endowments or other reserve funds; membership or affiliation campaigns, dinners, or special events; conferences and symposia and related travel; grants that further political doctrine; grants that further religious doctrine; grants to individuals; scholarships or sponsorships; individual medical procedures; medical, scientific, or academic research; grants to parochial or religious schools; grants to governmental agencies, except public schools; requests from individual public schools that have not coordinated the request with their central school district administration; requests from foundations/organizations that raise money for individual public schools; creation or installation of art objects; development, production, or distribution of books, newspapers, or video productions; grants for re-granting programs; requests for capital campaigns that have not met 75% of their goal; activities, projects, or programs that will have been completed before funding becomes available; and multi-year funding requests.

Geographic Focus: Colorado
Date(s) Application is Due: Feb 2; Jun 1; Oct 1
Contact: Jeff Hirota, Vice President; (303) 300-1790, ext. 129; fax (303) 300-6547; jhirota@denverfoundation.org
Internet: http://www.denverfoundation.org/page16399.cfm
Sponsor: Denver Foundation
55 Madison, 8th Floor
Denver, CO 80206

DeRoy Testamentary Foundation Grants   587

Established in 1979, the Foundation gives primarily in the state of Michigan. Giving primarily for youth development and services, education, human services, health care, and the arts. The Foundation offers support in the form of: scholarship funds; annual campaigns; building/renovation; continuing support; general/operating support; program development grants. There are no application deadlines. The board meets monthly.
Requirements: Michigan nonprofit organizations are eligible.
Restrictions: Grants are not made to individuals.
Geographic Focus: Michigan
Amount of Grant: 10,000 - 300,000 USD
Samples: National Bone Marrow Transplant Link, Southfield, MI, $10,000; Oakland Family Services, Pontiac, MI, $65,000; Interlochen Center for the Arts, Interlochen, MI, $300,000.
Contact: Julie Rodecker Holly, Vice President; (248) 827-0920; fax (248) 827-0922; deroyfdtn@aol.com
Sponsor: DeRoy Testamentary Foundation
26999 Central Park Boulevard, Suite 160N
Southfield, MI 48076

Deutsche Banc Alex Brown and Sons Charitable Foundation Grants   588

The Deutsche Banc Alex Brown and Sons Charitable Foundation awards one-year renewable grants to U.S. nonprofit organizations in its areas of interest, including arts and culture, community affairs, education, medicine, and science. Types of support include annual campaigns, capital grants, endowment funds, general operating grants, program development grants, and scholarship funds. Applicants should submit a letter of interest that briefly outlines the purpose of the grant prior to submission of a more detailed application. There are no specified annual deadlines.
Requirements: 501(c)3 tax-exempt organizations in Maryland and the Washington, DC, area are eligible to apply.
Restrictions: No support for private schools or churches. Grants are not made to individuals.
Geographic Focus: District of Columbia, Maryland
Amount of Grant: 1,000 - 100,000 USD
Samples: Baltimore Symphony Orchestra (MD)—for discretionary use, $1 million; Johns Hopkins Hospital (Baltimore, MD)—for discretionary use, $1 million; Baltimore Zoo (MD)—for discretionary use, $1 million.
Contact: Secretary; (202) 783-5476 or (202) 626-7000
Sponsor: Deutsche Banc Alex Brown and Sons Charitable Foundation
1440 New York Avenue NW
Washington, DE 20005-2111

DHHS ARRA Strengthening Communities Fund - State, Local, and   589
Tribal Government Capacity Building Grants

The purpose of this grant program is to build the capacity of government offices (or their authorized designee) that provide outreach to faith-based and community-based organizations and to assist nonprofit organizations in addressing the broad economic recovery issues present in their communities, including helping low-income individuals secure and retain employment, earn higher wages, obtain

better-quality jobs, and gain greater access to State and Federal benefits and tax credits. The Administration for Children and Families (ACF) will award funds to State, city, county, and Indian/Native American Tribal government offices (e.g., offices responsible for outreach to faith-based and community organizations or those interested in initiating such an effort), or their designees, to build their own capacity to partner with community-based and faith-based non-profits and to provide training and technical assistance to help nonprofit faith-based and community organizations better serve those in need and to increase nonprofit organizations' involvement in the economic recovery. Grantees will use program funds to provide free capacity building services to nonprofit organizations, such as a beneficiary benefits clearinghouse, outreach and education, facilitation of partnerships between and among nonprofits and other government agencies, and training and technical assistance to improve awareness of and access to ARRA efforts/benefits and to improve organizational capacity to be active participants in ARRA efforts/benefits. Grantees will also use program funds to build their own capacity to provide these services to nonprofits. The average projected award amount is $250,000 per project period.
Requirements: An applicant must be a State, city, county, or Indian/Native American Tribal government office or a designated private nonprofit organization authorized by such an office. All applicants, whether a government office or a private nonprofit organization, must be authorized by the State, city, county, or Indian/Native American Tribal government to apply for a SCF State, Local, and Tribal Government Capacity Building program grant through a statute, resolution, or executive order. Applicants must include a copy of the authorizing document in the application. If the document is not signed or approved prior to the application due date, a letter from the executive officer of the governing body may be submitted, with an approved statute, resolution, or executive order to be submitted by the start of the grant. This authorizing document must specify the role of the Authorized Entity as well as detail the support, access, and authority to be provided by the State, city, county, and Indian/Native American Tribal government with regard to the activities to be conducted under the grant. A State, city, county, or Indian/Native American Tribal government may designate only one authorized entity to apply for this program. All applicants must have a D&B Data Universal Numbering System (D-U-N-S) number.
Restrictions: Applications with requests that exceed the ceiling on the amount of individual awards will be deemed non-responsive and will not be considered for funding. These grants cannot be used to provide direct client services. Under the SCF State, Local, and Tribal Government Capacity Building program, organizations shall not use direct Federal grants or contracts to support inherently religious activities, such as religious instruction, worship, or proselytization. Therefore, any organization receiving funds must take steps to separate, in time or location, their inherently religious activities from the grant-funded activities. Some of the ways organizations may accomplish this include, but are not limited to, promoting only the Federally funded program in materials or websites created with any portion of the Federal funds. Further, participation in such inherently religious activity by individuals receiving services must be voluntary. Any criteria for selecting nonprofit organizations to receive training and technical assistance must be neutral to whether the nonprofits are religious or secular groups.
Geographic Focus: All States
Date(s) Application is Due: Jul 7
Contact: Thom Campbell, Office of Community Services Operations Center; (800) 281-9519; ocs@lcgnet.com
Internet: http://www.acf.hhs.gov/grants/open/HHS-2009-ACF-OCS-SN-0092.html
Sponsor: U.S. Department of Health and Human Services
370 L'Enfant Promenade SW
Washington, D.C. 20447

DHHS Health Centers Grants for Migratory and Seasonal   590
Farmworkers

The grants support the development and operation of migrant health centers and projects that provide primary health care services, supplemental health services, and environmental health services that are accessible to migrant and seasonal agricultural farm workers and their families as they move and work. Funds may be used for the planning, development, and operation of clearly defined migrant health centers and programs; for the acquisition and modernization of existing buildings; and for training related to the management of programs assisted through grants and contracts.
Requirements: Any public or nonprofit private entity may apply. Preference will be given to applications submitted by community-based organizations that are representative of the populations to be served.

Restrictions: For-profit organizations are ineligible.
Geographic Focus: All States
Amount of Grant: 50,000 - 2,500,000 USD
Contact: Grants Management Officer, Bureau of Primary Health Care; (301) 594-4235
Internet: http://www.bphc.hrsa.gov
Sponsor: U.S. Department of Health and Human Services
4350 East-West Highway
Bethesda, MD 20814

DHHS Individual Development Accounts for Refugees Project Grants   591
The Office of Refugee Resettlement invites qualified entities to submit competing grant applications for new projects that will establish, support, and manage Individual Development Accounts (IDAs) for eligible low-income refugee individuals and families. This program represents an anti-poverty strategy built on asset accumulation for low-income refugee individuals and families with the goal of promoting refugee economic independence. In particular, the objectives of this program are to: increase the ability of low-income refugees to save; promote their participation in the financial institutions of this country; assist refugees in advancing their education; increase home ownership; and assist refugees in gaining access to capital. These new projects will accomplish these objectives by establishing programs that combine the provision of matched savings accounts with financial training and counseling.
Requirements: Eligible applicants include states and private, nonprofit organizations.
Geographic Focus: All States
Amount of Grant: 5,000 - 19,000,000 USD
Contact: Office of Refugee Resettlement; (202) 401-9246; fax (202) 401-5487
Internet: http://www.acf.hhs.gov/programs/orr/programs/individual.htm
Sponsor: U.S. Department of Health and Human Services
370 L'Enfant Promenade SW
Washington, D.C. 20447

DHHS Oral Health Promotion Research Across the Lifespan   592
The National Institute of Dental and Craniofacial Research has invited proposals for improving the oral health of people of all ages. The research team must include someone with extensive experience in health promotion, behavioral and/or social science research. The health promotion intervention proposed for funding must be based on a previously conducted assessment of the epidemiology, social, behavioral and/or environmental factors related to the disease or condition under study. Research could focus on maternal and child health, adolescent and young adult health, or health of adults with complex diseases. For example, an applicant might propose to study approaches to involving families, social networks, communities, or neighborhoods in behaviors that promote and improve oral health; improving patient-provider communication related to oral preventive measures; or effective ways to train oral health professional students to communicate with diverse patient populations.
Requirements: Any person with the skills, knowledge, and resources necessary to carry out the proposed research as the project director/principal investigator (PD/PI) is invited to work with his/her organization to develop an application for support. Applications must be submitted electronically through Grants.gov (http://www.grants.gov) using the SF424 research and related forms and the SF424 application guide.
Geographic Focus: All States
Date(s) Application is Due: Mar 5; Jul 5; Nov 5
Contact: Maria Teresa Canto, (301) 594-5497; maria.canto@nih.gov
Internet: http://grants.nih.gov/grants/guide/pa-files/PA-07-225.html
Sponsor: National Institute of Dental and Craniofacial Research
45 Center Drive, Natcher Building
Bethesda, MD 20892

DHL Charitable Shipment Support   593
The corporation provides free shipment of materials supporting charitable programs. Applicants must submit a complete web questionnaire.
Requirements: Application by internet only.
Restrictions: Religious organizations are ineligible for religious sectarian activities, and political organizations are not eligible for political purposes.
Geographic Focus: All States
Contact: Technical Support; (800) 527-7298
Internet: http://www.dhl-usa.com
Sponsor: DHL International, Ltd.
1220 South Pine Island Road, Suite 600
Plantation, FL 33324

DHS ARRA Fire Station Construction Grants (SCG)   594
The Department of Homeland Security's Assistance to Firefighters Fire Station Construction Grants (SCG) will provide financial assistance directly to fire departments on a competitive basis to build new or modify existing fire stations in order for departments to enhance their response capability and protect the community they serve from fire and fire-related hazards.
Requirements: Non-Federal Fire Departments and state and local governments that fund/operate fire departments are eligible to apply. SCG seeks to support organizations lacking the tools and resources necessary to effectively protect the health and safety of the public and their emergency response personnel with respect to fire and all other hazards.
Geographic Focus: All States
Date(s) Application is Due: Jul 10
Contact: Help Desk; (866) 274-0960; firegrants@dhs.gov
Internet: http://www.firegrantsupport.com/afscg/
Sponsor: U.S. Department of Homeland Security
500 C Street SW
Washington, D.C. 20472

DHS ARRA Port Security Grant Program (PSGP)   595
The purpose of the FY 2009 ARRA PSGP is to create a sustainable, risk-based effort to protect critical port infrastructure from terrorism, particularly attacks using explosives and non-conventional threats that could cause major disruption to commerce. Funds will support increased port-wide risk management; enhanced domain awareness; and further capabilities to prevent, detect, respond to and recover from attacks involving improvised explosive devices (IEDs) and other non-conventional weapons. It is expected that about 200 awards will be granted from the estimated total program funding of $150,000,000.
Requirements: All entities covered by an Area Maritime Security Plans (AMSP) may submit an application for consideration of funding. A facility that is not expressly identified in an AMSP will be considered covered under an AMSP if the facility in question has had a risk analysis completed by the USCG utilizing the MSRAM tool. Congress has specifically directed DHS to apply these funds to the highest risk ports. In support of this, the ARRA PSGP includes a total of 147 specifically identified critical ports, representing approximately 95% of the foreign waterborne commerce of the United States. Applicants must provide a Dun and Bradstreet Data Universal Numbering System (DUNS) number with their application.
Geographic Focus: All States
Date(s) Application is Due: Jun 29
Contact: Program Director; (866) 927-5646; ASK-GMD@dhs.gov
Internet: http://www.fema.gov/government/grant/arra/index.shtm#2
Sponsor: U.S. Department of Homeland Security
500 C Street SW
Washington, D.C. 20472

DHS ARRA Transit Security Grant Program (TSGP)   596
The ARRA is an economic stimulus package that was designed to jumpstart the U.S. economy, create or save millions of jobs, and put a down payment on addressing long-neglected challenges nationally. Funds received under this Act are intended to support these goals, and unprecedented levels of transparency, oversight, and accountability are required of the expenditure of Act dollars. ARRA TSGP specifically will focus on the use of visible, unpredictable deterrence through the funding of Operational Packages for canine teams, mobile explosives detection screening teams, and Anti-Terrorism Teams both due to their effectiveness in reducing risk to transit systems and their potential for job creation. In addition, funding will be provided for capital projects including Multi-User High-Density Key Infrastructure Protection, Single-User High-Density Key Infrastructure Protection, Key Operating Asset Protection, and Other Mitigation Activities. These funds are intended to preserve and create jobs across the nation through projects that can be implemented quickly. Based on those considerations, the following project types are eligible: Priority 1a Operational Packages - Hiring of transit law enforcement officers to enhance visible, unpredictable deterrence efforts in transit (e.g., K-9 teams, mobile screening teams, and Anti-Terrorism teams); Priority 1b Support and Equipment for Operational Packages - Related support and equipment costs for new officers/capability; Priority 2 Shovel Ready Capital Projects for Asset Hardening - Capital Projects including Multi-User High-Density Key Infrastructure Protection, Single- User High-Density Key Infrastructure Protection, Key Operating Asset Protection, and Other Mitigation Activities that can certifiably begin within 90 days of release of funds and will be completed within 24 months from the release of funds date. Failure to meet the 90 day requirement may result in a loss of ARRA

TSGP funding for the specific project; Priority 3 Other Security Projects - Capital Projects including Multi-User High-Density Key Infrastructure Protection, Single-User High-Density Key Infrastructure Protection, Key Operating Asset Protection, and Other Mitigation Activities.

Requirements: With the exception of ferry systems, those eligible under the FY 2009 TSGP, as well as Amtrak are eligible for FY 2009 ARRA TSGP funds. Transit agencies eligible for FY 2009 TSGP funding were identified using a comprehensive, empirically-grounded risk analysis model. The risk methodology for the TSGP is consistent across modes and is linked to the risk methodology used to determine eligibility for the core DHS State and local grant programs. TSGP basic eligibility is derived from the Urban Areas Security Initiative (UASI). Eligibility for Operational Packages (Priority 1) is determined based on the number of authorized sworn positions for transit agency police departments and law enforcement agencies with dedicated transit bureaus. Eligible transit agencies and request thresholds were determined by the following transit police force or law enforcement provider characteristics: Transit police forces or law enforcement provider must have at least 100 authorized sworn positions dedicated to transit security; Funding requests are limited to no more than five percent (5%) of the force's current authorized sworn positions and the associated support equipment requests are based on number of officers requested. Law enforcement agencies with dedicated transit bureaus are eligible through the transit agency they provide security for; the transit agency itself is the grantee, and as such must apply on behalf of the law enforcement agency. To qualify for a Priority 2 Project, Shovel Ready Capital Projects for Asset Hardening, applicants must certify that the project can begin within 90 days of the release of funds. Applicants must also certify that the project will be completed within 24 months of the release of funds date.

Restrictions: Security service providers with unsworn law enforcement officers or guards are not eligible.

Geographic Focus: All States
Date(s) Application is Due: Jun 15
Contact: Program Director; (866) 927-5646; ASK-GMD@dhs.gov
Internet: http://www.fema.gov/government/grant/arra/index.shtm#1
Sponsor: U.S. Department of Homeland Security
500 C Street SW
Washington, D.C. 20472

Dick and Marsha Sands Family Ministry 597

Established in Maryland, the Dick and Marsha Sands Family Ministry has a primary interest in supporting human and social service programs, helping the needy, and the distribution of religious materials. There are no specific application materials or deadlines with which to adhere, and applicants should forward the completed proposal. Amounts range up to $1,000.

Geographic Focus: Florida, Maryland
Contact: Dick Sands, President; (410) 726-7224
Sponsor: Dick and Marsha Sands Family Ministry
12 Worcester Street, P.O. Box 351
Ocean City, MD 21843

Dining for Women Grants 598

Dining for Women funding is available for programs and/or projects that contribute to the empowerment of women and girls in less developed countries. Program and/or projects should be grassroots organizations that work with women and girls in the areas of health, education, environmental sustainability, and business development. Grants support one featured program each month that contributes to the mission to impact the lives, health and welfare of women and girls in developing countries. Awards are for one-to-two years, and total between $35,000 and $45,000.

Requirements: To be eligible, an applicant program must: support women and/or girls who face extreme challenges in developing countries; promote self-sufficiency, economic independence and/or good health for women and girls being supported; tie funding to direct impact on individuals' lives; provide evidence of long-term sustainability and program success; manage a DFW grant ranging between $35,000 and $45,000, which may be distributed over a two-year period; direct a minimum of 75% of expenses to programs; be a 501(c)3 U.S. nonprofit organization; operate independent of religious or political affiliation; provide informative organization website in English; and be able to provide educational materials, including a short video, that are relevant to the funded project/program.

Restrictions: Dining for Women does not fund: group trusts, foundations or other consolidated funding activity; governmental, political or religiously affiliated organizations; or major building projects, large capital expenditures, U.S. administrative fees or expenses and office costs.

Geographic Focus: All States
Date(s) Application is Due: Dec 31
Amount of Grant: 35,000 - 45,000 USD
Samples: Girls Empowerment Project, Heshima Kenya, Nairobi, $50,000 (over two years) - identifying and protecting separated and orphaned refugee children and youth living in Nairobi, Kenya; Midwives Save Lives, Haiti, $50,000 - to reduce maternal and neonatal mortality in Haiti by training Haitian women in the skills needed to save lives; One Heart World-Wide, Nepal, $50,000 - to decrease maternal and newborn mortality and morbidity in remote rural areas of the world.
Contact: Dr. Maggie Aziz; (864) 335-8401; grants@diningforwomen.org
Internet: http://www.diningforwomen.org/Programs/grants
Sponsor: Dining for Women
P.O. Box 25633
Greenville, SC 29616

District of Columbia Commission on the Arts City Arts Grants 599

The program encourages the growth of quality and diverse arts activities throughout the city, supports local artists, and makes arts experiences accessible to District residents. City Arts projects provide art exposure to the broader community or to persons traditionally underserved or separate from the mainstream due to geographic location, economic constraints, or disability. Eligible projects include, but are not limited to: festivals, concerts, visual arts exhibitions, literary readings, and salary support to enhance the cultural diversity of staff. Contact the program officer for deadline dates.

Requirements: Grants and awards are made to individuals and nonprofit 501(c)3 organizations based in the District of Columbia.
Geographic Focus: District of Columbia
Contact: Lionell Thomas, Assistant Director; (202) 724-5613; fax (202) 727-4135; lionell.thomas@dc.gov or dcart@dc.gov
Internet: http://dcarts.dc.gov
Sponsor: District of Columbia Commission on the Arts and Humanities
410 Eighth Street NW, 5th Floor
Washington, D.C. 20004

DJ and T Foundation Grants 600

The foundation supports low cost or free spay/neuter clinics in the United States. Preference will be given to grassroots-level, underfunded clinics that provide free or low-cost dog and cat spaying and neutering services. There are no application deadlines. Grant applications may be downloaded from the foundation's Web site.

Requirements: IRS 501(c)3 nonprofits operating a stationary and/or mobile clinic and nonprofits in the process of creating such a clinic are eligible.
Restrictions: The foundation does not underwrite voucher programs or other fees. Grants are not made to individuals.
Geographic Focus: All States
Amount of Grant: 15 - 26,597 USD
Samples: Colorado Humane Society (Boulder, CO)—for operating support; Adopt-A-Pet (Columbus, OH)—for operating support; Pasco Animal Welfare Society (FL)—for operating support.
Contact: William Prappas, (310) 278-1160; WillPrappas@msn.com
Internet: http://www.djtfoundation.org
Sponsor: DJ and T Foundation
9201 Wilshire Boulevard, Suite 204
Beverly Hills, CA 90210

DogTime Technology Grant 601

DogTime Media actively supports the efforts of rescue groups and shelters nationwide to significantly reduce the number of homeless and neglected pets in the country by providing authoritative advice to both novice and experienced pet guardians. DogTime Media donates to pet related causes through monthly grants and a variety of other programs. This grant will provide organizations dedicated to the rescue cause with access to essential technology services to help achieve their goals. Some of the basic web site services that the grant will cover include domain name setup, quick website setup, email service setup (forwarders or mailboxes), and easy access to site updates or content management. The grant will pay for one year of service. Rescues can reapply for grants in subsequent years.

Requirements: In order to apply, organizations must show that their focus is in preventing or rescuing homeless animals and have 501(c)3 status or be in the process of applying for 501(c)3 status. Organizations must not be proponents of the sale of animals through "puppy mills", irresponsible breeding, or pet stores. Organizations must be ready to prove the need for the $140 service.

Geographic Focus: All States
Amount of Grant: 155 - 155 USD
Samples: Athens Area Humane Society - Watkinsville, Georgia; Boston Terrier Rescue Group - Houston, Texas; For the Love of Pets - Streator, Illinois; Ginny's Pet Rescue - Pioneer, Tennessee; Hancock County Animal Shelter - Hawesville, Kentucky; Bark Ark Bully Rescue - Cincinnati, Ohio
Contact: Grants Officer; 415-830-9300; info@dogtime.com
Internet: http://dogtime.com/dog-shelter-grants/new/technology
Sponsor: DogTime Media
27 Maiden Lane, Suite 700
San Francisco, CA 94108

Dolan Children's Foundation Grants 602

The Dolan Children's Foundation was founded in New York in 1886 by Charles F. and Helen A. Dolan. Charles F. Dolan was the founder of the cable network HBO, and is the owner of Cablevision Systems Corporation, a cable television provider in New York City that also owns Madison Square Garden, Radio City Music Hall, the New York Knicks, and the New York Rangers. The Foundation awards community service grants with a focus on Long Island, New York. Areas of interest include: human services, disability services, mental health, schools, rehabilitation, hospitals, health facilities, and Catholic agencies and churches. Types of support include: general operating support, building and renovations; capital campaigns; equipment purchase and rental; land acquisition; program development; research; and matching grants. There are no application deadlines, though an application form is required. Recent awards have ranged from $50,000 to $400,000. Guidelines are available upon request.
Requirements: Schools and other nonprofits in New York City and Long Island are eligible. Applicants outside New York should call or write prior to submitting proposals.
Geographic Focus: New York
Amount of Grant: 50,000 - 400,000 USD
Samples: Children and Family Services, Manchester, New Hampshire, $80,000 - general operating support; Community of Hope, Washington, DC, $250,000 - general operating support; Lowell Schools, Bayside, New York, $95,000 - general operating support.
Contact: Robert Vizza, President; (516) 803-9200
Sponsor: Dolan Children's Foundation
340 Crossways Park Drive
Woodbury, NY 11797-2050

Donald and Sylvia Robinson Family Foundation Grants 603

The foundation awards grants to U.S. nonprofit organizations in its areas of interest, including animal and wildlife protection, arms control, arts (general, performing arts, and visual arts), environmental conservation and protection, eye diseases and eye research, family planning and human reproductive health, food distribution, international affairs, Israel, Jewish social services, and social service delivery programs. Types of support include annual campaigns, building construction/renovation, capital campaigns, and general operating support. There are no application deadlines or forms.
Requirements: National nonprofit organizations are eligible to apply.
Restrictions: Individuals are ineligible.
Geographic Focus: Pennsylvania
Amount of Grant: 500 - 5,000 USD
Samples: Phipps Conservatory and Botanical Gardens, Pittsburgh, PA, $5,000; Jewish Residential Services, Pittsburgh, PA, $5,000; Jewish Family and Childrens Service of Pittsburgh, Pittsburgh, PA, $500.
Contact: Donald Robinson, Treasurer; (412) 661-1200; fax (412) 661-4645
Sponsor: Donald and Sylvia Robinson Family Foundation
6507 Wilkins Avenue
Pittsburgh, PA 15217

Donald C. Brace Foundation Grants 604

The Donald C. Brace Foundation, named in honor of a co-founder of Harcourt Brace and Company Publishing, was established in Connecticut in 1987. The Foundation's primary fields of interest include: the arts; education; and support of other foundations. Giving occurs throughout the United States, with some emphasis on Hawaii, Idaho, and New Hampshire. A formal application is required, and can be secured by contacting the office directly. There are no identified annual deadlines. Most recent awards have ranged from $3,000 to $150,000.
Geographic Focus: All States
Amount of Grant: 3,000 - 150,000 USD
Samples: Caribbean Museum Center for the Arts, Frederiksted, Virgin Islands, $10,000 - general operations; Community Foundation of Teton Valley, Driggs,

Idaho, $25,000 - general operations; Assets School, Honolulu, Hawaii, $150,000 - general operations.
Contact: Robert A. Beer, (203) 426-3093
Sponsor: Donald C. Brace Foundation
30 Maltbie Road
Newtown, CT 06470-2508

Donald G. Gardner Humanities Trust Operational Grants 605

In 1944, Donald G. Gardner donated a painting by Frederick C. Frieseke, entitled Breakfast In The Garden, to the City of Ely, Minnesota. It was hung in the Ely Public Library in 1945. In 1989, the painting was sold for $510,000 and the Donald G. Gardner Humanities Trust was established for the enhancement, growth and improvement of: the Ely Public Library; the arts and artisans of Ely and surrounding area, to include the performing arts, the visual arts, and literature; the creating and funding of scholarships; educational and artistic grants; and the cultural and aesthetic environment of the City of Ely and its surrounding area. Specifically, Operational Grants provides funding to high-quality, established Ely-area arts organizations that produce or present fine arts activities or provide services to artists. Most recent awards have ranged from $500 to $2,000. The annual deadline for application submission is April 24.
Requirements: To be eligible to apply to this program, an arts organization or group must: be a federal non-profit, tax exempt 501(c)3 arts organization located in Ely or the surrounding area; be an arts producing, arts presenting, or artist service agency, dedicated primarily to the fine arts; be legally incorporated and registered as a non-profit in the State of Minnesota; have received at least two Trust project grants prior to making an application to this program; and have at least one designated administrative staff person (volunteer or paid).
Restrictions: The following organizations are not eligible to apply for this funding: schools and universities; for-profit organizations; and trust grant recipients with an overdue final report. Funding cannot be used to support activities that: require artists to pay excessive entry fees to exhibit or perform; are designed for a private audience which is not open to the general public; replace or substitute for basic or music curriculum in schools; serves as a benefit or fund raiser; or attempts to influence any state or federal legislation.
Geographic Focus: Minnesota
Date(s) Application is Due: Apr 24
Amount of Grant: 500 - 2,000 USD
Samples: Up North Arts, Ely, Minnesota, $1,000 - general operational funding; Ely Artwalk, Ely, Minnesota, $1,650 - general operational funding; Boundary Waters Choral Festival, Ely, Minnesota, $1,000 - general operational funding.
Contact: Keiko L. Williams, Executive Director; (218) 365-2639 or (218) 365-6764; info@gardnertrust.org
Internet: http://www.gardnertrust.org/grant.htm
Sponsor: Donald G. Gardner Humanities Trust
P.O. Box 720
Ely, MN 55731

Donald P. and Byrd M. Kelly Foundation Grants 606

The foundation awards grants to eligible nonprofit organizations in its areas of interest, including adult, elementary, preschool, higher, and secondary education; educational organizations; educational research; and minorities. Types of support include continuing support, endowment funds, general operating grants, and scholarship funds. Contact the office for application materials.
Requirements: Nonprofit organizations are eligible. Illinois nonprofits, with an emphasis on Chicago, receive preference.
Geographic Focus: Illinois
Samples: Big Shoulders Fund (Chicago, IL)—for general operating support, $25,000; Foundation Fighting Blindness (Hunt Valley, MD)—for general operating support, $76,191; Robert Crown Ctr for Health Education (Hinsdale, IL)—for general operating support, $12,500; Museum of Science and Industry (Chicago, IL)—for general operating support, $30,000.
Contact: Marcia Stone, Grants Coordinator; (630) 575-2344
Sponsor: Donald P. and Byrd M. Kelly Foundation
701 Harger Road
Oak Brook, IL 60523

Donald W. Reynolds Foundation Food Distribution Grants 607

The Charitable Food Distribution Initiative builds on the success of the Foundation's previous capital support of the Regional Food Bank of Oklahoma in Oklahoma City. This initiative awards planning grants and capital grants directly to qualified food banks. However; an additional high priority under the Charitable Food Distribution Initiative is to improve the broader and more collaborative work food banks can undertake to improve efficiency and

effectiveness. Application to the Charitable Food Distribution Initiative is by invitation only. Unsolicited requests will not be accepted, and applicants should begin by discussing needs with the Foundation.
Requirements: Organizations must first contact the Foundation to discuss their project before submitting a proposal.
Geographic Focus: Arkansas, Nevada, Oklahoma
Contact: Craig Willis, Program Director; (702) 804-6000; fax (702) 804-6099; craig.willis@dwrf.org or GeneralQuestions@dwrf.org
Internet: http://www.dwreynolds.org/Programs/Regional/Food.htm
Sponsor: Donald W. Reynolds Foundation
1701 Village Center Circle
Las Vegas, NV 89134-6303

Donald W. Reynolds Foundation Special Projects Grants 608

Special Projects of the Foundation are awarded at the discretion of the board and encompass areas outside of the established programs of the Foundation. While these grants might result in the construction of a facility, provide for the acquisition of equipment or fund a specific program, they are unique and considered for funding based upon their individual merits. Often, Special Projects present a unique opportunity to advance patriotism, entrepreneurship, or another special lifetime interest held by Donald W. Reynolds. Proposal invitations are usually generated directly by our Trustees. There is no application and no designated staff contact. Unsolicited proposals are rarely approved. Brief proposals may be sent to the Foundation, addressed to the attention of Special Projects.
Geographic Focus: All States
Samples: Arkansas Economic Acceleration Foundation, Little Rock, Arkansas, $4,000,000 - terminal funding for the Donald W. Reynolds Governor's Cup Business Plan Tri-State Competition and to provide prize money for the Arkansas, Nevada and Oklahoma competitions; Razorback Foundation, Fayetteville, Arkansas, $10,000,000 - design and construct the Football Operations Center building.
Contact: Courtney Latta Knoblock, Program Director; (702) 804-6000; fax (702) 804-6099; capitalquestions@dwrf.org or GeneralQuestions@dwrf.org
Internet: http://www.dwreynolds.org/Programs/Special/Special.htm
Sponsor: Donald W. Reynolds Foundation
1701 Village Center Circle
Las Vegas, NV 89134-6303

Dora Roberts Foundation Grants 609

The foundation awards general operating grants to eligible Texas organizations in its areas of interest, Arts, Social Services, Health and Education. Most grants are awarded in Big Spring, TX. There are no application forms. Trustees meet annually in the Fall to review all requests received prior to the deadline.
Requirements: The Foundation can distribute grants only to qualified charitable organizations in the State of Texas. Persons who represent an organization which they believe might qualify for our support are welcome to submit an application in letter form containing: a brief narrative history of the organization's purpose and work; a specific description of the program or project for which support is asked; a statement of the amount of funds requested; proof of tax exempt status; a list of Trustees or Directors and principal staff; and budgetary information pertaining to the requested grant.
Restrictions: The Foundation does not give or lend money to individuals.
Geographic Focus: Rhode Island
Date(s) Application is Due: Sep 30
Contact: Konnie Darrow, c/o JP Morgan Chase Bank, N.A., (817) 884-4772
Sponsor: Dora Roberts Foundation
P.O. Box 2050
Fort Worth, TX 76113

Doree Taylor Charitable Foundation 610

The mission of the Doree Taylor Charitable Foundation is to support charitable organizations that: provide relief to people the form of basic needs (including the provision of food, housing, shelter); promote the humane care of animals; provide health-care services for the underserved; and conduct Public radio or television. Occasional support will also be provided to colleges and universities as well as to environmental charitable organizations in Maine. The foundation will make grants throughout Maine, but has a priority for charitable organizations or projects located in the areas of Boothbay Harbor, Southport, and Brunswick. From time to time, the foundation may support organizations with a national scope. Grant requests for general operating support or program support are strongly encouraged and preferred; however, small capital requests may also be considered. The majority of grants from the Taylor Foundation are one year in duration; on occasion, multi-year support is awarded. Applicants

must apply online at the grant website. Applicants are strongly encouraged to do the following before applying: review the downloadable state application procedures for additional helpful information and clarifications; review the downloadable online-application guidelines at the grant website; review the foundation's funding history (link is available from the grant website); review the online application questions in advance; and review the list of required attachments. These will generally include: a list of board members, financial statements (audited, reviewed, or compiled by independent auditor); an organization summary; a list of other funding sources; an IRS Determination letter; and other required documents. All attachments must be uploaded in the online application as PDF, Word, or Excel files. The application deadline for the Doree Taylor Charitable Foundation is 11:59 p.m. on April 1. Applicants will be notified of grant decisions before August 31.
Requirements: 501(c)3 charitable organizations and municipalities which meet the mission criteria are eligible to apply.
Restrictions: The foundation will not contribute to endowments or consider grant requests from individuals, organizations attempting to influence policy through direct lobbying, or political campaigns.
Geographic Focus: All States, Maine
Date(s) Application is Due: Apr 1
Contact: Miki C. Akimoto; (866) 778-6859; miki.akimoto@baml.com
Internet: https://www.bankofamerica.com/philanthropic/fn_search.action
Sponsor: Doree Taylor Charitable Foundation
225 Franklin Street, 4th Floor, MA1-225-04-02
Boston, MA 02110

Doris and Victor Day Foundation Grants 611

The foundation supports local community organizations providing food, shelter, clothing, medical care, and education in Illinois/Iowa Quad Cities region. Preference will be given to preventive programs and projects that foster pride in the local community. Types of support include general operating support, building/renovation, equipment, emergency funds, seed grants, and scholarship funds.
Requirements: Illinois/Iowa Quad Cities region nonprofit organizations may apply.
Restrictions: The Foundation is committed to programs that are non-sectarian, and therefore, will not contribute toward programs and capital projects for religious purposes, except for modest contributions to the churches in which the Days held membership. However, clearly non-sectarian, community serving programs of religious organizations will be considered for funding.
Geographic Focus: Illinois, Iowa
Date(s) Application is Due: May 1
Samples: Transitions Mental Health Rehabilitation, $4,000—Client Home Renovation; Rock Island Economic Growth Corporation, $50,000—Neighborhood Stabilization Program; Martin Luther King Center, $175,000 — expansion and renovation.
Contact: Program Contact; (309) 788-2300; info@dayfoundation.org
Internet: http://www.dayfoundation.org/guide.htm
Sponsor: Doris and Victor Day Foundation Grants
1800 3rd Avenue, Suite 302
Rock Island, IL 61201-8019

Dorothy Babcock Family Charitable Foundation 612

The Dorothy Babcock Family Charitable Foundation was established in the State of New York in 2006, with the expressed purpose of providing grant support for Protestant agencies and churches in New York. Amounts range up to $5,000, and are given strictly for general operating support. There are no specified application forms or annual deadlines, and interested applicants should forward a written program overview directly to the Foundation in letter format. Full unsolicited applications are not accepted without prior invitation.
Requirements: Any 501(c)3 located in, or serving Protestant agencies of churches of, the State of New York should apply.
Geographic Focus: New York
Amount of Grant: Up to 5,000 USD
Contact: Dorothy B. Sheahan, President; (212) 715-9327 or (732) 205-2018
Sponsor: Dorothy Babcock Family Charitable Foundation
P.O. Box 1194
Water Mills, NY 11976-1194

Dorothy Hooper Beattie Foundation Grants 613

The Foundation primarily supports higher education, health care, and religious programs in and around the Greenville, South Carolina, region. Its program interests include: camps; cancer treatment; Catholicism; children and youth programs; higher education; health services; literacy; and the environment. Grants range from $620 to $6,500, and there are no specific deadlines or application forms.

Initial approach should be by letter, with telephone contacts discouraged. Mail applications to: Bank of America, 7 North Laurens Street, Greenville, SC 29601.
Geographic Focus: South Carolina
Amount of Grant: 620 - 6,500 USD
Samples: The Bernardine Fund St. Francis, Greenville, SC, $620; Upstate Forever, Greenville, SC, $1,345; Greenville Free Medical Clinic, Greenville, SC, $4,000; United Ministries, Greenville, SC, $6,500.
Contact: Mary W. Green, Bank of America Contact; (864) 271-5789
Sponsor: Dorothy Hooper Beattie Foundation
101 South Tryon Street
Charlotte, NC 28255

Dorrance Family Foundation Grants   **614**
The Dorrance Family Foundation was founded by Bennett Dorrance, co-owner of the Campbell Soup Company. The Foundation gives primarily in the states of Arizona, California, and Hawaii, offering support for projects that work to resolve societal, educational and environmental problems strategically and make communities a better place. Its two primary areas of interest are education and natural resource conservation. In the area of education, the Foundation awards grants for the funding of: academic needs of low income and/or underserved students; first generation graduates; innovation; literacy; primary, secondary, and post-secondary academics; quality teacher training and recruitment; and science and technology programs. In the area of conservation, the Foundations awards grants for the funding of: forests; innovation; marine and coastal areas; rivers, streams, wetlands, and watersheds; sustainable agriculture, land use, and land management; and wildlife habitats. The Foundation also supports arts and culture, children's medical research, science and other community needs. The Dorrance Family Foundation does not accept unsolicited grant applications. If your organization qualifies for a grant based on the Foundation's grantmaking focus and eligibility requirements, please submit a Letter of Inquiry.
Requirements: No formal application form is required, 501(c)3 non-profits operating in Arizona are eligible to apply for these grants. Applicants should submit a proposal consisting of a detailed description of project and amount of funding requested.
Restrictions: No funding available to individuals.
Geographic Focus: Arizona, California, Hawaii
Contact: Carolyn O'Malley; (480) 367-7000; info@dmbinc.com
Internet: http://www.dorrancefamilyfoundation.org/
Sponsor: Dorrance Family Foundation
7600 East Doubletree Ranch Road, Suite 300
Scottsdale, AZ 85258-2137

Dorr Foundation Grants   **615**
Dorr Foundation grants are made primarily for programs designed to develop new science curricula from sixth to 12th grade. Support is also given to special education projects for youth relating to conservation and the environment if such projects involve the school's curriculum, equipment purchase, program development, emergency funding, and seed money. In addition, some grants are made available to promote research and disseminate information on chemical, metallurgical, and sanitation engineering. Grants are awarded on a national basis, with emphasis in the Northeast states. Types of support include equipment, emergency funds, program development, seed money, curriculum development, scholarship funds, and research. Initial contact should be a phone call. There is no deadline for application submission. No response can be expected unless there is interest on the part of the trustees. Applications are accepted at any time. Typical awards range from $5,000 to $30,000.
Requirements: 501(c)3 tax-exempt organizations are eligible.
Restrictions: Grants are not made to individuals or for operation budgets, continuing support, annual campaigns, deficit financing, endowment funds, or conferences and seminars.
Geographic Focus: Connecticut, Maine, Massachusetts, New Hampshire, New York, Vermont
Amount of Grant: 5,000 - 30,000 USD
Samples: Maritime Museum, Norwalk, Connecticut, $20,000 - building STEM Academy for teachers; Maine Natural History Observatory, Gouldsboro, Maine, $15,000 - population counts of nesting Gulls and cormorants along the coast of Maine; Young Men's Leadership Academy, Kennedy, Texas, $5,561 - Ozone North and South project.
Contact: Barbara McMillan, Chairperson; (603) 433-6438
Sponsor: Dorr Foundation
84 Hillside Drive
Portsmouth, NH 03801-5328

Doug and Carla Salmon Foundation Grants   **616**
The Salmons moved to Appleton in 1972 to work in the medical field and raise their two children. In the late 1990s, Doug and Carla began to explore ways to give back to the community that had been so good to them. The Salmons also had a strong desire to help charitable organizations in the Fox Valley — particularly through capital campaigns and the development of administrative endowments. In 2002, Doug and Carla formed the Doug & Carla Salmon Foundation, a supporting organization within the Community Foundation for the Fox Valley Region. Through this partnership, they are able to fulfill their passion for sharing with others for generations to come. There are no specific deadlines or application forms. Applicants should begin by contacted the director via email or telephone.
Requirements: All 501(c)3 organizations serving the Fox Valley Region of Wisconsin are eligible to apply.
Geographic Focus: Wisconsin
Contact: Sue Detienne; (920) 832-0348; rdetienne@new.rr.com
Internet: https://www.cffoxvalley.org/Page.aspx?pid=403
Sponsor: Doug and Carla Salmon Foundation
660 W. Ridgeview Drive
Appleton, 54911

Douty Foundation Grants   **617**
The Foundation, established in 1968, supports projects in the fields of elementary and other education, youth, and community welfare, with special emphasis on services to disadvantaged people. Grants are sometimes made to small organizations for general operations. Preference is given to organizations that operate in Philadelphia and Montgomery counties, Pennsylvania.
Requirements: Organizations with annual budgets greater than $2 million are discouraged from applying for grants.
Restrictions: Grants for capital expenditures or endowments are not a priority for the Foundation, nor are grants for agency promotion, such as marketing, development, publication of annual reports or sponsorship of fund-raising events. Grants are not made for religious or political purposes.
Geographic Focus: Pennsylvania
Date(s) Application is Due: Feb 15; Mar 15; May 15; Oct 15
Amount of Grant: Up to 5,000 USD
Samples: ArtReach, Philadelphia, PA, $3,000—Museum and Arts Education Program; Brandywine Graphic Workshop, Philadelphia, PA, $2,500—after-school programs for Philadelphia high school students; Cunningham Community Center, Philadelphia, PA, $2,500—summer camp.
Contact: Judith L. Bardes; (610) 828-8145; fax (610) 834-8175; judy1@aol.com
Internet: http://www.grants-info.org/douty/index.htm
Sponsor: Douty Foundation
P.O. Box 540
Plymouth Meeting, PA 19462-0540

Dover Foundation Grants   **618**
The primary purpose of the foundation is to serve the interests of Cleveland County and other areas of North Carolina. Foundation grants seek to strengthen the spiritual, mental, and moral fiber of the community; give priority to those initiatives and programs that will elevate the life and educational opportunities of deserving recipients; and discover ways to encourage others to come together to address needs for the common welfare of the community. Types of support include general operating support, annual campaigns, capital campaigns, building/renovation, emergency funds, scholarship funds, and research. A formal grant request must be submitted by letter. The board of directors meets four times a year to consider grant awards—January, April, July, and October.
Requirements: Applicants must reside in North Carolina.
Restrictions: The foundation ordinarily does not make grants to organizations whose principal activities are outside the United States; political activities or entities; individuals or their projects; advertising; newsletters, magazines, or books; or trips or tours.
Geographic Focus: North Carolina
Amount of Grant: 500 - 25,000 USD
Samples: Gardner-Webb U, School of Business (Boiling Springs, NC)—to endow a faculty position at the School of Business, $500,000; Heineman Medical Research Center of Charlotte (Charlotte, NC)—for support, $50,000.
Contact: Hoyt Bailey, President; (704) 487-8888; fax (704) 482-6818; doverfnd@shelby.net
Sponsor: Dover Foundation
P.O. Box 208
Shelby, NC 28151

DPA Promoting Policy Change Advocacy Grants   **619**

The Drug Policy Alliance Advocacy Grants seek to broaden public and political support for drug policy reform and will fund strategic and innovative approaches to increase such support. Proposals should be designed to: educate the public and policymakers about the negative consequences of current local, state or national drug policies; promote better awareness and understanding of alternatives to current drug policies; and broaden awareness and understanding of the extent to which punitive prohibitionist policies are responsible for most drug-related problems around the country. Strategic, geographic or thematic collaborations are strongly encouraged. The Alliance prioritizes organizations focused on one or more of the following: public education campaigns and litigation to raise awareness of the negative consequences of current local, state, and national drug policies; and organizing and mobilizing constituencies that raise awareness about the negative consequences of local, state, and national drug policies. The Alliance also favors public education efforts that speak to: the failures and consequences of drug polices in the U.S. and the potential benefits of alternatives to prohibition; reducing over-reliance on the criminal justice system by raising awareness of the need for alternatives to incarceration and/or health-based approaches to drug use; discrimination in employment, housing, student loans and other benefits against those who use drugs or who have been convicted of drug law violations; the negative consequences of current drug policies on human rights; and efforts that mobilize people around the disproportionate impact of the drug war on communities of color and youth.

Requirements: Tax-exempt 501(c)3 organizations and organizations with 501(c)3 fiscal sponsors are eligible. The program provides both general support and project-specific grants. All grantmaking will be directed to organizations working within the United States, and possibly Canada, with particular emphasis on state-based activity. The Alliance will make grants to organizations that have been invited to apply and who demonstrate a clear ability and commitment to educate the public about the need for broad drug policy reform.

Geographic Focus: All States, Canada

Date(s) Application is Due: Jun 18

Amount of Grant: 15,000 - 25,000 USD

Contact: Asha Bandele, Grants Contact; (212) 613-8020; fax (212) 613-8021; abandele@drugpolicy.org or grants@drugpolicy.org

Internet: http://www.drugpolicy.org/about/jobsfunding/grants/index.cfm

Sponsor: Drug Policy Alliance

131 West 33rd Street, 15th Floor

New York, NY 10001

Dr. Bob and Jean Smith Foundation Grants   **620**

The foundation awards grants to Texas nonprofit organizations in its areas of interest, including arts and culture, higher education, medical education, medical research, and health care. Types of support include annual campaigns, building construction/renovation, capital campaigns, general operating support, matching/challenge grants, and scholarship funds. There are no application deadlines; the board meets quarterly.

Requirements: Texas nonprofit organizations are eligible. Preference is given to Dallas-based organizations.

Restrictions: Individuals are ineligible.

Geographic Focus: Texas

Amount of Grant: 100 - 500,000 USD

Samples: Southwestern Medical Foundation (Dallas, TX)—to conduct neuromuscular research at the U of Texas Southwestern Medical Ctr at Dallas, $1 million.

Contact: Sally Smith, Grants Administrator; (214) 521-3461

Sponsor: Dr. Bob and Jean Smith Foundation

3811 Turtle Creek Center, #2150 LB 53

Dallas, TX 75219

Dream Weaver Foundation   **621**

Established in 2000 in Georgia, the Dream Weaver Foundation offers grant funding primarily in Georgia and Florida. Its major fields of interest include: animals and wildlife; education (all levels); and human services. Funding is either directed at general operating costs or specific programs. There is no formal application requires, so interested parties should offer a proposal in the form of a two- or three-page letter. This format should be comprised of a general project description, the needed budgetary allowance, and copies of tax-free status letters. There are no specified annual deadlines. Most recently, grants have typically ranged from $1,000 to $5,000.

Requirements: 501(c)3 organizations from Georgia and Florida, or these supporting residents of these two states, are eligible to apply.

Restrictions: No grants are given to individuals

Geographic Focus: Florida, Georgia

Amount of Grant: 1,000 - 5,000 USD

Samples: New Horizons Services, Orange City, Florida, $5,000 - general welfare of dogs; The Place of Forsyth County, Cumming, Georgia, $5,000 - general operating costs; Stonecreek Church, Milton, Georgia, $3,500 - general operations.

Contact: Charles E. Weaver, President; (770) 781-2823 or (770) 889-2599

Sponsor: Dream Weaver Foundation

6315 Holland Drive

Cumming, GA 30041-4639

Dresher Foundation Grants   **622**

The foundation awards grants to eligible Maryland nonprofit organizations in its areas of interest, including capital campaigns, endowments, new or ongoing programs, operating support and scholarships. Summer camp and after-school program letters of inquiry are accepted for review only for the January and March deadlines. Letters of inquiry are accepted; full proposals are by request.

Requirements: Fund requests are generally limited to the Maryland jurisdictions of Baltimore City and Baltimore and Harford Counties. The Foundation will only make grants to organizations that are exempt from federal tax under section 501(c)3 of the IRS Code and that are not classified as private foundations under section 509(a) of the Code.

Restrictions: Support is not provided for: agencies that redistribute grant funds to nonprofits; annual giving; charter schools; public elementary or high schools; galas, special events, or golf tournaments; literacy programs; national or local chapters for specific diseases; one-time only events, seminars, or workshops; or political activities. The Foundation will not consider inquiries or proposals from any organization more than once every twelve months.

Geographic Focus: Maryland

Date(s) Application is Due: Jan 12; Mar 9; May 4; Aug 10; Oct 5

Samples: Johns Hopkins U (Baltimore, MD)—to establish a professorship in cardiac surgery in the department of medicine, $2 million.

Contact: Robin Platts, Executive Director; (410) 933-0384; robin@dresherfoundation.org

Internet: http://www.dresherfoundation.org

Sponsor: Dresher Foundation

4940 Campbell Boulevard, Suite 110

Baltimore, MD 21236

Dreyer's Foundation Large Grants   **623**

This grant focuses on young people from preschool to grade 12, primarily in Oakland and the East Bay. Grants will be awarded to K-12 public education and programs that help students to succeed in core academic subjects and graduate to post secondary education and/or vocational training. Priority will be given to programs, either in-school or after school, which are provided in sequential, consistent basis to students throughout the year. Organizations may request support for capital items, program expenses, operating expenses, start-up costs, materials, and/or supplies. Priority will be given to those programs/projects that support low and middle income youth and minority youth.

Requirements: Grants are awarded to nonprofit youth-serving organizations and K-12 public education organizations.

Restrictions: The Foundation does not fund basic health, clothing or shelter needs. An organization may submit only one proposal annually.

Geographic Focus: All States

Date(s) Application is Due: Jan 15

Amount of Grant: 3,000 USD

Contact: Large Grants Program Coordinator; (510) 450-4586

Internet: http://www.dreyersinc.com/dreyersfoundation/large_grants.asp

Sponsor: Dreyer's Foundation

5929 College Avenue

Oakland, CA 94618

DTE Energy Foundation Environmental Grants   **624**

The DTE Energy Foundation believes economic development and environmental protection are not mutually exclusive. Environmental grants focus on organizations and programs that: protect and restore the environment and enhance the quality of life in the communities that we serve or are home to our facilities; and build understanding of the environment and promote an understanding of the links between environmental stewardship and sustainable development, including education about renewable energy and energy efficiency, that reaches a broad audience. Grant amounts range from $500 to $100,000, and the application process is distinct for each of the following ranges: $500 to $2,000; $2,001 to $10,000; and any amount greater than $10,000. Applications must be submitted electronically by the stated deadlines.

Requirements: Eligible applicants must meet all of the following criteria: be located in or provide services to a community in which DTE Energy does business; and be a nonprofit (i.e. be exempt for federal income tax under section 501(c)3 of the Internal Revenue Code and not a private foundation, as defined in Section 509(a) of the Code).

Restrictions: The foundation does not provide support to: individuals; political parties, organizations or activities; religious organizations for religious purposes; organizations that are not able to demonstrate commitment to equality and diversity; student group trips; national or international organizations, unless they are providing benefits directly to our service-area residents; projects that may result in undue personal benefit to a member of the DTE Energy Foundation board, or to any DTE Energy employee; conferences unless they are aligned with DTE Energy's business interests; single purpose health organizations; or hospitals, for building or equipment needs.

Geographic Focus: Michigan

Date(s) Application is Due: Apr 13; Jul 13; Oct 12; Dec 28

Amount of Grant: 500 - 100,000 USD

Contact: Karla D. Hall; (313) 235-9271; foundation@dteenergy.com

Internet: http://www.dteenergy.com/dteEnergyCompany/community/foundation/whatWeSupport.html

Sponsor: DTE Energy Foundation

One Energy Plaza, 1046 WBC

Detroit, MI 48226-1279

DTE Energy Foundation Health and Human Services Grants 625

The DTE Energy Foundation is at the core of DTE Energy's commitment to the communities and customers it is privileged to serve. The DTE Energy Foundation is dedicated to strengthening the health and human services sector of these communities. Priority will be given to supporting organizations that are in the forefront of addressing the critical, acute human needs brought on by the economic downturn. Grant amounts generally range from $500 to $100,000, and the application process is distinct for each of the following ranges: $500 to $2,000; $2,001 to $10,000; and any amount greater than $10,000. Applications must be submitted electronically by the stated deadlines.

Requirements: Eligible applicants must meet all of the following criteria: be located in or provide services to a community in which DTE Energy does business; and be a nonprofit (i.e. be exempt for federal income tax under section 501(c)3 of the Internal Revenue Code and not a private foundation, as defined in Section 509(a) of the Code).

Restrictions: The Foundation does not provide support to: individuals; political parties, organizations or activities; religious organizations for religious purposes; organizations that are not able to demonstrate commitment to equality and diversity; student group trips; national or international organizations, unless they are providing benefits directly to our service-area residents; projects that may result in undue personal benefit to a member of the DTE Energy Foundation board, or to any DTE Energy employee; conferences unless they are aligned with DTE Energy's business interests; single purpose health organizations; hospitals, for building or equipment needs.

Geographic Focus: Michigan

Date(s) Application is Due: Apr 13; Jul 13; Oct 12; Dec 28

Amount of Grant: 500 - 100,000 USD

Samples: Center for Autism, Ann Arbor, Michigan, $100,000 - general operating support; Girl Scouts of Southeastern Michigan, Detroit, Michigan, $75,000 - general operating costs; Forgotten Harvest, Oak Park, Michigan, $60,000 - general operating costs.

Contact: Karla D. Hall; (313) 235-9271; foundation@dteenergy.com

Sponsor: DTE Energy Foundation

One Energy Plaza, 1046 WBC

Detroit, MI 48226-1279

DTE Energy Foundation Higher Learning Grants 626

In the area of Higher Learning grants, the DTE Energy Foundation's focus is on the following priorities: specific academic departments of engineering, science and business that prepare students to enter the professional workforce; programs and institutions that prepare students for technical and skilled trade careers in the energy industry; and programs that increase student retention and success in engineering, the sciences and business with a focus on women and minorities. Grant amounts generally range from $2,000 to $750,000, and the application process is distinct for each of the following ranges: $500 to $2,000; $2,001 to $10,000; and any amount greater than $10,000. Applications must be submitted electronically by the stated deadlines.

Requirements: Eligible applicants must meet all of the following criteria: be located in or provide services to a community in which DTE Energy does

business; and be a nonprofit (i.e. be exempt for federal income tax under section 501(c)3 of the Internal Revenue Code and not a private foundation, as defined in Section 509(a) of the Code).

Restrictions: The Foundation does not provide support to: individuals; political parties, organizations or activities; religious organizations for religious purposes; organizations that are not able to demonstrate commitment to equality and diversity; student group trips; national or international organizations, unless they are providing benefits directly to our service-area residents; projects that may result in undue personal benefit to a member of the DTE Energy Foundation board, or to any DTE Energy employee; conferences unless they are aligned with DTE Energy's business interests; single purpose health organizations; hospitals, for building or equipment needs.

Geographic Focus: Michigan

Date(s) Application is Due: Apr 13; Jul 13; Oct 12; Dec 28

Amount of Grant: 2,000 - 750,000 USD

Samples: University of Michigan, Ann Arbor, Michigan, $260,602 - ongoing costs; Wayne State University, Detroit, Michigan, $120,250 - ongoing costs; Western Michigan University Foundation, Kalamazoo, Michigan, $67,555 - general operating costs.

Contact: Karla D. Hall; (313) 235-9271; foundation@dteenergy.com

Internet: http://www.dteenergy.com/dteEnergyCompany/community/foundation/whatWeSupport.html

Sponsor: DTE Energy Foundation

One Energy Plaza, 1046 WBC

Detroit, MI 48226-1279

DTE Energy Foundation K -12 Education Grants 627

The DTE Energy Foundation's focus is on improving the quality of life in the communities they serve. Support is targeted on programs that increase the number of college undergraduates entering the STEM (Science, Technology, Engineering and Math) disciplines, thereby expanding the STEM workforce pipeline. Priority will be given to programs that: demonstrate proven effectiveness with increasing the number of college undergraduates in the STEM disciplines; provide an opportunity to improve skills in more than one STEM discipline; target high school age children; provide programs in underserved communities of DTE Energy's service area; and serve a large number of students (district-wide, multiple cities). Grant amounts generally range from $500 to $75,000, and the application process is distinct for each of the following ranges: $500 to $2,000; $2,001 to $10,000; and any amount greater than $10,000. Applications must be submitted electronically by the stated deadlines.

Requirements: Eligible applicants must meet all of the following criteria: be located in or provide services to a community in which DTE Energy does business; and be a nonprofit (i.e. be exempt for federal income tax under section 501(c)3 of the Internal Revenue Code and not a private foundation, as defined in Section 509(a) of the Code).

Restrictions: The Foundation does not provide support to: individuals; political parties, organizations or activities; religious organizations for religious purposes; organizations that are not able to demonstrate commitment to equality and diversity; student group trips; national or international organizations, unless they are providing benefits directly to our service-area residents; projects that may result in undue personal benefit to a member of the DTE Energy Foundation board, or to any DTE Energy employee; conferences unless they are aligned with DTE Energy's business interests; single purpose health organizations; hospitals, for building or equipment needs.

Geographic Focus: Michigan

Date(s) Application is Due: Apr 13; Jul 13; Oct 12; Dec 28

Amount of Grant: 500 - 75,000 USD

Contact: Karla D. Hall; (313) 235-9271; foundation@dteenergy.com

Internet: http://www.dteenergy.com/dteEnergyCompany/community/foundation/whatWeSupport.html

Sponsor: DTE Energy Foundation

One Energy Plaza, 1046 WBC

Detroit, MI 48226-1279

DTE Energy Foundation Leadership Grants 628

The foundation believes that leadership encompasses activity on two planes; personal and institutional. In the interest of building thriving communities, the foundation will place special emphasis on programs that promote and nurture leadership traits in young people. In addition, vibrant communities also benefit from the efforts of a core group of institutions dedicated to improving the community's way of life. Foundation focus is on: programs that provide unique experiences to equip individuals with leadership skills; initiatives that improve the strength, stability, sustainability and leadership of the nonprofit sector; and core institutions important to the quality of life in DTE Energy communities. Grant amounts generally range from $500 to $75,000, and the application process is distinct for each of the following ranges: $500 to $2,000; $2,001 to $10,000; and any amount greater than $10,000. Applications must be submitted electronically by the stated deadlines.

Requirements: Eligible applicants must meet all of the following criteria: be located in or provide services to a community in which DTE Energy does business; and be a nonprofit (i.e. be exempt for federal income tax under section 501(c)3 of the Internal Revenue Code and not a private foundation, as defined in Section 509(a) of the Code).

Restrictions: The foundation does not provide support to: individuals; political parties, organizations or activities; religious organizations for religious purposes; organizations that are not able to demonstrate commitment to equality and diversity; student group trips; national or international organizations, unless they are providing benefits directly to our service-area residents; projects that may result in undue personal benefit to a member of the DTE Energy Foundation board, or to any DTE Energy employee; conferences unless they are aligned with DTE Energy's business interests; single purpose health organizations; and hospitals, for building or equipment needs.

Geographic Focus: Michigan
Date(s) Application is Due: Apr 13; Jul 13; Oct 12; Dec 28
Amount of Grant: 500 - 100,000 USD
Contact: Karla D. Hall; (313) 235-9271; foundation@dteenergy.com
Internet: http://www.dteenergy.com/dteEnergyCompany/community/foundation/whatWeSupport.html
Sponsor: DTE Energy Foundation
One Energy Plaza, 1046 WBC
Detroit, MI 48226-1279

Duchossois Family Foundation Grants 629

The foundation focuses its efforts in the Chicago metropolitan area and gives primary consideration to nonprofit organizations that contribute to the community in the area of health. The foundation supports organizations involved with mental health/crisis services, cancer, HIV/AIDS, cancer research, AIDS research and, human services. A one-page summary-request letter should include a description of the organization and its specific needs and purposes, the amount requested, and a list of members of the board of directors and their business/professional affiliations.

Requirements: 501(c)3 tax-exempt public charities serving the Chicago metropolitan area are eligible.
Geographic Focus: Illinois
Contact: Iris Krieg, Executive Director; (312) 641-5765; iriskrieg1@aol.com
Sponsor: Duchossois Family Foundation (Chicago)
203 N Wabash Avenue, Suite 1800
Chicago, IL 60601

Duke Endowment Education Grants 630

The Education Division of the Duke Endowment awards grants to four specific institutions of higher education named in the trust indenture. Funds are provided annually both for general operating support and for special projects and programs. Application forms for individual grants are not required. Faculty and administrators at Duke University should contact the Office of the Provost, while faculty and administrators at the other eligible institutions should contact the Office of the President.

Requirements: The endowment awards education grants to four institutions: Davidson College, Duke University, Furman University, and Johnson C. Smith University.
Restrictions: The Endowment does not accept grant proposals from individual academic units or faculty members.
Geographic Focus: North Carolina, South Carolina
Contact: Susan L. McConnell, Program Officer; (704) 376-0291; fax (704) 376-9336; smcconnell@tde.org
Internet: http://www.dukeendowment.org/program-areas/higher-education
Sponsor: Duke Endowment
100 N Tryon Street, Suite 3500
Charlotte, NC 28202-4012

Duke Endowment Rural Churches Grants 631

The majority of grants awarded through this program go to individual rural United Methodist churches, defined as those churches in communities of fewer than 1,500 people. While North Carolina is becoming increasingly an urban state, almost 1,300 rural United Methodist churches meet eligibility requirements for Endowment grants. While the foundation makes many for capital projects such as sanctuaries and fellowship halls, recent years have seen the Endowment award an increasing number of grants for programs that help rural churches conduct ministries that meet the changing needs of modern communities. Grants are also made to the North Carolina and Western North Carolina Annual Conferences of the United Methodist Church, and to the districts of those conferences, for programs or projects addressing needs and concerns of groups of churches. The Endowment also awards grants to Duke University Divinity School, with special focus on programs that train and support pastors in rural churches.

Requirements: Nonprofit United Methodist in North Carolina and South Carolina in communities of less than 1,500 people.
Geographic Focus: North Carolina, South Carolina
Samples: Wesley Community Development, Iredell County, North Carolina; Sandy Plains United Methodist Church, Pembroke, North Carolina
Contact: W. Joseph Mann, Director, Rural Church Division; (704) 376-0291; fax (704) 376-9336; jmann@tde.org
Internet: http://www.dukeendowment.org/program-areas/rural-church
Sponsor: Duke Endowment
100 N Tryon Street, Suite 3500
Charlotte, NC 28202-4012

Duke Energy Foundation Economic Development Grants 632

The Duke Energy Foundation, along with employee and retiree volunteers, actively works to improve the quality of life in its communities, lending expertise in the form of leadership and financial support through grants to charitable organizations. The Foundation gives primarily in areas of company operations in Indiana, Kentucky, North Carolina, Ohio and South Carolina. In the area of economic development, the Foundation funds initiatives that support the company's economic development strategies and necessary skills to strengthen the workforce. Grants range from $1,000 to $1,250,000. A formal application is required, though there are no specified annual deadlines.

Requirements: Organizations with a 501(c)3 verification from the IRS or are a part of a governmental entity are eligible. All organizations applying for a grant must have: completed the Online Grant Application; a clear reason for making the contribution that relates to the areas of focus; and regular reports on the measurable results of the project.

Restrictions: Foundation funds are not provided for: organizations that discriminate by race, creed, gender, age or national origin; political activities and organizations; grants to individual agencies of the United Way or the Charlotte Arts and Science Council; capital campaigns and endowments, except in extremely rare and specialized situations that relate directly to our areas of expertise in business; individuals; athletics, including individual sports teams and all-star teams; underwriting of films, video and television productions; reducing the cost of utility service; sectarian or religious activities; conferences, trips or tours; fraternal, veteran or labor groups serving only their members; advertising; membership fees or association fees, either personal or corporate; dinners or tables at fund-raisers are rarely considered; family foundations.

Geographic Focus: Indiana, Kentucky, North Carolina, Ohio, South Carolina
Amount of Grant: 1,000 - 1,250,000 USD
Contact: Alisa McDonald; (704) 382-7200; fax (704) 382-7600
Internet: http://www.duke-energy.com/community/foundation/areas-of-focus.asp
Sponsor: Duke Energy Foundation
400 South Tryon Street, P.O. Box 1007
Charlotte, NC 28201-1007

Duluth-Superior Area Community Foundation Grants 633

The foundation supports a wide variety of activities in five interest areas: Arts, Community and Economic Development, Education, Environment, and Human Services. Consideration is given to regional needs, the availability of other funding sources, and level of foundation resources. The foundation concentrates its funding support towards new projects and organizational start-up for a limited time; however, some field of interest and donor advised funds consider requests for ongoing project or organizational support, and capital and equipment support.

Requirements: Eligible organizations include: those classified as charitable organizations under Section 501(c)3 of the Internal Revenue Code; or classified as an organization under Section 170(c)(1) of the Internal Revenue Code; located in or that provide services to residents within the seven counties of northeast Minnesota (Aitkin, Carlton, Cook, Itasca, Koochiching, Lake, and St. Louis) and/or the two counties in northwest Wisconsin (Bayfield, Douglas). Some funds have a specific geographic focus area.

Restrictions: The foundation does not make grants to/for: individuals (aside from scholarships initiated or managed by the Community Foundation), fundraising activities, requests from re-granting organizations for its own grant making activities, tickets for benefits, telephone solicitations, endowments, religious organizations for religious activities, medical research, debt retirement, political organizations or campaigns, organizations with significant activity considered influencing of legislation.

Geographic Focus: Minnesota, Wisconsin
Date(s) Application is Due: Feb 1; Apr 1; Aug 1; Oct 1
Amount of Grant: 1,000 - 10,000 USD
Samples: Hibbing Kinship Mentoring Program, Hibbing, Minnesota, $3,000; ISD 381 Lake Superior Public Schools, Two Harbors, Minnesota, $4,864—for Community Education Preschool scholarships, kindergarten transition activities and Weekly Readers for Preschool children; Minnesota Ballet, Duluth, Minnesota, $5,000—for operating support.
Contact: Katie Gellatly, (218) 726-0232; KGellatly@dsacommunityfoundation.com
Internet: http://www.dsacommunityfoundation.com/grants
Sponsor: Duluth-Superior Area Community Foundation
324 West Superior Street, Suite 212
Duluth, MN 55802

Dunspaugh-Dalton Foundation Grants 634

Since 1963, the Dunspaugh-Dalton Foundation, Inc. (DDF) has assisted qualifying, exempt 501(c)3 organizations in achieving charitable goals. The Foundation awards grants to eligible nonprofit organizations in the areas of higher, secondary, and elementary education; cpmmunity development; social services; youth services and programs; health associations and hospitals; cultural programs; and civic affairs. Types of support include capital campaigns, continuing support, endowment funds, matching funds, operating support, professorships, and special projects. There are no annual deadlines. The board meets monthly to consider requests.
Requirements: U.S. nonprofit organizations are eligible. The foundation primarily supports programs in California, Florida, and North Carolina.
Restrictions: Individuals are not eligible.
Geographic Focus: California, Florida, North Carolina
Amount of Grant: 5,000 - 50,000 USD
Contact: Sarah Lane Bonner, President; (305) 668-4192; fax (305) 668-4247; ddf@dunspaughdalton.org
Internet: http://www.dunspaughdalton.org/application-process.html
Sponsor: Dunspaugh-Dalton Foundation
1500 San Remo Avenue, Suite 103
Coral Gables, FL 33146

Dwight Stuart Youth Foundation Capacity-Building Initiative Grants 635

The Dwight Stuart Youth Foundation was endowed by Dwight L. Stuart (1924 - 1998). As a philanthropist, Mr. Stuart was honored for his work and generosity on behalf of underserved and disadvantaged children and youth. The foundation looks for projects and programs that provide direct services to underserved children and youth within Los Angeles County. The foundation's Capacity-Building Initiative builds on its regular grantmaking, which already has provided support for capacity building to a number of grantees. The Initiative's objective is to increase the foundation's commitment to strengthening youth-serving nonprofits in Los Angeles County, helping them achieve their missions by offering grant support for such purposes as staff training, creation of new staff positions such as development director, board training, facilities development and technology purchases. In addition, the Capacity-Building Initiative includes a Cornerstone Grants Program, which is by invitation only - you cannot apply for a Cornerstone grant and only current or past DSYF grantees are eligible to be invited. The purpose of these special grants is to provide up to three years of operating support (support for specific capacity-building activities also can be included) to a select group of youth-serving nonprofits in Southern California, based upon their demonstrated excellence and growth potential. Those invited to apply will be contacted by the Foundation.
Requirements: Nonprofit organizations with 501(c)3 status and in the Los Angeles County area are eligible to apply. The application process starts with a letter of inquiry. Letters of inquiry are accepted year round and are reviewed in the order they are received. If it is determined from your letter of inquiry that your request is consistent with the foundation's funding priorities and interests, you may be asked to participate in a conference call with foundation staff to further refine your request and clarify questions. During the conference call, if it is decided that your organization's objectives and activities match the foundation's criteria, you will be asked to submit a full proposal and application materials will be mailed to you at that time. Unsolicited full proposals are not accepted. Youth-serving nonprofits can apply for grant funds to support

capacity-building activities of their own choosing; these requests will be considered independent of any program requests, and you may ask for both program and capacity building support at the same time. If you are seeking capacity-building support, use the Quick Assessment Tool in the Resources section (see website) to help define your needs, and include brief responses to its five questions in your Letter of Inquiry. The maximum grant amount that can be requested for capacity building is $25,000. Submit your capacity building request separately from any program requests.
Restrictions: Funding is not available for individuals; private foundations; annual giving campaigns; buildings or capital campaigns; unrestricted endowments or deficit reduction; political parties, candidates, campaigns, or lobbying activities; fundraising activities, benefit sponsorship, advertisements, or tables; medical or health programs (this includes hospitals, clinics, and mental or physical trauma recovery programs). The foundation also does not fund programs for children and youth who are diagnosed as emotionally and/or developmentally disabled, or chronically and terminally ill; organizations which, in their constitution or practice, discriminate against a person or group on the basis of age, political affiliation, race, national origin, ethnicity, gender, disability, sexual orientation, or religious belief; programs outside Los Angeles County; institutions outside the United States of America.
Geographic Focus: California
Amount of Grant: Up to 25,000 USD
Contact: Wendy Chang; (310) 777-5050; fax (310) 777-5060
Internet: http://www.dsyf.org/grantmaking_capacitybuilding.asp
Sponsor: Dwight Stuart Youth Foundation
9595 Wilshire Boulevard, Suite 212
Beverly Hills, CA 90212

Dwight Stuart Youth Foundation Grants 636

The Dwight Stuart Youth Foundation was endowed by Dwight L. Stuart (1924 - 1998). As a philanthropist, Mr. Stuart was honored for his work and generosity on behalf of underserved and disadvantaged children and youth. The foundation looks for projects and programs that provide direct services to underserved children and youth within Los Angeles County. The four funding areas that are of interest are education enrichment, mentoring, leadership and school readiness.
Requirements: Nonprofit organizations with 501(c)3 status and in the Los Angeles County area are eligible to apply. The application process starts with a letter of inquiry. Letters of inquiry are accepted year round and are reviewed in the order they are received. If it is determined from your letter of inquiry that your request is consistent with the foundation's funding priorities and interests, you may be asked to participate in a conference call with foundation staff to further refine your request and clarify questions. During the conference call, if it is decided that your organization's objectives and activities match the foundation's criteria, you will be asked to submit a full proposal and application materials will be mailed to you at that time. Unsolicited full proposals are not accepted.
Restrictions: Funding is not available for individuals; private foundations; annual giving campaigns; buildings or capital campaigns; unrestricted endowments or deficit reduction; political parties, candidates, campaigns, or lobbying activities; fundraising activities, benefit sponsorship, advertisements, or tables; medical or health programs (this includes hospitals, clinics, and mental or physical trauma recovery programs). The foundation also does not fund programs for children and youth who are diagnosed as emotionally and/or developmentally disabled, or chronically and terminally ill; organizations which, in their constitution or practice, discriminate against a person or group on the basis of age, political affiliation, race, national origin, ethnicity, gender, disability, sexual orientation, or religious belief; programs outside Los Angeles County; institutions outside the United States of America.
Geographic Focus: California
Contact: Wendy Chang; (310) 777-5050; fax (310) 777-5060
Internet: http://www.dsyf.org/grantmaking_areas.asp
Sponsor: Dwight Stuart Youth Foundation
9595 Wilshire Boulevard, Suite 212
Beverly Hills, CA 90212

Dyson Foundation Management Assistance Program Mini-Grants 637

The purpose of the Dyson Foundation's Management Assistance Program (MAP) mini-grants is to help Mid-Hudson Valley nonprofits improve their internal operations, program development, administration, and management to better achieve their missions. Mini-grants enable nonprofit board, staff, and volunteer leaders to develop new skills by providing organizations with financial support to hire consultants to lead specific capacity building activities. Mini-grants may also be used to defray the cost of conferences, seminars, and other training opportunities for staff and board. Examples of how funds might be used include: facilitation of a strategic planning process; resource development planning; training for board members; developing a marketing and communication plan; establishing or improving fiscal systems; developing personnel policies or personnel management training; attending a relevant conference or seminar; and technology planning.

Requirements: 501(c)3 nonprofit organization or libraries based in the Mid-Hudson Valley (Columbia, Dutchess, Greene, Orange, Putnam, and Ulster counties) are eligible. Preference is given to organizations with operating budgets of less than $1 million.

Restrictions: MAP mini grants are not available for individuals, government entities, or public school systems. Consultancies and training opportunities already in progress or completed are not eligible for funding. Note that the Dyson Foundation does not generally provide management assistance funding to faith-based organizations.

Geographic Focus: New York

Amount of Grant: Up to 10,000 USD

Contact: Diana M. Gurieva, Executive Vice President; (845) 790-6312 or (845) 677-0644; fax (845) 677-0650; dgurieva@dyson.org or info@dyson.org
Jennifer Drake, Grants Program Coordinator; (845) 790-6318 or (845) 677-0644; fax (845) 677-0650; jdrake@dyson.org or info@dyson.org

Internet: http://www.dysonfoundation.org/mini-grant-program

Sponsor: Dyson Foundation

25 Halcyon Road

Millbrook, NY 12545-9611

Dyson Foundation Mid-Hudson Valley General Operating Support Grants   638

General operating support grants are sometimes referred to as core support or unrestricted grants. Many organizations use general operating support grants to cover day-to-day activities or ongoing expenses such as administrative salaries, utilities, office supplies, technology maintenance, etc. Other organizations use this type of funding to cover project costs, capital, technology purchases, and professional development. The use of these funds is totally at the discretion of the organization's board and/or executive staff, although the Foundation expects all organizational expenditures to be part of a board-approved annual budget. The first step in applying for a general operating support grant is to submit a letter of inquiry.

Requirements: 501(c)3 nonprofit organization or libraries based in the Mid-Hudson Valley (Columbia, Dutchess, Greene, Orange, Putnam, and Ulster counties) are eligible. To apply for a general operating support grant, an organization must: review the principles of best practice relative to nonprofit governance, finance, public disclosure, and programming; have been a recipient of a Dyson Foundation project grant within the past three years of their general operating support request; have a mission and programs that are consistent with core funding interests of the Dyson Foundation; and have demonstrated at least three years of stable executive leadership.

Restrictions: The Foundation places no restrictions on the use of these funds, unlike project or management technical assistance grants that are restricted by the Foundation to a particular project or activity. Colleges and universities, hospitals, faith-based institutions, and organizations with annual budgets in excess of $15 million dollars are not eligible to apply for general operating support grants.

Geographic Focus: New York

Amount of Grant: 1,000 - 1,000,000 USD

Contact: Diana M. Gurieva, Executive Vice President; (845) 790-6312 or (845) 677-0644; fax (845) 677-0650; dgurieva@dyson.org or info@dyson.org
Jennifer Drake, Grants Program Coordinator; (845) 790-6318 or (845) 677-0644; fax (845) 677-0650; jdrake@dyson.org or info@dyson.org

Internet: http://www.dysonfoundation.org/grantmaking/general-operating-support-grants

Sponsor: Dyson Foundation

25 Halcyon Road

Millbrook, NY 12545-9611

Dyson Foundation Nonprofit Strategic Restructuring Initiative Grants   639

Strategic restructuring is the establishment of an ongoing relationship between two or more independent organizations to increase administrative efficiency and/or further programmatic missions through shared, transferred, or combined services, resources, or programs. The results can range from jointly managed programs and consolidated administrative functions to full-scale mergers. The benefits can include reductions in duplicated services, improved efficiencies, and increased financial stability. The Dyson Foundation's Nonprofit Strategic Restructuring Initiative provides funding to help organizations through this process. Grants are made in the following four categories: preliminary exploration, planning, implementation, and post restructuring support.

Requirements: To be eligible for funding, one or more of the collaborating organizations must be a 501(c)3 nonprofit organization, a library or unit of government based in the Mid-Hudson Valley. The region includes: Columbia, Dutchess, Greene, Orange, Putnam, and Ulster counties.

Restrictions: Funding from the Strategic Restructuring Initiative is not available for individuals or private/independent schools. Grants do not support: dinners, fund raising events, tickets, or benefit advertising; direct mail campaigns; service clubs and similar organizations; debt or deficit reduction; governmental units; or international projects or to organizations outside of the United States.

Geographic Focus: New York

Amount of Grant: 10,000 - 35,000 USD

Contact: Diana M. Gurieva, Executive Vice President; (845) 790-6312 or (845) 677-0644; fax (845) 677-0650; dgurieva@dyson.org or info@dyson.org
Jennifer Drake, Grants Program Coordinator; (845) 790-6318 or (845) 677-0644; fax (845) 677-0650; jdrake@dyson.org or info@dyson.org

Internet: http://www.dysonfoundation.org/nonprofit-strategic-restructuring-initiative

Sponsor: Dyson Foundation

25 Halcyon Road

Millbrook, NY 12545-9611

Eastern Bank Charitable Foundation Grants   640

The goal of the foundation is to contribute to the health and vitality of northeastern Massachusetts communities served by Eastern Bank. The program provides financial support to nonprofit medical, cultural, educational, community service, or voluntary relief organizations operating within communities served by the bank. Types of support include capital grants, demonstration grants, development grants, endowments, general operating grants, and program grants. Requests for major gifts ($10,000-$25,000) must be submitted in the Associated Grantmakers of Massachusetts Application Form plus Eastern Bank donation request summary. Listed application deadlines are for major grants; there are no deadlines for community grants (less than $10,000). Guidelines are available online.

Requirements: Nonprofit organizations operating in northeastern Massachusetts communities served by Eastern Bank are eligible for funding.

Restrictions: Recipients of major gifts generally will be considered ineligible to reapply for a major gift for a period of three years.

Geographic Focus: Massachusetts

Date(s) Application is Due: May 1; Nov 1

Amount of Grant: 100 - 25,000 USD

Contact: Laura Kurzrok, Foundation Coordinator; (781) 598-7888; fax (978) 740-6329; Lkurzrok@easternbk.com

Internet: http://www.easternbank.com/a_charitable_foundation.html

Sponsor: Eastern Bank Charitable Foundation

1 Eastern Place, 195 Market Street

Lynn, MA 01901

Eastman Kodak American Greenways Awards   641

The program is a partnership project of Kodak, The Conservation Fund, and the National Geographic Society that provides small grants to stimulate the planning and design of greenways in communities throughout America. Grants may be used for activities such as mapping, ecological assessments, surveying, conferences, and design activities; developing brochures, interpretative displays, audiovisual productions, or public opinion surveys; hiring consultants, incorporating land trusts; and building foot bridges, bike paths, or other creative projects. In general, grants can be used for all appropriate expenses needed to complete a greenway project, including planning, technical assistance, legal, and other costs. The program also honors groups and individuals whose ingenuity and creativity foster creation of greenways. Applications are available online.

Requirements: Local, regional, and statewide nonprofit organizations are eligible. Public agencies also may apply, but community organizations will receive preference.

Geographic Focus: All States

Date(s) Application is Due: Jul 15

Amount of Grant: Up to 2,500 USD

Contact: Grants Administrator; (703) 525-6300; fax (703) 525-4610; kodakawards@conservationfund.org

Internet: http://www.conservationfund.org/awards_and_grants

Sponsor: Conservation Fund

1655 N Fort Myer Drive, Suite 1300

Arlington, VA 22209-2156

Eaton Charitable Fund Grants   642

The Fund is dedicated to supporting programs that improve the quality of life in communities where the company operates. The Fund gives primary consideration to requests for programs located in an Eaton community, recommended by an Eaton manager and where employees demonstrate leadership involvement. Programs selected for funding will have clearly defined objectives, measurable end results, and provide a positive return on the Funds investment. The Fund's primary interests are in support of community improvement, education, and arts and cultural programs. Program, project and capital grants are awarded. Capital grants are made for special purposes that meet specific community needs within the company's funding focus. On occasion, operating grants are awarded. Proposals should be sent to the manager of the Eaton facility located in an Eaton community.

Requirements: Applicant organizations must be 501(c)3 tax exempt charities and be located in communities where the company has operations.

Restrictions: Eaton does not make contributions to: annual operating budgets of United Way agencies or hospitals; medical research; endowment funds; debt retirement; religious organizations unless they are engaged in a significant program benefiting the entire community; fraternal or labor organizations; individuals or individual endeavors; fund raising benefits, sponsorships or other events.

Geographic Focus: Arkansas, Colorado, Florida, Georgia, Kansas, Kentucky, Louisiana, Maine, Maryland, Michigan, Minnesota, New Jersey, New York, North Carolina, Ohio, Pennsylvania, South Carolina, Texas, Wisconsin

Samples: 81,640 Eaton Multicultural Scholars Program, Cleveland, OH; $15,000 Habitat for Humanity, Sumter, SC; $7,500 United Performing Arts Fund, Milwaukee, WI; and $5,000 YMCA of North Oakland County, Rochester Hills, MI.

Contact: Grants Administrator; (216) 523-4944; fax (216) 479-7013

Internet: http://www.eaton.com/EatonCom/OurCompany/AboutUs/CorporateResponsibility/SocialCommitment/CorporateGiving/index.htm

Sponsor: Eaton Charitable Fund

1111 Superior Avenue

Cleveland, OH 44114-2584

eBay Foundation Community Grants   643

The mission of the Foundation is to make investments that improve the economic and social well-being of local communities. The Foundation works to fulfill its mission by collaborating with non-profit organizations and funding innovative programs primarily in microenterprise development. The Foundation also provides support to community organizations in areas where employees are located.

Requirements: 501(c)3 nonprofit organizations in communities where eBay has a major employment base, which includes San Jose, CA, and Salt Lake City, UT, are eligible.

Geographic Focus: California, Utah

Amount of Grant: 1,000 - 15,000 USD

Samples: Friends of Farm Drive (San Jose, CA)—for operating support of this organization, which is dedicated to improving the quality of life for residents of a neighborhood rampant with drug dealing and gang activity; U Research Expedition Program (U of California)—for scholarships to send California elementary and high school teachers on UREP trips, where they learn by working with university scientists and local residents in countries around the world, to increase awareness of current events and to foster understanding of different cultures among both students and teachers.

Contact: Grants Administrator; ebayfdn@cfsv.org

Internet: http://pages.ebay.com/community/aboutebay/foundation/grantapp.html

Sponsor: eBay Foundation

60 South Market Street, Suite 1000

San Jose, CA 95113

EcoLab Foundation Youth and Educaton Grants   644

The funds major focus is on youth and preparing children to grow up as contributing members of society. Programs of interest are those designed for learning readiness, and for mentoring troubled youth and students eager to learn about career opportunities in the business world.

Requirements: 501(c)3 nonprofit in Beloit, WI; City of Industry, CA; Elk Grove Village, IL; Garland, TX; Grand Forks, ND; Greensboro, NC; Hebron, OH; Huntington, IN; Joliet, IL; Martinsburg, WV; McDonough, GA; San Jose, CA; and Saint Paul, MN, are eligible.

Restrictions: Contributions will not be made to or in support of: individuals; sectarian/denominational religious organizations, except where funds are to be used in the direct interest of the whole community; loans or investments; political/lobbying organizations; industry, trade or professional association

memberships; disease-specific organizations; sports/athletic programs and facilities; and fundraising events/sponsorships.

Geographic Focus: California, Georgia, Illinois, Indiana, Minnesota, North Carolina, North Dakota, Ohio, Texas, West Virginia, Wisconsin

Date(s) Application is Due: Sep 21

Contact: Administrator; (651) 293-2658; ecolabfoundation@ecolab.com

Internet: http://www.ecolab.com/companyprofile/foundation/default.asp

Sponsor: EcoLab

370 Wabasha Street North

St. Paul, MN 55102

Ed and Carole Abel Foundation Grants   645

The Ed and Carole Abel Foundation was established in Oklahoma in 1990 by the Abel Law Firm, with funding centered in the states of Colorado, Missouri, and Oklahoma. The Foundations primary interest areas of support are: religion, human services, and community services. The type of funding provided typically supports general operations. There are no specified deadlines or application formats, and interested organization should begin by contacted the Foundation representatives directly. Most recently, awards have ranged from $200 to $10,000, though on occasion, funding has been as high as $20,000.

Geographic Focus: Colorado, Missouri, Oklahoma

Amount of Grant: 200 - 10,000 USD

Samples: Crossing Community Church, Oklahoma City, Oklahoma, $16,240 - general operations; Living Faith Ministry, Oklahoma City, Oklahoma, $5,000 - general operations; Living Hope Women's Ministry, Oklahoma City, $5,000 - general operations.

Contact: Carol Abel, Trustee; (405) 239-7046 or (800) 739-2235

Sponsor: Ed and Carole Abel Foundation

5917 N. Ann Arbor Avenue

Oklahoma City, OK 73122-7526

Edler G. Hawkins African American Culture Preservation Grants   646

Each year the foundation provides funding to nonprofit African American arts organizations in, but not limited to, the New York City metropolitan area. The foundation awards general operating and program support to organizations working in the following artistic disciplines: visual arts; dance; music; and theater. The foundation encourages organizations to submit proposals detailing programs for young people that focus on African American culture in classrooms and other arts education settings. Application and guidelines are available online.

Geographic Focus: New York

Date(s) Application is Due: May 7

Samples: Schomburg Ctr for Research in Black Culture, $10,000.

Contact: Grants Administrator; (212) 937-2020; eghf@eghf.org

Internet: http://www.eghf.org/grants04.htm

Sponsor: Edler G. Hawkins Foundation

Grand Central Station, P.O. Box 217

New York, NY 10163-0217

Edna Wardlaw Charitable Trust Grants   647

The Edna Wardlaw Charitable Trust awards general operating grants nationwide to nonprofit organizations in its areas of interest, including: children and youth services; community funds; cultural programs; human services; environmental and natural resources; conservation; health and hospitals; homelessness; international peace; and reproductive health. A formal application is not required, and the annual deadline is June 15. Grants typically range from $1,000 to $20,000.

Geographic Focus: All States

Date(s) Application is Due: Jun 15

Amount of Grant: 1,000 - 20,000 USD

Contact: Gregorie Guthrie, Secretary; (404) 419-3260 or (404) 827-6529

Sponsor: Edna Wardlaw Charitable Trust

One Riverside Building

Atlanta, GA 30327

Edward and Ellen Roche Relief Foundation Grants   648

The Edward & Ellen Roche Relief Foundation was established in 1953 to support organizations serving disadvantaged women and children. Recognizing the diverse array of programs that serve these populations, the Roche Relief Foundation has chosen to focus its limited resources on programs that address one or more of the following: housing needs of women and families; economic security of low-income women; violence against women; and child welfare. Grant requests for general operating support or program/project support are strongly encouraged. Applicants must apply online at the grant website. Applicants are strongly encouraged to do the following before applying: review the downloadable state application procedures for additional helpful information and clarifications; review the downloadable online-application guidelines at the grant website; review the foundation's funding history (link is available from the grant website); review the online application questions in advance; and review the list of required attachments. These will generally include: a list of board members, financial statements (audited, reviewed, or compiled by independent auditor); an organization summary; a list of other funding sources; an IRS Determination letter; and other required documents. All attachments must be uploaded in the online application as PDF, Word, or Excel files. The application deadline for the Edward & Ellen Roche Relief Foundation is 11:59 p.m. on July 31. Grant decisions will be made by December 31.

Requirements: Applicants must have 501(c)3 tax-exempt status and serve the residents of New York City.

Restrictions: The Roche Relief Foundation generally does not provide funding for projects in the areas of health care or disabilities, to individual schools or child care centers; or to organizations with annual budgets in excess of $10 million. In general, grant requests for endowment campaigns, capital projects, or research will not be considered. The foundation does not support requests from individuals, organizations attempting to influence policy through direct lobbying, or any political campaigns.

Geographic Focus: All States, New York, All Countries

Date(s) Application is Due: Jul 31

Samples: Global Partnerships, Seattle, Washington, $20,000, pilot program to use microfinance institutions as a delivery channel to provide essential health services to poor women and girls in Latin America; Hot Bread Kitchen, Brooklyn, New York, $20,000, for programs to train and build the long-term economic security of immigrant women in New York City; Good Shepherd Services, New York, New York, $15,000, Safe Homes Project.

Contact: Sara Rosen, Assistant; (646) 743-0425; sara.rosen@baml.com

Internet: https://www.bankofamerica.com/philanthropic/fn_search.action

Sponsor: Edward and Ellen Roche Relief Foundation

One Bryant Park, NY1-100-28-05

New York, NY 10036

Edward and Helen Bartlett Foundation Grants 649

Established by a single donor, Edward E, Bartlett, in Oklahoma in 1961, the Foundation primarily offers grant support for: education, particularly public schools; community programs and services; health care; children and youth; and social services. There are no specific application forms or deadlines with which to adhere, and applicants should begin by forwarding a letter of application to the contact listed. In the recent past, grant amounts have ranged between $5,000 to $150,000.

Requirements: Preference id given to non-profit 501(c)3 organizations located in, or serving the residents of, Oklahoma.

Restrictions: No grants are to individuals directly.

Geographic Focus: Oklahoma

Amount of Grant: 5,000 - 150,000 USD

Samples: Clarehouse, Tulsa, Oklahoma, $150,000; Creek County Literacy Program, Sapulpa, Oklahoma, $30,000; Retired Senior Volunteer Program of Tulsa, Tulsa, Oklahoma, $20,000.

Contact: Bruce A. Currie, (918) 586-5273

Sponsor: Edward and Helen Bartlett Foundation

P.O. Box 3038

Milwaukee, WI 53201-3038

Edward and Romell Ackley Foundation Grants 650

The Edward and Romell Ackley Foundation was established in Oregon in 2003 in support of Portland-based programs. The Foundation's primary areas of interest include: adoption; child welfare; diseases and conditions; human services; philanthropy; special hospital care; and youth development. Awards generally are given for operating support. Most recent grants have ranged from $2,500 to $25,000.

Requirements: Oregon-based 501(c)3 organizations serving the residents of Portland are eligible to apply.

Geographic Focus: Oregon

Amount of Grant: 2,500 - 25,000 USD

Contact: Robert H. Depew, Trustee; (503) 464-3580 or (503) 275-6564

Sponsor: Edward and Romell Ackley Foundation

P.O. Box 3168

Portland, OR 97208-3168

Edward N. & Della L. Thome Memorial Foundation Direct Services 651 Grants

The Edward N. and Della L. Thome Memorial Foundation was established in 2002 by Robert P. Thome to honor the memory of his parents, Edward and Della Thome. The mission of the foundation is twofold: to advance the health of older adults through (1) the support of direct service projects and (2) medical research on diseases and disorders affecting older adults. The goal of the foundation's direct services program is to support organizations in Maryland and Michigan that provide direct services addressing one or more of the following critical issues facing older adults: health care, housing, family services, neighborhood involvement, workforce opportunities, and aging with dignity at home. Grant requests for general operating support are strongly encouraged. Program support will also be considered. Program-related capital expenses may be included in general operating or program requests. To better support the capacity of nonprofit organizations, multi-year funding requests are encouraged. Applicants must apply online at the direct-services grant website above. Applicants are strongly encouraged to do the following before applying: review the downloadable state application procedures for additional helpful information and clarifications; review the downloadable online-application guidelines at the grant website; review the foundation's funding history (link is available from the grant website); review the online application questions in advance; and review the list of required attachments. These will generally include: a list of board members, financial statements (audited, reviewed, or compiled by independent auditor); an organization summary; a list of other funding sources; an IRS Determination letter; and other required documents. All attachments must be uploaded in the online application as PDF, Word, or Excel files. There is a rolling deadline for organizations applying for a direct services grant from the Thome Foundation. Applicants will generally be notified of grant decisions within six months of proposal submission. The research aspect of the foundation's mission is managed by the Medical Foundation, a Division of Health Resources in Action (HRIA). Applicants interested in applying for research funding through the Edward N. and Della L. Thome Memorial Foundation's research program will find application information at the Medical Foundation's website.

Requirements: The Thome Foundation direct services program is most interested in expanding services for older adults. Requests should clearly state how many previously-unserved older adults will now be served as a result of funding from the Thome Foundation. Applicants must have 501(c)3 tax-exempt status.

Restrictions: The foundation does not support requests from individuals, organizations attempting to influence policy through direct lobbying, or any political campaigns.

Geographic Focus: Maryland, Michigan

Contact: George Thorn; (312) 828-4154; ilgrantmaking@bankofamerica.com

Internet: https://www.bankofamerica.com/philanthropic/fn_search.action

Sponsor: Edward N. and Della L. Thome Memorial Foundation - BAML

231 South LaSalle Street, IL1-231-13-32

Chicago, IL 60604

Edward S. Moore Foundation Grants 652

The foundation awards grants to nonprofits in Connecticut and New York in its areas of interest, including youth, hospitals, education, cultural programs, museums, and Christian religion. Types of support include operating budgets, continuing support, annual campaigns, seed money, emergency funds, building funds, equipment, land acquisition, endowment funds, matching funds, internships, scholarship funds, special projects, and research. There are no application deadlines. The board meets in January, April, July, and October to consider proposals.

Requirements: Nonprofits in Connecticut and New York may apply.

Restrictions: Grants are not awarded to individuals or for deficit financing, publications, or conferences.

Geographic Focus: Connecticut, New York

Amount of Grant: 10,000 - 50,000 USD

Contact: John W. Cross III, President; (203) 629-4591

Sponsor: Edward S. Moore Foundation

30 Lismore Lane

Greenwich, CT 06831

Edwards Memorial Trust Grants 653

The Edwards Memorial Trust awards grants to eligible Minnesota nonprofit organizations in support of: health care for people without health insurance or who are under-insured; preventive health care for children; and programs for the disabled. Areas of support include health care and hospitals, mental health crisis services, social services, children and youth, and the disabled. Types of support include: building construction and renovation; equipment acquisition; general operating grants; and program development. A copy of

the tax determination letter and most recent audited financial statements must accompany all applications.
Requirements: Minnesota 501(c)3 tax-exempt organizations in the greater Saint Paul area are eligible.
Geographic Focus: Minnesota
Date(s) Application is Due: May 1; Nov 1
Amount of Grant: 2,000 - 50,000 USD
Contact: Grant Coordinator; (651) 466-8731
Sponsor: Edwards Memorial Trust
P.O. Box 64713
Saint Paul, MN 55164-0713

Edward W. and Stella C. Van Houten Memorial Fund Grants   654

Stella C. Van Houten resided in Bergen County, New Jersey. This foundation, providing funding for health and human services, education, education of medical professionals, and the care of children, was established in 1978 in memory of her husband and herself. The Van Houten's had a particular fondness for the Valley Hospital of Ridgewood, New Jersey and for the Rollins College in Florida. The Foundation continues to honor their preferences with grants to these two organizations in addition to grants to other organizations. The Foundation's mission is to: supports agencies, institutions and services in Passaic and Bergen Counties, New Jersey, having to do with the care or cure of sick or disabled persons or for the care of orphaned children or aged persons; educates students in the medical profession; support for educational purposes; support for the care of children. A target of 10% of the grants each year is for medical scholarships.
Requirements: Passaic and Bergen Counties, New Jersey non-profits are eligible to apply. The application form & guidelines are available online at the Wachovia website. The applications must be submitted by January 31 for a March meeting & August 1 for an October meeting.
Geographic Focus: New Jersey
Date(s) Application is Due: Jan 31; Aug 1
Amount of Grant: 6,000 - 100,000 USD
Samples: Therapeutic Learning Center, Ramsey, NJ, $6,000—speech therapy; William Paterson University Foundation, $20,000—scholarships for undergraduate, minority, and/or graduate nursing students; Christian Health Care Center Foundation, $100,000—to build a Great Room at Heritage Manor East.
Contact: Trustee, c/o Wachovia Bank; grantinquiries2@wachovia.com
Internet: https://www.wachovia.com/foundation/v/index.jsp?vgnextoid=00c7 8689fb0aa110VgnVCM1000004b0d1872RCRD&vgnextfmt=default
Sponsor: Edward W. and Suitella C. Van Houten Memorial Fund
190 River Road, NJ3132
Summit, NJ 07901

Edwin S. Webster Foundation Grants   655

The policy of the foundation is to support charitable organizations that are well known to the trustees, with emphasis on special projects and capital programs, or operating income for hospitals, medical research, education, youth agencies, cultural activities, and programs addressing the needs of minorities. Types of support include operating budgets, continuing support, annual campaigns, building funds, equipment, land acquisition, endowment funds, matching funds, scholarship funds, professorships, internships, fellowships, special projects, and research.
Requirements: The Foundation confines its grants primarily to the New England area. Grantees must provide evidence of their tax-exempt status. The AGM common proposal format, available on the Internet at http://agmconnect.org is suitable for submission of proposals but not required. There are no set deadlines, but for consideration at the spring meeting, proposals should arrive by May 1 and by November 1 for consideration at the fall meeting. Proposals received after the trustees meet will be held for consideration at the next meeting.
Restrictions: Grants are not made to organizations outside the United States or to individuals.
Geographic Focus: Massachusetts
Date(s) Application is Due: May 1; Nov 1
Amount of Grant: 15,000 - 50,000 USD
Samples: Massachusetts Institute of Technology, Office of Minority Education, Cambridge, MA, $40,000 - Mentor Advocate Partnership; Eastern Virginia Medical School, Norfolk, VA, $25,000 - general operations and interdisciplinary research; Museum of Science, Boston, MA, $50,000 - capital support for the Hayden Planetarium.
Contact: Michelle Jenney, Administrator; (617) 391-3087; fax (617) 426-7080; mjenney@gmafoundations.com
Sponsor: Edwin S. Webster Foundation
GMA Foundations, 77 Summer Street, 8th Floor
Boston, MA 02110-1006

Edwin W. and Catherine M. Davis Foundation Grants   656

The foundation awards grants to U.S. nonprofit organizations in its areas of interest, including arts, elderly, environment, higher education, housing, mental health, religion, social services,and youth. Types of support include annual campaigns, endowment funds, fellowships, operating grants, research grants, and scholarship funds. There are no application deadlines. The board meets in May or June; submit a proposal that is three pages or less in length.
Requirements: U.S. nonprofit organizations are eligible.
Geographic Focus: Washington
Amount of Grant: 1,000 - 10,000 USD
Contact: Gayle Roth; (651) 215-4408; fax (651) 228-0776
Sponsor: Edwin W. and Catherine M. Davis Foundation
30 East 7th Street, Suite 2000
Saint Paul, MN 55101-1394

Edwin W. Pauley Foundation Grants   657

The foundation awards grants to California nonprofit organizations in its areas of interest, including children and youth development and higher education. Types of support include annual campaigns, building construction/renovation, continuing support, general operating support, and professorships. There are no application deadlines or forms.
Requirements: California nonprofit organizations are eligible.
Restrictions: Grants are not made to individuals.
Geographic Focus: California
Amount of Grant: 10,000 - 50,000 USD
Samples: Pomona College (Claremont, CA)—to endow a professorship in environmental analysis, $1.5 million.
Contact: Stephen Pauley, President; (323) 954-3131
Sponsor: Edwin W. Pauley Foundation
5670 Wilshire Boulevard, Suite 1450
Los Angeles, CA 90036

Effie and Wofford Cain Foundation Grants   658

The Effie and Wofford Cain Foundation gives primarily for higher and secondary education, medical research, and public service organizations. Grants also are awarded to religious organizations (Baptist, Christian, Episcopal, Presbyterian, Salvation Army, and United Methodist), and for aid for the handicapped. Additional fields of interest include elementary and secondary education, early childhood development and education, medical school education, nursing school education, hospitals and general health care and health organizations, religious federated giving programs, government and public administration, African Americans, Latinos, the disabled, the aging, and economically disadvantaged and homeless. Types of support include general operating support, continuing support, annual campaigns, capital campaigns, building/renovations, equipment acquisition, endowment funds, program development, seed money, curriculum development, fellowships, internships, scholarship funds, research, and matching funds. Organizations may reapply for funding every other fiscal year.
Requirements: The foundation only makes grants to 501(c)3 tax-exempt organizations in Texas.
Restrictions: Individuals are ineligible.
Geographic Focus: Texas
Amount of Grant: 1,000 - 400,000 USD
Samples: People's Community Clinic, Austin, Texas, $50,500 - general support for medical care; East Texas Aboretum Abd Botanical Society, Athens, Texas, $351,000 - Henderson County Veterans Memorial; Heritage Society of Austin, Austin, Texas, $5,000 - general operating support.
Contact: Lynn Fowler, Executive Director; (512) 346-7490; fax (512) 346-7491; info@cainfoundation.org
Sponsor: Effie and Wofford Cain Foundation
4131 Spicewood Springs Road, Suite A-1
Austin, TX 78759-7490

Eileen Fisher Activating Leadership Grants for Women and Girls   659

As a socially conscious company, Eileen Fisher is dedicated to supporting women through social initiatives that address their well-being, to guiding our product and process towards sustaining the environment and to practicing business responsibly with absolute regard for human rights. For the current grant cycle, Eileen Fisher will fund programs that activate leadership qualities in women and girls. We are particularly interested in programs that: bring about self-discovery and personal transformation; help women and/or girls find their inner strength and trust their intuition; address any phase of a woman's and/or girl's life. Each year, grants of $5,000 or more are awarded, including grants for general support and seed funding for grassroots organizations. The application process opens on June 3, and all applications must be received no later than 12:00 noon EST of the deadline date.

Requirements: Applications will be accepted from 501(c)3 nonprofits with preference to organizations that: show an innovative, holistic, effective and direct approach to activating leadership among women and/or girls; form partnerships with other community organizations for deeper impact; demonstrate the long-term sustainability and viability of the organization; show a clear need for the funds and a plan for their use; demonstrate a long-term commitment to their work; establish resonance with the Eileen Fisher company mission and leadership practices; and, are located near the Eileen Fisher offices, retail stores or showrooms or, if outside the United States, via U.S.-based charities only. Grants are open to any applying organization, not just those who have received a grant previously.

Geographic Focus: All States
Date(s) Application is Due: Jul 18
Amount of Grant: 5,000 USD
Contact: Cheryl Campbell; (914) 721-4153; ccampbell@eileenfisher.com
Internet: http://www.eileenfisher.com/EileenFisherCompany/Company GeneralContentPages/SocialConciousness/Self_Image.jsp
Sponsor: Eileen Fisher Community Foundation
2 Bridge Street, Suite 230
Irvington, NY 10533

Eileen Fisher Women-Owned Business Grants   660

The Eileen Fisher Business Grant Program for Women Entrepreneurs was launched in 2004 with a single grant to commemorate the company's twentieth anniversary. The grant program seeks applicants from wholly women-owned businesses that combine the principles of social consciousness, sustainability and innovation to take their established businesses to the next stage of their business plan. In addition to the key social principles, each applicant is required to have a solid business plan and a strategy for long-term growth. Each of the five grant recipients receives a $12,500 grant plus mentoring from internal Eileen Fisher teams and a trip to New York City for a three-day workshop with Eileen Fisher committee members and past grant recipients.

Requirements: The guidelines for the annual Women-Owned Business Program are continuing to evolve, and the grant applications are typically open annually from early March through May. To apply, your business must be: innovative; 100 percent women-owned; producing products or services that foster environmental and economic health in the community; a for-profit business or a for-profit/nonprofit hybrid (social enterprise); and, in operation for at least three years and ready to move to the next stage of its business plan.

Geographic Focus: All States
Date(s) Application is Due: Jul 18
Amount of Grant: 12,500 - 12,500 USD
Contact: Cheryl Campbell; (914) 721-4153; ccampbell@eileenfisher.com
Internet: http://www.eileenfisher.com/EileenFisherCompany/Company GeneralContentPages/SocialConciousness/Women_Owned.jsp
Sponsor: Eileen Fisher Community Foundation
2 Bridge Street, Suite 230
Irvington, NY 10533

Eisner Foundation Grants   661

The Eisner Foundation exists to provide access and opportunity for disadvantaged children and the aging of Los Angeles County. The Eisner Foundation has been funding innovative and effective non-profit organizations that improve and enrich the lives of underserved children in Southern California since 1996. In 2008, the Foundation recognized that many of the same attributes that the children unfortunately possess physical and emotional vulnerability, extreme poverty, lack of advocacy on their behalf, minimal access to the arts, and general powerlessness also applied to many members of our rapidly aging population in the community. The Foundation elected to broaden the funding focus to include those at both ends of the spectrum of life, the young and the old. The Foundation's now dedicated to bringing about lasting changes in the lives of disadvantaged and vulnerable people starting and ending their lives in Los Angeles County.

Requirements: California nonprofit organizations serving Los Angeles and Orange Counties are eligible to apply. Applicants can apply at any time, but should know that these proposals will be reviewed and approved at the June or December board meetings. Applying to the Foundation is a two step process. The first step is to submit a Letter of Inquiry (see Eisner Foundation website for guidelines). If Letter of Inquiry meets the Foundation's criteria, a full application will be sent to the applicant for completion and submission, completing the second step.

Restrictions: Proposals for endowments are rarely excepted.
Geographic Focus: California
Amount of Grant: 5,000 - 100,000 USD
Samples: LA Scores, Los Angeles, CA, $100,000—to provide project support for an after-school program that combines creative writing, soccer, and community service; California Institute of the Arts, Los Angeles, CA, $1,250,000—to support the Community Arts Partnership program which provides new media arts education programs to local youth; Friendship Circle, Los Angeles, CA, $25,000—to provide support for an organization that addresses the challenges of families with special-needs children in the South Bay; Eisner Pediatric & Family Medical Center, Los Angeles, CA, $1,000,000—to support the endowment campaign for a pediatric and family medical center serving low-income, uninsured and under-insured families; Aquarium of the Pacific, Los Angeles, CA, $100,000—to provide support for a project that increases science learning access to Title I school communities in the South Bay; St. Barnabas Senior Center, Los Angeles, CA, $75,000—to support a program that provides education on sustained nutrition, adult day care, and other health promotion services for 3,000 seniors in the greater downtown Los Angeles area.
Contact: Trent Stamp; (310) 228-6808; trent.stamp@eisnerfoundation.org
Internet: http://www.eisnerfoundation.org/what_we_do/
Sponsor: Eisner Foundation
233 South Beverly Drive
Beverly Hills, CA 90212

Elaine Feld Stern Charitable Trust Grants   662

Established in Missouri in 1989, the Elaine Feld Stern Charitable Trust is currently managed by trustees of the Blue Ridge Bank and Trust. The Trust's primary fields of interest include: arts and culture, agriculture, food, health organizations, and human services. A formal application, which can be secured from the Trust office, is required. There are no annual application submission deadlines identified. Most recent grant awards have ranged from $1,000 to $25,000.

Requirements: Giving is limited to 501(c)3 organizations located in, or serving the residents of, the Kansas City, Missouri, area.
Restrictions: No support is provided for tax-supported institutions, individuals, for telethons, or conferences.
Geographic Focus: Missouri
Amount of Grant: 1,000 - 25,000 USD
Contact: J. Bryan Allee, (816) 358-5000 or (816) 795-9933
Sponsor: Elaine Feld Stern Charitable Trust
4200 Little Blue Parkway
Independence, MO 64057

Eli Lilly & Company Foundation Grants   663

Discretionary grants are awarded in two categories: nonprofit groups aligned with company interests, and grants in Indianapolis and several other communities with significant employee populations. Company-aligned giving focuses on public policy research, health and human services aligned with major therapeutic interests, and academic relations. Community-aligned giving focuses on culture, K-12 education and youth development, locally aligned healthcare organizations, fencerow neighborhood groups, and diversity. The foundation supports organizations within these categories that have a well-defined sense of purpose, a demonstrated commitment to maximizing available resources, and a reputation for meeting objectives and delivery quality programs and services.

Restrictions: Grants do not support individuals; endowments; debt reduction; religious or sectarian programs for religious purposes; bands or fraternal, labor, athletic, or veterans organizations; political contributions; beauty or talent contests; fundraising activities related to individual sponsorship; conferences or media productions; nonaccredited education groups; or memorials.
Geographic Focus: All States
Date(s) Application is Due: Jun 30; Dec 31
Samples: American National Red Cross (Washington, DC)—for relief efforts in South Asia and Africa, $1 million; Oklahoma Medical Research Foundation Foundation (Oklahoma City, OK)—to endow two professorships in biomedical research, $6 million.
Contact: Thomas King, President; (317) 276-3177; fax (317) 277-2025
Internet: http://www.lilly.com
Sponsor: Eli Lilly and Company Foundation
734 N LaSalle Street, #1167
Indianapolis, IN 46285

Elisabeth Severance Prentiss Foundation Grants 664

The foundation awards the majority of its support in the field of health and medicine. Scientific and medical research, hospitals, health projects, medical education, and care and support of the elderly are funded. Types of support include building programs, equipment needs, research, operating budgets, continuing support, seed grants, endowment funds, and projects/programs. Decision makers favor specific projects over general operating support. The maximum term of a commitment is five years, with preference for proposals for three years or less. Special consideration will be given to requests from applicants in the Cuyahoga County area. The board meets in June and December.

Requirements: Grants are awarded to promote and improve medical services in the greater Cleveland, OH, area.

Restrictions: Grants are not awarded to individuals for scholarships, fellowships, or grants in aid; or to organizations for fund-raising campaigns, surveys, assessments, studies, or planning activities.

Geographic Focus: Ohio

Date(s) Application is Due: May 15; Nov 15

Amount of Grant: 10,000 - 100,000 USD

Samples: University Hospitals of Cleveland (OH)—to create an inpatient psychiatric unit for children and adolescents at Rainbow Babies and Children's Hospital, $5 million.

Contact: Michael Galland, National City Bank Contact; (216) 222-2736

Sponsor: Elisabeth Severance Prentiss Foundation

P.O. Box 94651

Cleveland, OH 44104

Elizabeth & Avola W. Callaway Foundation Grants 665

The Elizabeth & Avola W. Callaway Foundation supports non-profit organizations primarily in the state of Georgia. General/operating support is available in the areas of : education; human services; Protestant agencies and; churches.

Requirements: Georgia 501(c)3 non-profits are eligible to apply, begin the application process by submitting a letter of inquiry to the Foundation. Letters of inquiry are accepted year round and should contain a detailed description of project and amount of funding requested.

Restrictions: No grants to individuals.

Geographic Focus: Georgia

Amount of Grant: 100 - 5,000 USD

Samples: Athens, Academy, Athens, GA, $1,200—education grant; First Methodist Church, Washinton, GA, $4,300—religious/education grant; Wills Memorial Hospital Foundation, Washington, GA, $1,750—public welfare grant.

Contact: Michael Benson, Grants Director; (706) 274-3392

Sponsor: Elizabeth and Avola W. Callaway Foundation

869 Callaway Road

Rayle, GA 30660-1421

Elizabeth Huth Coates Charitable Foundation Grants 666

Elizabeth Maddux was married to oilman George H. Coates from 1943 until his death in 1973. It was said that George provided the means while Elizabeth provided the philanthropic inspiration which she had learned from her parents growing up in San Antonio. A longtime supporter of the arts and education, she established the Elizabeth Huth Coates Charitable Foundation of 1992 to continue her legacy of support within the San Antonio area. The Foundation's primary fields of interest include: the arts; Catholicism; diseases; education; museums; Protestantism; and zoos. Most recently, awards have ranged from $5,000 to $300,000. The annual deadline for online application submission is December 31.

Requirements: Grants are directed to 501(c)3 organizations which fall within the principal charitable purposes of the foundation.

Geographic Focus: Texas

Date(s) Application is Due: Dec 31

Amount of Grant: 5,000 - 300,000 USD

Samples: Ballet San Antonio, San Antonio, Texas, $20,000 - general operating support (2014); Saint Mary's Hall, San Antonio, Texas, $300,000 - general operating support (2014); San Antonio Museum of Art, San Antonio, Texas, $200,000 - general operating support (2014).

Contact: Brian R. Korb, Senior Vice President; (210) 283-6700 or (210) 283-6500; bkorb@broadwaybank.com

Internet: http://www.broadwaybank.com/wealthmanagement/Foundation ElizabethHuthCoates.html

Sponsor: Elizabeth Huth Coates Charitable Foundation

P.O. Box 17001

San Antonio, TX 78217-0001

Elizabeth M. Irby Foundation Grants 667

The foundation awards grants to Mississippi nonprofits in its areas of interest, including arts and culture, elementary education, secondary education, higher education, social services, and Christian churches and religious organizations. Types of support include general operating support, continuing support, annual campaigns, capital campaigns, building construction/renovation, endowment funds, emergency funds, program development, research, scholarship funds, and matching funds. There are no application forms or deadlines.

Requirements: Mississippi nonprofit organizations may apply.

Restrictions: Individuals are ineligible.

Geographic Focus: Mississippi

Amount of Grant: 250 - 500,000 USD

Contact: Stuart Irby, President; (601) 989-1811

Sponsor: Elizabeth M. Irby Foundation

P.O. Box 1819

Jackson, MS 39215

Elizabeth Morse Genius Charitable Trust Grants 668

Established in 1992, the Elizabeth Morse Genius Charitable Trust honors the memory of Elizabeth Morse Genius, the daughter of Charles Hosmer Morse, a nineteenth century Chicago financier, industrialist, and land developer. The trust supports and promotes charitable organizations that: encourage the principles of individual self-reliance, self-sacrifice, thrift, industry, and humility; relieve human suffering through scientific research and education regarding disease; provide assistance to youths with troubled childhoods and emotional disorders; attend to the care of the elderly; provide assistance to humankind during times of natural and man-made disasters; foster individual self-worth and dignity, with a broad emphasis on the classical fine arts; develop physical health and spiritual well-being through vigorous athletic activity; and promote world peace and understanding through the improvement of national and international means of travel by air, rail, and sea. The majority of grants from the Genius Charitable Trust are one year in duration; on occasion, multi-year support is awarded. Applicants must first submit a letter of inquiry. Downloadable application guidelines are available at the Sponsor's website by clicking on the "Grant Application Process Button", or prospective applicants may also call the second phone number given to obtain application information. A synopsis of the grant, contact information, and a link to the trust's giving history is available at the grant website. The Elizabeth Morse Genius Charitable Trust has a rolling application deadline. In general, applicants will be notified of grant decisions three to four months after proposal submission.

Requirements: Nonprofits serving Chicago and Cook County are eligible.

Restrictions: The trust generally does not fund individuals; organizations outside the metropolitan Chicago city area; organizations attempting to influence policy through direct lobbying; capital campaigns; endowment campaigns; or political campaigns.

Geographic Focus: Illinois

Amount of Grant: 10,000 - 300,000 USD

Contact: Lauren MacDonald; (312) 828-6753; ilgrantmaking@ustrust.com

Internet: https://www.bankofamerica.com/philanthropic/fn_search.action

Sponsor: Elizabeth Morse Genius Charitable Trust

231 South LaSalle Street, IL1-231-13-32

Chicago, IL 60604

Ellen Abbott Gilman Trust Grants 669

The Ellen Abbott Gilman Trust, established in Massachusetts, has specified a number of fields of interest, including: aging centers and services; multipurpose art centers; children and youth services; education; human and community services; and museums. Support is restricted to the State of Massachusetts, and most often comes in the form of general operations. There are no specified application form or deadlines with which to adhere, and applicants should inquire directly to the Trust for more information.

Requirements: Applicants must be 501(c)3 organizations supporting the residents of Massachusetts.

Geographic Focus: Massachusetts

Amount of Grant: 1,000 - 3,000 USD

Samples: African and American Friendship, Roslindale, Massachusetts, $3,000 - for general operations; Outer Cape Health Services, Wellfleet, Massachusetts, $2,000 - for general operations; Young Achievers Outlook, Mattapan, Massachusetts, $2,000 - for general operations.

Contact: Walter G. Van Dorn; (617) 261-3100; walter.vandorn@klgates.com

Sponsor: Ellen Abbott Gilman Trust

KL Gates 1 Lincoln Street

Boston, MA 02111-2905

Ellie Fund Grants 670

The foundation awards grants to organizations located in Cuyahoga County, OH, whose activities benefit the county's residents. Applications outside of the area must be preapproved by a trustee. Preference is given to services for children within these priorities: crisis intervention, literacy, mental health, physical health, safety, and shelter. The trustees favor requests to support program development, as well as operating needs (especially for start-up, emergency, or bridge funding). Types of nonprofit organizations that receive support include start-up organizations; grassroots and community-based organizations; smaller organizations that do not receive wide public support; religious organizations, but only for secular programs that provide social services to the general community; and established organizations, but only for innovative programs. Organizations that have received a foundation grant for four consecutive years must go on a one-year hiatus before they can reapply for a grant.

Requirements: Grants are awarded only to tax-exempt, nonprofit organizations, and never to individuals.

Restrictions: Requests for annual appeals, fundraisers, symposia, and seminars will not be considered.

Geographic Focus: Ohio

Date(s) Application is Due: Aug 15

Amount of Grant: 1,000 - 7,500 USD

Contact: Management Services; (216) 621-2901; ellie@fmscleveland.com

Internet: http://www.fmscleveland.com/ellie/guidelines.cfm

Sponsor: Ellie Fund

1422 Euclid Avenue, Suite 627

Cleveland, OH 44115-1952

Elliot Foundation Inc Grants 671

The Elliot Foundation Inc. formerly known as Elliot Foundation for Medical Research and Education, Inc. is a independent foundation, operating primarily in the state of Indiana. The foundation offers funding in the form of general/operating support. The fields of interest include: Christian agencies & churches; crime/violence prevention; environment; natural resources; child abuses; education.

Requirements: Contact Foundation for more information.

Geographic Focus: Indiana

Contact: Richard E. Bond, Secretary; (575) 293-1165

Sponsor: Elliot Foundation

2210 East Jackson Boulevard

Elkhart, IN 46516-1165

Elmer L. and Eleanor J. Andersen Foundation Grants 672

The foundation exists to enhance the quality of the civic, cultural, educational, environmental, and social aspects of life in Minnesota, primarily in the metropolitan area of Saint Paul and Minneapolis. Types of support include general operating support, continuing support, annual campaigns, capital campaigns, building construction/renovation, endowment funds, program development, deficit reduction, publication, seed money, curriculum development, research, technical assistance, and matching funds. The board meets four times annually.

Requirements: Minnesota nonprofit organizations are eligible.

Geographic Focus: Minnesota

Date(s) Application is Due: Feb 1; May 1; Aug 1; Nov 1

Amount of Grant: 500 - 75,000 USD

Contact: Mari Oyanagi Eggum, Foundation Administrator; (651) 642-0127; fax (651) 645-4684; eandefdn@mtn.org

Sponsor: Elmer L. and Eleanor J. Andersen Foundation

2424 Territorial Road

Saint Paul, MN 55114

El Paso Community Foundation Grants 673

The Foundation is a facilitator linking the generosity of the region's donors to local non-profit organizations to meet the charitable needs of the El Paso area. In this capacity, the Foundation helps to provide funding for programs and initiatives of these organizations for the broader good of the El Paso Community. Major areas of interest are: arts and humanities; education; public benefit; health and disabilities; environment;animals and; human services. Types of support offered include: equipment acquisition; general/operating support; management development/capacity building; matching/challenge support; program development; scholarship funds; seed money; technical assistance. Priority is given to: more effective ways of doing things; projects where a moderate amount of grant money can have an impact; and projects that show collaboration with other organizations. Application deadlines are February 1 and August 1.

Requirements: Grant requests will be considered only from agencies located within or offering services to the citizens of our community, which includes far west Texas, southern New Mexico and northern Chihuahua, Mexico. Applicants must be exempt from income taxes under Section 501(c)3 of the Internal Revenue Service Code. Application form is available on the El Paso Community Foundation website.

Restrictions: Funding is not available for/to: individuals; capital campaigns; fundraising events or projects; religious organizations for religious purposes; annual appeals and membership contributions; organizations that are political or partisan in purpose; travel for individuals or groups; organizations outside the El Paso geographic area; endowment funds; past operating deficits.

Geographic Focus: Texas

Date(s) Application is Due: Feb 1; Aug 1

Amount of Grant: 3,000 - 10,000 USD

Samples: American Cancer Society, 42,000—provide local patients transportation to and from treatments; Angelo Catholic School, $11,000—teachers' salary; Animal Rescue League of El Paso, Inc., $8,000—animal rescue, rehabilitation and placement.

Contact: Bonita Johnson, Grants Manager; (915) 533-4020; fax (915) 532-0716; info@epcf.org

Internet: http://www.epcf.org/grant_guidelines

Sponsor: El Paso Community Foundation

P.O. Box 272

El Paso, TX 79943

El Pomar Foundation Awards and Grants 674

The Foundation is one of the largest and oldest private foundations in the Rocky Mountain West and contributes annually through direct grants and Community Stewardship Programs to support Colorado nonprofit organizations. The Foundation's primary focus is in health, human services, education, arts and humanities, and civic and community initiatives.

Requirements: The foundation makes grants to 501(c)3 nonprofit Colorado organizations and for activities that take place within the state.

Restrictions: The Foundation does not accept grant applications for: other foundations or nonprofits that distribute money to recipients of its own selection; endowments; individuals; organizations that practice discrimination of any kind; organizations that do not have fiscal responsibility for the proposed project; organizations that do not have an active 501(c)3 nonprofit IRS determination letter; camps, camp programs, or other seasonal activities; religious organizations for support of religious programs; cover deficits or debt elimination; cover travel, conferences, conventions, group meetings, or seminars; influence legislation or support candidates for political office; produce videos or other media projects; fund research projects or studies; primary or secondary schools (K-12).

Geographic Focus: Colorado

Amount of Grant: 500 - 500,000 USD

Samples: Four Miles Historical Park (Denver, CO)—to construct a visitors center on the history of Denver, $50,000; Saint Paul Catholic Church (Colorado Springs, CO)—to construct a community center, $333,333; Pikes Peak Hospice and Palliative Care (Colorado Springs, CO)—for a new system for managing patient information, $75,000; Colorado Assoc of Nonprofit Organizations (Denver, CO)—for general operating support for statewide nonprofit programs, $20,000.

Contact: Executive Office; (719) 633-7733 or (800) 554-7711; fax (719) 577-5702; grants@elpomar.org

Internet: http://www.elpomar.org/grant2.html

Sponsor: El Pomar Foundation

10 Lake Circle

Colorado Springs, CO 80906

Elsie H. Wilcox Foundation Grants 675

The Foundation provides partial support to programs and projects of tax-exempt, public charities in Hawaii to improve the quality of life in the state, particularly the island of Kauai. Areas of interest to the Foundation, include: education, health organizations, people with disabilities; human services, performing arts, theater, religion, YM/YMCAs & YM/YWHAs. Types of support include building/renovation; equipment; general/operating support. Grants average from $5,000 - $15,000.

Requirements: 501(c)3 nonprofit organizations in Hawaii are eligible to apply. The Foundation places a special emphasis on the island of Kauai. Contact Paula Boyce to acquire the cover sheet/application forms and any additional guidelines required to begin the application process. Proposals must be submitted by October 1st.

Restrictions: No grants to individuals, or for endowments.
Geographic Focus: Hawaii
Date(s) Application is Due: Oct 1
Amount of Grant: 5,000 - 15,000 USD
Samples: Girl Scouts of Hawaii, Honolulu, HI, $5,000—scholarships for Kauai girls in grades K-5; Bishop Museum, Honolulu, HI, $5,000—educational program support; American Cancer Society, Hawaii Pacific Division, Hawaii, Honolulu, HI, $5,000—quality of life services for cancer patients on Kauai.
Contact: Paula Boyce, c/o Bank of Hawaii; (808) 538-4944; fax (808) 538-4647; pboyce@boh.com
Internet: http://www.hawaiicommunityfoundation.org/index.php?id=290
Sponsor: Elsie H. Wilcox Foundation
Bank of Hawai'i, Foundation Administration Department 758
Honolulu, HI 96802-3170

Elsie Lee Garthwaite Memorial Foundation Grants 676
Established in 1943, the Foundation supports organizations primarily in Philadelphia, Chester, Montgomery and Delaware counties of Pennsylvania. Giving to organizations that: provide for the physical and emotional well-being of children and young people; seek to enable young people, particularly the needy, to reach their fullest potential through education, empowerment, and exposure to the arts; are smaller organizations, with budgets under $1 million per year.
Requirements: Non-profits are eligible in the Philadelphia, Chester, Montgomery and Delaware counties, PA. Contact the Foundation at least 30 days prior to deadlines with a Letter of Intent. An application form can be obtained from the Foundation after reviewing the Letter of Intent, unsolicited applications will not be excepted. Contact the Foundation for further guidelines.
Restrictions: No grants to individuals, public, private, or parochial schools, colleges and universities.
Geographic Focus: Pennsylvania
Date(s) Application is Due: Mar 31; Aug 31
Amount of Grant: 3,000 - 16,000 USD
Samples: United States Fund for UNICEF, New York, NY, $15,000 - for Pakistan earthquake victim relief; Citizen Schools, Boston, MA, $10,000 - for program support; Center for Grieving Children, Teens and Families, Philadelphia, PA, $3,000 - for general operating support;
Contact: Thomas Kaneda, Secretary; (610) 527-8101; fax (610) 527-7808
Sponsor: Elsie Lee Garthwaite Memorial Foundation
1234 Lancaster Avenue, P.O. Box 709
Rosemont, PA 19010-0709

Emerson Charitable Trust Grants 677
Established in 1944 in Missouri as the Emerson Electric Manufacturing Company Charitable Trust, the Foundation supports: arts and culture—fine arts and cultural institutions to enrich the diversity, creativity, and liveliness of the community; education—programs designed to promote educational systems at all levels; health and human services—programs designed to help individuals and families in times of need, including sickness, old age, family crisis, and natural disasters; civic affairs—programs designed to protect citizenry; further economic health of the community; and build and maintain assets such as parks and zoos; and youth—programs designed to give young people the opportunity to recognize their potential, confidence, and skills to achieve their dreams. The foundation awards college scholarships to children and step-children of employees of Emerson Electric. No specific application form is required, and initial approach should be the complete proposal,
Geographic Focus: All States
Amount of Grant: 5,000 - 300,000 USD
Samples: Alvin J. Siteman Ctr, Washington U School of Medicine and Barnes-Jewish Hospital (Saint Louis, MO)—for a new cancer-research facility and for cancer research, $6 million challenge grant.
Contact: Jo Ann Harmon; (314) 553-3722; fax (314) 553-1605
Internet: http://www.emerson.com/en-us/about_emerson/company_overview/pages/our_approach_to_corporate_philanthropy.aspx
Sponsor: Emerson Charitable Trust
8000 W Florissant Avenue, P.O. Box 4100
Saint Louis, MO 63136

Emily Hall Tremaine Foundation Grants 678
The foundation seeks to fund innovative projects that advance solutions to basic problems within society. Emphasis is placed on U.S. elementary and secondary education. The foundation also supports programs in the arts, environmental conservation, and learning disabilities. There are no application forms or deadlines. Unsolicited proposals rarely develop into a grant; submit informative letters of inquiry that highlight the organization's mission, goals, history, strategies, and programmatic scope.
Requirements: Education-related nonprofits may apply for grant support.
Geographic Focus: All States
Amount of Grant: 1,000 - 50,000 USD
Samples: Columbia U (New York, NY)—to teach two semesters of a course designed for Master of Fine Arts students to equip them with critical skills to manage their careers as a visual artist, $44,000; Side Street Projects (Los Angeles, CA)—t support the enhancement and implementation of a program to assist visual artists in Los Angeles with obtaining skills that will help them in their lives as artists, $45,000; Volunteer Lawyers for the Arts of Massachusetts (Boston, MA)—to support the development and implementation of a program to assist visual artists in Boston to obtain critical life and career management skills, $90,000.
Contact: Stewart Hudson, President; (203) 639-5544; fax (203) 639-5545; chevalier@tremainefoundation.org
Internet: http://www.tremainefoundation.org
Sponsor: Emily Hall Tremaine Foundation
290 Pratt Street
Meriden, CT 06450

Emma B. Howe Memorial Foundation Grants 679
The Emma B. Howe Memorial Foundation makes grants through the Minneapolis Foundation. The focus of all grants is to improve: the health and well-being of children, youth and families; opportunities for educational achievement; access to quality affordable housing; and economic vitality throughout the region. Information on the application process is available online.
Requirements: Eligible organizations include 501(c)3 nonprofits, public institutions; and emerging groups organized for nonprofit purposes.
Restrictions: Funds are not available for: individuals; organizations/activities outside of Minnesota; conference registration fees; memberships; direct religious activities; political organizations or candidates; direct fundraising efforts; telephone solicitations; courtesy advertising; financial deficits.
Geographic Focus: Minnesota
Samples: Kids in Distressed Situations (KIDS)—(New York, NY)—to provide donated products to low-income children and families in the Minneapolis area through Bridging Inc, $75,000 over three years.
Contact: Grants Manager; (612) 672-3836; grants@mplsfoundation.org
Internet: http://www.mplsfoundation.org/partners/emma.htm
Sponsor: Emma B. Howe Memorial Foundation
80 S Eighth Street
Minneapolis, MN 55402

Enterprise Rent-A-Car Foundation Grants 680
The Foundation's mission is to give back to and to strengthen the thousands of communities where employees and customers work and live. The Foundation supports four key focus areas: local causes by joining employees and providing a fifty percent match of contributions to United Way through the community; provides financial resources to worthwhile nonprofit initiatives that are actively supported by employees and customers; provides more sizable special grants to nonprofit groups or causes of significant strategic or social importance; and supports relief projects or causes the company deems important as they arise, such as natural disasters. A brief written proposal is requested. The Foundation Board meets three times each year.
Requirements: The Foundation provides grants only to qualified tax exempt 501(c)3 organizations in the United States.
Restrictions: Neither the Foundation nor the company donates vehicles or rentals. The Foundation considers the support of schools, churches, and sports teams a personal responsibility, and therefore discourages requests for Foundation support of these types of organizations.
Geographic Focus: All States
Date(s) Application is Due: Jan 19; Apr 6; Sep 7
Amount of Grant: 2,500 - 5,000 USD
Samples: Harris-Stowe State College—for the business-administration program, $1 million; Washington U (Saint Louis, MO)—to endow undergraduate scholarships and financial assistance for minority and other student's, as part of the university's campaign, $25 million.
Contact: Jo Ann Kindle, President; (314) 512-2754
Internet: http://206.196.101.205/what_we_believe/our_foundation.html
Sponsor: Enterprise Rent-A-Car Foundation
600 Corporate Park Drive
Saint Louis, MO 63105

Essex County Community Foundation Discretionary Fund Grants   **681**

The grant awards funds across the broad areas of nonprofit activity, including arts and culture, education, environment, health, social and community services and youth services. The Trustees will award Discretionary Fund grants to assist nonprofits with projects which strengthen the capacity of the organization to perform its work more effectively. ECCF is interested in helping organizations improve their infrastructure so that they can better serve their communities and clients. ECCF will consider projects which address capacity building such as: strengthening Board leadership; managing organizational change and growth; providing for strategic organizational planning; supporting leadership transition; strengthening fiscal management; and improving staff skills or other organizational functions which will improve the organization's long-term capacity.

Requirements: Eligible organizations must be Massachusetts 501(c)3 agencies that serve Essex County citizens with operating budgets of less than $500,000.

Restrictions: Funds are not available for: individuals; costs associated with programs or services provided to citizens outside of Essex County; sectarian or religious purposes; political purposes; debt or deficit reduction; capital campaigns for buildings, land acquisition or endowment; or to support academic research. Funding for equipment is limited to purchases that resolve a specific problem, are part of an overall capacity building project and will strengthen the operation of the organization. Equipment for programmatic purposes will not be granted. In general, staff salaries will not be eligible for funding unless the salary is directly tied to developing the capacity of the organization.

Geographic Focus: Massachusetts

Date(s) Application is Due: Feb 10

Amount of Grant: 1,000 - 5,000 USD

Contact: Julie Bishop, Vice President of Grants and Nonprofit Services; (978) 777-8876, ext. 28; fax (978) 777-9454; j.bishop@eccf.org or info@eccf.org

Internet: http://eccf.org/discretionary-fund-42.html

Sponsor: Essex County Community Foundation

175 Andover Street, Suite 101

Danvers, MA 01923

Essex County Community Foundation Emergency Fund Grants   **682**

This fund offers assistance, on a one-time basis, to non-profit organizations located within Essex County. The grants are for modest sums based on times of critical need. The fund assists non-profits with a short-term urgent funding need created by an unforeseen event that has or will significantly interrupt essential services such as natural disasters or emergency needs. Requests can be made at any time. Examples of unforeseen events include: natural disasters (e.g. fire, flood, tornado, storm damage, loss of utilities); and emergency needs (e.g. phase-out costs associated with closing a program due to a sudden loss of funding, equipment failure, civil disturbance).

Requirements: Requests may be submitted at any time by Massachusetts 501(c)3 agencies located in and serving Essex County citizens. To initiate a request an agency representative calls or emails the grants coordinator and provides an initial explanation of the emergency situation.

Restrictions: Generally, grants are not awarded: to bail out agencies because of mismanagement or poor planning; budget shortfalls; to assist individuals; for costs associated with programs or services provided to citizens outside of Essex County; for sectarian or religious purposes; for political purposes; to support ongoing program work; or to pay expenses which a group should have anticipated.

Geographic Focus: Massachusetts

Amount of Grant: Up to 5,000 USD

Contact: Julie Bishop, Vice President of Grants and Nonprofit Services; (978) 777-8876, ext. 28; fax (978) 777-9454; j.bishop@eccf.org or info@eccf.org

Internet: http://eccf.org/emergency-fund-43.html

Sponsor: Essex County Community Foundation

175 Andover Street, Suite 101

Danvers, MA 01923

Esther M. and Freeman E. Everett Charitable Foundation Grants   **683**

Established in Colorado in 2001, the Esther M. and Freeman E. Everett Charitable Foundation gives primarily in Colorado and Wisconsin. Its primary fields of interest include: the arts; children and youth services; education; community foundations; and human services. Since there are no specified application forms, applicants should submit a copy of their IRS determination letter, along with a brief overview of the program, program need, outcomes, and budget. There are no annual deadlines, and grant amounts typically range between $1,000 and $10,000.

Geographic Focus: Colorado, Wisconsin

Amount of Grant: 1,000 - 10,000 USD

Contact: Grant Administrator; (719) 227-6442

Sponsor: Esther M. and Freeman E. Everett Charitable Foundation

30 E. Pikes Peak Avenue

Colorado Springs, CO 80903

Ethel and Raymond F. Rice Foundation Grants   **684**

The foundation awards grants to eligible Kansas nonprofit organizations in its areas of interest, including arts and culture; elementary, secondary, and higher education; environmental programs; elderly and youth; and social services. Types of support include capital campaigns, equipment, general support, land acquisition, scholarship funds, and federated giving funds. An application form is required.

Requirements: 501(c)3 nonprofit organizations and colleges and universities, school districts, and schools in Kansas are eligible. The foundation focuses on the areas of Lawrence and Douglas counties.

Geographic Focus: Kansas

Amount of Grant: 1,000 - 150,000 USD

Contact: James Paddock, President; (785) 841-9961

Sponsor: Ethel and Raymond F. Rice Foundation

1617 St. Andrews Drive, 200A

Lawrence, KS 66047

Ethel Sergeant Clark Smith Foundation Grants   **685**

The activities of the Ethel Sergeant Clark Smith (ESCS) Memorial Fund focuses on grants to organizations located in Southeastern Pennsylvania, with primary emphasis on those serving community needs in Delaware County. Grants will be made for capital projects, operating expenses and special programs in amounts that are meaningful to the success of the individual endeavors of the organizations. However, operating expense grants are typically awarded for charities without capital requirement and under circumstances where continuing funding is not expected. Grants will be made in areas of medical, educational, cultural, arts, health and welfare, and such other areas as the trustee shall identify and determine from time to time, to be responsive to changes in community needs. Application forms are available online and must be submitted by March 1 or September 1 annually.

Requirements: Southeastern Pennsylvania 501(c)3 non-profit organizations with primary emphasis on those serving community needs in Delaware County, Pennsylvania are eligible to apply. Complete applications should include the following: one original copy of the Proposal which includes the purpose and general activities of the organization should be included as well as a description of the proposed project and its justification, a budget and timetable for the project are also required; one copy of audited financial statements for the last fiscal year (or if not audited, Internal Revenue Service form 990) plus an operating budget for the current period and budgets for future period if appropriate; copy of the Internal Revenue Service tax determination letter which shows the organization is tax-exempt under Section 501(c)3 and that it is not a private foundation under section 509 (a) of the Internal Revenue Code. Any organization that is awarded a grant will be required to sign a Grant Agreement Form prior to the distribution of funds. Approximately one year after a grant has been awarded, a Progress Report should be completed by the organization. This information must be submitted prior to the consideration of any new proposals.

Restrictions: Grants will not be considered for the following: deficit financing; construction or renovations to real estate not owned by the charitable entity; salaries; professional fund raiser fees; multi-year grants over three years; to any organization more than once in a given year; to any organization more than three years in succession; any organization receiving a grant over a three year period or in three successive years will not be eligible for a future grant until two years transpire after the three year period.

Geographic Focus: Pennsylvania

Date(s) Application is Due: Mar 1; Sep 1

Contact: Wachovia Bank, N.A., Trustee; grantinquiries4@wachovia.com

Internet: https://www.wachovia.com/foundation/v/index.jsp?vgnextoid=3b38 52199c0aa110VgnVCM1000004b0d1872RCRD&vgnextfmt=default

Sponsor: Ethel Sergeant Clark Smith Foundation

620 Brandywine Parkway, Mail Code PA 5042

West Chester, PA 19380

Ethyl Corporation Grants   **686**

The corporation supports nonprofit organizations internationally in company operating locations. Education grants are awarded to public and private institutions at the secondary, undergraduate, and graduate levels. The program matches employee grants of $25-$2500 and also supports but does not administer a scholarship fund. Economic education grants for all age

groups are awarded. Health and welfare grants support programs in the areas of health care, social services, recreation, and physical fitness. Requests also are considered for culture/arts and civic affairs, including federated giving. Types of support include general operating support, building funds, community advertising, employee-matching gifts, endowment support, professorships, and scholarships. Applicants should submit proposals, including a statement of purpose of the organization, a brief description of the organization and list of current board members, proof of tax-exempt status, and a brief statement on why Ethyl should contribute to the organization.
Requirements: Organizations in company-operating locations worldwide are eligible, including the United States, Australia, Belgium, Brazil, Canada, England, France, Germany, Japan, Russia, Saudi Arabia, and Singapore.
Restrictions: Grants are not awarded to religious organizations for religious purposes, individuals for personal gain, or fraternal groups.
Geographic Focus: All States
Date(s) Application is Due: Sep 1
Amount of Grant: 25 - 2,500 USD
Contact: Human Resources and External Affairs; (804) 788-5720; fax (804) 788-5636; contributions@ethyl.com
Internet: http://www.ethyl.com/About+Ethyl/Our+History.htm
Sponsor: Ethyl Corporation
P.O. Box 2189
Richmond, VA 23218

Eugene B. Casey Foundation Grants 687

The foundation awards grants to nonprofit organizations in the District of Columbia and Maryland. Nonprofit organizations of the Christian and Roman Catholic faiths also are eligible. Organizations receiving grants include colleges and universities, community service organizations, government agencies, medical centers, parochial schools, and religious groups. Types of support include capital grants and general support grants. There are no application forms or deadlines. Applicants should submit written proposals that include an annual report, the purpose for which the funds are requested, and the amount requested compared with the total sought.
Requirements: Nonprofits in Maryland or the District of Columbia are eligible.
Geographic Focus: District of Columbia, Maryland
Amount of Grant: 10,000 - 100,000 USD
Contact: Betty Brown Casey, Treasurer; (301) 948-4595
Sponsor: Eugene B. Casey Foundation
800 South Frederick Avenue, Suite 100
Gaithersburg, MD 20877-1701

Eugene M. Lang Foundation Grants 688

The foundation awards grants in New York and Pennsylvania in its areas of interest, including education (early childhood education and higher education), medical and health programs, arts, health organizations, medical research, minorities, and performing arts. Types of support include annual campaigns, conferences and seminars, continuing support, fellowships, general operating support, internship funds, professorships, program development, scholarship funds, and seed money. The foundation favors social services such as those helping homeless or single mothers. Locally based groups wanting support must involve a Lang family member. There are no application deadlines; initial approach should be by letter.
Requirements: Organizations in New York and Pennsylvania are eligible.
Restrictions: Grants are not made to individuals, or for building funds, equipment and materials, capital or endowment funds, deficit financing, publications, or matching gifts.
Geographic Focus: New York, Pennsylvania
Amount of Grant: 500 - 50,000 USD
Contact: Program Contact; (212) 949-4100
Sponsor: Eugene M. Lang Foundation
535 5th Avenue, Suite 906
New York, NY 10017

Eugene McDermott Foundation Grants 689

The foundation awards grants to Texas nonprofit organizations in its areas of interest, including children and youth, community development, education (early childhood through higher education), health care/organizations, international human rights, medical research, minorities, and social service delivery programs. Types of support include annual campaigns, building construction/renovation, capital campaigns, equipment/land acquisition, general operating grants, matching/challenge grants, professorships, programs/project support, research grants, scholarship funds, and seed grants. There are no application deadlines or forms. The board meets quarterly to consider requests.

Requirements: Texas nonprofit organizations are eligible.
Geographic Focus: Texas
Amount of Grant: 1,000 - 25,000 USD
Samples: Nasher Sculpture Center (Dallas, TX)—for endowment, $500,000; U of Texas Southwestern Medical Center (Dallas, TX)—to refurbish Medical School, $400,000; U of Texas Southwestern Medical Ctr (Dallas, TX)—to establish a chair in cardiothoracic anesthesiology, $1 million.
Contact: Grants Administrator; (214) 521-2924
Sponsor: Eugene McDermott Foundation
3808 Euclid Avenue
Dallas, TX 75205

Eulalie Bloedel Schneider Foundation Grants 690

The Foundation's mission is to support secular grassroots programs that enhance individual and family self-sufficiency and economic stability. Areas of interest are skill-building and training programs that empower at-risk youth, women and families to develop skills that would bring them towards economic self-sufficiency. The Foundation supports programs that provide job-related educational and skill building opportunities, and those seeking to build character and develop self-reliance and accountability. Artistic and cultural skill-building programs for youth and families that enhance educational and future career opportunities are also of interest.
Requirements: Washington 501(c)3 groups in Puget Sound area are eligible.
Restrictions: The Foundation will not support: groups outside the Puget Sound area; national organizations, even those with projects in the Pacific Northwest; human services or low-income services projects or organizations that are not specifically providing skill-building or training opportunities; programs with a religious or proselytizing approach or mission; educational and outreach programs of large artistic or cultural institutions; museum exhibits or related outreach programs for schools or communities; traditional academic-oriented literacy, tutoring, and mentorship programs; individual requests for research or scholarships; childcare centers, schools, or classroom projects; book, video, film, or home-page productions, unless the expenses occur within the context of a project that fits the foundation's major areas of interest; computer, software, or office equipment purchases unless clearly a component of a project that fits foundation areas of interest; and capital campaigns for building construction or renovations.
Geographic Focus: All States
Date(s) Application is Due: Feb 1; Aug 1
Amount of Grant: 1,000 - 3,500 USD
Samples: Creative Theatre Experience Olympia, WA)—to provide hands-on training for teen interns about behind-the-scenes work necessary to put on a show, $1500; Washington CASH (Seattle, WA)—general operations for this microcredit organization, $2500; Seattle Youth Garden Works (WA)—general operations for a market-gardening job-skills training program for homeless and low-income youth, $2500.
Contact: Therese Ogle; (206) 781-3472; oglefounds@aol.com
Internet: http://fdncenter.org/grantmaker/schneider
Sponsor: Eulalie Bloedel Schneider Foundation
6723 Sycamore Avenue NW
Seattle, WA 98117

Evan Frankel Foundation Grants 691

Although it was incorporated in 1978, the Evan Frankel Foundation became an active philanthropic entity according to Evan's wishes upon his death in 1991. The Foundation awards grants in its areas of interest, including higher education, the arts, humanities, health and science, social services, and the environment. Giving is primarily in Manhattan and Suffolk County, New York and Los Angeles, California. Most recent grants have ranged from as little as $500 up to $500,000. Applicants should submit a letter to request, outlining their program and budgetary needs.
Restrictions: Individuals are not eligible.
Geographic Focus: All States
Amount of Grant: 500 - 500,000 USD
Samples: A Place Called Home, Los Angeles, California, $117,000 - social services general operating costs; Harlem Educational Activities Fund, New York, New York, $49,000 - general operating support; East Hampton Library, East Hampton, New York, $204,750 - general operating support.
Contact: Ernest Frankel; (631) 329-0010; asff@hamptons.com
Internet: http://www.evanfrankelfoundation.org/
Sponsor: Evan Frankel Foundation
P.O. Box 5026
East Hampton, NY 11937

Evelyn and Walter Haas, Jr. Fund Gay and Lesbian Rights Grants 692

When Evelyn and Walter Haas, Jr. created this foundation in 1953, they were motivated by a set of values that still guide the organization today. With their vision of a just and caring society as its touchstone, the Fund supports initiatives and organizations that advance and protect fundamental rights and opportunities for all. The Fund is a leading supporter of gay and lesbian equality, based on our founders' vision of a just and caring society where all people are able to live, work and raise their families with dignity. There are three funding priorities in this area: achieving marriage equality in more states; advancing nondiscrimination protections at all levels of government; and building support for gay equality in communities of faith. Applicants should begin by contacting the fund with a two- to three-page letter of inquiry, outlining the proposal and an overall project budget.

Requirements: IRS 501(c)3 organizations in California not classified as private foundations under section 509(a) are eligible. Matching funds are required.

Restrictions: The fund generally does not make grants for capital campaigns, major equipment, basic research, conferences, publications, films or videos, deficit or emergency funding, scholarships, direct mail campaigns, fundraising events, annual appeals, or endowment contributions. Exceptions may be made for requests that form part of a larger effort in which the fund is engaged or for requests from organizations with which the fund has a long-term funding relationship. No exceptions will be made for aid to individuals.

Geographic Focus: All States

Contact: Clayton Juan; (415) 856-1400; fax (415) 856-1500; siteinfo@haasjr.org

Internet: http://www.haasjr.org/programs-and-initiatives/gays-and-lesbians

Sponsor: Evelyn and Walter Haas, Jr. Fund

114 Sansome Street, Suite 600

San Francisco, CA 94104

Evelyn and Walter Haas, Jr. Fund Immigrant Rights Grants 693

When Evelyn and Walter Haas, Jr. created this foundation in 1953, they were motivated by a set of values that still guide the organization today. With their vision of a just and caring society as its touchstone, the Fund supports initiatives and organizations that advance and protect fundamental rights and opportunities for all. The Fund has a long history of working to lift up the voice, leadership, and civic and political participation of immigrant communities. Building on this commitment, the Fund is joining with an array of partners to help build a diverse and powerful movement for immigrant rights and integration. There are three funding priorities in this area: strengthening public understanding about the need for comprehensive immigration reform at the national level; increasing civic participation among immigrants in California; and supporting public education about the need for immigrant-friendly state and local policies in California. Applicants should begin by contacting the fund with a two- to three-page letter of inquiry, outlining the proposal and an overall project budget.

Requirements: IRS 501(c)3 organizations in California not classified as private foundations under section 509(a) are eligible. Matching funds are required.

Restrictions: The fund generally does not make grants for capital campaigns, major equipment, basic research, conferences, publications, films or videos, deficit or emergency funding, scholarships, direct mail campaigns, fundraising events, annual appeals, or endowment contributions. Exceptions may be made for requests that form part of a larger effort in which the fund is engaged or for requests from organizations with which the fund has a long-term funding relationship. No exceptions will be made for aid to individuals.

Geographic Focus: California

Contact: Clayton Juan; (415) 856-1400; fax (415) 856-1500; siteinfo@haasjr.org

Internet: http://www.haasjr.org/programs-and-initiatives/immigrants

Sponsor: Evelyn and Walter Haas, Jr. Fund

114 Sansome Street, Suite 600

San Francisco, CA 94104

Evert B. and Ruth Finley Person Foundation Grants 694

The foundation supports nonprofits in Northern California, primarily Sonoma County, in the areas of music, musical arts, health associations, higher education, journalism, engineering, religion, and science education. Types of support include operating budgets, matching funds, and scholarship funds. There are no application deadlines.

Requirements: 501(c)3 nonprofits in northern California may apply.

Geographic Focus: California

Contact: Evert Person, Trustee; (707) 545-3136; fax (707) 575-5778

Sponsor: Evert B. and Ruth Finley Person Foundation

1400 N Dutton Avenue, Suite 12

Santa Rosa, CA 95401-4644

Every Voice in Action Foundation Grants 695

The Foundation is a private foundation based in Tucson, Arizona that makes grants to non-profit organizations to encourage and support youth voice in the Tuscon community. It defines youth voice as young people having an authentic voice in their lives and in the life of the community. This means the community recognizing youth as important resources, and encouraging them to express their unique perspectives and ideas. In addition to grant making, the Foundation operates and supports programs to teach youth about philanthropy and engage them in making grants that benefit other youth and the community.

Requirements: Tucson and Pima County, Arizona, serving nonprofit organizations are eligible.

Restrictions: Programs with a primary focus on academics, athletics, health, recreation, or other topics are not eligible if mentor relationships are a secondary focus or byproduct of the program.

Geographic Focus: Arizona

Amount of Grant: Up to 20,000 USD

Contact: Judith Anderson, President; (520) 615-2100; fax (520) 615-2112; judith@everyvoicefoundation.org

Internet: http://www.everyvoicefoundation.org/funding_areas.php

Sponsor: Every Voice in Action Foundation

2851 N Country Club Road

Tucson, AZ 85716

Ewing Marion Kauffman Foundation Grants and Initiatives 696

The vision of the Foundation is to foster a society of economically independent individuals who are engaged citizens, contributing to the improvement of their communities. The Foundation focuses its grant making and operations on two areas: advancing entrepreneurship and improving the education of children and youth. In entrepreneurship, the Foundation works nationwide to catalyze an entrepreneurial society in which job creation, innovation, and the economy flourish. In education, the Foundation works to improve the academic achievement of disadvantaged children and works with partners to support programs that directly impact a child's academic achievement, with a concentrated focus on math, science, and technology skills. The Foundation does not use a grant application form or formal application process. There are no proposal deadlines or established funding limits. Information regarding submission of a letter of inquiry is available online.

Requirements: The foundation only funds programs within the United States. The majority of education grants go to organizations within the Kansas City metropolitan area. The foundation's entrepreneurship efforts fund programs and activities nationally and within the Kansas City area.

Restrictions: The Foundation does not fund: requests from individuals, political, social, or fraternal organizations; endowments, special events, arts, or international programs; provide loans, start-up expenses or seed capital funding for private businesses or scholarships requested by individuals; proposals submitted via audiotape or videotape; institutions that discriminate on the basis of race, creed, gender, national origin, age, disability or sexual orientation in policy or in practice; programs in furtherance of sectarian religious activities, impermissible lobbying, legislative or political activities; programs targeted for people with a specific physical, medical or psychological condition; or medical research or profit-making enterprises.

Geographic Focus: All States

Samples: Center for a New American Security, Washington, DC, $25,000—support the Center for a New American Security's effort to make a meaningful contribution to our nation's debate over economic growth; Duke University, Pratt School of Engineering, Durham, NC, $40,000—support research on the contributions of immigrants to the U.S. economy and the role immigrant and native entrepreneurial and social networks play in fostering entrepreneurship and successful businesses.

Contact: Administrator; (816) 932-1000; fax (816) 932-1100; info@emkf.org

Internet: http://www.kauffman.org/grants.cfm

Sponsor: Ewing Marion Kauffman Foundation

4801 Rockhill Road

Kansas City, MO 64110-2046

Expect Miracles Foundation Grants 697

The MMLC Funding Award is given on an annual basis on behalf of the Miracle Maker Leadership Council to cancer fighting causes and patient care programs where such support is not always readily available. The proposed program should have the ability to materially impact an organization or a specific program of a qualified organization.

Requirements: Funding Award recipients must have 501(c)3 status as defined by the IRS. Applicants must provide service in at least one of the following areas: cancer patient care support programs and initiatives; cancer awareness and educational programs; or cancer prevention/health projects. Priority will be given to initiatives demonstrating sustainable benefits to the communities where the Foundation events are held and where Foundation supporters and the Miracle Maker Leadership Council (MMLC) members live.

Restrictions: Although there are no specific guidelines on the size, annual budget, or annual fundraising of a recipient organization, the program is not designed to assist in funding large institutional/national/society entities. The goal of the MMLC is to select programs and causes where funding is not always readily available. MMLC guidelines prohibit funding for the following: private pursuits; political parties, associations and representatives of advocacy groups; organizations that discriminate by race, creed, gender, sexual orientation, age, religion, or national origin; religious causes; advertising, promotion, or sponsorship; and donation to an individual or team fundraising initiative or program.

Geographic Focus: California, Connecticut, District of Columbia, Illinois, Maine, Maryland, Massachusetts, New Hampshire, New Jersey, New York, Pennsylvania, Rhode Island, Vermont

Date(s) Application is Due: Mar 5

Amount of Grant: Up to 27,000 USD

Contact: Alana Chin, (617) 391-9235; achin@expectmiraclesfoundation.org

Internet: http://www.expectmiraclesfoundation.org/

Sponsor: Expect Miracles Foundation

6 Quail Run

Hingham, MA 02043

F.B. Heron Foundation Grants 698

The foundation focuses on core wealth-creation strategies for low-income families and communities. Grantmaking is considered for programs that promote home ownerships, enterprise development, access to capital, quality and affordable child care, and comprehensive community development. There are no application deadlines or forms. Submit a two- to three-page letter of inquiry.

Requirements: U.S. 501(c)3 nonprofits may apply.

Geographic Focus: All States

Amount of Grant: 25,000 - 125,000 USD

Samples: Rosalie Manor, Inc. (Milwaukee, WI)—to support a First Time Parents program to promote health child development, $75,000; Wheelock College (Boston, MA)—for the Ctr for Career Development in Early Child Care, $50,000; Beyond Shelter (Los Angeles, CA)—for general support, $50,000.

Contact: Mary Jo Mullan, Program Officer, c/o Rockefeller and Company Inc; (212) 404-1800; fax (212) 404-1805

Internet: http://www.fbheron.org

Sponsor: F.B. Heron Foundation

100 Broadway, 17th Floor

New York, NY 10005

F.J. O'Neill Charitable Corporation Grants 699

The corporation awards general operating grants to eligible Ohio nonprofit organizations in its areas of interest, including higher and secondary education, medical research, and Roman Catholic organizations and churches. There are no application deadlines or forms.

Requirements: Ohio nonprofits serving the Cleveland area are eligible.

Geographic Focus: Ohio

Amount of Grant: 25,000 - 100,000 USD

Contact: Grants Administrator; (216) 464-2121

Sponsor: F.J. O'Neill Charitable Corporation

3550 Lander Road

Cleveland, OH 44124

Fairfield County Community Foundation Grants 700

As a community foundation, FCCF makes discretionary grants to nonprofits in the broad program areas of economic opportunity (including affordable housing, neighborhood development, and workforce development); children, youth and families; health and human services; the environment; arts and culture; and nonprofit organizational effectiveness. The Foundation is particularly interested in proposals focused on: economic opportunity; education and youth development; advancing school readiness in Fairfield County; organizational effectiveness; and regionalism. Applicants must first submit a letter of inquiry. Application information is available online.

Requirements: Nonprofit organizations in Fairfield County, CT, are eligible.

Restrictions: Funds are not used to provide support for religious or political purposes, deficit financing, annual appeals, fundraising events, open space purchases, for-profit, parochial, charter or private schools, or nonprofit endowments. Grants are not given to individuals.

Geographic Focus: Connecticut

Contact: Karen Brown, Vice President of Programs; (203) 750-3200; fax (203) 750-3232; kbrown@fccfoundation.org

Internet: http://www.fccfoundation.org/cm/grantseekers/what_we_fund.html

Sponsor: Fairfield County Community Foundation

383 Main Avenue

Norwalk, CT 06851-1543

Fales Foundation Trust Grants 701

The foundation provides financial support to social service agencies addressing issues of homelessness and hunger; and to artistic and cultural organizations in the city of Seattle, with strong emphasis in this category directed toward community-based arts programs related to issues of homelessness and hunger, providing arts opportunities for underserved constituencies. Types of support include general operating grants and special project grants. Preference is given to organizations receiving past support from the Fales Foundation. Application materials should be mailed to Cynthia Crawford, Trustee, Union Bank of California, The Private Bank, at the address listed. Guidelines are available online.

Requirements: Seattle 501(c)3 nonprofit organizations are eligible. Additional requirements for applicants include: successful program capability, sound fiscal policies, and responsible management; and in existence for five years or more.

Restrictions: The foundation will not support groups located outside the city of Seattle, even if the program serves a Seattle clientele or constituency; capital campaigns or expenditures; loans or investments; fundraising events; projects of a political or religious nature; individual requests for research or scholarships; computer, software, or office equipment purchases; projects of an individual artist, even if under the sponsorship of a 501(c)3 organization; video or film productions; or book publications.

Geographic Focus: All States

Date(s) Application is Due: Apr 1; Oct 1

Amount of Grant: 1,000 - 5,000 USD

Contact: Therese Ogle, Grants Consultant; (206) 781-3472; fax (206) 784-5987; oglefounds@aol.com

Internet: http://fdncenter.org/grantmaker/fales

Sponsor: Fales Foundation Trust

P.O. Box 3123

Seattle, WA 98114

Fallon OrNda Community Health Fund Grants 702

The purpose of the health fund is to advance projects that increase access to health care or health promotion services that improve the health status of vulnerable populations. Of particular interest are projects that result in: the support or creation of primary care outreach services to vulnerable populations; the development of continuing managed care services rather than episodic or uncoordinated care; and the removal of barriers that prevent people from receiving services such as lack of transportation, cultural competency of providers, language differences, or others. Grants may be for operational expenditures such as personnel costs, or for construction, renovation, equipment purchase or other physical improvements. Past grants have ranged from $6,500 to $30,000.

Requirements: Funding will not be provided for long-term underwriting of operational costs for any one program.

Geographic Focus: Massachusetts

Date(s) Application is Due: Feb 15

Amount of Grant: 6,500 - 30,000 USD

Contact: Lois Smith; (508) 755-0980, ext. 107; lsmith@greaterworcester.org

Internet: http://www.greaterworcester.org/grants/Fallon.htm

Sponsor: Greater Worcester Community Foundation

370 Main Street, Suite 650

Worcester, MA 01608-1738

Fan Fox and Leslie R. Samuels Foundation Grants 703

The foundation's areas of funding are the performing arts and healthcare. Healthcare funding supports patient-based and social service activities that directly help the elderly of New York City. The foundation supports performing arts organizations in the City of New York, principally, but not exclusively, in the borough of Manhattan. The foundation's primary mission is to support major performing arts institutions of national or international eminence. In addition to providing direct support, the foundation also assists presenting entities that have the requisite expertise, knowledge, and artistic judgment to present groups or individuals, new works, varied repertoire, and arts-in-education projects that will be contributions to the aesthetic and intellectual life of New York. Application guidelines are available on the Web site or upon request.

Requirements: The foundation funds organizations in the New York City area only. Only 501(c)3 tax-exempt organizations are invited to apply.

Restrictions: The foundation does not give grants to individuals or for scholarships, and does not support research, film, or video, nor does it fund education or social services. The foundation no longer actively solicits applications for support of arts-in-education programs at the primary and secondary level.

Geographic Focus: New York

Date(s) Application is Due: Mar 1; Jun 1; Dec 1

Amount of Grant: 25,000 - 250,000 USD

Samples: Hebrew Home for the Aged at Riverdale (New York, NY)—for a comprehensive center dedicated to preventing and treating elder abuse, including a shelter for abused senior citizens, $200,000 over two years; Jamaica Hospital Medical Ctr (New York, NY)—to establish an interdisciplinary family-medicine program for predominantly poor, minority, and elderly patients who do not have access to palliative-care services, $150,000; Metropolitan Jewish Health System (New York, NY)—to establish a palliative-medicine program based on home visits, $201,000 over two years; Calvary Hospital (New York, NY)—for a program to increase access to comprehensive hospice and palliative care for nursing-home residents, $250,000.

Contact: Joseph Mitchell, President; (212) 239-3030; fax (212) 239-3039; info@samuels.org

Internet: http://www.samuels.org

Sponsor: Fan Fox and Leslie R. Samuels Foundation

350 Fifth Avenue, Suite 4301

New York, NY 10118

Fannie E. Rippel Foundation Grants 704

The foundation aids, assists, funds, equips, and provides maintenance for corporations, institutions, associations, organizations, or societies maintained for the relief and care of aged women; provides funds for the building, equipping, and maintenance of hospitals; and provides funds for corporations, institutions, and other organizations existing for treatment of and/or research on heart disease or cancer. The foundation gives emphasis to the equipment and programmatic needs of major teaching medical centers and local rural hospitals, particularly where opportunities exist for leveraging the expertise or capabilities of the medical centers/rural hospitals. Programs should reach underserved rural and urban groups, advocate preventive care, present strategies to change behaviors of the people served, and promote humanistic medicine and mind-body-spirit connections in the healing process. Preference also is given to proposed projects where the benefits can be leveraged through challenge grants.

Requirements: Organizations, associations, institutions, and hospitals in the Northeast are eligible.

Restrictions: Grants are not awarded to individuals.

Geographic Focus: Connecticut, Maine, Massachusetts, New Hampshire, Rhode Island, Vermont

Amount of Grant: 50,000 - 300,000 USD

Contact: Leigh Scherrer, Foundation Associate; (973) 540-0101, ext. 305; fax (973) 540-0404; lscherrer@rippelfoundation.org

Internet: http://rippelfoundation.org/

Sponsor: Fannie E. Rippel Foundation

14 Maple Avenue, Suite 200

Morristown, NJ 07960

FAR Fund Grants 705

The FAR Fund Project is a New Orleans-based program exploring Hurricane Katrina's effects on New Orleans therapists and therapeutic practice. It was designed by and for clinicians. The project's mission is two fold: to offer support and concrete help to local clinicians, and to develop a model for better understanding how shared trauma affects therapists and therapy. Through this project, the FAR Fund wishes to unite and revitalize clinician communities following large-scale disasters wherever they occur, starting in New Orleans.

Requirements: The FAR Fund Project is open to New Orleans psychotherapists of all disciplines and theoretical orientations. Their mission is two-fold: to offer support and concrete help to local mental health clinicians, and to develop a psychodynamic model to better understand how shared trauma affects therapists and therapy.

Geographic Focus: Louisiana

Contact: Shirlee Taylor, Director; (212) 982-8400; fax (212) 982-8477; FARFund@mac.com

Sponsor: Far Fund

928 Broadway, Suite 902

New York, NY 10010

Faye McBeath Foundation Grants 706

The Faye McBeath Foundation is a private, independent foundation providing grants to tax-exempt nonprofit 501(c)3 organizations in the metropolitan Milwaukee, Wisconsin area, including Milwaukee, Waukesha, Ozaukee and Washington counties. The major areas of interest are: children; aging and elders; health; health education; civic and governmental affairs. The Foundation's Trustees are primarily interested in promising or established programs, operated by well-managed organizations. Benchmarks that will be applied to projects and organizations in all five interest areas are the following: strength of proposal - Foundation guidelines match; quality and creativity in project design, implementation and evaluation; quality of the applicant nonprofit's leadership and organizational capacity; potential to stretch or leverage McBeath funds; specific interests of Trustees and/or staff. The majority of grants support specific programs. On occasion, operating and capacity-building grants are awarded. Capital grants are limited to projects with community-wide impact that reflect the program interests of the Foundation. Any invited requests for operating or capacity-building support must include an organization's results-oriented annual plan, covering both programs and management. The trustees meet four times each year to consider grant proposals. Written notification of the Trustees' decision regarding a grant proposal will be sent within ten days of the meeting. Organizations awarded grants will receive written notification of grant conditions, payment dates and reporting requirements

Requirements: 501(c)3 nonprofit organizations in the metropolitan Milwaukee area are eligible. To begin the application process, submittal of a letter of intent, 1-2 pages long that includes: a brief description of the applicant organization, the program to be funded, the corresponding match between the Foundation's guidelines and the request, the amount requested and the estimated total project budget. Include the name and address of the organization, and the name, phone number and email address of a contact person. There are no deadlines for letters of intent. Upon receipt of a letter of intent, Foundation staff will formally acknowledge by email or letter. If the request is clearly outside the current program or geographical focus of the Foundation, a decline letter will be sent informing you of this determination. If you are formally invited by McBeath staff to submit a full proposal, you will be asked to use the Wisconsin Common Grant Application Form. The Foundation requires that a volunteer serving on the Board sign the application.

Restrictions: The Foundation does not award grants for annual fund drives, scholarships, support of individuals, sponsorship of fundraising events, or emergency funds. The Foundation does not consider or acknowledge general solicitation letters. Basic health sciences research is not funded by the Foundation. Single disease or condition organizations are typically not funded by the Foundation. An exception may be made for a creative project involving one or more of the following: service to multiple populations, collaboration and/or creation of a replicable model. There are no published deadlines for letters of intent or grant proposals. Proposal deadlines are established based upon discussion with Foundation staff. Organizations serving the disabled will be considered only if the project targets children or older adults. Any discussion of the availability of funding in a subsequent year should be initiated by the grantee and discussed with staff at least 60 days in advance of a project anniversary.

Geographic Focus: Wisconsin

Amount of Grant: 1,000 - 50,000 USD

Samples: Aurora Sinai Medical Center, Milwaukee, WI, 45,000—for improvement of access to Health Care Services; Greater Milwaukee Foundation, Milwaukee, WI, $25,000—for the Camps For Kids Forever Fund; NAMI Waukesha, Waukesha, WI, $10,000—for Housing Support and Advocacy Program.

Contact: Scott Gelzer, Executive Director; (414) 272-2626; fax (414) 272-6235; info@fayemcbeath.org

Internet: http://www.fayemcbeath.org/ProgramPriorities/index.html

Sponsor: Faye McBeath Foundation

101 West Pleasant Street, Suite 210

Milwaukee, WI 53212

Feldman Family Foundation Grants 707

Giving is concentrated in the areas of community development, social welfare, and Jewish causes. Types of support include annual campaigns, building construction/renovation, general operating support, program development, research, and scholarship funds. Initial contact should be by proposal letter. Foundation trustees meet in the spring and fall to review proposals under serious consideration. Applications are accepted at any time.

Requirements: Nonprofit organizations in California and Texas are eligible to apply. On rare occasions, grants are awarded outside of California and Texas.

Proposals must include full program information, statement of need, and copy of tax-exempt determination letter.

Restrictions: Grants will not be awarded to individuals.

Geographic Focus: California, Texas

Contact: Vice President; (972) 756-6032

Sponsor: Feldman Family Foundation

1431 Greenway Drive, Suite 360

Irving, TX 75038

FEMA Assistance to Firefighters Grants (AFG)   **708**

The program provides financial assistance directly to fire departments and nonaffiliated EMS organizations to enhance their abilities with respect to fire and fire-related hazards. The primary goal is to help fire departments and nonaffiliated EMS organizations meet their firefighting and emergency response needs. AFG seeks to support organizations that lack the tools and resources necessary to more effectively protect the health and safety of the public and their emergency response personnel with respect to fire and all other hazards. The project period for any award under AFG will be twelve months from the date of the award.

Requirements: The application will be accessible from the AFG website (www.firegrantsupport.com), the U.S. Fire Administration's (USFA) website (www.usfa.fema.gov), and grants.gov website (www.grants.gov). Paper applications will be accepted, but are discouraged due to the inherent delays associated with processing them. Fire departments or nonaffiliated EMS organizations operating in any of the 50 States plus the District of Columbia, the Commonwealth of the Northern Mariana Islands, the Virgin Islands, Guam, American Samoa, and Puerto Rico are eligible for funding. A fire department is defined as an agency or organization that has a formally recognized arrangement with a State, territory, local, or tribal authority (city, county, parish, fire district, township, town, or other governing body) to provide fire suppression to a population within a fixed geographical area on a first-due basis. A nonaffiliated EMS organization is defined as a public or private nonprofit emergency medical services organization that provides direct emergency medical services, including medical transport, to a specific geographic area on a first-due basis but is not affiliated with a hospital and does not serve a geographic area where emergency medical services are adequately provided by a fire department. Fire departments may submit applications for either or both of the following program areas: Firefighter Operations and Safety; Firefighter Vehicle Acquisition. EMS applicants may apply for assistance under either the Operations and Safety program area or the Vehicle Acquisition program area, or both using separate applications. Any eligible applicant, whether a fire department or a nonaffiliated EMS organization, may act as a host applicant and apply for large-scale or regional projects on behalf of itself and any number of organizations in neighboring jurisdictions. The only activities available for application under a regional project are training and equipment acquisition that positively affect interoperability.

Restrictions: Fire departments that are Federal, or contracted by the Federal Government, and are solely responsible under a formally recognized agreement for suppression of fires on Federal installations or land are ineligible for funding. Fire stations that are not independent entities, but are part of, controlled by, or under the day-to-day operational direction of a larger fire department or agency are not eligible for funding. Fire departments that are for-profit departments (i.e., do not have specific nonprofit status or are not municipally based) are not eligible for funding. Auxiliaries, fire service organizations or associations, and State/local agencies such as a forest service, fire marshals, hospitals, and training offices are not eligible for funding. Dive teams and search and rescue teams, or any similar organizations that do not provide medical transport, are not eligible for assistance as nonaffiliated EMS organizations.

Geographic Focus: All States

Date(s) Application is Due: May 4

Contact: Help Desk; (866) 274-0960; firegrants@dhs.gov

Internet: http://www.firegrantsupport.com/afg/

Sponsor: U.S. Department of Homeland Security

245 Murray Lane - Building 410, SW

Washington, D.C. 20528-7000

FHL Foundation Grants   **709**

The foundation supports efforts of eligible New Mexico nonprofit organizations to eliminate systems that support abuse and oppression of people and animals. Areas of interest include education to increase public understanding; discovery to uncover systems that allow abuse to happen; and service to provide care for victims of abuse. There are three levels of support: Level One for organizations new to the theory of attachment, or to provide ongoing support to organizations

actively applying attachment theory (whether at the program or project level); Level Two for organizations that are actively applying attachment theory to their programs but not necessarily their projects; and Level Three for organizations that are applying attachment theory to both their programs and their projects. Different levels of funding have different deadline dates.

Requirements: New Mexico nonprofit organizations are eligible.

Restrictions: Grants are not made to individuals.

Geographic Focus: New Mexico

Date(s) Application is Due: Feb 28; May 31; Aug 31; Nov 30

Amount of Grant: 1,000 - 20,000 USD

Contact: Administrator; (505) 247-2400; fhlfound@thuntek.net

Internet: http://www.fhlfoundation.com

Sponsor: FHL Foundation

P.O. Box 27650

Albuquerque, NM 87125

Field Foundation of Illinois Grants   **710**

The Foundation awards grants only to institutions and agencies operating in the fields of urban and community affairs, culture, education, community welfare, health, and environment, primarily serving the people of Chicago with extremely limited grant making in the metropolitan area. Preference will be given to funding innovative approaches for addressing program areas.

Requirements: Applicants must reside in Illinois. Grant applications are not provided; however, a formal proposal is required. The Foundation does not accept grant requests via email or fax.

Restrictions: No grants will be made to support: endowments; individuals; medical research or national health agency appeals; propaganda organizations or committees whose efforts are aimed at influencing legislation; printed materials, video or computer equipment; fund-raising events or advertising; appeals for religious purposes; other granting agencies or foundations for ultimate distribution to agencies or programs of its own choosing; custodian afterschool programs or tutoring; most disease specific programs, research or activities; or operating support of established neighborhood health centers or clinics, day care centers for children, or small cultural groups. Requests for computer equipment will not be considered.

Geographic Focus: Illinois

Date(s) Application is Due: Jan 15; May 15; Sep 15

Amount of Grant: 50,000 USD

Samples: Catholic Charities of the Archdiocese of Chicago (IL)—to support expansion of the Emergency Assistance Services program, $15,000; Jobs for Youth/Chicago (IL)—to support the Workforce Advancement Initiative, $10,000; Palliative Care Center and Hospice of the North Shore (IL)—to support the capital campaign for a new community facility, $25,000; Puerto Rican Alliance (IL)—to support the Community Arts Program, $10,000.

Contact: Joann Ross, (312) 831-0910; jross@fieldfoundation.org

Internet: http://www.fieldfoundation.org

Sponsor: Field Foundation of Illinois

200 S Wacker Drive, Suite 3860

Chicago, IL 60606

Fieldstone Foundation Grants   **711**

The Foundation was created to provide grants, leadership and development and service to nonprofit organizations working to support individuals in the communities where the company does business. The Foundation gives emphasis to programs that serve children and families and allocates its resources in four general areas: Humanitarian, Community and Education, Cultural Arts and Christian Ministries. Faxed and emailed proposals will not be accepted. Application information is available online.

Requirements: Funding is limited to non-profit organizations serving the communities where the company is currently operating: Orange, Riverside, and San Diego counties in Southern California and Salt Lake City in Utah.

Restrictions: Support will not be provided for individuals; political parties, candidates and partisan political organizations; veteran, labor, fraternal or athletic organizations except for specific projects that benefit the broad community; advertising; or individual churches. The Foundation does not make multi-year commitments or fund capital campaigns.

Geographic Focus: California, Utah

Date(s) Application is Due: Jun 30

Contact: Janine Mason, Executive Director; janinem@fieldstone-homes.com

Internet: http://www.fieldstone-homes.com/foundation

Sponsor: Fieldstone Foundation

14 Corporate Plaza Drive

Newport Beach, CA 92660

Finish Line Youth Foundation Founder's Grants 712

Finish Line Youth Foundation focuses funding on organizations that provide opportunities for youth participation in the following areas: Youth athletic programs - Community-based programs addressing active lifestyle and team building skills; Camps - Established camps with an emphasis on sports and active lifestyle, especially programs serving disadvantaged and special needs kids. These emergency funds grants would be awarded to qualifying organizations that have an emergency need that would somehow be keeping the organization from providing current services. Examples would be natural disasters or other unforeseen circumstances that require special funding to help build or develop facilities or equipment needs.

Requirements: Organizations operating near a Finish Line store with 501(c)3 tax-exempt status that provide opportunities for participation for children and young adults age 18 and under are eligible to apply. Preference is given to organizations whose activities provide direct services to individuals and produce tangible results, rather than those that are policy oriented. The foundation has a particular interest in the potential impact of the program/project and all the number of people who will benefit; the organization's fiscal responsibility and management qualifications; and, the ability of an organization to obtain the necessary additional funding to implement a program or project and to provide ongoing funding after the term of the grant has expired.

Restrictions: The Foundation will not make grants to: Organizations not currently exempt from federal taxation under section 501(c)3 of the Internal Revenue Code or created for eligible public purposes (such as public and private schools and state-funded universities and colleges); Political campaigns, or attempts to influence public officials; Organizations that unlawfully discriminate as to race, religion, income, gender, disability or national origin; Projects or programs aimed at promoting the teachings of a particular church or religious denomination, or construction projects of churches and other religious institutions; Fraternal, veterans or labor organizations; Foundations affiliated with a for-profit entity; Endowments; Organizations for on-going operating support; Start up organizations or programs; Reduce debt; Beauty or talent contests; Individuals; Sponsor teams, special events or fundraising activities; Medical, scientific or academic research; Pay for travel or trips.

Geographic Focus: All States
Amount of Grant: 5,000 - 25,000 USD
Contact: Roger Underwood; (317) 899-1022 x6741; Youthfoundation@finishline.com
Internet: http://www.finishline.com/store/youthfoundation/special-grants.jsp
Sponsor: Finish Line Youth Foundation
3308 N Mitthoeffer Road
Indianapolis, IN 46235

Fireman's Fund Insurance Company Heritage Grants 713

Fireman's Fund Insurance Company was founded in 1863 with a mission to donate a portion of its profits to support the fire service. The program continues that tradition today through its Heritage Grants program by awarding grants to fire service organizations for needed equipment, firefighter training and communication education programs. Funding is allocated in partnership with its employees and independent insurance agents, who assist in the direction of the grants.

Requirements: To apply, a nonprofit, tax-exempt organization should send a letter to the director setting forth the request for funding and the amount desired, enclosing a financial statement, IRS letter, and a list of board members.

Restrictions: The fund does not make grants for capital campaigns; endowment funds; general operating expenses; individuals; religious organizations; fraternal, veteran, or sectarian groups; medical research and health organizations; trips or tours; advertising; video, television, or film productions; fundraising events; sporting events; political organizations; subscription fees or admission tickets; or public sector services (with the exception of some school district programs).

Geographic Focus: All States
Amount of Grant: 5,000 - 25,000 USD
Contact: Executive Director; (866) 440-8716 or (415) 899-2000; fax (415) 899-3600; heritage@ffic.com
Internet: http://www.firemansfund.com/heritage/Pages/heritage.aspx
Sponsor: Fireman's Fund Insurance Company
777 San Marin Drive
Novato, CA 94998-1406

FirstEnergy Foundation Community Grants 714

The FirstEnergy Foundation's contributions to local nonprofit organizations help strengthen the social and economic fabric of our communities. Funded solely by FirstEnergy, the Foundation extends the corporate philosophy of providing community support. The Foundation traditionally funds these priorities: help improve the vitality of our communities and support key safety initiatives; promotion of local and regional economic development and revitalization efforts; and support of FirstEnergy employee community leadership and volunteer interests.

Requirements: 501(c)3 organizations within the FirstEnergy Corporation operating companies' service areas - Ohio Edison Company, the Cleveland Electric Illuminating Company, the Toledo Edison Company, Pennsylvania Power Company, Metropolitan Edison Company, Pennsylvania Electric Company, Jersey Central Power and Light Company, Monongahela Power Company, the Potomac Edison Company, West Penn Power Company, FirstEnergy Solutions Corporation, FirstEnergy Generation, and FirstEnergy Nuclear Operations - are eligible to apply.

Restrictions: Funding is not considered for: direct grants to individuals, political or legislative activities; organizations that receive sizable public tax funding; fraternal, religious, labor, athletic, social or veterans organizations - unless the contribution is earmarked for an eligible program or campaign open to all beneficiaries, including those not affiliated with the host organization; national or international organizations; organizations supported by federated campaigns, such as United Way; research; equipment purchases; loans or second party giving, such as endowments, debt retirement, or foundations; or public or private schools.

Geographic Focus: New Jersey, Ohio, Pennsylvania
Contact: Dee Lowery; (330) 761-4246 or (330) 384-5022; fax (330) 761-4302
Internet: http://www.firstenergycorp.com/community
Sponsor: FirstEnergy Foundation
76 South Main Street
Akron, OH 44308-1890

Fisa Foundation Grants 715

The foundation's mission is to build a culture of respect and improve the quality of life for three populations in southwestern Pennsylvania: women, girls, and people with disabilities. Emphasis is given to addressing gaps and unmet needs in the community. The foundation will consider support for new and ongoing programs and projects, operating needs, capacity building, equipment, and capital expenditures. Applicants are encouraged to submit a letter of inquiry outlining the needs to be addressed, a brief description of the proposed project or program, and the amount of the request. Letters of inquiry are reviewed on a monthly basis; full proposals are by invitation. Application and guidelines are available online.

Requirements: 501(c)3 and 509(a) nonprofit organizations in the 10-county southwestern Pennsylvania area, including Allegheny, Armstrong, Beaver, Butler, Fayette, Greene, Indiana, Lawrence, Washington and Westmoreland Counties, are eligible.

Restrictions: The foundation does not make grants in support of individuals; political campaigns or lobbying; religious organizations for religious purposes; travel, study and scholarships; services for people with disabilities that result from the aging process; renovations to improve physical accessibility of buildings; programs with the primary mission of serving individuals with mental illness; clinical research; or parenting programs, unless they specifically relate to parents with disabilities.

Geographic Focus: Pennsylvania
Amount of Grant: 5,000 - 75,000 USD
Contact: Mary Delaney, (412) 456-5550; fax (412) 456-5551; info@fisafoundation.org
Internet: http://www.fisafoundation.org/grtmk.ivnu
Sponsor: Fisa Foundation
1001 Liberty Avenue, Suite 650
Pittsburgh, PA 15222

Fisher Foundation Grants 716

The foundation awards grants to Connecticut nonprofits that benefit education, health and human services, housing, community needs, and arts and culture. The majority of grants are single year awards. Before submitting an application, a letter of inquiry or conversation with staff to discuss the specific purpose for which the funds are being requested is strongly recommended. Application information and guidelines are available online. Do not submit applications by fax or email.

Requirements: Nonprofits located in, and/or serving the residents of the Greater Hartford area, including: Andover, Avon, Bloomfield, Bolton, Canton, East Hartford, East Granby, East Windsor, Ellington, Enfield, Farmington, Glastonbury, Granby, Hartford, Hebron, Manchester, Marlborough, Newington, Rocky Hill, Simsbury, Somers, South Windsor, Suffield, Tolland, Vernon, West Hartford, Wethersfield, Windsor, and Windsor Locks are eligible.

Restrictions: Foundation policy does not allow funding for: organizations which are not tax-exempt under IRS Code section 501(c)3; organizations

which have the IRS private foundation designation; individuals; performances, conferences, retreats, one-time events, trips; annual campaigns.
Geographic Focus: Connecticut
Date(s) Application is Due: Jan 15; Apr 15; Sep 15
Contact: Beverly Boyle, Executive Director; (860) 570-0221; fax (860) 570-0225; bboyle@fisherfdn.org
Internet: http://www.fisherfdn.org/application/instructions.htm
Sponsor: Fisher Foundation
36 Brookside Boulevard
West Hartford, CT 06107

Fleishhacker Foundation Education Grants　　　**717**
The Foundation funds precollegiate education, K-12, with an emphasis on the K-8 level. The Foundation's general interest is in programs and projects which: take place at the school site, preferably during the school day; are innovative; involve coordination of programs and services which support the educational process; connect in-school learning to the student's home, community, and cultural life; are cost effective; and show potential for longevity. Application information is available online.
Requirements: Nonprofits in the San Francisco Bay area are eligible.
Restrictions: The foundation does not support: deficit financing; annual funds; endowment campaigns; capital campaigns over $10 million; youth who have dropped out of school; adult education; fundraising events; and travel.
Geographic Focus: California
Date(s) Application is Due: Jan 15; Jul 15
Amount of Grant: 5,000 - 10,000 USD
Contact: Christine Elbel; (415) 561-5350; info@fleishhackerfoundation.org
Internet: http://www.fleishhackerfoundation.org/education.html
Sponsor: Fleishhacker Foundation
P.O. Box 29918
San Francisco, CA 94129-0918

Fleishhacker Foundation Small Grants in the Arts　　　**718**
The particular emphasis of the Program is to support the development and presentation of the work of living Bay Area artists. New work is the first priority, however retrospectives and classical repertory of non-living artists will be considered. Grants may be awarded for: artists' fees for creative time; production costs for performances or film/video projects; exhibition/installation costs for visual, media, or interdisciplinary arts projects; activities that contribute to overall artistic development; and efforts to strengthen an organization's artistic impact within the community.
Requirements: Applicants must be: arts and cultural organizations incorporated as not-for-profit [501(c)3]; organizations residing and offering programming in the greater San Francisco Bay Area; able to demonstrate a consistent artistic presence in the Bay Area for at least 3 years; and of budget size between $100,000 and $750,000.
Restrictions: Not eligible for funding are: programs/projects whose fundamental purpose or benefit falls within the social services, health, youth, or community development fields; individuals (unless conducting a project under the sponsorship of an eligible nonprofit organization; organizations based outside the greater San Francisco Bay Area; or deficit financing, endowment campaigns, major capital campaign requests (campaigns over $10 million).
Geographic Focus: California
Date(s) Application is Due: Jan 15; Jul 15
Amount of Grant: 1,000 - 10,000 USD
Contact: Christine Elbel; (415) 561-5350; info@fleishhackerfoundation.org
Internet: http://www.fleishhackerfoundation.org/small.html
Sponsor: Fleishhacker Foundation
P.O. Box 29918
San Francisco, CA 94129-0918

Fleishhacker Foundation Special Arts Grants　　　**719**
Periodically grants which exceed the scope of the Small Grants Program are made to groups with budgets greater than $750,000. The project must clearly demonstrate potential for broad and long-term impact on the local community and the art form involved. This might involve: facility access or use, community-wide program initiatives, or exceptional artistic projects. Grants normally do not exceed $25,000.
Requirements: Applicants must be: arts and cultural organizations incorporated as not-for-profit [501(c)3]; organizations residing and offering programming in the greater San Francisco Bay Area; and able to demonstrate a consistent artistic presence in the Bay Area for at least 3 years.

Restrictions: Not eligible are capital campaigns over $1 million and endowment campaigns.
Geographic Focus: California
Date(s) Application is Due: Jan 15; Jul 15
Amount of Grant: Up to 25,000 USD
Contact: Christine Elbel; (415) 561-5350; info@fleishhackerfoundation.org
Internet: http://www.fleishhackerfoundation.org/special.html
Sponsor: Fleishhacker Foundation
P.O. Box 29918
San Francisco, CA 94129-0918

Flinn Foundation Grants　　　**720**
The foundation's grantmaking programs, limited to Arizona, include enhancing community-based solutions to local health care needs, especially those for children and youth; strengthening medical education and biomedical research programs in Arizona; strengthening Arizona's universities through an undergraduate scholarship program for outstanding Arizona high school students; and enhancing the visibility and long-term artistic mission of Arizona's principal visual and performing arts organizations. Types of support include program development, seed money, scholarship funds, and research grants.
Requirements: Arizona-based institutions or organizations whose programs are operated for the benefit of Arizona institutions and individuals are eligible to apply. Applications are accepted at any time. There is no application form, but a preliminary letter of inquiry or phone call is requested to determine the appropriateness of a full submission.
Restrictions: The foundation rarely provides grants to individuals, building projects (capital campaigns), purchase of equipment, endowment projects, annual fund-raising campaigns, ongoing operating expenses, or deficit needs. Requests to support conferences and workshops, publications, or the production of films and video are considered only when these activities are an integral component of a larger foundation initiative.
Geographic Focus: Arizona
Amount of Grant: 2,500 - 150,000 USD
Samples: Northern Arizona U (Flagstaff, AZ)—to expand teacher-preparation programs in the biological sciences, $517,100 over three years; Homeward Bound (Phoenix, AZ)—to coordinate access to health care services for disadvantaged children, $10,000; Ballet Arizona (Phoenix, AZ)—for 15 months of support, $200,000.
Contact: JoAnn Fazio; (602) 744-6800; fax (602) 744-6815; info@flinn.org
Internet: http://www.flinn.org/about/grants.cms
Sponsor: Flinn Foundation
1802 N Central Avenue
Phoenix, AZ 85004-1506

Florian O. Bartlett Trust Grants　　　**721**
The Florian O. Bartlett Trust was established in 1937 to support and promote quality educational, human services, and health care programming for underserved populations. The application deadline for the Florian O. Bartlett Trust is April 1. Applicants will be notified of grant decisions before June 30. Grant requests for general operating support are strongly encouraged. Program support will also be considered. Small, program-related capital expenses may be included in general operating or program requests. The majority of grants from the Bartlett Trust are 1 year in duration. On occasion, multi-year support is awarded.
Geographic Focus: Massachusetts
Date(s) Application is Due: Apr 1
Contact: Michealle Larkins; (866) 778-6859; michealle.larkins@baml.com
Internet: https://www.bankofamerica.com/philanthropic/fn_search.action
Sponsor: Florian O. Bartlett Trust
225 Franklin Street, 4th Floor, MA1-225-04-02
Boston, MA 02110

Florida Division of Cultural Affairs Endowment Grants　　　**722**
The purpose of Cultural Endowment grants is to create an endowment matching funds program that will provide operating resources to participating cultural organizations. The Cultural Endowment program is comprised of two components: cultural sponsoring organization (CSO) designation; and receipt of a $240,000 State Matching Share (SMS). Although both parts require the submission of application material, each contains eligibility criteria that are unique to the components. An organization may be designated as a CSO without submitting an application for an SMS. However, CSO designation is an eligibility criterion for the receipt of an SMS.
Requirements: Eligible organizations must be a not-for-profit, tax exempt Florida corporation or a tax exempt organization as defined in Section 501(c)3 or 501(c)4 of

the Internal Revenue Code of 1954. Eligible organizations must be able to provide a description and documentation of a program that qualifies it as a sponsoring organization within a cultural discipline. The description and documentation shall include printed performance or printed exhibition material such as brochures, programs, or catalogs. Applications for designation as a Cultural Sponsoring Organization may be submitted at any time. However, Cultural Sponsoring Organization designation is a criterion for eligibility to receive a State Matching Share. Designation must be recommended by the Florida Arts Council and approved by the Secretary of State before an organization can be considered eligible to receive a State Matching Share. Potential applicants are encouraged to contact the Division to inquire about the Florida Arts Council meeting schedule. An application must be received at least 30 days prior to a regular meeting of the council in order to be included on the agenda. Meetings are held four times a year; generally in March, June, September, and November. Applications for a State Matching Share must be received in the Office of the Division of Cultural Affairs (or the Department of State) by 5:00 p.m. of the deadline date. However, any application postmarked by the United States Postal Service no later than midnight of the deadline date, shall be deemed to have been timely received.
Restrictions: Ineligible programs and organizations are: Programs within the State University System and eligible for support under Section 240.257, Florida Statutes, the Florida Endowment Trust Fund for Eminent Scholars; Community colleges; Direct Support Organizations (i.e., Friends, Foundations, or Trusts) which is not primarily and directly responsible for conducting, creating, producing, presenting, staging, or sponsoring a cultural exhibit, performance, or event; federal, state, county, or city governments.
Geographic Focus: Florida
Amount of Grant: Up to 240,000 USD
Contact: Donald R. Blancett; (850) 245-6483; don.blancett@dos.myflorida.com
Internet: http://www.florida-arts.org/programs/endowment/
Sponsor: Florida Division of Cultural Affairs
500 South Bronough Street, 3rd Floor
Tallahassee, FL 32399-0250

Florida Division of Cultural Affairs General Program Support Grants 723
General Program Support (GPS) funding is designed to support the general program activities of an organization that is realizing its stated mission and furthering the state's cultural objectives by: conducting, creating, producing, presenting, staging, or sponsoring cultural exhibits, performances, educational programs, or events or providing professional services as a State Service Organization or Local Arts Agency. The Division offers three types of General Program Support: discipline-based program support for cultural and artistic programming; local arts agency program support for designated local arts agencies; and state service organization program support for cultural organizations that meet the definition of state service organization.
Requirements: Applicant organizations must be either a public entity or a Florida nonprofit, tax exempt corporation as of the application deadline. Grant request amounts must be matched at least 1:1 ($1 provided by the applicant for every $1 requested from the Division) with cash and in-kind (donated goods or services). Matching funds may be anticipated at the time of application, but must be received by the grant period end date (June 30). All expenses (both state grant and match) must be paid out (not merely encumbered) by the grant period end date.
Restrictions: Applicants must have submitted no other applications for the General Program Support or Specific Cultural Project programs in the current application cycle. No more than 25% of the Total Proposal Expenses may be in-kind. The following may not be used as match: state funds from any source (this includes any income that comes from an appropriation of state funds or grants from the State of Florida); or funds used as match for other Department of State grants.
Geographic Focus: Florida
Date(s) Application is Due: Jun 1
Amount of Grant: Up to 150,000 USD
Contact: Laura Lewis Blischke, Arts Administrator; (850) 245-6475; laura.blischke@dos.myflorida.com
Internet: http://www.florida-arts.org/programs/gps/
Sponsor: Florida Division of Cultural Affairs
500 South Bronough Street, 3rd Floor
Tallahassee, FL 32399-0250

Florida Division of Cultural Affairs Multidisciplinary Grants 724
Florida Division of Cultural Affairs discipline-based projects are discipline specific for organizations conducting cultural projects, realizing their stated mission, and furthering the state's cultural objectives. The Multidisciplinary discipline is for projects with programming that presents two or more separate artistic or cultural disciplines. Artistic and cultural disciplines include, but are not limited to: music; dance; theatre; creative writing; literature; architecture; painting; sculpture; folk arts; photography; crafts; media arts; and visual arts. The grant period start date is July 1 or the date the award agreement is executed, whichever is later. The grant period end date is June 30 unless an end date extension is approved by the Division. Multidisciplinary projects have a maximum request of $25,000.
Requirements: To meet the legal status requirement, an applicant organization must be either a public entity (Florida local government, entity of state government, school district, community college, college, or university) or a Florida nonprofit, tax exempt corporation as of the application deadline. Private schools, private community colleges, private colleges, and private universities are not public entities and must be nonprofit and tax exempt to meet the legal status requirement. Applicants must provide at least one dollar in cash and in-kind (donated goods or services) for every dollar requested from the division. Allowable expenses must be: directly related to the proposal; specifically and clearly detailed in the proposal budget; and incurred and paid within the grant start and end dates.
Restrictions: The following are non-allowable expenses for grant and matching funds: state funds from any source; funds used as match for other Department of State grants; expenses incurred or obligated before July 1 or after the grant period; lobbying or attempting to influence federal, state, or local legislation; building, renovation, or remodeling of facilities; capital expenditures (includes acquisitions, building projects, and renovations); costs associated with bad debts, contingencies (money set aside for possible expenses), fines and penalties, interest, taxes, and other financial costs; private entertainment, food, and beverages; plaques, awards, and scholarships; re-granting; contributions and donations; mortgage payments; or payments to current Department of State employees. No state funds may be used towards operational costs such as: phone; utilities; office supplies; equipment costing over $1,000; property improvements; fixtures; building maintenance; space rental; or other overhead or indirect costs.
Geographic Focus: Florida
Amount of Grant: Up to 25,000 USD
Contact: Laura Lewis Blischke, Program Manager; (850) 245-6475; llblischke@dos.state.fl.us
Internet: http://www.florida-arts.org/documents/guidelines/2012-2013.scp.guidelines.cfm#multidisciplinary
Sponsor: Florida Division of Cultural Affairs
500 South Bronough Street, 3rd Floor
Tallahassee, FL 32399-0250

Florida Division of Cultural Affairs Professional Theatre Grants 725
Florida Division of Cultural Affairs theatre disciplines support projects that promote excellence in theatre performance. The Professional Theatre discipline is for producing professional theatres. Organizations applying to the Professional Theatre discipline must compensate their artistic staff and actors. Professional Theatre panelists strongly emphasize the importance of payment to actors. Companies should be very specific when describing the financial compensation and/or benefits that are offered to artistic staff and actors. For information on minimum pay rates for actors and staff contact a theatrical union such as Actors Equity. The grant period start date is July 1 or the date the award agreement is executed, whichever is later. The grant period end date is June 30 unless an end date extension is approved by the Division. Projects have a maximum request of $25,000.
Requirements: To meet the legal status requirement, an applicant organization must be either a public entity (Florida local government, entity of state government, school district, community college, college, or university) or a Florida nonprofit, tax exempt corporation as of the application deadline. Private schools, private community colleges, private colleges, and private universities are not public entities and must be nonprofit and tax exempt to meet the legal status requirement. Applicants must provide at least one dollar in cash and in-kind (donated goods or services) for every dollar requested from the division. Allowable expenses must be: directly related to the proposal; specifically and clearly detailed in the proposal budget; and incurred and paid within the grant start and end dates.
Restrictions: The following are non-allowable expenses for grant and matching funds: state funds from any source; funds used as match for other Department of State grants; expenses incurred or obligated before July 1 or after the grant period; lobbying or attempting to influence federal, state, or local legislation; building, renovation, or remodeling of facilities; capital expenditures (includes acquisitions, building projects, and renovations); costs associated with bad debts, contingencies (money set aside for possible expenses), fines and penalties, interest, taxes, and other financial costs; private entertainment, food, and beverages; plaques, awards, and scholarships; re-granting; contributions and donations; mortgage payments; or payments to current Department of State employees.

No state funds may be used towards operational costs such as: phone; utilities; office supplies; equipment costing over $1,000; property improvements; fixtures; building maintenance; space rental; or other overhead or indirect costs.
Geographic Focus: Florida
Amount of Grant: Up to 25,000 USD
Contact: Sarah T. Stage, ; (850) 245-6459; sstage@dos.state.fl.us
Internet: http://www.florida-arts.org/documents/guidelines/2012-2013.scp. guidelines.cfm#theatre
Sponsor: Florida Division of Cultural Affairs
500 South Bronough Street, 3rd Floor
Tallahassee, FL 32399-0250

Florida Division of Cultural Affairs Specific Cultural Project Grants   726
The Specific Cultural Project (SCP) grant is designed to fund a cultural project, program, exhibition, or series taking place within the grant period (July 1 through June 30). The grant activities must support the mission of the organization and further the state's cultural objectives. The Division offers four project types: Arts In Education projects (promote arts and culture in education); Discipline-Based cultural or artistic projects; Culture Builds Florida projects (directly promote one or more elements of the state's cultural strategic plan); and, Underserved Cultural Community Development projects (assist with the development of underserved cultural organizations).
Requirements: An applicant organization must be either a public entity or a Florida nonprofit, tax exempt corporation as of the application deadline. Specific Cultural Projects have a maximum request of $25,000, except for Underserved Cultural Community Development projects. Grant request amounts must be matched at least 1:1 ($1 provided by the applicant for every $1 requested from the Division) with cash and in-kind (donated goods or services). No more than 25% of the Total Proposal Expenses may be in-kind. Matching funds may be anticipated at the time of application, but must be received by the grant period end date (June 30). All expenses (both state grant and match) must be paid out (not merely encumbered) by the grant period end date.
Restrictions: An organization may only submit one Specific Cultural Project or one General Program Support application for each annual grant cycle (July 1 to June 30). Grant funds may not be used for indirect or overhead expenses. All expenses must be directly related to the project detailed in the application. State funds from any source may not be used as match. This includes any income that comes from an appropriation or grant from the State of Florida. Funds used as match for other Department of State grants may not be used as match.
Geographic Focus: Florida
Date(s) Application is Due: Jun 1
Amount of Grant: Up to 25,000 USD
Contact: Sarah Stage, Arts Administrator; (850) 245-6459; fax (850) 245-6497; sarah.stage@dos.myflorida.com
Laura Lewis Blischke, Arts Administrator; (850) 245-6475; fax (850) 245-6497; laura.blischke@dos.myflorida.com
Internet: http://www.florida-arts.org/programs/scp/
Sponsor: Florida Division of Cultural Affairs
500 South Bronough Street, 3rd Floor
Tallahassee, FL 32399-0250

**Florida Division of Cultural Affairs Underserved Cultural   727
  Community Development Grants**
Underserved Cultural Community Development projects support the organizational development of underserved cultural organizations. There are three funding categories for Underserved Cultural Community Development projects: capacity building; consultant; and salary assistance. Capacity building funding provides up to $2,000 for projects that increase administrative or artistic capacity. Eligible projects include but are not limited to: staff and/or volunteer exchange; professional development opportunities such as attendance at seminars and workshops; plan development opportunities such as fundraising, marketing, and arts education; and equipment and technology needs. Consultant funding category provides up to $5,000 for retaining consultants that can provide specific administrative or artistic needs. The Salary Assistance funding category allows applicants to request up to $20,000 for the full or partial salary support for one or more positions.
Requirements: All applicants to this proposal type must meet the following criteria: meet basic eligibility requirements; be an underserved (rural, minority, or lacking in resources) cultural organization; have a Total Cash Income (from the applicant's most recently completed fiscal year) of $150,000 or less; and have at least one year of completed programming.
Restrictions: The following are non-allowable expenses for grant and matching funds: state funds from any source; funds used as match for other Department

of State grants; expenses incurred or obligated before July 1 or after the grant period; lobbying or attempting to influence federal, state, or local legislation; building, renovation, or remodeling of facilities; capital expenditures (includes acquisitions, building projects, and renovations); costs associated with bad debts, contingencies (money set aside for possible expenses), fines and penalties, interest, taxes, and other financial costs; private entertainment, food, and beverages; plaques, awards, and scholarships; re-granting; contributions and donations; mortgage payments; or payments to current Department of State employees. No state funds may be used towards operational costs such as: phone; utilities; office supplies; equipment costing over $1,000; property improvements; fixtures; building maintenance; space rental; or other overhead or indirect costs.
Geographic Focus: Florida
Amount of Grant: Up to 20,000 USD
Contact: Laura Lewis Blischke, Program Manager; (850) 245-6475; llblischke@dos.state.fl.us
Internet: http://www.florida-arts.org/documents/guidelines/2012-2013.scp. guidelines.cfm#ucd
Sponsor: Florida Division of Cultural Affairs
500 South Bronough Street, 3rd Floor
Tallahassee, FL 32399-0250

Fluor Foundation Grants   728
The Fluor Corporation achieves its contribution objectives through the Fluor Foundation and corporate giving. The Foundation's areas of interest are: education; human services; cultural outreach; and public/civic affairs. The Foundation considers requests for operating, program, capital or endowment support. Priority is given to funding organizations with employee volunteer participation. Application information is available online.
Requirements: Fluor's giving programs focus on community organizations in those locations around the world where the company has a presence. See website for local contact information: http://www.fluor.com/sustainability/community/fluor_giving/Pages/applying_for_fluor_foundation_grants.aspx
Restrictions: Funding is not available for: film production/publishing activities; individuals; sports organizations/programs; veterans, fraternal, labor or religious organizations; or lobbying/political organizations or campaigns.
Geographic Focus: Alaska, California, Louisiana, New Jersey, New York, North Carolina, Pennsylvania, South Carolina, Tennessee, Texas, Virginia, Washington, Albania, Andorra, Armenia, Australia, Austria, Azerbaijan, Belarus, Belgium, Bosnia & Herzegovina, Bulgaria, Canada, Caribbean, China, Croatia, Cyprus, Czech Republic, Denmark, Estonia, Finland, France, Georgia, Germany, Greece, Hungary, Iceland, Ireland, Italy, Japan, Kosovo, Latvia, Liechtenstein, Lithuania, Luxembourg, Macedonia, Malta, Mexico, Moldova, Monaco, Montenegro, New Zealand, Norway, Peru, Philippines, Poland, Poland, Portugal, Romania, Russia, Russia, San Marino, Serbia, Slovakia, Slovenia, Spain, Sweden, Switzerland, The Netherlands, Turkey, Ukraine, United Kingdom, Vatican City, Venezuela
Contact: Suzanne Esber, Executive Director of Community Relations; (949) 349-7847; fax (949) 349-7694; suzanne.esber@fluor.com
Internet: http://www.fluor.com/sustainability/community/fluor_giving/Pages/applying_for_fluor_foundation_grants.aspx
Sponsor: Fluor Foundation
3 Polaris Way
Aliso Viejo, CA 92698

FMC Foundation Grants   729
The foundation supports education, community improvement, urban affairs, health and human services, and public issues/economic education. Higher education is supported through scholarships and employee matching gifts. Education support tends to be in business, engineering, chemistry, and some minority education programs. Eligible applicants need to contact the FMC in their geograhic area. Each individual FMC location determines how their contributions will be given.
Requirements: Grants are awarded to 501(c)3 organizations in FMC-plant communities. US-based organizations with an international focus are also eligible.
Restrictions: Grants are not made to individuals.
Geographic Focus: Arizona, California, Delaware, Florida, Illinois, Louisiana, Maine, Maryland, Missouri, New Jersey, New York, North Carolina, Pennsylvania, Tennessee, Texas, West Virginia, Wyoming, Canada
Contact: Program Contact; (215) 299-6000; fax (215) 299-6140
Internet: http://www.fmc.com
Sponsor: FMC Foundation
1735 Market Street
Philadelphia, PA 19103

Foellinger Foundation Grants 730

The foundation awards grants primarily in Fort Wayne and Allen County, IN, to improve the quality of life in the areas of early child development, youth development, strengthening family services, strengthening organizations, and community concerns. Special emphasis is given to projects/programs that help children and their families, particularly those with the greatest economic need and least opportunity. By doing so, the Foundation hopes to help children and their families move from dependence to independence. In addition to programs and projects, the foundation also awards grants for general operating, capital, seed money, renovation projects, conferences and seminars, consulting services, equipment, challenge/matching, and planning purposes.

Requirements: Indiana organizations are eligible to apply.

Restrictions: The foundation does not fund scholarships, travel assistance, conference fees, religious groups, public or private elementary or secondary schools, sponsorships, special events, advertising, or endowments.

Geographic Focus: Indiana

Date(s) Application is Due: Feb 1; May 1; Nov 1

Amount of Grant: 10,000 - 100,000 USD

Samples: Public Broadcasting of Northeast Indiana (IN)—for general operating support; Arthur J. Blaising Social Services (IN)—for its after-school program and its 10-week summer day camp, $75,585; Turnstone (IN)—for a transportation program that serves elderly and disabled people, $187,500 over 18 months; Taylor U—for the Allen County Postsecondary Education Consortium, $219,690 over two years.

Contact: Cheryl Taylor; (219) 422-2900; fax (219) 422-9436; info@foellinger.org

Internet: http://www.foellinger.org

Sponsor: Foellinger Foundation

520 E Berry Street

Fort Wayne, IN 46802

Forest Foundation Grants 731

The Foundation awards grants to eligible Washington nonprofit organizations in its areas of interest, including community and economic development; environment; and youth development. The Foundation gives primarily to southwestern Washington counties, with emphasis on Pierce, Clallum, Cowlitz; Clark, Grays Harbor, Jefferson, Kitsap, Lewis, Mason, Pacific, Skamania; Thurston; and Wahkiakum. The Foundation Board meets six times per year. Organizations receive notification of funding in within 90 days.

Requirements: The Foundation should be initially approached with an email request for guidelines and instructions. Full proposals are by invitation only. Organizations should submit the following: copy of IRS Determination Letter; a brief history of organization and description of its mission; a listing of board of directors, trustees, officers and other key people and their affiliations; detailed description of project and amount of funding requested; a copy of the organization's current budget and/or project budget.

Restrictions: Grants do not funding for buildings or renovation projects.

Geographic Focus: Washington

Amount of Grant: 15,000 - 150,000 USD

Samples: Tacoma Rescue Mission, Tacoma, WA, $150,000 payable over one year; Tacoma Community College Foundation, Tacoma, WA, $100,000 payable over one year; Helping Hand House, Puyallup, WA, $20,000 payable over one year; Exodus Housing, Sumner, WA, $15,000 payable over one year.

Contact: Angela Baptiste; (253) 627-1634; fax (253) 627-6249

Sponsor: Forest Foundation

820 A Street, Suite 345

Tacoma, WA 98402

Forest Lawn Foundation Grants 732

The foundation awards grants in Los Angeles and Orange Counties, CA, to organizations serving youth and the disabled and to hospitals, welfare, and social service agencies. Types of support include continuing support, emergency funds, general purposes, matching funds, operating budgets, and special projects. Contact office for program availability.

Requirements: Nonprofit organizations in Los Angeles County and Orange County may apply.

Restrictions: Grants do not support federated appeals, political purposes, or projects/programs normally funded by the government.

Geographic Focus: California

Amount of Grant: 1,000 - 200,000 USD

Contact: Program Contact

Sponsor: Forest Lawn Foundation

1712 S Glendale Avenue

Glendale, CA 91205

Forever Young Foundation Grants 733

The Foundation serves children facing significant physical, emotional, and financial challenges. Grants are considered for organizations seeking to provide academic, athletic, and therapeutic opportunities currently unavailable to these children. The foundation has determined the best way to accomplish its mission is through the development and support of charitable organizations with a proven track record in delivering these services.

Requirements: In reviewing grant requests, FYF requires: requests to be from the Northern California, Utah, and Arizona region; the organization have a non-profit 501(c)3 tax-exempt charity status; goals fall under the mission of the Forever Young Foundation; organizations that do not discriminate by race, religion, color, creed, sex, or national origin; adequate financial resources for performance, the necessary experience, organizational, and technical qualifications, or a firm commitment, arrangement, or ability to obtain such, and; adequate financial management system and audit procedures that provide efficient and effective accountability and control of all property, funds, and other assets.

Geographic Focus: Arizona, California, Utah

Contact: Sterling Tanner, President & Executive Director; (800) 994-3837; sterling@foreveryoung.org

Internet: http://www.foreveryoung.org/donations.html?charityid=fore&homeurl=http://www.foreveryoung.org/foundation/

Sponsor: Steve Young Foundation

1424 S Stapley Drive

Mesa, AZ 85204

Foster Foundation Grants 734

The Foundation funds effective, nonprofit organizations that can provide tangible benefits and ongoing support to improve the quality of life for individuals, families and communities within the Pacific Northwest. The Foundation's primary field of interests are: basic human welfare issues, education, medical research, treatment and care and cultural activities. The Foundation places special emphasis on meeting the needs of the underserved and disadvantaged segments of the population, especially children, women and seniors.

Requirements: Eligible applicants must: be a nonprofit located in or serving the populations of the Pacific Northwest; address as their mission or project intent one of the Foundation's priority issues for funding; not have any delinquent final reports due to the Foundation from previous grant cycles.

Restrictions: The Foundation will not consider requests for: direct grants, scholarships or loans for the benefit of specific individuals; projects of organizations whose policies or practices discriminate on the basis of race, ethnic origin, sex, creed or sexual orientation; contributions or program support for sectarian or religious organizations whose activities benefit only their members; or loans.

Geographic Focus: Alaska, Idaho, Montana, Oregon, Washington

Contact: Jill Goodsell, Executive Director; (206) 726-1815; fax (206) 903-0628; info@thefosterfoundation.org

Internet: http://thefosterfoundation.org/Grants_Guide.asp

Sponsor: Foster Foundation

601 Union Street, Suite 3707

Seattle, WA 98101

Foundation Northwest Grants 735

Grants are awarded to organizations in the Inland Northwest—eastern Washington and northern Idaho—for charitable and educational purposes in the fields of music and drama; education; civic categories which include culture, education, civic and community development; and human services. The foundation has five distinct grant programs and types of support include matching funds, special projects, seed money, and occasional operating support and capital funding. Deadlines vary according to area and contributing sponsorship; contact program support for exact dates.

Requirements: Grant applications are accepted for projects that will enrich the quality of life in the communities of eastern Washington and northern Idaho. Eligible Washington counties include Adams, Asotin, Columbia, Ferry, Garfield, Lincoln, Pend Oreille, Spokane, Steven, and Whitman. Eligible Idaho counties include Benewah, Bonner, Boundary, Clearwater, Idaho, Kootenai, Latah, Lewis, Nez Perce, and Shoshone.

Restrictions: Grants do not support endowments, debt retirement, lobbying, sectarian religious purposes, individuals, travel, sports teams and classes, projects that taxpayers or commercial interests normally support, fundraising campaigns, publications or films (unless an integral part of a foundation-supported program), or nondonor-supported research.

Geographic Focus: Idaho, Washington

Amount of Grant: 2,500 - 7,500 USD

Contact: Program Contact; (509) 624-2606; fax (509) 624-2608; admin@
foundationnw.org
Internet: http://www.foundationnw.org
Sponsor: Foundation Northwest
221 Wall Street N, Suite 624
Spokane, WA 99201-0826

Foundations of East Chicago Education Grants   736

The Foundations of East Chicago, Indiana, is funded by the Resorts East
Chicago Casino and Hotel. The Foundations is committed to funding programs
and initiatives which support the education of its citizens – mind, body and spirit
– at every age. Such programs or projects are focused on addressing improvement
of the quality of educational achievement of East Chicago students.
Requirements: Applicants must be registered 501(c)3 organizations or schools
located in East Chicago, Indiana. If an applicant is not located in East
Chicago, it may still qualify if it complies with at least one of the following
requirements: the program that an applicant is applying for operates in East
Chicago; the funding that an applicant is applying for will go toward assisting
East Chicago residents.
Restrictions: All applications must be submitted via Foundations of East
Chicago website. The Foundations will not accept any applications in person.
Geographic Focus: Indiana
Amount of Grant: Up to 15,000 USD
Contact: Russell G. Taylor, Executive Director; (219) 392-4225; fax (219)
392-4245; grantinfo@foundationsofeastchicago.org
Internet: http://foundationsofeastchicago.org/apply-now
Sponsor: Foundations of East Chicago
100 W Chicago Avenue
East Chicago, IN 46312

Fourjay Foundation Grants   737

The Foundation supports only those organizations whose chief purpose is to
improve health and/or promote education, within Philadelphia, Montgomery,
and Bucks counties in southeastern Pennsylvania. The Fourjay Foundation
requires no specific application form. It will consider proposals that address
a well-defined need, offer a concrete plan of action, and request a specific
amount, from organizations whose staff has the ingenuity, commitment,
and motivation to carry out the proposal's objectives. Requests may be for
operating support, project specific funds, or capital funds.
Requirements: Organizations serving Philadelphia, Montgomery, and Bucks
Counties in southeastern Pennsylvania are eligible.
Restrictions: Funding is not available for: charities operating outside
Montgomery, Bucks, or Philadelphia counties; individuals; elementary or
secondary educational institutions; museums, musical groups, theaters, or
cultural organizations; religious organizations in support of their sacramental
or theological functions; political groups or related think tanks; athletic
organizations or alumni associations; libraries; public radio or television;
United Way or the YMCA; civic organizations; organizations that have
applied or been funded within the last 12 month period.
Geographic Focus: Pennsylvania
Date(s) Application is Due: Mar 1; Jun 1; Sep 1; Dec 1
Amount of Grant: 1,000 - 10,000 USD
Contact: Ann T. Bucci; (215) 830-1437; fax (215) 830-0157; abucci@fourjay.org
Internet: http://www.fourjay.org/grantGuidelines.asp
Sponsor: Fourjay Foundation
2300 Computer Avenue, Building G, Suite 1
Willow Grove, PA 19090-1753

Frances and Benjamin Benenson Foundation Grants   738

The foundation awards grants to nonprofit organizations in support of community
services, international ministries and missions, Jewish education, Jewish welfare,
and religious welfare. Types of support include general operating support and
scholarships. There are no application deadlines. Applications must be made in
writing, stating the purpose of the grant and the amount requested.
Requirements: Nonprofits of the Jewish and Roman Catholic faiths are eligible.
Restrictions: Grants are not made to individuals.
Geographic Focus: All States
Contact: Bruce W. Benenson, Vice President; (212) 867-0990; fax (212) 983-
1952; bbenenson@benensoncapital.com
Sponsor: Frances and Benjamin Benenson Foundation
708 Third Avenue, 28th Floor
New York, NY 10017

Francis A. and Jacquelyn H. Harrington Foundation Grants   739

The foundation supports requests from health, educational, and cultural
organizations that are providing solutions to, or prevention of, problems within
the immediate Worcester, MA, community area and that are receiving additional
support from other funding sources. Types of support include capital campaigns,
equipment acquisition, general operating support, and program development. A
proposal should be in letter form and should include the goals and objectives of
the request together with a plan for accomplishing the same. The trustees meet
twice each year, once in late summer to review requests received to date and
again in December to review requests and confirm grants. The foundation does
not make human service grants. Instead, all human service requests should be
sent to the Greater Worcester Community Foundation, where the foundation
has established the Francis A. and Jacquelyn H. Harrington Fund.
Requirements: The foundation provides grants to 501(c)3 tax-exempt
organizations that are based in the Worcester, MA, area.
Geographic Focus: Massachusetts
Date(s) Application is Due: Jun 1
Contact: Sumner Tilton Jr., Trustee; (508) 798-8621
Sponsor: Francis A. and Jacquelyn H. Harrington Foundation
370 Main Street, 12th Floor
Worcester, MA 01608

Francis Beidler Foundation Grants   740

Established in Illinois in 1997, the Francis Beidler Foundation offers support
for human service programs in Chicago, Illinois. Its primary fields of interest
include: children and youth services; education; health organizations; higher
education; children's museums; public affairs; and public safety. There are no
established deadlines or application formats. Applicants should begin the
process by submitting a letter describing the organization, a detailed overview
of the project, and amount of funding requested. Organizational literature
should accompany the application letter. Grants range up to $60,000.
Requirements: Organizations serving the Chicago area are eligible to apply.
Geographic Focus: Illinois
Amount of Grant: Up to 60,000 USD
Contact: Thomas B. Dorris, Trustee; (312) 922-3792
Sponsor: Francis Beidler Foundation
53 W. Jackson Boulevard, Suite 530
Chicago, IL 60604-3422

Francis Families Foundation Grants   741

In carrying out its mission, the foundation awards grants to educational and art
and cultural institutions in the greater Kansas City metropolitan area. Areas
of interest under education include child and youth development and higher
education. Under arts and culture, priority consideration is given to programs
that benefit major arts institutions, provide stability, enhance programming,
or assist the artistic or fiscal growth of such organizations; and educational arts
programming that has children as its focus. Support may be ongoing or a one-
time contribution and may include capital campaigns, pledges, general operations,
fellowships, or special projects. Interested persons should call or write to determine
whether their organization/project falls within foundation guidelines. Eligibility
varies between programs; contact program staff for eligibility.
Requirements: The applying entity must be tax-exempt under the IRS code and
geographically located within the greater Kansas City area (60 mile radius).
Restrictions: The foundation does not make grants to individuals.
Geographic Focus: Missouri
Date(s) Application is Due: Jul 28
Samples: Child and youth development programs and organizations (Kansas
City, KS)—$1.3 million total; Art and cultural programs and organizations
(Kansas City, KS)—$265,428 total.
Contact: Lyn Knox; (816) 531-0077; webmaster@francisfoundation.org
Internet: http://www.francisfoundation.org/application.htm
Sponsor: Francis Families Foundation
800 W 47th Street, Suite 717
Kansas City, MO 64112

Frank and Lydia Bergen Foundation Grants   742

The mission and goals of the Frank and Lydia Bergen Foundation are: to arrange
for musical entertainments, concerts and recitals of a character appropriate
for the education and instruction of the public in the musical arts. Paramount
consideration is given to traditional classical music programs; to aid worthy
students of music in securing a complete and adequate musical education; to aid
organizations in their efforts to present fine music to the public, provided that such
organizations are operated exclusively for educational purposes. Support is offered

in the form of: scholarships; program development; capital campaigns; financial aid; community outreach programs; community programs; artist-in-residency programs and; general operating support. Applications are due April 10, for the June meeting & August 15, for the October meeting. Grant applications forms are available online. Applicants will receive notice acknowledging receipt of the grant request, and subsequently be notified of the grant declination or approval.

Requirements: Qualifying tax-exempt 501(c)3 organizations are eligible to apply. There is no geographic restriction but applying organizations must be operating exclusively for educational purposes. Proposals should be submitted in the following format: completed Common Grant Application Form; an original Proposal Statement; an audited financial report and a current year operating budget;a copy of your official IRS Letter with your tax determination; a listing of your Board of Directors. Proposal Statements (second item in the above Format) should answer these questions: what are the objectives and expected outcomes of this program/project/request; what strategies will be used to accomplish your objective; what is the timeline for completion; if this is part of an on-going program, how long has it been in operation; what criteria will you use to measure success; if the request is not fully funded, what other sources can you engage; an Itemized budget should be included; please describe any collaborative ventures. Prior to the distribution of funds, all approved grantees must sign and return a Grant Agreement Form, stating that the funds will be used for the purpose intended. Progress reports and Completion reports must also be filed as required for your specific grant. All current grantees must be in good standing with required documentation prior to submitting new proposals to any foundation.

Restrictions: Grants are not made for political purposes, nor to organizations which discriminate on the basis of race, ethnic origin, sexual or religious preference, age or gender.

Geographic Focus: All States
Date(s) Application is Due: Apr 10; Aug 15
Amount of Grant: 3,000 - 60,000 USD
Samples: New Jersey Symphony Orchestra, $60,000—Greater Newark Youth/ Chamber Orchestras, program support; Newark School of the Arts, $20,000— financial aid and scholarship assistance for music students; Harmonium, A Classical Choral Society, Inc., $8,000—orchestra funding and artists' fees.
Contact: Gale Y. Sykes; (908) 598-3576; grantinquiries2@wachovia.com
Internet: https://www.wachovia.com/foundation/v/index.jsp?vgnextoid=9908 52199c0aa110VgnVCM1000004b0d1872RCRD&vgnextfmt=default
Sponsor: Frank and Lydia Bergen Foundation
190 River Road, NJ3132
Summit, NJ 07901

Frank B. Hazard General Charity Fund Grants 743

The Frank B. Hazard General Charity Fund was established in 1924 to support charitable organizations that work to improve the lives of "the poor, or the poor sick." Organizations receiving support from the fund must be managed and/or governed by individuals a majority of whom are of the Protestant religious faith. Grant requests for general operating support or program support are strongly encouraged. The majority of grants from the Hazard General Charity Fund are one year in duration. Applicants must apply online at the grant website. Applicants are strongly encouraged to do the following before applying: review the downloadable state application procedures for additional helpful information and clarifications; review the downloadable online-application guidelines at the grant website; review the trust's funding history (link is available from the grant website); review the online application questions in advance; and review the list of required attachments. These will generally include: a list of board members, financial statements (audited, reviewed, or compiled by independent auditor); an organization summary; a list of other funding sources; an IRS Determination letter; and other required documents. All attachments must be uploaded in the online application as PDF, Word, or Excel files. The application deadline for the Frank B. Hazard General Charity Fund is 11:59 p.m. on December 1. Applicants will be notified of grant decisions before January 31 of the following year.

Requirements: Applicants must have 501(c)3 tax-exempt status.
Restrictions: The Hazard General Charity Fund specifically supports charitable organizations that serve the people of Providence, Rhode Island. The fund does not support requests from individuals, organizations attempting to influence policy through direct lobbying, or any political campaigns.
Geographic Focus: Rhode Island
Date(s) Application is Due: Dec 1
Samples: Family Service, Providence, Rhode Island, $10,000; Community Preparatory School, Providence, Rhode Island, $17,000; Rhode Island Free Clinic, Providence, Rhode Island, $10,000.

Contact: Emma Greene; (617) 434-0329; emma.m.greene@baml.com
Internet: https://www.bankofamerica.com/philanthropic/fn_search.action
Sponsor: Frank B. Hazard General Charity Fund
225 Franklin Street, 4th Floor, MA1-225-04-02
Boston, MA 02110

Frank E. and Seba B. Payne Foundation Grants 744

The foundation awards grants in the Chicago, IL, area and in Pennsylvania in its areas of interest, including AIDS prevention, children and youth, cultural activities, education, and hospitals. Types of support include building construction/renovation, equipment acquisition, and general operating support.

Requirements: Nonprofit organizations in the greater Chicago, IL, metropolitan area and in Pennsylvania are eligible.
Restrictions: Grants are not made to individuals.
Geographic Focus: Illinois, Pennsylvania
Contact: M. Catherine Ryan, c/o Bank of America, (312) 828-1785
Sponsor: Frank E. Payne and Seba B. Payne Foundation
231 S LaSalle Street
Chicago, IL 60697

Frank G. and Freida K. Brotz Family Foundation Grants 745

The Foundation supports Wisconsin nonprofits of the Christian, Lutheran, and Roman Catholic faiths, including Salvation Army. Types of support include capital support and general support. Organizations eligible to receive support include colleges and universities, community service groups, hospitals, ministries, parochial schools and religious education organizations, religious welfare organizations, and youth organizations. There are no application forms or deadlines. Applicants should submit a brief letter of inquiry that contains a description of the organization, its purpose, purpose of grant, and proof of tax-exempt status.

Requirements: Grants are awarded to publicly supported, Section 170(c) IRS qualified organizations, primarily in the State of Wisconsin.
Restrictions: No grants are awarded to individuals or organizations that require expenditure responsibility under Treasury Regulations.
Geographic Focus: Wisconsin
Contact: Stuart W. Brotz; (920) 458-2121; fax (920) 458-1923
Sponsor: Frank G. and Freida K. Brotz Family Foundation
3518 Lakeshore Road, P.O. Box 551
Sheboygan, WI 53082-0551

Frank Reed and Margaret Jane Peters Memorial Fund I Grants 746

The Frank Reed & Margaret Jane Peters Memorial Fund I was established in 1935 to support and promote quality educational, human-services, and health-care programming for underserved populations. Special consideration is given to charitable organizations that serve youth and children. The Peters Memorial Fund I is a generous supporter of the Associated Grant Makers (AGM) Summer Fund. The AGM Summer Fund is a collaborative group of donors that provides operating support for summer camps serving low-income urban youth from Boston, Cambridge, Chelsea, and Somerville. Excluding the grant made to the AGM Summer Fund, the typical grant range is $10,000 to $40,000. Grant requests for general operating support are strongly encouraged. Program support will also be considered. Small, program-related capital expenses may be included in general operating or program requests. The majority of grants from the Peters Memorial Fund I are one year in duration; on occasion, multi-year support is awarded. Applicants must apply online at the grant website. Applicants are strongly encouraged to do the following before applying: review the downloadable state application procedures for additional helpful information and clarifications; review the downloadable online-application guidelines at the grant website; review the foundation's funding history (link is available from the grant website); review the online application questions in advance; and review the list of required attachments. These will generally include: a list of board members, financial statements (audited, reviewed, or compiled by independent auditor); an organization summary; a list of other funding sources; an IRS Determination letter; and other required documents. All attachments must be uploaded in the online application as PDF, Word, or Excel files. The application deadline for the Frank Reed & Margaret Jane Peters Memorial Fund I is 11:59 p.m. on September 1. Applicants will be notified of grant decisions before November 30.

Requirements: Applicants must have 501(c)3 tax-exempt status.
Restrictions: The fund does not support requests from individuals, organizations attempting to influence policy through direct lobbying, or any political campaigns.
Geographic Focus: Massachusetts
Date(s) Application is Due: Sep 1
Amount of Grant: 10,000 - 40,000 USD

Samples: Generations, Inc., Boston, Massachusetts, $20,000, general operating support; Boston Scholars Program, Boston, Massachusetts, $15,000, general operating support; Family Service, Lawrence, Massachusetts, $15,000, Youth Mentoring Department program development.
Contact: Miki C. Akimoto, Vice; (866) 778-6859; miki.akimoto@baml.com
Internet: https://www.bankofamerica.com/philanthropic/fn_search.action
Sponsor: Frank Reed and Margaret Jane Peters Memorial Fund I
225 Franklin Street, 4th Floor, MA1-225-04-02
Boston, MA 02110

Frank Reed and Margaret Jane Peters Memorial Fund II Grants   747

The Frank Reed & Margaret Jane Peters Memorial Fund II was established in 1935 to support and promote quality educational, human-services, and health-care programming for underserved populations. In the area of education, the fund supports academic access, enrichment, and remedial programming for children, youth, adults, and senior citizens that focuses on preparing individuals to achieve while in school and beyond. In the area of health care, the fund supports programming that improves access to primary care for traditionally underserved individuals, health education initiatives and programming that impact at-risk populations, and medical research. In the area of human services the fund tries to meet evolving needs of communities. Currently the fund's focus is on (but is not limited to) youth development, violence prevention, employment, life-skills attainment, and food programs. Grant requests for general operating support are strongly encouraged. Program support will also be considered. Small, program-related capital expenses may be included in general operating or program requests. The majority of grants from the Peters Memorial Fund II are one year in duration; on occasion, multi-year support is awarded. Applicants must apply online at the grant website. Applicants are strongly encouraged to do the following before applying: review the downloadable state application procedures for additional helpful information and clarifications; review the downloadable online-application guidelines at the grant website; review the foundation's funding history (link is available from the grant website); review the online application questions in advance; and review the list of required attachments. These will generally include: a list of board members, financial statements (audited, reviewed, or compiled by independent auditor); an organization summary; a list of other funding sources; an IRS Determination letter; and other required documents. All attachments must be uploaded in the online application as PDF, Word, or Excel files. The application deadline for the Frank Reed & Margaret Jane Peters Memorial Fund II is 11:59 p.m. on July 1. Applicants will be notified of grant decisions before September 30.
Requirements: Applicants must have 501(c)3 tax-exempt status.
Restrictions: In general, capital requests are not advised. The fund does not support endowment campaigns, events such as galas or award ceremonies, and costs of fundraising events. The fund does not support requests from individuals, organizations attempting to influence policy through direct lobbying, or any political campaigns.
Geographic Focus: Massachusetts
Date(s) Application is Due: Jul 1
Samples: Epiphany School, Dorchester, Massachusetts, $20,000, general operating support; Esther R. Sanger Center for Compassion, Wollaston, Massachusetts, $15,000, for general operating support; Boston Learning Center, Boston, Massachusetts, $20,000, general operating support.
Contact: Michealle Larkins; (866) 778-6859; michealle.larkins@baml.com
Internet: https://www.bankofamerica.com/philanthropic/fn_search.action
Sponsor: Frank Reed and Margaret Jane Peters Memorial Fund II
225 Franklin Street, 4th Floor, MA1-225-04-02
Boston, MA 02110

Frank S. Flowers Foundation Grants   748

The Frank S. Flowers Foundation primarily serves the Gloucester County, New Jersey area. The Foundation's area of interest include: Education—supporting public high schools of Gloucester County, New Jersey, to provide scholarships for college or graduate study, vocational or technical training; Youth—supporting chapters or councils or branches of Y.M.C.A. and Boys Scouts of America located in Gloucester and/or Salem Counties, grants are also considered for organizations having branches or offices in Gloucester County, New Jersey which treat and educate children with special needs; Health-Related—support to non-profit Gloucester County hospitals; Religious organizations—support to churches in the boroughs of Paulsboro and Wenonah, New Jersey. The Foundation also has a specific interest in The Shriner's Hospital for Crippled Children in Philadelphia, Pennsylvania and the Masonic Home Charity Foundation of New Jersey. Grants range from $1,000 - $8,000. Application

deadline date is February 15th, application available online. Requestors will receive a letter acknowledging the receipt of their request.
Requirements: Qualifying tax-exempt 501(c)3 organizations are eligible for grants if they meet the purpose of the foundation. Proposals should be submitted in the following format: completed Common Grant Application Form; an original Proposal Statement*; an audited financial report and a current year operating budget; a copy of your official IRS Letter with your tax determination; a listing of your Board of Directors. *Proposal Statement should answer these questions: what are the objectives and expected outcomes of this program/project/request; what strategies will be used to accomplish your objective; what is the timeline for completion; if this is part of an on-going program, how long has it been in operation; what criteria will you use to determine your success; if the request is not fully funded, what other sources can you engage. A Proposal budget should be included if this is for a specific program within your annual budget. Please describe any collaborative ventures.
Restrictions: Grants are not made for political purpose, nor to organizations which discriminate on the basis of race, ethnic origin, sexual or religious preference, age or gender.
Geographic Focus: New Jersey, Pennsylvania
Date(s) Application is Due: Feb 15
Amount of Grant: 1,000 - 8,000 USD
Samples: Holy Trinity Episcopal Church, Parking Lot Rehabilitation—$8,000; Deptford Township High School, $3,000—scholarships; Ronald McDonald House of Southern New Jersey, $5,000—general operations support.
Contact: Gale Y. Sykes, Trustee c/o Wells Fargo Bank; (908) 598-3576; grantinquiries2@wachovia.com
Internet: https://www.wachovia.com/foundation/v/index.jsp?vgnextoid=68d7 8689fb0aa110VgnVCM1000004b0d1872RCRD&vgnextfmt=default
Sponsor: Frank S. Flowers Foundation
190 River Road
Summit, NJ 07901

Frank Stanley Beveridge Foundation Grants   749

The foundation welcomes proposals in the areas of: animal care; arts, culture and humanities; civil rights, social action, advocacy; education; employment/jobs; environmental quality, protection and beautification; food, nutrition and agriculture; health; housing; human services; medical research; mental health; philanthropy; safety; recreation; religion; science; social services; and youth development. The board meets in October and April to consider requests. Multiyear grants are rare. Contact the foundation via the Web site only. No phone or written inquiries will be accepted.
Requirements: Applicants must be 501(c)3 nonprofit organizations or foundations in Massachusetts's Hampden and Hampshire Counties.
Restrictions: The Foundation prefers not to support: awards or prizes; commissioning of new artistic work; conferences/seminars; curriculum development; debt reduction; employee matching gifts; employee-related scholarships; endowment funds; exhibitions; faculty/staff development; fellowship funds; fellowships to individuals; film/video/radio production; foundation administered programs; general operating support; grants to individuals; income development; internship funds; management development; performance/production costs; professorships; program-related investment/loans; publications; scholarships to individuals; student aid; technical assistance.
Geographic Focus: Massachusetts
Date(s) Application is Due: Feb 1; Aug 1
Amount of Grant: 50,000 USD
Contact: Philip Caswell, President; (800) 229-9667; fax (561) 748-0644; administrator@beveridge.org or caswell@beveridge.org
Internet: http://www.beveridge.org/
Sponsor: Frank Stanley Beveridge Foundation
1340 U.S. Highway 1, Suite 102
Jupiter, FL 33469

Frank W. and Carl S. Adams Memorial Fund Grants   750

The Frank W. and Carl S. Adams Memorial Fund was established in 1925 to support and promote quality educational, human services, and health care programming for underserved populations. Annual gifts are also awarded to the Harvard University Medical School and the Massachusetts Institute of Technology for student scholarships. Grant requests for general operating support are strongly encouraged. Program support will also be considered. Small, program-related capital expenses may be included in general operating or program requests. To better support the capacity of nonprofit organizations, multi-year funding requests are strongly encouraged. The application deadline is December 1. Applicants will be notified of grant decisions before March 31.

Requirements: 501(c)3 organizations serving the residents of Massachusetts are eligible to apply.
Geographic Focus: Massachusetts
Date(s) Application is Due: Dec 1
Contact: Miki C. Akimoto; (866) 778-6859; miki.akimoto@baml.com
Internet: https://www.bankofamerica.com/philanthropic/fn_search.action
Sponsor: Frank W. and Carl S. Adams Memorial Fund
225 Franklin Street, 4th Floor, MA1-225-04-02
Boston, MA 02110

Fraser-Parker Foundation Grants 751

The Foundation awards funds in its areas of interest, including Christian religion organizations, education and higher education, and hospitals. There are no application forms and no deadlines.
Geographic Focus: All States
Amount of Grant: 5,000 - 50,000 USD
Samples: Visiting Nurse/Hospice Atlanta, Atlanta, Georgia, $25,000, chaplain residency training program; Colonial Williamsburg Foundation, Williamsburg, Virginia, $5,000, operating support; and University of Rochester, Rochester, New York, $65,000, therapeutic programs.
Contact: John Stephenson, Executive Director; (404) 827-6529
Sponsor: Fraser-Parker Foundation
3050 Peachtree Road NW, Suie 270
Atlanta, GA 30305

Fred & Gretel Biel Charitable Trust Grants 752

The Fred & Gretel Biel Charitable Trust was established in 2004 to support and promote quality educational, human-services, and health-care programming for underserved populations. Special consideration is given to organizations that provide food and clothing to low-income individuals and families. Consideration is also given to organizations that serve the economically disadvantaged through the provision of housing, legal assistance, or day-care services. Grant requests for general operating and capital support are encouraged. Grants from the Biel Charitable Trust are one year in duration. Application materials are available for download at the grant website. Applicants are strongly encouraged to review the state application guidelines for additional helpful information and clarifications before applying. Applicants are also encouraged to review the trust's funding history (link is available from the grant website). The application deadline for the Biel Charitable Trust is May 1. Applicants will be notified of grant decisions by June 30.
Requirements: The Biel Charitable Trust typically supports organizations serving the people of King and Snohomish Counties in the Puget Sound region of Washington. Occasionally grants will be made outside of the Puget Sound area. Applicant organizations must have 501(c)3 tax-exempt status.
Restrictions: Requests to assist with debt retirement or to correct an operating deficit will not be considered. Applicants who have received a grant for three consecutive years must wait two years before reapplying to the trust. The trust does not support requests from individuals, organizations attempting to influence policy through direct lobbying, or any political campaigns.
Geographic Focus: Washington
Date(s) Application is Due: May 1
Samples: Edmonds School District, Lynnwood, Washington, $2,500; Haller Lake Christian Health Clinic, Seattle, Washington, $5,000; North Helpline, Seattle, Washington, $2,500.
Contact: Nancy Atkinson, Vice President; (800) 848-7177 or (206) 358-0912; nancy.l.atkinson@baml.com
Internet: https://www.bankofamerica.com/philanthropic/fn_search.action
Sponsor: Fred and Gretel Biel Charitable Trust
800 5th Avenue
Seattle, WA 98104

Fred C. and Katherine B. Andersen Foundation Grants 753

Fred C. and Katherine B. Andersen Foundation, formerly known as the Andersen Foundation gives on a national basis for higher education. The foundation provides funds locally in Minnesota and western Wisconsin for all areas of interest, which include: arts; health care; higher education; hospitals; and youth development. Funding is available in the forms of: capital campaigns; general/operating support and; program development.
Requirements: 501(c)3 tax-exempt organizations are eligible. Giving is on a national basis although preference is given to requests from Minnesota.
Restrictions: The foundation does not make grants to institutions that receive federal funding.
Geographic Focus: All States

Date(s) Application is Due: Mar 18; Jul 22; Oct 21
Amount of Grant: 5,000 - 12,000,000 USD
Samples: Nichols College, Dudley Hall, Dudley, MA, $250,000—unrestricted, general grant; Bayport Public Library Foundation, Bayport, MN, $36,000—program support grant.
Contact: Mary Gillstrom, Director; (651) 264-5150
Sponsor: Fred C. and Katherine B. Andersen Foundation
P.O. Box 8000
Bayport, MN 55003-0080

Fred C. and Mary R. Koch Foundation Grants 754

The foundation mainly supports organizations in its geographic area of interest. Particular interest is given to education (programs that promote the application of economic and scientific principles to problem-solving); environmental stewardship (projects that apply innovative solutions to solve local environmental problems); and human services (projects that promote self-sufficiency, individual responsibility, tolerance, and respect for others) The foundation prefers to support specific projects with clearly defined parameters and measurable results rather than fund-raising events, endowments, capital campaigns, or general operating support.
Requirements: The foundation supports nonprofit, tax-exempt organizations and institutions in communities that have Koch employees and facilities: Kansas, Minnesota, Texas, Oklahoma, Louisiana, and Alberta, Canada.
Restrictions: Grants are not made to individuals.
Geographic Focus: All States, Canada
Contact: Susan Addington; (316) 828-2646; philanthropy@kochind.com
Internet: http://www.kochind.com/community/default.asp
Sponsor: Fred C. and Mary R. Koch Foundation
4111 E 37th Street N
Wichita, KS 67220

Freddie Mac Foundation Grants 755

The Foundation focus is on children whose families have limited resources and who are vulnerable to poor outcomes. The Foundation emphasizes the integration of services that focus on family strengthening and youth development in order to maximize the benefit to children and their families. Grants will be made for direct service projects, general operating support, capacity building, public awareness, planning and capital projects. The following funding priorities will be considered: the early years; elementary school years; junior high and high school years; children and families in crisis; and public awareness education. Proposals must be submitted online.
Requirements: Eligible organizations must be tax exempt under IRS code 501(c)3 and defined as a public charity. The Foundation's grantmaking program services the following metropolitan Washington, D.C. areas: District of Columbia; Virginia - the counties of Arlington, Fairfax, Loudoun and Prince William and the cities of Alexandria, Falls Church, Manassas Park, and Leesburg; Maryland - the counties of Charles, Frederick, Howard, Montgomery, and Prince George's.
Restrictions: The Foundation will not fund organizations that discriminate in the provision of services or in employment practices based on race, color, religion, ethnicity, sex, age, national origin, disability, sexual orientation, marital status, and any other characteristics protected by applicable law. Unless approved by the board, the Foundation does not fund: individuals; training in/promotion of religious doctrine; incurring a debt liability; endowment campaigns.
Geographic Focus: District of Columbia, Maryland, Virginia
Date(s) Application is Due: Sep 9
Amount of Grant: 5,000 - 50,000 USD
Samples: Distributed among nonprofit organizations to aid support-relief efforts following Hurricane Katrina, $10 million; CrossChildren's Law Ctr (Washington, DC)—to support the caregivers of children in the Washington, DC, foster-care system who are seeking adoption and guardianship, $90,000; Ctr for Multicultural Human Services (Falls Church, VA)—to acquire five transitional-housing units that will provide 16 homeless families in northern Virginia, many of whom are recent immigrants, with safe housing and intensive support services, $550,000; American National Red Cross (Washington, DC)—to assist tsunami-relief efforts, $150,000.
Contact: Ralph F. Boyd, President and CEO; fax (703) 918-8888; freddie_mac_foundation@freddiemac.com
Internet: http://www.freddiemacfoundation.org
Sponsor: Freddie Mac Foundation
8250 Jones Branch Drive, MS A40
McLean, VA 22102-3110

Frederick McDonald Trust Grants 756

The Frederick McDonald Trust was established in 1950 to support and promote quality educational, human-services, and health-care programming for underserved populations. Grant requests for general operating support, program, project and capital support will be considered. The majority of grants from the McDonald Trust are one year in duration. On occasion, multi-year support is awarded. Applicants must apply online at the grant website. Applicants are strongly encouraged to do the following before applying: review the downloadable state application procedures for additional helpful information and clarifications; review the downloadable online-application guidelines at the grant website; review the trust's funding history (link is available from the grant website); review the online application questions in advance; and review the list of required attachments. These will generally include: a list of board members, financial statements (audited, reviewed, or compiled by independent auditor); an organization summary; a list of other funding sources; an IRS Determination letter; and other required documents. All attachments must be uploaded in the online application as PDF, Word, or Excel files. The application deadline for the Frederick McDonald Trust is 11:59 p.m. on May 1. Applicants will be notified of grant decisions before August 31.

Requirements: Applicants must have 501(c)3 tax-exempt status.

Restrictions: Grants are made only to those organizations located in, or serving the people of Albany City. The trust does not support requests from individuals, organizations attempting to influence policy through direct lobbying, or any political campaigns.

Geographic Focus: New York

Date(s) Application is Due: May 1

Samples: Equinox, Albany, New York, $15,000; Albany Center for Economic Success, Albany, New York, $10,000; Girls, Inc. of the Greater Capital Region, Schenectady, New York, $15,000.

Contact: Christine O'Donnell, Vice President; (646) 855-1011; christine.l.o'donnell@baml.com

Internet: https://www.bankofamerica.com/philanthropic/fn_search.action

Sponsor: Frederick McDonald Trust

One Bryant Park, NY1-100-28-05

New York, NY 10036

Frederick S. Upton Foundation Grants 757

The foundation awards grants, primarily in southwestern Michigan. Areas of interest include arts, child welfare, education, youth programs, and religion. Types of support include annual campaigns building construction/renovation, capital campaigns, general operating support, and special projects. The application deadline is in mid-March, and there are no specific application forms.

Geographic Focus: Michigan

Date(s) Application is Due: Mar 15; Jun 15; Oct 15

Contact: Stephen E. Upton, President; (312) 732-4260; fax (269) 982-0323; fsuptonfdn@opexonline.com or uptonfoundation@comcast.net

Sponsor: Frederick S. Upton Foundation

100 Ridgeway Street

St. Joseph, MI 49085

Fred Meyer Foundation Grants 758

The Foundation is dedicated to enriching the quality of life in the communities where stores operate and where customers and associates live and work. The Foundation focuses grants on organizations that work toward youth development or hunger reduction. Grant recipients must be invited to apply by a Fred Meyer associate.

Requirements: Grants will be awarded to nonprofits in communities served by Fred Meyer Stores.

Restrictions: The Foundation does not accept unsolicited letters of inquiry.

Geographic Focus: Alaska, Idaho, Oregon, Washington

Samples: Perseverance Theater (Juneau, AK)—for a series of arts and cultural presentations for school-age children, $10,500; Community Transitional School (Portland, OR)—to purchase a school bus for this private alternative school serving homeless preschool through eighth-grade students in the Portland area, $25,000; Share Our Strength's Portland Operation Frontline (Portland, OR)—for a six-week class in which volunteer chefs teach basic cooking, food budgeting, and nutritional skills to low-income teenage parents, $15,000.

Contact: Manager; (503) 232-8844; foundation@fredmeyer.com

Internet: http://www.thekrogerco.com/corpnews/corpnewsinfo_charitable giving_fredmeyer.htm

Sponsor: Fred Meyer Foundation

3800 SE 22nd Avenue

Portland, OR 97202

Freeman Foundation Grants 759

The foundation's major objectives include strengthening the bonds between the United States and the Far East; preservation and protection of the forests, lands, and natural resources of the United States and land conservation and farmland preservation in Vermont; and development of a vibrant, international, free enterprise system. Giving primarily in VT for conservation and environment grants; Asian studies grants are awarded nationally. Grants are awarded four times annually.

Restrictions: Grants are not made to individuals.

Geographic Focus: All States

Samples: Johns Hopkins U (MD)—for the Freeman Southeast Asia Fellowships at the Paul H. Nitze School of Advanced International Studies, $1 million; Institute of International Education (New York, NY)—to rebuild schools devastated by the December tsunamis and provide educational resources to students in Indonesia and Thailand, $1.75 million.

Contact: George S. Tsandikos, (212) 649-5853; gtsandikos@rockco.com

Sponsor: Freeman Foundation

30 Rockefeller Plaza

New York, NY 10012

Fremont Area Community Foundation Amazing X Grants 760

The Amazing X Charitable Trust, a supporting organizaton of the Fremont Area Community Foundation, was established in the late 1970s by members of the Gerber family to benefit people with disabilities and to address general charitable needs in Newaygo County, Michigan. Grant requests are accepted for: projects or programs that serve people with disabilities; and projects or programs that address general charitable needs. Preferred programs are innovative, collaborative, and have a significant impact on the residents of Newaygo County. Grants range from $1,000 to $60,000, and applications are due each year by July 15.

Requirements: Michigan 501(c)3 organizations located in or supporting Newaygo County are eligible for funding. When submitting your proposal, include your organizations: mission, history, description of current programs, activities, and accomplishments; purpose of the grant (describe in detail and include supporting evidence); grant proposal budget form/narrative (form available at the Foundation's website). The following list of attachments must also be included: a copy of the current IRS 501(c)3 determination letter; roster of current governing board, including addresses and affiliations; finances: organization's current annual operating budget, including all expenses and revenues, audited financial statement (most recently completed), IRS Form 990 (most recently filed), annual report, if available; resumes and job descriptions of the key project personnel; organizational chart; letters of support (up to five).

Restrictions: In order to make the best use of available funds, the Foundation usually will not award grants for the following: grants to individuals; to pay off existing debts; religious programs that require religious affiliation and/or religious instruction to receive services; to further political campaigns; projects that begin prior to notification of Foundation funding; capital improvements on rental or individual private property; or programs or projects that subsidize or supplant funding for services considered general government obligations.

Geographic Focus: Michigan

Date(s) Application is Due: Jul 15

Amount of Grant: 1,000 - 60,000 USD

Samples: Arbor Circle, Newaygo, Michigan, $6,000 - in support of outpatient substance abuse counseling; Disability Connection of West Michigan, Muskegon, Michigan, $51,500 - support for advocacy, empowerment, accessibility, and education; Second Christian Reformed Church, Fremont, Michigan, $2,200 - support of the Fremont Friendship program

Contact: Vonda Carr; (231) 924-5350; fax (231) 924-5391; vcarr@tfacf.org

Internet: http://www.tfacf.org/grants/amazingx.html

Sponsor: Fremont Area Community Foundation

P.O. Box B

Fremont, MI 49412

Fremont Area Community Foundation Elderly Needs Grants 761

Overall, the Foundation is focusing its grantmaking resources primarily on expanding opportunities that enhance the well being of residents from the Newaygo County, Michigan area. The purpose of the Elderly Needs Fund is to make grants to support health and enrich aging for the elderly of Newaygo County. The strategies of the Fund include: promotion of the physical health of the elderly; promotion of the mental and emotional well being of the elderly and their caregivers; promotion of the social enrichment and prevention of the social isolation of the elderly; and promotion of the provision of basic human services for the elderly. Application deadlines are February 1 and September 1 each year.

Requirements: Michigan 501(c)3 organizations located in or supporting Newaygo County are eligible for funding. When submitting your proposal, include your organizations: mission, history, description of current programs, activities, and accomplishments; purpose of the grant (describe in detail and include supporting evidence); grant proposal budget form/narrative (form available at the Foundation's website). The following list of attachments must also be included: a copy of the current IRS 501(c)3 determination letter; roster of current governing board, including addresses and affiliations; finances: organization's current annual operating budget, including all expenses and revenues, audited financial statement (most recently completed), IRS Form 990 (most recently filed), annual report, if available; resumes and job descriptions of the key project personnel; organizational chart; letters of support (up to five).

Restrictions: In order to make the best use of available funds, the Foundation usually will not award grants for the following: grants to individuals; to pay off existing debts; religious programs that require religious affiliation and/or religious instruction to receive services; to further political campaigns; projects that begin prior to notification of Foundation funding; capital improvements on rental or individual private property; or programs or projects that subsidize or supplant funding for services considered general government obligations.

Geographic Focus: Michigan
Date(s) Application is Due: Feb 1; Sep 1
Amount of Grant: 10,000 - 250,000 USD
Samples: Catholic Charities West Michigan, Muskegon, Michigan, $56,000 - support for the Newaygo County Companion Program; Newaygo County Commission on Aging, White Cloud, Michigan, $252,000 - support for medical van services, respite, congregate meals, and home delivery of meals; Senior Sing A-Long, Newaygo, Michigan, $28,650 - support for the Tuned In program.
Contact: Vonda Carr; (231) 924-5350; fax (231) 924-5391; vcarr@tfacf.org
Internet: http://www.tfacf.org/grants/elderlyneeds.html
Sponsor: Fremont Area Community Foundation
P.O. Box B
Fremont, MI 49412

Fremont Area Community Foundation General Grants   762

The Fremont Area Community Foundation is focusing its grantmaking resources that enhance the well being of children, youth and families in Newaygo County, Michigan. The Foundation's areas of interest include: arts and culture; community development; education; the environment; and human services. Types of support offered include: building and renovation; capital campaigns; conferences and seminars; consulting services; continuing support; curriculum development; emergency funds; employee matching gifts; endowments; equipment; general operating support; management development; capacity building; matching or challenge support; program-related investments and loans; program development; program evaluation; scholarship funds; seed money; and technical assistance.

Requirements: Michigan 501(c)3 organizations located in or supporting Newaygo County are eligible for funding. When submitting your proposal, include your organizations: mission, history, description of current programs, activities, and accomplishments; purpose of the grant (describe in detail and include supporting evidence); grant proposal budget form/narrative (form available at the Foundation's website). The following list of attachments must also be included: a copy of the current IRS 501(c)3 determination letter; roster of current governing board, including addresses and affiliations; finances: organization's current annual operating budget, including all expenses and revenues, audited financial statement (most recently completed), IRS Form 990 (most recently filed), annual report, if available; resumes and job descriptions of the key project personnel; organizational chart; letters of support (up to five).

Restrictions: In order to make the best use of available funds, the Foundation usually will not award grants for the following: grants to individuals; to pay off existing debts; religious programs that require religious affiliation and/or religious instruction to receive services; to further political campaigns; projects that begin prior to notification of Foundation funding; capital improvements on rental or individual private property; or programs or projects that subsidize or supplant funding for services considered general government obligations.

Geographic Focus: Michigan
Date(s) Application is Due: Feb 1; Sep 1
Amount of Grant: Up to 500,000 USD
Contact: Vonda Carr; (231) 924-5350; fax (231) 924-5391; vcarr@tfacf.org
Internet: http://www.tfaf.org/grants.html
Sponsor: Fremont Area Community Foundation
P.O. Box B
Fremont, MI 49412

**Fremont Area Community Foundation Ice Mountain Environmental   763
   Stewardship Fund Grants**

In 2002, through the generosity of Great Spring Waters of America, the Ice Mountain Environmental Stewardship Fund was established at the Fremont Area Community Foundation. The Foundation serves the Newaygo County, Michigan region. Grants from the IMESF will be made to support the waters and water-dependent natural resources of the Muskegon River Watershed by assisting conservation, enhancement, and restoration projects that result in improvements to the physical, chemical, and biological integrity of the watershed. Proposals will be accepted for projects located in any county within the Muskegon River Watershed. Up to $50,000 is available annually for projects, typical grants are in the $5,000 to $20,000 range. The annual application deadline date is August 1.

Requirements: Michigan 501(c)3 organizations located in any county within the Muskegon River Watershed are eligible to apply. When submitting your proposal, include your organizations: mission, history, description of current programs, activities, and accomplishments; purpose of the grant (describe in detail and include supporting evidence); grant proposal budget form/narrative (form available at the Foundation's website). The following list of attachments must also be included: a copy of the current IRS 501(c)3 determination letter; roster of current governing board, including addresses and affiliations; finances: organization's current annual operating budget, including all expenses and revenues, audited financial statement (most recently completed), IRS Form 990 (most recently filed), annual report, if available; resumes and job descriptions of the key project personnel; organizational chart; letters of support (up to five).

Restrictions: In order to make the best use of available funds, the Foundation usually will not award grants for the following: grants to individuals; to pay off existing debts; religious programs that require religious affiliation and/or religious instruction to receive services; to further political campaigns; projects that begin prior to notification of Foundation funding; capital improvements on rental or individual private property; or programs or projects that subsidize or supplant funding for services considered general government obligations.

Geographic Focus: Michigan
Date(s) Application is Due: Aug 1
Amount of Grant: 5,000 - 20,000 USD
Contact: Vonda Carr; (231) 924-5350; fax (231) 924-5391; vcarr@tfacf.org
Internet: http://www.tfacf.org/grants/icemountain.html
Sponsor: Fremont Area Community Foundation
P.O. Box B
Fremont, MI 49412

Fremont Area Community Foundation Summer Youth Grants   764

The Summer Youth Initiative is a special grantmaking program of the Fremont Area Community Foundation which awards grants of up to $8,000 to provide summer programs for Michigan youth residing in Newaygo County. Priority will be given to programs that: involve a minimum of ten youth; last for a minimum of one week; provide education and recreation; be open and accessible to all interested youth; enhance participants' self-esteem; challenge participants' creativity; and involve participants in some physical exercise and teach healthy lifestyle. Grant applications and proper materials are due by February 1 each year.

Requirements: Organizations applying for a Summer Youth Initiative grant must: be designated as a 501(c)3 non-profit organization or utilize a 501(c)3 organization as a fiscal sponsor; conduct programs to benefit Newaygo County residents; be experienced youth program providers; have oversight of the program by personnel with appropriate credentials; have appropriate youth/staff ratio; provide a positive and safe environment; provide nutritious snack/meal if time warrants; not discriminate on the basis of race, sex, or religious preference; include a plan for evaluation with clearly stated goals and objectives; partner with colleagues and collaborate with other organizations when possible to avoid duplication of services and overlapping of projects.

Restrictions: Fremont Area Community Foundation will not fund: t-shirts; vacation bible schools; camps whose purpose is primarily athletics; and traditional or mandated summer school.

Geographic Focus: Michigan
Date(s) Application is Due: Feb 1
Amount of Grant: Up to 8,000 USD
Contact: Vonda Carr; (231) 924-5350; fax (231) 924-5391; vcarr@tfacf.org
Internet: http://www.tfacf.org/grants/summeryouth.html
Sponsor: Fremont Area Community Foundation
P.O. Box B
Fremont, MI 49412

Friedman Family Foundation Grants 765

The purpose of the family foundation is to fund programs that attempt to end the cycle of poverty. To this end, programs are sought that provide tools, support, and opportunity to people in need to overcome the root causes of their poverty, and in which the people to be helped are part of the design and decision making of the organization or project. Priority is given to organizations in the nine counties of the San Francisco Bay area of California. Occasionally projects are considered beyond this region if they offer lessons or benefits for the Bay area. Application deadlines vary; call for dates and application forms.

Requirements: California 501(c)3 nonprofit organizations or public entities with a board or advisory group that is reflective of the population or community being served are eligible.

Restrictions: The foundation generally does not fund films, videos, conferences, seminars, capital, scholarships, individuals, research, or special or fund-raising events.

Geographic Focus: California

Amount of Grant: 1,000 - 15,000 USD

Samples: Shefa Fund (Wyndmoor, PA)—to leverage investments from Jewish institutions and individuals for use by community development financial institutions, $100,000; Juma Ventures (San Francisco, CA)—for general support, $10,000.

Contact: Lisa Kawahara; (650) 342-8750; fax (650) 342-8750

Internet: http://www.friedmanfamilyfoundation.org

Sponsor: Friedman Family Foundation

204 E 2nd Avenue, PMB 719

San Mateo, CA 94401

Frist Foundation Grants 766

The foundation supports a variety of organizations in the fields of health, human services, civic affairs, education, and the arts. Grants support building the capacity of nonprofit organizations by strengthening their management structure and systems. Types of support include capital, management, operating, project, and technology grants. Deadline listed is for technology grants.

Requirements: 501(c)3 nonprofits in Davidson County, TN, area may apply.

Restrictions: The foundation does not support: individuals or their projects, private foundations, political activities, or advertising or sponsorships. The foundation does not ordinarily support: projects, programs, or organizations that serve a limited audience or a relatively small number of people; organizations during their first three years of operation; disease-specific organizations seeking support for national projects and programs; biomedical or clinical research; hospitals; organizations whose principal impact is outside of Middle Tennessee; endowments; social events or similar fund-raising activities; or religious organizations for religious purposes.

Geographic Focus: Tennessee

Date(s) Application is Due: Apr 1

Amount of Grant: 500 - 10,000 USD

Samples: Domestic Violence Intervention Ctr (TN)—to translate domestic violence educational materials into Spanish, $3000; Mockingbird Theatre (TN)—for general support, $5000; Metropolitan Nashville Public Schools (TN)—to establish a pilot reading program at Haywood Elementary School, $65,000; Faith Family Medical Clinic of Nashville (TN)—to help establish a medical clinic for low-income working people, $105,000.

Contact: Peter Bird, (615) 292-3868; fax (615) 292-5843; askfrist@ fristfoundation.org

Internet: http://www.fristfoundation.org/grants/general.asp

Sponsor: Frist Foundation

3100 W End Avenue, Suite 1200

Nashville, TN 37203

Frost Foundation Grants 767

The foundation awards grants in the areas of human service needs, environmental programs, and education programs in New Mexico and Louisiana. Preference will be given to programs that have potential for wider service or educational exposure than an individual community. The foundation encourages collaborations, mergers, and the formation of alliances among agencies within the community to reduce duplication of effort and to promote a maximum effective use of funds. Applicants are urged to call the foundation for guidelines before sending a proposal. Application information is available online.

Requirements: 501(c)3 nonprofits in Louisiana and New Mexico are eligible.

Geographic Focus: Louisiana, New Mexico

Date(s) Application is Due: Jun 1; Dec 1

Samples: Santa Fe Children's Museum, Santa Fe, New Mexico, $200,000; Share Your Care Adult Day Services, Albuquerque, New Mexico, $4,500; Lafayette Community Health Care Clinic, Lafayette, Louisiana, $15,000.

Contact: Mary Amelia Whited-Howell, President; (505) 986-0208; info@ frostfound.org

Internet: http://www.frostfound.org

Sponsor: Frost Foundation

511 Armijo, Suite A

Santa Fe, NM 87501

Fuller E. Callaway Foundation Grants 768

The foundation awards grants to nonprofit organizations and individuals in LaGrange and Troup County, Georgia. Grants are awarded in the areas of religion, higher and other education, social services, youth, and health. Types of support include: general operating budgets; annual campaigns; building funds; equipment; matching funds; and student aid. Letters of application from organizations are accepted and have deadlines at the end of December, March, June, and September.

Requirements: Nonprofit organizations and individuals in LaGrange and Troup County, Georgia, are eligible for support.

Geographic Focus: Georgia

Amount of Grant: 25,000 - 200,000 USD

Samples: Auburn University Foundation, Auburn, Alabama, $74,585 - scholarship fund contribution; Troup County Baptist Association, LaGrange, Georgia, $5,000 - general operations; Georgia Tech Alumni Association, Atlanta, Georgia, $250 - scholarship fund contribution.

Contact: H. Speer Burdette III, President; (706) 884-7348; fax (706) 884-0201; hsburdette@callaway-foundation.org

Internet: http://www.callawayfoundation.org/history.php

Sponsor: Fuller E. Callaway Foundation

209 Broome Street, P.O. Box 790

LaGrange, GA 30241

Fuller Foundation Arts Grants 769

The Fuller Foundation is a family foundation, inspired by its forward-thinking founder, Alvan T. Fuller. It's purpose is to support non-profit agencies which improve the quality of life for people, animals and the environment. The Foundation also funds the Fuller Foundation of New Hampshire which supports horticultural and educational programs for the public at Fuller Gardens. In funding the Arts, the Foundation seeks proposals from qualified agencies that carry on the life interests of Alan T. and Viola D. Fuller in this area. The Foundation expects its grants to encourage, through the agencies, hands-on and participatory collaborations between established cultural institutions, artists and communities. Specific program interests include: art for viewing and listening; art education in school; art and performing arts festivals; art (murals & sculpture) that beautifies or inspires a community; programs that bring symphony, opera and theater to the community; and adult and/or children's museum education programs. The geographic focus area is predominately the Boston area and the immediate seacoast area of New Hampshire. Through these grants the Foundation strives to effect change, make an impact on the community, and inspire good deeds. The two annual application submission deadlines are January 15 and June 15.

Requirements: Nonprofits in the Boston, Massachusetts, area and the immediate seacoast region of New Hampshire are eligible.

Restrictions: Funding is not available for: capital projects (unless in the opinion of the Trustees, the Foundation gift will have significant impact); individuals; or multiyear grants. Incomplete grants are not considered. Faxed or emailed grant requests will not be accepted.

Geographic Focus: Massachusetts, New Hampshire

Date(s) Application is Due: Jan 15; Jun 15

Amount of Grant: 3,500 - 7,500 USD

Contact: John T. Bottomley; (603) 964-6998; atfuller@aol.com

Internet: http://www.fullerfoundation.org/FullerFoundation/HomePage. cfm?page=arts

Sponsor: Fuller Foundation

P.O. Box 479

Rye Beach, NH 03871

Fuller Foundation Wildlife Grants 770

The Fuller Foundation is a family foundation, inspired by its forward-thinking founder, Alvan T. Fuller. It's purpose is to support non-profit agencies which improve the quality of life for people, animals and the environment. The Foundation also funds the Fuller Foundation of New Hampshire which supports horticultural and educational programs for the public at Fuller Gardens. In funding the Wildlife, Endangered Species, and their Environment, the Foundation seeks proposals from qualified agencies that will: educate the public

on wildlife and the adverse affects of encroachment on their habitat; support shelters, animal hospitals, animal habitats, and programs that insure a healthy wildlife population; protect endangered species, their environment and habitat from extinction or unnecessary human encroachment; and support programs which improve people's lives by interaction with animals. The geographic focus area is predominately the Boston area and the immediate seacoast area of New Hampshire. Through these grants the Foundation strives to effect change, make an impact on the community, and inspire good deeds. The two annual application submission deadlines are January 15 and June 15.
Requirements: Nonprofits in the Boston, Massachusetts, area and the immediate seacoast region of New Hampshire are eligible.
Restrictions: Funding is not available for: capital projects (unless in the opinion of the Trustees, the Foundation gift will have significant impact); individuals; or multi-year grants. Incomplete grants are not considered. Faxed or emailed grant requests will not be accepted.
Geographic Focus: Massachusetts, New Hampshire
Date(s) Application is Due: Jan 15; Jun 15
Amount of Grant: 3,500 - 7,500 USD
Contact: John T. Bottomley; (603) 964-6998; atfuller@aol.com
Internet: http://www.fullerfoundation.org/FullerFoundation/HomePage.cfm?page=wildlife
Sponsor: Fuller Foundation
P.O. Box 479
Rye Beach, NH 03871

Fuller Foundation Youth At Risk Grants 771
The Fuller Foundation is a family foundation, inspired by its forward-thinking founder, Alvan T. Fuller. It's purpose is to support non-profit agencies which improve the quality of life for people, animals and the environment. The Foundation also funds the Fuller Foundation of New Hampshire which supports horticultural and educational programs for the public at Fuller Gardens. In funding Youth at Risk, the Foundation seeks proposals from qualified agencies that involve a minimum of 25 youth, between the ages of 12 and 18, predominately at or below the poverty line, in programs that will: help prevent youth from experiencing the detrimental effects caused by the use of alcohol, tobacco and drugs through the early education of youth and parents; and challenge and empower youth at risk through peer leadership, outdoor adventure education programs, and alternative educational experiences. The Foundation funds programs which help youth reach their potential and lead productive lives. The Foundation favors programs that are year-round, or summer programs which re-enforce values and skills that are learned during the school year. The minimum number of participants is twenty-five. The geographic focus area is predominately the Boston area and the immediate seacoast area of New Hampshire. Through these grants the Foundation strives to effect change, make an impact on the community, and inspire good deeds. The two annual application submission deadlines are January 15 and June 15.
Requirements: Nonprofits in the Boston, Massachusetts, area and the immediate seacoast region of New Hampshire are eligible.
Restrictions: Funding is not available for: capital projects (unless in the opinion of the Trustees, the Foundation gift will have significant impact); individuals; or multi-year grants. Incomplete grants are not considered. Faxed or emailed grant requests will not be accepted.
Geographic Focus: Massachusetts, New Hampshire
Date(s) Application is Due: Jan 15; Jun 15
Amount of Grant: 3,500 - 7,500 USD
Contact: John T. Bottomley; (603) 964-6998; atfuller@aol.com
Internet: http://www.fullerfoundation.org/FullerFoundation/HomePage.cfm?page=youth
Sponsor: Fuller Foundation
P.O. Box 479
Rye Beach, NH 03871

Fund for New Jersey Grants 772
Grants support nonprofit organizations in New Jersey or organizations that benefit the state, with particular attention given to projects seeking to affect public policy. Although a few grants are provided for local activities, direct services, and general operating support, such proposals are considered usually at the fund's invitation. Grant applicants are asked to submit a single-page proposal cover sheet containing the following information: organization and contact person, summary of request, amount requested, and problem or need addressed by proposed activity. All proposals must be accompanied by a copy of the IRS tax-exemption letter, names and affiliations of the board of directors, and a budget. The board normally meets in March, June, September, and December to consider proposals.

Requirements: 501(c)3 tax-exempt organizations are eligible. Proposals are not accepted via email.
Restrictions: The fund does not accept proposals for support of individuals nor for capital projects such as acquisition, renovation, or equipment. The fund is unable to support day care centers, drug treatment programs, arts programs, health care delivery, or scholarships.
Geographic Focus: New Jersey
Amount of Grant: Up to 33,000,000 USD
Samples: CityWorks (Trenton, NJ)—for its efforts to develop commercial real-estate projects in selected urban neighborhoods, $100,000; New Jersey Community Capital (Trenton, NJ)—for a campaign intended to attract investments for community- and economic-development projects in low-income communities, $85,000; Pinelands Preservation Alliance (Southampton, NJ)—for advocacy efforts designed to help protect New Jersey's Pinelands region, $30,000; New Jersey Immigration Policy Network (Newark, NJ)—to support a coalition of civil-rights, community, immigrant, and labor groups that promote fair policies for recent immigrants, $100,000.
Contact: Mark Murphy, Executive Director; (732) 220-8656; fax (732) 220-8654; info@fundfornj.org
Internet: http://www.fundfornj.org/app_guide.html
Sponsor: Fund for New Jersey
94 Church Street, Suite 303
New Brunswick, NJ 08901

Fund for Santa Barbara Grants 773
The fund gives preference to projects working to address the root causes of social, economic, and environmental problems. Types of support include seed grants to new grassroots projects, general support, or project grants to small organizations, and grants to larger, more established organizations only for specific targeted purposes. Affirmative action considerations are among the criteria used in all funding decisions.
Requirements: Applications are invited from organizations that are working against discrimination based on race, sex/gender, age, religion, economic status, sexual orientation, physical/mental ability, ethnicity, language, or immigration status; struggling for the rights of workers; promoting self-determination in low-income and disenfranchised communities; promoting international peace and organizing locally for a just foreign policy; working on improving the environment, especially organizing a constituency usually without access or input to environmental concerns; and operating in a democratic manner, responsive to and directed by the constituency being served.
Restrictions: Grants do not support projects involved in electoral campaigns on behalf of candidates or parties; private (vs. public) interests; direct labor organizing; projects located outside of Santa Barbara County; projects providing direct services without a social change component; or direct support to individuals, capital ventures, or building improvements.
Geographic Focus: California
Date(s) Application is Due: Mar 12; Sep 9
Amount of Grant: Up to 10,000 USD
Contact: Fund Administrator; (805) 962-9164; fax (805) 965-0217; email@fundforsantabarbara.org
Internet: http://www.fundforsantabarbara.org/apply/apply.htm
Sponsor: Fund for Santa Barbara
924 Anacapa Street, Suite 4H
Santa Barbara, CA 93101-2192

Fund for the City of New York Grants 774
The Fund is dedicated to improving the quality of life in the city by supporting efforts to increase the efficiency and effectiveness of government agencies and the nonprofit organizations that are instrumental in promoting a healthy civic environment. The fund's programs concentrate on children and youth and community development and the urban environment. The grants provide project or general support for nonprofit organizations, including a number of watchdog and advocacy organizations. Short-term consultancy grants also are awarded to enable organizations to hire an additional person to help projects through difficult periods. Proposals must be received by April 15 to be considered for the spring cycle and August 15 to be considered for the fall cycle.
Requirements: Applicants are encouraged to contact the Foundation before submitting a letter of inquiry. Unsolicited proposals are not accepted.
Restrictions: Individuals, endowments, and capital campaigns are not eligible.
Geographic Focus: New York
Date(s) Application is Due: Apr 15; Aug 15
Contact: Barbara Cohn Berman, Vice President; (212) 925-6675; fax (212) 925-5675; bcohn@fcny.org

Internet: http://www.fcny.org/fcny/core/grants/
Sponsor: Fund for the City of New York
121 Avenue of the Americas, 6th Floor
New York, NY 10013

G. Harold and Leila Y. Mathers Charitable Foundation Grants　775
The foundation awards grants to support research in the basic life sciences. Requests for general operating support also will be considered. There are no application forms or deadlines. The board meets two or three times each year.
Requirements: U.S. research organizations are eligible.
Geographic Focus: All States
Amount of Grant: 10,000 - 200,000 USD
Contact: James Handelman; (914) 242-0465; bcheikin@mathersfoundation.org
Internet: http://www.mathersfoundation.org
Sponsor: G. Harold and Leila Y. Mathers Charitable Foundation
118 N Bedford Road, Suite 203
Mount Kisco, NY 10549-2555

G.N. Wilcox Trust Grants　776
The trust provides partial support to programs and projects of tax-exempt, public charities in Hawaii to improve the quality of life in the state, particularly the island of Kauai. Grants of one year's duration are awarded in categories of interest to the trust, including education, literacy programs and adult basic education, health, Protestant religion, delinquency and crime prevention, social services, youth services, and culture and the performing arts. Types of support include general operating grants, capital grants, equipment acquisition, seed grants, scholarship funds, and challenge/matching grants. Deadlines dates for general grants are: January 1; April 1; July 1; October 1. The deadline date for scholarships is February 15th.
Requirements: Giving is limited to Hawaii, with emphasis on the island of Kauai. To begin application process, contact Paula Boyce for additional guidelines.
Restrictions: Grants are not awarded to support government agencies (or organizations substantially supported by government funds), individuals, or for endowment funds, research, deficit financing, or student aid in scholarships or loans.
Geographic Focus: Hawaii
Date(s) Application is Due: Jan 1; Feb 15; Apr 1; Jul 1; Oct 1
Samples: Save our Seas—to support scholarships for youth to participate in the Second Annual Clean Oceans Conference, $2,954; Church of the Crossroads—to support the capital campaigns for renovations, $10,000; Hawaii Public Radio—to support the membership challenge grant, $3,000.
Contact: Paula Boyce, c/o Bank of Hawaii; (808) 538-4944; fax (808) 538-4647; pboyce@boh.com or emoniz@boh.com
Sponsor: G.N. Wilcox Trust
Bank of Hawai'i, Foundation Administration Department 758
Honolulu, HI 96802-3170

Gallo Foundation Grants　777
The foundation primarily supports nonprofits in Modesto, CA, in its areas of interest, including higher and other education, disabled, community funds, social services, and religion. Types of support include employee matching gifts and general operating budgets. There are no application deadlines or forms.
Requirements: Northern California nonprofits may submit grant requests.
Geographic Focus: California
Amount of Grant: 250 - 891,500 USD
Contact: Ronald Emerzian, (209) 341-3141
Sponsor: Gallo Foundation
P.O. Box 1130
Modesto, CA 95353

Gamble Foundation Grants　778
Founded in 1968, The Gamble Foundation is primarily interested in supporting organizations that serve disadvantaged children and youth in San Francisco, Marin and Napa counties. Within the field of youth development, the Foundation focuses on literacy, educational and personal enrichment programs designed to open doors of opportunity for at-risk youth in order to help them succeed in school and become productive, self-sufficient members of society. The Foundation is particularly interested in agricultural/environmental education, financial & computer literacy, vocational training and programs that prevent substance abuse and teen violence. To a lesser degree, the Foundation supports environmental organizations that focus on land preservation and sustainability, animal welfare and management, and pollution control. The foundation is interested in promoting green concepts that increase awareness of science based solutions that help reduce consumption of finite resources. The Foundation prefers to fund specific projects rather than annual appeals. Grants range from $5,000 to $20,000.

Requirements: Northern California 501(c)3 nonprofit organizations, with an emphasis on San Francisco, Marin, and Napa Counties, are eligible to apply. The Board meets in the spring each year and makes grants in late summer. The Foundation will accept proposals for the April meeting from January 25 - February 10. The Foundation encourages submission of proposals and attachments by email. For those submitting by email, the proposal and required attachments should be emailed in PDF format only. Send your proposals to Fiona Barrett at fbarrett@pfs-llc.net. If you do not receive an email within 24 hours confirming that your proposal has been received, please contact Fiona at (415) 561-6540, ext. 221. The Foundation will also accept a proposal submitted by mail as long as it is postmarked on or before February 10th. Proposals must include the following in the order listed: cover letter, on organization letterhead with address and phone number, including a brief summary of the request and a list of attachments (not more than one page); proposal narrative (not to exceed 5 pages); concise description of the organization (not more than two pages) including: relevant history, mission, geography and populations served; overview of programs; description of the project (not more than three pages) including: need, purpose, goals, timeline, project budget, including secured and projected sources of funding; financial statement, including actual revenue and expenses for the organization's most recently completed fiscal year; organizational budget for the present year, detailing proposed expenditures and projected sources of funding (not more than two pages); list of major public and private funders, identifying both secured and planned for funds; list of the Board of Directors, with affiliations; copy of the agency's IRS 501(c)3 tax-exempt determination letter. When submitting proposal, clasp the proposal materials with a single binder clip; do not use staples. Do not send audio-visual materials, binders, folders, or pamphlets unless requested. Receipt of proposals will be acknowledged with a written response within a reasonable period of time. Should additional information be required, applicants will be contacted.
Restrictions: In general, the Foundation does not support medical research, individuals, endowments, or capital improvements.
Geographic Focus: California
Date(s) Application is Due: Feb 10
Amount of Grant: 5,000 - 20,000 USD
Samples: WildCare: Terwilliger Nature Education and Wildlife Rehabilitation, San Rafael, CA, $20,000—for No Child Left Indoors program, providing outdoor education for Marin and San Francisco youth; Canal Alliance, San Rafael, CA, $25,000—for Youth Education and Development program, providing academic, leadership, and personal development for low-income San Rafael youth; Bay Area Discovery Museum, Sausalito, CA, $25,000—for Connections program.
Contact: Eric Sloan, Grants Manager; (415) 561-6540, ext. 205; fax (415) 561-6477; esloan@pfs-llc.net
Internet: http://www.pfs-llc.net/gamble/gamble.html
Sponsor: Gamble Foundation
1660 Bush Street, Suite 300
San Francisco, CA 94109

Gardiner Howland Shaw Foundation Grants　779
The Foundation is committed to awarding grants that can make a real difference in the way the justice system operates. The following are funding priorities: research, analysis, and journalism, that examine important criminal and juvenile justice issues and offer ways to improve the administrations of justice in Massachusetts; initiatives that demonstrate innovative approaches to the reintegration of adult and juvenile offenders leaving correctional and detention facilities; programs that demonstrate effective inter-agency and community collaboration models for crime prevention; initiatives that address the legal, social and rehabilitative needs of juvenile and adult offenders through advocacy, public education and training. Potential applicants are encouraged to telephone the office to discuss ideas prior to submitting a proposal.
Requirements: Nonprofit Massachusetts organizations are eligible.
Restrictions: The foundation does not support capital requests, the arts, endowments, grants to individuals, or scholarships.
Geographic Focus: Massachusetts
Date(s) Application is Due: Feb 1
Amount of Grant: 15,000 - 25,000 USD
Contact: Thomas Coury, Executive Director; (781) 455-8303; fax (781) 433-0980; admin@shawfoundation.org
Internet: http://www.shawfoundation.org/guidelines.php
Sponsor: Gardiner Howland Shaw Foundation
355 Boylston Street
Boston, MA 02116

Gardner Family Foundation Grants 780

Established in Virginia in 1999, the Gardner Family Foundation provides grant support in three primary areas: arts and culture; education; and human services. Most recent awards have ranged from $100 up to $11,500. Typically, this support is given in the form of general operating funds. Though most grants are given locally in Carlisle, Pennsylvania, awards have also been given to national organizations. Since there are no formal applications or annual deadlines for submission, interested parties should forward a proposal in letter form directly to the Foundation office.

Requirements: Recognized 501(c)3 organizations throughout the U.S. are eligible to apply.

Restrictions: Grant support is not given directly to individuals.

Geographic Focus: All States

Amount of Grant: 100 - 11,500 USD

Samples: Cumberland County Historical Society, Carlisle, Pennsylvania, $11,500 - general operating funds (2014); Alice Lloyd College, Pippa Passes, Kentucky, $100 - general operating funds (2014); Friends of Craighead House, Boiling Springs, Pennsylvania, $100 - general operating funds (2014).

Contact: Mary Adams, Secretary-Treasurer; (717) 245-0040

Sponsor: Gardner Family Foundation

P.O. Box 38, 1310 Holly Pike

Carlisle, PA 17013-4242

Gardner Foundation Grants 781

The Gardner Foundation was established in the State of New York in 1947, with a giving emphasis on Milwaukee, Wisconsin. The Foundation's major mission is to provide grant funding for a wide range of organizations supporting arts and culture, education, and youth services. Its primary fields of interest include: child welfare; community and economic development; elementary and secondary education; employment; homeless services; hospice care; human services; mental health care; museums; performing arts; and reproductive health care. That support typically comes in a variety of forms, which include: annual campaigns; capital and infrastructure; capital campaigns; continuing support; emergency funding; and general operating support. Most recent awards have ranged from $1,000 to $6,000. Application forms and application guidelines are provided. Annual deadlines are at minimum one month prior to Board meetings, which are generally scheduled in April, September, and December. April, September, and December

Requirements: 501(c)3 organizations and schools serving the Milwaukee, Wisconsin, area are eligible to apply.

Geographic Focus: Wisconsin

Date(s) Application is Due: Mar 1; Aug 1; Nov 1

Amount of Grant: 1,000 - 6,000 USD

Samples: 88 Nine Radio, Milwaukee, Wisconsin, $6,000 - general operating funds; Beyond Vision, Milwaukee, Wisconsin, $4,000 - general operating funds; Hunger Task Force, Milwaukee, Wisconsin, $4,000 - general operating funds.

Contact: Theodore Friedlander III, President; (414) 273-0308

Sponsor: Gardner Foundation of Milwaukee

322 E. Michigan Street, Suite 250

Milwaukee, WI 53202-5010

Gardner Foundation Grants 782

The Gardner Foundation was established in Louisville, Kentucky, in 1979, and giving is primarily centered around the city in which it began. The Foundation's major fields of interest include: the environment; religion; and youth development. Typical forms of support are for infrastructure and general operations. Awards have recently averaged between $250 and $10,000. A formal application can be secured from the Foundation office, and the annual deadline for its submission is May 1.

Requirements: 501(c)3 organizations either based in, or serving the residents of, Louisville, Kentucky, are eligible to apply.

Geographic Focus: Kentucky

Date(s) Application is Due: May 1

Amount of Grant: 250 - 10,000 USD

Samples: Cabbage Patch Settlement House, Louisville, Kentucky, $10,000 - general operations (2014); Nativity Academy of St. Bonaventure Church, Louisville, Kentucky, $10,000 - general operations (2014); Maryhurst School, Louisville, Kentucky, $5,000 - general operations (2014).

Contact: William A. Gardner, Jr., Vice President; (502) 894-4440

Sponsor: Gardner Foundation of Louisville

2301 River Road, Suite 301

Louisville, KY 40206-3040

Gardner Foundation Grants 783

The Gardner Foundation was established in the State of Nebraska in 1990, in support of programs in both the Wakefield, Nebraska, area and throughout South Carolina. The Foundation's primary fields of interest include: K-12 education; higher education; hospital care; orchestral music, and theater. Funding most often comes in the form of: infrastructure support; capital campaigns; endowment contributions; equipment purchases; fundraising efforts; and seed money. Most recently, awards have ranged from $2,000 to $90,000. An application form is required, and can be secured by contacting the Foundation office. The Board meets quarterly and, though there are no specific deadlines, complete applications should be forwarded ninety days prior to the upcoming meeting.

Requirements: 501(c)3 organizations serving a 75-mile radius of Wakefield, Nebraska, or the residents of South Carolina are eligible to apply.

Geographic Focus: Nebraska, South Carolina

Amount of Grant: 2,000 - 90,000 USD

Samples: AMI Kids, Seabrook, South Carolina, $10,000 - capital improvements (2014); Emerson Center, Emerson, Nebraska, $30,180 - support of outreach programs (2014); John Paul II Catholic School, Ridgeland, South Carolina, $90,000 - general operating support (2014).

Contact: Leslie A. Bebee, Vice President; (402) 287-2538

Sponsor: Gardner Foundation of Wakefield

P.O. Box 390, 307 Main Street

Wakefield, NE 68784-6026

Gardner W. and Joan G. Heidrick, Jr. Foundation Grants 784

The Gardner W. and Joan G. Heidrick, Jr. Foundation was established in the State of Texas in 1998, with the expressed purpose of providing support for nonprofit organizations in Texas. North Carolina, and Illinois. The Foundation's primary fields of interest include: higher education programs; human services; and recreation and sports. Typically, support is given in the form of general operating funds. Most recent grants have ranged from $20 to $1,000, with an average of ten awards given each year. A formal application is required, and can be secured directly from the Foundation office. There are no specified annual deadlines.

Requirements: 501(c)3 organizations serving residents of Texas, North Carolina, or Illinois are eligible to apply.

Geographic Focus: Illinois, North Carolina, Texas

Amount of Grant: 20 - 1,000 USD

Samples: American Diabetes, Charlotte, North Carolina, $100 - general operating funds; University of Chicago, Chicago, Illinois, $1,000 - general operations; University of Texas, Austin, Texas, $1,000 - general operations.

Contact: Gardner W. Heidrick, President; (704) 366-7880

Sponsor: Gardner W. and Joan G. Heidrick, Jr. Foundation

8919 Park Road, Suite 4019

Charlotte, NC 28210-2242

Gates Family Foundation Community Development & Revitalization Grants 785

The mission of the Foundation is to invest in Colorado-based projects and organizations primarily through capital grants which have meaningful impact and enhance the quality of life for those who live, work and visit the state. Funding goals in the area of Community Development and Revitalization include: investing in organizations that have the potential to reinforce and enhance the economic vitality of a community; supporting organizations that further the broad education of the population in the maintenance of the free enterprise system; supports educational programs that effectively teach the principles of entrepreneurship and business ethics; and supporting projects that involve partnerships between public and private sector organizations that seek to improve the economic and cultural health of communities.

Requirements: The Foundation: generally makes grants only to organizations in the state of Colorado; expects strong support for the project from the community; will grant funds only to properly documented tax-exempt organizations; and generally confines its grants to campaigns for capital improvement or projects.

Restrictions: The Foundation does not: provide loans, grants, or scholarships to individuals, or loans to organizations; make grants for projects that have been completed prior to the next trustees' meeting; make grants for conferences, meetings, or studies that are not initiated by the trustees; consider more than one proposal from an organization in a calendar year; make grants to other foundations or organizations engaged in grant making; grant funds for general operating support or to retire operating debt; make grants for the purchase of vehicles or office equipment; make grants directly to individual public schools or public school districts; make grants for the construction of medical facilities or for medical research; schedule interviews with the Foundation trustees unless the trustees initiate the meeting. The Foundation will not purchase tickets for fundraising dinners, parties, benefits, balls, or other social fundraising events.

Geographic Focus: Colorado

Date(s) Application is Due: Jan 15; Apr 1; Jul 15; Oct 1

Contact: Karen White Mather, Program Officer; (303) 722-1881; fax (303) 316-3038; info@gatesfamilyfoundation.org

Internet: http://www.gatesfamilyfoundation.org/www/gates.php?section= grant_applications&p=funding_priorities&fp=community

Sponsor: Gates Family Foundation

3575 Cherry Creek North Drive, Suite 100

Denver, CO 80209-3600

GATX Corporation Grants   786

Local community investment programs support organizations and projects that improve the quality of life in GATX communities across the US. Each year, GATX contributes to nonprofit organizations committed to the issues surrounding culture, education, the environment, families, healthcare and social services. GATX has active community investment committees in Buffalo, Chicago, and San Francisco, which serve their respective regions as well as several other locations. Types of support include challenge grants, employee matching gifts, general operating support, project grants, and seed grants. Applications are accepted year-round. Funding decisions are made by the contributions committee, which meets quarterly in February, May, August, and November. Proposals received after these dates will be held for a subsequent meeting.

Requirements: Eligible to apply are nonprofit 501(c)3 tax-exempt organizations located in company-operating areas and that serve the economically disadvantaged.

Restrictions: Grants are not awarded to individuals, political organizations, religious organizations, private foundations, capital campaigns, endowment funds, health research, national organizations, or for fund-raisers.

Geographic Focus: Illinois

Amount of Grant: 7,000 - 80,000 USD

Samples: Suzuki-Orff School for Young Musicians (Chicago, IL)—for the Clap, Sing, and Read program, which uses music to promote reading skills among at-risk children, $15,000; Chicago Anti-Hunger Federation (Chicago, IL)—for the Oliver's Kitchen Employment Training Program, which provides culinary training to formerly homeless and low-income individuals, $20,000; National Lekotek Ctr (Evanston, IL)—to provide learning and recreational services for disabled children in Chicago's West Humboldt Park neighborhood, as well as supportive services for their parents, $19,534.

Contact: Allison Dean; (312) 621-4274; community@gatx.com

Internet: http://www.gatx.com/common/about/community/about.asp

Sponsor: GATX Corporation

500 W Monroe

Chicago, IL 60661

Gaylord & Dorothy Donnelley Foundation Chicago Artistic Vitality   787
Grants

Making grants to organizations is the primary way that the Gaylord and Dorothy Donnelley Foundation fulfills its mission of land conservation, artistic vitality, and regionally significant collections in the Chicago region and lowcountry of South Carolina. The Chicago Artistic Vitality Grant program awards general operations grants to professional arts organizations of all disciplines in the Chicago region with annual expenses less than $1 million. General operations grant awards are based on the actual annual expenses of an organization's most recently completed fiscal year. Proposals for service, support, or technical assistance organizations are by invitation only. Obtain required application forms from the office. Annual deadlines are April 3 and July 31.

Requirements: IRS 501(c)3 organizations serving the Chicago region are eligible for this funding. The Chicago region includes 13 counties in three states: Illinois— Lake, McHenry, Kane, Cook, DuPage, Kendall, Grundy, and Will; Wisconsin— Kenosha, and Walworth; and Indiana—Lake, Porter, and LaPorte.

Restrictions: The Foundation usually will not support requests for individuals; endowments or capital campaigns; fund-raising events; publications, films, or videos; eradication of deficits or loans; conferences; or religious purposes.

Geographic Focus: Illinois

Date(s) Application is Due: Apr 3; Jul 31

Contact: Ellen Placey Wadey; (312) 977-2707; ewadey@gddf.org

Internet: http://gddf.org/grants/funding-guidelines/chicago-artistic-vitality

Sponsor: Gaylord and Dorothy Donnelley Foundation

35 E Wacker Drive, Suite 2600

Chicago, IL 60601-2102

Gaylord and Dorothy Donnelley Foundation Land Conservation   788
Grants

Making grants to organizations is the primary way that the Gaylord and Dorothy Donnelley Foundation fulfills its mission of land conservation, artistic vitality, and regionally significant collections in the Chicago region and lowcountry of South Carolina. The Land Conservation Grant program supports a variety of conservation organizations to protect and steward natural lands of strategic conservation value. Within the Chicago region, the Foundation has a particular interest in landscape-scale protection and stewardship within the following geographic focus areas: Calumet; the Forest Preserves of Cook County; Grand Kankakee; the Hackmatack National Wildlife Refuge; and the Midewin National Tallgrass Prairie. Within the lowcountry of South Carolina, the following geographic focus areas are of primary interest: South Lowcountry; the ACE Basin; Charleston Greenbelt; Sewee to Santee; and the Winyah Bay Watershed. Grants are available for the following, provided they contribute to landscape-scale conservation outcomes: land protection and stewardship; strategic land conservation partnerships; policy, planning and advocacy; and organizational capacity building. Applications are due three months prior to board meetings. Obtain required application forms from the office. Annual deadlines are April 3 and July 31. April 3 and July 31

Requirements: IRS 501(c)3 organizations serving the Chicago region or the South Carolina low country are eligible. The Chicago region includes 13 counties in three states: Illinois—Lake, McHenry, Kane, Cook, DuPage, Kendall, Grundy, and Will; Wisconsin—Kenosha, and Walworth; and Indiana—Lake, Porter, and LaPorte. Lowcountry of South Carolina counties include Beaufort, Colleton, Charleston, Berkeley, Georgetown, Dorchester, Jasper, Horry, and Hampton.

Restrictions: The Foundation usually will not support requests for individuals; endowments or capital campaigns; fund-raising events; publications, films, or videos; eradication of deficits or loans; conferences; or religious purposes. The Foundation does not make grants for the acquisition of land or conservation easements.

Geographic Focus: Illinois, Indiana, South Carolina, Wisconsin

Date(s) Application is Due: Apr 3; Jul 31

Contact: Susan Clark; (312) 977-2700; fax (312) 977-1686; sclark@gddf.org

Internet: http://gddf.org/grants/funding-guidelines/land-conservation

Sponsor: Gaylord and Dorothy Donnelley Foundation

35 E Wacker Drive, Suite 2600

Chicago, IL 60601-2102

Gaylord and Dorothy Donnelley Foundation Lowcountry Artistic   789
Vitality Grants

Making grants to organizations is the primary way that the Gaylord and Dorothy Donnelley Foundation fulfills its mission of land conservation, artistic vitality, and regionally significant collections in the Chicago region and lowcountry of South Carolina. The Lowcountry Artistic Vitality Grant program awards general operations grants to professional arts organizations of all disciplines. Obtain required application forms from the office. Annual deadlines are April 3 and July 31.

Requirements: RS 501(c)3 organizations serving the South Carolina low country are eligible. Lowcountry of South Carolina counties include Beaufort, Colleton, Charleston, Berkeley, Georgetown, Dorchester, Jasper, Horry, and Hampton. To be eligible, organizations must: be 501(c)3 public charities; have completed at least one full fiscal year of operations before applying; and demonstrate or strongly promise artistic vitality.

Restrictions: The Foundation usually will not support requests for individuals; endowments or capital campaigns; fund-raising events; publications, films, or videos; eradication of deficits or loans; conferences; or religious purposes. Organizations primarily focused on arts education or social service are not eligible.

Geographic Focus: South Carolina

Date(s) Application is Due: Apr 3; Jul 31

Contact: David Farren; (312) 977-2708; fax (312) 977-1686; dfarren@gddf.org

Internet: http://gddf.org/grants/funding-guidelines/lowcountry-artistic-vitality

Sponsor: Gaylord and Dorothy Donnelley Foundation

35 E Wacker Drive, Suite 2600

Chicago, IL 60601-2102

Gaylord and Dorothy Donnelley Foundation Regionally Significant   790
Collections Grants

Making grants to organizations is the primary way that the Gaylord and Dorothy Donnelley Foundation fulfills its mission of land conservation, artistic vitality, and regionally significant collections in the Chicago region and lowcountry of South Carolina. In both the Chicago Region and Lowcountry of South Carolina, the Foundation makes project grants for collections of regional significance; to help at critical junctures along a spectrum of conservation – from basic preservation through cutting edge mining and creative interpretation. Regionally significant collections – including art, artifacts, letters, photographs, maps, and books – are those that illuminate the unique culture, history and heritage of the Chicago region or the Lowcountry of South Carolina. GDDF may offer project support at any one or more of the following stages: stabilization; restoration; cataloguing or indexing; archival processing; finding aids; digitization; and interpretation. Applications are due three months prior to board meetings. Obtain required application forms from the office. Annual deadlines are April 3 and July 31.

Requirements: IRS 501(c)3 organizations serving the Chicago region or the South Carolina low country are eligible. The Chicago region includes 13 counties in three states: Illinois—Lake, McHenry, Kane, Cook, DuPage, Kendall, Grundy, and Will; Wisconsin—Kenosha, and Walworth; and Indiana—Lake, Porter, and LaPorte. Lowcountry of South Carolina counties include Beaufort, Colleton, Charleston, Berkeley, Georgetown, Dorchester, Jasper, Horry, and Hampton.

Restrictions: The Foundation usually will not support requests for individuals; endowments or capital campaigns; fund-raising events; publications, films, or videos; eradication of deficits or loans; conferences; or religious purposes. The Foundation generally does not support existing staff salaries or indirect costs; nor does in make grants for one-time exhibitions.

Geographic Focus: Illinois, South Carolina
Date(s) Application is Due: Apr 3; Jul 31
Contact: Susan Clark; (312) 977-2709; fax (312) 977-1686; sclark@gddf.org
Internet: http://gddf.org/grants/funding-guidelines/collections
Sponsor: Gaylord and Dorothy Donnelley Foundation
35 E Wacker Drive, Suite 2600
Chicago, IL 60601-2102

Gebbie Foundation Grants 791

The Foundation's mission is to support appropriate charitable and humanitarian programs to improve the quality of life, primarily in Chautauqua County, New York by focusing on: children, youth and education; arts; human services; and community development. The foundation's strategic focus is to rejuvenate downtown Jamestown, New York, through economic development. Types of funding include: annual campaigns; building/renovation; capital campaigns; continuing support; endowments; equipment; general/operating support; matching/challenge support; program-related investments/loans; scholarship funds; and seed money.

Requirements: Organizations requesting funding must be approved as (or sponsored by) a 501(c)3 organization. The Board meets quarterly and proposals are accepted throughout the year. Before preparing a complete proposal, applicants are urged to submit a letter of inquiry addressed to the Executive Director. The letter should contain a descriptive title for the project, the project's intent, objectives, outcome measures, short and long term funding needs, and other relevant factual information. After reviewing the letter of inquiry, a detailed proposal may be requested. It should not be assumed that such a request is an indication of funding. The full proposal should include a detailed narrative, budgets, a board list, an IRS determination letter, other funding sources and financial documentation. In addition, the proposal should describe expected future funding sources and should indicate whether and to what extent additional funding by the Foundation will be necessary for the proposed project to be successful. The Foundation will respond to all inquiries from eligible organizations.

Restrictions: Grants are not made to individuals or sectarian or religious organizations. Because the Foundation makes annual contributions to the United Way of Southern Chautauqua County, applications for assistance from United Way-funded agencies will not be considered unless there is a strong link to the strategic focus.

Geographic Focus: New York
Amount of Grant: 1,000 - 1,000,000 USD
Contact: John C. Merino, Executive Director; (716) 487-1062; fax (716) 484-6401; jmerino@gebbie.org or info@gebbie.org
Internet: http://www.gebbie.org
Sponsor: Gebbie Foundation
111 West Second Street, Suite 1100
Jamestown, NY 14701

Gene Haas Foundation 792

The Gene Haas Foundation was formed in 1999 to fund the needs of the local community and other deserving charities, at the discretion of its founder, Gene Haas. Of special importance to the Foundation are children's charities and organizations that feed the poor, especially within the local community of Ventura County. In addition, the Foundation provides scholarship funds

to community colleges and vocational schools for students entering technical training programs, especially machinist-based certificate and degree programs. Giving is primarily in California.

Requirements: The Gene Haas Foundation provides grants to organizations that are exempt under Internal Revenue Code Section 501(c)3 and currently are classified as a public charity pursuant to Internal Revenue Code Section 509(a)1, 2 or 3 (an "Exempt Public Charity"). Funds from the Gene Haas Foundation must be fully utilized within 2 years of date of grant. Funds that are not expended must be returned unless other arrangements are approved by the Gene Haas Foundation.

Restrictions: Grants provided by the Gene Haas Foundation, or the interest generated from those grants, may not be used to influence any legislation or the outcome of any election, to conduct a voter registration drive or to satisfy a charitable pledge or obligation of any person or organization.

Geographic Focus: California
Amount of Grant: Up to 100,000 USD
Contact: Gene F. Haas; (805) 278-1800; info@ghaasfoundation.org
Internet: http://ghaasfoundation.org/
Sponsor: Gene Haas Foundation
2800 Sturgis Road
Oxnard, CA 93030-8901

Genentech Corporate Charitable Contributions Grants 793

The Foundation's primary focus areas are health science education, patient education/advocacy, and community. The Foundation supports nonprofits through its contributions in two primary ways: project-specific or general support funding to organizations whose mission aligns with the Foundation's focus areas; and sponsorships of selected events that fall into the Foundation's focus areas. Interested applicant's are encouraged to submit applications online.

Requirements: Nonprofit organizations recognized by the IRS as tax exempt, public charities, located in the United States are eligible to apply. Eligible grantees may include public elementary and secondary schools, as well as public colleges and universities and public hospitals.

Restrictions: The Foundation does not provide funding to organizations that discriminate on the basis of age, political affiliation, race, national origin, ethnicity, gender, disability, sexual orientation or religious beliefs. Funding is not provided for: advertising journals or booklets; alumni drives; capital campaigns/building funds; continuing medical education; infrastructural requests (e.g. salaries, equipment); memorial funds; memberships; organizations based outside of the United States; political or sectarian organizations; professional sports events or athletes; religious organizations; scholarships; yearbooks.

Geographic Focus: California
Samples: To be distributed among 19 organizations (CA)—for science programs for students in the San Francisco Bay area, $1 million.
Contact: Program Manager; (650) 467-9494; give@gene.com
Internet: http://www.gene.com/gene/about/community/overview.jsp
Sponsor: Genentech
1 DNA Way
South San Francisco, CA 94080-4990

General Dynamics Corporation Grants 794

Corporate contributions funding goes to education, civic and public affairs, health and welfare, and arts and culture. Types of support include capital campaigns, general support, and operating funds. Grants are made nationally and communities where the company has operations. There is no formal application process. Interested applicants may submit a letter of application.

Geographic Focus: All States
Contact: Arlene Nestle, (703) 876-3305; fax (703) 876-3600
Internet: http://www.generaldynamics.com
Sponsor: General Dynamics Corporation
2941 Fairview Park Drive, Suite 100
Falls Church, VA 22042-4513

General Mills Foundation Grants 795

The Foundation was created to focus its philanthropic resources on community needs. Strategic objectives are to: demonstrably improve the quality of life in communities with GM facilities and employees; initiate innovative solutions and approaches to improve youth nutrition and fitness; and to support GM employees and retirees giving to United Way, education, and arts and culture organizations through gift matching. Funding priorities include: social services; youth nutrition and fitness; education; and arts and culture. Priority is given to organizations meeting the following criteria: their mission is closely related to the Foundation's priorities; programs or activities are based in communities with GM operations and employees; programs or activities involve GM employees and retirees; and services create sustainable community improvement. Applications are accepted at any time.

Requirements: U.S. and Canadian charitable 501(c)3 and 509(a) nonprofits in communities where General Mills operates (California, Georgia, Illinois, Indiana, Iowa, Maryland, Massachusetts, Missouri, Minnesota, Missouri, Montana, New Jersey, New York, Ohio, Oklahoma, Pennsylvania, Tennessee and Wisconsin) are eligible.

Restrictions: The Foundation does not support: organizations without 501(c)3 and 509(a) status; organizations that do not comply with the Foundation's non-discrimination policy; individuals; social, labor, veterans, alumni or fraternal organizations serving a limited constituency; travel by groups; recreational, sporting events or athletic associations; religious organizations for religious purposes; basic research; organizations seeking underwriting for advertising; political causes, candidates or legislative lobbying efforts; conferences, seminars and workshops; campaigns to eliminate or control specific diseases; publications, films or television programs; underwriting for program sponsorship.

Geographic Focus: Arizona, Arkansas, California, Georgia, Illinois, Indiana, Iowa, Maryland, Massachusetts, Michigan, Minnesota, Missouri, Montana, New Jersey, New Mexico, New York, Ohio, Oklahoma, Pennsylvania, Tennessee, Wisconsin

Contact: Christina L. Shea, President; (763) 764-2211; fax (763) 764-4114
Internet: http://www.generalmills.com/corporate/commitment/foundation.aspx
Sponsor: General Mills Foundation
1 General Mills Boulevard, P.O. Box 1113
Minneapolis, MN 55440

General Motors Foundation Grants Support Program 796

With a strong commitment to diversity in all areas, the targeted areas of focus for the Foundation are: education; health and human services; civic and community; public policy; arts and culture; and environment and energy. Primary consideration is given to requests that meet the following criteria: exhibit a clear purpose and defined need in one of the foundation's areas of focus; recognize innovative approaches in addressing the defined need; demonstrate an efficient organization and detail the organization's ability to follow through on the proposal; and, explain clearly the benefits to the foundation and the plant city communities. Paper applications are no longer accepted. Completion of an online eligibility quiz is the first step in the application process.

Requirements: Nonprofit, tax-exempt organizations and institutions are eligible to apply. Applications must be made online.

Restrictions: The Foundation not not support organizations that discriminate on the basis of race, religion, creed, gender, age, veteran status, physical challenge or national origin. Contributions are generally not provided for: individuals; religious organizations; political parties or candidates; U.S. hospitals and health care institutions (general operating support); capital campaigns; endowment funds; conferences, workshops or seminars not directly related to GM's business interests.

Geographic Focus: All States

Samples: American National Red Cross (Washington, DC)—for relief efforts in South Asia and Africa, $1 million; Pierre Chambon, College de France (Paris, France) and Ronald Evans, Salk Institute for Biological Studies (La Jolla, CA)—to honor their contributions to the diagnosis, prevention, and treatment of cancer, $250,000 jointly.

Contact: Grant Coordinator; (313) 556-5000
Internet: http://www.gm.com/company/gmability/community/guidelines/index.html
Sponsor: General Motors Foundation
300 Renaissance Center, P.O. Box 300
Detroit, MI 48265-3000

Genesis Foundation Grants 797

The Foundation funds projects and program in the areas of health and formal education, benefiting children 0 to 18 years old, as well as training programs in these two areas. Capital, operating, program and general grants are funded. Approximately eighty percent of grant-making is devoted to Colombian entities, with the remainder devoted to projects in the US, specifically in Southern Florida, Washington, D.C. and the New York Metropolitan area.

Requirements: Preliminary criteria to apply for a grant include: must be located in Colombia, Southern Florida, Washington, D.C. or the New York Metropolitan Area; must be incorporated as a non-profit, charitable institution in the appropriate jurisdiction; must have been in operation for a minimum of two (2) full years; must include at least three (3) people in decision-making process at all times; must benefit a minimum of 50 people per year; in Colombia, must have raised at a minimum the equivalent of U.S. $10,000 in the previous two years; in the U.S. must have raised a minimum of $20,000 in the previous two years; must have an independent financial auditor; must be able to provide audited financial statements for the previous three years; must be able to provide a budget for the organization and the project for which the grant is sought; must not be a political organization; and must not have a religious purpose.

Restrictions: Individuals and political or religious causes are ineligible.
Geographic Focus: District of Columbia, Florida, New York, Colombia
Date(s) Application is Due: Mar 15; Sep 15
Amount of Grant: 10,000 - 100,000 USD
Samples: Asociacion Social Popular (Bello, Colombia)—to purchase an educational facility, $35,000; Fundacion Estructurar (Bucaramanga, Colombia)—to provide education to working children, with an emphasis on training in design and graphic arts, $15,000; Fundacion Neumologica Colombiana (Bogota, Colombia)—to create an asthma center for children, $240,000; Nutrir (Bogota, Colombia)—to construct an additional facility that will provide nutritional and social services to underserved children, $40,000.

Contact: Grants Administrator; (212) 763-3703; fax (917) 591-7858; genesis@genesid-foundation.org
Internet: http://www.genesis-foundation.org
Sponsor: Genesis Foundation
140 East 45th Street, 2 Grant Central Tower 18th Floor, Suite A
New York, NY 10017

George and Ruth Bradford Foundation Grants 798

The foundation awards grants to local nonprofit organizations in the San Francisco Bay Area and Mendocino, California region. Areas of interest include: children and youth; families; education/higher education; environmental/wildlife conservation; housing and; social services. Types of support include general operating support and scholarship funds. T

Requirements: California nonprofit organizations in the San Francisco peninsula and Mendocino, California region are eligible to apply. There is no deadline date to adhere to. The Board meets monthly, letters of inquiry may be submitted throughout the year for review.

Restrictions: No grants to individuals.
Geographic Focus: California
Samples: Frank R. Howard Foundation, Willits, CA, $10,000-hospital building fund; Ukiah Valley Cultural & Recreation Center. Ukiah, CA, $5,000—youth recreation grant; MC Aids Volunteer Network, Ukiah, CA, $1,000—health services grant.

Contact: Myrna Oglesby, Director; (707) 462-0141; fax (707) 462-0160
Sponsor: George and Ruth Bradford Foundation
P.O. Box 720
Ukiah, CA 95482-0720

George and Sarah Buchanan Foundation Grants 799

Established in 2006, the George and Sarah Buchanan Foundation offers funding throughout the state of Virginia. Its primary fields of interest include: health care, health organizations, and religion. Support typically is given for general operations. There are no specified application formats or annual deadlines, and applicants should proceed by forwarding a proposal to the Foundation office. Recent grants have ranged from $250 to $20,000.

Requirements: Applicants should be 501(c)3 organizations either located in, or serving residents of, Virginia. Preference is given to the general Danville, Virginia, region.

Geographic Focus: Virginia
Amount of Grant: 250 - 20,000 USD
Samples: Averett University, Danville, Virginia, $20,000 - general operating support; Danville Cancer Association, Danville, Virginia, $20,000 - general operating support; Smile Train, Washington, DC, $250 - general operating support.

Contact: George Buchanan, Jr., (434) 797-3543
Sponsor: George and Sarah Buchanan Foundation
400 Bridge Street
Danville, VA 24541-1404

George A Ohl Jr. Foundation Grants 800

The purpose of the George A Ohl Jr. Foundation is to improve the well-being of the citizens of the State of New Jersey through science, health, recreation, education and increased good citizenship. Grants are made to organizations engaged in such work whether through research, publications, health, school or college activities. The Foundation's mission is the relief of the poor; the improvement of living conditions; the care of the sick, the young, the aged, the homeless, the incompetent and the helpless. The foundation will target: 35% of its grants to Community Redevelopment; 35% to Health and Human Services organizations; 15% for Arts and culture; 15% for Educational requests. Application deadlines are: January 22 for a March meeting and, June 15 for an August meeting. Application forms are available online. Applicants will receive notice acknowledging receipt of the grant request, and subsequently be notified of the grant declination or approval.

Requirements: New Jersey 501(c)3 nonprofit organizations are eligible to apply. Proposals should be submitted in the following format: completed Common Grant Application Form; an original Proposal Statement; an audited financial report and a current year operating budget; a copy of your official IRS Letter with your tax determination; a listing of your Board of Directors. Proposal Statements (second item in the above Format) should answer these questions: what are the objectives and expected outcomes of this program/project/request; what strategies will be used to accomplish your objective; what is the timeline for completion; if this is part of an on-going program, how long has it been in operation; what criteria will you use to measure success; if the request is not fully funded, what other sources can you engage; an Itemized budget should be included; please describe any collaborative ventures. Prior to the distribution of funds, all approved grantees must sign and return a Grant Agreement Form, stating that the funds will be used for the purpose intended. Progress reports and Completion reports must also be filed as required for your specific grant. All current grantees must be in good standing with required documentation prior to submitting new proposals to any foundation.

Restrictions: Grants are not made for political purposes, nor to organizations which discriminate on the basis of race, ethnic origin, sexual or religious preference, age or gender

Geographic Focus: New Jersey

Date(s) Application is Due: Jan 22; Jun 15

Amount of Grant: 3,000 - 35,000 USD

Samples: Mountainside Hospital Foundation, $35,000—Modernization of Internal Medicine Residents' Learning Center; Bloomfield College, $10,000—Improving Academic Success Through Technological Support Project; Medical Missions for Children, $5,000—Giggles Theater Programming Support (12 performances).

Contact: Wachovia Bank, N.A., Trustee; grantinquiries2@wachovia.com

Internet: https://www.wachovia.com/foundation/v/index.jsp?vgnextoid=e0f7 8689fb0aa110VgnVCM1000004b0d1872RCRD&vgnextfmt=default

Sponsor: George A Ohl Jr. Foundation

190 River Road, NJ3132

Summit, NJ 07901

George B. Page Foundation Grants 801

The foundation awards grants to Santa Barbara, CA, nonprofit organizations in support of programs for children and youth, youth development, clubs, and centers; athletics/sports, Special Olympics; community and economic development; education; human services; YM/YWCAs and YM/YWHAs. Types of support include annual campaigns; continuing support; debt reduction; emergency funds; general/operating support; program development; and seed money.

Requirements: Application forms are required, but organizations should initially call or write the Foundation to discuss the project, and request an application.

Restrictions: Funding is not available for individuals, endowment funds, or matching gifts.

Geographic Focus: California

Date(s) Application is Due: Oct 1

Amount of Grant: 2,000 - 50,000 USD

Contact: Sara Sorensen, Trustee; (805) 730-3634

Sponsor: George B. Page Foundation

P.O. Box 1299

Santa Barbara, CA 93102-1299

George B. Storer Foundation Grants 802

The foundation awards grants, primarily in Florida, in its areas of interest, including higher education, social services—particularly for the blind, youth organizations, conservation, hospitals, and cultural programs. Types of support include building construction/renovation, capital campaigns, general operating support, matching/challenge grants, and research grants. There are no application forms. Applications should be submitted between October 15 and the listed deadline.

Geographic Focus: All States

Date(s) Application is Due: Nov 15

Contact: Grants Administrator, c/o Thomas McDonald

Sponsor: George B. Storer Foundation

P.O. Box 1040

Tavernier, FL 33070

George E. Hatcher, Jr. and Ann Williams Hatcher Foundation Grants 803

The George E. Hatcher and Ann Williams Hatcher Foundation was created to support charitable organizations that provide for the relief of diseased people and the relief of human suffering which is due to disease, ill health, physical weakness, physical disability and/or physical injury. In addition, the foundation supports organizations that aid in the promotion and prolongation of life and that support the principle of dying with dignity. Grants from George E. Hatcher and Ann Williams Hatcher Foundation are primarily one year in duration; on occasion, multi-year support is awarded. Applicants must apply online at the grant website. Applicants are strongly encouraged to do the following before applying: review the downloadable state application procedures for additional helpful information and clarifications; review the downloadable online-application guidelines at the grant website; review the foundation's funding history (link is available from the grant website); review the online application questions in advance; and review the list of required attachments. These will generally include: a list of board members; financial statements (audited, reviewed, or compiled by independent auditor); an organization summary; a list of other funding sources; an IRS Determination letter; and other required documents. All attachments must be uploaded in the online application as PDF, Word, or Excel files. The George E. Hatcher and Ann Williams Hatcher Foundation application deadline is 11:59 p.m. on May 31. Applicants will be notified of grant decisions by letter within one to two months after the deadline.

Requirements: Disbursements are authorized to institutions or organizations located in the Middle Georgia area (Bibb County & surrounding communities) which provide health care and/or shelter for individuals (especially children) who cannot otherwise obtain such services due to circumstances beyond their control. A breakdown of number/percentage of people served by specific counties is required on the online application.

Restrictions: The foundation does not support requests from individuals, organizations attempting to influence policy through direct lobbying, or any political campaigns.

Geographic Focus: Georgia

Date(s) Application is Due: May 31

Samples: Macon Volunteer Clinic, Macon, Georgia, $25,000; Rebuilding Macon, Macon, Georgia, $25,000; Methodist Home of the South Georgia Conference, Macon, Georgia, $10,000.

Contact: Quanda Allen; (404) 264-1377; quanda.allen@baml.com

Internet: https://www.bankofamerica.com/philanthropic/fn_search.action

Sponsor: George E. Hatcher, Jr. and Ann Williams Hatcher Foundation

3414 Peachtree Road, N.E., Suite 1475, GA7-813-14-04

Atlanta, GA 30326-1113

George F. Baker Trust Grants 804

Grants are awarded nationwide, with preference given to nonprofits in the eastern United States, primarily for K-12, higher, and secondary education; hospitals; social services; private foundations; and zoos/zoological societies. Types of support include general operating support and matching funds. There are no application forms or deadlines. The board meets in June and November to consider requests.

Requirements: An application form is not required. Along with a letter of inquiry and brief outline of a proposal, applicants should submit the following: signature and title of chief executive officer; a copy of the organization's IRS determination letter; a detailed description of the project and amount of funding requested; and a listing of additional sources and amount of support. As a result of the enormous number of applications received and limited number of grants, only those applicants who receive a grant will be notified.

Restrictions: Funding is given primarily in Connecticut, Florida, Massachusetts, and New York. Grants are not made to individuals for scholarships or loans.

Geographic Focus: Connecticut, Florida, Massachusetts, New York

Amount of Grant: 1,000 - 50,000 USD

Contact: Rocio Suarez, Executive Director; (212) 755-1890; fax (212) 319-6316; rocio@bakernye.com

Sponsor: George F. Baker Trust

477 Madison Avenue, Suite 1650

New York, NY 10022

George Foundation Grants 805

The George Foundation strive to support organizations and programs that assist in developing strong, stable families across Fort Bend County region of Texas. The Foundation's areas of interest include: family stability; scholarships; foundation initiated programs, current programs include, Youth in Philanthropy (YIP), Leadership Excellence for Non-Profits, Integrated Mental Health Care, and Transportation. The Foundation prefers to fund the following types of grants to support Fort Bend organizations in their delivery of services to the community (listed in order of priority): program/project support; foundation initiated; general operating; capital. Proposal deadlines for making grant applications to the Foundation are January 15, April 15, July 15 and October 15 of each year. All proposals for capital support will be grouped together for review. The deadline for capital proposals will be October 15 of each year.

Requirements: Non-profit organizations in Fort Bend County, Texas may submit grant proposals.

Restrictions: The Foundation does not fund: grants to organizations that do not have a current 501(c)3 determination letter; churches or other organized religious bodies; grants to another organization that distributes money to recipients of its own selection, i.e., a regranting organization; regional, national or international programs; grants for research or studies; grants for travel, conferences, conventions, group meetings, or seminars; the purchase of event tickets, tables, ads or sponsorships; support to fairs and festivals; religious or private schools; request for funds to develop films, videos, books or other media projects; direct mail campaigns; loans of any kind; grants to individuals; grants to fraternal organizations; political interests of any kind; and institutions that discriminate on the basis of race, creed, gender, national origin, age, disability or sexual orientation in policy or in practice.

Geographic Focus: Texas

Date(s) Application is Due: Jan 15; Apr 15; Jul 15; Oct 15

Amount of Grant: 1,000 - 4,000,000 USD

Contact: Dee Koch, Grant Officer; (281) 342-6109; fax (281) 341-7635; dkoch@thegeorgefoundation.org

Internet: http://www.thegeorgefoundation.org

Sponsor: George Foundation

310 Morton Street, PMB Suite C

Richmond, TX 77469

George Frederick Jewett Foundation Grants 806

The foundation is concerned primarily with people and values. The grants program focuses on the future and on stimulating and supporting activities and projects of established, voluntary, nonprofit organizations that are of importance to human welfare. Grants are made in the fields of arts and humanities, conservation and preservation, education, health care and medical services, population, religion, and social welfare. The foundation may support research on and studies of important problems of public concern solely for the purpose of aiding in the gathering and presenting of facts that may assist the public to better understand such problems and to arrive at realistic and effective solutions to them. From time to time, support may be given to the scholarship, fellowship, and research programs of established institutions when sufficient evidence is available to establish clearly that the applicant organization is awarding such grants in accordance with the regulations established by the IRS. Grants are awarded to support activities in progress, research into potential projects, building and equipment, general operations, program development, seed funding, research, technical assistance, and matching funds. Inquiries for clarification of the foundation's policy and program emphasis are encouraged.

Requirements: Preference is given to public charities or nonprivate foundations. The foundation confines its grants largely to requests from eastern Washington and the San Francisco Bay area.

Restrictions: Grants do not support advertising; advocacy, athletic, international, religious, political, or veterans organizations; or individuals.

Geographic Focus: California, Washington

Amount of Grant: 5,000 - 50,000 USD

Contact: Ann Gralnek, (415) 421-1351; fax (415) 421-0721; ADGjewettf@aol.com or tfbjewettf@aol.com

Sponsor: George Frederick Jewett Foundation

235 Montgomery Street, Suite 612

San Francisco, CA 94104

George Gund Foundation Grants 807

The Foundation's long-standing interests include: arts; economic development; community revitalization; education; environment; and human services. The Foundation considers global climate change an urgent issue that cuts across all of the Foundation's programs. The Foundation takes seriously it's own responsibility and wants to hear from grant applicants what they are doing or considering to reduce or to eliminate their organizational impact on climate change. The Foundation also supports special projects grants, which currently include: Retinal Degenerative Diseases research grants, making an annual commitment for research on the causes, nature and prevention of inherited retinal degenerative diseases and; philanthropic services grants, offering support to organizations that strengthen the infrastructure of the nonprofit and philanthropic communities. The George Gund Foundation also supports capital grant requests but only for projects that are clearly aligned with their program priorities and that meet Green Building Council LEED (Leadership in Energy and Environmental Design) certification. The Foundation's green building policy covers both planning and construction grants. In addition, the Foundation supports opportunities that cross program boundaries and that integrate elements of the Foundation's interests. Although the Foundation's focus is centered in the Greater Cleveland, Ohio region, a portion of their grantmaking will continue to support state and national policy making that bolsters their work. Proposals should be mailed directly to the George Gund Foundation. All proposals are screened and evaluated by the staff before presentation at Trustee Meetings. Receipt of proposals will be acknowledged by mail.

Requirements: 501(c)3 nonprofit organizations are eligible to apply for funding, with a special interest in Greater Cleveland, Ohio region. Proposals are accepted three times: March 15, July 15 and November 15. Proposals are due the next business day if a deadline falls on a weekend. The grant application form is available on the George Gund Foundation website. All proposals must include a climate change statement, the Foundation's website includes resources to assist grantees with this task. Applicants also must include a completed Grant Application Cover Sheet, which is signed by the organization's board chair and executive director. Proposals should also include: organizational background; history; mission; types of programs offered; constituencies served; project description; justification of need; specific goals and objectives; activities planned to meet goals and objectives; project time line; qualifications of key personnel; methods of evaluation; project budget; anticipated expenses, including details about how Foundation funds would be used; anticipated income, including information about other sources approached for funding; organizational budget; previous and current year budget and proposed budget for project year(s) showing both income and expenses; the organization's most recent audited financial statement, do not include IRS 990 forms; supporting documents; list of current trustees; letters of support; readily available printed material about organization such as annual reports and brochures; IRS letter confirming Internal Revenue Code 501(c)3 status and classification as a public charity or information confirming status as a government unit or agency. The Foundation also will accept the Ohio Common Grant Form, available at www.ohiograntmakers.org, if organizations are using it to apply to multiple funders. Faxed or electronic proposals are not accepted.

Restrictions: Do not submit proposals in notebooks, binders or plastic folders and print proposals on both sides of each sheet of paper. The Foundation normally does not consider grants for endowments. Capital requests must meet the Foundation's program goals and also adhere to green building standards of environmental sustainability. Details on these requirements are available from the Foundation. Grants are not made for debt reduction or to fund benefit events. The Foundation does not make grants to individuals, nor does it administer programs it supports. Grants are limited to organizations located in the United States.

Geographic Focus: All States

Date(s) Application is Due: Mar 15; Jul 15; Nov 15

Contact: David Abbott, Executive Director; (216) 241-3114; fax (216) 241-6560; info@gundfdn.org

Internet: http://www.gundfdn.org/what.asp

Sponsor: George Gund Foundation

1845 Guildhall Building, 45 Prospect Avenue, West

Cleveland, OH 44115

George J. and Effie L. Seay Foundation Grants 808

The George J. & Effie L. Seay Foundation was established in 1957 to support and promote programs and services provided by qualifying charitable organizations in the Commonwealth of Virginia. Grants from the Seay Foundation are one year in duration. Application materials are available for download at the grant website. Applicants are strongly encouraged to review the state application guidelines for additional helpful information and clarifications before applying. Applicants are also encouraged to review the trust's funding history (link is available from the grant website). The George J. & Effie L. Seay Foundation has biannual deadlines of May 1 and November 1. Applicants for the May deadline will be notified of grant decisions by June 30. Applicants for the November deadline will be notified by February 28 of the following year.

Requirements: Applications must be mailed. Applicants must be classified by the Internal Revenue Service (IRS) as a 501(c)3 public charity.

Restrictions: Because requests for support usually exceed available resources, organizations are advised to apply to either the Morgan Trust or the Seay Foundation. An organization normally will not be considered for a subsequent grant from either the Morgan Trust or the Seay Foundation until at least 3

years after the date of the last grant payment. The Seay Foundation makes grants primarily for programs and projects designed to provide specific services or training. Requests for general operating grants will not be considered. The foundation does not support requests from individuals, organizations attempting to influence policy through direct lobbying, or any political campaigns.
Geographic Focus: Virginia
Date(s) Application is Due: May 1; Nov 1
Samples: Black History Museum and Cultural Center, Richmond, Virginia, $10,000, for exhibition guides and teacher workshops; School of the Performing Arts, Richmond, Virginia, $15,000; Virginia Historical Society, Richmond, Virginia, $20,000.
Contact: Sarah Kay, Vice President; (804) 788-2673; sarah.kay@baml.com
Internet: https://www.bankofamerica.com/philanthropic/fn_search.action
Sponsor: George J. and Effie L. Seay Foundation
1111 E. Main Street, VA2-300-12-92
Richmond, VA 23219

George K. Baum Foundation Grants   809
The foundation supports nonprofits in the greater Kansas City, MO, area in its areas of interest, including arts and cultural programs, education, health care, Jewish federated giving, and general charitable giving. There are no application deadlines or forms.
Requirements: Nonprofits in the metropolitan Kansas City area are eligible.
Geographic Focus: Missouri
Amount of Grant: Up to 392,000 USD
Contact: Jonathan Baum; (816) 474-1100 or (800) 821-7195; fax (816) 283-5171
Sponsor: George K. Baum Foundation
120 W 12th Street, Suite 800
Kansas City, MO 64105

George Kress Foundation Grants   810
Incorporated in Wisconsin in 1953, the George Kress Foundation awards grants to eligible Wisconsin nonprofit organizations in its areas of interest, including: arts and culture; boys and girls clubs; children and youth services; Christian agencies and churches; community and economic development; education; family services; health organizations; higher education; historic preservation; historical societies; hospitals; human services; libraries; recreation; United Ways and Federated Giving Programs; and YM/YWCAs and YM/YWHAs. Types of support include: annual campaigns; building and renovation; capital campaigns; continuing support; professorships; program development; and research. Preference is given to nonprofit organizations that benefit the communities of Green Bay and Madison. Most recent awards have ranged from $200 to $50,000. There are no specified annual deadlines for submission.
Requirements: Interested applicants should submit a letter of inquiry describing their proposed project.
Geographic Focus: Wisconsin
Amount of Grant: 200 - 50,000 USD
Samples: St. Vincent Health Systems, Little Rock, Arkansas, $25,000 - overall program support; Weidner Center, Green Bay, Wisconsin, $30,000 - overall program support; University of Wisconsin Foundation, Madison, Wisconsin, $50,000 - overall program support.
Contact: John Kress, President; (920) 327-5670 or (920) 433-3109
Sponsor: George Kress Foundation
1700 North Webster Avenue, P.O. Box 12800
Green Bay, WI 54307-2800

George P. Davenport Trust Fund Grants   811
Established in Maine in 1927, the Trust awards grants for education, religion, temperance and needy children. The focus of the Trust is on the economically disadvantaged. Types of support include: building and renovation, emergency funding, general operating funds, capacity building, matching/challenge funds, and seed money. It is recommended that applicants contact the Trust office to make an initial inquiry regarding projects before beginning the application process. Interested applicants should use the standard Maine Philanthropy Center common grant application which is available at mainephilanthropy.org. Grant applications are accepted all year, with no deadlines.
Requirements: Only nonprofit organizations serving the residents of Bath, Maine, and its surrounding area are eligible to apply.
Geographic Focus: Maine
Amount of Grant: 125 - 10,000 USD
Samples: Bath Elementary PTA, Bath, Maine, $6,550 - camp scholarships for youth; Brunswick Area Respite Care, Topsham, Maine, $10,000 - adult

disabilities of aging support; Good Shepherd Food Bank, Auburn, Maine, $5,000 - food for the needy.
Contact: Barry M. Sturgeon, Trustee; (270) 443-3431; fax (800) 665-5510; davenporttrust@verizon.net
Sponsor: George P. Davenport Trust Fund
65 Front Street
Bath, ME 04530-2508

George R. Wallace Foundation Grants   812
The foundation's fields of interest are culture, education, and the environment. Giving is primarily in the Fitchburg/Leominster, Massachusetts, area. Priority will be given to support education, particularly programs benefiting low income students. Grants will be awarded to support building/renovation, capital campaigns, endowment, general operating, multi-year pledges, special projects, and equipment. Initial contact should be by telephone or email inquiry. There is no set form of application, but letters should contain a concise statement of the purpose for which the grant is sought. All applicants should include the current year's operating budget; the most recent audited financial statements; a list of board members; and a copy of the IRS determination letter.
Requirements: Organizations in Massachusetts are eligible to apply.
Restrictions: Grants will not be awarded to individuals or for scholarships, fellowships, or loans.
Geographic Focus: Massachusetts
Amount of Grant: 10,000 USD
Contact: Lucia Thompson, (617) 570-1355; lthompson@goodwinprocter.com
Sponsor: George R. Wallace Foundation
Goodwin Procter LLP, Exchange Place
Boston, MA 02109-2881

George S. and Dolores Dore Eccles Foundation Grants   813
The foundation awards grants to eligible Utah organizations in its areas of interest, including arts, children and youth, economics, higher education, hospitals, medical research, performing arts, visual arts, and social services. Types of support include building construction/renovation, capital campaigns, equipment acquisition, general operating grants, matching/challenge grants, professorships, program development, research grants, and scholarship funds. A request for application is available online.
Requirements: Giving primarily in Utah.
Restrictions: Funding requests will not be considered from the following types of organizations: those that have not received a tax exemption letter establishing 501(c)3 status from the Internal Revenue Service, unless they are a unit of government, in which case such a letter is not required; other private foundations; those of a political nature that attempt to influence legislation and/or candidacy of persons for elected public office; conduit organizations, unified funds, or those that use funds to make grants to support other organizations; those that do not have fiscal responsibility for the proposed project. Funds will also not be considered for: contingencies, deficits, or debt reduction; general endowment funds; direct aid to individuals; conferences, seminars, or medical research; requests which do not fall within the Foundation's specified areas of interest.
Geographic Focus: Utah
Samples: Westminster College of Salt Lake City (UT)—for undergraduate scholarships, $1.2 million over three years.
Contact: Director; (801) 246-5340; fax (801) 350-3510; gseg@gseccles.org
Internet: http://www.gsecclesfoundation.org
Sponsor: George S. and Dolores Dore Eccles Foundation
79 South Main Street, 12th Floor
Salt Lake City, UT 84111

George W. Codrington Charitable Foundation Grants   814
The George W. Codrington Charitable Foundation gives primarily to nonprofit organizations in Ohio, but may consider other areas. The Foundation funds higher education, hospitals, museums, arts groups and performing arts, and youth programs. Types of support include annual and capital campaigns, continuing support, equipment, general/operating support, program development, and research.
Requirements: Application forms are not required. Applicants should submit three copies of the following: their IRS determination letter; a brief history of the organization and description of its mission; the geographic area to be served; a list of the board of directors, trustees, officers, and other key individuals with their affiliations; and a detailed description of the project and amount of funding requested. Proposals should be submitted one month before the board meets in April, June, September, and December. Organizations are notified of funding promptly after the board meeting.

Restrictions: Funding is not available for individuals, endowment funds, or loans.
Geographic Focus: Ohio
Amount of Grant: 1,000 - 50,000 USD
Contact: Craig Martahus; (216) 566-8674; tommie.robertston@thomasonhine.com
Sponsor: George W. Codrington Charitable Foundation
127 Public Square, 39th Floor
Cleveland, OH 44114-1216

George W. Wells Foundation Grants   815
The George W. Wells Foundation was established in 1934 to support and
promote quality educational, human-services, and health-care programming
for underserved populations. In the area of education, the fund supports
academic access, enrichment, and remedial programming for children, youth,
adults, and senior citizens that focuses on preparing individuals to achieve
while in school and beyond. In the area of health care, the fund supports
programming that improves access to primary care for traditionally underserved
individuals, health education initiatives and programming that impact at-risk
populations, and medical research. In the area of human services the fund tries
to meet evolving needs of communities. Currently the foundation's focus is on
(but is not limited to) youth development, violence prevention, employment,
life-skills attainment, and food programs. Special consideration is given to
charitable organizations that serve the people of Southbridge, Massachusetts,
and its surrounding communities. Grant requests for general operating support
are strongly encouraged. Program support will also be considered. Small,
program-related capital expenses may be included in general operating or
program requests. The majority of grants from the Wells Foundation are
one year in duration; on occasion, multi-year support is awarded. Applicants
must apply online at the grant website. Applicants are strongly encouraged to
do the following before applying: review the downloadable state application
procedures for additional helpful information and clarifications; review the
downloadable online-application guidelines at the grant website; review the
foundation's funding history (link is available from the grant website); review
the online application questions in advance; and review the list of required
attachments. These will generally include: a list of board members, financial
statements (audited, reviewed, or compiled by independent auditor); an
organization summary; a list of other funding sources; an IRS Determination
letter; and other required documents. All attachments must be uploaded in
the online application as PDF, Word, or Excel files. The application deadline
for the George W. Wells Foundation is 11:59 p.m. on October 15. Applicants
will be notified of grant decisions before December 31.
Requirements: Applicants must have 501(c)3 tax-exempt status.
Restrictions: The foundation does not support requests from individuals,
organizations attempting to influence policy through direct lobbying, or any
political campaigns.
Geographic Focus: Massachusetts
Date(s) Application is Due: Oct 15
Samples: Southern Worcester County Rehabilitation Center, Webster,
Massachusetts, $20,000, Assistance to establish a ceramics and crockery
business as adjunct to current day support and vocational program options;
Youth Opportunities Upheld, Worcester, Massachusetts, $18,500, Pregnant
and Parenting Teens Program; Family Health and Social Service Center,
Worcester, Massachusetts, $25,000, for Oral Health Services for low-income
residents in the Southbridge Area.
Contact: Miki C. Akimoto; (866) 778-6859; miki.akimoto@baml.com
Internet: https://www.bankofamerica.com/philanthropic/fn_search.action
Sponsor: George W. Wells Foundation
225 Franklin Street, 4th Floor, MA1-225-04-02
Boston, MA 02110

Georgia-Pacific Foundation Entrepreneurship Grants   816
Georgia-Pacific believes that self-sufficiency and economic empowerment are
two indispensable elements of every strong community. Entrepreneurs are
often the catalysts of these essential components. That is why the Foundation
believes that to create long-term value in GP communities, it must identify and
nurture the entrepreneurial spirit, especially among youth. The Foundation
partners with local elementary schools, high schools and universities that
encourage and inspire a student's entrepreneurial spirit and offer incentives
such as accreditation and/or certificate programs. It is particularly interested in
programs that help a student transition from a classroom environment to a real
working business model. The Foundation has supported programs that teach
practical economic principles, the benefits of a free enterprise system, and real-
world business skills to workers of any age. It realizes that student entrepreneurs,
when nurtured and developed, become adult entrepreneurs, creating value and

free markets. So, in addition to supporting educational programs for youth,
it also supports organizations that help build capacity in small, minority or
women owned businesses. There is no specific dollar amount for a request
for grants. The dollar amount varies based on the budget requested, program
value and Georgia-Pacific funds available. Types of support available include:
annual campaigns; building and renovation; capital campaigns; conferences
and seminars; continuing support; employee-related scholarships; employee
volunteer services; equipment; general operating support; in-kind gifts; program
development; scholarship funds; sponsorships; scholarships for individuals.
Requirements: Nonprofit organizations in Georgia-Pacific communities are
eligible to apply for funding. To find out whether a program qualifies for
consideration for a Georgia-Pacific Foundation grant, applicants should
complete the Eligibility Survey available online. The Georgia-Pacific
Foundation will accept proposals for grants and in-kind donations from
January 1 through October 31. It is recommended that applicants submit
proposals early in the grant cycle.
Restrictions: No support is given for discriminatory organizations, political
candidates, churches or religious denominations, religious or theological
schools, social, labor, veterans', alumni, or fraternal organizations not
of direct benefit to the entire community, athletic associations, national
organizations with local chapters already receiving support, medical or nursing
schools, or pass-through organizations. No grants to individuals (except for
scholarships), or for emergency needs for general operating support, political
causes, legislative lobbying, or advocacy efforts, goodwill advertising, sporting
events, general operating support for United Way member agencies, tickets or
tables for testimonials or similar benefit events, named academic chairs, social
sciences or health science programs, fundraising events, or trips or tours.
Geographic Focus: Alabama, Arkansas, California, Florida, Georgia, Illinois,
Indiana, Iowa, Kentucky, Louisiana, Massachusetts, Michigan, Mississippi,
New Jersey, New York, North Carolina, Ohio, Oklahoma, Oregon,
Pennsylvania, South Carolina, Tennessee, Texas, Virginia, Washington, West
Virginia, Wisconsin
Date(s) Application is Due: Oct 31
Contact: Curley M. Dossman, Jr., President; (404) 652-4182; fax (404) 749-
2754; cmdossma@gapac.com
Internet: http://gp.com/gpfoundation/entrepreneurship.html
Sponsor: Georgia-Pacific Foundation
133 Peachtree Street, NE, 39th Floor
Atlanta, GA 30303

Geraldine R. Dodge Foundation Arts Grants   817
The Dodge Foundation invites proposals for general operating or project-specific
support from organizations that: enhance the cultural richness of the community
in which they reside and contribute to New Jersey's creative economy. Priority
will be given to those that: pursue and demonstrate the highest standards of
artistic excellence; provide opportunities for meaningful connections between
people and art within their communities, and partner with others to expand
the inclusiveness and the impact of the arts; contribute to the diverse human
narrative by creating new work and/or re-imagining the classics; provide creative
opportunities and living wages for New Jersey artists; use the arts to revitalize
public places and natural spaces and/or help citizens engage in and advocate for
the environmental well-being of their communities. Letters of inquiry should
be received by August 1, with full proposals due by August 30.
Requirements: In order to be eligible for funding, an applicant must: be a
501(c)3 organization that makes its home in or has a significant impact on
New Jersey; demonstrate that it has the administrative and financial capacity
to achieve and assess the stated goals of the proposal; be led by an effective and
professional, paid staff; have a high-functioning board, with an expectation
of 100% of its trustees making an annual personal contribution; and strive
to make connections with other organizations, especially Dodge grantees,
working in the same community or on the same issues.
Restrictions: Funding is not provided for: higher education; health; religion;
capital programs; equipment purchases; indirect costs; endowment funds; and
deficit reduction. The Foundation does not make direct awards to individuals
or support lobbying efforts.
Geographic Focus: New Jersey
Date(s) Application is Due: Mar 1; Aug 30; Dec 3
Contact: Laura Aden Packer, Program Director; (973) 540-8442, ext. 105; fax
(973) 540-1211; lpacker@grdodge.org or info@grdodge.org
Internet: http://www.grdodge.org/what-we-fund/arts/
Sponsor: Geraldine R. Dodge Foundation
14 Maple Avenue, Suite 400
Morristown, NJ 07960

Geraldine R. Dodge Foundation Environment Grants 818

The Geraldine R. Dodge Foundation Environmental Grants program encourages comprehensive thinking about how to safeguard water and reinforce natural systems in order to promote more sustainable communities. The Foundation also supports ongoing, careful stewardship of the land, which includes efforts to support sustainable agriculture and develop regional food systems that offer plentiful access to fresh, local foods. It is particularly interested in empowering communities to identify their own unique challenges and opportunities, and to take ownership of thoughtful planning and decision-making. Furthermore, the Foundation believes that protecting limited resources must fundamentally include efforts to connect people to their natural environment. In particular, the Foundation strives to fulfill this vision for the Environment in New Jersey by funding organizations that: increase the quality, function and public accessibility of watersheds through land preservation, resource management, and stewardship; focus on urban greening, particularly through community-led design and decision making; and help develop regional food systems, including rural-to-urban farming connections and urban food market development. Letters of inquiry should be received by August 1, with full proposals due by August 30.

Requirements: In order to be eligible for funding, an applicant must: be a 501(c)3 organization that makes its home in or has a significant impact on New Jersey; demonstrate that it has the administrative and financial capacity to achieve and assess the stated goals of the proposal; be led by an effective and professional, paid staff; have a high-functioning board, with an expectation of 100% of its trustees making an annual personal contribution; and strive to make connections with other organizations, especially Dodge grantees, working in the same community or on the same issues.

Restrictions: Funding is not provided for: higher education; health; religion; capital programs; equipment purchases; indirect costs; endowment funds; and deficit reduction. The Foundation does not make direct awards to individuals or support lobbying efforts.

Geographic Focus: New Jersey
Date(s) Application is Due: Mar 1; Aug 30; Dec 3
Amount of Grant: 10,000 - 150,000 USD
Samples: Bayshore Discovery Project, Port Norris, New Jersey, $75,000 - general operating support for environmental education and stewardship programs; Greater Newark Conservancy, Newark, New Jersey, $90,000 - general operating support for environmental stewardship, education, community greening and urban agriculture programs; Isles, Trenton, New Jersey, $70,000 - urban agriculture and greening programs.
Contact: Margaret Waldock, Program Director; (973) 540-8442, ext. 117; fax (973) 540-1211; mwaldock@grdodge.org or info@grdodge.org
Internet: http://www.grdodge.org/what-we-fund/environment/
Sponsor: Geraldine R. Dodge Foundation
14 Maple Avenue, Suite 400
Morristown, NJ 07960

Geraldine R. Dodge Foundation Media Grants 819

The Dodge Foundation supports traditional and innovative uses of media to educate and engage the public around issues of importance to New Jersey and its citizens, as well as efforts to uncover abuses of power by the institutions the public trusts. The Foundation also believe that youth must be given a voice if they are to actively participate in civic affairs, and that communities thrive when their members are well-informed and seek to improve their lives as well as those of their neighbors. The Foundation strives to fulfill this vision for Media in New Jersey by funding organizations that: broaden and make more available New Jersey-centric news and programming; focus on investigative reporting of government, businesses and institutions; inform the public about issues related to the Foundation's priority funding areas; and empower youth and promote leadership through media production. Letters of inquiry should be received by August 1, with full proposals due by August 30.

Requirements: In order to be eligible for funding, an applicant must: be a 501(c)3 organization that makes its home in or has a significant impact on New Jersey; demonstrate that it has the administrative and financial capacity to achieve and assess the stated goals of the proposal; be led by an effective and professional, paid staff; have a high-functioning board, with an expectation of 100% of its trustees making an annual personal contribution; and strive to make connections with other organizations, especially Dodge grantees, working in the same community or on the same issues.

Restrictions: Funding is not provided for: higher education; health; religion; capital programs; equipment purchases; indirect costs; endowment funds; and deficit reduction. The Foundation does not make direct awards to individuals or support lobbying efforts.

Geographic Focus: New Jersey
Date(s) Application is Due: Mar 1; Aug 30; Dec 3
Amount of Grant: 7,500 - 125,000 USD
Samples: Montclair State University, Upper Montclair, New Jersey, $125,000 - the New Jersey Digital Media initiative; New Jersey Arts News, Summit, New Jersey, $20,000 - general operating support; Newark Public Radio, Newark, New Jersey, $55,000 - general operating support.
Contact: Molly de Aguiar, Director of Communications; (973) 540-8442, ext. 156; fax (973) 540-1211; mdeaguiar@grdodge.org or info@grdodge.org
Internet: http://www.grdodge.org/what-we-fund/media/
Sponsor: Geraldine R. Dodge Foundation
14 Maple Avenue, Suite 400
Morristown, NJ 07960

German Protestant Orphan Asylum Foundation Grants 820

The German Protestant Orphan Asylum (GP.O.A) Foundation Grants funding to support programs that serve children in Louisiana. The majority of those funded offer programs in the areas of education (tutoring, literacy, LEAP remediation, after school and summer programs, GED prep, early childhood education, child abuse prevention); enrichment (arts/music, mentoring, summer camps); life skills/pre-vocational training (parenting skills, work skills); and school-based health (mental health, vision screenings, immunizations, speech pathology). The Foundation makes grant decisions in May, August, November, and February. The Foundation's average grant award is $10,000 within a range of $1,000 to $40,000.

Requirements: A concept paper is required before submitting a proposal. Applicants should download, complete, then mail one original plus 12 copies of the one-page concept paper at least four months prior to their need for funds. The concept paper will be reviewed, and the organization will be notified whether a full proposal is invited. If a full proposal is invited, the organization should then download and fill out the GP.O.A Grant Proposal Form, and mail one original plus 12 copies to the Foundation by the deadline.

Restrictions: The Foundation does not fund building or renovation expenses, sponsorship of special events, individual scholarships, or programs which do not serve children in Louisiana. Equipment is rarely funded.

Geographic Focus: Louisiana
Amount of Grant: 4,000 - 40,000 USD
Contact: Lisa Kaichen, Foundation Manager; (985) 674-5328 or (504) 895-2361; fax (504) 674-0490; gpoafoundation@aol.com
Internet: http://www.gpoafoundation.org/amenities.html
Sponsor: German Protestant Orphan Asylum Association
P.O. Box 158
Mandeville, LA 70470

Gertrude and William C. Wardlaw Fund Grants 821

Established in 1936 in Georgia, the Gertrude and William C. Wardlaw Fund awards general operating grants to Georgia nonprofit organizations in its areas of interest, including: cultural activities; the arts; community development; education and higher education; and health care and hospitals. Specific application forms are not required, and there are no specified annual deadlines. Grants typically range from $2,500 to $50,000.

Requirements: Georgia nonprofit organizations are eligible to apply.
Geographic Focus: Georgia
Amount of Grant: 2,500 - 50,000 USD
Samples: Metro Atlant Task Force, Atlanta, Georgia, $50,000 - operating costs; Wardlaw School, Atlanta, Georgia, $20,000 - general operating costs; Viola White Water Foundation, Atlanta, Georgia, $2,500 - general operations.
Contact: Gregorie Guthrie, Secretary; (404) 419-3260 or (404) 827-6529
Sponsor: Gertrude and William C. Wardlaw Fund
One Riverside Building
Atlanta, GA 30327

Gibson Foundation Grants 822

The Foundation is committed to making the world a better place for children by creating, developing and supporting programs and other non-profit organizations in their efforts to advance education, music and the arts, the environment and health & welfare causes. The Foundation actively seeks out programs that will be a direct mission-fit and further its goals.

Requirements: Applicants must be 501(c)3 organizations.
Restrictions: The Foundation does not support religious or political affiliations, and does not award individual scholarships.
Geographic Focus: All States

Contact: Nina Miller, Executive Director; (615) 871-4500, ext. 2114; fax (615) 884-9597; nina.miller@gibson.com
Internet: http://www.gibson.com/en-us/Lifestyle/GibsonFoundation/
Sponsor: Gibson Foundation
309 Plus Park Boulevard
Nashville, TN 37217

Gil and Dody Weaver Foundation Grants   **823**
Established in Texas in 1980, the Gil and Dody Weaver Foundation offers support throughout the States of Texas, Oklahoma, and Louisiana, with some emphasis on the Dallas-Fort worth area. The Foundation's primary fields of interest include: cancer; children and youth services; education; health organizations; human services; social services; and recreational camps. Major types of support come in the form of: annual campaigns; general operating/ continual support; and scholarship funds. Although no formal application is required, the Foundation does provide specific application guidelines. These guidelines require a history of the organization, detailed information about the proposed project, and budgetary needs. The annual deadline is May 31, with final notifications by September 30. Recent grants have ranged from $1,000 to $20,000, with occasional higher amounts for special circumstances.
Requirements: 501(c)3 organization serving the residents of Texas, Oklahoma, and Louisiana, are welcome to apply.
Restrictions: No grants are given to individuals. No applications are accepted from organizations located in states other than Texas, Oklahoma, or Louisiana.
Geographic Focus: California, Louisiana, Mississippi, New Mexico, Oklahoma, Texas
Date(s) Application is Due: May 31
Amount of Grant: 1,000 - 20,000 USD
Samples: MD Anderson Cancer Center, Houston, Texas, $160,000 - cancer research; Camp McFadden, Ponce City, Oklahoma, $2,500 - operation support; Bookspring, Austin, Texas, $1,500 - Reach Out and Read program.
Contact: William R. Weaver, (214) 999-9497; fax (214) 999-9496
Sponsor: Gil and Dody Weaver Foundation
1845 Woodall Rodgers Freeway, Suite 1275
Dallas, TX 75201-2299

Gilroy and Lillian P. Roberts Charitable Foundation Grants   **824**
The foundation awards grants to eligible nonprofit organizations in its areas of interest, including arts and fine arts, health care and health organizations, higher education, Jewish temples and organizations, and social services. Types of support include annual campaigns, capital campaigns, continuing support, fellowships, general operating grants, professorships, program development, and scholarships. Most grants are awarded in Montgomery and Delaware Counties, PA. There are no application deadlines or forms.
Restrictions: Individuals are not eligible.
Geographic Focus: Pennsylvania
Amount of Grant: Up to 408,750 USD
Contact: Stanley Merves, Treasurer; (610) 668-1998
Sponsor: Gilroy and Lillian P. Roberts Charitable Foundation
101 W Elm Street, Suite 500
Conshohocken, PA 19428

Ginger and Barry Ackerley Foundation Grants   **825**
The Ginger & Barry Ackerley Foundation makes grants to public and private organizations that sponsor programs enhancing the education of young learners under the age of five, in the greater Puget Sound region. The Foundation focuses on organizations involved in skills support, literacy development, mentoring relationships and programs that connect school and home in order to produce specific and measurable results in early learning. Grants are usually made for capital drives, endowments and specific program objectives, not operating budgets. Grants are generally to be expended within one year, without expectation of further support. Priority will be given to requests that show specific plans for funding beyond the present.
Requirements: Washington State 501(c)3 tax-exempt organizations, with an active board of directors, with policy-making authority are eligible to apply. The board should demonstrate competence in the sound financial management of the organization. Organizations seeking grant support must receive an invitation from the Ackerley Foundation prior to submitting an application. To initiate the process, organizations that fit within the Foundation's mission and guidelines should submit a letter of inquiry describing the organization, the program the request is for, and the amount of funding sought. The process continues as follows: the Foundation arranges visits and meetings to learn more about the organization; suitable organizations are invited to apply for funding (Grant Request Summary form available online at the Foundation's website); all organizations must fulfill

the written application requirements. The Foundation evaluates funding requests twice annually, typically in March and October. Application deadlines will be established according to funding needs and program timing.
Restrictions: Funding is not available for: organizations that discriminate on the basis of race, color, creed, sex, marital status, or handicap; individuals, except scholarship recipients chosen by educational institutions; political candidates, organizations, or committees; religious organizations whose mission, policies or practices declare a purely denominational intent; debt retirement or operating deficits, loans, or investments; team sponsorships, individual athletic endeavors, or travel expenses; annual fund drives; administrative salaries.
Geographic Focus: Washington
Amount of Grant: 100 - 500,000 USD
Samples: Kidsquest Children's Museum, Bellevue, WA, $5,000—general support; First Place School, Seattle, WA, $100,000—general support; Kirlin Charitable Foundation, Bellevue, WA. $25,000—general support.
Contact: Twyla McFarlane, (206) 624-2888; fax (206) 623-7853; info@ ackerleyfoundation.com
Internet: http://www.ackerleyfoundation.org/apply/guidelines.html
Sponsor: Ginger and Barry Ackerley Foundation
4105 East Madison Street, Suite 210
Seattle, WA 98112

Ginn Foundation Grants   **826**
The foundation's mission is to address educational and community-based health care needs through supporting effective programs and services that bring about long-term solutions for individuals and the community, principally in Cuyahoga County, OH. The Foundation will consider not only grants to academic institutions, but also to organizations that meet non-academic educational needs, such as, programs that address issues of disease avoidance, child and family counseling, after-school training, arts, housing, and employment. Preference in all of these areas will be given to organizations and programs that serve low-income recipients. Faxed applications will not be considered. Application information is available online.
Requirements: Nonprofit organizations in Cuyahoga County, OH, may apply. Consideration will also be given to trustee-sponsored grants to similar types of organizations in the Chicago, Washington, DC, and Minneapolis-St. Paul metropolitan areas.
Restrictions: The foundation will not fund requests for support of advocacy activities. Nor will it make grants to endowment, capital, or annual fund campaigns. The foundation will not fund special events or attendance at conferences or symposia.
Geographic Focus: District of Columbia, Illinois, Minnesota, Ohio
Date(s) Application is Due: Mar 15; Sep 15
Amount of Grant: 5,000 - 30,000 USD
Samples: Bellflower Center for the Prevention of Abuse, Cleveland, OH, $10,000—general operating support for support services directly addressing healthy child development through the prevention & treatment of child abuse; Cleveland Playhouse, Cleveland, OH, $15,000—collaboration with Cleveland School of the Arts; Cleveland Hearing & Speech, Cleveland, OH, $15,000—Speech-Language Pathology Program.
Contact: Walter Pope Ginn, Trustee; info@ginnfoundation.org
Internet: http://www.ginnfoundation.org/index.html
Sponsor: Ginn Foundation
13938 A Cedar Road, P.O. Box 239
Cleveland Heights, OH 44118

Girl's Best Friend Foundation Grants   **827**
The foundation supports and promotes programs by and for girls and young women in Illinois (ages eight through 21). The foundation is dedicated to effecting change at the grassroots level by funding community-based organizations statewide. Types of grants made include general operating support, project specific support, planning or start-up support, technical assistance, and collaborative action research (research that lays the groundwork for policy changes conducted by a partnership between two nonprofits or a nonprofit contracting with a researcher or academic institution). When multiyear funding is requested, the foundation will consider making two-year grants if the requesting organization has received at least two previous grants from GBF, is seeking two years of funding for the same purpose, and has clearly demonstrated the need for a two-year grant. Applications are due the first Monday in August.
Requirements: Letters of intent will be accepted from 501(c)3 nonprofits for projects that serve or have a direct impact on girls living in the Chicago metropolitan area including Cook, DuPage, Kane, Lake, McHenry, and Will counties.
Restrictions: Organizations with budgets that exceed $650,000 may apply only for technical assistance and/or collaborative action research grants.

The foundation generally does not fund individuals, capital campaigns, debt reduction, scholarships, or government or religious organizations.
Geographic Focus: Illinois
Amount of Grant: 5,000 - 20,000 USD
Contact: Robin Dixon, Senior Program Officer; (312) 266-2842; fax (312) 266-2972; robin@girlsbestfriend.org or contact@girlsbestfriend.org
Internet: http://www.girlsbestfriend.org/apply/index.html
Sponsor: Girl's Best Friend Foundation
900 N Franklin, Suite 210
Chicago, IL 60610

Glaser Progress Foundation Grants 828
The foundation awards grants to U.S. nonprofit organizations in its areas of interest, including progress definition and measurement—efforts to improve understanding and measurement of human progress; animal advocacy—address issues such as wildlife cruelty, farm animals, vivisection, primate rights and protection, and use of technology for animal advocacy; and independent media—to support efforts to strengthen democracy by making independent voices heard. There are no application deadlines or forms. Application form is available online.
Requirements: U.S. 501(c)3 tax-exempt organizations are eligible.
Restrictions: Grants are not awarded to influence legislation or support candidates for political office.
Geographic Focus: All States
Amount of Grant: 1,000 - 25,000 USD
Samples: Yale U (New Haven, CT)—for the G-ECON Project, to explore the relationship between economics and geography, $100,000; Doris Day Animal Foundation (Washington, DC)—for general support of the Chimpanzee Collaboratory, $14,000; Independent Media Institute (San Francisco, CA)—to support AlterNet's online magazine and digest, $20,000; Columbia University (New York, NY)—to support the Access Project for the Global Fund to Fight AIDS, Tuberculosis, and Malaria, $450,000.
Contact: Melessa Rogers, (206) 728-1050; fax (206) 728-1123; melessa@glaserprogress.org or grants@glaserprogress.org
Internet: http://www.glaserprogress.org
Sponsor: Glaser Progress Foundation
P.O. Box 91123
Seattle, WA 98111

Global Fund for Children Grants 829
The Global Fund for Children's (GFC) mission is to advance the dignity of children and youth around the world through small grants to innovative community-based organizations working with some of the world's most vulnerable children and youth. The Fund selects its grantee partners based on their potential to grow in effectiveness and to become valuable resources or models for others. Selection criteria include exceptional leadership, sound management, strong community participation, innovative and effective programs, and direct engagement with the most vulnerable children. Fund focus is on four specific issues: learning, enterprise, safety, and healthy minds and bodies. Organizations may submit a letter of inquiry at any time. If a letter of inquiry falls within GFC's priorities, GFC will follow up with the organization to solicit a full proposal.
Requirements: Nonprofit organization worldwide are eligible.
Geographic Focus: All States
Amount of Grant: 5,000 - 20,000 USD
Samples: Anandan, Kolkata, India, $8,000—education grant; Benishyaka Association, Kigali, Rwanda, $15,000—academic scholarships; Children in the Wilderness, Lilongwe, Malawi, $15,000—education grant.
Contact: Andrew Barnes, Grants Manager; (202) 331-9003; fax (202) 331-9004; info@globalfundforchildren.org
Internet: http://www.globalfundforchildren.org/applyforagrant/index.html
Sponsor: Global Fund for Children
1101 Fourteenth Street, North West, Suite 420
Washington, D.C. 20005

Global Fund for Women Grants 830
The Global Fund for Women supports women's groups that advance the human rights of women and girls. Grants support women's groups based outside the United States by providing small, flexible, and timely grants for operating and project expenses. Grantees address issues that include but are not limited to building peace and ending gender-based violence; advancing health and sexual and reproductive rights; expanding civic and political participation; ensuring economic and environmental justice; increasing access to education; and fostering social change philanthropy. In addition urgent requests for support

to organize or participate in local, regional, or international meetings and conferences will be considered outside of the normal grant cycle. These types of requests must come from organizations, not individuals, and must be received at least eight weeks before the event. Funds for these types of grants are limited. Applications and guidelines are available online. Organizations should refer to the staff website for specific contacts according to their applicant origin.
Requirements: The applicant group must be based in a country outside the United States; demonstrate a strong commitment to women's equality and human rights that is clearly reflected in its activities; be a group of women working together; and be governed, directed, and led by women.
Restrictions: Grants do not support individuals; scholarships; academic research; groups based and working primarily or only in the United States; international organizations proposing projects with local partners; groups without a strong women's rights focus; groups headed and managed by men, or without women in the majority of leadership positions; groups whose sole purpose is to generate income or to provide charity to individuals; or political parties or election campaigns.
Geographic Focus: All Countries
Amount of Grant: 5,000 - 50,000 USD
Contact: Program Assistant; (415) 248-4800; fax (415) 202-4801
Internet: http://www.globalfundforwomen.org/apply-for-a-grant/types-of-grant
Sponsor: Global Fund for Women
222 Sutter Street, Suite 500
San Francisco, CA 94108

GNOF Bayou Communities Grants 831
In 2012 the Greater New Orleans Foundation (GNOF) established the Bayou Communities Foundation (BCF) that has, as its initial focus, the mission to improve life in the Louisiana parishes of Terrebonne and Lafourche, and that will work to strengthen local nonprofit capacity in compassionate and sustainable coastal communities in Louisiana for generations to come. The impetus to form BCF came from parish residents, who first organized among themselves and then approached GNOF, who had set up similar and successful foundations in St. Bernard, Plaquemines, and Jefferson Parishes after Hurricanes Katrina and Rita and the Gulf Oil Spill. BCF is set up as a GNOF donor-advised fund, an affiliate under GNOF's nonprofit umbrella. The new foundation will receive $500,000 in seed money for the next five years from the Gheens Foundation in Lafourche and has committed to raising $1 million in matching dollars. BCF has also commited to putting at least 90% of its first $100,000 from the Gheens Foundation back into the community through grants. As an affiliate foundation, BCF has access to the expertise of GNOF but makes independent decisions about BCF projects. Organizations interested in obtaining grants through BCF can contact GNOF for more information.
Geographic Focus: Louisiana
Contact: Josephine Everly, Senior Development Officer; (504) 598-4663; fax (504) 598-4676; josephine@gnof.org
Internet: http://www.gnof.org/
Sponsor: Greater New Orleans Foundation
1055 St. Charles Avenue, Suite 100
New Orleans, LA 70130

GNOF Community Revitalization Grants 832
134,000 housing units were damaged or destroyed by Hurricane Katrina and the subsequent levee failures, creating over $100 billion in damage in the greater New Orleans region. In 2007, leading local and national foundations created the $25-million Community Revitalization Fund at the Greater New Orleans Foundation (GNOF) which has since used the fund to support the development of nearly 9,000 housing units to help with the region's recovery. The aim of the fund is two-fold: to fill gaps in public spending with private philanthropy; and to leverage public resources such as Low-Income Housing Tax Credits, Community Development Block Grants, and HOME funds. The Revitalization Fund has a mandate to support activities that create or are a component of a working system that generates equitable and affordable housing and community development at scale for the greater New Orleans region. A working system functions in the following ways: it produces high-quality, diverse, mixed-income and mixed-use development that is architecturally, culturally, and ecologically appropriate, as well as environmentally sustainable; it engages a diversity of citizens in the community revitalization process and formalizes or sustains citizen engagement in community development; it promotes accountability in government and the effectiveness of public systems; it results in the creation of a number of housing units that is commensurate with the scale of the crisis at hand and at a pace that dignifies all displaced New Orleanians; and it increases the capacity of the locally-based housing

productions systems, including nonprofit and for-profit developers. The ultimate goal of the Revitalization Fund is a city of mixed-income and mixed-race neighborhoods of choice, each anchored by community facilities, schools, hospitals, pedestrian-friendly streets, and dynamic public open spaces available to and accessible by all residents. GNOF considers the efforts of New Orleanians who became "citizen planners" during post-Katrina planning processes an essential component of the working system and supports their move into leadership roles and into becoming effective stewards of the implementation process. The Community Revitalization Fund accepts Letters of Interest (LOIs) on a rolling basis. These should be submitted along with required supporting documentation via email to the address provided in the guidelines. Within one month of receiving an LOI, GNOF staff will respond in one of three ways: by requesting a full proposal; by requesting a meeting to discuss the project; or by declining the request. GNOF considers full proposals on a quarterly basis. Interested organizations are also encouraged to visit the GNOF website to obtain detailed guidelines on how to apply, background information on the Community Revitalization Fund, an explanation of its changing goals and strategies, and examples of the types of programs it will fund. A link to subscribe to the GNOF newsletter is available from GNOF's Apply-for-a-Grant web page. The newsletter keeps subscribers informed on all GNOF's upcoming funding opportunities.

Requirements: Requests for funding must do one or more of the following: address a specific need or barrier to housing development; contribute to the capacity of government, nonprofit, and/or for-profit developers to produce equitable, high-quality, mixed-income housing at scale (at least 50 units per year); increase expertise and/or capacity within the housing development industry; deliver important information and/or technical expertise on best practices in housing and community development; and collaborate across the public and private sectors to create innovative financing programs or housing policy that will increase the pace of the city's repopulation.

Geographic Focus: All States

Samples: Artspace Projects, Minneapolis, Minnesota, $150,000—to support Phase I of the redevelopment of the Andrew J. Bell School Campus in the Treme neighborhood that will include 73 unites of affordable live/work space for low income artists and their familes; Dr. Murphy W. McCaleb Educational Fund, New Orleans, Louisiana, $200,000—to support the construction of a 43-unit permanent supportive housing development in Central City; St. Paul's Episcopal Church, New Orleans, Louisiana, $1,000—to sponsor the attendance of families that have been served by the Homecoming Center to the Secret Millionaire event.

Contact: Ellen M. Lee, Sr. Vice President, Programs, Community Revitalization Program Director; (504) 598-4663; fax (504) 598-4676; ellen@gnof.org or crfund@gnof.org

Internet: http://www.gnof.org/community-revitalization-fund-grant/

Sponsor: Greater New Orleans Foundation
1055 St. Charles Avenue, Suite 100
New Orleans, LA 70130

GNOF Environmental Fund Grants 833

The Environmental Fund was established in 1994 using the settlement money from a legal dispute involving a phenol spill that tainted drinking water in the Mississippi River. The original gift of $6 million was invested and has grown to $10 million. It is currently administered by the Greater New Orleans Foundation (GNOF). The endowed fund's goal is to encourage ecological, economic, and cultural vitality, resilience and sustainability in the greater New Orleans region through environmentally focused policies, programs, and projects. People in greater New Orleans have been left to grapple with the environmental consequences of policies wrought by privileged groups with limited interests, many of whom left the area in the wake of Hurricanes Katrina and Rita. As the region's wetlands continue to disappear at a rate of 25 square miles per year, the impact of future storm surges will continue to rise; if it is to survive, the greater New Orleans community must rebuild itself with an emphasis on maximum resiliency and adapt itself in a sustainable way to the uniquely fluid environment that nourishes the region's neighborhoods, culture, economy and identity. The greater New Orleans community has come to understand that real solutions can only come about through decision-making processes that are open and deliberately inclusive. In fact GNOF believes that the foundation of community sustainability is community empowerment. From time to time GNOF will make available through a request for proposal (RFP), a certain sum that will promote a set of five regionally significant and relevant transformations: make the region a national leader in the protection and beneficial use of its water resources; turn the region into the most storm-resistant and resilient area in America; make the region the most innovative

and progressive energy center in America; make the region a place that is attractive, affordable, viable, and safe for businesses, workers, and their families; and keep the region as a place that celebrates its heritage but that is not captive to its past. GNOF accepts Environmental Fund applications only through its RFP process. Interested organizations are encouraged to subscribe to GNOF's email newsletter so they can be notified of future RFPs. The subscription link is available from GNOF's Apply-for-a-Grant web page which contains a comprehensive listing of GNOF's current and past funding opportunities. Interested organizations are also encouraged to visit the GNOF website to obtain detailed background information on the Environmental Fund, an explanation of its major goals and strategies, and examples of the types of programs it will fund.

Requirements: GNOF gives preference to locally-based nonprofits.

Geographic Focus: All States

Samples: Nature Conservancy of Louisiana, Baton Rouge, Louisiana, $118,250—to bring disparate interest groups to develop and promote a collective vision for the Lower Mississippi River; UNO Center for Hazards Assessment, Response and Technology, New Orleans, Louisiana, $25,000—to provide funding to create an online tool for coastal restoration projects; The Idea Village, New Orleans, Louisiana, $125,000—2011 Water Challenge.

Contact: Dr. Marco Cocito-Monoc, Director for Regional Initiatives; (504) 598-4663; fax (504) 598-4676; marco@gnof.org

Internet: http://www.gnof.org/the-environmental-fund-3/

Sponsor: Greater New Orleans Foundation
1055 St. Charles Avenue, Suite 100
New Orleans, LA 70130

GNOF IMPACT Grants for Arts and Culture 834

Through the IMPACT Program, the Greater New Orleans Foundation (GNOF) makes grants to organizations serving the Greater New Orleans region. The ultimate goal of the IMPACT Program is to create a resilient, sustainable, vibrant, and equitable region in which individuals and families flourish and in which the special character of the New Orleans region and its people is preserved, celebrated, and given the means to develop. Specifically GNOF hopes to accomplish the following objectives through its IMPACT grants: provide a much needed source of financial and other support to nonprofit organizations that are struggling in the current financial environment and that are important to the health and vibrancy of the region; develop a better sense of the nonprofit organizations serving the region so GNOF can more effectively match donor desires with effective charitable work; identify and nurture promising new leaders and initiatives, especially in those communities that are in greatest need; and gain knowledge that will help nonprofit leaders and GNOF staff develop better long-term strategies for addressing regional needs and taking best advantage of important opportunities. IMPACT grants are awarded in four categories: Arts and Culture, Youth Development, Education, and Health and Human Services. In the category of Arts and Culture GNOF supports organizations and programs that help preserve and grow the rich cultural heritage of the Greater New Orleans region and ensure that the originators and producers of creative goods and services can continue to enhance community life. Priority will be given to work that has the following goals: to improve the quality of life for artists and performers in the region; to demonstrate the importance of the arts and make the case for increased public support for the arts; and to form alliances and connections between grassroots-based organizations and the business community to expand income-producing opportunities for artists. Interested organizations must submit a letter of intent along with all attachments via one email by 5 p.m. on July 30. GNOF program staff will review all letters of intent and will contact those organizations that are invited to submit a full application for funding. Awards are announced in November. Deadlines may vary from year to year. Interested organizations should verify the current deadline at the GNOF website where they can also obtain complete guidelines and requirements as well as a downloadable application form and cover sheet. Prospective applicants can also subscribe to GNOF's email newsletter for announcements of future funding opportunities. The subscription link is available from GNOF's Apply-for-a-Grant web page which contains a comprehensive listing of GNOF's current and past funding opportunities.

Requirements: Nonprofit, tax-exempt organizations that serve the Greater New Orleans region are eligible to apply for funding. Organizations that are not tax-exempt but have a fiscal agent relationship with a 501(c)3 organization are also eligible.

Restrictions: Through its IMPACT program, the Greater New Orleans Foundation is unable to fund the following types of requests: requests for individual support, either through scholarships or other forms of financial assistance; special events or conferences; programs that promote religious doctrine; endowments; and scientific or medical research.

Geographic Focus: All States

Date(s) Application is Due: Jul 30

Amount of Grant: Up to 20,000 USD

Samples: Arts Council of New Orleans, New Orleans, Louisiana, $20,000—for general operating support; Sweet Home New Orleans, New Orleans, Louisiana, $20,000—for general operating support; Louisiana Cultural Economy Foundation, New Orleans, Louisiana, $25,000—for general operating support.

Contact: Roy Williams, Program Assistant; (504) 598-4663; fax (504) 598-4676; grants@gnof.org or roy@gnof.org

Internet: http://www.gnof.org/programs/impact/

Sponsor: Greater New Orleans Foundation

1055 St. Charles Avenue, Suite 100

New Orleans, LA 70130

GNOF IMPACT Grants for Education 835

Through the IMPACT Program, the Greater New Orleans Foundation (GNOF) makes grants to organizations serving the Greater New Orleans region. The ultimate goal of the IMPACT program is to create a resilient, sustainable, vibrant, and equitable region in which individuals and families flourish and in which the special character of the New Orleans region and its people is preserved, celebrated, and given the means to develop. Specifically GNOF hopes to accomplish the following objectives through its IMPACT grants: provide a much needed source of financial and other support to nonprofit organizations that are struggling in the current financial environment and that are important to the health and vibrancy of the region; develop a better sense of the nonprofit organizations serving the region so GNOF can more effectively match donor desires with effective charitable work; identify and nurture promising new leaders and initiatives, especially in those communities that are in greatest need; and gain knowledge that will help nonprofit leaders and GNOF staff develop better long-term strategies for addressing regional needs and taking best advantage of important opportunities. IMPACT grants are awarded in four categories: Arts and Culture, Youth Development, Education, and Health and Human Services. In the category of Education support is available to organizations that seek to ensure that all young people in public K-12 schools in GNOF's 13-parish service area attend high-performing schools. Priority will be given to work that has the following goals: to advance public education reforms in Orleans parish and other under served areas in GNOF's service area; to hold public agencies accountable for the success of our public schools; to improve student achievement by training and engaging key stakeholders in education (parents, school leaders, etc.) in the skills of organizing, policy research and analysis, policy advocacy, and the use of data in making policy recommendations; and conduct research and/or work with school leaders and other financial decision makers to address the financial sustainability issues within the charter school system. Interested organizations must submit a letter of intent along with all attachments via one email by 5 p.m. on July 30. GNOF program staff will review all letters of intent and will contact those organizations that are invited to submit a full application for funding. Awards are announced in November. Deadlines may vary from year to year. Interested organizations should verify the current deadline at the GNOF website where they can also obtain complete guidelines and requirements as well as a downloadable application form and cover sheet. Prospective applicants can also subscribe to GNOF's email newsletter for announcements of future funding opportunities. The subscription link is available from GNOF's Apply-for-a-Grant web page which contains a comprehensive listing of GNOF's current and past funding opportunities.

Requirements: Nonprofit, tax-exempt organizations that serve the thirteen parishes of Greater New Orleans are eligible to apply for funding. Organizations that are not tax-exempt but have a fiscal agent relationship with a 501(c)3 organization are also eligible.

Restrictions: Through its IMPACT program, the Greater New Orleans Foundation is unable to fund the following types of requests: requests for individual support, either through scholarships or other forms of financial assistance; special events or conferences; programs that promote religious doctrine; endowments; and scientific or medical research.

Geographic Focus: All States

Date(s) Application is Due: Jul 30

Amount of Grant: Up to 20,000 USD

Samples: Bureau of Governmental Research, New Orleans, Louisiana, $10,000—to provide general operating support; Loyola University, Chicago, Illinois, $20,000—to support the Place Matters Initiative; The Lens, New Orleans, Louisiana, $10,000—to support Charter School Reporting Corps.

Contact: Roy Williams, Program Assistant; (504) 598-4663; fax (504) 598-4676; grants@gnof.org or roy@gnof.org

Internet: http://www.gnof.org/programs/impact/

Sponsor: Greater New Orleans Foundation

1055 St. Charles Avenue, Suite 100

New Orleans, LA 70130

GNOF IMPACT Grants for Health and Human Services 836

Through the IMPACT Program, the Greater New Orleans Foundation (GNOF) makes grants to organizations serving the Greater New Orleans region. The ultimate goal of the IMPACT program is to create a resilient, sustainable, vibrant, and equitable region in which individuals and families flourish and in which the special character of the New Orleans region and its people is preserved, celebrated, and given the means to develop. Specifically GNOF hopes to accomplish the following objectives through its IMPACT grants: provide a much needed source of financial and other support to nonprofit organizations that are struggling in the current financial environment and that are important to the health and vibrancy of the region; develop a better sense of the nonprofit organizations serving the region so GNOF can more effectively match donor desires with effective charitable work; identify and nurture promising new leaders and initiatives, especially in those communities that are in greatest need; and gain knowledge that will help nonprofit leaders and GNOF staff develop better long-term strategies for addressing regional needs and taking best advantage of important opportunities. IMPACT grants are awarded in four categories: Arts and Culture, Youth Development, Education, and Health and Human Services. In the category of Health and Human Services, support is available to organizations that work to improve the health and living conditions of low-income families and their children, the disabled, the elderly, and other under served populations and help move them toward self-sufficiency. Priority will be given to work that increases Medicaid/LaCHIP or Medicare enrollment for indigent consumers of health-care services; advocates to preserve access to health care, to provide consumer protections, and/or to expand Medicaid coverage to increase access to comprehensive, quality primary care, mental health care, and preventive care for all; implements health education and outreach efforts to increase use of health-care services by the most under-served populations, African-American males in particular; uses health education to improve health literacy, influence attitudes, and improve health awareness so that indigent consumers of health care services can make better decisions and take preventive actions that will improve personal, family, and community health; and improve communication, coordination and collaboration between social-services providers to serve comprehensively the needs of low-income families, improving their chances of success in achieving self sufficiency. Interested organizations must submit a letter of intent along with all attachments via one email by 5 p.m. on July 30. GNOF program staff will review all letters of intent and will contact those organizations that are invited to submit a full application for funding. Awards are announced in November. Deadlines may vary from year to year. Interested organizations should verify the current deadline at the GNOF website where they can also obtain complete guidelines and requirements as well as a downloadable application form and cover sheet. Prospective applicants can also subscribe to GNOF's email newsletter for announcements of future funding opportunities. The subscription link is available from GNOF's Apply-for-a-Grant web page which contains a comprehensive listing of GNOF's current and past funding opportunities.

Requirements: Nonprofit, tax-exempt organizations that serve the thirteen parishes of Greater New Orleans are eligible to apply for funding. Organizations that are not tax-exempt but have a fiscal agent relationship with a 501(c)3 organization are also eligible.

Restrictions: Through its IMPACT program, the Greater New Orleans Foundation is unable to fund the following types of requests: requests for individual support, either through scholarships or other forms of financial assistance; special events or conferences; programs that promote religious doctrine; endowments; and scientific or medical research.

Geographic Focus: All States

Date(s) Application is Due: Jul 30

Amount of Grant: Up to 20,000 USD

Contact: Roy Williams, Program Assistant; (504) 598-4663; fax (504) 598-4676; grants@gnof.org or roy@gnof.org

Internet: http://www.gnof.org/programs/impact/

Sponsor: Greater New Orleans Foundation

1055 St. Charles Avenue, Suite 100

New Orleans, LA 70130

GNOF IMPACT Grants for Youth Development   837

Through the IMPACT Program, the Greater New Orleans Foundation (GNOF) makes grants to organizations serving the Greater New Orleans region. The ultimate goal of the IMPACT Program is to create a resilient, sustainable, vibrant, and equitable region in which individuals and families flourish and in which the special character of the New Orleans region and its people is preserved, celebrated, and given the means to develop. Specifically GNOF hopes to accomplish the following objectives through its IMPACT grants: provide a much needed source of financial and other support to nonprofit organizations that are struggling in the current financial environment and that are important to the health and vibrancy of the region; develop a better sense of the nonprofit organizations serving the region so GNOF can more effectively match donor desires with effective charitable work; identify and nurture promising new leaders and initiatives, especially in those communities that are in greatest need; and gain knowledge that will help nonprofit leaders and GNOF staff develop better long-term strategies for addressing regional needs and taking best advantage of important opportunities. IMPACT grants are awarded in four categories: Arts and Culture, Youth Development, Education, and Health and Human Services. In the category of Youth Development GNOF supports organizations that undertake the following types of projects: they facilitate access to high quality programs, activities, opportunities, and services for Greater New Orleans youth that will enhance their formal education, providing the cognitive, social, and emotional skills and abilities they need to become productive members of society; they provide professional development in the form of training, education, or tools to youth-development workers that will improve their knowledge, skills, and attitudes in the areas of case management, mentoring services, tutoring, and other remediation services or programs; they provide technical assistance and training to multiple youth-serving organizations to help them define and measure program outcomes and collect and track outcome and other data on participants and participation; they organize and/or increase the advocacy power of youth-serving organizations; and they develop a coordinated, comprehensive plan and strategies to address youth needs by engaging key stakeholders, promoting partnerships and strategic alliances, and identifying a diversified funding base. Interested organizations must submit a letter of intent along with all attachments via one email by 5 p.m. on July 30. GNOF program staff will review all letters of intent and will contact those organizations that are invited to submit a full application for funding. Awards are announced in November. Deadlines may vary from year to year. Interested organizations should verify the current deadline at the GNOF website where they can also obtain complete guidelines and requirements as well as a downloadable application form and cover sheet. Prospective applicants can also subscribe to GNOF's email newsletter for announcements of future funding opportunities. The subscription link is available from GNOF's Apply-for-a-Grant web page which contains a comprehensive listing of GNOF's current and past funding opportunities.

Requirements: Nonprofit, tax-exempt organizations that serve the thirteen parishes of Greater New Orleans are eligible to apply for funding. Organizations that are not tax-exempt but have a fiscal agent relationship with a 501(c)3 organization are also eligible.

Restrictions: Through its IMPACT program, the Greater New Orleans Foundation is unable to fund the following types of requests: requests for individual support, either through scholarships or other forms of financial assistance; special events or conferences; programs that promote religious doctrine; endowments; and scientific or medical research.

Geographic Focus: All States

Date(s) Application is Due: Jul 30

Amount of Grant: Up to 20,000 USD

Contact: Roy Williams, Program Assistant; (504) 598-4663; fax (504) 598-4676; grants@gnof.org or roy@gnof.org

Internet: http://www.gnof.org/programs/impact/

Sponsor: Greater New Orleans Foundation

1055 St. Charles Avenue, Suite 100

New Orleans, LA 70130

GNOF IMPACT Harold W. Newman, Jr. Charitable Trust Grants   838

Through the IMPACT Program, the Greater New Orleans Foundation (GNOF) makes grants to organizations serving the Greater New Orleans region. The ultimate goal of the IMPACT program is to create a resilient, sustainable, vibrant, and equitable region in which individuals and families flourish and in which the special character of the New Orleans region and its people is preserved, celebrated, and given the means to develop. Specifically GNOF hopes to accomplish the following objectives through its IMPACT grants: provide a much needed source of financial and other support to nonprofit organizations

that are struggling in the current financial environment and that are important to the health and vibrancy of the region; develop a better sense of the nonprofit organizations serving the region so GNOF can more effectively match donor desires with effective charitable work; identify and nurture promising new leaders and initiatives, especially in those communities that are in greatest need; and gain knowledge that will help nonprofit leaders and GNOF staff develop better long-term strategies for addressing regional needs and taking best advantage of important opportunities. IMPACT grants are awarded in four categories: Arts and Culture, Youth Development, Education, and Health and Human Services. In the category of Health and Human Services, special funding is available for organizations that provide health-care assistance to residents of New Orleans whose U.S. adjusted gross income for the preceding tax year, when added to any tax-exempt income and income from a spouse for that same year, is at least $75,000 but not more than $200,000. The health-care assistance must be for cancer, heart disease, or Alzheimer's. Interested organizations must submit a letter of intent along with all attachments via one email by 5 p.m. on July 30 and should indicate on the IMPACT application cover sheet that they are applying for funding from the Harold W. Newman, Jr. Charitable Trust. GNOF program staff will review all letters of intent and will contact those organizations that are invited to submit a full application for funding. Awards are announced in November. Deadlines may vary from year to year. Interested organizations should verify the current deadline at the GNOF website where they can also obtain complete guidelines and requirements as well as a downloadable application form and cover sheet. Prospective applicants can also subscribe to GNOF's email newsletter for announcements of future funding opportunities. The subscription link is available from GNOF's Apply-for-a-Grant web page which contains a comprehensive listing of GNOF's current and past funding opportunities.

Requirements: Nonprofit, tax-exempt organizations that serve the thirteen parishes of Greater New Orleans are eligible to apply for funding. Organizations that are not tax-exempt but have a fiscal agent relationship with a 501(c)3 organization are also eligible.

Restrictions: Through its IMPACT program, the Greater New Orleans Foundation is unable to fund the following types of requests: requests for support from individuals, either through scholarships or other forms of financial assistance; special events or conferences; programs that promote religious doctrine; endowments; and scientific or medical research.

Geographic Focus: All States

Date(s) Application is Due: Jul 30

Amount of Grant: Up to 20,000 USD

Contact: Roy Williams, Program Assistant; (504) 598-4663; fax (504) 598-4676; grants@gnof.org or roy@gnof.org

Internet: http://www.gnof.org/programs/impact/

Sponsor: Greater New Orleans Foundation

1055 St. Charles Avenue, Suite 100

New Orleans, LA 70130

GNOF Maison Hospitaliere Grants   839

In 1879 Coralie Correjolles organized 30 women into "La Société Hospitaliere des Dames Louisianaises" to provide food and medicine to the needy of New Orleans, many of whom had lost everything during the Civil War. The group became especially concerned by the plight of elderly ladies, who, due to the loss of their husbands in the war, were destitute and living in squalid conditions. Through its collection of 10 cent monthly dues over 14 years, the Société was able to raise the money for its first building, 822 Barracks Street, to provide residence for 20 women. Over the next 113 years Maison Hospitaliere evolved into a skilled nursing facility for both men and women. Hurricane Katrina scattered both residents and staff across the country, and in November 2006 the board decided to close the facility. When the Maison Hospitaliere sold its French Quarter complex for more than $4 million, the proceeds were incorporated into a Supporting Organization of the Greater New Orleans Foundation so that the Maison's mission could continue by making grants to organizations serving women and their families.

Requirements: Grants will be made available to 501(c)3 organizations that provide living assistance and care to indigent women in the Greater New Orleans area. These grants will support direct services to women in the form of either general operating support or program support. Grants will range up to $20,000. Proposals must be submitted by 5:00 pm of the deadline date.

Restrictions: Maison Hospitaliere will not consider capital projects, event sponsorship, or research requests. Faith-based organizations are welcome to apply for support for programs that do not include religious activities, such as religious worship, instruction, or proselytization.

Geographic Focus: Louisiana

Date(s) Application is Due: Sep 1
Amount of Grant: Up to 20,000 USD
Contact: Roy Williams; (504) 598-4663; fax (504) 598-4676; grants@gnof.org
Internet: http://www.gnof.org/maison-hospitaliere/
Sponsor: Greater New Orleans Foundation
1055 St. Charles Avenue, Suite 100
New Orleans, LA 70130

GNOF Metropolitan Opportunities Grants 840
In 2011, the Ford Foundation and the Greater New Orleans Foundation (GNOF) formed a partnership called the Metropolitan Opportunities Initiative. As part of a national initiative of the Ford Foundation, Metropolitan Opportunities enables GNOF to adopt and encourage a holistic approach to community revitalization on a regional scale—in this case, the entire thirteen-parish area that comprises Greater New Orleans—rather than on just one neighborhood or one block. The Metropolitan Opportunities Initiative is focused on three core areas: access to affordable housing, metropolitan land-use innovation, and access to economic opportunity. The specific goals of the Initiative are to connect people to opportunities for safe, affordable housing and efficient, effective transit, and to promote economic and workforce development. Interested organizations can contact GNOF with any questions about Metropolitan Opportunities and visit the GNOF website to obtain more detailed information about the initiative as well as its past grantees. Organizations can also subscribe to GNOF's email newsletter for announcements of future funding opportunities. The subscription link is available from GNOF's Apply-for-a-Grant web page which contains a comprehensive listing of GNOF's current and past funding opportunities.
Geographic Focus: All States
Amount of Grant: 10,000 - 300,000 USD
Contact: Ryan Albright, Metropolitan Opportunities Program Officer; (504) 598-4663; fax (504) 598-4676; albright@gnof.org
Internet: http://www.gnof.org/programs/metropolitan-opportunities-initiative/
Sponsor: Greater New Orleans Foundation
1055 St. Charles Avenue, Suite 100
New Orleans, LA 70130

GNOF Plaquemines Community Grants 841
Plaquemines Parish is the "big toe of Louisiana's boot" protruding into the Gulf of Mexico. On August 29, 2005, Hurricane Katrina struck on the west bank of Plaquemines Parish. The 20-foot storm surge hit the southern coastline and gradually inundated the entire parish as it moved northward. A month later, Hurricane Rita's three-foot storm surge caused more damage to the already weakened parish levees, resulting in more flooding. In 2006 the Greater New Orleans Foundation (GNOF) established an affiliate community foundation in Plaquemines Parish, because GNOF believed that the rebuilding process in devastated areas should be led by those who live and work in them. GNOF seeded the Plaquemines Community Foundation (PCF) with $500,000, distributed over a period of five years, with the agreement that PCF would set aside 10% of the seed money as an endowment. The mission of PCF is to improve the quality of life for all citizens of the Plaquemine parish. PCF's board identifies current and emerging needs and addresses those needs through grants, and also fosters relationships with donors to build permanent endowments. Since its inception, the PCF has awarded grants to support education programs and agricultural initiatives. It has also partnered with the Saint Bernard Community Foundation to create the Southeast Louisiana Fisheries Assistance Center, which currently serves as a clearing house for local fishermen to receive free business planning, financial assistance (in the form of grants and low-interest loans), fishing licenses, and industry-specific training services. Plaquemine organizations interested in obtaining grants through PCF can contact GNOF for more information.
Geographic Focus: Louisiana
Samples: The Plaquemines Parish Economic Development and Tourism Department, Belle Chasse, Louisiana, $9,000— to fund an alternative crop project by the Lousiana State University Agricultural Center to increase crop diversity and profitability; The Plaquemines Community CARE Center, Belle Chasse, Louisiana, $50,000—to help support human services programs in the aftermath of the Gulf Oil Spill; Woodlands Trail and Park, Belle Chasse, Louisiana—for the organization's Ecosystem Restoration Project.
Contact: Dr. Marco Cocito-Monoc, Director for Regional Initiatives; (504) 598-4663; fax (504) 598-4676; marco@gnof.org
Perry A. Triche, Chair, Plaquemines Community Foundation Board; (504) 598-4663; fax (504) 598-4676

Internet: http://www.gnof.org/overview-6/
Sponsor: Greater New Orleans Foundation
1055 St. Charles Avenue, Suite 100
New Orleans, LA 70130

Golden Heart Community Foundation Grants 842
The Golden Heart Community Foundation's grantmaking priorities are still in development, but it will support projects that strengthen the Fairbanks community. The Foundation will include organizations and programs that serve youth, the elderly, recreation, safety, vulnerable populations, and arts and culture. Preference will be given to applications which have the potential to impact a broad range of area residents. Applications should describe measurable outcomes and other sources of support, collaboration and/or cooperation. Applications should also address the sustainability of the proposed program or project for which funding is desired. Currently, no annual deadlines have been established.
Requirements: The Foundation seeks applications from qualified tax-exempt 501(c)3 organizations (or equivalent organizations) in the greater Fairbanks area. Equivalent organizations may include tribes, local or state governments, schools, or Regional Educational Attendance Areas.
Restrictions: Individuals, for profit, and 501(c)4 and (c)6 organizations, non-Alaska based organizations and state or federal government agencies are not eligible for competitive grants. Applications for religious indoctrination or other religious activities, endowment building, deficit financing, fundraising, lobbying, electioneering and activities of a political nature will not be considered, nor will proposals for ads, sponsorships, or special events.
Geographic Focus: Alaska
Contact: Ricardo Lopez, Affiliate Program Officer; (907) 249-6707; fax (907) 334-5780; rlopez@alaskacf.org
Internet: http://goldenheartcf.org/grants-community-projects/
Sponsor: Golden Heart Community Foundation
P.O. Box 73183
Fairbanks, AK 99707-3183

Golden LEAF Foundation Grants 843
The mission of the foundation is to support organizations that promote the social welfare of North Carolina's citizens and to receive and distribute funds to lessen the economic impact of changes in the state's tobacco economy. The Foundation looks for projects with the following characteristics: serving unmet needs in communities; supporting new technology, crops, and applications to increase the areas advantage in agriculture; job creation and retention in rural tobacco-dependent counties; creation, expansion and improvement of business activity in rural tobacco-dependent counties; training/workforce preparedness initiatives; and public infrastructure improvement projects. Applicants seeking funding are encouraged to contact the Foundation for more information regarding the grants application process and funding priorities.
Requirements: Government and 501(c)3 tax-exempt organizations in North Carolina are eligible to apply.
Restrictions: Grants will not be awarded to: endowments; capital campaigns; construction projects - except as noted; infrastructure - except as noted; debt relief; revolving loan funds; purchase of land; after-school or day care programs; general employability training programs; general use community centers/facilities.
Geographic Focus: North Carolina
Date(s) Application is Due: Aug 1
Contact: Grants Administrator; (888) 684-8404 or (252) 442-7474; fax (252) 442-7404; info@goldenleaf.org
Internet: http://www.goldenleaf.org
Sponsor: Golden LEAF (Long-term Economic Advancement Foundation) Foundation
107 SE Main Street, Suite 500
Rocky Mount, NC 27801

Goldseker Foundation Community Affairs Grants 844
The Goldseker Foundation maintains a two-track grantmaking program that designates three priority areas but retains the ability to initiate and respond to new ideas and opportunities within our established program areas. In each of the priority grant areas, the Foundation is a directly engaged and active partner. Grants include a mix of Foundation initiatives and projects submitted independently by potential grantees. Community affairs grants cut across a number of areas, including foreclosure prevention, economic development, and improving and strengthening organizations that make living and working in Baltimore City and its metropolitan region attractive to long term residents, businesses, and talented newcomers.

Requirements: To be considered for funding, an organization must meet all of the following requirements: must be nonprofit organizations as defined in Section 501(c)3 and Section 509(a) of the Internal Revenue Code; must carry on their work principally in metropolitan Baltimore; and, applicants may not discriminate on the basis of race, creed, color, physical handicap, or gender. Because the Foundation is not normally a long-term source of funds, applicants are encouraged to demonstrate how proposed activities will be sustained. Applicants are expected to demonstrate adequate administrative capacity and financial stability and to describe evaluation criteria and methods in their requests.

Restrictions: The Foundation does not provide funds for endowments; individuals; building campaigns; deficit financing; annual giving; publications; arts and culture; religious programs or purposes; political action groups; specific disabilities or diseases; or, projects normally financed by government.

Geographic Focus: Maryland

Contact: Laurie Latuda Kinkel, Program Officer; (410) 837-6115; fax (410) 837-7927; lmlatuda@goldsekerfoundation.org

Internet: http://www.goldsekerfoundation.org/_grants?program_area_id=5

Sponsor: Morris Goldseker Foundation

1040 Park Avenue, Suite 310

Baltimore, MD 21201

Goodrich Corporation Foundation Grants 845

The Foundation makes charitable grants in four categories: education; arts and culture; civic and community; and health and human services. Preference shall be given to requests for projects or programs in areas having a significant number of employees, employees serving on boards of charitable organizations or other noticeable corporate presence. The Foundation staff accepts and reviews grant requests quarterly. To request funding, applicants will need to complete the application form which is available online. Telephone and email requests or inquiries are not accepted.

Requirements: 501(c)3 tax-exempt organizations are eligible.

Restrictions: The foundation generally will not support: multiyear grants in excess of five years; individuals, private foundations, endowments, churches or religious programs, fraternal/social/ labor/veterans organizations; groups with unusually high fundraising or administrative expenses; political parties, candidates, or lobbying activities; travel funds for tours, exhibitions, or trips by individuals or special interest groups; organizations that discriminate because of race, color, religion, national origin, or areas covered by applicable federal, state, or local laws; local athletic/sports programs or equipment, courtesy advertising benefits, raffle tickets and other fundraising events; organizations that receive sizable portions of their support through municipal, county, state, or federal dollars; individual United Way agencies that already benefit from Goodrich contributions to the United Way; or international organizations.

Geographic Focus: All States

Date(s) Application is Due: Feb 1; Aug 1

Contact: Foundation Contact, Foundation Contact; (704) 423-7011

Internet: http://www.goodrich.com/CDA/GeneralContent/0,1136,59,00.html

Sponsor: Goodrich Foundation

Four Coliseum Center, 2730 West Tyvola Road

Charlotte, NC 28217-4578

Good Works Foundation Grants 846

The Foundation was established to support good works wherever they are found and encourage innovative programs which involve collaboration in education, the arts, and the environment. In particular, the Foundation focuses on initiatives and programs that impact children, especially the culture and environment in which they learn and grow. The Foundation generally meets quarterly to evaluate requests for funding programs. Guidelines and application information is available online.

Requirements: 501(c)3 tax-exempt organizations in the Santa Monica and West Los Angeles area are eligible.

Restrictions: No fax or email proposals are accepted. You may not apply for fellowships, capital expenditures, construction, or endowment.

Geographic Focus: California

Contact: Laura Donnelley-Morton, (310) 828-1288; fax (310) 829-6090; info@goodworks.org

Internet: http://www.goodworks.org/pages/guidelines

Sponsor: Good Works Foundation

2101 Wilshire Boulevard, Suite 225

Santa Monica, CA 90403

Google Grants Beta 847

The Google Grants program supports organizations sharing their philosophy of community service to help the world in areas such as science and technology, education, global public health, the environment, youth advocacy, and the arts. Google Grants has awarded AdWords advertising to non-profit groups whose missions range from animal welfare to literacy, from supporting homeless children to promoting HIV education. Recipients use their award of free AdWords advertising on Google.com to raise awareness and increase traffic. Application available online only.

Requirements: In the United States - Organizations must have current 501(c)3 status, as assigned by the Internal Revenue Service to be considered for a Google Grant. Outside the U.S - currently accepting applications from eligible charitable organizations based in Australia, Brazil, Canada, Denmark, France, Germany, India, Ireland, Italy, Japan, the Netherlands, Spain, Sweden, Switzerland and the UK.

Restrictions: Organizations already participating in the Google AdSense program are not eligible for Google Grants consideration. In addition, organizations that are either religious or political in nature are not eligible, including those groups focused primarily on lobbying for political or policy change.

Geographic Focus: All States

Samples: Three award recipients have achieved these results: - Room to Read, which educates children in Vietnam, Nepal, India and Cambodia, attracted a sponsor who clicked on its AdWords ad. He has donated funds to support the education of 25 girls for the next 10 years. - The U.S. Fund for UNICEF's e-commerce site, Shop UNICEF, has experienced a 43 percent increase in sales over the previous year. - CoachArt, supporting children with life-threatening illnesses through art and athletics programs, has seen a 60 to 70 percent increase in volunteers.

Contact: Google Grants Team Contact; googlegrants@google.com

Internet: http://www.google.com/grants/

Sponsor: Google

1600 Amphitheatre Parkway

Mountain View, CA 94043

Grace and Franklin Bernsen Foundation Grants 848

The Grace and Franklin Bernsen Foundation provide grants primarily within the metropolitan Tulsa, Oklahoma area. Areas of interest supported are: religious; charitable; scientific; literary and; educational purposes. Grant applications for programs and projects that will provide a defined benefit such as capital projects, building programs, specific program needs or ongoing operations from time to time are all considered. Grant applications from elementary or secondary education institutions will be considered if they involve programs for at-risk, handicapped or learning-disabled children; or if they are innovative and apply to all schools in the system.

Requirements: Applicant should submit a narrative summary no more than three pages in length. This letter should be addressed to the Trustees of the Foundation, see website for detailed description of narrative requirements. IRS 501(c)3 non-profit organizations in the metropolitan Tulsa, Oklahoma area are eligible to apply. Application may be made at any time for support of activities consistent with the Foundation's guidelines. The Foundation's Board meets monthly to review grant applications. Applications received on or before the 12th day of the month (unless the 12th falls on a Saturday, Sunday, or a holiday, in which event applications are due on the preceding business day) preceding a next regularly scheduled Board meeting are normally considered at such meeting.

Restrictions: Grant applications for individuals are not considered. The Foundation discourages applications for general support or reduction of debt, or for continuing or additional support for the same programs. The Foundation will only review one grant request per agency during our fiscal year

Geographic Focus: Oklahoma

Amount of Grant: 2,000 - 1,000,000 USD

Samples: Parent Child Center of Tulsa, Tulsa, OK, $10,000—program funds; St. John Medical Center Foundation, Tulsa, OK, $106,000—funds for programs and capital improvements; Tulsa Air & Space Museum, Tulsa, OK, $10,000—provide funds for capital improvements.

Contact: Margaret Skyles, Administrator; (918) 584-4711; fax (918) 584-4713; mskyles@bernsen.org or info@bernsen.org

Internet: http://www.bernsen.org/grant.html

Sponsor: Grace and Franklin Bernsen Foundation

15 West Sixth Street, Suite 1308

Tulsa, OK 74119-5407

Grace Bersted Foundation Grants 849

The Grace Bersted Foundation was established in 1986 to support and promote quality education, human services, and health care programming for underserved populations. Special consideration is given to charitable organizations that serve the needs of children or the disabled. Applicants must apply online at the grant website. Applicants are strongly encouraged to do the following before applying: review the downloadable state application procedures for additional helpful information and clarifications; review the downloadable online-application guidelines at the grant website; review the foundation's funding history (link is available from the grant website); review the online application questions in advance; and review the list of required attachments. These will generally include: a list of board members, financial statements (audited, reviewed, or compiled by independent auditor); an organization summary; a list of other funding sources; an IRS Determination letter; and other required documents. All attachments must be uploaded in the online application as PDF, Word, or Excel files. The deadline for application to the Foundation August 1, and grant decisions will be made by November 1.

Requirements: Applicant organizations must have 501(c)3 tax-exempt status and an office located in one of the following counties: DuPage, Kane, Lake, or McHenry.

Restrictions: The foundation does not support requests from individuals, organizations attempting to influence policy through direct lobbying, or any political campaigns.

Geographic Focus: Illinois
Date(s) Application is Due: Aug 1
Contact: Debra L. Grand; (312) 828-2055; ilgrantmaking@ustrust.com
Internet: https://www.bankofamerica.com/philanthropic/fn_search.action
Sponsor: Grace Bersted Foundation
231 South LaSalle Street, IL1-231-13-32
Chicago, IL 60604

Great Clips Corporate Giving 850

Each month, Great Clips selects one independent charity and rewards their dedication to greatness in their community with a $1,500 donation. Charities entered will also have the chance to get even more funds at the end of the year. Each charity will receive an additional donation from Great Clips based on the number of votes they receive on EverythingGreat.com.

Requirements: Nonprofit organizations in the United States and Canada may enter the monthly contests. Organizations must include their 501(c)3 number or registration document with the Charities Directorate of the Canada Revenue Agency (in Canada) within the application. The program nominated must align with Great Clips' mission of supporting organizations that inspire us with their creativity, passion and greatness and must positively impact communities where Great Clips salons are located.

Restrictions: The Great Clips Great Giving Program does not provide funding for: political organizations, fraternal groups or social clubs that engage in any kind of political activity; religious organizations, unless they serve the general public in a significant non-denominational way; individuals or individual families; organizations located outside Great Clips markets; capital campaigns; private foundations; sponsorships for music, film and art festivals; support for business expositions/conferences; scholarships; charities that are already supported from government organizations or national charities (e.g. Red Cross, United Way, Children's Miracle Network, etc.); organizations that discriminate on the basis of race, color, gender, sexual orientation, age, religion, physical disability, or national or ethnic origin; or, 501(c)3 organizations or programs/projects that have been in place for less than one year.

Geographic Focus: All States
Amount of Grant: 1,500 USD
Contact: Corporate Giving Manager; (800) 999-5959; fax (952) 844-3444
Internet: http://everythinggreat.greatclips.com/great-giving/
Sponsor: Great Clips, Inc.
4400 West 78th Street, Suite 700
Minneapolis, MN 55435

Greater Columbus Arts Council Operating Grants 851

GCAC grants fund the operation of arts organizations that demonstrate high-quality artistic programming, stable artistic and administrative staffing, healthy financial structures, and significant impact on the city's economy and tourism. Operating support grants allow the organization to develop and maintain managerial and artistic capacity through methods the organization deems most valuable. Operating support grants are unrestricted as to use.

Requirements: Applicant organizations must have had 501(c)3 status for at least three consecutive years prior to the date of application, demonstrate that the organization's primary focus and actual operation are artistic in nature, provide cultural programming of the highest caliber, employ professional management staff, demonstrate a wide-ranging impact on the city of Columbus, operate with a community-based board of trustees, operate with a clearly articulated artistic plan, and demonstrate fiscal accountability.

Geographic Focus: Ohio
Date(s) Application is Due: Feb 1
Samples: Actors' Theater Company (Columbus, OH)—for general operating support, $15,544; Columbus Symphony Orchestra (Columbus, OH)—for general operating support, $208,083; The Thurber House (Columbus, OH)—for general operating support, $44,103.
Contact: Program Officer, Community Funding; (614) 224-2606; fax (614) 224-7461; grants@gcac.org
Internet: http://www.gcac.org/org/guidelines_operating_support.php
Sponsor: Greater Columbus Arts Council
100 E Broad Street, Suite 2250
Columbus, OH 43215

Greater Saint Louis Community Foundation Grants 852

The Greater Saint Louis Community Foundation (GSLCF) was founded in 1915, one year after the first community foundation was established in Cleveland, Ohio. Currently GSLCF administers over 400 individual charitable funds that total $170 million in assets. These funds annually make over $17 million in grants that shape the greater Saint Louis region, touch communities across the nation, and reach across the globe. Historically, the mission of GSLCF has been two-fold: to serve donors and ensure that their dollars work in line with the goals that are important to them; and to promote charitable giving through community investment in nonprofit organizations capable of addressing community issues in measurable ways. To this end GSLCF maintains an online database YOURGivingLink to help donors find deserving nonprofit organizations that match their giving interests. Nonprofits are encouraged to register their organizations with the database; the link is available at the GSLCF website.

Requirements: While the Foundation predominately supports St. Louis area nonprofits, grants are also made to national and international charities.

Geographic Focus: Illinois, Missouri
Contact: Amy Basore Murphy, Director of Scholarships and Donor Services; (314) 588-8200, ext. 139 or (314) 880-4965; fax (314) 588-8088; amurphy@stlouisgives.org
Internet: http://www.stlouisgives.org/charities/
Sponsor: Greater Saint Louis Community Foundation
319 North Fourth Street, Suite 300
Saint Louis, MO 63102-1906

Greater Tacoma Community Foundation Fund for Women and Girls Grant 853

The mission of the fund is to promote the power of generosity among women and fund opportunities for women and girls in Pierce County. Distributions from the Fund shall provide assistance to programs that promote intellectual, physical, emotional, social, economic, and cultural growth of women and girls of all ages. Grants will be considered for general operations, equipment, and project support. Application information is available online.

Requirements: Grants will be made to organizations, located primarily in, and serving women and girls of, the greater Tacoma-Pierce County area.

Restrictions: Grants will not be made for annual campaigns, fund raising events, travel expenses, political or lobbying activities, religious organizations for sacramental/theological purposes, endowments, or publications except those that grow out of research and experiments underwritten by the Foundation. Grants will not be awarded for deficit reduction. Grant requests from agencies that are discriminatory to race, sex, age, national origin, religion, physical or mental handicap, veteran status or sexual orientation will not be considered.

Geographic Focus: Washington
Date(s) Application is Due: May 15; Jun 15
Amount of Grant: 1,700 USD
Contact: Sherrana Kempton, (253) 383-5622; sherrana@gtcf.org
Internet: http://www.tacomafoundation.org/newsarticle.cfm?articleid=67374&ptsidebaroptid=0&returnto=page19700.cfm&returntoname=Fund%20for%20Women%20and%20Girls&siteid=1735&pageid=19538&sidepageid=19700&banner1img=banner%5F1%2EJPG&banner2img=banner%5F2%2EJPG&bannerb
Sponsor: Greater Tacoma Community Foundation
950 Pacific Avenue, Suite 1220, P.O. Box 1995
Tacoma, WA 98402

Greater Tacoma Community Foundation Grants   854

The Foundation invests in the community through grants to vital nonprofit agencies in Pierce County. While grants are made across all fields, principal funding areas include: arts and culture; civics; education; the environment; health; and human services. The Foundation also makes capital, equipment, project and operating support grants. Application information is available online.

Requirements: Eligible applicants must meet the following criteria: attest to non-discrimination on the basis of race, sex, age, national origin, religion, physical or mental handicap, veteran status or sexual orientation; provide a service primarily for residents of Pierce County; qualify as tax-exempt under section 501(c)3 of the IRS Code; and apply no more than once a year for any one governing or umbrella organization.

Restrictions: Grants will not be made for: fundraising events or fundraising feasibility projects; individuals; religious organizations for sacramental/ theological purposes; production of books, videos, films, or other publications; annual campaign appeals; travel; political or lobbying activities; endowments; debt reduction; events or programs that occur prior to the board of directors decision/notification dates.

Geographic Focus: Washington

Samples: Kids in Distressed Situations (New York, NY)—to provide donated products to low-income children and families in Tacoma and Pierce County, WA, through the Emergency Food Network, $25,000.

Contact: Rose Lincoln Hamilton, President & CEO; (253) 383-5622; fax (253) 272-8099; rlincoln@gtcf.org

Internet: http://www.tacomafoundation.org

Sponsor: Greater Tacoma Community Foundation

950 Pacific Avenue, Suite 1220, P.O. Box 1995

Tacoma, WA 98402

Greater Worcester Community Foundation Jeppson Memorial Fund   855
for Brookfield Grants

The Fund provides money to civic and community projects that help improve the lives of residents and enrich the cultural environment. The Fund provides support for: cultural or artistic performances; public seminars; festivals or exhibitions; services that help frail or vulnerable citizens, or that contribute to public health and safety; opportunities for educational enrichment; youth involvement in recreation, sports and the arts; and projects that foster community awareness and connections among different groups. Application information is available online.

Requirements: Any nonprofit or civic organization that serves the residents of Brookfield may apply.

Restrictions: Grant funds may not be used for expenses already incurred by the applicant. Fund awards are not intended to replace municipal funds.

Geographic Focus: Massachusetts

Date(s) Application is Due: Jul 15

Contact: Pamela B. Kane, (508) 755-0980; pkane@greaterworcester.org

Internet: http://www.greaterworcester.org/grants/Jeppson.htm

Sponsor: Greater Worcester Community Foundation

370 Main Street, Suite 650

Worcester, MA 01608-1738

Greenburg-May Foundation Grants   856

Grants are almost entirely awarded for medical research, primarily in the fields of cancer, heart, and neurological research. In addition, some support is given to hospitals, Jewish welfare funds, temple support, and the aging. Types of support include general operating support, continuing support, annual campaigns, endowment funds, emergency funds, program development, internships, scholarship funds, research, and consulting services. Organizations in Florida and New York City receive the largest part of the funds. Applications may be submitted at any time.

Requirements: Nonprofits in southern Florida and New York are eligible.

Restrictions: Grants are not given to individuals or for endowment funds, special projects, publications, or conferences, and generally not for scholarships and fellowships.

Geographic Focus: Florida, New York

Amount of Grant: Up to 295,282 USD

Samples: Miami Jewish Home and Hospital for the Aged (Miami, FL)—$75,200; Greater Miami Opera (Miami, FL)—$4,220.

Contact: Isabel May, President; (305) 864-8639

Sponsor: Greenburg-May Foundation

P.O. Box 54-5816

Miami Beach, FL 33154

GreenPoint Foundation Grants   857

The foundation awards grants in operating communities to organizations dedicated to increasing the availability of affordable housing and that meet basic health and human service needs. Submit grant requests on organization letterhead, which is signed by an officer, and include specific details, including budget, about the project or event; the organization's mission statement; details regarding the organization's services to low- to moderate-income individuals and/or its activities to revitalize/stabilize low- to moderate-income areas (include statistics if possible); and the IRS determination letter with the organization's federal (not state) tax ID number.

Requirements: 501(c)3 nonprofits that serve the needs of the communities in which GreenPoint Bank does business are eligible.

Restrictions: Grants do not support capital campaigns, endowments, scholarship funds, special events, other short-term projects, religious organizations, or membership organizations.

Geographic Focus: New York

Amount of Grant: Up to 28,000,000 USD

Samples: Families of employees of Keefe, Bruyette and Woodf (New York, NY)—for families of employees killed in the September 11 attacks on the World Trade Center, $250,000; American Red Cross, Disaster Relief Fund (Washington, DC)—to provide disaster-relief services to victims of the September 11 terrorist attacks, $25,000.

Contact: Gwen Perry, Foundation Manager; (212) 834-1215; fax (212) 834-1406; gperry@GreenPoint.com

Internet: http://www.greenpoint.com/index.cfm?spPathname=static/com-grants5less.htm

Sponsor: GreenPoint Foundation

90 Park Avenue, 4th Floor

New York, NY 10016

Greenspun Family Foundation Grants   858

The Greenspun Family Foundation supports many causes with an emphasis on education, health, children, Jewish issues, and the greater Las Vegas community. Preference is given to requests from the Las Vegas area. There are no application forms or deadlines. Applicants should submit a letter of inquiry. Information about current programs supported is available at the Foundation website.

Geographic Focus: Nevada

Amount of Grant: 50,000 - 2,000,000 USD

Samples: University of Nevada at Las Vegas, Las Vegas, Nevada, $2.2 million, payable over one year; Nevada Cancer Institute, Las Vegas, Nevada, $1,000,000, payable over one year; Clark County Public Education, Las Vegas, Nevada, $50,000, payable over one year.

Contact: Dr. Brian Cram, Director; (702) 259-2323 or (702) 259-4023; fax (702) 259-4019; brian.cram@lasvegassun.com

Internet: http://www.thegreenspuncorp.com/philanthropy.php

Sponsor: Greenspun Family Foundation

901 North Green Valley Parkway, Suite 210

Henderson, NV 89074

Grotto Foundation Project Grants   859

The Grotto Foundation works to improve the education and economic, physical and social well-being of citizens, with a special focus on families and culturally diverse groups. The Foundation funds support agencies and institutions dedicated to improving the quality of parenting and well-being of infants and children from birth to six years of age. The Foundation is further interested in increasing public understanding of American cultural heritage, the cultures of nations and the individual's responsibility to fellow human beings.

Requirements: Detailed applications for Native American grants are available online. Applicants are encouraged to contact the Foundation and discuss their early childhood development to be certain it is appropriate for funding.

Restrictions: Policy precludes grants being awarded for capital fund projects, travel, publication of books or manuscripts, undergraduate research projects, or grants to individuals.

Geographic Focus: Minnesota

Date(s) Application is Due: Jan 15; Mar 15; Jul 15; Nov 15

Amount of Grant: Up to 10,000 USD

Contact: Jennifer Kolde, Grants Manager; (651) 209-8010; fax (651) 209-8014; jkolde@grottofoundation.org

Internet: http://www.grottofoundation.org

Sponsor: Grotto Foundation

1315 Red Fox Road, Suite 100

Arden Hills, MN 55112

Grundy Foundation Grants 860

The Grundy Foundation's endowment, which sustains the operations of both the museum and library, also provides grantmaking. Grant support is given to projects that benefit the people and institutions of Pennsylvania. Upon availability, the Board of Trustees generally restricts grantmaking to Bucks County public charities, with special consideration to those of Bristol Borough. Grant applications are awarded primarily for capital projects to serve a wide area rather than a single neighborhood. Grantmaking activities include community development, arts and culture, education, environment, health, and human services. The average grant is $2,500.

Requirements: There are no applications or specific deadlines. The Foundation accepts and reviews written requests for funding throughout the year. In general, organizations having other support for core operating expenses and long-term costs of new projects are given priority. Organizations are encouraged to contact the Foundation prior to submission of a grant application. Prospective grantees may use the forms developed by the Delaware Valley Grant makers, if preferred. At a minimum, each proposal must include: One-page summary with contact name, executive director's name, organization name, address, telephone, email, and fax; project summary; amount requested; and total project budget amount; detailed proposal with mission and history of the organization; complete description of the proposed project; project budget, including other sources of support, with indication of whether support is in hand, pledged, requested, or to be requested; expected sources of support for this project in the future; and expected arrangements for future maintenance and repairs; the organization's financial report of IRS 990 filing for the most recent fiscal year (audited reports are preferred); copy of IRS 501(c)3 letter of determination or proof that the organization is a government agency; a list of officers and directors; a copy of report of the organization's activities over the most recent fiscal year. Proposals can be mailed, faxed or sent electronically (faxes and email versions require prior Foundation approval). Videotaped proposals will not be accepted.

Restrictions: The Foundation does not make grants to nonpublic schools, individuals, religious organizations, or for endowments, loans, research, or political activities.

Geographic Focus: Pennsylvania

Contact: Eugene Williams, Executive Director; (215) 788-5460; fax (215) 788-0915; info@grundyfoundation.com

Internet: http://www.grundymuseum.org/

Sponsor: Grundy Foundation

680 Radcliffe Street, P.O. Box 701

Bristol, PA 19007

Gulf Coast Foundation of Community Capacity Building Grants 861

The Capacity Building Grants program offers Grant Writer Assistance funding, which helps local nonprofits that are unable to compete for grant opportunities because of complex, lengthy grant applications. Funds may be used to hire an experienced grant writer with the capabilities to attract dollars from regional or national funders and private or government programs. Requests for grant writing assistance will be judged on the following criteria: amount is significant enough to warrant the use of grant funds to hire a grant writer; the source of the grant is non-local; the expertise of the selected grant writer is appropriate; the agency has a reasonable chance of receiving the grant; the cost to hire a grant writer would have been prohibitive to the agency if these funds were not available; and all fund requests will require a minimum 50 percent cash match by the agency.

Requirements: The Foundation will make grants to qualified organizations classified as 501(c)3 tax-exempt public charities by the Internal Revenue Service in the counties of Brevard, Charlotte, Citrus, Collier, DeSoto, Glades, Hardee, Hendry, Hernando, Highlands, Hillsborough, Indian River, Lake, Lee, Manatee, Okeechobee, Orange, Osceola, Pasco, Pinellas, Polk, Sarasota, Seminole, Sumter, and St. Lucie.

Geographic Focus: Florida

Contact: Kirstin Fulkerson; (941) 486-4600; info@gulfcoastcf.org

Internet: http://www.gulfcoastcf.org/resources.php

Sponsor: Gulf Coast Foundation of Community

601 Tamiami Trail South

Venice, FL 34285

Gulf Coast Foundation of Community Operating Grants 862

Through grants and strategic community initiatives, Gulf Coast invests in the work of effective nonprofit organizations that improve quality of life in our region. The Foundation will award operating grants over $10,000, with grant funds to be expended within one year of approval. Currently, the Foundation has four grant cycles for operating grants, which fund the core operating needs of nonprofits

and help make them stronger. This includes staff and training, database and accounting systems, marketing and fundraising operations. Organizations that want to diversify income streams and generate new revenue sources may apply for an operating – earned revenue grant. Examples of successful proposals in this category include using existing facilities to generate rental income or marketing and selling a packaged program/service to other organizations. Groups that want to reduce operating costs may apply for an operating – efficiency grant. Examples of successful proposals in this category include consolidating services with other nonprofits, implementing new or improved technologies such as databases or financial systems, or "greening" offices.

Requirements: The Foundation will make grants to qualified organizations classified as 501(c)3 tax-exempt public charities by the Internal Revenue Service in the counties of Brevard, Charlotte, Citrus, Collier, DeSoto, Glades, Hardee, Hendry, Hernando, Highlands, Hillsborough, Indian River, Lake, Lee, Manatee, Okeechobee, Orange, Osceola, Pasco, Pinellas, Polk, Sarasota, Seminole, Sumter, and St. Lucie. All operating – earned revenue grant applications must provide realistic revenue estimates that result in a return on investment that exceeds the grant amount. Operating – efficiency grant applications must provide a cost?benefit analysis showing how proposed funding approaches will produce cost savings.

Geographic Focus: Florida

Samples: Special Operations Warrior Foundation, $500,000 - immediate financial assistance for special operations personnel, who have been severely wounded, to have his/her family travel and be bedside; Charlotte Behavioral Health Care, $200,000 - addressing mental health, substance abuse, and related psychosocial needs of veterans and their families.

Contact: Kirstin Fulkerson, Philanthropic Advisor; (941) 486-4600; fax (941) 486-4699; info@gulfcoastcf.org

Internet: http://www.gulfcoastcf.org/resources.php

Sponsor: Gulf Coast Foundation of Community

601 Tamiami Trail South

Venice, FL 34285

Guy's and St. Thomas' Charity Grants 863

The Charity's grants program supports both small (under 20,000 British pounds) and large (between 20,000 and 1 million British pounds) projects under three themes: staff benefits and development; clinical and service innovation; and buildings and the environment. Applications for grants under 20,000 British pounds are considered by the Small Grants Committee, and grants over 20,000 British pounds are assessed by the New Services and Innovations Committee. The small grants deadline dates are: August, 14; September, 25; October 16. Deadline dates for the large grants are: December, 1; March, 6; June, 5; September, 4; November, 20.

Requirements: The Charity only considers applications from anyone working in one of the four NHS Trusts in Lambeth or Southwark, although there are some restrictions for mental health staff.

Geographic Focus: All States, United Kingdom

Date(s) Application is Due: Mar 6; Jun 5; Aug 14; Sep 4; Sep 25; Oct 16; Nov 20; Dec 1

Amount of Grant: 20,000 - 1,000,000 GBP

Samples: Julie Brown, Midwifery Practice Leader for Parent Education, 5,000 pounds; Dr. Danielle Harari, Consultant Physician in Elderly Medicine, 20,000 pounds; Improving dermatology training for primary care professionals, NHS Foundation Trust, 254,000 pounds.

Contact: Anne Rigby; 020 7188 1227; anne.rigby@gsttcharity.org.uk

Internet: http://www.gsttcharity.org.uk/grants/index.html

Sponsor: Guy's and St. Thomas' Charity

Freepost Lon 15724

London, SE1 9YA England

Guy I. Bromley Trust Grants 864

The Guy I. Bromley Trust was established in 1964 to support and promote quality educational, cultural, human-services, and health-care programming. In the area of education the trust supports programming that: promotes effective teaching; improves the academic achievement of, or expands educational opportunities for disadvantaged students; improves governance and management; strengthens nonprofit organizations, school leadership, and teaching; and bolsters strategic initiatives of area colleges and universities. In the area of culture the trust supports programming that: fosters the enjoyment and appreciation of the visual and performing arts; strengthens humanities and arts-related education programs; provides affordable access; enhances artistic elements in communities; and nurtures a new generation of artists. In the area of human services, the trust supports programming that: strengthens agencies that deliver critical human

services and maintains the community's safety net; and helps agencies respond to federal, state, and local public policy changes. In the area of health the trust supports programming that: improves the delivery of health care to the indigent, uninsured, and other vulnerable populations; and addresses health and health-care problems that intersect with social factors. Grant requests for general operating support and program support will be considered. Grants from the trust are one year in duration. There are no application deadlines for the Bromley Trust. Proposals are reviewed on an ongoing basis. Downloadable application materials are available at the grant website. Applicants are encouraged to review the downloadable state guidelines at the grant website for further information and clarification before applying. Applicants are also encouraged to view the trust's funding history (link is available at the grant website).
Requirements: Applicants must have 501(c)3 tax-exempt status and serve the residents of Atchison, Kansas and the Greater Kansas City Metropolitan area. Applications must be mailed.
Restrictions: Grant requests for capital support will not be considered. The trust does not support requests from individuals, organizations attempting to influence policy through direct lobbying, or any political campaigns.
Geographic Focus: All States
Samples: Humane Society of Atchison, Atchison, Kansas, $5,000; Benedictine College, Atchison, Kansas, $30,000; Community of Christ, Independence, Missouri, $30,000.
Contact: Spence Heddens, Market President; (816) 292-4301; Spence. heddens@baml.com
Internet: https://www.bankofamerica.com/philanthropic/fn_search.action
Sponsor: Guy I. Bromley Trust
1200 Main Street, 14th Floor, P.O. Box 219119
Kansas City, MO 64121-9119

GVF Elgin Grant Works   865
The foundation awards a limited number of general operating grants per year to Elgin-based nonprofit organizations. Organizations may apply for renewed support for two additional years. After the third year of funding, a full calendar year must elapse before an organization may apply for another general operating grant. Application deadlines are the first Friday in February, June, and October. Application and guidelines are available online.
Requirements: Eligible organizations are 501(c)3; based in Elgin, IL, providing services to Elgin residents; and have a dedicated Elgin budget; have an annual operating budget between $50,000 and $4 million; are well managed and fiscally sound; have a balanced budget or an operating deficit of less than 10 percent; have at least one paid staff person; have been in business and operating as a 501(c)3 nonprofit for at least three years; are willing to abide by the grant agreement; and are willing to submit a final report.
Restrictions: Grants are not available to support endowments, organizations not based in Elgin, fundraising events, debt or deficit reduction, grantmaking organizations, federated funds, scholarships, political campaigns, religious purposes, or individuals.
Geographic Focus: Illinois
Date(s) Application is Due: Feb 3; Jun 3; Oct 7
Amount of Grant: Up to 10,000 USD
Samples: Elgin Children's Chorus (IL)—general operating support, $10,000; The Literacy Connection (Elgin, IL)—general operating support, $10,000; Little Angels Parents ARC (Elgin, IL)—general operating support, $10,000; Sybaquay Girl Scout Council (Elgin, IL)—general operating support, $10,000.
Contact: Grants Administrator; (847) 289-8575; fax (847) 289-8576; info@grandvictoriafdn.org
Internet: http://www.grandvictoriafdn.org
Sponsor: Grand Victoria Foundation
60 S Grove Avenue
Elgin, IL 60120

H&R Block Foundation Grants   866
The foundation supports the arts and culture, community development, education, and health and human services. Grants for operational support; special projects; and capital improvements for construction, renovation, and equipment will be considered. The foundation usually makes one-year grants but may consider requests for up to five years for special project funding. Guidelines and application are available online.
Requirements: 501(c)3 tax-exempt organizations are eligible. Major emphasis is placed on support of activities in the Kansas City metropolitan area.
Restrictions: Except in most unusual circumstances, the foundation does not make grants to individuals or businesses; publications; projects for which the foundation must exercise expenditure responsibility; single-disease agencies;

travel or conferences; historic preservation; or telethons, dinners, advertising, or other fundraising events.
Geographic Focus: Kansas, Missouri
Date(s) Application is Due: Jan 28; Apr 29; Jul 29; Oct 14
Amount of Grant: 500 USD
Contact: Grants Administrator; (816) 932-8324; fax (816) 753-1585; foundation@hrblock.com
Internet: http://www.hrblockfoundation.org/grants/index.html
Sponsor: HandR Block Foundation
4400 Main Street
Kansas City, MO 64111

H.A. and Mary K. Chapman Charitable Trust Grants   867
H. Allen Chapman was born in Colorado in 1919. In 1976, he established the H.A. and Mary K. Chapman Charitable Trust, a perpetual charitable private foundation that maintains endowments to fund charitable grants to public charities. The trustees and staff that administer the foundation also provide public stewardship through service to charitable organizations and causes. A major charitable focus of H. A. Chapman during his life, and the lives of his philanthropic parents, James A. and Leta Chapman, was education and medical research. Though not limited geographically, most grants and public service are within Oklahoma. Grants to human services and civic and community programs and projects are primarily focused in the area of Tulsa. There are two steps in the process of applying for a grant. The first is a Letter of Inquiry from the applicant. This letter is used to determine if the applicant will be invited to take the second step of submitting a formal Grant Proposal.
Requirements: IRS 501(c)3 non-profits are eligible to apply.
Restrictions: Grant requests for the following purposes are not favored: endowments, except as a limited part of a capital project reserved for maintenance of the facility being constructed; deficit financing and debt retirement; projects or programs for which the Chapman Trusts would be the sole source of financial support; travel, conferences, conventions, group meetings, or seminars; camp programs and other seasonal activities; religious programs of religious organizations; project or program planning; start-up ventures are not excluded, but organizations with a proven strategy and results are preferred; purposes normally funded by taxation or governmental agencies; requests made less than nine months from the declination of a previous request by an applicant, or within nine months of the last payment made on a grant made to an applicant; requests for more than one project.
Geographic Focus: Oklahoma
Amount of Grant: Up to 300,000 USD
Samples: Gilcrease Museum Management, Tulsa, Oklahoma, $250,000 - general operating funds; Tulsa Air and Space Museum, Tulsa, Oklahoma, $35,000 - general operating support; Friends of the Fairgrounds Foundation, Tulsa, Oklahoma, $15,000 - general operating funds.
Contact: Andrea Doyle, Program Officer; (918) 496-7882; fax (918) 496-7887; andie@chapmantrusts.com
Internet: http://www.chapmantrusts.org/grants_programs.html
Sponsor: H.A. and Mary K. Chapman Charitable Trust
6100 South Yale, Suite 1816
Tulsa, OK 74136

H.J. Heinz Company Foundation Grants   868
The Foundation is committed to promoting the health and nutritional needs of children and families. Priority is given to programs in communities where Heinz operates with a special focus given to southwestern Pennsylvania. The Foundation proactively donates funds to develop and strengthen organizations that are dedicated to nutrition and nutritional education, youth services and education, diversity, healthy children and families, and quality of life. Application information is available online.
Requirements: Only organizations that have 501(c)3 tax status under the U.S. Internal Revenue Code are eligible for support domestically. International organizations are encouraged to submit a letter of inquiry prior to preparing a full proposal to determine eligibility. International organizations will need to provide a 501(c)3 determination letter from the United States Internal Revenue Service or sufficient documentation to demonstrate that the non-U.S. grantee is the equivalent of a U.S. public charity. Documentation should be provided in English. The Foundation will also accept proposals in the Common Grant Application Format. All proposals must be submitted in writing. Electronic submissions are not accepted at this time.
Restrictions: The Foundation will not provide grants to individuals nor make multi-year pledges except for major capital or grant campaigns. Generally, the Foundation does not make loans and does not provide grants for individuals,

equipment, conferences, travel, general scholarships, religious programs, political campaigns, and unsolicited research projects.
Geographic Focus: All States
Samples: King Edwards Memorial Hospital, Subiacio, Perth, Australia, $28,000—Micronutrient long-term development study; The Children's Medical & Research Foundation, Dublin, Ireland, $25,000—new adolescent Hematology/Oncology unit; Pittsburgh Public Theater, Pittsburgh, PA, $30,000—program support.
Contact: Tammy B. Aupperle, Program Director; (412) 456-5773; fax (412) 442-3227; heinz.foundation@hjheinz.com
Internet: http://www.heinz.com/sustainability.aspx/social/heinz-foundation.aspx
Sponsor: H.J. Heinz Company Foundation
P.O. Box 57
Pittsburgh, PA 15230-0057

H. Leslie Hoffman and Elaine S. Hoffman Foundation Grants 869
The foundation awards general operating grants to California non-profits, primarily focusing on education. Additional funding is also available in the following areas of interest: arts; social services; hospitals; health organizations; children/youth services, including children's hospitals and, social services. There are no application forms or deadlines.
Requirements: California IRS 501(c)3 non-profits are eligible to apply. The majority of grants are funded in the Los Angeles area with a special emphasis on Pasadena.
Restrictions: Individuals are ineligible.
Geographic Focus: California
Amount of Grant: 1,000 - 200,000 USD
Samples: All Saints Church, Pasadena, CA, $10,000—general funding; Hillsides Home For Children, Pasadena, CA, $5,000—general funding; Descanso Gardens, Lacanada, CA, $1,000—annual benefit.
Contact: J. Kristoffer Popovich, Treasurer; (626) 793-0043
Sponsor: H. Leslie Hoffman and Elaine S. Hoffman Foundation
225 S Lake Avenue, Suite 1150
Pasadena, CA 91101-3005

Haddad Foundation Grants 870
The Haddad Foundation, established in West Virginia in 2003, offers grant support primarily in Boone and Kanawha counties of West Virginia. Its identified fields of interest include: children and youth services; higher education; and human services. Funding comes in the form of general operations support. There are no specific application forms or deadlines with which to adhere, and initial approach should be with a letter of application. Amounts range up to $10,000.
Requirements: Applicants must be a 501(c)3 organization that serves the residents of either Boone or Kanawha counties, West Virginia.
Geographic Focus: West Virginia
Amount of Grant: Up to 10,000 USD
Samples: Smile Train, New York, New York, $10,000 - general operating support; University of South Florida, Tampa, Florida, $6,400 - general operating support.
Contact: Susan L. Haddad, Director; (304) 925-5418
Sponsor: Haddad Foundation
707 Virginia Street East, Suite 900
Charleston, WV 25301-2716

HAF Technical Assistance Program (TAP) Grants 871
The Technical Assistance Program is a small award program which provides nonprofits with one-on-one technical assistance in a variety of forms, such as consultants, training workshops, self-pace manuals, software, or any other form identified by applicants. Awards typically range from $500 to $2,000. Funds must be used to improve the organization, its leadership or operations. Areas of assistance may include the following: strategic planning; board development; community organizing training; increasing organizational diversity; financial management, operational assessments, board development; program assessments; personnel issues; collaboration building; executive coaching; succession planning; exit strategy planning; fundraising planning; and involving those who serve in program planning, development and evaluation. Applications and information are confidential, and will not affect other potential Humboldt Area Foundation grant funding. Grant applications are accepted on the first of each month, with grants paid directly to a consultant to cover the costs of their consulting services. Additional information is available at the website.

Requirements: Funding is available to organizations and community groups in Humboldt, Del Norte, and Trinity counties.
Restrictions: TAP will not pay for grant writing, programmatic development or for duties that are typically handled by staff (e.g. data entry). Organizations less than a year old and government entities are not eligible to apply.
Geographic Focus: California
Date(s) Application is Due: Jan 1; Feb 1; Mar 1; Apr 1; May 1; Jun 1; Jul 1; Aug 1; Sep 1; Oct 1; Nov 1; Dec 1
Amount of Grant: 500 - 2,000 USD
Contact: Amy Jester, Program Manager, Health and Nonprofit Resources; (707) 442-2993, ext. 374; fax (707) 442-9072; amyj@hafoundation.org
Internet: http://www.hafoundation.org/index.php?option=content&task=view&id=74
Sponsor: Humboldt Area Foundation
373 Indianola Road
Bayside, CA 95524

Hagedorn Fund Grants 872
William Hagedorn directed that the remainder of his estate be dedicated to this fund, in memory of his late wife, Tillie Hagedorn, that would support religious or charitable organizations in the New York City region. Funding interests include: health (including cancer, HIV/AIDS, blindness), gardens, social services, youth, education, senior services and housing and community development. All applications to the Hagedorn Fund must be submitted online, additional information is available at the Hagedorn Fund website.
Requirements: New York nonprofit organizations are eligible to apply.
Restrictions: No grants are made to individuals or private foundations or for matching gifts or loans.
Geographic Focus: New York
Date(s) Application is Due: Sep 1
Amount of Grant: 5,000 - 45,000 USD
Samples: Cornell University, New York, NY, $10,000; Brooklyn Botanic Garden Corporation, Brooklyn, NY, $20,000; Riverdale Presbyterian Church, Bronx, NY, $20,000.
Contact: Erin K. Hogan, Fund Manager; (212) 464-2476; fax (212) 464-2305; erin.k.hogan@jpmorgan.com
Internet: http://fdncenter.org/grantmaker/hagedorn
Sponsor: Hagedorn Fund
270 Park Avenue, 16th Floor
New York, NY 10017

Hahl Proctor Charitable Trust Grants 873
Before moving to Midland, Hahl Proctor studied voice in a Chicago school of music. Although very active in the ranching industry, she continued to pursue her music interests through her church and other civic organizations. In addition to her vocation and avocation, Hahl was an attractive, popular, and generous woman who loved to entertain. She established a trust in her will to provide a continuous source of financial assistance to worthwhile charities. The trust focuses on charitable organizations dedicated to children and families, the arts, and education. Applicants must apply online at the grant website. Applicants are strongly encouraged to do the following before applying: review the downloadable state application procedures for additional helpful information and clarifications; review the downloadable online-application guidelines at the grant website; review the trust's funding history (link is available from the grant website); review the online application questions in advance; and review the list of required attachments. These will generally include: a list of board members, financial statements (audited, reviewed, or compiled by independent auditor); an organization summary; a list of other funding sources; an IRS Determination letter; and other required documents. All attachments must be uploaded in the online application as PDF, Word, or Excel files. The application deadline is 11:59 p.m. on May 15.
Requirements: Applicants must have 501(c)3 tax-exempt status and serve residents of the Permian Basin Area.
Restrictions: The trust does not support requests from individuals, organizations attempting to influence policy through direct lobbying, or any political campaigns.
Geographic Focus: Texas
Date(s) Application is Due: May 15
Amount of Grant: 2,000 - 20,000 USD
Contact: Mark J. Smith, Philanthropic Relationship Manager; (817) 390-6028; tx.philanthropic@baml.com
Internet: https://www.bankofamerica.com/philanthropic/fn_search.action
Sponsor: Hahl Proctor Charitable Trust
500 West 7th Street, 15th Floor, TX1-497-15-08
Fort Worth, TX 76102-4700

Halliburton Foundation Grants 874

The foundation supports education at all levels and charitable organizations in the following ways: matching US- based employee donations on a two-for-one basis up to $20,000 annually per employee for accredited junior colleges, colleges, and universities; matching US-based employee donations to accredited elementary and secondary schools on a two-for-one basis up to $500 annually per employee; making direct donations to US-based elementary and secondary schools and colleges and universities; and recognizing and supporting active US-based employee volunteerism with direct donations through the Halliburton Volunteer Incentive Program. The corporate giving program makes donations to tax-exempt nonprofit organizations dedicated to education, health/welfare, civic issues, and arts and culture. The board meets quarterly. There are no application deadlines or forms.

Geographic Focus: Arizona, Texas
Amount of Grant: 250 - 20,000 USD
Contact: Margaret Carriere, (713) 676-3717; fhoufoundation@halliburton.com
Internet: http://www.halliburton.com/about/community.jsp
Sponsor: Halliburton Foundation
4100 Clinton Drive, Building 1, 7th Floor
Houston, TX 77020

Hallmark Corporate Foundation Grants 875

The mission of the Foundation is to help create communities where: all children have the chance to grow up as healthy, productive and caring persons; vibrant arts and cultural experiences enrich the lives of all citizens; there is a strong infrastructure of basic institutions and services, especially for persons in need; and all citizens feel a responsibility to serve their community. Proposals are accepted and reviewed throughout the year. There are no deadlines. The application process can be completed online using the Hallmark General Grant Application, which is available on the Hallmark website.

Requirements: IRS Non-profit 501(c)3 organizations are eligible to apply in the following areas: Kansas City metropolitan area; Center, Texas; Columbus, Georgia; Enfield, Connecticut; Lawrence, Kansas; Leavenworth, Kansas; Liberty, Missouri; Metamora, Illinois and; Topeka, Kansas.
Restrictions: Funding is not available for: individuals for any purpose, including travel, starting a business or paying back loans; religious organizations unless they can demonstrate that services are provided to the community-at-large and separated from religious purposes; fraternal, international and veterans organizations; sports teams and athletic organizations; individual youth clubs, troops, groups or school classrooms; social clubs; disease-specific organizations whose local chapters primarily raise funds for national research; past operating deficits; endowment or foundation funds; conferences; scholarly or health-related research; scholarship funds.
Geographic Focus: Connecticut, Georgia, Illinois, Kansas, Missouri, Texas
Contact: Community Development Manager; (816) 545-6906; contributions@hallmark.com.
Internet: http://corporate.hallmark.com/Community/Community-Involvement-Program-Guidelines
Sponsor: Hallmark Corporate Foundation
Mail Drop 323, P.O. Box 419580
Kansas City, MO 64141-6580

Hamilton Family Foundation Grants 876

The Foundation provides financial support primarily in the area of education, grades K-12 with a particular emphasis on literacy projects in underserved Philadelphia area schools. The Foundation considers applications for high school enrichment projects, as well as academically based after-school, arts and culture, and summer programs. Colleges and universities are not generally considered. The grant application is available online.

Requirements: Nonprofit organizations in Pennsylvania's Chester, Camden, Montgomery, and Delaware Counties are eligible.
Restrictions: Grant requests for individuals, bricks and mortar projects, endowments, and other foundations are not processed.
Geographic Focus: Pennsylvania
Date(s) Application is Due: Feb 1; May 1; Aug 1; Nov 1
Amount of Grant: 3,000 - 15,000 USD
Contact: Nancy Wingo, (610) 975-0517; fax (610) 293-0967; nwingo@HamiltonFamilyFoundation.org
Internet: http://www.hamiltonfamilyfoundation.org/guidelines.html
Sponsor: Hamilton Family Foundation
200 Eagle Road, Suite 316
Wayne, PA 19087

Handsel Foundation Grants 877

The Handsel Foundation provides grants to organizations working to end companion animal cruelty, neglect, and overpopulation. It is most interested in supporting organizations with effective plans to reduce animal suffering through targeted spay/neuter programs to address companion animal overpopulation. These projects will be given special consideration, particularly for larger grants. The foundation occasionally provides grants for adoption and/or education programs relating to companion animals. However, these grants are rare and typically small relative to our spay/neuter grants.

Requirements: Prospective grant recipients must meet the following criteria: only 501(c)3 nonprofit organizations will be considered, as defined by the IRS; organization must have been in operation for at least one year; total expenses of less than $1 million for latest fiscal year; and must be seeking funds for programs in Oregon, Washington, or California.
Geographic Focus: All States
Date(s) Application is Due: Mar 31; Jun 30; Sep 30; Dec 31
Amount of Grant: 3,000 - 25,000 USD
Contact: Grants Coordinator; (206) 905-9887; inquiries@handselfdn.org
Internet: http://www.handselfdn.org/howtoapply.htm
Sponsor: Handsel Foundation
P.O. Box 6476
Olympia, WA 98507-6476

Harder Foundation Grants 878

The foundation focuses grant making on environmental efforts. The foundation's four main interest areas are large forest ecosystem protection, grizzly bear habitat preservation in the 48 contiguous states, wild salmon recovery in the Pacific Northwest, and protection of the Everglades. Funded projects usually offer long-term protection of specific public lands and waterways and may concentrate on a particular environmental problem. The foundation gives priority to advocacy projects of statewide or regional significance aiming to protect undeveloped habitat areas facing immediate threats. Types of support include operating budgets, continuing support, annual campaigns, seed grants, land acquisition, endowment funds, and matching funds.

Requirements: Nonprofit environmental groups or projects in Alaska, Colorado, Florida, Idaho, Montana, Nevada, Oregon, Utah, Washington, and Wyoming are eligible.
Restrictions: Local projects with limited scope, environmental education programs, and public policy development are not funded.
Geographic Focus: Alaska, Colorado, Florida, Idaho, Montana, Nevada, Oregon, Utah, Washington, Wisconsin
Amount of Grant: 10,000 - 50,000 USD
Contact: Mary Martin, Office Manager; (253) 593-2121; fax (253) 593-2122; grants@theharderfoundation.org
Sponsor: Harder Foundation
401 Broadway Avenue, Suite 303
Tacoma, WA 98402

Harmony Grove Foundation Grants 879

The Harmony Grove Foundation was established in Georgia with the specific mission to support community development, economic development, libraries, human services, and other worthwhile programs in the Jackson County, Georgia, region. Past project support has included: expansion of the Commerce Public Library; the Hardman Preservation Microfilming Project; and the Community Gardens of Commerce. Most recently, awards have ranged from $25,000 to $100,000. There is no official application format, so interested parties should begin by contacting the Foundation office directly. No application deadlines for submission have been identified.

Requirements: Any 501(c)3 serving residents of the Commerce, Georgia, metro area is eligible to apply.
Restrictions: No grants are provided directly to individuals.
Geographic Focus: Georgia
Amount of Grant: 25,000 - 100,000 USD
Contact: Charles W. Blair, Jr., Treasurer; (706) 335-7195 or (706) 335-8205
Sponsor: Harmony Grove Foundation
86 Forest Hills Court
Commerce, GA 30529

Harold and Arlene Schnitzer CARE Foundation Grants 880

The Foundation's principal purpose is to assist with Jewish, cultural, youth, education, medical, social service, and community activities. Foundation focus is on proposals for projects that enhance the quality of life in Oregon and Southwest Washington. The Foundation funds grant requests for operating expenses, special projects, matching grants, multiple-year grants and capital campaigns as well as for purchase of specific items. There is no formal application form. Interested applicants may contact the Foundation for guidelines.

Requirements: Nonprofit organizations in Oregon and Washington are eligible. Organizations located in Portland are given first funding priority. Approximately 90% of grant funds stay in the Portland metropolitan area.

Restrictions: The Foundation does not provide funds for individuals, non tax-exempt organizations, other private foundations or political groups.

Geographic Focus: Oregon, Washington

Date(s) Application is Due: Feb 28; May 31; Aug 31; Nov 30

Amount of Grant: 1,000 - 5,000,000 USD

Samples: Mittleman Jewish Community Center, Portland, OR, $400,000— for operating support; Oregon Health and Science University Foundation, Portland, OR, $5,500,000— for Diabetes Center; Give Them Wings, Hood River, OR, $25,000—for Wyeth Work Camp renovation.

Contact: Barbara Hall, Vice President; (503) 973-0286; fax (503) 450-0810

Sponsor: Harold and Arlene Schnitzer Foundation

P.O. Box 2708

Portland, OR 97208-2708

Harold Simmons Foundation Grants 881

The foundation awards grants to Texas nonprofit organizations, with emphasis on social services, religion, health, the arts, and youth. Grants also support community programs and projects, child development, and adult basic education/literacy programs. The foundation also supports international development and relief efforts in Third World countries. Grants are awarded for general operating support, annual campaigns, capital campaigns, building construction/renovation, continuing support, seed money, and program development. Application forms are not required, and there are no deadline dates.

Requirements: Dallas, TX, nonprofits are eligible.

Restrictions: Grants are not awarded to support individuals or for endowment funds or loans.

Geographic Focus: Texas

Samples: Children's Medical Ctr Dallas (TX)—to establish a hospital within the medical center devoted to the needs of child cardiac patients, $5 million; U of Texas Southwestern Medical Ctr (Dallas)—to enhance the Simmons Comprehensive Cancer Center, including supporting the work of its newly recruited director, $15.4 million.

Contact: Lisa Simmons Epstein, President; (972) 233-2134

Sponsor: Harold Simmons Foundation

5430 LBJ Freeway, Suite 1700

Dallas, TX 75240-2697

Harold Whitworth Pierce Charitable Trust Grants 882

The trust awards grants to Boston-area nonprofit organizations in its areas of interest, including green and public spaces—projects that support community gardens, parks, and other natural areas, and projects that enhance space for recreation; capital projects—projects that reduce the operating costs for an institution and projects that improve and/or restore the physical heritage of Boston; and research—environmental research and/or for making the results of such research available for public policy. Occasionally other areas are supported. Types of support include program development, seed money, capital projects, and operating grants on occasion. The first step in the application process is a phone call to determine whether the project is eligible. The listed application deadlines are for concept letters (two-page maximum). Full proposals are by invitation.

Requirements: 501(c)3 organizations in the Boston, MA, area are eligible.

Restrictions: Grants do not support scholarships, individuals, fund-raising events or training, films, videos, travel, or advocacy.

Geographic Focus: Massachusetts

Date(s) Application is Due: Mar 1; Sep 15

Amount of Grant: 1,000 - 100,000 USD

Contact: Elizabeth Nichols, (617) 523-8368; fax (617) 523-8949; piercetrust@nichols-pratt.com

Sponsor: Harold Whitworth Pierce Charitable Trust

50 Congress Street, Suite 832

Boston, MA 02109

Harris and Eliza Kempner Fund Grants 883

The foundation provides grants primarily in the Galveston, TX, area to qualifying organizations in the broad areas of the arts, historic preservation, community development, education, health, and human services. The foundation gives preference to requests for seed money, operating funds, small capital needs, and special projects partnering with other funding sources. Application information is available online.

Requirements: Grants are made primarily to Texas qualifying organizations in the greater Galveston area.

Restrictions: Funding is not available for: fund-raising benefits; direct mail solicitations; grants to individuals; and grants to non-USA based organizations.

Geographic Focus: Texas

Date(s) Application is Due: Mar 15; Oct 15

Samples: Galveston Art League, Galveston, TX, $5,000—matching grant to purchase gallery space; Avenue L Missionary Baptist Church, Galveston, TX, $20,000—renovation and restoration repairs to Fellowship Hall; Galveston Island Swim Team, Galveston, TX, $$4,600—program expansion to include all Galveston Island youth.

Contact: Harrette N. Howard, Grants Administrator; (409) 762-1603; fax (409) 762-5435; information@kempnerfund.org

Internet: http://www.kempnerfund.org/app/programs.html

Sponsor: Harris and Eliza Kempner Fund

2201 Market Street, Suite 601

Galveston, TX 77550-1529

Harris Bank Foundation Grants 884

Grants are made to a broad range of cultural, educational, community, and civic organizations in Chicago, IL, including organizations that help ethnic and/or minority groups. Education grants are made to private four-year institutions to help defray operating expenses, limited to colleges and universities within Cook County that provide comprehensive accredited programs. Education-related grants considered are unrestricted for operating expenses of recognized, nonprofit Chicago educational institutions other than schools, such as museums, public television, career development programs, and so forth. Culture and fine arts grants are given to organizations that foster an appreciation of the arts such as opera companies, art institutes, and symphony orchestras. Health care grants are available to local health organizations that increase minority community access to primary health care. The bank will fund programming for handicapped, drug rehabilitative, and other health care services on a selective basis. For civic affairs grants, the foundation considers organizations whose work and service enhance the business and community spirit of greater Chicago. Harris Bank also supports the revitalization of Chicago's neighborhoods throughout the city, makes grants for initial expenses of new organizations or new projects of established organizations that provide social services, especially to minority groups, and also provides funding for capital expenses of metropolitan organizations whose objectives are to respond to charitable, educational, scientific, medical, or cultural needs. Grants are approved at bimonthly meetings, usually on a yearly basis; however, the committee may approve multiple-year grants.

Requirements: Grants are given only to tax-exempt organizations located in the Chicago metropolitan area. A proposal should include a statement of the proposed project; project budget and potential funding sources; background information about the organization; evidence of tax-exempt status; and current, audited financial statements.

Restrictions: Grants are not made for or to political activities, individuals, individual sectarian or religious organizations, fraternal organizations, nor for testimonial drives, advertisements in souvenir or program books, or raffle tickets.

Geographic Focus: Illinois

Amount of Grant: 5,000 - 20,000 USD

Samples: Art Institute of Chicago (IL)—for general operating support, $14,000; YMCA of Metropolitan Chicago (IL)—for Duncan YMCA renovation and expansion, $10,000; Habitat for Humanity Uptown Chicago (IL)—for general operating support, $10,000.

Contact: Mary Houpt; (312) 461-5834; fax (312) 293-4702

Sponsor: Harris Bank Foundation

111 W Monroe Street, P.O. Box 755

Chicago, IL 60690

Harry A. and Margaret D. Towsley Foundation Grants 885

In 1959, Margaret Towsley created the Harry A. and Margaret D. Towsley Foundation with an initial gift of $4 Million in Dow Chemical Company stock. While the Foundation's initial goals were typical of general family foundations, its mission later became focused on programs promoting education, health care, shelter, and nutrition for children. As its assets grew, its areas of concentration expanded into college and university education, medical education, planned parenthood, and interdisciplinary programs with the schools of law and social work. These areas reflected Dr. and Mrs. Towsley's common interest in teaching. The foundation currently awards grants to Michigan organizations in its areas of interest, including environment,

medical and preschool education, social services, continuing education, and research in the health sciences. Types of support include annual campaigns, building construction and renovation, capital campaigns, continuing support, employee matching gifts, endowments, general operating support, matching/ challenge support, professorships, program development, research, and seed grants. There are no application forms; submit a letter of inquiry between January and the listed application deadline.
Restrictions: Grants are not awarded to individuals or for travel, scholarships, fellowships, conferences, books, publications, films, tapes, audio-visual or communication media, or loans.
Geographic Focus: Michigan
Date(s) Application is Due: Mar 31
Contact: Lynn Towsley White; (989) 837-1100; fax (989) 837-3240
Sponsor: Harry A. and Margaret D. Towsley Foundation
140 Ashman Street, P.O. Box 349
Midland, MI 48640

Harry and Helen Sands Charitable Trust Grants　　886
Established in Milwaukee, Wisconsin, in 2007, the Harry and Helen Sands Charitable Trust offers its support primarily in West Virginia. Its primary field of interest is to assist in the funding of Christian churches and agencies through general operations money. Applicants should adhere to the Foundation guidelines by first requesting a formal application and submitting the completed request by the annual November 1 deadline.
Requirements: Applicants must be 501(c)3 or Christian organizations either located in, or serving the residents of, Wheeling, West Virginia.
Geographic Focus: West Virginia
Date(s) Application is Due: Nov 1
Amount of Grant: Up to 5,000 USD
Samples: Soup Kitchen of Greater Wheeling, Wheeling, West Virginia, $4,000; Wheeling Health Right, Wheeling, West Virginia, $4,000; Kings Daughters Child Care Centers, Wheeling, West Virginia, $2,500.
Contact: Debbie Broemsen, Trust Administrator; (866) 300-6222; fax (800) 883-7695; debbie.x.broemsen@jpmorgan.com
Sponsor: Harry and Helen Sands Charitable Trust
P.O. Box 3038
Milwaukee, WI 53201-3038

Harry and Jeanette Weinberg Foundation Grants　　887
The foundation awards grants to support organizations in the areas of aging/ gerontology, disabled, disadvantaged (economically), food distribution, and social services. Types of support include building construction/renovation, capital campaigns, challenge/matching grants, endowments, general operating support, and material acquisition. Submit a letter of inquiry at any time.
Restrictions: Grants are not awarded to higher education or museums.
Geographic Focus: All States
Amount of Grant: 10,000 - 1,000,000 USD
Samples: Punahou School (Honolulu, HI)—to construct Case Middle School, $3 million; Metropolitan Career Ctr (Philadelphia, PA)—for general operating support of its work with low-income and unemployed people, $330,000 over three years; Strive (New York, NY)—to strengthen and expand its job training and placement network, and for endowment, $5 million challenge grant.
Contact: Grants Administrator; (410) 654-8500
Internet: http://www.hjweinbergfoundation.org
Sponsor: Harry and Jeanette Weinberg Foundation
7 Park Center Court
Owings Mills, MD 21117

Harry Bramhall Gilbert Charitable Trust Grants　　888
The Harry Bramhall Gilbert Charitable Trust supports tax-exempt organizations that contribute to the health, education, and cultural life of the Tidewater, Virginia region. The Trust currently and substantially funds nonprofits based in the cities of Norfolk, Chesapeake, and Virginia Beach, Virginia. To apply, submit a letter to the Trust (no application form is required) containing the following information: copy of IRS Determination Letter; copy of most recent annual report/audited financial statement/990; listing of board of directors, trustees, officers and other key people and their affiliations; detailed description of project and amount of funding requested. Include two copies.
Requirements: Virginia nonprofit organizations based in the cities of Norfolk, Chesapeake, and Virginia Beach are eligible.
Restrictions: No support for religious or political organizations.
Geographic Focus: Virginia
Date(s) Application is Due: Sep 30

Amount of Grant: 2,500 - 100,000 USD
Samples: Chesapeake Public Library Foundation, Chesapeake, VA, $5,000— for additions to collections of books, magazines, newspapers, computers, and software at Central Library; University of Virginia, Charlottesville, VA, $100,000—for merit scholarships for undergraduate students in their fourth-year at UVA meeting certain criteria, who have graduated from Public High School of City of Chesapeake, VA; Virginia Symphony, Norfolk, VA, $25,000—for general support and the Virginia Symphony Endowment Fund.
Contact: Stuart D. Glasser, Treasurer; (757) 204-4858; sdglasser@cox.net
Internet: http://fdncenter.org/grantmaker/gilbert
Sponsor: Harry Bramhall Gilbert Charitable Trust
316 Scone Castle Loop
Chesapeake, VA 23322

Harry C. Trexler Trust Grants　　889
The trust supports charitable organizations located in the city of Allentown or in Lehigh County, Pennsylvania. The trust provides that one-fourth of the income shall be added to the corpus, one-fourth paid to the city of Allentown for park purposes, and the remainder distributed to such charitable organizations and objects as shall be of the most benefit to humanity, but limited to Allentown and Lehigh County, Pennsylvania, particularly for hospitals, churches, institutions for the care of the crippled and orphans, youth agencies, social services, cultural programs, and support of ministerial students at two named Pennsylvania institutions. Types of support include: building construction/renovation, capital campaigns, continuing support, land acquisition, equipment acquisition, program development, general operating support, and matching/challenge grants.
Requirements: Potential grantees are nonprofit organizations located in Allentown or Lehigh County, PA, and rendering exclusive or substantial services to the people residing therein.
Restrictions: Grants are not made to individuals or for endowment funds, research, scholarships, or fellowships.
Geographic Focus: Pennsylvania
Date(s) Application is Due: Dec 1
Amount of Grant: 1,000 - 100,000 USD
Samples: Allentown Art Museum, Allentown, PA, $200,000—to construct a new wing; Lehigh Valley Public Telecommunications Corporation, Allentown, PA, $15,000—underwrite a reading program in the Allentown School District; Sacred Heart Hospital, Allentown, PA, $80,000—underwrite the operating expenses of the Parish Nurse Program in center-city Allentown.
Contact: Janet Roth, Executive Director; (610) 434-9645; fax (610) 437-5721
Internet: http://www.TrexlerTrust.org/
Sponsor: Harry C. Trexler Trust
33 South 7th Street, Suite 205
Allentown, PA 18101

Harry Frank Guggenheim Foundation Research Grants　　890
The Foundation invites proposals in any of the natural sciences, social sciences or humanities that promise to increase understanding of the causes, manifestations, and control of human violence and aggression. Highest priority is given to research that can increase understanding and improve urgent problems of violence and aggression in the modern world. Questions that interest the foundation concern violence and aggression in relation to social change, intergroup conflict, war, terrorism, crime, and family relationships, among other subjects. Priority will also be given to areas and methodologies not receiving adequate attention and support from other funding sources. Applicants may be citizens of any country. Most awards fall within the range of $15,000 to $40,000 per year for periods of one or two years. Applications for larger amounts and longer durations must be very strongly justified. Applications must be received by August 1, with a decision given in December.
Requirements: Applicants must mail two copies of the typed application in English to the Foundation. Applications may not be faxed or emailed. Along with two copies of the application, applicants must include the following: title page; abstract and survey; budget and its justification; personnel; research plan; other support; protection of subjects; and referee comments. Applicants should refer to the Foundation website for specific instructions on how to submit each of the attachments, and contact the Foundation if they have any questions.
Restrictions: Research with no relevance to understanding human problems will not be supported, nor will proposals to investigate urgent social problems where the Foundation cannot be assured that useful, sound research can be done. While almost all recipients of the Foundation grants possess a Ph.D., M.D., or equivalent degree, there are no formal degree requirements for the grant. The grant, however, may not be used to support research undertaken

as part of the requirements for a graduate degree. Applicants need not be affiliated with an institution of higher learning, although most are college or university professors. The foundation awards research grants to individuals (or a few principal investigators at most) for individual projects, but does not award grants to institutions for institutional programs. Individuals who receive research grants may be subject to taxation.

Geographic Focus: All States, All Countries
Date(s) Application is Due: Aug 1
Amount of Grant: 15,000 - 40,000 USD
Contact: Officer; (646) 428-0971; fax (646) 428-0981; info@hfg.org
Internet: http://www.hfg.org/rg/guidelines.htm
Sponsor: Harry Frank Guggenheim Foundation
25 West 53rd Street
New York, NY 10019-5401

Harry S. Black and Allon Fuller Fund Grants 891

The Harry S. Black and Allon Fuller Fund was established in 1930 to support quality health-care and human-services programming for underserved populations. The grantmaking focus is in the areas of health care and physical disabilities. The fund supports access to health care; health education; health/wellness promotion and disease prevention; health policy analysis and advocacy; access programs for physically disabled individuals; disability policy analysis and advocacy; workforce development programs; and programs that improve quality of life for the disabled. Emphasis will be placed on programs serving low-income communities. Grant requests for general operating support or program/project support are strongly encouraged. Applicants must apply online at the grant website. Applicants are strongly encouraged to do the following before applying: review the downloadable state application procedures at the grant website; review the downloadable online-application guidelines at the grant website; review the foundation's funding history (link is available from the grant website); review the online application questions in advance; and review the list of required attachments. These will generally include: a list of board members, financial statements (audited, reviewed, or compiled by independent auditor); an organization summary; a list of other funding sources; an IRS Determination letter; and other required documents. All attachments must be uploaded in the online application as PDF, Word, or Excel files. The Harry S. Black and Allon Fuller Fund has a deadline of June 30. Grant decisions will be made by December 31.

Requirements: Nonprofit organizations must be geographically located within the city limits of New York City or Chicago to be eligible to apply.
Restrictions: The fund generally does not support the following: projects in the areas of health care specific to medical/academic research; organizations or programs that primarily provide mental health services; programs that primarily provide services to either the mentally or developmentally disabled; endowment campaigns; and capital projects. The fund does not support requests from individuals, organizations attempting to influence policy through direct lobbying, or any political campaigns.
Geographic Focus: Illinois, New York
Date(s) Application is Due: Jun 30
Contact: George Suttles; (646) 743-0425; george.suttles@ustrust.com
Internet: https://www.bankofamerica.com/philanthropic/fn_search.action
Sponsor: Harry S. Black and Allon Fuller Fund
114 West 47th Street, NY8-114-10-02
New York, NY 10036

Harry W. Bass, Jr. Foundation Grants 892

The Dallas-based Harry W. Bass, Jr. Foundation seeks to enrich the lives of the citizens of Texas by providing support to qualified organizations in the areas of education, health, human services, civic & community, science, research, arts and culture. Grant applications for specific programs or projects, capital projects or, less often, general operations are considered. Endowment gifts are rare. The Harry W. Bass, Jr. Foundation also considers program-related investments as part of its grant-making activities. The foundation strives to be responsive to the needs of all eligible organizations and considers requests of any amount. There is no formal application form. Grant requests are accepted at any time throughout the year. Each organization is limited to one application within a twelve-month period. Requests are usually processed within three to four months. Electronic grant applications should be submitted to dcalhoun@hbrf.org (no file attachments, please). For more information, contact the Harry W. Bass, Jr. Foundation.

Requirements: Texas 501(c)3 tax-exempt organizations are eligible.
Restrictions: In general, grants are not made for purposes of: church or seminary construction; annual fundraising events or general sustentation

drives; professional conferences and symposia; out-of-state performances or competition expenses; to other private foundations. Unsolicited grant requests are restricted to organizations based in the Greater Dallas area. In the event a grant is approved, the recipient organization will be unable to submit another grant request for two years due to the foundation policy of not providing subsequent year grants.

Geographic Focus: Texas
Samples: Southwestern Medical Foundation, $3,000,000—Heart, Lung & Vascular Center of Excellence at UT Southwestern University Hospital - St. Paul; Child Protective Services Community Partners, $10,000—Rainbow Room; Health & Human Services Grant; Wilkinson Center, $20,000— CLIMB After-School and Summer Program.
Contact: F. David Calhoun, Executive Director; (214) 599-0300; fax (214) 599-0405; dcalhoun@hbrf.org
Internet: http://www.harrybassfoundation.org/about.asp
Sponsor: Harry Bass Foundation
4809 Cole Avenue, Suite 252
Dallas, TX 75205

Hartford Aging and Health Program Awards 893

The foundation's two principal programs are Health Care Cost and Quality and Aging and Health. The Health Care Cost and Quality program supports the community health management initiative, health care quality measures, and reducing inappropriate health care services. The Aging and Health program supports strengthening physicians' knowledge of geriatrics, reducing medication problems of the elderly, and demonstrating integrated financing and service delivery for comprehensive geriatric services. Types of support include operating budgets, continuing support, projects/programs, research, publications, and conferences and seminars. The foundation also welcomes inquiries regarding projects that may not fit these specific interests but would further its broad goal of improving health care in America. Types of support include general operations, continuing support, projects/programs, research, publications, and conferences and seminars. Applications are accepted at any time and are reviewed four times each year when the board meets.

Requirements: U.S. health, education, and social service organizations may apply.
Restrictions: Requests will be denied for general research or for projects lasting more than three years.
Geographic Focus: All States
Samples: New York Academy of Medicine (NY)—to help start rotational field-training components, with a focus on working with older adults, in programs that offer master's degrees in social work, $5.1 million over four years; U of California (San Diego, CA) and U of Pittsburgh (PA)—to create new centers of excellence in geriatric medicine in order to increase the number of physician faculty members in the field of geriatrics, $450,000 each over three years; American Federation for Aging Research (New York, NY)—for the Medical Student Summer Research Training in Aging Program, $1.9 million over five years.
Contact: Corinne Rieder, Executive Director; (212) 832-7788; fax (212) 593-4913; mail@jhartfound.com
Internet: http://www.jhartfound.org
Sponsor: John A. Hartford Foundation
55 E 59th Street, 16th Floor
New York, NY 10022-1178

Hartford Foundation Regular Grants 894

The Foundation awards grants for a broad range of purposes to a wide variety of nonprofit organizations in social services, health, education, early childhood and youth services, arts and culture, housing and neighborhood development, and other charitable fields. These grants: enhance or strengthen existing activities; provide start-up for organizations and new programs; provide support for capital improvements. Interested applicants are encouraged to phone a program contact to discuss their project before beginning the application process.

Requirements: Nonprofit organizations in the following Connecticut towns are eligible to apply for funding: Andover, Avon, Bloomfield, Bolton, Canton, East Granby, East Hartford, East Windsor, Ellington, Enfield, Farmington, Glastonbury, Granby, Hartford, Hebron, Manchester, Marlborough, Newington, Rocky Hill, Simsbury, Somers, South Windsor, Suffield, West Hartford, Wethersfield, Windsor, Windsor Locks, Tolland, and Vernon. Proposals for statewide programs may be considered when there is a substantial benefit to residents of these communities.
Restrictions: The Foundation does not make grants from its unrestricted funds for: sectarian or religious activities; grants directly to individuals; grants to private foundations; endowments or memorials; direct or grass-roots lobbying

efforts; conferences; research; or informational activities on topics that are primarily national or international in perspective. In addition, the Foundation generally does not make grants for: federal, state, or municipal agencies or departments supported by taxation; sponsorship of or support for one-time events; liquidation of obligations incurred at a previous date; or sustaining support for recurring operating expenses.

Geographic Focus: Connecticut
Amount of Grant: Up to 500,000 USD
Samples: Town of Farmington, Farmington, CT, $19,749 - for construction of a tower and zip line at the youth center and for the Farmington High School's McDonough School Math and Literacy Tutoring Program; The ARC of the Farmington Valley, Inc., Canton, CT, $375,000 - for remodeling, code compliance, and upgrades to the Alleluia property.
Contact: Cheryl L. Gerrish, Grants Manager; (860) 548-1888; fax (860) 524-8346; gerrish@hfpg.org or hfpg@hfpg.org
Internet: http://www.hfpg.org/GrantmakingPrograms/Overview/tabid/163/Default.aspx
Sponsor: Hartford Foundation
10 Columbus Boulevard, 8th Floor
Hartford, CT 06106

Hartford Foundation Transitional Operating Support Grants 895

The Foundation offers transitional operating support grants to enable well-run nonprofits that have experienced unexpected income shortfalls to continue important community programs. Support is designed for programs that: address critical needs, especially those involving disadvantaged or vulnerable populations; have been operated competently and demonstrate evidence of positive effects on the lives of the population served; and would be particularly difficult or expensive to reestablish if they ceased operations. Interested applicants should call the Foundation and speak with a program officer.
Requirements: Nonprofit organizations in the following Connecticut towns are eligible to apply for funding: Andover, Avon, Bloomfield, Bolton, Canton, East Granby, East Hartford, East Windsor, Ellington, Enfield, Farmington, Glastonbury, Granby, Hartford, Hebron, Manchester, Marlborough, Newington, Rocky Hill, Simsbury, Somers, South Windsor, Suffield, West Hartford, Wethersfield, Windsor, Windsor Locks, Tolland, and Vernon. Proposals for statewide programs may be considered when there is a substantial benefit to residents of these communities.
Restrictions: The Foundation does not make grants from its unrestricted funds for: sectarian or religious activities; grants directly to individuals; grants to private foundations; endowments or memorials; direct or grass-roots lobbying efforts; conferences; research; or informational activities on topics that are primarily national or international in perspective. In addition, the Foundation generally does not make grants for: federal, state, or municipal agencies or departments supported by taxation; sponsorship of or support for one-time events; liquidation of obligations incurred at a previous date; or sustaining support for recurring operating expenses.
Geographic Focus: Connecticut
Amount of Grant: Up to 200,000 USD
Contact: Cheryl L. Gerrish, Grants Manager; (860) 548-1888; fax (860) 524-8346; gerrish@hfpg.org or hfpg@hfpg.org
Internet: http://www.hfpg.org/GrantmakingPrograms/AboutOurGrantmaking/TypesofGrants/tabid/168/Default.aspx#transitionaloperating
Sponsor: Hartford Foundation
10 Columbus Boulevard, 8th Floor
Hartford, CT 06106

Harvest Foundation Grants 896

Formed by the sale of Memorial Health Systems, the foundation is managing an endowment to invest in programs and initiatives that will address local challenges in the areas of health, education, and welfare in Martinsville/Henry County. The foundation is committed to honoring the legacy of Memorial Hospital by emphasizing prevention, safety and access to health care; by facilitating opportunities for local citizens to help their community reach its potential; and by improving the learning environment for citizenship, academic, and vocational preparedness. Application and guidelines are available online.
Requirements: To be eligible for consideration, an organization must: be located within, or have its program focused within Martinsville and/or Henry County; have a letter from the IRS stating its 501c3 status; and propose a project within one of the Foundation's three interest areas of health, education or welfare.
Restrictions: The foundation does not fund organizations that discriminate based upon race, creed, gender, or sexual orientation; scholarships, fellowships, or grants to individuals; sectarian religious activities, political lobbying, or legislative activities; profit-making businesses; emergency needs or extremely time sensitive requests; or direct replacement of discontinued government support.
Geographic Focus: Virginia
Samples: Dan River Basin Association, $8,000— to enhance the Uptown Spur Trail; Boy Scouts of America, Blue Ridge Mountains Council, $45,300—to launch the Scoutreach Program aimed at recruiting underserved boys in Martinsville/Henry County to join the Boy Scouts; MARC Workshop, Inc., $241,900—funding paid over 3 years to start-up a mobile employment program for disabled adults, creating competitive, minimum wage jobs for special education students graduating out of the public school system.
Contact: Allyson Rothrock, Executive Director; (276) 632-3329; fax (276) 632-1878; arothrock@theharvestfoundation.org
Internet: http://www.theharvestfoundation.org/page.cfm/topic/strategic-map
Sponsor: Harvest Foundation
1 Ellsworth Street, P.O. Box 5183
Martinsville, VA 24115

Hattie M. Strong Foundation Grants 897

The Foundation awards grants in support of projects designed to provide educational opportunities and services to youth and adults in the Greater Washington Area, with a concentration on programs in Washington, D.C. The Foundation considers innovative and effective programs that strengthen academic education (enrichment and remedial), promote literacy, and provide vocational skills training. Organizations interested in submitting a proposal for consideration by the Board should first contact the Foundation for written materials explaining the Foundation's proposal procedure and requirements.
Requirements: Nonprofit organizations serving the Washington, DC, metropolitan area may apply.
Restrictions: Funding is not available for building or endowment funds, requests for equipment, research, conferences, special events or benefits, projects designed to educate the general public, or programs of national or international scope. The Foundation does not make grants to individuals nor does it give scholarships.
Geographic Focus: District of Columbia
Date(s) Application is Due: Jan 15; Apr 15; Jul 15; Oct 15
Samples: Campagna Ctr (Alexandria, VA)—to support the Reading Specialist Program for first- to third-grade students at Mount Vernon Elementary School, $6000; Carlos Rosario Adult and Career Ctr (Washington, DC)—for general support to expand this adult education program, $6500.
Contact: Grants Director; (202) 331-1619; fax (202) 466-2894; hmsf@hmstrongfoundation.org
Internet: http://www.hmstrongfoundation.org
Sponsor: Hattie M. Strong Foundation
1620 I Street NW, Suite 700
Washington, D.C. 20006-4005

Hatton W. Sumners Foundation for the Study and Teaching of Self 898
Government Grants

The Foundation's purpose is to encourage the study, teaching and research in the science and art of self-government so that citizens understand the fundamental principles of democracy in shaping governmental policies. Working through qualified, tax-exempt organizations, the Foundation seeks to reach, educate, and motivate the general public and the current and future leaders of American society. The Foundation gives to youth organizations and higher education. Types of support include: conferences and seminars; continuing support; curriculum development; endowments; fellowships; general operating support; internship funds; matching and challenge support; and research. Application information is available at the Foundation website. Grant applications will be accepted from January 1st through August 1st of each year. Final decisions on grant proposals are made by the Trustees in October of each year.
Requirements: Grants are made only to 501(c)3 tax-exempt organizations in Texas, New Mexico, Oklahoma, Louisiana, Arkansas, Kansas, Nebraska and Missouri.
Restrictions: The Foundation does not fund religious organizations or individuals.
Geographic Focus: Arkansas, Kansas, Louisiana, Missouri, Nebraska, New Mexico, Oklahoma, Texas
Date(s) Application is Due: Aug 1
Contact: Hugh Akin, Executive Director; (214) 220-2128; fax (214) 953-0737; hugh@hattonsumners.org or info@hattonsumners.org
Internet: http://www.hattonsumners.org
Sponsor: Hatton W. Sumners Foundation for the Study and Teaching of Self Government
325 North St. Paul Street, Suite 3920
Dallas, TX 75201

Hawaii Community Foundation Geographic-Specific Fund Grants   899

With its Geographic-Specific program, the Foundation supports grant making in Ewa Beach, Kamuela, Kauai, Lanai, Maui, and West Hawaii via eleven distinct funds. Generally, these funds hope to improve the lives of residents living within these distinct geographic regions of Hawaii. Funding levels and deadlines vary throughout the course of year by fund, and applicants should visit the website for specific details.

Requirements: Nonprofit, tax-exempt 501(c)3 organizations, public schools, or units of government are eligible to apply. The Richard Smart Fund program supports projects that benefit the Waimea community.

Geographic Focus: Hawaii

Contact: Georgianna deCosta, Philanthropic Services Assistant; (808) 537-6333 or (888) 731-3863; gdecosta@hcf-hawaii.org

Internet: http://hawaiicommunityfoundation.org/index.php?id=71&categoryID=22

Sponsor: Hawai'i Community Foundation

1164 Bishop Street, Suite 800

Honolulu, HI 96813

Hawaii Community Foundation Health Education and Research   900
Grants

The program provides support from three distinct funds: Tobacco Prevention & Control Trust Fund; the Leahi Fund Research Fund; and the Medical Research Program. Funding will be provided for medical education and research in the fields of: cancer; heart disease; lung disease and research. Priority is given to projects that: demonstrate a foreseeable benefit to the people of Hawaii; support new investigators in Hawaii; and support collaborative efforts. Proposal submission information is available online.

Requirements: To be eligible for consideration an organization must be a 501(c)3 organization or a unit of government. The Principal Investigator must be based in Hawaii and conducting the research in Hawaii.

Geographic Focus: Hawaii

Date(s) Application is Due: Feb 27; Jul 17; Aug 14; Sep 10

Amount of Grant: 25,000 - 50,000 USD

Contact: Christel Wuerfel, Philanthropic Services Assistant; (808) 537-6333 or (888) 731-3863; cwuerfel@hcf-hawaii.org

Internet: http://www.hawaiicommunityfoundation.org/index.php?id=71&categoryID=23

Sponsor: Hawai'i Community Foundation

1164 Bishop Street, Suite 800

Honolulu, HI 96813

Hawaii Community Foundation Human Services Grants   901

The purpose of the Foundation's Human Services program is to support children and youth, and family strengthening. Six distinct funds have been established to support various facets of the program, including: the Hawaii Children's Trust Fund (awareness & prevention); the Oscar and Rosetta Fish Fund for Speech Therapy; the Persons In Need (PIN) Program; the Reverend Takie Okumura Family Fund for Children and Youth; the Theodore A. Vierra Fund and Kitaro Watanabe Fund; and the Victoria S. and Bradley L. Geist Foundation Supporting Enhancements for Foster Children. Deadlines and funding levels of each program vary, and applicants should contact the Foundation for further details.

Requirements: Nonprofit, tax-exempt 501(c)3 organizations, public schools, or units of government are eligible to apply.

Geographic Focus: Hawaii

Amount of Grant: 3,000 - 10,000 USD

Contact: Jennifer Murphy, Program Officer; (808) 537-6333 or (888) 731-3863; csutherland@hcf-hawaii.org

Internet: http://hawaiicommunityfoundation.org/index.php?id=71&categoryID=24

Sponsor: Hawai'i Community Foundation

1164 Bishop Street, Suite 800

Honolulu, HI 96813

Haymarket People's Fund Sustaining Grants   902

Haymarket People's Fund is an anti-racist and multi-cultural foundation committed to strengthening the movement for social justice in New England. Through grant making, fundraising, and capacity building, it supports grassroots organizations that address the root causes of injustice. Haymarket also organizes to increase sustainable community philanthropy throughout the region. Applications are evaluated according to the following criteria: self-determination and accountability; leadership development; anti-racism and anti-oppression values and practices; organizing for systemic change; movement building; diversified funding base; and limited access to traditional funding. Sustaining grants range up to $10,000 for grassroots, social

change organizations (start-ups or established) that meet funding criteria. Organizations must request an application from Haymarket, and return it and all supporting materials through regular mail.

Requirements: Both incorporated organizations (with or without established 501(c)3 status) and unincorporated organizations may apply. Applicants must conduct work within New England (Connecticut, Maine, Massachusetts, New Hampshire, Rhode Island, and Vermont).

Restrictions: Haymarket does not fund: organizations providing direct services that focus on meeting people's basic needs or that focus on individual empowerment or self-help; publications, reports, workshops, classes, conferences, media events, arts and theater productions unless they are part of an ongoing community organizing effort or are accountable to social change movements; groups or work focused outside of New England; legal or research expenses; capital campaigns or endowment drives; individuals or individual projects; projects sponsored by a government agency; organizations with budgets over $350,000; small businesses, alternative business, or business associations; other foundations; elections; union organizing work, unless it benefits a wider community; and civil disobedience or other actions that involve breaking the law.

Geographic Focus: Connecticut, Maine, Massachusetts, New Hampshire, Rhode Island, Vermont

Date(s) Application is Due: Dec 5

Amount of Grant: Up to 10,000 USD

Contact: Jaime Smith, Grants Organizer; (617) 522-7676, ext. 115; fax (617) 522-9580; jaime@haymarket.org

Internet: http://www.haymarket.org/grantmaking/grants-process

Sponsor: Haymarket People's Fund

42 Seaverns Avenue

Boston, MA 02130

Haymarket Urgent Response Grants   903

Haymarket People's Fund is an anti-racist and multi-cultural foundation committed to strengthening the movement for social justice in New England. Through grant making, fundraising, and capacity building, it supports grassroots organizations that address the root causes of injustice. Haymarket also organizes to increase sustainable community philanthropy throughout the region. Applications are evaluated according to the following criteria: self-determination and accountability; leadership development; anti-racism and anti-oppression values and practices; organizing for systemic change; movement building; diversified funding base; and limited access to traditional funding. Haymarket makes Urgent Response grants of up to $1,000/year to help grassroots, social change organizations respond quickly to unforeseen crises or opportunities that critically affect their organization and constituency. This includes unexpected events, political crises, or organizing opportunities. Grants are not to be used for ongoing program work (including expenses the organization should have anticipated), for financial crises or a shortfall in projected funding, or because the group missed a funding deadline. Organizations must call to discuss their project and request an application. Haymarket will send an application if they feel the project meets their criteria. The application and all supporting materials must be returned through regular mail.

Requirements: Organizations are not required to have tax-exempt status if their work falls within what the IRS defines as charitable or educational tax exempt activities.

Restrictions: Haymarket does not fund: organizations providing direct services that focus on meeting people's basic needs or that focus on individual empowerment or self-help; legal or research expenses; capital campaigns or endowment drives; individuals or individual projects; projects sponsored by a government agency; organizations with budgets over $350,000; small or alternative businesses or business associations; other foundations; elections; union organizing work, unless it benefits a wider community; and civil disobedience or other actions that involve breaking the law.

Geographic Focus: Connecticut, Maine, Massachusetts, New Hampshire, Rhode Island, Vermont

Date(s) Application is Due: Dec 5

Amount of Grant: Up to 1,000 USD

Contact: Jaime Smith, Grants Organizer; (617) 522-7676, ext. 115; fax (617) 522-9580; jaime@haymarket.org

Internet: http://www.haymarket.org/grantmaking/grants-process

Sponsor: Haymarket People's Fund

42 Seaverns Avenue

Boston, MA 02130

Hazel and Walter T. Bales Foundation Grants 904

Established in Indiana in 1989, the Hazel and Walter T. Bales Foundation provides funding for programs in Clark and Floyd counties, Indiana, as well as Jefferson County, Kentucky. The Foundations primary fields of interest include: children and youth services; hospitals; human services; Protestant agencies and churches; and the Salvation Army. Types of funding include: building construction and renovation; continuing support; curriculum development; and matching grants. There are no specific deadlines, and applicants should send a letter of application directly to the Foundation office. Most recent grant awards have ranged from $350 to $13,500.

Geographic Focus: Indiana, Kentucky
Amount of Grant: 350 - 13,500 USD
Contact: Lori Lewis, President; (812) 282-2586
Sponsor: Hazel and Walter T. Bales Foundation
630 Broadway
Jeffersonville, IN 47130-8203

HCA Foundation Grants 905

The Foundation is committed to the care and improvement of human life. Grants are made in the areas of health and well being, childhood and youth development, and the arts. Preference will be given to requests from organizations where an HCA employee volunteers or serves on the board. New applicants are asked to send a one-or two-page letter of inquiry to the Foundation, describing the proposed project, its goals and objectives and the approximate level of funding required. Foundation staff will review each request and will notify the organization as to whether the project coincides with funding priorities.

Requirements: 501(c)3 nonprofit organizations are eligible. Because the foundation focuses its giving in Middle Tennessee, all requests outside of the Nashville area should be submitted to the closest HCA facility location or division office. Organizations must have a full updated GivingMatters.com profile to be considered for funding. For more information please go to www.givingmatters.com.

Restrictions: Funding is not available for: individuals or their projects; private foundations; political activities; advertising or sponsorships of events; social events or similar fund-raising activities. The Foundation does not ordinarily support: organizations in their first three years of operation and organizations involved in research, sports, environmental, wildlife, civic and international affairs. The Foundation does not accept proposals from individual churches or schools, but will support broad faith-based initiatives consistent with it's mission and guidelines.

Geographic Focus: Tennessee
Date(s) Application is Due: Mar 12; Jun 11; Sep 10; Dec 12
Amount of Grant: 20,000 - 100,000 USD
Samples: Campus for Human Development Public Charity, Nashville, TN, $100,000—capital funding; Second Harvest Food Bank Middle Tennessee, Nashville, TN, $35,000—general operating; Mental Health Association of Middle, Tennessee, Nashville, TN, $20,000—program funding.
Contact: Lois Abrams, Grants Manager; (615) 344-2390; fax (615) 344-5722; lois.abrams@hcahealthcare.com
Internet: http://www.hcacaring.org/CustomPage.asp?guidCustomContentID =BBB7D8F2-B906-4302-A164-07643DB2582E
Sponsor: HCA Foundation
1 Park Plaza, Building 1, 4th Floor East
Nashville, TN 37203

Head Start Replacement Grantee: Colorado 906

The Administration for Children and Families solicits applications from local public or private non-profit organizations, including faith-based organizations or local for-profit organizations, that wish to compete for funds that are available to provide Head Start services to children and families residing in the City of Alamosa, Colorado. The intent of this announcement is to provide for the continuation of services as previously provided by the former grantee, Alamosa Head Start, Inc. Funds in the amount of $987,663 annually will be available to provide Head Start program services to eligible children and their families. The former grantee was funded for a total enrollment of 161 children and families. Interested applicants should call the ACYF Operations Center at (866) 796-1591 to receive pre-application materials and additional information.

Requirements: Eligibility is limited to local public or private non-profit organizations, including faith-based organizations or local for-profit organizations, that can provide Head Start services to children and families residing in the City of Alamosa, Colorado.

Restrictions: Grantees are required to meet a non-Federal share of the project costs, in accordance with section 640(b) of the Head Start Act. Grantees must provide at least 20 percent of the total approved cost of the project.

Geographic Focus: Colorado
Date(s) Application is Due: Mar 28
Amount of Grant: 987,663 USD
Contact: Karen McKinney; (866) 796-1591; OHS@dixongroup.com
Internet: http://www.acf.hhs.gov/grants/open/HHS-2007-ACF-OHS-CH-0801.html
Sponsor: Administration for Children and Families
ACYF Operations Center, 118 Q Street NE
Washington, D.C. 20002

Head Start Replacement Grantee: Florida 907

The Administration for Children and Families solicits applications from local public or private non-profit organizations, including faith-based organizations or local for-profit organizations, that wish to compete for funds that are available to provide Head Start services to children and families residing in Polk County, Florida. The intent of this announcement is to provide for the continuation of services as previously provided by the former grantee, the Polk County Opportunity Council, Inc. Funds in the amount of $6,896,580 annually will be available to provide Head Start program services to eligible children and their families. The former grantee was funded for a total enrollment of 942 children and families. Interested applicants should call the ACYF Operations Center at (866) 796-1591 to receive pre-application materials and additional information.

Requirements: Applicants should propose a design or designs that best address the needs of the proposed service area. Applicants have flexibility in determining the appropriate number of children to be served by the various program options (center-based, home-based, or combination) and program designs (hours per day, days per week, weeks per year). Preference will be given to applicants who can demonstrate efficient management of several or all of the service areas.

Restrictions: Grantees are required to meet a non-Federal share of the project costs, in accordance with section 640(b) of the Head Start Act. Grantees must provide at least 20 percent of the total approved cost of the project.

Geographic Focus: Florida
Date(s) Application is Due: Apr 13
Amount of Grant: 69,000,000 USD
Contact: Karen McKinney; (866) 796-1591; OHS@dixongroup.com
Internet: http://www.acf.hhs.gov/grants/open/HHS-2007-ACF-OHS-CH-0402.html
Sponsor: Administration for Children and Families
ACYF Operations Center, 118 Q Street NE
Washington, D.C. 20002

Head Start Replacement Grantee: West Virginia 908

The Administration for Children and Families solicits applications from local public or private non-profit organizations, including faith-based organizations or local for-profit organizations, that wish to compete for funds that are available to provide Head Start services to children and families residing in Calhoun, Doddridge, Pleasants, Tyler, Wirt and/or Wood Counties, West Virginia. The intent of this announcement is to provide for the continuation of services as previously provided by the former grantee, Family Development, Inc. Applicants may apply to operate a Head Start program for one or more of the listed areas. Interested applicants should call the ACYF Operations Center at (866) 796-1591 to receive pre-application materials and additional information.

Requirements: Applicants should propose a design or designs that best address the needs of the proposed service area. Applicants have flexibility in determining the appropriate number of children to be served by the various program options (center-based, home-based, or combination) and program designs (hours per day, days per week, weeks per year). Preference will be given to applicants who can demonstrate efficient management of several or all of the service areas.

Restrictions: Grantees are required to meet a non-Federal share of the project costs, in accordance with section 640(b) of the Head Start Act. Grantees must provide at least 20 percent of the total approved cost of the project.

Geographic Focus: West Virginia
Date(s) Application is Due: Apr 23
Amount of Grant: Up to 23,000,000 USD
Contact: Karen McKinney; (866) 796-1591; OHS@dixongroup.com
Internet: http://www.acf.hhs.gov/grants/open/HHS-2007-ACF-OHS-CH-0303.html
Sponsor: Administration for Children and Families
ACYF Operations Center, 118 Q Street NE
Washington, D.C. 20002

Healthcare Georgia Foundation Grants
909

The foundation's mission is to advance the health of all Georgians and to expand access to affordable, quality healthcare for underserved individuals and communities. Grantmaking priority areas include addressing health disparities, strengthening nonprofit health organizations, and expanding access to primary healthcare. The foundation will award grants that support: policy development and advocacy, research and evaluation, technical assistance/capacity building, organizational improvement, leadership development and recognition, direct service delivery, professional development and training, and public education and awareness. The grant application process begins with the submission of a two-page letter of inquiry that describes the funding request specifying who, what, where, when, for whom, and for what cost. Full proposals are by invitation.

Requirements: Georgia organizations, including community-based/health service, education, government, public policy, and other nonprofits, are eligible.

Geographic Focus: Georgia

Samples: Lowndes County Partnership for Health (Atlanta, GA)—to expand the Well Workplace health promotion program, to implement a strategic plan, and to help a church-based program become a self-sustaining, community-based nonprofit group, $145,000; National Council of La Raza-Atlantic Program Office (GA)—for the Georgia Latino/Hispanic Health Agenda and Leadership Project, $235,000; Planned Parenthood of Georgia (Atlanta, GA)—to strengthen its ability to provide health services to low-income women and to enhance the self-sustainability of its programs in Augusta, $50,000; Meridian Educational Resource Group (Atlanta, GA)—to establish a fitness, health-promotion, and weight-loss program for children served by the Whitefoord and Coan School Health Clinics, $150,000.

Contact: Grants Administrator; (404) 653-0990; fax (404) 577-8386; info@healthcaregeorgia.org

Internet: http://www.healthcaregeorgia.org

Sponsor: Healthcare Georgia Foundation

50 Hurt Plaza, Suite 550

Atlanta, GA 30303

Health Foundation of Greater Indianapolis Grants
910

The foundation promotes health care for children, youth, and families in Marion County, IN, and seven contiguous Indiana counties. Programs of interest include school-based health, adolescent health, and HIV/AIDS Grants also are awarded to support the development of health careers and to promote cooperative effort between health professionals. Types of support include general operations, building/renovations, equipment, program/project development, conferences and seminars, seed money, technical assistance, and matching funds. Prior to submitting a proposal, contact Stephen L. Everett, Vice President of Programs, to determine if your program and proposal matches The Health Foundation of Greater Indianapolis' funding priorities and application guidelines.

Requirements: Grants are awarded to neighborhood-based service centers in Indiana's Marion County and the seven contiguous counties of Boone, Hamilton, Hancock, Hendricks, Johnson, Morgan and Shelby. Applicants must be a 501(c)3 group, organization or agency that provides health-related programs or services.

Restrictions: Grants will not be provided for: individuals; sectarian religious organizations; research projects; purchase of advertising or tickets to events; production and design of educational materials already available; endowments; short or long term loans or payment of financial obligations.

Geographic Focus: Indiana

Amount of Grant: 10,000 - 100,000 USD

Contact: Stephen Everett, Program Officer; (317) 630-1805; fax (317) 630-1806; severett@thfgi.org

Internet: http://www.thfgi.org

Sponsor: Health Foundation of Greater Indianapolis

429 East Vermont Street, Suite 300

Indianapolis, IN 46202

Health Foundation of Southern Florida Responsive Grants
911

The foundation awards Responsive Grants through two grant cycles per year. With exceptions, the foundation focuses on providing one to three year grants that do not exceed $300,000 annually. The majority of grants are funded in the $50,000 to $150,000 range over one or two years. Funding is provided in four categories: Project Planning; Health Services; Organizational Capacity Building and Health System/Health Policy Development.

Requirements: Though the foundation welcomes proposal applications anytime, the applications are reviewed on a semi-annual basis. Applicant organizations must be tax-exempt nonprofit under section 501(c)3 of the Internal Revenue Code or a local or state governmental agency. The project

must serve exclusively the residents of Broward, Miami-Dade and/or Monroe counties. Initially, a preliminary proposal is required (see the sponsor's website for specific details). If approved, the sponsor will then invite a full proposal. Download the sponsor's grant guide from the website.

Restrictions: The foundation does not fund: Biomedical research or other research that will not impact local residents within the immediate future (1-3 years) or that does not have a direct application to implementing a community-driven health intervention; Capital campaigns of over $1 million (versus grants toward specific health-related equipment or the 'build out' of a specific health-focused space); Secondary and tertiary services (versus preventive and primary medical, oral and behavioral health care services); Health promotion and/or health care with a high per capita cost (this figure will vary depending upon the type of intervention, but over $1,000 per person/year cost may be a rule of thumb); Service expansion or new projects without viable sustainability (unable to reach sustainability without the foundation's resources within a four-year period).

Geographic Focus: Florida

Date(s) Application is Due: Mar 13; Apr 24

Amount of Grant: Up to 300,000 USD

Contact: Eliane Morales, (305) 374-7200; emorales@hfsf.org

Internet: http://www.hfsf.org/ORIGHTML/responsive.html

Sponsor: Health Foundation of South Florida

2 South Biscayne Boulevard

Miami, FL 33131

Hearst Foundations Culture Grants
912

The Hearst Foundations fund non-profit organizations working in the fields of culture, education, health, and social services. The Foundations have two offices, one in New York which manages funding for non-profits headquartered east of the Mississippi River and one in San Francisco which manages funding for non-profits to the west. About 80% of the Foundations' total funding goes to prior grantees; the Foundations receive approximately 1,200 grant requests annually. The Foundations' cultural funding comprises 25% of their total giving; 60% of the Foundations' cultural funding goes to organizations having budgets over ten-million dollars. In the area of culture, the Foundations look for institutions that offer meaningful programs in the arts and sciences. Preference is given to artist development and training, arts-education programs that address the lack of arts programming in K-12 curricula, and science-education programs that focus on developing academic pathways in science, technology, engineering, and math. Requests which enable engagement by young people and which create a lasting impression are given higher priority. The Foundations provide program, capital, and, on a limited basis, general and endowment support. Requests are accepted year round. These must be submitted via the Foundations' online application portal. Each request goes through an evaluation process that generally spans four to six weeks. The Foundations conduct a site visit of semi-finalists and may also consult with experts in a given field. Applicants will receive an email confirmation of receipt of submission and can follow the status of their request through the online system. Instructions for using the system, guidelines (in the form of an FAQ), and the link to the Foundations' online portal are at the Foundations' website.

Requirements: Grants are made only to 501(c)3 organizations. Well-established nonprofits that primarily serve large demographic and/or geographic constituencies are preferred. Within those, the Foundations identify organizations which achieve truly differentiated results relative to other organizations making similar efforts for similar populations. The Foundations also look for evidence of sustainability beyond their support.

Restrictions: Organizations must wait one year from the date of their notice of decline before the Foundations will consider another request. Grantees must wait a minimum of three years from their grant award date before the Foundations will consider another request. The Foundations do not fund individuals or the following types of requests: those from organizations operating outside the United States; those from organizations with operating budgets under one million dollars; those from organizations involved in publishing, radio, film, or television; those from local chapters of organizations; those from organizations lacking demonstrable long-term impact on populations served; requests to fund tours, conferences, workshops, or seminars; requests to fund advocacy or public-policy research; requests to fund special events, tickets, tables, or advertising for fundraising events; requests for seed money or to fund start-up projects; and request to fund program-related investments.

Geographic Focus: All States

Amount of Grant: Up to 1,000,000 USD

Samples: Arab Community Center for Economic & Social Services Access, Dearborn, Michigan, $50,000—toward the SURA Arts Academy educational programs at the Arab-American National Museum; Cambria Library,

Cambria, California, $70,000—towards the capital campaign for a new library; Center of Creative Arts, St. Louis, Missouri, $100,000—to support the Urban Arts Outreach programs.
Contact: Mason Granger, Director of Grants; (212) 649-3750; fax (212) 586-1917; hearst.ny@hearstfdn.org
Internet: http://www.hearstfdn.org/funding-priorities/
Sponsor: Hearst Foundations
300 West 57th Street, 26th Floor
New York, NY 10019-3741

Hearst Foundations Education Grants   913
The Hearst Foundations fund non-profit organizations working in the fields of culture, education, health, and social services. The Foundations have two offices, one in New York which manages funding for non-profits headquartered east of the Mississippi River and one in San Francisco which manages funding for non-profits to the west. About 80% of the Foundations' total funding goes to prior grantees; the Foundations receive approximately 1,200 grant requests annually. The Foundations' education funding comprises 30% of their total giving; 80% of the Foundations' education funding goes to organizations having budgets over ten-million dollars. In the area of education, the Foundations' focus is largely on higher education, but they also fund innovative models of early childhood and K-12 education as well as professional development. Preference is given to higher education scholarships, professional development for faculty, and, on a limited basis, scholarships for post-graduate education. The Foundations provide program, capital, and, on a limited basis, general and endowment support. Requests are accepted year round. These must be submitted via the Foundations' online application portal. Each request goes through an evaluation process that generally spans four to six weeks. The Foundations conduct a site visit of semi-finalists and may also consult with experts in a given field. Applicants will receive an email confirmation of receipt of submission and can follow the status of their request through the online system. Instructions for using the system, guidelines (in the form of an FAQ), and the link to the Foundations' online portal are at the Foundations' website.
Requirements: The Foundations look for educational institutions demonstrating uncommon success in preparing students to thrive in a global society. Grants are made only to 501(c)3 organizations.
Restrictions: Organizations must wait one year from the date of their notice of decline before the Foundations will consider another request. Grantees must wait a minimum of three years from their grant award date before the Foundations will consider another request. The Foundations do not fund individuals or the following types of requests: those from organizations operating outside the United States; those from organizations with operating budgets under one million dollars; those from organizations involved in publishing, radio, film, or television; those from local chapters of organizations; those from organizations lacking demonstrable long-term impact on populations served; requests to fund tours, conferences, workshops, or seminars; requests to fund advocacy or public-policy research; requests to fund special events, tickets, tables, or advertising for fundraising events; requests for seed money or to fund start-up projects; and request to fund program-related investments.
Geographic Focus: All States
Amount of Grant: Up to 200,000 USD
Samples: 826 National, San Francisco, California, $50,000—general operating support to enhance programming and national expansion efforts; Albright College, Reading, Pennsylvania, $80,000—to enable twenty historically underrepresented students to experience high-impact undergraduate science research experiences; Bradley University, Peoria, Illinois, $100,000—toward the Business and Engineering Convergence Center.
Contact: Mason Granger, Director of Grants; (212) 649-3750; fax (212) 586-1917; hearst.ny@hearstfdn.org
Internet: http://www.hearstfdn.org/funding-priorities/
Sponsor: Hearst Foundations
300 West 57th Street, 26th Floor
New York, NY 10019-3741

Hearst Foundations Social Service Grants   914
The Hearst Foundations fund non-profit organizations working in the fields of culture, education, health, and social service. The Foundations have two offices, one in New York which manages funding for non-profits headquartered east of the Mississippi River and one in San Francisco which manages funding for non-profits to the west. About 80% of the Foundations' total funding goes to prior grantees; the Foundations receive approximately 1,200 grant requests annually. The Foundations' social-service funding comprises 15% of their total giving; 60% of the Foundations' social-service giving goes to organizations

having budgets over five-million dollars. In the area of social service, the Foundations fund direct-service organizations that tackle the roots of chronic poverty by applying effective solutions to the most challenging social and economic problems. Preference is given to affordable-housing, job-creation and job-training, literacy, and youth-development programs. In limited cases, the Foundations fund organizations focusing on domestic abuse, food delivery and food banks, sexual abuse, and substance abuse. The Foundations fund requests for program, capital, and general support. Requests are accepted year round. These must be submitted via the Foundations' online application portal. Each request goes through an evaluation process that generally spans four to six weeks. The Foundations conduct a site visit of semi-finalists and may also consult with experts in a given field. Applicants will receive an email confirmation of receipt of submission and can follow the status of their request through the online system. Instructions for using the system, guidelines (in the form of an FAQ), and the link to the Foundations' online portal are at the Foundations' website.
Requirements: Grants are made only to 501(c)3 organizations. Initiatives of an organization's national headquarters are preferred over those of local chapters. The Foundations give high priority to programs that have proven successful in facilitating economic independence and in strengthening families and that have the potential to scale productive practices in order to reach more people in need.
Restrictions: Organizations must wait one year from the date of their notice of decline before the Foundations will consider another request. Grantees must wait a minimum of three years from their grant award date before the Foundations will consider another request. The Foundations do not fund individuals or the following types of requests: those from organizations operating outside the United States; those from organizations with operating budgets under one million dollars; those from organizations involved in publishing, radio, film, or television; those from organizations lacking demonstrable long-term impact on populations served; requests to fund tours, conferences, workshops, or seminars; requests to fund advocacy or public-policy research; requests to fund special events, tickets, tables, or advertising for fundraising events; requests for seed money or to fund start-up projects; and request to fund program-related investments.
Geographic Focus: All States
Amount of Grant: Up to 100,000 USD
Samples: Arab-American Family Support Center, Brooklyn, New York, $50,000—general support; Alliance House Inc., Salt Lake City, Utah, $35,000—to provide housing for people who are homeless or at risk of homelessness because of mental illness; Alt Consulting, Memphis, Tennessee, $50,000—toward rural and minority economic and business development programs in the Delta.
Contact: Mason Granger, Director of Grants; (212) 649-3750; fax (212) 586-1917; hearst.ny@hearstfdn.org
Internet: http://www.hearstfdn.org/funding-priorities/
Sponsor: Hearst Foundations
300 West 57th Street, 26th Floor
New York, NY 10019-3741

Heckscher Foundation for Children Grants   915
The Heckscher Foundation for Children was founded in 1921 to promote the welfare of children, primarily in New York City. Funding organizations serving youth in the fields of education, family services, job training, health, arts and recreation. The Foundation's giving takes the form of program support, capacity-building, capital projects and general operating support. The Foundation does not participate in annual appeals, endowments, fundraising events or political efforts. The Heckscher Foundation provides support in the following categories: Education & Academic Support; Arts; Social Services; Health; Recreation and; Workforce Development. The Foundation accepts applications online only. To begin the application process. fill out the application template provided online. Do not submit additional information or materials unless asked to do so. All inquiring organizations will be notified of the outcome of the Foundation's review, and any further necessary materials will be requested at that time.
Requirements: 501(c)3 nonprofit organizations are eligible.
Restrictions: Funding is not available for annual appeals, endowments, fundraising events or political efforts.
Geographic Focus: New York
Amount of Grant: 25,000 - 500,000 USD
Contact: Virginia Sloane, President; (212) 744-0190; fax (212) 744-2761
Internet: http://fdncenter.org/grantmaker/heckscher
Sponsor: Heckscher Foundation for Children
123 East 70th Street
New York, NY 10021

Heinz Endowments Grants 916

The endowments support efforts to make southwestern Pennsylvania a premier place to live and work, a center of learning and educational excellence, and a home to diversity and inclusion. Committed to helping its region thrive as a whole community—economically, ecologically, educationally and culturally—the foundation works within Pennsylvania and elsewhere in the nation to develop solutions to challenges that are national and even international in scope. Fields of emphasis include arts and culture; children, youth and families; economic opportunity; education; the environment; and innovation economy. The two-step application process begins with submitting an online letter of inquiry (LoI) available at the Heinz website. The second step is a formal application process for those requests that are determined to meet the endowments' basic funding criteria. Information for submission of an LOI is available online.

Requirements: Grants are limited to 501(c)3 nonprofit organizations and 509(a) public charities in Pennsylvania and generally to the southwestern Pennsylvania region.

Restrictions: Individuals and for-profit organizations are not eligible.

Geographic Focus: Pennsylvania

Date(s) Application is Due: Feb 1; Aug 1

Contact: Program Contact; (412) 281-5777; fax (412) 281-5788

Internet: http://www.heinz.org/programs.aspx

Sponsor: Heinz Endowments

30 Dominion Tower, 625 Liberty Avenue

Pittsburgh, PA 15222-3115

Helen and Merrill Bank Foundation Grants 917

The foundation awards general operating grants to nonprofit organizations nationwide, including religious organizations (Christian, Jewish, and Salvation Army), hospitals, museums, organizations serving the disabled, parochial schools, temples, and organizations addressing issues affecting women. The foundation requests applications be made in writing. Include a description of the organization and activities for which funds are sought. There are no application deadlines.

Requirements: Nonprofit organizations in Florida and Maryland are eligible.

Geographic Focus: Florida, Maryland

Amount of Grant: Up to 548,025 USD

Samples: Raymond F. Kravis Ctr for the Performing Arts (West Palm Beach, FL)—for operating support, $79,150; Temple Israel (Boston, MA)—for operating support, $45,000.

Contact: Herbert Bank, (410) 363-6767

Sponsor: Helen and Merrill Bank Foundation

8 Roland Mews

Baltimore, MD 21210

Helena Rubinstein Foundation Grants 918

The Foundation supports programs in education, community services, arts/arts in education, and health with emphasis on projects which benefit women and children. Grants are primarily targeted to organizations in New York City. Although general operating grants are made, the Foundation prefers to support specific programs. Grant proposals are accepted throughout the year. There is no formal application form; however, the New York Common Application Form may be used. Organizations seeking funds are asked not to make telephone inquiries, but to submit a brief letter outlining the project.

Requirements: U.S. nonprofit organizations are eligible.

Restrictions: Support is not offered to individuals, or for film or video projects. Grants are rarely made to endowment funds and capital campaigns. The foundation does not make loans and cannot provide emergency funds. Funding of new proposals is limited by ongoing commitments and fiscal constraints.

Geographic Focus: New York

Contact: Diane Moss, President; (212) 750-7310

Internet: http://www.helenarubinsteinfdn.org/guide.html

Sponsor: Helena Rubinstein Foundation

477 Madison Avenue, 7th Floor

New York, NY 10022-5802

Helen Bader Foundation Grants 919

Throughout her life, Helen Bader sought to help others. She played many roles - student, mother, businesswoman, and social worker - believing that everyone should have the opportunity to reach their fullest potential. Growing up in the railroad town of Aberdeen, South Dakota, Helen learned the value of hard work and self-reliance. The Great Depression and the sacrifices of World War II also taught her the importance of reaching out to those in need. Helen attended Downer College in Milwaukee, earning a degree in botany. She married Alfred

Bader, a chemist from Austria, and together they started a family and created a business, the Aldrich Chemical Company. From the 1950s to the 1970s, their hard work helped build one of Wisconsin's most successful start-up enterprises of the era. The Baders' eventual divorce led Helen to again become self-reliant. She subsequently finished her Master of Social Work at the University of Wisconsin-Milwaukee. While doing her field work with the Legal Aid Society of Milwaukee, Helen met and helped many people in need, including single mothers and adults with mental illness. In the process, she gained a deeper appreciation for their everyday struggles. After graduation, she worked at the Milwaukee Jewish Home, where working with older adults brought home the many issues of aging. At a time when Alzheimer's disease was almost a complete mystery, she helped open the resident' minds and hearts through dance and music. Helen felt that the residents' quality of life depended upon the small details, so she was happy to run errands or escort them to the symphony. She found herself touched by the arts and studied the violin and guitar at the Wisconsin Conservatory of Music. Helen eventually faced cancer. As the illness began to sap her physical strength, she shared a wish with her family: to continue to aid those in need. She died in 1989. After her death, patterns of Helen's quiet style of philanthropy became more apparent. When she had come across an organization that impressed her, she would just pull out her checkbook without a lot of fanfare. In her name, the Helen Bader Foundation (HBF) supports worthy organizations working in key areas affecting the quality of life in Milwaukee, the state of Wisconsin, and Israel. The foundation also seeks to inspire the generosity in others, as every individual can make a difference through gifts of time, talent, and resources. The foundation will consider multiple-year requests with 24 or 36 month terms. Multi-year grants are subject to annual review before funds for subsequent years are released. The application deadline for the online preliminary proposal is January 5. The application deadline for organizations invited to complete a full proposal is February 2. The link to the online application system is available at the grant website. Application deadlines may vary from year to year. Prospective applicants are encouraged to visit the grant website to verify current deadline dates.

Requirements: Grants are awarded for projects consistent with one or more of the Helen Bader Foundation's program areas: Alzheimer's and aging (national in scope, with priority given to Wisconsin); economic development (restricted to the city of Milwaukee); community partnerships for youth (restricted to the city of Milwaukee); community initiatives (restricted to greater Milwaukee); arts (restricted to the city of Milwaukee); and directed grants and initiatives such as aid and support to Israel (for which proposals must be staff-solicited). Grants are given only to U.S. organizations which are tax exempt under Section 501(c)3 of the Internal Revenue Code or to government entities; grants will only be approved for foreign entities which meet specific charitable status requirements.

Restrictions: The Foundation does not provide direct support for individuals, such as individual scholarships.

Geographic Focus: All States, All Countries

Date(s) Application is Due: Jan 5; Feb 25

Amount of Grant: 10,000 - 100,000 USD

Samples: Aging & Disabiity Resource Center of Portage County, Stevens Point, Wisconsin, $12,000, creation of an Early Memory Loss Program to serve central Wisconsin; Arts at Large, Inc., Milwaukee, Wisconsin, $412,000, inclusive arts programming for low-income children attending six Milwaukee Public Schools in grades K-8 and their affiliated Community Learning Centers; Ben-Gurion University of the Negev, Beer Sheva, Israel, $10,000, Summer School Science Camp for 50 seventh grade Bedouin students from Abu Basma schools.

Contact: Tamara Hogans, Grants Manager; (414) 224-6464; fax (414) 224-1441; tammy@hbf.org or info@hbf.org

Internet: http://www.hbf.org/apply.htm

Sponsor: Helen Bader Foundation

233 North Water Street, Fourth Floor

Milwaukee, WI 53202

Helen K. and Arthur E. Johnson Foundation Grants 920

The foundation makes grants to a wide variety of nonprofit organizations in an attempt to solve community problems and enrich the quality of life in Colorado in the following areas: education, youth, health, community and social services, civic and cultural, and senior citizens. Requests are welcomed throughout the year. However, to be considered at the next board meeting, complete written proposals must be received by the listed application deadline dates. Proposal submission information is available online.

Requirements: IRS 501(c)3 tax-exempt organizations serving Colorado residents may apply.

Restrictions: Funding is not available for: loans or fund endowments; individuals; conferences; scholarships to individuals; multiple year grants; fundraising dinners or special events. The Foundation does not support organizations whose primary purpose is to influence (directly or indirectly) the legislative or judicial process in any manner or for any cause. In addition, the Foundation will not consider grant requests that pass through the nominal grant recipient to another organization.
Geographic Focus: Colorado
Date(s) Application is Due: Jan 1; Apr 1; Jul 1; Oct 1
Samples: Little Sisters of the Poor, Denver, CO, $250,000—for heating and air conditioning system; Educare Colorado, Denver, CO, $100,000—for program support.
Contact: John H. Alexander, President; (800) 232-9931 or (303) 861-4127; fax (303) 861-0607; info@johnsonfoundation.org
Internet: http://www.johnsonfoundation.org
Sponsor: Helen K. and Arthur E. Johnson Foundation
1700 Broadway, Suite 1100
Denver, CO 80290-1718

Helen Pumphrey Denit Charitable Trust Grants 921

The Helen Pumphrey Denit Trust for Charitable and Educational Purposes was established in 1988 to support charitable organizations that promote quality education, culture, human service, health service and arts opportunities. The grants are primarily made to organizations in the Baltimore region. Special consideration is given to the following three organizations: Montgomery General Hospital in Onley, Maryland; The George Washington University in Washington, D.C; and The Wesley Theological Seminary in Washington, D.C. Grants for capital and program support are encouraged. Requests for general operating support will be received, but they will be given lower priority than other grants that have more specific purposes. Grants are primarily one year in duration. On occasion, multi-year grants will be awarded. Applicants must apply online at the grant website. Applicants are strongly encouraged to do the following before applying: review the downloadable state application procedures for additional helpful information and clarifications; review the downloadable online-application guidelines at the grant website; review the trust's funding history (link is available from the grant website); review the online application questions in advance; and review the list of required attachments. These will generally include: a list of board members; financial statements (audited, reviewed, or compiled by independent auditor); an organization summary; a list of other funding sources; an IRS Determination letter; and other required documents. All attachments must be uploaded in the online application as PDF, Word, or Excel files. The Helen Pumphrey Denit Trust has an application deadline of 11:59 p.m. on February 1. The applicants will be notified of grant decisions by June 30.
Requirements: Applicants must have 501(c)3 tax-exempt status and serve residents of Baltimore and surrounding communities.
Restrictions: The trust does not support requests from individuals, organizations attempting to influence policy through direct lobbying, or any political campaigns.
Geographic Focus: Maryland
Date(s) Application is Due: Feb 1
Samples: George Washington University, Washington, D.C., $50,000; Walters Art Museum, Baltimore, Maryland, $20,000; Montgomery General Hospital, Olney, Maryland, $50,000.
Contact: Sarah Kay, Vice President; (804) 788-2673; sarah.kay@baml.com
Internet: https://www.bankofamerica.com/philanthropic/fn_search.action
Sponsor: Helen Pumphrey Denit Charitable Trust
1111 E. Main Street, VA2-300-12-92
Richmond, VA 23219

Helen S. Boylan Foundation Grants 922

The Helen S Boylan Foundation is a private family foundation established in 1982 to continue the family tradition of commitment to enhancing the quality of life of the community through grants to qualified charitable organizations. In carrying out its mission, the Foundation considers a wide range of proposals within the following areas: arts, education, health, human services, environment, and public interest. Generally, grants are limited to projects that benefit the citizens of Jasper County, Missouri, Smith County, Texas and, Kansas City, Metropolitan area. Occasionally, projects that benefit the state of Missouri as a whole may be considered as well. The Foundation prefers to support proposals for new initiatives, special projects, expansion of current programs, capital improvements or building renovations. Grants from the Foundation are usually awarded for one year only. For projects in those areas in which the Foundation has a special interest, requests for multi-year funding and general operating

support may be considered. The Board of Directors meet four times a year to consider grant requests. Applications must be received by March 31, June 30, September 30 or December 31 to be acted upon at the following meeting.
Requirements: IRS 501(c)3 nonprofit organizations operating in the Carthage, Kansas City Metro and Lindale Texas area are eligible to apply for funding. Application form is available online at the Foundation's website.
Restrictions: No support for political organizations or religious activities. No grants to individuals, or for annual campaigns or endowments.
Geographic Focus: Missouri, Texas
Date(s) Application is Due: Mar 31; Jun 30; Sep 30; Dec 31
Amount of Grant: 500 - 50,000 USD
Samples: Lindale Independant Schools, Lindale, TX, $52,000—supplies, systems, books, programs; Heartland Hoops, Kansas City, MO, $10,000—uniforms & fees; Art Central, Carthage, MO, $7,500—children's art camp.
Contact: James R. Spradling, President; (417) 358-4033; fax (417) 358-5937; spradlinglaw@hotmail.com
Internet: http://www.boylanfoundation.org/
Sponsor: Helen S. Boylan Foundation
320 Grant Street, P.O. Box 731
Carthage, MO 64836

Helen Steiner Rice Foundation Grants 923

The Foundation awards grants to worthy charitable programs that assist the needy and the elderly. Essential objectives for grant consideration are: basic necessities and human needs for the poor and elderly; preference for meeting the immediate needs of the poor; and innovative approaches. Organizations in the Greater Cincinnati area should use the contact information for Cincinnati. Organizations in Lorain County should contact: Linda Weaver, Community Foundation Center of Lorain County, (440) 277-0142, Ext. 23. Application forms and instructions are available online.
Requirements: Nonprofit organizations in the greater Cincinnati area and Lorain, OH, may submit grant applications.
Restrictions: Funding is not available for building or endowment programs, direct gifts to individuals, or capital fund drives.
Geographic Focus: Ohio
Date(s) Application is Due: Jul 1
Contact: James D. Huizenga, Director; (513) 241-2880; fax (513) 768-6122; huizengai@greatercincinnatifdn.org or hrice@cincymuseum.org
Internet: http://www.helensteinerrice.com/grants.html
Sponsor: Helen Suiteiner Rice Foundation
200 West Fourth Street
Cincinnati, OH 45202-2602

Helen V. Brach Foundation Grants 924

Established in 1974 in Illinois by the wife of Frank Brach, principal owner of the E.J. Brach and Sons Candy Company of Chicago, the foundation operates to prevent cruelty to animals or to children; for religious, charitable, scientific, literary, and education purposes; and for public safety testing through support of Midwest 501(c)3 tax-exempt organizations carrying out programs and activities in these areas. Brach provides grants nationally and has wide-ranging interests. For example, it supports homeless and women's emergency shelters, teen pregnancy prevention programs, parenting education, summer school for disadvantaged children, job training for welfare mothers, orphanages, and scholarships for economically disadvantaged students. Types of support include annual campaigns, building construction and renovation, equipment, general operating support, publications, research, and special projects. The foundation ordinarily does not make multi-year grants or commitments. Applicants are required to complete in full a brief application form, which may be obtained from the office. The board of directors gives final consideration to all applications received in a given year at the board's meeting, which is usually held in March.
Requirements: Although 501(c)3 nonprofits from across the nation are eligible, giving is primarily made in the Midwest, as well as California, Massachusetts, Ohio, Pennsylvania, and South Carolina.
Restrictions: Grants are not made to individuals or to organizations outside the United States. Typically grants are not made in excess of 10 percent of a group's operating budget, which automatically excludes start-up grants.
Geographic Focus: All States
Date(s) Application is Due: Dec 31
Amount of Grant: 5,000 - 25,000 USD
Contact: John P. Hagnell; (312) 372-4417; fax (312) 372-0290
Sponsor: Helen V. Brach Foundation
55 W Wacker Drive, Suite 701
Chicago, IL 60601-1609

Hendricks County Community Foundation Grants 925

The Hendricks County Community Foundation Grants provide funding for organizations or charitable projects that serve in the following program areas: arts and culture; community development; education; environment; health and human services; and youth. These grants enable organizations to provide effective programs and respond to needs of people in the Hendricks County community.

Requirements: A letter of intent should be submitted to the organization between December 1 and January 11. The Foundation uses the following criteria when reviewing applications: sustainability; effective operations; proven success; strong leadership; innovation and creativity; accessibility; collaboration; and engagement.

Restrictions: The Foundation will not fund: bands, sports teams, or other groups without a philanthropic project; annual appeals, galas or membership contributions; fundraising events such as golf tournaments, walk-a-thons, and fashion shows; grants to individuals; projects aimed at promoting a particular religion or construction projects for religious institutions; operating, program and construction costs at schools, universities and private academies unless there is a significant opportunity for community use or collaboration; organizations or projects that discriminate based upon race, ethnicity, age, gender, sexual orientation; political campaigns or direct lobbying efforts by 501(c)3 organizations; post-event, after-the-fact situations or debt retirement; medical, scientific or academic research; publications, films, audiovisual and media materials, programs produced for artistic purposes or produced for resale.

Geographic Focus: Indiana

Amount of Grant: 500 - 17,500 USD

Samples: Farmers and Hunters Feeding the Hungry, general operating expenses, $3,000; Hendricks County Senior Services, transportation for the elderly and disabled, $5,000; Kingsway Community Care Center, general operating expenses, $2,500.

Contact: Susan Rozzi, Associate Director; (317) 718-1200; fax (317) 718-1033; janet@hendrickscountycf.org

Internet: http://www.hendrickscountycf.org/grants/oppfund_grants/index.shtml

Sponsor: Hendricks County Community Foundation

5055 East Main Street, Suite A

Avon, IN 46123

Henrietta Tower Wurts Memorial Foundation Grants 926

The Foundation supports organizations which are engaged in helping or caring for people in need, or alleviating the conditions under which they live, primarily for the elderly, women, family and child welfare services. Giving is limited to Philadelphia, Pennsylvania.

Requirements: Non-profits in Philadelphia, Pennsylvania are eligible. The initial approach should be a letter requesting an application form from the Foundation.

Restrictions: No grants to individuals, or for endowment funds, scholarships, fellowships, or matching gifts; no loans. Organizations or programs serving disadvantaged youth and the elderly in Philadelphia, Pennsylvania must have an annual budget of less than 3 million.

Geographic Focus: Pennsylvania

Date(s) Application is Due: Feb 1; May 1; Sep 1

Amount of Grant: 1,000 - 7,000 USD

Samples: Empowerment Group, Philadelphia, PA, $7,000; Juvenile Law Center, Philadelphia, PA, $5,000; Supportive Older Womens Network, Philadelphia, PA, $4,000;

Contact: Andrew Swinney, President; (215) 563-6417

Sponsor: Henrietta Tower Wurts Memorial Foundation

1234 Market Street, Suite 1800

Philadelphia, PA 19107-3704

Henry A. and Mary J. MacDonald Foundation 927

Established in 1998 in Pennsylvania, the Henry A. and Mary J. MacDonald Foundation offers funding in its primary field of interest, health care. A formal application is required, though there are no annual deadlines. Applicants should begin by contacting the Foundation directly. Most recently, grants have averaged about $3,000, though there are no limitations on award ceilings other than availability of funds.

Restrictions: No grants are given to individuals.

Geographic Focus: All States

Amount of Grant: 2,000 - 5,000 USD

Contact: James D. Cullen, President; (814) 870-7705

Sponsor: Henry A. and Mary J. MacDonald Foundation

100 State Street, Suite 700

Erie, PA 16507-1498

Henry and Ruth Blaustein Rosenberg Foundation Arts and Culture 928 Grants

The Henry and Ruth Blaustein Rosenberg Foundation provides support primarily in the Baltimore, Maryland region. In the area of Arts and Culture, the Foundation's primary goal is to enable cultural institutions in the Baltimore metropolitan area to reach underserved youth and to diversify audiences. Typically, awards range from $10,000 to $500,000, and the majority of grants are multi-year in nature. There are nor specified annual deadlines or application forms.

Requirements: 501(c)3 tax-exempt charitable organizations located in or primarily serving the metropolitan Baltimore area are eligible to apply. An initial application should include the following: information about the program(s) for which funding is requested; need, purpose, activities, and evaluation plan of the proposed program(s); program budget (including sources of anticipated income as well as expenditures) and timeline; dollar amount of funding requested; history, mission, and key accomplishments of your organization; information on Board members and key staff; current institutional operating budget (including major sources of revenue as well as expenditures); copy of an IRS tax status determination letter or information about your fiscal agent.

Restrictions: The foundation does not: make grants or scholarships to individuals; accept unsolicited proposals for academic, scientific, or medical research; or support direct mail, annual giving, membership campaigns, fundraising and commemorative events. The foundations rarely make capital grants unless there is a prior relationship with the applicant organization.

Geographic Focus: Maryland

Amount of Grant: 10,000 - 500,000 USD

Samples: Arts Education in Maryland Schools, Baltimore, Maryland, $20,000 - a two-year award to support advocacy efforts to promote the teaching of art and music in public schools (2014); Baltimore Symphony Orchestra, Baltimore, Maryland, $500,000 - a five-year award to support The Campaign for the BSO's Second Century (2014); National Aquarium in Baltimore, Baltimore, Maryland, $200,000 - a five-year award to support the Campaign for the Future of the National Aquarium (2014).

Contact: Henry A. Rosenberg, Jr., President; (410) 347-7201; fax (410) 347-7210; info@blaufund.org

Internet: http://www.blaufund.org/foundations/henryandruth_f.html

Sponsor: Henry and Ruth Blaustein Rosenberg Foundation

One South Street, Suite 2900

Baltimore, MD 21202

Henry and Ruth Blaustein Rosenberg Foundation Health Grants 929

The Henry and Ruth Blaustein Rosenberg Foundation provides support primarily in the Baltimore, Maryland region. In the area of Health, the primary goal is to promote quality treatment and supportive care at selected health institutions serving the Baltimore community. Typically, awards range from $100,000 to $250,000, and the majority of grants are multi-year in nature. There are nor specified annual deadlines or application forms.

Requirements: 501(c)3 tax-exempt charitable organizations located in or primarily serving the metropolitan Baltimore area are eligible to apply. An initial application should include the following: information about the program(s) for which funding is requested; need, purpose, activities, and evaluation plan of the proposed program(s); program budget (including sources of anticipated income as well as expenditures) and timeline; dollar amount of funding requested; history, mission, and key accomplishments of your organization; information on Board members and key staff; current institutional operating budget (including major sources of revenue as well as expenditures); copy of an IRS tax status determination letter or information about your fiscal agent.

Restrictions: The Foundation does not accept unsolicited proposals for health research. The foundation does not: make grants or scholarships to individuals; accept unsolicited proposals for academic, scientific, or medical research; or support direct mail, annual giving, membership campaigns, fundraising and commemorative events. The foundations rarely make capital grants unless there is a prior relationship with the applicant organization.

Geographic Focus: Maryland

Amount of Grant: 100,000 - 250,000 USD

Samples: American Heart Association: Mid Atlantic Affiliate, Glen Allen, Virginia, $150,000 - three-year award to support the establishment of the Simple Cooking with Heart Kitchen in Baltimore (2014); Kennedy Krieger Institute, Baltimore, Maryland, $250,000 - five-year award to support a capital campaign (2014); LifeBridge Health, Baltimore, Maryland, $100,000 - support for the ER-7 Capital Campaign at Northwest Hospital (2014).

Contact: Henry A. Rosenberg, Jr., President; (410) 347-7201; fax (410) 347-7210; info@blaufund.org

Internet: http://www.blaufund.org/foundations/henryandruth_f.html

Sponsor: Henry and Ruth Blaustein Rosenberg Foundation
One South Street, Suite 2900
Baltimore, MD 21202

Henry & Ruth Blaustein Rosenberg Foundation Youth Development Grants   930

The Henry and Ruth Blaustein Rosenberg Foundation provides support primarily in the Baltimore, Maryland region. In the area of Youth Development, the goals are to promote recreation, learning, and leadership development through after-school programs; prevent teen pregnancy; and advocate for policies and practices that improve outcomes for youth. Typically, awards range from $10,000 to $75,000, and the majority of grants are multi-year in nature. There are nor specified annual deadlines or application forms.

Requirements: 501(c)3 tax-exempt charitable organizations located in or primarily serving the metropolitan Baltimore area are eligible to apply. An initial application should include the following: information about the program(s) for which funding is requested; need, purpose, activities, and evaluation plan of the proposed program(s); program budget (including sources of anticipated income as well as expenditures) and timeline; dollar amount of funding requested; history, mission, and key accomplishments of your organization; information on Board members and key staff; current institutional operating budget (including major sources of revenue as well as expenditures); copy of an IRS tax status determination letter or information about your fiscal agent.

Restrictions: The foundation does not: make grants or scholarships to individuals; accept unsolicited proposals for academic, scientific, or medical research; or support direct mail, annual giving, membership campaigns, fundraising and commemorative events. The foundations rarely make capital grants unless there is a prior relationship with the applicant organization.

Geographic Focus: Maryland

Amount of Grant: 10,000 - 75,000 USD

Samples: Digital Harbor Foundation, Baltimore, Maryland, $10,000 - support for Maker Foundations, a STEM after school program for middle and high school students (2014); Next One Up Foundation, Baltimore, Maryland, $30,000 - two-year award to support mentoring and coaching of Baltimore City lacrosse players (2014); YMCA of Central Maryland, Baltimore, Maryland, $75,000 - a three-year award to support the Campaign to Rebuild the Towson Family Center YMCA (2014).

Contact: Henry A. Rosenberg, Jr., President; (410) 347-7201; fax (410) 347-7210; info@blaufund.org

Internet: http://www.blaufund.org/foundations/henryandruth_f.html

Sponsor: Henry and Ruth Blaustein Rosenberg Foundation
One South Street, Suite 2900
Baltimore, MD 21202

Henry J. Kaiser Family Foundation Grants   931

The foundation concentrates giving in the following areas: U.S. government's role in health, health of low-income and minority groups with major emphasis on HIV/AIDS policy, reproductive health policy, and health system innovation and reform in California. The foundation also operates a major program to improve health and health care and promote social justice in South Africa. Grants are awarded for one to three years and support a range of activities, including policy analysis, applied research to define and measure public health problems, demonstration and pilot projects, and communications activities that help sharpen health care debates and improve quality of health information. Prospective applicants should submit a preliminary letter (two to three pages in length) that briefly describes the proposed project, along with an estimate of the total budget and the amount requested from the foundation. There are no deadlines and no application forms. Inquiries for projects in South Africa may be addressed to Dr. Michael Sinclair, Senior Vice President, The Henry J. Kaiser Family Foundation, 1450 G St NW, Suite 250, Washington, D.C. 20005, (202) 347-5270, fax: (202) 347-5274.

Requirements: Grants in response to unsolicited proposals are made only to governmental agencies and to private organizations with IRS 501(c)3 tax-exempt status.

Restrictions: The foundation does not award grants to individuals. Support is not given to ongoing general operating expenses, indirect costs, capital campaigns, annual appeals or other fundraising events, construction, purchase or renovation of facilities, or equipment purchases.

Geographic Focus: All States

Amount of Grant: 1,000 - 500,000 USD

Samples: Alliance for Justice (Washington, DC)—for general operating support, $600,000 over three years; U of Florida, Tropical Conservation and Development Program (Gainesville, FL)—for a community-based conservation and training program for organizations working in protected areas of Colombia and Ecuador,

$240,000 over three years; U of California at Los Angeles (CA)—for the Network on Youth Mental Health Care, $5 million over four years; Ctr for Defense Information (Washington, DC)—for policy research and advocacy on nuclear-weapons systems and their vulnerabilities, $650,000 over three years.

Contact: Renee Wells; (415) 854-9400; fax (415) 854-4800; rwells@kff.org

Internet: http://www.kff.org

Sponsor: Henry J. Kaiser Family Foundation
2400 Sand Hill Road
Menlo Park, CA 94025

Henry P. Kendall Foundation Grants   932

The foundation focuses almost entirely on the environment and securing its physical, biological, and aesthetic wealth for future generations. Geographic priorities for grants are New England and the Maritime Provinces of Eastern Canada and the Pacific Northwest, including Western Canada and Alaska. Current program themes include Gulf of Maine ecosystem, Northeastern landscape, Northeast climate change initiative, North country institution capacity-building, Yellowstone to Yukon conservation, watershed innovations in North America, public lands management, and special project initiatives. The foundation provides funding for general operating needs and for specific programs and initiatives. Activities funded include advocacy, public education, policy research and analysis, on-the-ground resource management experiments, and institutional development. Grants are normally made for one or two years. Unsolicited proposals and inquiries will not be reviewed.

Restrictions: Grants do not support endowments or capital fund campaigns, land acquisition, television and film projects, fellowships, basic scientific research, building construction or maintenance, equipment, debt reduction, or conferences unrelated to current foundation institutional grants. Nor does the foundation normally fund waste clean-ups, toxics or air/water pollution prevention or pollution monitoring initiatives, individual land trusts, or species-specific preservation efforts.

Geographic Focus: Alaska, Canada

Date(s) Application is Due: Feb 1; May 1; Oct 1

Amount of Grant: 20,000 - 50,000 USD

Samples: Alaska Conservation Foundation (Anchorage, AK)—to create a strategic transition fund dedicated to strengthening and expanding efforts to build a popular majority for conservation values—terrestrial and marine—throughout Alaska over the next two decades, $100,000; Earth Day Network (Seattle, WA)—to support preparatory organizing efforts in New England for Earth Day 2000, $35,000; Montana Wilderness Assoc (Helena, MT)—for general support to advance the protection of public wildlands and naturally functioning ecosystems in the Montana portion of the Yellowstone to Yukon landscape, $40,000.

Contact: Jennifer Patrick; (617) 951-2525; fax (617) 443-1977

Internet: http://www.kendall.org/grants/types.html

Sponsor: Henry P. Kendall Foundation
176 Federal Street
Boston, MA 02110

Henry W. Bull Foundation Grants   933

Established in 1960 in California, the foundation was established by Maud Bull in memory of her husband, Henry W. Bull. The foundation grants awards on a nationwide basis, giving primarily in the areas of: arts/performing arts; education; health and; human services. Types of support include annual campaigns, building construction/renovation, capital campaigns; program development, equipment acquisition, matching/challenge grants; general operating support, continuing support, and research. There is no formal grant application form. Submit a simple, concise statement of needs and objectives with pertinent supportive data, c/o Janice Gibbons, Santa Barbara Bank & Trust, P.O. Box 2340, Santa Barbara, CA, 93120-2340.

Requirements: 501(c)()3 nonprofits are eligible.

Restrictions: No grants to individuals or private foundations.

Geographic Focus: All States

Date(s) Application is Due: Apr 1; Sep 1

Amount of Grant: 500 - 20,000 USD

Samples: Shiloh Christian Childrens Ranch, Shelbina, MO, $2,000—general support; FamiliesFirst, Davis, CA, $3,000—to help expand child abuse prevention program; Dunn School, Los Olivos, CA, $10,000—purchase of new biology countertops, data collection equipment and laptop computers for Science Department.

Contact: Janice Gibson, Vice-President, Santa Barbara Bank & Trust; (805) 899-8405; fax (805) 884-1404

Sponsor: Henry W. Bull Foundation
P.O. Box 2340
Santa Barbara, CA 93120-2340

Herbert A. and Adrian W. Woods Foundation Grants   **934**

The Herbert A. and Adrian W. Woods Foundation was established on June 9, 1999 upon the death of Mrs. Adrian W. Woods. Mrs. Woods had a long history of charitable giving in the St. Louis community and wanted to establish this foundation to continue that legacy of giving. The Foundation supports charitable organizations primarily in the greater St. Louis, Missouri area. The Trustees will consider the donor's past giving history and any special needs of any of the charities she has given to in the past. The Trustees will also consider requests from charitable organizations that fall into one or more of the following categories: abused, neglected, or troubled children; the poor; the Episcopal Church and affiliates, including outreach programs; arts and culture in the Metropolitan St. Louis area; animal welfare (in Missouri); and victims of illness or disability, including research in this area. The following types of requests may be submitted: special projects; capital campaign requests (capital grants are awarded only as a source of support among a broad community of funders); challenge or matching grants; and general operation funding. Applicants must apply online at the grant website. Applicants are strongly encouraged to do the following before applying: review the downloadable state application procedures for additional helpful information and clarifications; review the downloadable online-application guidelines at the grant website; review the foundation's funding history (link is available from the grant website); review the online application questions in advance; and review the list of required attachments. These will generally include: a list of board members, financial statements (audited, reviewed, or compiled by independent auditor); an organization summary; a list of other funding sources; an IRS Determination letter; and other required documents. All attachments must be uploaded in the online application as PDF, Word, or Excel files. The application deadline for this foundation is 11:59 p.m. on September 1. Final decisions about grant rewards will be made by November 30.

Requirements: Applicants must have 501(c)3 tax-exempt status.

Restrictions: The fund will not consider requests for multi-year grants (pledges) or endowment creation and funding. The fund does not support requests from individuals, organizations attempting to influence policy through direct lobbying, or any political campaigns.

Geographic Focus: Missouri

Date(s) Application is Due: Sep 1

Samples: Grace Hill Settlement House, Saint Louis, Missouri, $20,000; Humane Society of Missouri, Saint Louis, Missouri, $15,000; Central Institute for the Deaf, Saint Louis, Missouri, $5,000.

Contact: Shanise Evans; (314) 466-8027; shanise.evans@baml.com

Internet: https://www.bankofamerica.com/philanthropic/fn_search.action

Sponsor: Herbert A. and Adrian W. Woods Foundation

100 North Broadway MO2-100-07-15

Saint Louis, MO 63102-2728

Herbert and Gertrude Latkin Charitable Foundation Grants   **935**

The foundation awards grants to eligible California nonprofit organizations to assist and promote the welfare and health of the elderly. Areas of interest include human services, aging centers and services, and family services. Additional focus areas include animal cruelty, child abuse, emergency medical services, and scholarships to college students. Types of support include general operating support, emergency funds, and equipment acquisition.

Requirements: California nonprofit organizations serving Santa Barbara County are eligible.

Geographic Focus: California

Date(s) Application is Due: Apr 1; Oct 1

Amount of Grant: 1,000 - 16,000 USD

Contact: Janice Gibbons, (805) 564-6211

Sponsor: Herbert and Gertrude Latkin Charitable Foundation

P.O. Box 2340

Santa Barbara, CA 93120-2340

Herbert H. and Grace A. Dow Foundation Grants   **936**

The Foundation has charter goals to improve the educational, religious, economic and cultural lives of Michigan's people. Priority is given to organizations that: have clearly stated objectives, strong and purposeful management and are publicly accountable; have needs which are in areas not normally funded by governmental or public financing; are not hesitant to explore, initiate, volunteer, or execute original ideas or concepts; are willing to collaborate with other persons or organizations to give synergy to a common objective or goal; have purposes which tend to advance private enterprise and the preservation of a free, open and self-resourceful society. There is no formal application form, though grant seekers will find detailed submission information online.

Requirements: Only organizations in Michigan are eligible to apply.

Restrictions: The Foundation does not make grants directly to individuals. It cannot legally support: organizations to which contributions are not tax deductible, according to Internal Revenue Service regulations; organizations that practice discrimination by race, sex, creed, age or national origin; political organizations or organizations whose purposes are to influence legislation.

Geographic Focus: Michigan

Contact: Macauley Whiting Jr., President; (989) 631-3699; fax (989) 631-0675; grants@hhdowfoundation.org

Internet: http://www.hhdowfdn.org/guidelines.html

Sponsor: Herbert H. and Grace A. Dow Foundation

1018 West Main Street

Midland, MI 48640-4292

Herman Abbott Family Foundation Grants   **937**

The Foundation, established in 1996 in New York, supports the arts, performing arts, and Jewish agencies and temples. Grant funding most often comes in the form of general operating support. There are no specified application formats or deadlines with which to adhere, and applicants should approach the foundation initially in writing. Awards average about $25,000.

Geographic Focus: All States

Amount of Grant: Up to 35,000 USD

Contact: David Y. Bailey, Treasurer; (203) 481-1120; fax (203) 488-3027

Sponsor: Herman Abbott Family Foundation

1224 Main Street, Lockworks Square

Branford, CT 06405-3778

Herman Goldman Foundation Grants   **938**

The Herman Goldman Foundation strives to enhance the quality of life through innovative grants in four main areas: 1) health — to achieve effective delivery of physical and mental health care services; 2) social justice — to develop organizational, social, and legal approaches to those who are aid deprived or handicapped; 3) education — for new or improved counseling for effective preschool, vocational and paraprofessional training; and 4) the arts — to increase opportunities for talented youth to receive training and for less affluent individuals to attend quality presentations. Grantmaking is primarily to 501(c)3 organizations in the metropolitan New York area. Types of support include: annual campaigns; building and renovation; capital campaigns; continuing support; endowments; general operating support; program development; internship funds; research; and seed money.

Requirements: Applicants should submit a proposal along with a copy of the organization's IRS determination letter. There are no deadlines. The board meets monthly, with grants considered in April, July, and November. Organizations are notified within two to three months of submission.

Restrictions: The Foundation does not fund religious organizations, individuals, or emergency funds.

Geographic Focus: New York

Contact: Richard Baron; (212) 797-9090; goldfound@aol.com

Sponsor: Herman Goldman Foundation

44 Wall Street, Suite 1212

New York, NY 10005-2401

HFSF Grants   **939**

The foundation conducts two separate grant programs: responsive grants and strategic initiative grants. With exceptions, the foundation will focus on developing one- to two-year grants. The following responsive grant categories have been established: project planning—to support the planning of projects requiring outside expertise, significant amounts of inter-agency collaboration, or other aspects needing additional resources to develop; health system/health policy development—to support a variety of activities specifically designed to improve public policies, infrastructure, and/or inter-agency procedures leading to increased system effectiveness, efficiency, sustainability, and overall capacity; organizational capacity building/core operating support—to organizations with a clear plan for increasing their agencies' effectiveness, efficiency, and sustainability; and health services—to support a range of preventive and primary health care services. The listed deadlines are for preliminary proposals; full proposals are by invitation. Application and guidelines are available online.

Requirements: 501(c)3 organizations serving southern Florida are eligible.

Geographic Focus: Florida

Date(s) Application is Due: Mar 31; Oct 22

Amount of Grant: 50,000 - 300,000 USD

Samples: Broward House (Fort Lauderdale, FL)—to support operational efficiency and improve its technology, $86,380; Community Committee for Developmental Handicaps (Miami, FL)—to develop a plan designed to strengthen its board development, marketing, staffing, and technology, $23,925; Human Services Coalition (Miami, FL)—to increase organizational capacity by improving communications and increasing membership, revenue, and donations, $20,000; Florida International U, Ctr on Aging (FL)—for efforts to improve the health of older adults who are at high risk for poor health due to obesity and physical inactivity, $263,394.

Contact: Peter Wood, Chief Program Officer; (305) 374-2282; fax (305) 374-7003; pwood@hfsf.org

Internet: http://www.hfsf.org

Sponsor: Health Foundation of South Florida

601 Brickell Key Drive, Suite 901

Miami, FL 33131

High Meadow Foundation Grants   940

The foundation grants funds in support of the performing arts, especially theater and music, and other cultural organizations. Organizations supported are usually located in Berkshire County, MA. Types of support include continuing support, annual campaigns, capital campaigns, building construction/renovation, equipment acquisition, emergency funds, program development, employee-related scholarships, and matching funds. Applications are accepted at any time. Forms are not necessary; a letter outlining the proposed project should include budget and administrative information.

Requirements: Western Massachusetts 501(c)3 tax-exempt organizations in Berkshire County are eligible.

Geographic Focus: Massachusetts

Samples: Massachusetts Museum of Contemporary Art, North Adams, MA, $100,000; Berkshire Theater Festival, Stockbridge, MA, $60,000; Lenox Library Association, Lenox, MA, $10,000;

Contact: Jane Fitzpatrick, Treasurer; (413) 298-5565 or (413) 243-1474; fax (413) 298-4058

Sponsor: High Meadow Foundation

30 Main Street

Stockbridge, MA 01262

Hillman Foundation Grants   941

The foundation provides grants to nonprofit organizations in the city of Pittsburgh and the southwestern Pennsylvania region for programs and projects designed to improve the quality of life in the area. The foundation's areas of interest include community affairs, social services, culture and the arts, education at all levels, and youth services including medical and health. Grants range widely in size and are allocated for large and small capital projects, endowment, new and expanding programs, and on a limited basis, operating support. Applications should include an annual budget of the organization, project information, and evidence of tax-exempt status. Application information is available online.

Requirements: The Foundation considers requests only from organizations classified as tax-exempt under Section 501(c)3 of the U.S. Internal Revenue Code and designated as public charities under Section 509(a).

Restrictions: Grants are not made to individuals, organizations located outside of the United States, for travel expenses for groups, or in support of events, sponsorships and meetings such as conferences, institutes and seminars.

Geographic Focus: Pennsylvania

Samples: Strong Women, Strong Girls, INc., $10,000—towards program for at-risk and low-income girls; Greater Pittsburgh Community Food Bank, $65,000—toward food pantry and outreach program; Carnegie Institute/Museum of Natural History, $50,000—towards purchase of bournonite, amazonite, smoky quarts and rhodochrosite mineral specimens.

Contact: David K. Roger, President; (412) 338-3466; fax (412) 338-3463; foundation@hillmanfo.com

Internet: http://www.hillmanfdn.org/grantprograms.html

Sponsor: Hillman Foundation

330 Grant Street, Suite 2000

Pittsburgh, PA 15219

Hilton Hotels Corporate Giving Program Grants   942

Hilton makes charitable contributions to nonprofit organizations involved with K-12 education, youth development, public policy, homelessness, and civic affairs. Support is given primarily in areas of company operations, with emphasis on California, including Los Angeles and San Francisco, and Tennessee, including Memphis; giving also to national organizations. Contact Ellen Gonda for additional information at: corporate_communications@hilton.com.

Requirements: 501(c)3 tax-exempt organizations are eligible.

Restrictions: No support for sport teams, religious organizations not of direct benefit to the entire community, government-supported organizations (over 20 percent of budget), hospitals, private schools, pre-schools, or day care facilities, film and video production, or promotional materials. No grants to individuals (except for employee-related scholarships), or for fellowships, sports activities, debt reduction, capital campaigns or endowments, film or video projects, or promotional merchandise.

Geographic Focus: California, Tennessee

Contact: Ellen Gonda, Senior Vice President; (310) 278-4321; fax (310) 205-7678; corporate_communications@hilton.com

Internet: http://www.hiltonworldwide.com

Sponsor: Hilton Hotels Corporation

9336 Civic Center Drive

Beverly Hills, CA 90210-3604

Hirtzel Memorial Foundation Grants   943

The foundation awards grants to eligible organizations in New York and Pennsylvania in its areas of interest, including medical research and health care; community and neighborhood improvement; higher education; and social and human services. Types of support include building construction and renovation, capital campaigns, scholarships, equipment acquisition, general operating support, research, and scholarships. There are no application deadlines; contact the office for appropriate forms.

Requirements: New York nonprofit organizations in Ripley, Chautauqua County, and Pennsylvania nonprofit organizations in North East, Erie County, are eligible.

Geographic Focus: New York, Pennsylvania

Amount of Grant: 750 - 250,000 USD

Contact: Laurie Moritz, Grants Administrator, c/o Mellon Financial Corporation; (412) 234-0023

Sponsor: Orris C. Hirtzel and Beatrice Dewey Hirtzel Memorial Foundation

P.O. Box 185

Pittsburgh, PA 15230

Historic Landmarks Legal Defense Grants   944

While the foundation regards legal action as a last resort, it is recognized that it is sometimes required to save endangered structures and support preservation processes. The defense grants cover 80% of the total cost of legal counsel up to $2,000.

Requirements: Nonprofit preservation organizations may request grants of up to $2,000 for legal fees to defend or compel conformance with a local preservation ordinance, enforce protective covenants, or seek an injunction to prevent the demolition of a historic building.

Restrictions: Limited to Indiana only.

Geographic Focus: Indiana

Amount of Grant: Up to 2,000 USD

Contact: Carla Jones, Receptionist, State Headquarters; (317) 639-4534; fax (317) 639-6734; info@historiclandmarks.org

Internet: http://www.historiclandmarks.org/help/grants.html

Sponsor: Historic Landmarks Foundation of Indiana

340 W Michigan Street

Indianapolis, IN 46202

HNHfoundation Grants   945

The foundation awards general operating and program support to New Hampshire healthcare organizations. Preference will be given to programs providing services to children and youth. There are no application deadlines; obtain application forms and procedures from the office.

Requirements: New Hampshire nonprofit organizations are eligible.

Geographic Focus: New Hampshire

Amount of Grant: 250 - 250,000 USD

Samples: Home Health and Hospice Care (Nashua, NH)—to support an outreach program for uninsured children, $10,000; North Country Health Consortium (NH)—for health insurance for small businesses, $35,361; Community Health Access Network (Newmarket, NH)—to support chronic-disease education programs, $34,433.

Contact: Sandi Van Scoyoc, President; (603) 229-3260; fax (603) 229-3259; info@hnhfoundation.org

Internet: http://www.hnhfoundation.org

Sponsor: HNHfoundation

14 Dixon Avenue

Concord, NH 03301

Hoglund Foundation Grants 946

The foundation supports nonprofits working in the areas of education, health science and services, social services, and children's health and development. Grants are made primarily in Dallas, and Houston, Texas, with a limited number of grants awarded outside of this area. Types of support include project support, capital support, and general operating support. Application guidelines are available on the foundation's Web site.

Requirements: To be eligible for consideration, an organization must provide proof that they have received a determination letter from the Internal Revenue Service indicating that it is a tax exempt organization as described in Section 501(c)3 of the Internal Revenue Code of 1986 and is treated as other than a private foundation as within the meaning of Section 509(a) of the Code. An organization may also qualify under Section 170(c)(1) if the grant requested is to be used exclusively for public purposes as described in the Code.

Restrictions: Grants are not made to individuals.

Geographic Focus: Texas

Date(s) Application is Due: Mar 15; Jul 15; Nov 15

Amount of Grant: 1,000 - 200,000 USD

Contact: Kelly Compton, Executive Director; (214) 987-3605; fax (214) 363-6507; info@hoglundfoundation.org

Internet: http://www.hoglundfoundation.org/grants.html

Sponsor: Hoglund Foundation

5910 North Central Expressway, Suite 255

Dallas, TX 75206

Homeland Foundation Grants 947

The foundation awards grants to nonprofit organizations in its areas of interest, including the environment and natural resource conservation—primarily the U.S. West Coast (including Baja, CA, and Hawaii)and the Caribbean and Western Pacific; and women's issues—physical, mental, and financial health—in California's Los Angeles and Orange Counties. Types of support include general operating grants, program grants, continuing support, and multiyear grants. The board meets quarterly; contact the office for guidelines prior to submitting proposals.

Requirements: 501(c)3 nonprofit organizations are eligible.

Restrictions: Grants are not awarded to support political campaigns, individuals, scholarships, fellowships, or film or video projects.

Geographic Focus: California, Hawaii

Date(s) Application is Due: Mar 1; Jun 1; Sep 1; Dec 1

Amount of Grant: 1,000 - 328,000 USD

Contact: Glenda Menges; (949) 494-0365; fax (949) 494-8395

Sponsor: Homeland Foundation

412 N Pacific Coast Highway, PMB 359

Laguna Beach, CA 92651

Homer A. Scott and Mildred S. Scott Foundation Grants 948

The foundation awards grants to Wyoming nonprofit organizations in its areas of interest, including children and youth, higher education, and social services. Types of support include employee matching gifts and matching funds. Preference is given to requests that intervene in and prevent the problems of young people, build public awareness of youth issues, promote coordination and communication among programs serving young people, develop leadership skills, build self-esteem, and can become sustainable. Application deadlines vary; contact program staff for exact dates. Application forms must be obtained from the office. The board meets quarterly to consider requests.

Requirements: Sheridan, WY, nonprofit organizations are eligible.

Restrictions: No grants to individuals.

Geographic Focus: Montana, Wyoming

Contact: Lynn Mavrakis, Executive Director; (307) 672-1448; fax (307) 672-1443; lynn.mavrakis@fib.com

Sponsor: Homer A. Scott and Mildred S. Scott Foundation

P.O. Box 2007

Sheridan, WY 82801-2007

Honor the Earth Grants 949

As a unique national Native initiative, Honor the Earth works to raise public awareness, and raise and direct funds to grassroots Native environmental groups. Honor the Earth's Board encourages proposals on Native environmental justice, sustainable development, and cultural preservation, with a grant limit of $5,000. The organization's focus will remain on sustainable Indigenous communities support. Their work also focuses on opposition to fossil fuels extraction and destructive mining practices. Additional information, guidelines, and information on previously funded projects is available at the website. Applicants are encouraged to check back periodically for grant funding

through the Building Resilience program. Proposals may be submitted in hard copy or by email. Faxed proposals cannot be accepted.

Requirements: Grants are awarded solely to organizations that are led and managed by Native peoples. Priority is given to grassroots, community-based organizations and groups with a lack of access to federal and/or tribal funding resources.

Restrictions: Funding is not available for individuals.

Geographic Focus: All States, Canada

Date(s) Application is Due: Nov 9

Amount of Grant: 1,000 - 5,000 USD

Contact: Winona LaDuke, Executive Director; (218) 375-3200; HonorGrants@honorearth.org or info@honortheearth.org

Internet: http://www.honorearth.org/grantmaking

Sponsor: Honor the Earth

607 Main Avenue

Callaway, MN 56521

Horace A. Kimball and S. Ella Kimball Foundation Grants 950

Although the Horace A Kimball and S. Ella Kimball Foundation was not legally established until July of 1956, its roots along with those of its sister organization, the Phyllis Kimball Johnstone and H. Earle Kimball foundation, go back to the early 1900s. It was then that Horace A. Kimball of Providence, Rhode Island, a retired woolen manufacturer, acquired controlling interest of the Clicquot Club Beverage Company of Millis, Massachusetts. Today, the Kimball Foundation makes grants almost exclusively to Rhode Island operatives (charities) or those benefitting Rhode Island residents and causes. Although, the Foundation considers gifts to all areas in the state, greater emphasis is placed on South County. Areas of interest for the Foundation are: human services; the environment; and health care. Most recent awards have ranged from $2,500 to $25,000. Interested parties can apply either with a mailed hard copy or by using the online application format.

Requirements: The Foundation will consider any organization which has proper 501(c)3 and 509(a) IRS tax classification status.

Restrictions: No support for religious organizations. No grants to individuals, or for feasibility studies, capital projects or multi-year commitments.

Geographic Focus: Rhode Island

Date(s) Application is Due: Jul 15

Amount of Grant: 1,000 - 50,000 USD

Samples: Chorus of Westerly, Westerly, Rhode Island, $13,000 - roof repairs; Education Exchange, Peace Dale, Rhode Island, $25,000 - testing equipment purchase; Wood Valley Health Services, Hope Valley, Rhode Island, $3,700 - general program support.

Contact: Thomas F. Black III, President; (401) 364-3565 or (401) 348-1234

Internet: http://www.hkimballfoundation.org/index2.htm

Sponsor: Horace A. Kimball and S. Ella Kimball Foundation

130 Woodville Road

Hope Valley, RI 02832

Horace Moses Charitable Foundation Grants 951

The Horace Moses Charitable Foundation was established in 1923 to support and promote quality educational, human-services, and health-care programming for underserved populations. Special consideration is given to charitable organizations that serve the community of Springfield and its surrounding communities. Grant requests for general operating support are strongly encouraged. Program support will also be considered. Small, program-related capital expenses may be included in general operating or program requests. The majority of grants from the Moses Charitable Foundation are one year in duration; on occasion, multi-year support is awarded. Applicants must apply online at the grant website. Applicants are strongly encouraged to do the following before applying: review the downloadable state application procedures for additional helpful information and clarifications; review the downloadable online-application guidelines at the grant website; review the foundation's funding history (link is available from the grant website); review the online application questions in advance; and review the list of required attachments. These will generally include: a list of board members, financial statements (audited, reviewed, or compiled by independent auditor); an organization summary; a list of other funding sources; an IRS Determination letter; and other required documents. All attachments must be uploaded in the online application as PDF, Word, or Excel files. The application deadline for the Horace Moses Charitable Foundation is 11:59 p.m. on April 1. Applicants will be notified of grant decisions before June 30.

Requirements: Applicants must have 501(c)3 tax-exempt status.

Restrictions: The foundation does not support requests from individuals, organizations attempting to influence policy through direct lobbying, or any political campaigns.

Geographic Focus: Massachusetts
Date(s) Application is Due: Apr 1
Samples: Big Brothers Big Sisters of Hampden County, Springfield, Massachusetts, $15,000, Continuing Support; Open Pantry Community Services, Springfield, Massachusetts, $10,000, for Loaves and Fishes Community Kitchen; Drama Studio, Springfield, Massachusetts, $2,500, Acting Training and Community Outreach Program.
Contact: Michealle Larkins, Vice President; (866) 778-6859; michealle.larkins@baml.com
Internet: https://www.bankofamerica.com/philanthropic/fn_search.action
Sponsor: Horace Moses Charitable Foundation
225 Franklin Street, 4th Floor, MA1-225-04-02
Boston, MA 02110

Horizon Foundation for New Jersey Grants   952

The Foundation's purpose is to promote health, well-being, and quality of life in New Jersey communities. Foundation goals are to improve health by promoting quality health care programs and access and to enhance arts and cultural opportunities. Application information is available online. Only electronic grant applications will be accepted. Application are accepted between January 1 and September 31.
Requirements: 501(c)3 tax-exempt organizations in New Jersey communities located in and served by Horizon Blue Cross Blue Shield of New Jersey are eligible.
Restrictions: Funding is not available for: capital campaigns; endowments; hospitals or hospital foundations; individuals; political causes; political candidates; political organizations; political campaigns.
Geographic Focus: New Jersey
Amount of Grant: 10,000 - 50,000 USD
Samples: ChoiceOne Pregnancy & Sexual Health Resource Centers, Lawrenceville, NJ, $25,000—to support the Sexually Transmitted Diseases Education and Prevention component of its Straight Talk Program; Family Guidance Center, Hamilton, NJ, $15.000—to support its Behavioral Health Services-Depression Recovery Program; American Repertory Ballet, New Brunswick, HJ, $7,500—to support the Dance Power Program.
Contact: Michele Berry; Foundation_Info@horizonblue.com
Internet: http://www.horizon-bcbsnj.com/foundation/about/funding.html?WT.svl=leftnav
Sponsor: Horizon Foundation for New Jersey
Three Penn Plaza East, PP-15V
Newark, NJ 07105-2200

Horizons Community Issues Grants   953

Grants support program activities or projects serving lesbian, gay, bisexual, and transgender (LGBT) people of all ages in designated California counties focusing on the following issue areas: arts and culture; advocacy, awareness, and civil rights; children, youth, and families; and community and social services. Application information is available online.
Requirements: To be eligible, an organization must: be a nonprofit, 501(c)3 organization, or provide documentation that the organization is sponsored under a fiscal agent umbrella that has 501(c)3 status. Organizations or programs must request support for one or more of the following counties: Alameda; Contra; Costa; Marin; Napa; San Francisco; San Mateo; Santa Clara; Solano; Sonoma.
Restrictions: The following are not eligible for support: costs incurred prior to the date of the grant award; government agencies; capital support, including construction and renovation; fundraising or event sponsorship; individuals; Non-LGBT organizations with budget over $1 million.
Geographic Focus: California
Amount of Grant: 10,000 - 20,000 USD
Contact: Jewelle Gomez, Program Officer; (415) 398-2333, ext. 116; jgomez@horizonsfoundation.org
Internet: http://www.horizonsfoundation.org/page/organizations/ci
Sponsor: Horizons Foundation
870 Market Street, Suite 728
San Francisco, CA 94102

Hormel Family Foundation Business Plan Award   954

The purpose of this competition is to stimulate entrepreneurship and economic development in McCook, Nebraska. Competition is different from many other business plan competitions in the sense that the prize is not a simple cash award, but an actual investment by which the Hormel Family Foundation becomes a shareholder in the winning business. In addition to the $25,000 investment, the winner will receive business, legal and advertising services valued at $10,000. The Foundation views this competition not only as an investment in an individual or team, but primarily in the community of McCook.
Requirements: The proposed business must be located in or near McCook, Nebraska. Business owners located outside McCook city limits must be willing to relocate their business to McCook, or within a proximity acceptable to the Foundation. The business plan must be an original idea, and must be written by the applicant(s). Any copyright or intellectual property infringement will result in immediate disqualification and possible legal action. While the operations of the business must be based in the McCook area, and any tax dollars earned by the business must benefit McCook, sales of proposed products or services are not limited to McCook. This is important to note, especially in the case of internet-based businesses and businesses that might distribute products throughout the United States.
Restrictions: Applicants must be: local business owners interested in expanding or improving their existing business; any individual or team with a brand new business idea, willing to launch their business in McCook; or business owners elsewhere who are willing to relocate their business to McCook.
Geographic Focus: Nebraska
Amount of Grant: 35,000 USD
Contact: Susan Harris-Broomfield, Project Manager; (308) 340-0856; susan@hormelfamilyfoundation.com
Internet: http://www.hormelfamilyfoundation.com/businessplancompetition.html
Sponsor: Hormel Family Foundation
1 Prairie Hills Road
McCook, NE 69001

Houston Arts Alliance General Operating Support Expansion for   955
Organizations

The Houston Arts Alliance General Operating Support Expansion for Organizations funding program provides operating support for multicultural arts organizations that present a regular season of arts or cultural programs that serve residents, visitors and tourists to Houston. While the grants are awarded for operating support, grantees are required to spend the grant funds only for the allowed purposes of the Hotel Occupancy Tax. Organizations approved for a grant will enter into an agreement with Houston Arts Alliance that outlines the arts activities that will be supported through grant evaluations and accountability requirements. The maximum amount awarded for a General Operating Support or General Operating Support Expansion grant is $100,000. Applications will be accepted from February 20 through March 21.
Requirements: Houston 501(c)3 nonprofit cultural arts or university arts organizations are eligible. Applicants must: provide operating support for organizations that present a regular season of arts or cultural programs that serve residents, visitors and tourists to Houston; be deeply rooted in and reflective of a minority, inner-city, tribal or disabled community; be devoted to primarily providing art to its minority, inner-city, tribal or disabled community; have 50% or more of the organization's board of directors representative of the minority, inner-city, tribal or disabled community; provide operating support for multicultural arts organizations that present a regular season of arts or cultural programs that serve residents, visitors and tourists to Houston; have two year operating revenue of $50,000 or more; and have received two consecutive prior years of Houston Arts Alliance funding in any grant category.
Restrictions: First-time and former applicant organizations that have not received a Houston Arts Alliance General Operating Grant in the past two years will be considered first-time applicants and are not eligible for General Operating Support.
Geographic Focus: Texas
Date(s) Application is Due: Mar 21
Amount of Grant: Up to 100,000 USD
Contact: Diem Jones; (713) 527-9330; fax (713) 630-5210; diem@haatx.com
Internet: http://www.houstonartsalliance.com/grants/organizations/gos/
Sponsor: Houston Arts Alliance
3201 Allen Parkway, Suite 250
Houston, TX 77019-1800

Houston Arts Alliance General Operating Support for Organizations   956

The Houston Arts Alliance General Operating Support for Organizations funding program provides operating support for arts and cultural organizations that present regular seasons of arts or cultural programs that serve residents, visitors and tourists to Houston. While the grants are awarded for operating support, grantees are required to spend the grant funds only for the allowed purposes of the Hotel Occupancy Tax. Organizations approved for a grant will enter into an agreement with Houston Arts Alliance that outlines the arts activities that will be supported through grant evaluations and accountability requirements. The maximum amount awarded for a General Operating Support grant is $100,000. Applications will be accepted from February 20 through March 21.

Requirements: Houston 501(c)3 nonprofit cultural arts or university arts organizations are eligible. Applicants must: provides operating support for organizations that present a regular season of arts or cultural programs that serve residents, visitors and tourists to Houston; have a two year average operating revenue of $50,000 or more; and have received two consecutive prior years of Houston Arts Alliance funding in any grant category.

Restrictions: First-time and former applicant organizations that have not received a Houston Arts Alliance General Operating Grant in the past two years will be considered first-time applicants and are not eligible for General Operating Support.

Geographic Focus: Texas
Date(s) Application is Due: Mar 21
Amount of Grant: Up to 100,000 USD
Contact: Diem Jones; (713) 527-9330; fax (713) 630-5210; diem@haatx.com
Internet: http://www.houstonartsalliance.com/grants/organizations/gos/
Sponsor: Houston Arts Alliance
3201 Allen Parkway, Suite 250
Houston, TX 77019-1800

Howard County Community Foundation Grants 957

The foundation awards grants to Maryland nonprofit organizations in its areas of interest, including human services, arts and culture, and education and community affairs. The board meets monthly. Project grants are reviewed in March, and operating grants are reviewed in November. Contingency grants are available year-round. Contact the office for application forms and deadlines.

Requirements: Howard County, MD, nonprofit organizations are eligible.
Restrictions: Grants do not support individuals, sectarian religious purposes, or medical research.
Geographic Focus: Maryland
Contact: Program Contact; (410) 730-7840; fax (410) 997-6021; info@columbiafoundation.org
Internet: http://www.columbiafoundation.org/nonprofits/index.html
Sponsor: Columbia Foundation/Howard County Community Foundation
10227 Wincopin Circle, Suite G-15
Columbia, MD 21044

Howard Gilman Foundation Grants 958

The foundation is dedicated to the preservation of natural and cultural resources, with a focus on environmental, especially animal, conservation; the preservation and advancement of artistic and cultural endeavors; and medical research, especially in the fields of HIV/AIDS, cardiology, and sports medicine. The arts and culture component of the program is focused primarily in the New York metropolitan area. Types of support include general operating grants, program grants, research grants, and seed money grants. Staff prefer to respond to a brief letter of inquiry outlining the project's aim and general budgetary requirements before asking potential grantees to prepare full proposals.

Requirements: 501(c)3 nonprofit organizations are eligible.
Restrictions: Religious and political agencies are ineligible.
Geographic Focus: New York
Amount of Grant: 1,000 - 100,000 USD
Samples: Brooklyn Academy of Music (Brooklyn, NY)—for endowment and operating support, $5 million.
Contact: Harry Brown, Program Associate; (212) 307-1073; fax (212) 262-4108; hbrown@gilman.com
Sponsor: Howard Gilman Foundation
111 W 50th Street, 40th Floor
New York, NY 10020

Howard H. Callaway Foundation Grants 959

The Howard H. Callaway Foundation offers support in the form of general operation grants primarily in the state of Georgia. The Foundations areas of interest include: athletics/sports, baseball; federated giving programs; higher education; human services and; public affairs. Applications are accepted year round, submit a letter of inquiry to the Foundation to begin the application process.

Requirements: Georgia 501(c)3 non-profit organizations are eligible for funding. There is neither a deadline date to adhere to nor, is there a specific application form to submit. Begin the application process by submitting a letter of inquiry to the Foundation containing: copy of IRS Determination Letter; descriptive literature about organization; detailed description of project and amount of funding requested.

Restrictions: No grants to individuals.

Geographic Focus: Georgia
Amount of Grant: 5,000 - 25,000 USD
Contact: Howard H. Callaway, President; (706) 663-5075
Sponsor: Howard H. Callaway Foundation
P.O. Box 1326
Pine Mountain, GA 31822-1326

HRK Foundation Grants 960

The foundation focuses its resources on single-year funding for special projects in the areas of health care, AIDS, and children and youth services. Within the Twin Cities metro area, the Saint Croix Valley, and Ashland and Bayfield Counties of Wisconsin, the board will consider programming related to the issue of AIDS and programming that addresses children's health issues. Within the Saint Croix Valley and Ashland and Bayfield Counties in Wisconsin, the board will consider local community-specific projects. Types of support include general operating support, seed funding, community development, matching/challenge grants, equipment acquisition, and annual campaigns. Requests are considered two times each year.

Requirements: The foundation makes grants only to qualified IRS 501(c)3 organizations that specifically benefit people in the area surrounding Bayport and Saint Paul, MN, and western Wisconsin.
Restrictions: The foundation does not make loans or provide grants to individuals.
Geographic Focus: Minnesota, Wisconsin
Date(s) Application is Due: Mar 15; Sep 15
Amount of Grant: 1,000 - 25,000 USD
Contact: Kathleen Fluegel, Foundation Director; (866) 342-5475 or (612) 293-9001; fax (612) 298-0551; info@HRKFoundation.org
Internet: http://www.hrkfoundation.org/grants/index.htm
Sponsor: HRK Foundation
345 St. Peter Street, Suite 1200
Saint Paul, MN 55102-1639

Huber Foundation Grants 961

The Foundation focuses its grants program on three specific aspects of reproductive rights: keeping abortion safe, legal, and preferably increasingly rare; contraceptive choice and availability; and relevant education. The Foundation's major interest lies in funding organizations that will impact these issues on a national level. There is no formal application procedure. A letter describing the project, a budget for the project, and proof of tax-exempt status is required. Though the Foundation board meets four times annually, there are no fixed deadline dates.

Requirements: U.S. nonprofits, including advocacy groups, hospitals, legal defense groups, family planning agencies, educational organizations, universities, and women's groups may submit grant applications.
Restrictions: The foundation does not encourage proposals for projects that are local or regional in scope. It will not consider grants to individuals, foreign organizations, capital campaigns, scholarships, endowment funds, research, international projects, or film productions.
Geographic Focus: All States
Amount of Grant: 10,000 - 100,000 USD
Contact: Lorraine Barnhart, Executive Director; (732) 933-7700
Sponsor: Huber Foundation
P.O. Box 277
Rumson, NJ 07760-0277

Hudson Webber Foundation Grants 962

The purpose of the Foundation is to improve the vitality and quality of life of the metropolitan Detroit community. The Foundation concentrates its giving primarily within the City of Detroit and has a particular interest in the revitalization of the urban core because this area is a focus for community activity and pride and is of critical importance to the vitality of the entire metropolitan community. The Foundation presently concentrates its efforts and resources in support of projects within five program missions: Detroit Physical Revitalization; Economic Development; The Arts; Safe Community; and the Detroit Medical Center. A brief letter signed by a senior officer of the requesting organization is the preferred form of application. Information for completing the letter of request are available online.

Requirements: The foundation concentrates its giving within Detroit.
Geographic Focus: Michigan
Contact: Katy Locker; (313) 963-7777; HWF@hudson-webber.org
Internet: http://www.hudson-webber.org/HowToApply_Instructions.html
Sponsor: Hudson Webber Foundation
333 West Fort Street, Suite 1310
Detroit, MI 48226-3134

HUD Supportive Housing Program Grants   963

The program is designed to promote the development of supportive housing and supportive services, including innovative approaches to assist homeless persons in the transition from homelessness and to enable them to live as independently as possible. Funds may be used to provide transitional housing, permanent housing, supportive housing, supportive services for homeless individuals not provided in conjunction with supportive housing, or facilities in which supportive services are provided. Seven types of assistance may be provided, including: acquisition of structures for use as supportive housing or in providing supportive services; rehabilitation of structures for use as supportive housing or in providing supportive services; new construction of buildings for use as supportive housing under limited circumstances; leasing of structures for use as supportive housing or in providing supportive services; operating costs of supportive housing; costs of providing supportive services to homeless persons; and administrative costs not to exceed five percent of the SHP grant. Funding of up to 75 percent of the annual operating costs is allowed for the first two years. Funding of up to 80 percent for supportive services cost and, the program provides grants for leasing costs for up to three years.

Requirements: States, local governments, other governmental entities; Native American tribes; private nonprofit organizations; and public, nonprofit community mental health associations are eligible to apply.

Geographic Focus: All States

Amount of Grant: 200,000 - 400,000 USD

Contact: Mark Johnston; (202) 708-4300; Mark.Johnston@hud.gov

Internet: http://www.hud.gov/offices/cpd/homeless/programs/shp/index.cfm

Sponsor: U.S. Department of Housing and Urban Development

451 Seventh Street SW

Washington, D.C. 20410

Huffy Foundation Grants   964

The Huffy Foundation gives primarily to areas in which the company has operations in California, Ohio, Pennsylvania, and Wisconsin. These areas include: the visual arts; museums; performing arts; theater; arts/cultural programs; all levels of education; hospitals (general); health care and associations; recreation; children and youth services; and federated giving (United Way). Types of support include general and operating support; continuing support; annual campaigns; capital campaigns; building/renovation programs; emergency funds; program development; seed money; consulting services; employee matching gifts; and matching funds. Requests should include a description of the organization, its history and purpose, a description of the people it serves, and a summary of total budget and funding.

Requirements: The Foundation provides a brochure which delineates the application and grant guidelines. There is no application form. The Foundation recommends that the initial approach be in the form of a letter or a proposal. One copy of the letter/proposal should be submitted. There are no deadlines. The Board meets in February, May, August and November.

Restrictions: Grants are not made to individuals, in support of political activities or of religious organizations for religious purposes, or organizations that are not tax exempt. Grants are seldom made for medical research; to endowments; or for operating funds for organizations located outside the corporation communities.

Geographic Focus: California, Ohio, Pennsylvania, Wisconsin

Contact: Pam Booher, Secretary; (937) 866-6251

Sponsor: Huffy Foundation

225 Byers Road

Miamisburg, OH 45342

Hugh J. Andersen Foundation Grants   965

The mission of the Hugh J. Andersen Foundation is to give back to our community through focused efforts that foster inclusivity, promote equality, and lead to increased human independence, self sufficiency and dignity. To fulfill this mission, the Foundation acts as a grantmaker, innovator, and convener. The Foundation's primary geographic area of focus is the St. Croix Valley: Washington County in Minnesota and Pierce, Polk and St. Croix Counties in Wisconsin. Secondarily, there is an interest in St. Paul, Minnesota. From time to time the Foundation may consider programs in other parts of the Metro Area and Greater Minnesota. Please contact the Program Director prior to submitting a proposal to determine if the program might be of interest to the Foundation. The Board generally considers requests in June, September, December and February. Faxed or emailed applications will not be considered.

Requirements: The Hugh J. Andersen Foundation awards grants only to qualified charitable organizations that are designated as tax exempt under Internal Revenue Service Code 501(c)3 and are not classified as private foundations.

Restrictions: The Hugh J. Andersen Foundation: does not make loans, and does not provide grants or scholarships to individuals; does not provide grants for lobbying activities, fundraising dinners and events, or travel; will generally not consider the following types of organizations and programs for funding: agencies/divisions/councils/programs that have counterparts in St. Paul or the St. Croix Valley; arts organizations exclusively focused on music, dance or visual arts; athletic teams; business/economics education; child care centers; civic action groups; debt or after the fact situations; immigration/refugee issues and programs; independent media productions; political/voter education; private or alternative schools; religious institutions. In addition, the Foundation: will generally not fund the entire project budget, but prefers to be part of an effort supported by a number of sources; considers major endowment and capital requests for funding to be a low priority; does not provide funding through fiscal agents; considers letters of inquiry. Letters of inquiry are reviewed at the Foundation's next board meeting. If the board determines that the request falls within its guidelines and interests, a full proposal will be requested from the applicant for review at the following board meeting.

Geographic Focus: Minnesota, Wisconsin

Date(s) Application is Due: Mar 15; Jun 15; Aug 15; Nov 15

Contact: Brad Kruse, Program Director; (651) 275-4489 or (888) 439-9508; fax (651) 439-9480; hjafdn@srinc.biz

Internet: https://www.srinc.biz/hja/documents/HJAGuidelines09-10.pdf

Sponsor: Hugh J. Andersen Foundation

White Pine Building, 342 Fifth Avenue North

Bayport, MN 55003

Huie-Dellmon Trust Grants   966

The trust awards grants to Louisiana nonprofits in its areas of interest, including hospitals, higher and secondary education, libraries, and Protestant churches and organizations. Types of support include general operating support, capital campaigns, building construction/renovation, equipment acquisition, program development, scholarship funds, research, and matching funds. There are no application forms or deadlines.

Requirements: Central Louisiana nonprofit organizations are eligible.

Geographic Focus: Louisiana

Amount of Grant: 1,000 - 100,000 USD

Contact: Richard Crowell Jr., Trustee; (318) 748-8141

Sponsor: Huie-Dellmon Trust

P.O. Box 330

Alexandria, LA 71309-0330

Huisking Foundation Grants   967

The foundation awards grants in its areas of interest, including Catholic higher and secondary education, church support and social services, hospitals, and religion associations. Types of support include general operating support, building construction/renovation, research grants, endowment funds, scholarship funds, special projects, and continuing support. The board meets in April and November; letters of intent are due in February and August.

Geographic Focus: All States

Contact: Frank Huisking, Treasurer; (203) 426-8618

Sponsor: Huisking Foundation

291 Peddlers Road

Guilford, CT 06437

Hulman & Company Foundation Grants   968

The Hulman & Company Foundation was established in 1998 in the state of Indiana. The Foundation giving primarily in Indianapolis and the Terre Haute area. The Foundation supports community foundations and organizations involved with engineering education, animal welfare, and youth services.

Requirements: Contact the Foundations office with a proposal for initial approach, no application form required.

Restrictions: NO grants available to individuals.

Geographic Focus: Indiana

Contact: Jeffrey G. Belskus, Treasurer; (812) 232-9446

Sponsor: Hulman and Company Foundation

P.O. Box 150

Terre Haute, IN 47808-0150

Human Source Foundation Grants   969

The Human Source Foundation is organized to support charitable and educational initiatives that improve the human condition. The Foundation provides assistance and financial support for programs involved with education, human services, and youth development. Giving is restricted to the state of

Texas, primarily in Denton and Fort Worth counties. There are no specific deadlines or application forms, and applicants should begin by forwarding a letter of request.

Requirements: Tax-exempt 501(c)3 organizations serving Texas, primarily Denton and Fort Worth counties, are eligible to apply.

Geographic Focus: Texas

Contact: Mary G. Palko; (817) 926-2799; fax (817) 926-5202; mary@ftw.com

Sponsor: Human Source Foundation

2409 Winton Terrace West, P.O. Box 100423

Fort Worth, TX 76185-0423

Hyams Foundation Grants   970

The Foundation's mission is to increase economic and social justice and power within low-income communities in Boston and Chelsea, Massachusetts. The Foundation's focus is on four community priorities or outcomes: increased civic engagement, with a special focus on immigrant communities; more affordable housing, especially for very low-income families; increased family economic self-sufficiency; and expanded opportunities for low-income, older teens. Application information is available online.

Requirements: Massachusetts 501(c)3 charitable organizations are eligible. The foundation will give priority to programs that have a substantial impact on low-income neighborhoods/populations in Boston, and Chelsea.

Geographic Focus: Massachusetts

Date(s) Application is Due: Mar 1; Sep 1; Dec 1

Amount of Grant: 20,000 - 50,000 USD

Contact: Susan Perry, (617) 426-5600, ext. 307; fax (617) 426-5696; sperry@hyamsfoundation.org

Internet: http://www.hyamsfoundation.org

Sponsor: Hyams Foundation

50 Federal Street, 9th Floor

Boston, MA 02110

I.A. O'Shaughnessy Foundation Grants   971

The Foundation is concerned that too many schools lack sufficient resources; that students in high-poverty areas have lower achievement scores, higher drop-out rates, and lower rates of college graduation; that low-income families lack the resources to choose better schools; and that the gap between the rich and the poor is increasing. The Foundation has set its current funding interest to help address these critical matters of public concern. The Foundation is currently interested in making grants to support high quality education that prepares students in disadvantaged communities for educational and life success. Priority is given to organizations that provide support networks; remove impediments to student success; are broadly supported by the community, and have a record of demonstrated success. Additional guidelines and application forms are available at the foundation's website.

Requirements: Eligible applicant must be: nonprofit organizations; mission-consistent; fiscally sound; demonstrate a need; and capable and accountable.

Restrictions: The Foundation will not fund: grants that are not consistent with Foundation values; national or umbrella organizations that raise funds through broad-based solicitations to the general public; organizations that become overly dependent on the Foundation for on-going operational support; capital campaign gifts exceeding 20% of the campaign goal; political campaigns, events, or organizations whose purpose is to promote political candidates; lobbying; individuals.

Geographic Focus: Illinois, Kansas, Minnesota, Texas

Samples: Chicago Communities in Schools, $15,000; Church of St. Michael Stillwater, $200,000; Museum of New Mexico Foundation, $88,000.

Contact: Eileen A. O'Shaughnessy, Secretary; (952) 698-0959; fax (952) 698-0958; info@iaoshaughnessyfdn.org

Internet: http://www.iaoshaughnessyfdn.org/guidelines.htm

Sponsor: I.A. O'Shaughnessy Foundation

2001 Killebrew Drive, Suite 120

Bloomington, MN 55425

Ian Hague Perl 6 Development Grants   972

In May 2008 The Perl Foundation (TPF) received an unprecedented gift from Ian Hague, a finance executive in New York. The amount of the gift was $200,000 and was given to TPF to support Perl 6 development. Roughly half of the donation would be used to develop TPF's own capabilities to further search for Perl 6 support, and the balance would be used to directly and indirectly support developers working on Perl 6. The nominal maximum monthly payment is $5,000 for full-time work on the grant. This amount is not changed based on changes to the schedule of the grant once the grant is in process. Payments for varying levels of part-time work will be pro-rated against this nominal amount.

Requirements: Grants will be made to projects which obviously and concretely advance the completion of a Perl 6 implementation. Other Perl 6 projects, while potentially very worthwhile, are not the focus of Hague grants. The main goal is the release of a Perl 6 implementation, so critical path elements have preference. In order to demonstrate the criticality of your grant, supporting documentation of a complete project milestone list for your implementation will be very useful. Obviously, grants that support well-documented and well planned implementations have preference.

Restrictions: Residents and nationals of countries that are prohibited by U.S. law from engaging in commerce, are ineligible to participate.

Geographic Focus: All States

Amount of Grant: Up to 15,000 USD

Contact: Richard Dice, President; rdice@perlfoundation.org

Internet: http://www.perlfoundation.org/ian_hague_perl_6_development_grants

Sponsor: Perl Foundation

6832 Mulderstraat

Grand Ledge, MI 48837

IBM Community Development Grants   973

IBM's philanthropic resources are allocated to specific projects and programs that fit within our targeted areas of interest. IBM realizes the power and importance of education. Wherever IBM does business around the globe, the Corporation forms connections to communities and supports a range of civic and nonprofit activities that help those in need through its Community Development grants. In all of its efforts, the Corporation demonstrates how technology can enrich and expand access to services and assistance. Nonprofit organizations wishing to submit unsolicited proposals to IBM should make an initial inquiry in the form of a two-page letter. In the event that the proposal is of interest to IBM, additional information will be requested. The letter should include the following information: a brief statement fully describing the mission of the organization, the amount of money requested, and the purpose of the contribution; a description of the problem you wish to address, the solution you propose, and how IBM technology, and IBM volunteers, if appropriate, will be incorporated; proposed project budget with all other anticipated sources of income; plans to measure and evaluate program results; and the name, address and telephone number of the project contact person.

Requirements: IBM only considers requests submitted by organizations which have a tax-exempt classification under Sections 170(c) or 501(c)3 of the U.S. Internal Revenue Code. Priority is assigned to requests involving IBM technology or the volunteer efforts of its employees. In making a grant decision, they also consider what other types of IBM support (Matching Grants, Fund for Community Service, United Way) an organization may already be receiving. Videotapes and other supplemental materials are strongly discouraged at the initial stage of application.

Restrictions: IBM does not make equipment donations or grants from corporate philanthropic funds to: individuals, political, labor, religious, or fraternal organizations or sports groups; fund raising events such as raffles, telethons, walk-a-thons or auctions; capital campaigns, construction and renovation projects; chairs, endowments or scholarships sponsored by academic or nonprofit institutions; special events such as conferences, symposia or sports competitions; or, organizations that advocate, support, or practice activities inconsistent with IBM's non-discrimination policies, whether based on race, color, religion, gender, gender identity or expression, sexual orientation, national origin, disability, age or status as a protected veteran.

Geographic Focus: All States

Contact: Ann Cramer, Director; (404) 238-6660; fax (404) 238-6138; acramer@us.ibm.com or alfredat@us.ibm.com

Internet: http://www.ibm.com/ibm/ibmgives/grant/index.shtml

Sponsor: IBM Corporation

4111 Northside Parkway NW

Atlanta, GA 30327-3098

Icahn Family Foundation Grants   974

Established in 1996, the Foundation awards grants in primarily for education, higher education, and medical schools. Areas of interest include arts, children and youth services, and education. Of particular interest are elementary and secondary education, as well as education reform. There are no application forms or deadlines with which to adhere, and organizations interested in appealing for funding should submit a copy of their IRS Determination Letter, a detailed description of the project, and the amount of funding requested.

Geographic Focus: New Jersey, New York

Amount of Grant: Up to 500,000 USD

Samples: Princeton University (Princeton, NJ)—for Carl C. Icahn Laboratory for Genomics, $3,650,000; Mount Sinai School of Medicine of New York University (New York, NY)—for medical research, $1,010,000.
Contact: Gail Golder-Icahn; (212) 702-4300; fax (212) 750-5815
Sponsor: Icahn Family Foundation
767 Fifth Avenue, 47th Floor
New York, NY 10153

Idaho Power Company Corporate Contributions   975

The company awards grants in company operating territories in its areas of interest, including arts and culture, civic and community, education, and health and human services. Types of support include building construction/renovation, capital campaigns, continuing support, equipment, general operating support, matching gifts, scholarships, and sponsorships. The corporate contribution request form is available online. There are no application deadlines.
Requirements: Nonprofits in southern Idaho and eastern Oregon are eligible.
Restrictions: Grants do not support: individuals; loans or investments; churches or religious organizations for purposes of religious advocacy; tickets for contests, raffles, or other prize-oriented activities; organizations that discriminate for any reason, including race, color, religion, creed, age, sex, or national origin; individual school programs or projects with limited participation; fraternal or labor organizations; unrestricted operating funds; special occasion good-will advertising.
Geographic Focus: Idaho, Oregon
Contact: Contribution Program Manager; (208) 388-2200
Internet: http://www.idahopower.com/aboutus/community/corporateContributions.htm
Sponsor: Idaho Power Company
P.O. Box 70
Boise, ID 83707

Ida S. Barter Trust Grants   976

The Ida S. Barter Trust was established in 1953 to support and promote quality educational, human services, and health care programming for underserved populations. Grant requests for general operating support are strongly encouraged. Program support will also be considered. Small, program-related capital expenses may be included in general operating or program requests. The application deadline is April 1, and applicants will be notified of grant decisions before June 30. The majority of grants from the Barter Trust are 1 year in duration. On occasion, multi-year support is awarded.
Geographic Focus: Massachusetts
Date(s) Application is Due: Apr 1
Contact: Michealle Larkins; (866) 778-6859; michealle.larkins@baml.com
Internet: https://www.bankofamerica.com/philanthropic/fn_search.action
Sponsor: Ida S. Barter Trust
225 Franklin Street, 4th Floor, MA1-225-04-02
Boston, MA 02110

Iddings Foundation   977

Grants are given to Ohio nonprofits for operating budget support, capital improvements, upper-class collegiate scholarships to designated institutions, expansion of programs, and equipment in the areas of physical and mental health; education; culture and the environment; community welfare; and human services. Types of support include challenge/matching grants, equipment acquisition, demonstration grants, development grants, seed grants, annual campaigns, conferences and seminars, publication, and scholarship funds. and project grants. Proposals are reviewed quarterly; the distribution committee meets the month following the application deadline date.
Requirements: Applicants must be Ohio-based, tax-exempt organizations whose purpose is to improve the community environment and lives of the citizens, and whose primary focus is on the greater Dayton area.
Restrictions: Grants are not made to individuals or to organizations outside Ohio. Additionally, there will be no endowment support.
Geographic Focus: Ohio
Date(s) Application is Due: Mar 1; Jun 1; Sep 1; Nov 1
Amount of Grant: 500 - 50,000 USD
Samples: AIDS Foundation of Miami Valley (OH)—for staff support over two years, $19,125; Miami Valley Literacy Council (OH)—for salary support of a curriculum director, $5000.
Contact: Maribeth Graham; (937) 224-1773; fax (937) 224-1871
Sponsor: Iddings Benevolent Trust
Ketting Tower, Suite 1620
Dayton, OH 45423

IDEM Section 319(h) Nonpoint Source Program Grants   978

This program funds projects that will work on a watershed level to reduce nonpoint source pollution in Indiana's lakes, rivers, and streams. Nonpoint source pollution does not come from a pipe. It results when water (rain or snowmelt) moves across land, such as city streets, agricultural fields and residential backyards, and picks up dirt, fertilizers, pesticides, animal wastes, road salt, motor oil and other pollutants. Nonpoint source pollution is also caused by wind, which like rain, can pick up soil particles and deposit them in lakes and streams. These pollutants have harmful effects on drinking water supplies, recreation, fisheries and wildlife. Nonpoint source pollution is the leading cause of water quality problems in Indiana and is responsible for many of the impairments identified on the 303(d) List of Impaired Waterbodies. Funding for selected projects will be provided by Clean Water Act Section 319 grant funds and match is provided by grant recipients and partners.
Requirements: To be considered for funding, the project sponsor (the entity responsible for the project and its overall success), must be one of the following: 1) Municipality; 2) County Government; 3) State Government; 4) Federal Government; 5) College/University; 6) Nonprofit 501(c)3. The program provides funding and technical assistance to groups that work on the watershed level with citizens to develop locally-based solutions to nonpoint source pollution. Specific ways to address nonpoint source water pollution include education/outreach on watershed management, information gathering activities such as conducting watershed inventories and water quality assessments for the purpose of developing comprehensive watershed management plans and implementing those plans, including implementation of best management practices that directly reduce sources of nonpoint source pollution. IDEM provides sixty percent (60%) of an approved project's total cost with Section 319 funds. A grant recipient must provide the remaining forty percent (40%) of the total project cost as match. Match may be in-kind services or cash. Match cannot come from any federal funding sources. Guidelines and application forms are available for download at the website. Do not use forms from previous years - they will not be accepted by IDEM.
Restrictions: The following is a list of activities that cannot be funded with Section 319 funds and cannot be counted as matching funds for a Section 319 grant: Permit fees; Food for meetings or other events; Purchase of agricultural equipment, or other large pieces of equipment (equipment modifications and leasing are allowable); Purchase of land or land easements (these activities can be counted as matching funds in some cases); Any project which is directed at water quantity rather than water quality, such as dredging, drainage, or flood control; Any practices, equipment, or supplies used to fulfill the requirements of any federal permit (NPDES permit, Section 401 Water Quality Certification, permits from the U.S. Army Corps of Engineers, as examples) or to comply with IDEM's Confined Feeding Operation rule or permit requirements, or to meet enforcement requirements; Wetland mitigation sites; Incentive payments or yield losses; Nonpoint source best management practices not sanctioned by IDEM or not sanctioned by a partner agency of IDEM; Practices not installed in accordance with standards and specifications developed by NRCS, IDNR or other recognized standards; Office furniture; Sales tax. Additionally, the following will not be funded by this grant program: Septic system pump outs, repairs, rehabilitations, or demonstrations of alternative septic systems; Projects whose sole purpose is data collection, research, demonstration of best management practices, or education/outreach. However, these activities may be incorporated as elements into a proposal that meets one of the three priorities.
Geographic Focus: Indiana
Date(s) Application is Due: Sep 1
Contact: Laura Bieberich, Team Leader; (317) 233-1863
Internet: http://www.in.gov/idem/resources/grants_loans/319h/index.html
Sponsor: Indiana Department of Environmental Management
Indiana Government Center North, 100 N Senate Avenue, 50-01
Indianapolis, IN 46204-2251

IEDC Industrial Development Grant Fund (IDGF)   979

The IED.C. provides financial support for infrastructure improvements in conjunction with projects creating jobs and generating capital investment in Indiana. This grant provides money to local governments for off-site infrastructure projects associated with an expansion of an existing Indiana company or the location of a new facility in Indiana. State funding through the IDGF program must be matched by a combination of local government and company financial support. The grant may be awarded to communities or other eligible applicants who have a commitment letter from representatives of the affected industry/industries indicating their plans to locate or expand a facility. Applicants will be reviewed based on the number and quality of jobs being created, the community's economic need, a local match of funding and capital investment being made by the company. Typically this grant does not exceed 50% of the total project costs.

Requirements: Eligible applicants include the following entities: City; Town; County; Special taxing district; An economic development commission; Nonprofit corporation; Corporation established under I.C. 23-17 for the purpose of distributing water for domestic and industrial use; Regional water, sewage, or solid waste district; Conservancy district that includes in its purpose the distribution of domestic water or the collection and treatment of waste. Projects which may qualify include: (1) Construction of airports, airport facilities, and tourist attractions; (2) Construction, extension, or completion of: (a) Sanitary sewer lines, storm sewers, and other related drainage facilities; (b) Waterlines; (c) Roads and storms; (d) Sidewalks; (e) Rail spurs and sidings; and (f) Information and high technology infrastructure; (3) Leasing, purchase, construction, repair, and rehabilitation of property, both real and personal; and (4) Preparation of surveys, plans, and specifications for the construction of publicly owned and operated facilities, utilities, and services.

Restrictions: Funds are limited to existing Indiana companies or the location of a new facility in Indiana.

Geographic Focus: Indiana
Contact: Charlie Sparks; (317) 233-5122; fax (317) 232-4146; csparks@iedc.in.gov
Internet: http://www.in.gov/iedc/incentives/idgf.html
Sponsor: Indiana Economic Development Corporation
1 North Capitol Avenue, Suite 700
Indianapolis, IN 46204

IEDC International Trade Show Assistance Program   980

The program provides financial assistance for small Indiana businesses to participate in international trade shows. TSAP is designed to promote Indiana exports by encouraging companies to explore overseas markets. The maximum amount of funding is $5,000, or 100% of exhibit space rental fees, whichever is less. The State Fiscal Year runs from July 1 through June 30.

Requirements: Small businesses eligible for this program are to be defined as a manufacturing concern with worldwide employment of 500 employees or less within the preceding 12 months (this includes parent companies, subsidiaries, divisions of, etc.). Firms must be prequalified with the IED.C. in order to receive reimbursement. To receive this assistance, firms must: promote their company's products at an applicable trade show, exposition or fair; have an official company representative attend the show; have less than 500 employees worldwide; manufacture at least 51% of their product in Indiana; provide market research for applicable market. NOTE: Full stay at the show is required. Those companies not exhibiting ALL days of the show are disqualified from receiving funding from TSAP. See the website for detailed guidelines and application instruction.

Restrictions: Funding for trade shows is limited to one (1) show per company per fiscal year. Also, companies may not receive funding to attend the same show every year and may not exhibit by catalog only.

Geographic Focus: Indiana
Amount of Grant: Up to 5,000 USD
Contact: Steve Akard, Director, Office of International Development; (317) 234-2083; fax (317) 232-4146; sakard@iedc.in.gov
Internet: http://www.in.gov/iedc/incentives/tradeShow.html
Sponsor: Indiana Economic Development Corporation
1 North Capitol Avenue, Suite 700
Indianapolis, IN 46204

IEDC Skills Enhancement Fund (SEF)   981

The fund is a tool to encourage companies to invest in their existing workforce and train new employees. SEF provides reimbursement for eligible training expenses over a two year term. Companies may reapply for additional SEF Funds after their initial two year term. The maximum amount awarded through the SEF program typically does not exceed 50% of a company's training budget.

Requirements: Companies may claim reimbursement for training expenses that result in improved basic or transferable skills. Company specific and quality assurance training expenses are also eligible.

Restrictions: IED.C. typically does not provide reimbursement for training that is required by law. Those businesses that receive SEF training assistance must commit to continue their operations at the location where the SEF training assistance is provided for at least five years after the date that the training grant is completed.

Geographic Focus: Indiana
Contact: Karen Northrop, Business Development Specialist; (317) 232-0160; fax (317) 232-4146; knorthrop@iedc.in.gov
Internet: http://www.in.gov/iedc/incentives/sef.html

Sponsor: Indiana Economic Development Corporation
1 North Capitol Avenue, Suite 700
Indianapolis, IN 46204

Illinois Arts Council Community Arts Access Grants   982

The Illinois Arts Council Community Arts Access provides the opportunity for local arts agencies to distribute state funds in their own service areas according to their assessment of local needs. The Illinois Arts Council provides technical assistance and consultation to organizations seeking assistance in ADA Compliance.

Geographic Focus: Illinois
Contact: Jennifer Armstrong, Program Director; (312) 814-4993; fax (312) 814-1471; j.armstrong@illinois.gov
Internet: http://www.arts.illinois.gov./grants-programs/funding-programs/community-arts-access
Sponsor: Illinois Arts Council
100 W Randolph Street, Suite 10-500
Chicago, IL 60601-3230

Illinois Arts Council Local Arts Agencies Program Grants   983

Program Grant funds provide artistic and operational support to established organizations that make a significant local, regional, or statewide impact on the quality of life in Illinois. Local Arts Agencies Program Grants are designed to provide project and/or operational support to Illinois local arts agencies (defined as a community-based organization or an agency of city or county government that supports the growth and development of all of the arts in the identified area of service). Available funding ranges from $500 to $30,000, depending upon the applicant organization's overall past operating budget.

Requirements: Nonprofit organizations applying for funding must be chartered in the state of Illinois.

Geographic Focus: Illinois
Date(s) Application is Due: Mar 15
Amount of Grant: 500 - 30,000 USD
Contact: Jennifer Armstrong, Director; (312) 814-4993; fax (312) 814-1471; j.armstrong@illinois.gov
Internet: http://www.arts.illinois.gov/Program%20Grant%3A%20Local%20Arts%20Agencies
Sponsor: Illinois Arts Council
100 W Randolph Street, Suite 10-500
Chicago, IL 60601-3230

Illinois Arts Council Multidisciplinary Program Grants   984

Program Grant funds provide artistic and operational support to established organizations that make a significant local, regional, or statewide impact on the quality of life in Illinois. Multidisciplinary Program Grants are designed to support organizations offering programming that involves or fuses two or more distinct artistic disciplines. Programs should be distinct, not supplemental in nature, and must integrally involve each of the participating art forms rather than be in service to a single art form. Grants are available for ongoing programming, new projects, staff, production costs, marketing, and audience development. Available funding ranges from $500 to $30,000, depending upon the applicant organization's overall past operating budget.

Requirements: Nonprofit organizations applying for funding must be chartered in the state of Illinois.

Geographic Focus: Illinois
Date(s) Application is Due: Mar 15
Amount of Grant: 500 - 30,000 USD
Contact: Encarnacion Teruel, Director; (312) 814-6753; fax (312) 814-1471; encarnacion.teruel@illinois.gov
Internet: http://www.arts.illinois.gov/Program%20Grant%3A%20Multi-Disciplinary
Sponsor: Illinois Arts Council
100 W Randolph Street, Suite 10-500
Chicago, IL 60601-3230

Illinois Arts Council Music Program Grants   985

Program Grant funds provide artistic and operational support to established organizations that make a significant local, regional, or statewide impact on the quality of life in Illinois. Music Program Grants are designed to support professional, regional, and community companies including opera, vocal ensembles, orchestras, chamber music, jazz ensembles, contemporary and early music groups, and concert and wind bands. Available funding ranges from $500 to $30,000, depending upon the applicant organization's overall past operating budget.

Requirements: Nonprofit organizations applying for funding must be chartered in the state of Illinois.
Geographic Focus: Illinois
Date(s) Application is Due: Mar 15
Amount of Grant: 500 - 30,000 USD
Contact: Walter Buford, Director; (312) 814-4992; fax (312) 814-1471; walter. buford@illinois.gov
Internet: http://www.arts.illinois.gov/Program%20Grant%3A%20Music
Sponsor: Illinois Arts Council
100 W Randolph Street, Suite 10-500
Chicago, IL 60601-3230

Illinois Arts Council Partners in Excellence Grants   986
Recognizing that Illinois is the home of creative arts institutions of regional and national significance; the Illinois Arts Council has implemented the Partners in Excellence Program (PIE). The PIE Program provides general operating support to designated organizations of scale and significance in all regions of the state. Check the listing of designated organizations at the website before making application.
Requirements: Only designated organizations in Illinois can apply.
Geographic Focus: Illinois
Date(s) Application is Due: Mar 15
Contact: Walter Buford, Program Director; (312) 814-4992; fax (312) 814-1471; walter.buford@illinois.gov
Internet: http://www.arts.illinois.gov./grants-programs/funding-programs/partners-excellence
Sponsor: Illinois Arts Council
100 W Randolph Street, Suite 10-500
Chicago, IL 60601-3230

Illinois Arts Council Theater Program Grants   987
Program Grant funds provide artistic and operational support to established organizations that make a significant local, regional, or statewide impact on the quality of life in Illinois. Theatre Program grants are designed to support professional, regional, and community companies, including experimental, street, and children's theater. This includes experimental, musical theatre, street performance, and theatre for young audiences. Available funding ranges from $500 to $30,000, depending upon the applicant organization's overall past operating budget.
Requirements: Nonprofit organizations applying for funding must be chartered in the state of Illinois.
Geographic Focus: Illinois
Date(s) Application is Due: Mar 15
Amount of Grant: 500 - 30,000 USD
Contact: Walter Buford, Director; (312) 814-4992; fax (312) 814-1471; walter. buford@illinois.gov
Internet: http://www.arts.illinois.gov/Program%20Grant%3A%20Theater
Sponsor: Illinois Arts Council
100 W Randolph Street, Suite 10-500
Chicago, IL 60601-3230

Illinois Humanities Council Community General Support Grants   988
The Illinois Humanities Council (IHC) funds public humanities programs for Illinois audiences that are shaped by and significantly involve humanities scholars and/or other community experts. The IHC's priority is to support programs developed by, for, or aimed at reaching new or historically neglected audiences. Applications are invited from organizations that serve these communities and strongly encourage other applicants to extend their proposed programs to include such audiences. General Support Grants have a maximum of $5,000 and can support programming and activities in general, as opposed to targeting funds only for a specific project.
Requirements: All nonprofit organizations serving Illinois audiences are eligible. Organizations need to demonstrate that they are primarily a humanities organization; engagement with the humanities must be evident in their mission and in their programs and activities. All project grant applications must: be rooted in one or more of the humanities disciplines; integrally feature humanities experts in all phases or the project; be public; be sponsored by a nonprofit organization; and comply with federal debarment and nondiscrimination statutes. Applications for any of the grant categories are welcome at each deadline. If you plan to apply for a grant, contact a program officer at least one month ahead of the application deadline to discuss your project. Additionally, the IHC conducts grant and resource workshops several times a year throughout the state. Workshops are held at the offices in Chicago

on the third Fridays of May and November and in the fall and spring in central, eastern, western and southern Illinois communities. Notifications will be sent approximately 8 weeks after the deadline.
Restrictions: Organizations that have run humanities projects but whose primary purpose involves something other than the public humanities are not eligible for general support grants. General Support grants are not intended for new start-up organizations. The council does not fund: advocacy or social action; projects for fund raising purposes; construction or restoration costs; purchase of permanent equipment; library or museum acquisitions; individuals, research, or other endeavors intended primarily for the scholarly community; curriculum development or revisions; academic courses for credit; performing arts as ends in themselves; projects directed primarily to children or students in formal school settings; more than 50 percent of total project costs; indirect costs of sponsoring organizations; food and beverage costs for audiences or alcoholic beverages; or expenses incurred or paid out before an IHC grant award is made.
Geographic Focus: Illinois
Date(s) Application is Due: Jan 15; Apr 15; Jul 15; Oct 15
Amount of Grant: Up to 5,000 USD
Contact: Ryan M. Lewis; rml@prairie.org or ihc@prairie.org
Internet: http://www.prairie.org/programs/community-grants-program
Sponsor: Illinois Humanities Council
17 North State Street, Suite 1400
Chicago, IL 60602-3298

Illinois Tool Works Foundation Grants   989
The corporate foundation awards grants in areas of company operations, with emphasis on Chicago, Ilinoise. Grants support organizations that focus on: education, the arts, health and human services, social welfare, housing, environmental and youth issues. The Foundation contributes financial support to not-for-profit organizations through two major giving programs: a direct-giving program and a three-for-one matching gift program for employees.
Requirements: Not-for-profit organizations are eligible to apply.
Geographic Focus: All States
Amount of Grant: 5,000 - 1,000,000 USD
Contact: Mary Ann Mallahan, Secretary; (847) 724-7500; fax (847) 657-4261; mmallahan@itw.com
Internet: http://www.itwinc.com/itw/corporate_citizenship/itw_foundation
Sponsor: Illinois Tool Works Foundation
3600 West Lake Avenue
Glenview, IL 60026

IMLS Grants to State Library Administrative Agencies   990
Through the program, the Institute of Museum and Library Services provides funds to State Library Administrative Agencies (SLAAs) using a population-based formula. State libraries may use the appropriation to support statewide initiatives and services. They also may distribute the funds through subgrant competitions or cooperative agreements to public, academic, research, school, and special libraries in their state.
Requirements: State library administrative agencies located in one of the 50 states of the United States, the District of Columbia, the Commonwealth of Puerto Rico, Guam, American Samoa, the U.S. Virgin Islands, the Commonwealth of the Northern Mariana Islands, the Republic of the Marshall Islands, the Federated States of Micronesia, and the Republic of Palau are eligible to submit five-year plans.
Geographic Focus: All States
Date(s) Application is Due: Apr 1
Amount of Grant: 1 - 2,000,000 USD
Contact: Laurie C. Brooks; (202) 653-4650; stateprograms@imls.gov
Internet: http://www.imls.gov/programs/programs.shtm
Sponsor: Institute of Museum and Library Services
1800 M Street NW, 9th Floor
Washington, D.C. 20036-5802

Imperial Charitable Trust Grants   991
Imperial Charitable Trust Grants are primarily offered to nonprofits and schools in Virginia and West Virginia. The Foundation's primary fields of interest include: education; elementary and secondary education; and higher education. Support typically comes in the area of general operations funding. An formal application is required, though applicants should begin by contacting the Trust with a letter describing the program and specific budgetary needs. Grants range up to $18,000, and there are no annual deadlines.
Restrictions: Grants are not given to individuals.
Geographic Focus: Virginia, West Virginia

Amount of Grant: Up to 18,000 USD

Samples: Academy of Fine Arts, Lynchburg, Virginia, $5,000 - general operations; Corporation for Jefferson's Poplar Forest, Forest, Virginia, $5,000 - general operations; Virginia Foundation for Independent Colleges, Richmond, Virginia, $16,000 - general operations.

Contact: C. Lynch Christian, III, Trustee; (434) 845-5918

Sponsor: Imperial Charitable Trust

P.O. Box 638

Lynchburg, VA 24505-0638

Inasmuch Foundation Grants   **992**

The foundation was established for charitable, scientific, and educational projects primarily in Oklahoma; however, select projects in Colorado Springs, CO, also are supported. The foundation consistently provides funding and support to educational, health and human service, cultural, artistic, historical, and environmental concerns. This funding is not available to individuals, but is available to formal organizations seeking capital and support for existing programs that meet the emerging needs of the community. In order to initiate a proposal, submit a one-page letter of inquiry by the listed application deadlines. Application information is available online.

Restrictions: The foundation does not fund endowments or scholarships.

Geographic Focus: Colorado, Oklahoma

Date(s) Application is Due: Feb 15; Aug 15

Samples: Colorado College (Colorado Springs, CO)—to construct a facility for arts education and performances, $4 million.

Contact: Program Contact; (405) 604-5292

Internet: http://www.inasmuchfoundation.org/application.html

Sponsor: Inasmuch Foundation

210 Park Avenue, Suite 3150

Oklahoma City, OK 73102

Independence Community Foundation Education, Culture & Arts   **993**
  Grant

The Foundation recognizes that cultural and educational institutions create positive change in communities. The Foundation provides program and project support to institutions that seek to bolster economic and social development, and act as stabilizing forces in their communities. Interested applicants should submit a letter of inquiry. Application information is available online.

Requirements: Program or project grants are made on a competitive basis to nonprofit organizations located within New York City, Nassau, Suffolk and Westchester counties in New York, and Essex, Bergen, Union, Hudson, Middlesex, Ocean, and Monmouth counties in New Jersey.

Restrictions: Funding is not available to support individual artists.

Geographic Focus: New Jersey, New York

Date(s) Application is Due: Mar 30; Sep 30

Contact: Program Contact; (718) 722-2300; inquiries@icfny.org

Internet: http://www.icfny.org/education_arts.html

Sponsor: Independence Community Foundation

182 Atlantic Avenue

Brooklyn, NY 11201

Independence Foundation Grants   **994**

The foundation awards grants to Philadelphia nonprofit organizations in its areas of interest, including community-based nurse managed health care, health promotion, family planning, and comprehensive health care services where issues of quality, access, and cost are considered; arts and culture; legal aid; and assistance to the disadvantaged. Types of support include development grants, endowments, general operating grants, professorships, program development grants, seed money grants, and scholarships. A brief letter outlining a proposed project is a prerequisite to a formal application.

Requirements: 501(c)3 tax-exempt organizations serving Philadelphia and the surrounding counties including Bucks, Chester, Delaware, and Montgomery are eligible.

Restrictions: Grants will not be made to individuals or for building and development funds or to support travel, research, or publications.

Geographic Focus: Pennsylvania

Amount of Grant: 1,000 - 100,000 USD

Contact: Grants Administrator; (215) 985-4009; fax (215) 985-3989

Internet: http://www.independencefoundation.org

Sponsor: Independence Foundation

200 S Broad Street, Suite 1101

Philadelphia, PA 19102

Indiana 21st Century Research and Technology Fund Awards   **995**

The Indiana 21st Century Research and Technology Fund of the Indiana Economic Development Corporation (IEDC) is open to proposals from all public and private entities for technology-based commercialization activities encompassing science/technology creation, innovation, and transfer intended to have commercial impacts. The fund intends to increase the numbers, and rates of development, of new and expanding technology-based companies by funding promising opportunities that, in some cases, the financial markets might find too risky. The Fund makes awards in two broad categories: Science and Technology Commercialization and Centers of Excellence. In addition, the Fund provides cost-share on behalf of Federal proposals submitted by Indiana-based entities. Generally awards are made in multiples of $50,000 up to $2,000,000. Support for awards in excess of $2,000,000 will be rare.

Requirements: The IED.C. defines a technology-based company as one that is involved in transferring advanced technology into products, developing technologies with the near-term intention of creating products, or using new or advanced technologies in its design, development, and/or manufacturing of products. The Fund emphasizes the creation of academic-sector - commercial-sector partnerships. In making awards, the Fund expects significant leverage from the partners involved in the projects. Important: before applying, contact Fund staff (email preferred) to discuss your interest in submitting a proposal and to discuss your technology and commercialization goals. While not a review criterion, the fund encourages the inclusion of interns from any academic institution, or participating commercial sector partner, in order to increase project-related involvement of students at all levels.

Restrictions: Only direct costs will be supported. Institutions will not be provided indirect (overhead) cost support. Entities with previous Fund awards that are not current with regard to financial or technical reporting requirements will be disqualified from making new submissions to the Fund. Resubmissions of previously declined proposals will be considered only if substantive changes have been made to the proposal. Fund staff will determine whether to review resubmissions.

Geographic Focus: Indiana

Samples: 2K Corporation: $400,000 - Commercialization of a Neutron Based Explosives Detection Device (Car Bomb Detection). Arxan Technologies, Inc.: $1,944,096 - Protecting Critical IP in the 21st Century: Advancing Anti-Tamper Technologies. BioVitesse Inc.: $1,300,000 - Rapid Detection and Identification of Live Bacteria. CIS LLC: $1,075,000 - Commercialization of Satellite Radio for Cell Phone Applications.

Contact: Carla Phelps; (317) 233- 4336; cphelps@21fund.org

Internet: http://www.21fund.org/

Sponsor: Indiana Economic Development Corporation

1 North Capitol Avenue, Suite 900

Indianapolis, IN 46204

Indiana Arts Commission Organization Support Grants   **996**

The Indiana Arts Commission Regional Initiative Grant (RIG) Arts Operating Support I and II program will provide annual operating support for the ongoing artistic and administrative functions of eligible arts organizations that provide quality arts activities with special attention to underserved communities (an underserved community is one in which individuals lack access to arts programs due to geography, economic conditions, ethnic background, disability, or age). Eligible arts organizations are organizations for which providing arts activities or services is the primary mission and purpose.

Requirements: AOS I and AOS II applicants are required to submit a Notice of Intent to Apply form for eligibility by January 9.

Restrictions: Funding will not be awarded for the following: organizations whose primary purpose is not arts-based; organizations whose primary purpose is educational or instructional (e.g., schools, universities, colleges, etc.); entities that receive state operating support directly from the general assembly; any organization whose sole or primary purpose is to fund raise (e.g., "friends of" groups, foundations, etc.) for an otherwise ineligible organization; any organization with an outstanding Final Grant Report due to the Regional Arts Partner/Indiana Arts Commission; or an organization may not apply for IAC-based funding from both the IAC and a Regional Arts Partner or IAC administered Regional Initiative Grant program in the same fiscal year.

Geographic Focus: Indiana

Contact: Sarah Fronczek, Program Manager; (317) 232-1274 or (317) 232-1268; fax (317) 232-5595; sfronczek@iac.in.gov

Internet: http://www.in.gov/arts/regionalinitiativegrant.htm

Sponsor: Indiana Arts Commission

100 North Senate Avenue, Room N505

Indianapolis, IN 46204

Indianapolis Preservation Grants 997

Grants are available for professional architectural and engineering feasibility studies and other preservation consulting services, as well as organizational development and fundraising projects. The foundation makes the preservation grants on a four-to-one matching basis, with four dollars from us matching each local cash dollar. Grants will fund 80% of the total project cost up to $2,000.

Requirements: Nonprofit community preservation organizations and historic neighborhood foundations in Marion County are eligible to apply.

Restrictions: The grants may not be used for physical restoration work.

Geographic Focus: Indiana

Amount of Grant: Up to 2,000 USD

Contact: Chad Lethig, Indianapolis Preservation Coordinator, Central Regional Office; (317) 639-4534; fax (317) 639-6720; flip@historiclandmarks.org

Internet: http://www.historiclandmarks.org/help/grants.html

Sponsor: Historic Landmarks Foundation of Indiana

340 W Michigan Street

Indianapolis, IN 46202

Indiana Preservation Grants 998

Grants are available for professional architectural and engineering feasibility studies and other preservation consulting services, as well as organizational development and fundraising projects. The foundation makes the preservation Grants on a four-to-one matching basis, with four dollars from us matching each local cash dollar. Grants will fund 80% of the total project cost up to $2,500.

Requirements: Nonprofit organizations in Indiana are eligible to apply. Contact the Historic Landmarks regional office that serves your community (see website for list of regional offices or contact the state headquarters office) for guidelines and forms.

Restrictions: The grants may not be used for physical restoration work.

Geographic Focus: Indiana

Amount of Grant: Up to 2,500 USD

Samples: Clinton, IN (Vermillion County) $3,040 grant for a feasibility study led to a $700,000 restoration of the town's 1905 passenger depot.

Contact: Carla Jones, Receptionist, State Headquarters; (317) 639-4534; fax (317) 639-6734; info@historiclandmarks.org

Internet: http://www.historiclandmarks.org/help/grants.html

Sponsor: Historic Landmarks Foundation of Indiana

340 W Michigan Street

Indianapolis, IN 46202

Indiana Recycling Grants 999

Indiana Recycling Grants are designed to help start or expand source reduction, recycling, and recycling education programs in Indiana. Funds are available for the costs associated with establishing curbside recycling, drop-off recycling, recycling processing, and yard waste collection and management. These grants are intended to create sustainable projects with no state funding for ongoing program costs.

Requirements: A matching contribution of 50% of the total project cost is required. Solid waste management districts, counties, municipalities, townships, schools, and nonprofit organizations with 501(c) status are eligible. Detailed guidelines, application and forms are available at the website.

Restrictions: Limited to Indiana only.

Geographic Focus: Indiana

Date(s) Application is Due: May 25; Sep 28

Contact: Kristin Brier; (800) 988-7901; kbrier@idem.in.gov

Internet: http://www.in.gov/recycle/funding/irg.html

Sponsor: Indiana Department of Environmental Management

100 North Senate Avenue, MC 64-01

Indianapolis, IN 46204-2251

Inland Foundation Inc Grants 1000

Nonprofit organizations located in communities where Inland Container has facilities and employees are invited to apply for grants in the areas of community services, education, art and culture, and health. Types of support include employee-related scholarships, annual campaigns, continuing support, general operating budgets, and special projects. Proposals should consist of a brief letter that includes a description of the sponsoring organization and project; statement of the importance of the project and why it meets the foundation's guidelines; geographical area served by the project; total funds needed and the amount requested from the foundation; other sources of income and funding; and proof of the organization's tax-exempt status. Grant proposals are accepted throughout the year.

Requirements: Grants are awarded to nonprofits in plant locations, including Fort Smith, AR; Buena Park, El Centro, Los Angeles, Neward, Santa Fe Springs, and Tracy, CA; Denver, CO; Orlando, FL; Rome, GA; Chicago, IL; Crawfordsville, Evansville, Indianapolis, and Newport, IN; Garden City and Kansas City, KS; Louisville and Maysville, KY; Minden, LA; Minneapolis, MN; Hattiesburg, MS; Saint Louis, MO; Edison and Spotswood, NJ; Middletown, OH; Biglerville, and Hazleton, PA; Vega Alta, Puerto Rico; Lexington and Rock Hill, SC; Elizabethton and New Johnsonville, TN; Dallas, Edinburg, and Orange, TX; and Petersburg, VA.

Restrictions: The foundation does not make grants to individuals, religious organizations for sectarian purposes, or individual professors or departments within universities.

Geographic Focus: All States

Amount of Grant: 1,000 - 30,000 USD

Contact: Evonne Nerren, Secretary/Treasurer; (936) 829-1721

Internet: http://www.templeinland.com

Sponsor: Inland Foundation

303 S Temple Drive

Diboll, TX 75941

Intergrys Corporation Grants 1001

Integrys supports the giving initiatives of Wisconsin Public Service Foundation in Michigan, Minnesota and Wisconsin. Other significant giving by Integrys occurs through programs operated by Peoples Gas and North Shore Gas in Illinois, including the city of Chicago and its 54 suburban communities in northeastern Illinois. Areas of interest include: arts and culture; education (all levels); human services and health; community and neighborhood development; and the environment. Employee volunteers allow staff to give back to the neighborhoods they cherish. Matching funds energize charitable involvement. Categories of giving include health and welfare, civic and community, higher education, and cultural. Most corporate contributions are in the form of unrestricted grants. Types of support include capital grants, endowments, general operating grants, matching gifts, and program grants. Before eligibility is determined, consideration will be given to the background of the organization, the organization's legal status, how the program will benefit the community, whether the organization receives broad community support, the quality of the organization's leadership, and the organization's financial status.

Requirements: Organizations in Illinois, Michigan, Minnesota, and Wisconsin are eligible.

Restrictions: Contributions will not be made to individuals; organizations that discriminate by race, color, creed, or national origin; political organizations or campaigns; organizations whose prime purpose is to influence legislation; religious organizations for religious purposes; agencies owned and operated by local, state, or federal governments; or for trips or tours, or special-occasion or goodwill advertising.

Geographic Focus: Illinois, Michigan, Minnesota, Wisconsin

Amount of Grant: Up to 5,000 USD

Contact: Community Contributions Officer; (312) 240-7516 or (800) 699-1269; fax (312) 240-4389

Internet: http://www.integrysgroup.com/corporate/corporate_giving.aspx

Sponsor: Intergrys Corporation

130 E Randolph Drive, 18th Floor

Chicago, IL 60601

Iosco County Community Foundation Common Grants 1002

Iosco County Community Foundation Common Grants are awarded from the Iosco County Community Needs Fund to non-profits that serve Iosco County. Grants are used to fund programs and projects that benefit this geographical area. Specific funding for programs benefiting health for youth under the age of 18 and senior citizens over the age of 65 is awarded from the Iosco County Tobacco Settlement Fund in conjunction with Common Grants. Applicants may submit requests up to a maximum of $3,000 per application cycle unless otherwise indicated. Mini-grants up to $300 are available. The annual deadline for application submission is May 1.

Requirements: IRS 501(c)3 nonprofit organizations, schools, churches (for non-sectarian purposes), cities, townships, and other governmental units serving Iosco County are eligible to apply. An organization may apply each year for a grant.

Restrictions: No program may be funded for more than two (2) consecutive grant cycles or two (2) years, whichever is longer. The Community Foundation will not support the sustained funding of any program. Grants are not given to individuals, except for awards or scholarships from designated donor funds.

Geographic Focus: Michigan

Date(s) Application is Due: May 1

Amount of Grant: Up to 3,000 USD
Samples: AuSable-Oscoda Historical Society, Oscoda, Michigan, $3,000 - J.D. Hawks Historical Photo Album Restoration (2014); Iosco County Sheriff Department, Tawas City, Michigan, $2,500 - Hale Area Citizen's Patrol (2014); Third Level Crisis Intervention Center, Traverse City, Michigan, $2,500 - Northeast Michigan Youth Services Street Outreach Program (2014).
Contact: Barbara Frantz, Executive Director; (989) 354-6881 or (877) 354-6881; fax (989) 356-3319; bfrantz@cfnem.org
Internet: http://www.cfnem.org/ICCF/Common.aspx
Sponsor: Iosco County Community Foundation
111 Water Street, P.O. Box 495
Alpena, MI 49707

Iowa Arts Council Operational Support Grants for Major and Mid-Size Arts Organizations   1003

A limited number of grants are awarded annually for operational support to major and midsize arts organizations providing cultural and managerial excellence on a continuing basis to the citizens of Iowa. Organizations receiving Operational Support grants are required to demonstrate the ability to cash match the award. Application forms will be mailed to organizations on request or on receipt of the required letter of intent. Applicants who are currently in the operating support grant cycle must submit an Interim Application for the second year of funding on or before May 1. Contact program staff for current funding schedule.
Requirements: Organizations must be located and incorporated in Iowa, federally tax-exempt, and must have had an annual cash operating budget of between $50,000 and $250,000 (for midsize) for at least three years before filing an application. Applicant organizations must be unattached to an educational institution, must operate year-round, and must have at least one professional staff member.
Restrictions: Organizations requesting operational support are not eligible to apply for project grants.
Geographic Focus: Iowa
Date(s) Application is Due: May 1
Amount of Grant: 3,000 - 22,000 USD
Contact: Bruce Williams, Program Contact; (515) 281-4406; bruce.williams@iowa.g or bruce.williams@dca.state.ia.us
Internet: http://www.iowaartscouncil.org/funding/overview.shtml
Sponsor: Iowa Arts Council
600 E Locust, Capitol Complex
Des Moines, IA 50319-0290

IREX Kosovo Civil Society Project (KCSP) Grants   1004

The Program is aimed at assisting Kosovo's Nongovernmental Organization (NGO) community in becoming a truly indigenous, viable sector that plays an important role in representing and serving Kosovo's diverse citizenry and shaping public policy. IREX works with individual NGOs and coalitions to strengthen their capacity to advocate for public policy issues while progressing toward forming an inclusive, transparent, and credible Kosovo network of NGOs. In partnership with the Advocacy Training and Resource Center (ATRC), the Program provides grants to support issue-specific campaigns, coalition-building and training on effective advocacy, coalition-building techniques, and public relations through the media.
Geographic Focus: All States
Samples: Building Partnerships for Economic Development—this project promotes partnerships among local government, the NGO sector and the business community in order to attract more foreign investment in the Gjakove region, $100,000; Municipal Court as a Place of Justice—the project provides space for Kosovar nongovernmental organizations to participate with policymakers in the creation of future laws related to the status of women in Kosovo, $100,000.
Contact: Officer; (202) 628-8188; fax (202) 628-8189; kcsp@irex.org
Internet: http://www.irex.org/programs/kcsp/index.asp
Sponsor: International Research and Exchanges Board
2121 K Street NW, Suite 700
Washington, D.C. 20037

IREX Russia Civil Society Support Program (CSSP) Grants   1005

The Program is aimed at strengthening the nongovernmental organization (NGO) sector in Russia, particularly in the Russian Far East. CSSP promotes an environment where the government actively reaches out to involve NGOs in policy development and, in turn, NGOs demonstrate the skills and capacity to advocate their positions in a constructive manner. Small grants support NGO coalitions and alliances for advocacy projects benefiting their constituents. To date, regional and inter-regional coalitions have been initiated to advocate for housing rights, welfare of disabled children, education reform, and environmental protection in twenty regions of the Russian Federation.
Geographic Focus: All States, Russia
Contact: Program Officer; (202) 628-8188; fax (202) 628-8189; csd@irex.org
Internet: http://www.irex.org/programs/cssp/index.asp
Sponsor: International Research and Exchanges Board
2121 K Street NW, Suite 700
Washington, D.C. 20037

IREX Small Grant Fund for Civil Society Projects in Africa and Asia   1006

IREX will provide a select number of grants of up to US$10,000 to local private, nongovernmental institutions in Africa and Asia. Proposed project must focus on strengthening civic engagement in one of the following ways: institutional development of civil society organizations, to include support for training and technical assistance. Preference given to organizations and/or initiatives focused on advocacy, transparency and accountability, anti-corruption and/or citizen participation; women's empowerment initiatives that promote the full participation of women in all levels of economic, political and /or social life (special use of technology is encouraged); and vocational training or educational programs addressing child labor or trafficking, child soldiers, HIV/AIDS, learning disabilities or special needs. In lieu of a formal application or proposal, IREX requests that interested organizations submit a brief letter of inquiry, of no more than two pages, to help determine whether the proposed project would address IREX's present interests. Inquiry letters will be reviewed on a rolling basis and if they meet current interests, the grant seeker will be asked to submit a formal proposal. Inquiry letters can be sent by mail, fax or email.
Requirements: Applicants must be a private nongovernmental organization based solely in Africa or Asia.
Restrictions: The Program will not fund: grants to individuals; grants for university study, graduate study or research; or grants to attend conferences, trainings or workshops.
Geographic Focus: All States, Algeria, Angola, Benin, Botswana, Burkina Faso, Burundi, Cameroon, Cape Verde, Central African Republic, Chad, Comoros, Congo, Congo, Democratic Republic of, Cote d' Ivoire (Ivory Coast), Djibouti, Egypt, Equatorial Guinea, Eritrea, Ethiopia, Gabon, Gambia, Ghana, Guinea, Guinea-Bissau, Kenya, Lesotho, Liberia, Libya, Madagascar, Malawi, Mali, Mauritania, Mauritius, Morocco, Mozambique, Namibia, Niger, Nigeria, Rwanda, Sao Tome & Principe, Senegal, Seychelles, Sierra Leone, Somalia, South Africa, Sudan, Swaziland
Amount of Grant: Up to 10,000 USD
Contact: Officers; (202) 628-8188; fax (202) 628-8189; sgfcsd@irex.org
Internet: http://www.irex.org/programs/sgf/index.asp
Sponsor: International Research and Exchanges Board
2121 K Street NW, Suite 700
Washington, D.C. 20037

IREX Small Grant Fund for Media Projects in Africa and Asia   1007

IREX will provide a select number of grants of up to US$10,000 to local private, nongovernmental institutions in Africa and Asia. Proposed project must focus on promoting professionalism and independence in media in one of the following ways: journalism training, to include basic reporting skills, environmental reporting, business and economics reporting, investigative reporting, and other specialized reporting skills; media advocacy, to include education on the value of professional media, development of media legislation, community outreach, and training in issues related to free media; and institutional development of media and media-related institutions, to include support for equipment and operational costs. In lieu of a formal application or proposal, IREX requests that interested organizations submit a brief letter of inquiry, of no more than two pages, to help determine whether the proposed project would address IREX's present interests. Inquiry letters will be reviewed on a rolling basis and if they meet current interests, the grant seeker will be asked to submit a formal proposal. Inquiry letters can be sent by mail, fax or email.
Requirements: Applicants must be a private nongovernmental organization based solely in Africa or Asia.
Restrictions: The Program will not fund: grants to individuals; grants for university study, graduate study or research; or grants to attend conferences, trainings or workshops.
Geographic Focus: All States, Algeria, Angola, Benin, Botswana, Burkina Faso, Burundi, Cameroon, Cape Verde, Central African Republic, Chad, Comoros, Congo, Congo, Democratic Republic of, Cote d' Ivoire (Ivory Coast), Djibouti, Egypt, Equatorial Guinea, Eritrea, Ethiopia, Gabon, Gambia, Ghana, Guinea, Guinea-Bissau, Kenya, Lesotho, Liberia, Libya, Madagascar, Malawi, Mali, Mauritania, Mauritius, Morocco, Mozambique,

Namibia, Niger, Nigeria, Rwanda, Sao Tome & Principe, Senegal, Seychelles, Sierra Leone, Somalia, South Africa, Sudan, Swaziland
Amount of Grant: Up to 10,000 USD
Contact: Officers; (202) 628-8188; fax (202) 628-8189; sgfmdd@irex.org
Internet: http://www.irex.org/programs/sgf/index.asp
Sponsor: International Research and Exchanges Board
2121 K Street NW, Suite 700
Washington, D.C. 20037

Irving and Harriet Sands Foundation Grants   1008
The Irving and Harriet Sands Foundation (formerly known as the Sands Family Foundation) was established in 1991 by Irving Sands. Giving is limited primarily in Florida, Boston, Massachusetts, Akron, Ohio, and Seattle, Washington. Specific fields of interest include Jewish agencies and synagogues. There are no specific deadlines or application forms with which to adhere, and applicants should begin by forwarding a narrative request by mail.
Geographic Focus: Florida, Massachusetts, Ohio, Washington
Amount of Grant: Up to 1,000 USD
Samples: Atlantic Street Center, Seattle, Washington, $1,000; Food Lifeline, Shoreline, Washington, $1,000; Dale Turner Family YMCA, Shoreline, Washington, $1,000.
Contact: Richard Sands; (617) 283-0027; richsands1@rich-sands.com
Sponsor: Irving and Harriet Sands Foundation
37 Beverly Road
Arlington, MA 02474

Irving S. Gilmore Foundation Grants   1009
The Irving S. Gilmore Foundation endeavors to develop and to enrich the Greater Kalamazoo community of Michigan and, its residents by supporting the work of nonprofit organizations. The Foundation's funding priorities are: health and well-being; arts; human services; education; community development; culture and humanities. Organizations that are first time Foundation applicants or have not received Foundation funding since 2007 must contact the Foundation at least four weeks prior to an applicable submission deadline.
Requirements: The Foundation supports Kalamazoo County projects, programs, and purposes carried out by charitable institutions, primarily public charities and governmental entities.
Restrictions: Grants are not made to individuals.
Geographic Focus: Michigan
Date(s) Application is Due: Jan 4; Mar 1; May 3; Jul 1; Sep 1; Nov 1
Samples: Michigan Festival of Sacred Music—Operational Support; Hospice Care of Southwest Michigan—Capital Campaign; Volunteer Services of Greater Kalamazoo— BoardConnect Program.
Contact: Janice C. Elliott; (269) 342-6411; fax (269) 342-6465
Internet: http://www.isgilmorefoundation.org/communityinvolvement.htm
Sponsor: Irving S. Gilmore Foundation
136 East Michigan Avenue, Suite 900
Kalamazoo, MI 49007-3912

Irvin Stern Foundation Grants   1010
The Irvin Stern Foundation awards grants to nonprofits, primarily in the following areas of interest: human services; civic affairs; the arts; and Jewish welfare. Other grant requests should be within the Foundation's additional areas of interest which include: aiding the under-served, the poor and disadvantaged; improving the quality of life in urban communities; and enhancing Jewish community, education and spirituality. Since there are no specified application forms, interested applicants should submit an online letter of inquiry or application letters mailed to the Foundation office. The Foundation's two annual deadlines for application submission are March 1 and September 1. Most recently, awards have ranged from $1,000 to $120,000.
Requirements: The Foundation makes grants to 501(c)3 tax-exempt organizations.
Restrictions: The Foundation does not contribute to endowments, capital campaigns, capital construction projects, and academic or medical research programs of any kind.
Geographic Focus: All States
Date(s) Application is Due: Mar 1; Sep 1
Amount of Grant: 1,000 - 120,000 USD
Contact: Christine Flood; (312) 321-9402; christine@irvinstern.org
Internet: http://irvinstern.org/guidelines/
Sponsor: Irvin Stern Foundation
4 East Ohio Street, Studio 6
Chicago, IL 60611

Island Foundation Grants   1011
Grants are awarded in the New England states for the support of arts and culture, civic and public affairs, community development, elementary and secondary education, environmental advocacy as it relates to alternatives in wastewater technology, and social services. Types of support include general operating budgets, matching funds, special projects, and research. Interested persons should request a copy of the foundation's annual report and guidelines before submitting their request.
Requirements: Nonprofit organizations in Maine, Massachusetts, and Rhode Island are eligible for grant support.
Restrictions: Grants do not support individuals, international organizations, religious organizations, special events, benefit dinners, or political campaigns.
Geographic Focus: Maine, Massachusetts, Rhode Island
Amount of Grant: Up to 17,000,000 USD
Samples: Woods Hole Oceanographic Institution (Woods Hole, MA)—to support research on solar aquatic systems, $231,000; Coalition for Buzzards Bay (Buzzards Bay, MA)—for the protection of Buzzards Bay, $45,000.
Contact: Julie Early, Executive Director; (508) 748-2809; fax (508) 748-0991; islandfdn@earthlink.net
Sponsor: Island Foundation
589 Mill Street
Marion, MA 02738

Ittleson Foundation AIDS Grants   1012
In regards to AIDS, the foundation is particularly interested in new model, pilot, and demonstration efforts: addressing the needs of underserved at-risk populations and especially those programs recognizing the overlap between such programs; responding to the challenges facing community-based AIDS service organizations and those organizations addressing systemic change; providing meaningful school-based sex education; making treatment information accessible, available and easily understandable to those in need of it; or, addressing the psycho-social needs of those infected and affected by AIDS, especially adolescents.
Requirements: Tax-exempt organizations may apply.
Restrictions: The foundation generally does not provide funds for capital building projects, endowments, grants to individuals, scholarships or internships (except as part of a program), direct service programs (especially outside New York City), projects that are local in focus and unlikely to be replicated, continuing or general support, projects and organizations that are international in scope or purpose, or biomedical research.
Geographic Focus: All States
Date(s) Application is Due: Sep 1
Samples: AIDS Alliance for Children Youth and Family, Washington, DC, $5,000—to transform the National Consumer Leadership Corps Training Program into one that can be replicated by local AIDS organizations around the nation; Cesar E. Chavez Institute, New York, NY, $40,000—one-time grant to develop new family interventions and a new family-related model of care to reduce risk for HIV and mental health problems in lesbian, gay, bisexual and transgender (LGBT) youth.
Contact: Anthony C. Wood; (212) 794-2008; fax (212) 794-0351
Internet: http://www.ittlesonfoundation.org/aids.html
Sponsor: Ittleson Foundation
15 E 67th Street, 5th Floor
New York, NY 10021

Ittleson Foundation Environment Grants   1013
The foundation supports innovative pilot, model and demonstration projects that will help move individuals, communities, and organizations from environmental awareness to environmental activism by changing attitudes and behaviors. This program seeks to encourage and nurture environmental action through: supporting the present generation of environmental activists, whether professionals or volunteers through education, training and other activities; educating and engaging the next generation of environmentalists with a special interest in supporting the training of those who are teaching that generation; strengthening the infrastructure of the environmental movement with a particular focus on efforts at the grassroots and statewide levels; activating new constituencies, particularly those focused on environmental equity issues.
Requirements: Tax-exempt organizations may apply.
Restrictions: The foundation generally does not provide funds for capital building projects, endowments, grants to individuals, scholarships or internships (except as part of a program), direct service programs (especially outside New York City), projects that are local in focus and unlikely to be replicated, continuing or general support, projects and organizations that are international in scope or purpose, or biomedical research.

Geographic Focus: All States
Date(s) Application is Due: Sep 1
Samples: Antioch University New England, Keene, NH, $45,000—to advance the emerging field of Conservation Psychology; Cornell University Cooperative Extension, New York, NY, $40,000—one-time grant for the Participatory Development of an Urban Forestry Community Engagement Model involving the public in the planning planting and stewardship of urban forestry efforts.
Contact: Anthony C. Wood; (212) 794-2008; fax (212) 794-0351
Internet: http://www.ittlesonfoundation.org/enviro.html
Sponsor: Ittleson Foundation
15 E 67th Street, 5th Floor
New York, NY 10021

Ittleson Foundation Mental Health Grants 1014

For this program, the foundation is interested in innovative, pilot, model and demonstration projects that are: fighting the stigma associated with mental illness and working to change the public's negative perception of people who have mental illness; utilizing new knowledge and current technological advances to improve programs and services for people who have mental illness; bringing the full benefits of this new knowledge and technology to those who presently do not have access to them; or, advancing preventative mental health efforts, especially those targeted to youth and adolescents, with a special focus on strategies that involve parents, teachers, and others in close contact with these populations.
Requirements: Tax-exempt organizations may apply.
Restrictions: The foundation generally does not provide funds for capital building projects, endowments, grants to individuals, scholarships or internships (except as part of a program), direct service programs (especially outside New York City), projects that are local in focus and unlikely to be replicated, continuing or general support, projects and organizations that are international in scope or purpose, or biomedical research.
Geographic Focus: All States
Date(s) Application is Due: Sep 1
Contact: Anthony C. Wood; (212) 794-2008; fax (212) 794-0351
Internet: http://www.ittlesonfoundation.org/mental.html
Sponsor: Ittleson Foundation
15 E 67th Street, 5th Floor
New York, NY 10021

J.B. Reynolds Foundation Grants 1015

The foundation makes grants in the local Kansas City, MO, area, up to a 150-mile radius of the city. Grants are awarded for building and equipment, community development, medical research, social welfare, and the arts and humanities. Some support is given to colleges and universities. Additional types of support include general operating support, continuing support, annual campaigns, endowment funds, publications, and research. The board meets in April and December of each year to consider letters of requests, and only invited proposals are reviewed. All grants are awarded in December.
Requirements: 501(c)3 organizations in the Kansas City area may submit applications.
Geographic Focus: Missouri
Amount of Grant: 5,000 - 50,000 USD
Contact: Richard L. Finn; (816) 753-7000; fax (816) 753-1354
Sponsor: J.B. Reynolds Foundation
P.O. Box 219139
Kansas City, MO 64141-6139

J. F. Maddox Foundation Grants 1016

The mission of the Foundation is to significantly improve the quality of life in southeastern New Mexico. The Foundation is most interested in supporting initiatives that strive to obtain well-planned project outcomes. The Foundation has redirected its focus toward economic and community development initiatives in an effort to provide opportunities for long-term economic vitality within Lea County. Application information is available online.
Requirements: Nonprofit organizations and governmental agencies seeking grants for the explicit benefit of Lea County, New Mexico are eligible.
Restrictions: Grants are not made to individuals, for the express benefit of an individual, or to other private foundations.
Geographic Focus: New Mexico
Amount of Grant: 5,000 - 700,000 USD
Samples: New Mexico Junior College, Hobbs, NM, $2,500—to provide funding to bus Lea County, New Mexico elementary children to the Western Heritage Museum to tour the museum and participate in hands-on activities related to the Handmade Books of New Mexico exhibit; City of Hobbs, Hobbs, NM, $25,000—to purchase outdoor movie theatre equipment for the

annual outdoor summer movie series event held in Del Norte Park; City of Hobbs, Senior Center, Hobbs, NM, $5,000—a matching grant to help replace computers in the Senior Center computer lab.
Contact: Jennifer Townsend, Grants Manager; (575) 393-6338, ext. 23; fax (575) 397-7266; jtownsend@jfmaddox.org
Internet: http://www.jfmaddox.org/areas_of_emphasis.asp
Sponsor: J. F. Maddox Foundation
P.O. Box 2588
Hobbs, NM 88241-2588

J.H. Robbins Foundation Grants 1017

The J.H. Robbins Foundation was established in 1983 in California, and was reclassified as a private operating foundation in 1994. Currently, the Foundation's primary fields of interest include: health care; human services; and safety/disaster program support. The type of support most often given is for general operations. Though a formal application is required, there are no specific annual deadlines for submission, and interested parties should begin by contacting the Foundation directly. Recent awards have ranged from $500 to as much as $7,500.
Requirements: 501(c)3 nonprofit organizations throughout the San Mateo, California, region are eligible to apply.
Geographic Focus: California
Amount of Grant: 500 - 7,500 USD
Contact: Aron H. Hoffman, Treasurer; (650) 343-5300
Sponsor: J.H. Robbins Foundation
503 Princeton Road
San Mateo, CA 94402

J. Homer Butler Foundation Grants 1018

The foundation awards grants to Roman Catholic nonprofits nationwide and internationally, with a focus on New York. Recipient organizations include child welfare organizations, churches, community service organizations, health care organizations and hospitals, international ministries and relief organizations, missions, parochial schools and religious education organizations, seminaries, and women affairs organizations. Types of support include emergency funds, general support grant, multiyear grants, project development grants, special project grants, and scholarships. Application must be made in writing.
Geographic Focus: All States
Date(s) Application is Due: Jun 30; Dec 31
Amount of Grant: 1,000 - 3,000 USD
Contact: Grant Administrator; (212) 242-7340; fax (718) 442-5088
Sponsor: J. Homer Butler Foundation
30 W 16th Street
New York, NY 10011

J.M. McDonald Foundation Grants 1019

Grants are awarded to nonprofit organizations for educational purposes; for the aged, orphans, and children who are sick, infirm, blind, or crippled; for youth and child care in an effort to combat juvenile delinquency; and to aid underprivileged, mentally or physically handicapped children. Grants are also given for building funds, equipment, and general purposes to educational institutions and hospitals. Application guidelines will be sent upon written request.
Requirements: New York organizations classified as IRS 509(a) tax-exempt are eligible to apply.
Restrictions: Grants are not made to individuals, or for seminars, workshops, endowment funds, fellowships, travel, exhibits, or conferences.
Geographic Focus: New York
Date(s) Application is Due: Apr 15; Sep 15
Amount of Grant: 5,000 - 100,000 USD
Contact: Donald McJunkin, President; (303) 674-9300; fax (303) 674-9216
Sponsor: J.M. McDonald Foundation
P.O. Box 3219
Evergreen, CO 80437

J. Spencer Barnes Memorial Foundation Grants 1020

The J. Spencer Barnes Memorial Foundation was established in Michigan in 1999, with the intent of funding programs in and around Grand Rapids, Michigan. Its primary fields of interest include diabetes, with target populations being children and youth, as well as the general population afflicted with the disease. The major types of support are income development and program development. There are no specific application forms or annual deadlines, and applicants should begin by forwarding a proposal to the office listed. Amounts range from $500 to $2,000.

Requirements: Nonprofits in California are eligible to apply.
Geographic Focus: Michigan
Amount of Grant: 500 - 2,000 USD
Contact: Robert C. Woodhouse, Jr., President; (616) 949-4854
Sponsor: J. Spencer Barnes Memorial Foundation
3073 East Fulton Street
Grand Rapids, MI 49506-1813

J.W. and Ida M. Jameson Foundation Grants 1021
The foundation supports higher and theological education, hospitals, medical research, cultural programs, and Protestant and Catholic religion. Types of support include research and general operating budgets. Applicants should submit a proposal.
Requirements: California nonprofits may submit applications.
Geographic Focus: California
Date(s) Application is Due: Feb 1
Amount of Grant: 5,000 - 50,000 USD
Contact: Les Hugn, President; (626) 355-6973
Sponsor: J.W. and Ida M. Jameson Foundation
P.O. Box 397
Sierra Madre, CA 91025

J.W. Gardner II Foundation Grants 1022
The J.W. Gardner II Foundation was established in Illinois in 2002, with an aim to support nonprofit residents of Quincy, Illinois. The Foundation's primary fields of interest include: adult and child mentor programs; animal welfare; child welfare; education; housing development; human services; museums; and scouting programs. Most recent awards have ranged from $1,500 to $50,000, with an average of ten to twelve grants given each year. Most often, these awards are in the form of general operating support. A formal application is required, and should reach the Foundation office by the annual June 30 deadline.
Requirements: 501(c)3 organizations serving Quincy, Illinois, specifically are eligible to apply.
Geographic Focus: Illinois
Date(s) Application is Due: Jun 30
Amount of Grant: 1,500 - 50,000 USD
Samples: Quincy Symphony Orchestra, Quincy, Illinois, $1,500 - general operating expense; Cheerful Home Association, Quincy, Illinois, $50,000 - general operating expense; Horizons Social Service, Quincy, Illinois, $20,000 - general operating expense.
Contact: John G. Stevenson, Jr., Director; (217) 277-2526 or (217) 224-0401
Sponsor: J.W. Gardner II Foundation
510 Maine Street, 9th Floor, P.O. Box 140
Quincy, IL 62306-3941

J.W. Kieckhefer Foundation Grants 1023
The Kieckhefer Foundation awards grants to nation-wide 501(c)3 organizations in support of medical research, hospices, and health agencies; family planning services; social services; higher education; youth and child welfare agencies; ecology and conservation; community funds; and cultural programs. Types of support include the following: annual campaigns; building renovation; conferences and seminars; continuing support; emergency funds; endowments; equipment; general operating support; land acquisition; matching and challenge support; program development; publication; and research.
Requirements: Applications are not accepted. Organizations should submit a letter of inquiry to the Foundation, with a description of their project and amount requested.
Restrictions: Grants are not awarded to individuals.
Geographic Focus: All States
Contact: John I. Kieckhefer, Trustee; (928) 445-4010
Sponsor: J.W. Kieckhefer Foundation
116 East Gurley Street
Prescott, AZ 86301-3821

J. Walton Bissell Foundation Grants 1024
The J. Walton Bissell Foundation Grants support 501(c)3 organizations in Connecticut, with emphasis on Hartford. The Foundation gives primarily to the arts and social services, including child welfare and programs for the blind. Funding requests should be submitted four months before funding is needed. Types of support include general operating support, program development, and seed money.
Requirements: Applicants should submit a letter of inquiry, along with a copy of their IRS determination letter, and a copy of their annual report, audited financial statement, or 990.

Restrictions: The Foundation does not grant funding to individuals or endowments.
Geographic Focus: Connecticut
Contact: J. Danford Anthony, Jr., President; (860) 586-8201
Sponsor: J. Walton Bissell Foundation
P.O. Box 370067
West Hartford, CT 06137

J. Willard and Alice S. Marriott Foundation Grants 1025
The J. Willard and Alice S. Marriott Foundation is a private family foundation dedicated to helping youth secure a promising future, especially through education on the secondary and higher education levels, mentoring and youth leadership programs. Equally important are organizations that help provide relief from hunger and disasters; support people with disabilities; and create gainful employment opportunities for vulnerable youth and adults. The Foundation awards grants to nonprofit organizations in its areas of interest: scholarship programs; inner city work and; youth programs, with special interest in employment opportunities for young people with disabilities. Interested applicants should prepare a written request which should include a project narrative and attachments. The Board of Trustees meets two times each year, usually in the Spring and Fall.
Requirements: Nonprofit organizations in Maryland, Virginia and the District of Columbia are eligible to apply.
Restrictions: Individuals are ineligible.
Geographic Focus: District of Columbia, Maryland, Virginia
Contact: Arne Sorenson, President; (301) 380-2246; fax (301) 380-8957; kimberly.howes@marriott.com
Sponsor: J. Willard and Alice S. Marriott Foundation
10400 Fernwood Road
Bethesda, MD 20917

J. Willard Marriott, Jr. Foundation Grants 1026
Established in 1992 in Maryland in the name of the Executive Chairman of Marriott International, the J. Willard Marriott, Jr. Foundation primarily supports residents of New Hampshire, Maryland, and the District of Columbia, although funding is occasionally provided to those outside of this region. Giving is primarily in the areas of health and education, including scholarship awards only to residents of the State of New Hampshire who received their primary and/or secondary education through home schooling and are enrolled in an accredited college or university. Initial approach should be by letter, with all applications being postmarked no later than August 31. Typical awards range from $200 to $5,000.
Geographic Focus: District of Columbia, Maryland, New Hampshire
Date(s) Application is Due: Aug 31
Amount of Grant: 200 - 5,000 USD
Samples: Special Olympics, Linthicum Heights, Maryland, $500 - general operations; U.S. Naval Academy Foundation, Annapolis, Maryland, $5,000 - general operation support; New Hampshire Boat Museum, Wolfeboro Falls, New Hampshire, $1,000 - general operations.
Contact: Steven J. McNeil, (301) 380-1765 or (301) 380-3000
Sponsor: J. Willard Marriott, Jr. Foundation
1 Marriott Drive, P.O. Box 925
Washington, D.C. 20058-0003

Jack H. and William M. Light Charitable Trust Grants 1027
The Jack H. and William M. Light Charitable Trust was established in Texas in 1998, and makes grant distributions to San Antonio area non-profits on a semiannual basis. Its primary field of interest is human services, particularly the welfare of children in the broadest sense, with an effort to support organizations involved in the health, mental health, and education of children. Types of support include: annual campaigns; capital and infrastructure; capital campaigns; curriculum development; emergency funding; endowment contributions; equipment purchase; general operations; program development; and research. Most recently, awards have ranged from $2,500 to $30,000. The annual deadlines for online application submission are April 30 and October 31.
Requirements: Grants are directed to 501(c)3 organizations which fall within the principal charitable purposes of the foundation, and which have a direct impact on the residents of Bexar, Denton and Harris counties in Texas.
Geographic Focus: Texas
Date(s) Application is Due: Apr 30; Oct 31
Amount of Grant: 2,500 - 30,000 USD
Samples: Houston Pi Beta Phi Foundation, Houston, Texas, $20,000 - general operating support; Camp Allen Conference and Retreat Center, Navasota,

Texas, $25,000 - general operating support; Texas Children's Hospital, Houston, Texas, $30,000 - support of the Care Survival Portal.
Contact: Brian R. Korb, Senior Vice President; (210) 283-6700 or (210) 283-6500; bkorb@broadwaybank.com
Internet: http://www.broadwaybank.com/wealthmanagement/Foundation WilliamMLight.html
Sponsor: Jack H. and William M. Light Charitable Trust
P.O. Box 17001
San Antonio, TX 78217-0001

Jackson Foundation Grants   **1028**
The Jackson Foundation was established October 1960 pursuant to the last will of Maria C. Jackson. Its purpose is to respond to the requests deemed appropriate to promote the welfare of the public of the City of Portland or the State of Oregon, or both. The Foundation considers projects located outside the Portland metropolitan area only if the project is of statewide appeal, rather than of local concern.
Requirements: Grants are awarded to nonprofit 501(c)3 tax-exempt agencies located within the state of Oregon.
Restrictions: Funding is not available for individuals or private businesses. Grants are generally not made to a K-12 school. Do not contact the Foundation by phone to check the status of an application.
Geographic Focus: Oregon
Date(s) Application is Due: Mar 31; Jun 30; Sep 30; Dec 31
Amount of Grant: 1,000 - 25,000 USD
Samples: Emanuel Medical Center Foundation (Portland, OR)—for general support, $10,000; Portland Community College Foundation (OR)—for program support, $5000.
Contact: Robert H. Depew, c/o U.S. Bank, (503) 275-4414
Internet: http://www.thejacksonfoundation.com
Sponsor: Jackson Foundation
P.O. Box 3168
Portland, OR 97208

Jacob and Charlotte Lehrman Foundation Grants   **1029**
The foundation makes grants to establish scholarships and fellowships at institutions of learning and to foster research in medicine and science. Grants are also given for Jewish welfare funds, care of the aged and sick, the establishment of trade schools, the fostering of religious observance, recreation, and aid to refugees. Additional types of support include general operating grants and matching funds. The Foundation Board generally makes grants once a year, typically in October. The deadline for RFPs as well as proposals submitted from current grant recipients is April 1.
Requirements: Grants are made primarily to organizations in the greater metropolitan Washington, DC, area.
Restrictions: Grants are not made to individuals.
Geographic Focus: District of Columbia
Date(s) Application is Due: Apr 1
Amount of Grant: 1,000 - 10,000 USD
Contact: Robert Lehrman, Vice President; (202) 338-8400; fax (202) 338-8405; info@lehrmanfoundation.org
Internet: http://www.lehrmanfoundation.org
Sponsor: Jacob and Charlotte Lehrman Foundation
1027 33rd Street NW, 2nd Floor
Washington, D.C. 20007

Jacob and Hilda Blaustein Foundation Grants   **1030**
The Foundation promotes social justice and human rights through its five program areas: Jewish life; strengthening Israeli democracy; health and mental health; educational opportunity; and human rights. Support is provided to organizations in the United States and abroad, with a preference to the Baltimore, Maryland area. The Foundation supports organizations that promote systemic change; involve constituents in planning and decision-making; encourage volunteer and professional development; and engage in ongoing program evaluation. Additional guidelines and application information is available online.
Requirements: Nonprofit organizations are eligible to apply.
Restrictions: Support is unavailable for the following: individuals; scholarships to individuals; unsolicited proposals for academic, scientific, or medical research; direct mail; annual giving; membership campaigns; fundraising; commemorative events.
Geographic Focus: Maryland
Samples: The Foundation for Jewish Campus Life, Washington, DC, $150,000—support offered over a two year period, for Tzedek Hillel, a program

that promotes social justice activities among Jewish college students across the country, and support for the Tzedek Leadership Mission to Israel; Fund for Educational Excellence, Baltimore, MD, $250,000—support for over five years, for the implementation of a reform plan for Baltimore's neighborhood high schools; Mental Disability Rights International, Washington, DC, $70,000—support paid over two years, to promote the human rights of people with mental disabilities worldwide.
Contact: Betsy Ringel, Executive Director; (410) 347-7103; fax (410) 347-7210; info@blaufund.org
Internet: http://www.blaufund.org/foundations/jacobandhilda_f.html
Sponsor: Jacob and Hilda Blaustein Foundation
10 E Baltimore Street, Suite 1111
Baltimore, MD 21202

Jacobs Family Foundation Village Neighborhoods Grants   **1031**
The Foundation primarily serves the four neighborhoods immediately surrounding The Village at Market Creek: Chollas View, Emerald Hills, Lincoln Park, and Valencia Park; proposals are considered from throughout the Fourth City Council District of southeastern San Diego. The Neighborhood Grants Program funds programs or strategies that: strengthen and expand health, environmental, education and family resources; foster opportunities for ownership and building assets through economic and business development; create vibrant places and spaces which express and enhance the cultures and environment of the community; and/or strengthen the ability of the community to get things done and include the voice of residents in decision-making, advocacy, and planning. The Village Neighborhoods Fund makes grants to resident groups and neighborhood organizations that serve or support The Village at Market Creek. Funding is also available for a limited number of grants that support projects outside the neighborhoods that demonstrate innovative community and economic development strategies and a commitment to share what works, what doesn't, and why. Applications are excepted year round, however unsolicited applications are not. Call the Foundation to discuss your project. If the project meets the Foundations criteria, you may be asked to send a brief letter of interest and/or complete a full Village Neighborhoods Fund application.
Requirements: 501(c)3 non-profits may apply that: work with the Jacobs Center to develop The Village at Market Creek in southeastern San Diego; provide programs or services that benefit the neighborhoods surrounding The Village at Market Creek; or provides neighborhood strengthening strategies or models that can inform and advance The Village at Market Creek work.
Geographic Focus: California
Amount of Grant: 10,000 - 75,000 USD
Contact: Program Contact; (619) 527-6161 or (800) 550-6856; fax (619) 527-6162; communications@jacobscenter.org
Internet: http://www.jacobsfamilyfoundation.org/how.htm
Sponsor: Jacobs Family Foundation
Joe & Vi Jacobs Center, 404 Euclid Avenue
San Diego, CA 92114

James & Abigail Campbell Family Foundation Grants   **1032**
The James & Abigail Campbell Family Foundation embraces the values and beliefs of James and Abigail Campbell by investing in Hawwaii's people and the communities that nuture them. The Foundation supports projects in the following areas: Youth—programs that address the challenges of young people; Education—support for public schools, early childhood education and environmental stewardship; Hawaiian—support for programs that promote values and the health and welfare of Hawaiians. Priority is given to programs located in or serving communities in the following areas of West Oahu: Ewa/Ewa Beach, Kapolei, Makakilo and the Wai'anae Coast. The following types of requests are eligible for consideration: support for special projects that are not part of an organization's ongoing operations; program support when unforeseen circumstances have affected the financial base of an organization; financial assistance to purchase items such as office equipment and to fund minor repairs and renovations. Grants range from $5,000 - $50,000. Your grant application must be postmarked by February 1 for the April/May meeting, August 1 for the October/November meeting.
Requirements: The Foundation will only consider requests from organizations which qualify as non-profit, tax-exempt public charities under Section 501(c)3 and 170(b) of the Internal Revenue Code. To apply for a grant, summarize the following information in a two - three page proposal letter: the nature and purpose of your organization; the objectives of your program, include the grant amount requested and the proposed use of funds; a brief outline on how you plan to accomplish your objectives; a statement of a community

problem, need or opportunity that this project will address; the duration for which Foundation funds are needed; other sources of funding currently being sought and future funding sources; methods used to measure the program's effectiveness. In addition to the proposal letter, submit a copy of the following: Internal Revenue Service notification of tax-exempt status; most recent annual financial statement; list of the current Board of Directors; the project's proposed budget; one (1) copy of your complete grant proposal package.
Restrictions: The Foundation will not consider funding for: individuals, endowments, sectarian or religious programs, loans, political activities or highly technical research projects. Only one request per organization will ordinarily be considered in a calendar year. Funds are usually not committed for more than one year at a time.
Geographic Focus: Hawaii
Date(s) Application is Due: Feb 1; Aug 1
Amount of Grant: 5,000 - 50,000 USD
Contact: D. Keola, Grant Manager; (808) 674-3167; fax (808) 674-3349; keolal@jamescampbell.com
Internet: http://www.campbellfamilyfoundation.org/grant_procedures.cfm
Sponsor: James and Abigail Campbell Family Foundation
1001 Kamokila Boulevard
Kapolei, HI 96707

James A. and Faith Knight Foundation Grants   1033
Primarily serving Jackson and Washtenaw counties, Michigan, the Foundation is dedicated to improving communities by providing grant support to qualified nonprofit organizations including, but not limited to, those that address the needs of women and girls, animals and the natural world, and internal capacity. In general, the foundation supports organizations that believe in good nonprofit practices including sound financial management, developed governance practices, and clarity of mission. Attention to gender, diversity, and outcomes are important. Giving is primarily for human services, including a neighborhood center, women's organizations, and family services; support also for nonprofit management, the United Way, housing, the arts, education, and environmental conservation. Fields of interest include: adult education and literacy; basic skills; GED; arts; environment and natural resources; family services; housing development; human services; nonprofit management; and women's services. There are two annual deadlines, and initial approach should be by letter.
Requirements: Giving is limited to Michigan, with emphasis on Jackson and Washenaw counties.
Restrictions: No support is offered for religious or political organizations. No grants to individuals, or for conferences or special events, or for annual campaigns.
Geographic Focus: Michigan
Date(s) Application is Due: Jan 28; Sep 16
Samples: Center for the Childbearing Year, Ann Arbor, Michigan, $23,000—to increase capacity of the Doulas Care program, with targeted emphasis to improve maternal/infant health outcomes and develop a health career pathway for women; Dahlem Conservancy, Jackson, Michigan, $18,000—to purchase a van to initiate outreach programs.
Contact: Margaret A. Talburtt, Executive Director; (734) 769-5653; fax (734) 769-8383; peg@KnightFoundationMi.org or info@knightfoundationmi.org
Internet: http://www.knightfoundationmi.org/guidelines.htm
Sponsor: James A. and Faith Knight Foundation
180 Little Lake Drive, Suite 6B
Ann Arbor, MI 48103-6219

James and Elsie Nolan Charitable Trust Grants   1034
The trust awards grants, primarily in southeastern Alaska, in its areas of interest, including museums, hospitals, and public administration. General operating and project grants are awarded. There are no application deadlines. The board meets in early October.
Requirements: Alaska nonprofit organizations are eligible.
Restrictions: Individuals are ineligible.
Geographic Focus: Alaska
Amount of Grant: Up to 22,000,000 USD
Samples: Catholic Community Services of Juneau (AK)—for wheelchair-accessible vehicles, $17,000; Junior Achievement in Anchorage (AK)—for computer equipment; Wrangell Medical Ctr (AK)—for mammogram machine and endoscopes, $105,000; Irene Ingle Public Library (Wrangell, AK)—for library book purchases and a learning project, $4164.
Contact: Gwendolyn Feltis, c/o Wells Fargo Bank Alaska, N.A., N.A.
Sponsor: James and Elsie Nolan Charitable Trust
P.O. Box 927
Wrangell, AK 99929

James Ford Bell Foundation Grants   1035
The Foundation supports organizations primarily in Minnesota. Emphasis is on cultural programs, support is also available for wildlife preservation and conservation, youth agencies, the environment, education, health and human services. A high priority is given to projects with historical connections to the Bell Family. The Trustees meet in the Spring and Fall. Contact the Foundation prior to sending in a proposal. Unsolicited requests for funds are not accepted.
Requirements: Nonprofit organizations in Minnesota are eligible to apply.
Restrictions: No grants are made directly to individuals, nor for scholarships, fellowships, or political campaigns. No funding is available to units of local government. The Foundation does not respond to requests for memberships, annual appeals, or special events and fundraisers.
Geographic Focus: Minnesota
Contact: Ellen George; (612) 377-8400; fax (612) 377-8407; ellen@fpadvisors.com
Internet: http://www.fpadvisors.com/jamesfordbell/jamesfordbell.htm
Sponsor: James Ford Bell Foundation
1818 Oliver Avenue South
Minneapolis, MN 55405-2208

James Irvine Foundation Creative Connections Grants   1036
The Creative Connections Fund supports creativity and the expansion of diverse, relevant cultural offerings in local communities across California and primarily outside San Francisco, San Mateo and Santa Clara counties. The Fund targets small and midsize arts organizations and offers project grants of up to $50,000, over a maximum of 24 months, through an open, competitive review process. The Creative Connections Fund aims to support small and midsize arts organizations with a diversity of projects and ideas. The Foundation's rationale is two-fold. First, small organizations play an important role in the arts ecosystem. They have close ties to the communities they serve, present aesthetics that have particular relevance to their audiences, and involve local artists. In this way, community-based arts organizations support grassroots creativity and add to the cultural offerings of the neighborhoods and cities they serve, which, in turn, adds to the cultural vibrancy of the state. Second, because we frequently partner with organizations that have annual budgets greater than $2 million, the Creative Connections Fund is an important complement to our invitational portfolio and a way to reach arts organizations of all artistic disciplines and aesthetics, located in all geographic locations in California. See Foundations website for additional guidelines.
Requirements: To be considered for a grant organizations and requests must meet all the following requirements: 501(c)3 status or an established relationship with an approved fiscal sponsor; California focus; no more than 50 percent of revenue from government sources; annual revenue of at least $100,000; grant request of no more than $50,000 or 10% of organizations annual budget; no active grant or outstanding reports due to the Foundation.
Restrictions: Irvine does not make direct grants to individual artists.
Geographic Focus: California
Amount of Grant: 50,000 USD
Contact: Fund Coordinator; (800) 374-6851; artsfund@irvine.org
Internet: http://www.irvine.org/grantmaking/our-programs/arts-program/fundingguidelines/creativeconnectionsfund
Sponsor: James Irvine Foundation
575 Market Street, Suite 3400
San Francisco, CA 94105

James J. and Joan A. Gardner Family Foundation Grants   1037
Established in Cincinnati, Ohio, in 1994, the James J. and Joan A. Gardner Family Foundation was named in honor of James Joseph Gardner, a civic-minded leader, a philanthropist, and an exemplary and loving caregiver to his wife, Joan, who suffers from Parkinson's disease. The Foundation's major purpose is to provide support for higher education, Christian and Roman Catholic churches and organizations, social services, and health organizations. With that in mind, its primary fields of interest include: Catholicism; Christianity; diseases and conditions (particularly Parkinson's); education; higher education; human services; and right to life causes. Currently, the geographic focus is on Ohio and Florida. An application form is required, along with a brief history of the applicant organization, its mission, and budgetary needs. Most recent awards have ranged from $1,000 to $50,000. There are no identified annual deadlines.
Requirements: Nonprofit 501(c)3 organizations and educational programs in both the State of Florida and the Cincinnati, Ohio, region are welcome to apply.
Geographic Focus: All States
Amount of Grant: 1,000 - 50,000 USD

Samples: Boys Hope, Girls Hope, Cincinnati, Ohio, $50,000 - general operating funds; Admiral Farragut Academy, St. Petersburg, Florida, $10,000 - general operating funds; Alex's Lemonade Stand, Wynnewood, Pennsylvania, $1,000 - general operating funds.
Contact: Regina L. Estenfelder; (513) 459-1085; fax (513) 573-0778
Sponsor: James J. and Joan A. Gardner Family Foundation
6847 Cintas Boulevard, Suite 120
Mason, OH 45040-9152

James L. and Mary Jane Bowman Charitable Trust Grants   1038

Established in 1997 in Virginia through a donation by James L. Bowman, the James L. and Mary Jane Bowman Charitable Trust Supports both education and libraries within Virginia. The Trust's primary fields of interest include: Christian agencies and churches, higher education, human services, public libraries, and recreation. There are no specific application forms or deadlines with which to adhere, and applicants should forward a letter of application that includes a needs statement, population to be served, and the project budget.
Requirements: 501(c)3 nonprofit organizations Serving residents of Virginia are eligible.
Restrictions: The foundation does not award grants to individuals in the form of scholarships or other direct support; orpolitical causes or candidates.
Geographic Focus: Virginia
Date(s) Application is Due: Apr 1
Amount of Grant: 1,000 - 15,000 USD
Samples: Lord Fairfax Community College, Middletown, Virginia, $19,151 - general operations support; Blue Ridge Hospice, Winchester, Virginia, $10,000 - to provide hospice care for local chronically ill patients; Museum of the Shenandoah Valley, Winchester, Virginia, $6,500 - to preserve regional art, history, and culture.
Contact: Beverley B. Shoemaker; (540) 869-1800; fax (540) 869-4225
Sponsor: James L. and Mary Jane Bowman Charitable Trust
P.O. Box 480
Stephens City, VA 22655-0480

James L. Stamps Foundation Grants   1039

The foundation awards grants to nonprofits primarily in southern California to support Protestant religion schools, churches, seminaries, and organizations. Types of support include operating budgets, continuing support, emergency funds, matching funds, special projects, and scholarship funds for Christian colleges only. There are no application deadline dates or forms. Applicants should submit a letter of request. The board meets bimonthly beginning in February.
Requirements: Southern California nonprofit organizations may apply.
Geographic Focus: California
Amount of Grant: 1,000 - 50,000 USD
Contact: Delores Boutault, Manager; (714) 568-9740
Sponsor: James L. Stamps Foundation
2000 E 4th Street, Suite 230
Santa Ana, CA 92705-3814

James R. Dougherty Jr. Foundation Grants   1040

The James R. Dougherty, Jr. Foundation, established in 1950, gives to organizations primarily in Texas. Areas of interest include: family services, domestic violence, human services and women. Support is offered in the form of: annual campaigns, building/renovation, capital campaigns, continuing support, curriculum development, endowments, equipment, general/operating support, income development, management development/capacity building, matching/challenge support, program development, program evaluation, research, scholarship funds, seed money and, technical assistance grants. The board meets twice a year, in the Spring and Fall. No application form is required, contact the Foundation, before submitting a proposal.
Requirements: Nonprofit organizations in Texas are eligible to apply.
Geographic Focus: Texas
Date(s) Application is Due: Mar 1; Sep 1
Contact: Daren Wilder, Grants Administrator; (512) 358-3560
Sponsor: James R. Dougherty Jr. Foundation
P.O. Box 640
Beeville, TX 78104-0640

James R. Thorpe Foundation Grants   1041

The Foundation is interested in supporting organizations, programs or projects which address the needs of the Elderly and Youth. The Thorpe Foundation is most likely to make general operating or program support grants. In the area of Youth, the Foundation supports organizations and programs that: engage youth in the arts; encourage character development; support academic and social development; provide safety and support to youth. In the area of the Elderly, the Foundation fosters the vital aging of seniors through support of services which help them to live independently. The Foundation will give special consideration to services which address the needs of economically disadvantaged seniors, immigrant seniors and the frail elderly. The Foundation supports organizations and programs that: provide transportation services; assist seniors in remaining in their own homes; educate seniors about housing options; provide social and recreational opportunities for seniors. Additional guidelines are available at: http://www.jamesrthorpefoundation.org/2010procedures.html.
Requirements: The Thorpe Foundation supports 501(c)3 non-profit organizations located in and serving the Minneapolis and the western Minneapolis metro suburbs of the Twin Cities.
Restrictions: The Foundation does not: make multi-year grants or fund individuals; make grants in the east metro area, greater Minnesota, or outside the State of Minnesota; make grants through fiscal agents; support endowment drives, conferences, seminars, tours, or fundraising events; support organizations with operating budgets over $2 million; support organizations with no paid staff.
Geographic Focus: Minnesota
Date(s) Application is Due: Mar 1; Sep 1
Contact: Kerrie Blevins, Foundation Manager; (612) 822-3412; kerrieblevins@jamesrthorpefoundation.org
Internet: http://www.jamesrthorpefoundation.org/2010guidelines.html
Sponsor: James R. Thorpe Foundation
318 West 48th Street
Minneapolis, MN 55419

Jane's Trust Grants   1042

The Jane's Trust has particular interest in organizations and projects which primarily benefit underserved populations and disadvantaged communities. Jane's Trust will support grants for general operating purposes, as well, as it's Fields of Interest, which are: arts and culture, education, the environment, health and welfare. The Trust will make grants in the states of Florida, with a preference for southwest and central Florida; Massachusetts, with a preference for greater Boston and eastern Massachusetts; and in the northern New England states of Maine, New Hampshire and Vermont. Preference will be given to organizations located in those states for projects which will primarily provide benefits within those states. The application process begins by submitting of a concept paper. Guidelines are available at the Trusts website.
Requirements: 501(c)3 tax-exempt organizations in Florida, Maine, Massachusetts, New Hampshire, and Vermont are eligible.
Restrictions: Jane's Trust will not support: loans to charitable organizations; attempts to influence legislation; requests from individuals. Please note: Jane's Trust will normally not support public entities, such as municipalities, municipal departments, or public schools directly, but will entertain applications from tax-exempt fiscal agents or partners for collaborative projects with municipalities or schools. This does not apply to public colleges and universities.
Geographic Focus: Florida, Maine, Massachusetts, New Hampshire, Vermont
Date(s) Application is Due: Jan 25; Jul 15
Amount of Grant: 50,000 - 1,000,000 USD
Contact: Susan Fish, Grants Administrator; (617) 227-7940, ext. 775; fax (617) 227-0781; sfish@hembar.com
Internet: http://www.hembar.com/selectsrv/janes/index.html
Sponsor: Hemenway and Barnes LLP
60 State Street
Boston, MA 02109-1899

Jane and Jack Fitzpatrick Fund Grants   1043

The Jane and Jack Fitzpatrick Fund was established in Massachusetts in 2005 with the identified purpose of supporting higher education within the State of Massachusetts. The Foundation's primary fields of interest include: arts and art services, economic development, higher education, historic preservation, historical societies, and museums. Types of funding include: building and renovation, equipment purchase, general operating support, management development, and capacity building. A formal application is required, although interested parties should begin by forwarding a letter of interest describing the need in general terms. There are no specified annual deadlines.
Geographic Focus: Massachusetts
Amount of Grant: 50,000 - 100,000 USD
Contact: Jane P. Fitzpatrick, Trustee; (413) 298-1605 or (413) 298-1036
Sponsor: Jane and Jack Fitzpatrick Fund
P.O. Box 1164
Stockbridge, MA 01262-1164

Jane Bradley Pettit Foundation Arts and Culture Grants   1044

The Jane Bradley Pettit Foundation awards grants to initiate and sustain projects in the Greater Milwaukee community, with a focus on programs and projects that serve low-income and disadvantaged individuals, women, children, and the elderly. The Foundation supports the ongoing expenses of arts and cultural organizations through projects which offer guidance as well as individual and social development of young people. An initial application should be in the form of a letter of intent.

Requirements: Milwaukee-area charitable organizations are eligible.
Geographic Focus: Wisconsin
Date(s) Application is Due: Jan 15; May 15; Sep 15
Amount of Grant: 5,000 - 40,000 USD
Samples: Arts at Large, Milwaukee, Wisconsin, $10,000 - for general operations; Milwaukee Repertory Theater, Milwaukee, Wisconsin, $10,000 - for general operations; Renaissance Theaterworks, Milwaukee, Wisconsin, $5,000 - for general operations.
Contact: Heidi Jones, Director of Administration; (414) 982-2880 or (414) 982-2874; fax (414) 982-2889; hjones@staffordlaw.com
Internet: http://www.jbpf.org/guidelines/index.html
Sponsor: Jane Bradley Pettit Foundation
1200 N. Mayfair Road, Suite 430
Wauwatosa, WI 53226-3282

Jane Bradley Pettit Foundation Community & Social Development Grants   1045

The Jane Bradley Pettit Foundation awards grants to initiate and sustain projects in the Greater Milwaukee community, with a focus on programs and projects that serve low-income and disadvantaged individuals, women, children, and the elderly. The Foundation has designated two areas for special consideration in the area of Community and Social Development Grants: early childhood development and assistance to women and children in poverty. The Foundation also supports programs which enable youth to develop leadership skills, character and self-esteem. An initial application should be in the form of a letter of intent.

Requirements: Milwaukee-area charitable organizations are eligible.
Geographic Focus: Wisconsin
Date(s) Application is Due: Jan 15; May 15; Sep 15
Amount of Grant: 5,000 - 100,000 USD
Contact: Heidi Jones, Director of Administration; (414) 982-2880 or (414) 982-2874; fax (414) 982-2889; hjones@staffordlaw.com
Internet: http://www.jbpf.org/guidelines/index.html
Sponsor: Jane Bradley Pettit Foundation
1200 N. Mayfair Road, Suite 430
Wauwatosa, WI 53226-3282

Jane Bradley Pettit Foundation Health Grants   1046

The Jane Bradley Pettit Foundation awards grants to initiate and sustain projects in the Greater Milwaukee community, with a focus on programs and projects that serve low-income and disadvantaged individuals, women, children, and the elderly. In the area of Health, the Foundation gives priority to community-based health care and prevention programs which address the physical and mental health needs of families, children, persons at-risk and the elderly. Support and advocacy for victims of abuse and neglect are also a priority. An initial application should be in the form of a letter of intent.

Requirements: Milwaukee-area charitable organizations are eligible.
Geographic Focus: Wisconsin
Date(s) Application is Due: Jan 15; May 15; Sep 15
Amount of Grant: 5,000 - 100,000 USD
Contact: Heidi Jones, Director of Administration; (414) 982-2880 or (414) 982-2874; fax (414) 982-2889; hjones@staffordlaw.com
Internet: http://www.jbpf.org/guidelines/index.html
Sponsor: Jane Bradley Pettit Foundation
1200 N. Mayfair Road, Suite 430
Wauwatosa, WI 53226-3282

Janice Gardner Foundation   1047

The Janice Gardner Foundation was established by George James Gardner in Minneapolis, Minnesota, during the mid-1970s. Shortly after the death of his wife, Janice in 1975, George established and funded the Foundation in her memory. This Foundation was incorporated to be operated exclusively for religious, charitable, scientific, literary and educational purposes including the encouragement of art and the prevention of cruelty to animals. Through the Foundation, George was able to generously and continually support the Basilica of St. Mary, the Methodist Hospital Foundation, the scholarship program at the University of St. Thomas, as well as numerous other deserving organizations. Currently, the Foundation major field of interest is the support of Roman Catholic education, agencies, and churches, as well as human service programs throughout the State of Minnesota. Most recently, awards have ranged from $4,000 to as much as $75,000, with an average annual distribution of $300,000 to approximately fifteen organizations. Although there is no annual deadline for submission, a formal application is required, and should be secured from the Foundation office.

Requirements: Roman Catholic agencies, churches, and educational programs throughout Minnesota are eligible to apply.
Geographic Focus: Minnesota
Amount of Grant: 4,000 - 75,000 USD
Samples: Archdiocese of St. Paul, St. Paul, Minnesota, $55,000 - support of the Growing in Faith campaign (2014); Hope Interfaith Center, Mankato, Minnesota, $20,000 - general operations (2014); Sharing and Caring Hands, Minneapolis, Minnesota, $20,000 - general operations (2014).
Contact: Barbara Illies, Director; (651) 731-0160
Sponsor: Janice Gardner Foundation
60 South 6th Street, Suite 3700
Minneapolis, MN 55402-4437

Jaquelin Hume Foundation Grants   1048

The Jacquelin Hume Foundation Grants primarily support K-12 education reform efforts that are national in scope. Grants will be made for general operations, project development, and research. Special projects are generally preferred. One request per organization per year will be considered.

Requirements: An application form is not required. Applicants should submit a one-page letter of inquiry along with the following: the qualifications of key personnel; a copy of the IRS determination letter; a copy of the most recent annual report, audited financial statement, or 990; a detailed description of the project and amount of funding requested; a listing of the board of directors, trustees, officers and other key people, with their affiliations; and a list of past and present donors.
Restrictions: The Foundation does not support organizations outside the U.S. or grants to individuals.
Geographic Focus: All States
Date(s) Application is Due: Mar 15; Sep 15
Contact: Gisele Huff, Executive Director; (415) 705-5115
Sponsor: Jaquelin Hume Foundation
600 Montgomery Street, Suite 2800
San Francisco, CA 94111-2803

Jayne and Leonard Abess Foundation Grants   1049

The Jayne and Leonard Abess Foundation was established in Miami, Florida, in 2004, by the son of City National Bank co-founder, Leonard L. Abess, Sr. The Foundation supports a variety of causes both locally and nationally. Areas of interest include: design arts education, writer's, employment training, human services programs, Jewish agencies and temples, children with special needs, and higher education. The primary type of support is general operating funds. There are no specific applications or deadlines with which to adhere, and applicants should contact the Foundation office directly in writing. This initial contact should include a detailed description of the program, and a budget narrative. Most recently, awards have ranged from $1,000 to $100,000.

Geographic Focus: All States
Amount of Grant: 1,000 - 100,000 USD
Contact: Leonard L. Abess; (212) 632-3000; informed@ftci.com
Sponsor: Jayne and Leonard Abess Foundation
600 Fifth Avenue
New York, NY 10020-2302

Jean and Louis Dreyfus Foundation Grants   1050

The Jean and Louis Dreyfus Foundation was established in 1979 from the estate of Louis Dreyfus, a music publisher, and that of his wife, Jean. The mission of the Foundation is to enhance the quality of life of New Yorkers, particularly the aging and disadvantaged. The Foundation disburses grants mainly within the five boroughs of New York City, and supports programs in the arts, health and social services (including youth agencies, women, and the elderly), and education (including literacy). Support is given for program development and matching funds. Application forms are not required. The board meets each year in the spring and in the fall. Initial inquiries should consist of a one or two page letter describing the organization and outlining the project in question. The January 15th and July 15th deadlines are for Letters of Intent.

Requirements: New York City nonprofits are eligible.
Restrictions: Grants are never made to individuals.

Geographic Focus: New York
Date(s) Application is Due: Jan 15; Jul 15
Contact: Jessica Keuskamp, Program Director; (212) 599-1931; fax (212) 599-2956; jldreyfusfdtn@hotmail.com
Internet: http://foundationcenter.org/grantmaker/dreyfus/guide.html
Sponsor: Jean and Louis Dreyfus Foundation
420 Lexington Avenue, Suite 626
New York, NY 10170

Jean and Price Daniel Foundation Grants 1051

The Jean and Daniel Price Foundation, established in Texas in 1985, has the primary purpose of supporting historical preservation programs. The Foundation's current fields of interest include: historical societies, libraries, archives, protestant agencies and churches, and public health initiatives. Types of support include building and renovation, general operating support, land acquisition, and program development. There are no specific application forms or deadlines with which to adhere, and potential applicants should contact the office initially by letter. Past grants have ranged from $5,000 to $100,000.
Requirements: Applicants should be 501(c)3 organizations located in, or serving the residents of, Texas.
Geographic Focus: Texas
Amount of Grant: 5,000 - 100,000 USD
Samples: Coppell Historical Society, Coppell, Texas, $50,000 - historical preservation projects; Texas Governor's Mansion Restoration Project, Austin, Texas, $100,000 - restoration and preservation; Wallisville Heritage Park, Wallisville, Texas, $10,000 - general operating expenses.
Contact: Jean Daniel Murph, President; (936) 336-7355
Sponsor: Jean and Price Daniel Foundation
P.O. Box 789
Liberty, TX 77575-0789

JELD-WEN Foundation Grants 1052

The Foundation seeks to improve the quality of life in company-operating areas and awards grants in the areas of capital campaigns, education, youth activities, community development, health and medical, and arts and humanities. Types of support include building construction/renovation, equipment, general operating support, land acquisition, matching/challenge support, program development, scholarship funds, and seed money. Prescreening and application information are available online.
Requirements: Nonprofits in the Foundation's area of operations.
Geographic Focus: All States
Amount of Grant: 1,000 - 1,000,000 USD
Samples: Knox Community Hospital, Mt. Vernon, OH, $500,000—grant to help build an outpatient cancer treatment center; Crater Lake Science and Learning Center, Crater Lake, OR, $500,000—to help build the Science and Learning Center at Crater lake National Park; Yakima Valley Museum, Yakima, WA, $250,000—to upgrade and improve the museum facility.
Contact: Foundation Headquarters; (503) 478-4478; fax (503) 478-4474
Internet: http://www.jeld-wenfoundation.org/
Sponsor: Jeld-Wen Foundation
200 SW Market Street, Suite 550
Portland, OR 97201

Jenkins Foundation: Improving the Health of Greater Richmond Grants 1053

The foundation is committed to expanding access to community-based services through programs and organizations that have the potential to make a significant impact on the quality of health, especially for the youth in its local area.
Requirements: The current areas of focus are: Expanding access to health care services for the uninsured and underserved; Substance abuse prevention services that promote healthy lifestyles and increase availability of services; Violence prevention services that promote safe and healthy environments for children and their families and work toward the elimination of violence in the local communities; In addition, the foundation is committed to the long-term viability of the organizations it supports, and will consider capacity building grants that strengthen an agency's ability to better serve its clients. The foundation will also consider a limited number of proposals outside the above stated focus areas.
Restrictions: Proposals will be accepted from charitable organizations, which serve the residents of the City of Richmond and the counties of Chesterfield, Hanover, Henrico, Goochland, and Powhatan.
Geographic Focus: Virginia
Date(s) Application is Due: May 5; Nov 5
Amount of Grant: Up to 50,000 USD

Contact: Elaine Summerfield, Program Officer; (804) 330-7400; fax (804) 330-5992; esummerfield@tcfrichmond.org
Internet: http://www.tcfrichmond.org/Page2954.cfm#Jenkins
Sponsor: Community Foundation Serving Richmond and Central Virginia
7501 Boulders View Drive, Suite 110
Richmond, VA 23225

Jerome Foundation Grants 1054

The Foundation supports programs in dance, literature, media arts, music, theater, performance art, the visual arts, multidisciplinary work and arts criticism. The Foundation seeks to support artists who exhibit significant potential yet are not recognized as established creators by fellow artists and other arts professionals. Examples of recognition include exhibitions, reviews, commissions, performances, grant awards, residencies, fellowships, publications and productions. Applications are available online.
Requirements: Artists and nonprofit, tax-exempt organizations in Minnesota and New York are eligible.
Geographic Focus: Minnesota, New York
Samples: Aperture Foundation (New York, NY)—to publish the work of emerging photographers, $30,000 over two years; SASE, the Write Place (Minneapolis, MN)—for fellowships and mentoring for emerging writers, $49,500; Art in General (New York, NY)—for commissions, exhibitions, residencies, and artists' services, $38,000 over two years; Zeitgeist (Saint Paul, MN)—for a program for musicians and composers, $27,000 over two years.
Contact: Program Contact; (800) 995-3766 or (651) 224-9431; fax (651) 224-3439; info@jeromefdn.org
Internet: http://www.jeromefdn.org
Sponsor: Jerome Foundation
400 Sibley Street, Suite 125
Saint Paul, MN 55101-1928

Jerome Robbins Foundation Grants 1055

Jerome Robbins established the Foundation in 1958, in honor of his mother, with the intent to support dance, theater, and their associative arts. In the 1980's, following the outbreak of AIDS, he directed Foundation resources almost exclusively to the AIDS crisis and still later, in letters left to the board, he conveyed his wish that the Foundation once again extend its resources to the performing arts - dance and theater especially. In line with the founder's life, financial support is offered - primarily in the New York City metro area - for dance, theater and groups dedicated to serving those with HIV and AIDS with an emphasis on the artistic community. Applications may take three to four months to evaluate and funds for specific projects are not granted retroactively. Fiscal sponsorship is acceptable. Unless otherwise specified, Foundation grants apply to general operating costs. Between one hundred and two hundred awards are given annually, ranging from $1,000 to $50,000 each.
Requirements: All suggestions for proposals must be submitted via email, and must be in the form of two pdf files and contain only the following information: no more than two pages outlining the organization's activities and the nature of the request; the organization's or project's latest budget; current funding sources; the organization's address; the organization's IRS statement of tax-exempt status (applies only to new proposals); and the organization's latest audited financial statement or tax return, submitted as a separate and second pdf file. If interested, the Foundation will invite a full proposal.
Geographic Focus: All States
Amount of Grant: 1,000 - 50,000 USD
Samples: Bailey House, New York, New York, $36,250 - general operating support; American Friends of The Paris Opera and Ballet, New York, New York, $25,000 - general operating support; Pennsylvania Ballet, Philadelphia, Pennsylvania, $15,000 - general operating support.
Contact: Christopher Pennington, Executive Director; (212) 367-8956; fax (212) 367-8966; pennington@jeromerobbins.org
Internet: http://www.jeromerobbins.org/foundation
Sponsor: Jerome Robbins Foundation
156 W. 56th Street, Suite 900
New York, NY 10019

Jerry L. and Barbara J. Burris Foundation Grants 1056

The Jerry L. and Barbara J. Burris Foundation was established in Indiana in 1994. Its primary fields of interest include: the arts; cancer research; children and youth services; education; hospitals; human services; museums; Protestant agencies and churches; and zoological societies. Funding typically comes in the form of general operating support and scholarship funding. There are no specific applications or annual deadlines, so applicants should begin by contacting the Foundation directly.

Geographic Focus: Florida, Indiana
Amount of Grant: 1,000 - 10,000 USD
Samples: Shelter for Abused Women and Children, Naples, Florida, $9,000 - general operating fund; Butler University, Indianapolis, Indiana, $10,000 - scholarship fund; Indianapolis Zoological Society, Indianapolis, Indiana, $6,500 - general operating fund.
Contact: Barbara J. Burris, President; (317) 843-5678
Sponsor: Jerry L. and Barbara J. Burris Foundation
P.O. Box 80238
Indianapolis, IN 46280-0238

Jessie Ball Dupont Fund Grants   1057

The fund is a national foundation having a special, though not exclusive, interest in issues affecting the South. Grants awarded include competitive grants—program grants, institutional development, and capacity building; and feasibility grants—smaller grants that enable institutions to carefully explore and develop new concepts and programs. Areas of interest include six focus areas: strengthening the independent sector; organizing and nurturing philanthropy; building assets of people, families, and communities; building the capacity of eligible organizations; stimulating community problem solving; and helping people hold their communities accountable. The fund supports four initiatives: the religion initiative, the nonprofit initiative, the small liberal arts colleges initiative, and the independent schools initiative. Types of support include general operating support, building construction/renovation, equipment acquisition, program development, seed money grants, publication, consulting services, professorships, curriculum development, matching funds, and technical assistance. Grants are awarded generally for one year. The trustees meet in January, March, May, July, September, and November to consider requests.
Amount of Grant: 2,000 - 5,000 USD
Samples: Jacksonville Symphony Assoc (FL)—to implement a strategic marketing program, $50,000; Historical Society of Delaware (Wilmington, DE)—to hire a consultant to lead a community-based strategic-planning process, $52,690; Episcopal Diocese of Southern Ohio (Cincinnati, OH)—to support a partnership with Scioto Christian Ministries to conduct a needs-assessment in Ohio's Scioto County, $28,000; U of Richmond (VA)—to support the creation of an Internet-based resource center that will serve community organizations in the Northern Neck region of Virginia, $219,975.
Contact: Geana Potter, Grants Manager; (904) 353-0890 or (800) 252-3452; fax (904) 353-3870; contactus@dupontfund.org
Internet: http://www.dupontfund.org
Sponsor: Jessie Ball Dupont Fund
One Independent Drive, Suite 1400
Jacksonville, FL 32202-0511

Jessie Smith Noyes Foundation Grants   1058

The foundation is committed to preventing damage to the natural systems upon which all life depends and to strengthening individuals and institutions committed to protecting natural systems and ensuring a sustainable society. The foundation makes grants primarily in the interrelated areas of environment and reproductive rights. The program components include toxics, sustainable agriculture (both with emphasis on southern and Rocky Mountain states), and U.S. reproductive rights. In addition, a few grants are made in four areas of special concern: sustainable communities, U.S. environmental justice, strengthening the U.S. nonprofit sector, and environmental issues in the metropolitan New York region. Letters of inquiry are received at any time; proposals will be requested from the foundation after review.
Requirements: 501(c)3 tax-exempt organizations are eligible.
Restrictions: Normally, the foundation will not consider requests for direct service, endowments, loans or scholarships to individuals, capital construction funds, conferences, media events, production of media and TV programming, or general fund-raising drives. General research projects are not funded per se.
Geographic Focus: All States
Samples: Northwest Women's Law Ctr (Seattle, WA)—for its contributions to the field of reproductive-health care and rights in Alaska, Idaho, Montana, Oregon, and Washington State, $100,000.
Contact: Millie Buchanan, Program Officer; (212) 684-6577; fax (212) 689-6549; noyes@noyes.org
Internet: http://www.noyes.org
Sponsor: Jessie Smith Noyes Foundation
6 E 39th Street, 12th Floor
New York, NY 10016-0112

Jewish Fund Grants   1059

The Fund awards grants to sustain, enrich, and address the overall health care needs of both the Jewish community and general community in the metropolitan Detroit area. The Fund is particularly interested in supporting projects that: address health care and social welfare needs of vulnerable/at-risk populations within the Jewish community; respond to priority capital and equipment needs of the Detroit Medical Center/Sinai Hospital; improve the health and well-being of vulnerable/at risk populations in the general community; support inclusion of people with special needs into the general activities of the community; enhance positive relationships between the Jewish community and the Detroit community. Highest priority is given to requests for programs that: address a critical need; impact the lives of residents of the Wayne, Oakland and Macomb counties; have a defined plan for sustaining the program beyond the grant period; include a financial or in-kind contribution from the organization; involve collaboration with others; have an outcomes-based evaluation plan; and can be funded and replicated by others. Samples of previously funded grants are available on the Fund website.
Requirements: The Jewish Fund will make grants to 501(c)3 organizations and other non-profits qualified as tax exempt under the Internal Revenue Code. Applicant organizations must provide a current audited financial statement. Applicants are encouraged to contact the Fund and discuss their proposed project with the executive director before applying for funding.
Restrictions: The Fund will usually not support: grants made directly to individuals; loans; grants to support religious activities or sectarian education; overseas projects; capital projects or equipment purchases (except equipment at the DMC/Sinai); endowments, annual fund drives, and fundraising events; and past operating deficits.
Geographic Focus: Michigan
Contact: Margo Pernick; (248) 203-1487; fax (248) 645-7879
Internet: http://thejewishfund.org/grant-request-guidelines.html
Sponsor: Jewish Fund
6735 Telegraph Road
Bloomfield Hills, MI 48301-2030

Jim Moran Foundation Grants   1060

The Jim Moran Foundation Grants award funding to 501(c)3 organizations in Florida. The Foundation seeks to improve the quality of life for youth and families through the support of innovative programs and opportunities that meet the ever-changing needs of the community. The Foundation's funding focuses include: education; elder care programs; family strengthening programs; meaningful after school programs; and youth transitional living programs. Proposals for programs that improve the quality of life for those who are at-risk and economically disadvantaged (without extenuating medical or developmental disabilities) will receive priority consideration. Grants are primarily awarded to the Florida counties of Broward, Palm Beach, and Duval. Applicants submit an online letter of inquiry, and will be notified within 90 days if they qualify to submit the online application.
Requirements: The Foundation will consider only organizations that have received 501(c)3 tax-exempt status under the IRS code. Additionally, the organization must be appropriately recognized by state statutes, laws and regulations that govern tax exempt organizations.
Restrictions: The Foundation will consider requests for operating dollars, but only if they do not exceed 50% of the grant request. The Foundation will not consider requests for capital campaigns, capacity building, healthcare or medical research, or event sponsorships.
Geographic Focus: Florida
Contact: Melanie Burgess, Executive Director; (954) 429-2122; fax (954) 429-2699; information@jimmoranfoundation.org
Internet: http://www.jimmoranfoundation.org/GrantApplication.aspx
Sponsor: Jim Moran Foundation
100 Jim Moran Boulevard
Deerfield Beach, FL 33442

Joan Bentinck-Smith Charitable Foundation Grants   1061

Established in 1994, the Joan Bentinck-Smith Charitable Foundation offers funding support primarily within its home state of Massachusetts. Its major fields of interest include: children and youth services; education; housing and shelter; human services; and the support of local YMCAs and YWCAs. There are no specified application forms or annual deadlines, so applicants should begin by contacting the Foundation directly. Recent grants have ranged from $500 to $15,000.
Requirements: The Foundation offers funding to 501(c)3 organizations located within, or supporting the residents of, Massachusetts
Geographic Focus: Massachusetts

Amount of Grant: 500 - 15,000 USD

Samples: Cape Cod Council of Churches, Hyannis, Massachusetts, $1,000 - in support of the Visiting Nurse Association; Greater Boston Food Bank, Boston, Massachusetts, $15,000 - in support of the Cape Cod Island Food Bank program; One Youth World Project, Boston, Massachusetts, $2,000 - for operating support.

Contact: Joan Bentinck-Smith, Trustee; (508) 420-4250

Sponsor: Joan Bentinck-Smith Charitable Foundation

1340 Main Street

Osterville, MA 02655-0430

Joe W. and Dorothy Dorsett Brown Foundation Grants   1062

The Joe W. and Dorothy Dorsett Brown Foundation awards grants to nonprofit organizations in Louisiana and the Gulf Coast of Mississippi. Areas of interest include medical research; housing for the homeless; support for organizations who care for the sick, hungry or helpless; religious and educational institutions; and organizations and groups concerned with improving the local community. Types of support include: operating budgets; research; and student aid. The foundation also supports service learning, a learn-by-doing approach to the curriculum. Students receive practical, hands-on experience in the subject matter studied by meeting identified community needs through active participation. The listed annual deadline date for application submission is August 31.

Requirements: Louisiana and Mississippi nonprofit organizations, with a focus on South Louisiana, the New Orleans area, and the Mississippi Gulf Coast, are eligible. Service Learning grant applications are available yearly to sixth through 12th grades in the following parishes: Orleans, Jefferson, Plaquemines, Saint Bernard, Saint Charles, Tangipahoa, Saint James, Saint John, Saint Tammany, and Washington.

Geographic Focus: Louisiana, Mississippi

Date(s) Application is Due: Aug 31

Amount of Grant: 5,000 - 25,000 USD

Contact: Beth Buscher, (504) 834-3433, ext. 200 or (504) 834-3441; bethbuscher@thebrownfoundation.org

Internet: http://www.thebrownfoundation.org

Sponsor: Joe W. and Dorothy Dorsett Brown Foundation

320 Hammond Highway, Suite 500

Metairie, LA 70005

John and Margaret Post Foundation Grants   1063

The John and Margaret Post Foundation provides support to charitable organizations, which benefit the quality of life for families and society in general and primarily in Northwest New Jersey. The Foundations mission: first consideration for grants is given to organizations based in Northwest New Jersey, or the New Jersey chapters of national organizations; proposals are occasionally considered from groups outside of the state. Priority for funding will be given in the following order: capital needs, specific programs and general operating expenses for smaller organizations who do not have endowments that provide operating support or that can be considered grass roots. Application deadlines are April 1st for a June meeting & October 1st for a December meeting. Grants average $20,000.

Requirements: 501(c)3 organizations based in Northwest New Jersey, or the New Jersey chapters of national organizations are eligible to apply for funding. Contact the Foundation via email for Application Form and Instructions.

Geographic Focus: New Jersey

Date(s) Application is Due: Apr 1; Oct 1

Amount of Grant: 20,000 USD

Contact: Gale Y. Sykes; (908) 598-3576; grantinquiries2@wachovia.com

Internet: https://www.wachovia.com/foundation/v/index.jsp?vgnextoid=af87 8689fb0aa110VgnVCM1000004b0d1872RCRD&vgnextfmt=default

Sponsor: John and Margaret Post Foundation

190 River Road, NJ3132

Summit, NJ 07901

John D. and Catherine T. MacArthur Foundation Media Grants   1064

The goal of the foundation's media grantmaking is to improve the diversity of viewpoints and high-quality documentary content available in radio and television and to use media, especially television and radio production, to further the goals of the other foundation programs. The primary focus of funding is independent documentary film. The foundation usually supports films and programming that address subject matter close to MacArthur's grantmaking strategies; but also it occasionally supports projects on other subjects of overall relevance to the foundation's mission. The foundation also supports outreach efforts, especially related to films it has supported in the production stage

and organizations serving filmmakers. Grants may be used for strategic planning, general operating support, publications, and to convene members of the field. Funding for public radio is intended to maintain and strengthen its program—production infrastructure. The program supports the production and distribution infrastructure of public radio through grants to selected national networks including National Public Radio and Public Radio International.

Requirements: Eligible applicants are media centers, which the foundation defines as organizations that provide community-based and independent producers with access to training and resources needed to produce, exhibit, and distribute film and video; and media organizations, which work at the national level to support independent producers, provide services to the field or support the exhibition of independent media. The foundation is particularly interested in projects that collaborate with nonprofit organizations, public institutions, and disadvantaged communities.

Restrictions: The foundation does not support film festivals, children's programming, or public affairs series. Funds are not provided for individual radio series or individual stations.

Geographic Focus: All States

Date(s) Application is Due: Sep 30

Amount of Grant: Up to 55,000,000 USD

Samples: Lichtenstein Creative Media (Cambridge, MA)—to produce a documentary film examining the intersection of the education, foster-care, juvenile- justice, and mental-health systems, $300,000; West Wind Productions (San Francisco, CA)—to produce a film about the multinational efforts to bring former Chilean dictator Augusto Pinochet and his associates to trial, $300,000; WGBH Educational Foundation (Boston, MA)—for the Frontline/World documentary series, $500,000 over two years; WNET (New York, NY)—for Wide Angle, a television series that features documentary films on international issues, $550,000 over two years.

Contact: Office of Grants Management; (312) 726-8000; fax (312) 920-6258; 4answers@macfdn.org

Internet: http://www.macfound.org/programs

Sponsor: John D. and Catherine T. MacArthur Foundation

140 S Dearborn Street, Suite 1100

Chicago, IL 60603-5285

John D. and Katherine A. Johnston Foundation Grants   1065

The John D. and Katherine A. Johnston Foundation was established in 1928 to support charitable organizations that work to improve the lives of physically disabled children and adults. Special consideration is given to organizations that serve low-income individuals. Preference is given to charitable organizations that serve the people of Newport, Rhode Island. Capital requests that fund handicapped assistive devices (wheelchairs, walkers, etc.) or adaptive equipment (lift installation, ramp installation, etc.) are strongly encouraged. Grant requests for general operating or program support will also be considered. The majority of grants from the Johnston Foundation are one year in duration. The Johnston Foundation shares a mission and grantmaking focus with the Vigneron Memorial Fund. Both foundations have the same proposal deadline date of 11:59 p.m. on April 1. Applicants will be notified of grant decisions before May 31. Applicants must apply online at the grant website. Applicants are strongly encouraged to do the following before applying: review the downloadable state application procedures for additional helpful information and clarifications; review the downloadable online-application guidelines at the grant website; review the foundation's funding history (link is available from the grant website); review the online application questions in advance; and review the list of required attachments. These will generally include: a list of board members, financial statements (audited, reviewed, or compiled by independent auditor); an organization summary; a list of other funding sources; an IRS Determination letter; and other required documents. All attachments must be uploaded in the online application as PDF, Word, or Excel files.

Requirements: Applicants must have 501(c)3 tax-exempt status.

Restrictions: The foundation does not support requests from individuals, organizations attempting to influence policy through direct lobbying, or any political campaigns.

Geographic Focus: Rhode Island

Date(s) Application is Due: Apr 1

Samples: Rhode Island Hospital Foundation, Providence, Rhode Island, $7,500; CranstonArc, Cranston, Rhode Island, $4,000; Meals on Wheels of Rhode Island, Providence, Rhode Island, $3,500.

Contact: Emma Greene; (617) 434-0329; emma.m.greene@baml.com

Internet: https://www.bankofamerica.com/philanthropic/fn_search.action

Sponsor: John D. and Katherine A. Johnston Foundation

225 Franklin Street, 4th Floor, MA1-225-04-02

Boston, MA 02110

John Deere Foundation Grants 1066

The foundation invests in programs in education, health/human services, community improvement, arts and culture. Types of support include annual campaigns, building construction/renovation, continuing support, fellowships, general operating support, scholarship funds, and seed money grants. Foundation interest also includes support for Third World development through US-based nonprofits with international building funds, research grants, general operating purposes, and continuing support. There are no application deadlines.

Requirements: Nonprofit organizations in communities with major John Deere operating units, and employee presence are eligible. Eligible U.S. locations are: Augusta, GA; Quad City Region, IL; Des Moines, IA, Dubuque, IA, Iowa Quad Cities, IA, Ottumwa, IA, Waterloo, IA, Coffeyville, KS, Lenexa, KS, Thibodaux, LA, Springfield, MO, Cary, NC, Fuquay-Varina, NC, Fargo, ND, Greeneville, TN, Madison, WI, Horicon, WI. Exceptions include: accredited colleges and universities; organizations focused on international development initiatives related to John Deere Solutions for World Hunger initiative. Because John Deere dealerships are owned and operated independently, their communities are not included in this geographic scope. Also eligible to apply are organizations and institutions of national or international scope that reflect the foundation's concerns.

Restrictions: Funds are not available for the following organizations or purposes: individual initiatives, including scholarships; sports teams, racing teams, athletic endeavors or scholarships designated for athletes; faith-based organizations for sectarian purposes; political candidates, campaigns or organizations; private clubs, fraternities or sororities; other foundations for purposes of building endowment; tax-supported entities.

Geographic Focus: Georgia, Illinois, Iowa, Kansas, Louisiana, Missouri, North Carolina, Tennessee, Wisconsin, Belarus, Brazil, Canada, Estonia, Latvia, Lithuania, Moldova, Ukraine

Contact: Amy Nimmer, Director; (309) 765-8000

Internet: http://www.deere.com/en_US/globalcitizenship/socialinvestment/index.html

Sponsor: John Deere Foundation

1 John Deere Place

Moline, IL 61265-8098

John Edward Fowler Memorial Foundation Grants 1067

The foundation makes grants to qualified charitable organizations providing grassroots programs for people in need in the Washington, DC, metropolitan area. Preference is given to programs that address the issues of homelessness, hunger, at-risk children and youth (pre-school through high school), adult literacy, free medical care (prenatal to seniors), seniors aging in place, job training and placement. Types of support include general operating support, building construction/renovation, equipment acquisition, program development, and matching funds. The foundation is interested in supporting smaller, well-managed nonprofit organizations that have innovative ideas about how to help people help themselves. Contact the office for application forms. There are no application deadlines.

Requirements: Organizations in Washington, DC, and its close Maryland and Virginia suburbs are eligible.

Restrictions: Grants are not made outside the metropolitan Washington, DC, area, or to/for national health organizations; government agencies; medical research; public school districts; individuals; or arts (except for intensive arts-in-education programs that directly benefit at-risk children and youth).

Geographic Focus: District of Columbia, Maryland, Virginia

Amount of Grant: 5,000 - 20,000 USD

Samples: Carpenter's Shelter, Alexandria, VA, $20,000 - housing with intensive supportive services for homeless adults and children; Bucknell University, Lewisburg, PA, $10,000 - general support; All Souls' Episcopal Church, Mechanicsville VA, $15,000 - Orphans Program of the Maseno Mission in Kenya.

Contact: Suzanne Martin, Grant Consultant; (301) 654-2700

Internet: http://fdncenter.org/grantmaker/fowler/about.html

Sponsor: John Edward Fowler Memorial Foundation

4340 East-West Highway, Suite 206

Bethesda, MD 20814

John Gogian Family Foundation Grants 1068

The Gogian Foundation supports nonprofit organizations in Los Angeles County that provide services and solutions for developmentally disabled adults and children, concentrating on life skills and vocational training, residential group homes, employment, day services, after school programs, and therapeutic services. The Foundation also supports organizations that provides services for abused or neglected youth including: residential group homes; emancipating foster youth; therapeutic, social, and educational services; institutionalized or incarcerated youth; domestic violence; and family preservation. The Foundation makes grants for new, expanding, or sustaining core programming. It also supports improvements, equipment, and vehicle capital expenditures.

Requirements: Applicants must submit the online Letter of Inquiry to request funding, but submit the filled out form by U.S. mail. Organizations will be notified of the outcome of their LOI within 45 of submittal deadline.

Restrictions: The Foundation does not fund the following: national organizations or their affiliates; individuals; care of animals; arts; culture; research; reduction of existing debt; funding of endowments; lending of funds; fundraising events; or political campaigns or projects designed to influence legislation.

Geographic Focus: California

Date(s) Application is Due: Jan 20; Jun 22

Amount of Grant: 5,000 - 20,000 USD

Contact: Lindsey Stammerjohn; (310) 325-0954; jgff@gogianfoundation.org

Internet: http://www.gogianfoundation.org/grant/index.html

Sponsor: John Gogian Family Foundation

3305 Fujita Street

Torrance, CA 90505

John H. and Wilhelmina D. Harland Charitable Foundation 1069
Children and Youth Grants

The John H. and Wilhelmina D. Harland Charitable Foundation offers support for: children and youth programs; community services; and arts, culture, and the environment. In the area of children and youth, support is offered for early childhood education, after school and summer programs for Elementary and Middle School Students, and programs that enhance success in public schools. The focus is local rather than regional or national, and priority is given to institutions in metropolitan Atlanta, Georgia. Grants awards support: building and renovation; capital campaigns; equipment; general operating support; challenge support; and scholarship funds. The Foundation prefers a telephone call as opposed to a letter of inquiry for the initial approach. January 10 is the deadline for the spring grant cycle and August 8 is the deadline for the fall grant cycle.

Requirements: Grant support is available to nonprofit organizations in Georgia, with emphasis on the metropolitan Atlanta area.

Restrictions: Grants are not awarded to individuals.

Geographic Focus: Georgia

Date(s) Application is Due: Jan 10; Aug 8

Amount of Grant: 4,000 - 25,000 USD

Samples: Adaptive Learning Center, Atlanta, Georgia, $20,000 - Inclusion Education Program in partnership with Our House; Moving in the Spirit, Atlanta, Georgia, $12,500 - in support of the Girls Leadership Track; Scottdale Child Development Center and Family Resource Center, Atlanta, Georgia, $20,000 - tuition assistance for early childhood education program.

Contact: Jane Hardesty, Executive Director; (404) 264-9912; info@harlandfoundation.org

Internet: http://harlandfoundation.org/index.php?option=com_content&view=article&id=48&Itemid=55

Sponsor: John H. and Wilhelmina D. Harland Charitable Foundation

Two Piedmont Court, Suite 710

Atlanta, GA 30305-1567

John I. Smith Charities Grants 1070

The foundation supports nonprofit organizations, primarily in South Carolina. With its areas of interest, including: the visual and performing arts, higher education, medical education, theological education, literacy education and basic skills, Christian agencies and churches, child welfare, and programs for the disabled. Grants support general operations, capital campaigns, endowment funds, scholarship funds, and emergency funds. Application forms are not required. The board meets on a quarterly basis. Mail applications to: P.O. Box 1687, Greer, SC 29652

Requirements: Nonprofits in South Carolina are eligible to apply.

Geographic Focus: South Carolina

Amount of Grant: 2,500 - 200,000 USD

Samples: Furman University, Greenville, SC, $100,000; Alliance for Quality Education, Greenville, SC, $27,000; Columbia Theological Seminary, Decatur, GA, $200,000.

Contact: Jefferson Smith, President; (864) 879-2455

Sponsor: John I. Smith Charities

P.O. Box 40200, FL9-100-10-19

Jacksonville, FL 32203-0200

John J. Leidy Foundation Grants 1071

The John J. Leidy Foundation was established in 1957. The foundation gives primarily in the metropolitan Baltimore, Maryland, area. Funding is available to people with disabilities, education, health, social services, and Jewish organizations in the form of, scholarship funds, building/renovation, equipment, general/operating support, and program development grants.

Requirements: Maryland non-profits are eligible to apply.

Restrictions: No grants to individuals.

Geographic Focus: Maryland

Contact: Robert L. Pierson; (410) 821-3006; Leidyfd@attglobal.net

Sponsor: John J. Leidy Foundation

305 W Chesapeake Avenue, Suite 308

Towson, MD 21204-4440

John Jewett and Helen Chandler Garland Foundation Grants 1072

Established in 1959, the John Jewett & Helen Chandler Garland Foundation gives primarily in California, with emphasis on southern California. The foundations area of interest include: the arts, education, health care, children and social services. There are no application deadlines.

Requirements: California nonprofit organizations are eligible.

Restrictions: No telephone inquiries excepted, submit a letter of inquiry as your initial approach.

Geographic Focus: California

Amount of Grant: 2,500 - 610,000 USD

Samples: Huntington Library, Friends of the, San Marino, CA, $800,000 - for general support and educational programs at Botanical Center; Marlborough School, Los Angeles, CA, $25,000 - for general support and minority scholarships; Boys and Girls Clubs of Pasadena, Pasadena, CA, $110,000 - for general support and to make swimming pool accessible year-round.

Contact: Lisa M. Hausler, Manager

Sponsor: John Jewett and Helen Chandler Garland Foundation

P.O. Box 550

Pasadena, CA 91102-0550

John M. Ross Foundation Grants 1073

The John M. Ross Foundation provides funding to nonprofit organizations operating in the state of Hawaii. Funding priorities include youth services, scholarship funds and federated giving programs, offering support in the form of general/operating grants & scholarships. Grant proposals are due February 1st. Applicants are notified in writing of the Committee's action on their requests. Grants range from $250 - $10,000.

Requirements: Nonprofit organizations operating in the State of Hawaii are eligible. To begin the application process, contact the Foundation's administrative office for a Funding Cover Sheet (FCS) and application form. The (FCS) must accompany each grant proposal. The proposal should be no more then 3 pages in length. Include the following information and documentation with your proposal: 1 copy of IRS determination letter, charter, and bylaw, and annual report and financial statements; how project will be sustained once grantmaker support is completed; qualifications of key personnel; statement of problem project will address; population served; copy of IRS Determination Letter; copy of most recent annual report/audited financial statement/990; how project's results will be evaluated or measured; listing of board of directors, trustees, officers and other key people and their affiliations; detailed description of project and amount of funding requested; organization's charter and by-laws; copy of current year's organizational budget and/or project budget; listing of additional sources and amount of support; 4 copies of proposal. Mail proposal to: John M. Ross Foundation c/o Bank of Hawaii, Corporate Trustee Foundation Administration #758 P. O. Box 3170 Honolulu, Hawaii 96802-3170.

Restrictions: No grants are made for endowments or capital campaigns. The recipient of a grant will be required to submit a narrative report on what has been accomplished as a result of the grant, and a fiscal accounting of the grant expenditures.

Geographic Focus: Hawaii

Date(s) Application is Due: Feb 1

Amount of Grant: 250 - 10,000 USD

Samples: YWCA of Hawaii Island, Hilo, HI, $5,000—operational & program Support for Hamakua youth; Aloha Performing Arts Company, Kealakekua, HI, $6,893—Aloha Teen Theatre production of "A Christmas Story"; University of Hawaii Foundation, Honolulu, HI, $10,000—scholarship.

Contact: Paula Boyce; (808) 694-4945; paula.boyce@boh.com

Sponsor: John M. Ross Foundation

P.O. Box 3170

Honolulu, HI 96802-3170

John M. Weaver Foundation Grants 1074

Established in California in 1997, the John M. Weaver Foundation offers funding support for animals and wildlife, education, and human services throughout the State. There is no specified application form, and no annual deadlines. Interested parties should contact the Foundation directly with a two- or three-page query letter, describing their project, budgetary needs, and overall timeline. Recent grants have been funded in the amount of $100 to $1,200.

Requirements: Any 501(c)3 located in, or serving the residents of, California are eligible to apply.

Geographic Focus: California

Amount of Grant: 100 - 1,200 USD

Samples: Hanna Boys Center, Sonoma, California, $1,200 - care and education of children; Westmont College, Santa Barbara, California, $300 - enhancement of the athletic program; Valley Christian High School, San Jose, California, $200 - education of high school students.

Contact: John M. Weaver, President; (408) 268-6471

Sponsor: John M. Weaver Foundation

4760 Sherbourne Drive

San Jose, CA 95124-4845

John P. McGovern Foundation Grants 1075

The John P. McGovern Foundation, established in 1961, supports the charitable interests of the donor to support the activities of established nonprofit organizations, which are of importance to human welfare with special focus on children and family health education and promotion, treatment and disease prevention. The Foundation gives primarily in Texas with an emphasis on the Houston area, but also provides funding in the Southwest region as well. The types of support offered are: building/renovation; conferences/seminars; continuing support; curriculum development; emergency funds; endowments; general/operating support; matching/challenge support; professorships; publication; research; and scholarship funds.

Requirements: Non-profits in Texas are eligible to apply.

Geographic Focus: Texas

Date(s) Application is Due: Aug 31

Amount of Grant: 10,000 - 100,000 USD

Samples: University of Texas Health Science Center, Houston, TX. $1,500,000 - for John P. McGovern, MD, Center for Health, Humanities, and Human Spirit/Certificate Program Endowment Fund; Community Family Centers, Houston, TX. $200,000- for John P. McGovern Community Sports and Recreation Building; Salvation Army of Houston, Houston, TX. $150,000 - for general operating fund.

Contact: Kathrine G. McGovern; (713) 661-4808; fax (713) 661-3031

Sponsor: John P. McGovern Foundation

2211 Norfolk Street, Suite 900

Houston, TX 77098-4044

John R. Oishei Foundation Grants 1076

The foundation's primary mission is to support medical research and care and education, as well as cultural and social needs existing in the Buffalo Niagara region. The foundation favors creative programs that attempt to advance from the status quo, are strategically sound, and are strongly focused on excellence. Programs that provide opportunities for foundation support to be leveraged into greater support from other sources will be especially favored. The foundation generally does not fund operating expenses, though occasional exceptions may be made for organizations that address basic human needs. Requests for capital funds will not be considered unless they are an integral part of an otherwise eligible proposal. Contact the foundation to discuss eligibility before submitting an application. Grant applications are accepted throughout the year.

Requirements: It is the general policy of the foundation to confine its support to activities located in the Buffalo, NY, metropolitan region.

Restrictions: Grants do not support endowments; capital requests (buildings or equipment); deficit funding or loans; individual scholarships or fellowships (except within specific foundation programs); travel, conferences, seminars, or workshops; fundraising events; or 509(a) private foundations.

Geographic Focus: New York

Amount of Grant: 100,000 - 200,000 USD

Contact: Blythe T. Merrill, Senior Program Officer; (716) 856-9490, ext. 3; fax (716) 856-9493; btmerrill@oisheifdt.org

Internet: http://www.oisheifdt.org/Home/Fund/WhatWeFundOverview

Sponsor: John R. Oishei Foundation

1 HSBC Center, Suite 3650

Buffalo, NY 14203-2805

John Reynolds and Eleanor B. Allen Charitable Foundation Grants 1077

The Foundation, established in Florida in 2004, is a 501(c)3 dedicated to supporting performing arts programs, particularly instrumental music, as well as other charitable organizations operating in and around Wauchula, Florida. The brainchild of W. Reynolds Allen, founding partner of a Labor and Employment Law firm, the Foundation is interested in offering its support throughout southern Florida. There are no specific application formats or deadlines, and applicants should contact the Foundation for further instructions. Unsolicited or unapproved applications are not accepted.

Requirements: Applicants should be located in Florida.

Geographic Focus: Florida

Amount of Grant: Up to 1,000 USD

Contact: W. Reynolds Allen, (813) 251-1210; rallen@anblaw.com

Sponsor: John Reynolds and Eleanor B. Allen Charitable Foundation

324 S Hyde Park Avenue, Suite 225

Tampa, FL 33606-4127

John S. and James L. Knight Foundation Communities Grants 1078

The program aims to improve the quality of life in 26 U.S. communities where the Knight brothers owned newspapers. Grants support six priority areas: education—to gain economic self-sufficiency, remain active learners, be good parents, and effective citizens in a democracy; well-being of children and families; housing and community development—to provide affordable, decent housing in safe, drug-free neighborhoods and to provide services for the homeless as well as affordable opportunities for home ownership; economic development—to help all adults gain access to jobs; civic engagement/positive human relations—to encourage residents to be good citizens, form ties to local institutions, and strengthen relationships with one another; and vitality of cultural life—to provide access to a wide variety of arts and cultural pursuits for all and to nourish creativity in children, youth, and adults. The foundation will work with local advisory committees to craft customized strategies for each Knight community, based on the priority areas, and to identify appropriate nonprofit partners. The foundation encourages interested organizations to send a one- to two-page letter of inquiry before submitting a proposal.

Requirements: Nonprofit organizations and institutions are eligible. The proposed project must serve at least one of the following target areas: Long Beach or San Jose, CA; Boulder, CO; Boca Raton, Bradenton, Miami, or Tallahassee, FL; Columbus, Macon, or Milledgeville, GA; Fort Wayne or Gary, IN; Wichita, KS; Lexington, KY; Detroit, MI; Duluth or Saint Paul, MN; Biloxi, MS; Charlotte, NC; Akron, OH; Philadelphia or State College, PA; Columbia or Myrtle Beach, SC; and Aberdeen, SD. Applicant organizations may be located outside of the project target area.

Geographic Focus: California, Colorado, Florida, Georgia, Indiana, Kansas, Kentucky, Minnesota, Mississippi, North Carolina, Ohio, Pennsylvania, South Carolina, South Dakota

Contact: Anne Corriston, Program Director; (305) 908-2600 or (305) 908-2673; fax (305) 908-2698; publications@knightfdn.org

Internet: http://www.knightfoundation.org/programs/communities/

Sponsor: John S. and James L. Knight Foundation

200 S Biscayne Boulevard, Suite 3300

Miami, FL 33131-2349

Johns Manville Fund Grants 1079

The Johns Manville Fund, Inc. gives primarily in areas of company operations in Denver, Colorado, Etowah, Tennessee, and in Canada. The Fund offers support in the areas of: the arts; education; health care; human services; youth services and the American Red Cross. The grants are offered in the form of employee-related scholarships, employee volunteer services, general/operating support, and program development. Contact the Johns Manville Fund, Inc. for a Informational brochure, including application guidelines.

Requirements: Non-profits operating in Denver, Colarado, Etowah, Tennessee, and in Canada are eligible.

Restrictions: No support for religious organizations not of direct benefit to the entire community, hospitals, or non-special needs private educational organizations. No grants for special events.

Geographic Focus: Colorado, Tennessee, Canada

Amount of Grant: 1,000 - 27,000 USD

Contact: Manager; (303) 978-3863; fax (303) 978-2108

Internet: http://www.jm.com/corporate/careers/1241.htm

Sponsor: Johns Manville Fund

717 17th Street

Denver, CO 80202-3330

Johnson & Johnson Corporate Contributions Grants 1080

Johnson & Johnson and its many operating companies support community-based programs that improve health and well-being. The Company works with community-based partners that have the greatest insight into the needs of local populations and the strategies that stand the greatest chances of success. Giving focuses on: saving and improving the lives of women and children; building on the skills of people who serve community health needs, primarily through education; and preventing diseases and reducing stigma and disability in underserved communities where we have a high potential for impact.

Requirements: Grants are awarded to nonprofit and tax-exempt local, national, and international organizations and institutions.

Restrictions: Grants are not awarded to individuals, for deficit funding, capital or endowment funds, demonstration projects, or publications.

Geographic Focus: All States

Contact: Shaun Mickus, (732) 524-2086; smickus@corus.jnj.com

Internet: http://www.jnj.com/connect/caring/corporate-giving/

Sponsor: Johnson and Johnson

1 Johnson & Johnson Plaza

New Brunswick, NJ 08933-0001

Johnson Controls Foundation Arts and Culture Grants 1081

The Johnson Controls Foundation provides financial gifts to select U.S.-based organizations located in the communities in which the company has a presence. In the area of arts and culture, the Foundation supports organizations in the areas of visual, performing and literary arts, public radio and television, libraries, museums, and related cultural activities.

Requirements: In evaluating requests for funds, the Advisory Board has developed policies and guidelines for giving in Culture and the Arts. Contributions will be given to visual, performing, and literary arts, public radio and television, libraries, museums, and other related cultural activities. Priority will be extended to those serving communities in which Johnson Controls employees live and work, and to those in which these employees are involved with their time and/or funds.

Restrictions: In general, no grants will be made to any political campaign or organization; any municipal, state, federal agency, or department, or to any organization established to influence legislation; any private individual for support of personal needs; any sectarian institutions or programs whose services are limited to members of any one religious group or whose funds are used primarily for the propagation of a religion; for testimonial dinners, fund raising events, tickets to benefits, shows, or advertising; to provide monies for travel or tours, seminars and conferences or for publication of books and magazines or media productions; for specific medical or scientific research projects; foreign-based institutions nor to institutions or organizations for use outside of the United States; fraternal orders or veteran groups; private foundations or to endowment funds. The foundation does not donate equipment, products or labor.

Geographic Focus: All States

Amount of Grant: 500 - 40,000 USD

Contact: Charles A. Harvey, President; (414) 524-1200 or (414) 524-2296

Internet: http://www.johnsoncontrols.com/publish/us/en/about/our_ community_focus/johnson_controls_foundation.html

Sponsor: Johnson Controls Foundation

5757 North Green Bay Avenue, P.O. Box 591

Milwaukee, WI 53201

Johnson Controls Foundation Civic Activities Grants 1082

The Johnson Controls Foundation provides financial gifts to select U.S.-based organizations located in the communities in which the company has a presence. In the area of civic activities, the Foundation provides assistance to programs in the areas of justice and law, community and neighborhood improvements, the environment, civic activities and equal opportunity, citizenship and safety.

Requirements: In evaluating requests for funds, the Advisory Board has developed policies and guidelines for giving in civic activities. Contributions will be given to programs in the areas of justice and law, community and neighborhood improvements, the environment, civil rights and equal opportunity, citizenship and safety. Requests to finance office equipment and computer systems do not have a high priority.

Restrictions: In general, no grants will be made to any political campaign or organization; any municipal, state, federal agency, or department, or to any organization established to influence legislation; any private individual for support of personal needs; any sectarian institutions or programs whose services are limited to members of any one religious group or whose funds are used primarily for the propagation of a religion; for testimonial dinners, fund raising events, tickets to benefits, shows, or advertising; to provide monies for travel or tours, seminars and conferences or for publication of books and magazines or media productions; for specific medical or scientific research projects; foreign-based institutions nor to institutions or organizations for use outside of the United States; fraternal orders or veteran groups; private foundations or to endowment funds. The foundation does not donate equipment, products or labor.

Geographic Focus: All States
Date(s) Application is Due: Aug 30
Contact: Charles A. Harvey, President; (414) 524-1200 or (414) 524-2296
Internet: http://www.johnsoncontrols.com/publish/us/en/about/our_community_focus/johnson_controls_foundation.html
Sponsor: Johnson Controls Foundation
5757 North Green Bay Avenue, P.O. Box 591
Milwaukee, WI 53201

Johnson Controls Foundation Health and Social Services Grants   1083

The Johnson Controls Foundation provides financial gifts to select U.S.-based organizations located in the communities in which the company has a presence. Operating support for organizations in the health and social services category largely occurs in communities where Johnson Controls has a local presence and is often directed through contributions to United Way.

Requirements: In evaluating requests for funds, the Advisory Board has developed policies and guidelines for giving in health and social services. Contributions will be given financial assistance to federated drives, hospitals, youth agencies and other health and human service agencies. Ordinarily, operating support of health and social service agencies is reserved for Johnson Controls communities, and generally directed through contributions to United Way.

Restrictions: In general, no grants will be made to any political campaign or organization; any municipal, state, federal agency, or department, or to any organization established to influence legislation; any private individual for support of personal needs; any sectarian institutions or programs whose services are limited to members of any one religious group or whose funds are used primarily for the propagation of a religion; for testimonial dinners, fund raising events, tickets to benefits, shows, or advertising; to provide monies for travel or tours, seminars and conferences or for publication of books and magazines or media productions; for specific medical or scientific research projects; foreign-based institutions nor to institutions or organizations for use outside of the United States; fraternal orders or veteran groups; private foundations or to endowment funds. The foundation does not donate equipment, products or labor.

Geographic Focus: All States
Date(s) Application is Due: Apr 30
Amount of Grant: 1,000 - 150,000 USD
Contact: Charles A. Harvey, President; (414) 524-1200 or (414) 524-2296
Internet: http://www.johnsoncontrols.com/publish/us/en/about/our_community_focus/johnson_controls_foundation.html
Sponsor: Johnson Controls Foundation
5757 North Green Bay Avenue, P.O. Box 591
Milwaukee, WI 53201

Johnson Foundation Wingspread Conference Support Program   1084

The Johnson Foundation at Wingspread sponsors grants to partially fund conferences focusing on subjects in the public interest, primarily health issues and the environment. Meeting facilities include Wingspread, the home designed by Frank Lloyd Wright, and formerly owned by Herbert Fisk Johnson of the Johnson and Johnson family. Conferences are intensive, one- to four-day meetings of small groups convened in partnership with nonprofit organizations, public agencies, universities, and other foundations. Strategic interests of the Foundation are education, sustainable development and environment, democracy and community, and family. The Foundation's usual contribution to a conference sponsored by one or more other organizations consists of the provision of the full conference facilities of Wingspread, planning and logistical support by the staff, meals and other amenities for the period of the meeting.

Requirements: To be invited to submit a full proposal, applicants first must submit a brief concept letter, consisting of: a clear statement of purpose; a draft agenda; the identification of key participants; and an estimated budget and schedule. The letter should describe how the conference will enhance collaboration and community, include diverse opinions and perspectives, identify solutions, and result in action.

Geographic Focus: All States
Contact: Coordinator; (262) 639-3211; fax (262) 681-3327; info@johnsonfdn.org
Internet: http://www.johnsonfdn.org/guidelines.html
Sponsor: Johnson Foundation
33 East Four Mile Road
Racine, WI 53402

John W. Boynton Fund Grants   1085

The John W. Boynton Fund was established in 1952 by Dora Carter Boynton in memory of her husband. He had a thriving business in tinware in Templeton, MA, and later in his life was a resident of Athol, MA. In her will, Mrs. Boynton asked that "organizations which benefit poor, needy, and deserving persons and particularly those of advanced years and gentility" be considered. She also expressed a desire that special consideration be given to charitable organizations serving the Town of Athol. Grant requests for new or special programs and capital projects are preferred. General operating support also will be considered. In come cases, general operating grants are made to make up for a temporary loss of public or private funding. A typical grant is $5,000. Applicants must apply online at the grant website. Applicants are strongly encouraged to do the following before applying: review the downloadable state application procedures for additional helpful information and clarifications at the grant website; review the downloadable online-application guidelines at the grant website; review the foundation's funding history (link is available from the grant website); review the online application questions in advance; and review the list of required attachments. These will generally include: a list of board members, financial statements (audited, reviewed, or compiled by independent auditor); an organization summary; a list of other funding sources; an IRS Determination letter; and other required documents. All attachments must be uploaded in the online application as PDF, Word, or Excel files. The application deadline is 11:59 p.m. on July 15. Applicants will be notified of decisions by the end of September.

Requirements: Applicants must have 501(c)3 tax-exempt status and serve the residents of Greater Boston.

Restrictions: The fund does not support requests from individuals, organizations attempting to influence policy through direct lobbying, or any political campaigns.

Geographic Focus: Massachusetts
Date(s) Application is Due: Jul 15
Amount of Grant: 2,500 - 25,000 USD
Samples: Friends of the Athol Council on Aging, Athol, Massachusetts, $60,000; Associated Grant Makers, Boston, Massachusetts, $5,000; Womens Lunch Place, Boston, Massachusetts, $3,000.
Contact: Michealle Larkins, Vice President; (866) 778-6859; michealle.larkins@baml.com
Internet: https://www.bankofamerica.com/philanthropic/fn_search.action
Sponsor: John W. Boynton Fund
225 Franklin Street, 4th Floor, MA1-225-04-02
Boston, MA 02110

John W. Speas and Effie E. Speas Memorial Trust Grants   1086

The John W. Speas and Effie E. Speas Memorial Trust was established in 1943 to support and promote quality educational, cultural, human-services, and health-care programming. In the area of arts, culture, and humanities, the trust supports programming that: fosters the enjoyment and appreciation of the visual and performing arts; strengthens humanities and arts-related education programs; provides affordable access; enhances artistic elements in communities; and nurtures a new generation of artists. In the area of education, the trust supports programming that: promotes effective teaching; improves the academic achievement of, or expands educational opportunities for, disadvantaged students; improves governance and management; strengthens nonprofit organizations, school leadership, and teaching; and bolsters strategic initiatives of area colleges and universities. In the area of health, the trust supports programming that improves the delivery of health care to the indigent, uninsured, and other vulnerable populations and addresses health and health-care problems that intersect with social factors. In the area of human services, the trust funds programming that: strengthens agencies that deliver critical human services and maintains the community's safety net and helps agencies respond to federal, state, and local public policy changes. In the area of community improvement, the trust funds capacity-building and infrastructure-development projects including: assessments, planning, and implementation of technology for management and programmatic functions within an organization; technical assistance on wide-ranging topics, including grant writing, strategic planning, financial management services, business development, board and volunteer management, and marketing; and mergers, affiliations, or other restructuring efforts. Grant requests for general operating support and program support will be considered. Grants from the foundation are one year in duration. Application materials are available for download at the grant website. Applicants are strongly encouraged to review the state application guidelines for additional helpful information and clarifications before applying. Applicants are also encouraged to review the foundation's funding history (link is available from the grant website). There are no application deadlines for the Speas Memorial Trust. Proposals are reviewed on an ongoing basis.

Requirements: Applicants must have 501(c)3 tax-exempt status and serve the residents of the Greater Kansas City Metropolitan area. Applications must be mailed.
Restrictions: Grant requests for capital support will not be considered. The trust does not support requests from individuals, organizations attempting to influence policy through direct lobbying, or any political campaigns.
Geographic Focus: Missouri
Samples: TLC for Children and Families, Olathe, Kansas, $25,000, Technology Capacity Building Project; Truman Medical Center Charitable Foundation, Kansas City, Missouri, $200,000, joint venture between Truman and Children's Mercy in support of Don Chisholm Hospital Hill Center; Mid-America Regional Council Community Services Corporation, Kansas City, Missouri, $100,000, Kansas City Bi-State Health Information Exchange.
Contact: Spence Heddens; (816) 292-4301; Spence.heddens@baml.com
Internet: https://www.bankofamerica.com/philanthropic/fn_search.action
Sponsor: John W. Speas and Effie E. Speas Memorial Trust
1200 Main Street, 14th Floor, P.O. Box 219119
Kansas City, MO 64121-9119

Joseph Alexander Foundation Grants   1087
Established in 1960 in New York, the Foundation supports primarily in the New York region. Fields of interest include the following: higher education; health organizations; medical research, particularly optic nerve research; social services; and Jewish organizations. Types of support also include the following: annual campaigns; building/renovation; capital campaigns; conferences/seminars; curriculum development; endowments; equipment; exchange programs; general/operating support; program development; research; and scholarship funds. Applicants should submit a letter requesting application guidelines before submitting a proposal. There is no deadline, but the board meets in January, April, July, and October.
Requirements: Nonprofit organizations are eligible to apply.
Restrictions: Grants are not made to individuals.
Geographic Focus: New York
Amount of Grant: 5,000 - 50,000 USD
Samples: Salk Institute for Biological Studies, La Jolla, California, $40,000, payable over one year; University of Pennsylvania, Philadelphia, Pennsylvania, $50,000, payable over one year; Hebrew Free Burial Association, New York, New York, $3,500, payable over one year.
Contact: Robert Weintraub, President; (212) 355-3688
Sponsor: Joseph Alexander Foundation
110 East 59th Street
New York, NY 10022-1304

Joseph Drown Foundation Grants   1088
The foundation makes contributions in the areas of education; community, health and social services; and arts and humanities. It supports programs dealing with such issues as the high school drop-out rate, teen pregnancy, lack of sufficient health care, substance abuse, and violence. Types of support include general operating support, program development, seed money, scholarship funds, and matching funds. Most grant making is limited to programs or organizations in California. Requests are considered each year at March, June, September, and December meetings. The foundation makes grants for both operating support and program support but does not make multiyear commitments. No special application form is required. Proposal should include a letter with information about the organization and the project, a copy of 501(c)3 determination letter, a budget for the organization and the project, the most recent audited financial statements, a copy of the most recent IRS Form 990, and a list of the current board of directors. Any additional materials, such as an annual report, may be attached. Questions should be directed to the program director; proposals should be sent to the foundation president.
Requirements: California 501(c)3 organizations may apply.
Restrictions: The foundation does not provide funds to individuals, endowments, capital campaigns, or annual funds. The foundation does not underwrite annual meetings, conferences, or special events, nor does it fund religious programs or purchase tickets to fund-raising events.
Geographic Focus: California
Date(s) Application is Due: Jan 15; Apr 15; Jul 15; Oct 15
Amount of Grant: 10,000 - 100,000 USD
Samples: The Henry Mancini Institute, Los Angeles, CA, $15,000 - for support of the Community Outreach Initiative; The Museum of Tolerance, Los Angeles, CA, $50,000 - for Tolerance Youth Education programs; Friends of the Semel Institute for Neuroscience, Los Angeles, CA, $40,000 - for a postdoctoral fellowship; Los Angeles Leadership Academy, Los Angeles, CA, $30,000 - for a literacy coordinator and development director in initial year of operation.

Contact: Alyssa Eichelberger, Program Administrator; (310) 277-4488, ext. 100; fax (310) 277-4573; alyssa@jdrown.org
Internet: http://www.jdrown.org
Sponsor: Joseph Drown Foundation
1999 Avenue of the Stars, Suite 1930
Los Angeles, CA 90067

Joseph H. and Florence A. Roblee Foundation Grants   1089
The foundation awards grants to enable organizations to promote change by addressing significant social issues in order to improve the quality of life and help fulfill the potential of individuals. The foundation arises out of a Christian framework, and values ecumenical endeavors. The foundation particularly supports programs which work to break down cultural, racial, and ethnic barriers. Organizations and churches are encouraged to collaborate in achieving positive change through advocacy, prevention, and systemic improvements.
Requirements: Giving limited to nonprofit organizations in the greater bi-state St. Louis region, and Miami/Dade, FL. Contact Foundation for additional guidelines.
Restrictions: Support is not given to individuals or for annual campaigns, research, or loans.
Geographic Focus: Florida, Illinois, Missouri
Date(s) Application is Due: Jan 15; Jun 15
Amount of Grant: 1,000 - 30,000 USD
Samples: Planned Parenthood of the Saint Louis Region, Saint Louis, MO, $20,000 - for comprehensive sex education programs for area teens; Christian Activity Center, East Saint Louis, IL, $15,000 - for Bridging the Gap after-school homework room program; Switchboard of Miami, Miami, FL, $30,000 - for Kevin Kline Suicide Awareness Initiative;
Contact: Peggy Thomas c/o Bank of America, N.A., Bank of America; (314) 466-1304; kathydc@robleefoundation.org.
Sponsor: Joseph H. and Florence A. Roblee Foundation
P.O. Box 14737, MO2-100-07-19
Saint Louis, MO 63178-4737

Josephine S. Gumbiner Foundation Grants   1090
The charitable foundation functions for the benefit of women and children in the Long Beach area. The funder supports a wide array of programs, such as the arts; day care; education health care intervention, prevention, and direct services; housing; and recreation. Organizations are not be eligible for funding more than once in any 12-month period. As a general rule, the foundation will not grant funding to any organization for more than three consecutive years. The two-step application process begins with requesting a letter of intent questionnaire, which should be requested through email. Full applications are by invitation. There are no application deadlines. The board meets three or four times each year.
Requirements: Southern California nonprofit organizations are eligible.
Restrictions: Grants do not support political campaigns, lobbying efforts, programs that supplant tradition schooling, pass-through organizations, or groups with endowments greater than $5 million.
Geographic Focus: California
Amount of Grant: 5,000 - 50,000 USD
Samples: Children's Dental, CA, $20,000 - I.V. Sedation for L.B. Children Program; Children Today, Long Beach, CA, $15,000 - LCSW Support; Helpline Youth Counseling, Norwalk, CA, $15,000 - L.B. Gang Prevention Program.
Contact: Administrator; (562) 437-2882; fax (562) 437-4212; julie@jsgf.org
Internet: http://www.jsgf.org/
Sponsor: Josephine S. Gumbiner Foundation
333 West Broadway, Suite 302
Long Beach, CA 90802

Joseph S. Stackpole Charitable Trust Grants   1091
The Joseph S. Stackpole Charitable Trust was established in 1957 to support and promote quality educational and human-services programming for underserved populations. Preference is given to charitable organizations that serve the people of Hartford County, Connecticut. The Stackpole Charitable Trust makes approximately 10-15 grants each year. The grant range is $1000-$1500 and grants are one year in duration. Applicants must apply online at the grant website. Applicants are strongly encouraged to do the following before applying: review the downloadable state application procedures for additional helpful information and clarifications; review the downloadable online-application guidelines at the grant website; review the trust's funding history (link is available from the grant website); review the online application questions in advance; and review the list of required attachments. These will generally include: a list of board members, financial statements (audited, reviewed, or compiled by independent auditor); an organization summary; a list of other

funding sources; an IRS Determination letter; and other required documents. All attachments must be uploaded in the online application as PDF, Word, or Excel files. The deadline for application to the Joseph S. Stackpole Charitable Trust is 11:59 p.m. on August 15. Applicants will be notified of grant decisions by letter within two to three months after the proposal deadline.

Requirements: First time applicants are asked to contact the Program Officer before applying to the Stackpole Charitable Trust. Applicants must be classified by the Internal Revenue Service (IRS) as a 501(c)3 public charity.

Restrictions: Grant requests for capital projects will not be considered. Applicants will not be awarded a grant for more than 3 consecutive years. The trust does not support requests from individuals, organizations attempting to influence policy through direct lobbying, or any political campaigns.

Geographic Focus: Connecticut
Date(s) Application is Due: Aug 15
Amount of Grant: 1,000 - 1,500 USD
Samples: Hartford Areas Rally Together, Hartford, Connecticut, $1,500, HOME Program (to create successful homeowners by educating individuals about the process of home purchase and home ownership); ConnectiKids, Hartford, Connecticut, $1,500, Tutoring/Mentoring and Arts/Enrichment programs (general operations); Bridge Family Center, West Hartford, Connecticut, $1,000, for youth shelters/short-term assessment and respite (STAR) homes.
Contact: Kate Kerchaert, Senior Foundation Officer; (860) 657-7016; kate. kerchaert@baml.com
Internet: https://www.bankofamerica.com/philanthropic/fn_search.action
Sponsor: Joseph S. Stackpole Charitable Trust
200 Glastonbury Boulevard, Suite # 200, CT2-545-02-05
Glastonbury, CT 06033-4056

Jostens Foundation Community Grants 1092

Jostens provides support to organizations that enhance the lives of youth and promote educational opportunities that significantly and positively impact children from birth through college. The foundation meets quarterly to review all Community Grant requests.

Requirements: Nonprofit organizations with 501(c)3 status are eligible. The foundation gives priority to organizations where Jostens facilities and employees are located and gives priority to nonprofit organizations that involve Jostens employees.

Restrictions: In general, grants are not made to support educational institutions or for scholarships, political organizations, churches or religious groups, fundraising events, or endowment funds.

Geographic Focus: All States
Date(s) Application is Due: Mar 9; Jun 8; Sep 7; Dec 7
Amount of Grant: 500 - 10,000 USD
Contact: Mary Klimek, (952) 830-3235; foundation@jostens.com
Internet: http://www.jostens.com/company/community/index.asp
Sponsor: Jostens Foundation
5601 American Boulevard W
Minneapolis, MN 55437

Joukowsky Family Foundation Grants 1093

The Joukowsky Family Foundation supports secondary and higher education, cultural, social, archaeological and historical activities in the northeastern United States. Types of support include capital campaigns; continuing support; endowments; fellowships; general/operating support; and scholarships. The Foundation contributes to pre-selected organizations. Unsolicited proposals are not accepted.

Requirements: Nonprofit 501(c)3 organizations are eligible to apply.
Geographic Focus: Connecticut, Maine, Massachusetts, New Hampshire, New Jersey, New York, Pennsylvania, Rhode Island, Vermont
Amount of Grant: 5,000 - 2,000,000 USD
Contact: Nina Koprulu; (212) 355-3151; fax (212) 355-3147
Internet: http://www.joukowsky.org/guidelines.html
Sponsor: Joukowsky Family Foundation
620 Park Avenue, 5th Floor
New York, NY 10022

Journal Gazette Foundation Grants 1094

The foundation awards grants to northeastern Indiana nonprofit organizations in its areas of interest, including community funds, education, higher education, health organizations and hospitals, social services, Christian agencies and churches, and youth. Types of support include general operations and capital campaigns. There are no application deadlines; the board meets quarterly.

Requirements: Indiana nonprofit organizations are eligible. Preference is given to requests from northeastern Indiana.

Restrictions: Grants are not made to individuals.
Geographic Focus: Indiana
Amount of Grant: 25 - 112,000 USD
Contact: Jerry Fox, (260) 424-5257
Sponsor: Journal Gazette Foundation
701 S Clinton
Fort Wayne, IN 46802-1883

Jovid Foundation Employment Training Grants 1095

The Jovid Foundation is a philanthropic foundation incorporated in 1990 in the District of Columbia. The Foundation's primary interest is in supporting District of Columbia nonprofit organizations that help District residents in or at risk of long-term poverty to become more self-sufficient. Because the Foundation is small and seeks to make a positive difference, it is particularly interested in funding neighborhood-based efforts that provide employment training programs and services to low-income D.C. adults that help them obtain and retain permanent jobs. In addition, a small number of grants may be made from a discretionary fund. Because the Foundation does not have the staff to review lengthy submissions, it does not accept unsolicited proposals that are already fully developed. The Foundation requests a letter of inquiry (LOI) describing the proposed project. Even if your organization has received funding from Jovid in the past, a new letter of inquiry must first be submitted. Annual deadlines for Letters of Inquiry are January 7, April 8, and August 12. If a full proposal is requested, annual application deadlines are February 11, May 6, and September 9.

Requirements: Washington, DC, nonprofits are eligible to apply.
Geographic Focus: District of Columbia
Date(s) Application is Due: Feb 11; May 6; Sep 9
Amount of Grant: Up to 20,000 USD
Samples: Byte Back, Washington, DC, $20,000 - support for computer training; Concerned Black Men, Washington, DC, $10,000 - support for the Family Services Center; Employment Justice Center, Washington, DC, $7,500 - support of the Legal Services Program.
Contact: Bob Wittig, Executive Director; (202) 686-2616; fax (202) 686-2621; jovidfoundation@gmail.com
Internet: http://fdnweb.org/jovid/employment-training-program/
Sponsor: Jovid Foundation
5335 Wisconsin Avenue NW, Suite 440
Washington, D.C. 20015-2003

Joyce Foundation Democracy Grants 1096

The Joyce Foundation has long been interested in ensuring the vibrancy of American democracy, from funding presidential debates to supporting work on such concerns as voter registration and full participation in the U.S Census. Beginning in the mid-1990s, the Foundation focused its efforts on combating the overwhelming influence of big money on most areas of American public life. The Foundation has supported the growth of a strong network of public interest groups in Midwest states, which collaborate through the Midwest Democracy Network; and it has also funded national groups ranging from the Brookings Institution to the Cato Institute. More recently, Joyce's grant making has expanded beyond campaign finance reform to include such issues as fair and open redistricting, protection of voting rights, governmental ethics, and judicial independence – all essential elements of a strong democracy.

Requirements: The overriding goal of the Democracy Program is to preserve and strengthen those values and qualities that are the foundation of a healthy democratic political system: honesty, fairness, transparency, accountability, competition, and maximizing informed citizen participation. Accordingly, the Foundation seeks to create political cultures in Illinois, Michigan, Minnesota, Ohio and Wisconsin which make it possible for more citizens, not just those who are wealthy and well-connected, to run for public office; offer voters real candidate and policy choices at election time; protect voting rights; respect the independence and impartiality of the courts; guarantee the fairness and reliability of elections; and provide citizens with the information needed to make reasoned decisions. To promote these ends, the Foundation supports organizations and coalitions in the Midwest that are willing and have the skills to: (1) Contribute to the development and promotion of broad, multi-issue political reform agendas within the target states, including improvements in the laws and practices governing campaign finance, elections, redistricting, judicial selection, voting rights, and local news coverage of government and politics. (2) Engage in activities necessary for effective advocacy including: policy research and development; public and policy maker education; civic engagement, particularly in underrepresented communities; coalition building; news media outreach; and participation in official proceedings, including litigation. (3) Work collaboratively with other reform and civic groups, academic and legal

experts, and policy makers to advance shared goals within their states and across the region. (4) Participate in activities designed to enhance their capacities in the areas of strategic planning, organizing, coalition building, fundraising, advocacy, and communications. A letter of interest (LOI) should be submitted first. If acceptable, applicants will be requested to submit a full proposal. Applicants are strongly encouraged to plan their application and proposal submission process for the April or July meetings, since most grant funds will be distributed at those times. Grants to non-Midwest organizations must be for projects that strengthen the capacity of state-based groups as advocates for comprehensive political reforms, including campaign finance, redistricting, judicial, governmental ethics, lobbying and media reforms.
Geographic Focus: Illinois, Michigan, Minnesota, Ohio, Wisconsin
Date(s) Application is Due: Apr 8; Aug 14; Dec 3
Contact: Veronica Salter, Grants Manager; (312) 782-2464; fax (312) 595-1350; info@joycefdn.org or vsalter@joycefdn.org
Internet: http://www.joycefdn.org/programs/democracy/
Sponsor: Joyce Foundation
321 North Clark Street, Suite 1500
Chicago, IL 60654

Joyce Foundation Gun Violence Prevention Grants   1097

Gun violence claims 30,000 persons in the United States every year, including lives lost in gun homicides, suicides, and accidental shootings. An additional 60,000 Americans are injured by guns annually. This public health and public safety crisis takes an enormous toll on families, and offends the right of all Americans to be safe in their communities. The Joyce Foundation works with law enforcement, policy makers and advocates to develop common sense gun violence reduction and prevention policies that keep our communities safe. The Foundation supports local, state, regional, and national projects that: (1) Advance state-based policy advocacy and organizing to secure effective gun violence prevention policies and practices; (2) Improve public engagement in support of effective gun violence prevention policies and practices; (3) Build effective coalitions to secure support for gun violence prevention policy reform among groups most impacted by gun violence; (4) Support Second Amendment legal strategies to uphold effective gun violence prevention policies and practices; and, (5) Encourage policy-oriented research and data collection to support effective gun violence prevention policies and practices.
Requirements: Grant making focuses on initiatives that promise to have an impact on the Great Lakes region, specifically the states of Illinois, Indiana, Michigan, Minnesota, Ohio, and Wisconsin. The Joyce Foundation is committed to improving public policy through its grant program. Accordingly, the Foundation welcomes grant requests from organizations that engage in public policy advocacy. Federal tax law prohibits private foundations from funding lobbying activities. The Foundation may support organizations engaged in public policy advocacy by either providing general operating support or by funding educational advocacy such as nonpartisan research, technical assistance, or examinations of broad social issues. A letter of interest (LOI) should be submitted first. If acceptable, applicants will be requested to submit a full proposal. Applicants are strongly encouraged to plan their application and proposal submission process for the April or July meetings, since most grant funds will be distributed at those times.
Restrictions: The Foundation does not generally support capital proposals, endowment campaigns, religious activities, commercial ventures, direct-service programs, or scholarships.
Geographic Focus: All States
Date(s) Application is Due: Apr 8; Aug 14; Dec 3
Contact: Veronica Salter, Grants Manager; (312) 782-2464; fax (312) 595-1350; info@joycefdn.org or vsalter@joycefdn.org
Internet: http://www.joycefdn.org/programs/gun-violence-prevention/
Sponsor: Joyce Foundation
321 North Clark Street, Suite 1500
Chicago, IL 60654

Joy Family Foundation Grants   1098

The foundation awards grants to nonprofit organizations and individuals in the city of Buffalo, NY, and the counties of Erie and Niagara, NY, to improve the quality of life. Grants are awarded in support of human and family services, education and literacy, AIDS research, substance abuse, alcoholism, the aging, the economically disadvantaged, hospitals, women and children, and Roman Catholic churches and organizations. Grants will be awarded for programs and projects, general operating support, capital campaigns, building/renovation, technical assistance, and consulting services. The board meets quarterly.
Requirements: New York nonprofit organizations are eligible.

Geographic Focus: New York
Amount of Grant: 100 - 100,000 USD
Contact: Marsha Sullivan, Executive Director; (716) 633-6600; fax (716) 633-0600; info@joyfamilyfoundation.org
Internet: http://www.joyfamilyfoundation.org
Sponsor: Joy Family Foundation
5436 Main Street, Suite 1
Williamsville, NY 14221

JP Morgan Chase Arts and Culture Grants   1099

The foundation supports programs in the New York tri-state region, across the nation, and around the world that strengthen communities where JP Morgan Chase employees live and work. In its Arts and Culture grantmaking, the Foundation looks for opportunities to integrate the arts into children's educational opportunities and position arts organizations and artists as key drivers of local economic renewal. The Foundation supports: arts programs in schools and after school; building the capacity of community-based arts institutions; initiatives that stimulate the creation and growth of local cultural economies; broadening of access to artistic excellence and diversity by partnering with major arts and culture groups.
Requirements: Only charitable, not-for-profit organizations are eligible to apply. Refer to the website in order to identify the region in which your program will be administered.
Restrictions: The following types of organizations, activities or purposes are not funded: programs outside the geographic markets we serve; individuals; fraternal organizations; athletic teams or social groups; public agencies; private schools; public schools (K-12), unless in partnership with a qualified not-for-profit organization; parent-teacher associations; scholarships or tuition assistance; higher education, unless program is specifically within guidelines; fundraising events (e.g. golf outings, school events); advertising, including ads in event, performance or athletic programs; volunteer-operated organizations; funds to pay down operating deficits; programs designed to promote religious or political doctrines; endowments or capital campaigns (exceptions are made by invitation only); organizations that discriminate on the basis of race, sex, sexual orientation, age or religion; health or medical-related organizations, unless program fits within stated giving guidelines.
Geographic Focus: Arizona, California, Colorado, Connecticut, Delaware, Florida, Illinois, Indiana, Kentucky, Louisiana, Michigan, New Jersey, New York, Ohio, Oklahoma, Texas, Utah, West Virginia, Wisconsin
Contact: Kimberly B. Davis, President; (212) 270-6000
Internet: http://www.jpmorganchase.com/corporate/Corporate-Responsibility/corporate-philanthropy.htm
Sponsor: JP Morgan Chase & Company
270 Park Avenue
New York, NY 10017

JP Morgan Chase Community Development Grants   1100

Working with best-in-class community-based partners, the JP Morgan Chase goal is to help stabilize families living in high-poverty neighborhoods and to make that stability echo through a neighborhood in a manner that improves educational and job opportunities, reduces crime and dramatically raises the community's quality of life. The program supports both resident-focused programs and community-focused programs. Resident-focused programs that address workforce development, asset building, and financial literacy, will support: continuing education courses; adult literacy outreach; job training; money management basics; credit repair; EITC workshops; home ownership and home buyer workshops; and foreclosure prevention programs. Community-focused programming addresses economic development and affordable housing issues.
Requirements: Only charitable, not-for-profit organizations are eligible to apply. Refer to the website in order to identify the region in which your program will be administered.
Restrictions: The following types of organizations, activities or purposes are not funded: programs outside the geographic markets we serve; individuals; fraternal organizations; athletic teams or social groups; public agencies; private schools; public schools (K-12), unless in partnership with a qualified not-for-profit organization; parent-teacher associations; scholarships or tuition assistance; higher education, unless program is specifically within guidelines; fundraising events (e.g. golf outings, school events); advertising, including ads in event, performance or athletic programs; volunteer-operated organizations; funds to pay down operating deficits; programs designed to promote religious or political doctrines; endowments or capital campaigns (exceptions are made by invitation only); organizations that discriminate on the basis of race, sex, sexual orientation, age or religion; health or medical-related organizations, unless program fits within stated giving guidelines.

Geographic Focus: Arizona, California, Colorado, Connecticut, Delaware, Florida, Illinois, Indiana, Kentucky, Louisiana, Michigan, New Jersey, New York, Ohio, Oklahoma, Texas, Utah, West Virginia, Wisconsin
Contact: Kimberly B. Davis, President; (212) 270-6000
Internet: http://servicelearning.org/resources/funding_sources/index.php?popup_id=898
Sponsor: JP Morgan Chase & Company
270 Park Avenue
New York, NY 10017

JPMorganChase Regrant Program for Small Ensembles   1101
This joint grant initiative of Meet The Composer and JPMorganChase is dedicated to general operating support for professional music organizations and music presenters with annual budgets of $300,000 or less. The goal of this program is to encourage the work of small New York City based music organizations and music presenters (Bronx, Brooklyn, Manhattan, Queens and Staten Island). The purpose of general operating support is to provide unrestricted support for ongoing institutional operating activities of organizations whose central mission is the creation, production, and performance of musical programming. Guidelines and application instructions are available online.
Requirements: 501(c)3 tax-exempt organizations in the five boroughs of New York City, with organized music programs for at least three years, and an annual budget of less than $300,000 are eligible. Eligible organizations must have an existing organizational structure and an on-going artistic product.
Geographic Focus: All States
Date(s) Application is Due: Mar 4
Amount of Grant: Up to 5,000 USD
Contact: Grants Administrator; (212) 645-6949, ext. 101; mtrevino@meetthecomposer.org
Internet: http://www.meetthecomposer.org/programs/fundforsmall.html
Sponsor: Meet the Composer
75 Ninth Avenue, Floor 3R, Suite C
New York, NY 10011

JSPS Postdoctoral Fellowship for Foreign Researchers   1102
To facilitate cooperative research between young foreign researchers and hosting Japanese researchers, fellowships are awarded to enable postdoctoral researchers to undertake research at Japanese universities and institutions. The program also supports short-term fellowships of 15 days to 11 months. The fellowship includes round-trip airfare, a monthly stipend of @Y270,000, and an additional settling-in allowance. In addition, JSPS may provide a special research grant up to @Y1.5 million, depending on need of applicants.
Requirements: Fellowships are available to citizens of countries that have diplomatic relations with Japan. Candidates must hold the doctorate degree when the fellowship goes into effect; the degree must have been received within six years prior to April of the fiscal year in which the fellowship commences. The candidate must have arranged in advance a research plan with his/her Japanese host researcher, who must be employed at a Japanese university/research institution.
Geographic Focus: All States
Amount of Grant: 5,000 - 13,000 USD
Contact: Program Administrator, Foreign Fellowship Division; 81-3-3263-1721; fax 81-3-3263-1854
Internet: http://www.jsps.go.jp/english/e-fellow/postdoctoral.html#short
Sponsor: Japan Society for the Promotion of Science
Nihon Gakujutsu Shinko-kai, 5-3-1, Kojimachi, Chiyoda-ku
Tokyo, 102-8471 Japan

Judith and Jean Pape Adams Charitable Foundation Tulsa Area Grants   1103
The Foundation was established in 2004 as a private foundation and is involved in making distributions to charitable organizations on an annual basis. It encompasses two areas of support: organizations and agencies predominantly in Tulsa County, Oklahoma, and national Amyotrophic Lateral Sclerosis (ALS) research. For the former, primary areas of interest include arts and culture, human services and education. Support is given for operations, programs, capital projects, and maintenance reserve funding. The annual deadline is August 15.
Requirements: Public agencies serving the Tulsa, Oklahoma, region that are classified as a charitable organization described in Section 501(c)3 of the Internal Revenue Code and as a public charity under Section 509(a) of the Internal Revenue Code may apply.
Geographic Focus: Oklahoma
Date(s) Application is Due: Aug 15
Amount of Grant: 500 - 250,000 USD

Samples: Oklahoma Humanities Council, Oklahoma City, Oklahoma, $1,250 - operating support; Clarehouse, Tulsa, Oklahoma, $20,000 - operating support; Safari Joe's Wildlife Ranch, Adair, Oklahoma - operating support.
Contact: Marcia Y. Manhart, Executive Director; (830) 997-7347; fax (830) 997-9888; mmanhart@jjpafoundation.com
Sue Mayhue, (316) 383-1795
Internet: http://www.jjpafoundation.com/guidelines.html
Sponsor: Judith and Jean Pape Adams Charitable Foundation
7030 South Yale Avenue, Suite 600
Tulsa, OK 74136

Julius N. Frankel Foundation Grants   1104
The Julius N. Frankel Foundation supports Chicago-area nonprofits in the areas of: arts and performing arts; children and youth service; higher education; hospitals; human services; and medical school education. Recipients have included hospitals, universities, cultural organizations, and social service providers, with an emphasis on large, established organizations. There are no specified application formats or deadlines, though the Board meets at least five times annually. Most recent grant awards have ranged from $25,000 to $200,000. The initial approach should be by letter, detailing the program and budgetary needs.
Requirements: Chicago-area nonprofits are eligible to apply.
Restrictions: Individuals are not eligible.
Geographic Focus: Illinois
Amount of Grant: 25,000 - 200,000 USD
Samples: Chicago Opera Theater, Chicago, Illinois, $45,000 - general operations; Chicago Symphony Orchestra, Chicago, Illinois, $150,000 - general support; Lawrence Hall Youth Services, Chicago, Illinois, $50,000 - general operating support.
Contact: Hector Ahumada, Trustee; (312) 461-5154
Sponsor: Julius N. Frankel Foundation
111 W. Monroe Street, Tax Division 10C
Chicago, IL 60603-4096

K. M. Hunter Charitable Foundation Social Welfare Grants   1105
The Foundation provides a number of major grants to social and health services programs in Ontario. In addition, a series of smaller grants are given to organizations, including housing shelters and hospices for the sick. The Foundation requests that applicants make all contacts through its published email address. There are no specific applications or deadlines, and the Board meets two or three times annually to make its funding decisions.
Requirements: Grants are made to registered charitable organizations based in Ontario, with the exception of grants that support AIDS in Africa.
Geographic Focus: Canada
Contact: Judith Hunter; (416) 365-6600; turtlart@gmail.com
Internet: http://www.kmhunterfoundation.ca/social.html
Sponsor: K.M. Hunter Charitable Foundation
P.O. Box 38, Station E
Toronto, ON M6H 4E1 Canada

K.S. Adams Foundation Grants   1106
Established in Oklahoma in 1953, the K.S. Adams Foundation offers support primarily in the Bartlesville, Oklahoma region. The Foundation's major fields of interest include: community and economic development, education, philanthropy, and volunteerism. Types of funding come in the form of annual campaign contributions and continuing financial support. A formal application is not required, and interested parties should forward a letter of application. Recently, grants have ranged between $500 and $10,000. There are no specified annual deadlines.
Geographic Focus: Oklahoma
Contact: Trustee; (918) 337-3470 or (918) 337-3279
Sponsor: K.S. Adams Foundation
P.O. Box 1156
Bartlesville, OK 74005

Kaman Corporate Giving Program Grants   1107
The corporate giving program focuses on the needs of the handicapped and disabled, but funding is provided to cover a broad range of human needs. Grants are made for capital building, renovation campaigns, and selected operating programs. The majority of grants are awarded to nonprofits in the Hartford, CT, area. Requests are accepted throughout the year. Requests for funding should include the organization's latest financial report; a description of (and budget for) the project to be funded; information concerning the status of funding toward the goal; a listing of the organization's board of directors and key staff; and the name,

address, and phone number of the person to be contacted for further information. Other material the organization feels would be helpful is welcomed.

Requirements: Nonprofits in the greater Hartford region of Connecticut are eligible.

Restrictions: Grants do not support endowment funds, recipients of state grants, agencies receiving funds from the United Way/Combined Health Appeal, or galas and events.

Geographic Focus: Connecticut

Amount of Grant: 25,000 - 500 USD

Contact: Russell Jones, Vice President; (860) 243-6308; fax (860) 243-6365; info.kaman-corp@kaman.com

Internet: http://www.kaman.com

Sponsor: Kaman Corporation

1332 Blue Hills Avenue

Bloomfield, CT 06002

Kansas Arts Commission Operational Support for Arts and Cultural   1108 Organizations

Through operational support grants, the Commission offers financial assistance to nonprofit arts and cultural organizations with at least a three-year history of incorporation or operation as an independent entity. The award is based upon a percentage of the organization's projected expense budget and the amount of funds available for distribution in this program category. Arts organizations may apply for support of general operating, program, and administrative expenses; and on attached application components, arts organizations may apply for support of arts in education activities, and for support of Kansas touring program events. The purpose of the operational support grants is to strengthen the administrative and programming capability of arts organizations; enable arts organizations to provide high-quality, accessible arts activities, programs, and services to their constituencies; support arts organizations in planning and development of long-term goals; and augment, not supplant, local support for arts organizations.

Requirements: Single or multidisciplinary arts and cultural organizations based in Kansas are eligible to apply. Organizations must have as their primary missions planning, development, support or presentation of arts and cultural programs and services, as evidenced by their mission statement, total fiscal operations, and total activities.

Geographic Focus: Kansas

Date(s) Application is Due: Mar 4

Amount of Grant: 2,000 USD

Contact: Raena Sommers, Grants Administrator; (785) 296-4089; fax (785) 296-4989; raena@arts.state.ks.us

Internet: http://arts.ks.gov/grants/os/index.shtml

Sponsor: Kansas Arts Commission

700 SW Jackson, Jayhawk Tower, Suite 1004

Topeka, KS 66603-3774

Karma Foundation Grants   1109

The foundation awards grants on an international basis to support the following broad interest areas: arts and culture, education and literacy, health and human services, and development and enrichment of Jewish life. Types of support include operating expenses, special projects, capital grants, seed grants, equipment and materials. and disaster relief. The foundation also provides technical assistance and assists in proposal development. There are no application deadlines.

Requirements: National and international nonprofits are eligible.

Restrictions: Grants do not support travel expenses for bands or sports teams, political or lobbying activities, advertising for fundraising events, litigation, charter schools, or loans.

Geographic Focus: California, New Jersey, Wisconsin

Amount of Grant: 500 - 25,000 USD

Contact: Dina Karmazin Elkins, Executive Director; (609) 924-5939; fax (609) 924-2714; info@karmafoundation.org

Internet: http://www.karmafoundation.org

Sponsor: Karma Foundation

140 Arreton Road

Princeton, NJ 08540

Kate B. Reynolds Charitable Trust Health Care Grants   1110

The Trust responds to health care and wellness needs and invests in solutions that improve the quality of health for financially needy residents throughout North Carolina. The Health Care Division seeks impact through two program areas: providing treatment and supporting prevention. The trust requires advanced consultation by phone or in writing. Application materials are available online, but applications are not accepted electronically.

Requirements: 501(c)3 organizations in North Carolina are eligible.

Restrictions: Grants are not awarded to individuals.

Geographic Focus: North Carolina

Date(s) Application is Due: Mar 15; Sep 15

Amount of Grant: 20,000 - 200,000 USD

Contact: John H. Frank, Director; (336) 397-5502 or (866) 551-0690; fax (336) 723-7765; john@kbr.org

Internet: http://www.kbr.org/health-care-division-fund.cfm

Sponsor: Kate B. Reynolds Charitable Trust

128 Reynolda Village

Winston-Salem, NC 27106-5123

Kate B. Reynolds Charitable Trust Poor and Needy Grants   1111

Through the Poor and Needy Division, the trust responds to basic life needs and invests in solutions that improve the quality of life for financially needy residents of Forsyth County. The Poor and Needy division seeks impact through two program areas by providing operating funds: Providing Basic Needs and Increasing Self Reliance. The Grant Application Process is a two-step process involving consultation with a staff Program Officer, followed by formal submission of a grant application. The consultation can be scheduled by calling our Winston-Salem offices.

Requirements: Nonprofit 501(c)3 organizations in Forsyth County, North Carolina, are eligible.

Restrictions: Grants are not awarded to individuals.

Geographic Focus: North Carolina

Date(s) Application is Due: Jan 15; Jul 15

Contact: Joyce T. Adger, Program Director; (336) 397-5503 or (336) 723-1456; fax (336) 723-7765; joyce@kbr.org

Internet: http://www.kbr.org/poor-and-needy-division-fund.cfm

Sponsor: Kate B. Reynolds Charitable Trust

128 Reynolda Village

Winston-Salem, NC 27106-5123

Katharine Matthies Foundation Grants   1112

The Katharine Matthies Foundation was established in 1987 to support and promote quality educational, human-services, and health-care programming for underserved populations. Special consideration is given to organizations that work to prevent cruelty to children and animals. The majority of grants from the Matthies Foundation are one year in duration; on occasion, multi-year support is awarded. Applicants must apply online at the grant website. Applicants are strongly encouraged to do the following before applying: review the downloadable state application procedures for additional helpful information and clarifications; review the downloadable online-application guidelines at the grant website; review the foundation's funding history (link is available from the grant website); review the online application questions in advance; and review the list of required attachments. These will generally include: a list of board members, financial statements (audited, reviewed, or compiled by independent auditor); an organization summary; a list of other funding sources; an IRS Determination letter; and other required documents. All attachments must be uploaded in the online application as PDF, Word, or Excel files. The deadline for application to the Katherine Matthies Foundation is 11:59 p.m. on May 1. Applicants will be notified of grant decisions by letter within three to four months after the proposal deadline.

Requirements: Applicant organizations must have 501(c)3 tax-exempt status and serve the people of the following Connecticut towns: Seymour, Ansonia, Derby, Oxford, Shelton, or Beacon Falls. A breakdown of number/percentage of people served by specific towns will be required in the online application. Special consideration will be given to organizations that serve the people of Seymour, Connecticut.

Restrictions: The Matthies Foundation specifically serves people of the Lower Naugatuck Valley. The foundation does not support requests from individuals, organizations attempting to influence policy through direct lobbying, or any political campaigns.

Geographic Focus: Connecticut

Date(s) Application is Due: May 1

Contact: Amy Lynch; (860) 657-7015; amy.r.lynch@baml.com

Internet: https://www.bankofamerica.com/philanthropic/fn_search.action

Sponsor: Katharine Matthies Foundation

200 Glastonbury Boulevard, Suite # 200

Glastonbury, CT 06033-4056

Katherine Mabis McKenna Foundation Grants 1113

The foundation awards grants to eligible Philadelphia nonprofit organizations in its areas of interest, including education, arts and culture, philanthropy, human services, environment, and community development. Types of support include annual campaigns, building construction/renovation, capital campaigns, equipment acquisition, general operating grants, program development, and seed grants. There are no application forms. The foundation prefers to receive proposals between January and July.

Requirements: Philadelphia nonprofit organizations are eligible. Preference is given to requests from Westmoreland County.

Geographic Focus: Pennsylvania

Date(s) Application is Due: Oct 1

Amount of Grant: 2,500 - 50,000 USD

Contact: Linda McKenna Boxx, (724) 537-6900

Sponsor: Katherine Mabis McKenna Foundation

P.O. Box 186

Latrobe, PA 15650

Kathryne Beynon Foundation Grants 1114

Founded in California in 1967, the Kathryne Beynon Foundation provides support primarily for: hospitals (with a special interest in Asthma); youth agencies; child welfare; Roman Catholic church; higher education, Types of support include: general operating support; building construction/renovation; endowment funds; and scholarship funds. The Board meets quarterly to review grant requests. Applicants should contact the office in writing, outlining their proposal. Application is by invitation only, and there is no deadline date when submitting grant proposals. Contact the Foundation directly for additional guidelines before submitting a full proposal.

Requirements: 501(c)3 southern California tax-exempt organizations are eligible. Preference is given to requests from Pasadena. There are no: deadline dates; formal application form required to submit proposal.

Restrictions: No support to individuals.

Geographic Focus: California

Amount of Grant: 500 - 50,000 USD

Samples: Artists of America, San Pedro, CA, $17,800—Laurel Elementary School, Prep art classes; Assistance League of Southern California, Hollywood, CA, $4,000—children's club/ day nursery; Scripps College, Claremont, CA, $20,000—science scholarship program.

Contact: Robert D. Bannon, Trustee; (626) 584-8800

Sponsor: Kathryne Beynon Foundation

1111 South Arroyo Parkway, Suite 470

Pasadena, CA 91105-3239

Kawabe Memorial Fund Grants 1115

The Kawabe Memorial Fund was established in 1971 to support and promote quality human-services programming for the economically disadvantaged, children and the elderly. The Fund also provides capital grants to churches as well as scholarships to support teachers and the clergy. The Kawabe Memorial Fund typically supports organizations serving the people of the Puget Sound area. Grant requests for general operating support are strongly encouraged. Program support will also be considered. Small, program-related capital expenses may be included in general operating or program requests. Grants from the Kawabe Memorial Fund are one year in duration. Application materials are available for download at the grant website. Applicants are strongly encouraged to review the state application guidelines for additional helpful information and clarifications before applying. Applicants are also encouraged to review the foundation's funding history (link is available from the grant website). Applications to the Kawabe Memorial Fund are due on the first Friday in February, May or September. Proposals must be post-marked on or before the application deadline and mailed to the address given in the downloadable state guidelines document. In general, applicants will be notified of grant decisions 3 to 4 months after proposal submission.

Geographic Focus: Washington

Samples: Asian Counseling and Referral Service, Seattle, Washington, $3,000; Buddhist Churches of America, Tacoma, Washington, $9,950; Shalom Zone Nonprofit Association, Seattle, Washington, $2,000.

Contact: Nancy Atkinson; (800) 848-7177; nancy.l.atkinson@baml.com

Internet: https://www.bankofamerica.com/philanthropic/fn_search.action

Sponsor: Kawabe Memorial Fund

800 5th Avenue, WA1-501-33-23

Seattle, WA 98104

KDA Horticulture Advertising Cost-Share Grants 1116

The Kentucky Department of Agriculture works with the Kentucky Horticulture Council to administer the advertising and market development grants program. These grants are provided by the Kentucky Agriculture Development Board through funding from Kentucky's Tobacco Settlement funds. The selling of Kentucky-grown horticultural products must be the main focus of the advertising and promotional efforts.

Requirements: To qualify all horticulture products must be Kentucky-grown, and applicants must be Kentucky Proud Members. Successful applicants receive a 50 percent cash match of up to $1,250 for the calendar year if all guidelines are followed for promoting and advertising Kentucky Proud products.

Restrictions: Any expense cost shared as a part of this program is not eligible for cost-share in the Kentucky Proud Promotional Grant program. With limited funds, some items do not fit under the program purpose. The following is a list of things not reimbursable under the program. This is not an all-inclusive list but should serve as a guide: Equipment whose primary purpose is something other than advertisement, such as tents, baskets, printers, trucks, signs with non-permanent lettering, grills, etc; supplies that may or may not be used for advertising, such as paper, ink, CDs, labels, etc; customer giveaways that are not personalized to the business, including food; items in the Kentucky Proud at-cost program; ads that do not sell horticulture products as the primary purpose of the ad; membership dues; any items not using the Kentucky Proud logo or the appropriate words; sponsorships of ball teams, fairs, events beyond the cost of the ad itself; commercially produced value-added products. (i.e. pickles, jams, jellies, sauces, soup mixes, etc.).

Geographic Focus: Kentucky

Date(s) Application is Due: Dec 31

Amount of Grant: Up to 1,250 USD

Contact: Roger Snell, (502) 564-4983; Roger.Snell@ky.gov

Internet: http://www.kyagr.com/marketing/advertising-market-development.html

Sponsor: Kentucky Department of Agriculture

100 Fair Oaks Lane

Frankfort, KY 40601

Keith Campbell Foundation for the Environment Grants 1117

The foundation awards grants to Maryland nonprofit organizations serving children in the areas of culture and social services delivery. Types of support include building construction/renovation, equipment acquisition, program development, and general operating grants. Grants are awarded for one year. Submit a brief (two-page maximum) proposal describing the request and organization.

Requirements: Maryland 501(c)3 tax-exempt organizations are eligible. The majority of grants are awarded in the Baltimore area.

Restrictions: Grants are not made to individuals.

Geographic Focus: Maryland

Amount of Grant: 150 - 500,000 USD

Contact: Keith Campbell, President; (410) 825-0545, ext. 103

Sponsor: Keith Campbell Foundation for the Environment

210 W Pennsylvania Avenue, Suite 770

Towson, MD 21204

Kellwood Foundation Grants 1118

The foundation makes grants to 501(c)3 charitable scientific, educational, and literary organizations for programs that provide basic human needs and improve the quality of life. Primary focus areas include cultural and performing arts; education; health services; and social welfare, civic, and community programs. Types of support include general operating support, annual campaigns, capital campaigns, program development, and employee matching gifts. The board meets in March, June, September, and December to consider requests. Requests should be submitted on organization letterhead and contain the name, address, and phone number of the contact person; statement of the problem to be addressed; identification of geographic area and number of people served; statement of the purpose for which funds are requested; specific dollar request; explanation of how the program differs from others providing similar services in the same geographic area; annual organizational budget; identification of sources of annual operating funds; identification of board of directors and key staff members; and copy of IRS 501(c)3 determination letter.

Requirements: Giving is primarily made to the greater St. Louis, MO, area.

Geographic Focus: Missouri

Amount of Grant: 25 - 70,000 USD

Contact: Terri Grandcolas, (314) 576-3431; fax (314) 576-3439

Sponsor: Kellwood Foundation

600 Kellwood Parkway

Chesterfield, MO 63017

Kelsey Trust Grants 1119

The trust awards grants within its geographical territory to support organizations in its primary areas of interest, including child development education, adult basic education and literacy, vocational education, health care and health organizations, the environment and conservation, and services for children and families. Grants are awarded for general operating support, program development, seed money, scholarship funds, matching funds, and emergency funds.

Requirements: Nonprofit organizations in the Lake Champlain Valley drainage basin; eastern Adirondacks, in New York; and western Vermont, north of Rutland, may submit applications for grant support.

Restrictions: The trust does not typically make grants for most capital projects, debt reduction, normal operating budgets, to individuals, for sectarian religious purposes, for endowments, or where the trust may become a predominant source of support.

Geographic Focus: New York, Vermont
Date(s) Application is Due: Feb 1; Sep 1
Amount of Grant: 2,500 - 10,000 USD
Contact: Paula Johnson; (802) 388-3355
Internet: http://www.vermontcf.org/guidelines-forms/kelsey-trust.html
Sponsor: Kelsey Trust
P.O. Box 30
Middlebury, VT 05753

Kelvin and Eleanor Smith Foundation Grants 1120

The foundation awards grants to northeast Ohio nonprofits in its areas of interest, including nonsectarian education, the performing and visual arts, health care, and environmental conservation and protection. Types of support include general operating support, continuing support, annual campaigns, capital campaigns, building construction/renovation, and equipment acquisition. Since there are no required application forms, each proposal include a cover letter that outlines the reason for the request and the dollar amount. Organizations who have previously received funding from this Foundation may submit a proposal annually. There are no specified annual deadlines.

Requirements: Nonprofits in the greater Cleveland, OH, area are eligible.
Restrictions: Grants are not made in support of individuals or for endowment funds, scholarships, fellowships, matching gifts, or loans.
Geographic Focus: Ohio
Amount of Grant: 3,000 - 150,000 USD
Contact: Carol W. Zett, Grants Manager; (216) 591-9111; fax (216) 591-9557; cwzett@kesmithfoundation.org
Internet: http://www.kesmithfoundation.org/grantguidelines.html
Sponsor: Kelvin and Eleanor Smith Foundation
30195 Chagrin Boulevard, Suite 275
Cleveland, OH 44124

Kenneth King Foundation Grants 1121

The foundation awards grants to Colorado nonprofit organizations in its areas of interest, including agriculture, arts and culture, civic and public affairs, community development, disabled, disadvantaged (economically), education (elementary, secondary, and higher), environment, healthcare, international (Hungary, Russia), religion, social services, technology, and women's issues. Types of support include general operating support, matching/challenge grants, program development, research grants, and scholarship funds. Guidelines are available online.

Requirements: Colorado 501(c)3 nonprofit organizations are eligible. Organizations that received more than $1500 in the previous year should contact the office by phone or email before submitting a proposal.
Restrictions: Capital requests will not be considered.
Geographic Focus: Colorado
Date(s) Application is Due: Mar 1
Amount of Grant: 300 - 200,000 USD
Contact: Janice Fritsch, Program Contact; (303) 832-3200; fax (303) 832-4176; jfritsch@kennethkingfoundation.org
Internet: http://www.kennethkingfoundation.org
Sponsor: Kenneth King Foundation
900 Pennsylvania Street
Denver, CO 80203-3163

Kenneth T. and Eileen L. Norris Foundation Grants 1122

The foundation supports Los Angeles County nonprofits in the areas of: medicine—to improve access to health care, increase knowledge through research, and provide facilities for those activities to take place; youth—to provide constructive activities, positive role models, and opportunities for disadvantaged, disabled, and misguided children; community—to support law enforcement agencies, good citizenship, and environmental conservation; culture—to support museums, symphony orchestras, and dance and theater companies; and education and science—to focus on private education, especially secondary and college levels. Types of support include general operating support, continuing support, building construction and/or renovation, equipment acquisition, endowment funds, program development, professorships, scholarship funds, research, and matching funds. Education/science and medicine projects are accepted between May 1 and June 30; youth requests are accepted between February 15 and March 31; cultural (the arts) and community requests are accepted between December 1 and January 31; and medicine proposals are due between May 1 and June 30.

Requirements: Grants are awarded to organizations in southern California.
Geographic Focus: California
Date(s) Application is Due: Jan 31; Mar 31; Jun 30
Amount of Grant: 5,000 - 25,000 USD
Contact: Lisa D. Hansen; (562) 435-8444; fax (562) 436-0584; grants@ktn.org
Internet: http://www.norrisfoundation.org/grant.html
Sponsor: Kenneth T. and Eileen L. Norris Foundation
11 Golden Shore, Suite 450
Long Beach, CA 90802

Kenny's Kids Grants 1123

The foundation awards grants to U.S. nonprofits in company-operating locations with a focus on programs that improve life for children and young adults. The primary target of grants is giving support to organizations which seek to give youth greater opportunities outside of the classroom to learn and grow, to teach them skills that will enable them to thrive in a technology-oriented society, and to offer them the guidance and attention necessary to develop such skills. Also consideration for youth-oriented organizations and other organizations that promote the welfare of youth, such as those that offer hope and encouragement to the sick and terminally ill, protect those who have suffered from abuse, and offer after-school programs for the underprivileged. There are no application deadlines. Allow eight to 12 weeks for proposal review.

Requirements: Nonprofits in company operating areas of Illinois are eligible.
Restrictions: No support for private foundations, schools (public or private), or corporations. Grants are not made to individuals, or for political campaigns, film, video, or audio productions.
Geographic Focus: Illinois
Amount of Grant: Up to 573,902 USD
Contact: Nicholas Pontikes, President
Sponsor: Kenny's Kids
1212 W Lill Street
Chicago, IL 60614

Kentucky Arts Council Partnership Grants 1124

The Kentucky Arts Partnership Grants provide unrestricted operating support to arts organizations to ensure that year-round participation in the arts is available to the people of Kentucky. The amount funded is derived from a formula based on the organization's operating revenues, the panelists' assessment of the application, and the funds available for the program. Additional guidelines, along with the application and a complete list of previously funded projects, are available at the website.

Requirements: Kentucky nonprofit organizations that have had IRS tax-exempt status for at least one year prior to the application deadline, and whose primary purpose is to provide year-round arts services and programs directly for the benefit of the public are eligible to apply.
Restrictions: Internal programs of academic institutions and state or other agencies supported primarily with state or federal funds are not eligible. Partnership Grants cannot be used for the following purposes: purchase of equipment, property, library holdings or acquisitions; capital improvements, facility construction, structural renovations and restorations; publications or recordings for commercial purposes; scholarships or other activities related to academic credit or degrees; activities intended primarily for fundraising; food, beverages or other refreshments; or requests designed to reduce or eliminate existing deficits.
Geographic Focus: Kentucky
Date(s) Application is Due: Jan 15
Amount of Grant: Up to 120,000 USD
Contact: Daniel Strauss, Senior Program Analyst; (502) 564-8110, ext. 474 or (888) 833-2787; fax (502) 564-2839; dan.strauss@ky.gov
Internet: http://artscouncil.ky.gov/Grants/KAP.htm
Sponsor: Kentucky Arts Council
500 Mero Street, 21st Floor, Capital Plaza Tower
Frankfort, KY 40601-1987

Kessler Foundation Community Employment Grants 1125

Kessler Foundation's Community Employment Grant Program seeks to support projects, programs, capacity building, pilot initiatives, and creative solutions that focus on job placement, education, training and retention for New Jersey citizens with disabilities. These solutions improve the employment landscape and lead to full-time or part-time employment, which provides independence and economic self-sufficiency, important factors towards living a purposeful life. Community Employment Grants are awarded for one year. Funding ranges from $25,000 - $50,000. Organizations may apply for indirect cost expenses up to 8% in their project budgets.

Requirements: Nonprofit organizations serving New Jersey residents that are tax-exempt according to the Internal Revenue Code may apply for a Community Employment Grant. This includes nonprofit organizations, public/private schools and public institutions. The Foundation will accept applications from non-NJ based groups as long as the proposed grant projects are based in NJ and serve NJ residents. Some areas of interest are transition to work for youth and adults, vocational training and workplace preparation, employment-related transportation issues, and strategies to support recruitment, hiring, placement and retention. Other related projects or programs may be considered and/or funded at the discretion of our Board of Trustees. It is very important to have a plan for sustaining a funded project beyond the grant period if the proposed project will be ongoing. Additionally, Kessler Foundation is also interested in knowing how the grant will be judged effective at the end of the grant period. Since an affiliation with rehabilitative medicine has been a significant part of Kessler Foundation's history, a priority is placed on serving individuals with mobility disabilities, traumatic brain injury, spinal cord injury, multiple sclerosis, stroke, cerebral palsy, spina bifida, epilepsy or other impairments primarily from neuromuscular disorders. The Foundation requires that 65% of the target grant population meet these criteria.

Restrictions: Any organization awarded a Community Employment Grant for the past three (3) consecutive years is not eligible to apply for this program. Kessler Foundation will not fund projects that discriminate in hiring staff or providing services on basis of race, gender, religion, marital status, sexual orientation, age, or national origin. The foundation does not fund projects for which the primary diagnosis of disability is related to autism, developmental/intellectual disabilities, mental illness, post-traumatic stress, learning disabilities, chemical dependency, or sensory impairments of vision and/or hearing.

Geographic Focus: New Jersey
Date(s) Application is Due: Mar 1
Amount of Grant: 25,000 - 50,000 USD
Samples: Alliance Center for Independence, Edison, NJ - To provide a 12-session program designed to give 40 individuals ages 21 and over the tools to prepare them for meaningful employment: $25,000. Alternatives, Inc., Raritan, NJ - To provide job-training and accommodation assistance to people with disabilities in a retail setting: $40,000. The Arc of Union County, Springfield, NJ - To provide training and employment opportunities for individuals with disabilities in an ecologically-conscious retail business, selling new and used sports equipment: $40,000.
Contact: Elaine Katz, Vice President of Grants; (973) 324-8367; fax (973) 324-8373; KFgrantprogram@KesslerFoundation.org
Internet: http://kesslerfoundation.org/grantprograms/communityemploymentgrants.php
Sponsor: Kessler Foundation
300 Executive Drive, Suite 70
West Orange, NJ 07052

Kessler Foundation Signature Employment Grants 1126

Kessler Foundation awards Signature Employment Grants yearly to support non-traditional solutions and/or social ventures that increase employment outcomes for individuals with disabilities. Signature Employment Grants are awarded nationally to fund new pilot initiatives, demonstration projects or social ventures that lead to the generation of new ideas to solve the high unemployment and underemployment of individuals with disabilities. Preference is given for interventions that overcome specific employment barriers related to long-term dependence on public assistance, advance competitive employment in a cost-effective manner, or launch a social enterprise or individual entrepreneurship project. Signature grants are not intended to fund project expansions or bring proven projects to new communities, unless there is a significant scale, scope or replicable component. Innovation lies at the core of all signature employment grants. Organizations may apply for up to two years of funding. Yearly funding ranges from $100,000 - $250,000, with maximum project funding at $500,000.

Requirements: The Signature Employment Grant program begins with online concept submission. The concept is scored and reviewed for originality, creativity, feasibility, collaborative stakeholder team. A selected group of candidates will then be invited to submit a full grant proposal. Nonprofit organizations that are tax-exempt according to the Internal Revenue Code may apply for funding. This includes U.S. based non-profit organizations, public/private schools and public institutions, such as universities and government. Application is open to eligible organizations in any state or territories. Priority is placed on serving individuals with mobility disabilities, traumatic brain injury, spinal cord injury, multiple sclerosis, stroke, cerebral palsy, spina bifida, epilepsy or other related impairments. The Foundation requires that 65% of the target grant population meet these criteria. Although matching funds are not required, applicants with additional cash funding provided by the applicant or collaborator(s) will be scored higher. A proven track record managing collaborative grant projects is also desirable.

Restrictions: Kessler Foundation will not fund projects that discriminate in hiring staff or providing services on basis of race, gender, religion, marital status, sexual orientation, age, or national origin. The foundation does not fund projects for which the primary diagnosis of disability is related to autism, developmental/intellectual disabilities, mental illness, post-traumatic stress, learning disabilities, chemical dependency, or sensory impairments of vision and/or hearing.

Geographic Focus: All States
Date(s) Application is Due: May 24
Amount of Grant: 100,000 - 500,000 USD
Samples: APSE, Rockville, MD - To partner with OfficeMax to create a job training model that will allow individuals with significant disabilities to receive the pre-training necessary to close the "skill gap" that has prevented many individuals from successful employment in the past, although they posses amazing potential: $323,333. The Center for Head Injury Services, St. Louis, MO - To create Destination Desserts, a purpose driven, social enterprise business that will provide opportunities for training and employment for people with brain injuries: $500,000. National Disability Institute, Washington, D.C. - To facilitate the connection between employer and qualified job seeker with a disability by forming a collaborative employment model in the financial services sector, through the use of applicant training and certification, capacity building, and Vocational Rehabilitation Work Try-Out and On-The-Job training: $484,452.
Contact: Elaine Katz, Vice President of Grants; (973) 324-8367; fax (973) 324-8373; KFgrantprogram@KesslerFoundation.org
Internet: http://kesslerfoundation.org/grantprograms/signatureemploymentgrants.php
Sponsor: Kessler Foundation
300 Executive Drive, Suite 70
West Orange, NJ 07052

KFC Allied Health Research Grants 1127

The foundation supports research into the incidence and cure of kidney and urinary tract disease, patient services, and public education. Preference will be given to allied health personnel undertaking research related to the kidney and urinary tract and to a new research project not supported by any other agency. Applications from investigators in related specialty areas also are considered. Types of support include capital grants, fellowships, general operating grants, program development grants, scholarships, and travel assistance. One- and two-year renewable grants are awarded.

Requirements: Application is open to individuals affiliated with Canadian universities for research conducted within Canada.
Restrictions: Grants will not be awarded for equipment only.
Geographic Focus: All States, Canada
Date(s) Application is Due: Oct 15
Amount of Grant: Up to 50,000 CAD
Contact: National Research Programs Manager; (514) 369-4806, ext. 223 or (800) 361-7494, ext. 223; research@kidney.ca
Internet: http://www.kidney.ca/english/research/allied-funding-03.htm
Sponsor: Kidney Foundation of Canada
300-5165 Sherbrooke Street W
Montreal, QC H4A 1T6 Canada

KFC Biomedical Research Grants 1128

The program fosters and encourages research about the kidney and urinary tract and the understanding of kidney diseases. Types of support include general operating grants, research grants, materials and supplies, and travel assistance. One- and two-year renewable grants are offered.

Requirements: Canadian citizens or landed immigrants may apply. Research must be conducted in Canada by individuals holding staff appointments at Canadian universities or academic institutions.
Restrictions: Requests for equipment only are denied.
Geographic Focus: All States, Canada

Date(s) Application is Due: Oct 15
Contact: National Research Programs Manager; (514) 369-4806, ext. 225 or (800) 361-7494, ext. 225; fax (514) 369-2472; research@kidney.ca
Internet: http://www.kidney.ca/english/research/biomed-funding-03.htm
Sponsor: Kidney Foundation of Canada
300-5165 Sherbrooke Street W
Montreal, QC H4A 1T6 Canada

Kimball International-Habig Foundation Arts and Culture Grants   1129

The Kimball-Habig Foundation was established by company founder, Arnold F. Habig, in 1951 for the purpose of supporting charitable causes within the communities in which Kimball operates, or from which it draws employees. The Foundation is funded by a percentage of profit earnings by the company. In keeping with the corporate philosophy and guiding principles, the Foundation is committed to helping the communities in which they operate to become even better places to live. Supporting that goal, the foundation focuses its funding and resources on grants to organizations and programs that most directly benefit those U.S. communities in which Kimball has operations or facilities, or from which it draws employees. The Foundation recognizes the importance of the visual, written and performing arts to enhance the human spirit, and supports opportunities to provide exposure to the arts among its youth, school systems and communities at large. Requests are considered that: promote or provide for artistic exposure in the community school systems; and promote or provide for performances or exhibits in local communities. Awards are typically for general operating support. Though there are no specific deadlines, the Board meets quarterly, during the last week in March, June, September, and December, to award grants applied for during the previous 90 days.

Requirements: All requests for funding made to the Kimball Foundation must be made using the online request form. All requests must be in writing (via this online form), and absolutely no verbal or phone call requests will be processed or acknowledged. Major requests (those over $2,000) are reviewed, assessed and approved quarterly. Standard requests (those under $2,000) are reviewed and approved monthly. Standard requests are reviewed by the foundation board on or about the 25th of each month.

Geographic Focus: California, Florida, Idaho, Indiana, Kentucky, China, Mexico, Poland

Contact: Dean Vonderheide, President; (812) 482-8255 or (812) 482-8701; habigfoundation@kimball.com

Internet: http://www.kimball.com/foundation.aspx

Sponsor: Kimball International-Habig Foundation
1600 Royal Street
Jasper, IN 47549-1001

Kimball International-Habig Foundation Education Grants   1130

The Kimball-Habig Foundation was established by company founder, Arnold F. Habig, in 1951 for the purpose of supporting charitable causes within the communities in which Kimball operates, or from which it draws employees. The Foundation is funded by a percentage of profit earnings by the company. In keeping with the corporate philosophy and guiding principles, the Foundation is committed to helping the communities in which they operate to become even better places to live. Supporting that goal, the foundation focuses its funding and resources on grants to organizations and programs that most directly benefit those U.S. communities in which Kimball has operations or facilities, or from which it draws employees. To improve education for children, from preschool through high school, and for adults via continuing education and development, Kimball supports programs that foster: critical thinking skills; reading and comprehension; and technology and business interests. Awards are typically for general operating support. Though there are no specific deadlines, the Board meets quarterly, during the last week in March, June, September, and December, to award grants applied for during the previous 90 days.

Requirements: All requests for funding made to the Kimball Foundation must be made using the online request form. All requests must be in writing (via this online form), and absolutely no verbal or phone call requests will be processed or acknowledged. Major requests (those over $2,000) are reviewed, assessed and approved quarterly. Standard requests (those under $2,000) are reviewed and approved monthly. Standard requests are reviewed by the foundation board on or about the 25th of each month.

Geographic Focus: California, Florida, Idaho, Indiana, Kentucky, China, Mexico, Poland

Contact: Dean Vonderheide, President; (812) 482-8255 or (812) 482-8701; habigfoundation@kimball.com

Internet: http://www.kimball.com/foundation.aspx

Sponsor: Kimball International-Habig Foundation
1600 Royal Street
Jasper, IN 47549-1001

Kimball International-Habig Foundation Health and Human   1131
Services Grants

The Kimball-Habig Foundation was established by company founder, Arnold F. Habig, in 1951 for the purpose of supporting charitable causes within the communities in which Kimball operates, or from which it draws employees. The Foundation is funded by a percentage of profit earnings by the company. In keeping with the corporate philosophy and guiding principles, the Foundation is committed to helping the communities in which they operate to become even better places to live. Supporting that goal, the foundation focuses its funding and resources on grants to organizations and programs that most directly benefit those U.S. communities in which Kimball has operations or facilities, or from which it draws employees. In the area of health and human services, the Foundation's main focus is to improve the human condition and help to alleviate suffering by assisting local community organizations, charities, faith-based initiatives, and social services, in their efforts by considering the following types of requests: care and protection of children and infants; care and protection of at-risk women and families; care and protection of the elderly and infirmed; provision of healthcare, medical, and counseling services; and provision of basic social and support services. Awards are typically for general operating support. Though there are no specific deadlines, the Board meets quarterly, during the last week in March, June, September, and December, to award grants applied for during the previous 90 days.

Requirements: All requests for funding made to the Kimball Foundation must be made using the online request form. All requests must be in writing (via this online form), and absolutely no verbal or phone call requests will be processed or acknowledged. Major requests (those over $2,000) are reviewed, assessed and approved quarterly. Standard requests (those under $2,000) are reviewed and approved monthly. Standard requests are reviewed by the foundation board on or about the 25th of each month.

Geographic Focus: California, Florida, Idaho, Indiana, Kentucky, China, Mexico, Poland

Contact: Dean Vonderheide, President; (812) 482-8255 or (812) 482-8701; habigfoundation@kimball.com

Internet: http://www.kimball.com/foundation.aspx

Sponsor: Kimball International-Habig Foundation
1600 Royal Street
Jasper, IN 47549-1001

Kimball International-Habig Foundation Religious Institutions   1132
Grants

The Kimball-Habig Foundation was established by company founder, Arnold F. Habig, in 1951 for the purpose of supporting charitable causes within the communities in which Kimball operates, or from which it draws employees. The Foundation is funded by a percentage of profit earnings by the company. In keeping with the corporate philosophy and guiding principles, the Foundation is committed to helping the communities in which they operate to become even better places to live. Supporting that goal, the foundation focuses its funding and resources on grants to organizations and programs that most directly benefit those U.S. communities in which Kimball has operations or facilities, or from which it draws employees. Faith-based projects and programs aimed at alleviating human suffering, improving the human condition, promoting self-worth, and instilling values, regardless of denominational affiliation. The Foundation no longer considers requests for new buildings, expansion or renovation projects or to affiliated capital campaigns. Instead, it only supports true service ministry activities. Awards are typically for general operating support. Though there are no specific deadlines, the Board meets quarterly, during the last week in March, June, September, and December, to award grants applied for during the previous 90 days.

Requirements: All requests for funding made to the Kimball Foundation must be made using the online request form. All requests must be in writing (via this online form), and absolutely no verbal or phone call requests will be processed or acknowledged. Major requests (those over $2,000) are reviewed, assessed and approved quarterly. Standard requests (those under $2,000) are reviewed and approved monthly. Standard requests are reviewed by the foundation board on or about the 25th of each month.

Geographic Focus: California, Florida, Idaho, Indiana, Kentucky, China, Mexico, Poland

Contact: Dean Vonderheide, President; (812) 482-8255 or (812) 482-8701; habigfoundation@kimball.com

Internet: http://www.kimball.com/foundation.aspx

Sponsor: Kimball International-Habig Foundation
1600 Royal Street
Jasper, IN 47549-1001

Kimberly-Clark Foundation Grants   1133

The foundation supports nonprofits within 50 miles of a Kimberly-Clark manufacturing plant or facility in a wide range of areas, including social welfare, medicine, and health; education; and civic and cultural activities. In the social welfare and health category, grants have supported groups such as boys' and girls' clubs, the Salvation Army, and visiting nurse associations. Educational funding includes NAACP and higher education institutions. The category of civic and cultural activities includes support for public broadcasting, museums, performing arts, and environmental groups. Types of support include annual campaigns, building construction funds, continuing support, equipment acquisition, operating budgets, seed grants, scholarship funds, and capital campaigns. Requests for the company's application form must be in writing.
Requirements: Nonprofits in Kimberly-Clark locations are eligible.
Geographic Focus: All States
Amount of Grant: 1,000 - 75,000 USD
Samples: Marquette U (Milwaukee, WI)—for the Raynor Library's Information Commons and the Thompson Center for Excellence in Education, $1.1 million over five years; U.S. Fund for Unicef (New York, NY)—to provide education, health, legal, and mental-health services to African children orphaned because of AIDS, $2.6 million over four years; UNICEF—to provide services to the more than 13 million children worldwide orphaned as a result of AIDS, including health and nutritional services, community care, group homes, access to education, grief counseling, and legal advice on how to keep siblings together, $2.6 million.
Contact: Carolyn Mentesana; (972) 281-1200; fax (972) 281-1490
Internet: http://www.kimberly-clark.com/aboutus/kc_foundation.asp
Sponsor: Kimberly-Clark Foundation
P.O. Box 619100
Dallas, TX 75261-9100

Kind World Foundation Grants   1134

The foundation's purpose is to encourage and support charitable programs and activities that enhance the quality of life and best serve the public good. Funding priorities are environmental concerns, animal welfare, human services, education, and the arts. Types of support include general operating support, continuing support, annual campaigns, capital campaigns, building construction/renovation, equipment acquisition, endowment funds, seed grants, research, consulting services, and matching funds. Although the foundation supports regional and national programs, major grants are usually limited to the greater Siouxland area, including northwest Iowa, southeast South Dakota, and northeast Nebraska. Challenge grants and matching gift proposals receive special consideration. Proposals may be submitted at any time and are reviewed by the board of directors on a revolving basis. The board meets in January, April, July, October, and as needed. It is suggested that applicants contact the office prior to submitting a formal application.
Geographic Focus: California, Iowa
Amount of Grant: 500 - 250,000 USD
Contact: Arlene Curry; (605) 232-9139; acurry@kindworld.org
Sponsor: Kind World Foundation
P.O. Box 980
Dakota Dunes, SD 57049

Kinsman Foundation Grants   1135

The Kinsman Foundation awards grants to eligible nonprofit organizations in its areas of interest, including: historic preservation; arts, culture, and humanities; and animals and wildlife; and health care policy. Types of support include annual budgetary support, building construction and renovation, capital campaigns, challenge/matching grants, conferences and seminars, consulting services, continuing support, curriculum development, endowments, equipment acquisition, general operating support, internships, program development, publication, research, seed grants, and technical assistance. The Foundation is in the process of eliminating its formal grant application in favor of collecting information in whatever format is most convenient to the applicant. Applications for the Betty Kinsman Fund are due February 15 of each year. For Historic Preservation and Native Wildlife Rehabilitation and Appreciation grants, inquiries less than $10,000 are processed throughout the year.
Requirements: Oregon and southern Washington nonprofits are eligible.
Geographic Focus: Oregon, Washington
Contact: Sara Bailey, Grants Associate; (503) 654-1668; fax (503) 654-1759; sara@kinsmanfoundation.org or grants@kinsmanfoundation.org
Internet: http://www.kinsmanfoundation.org/guidelines/index.htm
Sponsor: Kinsman Foundation
3727 SE Spaulding Avenue
Milwaukie, OR 97267-3938

Kiplinger Foundation Grants   1136

The foundation awards grants to educational, health, welfare, civic, and cultural organizations, primarily in the Washington, DC, area. Building grants are also awarded to organizations in these areas of endeavor. The foundation also provides matching grants on a two-to-one basis to secondary schools and college-level institutions on behalf of Kiplinger Washington Editors employees and retirees of up to $5000 per year per employee or retiree. Areas of particular interest to the foundation include the arts and programs that provide better conditions for troubled and deprived youth. Grants also support annual campaigns, capital campaigns, continuing support, endowment funds, and special projects. Application should be a brief letter of proposal outlining the project for which funds are sought and objectives that the project should accomplish. Most grants are made for a period of one year.
Requirements: Organizations with IRS 501(c)3 status in the greater Washington, D.C. area are eligible.
Restrictions: The foundation does offer money for seed grants nor does it support scholarships.
Geographic Focus: District of Columbia
Amount of Grant: Up to 15,000,000 USD
Contact: Andrea Wilkes; (202) 887-6559; foundation@kiplinger.com
Sponsor: Kiplinger Foundation
1729 H Street NW
Washington, D.C. 20006

Kirkpatrick Foundation Grants   1137

The Kirkpatrick Foundation lends support to organizations with projects and programs that compliment the vision and mission of the Foundation, within the primary fields of interest of arts and culture, education, natural and built environments, animal research, and conservation. The Foundation encourages preliminary discussion to explore potential project proposals. Grant proposals are considered only from not-for-profit organizations qualified as public charities under Section 501(c)3 of the IRS. Organizations should have at least a three-year track record of programming and have maintained current financial records, a working board of directors and management, governance and accountability structures in place. The Foundation also considers requests from public and private educational institutions and faith-based educational programs. Priority is given to organizations serving Oklahoma with particular emphasis placed on programs and services directly benefiting citizens of the Oklahoma City metropolitan area.
Requirements: Organizations are encouraged to contact the Foundation before beginning the grant application process to determine if the project idea is compatible with Foundation interest areas. First time applicants must complete an on-line eligibility quiz to access the Small Grant Application or Letter of Inquiry. A small proposal of $5,000 or less may be submitted by completing the electronic Small Grant Application. These requests may be submitted throughout the year for future projects not already funded by the Foundation. Small grant requests will typically receive notification of a funding decision within 30 days of submitting the application. The Large Grant application procedure is a two-step electronic process beginning with a Letter of Inquiry. There is no set upper limit on the amount requested, but organizations should seek advice from Foundation staff on an appropriate range, and see the website for further instructions for submission.
Restrictions: Capital campaigns and endowments are not regularly funded. Grants may not be used to fund indirect costs or foundation fees. Grants are also not awarded to: individuals; lobbying organizations; medical and health related causes; social welfare; school trips including for marching bands; and athletic programs.
Geographic Focus: Oklahoma
Date(s) Application is Due: Jan 15; Jul 15
Amount of Grant: 1,000 - 130,000 USD
Contact: Meaghan Hunt Wilson, Program Associate; (405) 608-0934; fax (405) 608-0942; mhuntwilson@kirkpatrickfoundation.com
Internet: http://www.kirkpatrickfoundation.com/Grants/tabid/58/Default.aspx
Sponsor: Kirkpatrick Foundation
1001 West Wilshire Boulevard, Suite 201
Oklahoma City, OK 73116

Kitsap Community Foundation Grants   1138

The foundation strives to address basic human needs in the Kitsap community. The foundation is primarily interested in funding programs in its focus areas that build on existing strengths of an organization; focus areas include arts and culture, civic and community improvement, education, social services, health, recreation, environment, and youth. Grants will be considered for general operational support and for capital needs of qualified institutions or organizations. Decisions are based on a number of factors including, but not limited to the number of people served, the potential for funding from other sources, whether the grant falls within the funding priority areas, the originality of the project, whether any other services of its kind exist, and the demonstrated need of the organization. Application guidelines and procedures are available online.

Requirements: Washington 501(c)3 nonprofit organizations in Kitsap County and its neighboring communities are eligible.

Restrictions: Generally, the foundation does not make grants to annual campaign appeals; endowments; individuals; political or lobbying activities; religious organizations for sacramental or theological purposes; publications except those that grow out of research and experiments underwritten by the foundation; or deficit reduction.

Geographic Focus: Washington

Date(s) Application is Due: Feb 15

Amount of Grant: Up to 2,000 USD

Contact: Executive Director; (360) 698-3622; kcf@kitsapfoundation.org

Internet: http://www.kitsapfoundation.org/grantgd.html

Sponsor: Kitsap Community Foundation

P.O. Box 3670

Silverdale, WA 98383

Klingenstein Fellowship Awards in the Neurosciences   1139

The purpose of these awards is to support, in the early stages of their careers, young investigators engaged in basic or clinical research that may lead to a better understanding of epilepsy. The fund recognizes that to accomplish this goal it is necessary to encourage a variety of new approaches. Several areas within the neurosciences are of particular interest to the fund: Cellular and molecular neuroscience—Studies of the mechanisms of neuronal excitability and development, and of the genetic basis of seizure disorders. Neural systems—Studies of the integrative function of the nervous system. Clinical research—Studies designed to improve the prevention, diagnosis, treatment and our understanding of the causes of epilepsy. Application may be made at any time.

Requirements: Applicants must hold the PhD and/or MD degrees, and have completed all research training, including post-doctoral training. U.S. citizenship is not a requirement, but it is expected that candidates will be permanent residents of the U.S. and that their research will be carried out in U.S. institutions.

Restrictions: The fund does not contribute to endowments and rarely contributes to buildings or other kinds of capital projects.

Geographic Focus: All States

Date(s) Application is Due: Dec 10

Samples: Teachers College Columbia U (New York, NY)—for program support, $578,595; American Jewish Committee (New York, NY)—for work on issues of separation of church and state, $40,000; Foundation for Biomedical Research (Washington, DC)—for animal biomedical research, $25,000.

Contact: Kathleen Pomerantz, Vice President; (212) 492-6181; kathleen. pomerantz@klingenstein.com

Internet: http://www.klingfund.org

Sponsor: Esther A. and Joseph Klingenstein Fund

787 7th Avenue, 6th Floor

New York, NY 10019

Klingenstein Third Generation Foundation Grants in Depression   1140

The foundation strives to improve the lives of families afflicted by clinical depression, including childhood and adolescent depression, and Attention Deficit/Hyperactive Disorder (ADHD). Grants are awarded in the areas of intervention and referral, prevention, public education/training, and infrastructure. The foundation will consider making capital grants, operating grants, challenge grants, seed grants, and grants given over more than a one-year period. The foundation also sponsors fellowships for postdoctoral research in depression. Funding proposals will be accepted from any geographic area, but the board expects to fund primarily in the New York, Chicago, and District of Columbia metropolitan areas. There is no formal application procedure or form. Applicants should submit a brief letter that succinctly describes the project and the amount sought and explains why the project is significant. The foundation will request a more detailed proposal.

Requirements: U.S. tax-exempt organizations are eligible.

Restrictions: Grants do not support direct services, unless they include a research or program evaluation component, or unless they represent the application of research findings to a clinical setting.

Geographic Focus: All States

Amount of Grant: 5,000 - 35,000 USD

Samples: American Academy of Child and Adolescent Psychiatry (Washington, DC)—for general support, $15,000; Columbia U, Carmel Hill Ctr for Early Diagnosis and Treatment (New York, NY)—to create brochures on mental-

health disorders written in different languages and at a low reading level, $15,000; State U of New York (Buffalo, NY)—fellowship support for James Waxmonsky, for research on child and adolescent depression, $30,000 over two years.

Contact: Sally Klingenstein Martell, Executive Director; (212) 492-6179; fax (212) 492-7007; sally@ktgf.org

Internet: http://www.ktgf.org/depress.html

Sponsor: Klingenstein Third Generation Foundation

787 Seventh Avenue, 6th Floor

New York, NY 10019-6016

Knight Foundation Grants - Georgia   1141

The Foundation, established in 1992, serves a variety of programs and organizations in Savannah, Georgia. Its primary fields of interest include: children and youth services; human services; and Protestant churches and agencies. The primary type of support provided is by way of general operations funding. Applicants should submit: a detailed description of project and amount of funding requested; and the name, address and phone number of organization. The annual deadline is December 1st.

Restrictions: No funding is provided to individuals, and giving is primarily limited to 501(c)3 non-profits operating in Savannah, Georgia.

Geographic Focus: Florida, Georgia

Date(s) Application is Due: Dec 1

Amount of Grant: Up to 10,000 USD

Contact: Stuart G. Knight, President; (912) 925-8092

Sponsor: Knight Foundation

28 Sherborne Road

Savannah, GA 31419-3261

Koessler Family Foundation Grants   1142

The family foundation awards grants to western New York nonprofits, with emphasis on Buffalo, NY. Areas of interest include higher education, hospitals, and hospices. Types of support include general operating support, building construction/renovation, capital campaigns, and matching grants. Submit a letter of request.

Requirements: Western New York nonprofits are eligible.

Geographic Focus: New York

Date(s) Application is Due: Nov 30

Amount of Grant: Up to 342,000 USD

Samples: Canisius College (Buffalo, NY)—for its capital campaign, $1 million matching grant; Childrens Hospital of Buffalo (Buffalo, NY)—for general support, $60,000; Kenmore Mercy Foundation (Kenmore, NY)—to construct a new patient tower, $24,000.

Contact: Stephen Juhasz, Grant Manager

Sponsor: Kenneth L. and Katherine G. Koessler Family Foundation

124 Brantwood Road

Snyder, NY 14226

Kongsgaard-Goldman Foundation Grants   1143

The foundation provides support to a wide range of nonprofit organizations in the Pacific Northwest in the areas of human rights, civic development, environmental protection and conservation, and the arts and humanities. Grants are awarded for both general operating support and special projects. Small technical assistance grants are also made throughout the year to assist organizations with training and skill development, expert consultation, leadership development, and networking. Preapplications must be submitted. Deadlines for preapplications are March 16 and September 16; proposals are due April 30 and October 31. There are no application forms.

Requirements: Organizations classified as 501(c)3 or 149(1)f (Canada) may apply. Grants are limited to organizations in the Pacific Northwest (Washington, Oregon, Idaho, Alaska, Montana) and British Columbia, Canada.

Restrictions: Grants are not awarded to support direct services, clinical and health services, medical research grants to individuals, wildlife rehabilitation programs, land acquisition, or funding of individual scholarships or fellowships.

Geographic Focus: Alaska, Idaho, Montana, Oregon, Washington, Canada

Date(s) Application is Due: Mar 16; Apr 30; Sep 16; Oct 31

Amount of Grant: Up to 1,500 USD

Contact: Aana Agee, Administrator; (206) 448-1874; fax (206) 448-1973; kgf@kongsgaard-goldman.org

Internet: http://www.kongsgaard-goldman.org/program.html

Sponsor: Kongsgaard-Goldman Foundation

1932 First Avenue, Suite 602

Seattle, WA 98101

Kopp Family Foundation Grants 1144

The Kopp Family Foundation supports programs in Minnesota that impact youth, women, the elderly, and emergency human services; elementary and secondary education; and Roman Catholic churches and organizations. There are no specific deadlines and the Foundation board meets six times a year.

Requirements: The Foundation accepts the Minnesota Common Grant application form. Organizations should initially submit a letter of inquiry, then wait for approval to submit a proposal application. Applicants should receive funding notification within two months of submission.

Geographic Focus: Minnesota

Amount of Grant: 2,000 - 50,000 USD

Samples: St. Stephens Human Services, Minneapolis, MN, $10,000, payable over one year; Project for Pride in Living, Minneapolis, MN, $50,000, payable over one year; Minneapolis Community and Technical College Foundation, $50,000.

Contact: Lindsey Lang, Administrator; (952) 841-0438; fax (952) 841-0411; foundation@koppinvestments.com

Sponsor: Kopp Family Foundation

8400 Normandale Lake Boulevard

Bloomington, MN 55437-3837

Koret Foundation Grants 1145

The Koret Foundation supports projects in the San Francisco Bay Area (Alameda, Contra Costa, Marin, San Francisco, San Mateo, and Santa Clara Counties) related to the following: arts and culture; community development; higher education; Jewish life and culture; primary and secondary education; and youth development. It also supports projects in Israel related to economic development, higher education, and security.

Requirements: Applicants should review grant guidelines, then submit the following: a letter of inquiry; timetable for implementation and evaluation of project; population and geographic area to be served; copy of IRS determination letter; copy of most recent annual report/audited financial statement/990; how project's results will be evaluated or measured; descriptive literature about organization; listing of board of directors, trustees, officers and other key people and their affiliations; detailed description of project and amount of funding requested; and a copy of he current year's organizational budget and/or project budget.

Restrictions: Giving is limited to the Bay Area counties of San Francisco, Alameda, Contra Costa, Marin, Santa Clara, and San Mateo, California. Giving also in Israel and on a national basis for Jewish funding requests. No support for private foundations, or veterans, fraternal, military, religious, or sectarian organizations whose principal activity is for the benefit of their own membership. Funding is not available for individuals, endowment funds, or deficit financing.

Geographic Focus: All States, Israel

Contact: Marina Lum, Grants Manager; (415) 882-7740; fax (415) 882-7775; info@KoretFoundation.org

Internet: http://www.koretfoundation.org/apply/application.shtml

Sponsor: Koret Foundation

33 New Montgomery Street, Suite 1090

San Francisco, CA 94105-4526

Kovler Family Foundation Grants 1146

The Kovler Family Foundation awards grants in the areas of the arts, children/youth services, medical research (particularly diabetes), education, human services, higher education, human services, and Jewish federated giving programs. General operating or research grants are awarded primarily in the Chicago metropolitan area. There are no application forms. Applicants should submit a one to two page written proposal letter with a copy of their IRS determination letter by mid-November. Typical grant awarded is between $1,000-$5,000.

Requirements: Illinois nonprofit organizations are eligible to apply.

Restrictions: The Foundation does not award grants to individuals.

Geographic Focus: Illinois

Contact: Jonathan Kovler, President and Treasurer; (312) 664-5050

Sponsor: Kovler Family Foundation

875 North Michigan Avenue

Chicago, IL 60611-1958

Kroger Foundation Diversity Grants 1147

The Kroger Foundation provides financial support to local schools, hunger relief agencies, and nonprofit organizations in communities where the company operates stores or manufacturing facilities. Kroger focuses its charitable giving in the following areas: hunger relief; education; diversity; grassroots community support; and women's health. Types of support include grants for general operation, capital gains, and seed money. Diversity grants support organizations that advocate and support the advancement of women and people of color, including local chapters of YWCA, NCCJ, Urban League, and NAACP. At the local level, the Foundation has supported Latino and Native American festivals, the Arab American and Chaldean Council in Detroit, and the Midwest Black Family Reunion in Cincinnati. A list of previously funded projects and organizations across the county is available at the website.

Requirements: Grant applications are not available. Nonprofit organizations may submit grant proposals at any time through the community relations departments at their local Kroger retail store, or contact the fiscal administrator at the corporate office for more information. Proposals must include an IRS tax-exempt letter, a statement of goals and objectives, and a board of trustrees list. Support is provided to programs that address a clearly identified need in the community, with specific goals and objectives. Organizations should reflect a strong base of community support.

Restrictions: Only organizations that serve the geographic areas where Kroger owned company operate are eligible to apply. Funding is not available for the following: national or international organizations; for profit organizations; conventions or conference luncheons or dinners; other foundations, except those associated with educational initiatives; endowment campaigns; ongoing operating funding, especially for agencies receiving United Way support (or other federation type support such as a fine arts fund); medical research organizations; sponsorship of golf or other sports events; religious organizationhs or institutions, if the project is for sectarian purposes; individuals; program advertisements; or membership dues.

Geographic Focus: All States

Contact: Fiscal Administrator; (513) 762-4449; fax (513) 762-1295

Internet: http://www.thekrogerco.com/docs/default-document-library/click-here.pdf

Sponsor: Kroger Foundation

1014 Vine Street

Cincinnati, OH 45202-1100

Kroger Foundation Education Grants 1148

The Kroger Foundation provides financial support to local schools, hunger relief agencies, and nonprofit organizations in communities where the company operates stores or manufacturing facilities. Kroger focuses its charitable giving in the following areas: hunger relief; education; diversity; grassroots community support; and women's health. Types of support include grants for general operation, capital, and seed money. Education grants focus on K-12 programs, providing library books, technology centers, science programs, and academic competitions. They also assist local arts, music, sports, and enrichment programs. Samples of previous support are posted on the Foundation website.

Requirements: Grant applications are not available. Nonprofit organizations may submit grant proposals at any time through the community relations departments of their local Kroger retail store, or contact the fiscal administrator at the corporate office for more information. Proposals must include an IRS tax-exempt determination letter, a statement of goals and objectives, and a list of the board of trustees. Support is provided only to programs that address a clearly identified need in the community, with clearly defined goals and objectives. Organizations should reflect a strong base of community support.

Restrictions: Only organizations that serve the geographic areas where Kroger owned companies operate are eligible to apply. Funding is not available for the following: national or international organizations; for profit organizations; conventions or conferences dinners or luncheons; other foundations, except those associated with educational initiatives; endowment campaigns; ongoing operating funding, especially for agencies receiving United Way support (or other federation type support such as a Fine Arts Fund); medical research organizations; sponsorship of golf or other sports events; religious organizations or institutions, if the project is for sectarian purposes; individuals; program advertisements; or membership dues.

Geographic Focus: All States

Contact: Foundation Administrator; (513) 762-4449; fax (513) 762-1295

Internet: http://www.thekrogerco.com/docs/default-document-library/click-here.pdf

Sponsor: Kroger Foundation

1014 Vine Street

Cincinnati, OH 45202-1100

Kroger Foundation Grassroots Community Support Grants 1149

The Kroger Foundation provides financial support to local schools, hunger relief agencies, and nonprofit organizations in communities where the company operates stores or manufacturing facilities. Kroger focuses its charitable giving in the following areas: hunger relief; education; diversity; grassroots community support; and women's health. Types of support includes grants for general operation, capital gains, and seed money. The Grassroots Community Support Grants concentrate on addressing local needs such as assisting with a

community environmental issue, building a skateboarding park, or supporting regional youth music or sports programs. The Foundation also offers financial aid when natural disasters such as hurricans strike by supporting the American Red Cross and Salvation Army. Samples of additional project support throughout the U.S. is listed at the Foundation's website.
Requirements: Grant applications are not available. Nonprofit organizations may submit grant proposals at any time through the community relations departments of their local Kroger retail store, or contact the fiscal administrator at the corporate office for more information. Proposals must include an IRS tax-exempt letter, a statement of goals and objecties, and a list of the board of trustees. Support is provided only to programs that address a clearly identified need in the community, with specific goals and objecties. Organizations should reflect a strong base of community support.
Restrictions: Only organizations that serve the geographic areas where Kroger owned companies operate are eligibly to apply. Funding is not available for the following: national or international organizations; for profit organizations; conventions or conferences luncheons or dinner; other foundation, except those associated with educational initiatives; endowment campaigns; ongoing operating funding, especially for agencies receiving United Way support (or other federation type support such as a Fine Arts Fund); medical research organizations; religious organizations or institutions, if the project is for sectarian purposes; individuals; programs advertisements; or membership dues.
Geographic Focus: All States
Contact: Fiscal Administrator; (513) 762-4449; fax (513) 762-1295
Internet: http://www.thekrogerco.com/docs/default-document-library/click-here.pdf
Sponsor: Kroger Foundation
1014 Vine Street
Cincinnati, OH 45202-1100

Kroger Foundation Hunger Relief Grants   1150
The Kroger Foundation provides financial support to local schools, hunger relief agencies, and nonprofit organizations in communities where the company operates stores or manufacturing facilities. Kroger focuses its charitable giving in the following areas: hunger relief; education; diversity; grassroots community support; and women's health. Types of support include grants for general operation, capital gains, and seed money. The Foundation's hunger relief grants support local food banks by purchasing trucks and refrigerators, buying computers to improve their logistics operations, and funding new projects. Kroger is a key partner with Second Harvest, the nation's largest hunger relief organization. Samples of previously funded organizations and projects throughout the U.S. are listed on the Foundation's website.
Requirements: Grant applications are not available. Nonprofit organizations may subject grant proposals at any time through the community relations departments of their local Kroger retail store, or contact the fiscal administrator at the corporate office for more information. Proposals must include an IRS tax-exempt letter, a statement of goals and objectives, and a list of the board of trustees. Support is provided only to programs that address a clearly identified need in the community, with specific goals and objectives. Organizations should reflect a strong base of community support.
Restrictions: Only organizations that serve the geographic areas where Kroger owned companies operate are eligible to apply. Funding is not available for the following: national or international organzations; for profit organizations; conventions or conference luncheons or dinners; other foundations, except those associated with educational initiatives; endowment campaigns; ongoing operating funding, especially for agencies receiving United Way support (or other federation type support such as a Fine Arts Fund); medical research organizations; sponsorship of sporting events; religious organizations or institutions, if the project is for sectarian purposes; individuals; program advertisements; or membership dues.
Geographic Focus: All States
Contact: Fiscal Administrator; (513) 762-4449; fax (513) 762-1295
Internet: http://www.thekrogerco.com/docs/default-document-library/click-here.pdf
Sponsor: Kroger Foundation
1014 Vine Street
Cincinnati, OH 45202-1100

Kroger Foundation Women's Health Grants   1151
The Kroger Foundation provides financial support to local schools, hunger relief agencies, and nonprofit organizations in communities where the company operates stores or manufacturing facilities. Kroger focuses on its charitable giving in the following areas: hunger relief; education; diversity; grassroots community support; and women's health. Types of support includes grants for general operation, capital gains, and seed money. The Foundation focuses

on women's health, especially breast cancer, because of its impact on women and their family members. The Foundation makes grants to organizations that provide services to women and their families, in addition to funding important research, such as the American Cancer Society and the Susan G. Komen Breast Cancer Foundation. The Foundation also supports the American Heart Association and Red Dress Campaign to educate women about the importance of heart healthy living. Samples of additional organizations and previously funded projects throughout the U.S. are listed on the Foundation website.
Requirements: Grant applications are not available. Nonprofit organizations may submit grant proposals at any time through the community relations departments of their local Kroger retail store, or contact the fiscal administrator at the corporate office for more information. Proposals must include an IRS tax-exempt letter, a statement of goals and objectives, and a list of the board of trustees. Support is provided only to programs that address a clearly identified need in the community, with specific goals and objectives. Organizations should reflect a strong base of community support.
Restrictions: Only organizations that serve the geographic areas where Kroger owned companies operate are eligible to apply. Funding is not available for the following: national or international organizations; for profit organizations; conventions or conferences luncheons or dinners; other foundations, except those associated with educational initiatives; endowment campaigns; ongoing operating funding, especially for agencies receiving United Way support (or other federation type support such as a Fine Arts Fund); medical research organizations; sponsorship of sporting events; religious organizations or institutions, if the project is for sectarian purposes; individuals; program advertisements; or membership dues.
Geographic Focus: All States
Contact: Fiscal Administrator; (513) 762-4449; fax (513) 762-1295
Internet: http://www.thekrogerco.com/docs/default-document-library/click-here.pdf
Sponsor: Kroger Foundation
1014 Vine Street
Cincinnati, OH 45202-1100

L. W. Pierce Family Foundation Grants   1152
Established in 1997, The Foundation supports organizations involved with health, social, and educational services in the areas of alcohol and drug abuse, hospice care and children's welfare. Giving is limited to the Vero Beach, FL and Philadelphia, PA areas.
Requirements: Non-profits in the Vero Beach, Florida, and Philadelphia, Pennsylvania areas are eligible.
Restrictions: No grants to individuals.
Geographic Focus: Florida, Pennsylvania
Date(s) Application is Due: Mar 1
Amount of Grant: 1,000 - 50,000 USD
Samples: Homeless Family Center, Vero Beach, FL, $50,000; Senior Resource Association, Vero Beach, FL, $20,000; Thomas Jefferson University, Philadelphia, PA, $20,000;
Contact: Constance Buckley, President; (610) 862-2105; fax (610) 862-2120
Sponsor: L. W. Pierce Family Foundation
8 Tower Bridge, Suite 1060, 161 Washington Street
Conshohocken, PA 19428-2060

La-Z-Boy Foundation Grants   1153
The foundation makes grants to nonprofit organizations in communities where it maintains plants and within a 15-mile radius of its corporate headquarters in Monroe, MI. Grants are awarded to public charities, civic organizations, and hospitals and health organizations. Support is given for general operating costs, building construction/renovation, education programs, and preservation/restoration. Potential applicants are asked to write to the office and describe the purpose of their project, time span, estimated costs, and benefits. Requests are reviewed at quarterly staff meetings held in March, June, September, and December.
Requirements: 501(c)3 nonprofit charities are eligible. Grants are awarded primarily in communities of company operations, including Siloam Springs, AR; Redlands, CA; Monroe, MI; Neosho, MO; Newton and Leland, MS; Lincolnton, NC; Florence, SC; Dayton, TN; and Tremonton, UT.
Geographic Focus: Arkansas, California, Michigan, Mississippi, Missouri, North Carolina, South Carolina, Tennessee, Utah
Date(s) Application is Due: Mar 1; Jun 1; Sep 1; Dec 1
Amount of Grant: 250 - 50,000 USD
Contact: Donald Blohm, Administrator; (734) 242-1444; fax (734) 457-2005
Internet: http://www.la-z-boy.com
Sponsor: La-Z-Boy Foundation
1284 N Telegraph Road
Monroe, MI 48162

Laclede Gas Charitable Trust Grants 1154

The Trust represents Laclede Gas Company's recognition of its civic responsibility to those in its service area. Areas of interest include human needs and services; education and educational institutions; arts and culture; and civic and community projects. The Trust funds operating support, special projects and annual support. Application forms are available on the website. There are no deadlines. The Trustees of the Charitable Trust meet at least semi-annually.

Requirements: Eligible applicants must be 501(c)3 organizations. Only organizations in the Laclede Gas Company's service area are eligible. The service area includes the city of St. Louis and ten other counties in Eastern Missouri. See the website for a map specifying the service area.

Restrictions: The following is not eligible: individuals, family support or family reunions; advertising; political, labor, fraternal or religious organizations or civic clubs; individual K-8 schools or school-affiliated clubs or events (public or private); sports, athletic events or athletic programs; travel related events, including student trips or tours; development or production of books, films, videos or television programs; and endowment or memorial campaigns. No contribution will be made to an organization if the contribution may impair the independence of a member of Laclede's Board of Directors.

Geographic Focus: Missouri

Samples: Academy of Science, St. Louis, Missouri, $3,000 - operating support; Barnes Jewish Foundation, St. Louis, Missouri, $40,000 - operating support; and YMCA of reater St. Louis, $60,000 - operating support.

Contact: Grants Administrator; (314) 421-1979

Internet: http://www.lacledegas.com/service/trust.php

Sponsor: Laclede Gas Charitable Trust

720 Olive Street, Room 1517

Saint Louis, MO 63101

LaGrange Independent Foundation for Endowments (L.I.F.E.) 1155

LaGrange Independent Foundation for Endowments, or L.I.F.E., is a philanthropic group of young people in LaGrange County. Representatives from four county schools are selected when they enter grade 8 and serve throughout their high school career as the advisory committee for the donor advised non-permanent fund held by the foundation. Grant applications submitted to the LCCF office are evaluated by the L.I.F.E Youth Pod in order to select recommended recipients.

Requirements: Nonprofit organizations including schools in LaGrange county are eligible to apply. Grants are awarded during the school year. The application is available at the foundation's website.

Geographic Focus: Indiana

Samples: LaGrange Communities Youth Centers, after school programming for youth: Lakeland High School, Protective suits for use in Sheriff's Dept. Rape Agression Defense (RAD) training for women: Prairie Heights Leo Club: Boomerang Backpack program for young people in elementary schools.

Contact: Laura Lemings, Executive Director; (260) 463-4363; fax (260) 463-4856; llemings@lccf.net

Internet: http://www.lccf.net/life.html

Sponsor: LaGrange County Community Foundation

109 E Central Avenue, Suite 3

LaGrange, IN 46761

Land O'Lakes Foundation Mid-Atlantic Grants 1156

The Land O'Lakes Foundation Mid-Atlantic Grants were developed specifically for the company's dairy communities in Maryland, New Jersey, New York, Pennsylvania, and Virginia. The program works to improve quality of life by supporting worthy projects and charitable endeavors initiated by our Mid-Atlantic dairy-member leaders. Community organizations applying for grants may be eligible for donations of $500 to $5,000 for local projects and programs. Funds could be used to support such worthwhile projects as: backing local food pantries or emergency feeding efforts; aiding 4-H or FFA programs; building a new park pavilion for the community; establishing a local wetland preserve; or purchasing books for the community library. Application procedures are available online.

Requirements: Applications are initiated by Land O'Lakes farmer-members. An Area Procurement Specialist (APS) review is also part of this process. To be considered, grant proposals must demonstrate how the donation will be used to help improve community quality of life. Mid-Atlantic grants are generally restricted to organizations that have been granted tax-exempt status under Section 501(c)3 of the Internal Revenue Code. The Foundation awards grants to projects that best address the following areas: hunger relief; youth and education; rural leadership; civic improvements; soil and water preservation; and art and culture.

Restrictions: Grants will not be awarded for the following purposes: scholarship funds, gifts or fund raisers for individuals, or non-public religious use.

Geographic Focus: Maryland, New Jersey, New York, Pennsylvania, Virginia

Amount of Grant: 500 - 5,000 USD

Contact: Martha Atkins-Sakry, Executive Assistant; (651) 481-2470 or (651) 481-2212; MLAtkins-Sakry@landolakes.com

Internet: http://www.landolakesinc.com/company/corporateresponsibility/foundation/midatlanticgrants/default.aspx

Sponsor: Land O'Lakes Foundation

P.O. Box 64101

St. Paul, MN 55164-0150

Lannan Foundation Indigenous Communities Program Grants 1157

The program is designed to help Native Americans renew institutions and traditions. Funding priority is given to rural indigenous projects that are consistent with traditional values in the areas of education, Native cultures, the revival and preservation of languages, legal rights, and environmental protection. The foundation will consider multiyear requests for funding of project costs, operating costs, technical assistance, and collaborative activities that build organizational strength and community capacity. There are no application forms or deadlines; submit a letter of inquiry.

Geographic Focus: All States

Amount of Grant: 5,000 - 50,000 USD

Samples: Fort Yuma-Quechan Indian Tribe (Yuma, AZ)— for initiative to stop gold mine, $200,000; Pueblo of Zuni (Zuni, NM)—for legal support to stop coal mine and protect sacred lake, $200,000; Lost Children School (Browning, MT)—for a program where students in grades 5-8 are immersed in the Blackfoot language.

Contact: Administrator; (505) 986-8160; fax (505) 986-8195; info@lannan.org

Internet: http://ee.lannan.org/lf/about/grant-guidelines

Sponsor: Lannan Foundation

313 Read Street

Santa Fe, NM 87501-2628

Laura B. Vogler Foundation Grants 1158

The Vogler Foundation supports innovative programs and projects in New York City and Long Island in the areas of education, health care, and social services. The Foundation is particularly interested in organizations that serve and support children, the elderly, and the disadvantaged. Types of support include general operating support, program development, research grants, and seed money grants. Grants provide one-time, nonrenewable support. Most recent grant awards have ranged from $2,500 to $5,000. The annual deadlines for applications are March 1, July 1, and November 1.

Requirements: Nonprofit 501(c)3 organizations in New York City and Long Island, New York, may submit proposals.

Restrictions: Grants are not awarded to support building or endowment funds, annual fund-raising campaigns, or matching gifts. Requests for funds for conferences, seminars, or loans are not accepted.

Geographic Focus: New York

Date(s) Application is Due: Mar 1; Jul 1; Nov 1

Amount of Grant: 2,500 - 5,000 USD

Samples: Brooklyn Public Library, Brooklyn, New York, $3,000 - support of a creative aging program for adults 55-years-old and older (2015); Cathedral Church of St. John the Divine, New York, New York, $3,500 - fighting poverty (2015); Jewish Guild for the Blind, New York, New York, $5,000 - rehabilitation services to visually impaired/blind children (2015).

Contact: Lawrence L. D'Amato, President; (718) 423-3000; fax (631) 251-7162; voglerfound@gmail.com

Internet: https://sites.google.com/site/voglerfoundation/

Sponsor: Laura B. Vogler Foundation

51 Division Street, P.O. Box 501

Sag Harbor, NY 11963

Laura Jane Musser Little Falls/Morrison County Grants 1159

The Laura Jane Musser Fund wants to help the citizens of Little Falls and Morrison County continue to develop and maintain strong, vibrant, and healthy communities. Musser Fund grants in this area are available through two distinct programs – the General Operating Support Program and the Small Grants Program. An organization may not apply to both grant programs in one year. Grants in this program may be up to $10,000 per year for up to three consecutive years. Grants are provided in order to help increase sustainable, organizational strength and the ability of organizations to meet the needs of their communities.

Requirements: Non-profit, 501(c)3 charitable organizations located in Morrison County, Minnesota are eligible to apply. Priority is placed on organizations that: are working to increase the community's access to their services through scholarships, hands-on activities, community venues, workshops, discounts and other innovations; are working in measurable ways to increase their sustainability; demonstrate capacity to engage their community in their services; and demonstrate support from their community (through volunteerism, membership, in-kind, or other types of support).
Restrictions: After three consecutive years of funding, grantees are not eligible for further Musser Fund support for at least a one year period. All types of Laura Jane Musser Fund grants count towards this three-year limit. Grants will not support capital campaigns, festivals and conferences, or advocacy.
Geographic Focus: Minnesota
Date(s) Application is Due: Mar 20
Amount of Grant: Up to 10,000 USD
Contact: Mary Karen Lynn-Klimenko, Grants Program Manager; (612) 825-2024; ljmusserfund@earthlink.net
Internet: http://www.musserfund.org/index.asp?page_seq=35
Sponsor: Laura Jane Musser Fund
318 West 48th Street
Minneapolis, MN 55419

Laurel Foundation Grants 1160
Laurel Foundation Grants focus on programs in Pittsburgh and southwestern Pennsylvania that offer long-term benefits for participants and the community. The Foundation favors programs from nonprofit organizations that foster individual responsibility and self-sufficiency; exhibit a commitment to sound fiscal and program management; implement collaborative efforts; and demonstrate measurable outcomes. Types of funding include those that concentrate in the fields of arts and culture; education; environment; and public/society benefit. Organizations are advised to carefully review the Foundation website to gauge its possible interest prior to submitting a full proposal. If there is uncertainty, a brief, one-page letter of inquiry may be sent to the President, including a summary of the project and related costs.
Requirements: Nonprofit organizations in Pittsburgh and southwestern Pennsylvania may submit applications. The Board meets in June and December. Proposals submitted for consideration at these meetings must be received by April 1 and October 1. Proposals may follow the format of the Common Grant Application, which can be accessed at the Grantmakers of Western Pennsylvania website.
Restrictions: Individuals are not eligible for funding, nor are grants made for scholarships or fellowships. Social and cultural organizations whose services fall outside the Greater Pittsburgh area are not encouraged to submit a request. Laurel Foundation does not ordinarily approve multi-year grants, preferring instead to monitor the status of a program prior to additional funding approval.
Geographic Focus: Pennsylvania
Date(s) Application is Due: Apr 1; Oct 1
Amount of Grant: 5,000 - 55,000 USD
Contact: Elizabeth Tata; (412) 765-2400; laurelcontact@laurelfdn.org
Internet: http://www.laurelfdn.org/grants_program.html
Sponsor: Laurel Foundation
2 Gateway Center, Suite 1800
Pittsburgh, PA 15222

Laurie H. Wollmuth Charitable Trust Grants 1161
The Laurie H. Wollmutch Charitable Trust was established in New York in 2000, following the sudden and tragic death of an executive of Goldman Sachs. with the expressed purpose to support religious organizations, youth programs, and education. Its primary region of giving is centered in the State of New Jersey. Since there are no formal application materials required, interested parties should forward a proposal letter, which includes a detailed description of project and amount of funding requested. There are no annual deadlines. Most recently, awards have ranged from $500 to $15,000.
Geographic Focus: New Jersey
Amount of Grant: 500 - 15,000 USD
Samples: New Jersey Rockets Youth Hockey association, Berkeley Heights, New Jersey, $500 - general operating support (2014); Pingry School, Martinsville, New Jersey, $15,000 - general operating support (2014).
Contact: Rory Deutsch, Trustee; (212) 382-3300
Sponsor: Laurie H. Wollmutch Charitable Trust
500 Fifth Avenue, Suite 1200
New York, NY 10110

Lavelle Fund for the Blind Grants 1162
The fund is dedicated to supporting programs that promote the spiritual, moral, intellectual, and physical development of blind and low-vision people of all ages, together with programs that help people avoid vision loss. Priority is given to agencies that concentrate on serving the New York City metropolitan area. The fund gives preference to program creation, expansion, or improvement. (General operating support is rarely provided.) Capital support is generally awarded only in connection with specific program support needs. Application guidelines are available online.
Requirements: 501(c)3 tax-exempt organizations are eligible.
Restrictions: The fund does not make grants to: individuals; medical research programs; conferences or media events (unless they are an integral part of a broader program of direct service); efforts to influence legislation or elections; or organizations seeking support for deficit reduction or emergency funding.
Geographic Focus: All States
Samples: Cancer Care (New York, NY)—to create a financial-assistance and support program for people with ocular cancers, $122,750 over 18 months; Catholic Near East Welfare Assoc (New York, NY)—for projects at five Palestinian schools for the blind or at vision-rehabilitation groups in the Jerusalem area and the West Bank and Gaza, $209,316 over three years; International Trachoma Initiative (New York, NY)—for a program that will provide sight-saving surgeries in Mali and Niger, two countries with extremely high rates of trachoma, $300,000 Over two years; Recording for the Blind and Dyslexic (Princeton, NJ)—to create 300 digitally recorded textbooks on mathematics, science, and technology, $320,000 over two years.
Contact: Andrew Fisher; (212) 668-9801; afisher@lavellefund.org
Internet: http://fdncenter.org/grantmaker/lavellefund
Sponsor: Lavelle Fund for the Blind
80 Maiden Lane, Suite 1207
New York, NY 10038

Lawrence J. and Anne Rubenstein Charitable Foundation Grants 1163
The Foundation, established in 1963, supports organizations involved with early childhood services, and higher education, support also for programs for school preparedness. Giving primarily in Boston, MA and Philadelphia, PA. Contact the Foundation for further application information and guidelines.
Requirements: Nonprofits operating in the Boston, MA and Philadelphia, PA area are eligible.
Restrictions: No grants to individuals.
Geographic Focus: Massachusetts, Pennsylvania
Date(s) Application is Due: Apr 1; Oct 1
Samples: Dorchester Community Council, Dorchester, MA, $34,000 - for Pre-K literacy; Hebrew SeniorLife, Boston, MA, $20,000 - for senior fitness program; Camp Sunshine at Sebago Lake, Casco, ME, $15,000 - for general support;
Contact: Susan W. Hunnewell, Foundation Contact c/o Ridgeway Advisors; (617) 279-8052; fax (617) 279-8059; shunnewelle@ridgewayadvisors.com
Sponsor: Lawrence J. and Anne Rubenstein Charitable Foundation
10 Post Office Square
Boston, MA 02109-4615

Lee and Ramona Bass Foundation Grants 1164
The Foundation was established in 1993 to support nonprofit organizations that provide important services for people, primarily within the state of Texas. Funding is provided in the following categories: schools, colleges and universities within Texas, with emphasis placed upon faculty development and liberal arts programs; community programs and projects, particularly related to the arts and the environment, such as museums, zoos, and educational/research institutions; and national and regional conservation programs. Preliminary inquiries are requested, in the form of a letter briefly describing the organization and the program or project. Formal proposals are accepted only after the Foundation has responded to the preliminary inquiry.
Requirements: Eligible applicants must have 501(c)3 organizations.
Restrictions: No grants are made to individuals.
Geographic Focus: All States
Samples: Intercollegiate Studies Institute, Wilmington, Delaware, $700,000 (over 2 years) - support for the Western Civilization Program and the website marketing program; and The Peregine Fund, Inc., Boise, Idaho, $1,500,000 (over 3 years) - recovery of the Northern Aplomado Falcon.
Contact: Valleau Wilkie Jr., Executive Director; (817) 336-0494; fax (817) 332-2176; cjohns@sidrichardson.org
Internet: http://www.leeandramonabass.org/grantguidlines.html
Sponsor: Lee and Ramona Bass Foundation
309 Main Street
Fort Worth, TX 76102

Leicester Savings Bank Fund 1165

The Fund supports projects that improve the quality of life and build a stronger community in Leicester, Massachusetts. To receive funding, applicants must state how they will use the grant to do the following: make a positive difference for the Leicester community's vulnerable citizens; improve Leicester community life through community development, education, recreation, the arts, or human services; and attract other resources or secure matching funds from public or private sources. Grants are available for capital expenditures (to acquire or renovate property or equipment) or for operating expenses of specific programs or projects undertaken by associations or organizations.

Requirements: Any non-municipal association or nonprofit organization that serves residents of Leicester is invited to apply.

Restrictions: Grants will generally not be awarded to individuals or to municipal agencies.

Geographic Focus: Massachusetts

Date(s) Application is Due: Apr 15

Contact: Pamela B. Kane, (508) 755-0980; pkane@greaterworcester.org

Internet: http://www.greaterworcester.org/grants/LSB.htm

Sponsor: Greater Worcester Community Foundation

370 Main Street, Suite 650

Worcester, MA 01608-1738

Leland Fikes Foundation Grants 1166

Grants are awarded for medical research, mental health programs, social welfare, education, reproductive health care, and arts and culture. Building programs and equipment acquisition are supported in these areas. Support is rarely given to programs located outside of the Dallas area. Additional types of support include general operating support, continuing support, annual campaigns, capital campaigns, endowment funds, emergency funds, program development, professorships, seed money grants, scholarship funds, research, and matching funds. Contact the foundation for guidelines.

Requirements: Giving is primarily to Texas organizations.

Restrictions: Grants are not awarded to individuals.

Geographic Focus: Texas

Amount of Grant: 5,000 - 75,000 USD

Samples: Saint Marks School of Texas (Dallas, TX)—for capital campaign, $200,000; Texas Partnership for End-of-Life Care (Austin, TX)—for general support, $175,000; Planned Parenthood (TX)—for operating support.

Contact: Nancy Solana, (214) 754-0144

Sponsor: Leland Fikes Foundation

3050 Lincoln Plaza, 500 N Akard Street

Dallas, TX 75201

Lena Benas Memorial Fund Grants 1167

The Lena Benas Memorial Fund was established in 1986 to provide for the health, human services, and housing needs of underserved people living in Litchfield, Connecticut, and its surrounding communities. The annual deadline for application to the Fund is November 1, and applicants will be notified of grant decisions by letter within 2 months after the proposal deadline. Special consideration is given to organizations that provide housing maintenance and human services programming to needy populations.

Requirements: Preference is given to organizations serving the people of Litchfield, Connecticut. Organizations serving the towns contiguous to Litchfield, including Cornwall, Goshen, Harwinton, Morris, Thomaston, Torrington, Warren, Washington, and Watertown will also be considered.

Restrictions: Grants from the Benas Memorial Fund are 1 year in duration.

Geographic Focus: Connecticut

Date(s) Application is Due: Nov 1

Contact: Kate Kerchaert, Senior Foundation Officer; (860) 657-7016; kate.kerchaert@ustrust.com

Internet: https://www.bankofamerica.com/philanthropic/fn_search.action

Sponsor: Lena Benas Memorial Fund

200 Glastonbury Boulevard, Suite #200, CT2-545-02-05

Glastonbury, CT 06033-4056

Leo Burnett Company Charitable Foundation Grants 1168

The charitable foundation supports at-risk youth projects and literacy programs in Chicago. The foundation currently is not making discretionary grants other than to local, major cultural institutions. Past support has been given in the areas of environmental affairs, wildlife protection, international affairs, and international relief efforts. Types of support include employee matching gifts, operating support, and project support. There are no application deadlines. Proposals are reviewed throughout the year.

Requirements: Illinois nonprofit organizations are eligible.

Geographic Focus: Illinois

Contact: Chris Kimball, (312) 220-5959; belief@leoburnett.com

Internet: http://www.leoburnett.com

Sponsor: Leo Burnett Company Charitable Foundation

35 Wacker Drive

Chicago, IL 60601

Leo Goodwin Foundation Grants 1169

The Leo Goodwin Foundation offers grants in the areas of arts, culture, humanities; education; health; human services; and public benefit. Types of support include: capital campaigns for museums and performing arts centers; literacy programs and educational foundations; community college scholarships; cancer research institutes; boys and girls clubs; and child care organizations. There are no deadlines, and organizations may apply at any time. The trustees meet once a month to assess requests for funding.

Requirements: Applicants must be 501(c)3 nonprofit organizations in the state of Florida. All requests must be submitted with the following information: cover letter stating purpose of program and amount requested; objectives, demographics - social and economic status, age, gender, etc; how funds will be used; operating budget, current audited statement and tax return; IRS 501(c)3 status letter; non-recovation statement; funding sources with amounts received; names and information of governing board members; outcome measures and results; and strategic partners or alliances in delivery of services.

Restrictions: Individuals are not eligible.

Geographic Focus: Florida

Amount of Grant: 1,000 - 25,000 USD

Contact: Helen Furia, Trustee; (954) 772-6863; hfurialgj@bellsouth.net

Internet: http://leogoodwinfoundation.org/

Sponsor: Leo Goodwin Foundation

800 Corporate Drive, Suite 500

Fort Lauderdale, FL 33334-3621

Leo Niessen Jr., Charitable Trust Grants 1170

Leo Niessen lived in Abington Township, Montgomery County, Pennsylvania. In 1993, his Foundation was funded from a testamentary bequest. He was a charitable man, who also made substantial philanthropic gifts to Holy Redeemer Hospital during his lifetime. He had a special affinity for Red Cloud Indian School of Pine Ridge, South Dakota. To this day, the Co-trustees of his Foundation continue to support this school, as well as the Hospital and The Society for the Propagation of the Faith. All grants are made in the memory of Leo Niessen and his family. The Foundation also supports organizations: that provide health services for all ages; which educate the needy and educable at all academic levels, without regard to age; working for and on behalf of youth and the elderly, and which provide assistance to the homeless and economically disadvantaged; which provide spiritual and emotional guidance. Application Deadlines are, January 31 and July 31. Application forms are available online. Applicants will receive notice acknowledging receipt of the grant request, and subsequently be notified of the grant declination or approval.

Requirements: Pennsylvania 501(c)3 nonprofit organizations are eligible to apply. Proposals should be submitted in the following format: completed Common Grant Application Form; an original Proposal Statement; an audited financial report and a current year operating budget; a copy of your official IRS Letter with your tax determination; a listing of your Board of Directors. Proposal Statements (second item in the above Format) should answer these questions: what are the objectives and expected outcomes of this program/project/request; what strategies will be used to accomplish your objective; what is the timeline for completion; if this is part of an on-going program, how long has it been in operation; what criteria will you use to measure success; if the request is not fully funded, what other sources can you engage; an Itemized budget should be included; please describe any collaborative ventures. Prior to the distribution of funds, all approved grantees must sign and return a Grant Agreement Form, stating that the funds will be used for the purpose intended. Progress reports and Completion reports must also be filed as required for your specific grant. All current grantees must be in good standing with required documentation prior to submitting new proposals to any foundation.

Restrictions: Grants are not made for political purposes, nor to organizations which discriminate on the basis of race, ethnic origin, sexual or religious preference, age or gender. The Niessen Foundation normally does not consider grants for endowment.

Geographic Focus: Pennsylvania

Date(s) Application is Due: Jan 31; Jul 31

Amount of Grant: 10,000 - 60,000 USD

Contact: Wachovia Bank, N.A., Trustee; grantinquiries3@wachovia.com
Internet: https://www.wachovia.com/foundation/v/index.jsp?vgnextoid=3458
52199c0aa110VgnVCM1000004b0d1872RCRD&vgnextfmt=default
Sponsor: Leo Niessen Jr., Charitable Trust
Wachovia Bank, N A. PA 1279, 1234 East Broad Street
Philadelphia, PA 19109-1199

Leon Lowenstein Foundation Grants 1171

The foundation awards grants to eligible organizations in its areas of interest, including education, medical research, and disaster relief. Types of support include research grants, general operating support, program development, and seed funding. There are no application deadlines or forms. The board meets twice each year to consider requests.
Requirements: Nonprofit organizations are eligible. Preference will be given to requests from the New York City metropolitan area.
Geographic Focus: All States
Samples: U of Pennsylvania (Philadelphia, PA)—to create a loan-forgiveness fund for MBA graduates of the Wharton School who pursue careers at public and nonprofit institutions, $2.5 million.
Contact: Executive Director; (212) 319-0670; fax (212) 688-0134
Sponsor: Leon Lowenstein Foundation
126 E 56th Street
New York, NY 10022

Leonsis Foundation Grants 1172

The Leonsis Foundation primarily focuses on innovative programs that create opportunities for children under the age of 18. The Foundation is particularly interested in educational and mentoring programs which incorporate Internet technology. Types of support include continuing support; general operating support; scholarship funds; and program development
Requirements: Organizations submit a letter of inquiry about their program before a proposal is accepted. There are no deadline dates.
Restrictions: Funding is not available for individuals.
Geographic Focus: District of Columbia, Maryland, Virginia
Contact: Ellen Kennedy Folts, Grants Administrator; (202) 266-2294; fax (202) 347-5580; leonsisfdn@aol.com
Internet: http://www.leonsisfoundation.org
Sponsor: Leonsis Foundation
627 North Glebe Road, Suite 850
Arlington, VA 22203-2110

Levi Strauss Foundation Grants 1173

The Levi Strauss Foundation Community Partnership program awards contributions to nonprofit community agencies in the following areas: reducing poverty; youth and women; economic development (job creation and community-based economic development); job training, placement, and access; leadership development aimed at strengthening the economic development capacity of community organizations; international education, health care, and peace; and microenterprise. The program also supports AIDS and disease prevention (assistance to people with AIDS and their caregivers); risk reduction education for those with high-risk behaviors; and services to populations severely affected by AIDS. Contributions are also made in the field of social justice (programs that seek to remove racial and other discriminatory barriers, ease tension between groups, promote diversity in community leadership, and prevent violent acts of racial and cultural prejudice). Types of support include matching funds, continuing support, seed money, equipment, exchange programs, employee-related scholarships, employee matching gifts, technical assistance, special projects, and operating budgets. Contact the foundation for more information and application guidelines.
Requirements: Giving is on a national basis with emphasis on areas of company operations. Agencies receiving funding must be accredited charitable organizations or public entities and have boards or advisory groups that reflect the population or communities being served.
Restrictions: The company does not fund projects by individuals or for political, sectarian, or religious purposes; tickets for dinners or other special events; requests for sponsorships; or courtesy advertising. Research and conferences are generally not considered for funding unless they are an integral part of a larger effort that the company is supporting. The foundation does not accept unsolicited proposals.
Geographic Focus: All States
Samples: American Institute for Public Service (Wilmington, DE)—for support for 2003 Jefferson Awards, $20,000; The Asia Foundation (San Francisco, CA)— for the Labor Projects Workshop, $27,000; Citizens'

Scholarship Foundation of America (Saint Peter, MN)—for the Families of Freedom Scholarship Fund, to provide undergraduate scholarships for the spouses and children of people injured or killed as a result of the September 11 terrorist attacks, $500,000.
Contact: Theresa Fay-Bustillos, Executive Director; (415) 501-3577; fax (415) 501-6575; lsf@levi.com
Internet: http://www.levistrauss.com/responsibility/foundation/guidelines.htm
Sponsor: Levi Strauss Foundation
1155 Battery Street, P.O. Box 7215
San Francisco, CA 94111

Lewis H. Humphreys Charitable Trust Grants 1174

The Lewis H. Humphreys Charitable Trust was established in 2004 to support and promote quality educational, cultural, human-services, and health-care programming for underserved and disadvantaged populations. In the area of arts, culture, and humanities, the trust supports programming that: fosters the enjoyment and appreciation of the visual and performing arts; strengthens humanities and arts-related education programs; provides affordable access; enhances artistic elements in communities; and nurtures a new generation of artists. In the area of education, the trust supports programming that: promotes effective teaching; improves the academic achievement of, or expands educational opportunities for, disadvantaged students; improves governance and management; strengthens nonprofit organizations, school leadership, and teaching; and bolsters strategic initiatives of area colleges and universities. In the area of health, the trust supports programming that improves the delivery of health care to the indigent, uninsured, and other vulnerable populations and addresses health and health-care problems that intersect with social factors. In the area of human services, the trust funds programming that: strengthens agencies that deliver critical human services and maintains the community's safety net and helps agencies respond to federal, state, and local public policy changes. In the area of community improvement, the trust funds capacity-building and infrastructure-development projects including: assessments, planning, and implementation of technology for management and programmatic functions within an organization; technical assistance on wide-ranging topics, including grant writing, strategic planning, financial management services, business development, board and volunteer management, and marketing; and mergers, affiliations, or other restructuring efforts. Grant requests for general operating support, program support, and capital support will be considered. Grant requests for capital support, such as for buildings, land, and major equipment should meet a compelling community need and offer a broad social benefit. Grants from the trust are one year in duration. Application materials are available for download at the grant website. Applicants are strongly encouraged to review the state application guidelines for additional helpful information and clarifications before applying. Applicants are also encouraged to review the trust's funding history (link is available from the grant website). Grant applications can be submitted between August 1 and September 30. Applicants will be notified of grant decisions by November 30.
Requirements: Applicants must have 501(c)3 tax-exempt status and serve the residents of Kansas. Grant application materials must be mailed.
Restrictions: The trust does not support requests from individuals, organizations attempting to influence policy through direct lobbying, or any political campaigns.
Geographic Focus: Kansas
Date(s) Application is Due: Sep 30
Samples: Kansas Childrens Discovery Center, Topeka, Kansas, $50,000; Hetlinger Developmental Services, Emporia, Kansas, $50,000; Boy Scouts of America, Topeka, Kansas, $75,000.
Contact: James Mueth; (816) 292-4342; james.mueth@baml.com
Internet: https://www.bankofamerica.com/philanthropic/fn_search.action
Sponsor: Lewis H. Humphreys Charitable Trust
1200 Main Street, 14th Floor, P.O. Box 219119
Kansas City, MO 64121-9119

Liberty Hill Foundation Seed Fund Grants 1175

The hallmark of Liberty Hill's grant making is its Seed Fund, providing one-year grants of $10,000 to $20,000 to organizations tackling social, racial and economic justice issues that are often too new or too controversial to attract funding from more traditional sources. The Seed Fund is often the catalyst that turns someone's vision for a better future into a solid plan of action capable of changing lives as well as communities.
Requirements: Los Angeles County, California, grassroots, proactive, community organizations that are committed to diversity, with a record of leadership development through a democratic process, are eligible.

Restrictions: The foundation does not fund social service providers that do not have a strong community organizing component, projects directed at constituencies outside Los Angeles County, individual efforts, film projects, groups that received foundation funding in the previous funding cycle, direct union organizing, nor businesses or profit-making ventures. Liberty Hill generally does not fund travel expenses, equipment purchases, or research.
Geographic Focus: California
Date(s) Application is Due: Aug 15
Amount of Grant: 10,000 - 20,000 USD
Contact: James Williams, (310) 453-3611, ext. 114; fax (310) 453-7806; jwilliams@libertyhill.org or info@libertyhill.org
Internet: http://libertyhill.org/donor/seed.html
Sponsor: Liberty Hill Foundation
2121 Cloverfield Boulevard, Suite 113
Santa Monica, CA 90404

Lied Foundation Trust Grants 1176
The foundation awards grants primarily to Nebraska and Nevada nonprofits in its areas of youth organizations, higher education, and arts and culture. The foundation favors programs that have some educational aspect to them. Types of support include building construction/renovation, equipment acquisition, program development, endowment funds, and scholarship funds.
Requirements: Nonprofit organizations in Nevada, Nebraska, Kansas and Iowa may apply. There is no specific form to complete.
Geographic Focus: Iowa, Kansas, Nebraska, Nevada
Contact: Christina Hixson, Trustee; (702) 878-1559
Sponsor: Lied Foundation Trust
3907 West Charleston Boulevard
Las Vegas, NV 89102

Lifebridge Foundation Grants 1177
U.S. nonprofit organizations receive foundation support for a wide range of environmental, educational, and arts projects that create bridges of understanding among diverse populations. Past grants have funded studies in parapsychology, land purchase for a shamanic learning center, and research on the survival of the personality after death. The foundation makes grants for projects, general operating support, seed money, and challenge/matching purposes. Funding generally extends for a maximum of three years.
Requirements: Nonprofit organizations, individuals sponsored by nonprofit organizations, and individuals working independently on specific projects are eligible for funding. The foundation generally preselects its grantees, but also accepts introductory letters. A letter should be no more than three pages and should describe how the organization or project specifically reflects foundation's purposes and aims. Do not include any other supporting materials. Individuals seeking support for a specific project should include a resume or brief biography only.
Restrictions: No introductory letters sent via email will be accepted.
Geographic Focus: All States
Amount of Grant: 2,000 - 10,000 USD
Contact: Robert Silverstein, Communications Manager; (212) 757-9711; fax (212) 757-0246; LifebridgeNYC@aol.com
Internet: http://www.lifebridge.org/policy.htm
Sponsor: Lifebridge Foundation
P.O. Box 793, Times Square Station
New York, NY 10108

Lightner Sams Foundation of Wyoming Grants 1178
The foundation awards grants primarily to Texas nonprofit organizations in its areas of interest, including arts and culture, education, women, and social services. Types of support include general operating support, continuing support, annual campaigns, capital campaigns, building construction/renovation, equipment acquisition, and matching funds. There are no application deadlines or forms. The board meets quarterly to consider requests.
Requirements: Giving is limited to the Dallas, TX metroplex area.
Restrictions: Grants are not made to individuals.
Geographic Focus: Texas
Date(s) Application is Due: Feb 1; Jun 1; Oct 1
Amount of Grant: 300 - 42,000 USD
Contact: Larry Lightner, (972) 458-8811; fax (972) 458-8812; foundation@lightnersams.org
Sponsor: Lightner Sams Foundation of Wyoming
5400 LBJ Freeway, Suite 515
Dallas, TX 75240

Lillian S. Wells Foundation Grants 1179
The Lillian S. Wells Foundation established in 1976, primarily supports the Fort Lauderdale, Florida, and Chicago, Illinois regions with funding interests that include: medical research, with emphasis on brain cancer research, women's health, substance abuse, and at-risk youth. Additional funding for education and the arts. Contact the Foundation for an application form, the Board meets quarterly in January, April, July, and October.
Requirements: Nonprofit organizations in Chicago, Illinois and Fort Lauderdale, Florida area are eligible to apply.
Geographic Focus: Florida, Illinois
Date(s) Application is Due: Mar 15; Jun 15; Sep 15; Dec 15
Amount of Grant: 1,000 - 1,900,000 USD
Contact: Patricia F. Mulvaney; patricia.mulvaney@thewellsfamily.net
Sponsor: Lillian S. Wells Foundation
600 Sagamore Road
Fort Lauderdale, FL 33301-2215

Lilly Endowment Giving Indiana Funds for Tomorrow Grants 1180
The Giving Indiana Funds for Tomorrow (GIFT) Grants strive to expand the concept of community foundations to Indiana counties and to increase the endowments of existing community foundations in the state. The GIFT Grants also build the capacity of Indiana communities to be self-reliant and better able to shape their own destinies by having local control over their own resources. The Indiana Grantmakers Alliance Foundation (IGAF) provides technical assistance for the GIFT initiative, which includes an annual calendar of programs and on-site visits for community foundations. Technical assistance and training are available to all participants, including board members, staff and volunteers. Organizations are encouraged to
Requirements: Applicants are encouraged to submit a letter of inquiry to see if their project is appropriate for the GIFT grant. Inquiry letters must be submitted through the mail; emailed or faxed letters will not be considered.
Restrictions: Only Indiana organizations are eligible to apply. The Endowment generally does not support loans or cash grants to private individuals; requests to discharge pre-existing debts of individuals or organizations; health-care projects; mass media projects; libraries; or organizations outside of Indianapolis.
Geographic Focus: Indiana
Contact: Ace Yakey, Program Director; (317) 916-7307
Internet: http://www.lillyendowment.org/cd_gift.html
Sponsor: Lilly Endowment
2801 N Meridian Street, P.O. Box 88068
Indianapolis, IN 46208-0068

Lincoln Community Foundation Grants 1181
The foundation offers program, capital, and quick response grants. Program grants are available to fund the creation of new programs or the enhancement of existing programs within nonprofit organizations. These grants are given in support of programs that focus on the areas of basic needs, children and youth, older adults, human diversity, family issues, environmental enhancement and cultural arts. Capital grants are available to help nonprofit organizations fund the construction of a new facility or facility addition, the renovation or purchase of an existing facility, and/or the purchase of equipment (including furnishings and computer equipment). Quick response grants are available to nonprofit organizations to provide quick solutions to unexpected needs or special opportunities. These grants give nonprofits the opportunity to meet requests that could not typically be responded to due to the traditional application process and timeline or lack of funding sources. Deadlines listed are for program grants.
Requirements: IRS 501(c)3 organizations serving the Lincoln area are eligible.
Restrictions: Grants are not awarded to individuals, and requests are generally not considered for religious purposes, political purposes, endowments, programs outside the Lincoln/Lancaster County area, routine operating expenses, large capital expenditures, budget deficits, and projects with future annual commitments.
Geographic Focus: Nebraska
Date(s) Application is Due: Jun 1; Dec 1
Amount of Grant: 50 - 50,000 USD
Contact: Debra Shoemaker, Program Director; (402) 474-2345; fax (402) 476-8532; debs@lcf.org or lcf@lcf.org
Internet: http://www.lcf.org
Sponsor: Lincoln Community Foundation
215 Centennial Mall S, Suite 200
Lincoln, NE 68508

Linden Foundation Grants 1182

The Linden Foundation funds direct program support, general operating support, and occasionally very modest capital needs associated with a particular program. Existing programs, expansion of successful pilot programs, and new programs may all be considered for funding. The Foundation generally makes initial grants for amounts up to $10,000. The Foundation prefers to fund partial support for a project and welcomes the opportunity to join with other philanthropic funders in underwriting an endeavor. Please note that the Linden Foundation is not currently accepting any new inquiries or applications.

Requirements: The Linden Foundation will invite selected organizations to submit proposals. No unsolicited Full Proposals will be considered. Please note that most of the Foundation's grants budget is allocated to renewed funding since much of the Foundation's funding is multi-year. All grant applicants must be non-profit, 501(c)3 organizations, generally serving disadvantaged, low-income communities in the following areas: the northern side of the greater Boston area, with emphasis on communities inside Route 128 and the North Shore to the Gloucester area; and, the counties of the Lakes Region and northern New Hampshire.

Restrictions: No grants will be made to individuals, public schools, charter schools, colleges, or universities. No grants will be made to support community organizing, political lobbying efforts, or stand-alone enrichment activities, such as tickets to artistic and musical performances. Due to limited funding, no grants will be made for computer centers or general operating support for community centers.

Geographic Focus: Massachusetts, New Hampshire
Date(s) Application is Due: Jun 1; Dec 1
Contact: Ruth Victorin, Foundation Assistant; (617) 426-7080 ext. 288; fax (617) 426-7087; rvictorin@gmafoundations.com
Internet: http://www.lindenfoundation.org/grants.html
Sponsor: Linden Foundation
77 Summer Street, 8th Floor
Boston, MA 02110-1006

Lippard-Clawiter Foundation Grants 1183

The foundation awards grants in Chouteau County in its areas of interest, including children and youth services, community development, and recreation. Types of support include general operating support and equipment acquisition.

Requirements: Chouteau County, MT, nonprofits are eligible.
Restrictions: Individuals are ineligible.
Geographic Focus: Montana
Amount of Grant: Up to 275,000 USD
Samples: Chouteau County Fair Board (Fort Benton, MT)—for renovation of fair ground buildings and for chairs, $25,000; Chouteau County Free Library Foundation (Fort Benton, MT)—for installation of elevator, $15,000.
Contact: Rodney Thorne, Secretary-Treasurer; (406) 727-0888
Sponsor: Lippard-Clawiter Foundation
P.O. Box 1605
Great Falls, MT 59403

Little River Foundation Grants 1184

The foundation supports nonprofit organizations in the Mid-Atlantic states, primarily New Jersey, New York, and Pennsylvania. Grants are awarded for hospitals, AIDS research, substance abuse services, higher education, secondary education, early childhood education, adult basic education, building funds, literacy programs, animal welfare, legal education, international studies in Africa, environmental conservation, legal services, religious organizations, and community funds. Grants are awarded for general operating support, annual campaigns, endowment funds, conferences and seminars, research, and building construction/renovations. Application forms are not required. The board meets each year in the fall.

Requirements: Only residents of Maryland, New Jersey, New York, Pennsylvania, and Virginia may apply.
Geographic Focus: California, New York, Virginia
Amount of Grant: 100 - 175,000 USD
Samples: Grace Episcopal Church (The Plains, VA)—for facilities improvement, $25,000; Piedmont Environmental Council (Warrenton, VA)—for the building program, $87,000; Johns Hopkins U (Baltimore, MD)—for brain tumor research, $25,000; Princeton U (Princeton, NJ)—for annual support, $25,000.
Contact: Dale Hogoboom, Assistant Treasurer
Sponsor: Little River Foundation
101 Park Avenue, Suite 3500
New York, NY 10178-0061

Livingston Memorial Foundation Grants 1185

The foundation awards grants to promote medical and health-related services of benefit to the underserved and uninsured people of Ventura County, CA. General operating grants support well-established programs that continue to have positive results. Special projects grants support organizations that can demonstrate the need for assistance in funding a special project or with the cost of medical equipment that promises significant positive results. Organizations should submit a brief letter of inquiry that includes a concise statement of the need for the funds, the amount requested, pertinent factual information, and state the desired type of grant. Include a copy of the tax-exemption letter.

Requirements: California nonprofits serving Ventura County are eligible.
Restrictions: Grants are not awarded to individuals or for projects normally financed from government sources, conferences, seminars, workshops, exhibits, travel, or publication.
Geographic Focus: California
Amount of Grant: 2,500 - 156,000 USD
Contact: Laura McAvoy, (805) 495-7489; Lmcavoy@jdplaw.com
Sponsor: Livingston Memorial Foundation
2815 Townsgate Road, Suite 200
Westlake Village, CA 91361

Liz Claiborne Foundation Grants 1186

Liz Claiborne Inc.'s founders established the Liz Claiborne Foundation to serve as the company's center for charitable activities. The Liz Claiborne Foundation is a separate nonprofit legal entity, which supports organizations in the U.S. communities where Liz Claiborne Inc.'s primary offices are located. These include the five boroughs of New York City; Hudson County, New Jersey; and Los Angeles County, California. In addition, a small portion of the grants may be directed to national organizations addressing critical issues for women, specifically women's economic independence. The mission of the Liz Claiborne Foundation is as follows: Established in 1981, the Liz Claiborne Foundation supports nonprofit organizations working with women to achieve economic independence by supporting multi-dimensional programs that offer essential job readiness training and increase access to tools that help women, including those affected by domestic violence, transition from poverty into successful independent living.

Requirements: Non-profits in the five boroughs of New York City; Hudson County, New Jersey; and Los Angeles County, California are eligible to apply for funding.
Restrictions: Religious organizations and individuals are ineligible for grants.
Geographic Focus: California, New Jersey, New York
Contact: Melanie Lyons, Vice President; (212) 626-5704; fax (212) 626-5304
Internet: http://www.lizclaiborneinc.com/foundation/default.asp
Sponsor: Liz Claiborne Foundation
1440 Broadway
New York, NY 10018

Lloyd A. Fry Foundation Arts Learning Grants 1187

The Lloyd A. Fry Foundation supports organizations with the strength and commitment to address persistent problems of urban Chicago resulting from poverty, violence, ignorance, and despair. The Foundation's Arts Learning funding focuses on programs for low-income Chicago children and youth that use the arts as a means to improve learning and provide life-enriching experiences. With this program, the Foundation supports arts education for students and professional development for arts educators, including classroom teachers. Most recent grants have ranged from $20,000 to $150,000.

Requirements: Grants are made only to tax-exempt organizations and are rarely made to organizations outside the Chicago metropolitan area.
Restrictions: The foundation does not fund government entities, political or religious activities, fundraising events, or medical research.
Geographic Focus: Illinois
Date(s) Application is Due: Jun 1; Sep 1
Amount of Grant: 20,000 - 150,000 USD
Samples: American Theater Company, Chicago, Illinois, $25,000 - in support of the American Mosaic theater education program; Chicago Children's Choir, Chicago, Illinois, $65,000 - support of the Neighborhood Choir Program for the creation of a professional development program for Chicago public school music teachers; Ingenuity, Chicago, Illinois, $150,000 - for the development and implementation of strategies to expand arts learning in Chicago.
Contact: Unmi Song, President; (312) 580-0310; fax (312) 580-0980; usong@fryfoundation.org
Internet: http://www.fryfoundation.org/grants/arts-learning/
Sponsor: Lloyd A. Fry Foundation
120 South LaSalle Street, Suite 1950
Chicago, IL 60603-3419

Lloyd A. Fry Foundation Education Grants 1188

The Lloyd A. Fry Foundation supports organizations with the strength and commitment to address persistent problems of urban Chicago resulting from poverty, violence, ignorance, and despair. The Foundation is committed to increasing the academic achievement of low-income students in Chicago public schools. Teacher professional development, principal preparation programs, and rigorous academic enrichment programs are among the activities it funds to support this goal. The Foundation also considers grant requests for policy advocacy when the connection to academic achievement is clear. Most recent grants have ranged from $18,000 to $75,000.

Requirements: Grants are made only to tax-exempt organizations and are rarely made to organizations outside the Chicago metropolitan area.

Restrictions: The foundation does not fund government entities, political or religious activities, fundraising events, or medical research.

Geographic Focus: Illinois

Date(s) Application is Due: Mar 1; Jun 1; Dec 1

Amount of Grant: 15,000 - 75,000 USD

Samples: Academy for Urban School Leadership, Chicago, Illinois, $75,000 - for Urban Teaching Residency Program, an alternative teacher preparation program; Ada S. McKinley Community Services, Chicago, Illinois, $18,000 - for Talent Search, an academic support, college preparation and placement program for Chicago public school students; Association of Illinois Middle-Grades Schools, Normal, Illinois, $47,500 - for the Chicago School Transformation Network to build the capacity of middle school math and literacy instructors.

Contact: Unmi Song, President; (312) 580-0310; fax (312) 580-0980; usong@fryfoundation.org

Internet: http://www.fryfoundation.org/guidelines.html

Sponsor: Lloyd A. Fry Foundation

120 South LaSalle Street, Suite 1950

Chicago, IL 60603-3419

Lloyd G. Balfour Foundation Attleboro-Specific Charities Grants 1189

The Lloyd G. Balfour Foundation was established in 1973. The Foundation's 3 primary focus areas reflect Mr. Balfour's strong affinity for the employees of the Balfour Company; his commitment to the city of Attleboro, Massachusetts; and his lifelong interest in education. The Foundation supports organizations that specifically serve the people of Attleboro, with special consideration given to organizations that provide educational, human services, and health care programming for underserved populations. The application deadline for Attleboro-specific charities is February 1.

Requirements: 501(c)3 organizations serving the residents of Attleboro, Massachusetts, Maine, New Hampshire, Rhode Island, and Vermont are eligible to apply.

Geographic Focus: Massachusetts

Date(s) Application is Due: Feb 1

Amount of Grant: 75,000 - 200,000 USD

Contact: Miki C. Akimoto; (866) 778-6859; miki.akimoto@baml.co

Internet: https://www.bankofamerica.com/philanthropic/fn_search.action

Sponsor: Lloyd G. Balfour Foundation

225 Franklin Street, 4th Floor, MA1-225-04-02

Boston, MA 02110

Lloyd G. Balfour Foundation Educational Grants 1190

The Lloyd G. Balfour Foundation was established in 1973. The Foundation's 3 primary focus areas reflect Mr. Balfour's strong affinity for the employees of the Balfour Company; his commitment to the city of Attleboro, Massachusetts; and his lifelong interest in education. The Foundation funds educational organizations, especially those that promote college readiness, access, and success for underserved populations. There is a rolling deadline for organizations applying for a general education grant from the Balfour Foundation. Educational organizations are strongly encouraged to submit grant requests for general operating support. Program support will also be considered. Small, program-related capital expenses may be included in general operating or program requests. To better support the capacity of nonprofit organizations, multi-year funding requests are strongly encouraged.

Geographic Focus: Connecticut, Maine, Massachusetts, New Hampshire, Rhode Island, Vermont

Contact: Miki C. Akimoto, Vice President; (866) 778-6859; miki.akimoto@baml.co

Internet: https://www.bankofamerica.com/philanthropic/fn_search.action

Sponsor: Lloyd G. Balfour Foundation

225 Franklin Street, 4th Floor, MA1-225-04-02

Boston, MA 02110

Loews Foundation Grants 1191

The foundation supports Jewish causes and organizations in Israel. Types of support include matching gifts, general support grants, and scholarships.

Requirements: Organizations in Israel are eligible to apply.

Geographic Focus: All States

Amount of Grant: 1,000 - 50,000 USD

Contact: Candace Leeds, (212) 521-2650; fax (212) 521-2634

Sponsor: Loews Foundation

655 Madison Avenue

New York, NY 10021

Logan Family Foundation 1192

The Logan Family Foundation provides funding throughout the Indianapolis area in its primary fields of interest, which include: human services; religion; and science education. An application form, which can be secured directly from the Foundation office, is required. It should include a detailed description of the project, as well as the amount of funding requested. There are no annual deadlines.

Requirements: any 501(c)3 organization serving residents of the Indianapolis metro area are eligible to apply.

Geographic Focus: Indiana

Amount of Grant: Up to 2,500 USD

Samples: Noah's Ark, Nashville, Tennessee, $1,200 - general operating fund (2014); Miracle Place, Indianapolism Indiana, $565 - general operating fund (2014).

Contact: Patrick C. Logan, President; (317) 359-5357

Sponsor: Logan Family Foundation

5347 Fletcher Court

Indianapolis, IN 46226-1430

Lotus 88 Foundation for Women and Children Grants 1193

The foundation's mission is to promote the empowerment of women and children through supporting their economic, emotional, and spiritual development. The foundation's focus area is American Indian Country. Grants are awarded in Indian Country for two strategic purposes: revitalizing the council tipis as spiritual, cultural, and service centers; and providing the basic needs through community building. Community building grants are intended to promote and support community building in Indian Country to improve basic living conditions and to encourage a more positive future. Tipi project grants are made to help tribal women living on reservation or off reservation in building community. Grants support cultural and social services, tribal gatherings, educational programs, healing and purification ceremonies, and retreats. Each proposal should identify the specific needs and uses for the tipi and should identify a nonprofit program partner working in the tribal area who will work with the foundation on the project. Contact the Foundation directly for application and additional guideline information.

Requirements: Projects in American Indian communities are eligible.

Geographic Focus: All States

Contact: Patricia Stout; (510) 841-4123; fax (510) 841-4093; benita@lotus88.org

Internet: http://lotus88.net/

Sponsor: Lotus 88 Foundation for Women and Children

127 University Avenue, P.O. Box 10728

Berkeley, CA 94710

Louie M. and Betty M. Phillips Foundation Grants 1194

The Foundation supports a variety of organizations in the fields of health, human services, civic affairs, education, and the arts. Types of support include annual operating grants for selected organizations contributing significantly to the Nashville area; one-year project and program grants for specific projects or equipment; and capital support (five-years maximum) for major capital projects of organizations with strong records of community service. The application and a list of previously funded projects are available at the Foundation website.

Requirements: Nonprofit organizations are eligible. With rare exceptions, grants are limited to organizations in the greater Nashville area.

Restrictions: The Foundation does not support individuals or their projects, private foundations, political activities, advertising, or sponsorships. In general, the Foundation does not support projects, programs, or organizations that serve a limited audience; disease-specific organizations; biomedical or clinical research; organizations whose principal impact is outside the Nashville area; or tax-supported institutions.

Geographic Focus: Tennessee

Date(s) Application is Due: Jun 1; Nov 1

Amount of Grant: 500 - 35,000 USD

Samples: Walden's Puddle Wildlife Rehabilitation Center, Nashville, Tennessee, operating support, $10,000; Safe Haven Family Shelter, Nashville,

Tennessee, operating support, $5,000; Men of Valor, Nashville, Tennessee, capital and operating support, $35,000; Boys and Girls Club of Davidson County, Nashville, Tennessee, capital and operating support, $12,500.
Contact: Louie Buntin, Grant Coordinator; (615) 385-5949; fax (615) 385-2507; louie@phillipsfoundation.org
Internet: http://www.phillipsfoundation.org
Sponsor: Louie M. and Betty M. Phillips Foundation
3334 Powell Avenue, P.O. Box 40788
Nashville, TN 37204

Louis and Elizabeth Nave Flarsheim Charitable Foundation Grants   1195
The Louis & Elizabeth Nave Flarsheim Charitable Foundation was established to support and promote quality educational, cultural, human-services, and health-care programming. In the area of arts, culture, and humanities, the foundation supports programming that: fosters the enjoyment and appreciation of the visual and performing arts; strengthens humanities and arts-related education programs; provides affordable access; enhances artistic elements in communities; and nurtures a new generation of artists. In the area of education, the foundation supports programming that: promotes effective teaching; improves the academic achievement of, or expands educational opportunities for, disadvantaged students; improves governance and management; strengthens nonprofit organizations, school leadership, and teaching; and bolsters strategic initiatives of area colleges and universities. In the area of health, the foundation supports programming that improves the delivery of health care to the indigent, uninsured, and other vulnerable populations and addresses health and health-care problems that intersect with social factors. In the area of human services, the foundation funds programming that: strengthens agencies that deliver critical human services and maintains the community's safety net and helps agencies respond to federal, state, and local public policy changes. In the area of community improvement, the foundation funds capacity-building and infrastructure-development projects including: assessments, planning, and implementation of technology for management and programmatic functions within an organization; technical assistance on wide-ranging topics, including grant writing, strategic planning, financial management services, business development, board and volunteer management, and marketing; and mergers, affiliations, or other restructuring efforts. Grant requests for general operating support and program support will be considered. Grants from the foundation are one year in duration. Application materials are available for download at the grant website. Applicants are strongly encouraged to review the state application guidelines for additional helpful information and clarifications before applying. Applicants are also encouraged to review the foundation's funding history (link is available from the grant website). There are no application deadlines for the Flarsheim Charitable Foundation. Proposals are reviewed on an ongoing basis.
Requirements: The Flarsheim Foundation supports organizations that serve the residents of Kansas City, Missouri. Applications must be mailed.
Restrictions: Grant requests for capital support will not be considered.
Geographic Focus: Missouri
Samples: Paul Mesner Puppets, Kansas City, Missouri, $10,000; Kansas City Chorale, Kansas City, Missouri, $5,000; Jewish Community Center Charitable Supporting Foundation, Overland Park, Kansas, $2,500.
Contact: Spence Heddens, Market President; (816) 292-4301; Spence.heddens@baml.com
Internet: https://www.bankofamerica.com/philanthropic/fn_search.action
Sponsor: Louis & Elizabeth Nave Flarsheim Charitable Foundation
1200 Main Street, 14th Floor, P.O. Box 219119
Kansas City, 64121-9119

Louis Calder Foundation Grants   1196
The Louis Calder Foundation seeks to promote the educational and scholastic development of children and youth by improving academic content at charter and parochial schools and at community based organizations. The Foundation's grant making will focus on opportunities for schools and community based organizations in communities within the Northeast Corridor with populations no greater than 500,000 to undertake such efforts during the regular school hours as well as the out-of-school or extended-day hours. New and existing charter schools, parochial schools and community based organizations are invited to submit a letter of inquiry with a summary of their plans to improve or initiate programs and projects designed to deliver classical education in areas of literacy, history, ethics, mathematics and the sciences. The Foundation has no formal application form and requests that organizations use the Philanthropy New York Common Application Form (available at the Foundation's website).
Requirements: New and existing charter schools, parochial schools and community based organizations are invited to submit a letter of inquiry with a

summary of their plans to improve or initiate programs and projects designed to deliver classical education in areas of literacy, history, ethics, mathematics and the sciences. There is no application deadline when applying for funding.
Restrictions: The Foundation does not provide long term continuing program support and requests for renewed support are considered on the basis of reports received, site visits and Foundation priorities.
Geographic Focus: All States
Amount of Grant: 5,000 - 600,000 USD
Samples: Achievement First, Inc., New Haven, Connecticut, $300,000 - program expansion; Friends of Catholic Urban Schools, St. Paul, Minnesota, $229,000 - curriculum development in three consortium schools; Core Knowledge Foundation, Charlottesville, Virginia, $600,000 - Core Knowledge Language Arts K-2 curriculum.
Contact: Holly Nuechterlein, Grant Program Director; (203) 966-8925; fax (203) 966-5785; proposals@calderfdn.org
Internet: http://www.louiscalderfdn.org/gguide.html
Sponsor: Louis Calder Foundation
175 Elm Street
New Canaan, CT 06840

Louisiana State Arts Council General Operating Support Program   1197
The program provides support for organizations whose programming has major impact on their communities and on the state's cultural environment. There are two funding levels. Level One provides support for organizations whose annual budget is $500,000 or more and who have paid, professional staff responsible for the administrative and artistic functions of the organization. Level Two provides support for organizations whose budget is at least $250,000 but less than $500,000. Organizations intending to use grant money for the hiring of a director or supplementing a director's salary should contact the division staff for special technical assistance before making application. First-time applicants should also contact the staff for special technical assistance before applying.
Requirements: Louisiana nonprofit 501(c)3 organizations are eligible. Applicants for both Level One and Level Two funding must have been incorporated as an arts producing and programming organization for at least three years prior to the application deadline; have an independent governing board empowered to formulate policies and execute programs; have significant educational outreach for children and adults; provide a full season of 26 weeks or more of public programming to include production or exhibitions, educational activities, outreach programs, and free public performances; have produced at least one free community performance during the preceding year; and provided with the application a complete copy of an independent financial audit for the organization's prior year if such audit has not been previously submitted. In addition, Level One applicants must provide a copy of the organization's long-range plan with application. Level Two applicants must provide a three-year, long-range plan with their application addressing the following areas: artistic program, educational outreach, fund raising and development, personnel/staff development, financial development, and marketing. Grants must be matched by cash reflected in the operating budget approved by the organization's governing board.
Restrictions: Grants will not be made to fund exhibitions or productions by children or students in grades K-12 or performances or exhibitions primarily for student audiences. In addition, the program does not support projects that pay children or students in grades K-12 or in undergraduate degree programs. Applicants for these grants are not eligible to apply for funding under the project assistance program.
Geographic Focus: Louisiana
Date(s) Application is Due: Mar 1
Contact: Program Officer; (225) 342-8180; arts@crt.state.la.us
Internet: http://www.crt.state.la.us/arts/04_06Guidedwnld.htm
Sponsor: Louisiana State Arts Council and Division of the Arts
P.O. Box 44247
Baton Rouge, LA 70804-4247

Louisiana State Arts Council Local Arts Agency Level One Grants   1198
A local arts agency (LAA) is a government agency or nonprofit community organization, officially designated by municipal or parish governments to provide financing, services, or other programs for arts organizations and individual artists within a city, parish, or region of adjacent parishes. The Level One program is designed for established local arts agencies that provide diverse programs and services in their communities or region. There should be a significant relationship between local government and the LAA. Grant applications and plans submitted must indicate the impact of LAA activities on the economy of the community or region. This program is designed for mature organizations with a record of successful service and administrative

competence. General support funds may be used at the discretion of the agency for a variety of purposes such as arts programs, salaries, artist fees, supplies, or operating expenses. Applicants may request general support grants of up to 25 percent of the agency's actual cash operating revenues for the prior fiscal year (excluding grants from the division).

Requirements: Louisiana 501(c)3 nonprofit organizations may apply. In addition, Level One applicants must be officially designated by the municipal or parish governing body with jurisdiction over the service area to act on its behalf as the local arts agency; have at least one full-time, paid professional staff member; have a governing board with the responsibility and the legal power to set agency policy; have had annual operating revenues of $100,000 or more for the preceding fiscal year; provide, with the application, a complete copy of an independent financial audit for the organization's prior year (if such audit has not previously been submitted); and provide a copy of the current community cultural plan.

Geographic Focus: Louisiana
Date(s) Application is Due: Mar 1
Amount of Grant: Up to 250,000 USD
Contact: Officer; (225) 342-8180; fax (225) 342-8173; arts@crt.state.la.us
Internet: http://www.crt.state.la.us/arts/04_06Guidedwnld.htm
Sponsor: Louisiana State Arts Council and Division of the Arts
P.O. Box 44247
Baton Rouge, LA 70804-4247

Louisiana State Arts Council Local Arts Agency Level Two Grants   1199

A local arts agency (LAA) is a government agency or nonprofit community organization, officially designated by municipal or parish governments to provide financing, services, or other programs for arts organizations and individual artists within a city, parish, or region of adjacent parishes. The Level Two program is designed to support smaller local arts agencies in early stages of development and communities committed to establishing an LAA. Grants may be used for planning, operations, special projects, or organizational and professional staff development. An application for a maximum grant must indicate cash resources of at least $25,000. Grants must be matched dollar for dollar in either cash or a combination of cash and in-kind contributions.

Requirements: Louisiana 501(c)3 nonprofit organizations may apply. In addition, Level Two applicants must be officially designated by the municipal or parish governing body with jurisdiction over the service area to act on its behalf as the local arts agency; have a governing board with the responsibility and the legal power to set agency policy; have had annual operating revenues of not more than $100,000 for the preceding fiscal year; and provide a copy of current community cultural plans.

Geographic Focus: Louisiana
Date(s) Application is Due: Mar 1
Amount of Grant: 10,000 USD
Contact: Officer; (225) 342-8180; fax (225) 342-8173; arts@crt.state.la.us
Internet: http://www.crt.state.la.us/arts/04_06Guidedwnld.htm
Sponsor: Louisiana State Arts Council and Division of the Arts
P.O. Box 44247
Baton Rouge, LA 70804-4247

Louis R. Lurie Foundation Grants   1200

The foundation awards one-year renewable grants to nonprofits in the metropolitan Chicago area and in the San Francisco Bay area to support local arts, community services, education, and health care programs. Types of support include program development, seed money, equipment, and general operating support. Applications are accepted by invitation only.

Requirements: Nonprofits serving the metropolitan Chicago area and the San Francisco Bay area are eligible for grant support.
Geographic Focus: California, Illinois
Contact: Nancy Terry, Administrator; (415) 392-2470
Internet: http://fdncenter.org/grantmaker/lurie
Sponsor: Louis R. Lurie Foundation
555 California Street, Suite 5100
San Francisco, CA 94104

Lowe Foundation Grants   1201

The foundation awards grants to organizations in Texas, primarily for programs that support the critical needs of women and children. The arts and higher education also receive support. Grants are awarded to support capital campaigns, building construction/renovation, and general operations. The board meets in April of each year. The December 1 deadline listed is for pre-proposals, with full proposals by request due on December 31.

Requirements: 501(c)3 organizations in Texas may apply for grant support.
Geographic Focus: Texas
Date(s) Application is Due: Dec 1; Dec 31
Amount of Grant: 5,000 - 225,000 USD
Samples: U of Texas Southwestern Medical Ctr at Dallas (Dallas, TX)—to endow a professorship in pediatric critical care, $100,000.
Contact: Clayton Maebius, Trustee; (512) 322-0041; fax (512) 322-0061; info@thelowefoundation.org
Internet: http://www.thelowefoundation.org/guidelines.htm
Sponsor: Lowe Foundation
1005 Congress Avenue, Suite 895
Austin, TX 78701

Lowell Berry Foundation Grants   1202

Mr. Lowell W. Berry established The Lowell Berry Foundation in 1950 with the primary purpose of assisting in strengthening Christian ministry at the local church level. Mr. Berry's secondary purpose was that of assisting social service programs in the areas in California where he lived and operated his business. Guidelines are available at the Foundation's website.

Requirements: 501(c)3 organizations may apply, The Foundation provides funding primarily in Contra Costa and Alameda counties of California.
Restrictions: No grants to individuals, or for building or capital funds, equipment, seed money, or land acquisition.
Geographic Focus: California
Amount of Grant: 5,000 - 200,000 USD
Samples: Fuller Theological Seminary, Pasadena, CA, $115,000—Fellowship Program & Lowell Berry Institute; Hawaiian Islands Ministries, Honolulu, HI, $60,000—Bay Area Conference; Faith Network of the East Bay, Oakland, CA, $25,000—Urban School Adoption Program.
Contact: Katherine Sanders, Office Manager; (925) 284-4427; fax (925) 284-4332; info@lowellberryfoundation.org
Internet: http://www.lowellberryfoundation.org/process.html
Sponsor: Lowell Berry Foundation
3685 Mount Diablo Boulevard, Suite 269
Lafayette, CA 94549-3776

Lubbock Area Foundation Grants   1203

The Lubbock Area Foundation is a nonprofit community foundation that manages a pool of charitable endowment funds, the income from which is used to benefit the South Plains community through grants to nonprofit organizations, educational programs and scholarships. Funding priorities are: art and culture; social services; civic and community; education; social services; health and human services. Grants may be made for start-up funding, general operating support, program support and demonstration programs. Typical grant awards range from $500 - $2,500 with $5,000 as the maximum from the unrestricted funds. Grant application and additional guidelines are available on the Foundation's website.

Requirements: The Foundation restricts its support to organizations in Lubbock and the surrounding South Plains area which are 501(c)3 or the government equivalent.
Restrictions: The Foundation does not make grants to individuals, for political purposes, to retire indebtedness or for payment of interest or taxes.
Geographic Focus: Texas
Date(s) Application is Due: Jan 1; Mar 1; May 1; Jul 1; Sep 1; Nov 1
Amount of Grant: 500 - 5,000 USD
Samples: Louise Hopkins Underwood Center for the Arts Clay Studio, Lubbock, TX, $8,500—Firehouse Theatre and Marketing Staff Salaries; The Haven Animal Care Shelter, Lubbock, TX—$8,000— funding for veterinary care for animals; Lubbock Children's Health Clinic, Lubbock, TX, $3,600—Pharmacy Assistance Program.
Contact: Kathleen Stocco; (806) 762-8061; fax (806) 762-8551
Internet: http://www.lubbockareafoundation.org/grant.shtml
Sponsor: Lubbock Area Foundation
1655 Main Street, Suite 202
Lubbock, TX 79401

Lubrizol Corporation Community Grants   1204

The Lubrizol Corporation has a long-standing commitment to the local communities in which it operates. The Corporation believes that enhancing the quality of life and building and maintaining positive relationships is the right thing to do. It all began with its founders' corporate philosophy, whose legacy is a culture of active community support. Today, the Corporation continues their model by providing dollars and people to support a wide variety of educational, cultural and charitable organizations. One of the ways that Lubrizol and its employees provide support to its local communities is through various charitable outreach efforts. Employees volunteer their time to offer assistance to local organizations, making use of their individual skills. An annual event in Northeast Ohio that exemplifies this type of charitable outreach is the Building Bonds event. Applicants should contact the Corporate Community Involvement office for further guidelines.

Requirements: IRS 501(c)3 organizations in or serving the following regions may apply: Wickliffe, Ohio; Cleveland, Ohio; Brussels, Belgium; and Hong Kong.

Geographic Focus: Ohio, Belgium, Hong Kong

Contact: Karen Lerchbacher, Administrator; (440) 347-1797; fax (440) 347-1858; karen.lerchbacher@lubrizol.com

Internet: http://www.lubrizol.com/CorporateResponsibility/Community.html

Sponsor: Lubrizol Corporation

29400 Lakeland Boulevard

Wickliffe, OH 44092-2298

Lubrizol Foundation Grants 1205

The Lubrizol Foundation makes grants in support of education, health care, human services, civic, cultural, youth and environmental activities of a tax-exempt, charitable nature. Scholarships, fellowships, and awards are generally made in the fields of chemistry and chemical and mechanical engineering at colleges and universities. Types of support include the following: annual campaigns; building/renovation; capital campaigns; continuing support; employee matching gifts; employee volunteer services; equipment; fellowships; general/operating support; scholarship funds. Priority is given to the greater Cleveland, Ohio and Houston, Texas areas. The Lubrizol Foundation typically reviews and decides upon requests quarterly. There are no deadlines by which you need to submit your proposal. Proposals may be submitted via postal mail or email, but not by fax. Applicants will receive written notification of the decision on their proposal.

Requirements: Written applications of established Ohio and Texas nonprofit charitable organizations will be considered on a case by case basis. Grant proposals should include the following: a cover letter that summarizes the purpose of the request, signed by the executive officer of the organization or development office; a narrative of specific information related to the subject of the request; current audited financial statements and a specific project budget, if applicable; documentation of the organization's Federal tax-exempt status, e.g., a copy of the 501(c)3 determination letter. Additional descriptive literature (e.g., an annual report, brochures, etc.) that accurately characterizes the overall activities of the organization is appreciated. Upon review, further information may be requested including an interview and site visit.

Restrictions: Grants are not made for religious or political purposes, to individuals nor, generally, to endowments.

Geographic Focus: Ohio, Texas

Amount of Grant: 2,000 - 250,000 USD

Samples: Big Brothers Big Sisters of Greater Cleveland, Cleveland, OH, $2,500 - for operating support; American Red Cross, Houston, Texas, $25,000 - for Hurricane Ike Disaster Relief Fund; Hospice of the Western Reserve, Cleveland, OH, $250,000 - toward construction of new faculty.

Contact: Karen Lerchbacher, Administrator; (440) 347-1797; fax (440) 347-1858; karen.lerchbacher@lubrizol.com

Internet: http://www.lubrizol.com/CorporateResponsibility/Lubrizol-Foundation.html

Sponsor: Lubrizol Foundation

29400 Lakeland Boulevard, 053A

Wickliffe, OH 44092-2298

Lucile Horton Howe and Mitchell B. Howe Foundation Grants 1206

The foundation supports youth organizations, social services, medical research, hospitals, religion, child welfare, drug abuse, education, and family services. Types of support include continuing support, general operating funds, and research. Requests from qualified organizations must be received prior to the second Tuesday of March for the grant year. There is only one consideration meeting a year.

Requirements: Only nonprofit organizations in the Prox-Pasadena area and the San Gabriel Valley of California are eligible. A brief letter and a copy of the organizations 501(c)3 form are the requirements for application.

Restrictions: No restricted grants will be funded by the foundation.

Geographic Focus: California

Date(s) Application is Due: Feb 28

Amount of Grant: 1,000 - 300,000 USD

Contact: Mitchell B. Howe; (626) 792-2771; lhmbhowefoun@earthlink.net

Sponsor: Lucile Horton Howe and Mitchell B. Howe Foundation

180 South Lake Avenue

Pasadena, CA 91101-4932

Lucille Lortel Foundation New York City Theater Grants 1207

The foundation awards general operating grants to small and mid-size nonprofit theater companies in New York City. The grants are paid in two annual installments. Annual deadline dates may vary; contact program staff for exact dates.

Requirements: An applicant theater must have been in operation as a professional, nonprofit, producing organization in New York, NY, for at least three years; have a current annual operating budget of $200,000 to $2.5 million; and have at least one paid professional manager or director.

Geographic Focus: New York

Date(s) Application is Due: Oct 25

Amount of Grant: 2,500 - 25,000 USD

Samples: 49 small and mid-size nonprofit theaters in New York City that were affected by the attacks on the World Trade Center (NY)—for operating support, $1 million total.

Contact: Shawn Willett, (212) 924-2817, ext. 208; fax (212) 989-0036; grants@lortel.org

Internet: http://www.lortel.org

Sponsor: Lucille Lortel Foundation

322 Eighth Avenue, 21st Floor

New York, NY 10001

Lucy Downing Nisbet Charitable Fund Grants 1208

The Lucy Downing Nisbet Charitable Fund was established in 2002 to support and promote educational, health-and-human-services, and arts programming for underserved populations. The Foundation specifically serves organizations located in and serving the people of Vermont. Special consideration is given to organizations in the area of healthcare/nursing, domestic violence awareness, heart disease, and endangered species, and organizations located in and serving the people of Morrisville, Vermont. Grants are one year in duration. Applicants must apply online at the grant website. Applicants are strongly encouraged to do the following before applying: review the downloadable state application procedures for additional helpful information and clarifications; review the downloadable online-application guidelines at the grant website; review the foundation's funding history (link is available from the grant website); review the online application questions in advance; and review the list of required attachments. These will generally include: a list of board members, financial statements (audited, reviewed, or compiled by independent auditor); an organization summary; a list of other funding sources; an IRS Determination letter; and other required documents. All attachments must be uploaded in the online application as PDF, Word, or Excel files. The Lucy Downing Nisbet Charitable Fund application deadline is 11:59 p.m. on January 15. Applicants will be notified of grant decisions by letter within two to three months of the deadline.

Requirements: The foundation specifically serves organizations located in and serving the people of Vermont. Applicants must have 501(c)3 tax-exempt status.

Restrictions: The trustees do not make grants for deficit financing, annual giving, endowments or capital projects. The fund does not support requests from individuals, organizations attempting to influence policy through direct lobbying, or any political campaigns.

Geographic Focus: Vermont

Date(s) Application is Due: Jan 15

Amount of Grant: 5,000 - 20,000 USD

Samples: Copley Health Systems, Morrisville, Vermont, $58,400, to provide computerized Physician's Order Entry component of Electronic Medical Record Software and to fund Nursing Education; Vermont Foodbank, South Barre Vermont, $20,000, for USDA Summer Food Service Program in high-poverty and extremely rural area; River Arts of Morrisville, Morrisville, Vermont, $8,000, Arts for Everyone archive.

Contact: Amy Lynch, Senior Foundation Manager; (860) 657-7015; amy.r.lynch@baml.com

Internet: https://www.bankofamerica.com/philanthropic/fn_search.action

Sponsor: Lucy Downing Nisbet Charitable Fund

200 Glastonbury Boulevard, Suite # 200, CT2-545-02-05

Glastonbury, CT 06033-4056

Lucy Gooding Charitable Foundation Trust 1209

The trust awards grants to eligible Florida nonprofit organizations in its areas of interest, including child welfare, disabled children, disadvantaged people, homelessness, and hospices. Types of support include building construction/renovation, capital campaigns, equipment and land acquisition, general operating support, seed grants, and United Way. Contact the office for required application form.

Requirements: Florida 501(c)3 nonprofit organizations serving the Jacksonville area are eligible.

Geographic Focus: Florida
Date(s) Application is Due: Sep 30
Amount of Grant: 2,500 - 25,000,000 USD
Samples: Wolfson Children's Hospital (Jacksonville, FL)—to establish a pediatric neurosurgery center, $5 million; Community Foundation in Jacksonville (FL)—to endow a fund to support organizations that serve children or provide relief services, with an emphasis on Florida's Clay and Duval Counties, $25 million.
Contact: Bonnie Smith; (904) 786-4796; bhsmith@bellsouth.net
Sponsor: Lucy Gooding Charitable Foundation Trust
P.O. Box 37349
Jacksonville, FL 32236-7349

Lumina Foundation for Education Grants 1210

The Lumina Foundation for Education believes that education provides the basis for individual opportunity, economic vitality and social stability. With its partners, Lumina strives to meet workforce demands and close gaps in attainment for groups not historically well-served by higher education. Lumina's overarching goal is to increase the higher education attainment rate of the United States to 60 percent by 2025. This will represent an increase of 23 million graduates above current levels of production. The Foundation's proactive portfolio focuses on: increasing awareness of the benefits of higher education; improving student access to and preparedness for college; improving student success in college; and productivity across the higher education system. Note that Foundation grants vary in size by their scope but that grants resulting from unsolicited inquiries typically range from $50,000-$250,000. The usual duration for a grant is one to three years.
Requirements: IRS 501(c)3 or 509(a)(1, 2, or 3) tax-exempt organizations and public school organizations are eligible.
Restrictions: The foundation will not award grants that support corporate sponsorships and fundraising events; fund partisan political or lobbying efforts; or provide direct support for individuals, including scholarships or institutional scholarship funds.
Geographic Focus: All States
Amount of Grant: 50,000 - 250,000 USD
Contact: Candace Brandt, Grants Management Associate; (800) 834-5756 or (317) 951-5300; fax (317) 951-5063
Internet: http://www.luminafoundation.org/grants.html
Sponsor: Lumina Foundation for Education
30 South Meridian Street, Suite 700, P.O. Box 1806
Indianapolis, IN 46204

Lumpkin Family Foundation Healthy People Grants 1211

Historically, the Lumpkin Family Foundation has supported entities that provide services that help keep people in its geographic area healthy. Requests will be evaluated on how well they accomplish one or more of the following: support the creativity of nonprofit organizations by seeding new projects and encouraging experimentation and innovation; support organizations demonstrating outstanding leadership in their field or community; promote the effectiveness of organizations and the nonprofit sector by supporting planning, learning and the professional development of staff and board leaders; facilitate collaboration across traditional organization or sector boundaries for community benefit; and develop public understanding of issues and promote philanthropic support necessary to address issues of community importance.
Requirements: Grants are awarded to nonprofits that serve the community without discrimination on the basis of race, sex, or religion. Special consideration will be given to organizations and programs in East Central Illinois.
Restrictions: Proposals will not be considered from organizations that are not 501(c)3 tax-exempt; organizations whose primary purpose is to influence legislation; political causes, candidates, organizations or campaigns; individuals; or religious organizations, unless the particular program will benefit a large portion of the community and does not duplicate the work of other agencies in the community.
Geographic Focus: All States
Amount of Grant: 1,000 - 50,000 USD
Contact: Bruce Karmazin, (217) 234-5915 or (217) 235-3361; fax (217) 258-8444; Bruce@lumpkinfoundation.org
Internet: http://www.lumpkinfoundation.org/bWHATbwefund/HealthyPeople.aspx
Sponsor: Lumpkin Family Foundation
121 South 17th Street
Mattoon, IL 61938

Lutheran Foundation Grants 1212

The foundation awards Regular, Partnership, and Emergency Grants. Regular grants are available to any congregation or nonprofit organization in northeast Indiana. Regular grants are awarded four times a year. The foundation will consider funding of one-time grants, single-year grants, and multi-year grants that do not exceed three years. Partnership grants are available to each of the foundation's member congregations. They are designed to assist congregations with their outreach ministries and also to enrich the internal life of their own membership. Emergency grants are designed to address unforeseen circumstances that disrupt the ongoing ministry or service provided by churches and organizations. The foundation also encourages, promotes, and supports Lutheran and Christian educational opportunities. Guidelines and application are available online.
Requirements: The foundation awards grants to ministries located in 10 counties in northeast Indiana, including Adams, Allen, DeKalb, Huntington, LaGrange, Noble, Steuben, Wabash, Wells, and Whitley counties.
Restrictions: Proposals for projects that have been completed, deficit financing, fundraising, and promotional items are not considered. In addition, the foundation does not fund individuals, endowments, other funds, or the general operating expenses of congregations or medical procedures that are destructive of life.
Geographic Focus: Indiana
Amount of Grant: Up to 10,000 USD
Samples: Allen County Non-Public School Assoc (Fort Wayne, IN)—to fund school nurse program expenses for parochial and independent schools $57,565 three-year grant; Bethlehem Evangelical Lutheran Church and School (Fort Wayne, IN)—for renovations to cafeteria, basement classrooms, and Fellowship Hall for handicap accessibility $9870 matching grant; Camp Lutherhave (Albion, IN)—to purchase multi-passenger van, $22,000; Cancer Services of Allen County (Fort Wayne, IN)—for operational support, $75,000 three-year grant.
Contact: Terri Kortokrax, (800) 677-2451 or (260) 458-2112, ext. 302; fax (260) 458-3069; tkortokrax@thelutheranfoundation.org
Internet: http://www.thelutheranfoundation.org/grants.htm
Sponsor: Lutheran Foundation
3024 Fairfield Avenue, Suite 200
Fort Wayne, IN 46807-1697

Luther I. Replogle Foundation Grants 1213

The foundation focuses its giving on the following areas: programs addressing the needs of youth and children living in, or at risk of, long-term poverty (especially children of inner-city residents and migrant workers); programs to improve educational opportunities for inner-city children, including enrichment programs in the arts and sciences, alternative schools, after-school tutoring and mentoring, and scholarship programs; programs for affordable and supportive housing that reach groups of people frequently left out of traditional shelter programs, including single mothers and families with children, the elderly, ex-offenders, and youth; projects, lectures, and fellowships in classical archaeology; projects and institutions working for the conservation of maps and globes, and dissemination and education in the area of geography; and a modest budget for support of the arts. Types of support include direct service efforts; advocacy at the local, state, and/or federal levels; general operating support, new projects, and capital campaigns (limited). The board meets twice a year to make funding decisions, once in the autumn and once in the spring. Guidelines and application are available online.
Requirements: 501(c)3 nonprofits in Chicago, IL; Minneapolis, MN; Palm Beach County, FL; and Washington, DC, are eligible. Preference is given to organizations with small or modest operating budgets
Geographic Focus: District of Columbia, Florida, Illinois, Minnesota
Date(s) Application is Due: Mar 15; Sep 15
Amount of Grant: 500 - 45,000 USD
Contact: Gwenn Gebhard; (202) 296-3686; fax (202) 296-3948; info@lirf.org
Internet: http://www.lirf.org
Sponsor: Luther I. Replogle Foundation
1111 19th Street NW, Suite 900
Washington, D.C. 20036

Lydia deForest Charitable Trust Grants 1214

The Lydia Collins deForest Charitable Trust was established in 2002. The deForest Charitable Trust specifically supports: organizations that provide services to those who are visually limited; churches and organizations affiliated with the Protestant Episcopal Church in the United States and other religious organizations in union with or recognized by the Episcopal Church; and organizations that provide services to those who are homeless, unemployed, or substance-dependent. Special consideration is given to the following 3 organizations: The Lighthouse, Inc., in New York, New York; the

Calvary Episcopal Church of Summit, New Jersey; and the Salvation Army in Union, New Jersey. Grant requests for general operating support are strongly encouraged. Program support will also be considered. Small, program-related capital expenses may be included in general operating or program requests. To better support the capacity of nonprofit organizations, multi-year funding requests are encouraged. Applicants must apply online at the grant website. Applicants are strongly encouraged to do the following before applying: review the downloadable state application procedures for additional helpful information and clarifications; review the downloadable online-application guidelines at the grant website; review the trust's funding history (link is available from the grant website); review the online application questions in advance; and review the list of required attachments. These will generally include: a list of board members, financial statements (audited, reviewed, or compiled by independent auditor); an organization summary; a list of other funding sources; an IRS Determination letter; and other required documents. All attachments must be uploaded in the online application as PDF, Word, or Excel files. The application deadline for the deForest Charitable Trust is August 31. Applicants will be notified of grant decisions before February 28 of the following year.

Requirements: Applicants must have 501(c)3 tax-exempt status and serve the people of New Jersey. Occasional support is given to organizations within the Metro New York City area.

Restrictions: The Trust does not support requests from individuals, organizations attempting to influence policy through direct lobbying, or any political campaigns.

Geographic Focus: New Jersey

Date(s) Application is Due: Aug 31

Contact: Anne Bridgette Hennessy, Senior Philanthropic Relationship Manager; (646) 855-2270; anne.hennessy@ustrust.com

Internet: https://www.bankofamerica.com/philanthropic/fn_search.action

Sponsor: Lydia Collins deForest Charitable Trust

114 West 47th Street, NY8-114-10-02

New York, NY 10036

Lynde and Harry Bradley Foundation Grants 1215

The foundation aims to encourage projects that focus on cultivating a renewed, healthier, and more vigorous sense of citizenship among the American people and among peoples of other nations. Projects likely to be supported will generally treat free people as self-governing, personally responsible citizens, not as victims or clients; aim to restore the intellectual and cultural legitimacy of common sense, the wisdom of experience, everyday morality, and personal character; seek to reinvigorate and re-empower the traditional, local institutions—families, schools, churches, and neighborhoods—that provide training in and room for the exercise of genuine citizenship, that pass on everyday morality to the next generation, and that cultivate personal character; and encourage decentralization of power and accountability away from centralized, bureaucratic, national institutions back to states, localities, and revitalized mediating structures. Eligible projects may address any arena of public life—economics, politics, culture, or civil society; the problem of citizenship at home or abroad; Milwaukee and Wisconsin community and state projects that aim to improve the life of the community through increasing cultural and educational opportunities, grassroots economic development, and social and health services; the resuscitation of citizenship in the economic, political, cultural, or social realms; policy research and writing about approaches encouraging that resuscitation; academic research and writing that explore the intellectual roots of citizenship; and popular writing and media projects that illustrate for a broader public audience the themes of citizenship. The foundation supports programs that research the needs of gifted children and techniques of providing education for students with superior skills and/or intelligence; research programs investigating how learning occurs in gifted children; and demonstration programs of instruction.

Requirements: As an initial step, tax-exempt and nonprofit organizations should prepare a brief letter of inquiry presenting a concise description of their project, its objectives and significance, and the qualifications of the organizations and individuals involved. If the project appears to fall within the foundation's mandate, the applicant will be invited to submit a formal proposal. If invited to submit a formal proposal, the applicant should submit another letter. It should include a more-thorough, yet still concise description of the project, its objectives and significance, and the qualifications of the groups and individuals involved in it. It should also include a project budget, the specific amount being sought from Bradley, and a list of its other sources of support, philanthropic or otherwise.

Restrictions: The foundation favors projects that are normally not financed by public funds and will consider requests from religious organizations that are not denominational in character. Grants without significant importance to the foundation's areas of interest will only under special conditions be considered for endowment or deficit financing proposals. Grants will not be made to individuals, for overhead costs, or for fund-raising counsel.

Geographic Focus: All States

Date(s) Application is Due: Feb 1; May 1; Aug 1; Nov 1

Amount of Grant: 25,000 - 300,000 USD

Contact: Daniel P. Schmidt; (414) 291-9915; fax (414) 291-9991

Internet: http://www.bradleyfdn.org/program_interests.asp

Sponsor: Lynde and Harry Bradley Foundation

1241 North Franklin Place

Milwaukee, WI 53202-2901

Lyndhurst Foundation Grants 1216

The foundation concentrates its funding on a variety of strategic partnerships that serve to strengthen and enhance the design, animation, ecology, and livability of metropolitan Chattanooga and advance the protection and restoration of the region's forests, watersheds, and natural systems. Contact the Foundation before submitting any requests.

Requirements: Any Chattanooga-based nonprofit is eligible to apply.

Geographic Focus: All States

Date(s) Application is Due: Jan 11; Apr 1; Jul 5; Sep 30

Amount of Grant: 1,000 - 1,200,000 USD

Samples: Allied Arts of Greater Chattanooga, Chattanooga, TN, $100,000—to galvanize broad participation in and widespread support for the arts in Chattanooga and Hamilton County; American Trails, Redding, CA, $10,000—for support of the 2010 National Trails Symposium and assistance for local planning and marketing activities in advance of the event; Chattanooga Community Kitchen, Chattanooga, TN, $50,000—general support for food, shelter, and other basic services as provided by the Chattanooga Community Kitchen.

Contact: Benic M. Clark III, President; (423) 756-0767; fax (423) 756-0770; bclark@lyndhurstfoundation.org

Sponsor: Lyndhurst Foundation

517 E Fifth Street

Chattanooga, TN 37403-1826

Lynn and Rovena Alexander Family Foundation Grants 1217

The Lynn and Rovena Alexander Family Foundation was established in Lubbuck, Texas, in 2003, and primarily serves the residents of Lexington, Kentucky, and San Angelo, Texas. The Foundation's major fields of interest include: elementary education, secondary education, higher education, human services, and Christian agencies and churches. Along with the formal application, interested parties should submit: a copy of their IRS Determination Letter; a brief history of organization and description of its mission; a copy of most recent annual report or audited financial statement; a detailed description of project and amount of funding requested; and a copy of the current year's organizational budget and project budget. Most recent funding has ranged from $2,500 to $125,000. There are two annual deadlines for applicants, including February 1 and September 1.

Requirements: Organizations located in, or serving the residents of, Lexington, Kentucky, and San Angelo, Texas, are eligible to apply.

Geographic Focus: Kentucky, Texas

Date(s) Application is Due: Feb 1; Sep 1

Amount of Grant: 2,500 - 125,000 USD

Samples: Southland Christian Church, Lexington, Kentucky, $125,000 - religious purposes; Kentucky Children's Hospital, Lexington, Kentucky, $10,000 - medical education and operations; Lexington Leadership, New Life, Lexington, Kentucky, $2,500 - general medical program operations.

Contact: Kimberly L. King, Director; (325) 374-0050 or (806) 795-0470

Sponsor: Lynn and Rovena Alexander Family Foundation

P.O. Box 1160

Nicholasville, KY 40340-1160

M.B. and Edna Zale Foundation Grants 1218

The M.B. & Edna Zale Foundation honors the tradition of its founders through grants that stimulate change. To accomplish this mission, the Foundation acts as a catalyst for collaboration and makes grants in communities where the Directors live or have an interest. Grants are made primarily in the communities of Dallas (Dallas County) and Houston (Harris County), Texas; Boca Raton, Florida; Portland, Oregon; and New York, including Long Island. The Foundation has an interest in four areas of funding: community services; health; education; Jewish heritage.

Requirements: 501(c)3 nonprofits organizations in the communities of Dallas (Dallas County) and Houston (Harris County), Texas; Boca Raton, Florida; Portland, Oregon; and New York, including Long Island are eligible. Contact the Foundation for further application information and guidelines.
Restrictions: The Foundation does not ordinarily provide: major support for the arts; grants to individuals; scholarships and fellowships to individuals (except through colleges and universities).
Geographic Focus: Florida, New York, Oregon, Texas
Amount of Grant: 2,000 - 100,000 USD
Contact: Leonard Krasnow, President; (214) 855-0627; fax (972) 726-7252; mail@zalefoundation.org
Sponsor: M.B. and Edna Zale Foundation
6360 LBJ Highway, Suite 205
Dallas, TX 75240

M. Bastian Family Foundation Grants 1219

The foundation supports nonprofit organizations in its areas of interest, including music, the arts, higher education, health care and health organizations, religion (Christian and Latter-day Saints), social services, and wildlife conservation. Types of support include general operating support and scholarship funds. Contact the office for application forms. There are no application deadlines.
Requirements: Funding focus is primarily in Utah.
Restrictions: Grants are not made to individuals.
Geographic Focus: All States
Amount of Grant: 2,000 - 200,000 USD
Samples: Brigham Young U (Provo, UT)—for scholarship endowment, $200,000; Pediatric AIDS Foundation (Los Angeles, CA)—for general support, $20,000; American Diabetes Assoc (Alexandra, VA)—for research, $100,000.
Contact: McKay Matthews, Program Contact; (801) 225-2455
Sponsor: M. Bastian Family Foundation
51 W Center Street, Suite 305
Orem, UT 84057

M.E. Raker Foundation Grants 1220

The foundation was established in 1984, serving the Allen County, Indiana area. Areas of interest include: children/youth, services; education; environment; natural resources; health care; historic preservation/historical societies; human services people with disabilities. Support is offered in the following areas: building/renovation; general/operating support; matching/challenge support; Program development. No support for the arts or to individuals.
Requirements: Indiana nonprofit organizations are eligible. Emphasis is given to requests from Fort Wayne. Send a letter requesting an application to the foundation office. Application form required for grant proposals.
Geographic Focus: Indiana
Amount of Grant: 5,000 - 40,000 USD
Contact: Jennifer Pickard, Grants Coordinator; (260) 436-2182
Sponsor: M.E. Raker Foundation
6207 Constitution Drive
Fort Wayne, IN 46804-1517

Mabel A. Horne Trust Grants 1221

The Mabel A. Horne Trust was established in 1957 to support and promote quality educational, human-services, and health-care programming for underserved populations. Grant requests for general operating support are strongly encouraged. Program support will also be considered. Small, program-related capital expenses may be included in general operating or program requests. The majority of grants from the Horne Trust are one year in duration; on occasion, multi-year support is awarded. Applicants must apply online at the grant website. Applicants are strongly encouraged to do the following before applying: review the downloadable state application procedures for additional helpful information and clarifications; review the downloadable online-application guidelines at the grant website; review the trust's funding history (link is available from the grant website); review the online application questions in advance; and review the list of required attachments. These will generally include: a list of board members, financial statements (audited, reviewed, or compiled by independent auditor); an organization summary; a list of other funding sources; an IRS Determination letter; and other required documents. All attachments must be uploaded in the online application as PDF, Word, or Excel files. The application deadline for the Mabel A. Horne Trust is 11:59 p.m. on February 1. Applicants will be notified of grant decisions before May 31.
Requirements: Applicants must have 501(c)3 tax-exempt status.

Restrictions: The trust does not support requests from individuals, organizations attempting to influence policy through direct lobbying, or any political campaigns.
Geographic Focus: Massachusetts
Date(s) Application is Due: Dec 1
Contact: Philanthropic Relationship Manager; (866) 778-6859; ma.grantmaking@ustrust.com
Internet: https://www.bankofamerica.com/philanthropic/fn_search.action
Sponsor: Mabel A. Horne Trust
225 Franklin Street, 4th Floor, MA1-225-04-02
Boston, MA 02110

Mabel Y. Hughes Charitable Trust Grants 1222

The Mabel Y. Hughes Charitable Trust was established under the last will and testament of Mabel Y. Hughes, a resident of Denver, Colorado, who died on April 9, 1969. Her legacy of giving continues through grants to charitable organizations in the state of Colorado. The Trust awards funding to nonprofit organizations in its areas of interest, including: children and youth services; education; family services; health care; higher education; human services; children's and art museums; performing arts centers; performing arts, opera; and reproductive health and family planning. Types of support include: annual campaigns; continuing support; emergency funds; endowments; equipment; general/operating support; program development; research; and seed money. Approximately fifty awards are given each year, with the average grant size ranging from $5,000 to $25,000. Applications must be submitted by March 1, July 1 or November 1 to be reviewed at the grant meeting that occurs after each deadline.
Requirements: Organizations should submit a letter of inquiry to the Trust, and if their project is appropriate for funding, they will be asked to submit a proposal.
Restrictions: The Trust does not support funding for individuals, deficit financing, scholarships, fellowships, or loans.
Geographic Focus: Colorado
Date(s) Application is Due: Mar 1; Jul 1; Nov 1
Amount of Grant: 5,000 - 30,000 USD
Contact: Peggy Toal, Private Client Services; (720) 947-6725 or (888) 234-1999; fax (877) 746-5889; grantadministration@ wellsfargo.com
Sponsor: Mabel Y. Hughes Charitable Trust
1740 Broadway
Denver, CO 80274

MacArthur Foundation Chicago Arts and Culture General Operations Grants 1223

The MacArthur Foundation's support for arts and culture in the Chicago area is an expression of its civic commitment to Chicago. MacArthur provides multi-year, general operating support to Chicago-area theaters, dance groups, music organizations, art programs, film centers, museums, and libraries. Additional grants support short-term projects that benefit a set of organizations or the field as a whole. In reviewing proposals from arts groups, the Foundation considers: quality of the organization's artistic program; strength of its board and staff leadership; impact on the organization's neighborhood, the city or the region; sizes and types of audiences served; and community and educational outreach activities.
Requirements: Applicants must be Chicago-based theaters, dance groups, music organizations, art programs, film centers, museums, or libraries.
Geographic Focus: Illinois
Contact: Deepa Gupta, Program Officer; (312) 726-8000; fax (312) 920-6258; dgupta@macfound.org or 4answers@macfound.org
Internet: http://www.macfound.org/info-grantseekers/grantmaking-guidelines/arts-grant-guideline/
Sponsor: John D. and Catherine T. MacArthur Foundation
140 S Dearborn Street, Suite 1100
Chicago, IL 60603-5285

MacDonald-Peterson Foundation Grants 1224

Established in 1995 in Texas, the MacDonald-Peterson Foundation offers funding for health and human services programs in Texas. The Foundation's primary fields of interest include: children's services; Christian agencies and churches; community and economic development; food banks; health organizations; higher education; hospitals; human services; medical research; mental health counseling and support groups; performing arts (orchestras); and youth development and community service clubs. There is no specified application format or annual deadlines, so applicants should begin the process by contacting the Foundation directly. Awards generally range from $5,000 to $20,000, and are given for general operations.

Requirements: Any 501(c)3 organization in, or serving the residents of, Texas are eligible to apply.
Geographic Focus: Texas
Contact: Guy Tabor, (713)579-2355
Sponsor: MacDonald-Peterson Foundation
1 Riverway, Suite 1000
Houston, TX 77056-1944

Macquarie Bank Foundation Grants   1225

The Foundation is one of Australia's oldest and largest corporate foundations contributing more than $150 million to more than 1500 community organizations world-wide since 1985. The Foundation focuses its resources in five core areas - the arts, education, environment, health, and welfare. The Foundation is also committed to projects specifically aimed at supporting indigenous communities. The Foundation's funding criteria is flexible and open. It welcomes applications from a diverse range of community organizations that are working in innovative ways to provide long-term benefits. Funding levels are flexible and are dictated by the needs of the organization and funding availability. Each application is assessed on its individual merit, with priority given to programs which support a broad section of the community at a regional, state or national level; have the involvement or potential for involvement of Macquarie Bank staff through volunteering, fundraising, pro bono work and board and/or management committee involvement; are located in cities/countries where Macquarie Bank staff are located; and deliver long-term benefits and build community sustainability. Prospective applicants are encouraged to check the Foundation website or contact Foundation Staff for more information on how to apply.
Geographic Focus: All States, All Countries
Amount of Grant: 100 - 500,000 USD
Contact: Heather Matwejev; +61 2 8232 6951; fax +61 2 8232 0019; heather.matwejev@macquarie.com or foundation@macquarie.com
Internet: http://www.macquarie.com/mgl/com/foundation/about/application-guidelines
Sponsor: Macquarie Bank Foundation
GP.O. Box 4294
Sydney, NSW 1164 Australia

Maddie's Fund Medical Equipment Grants   1226

Maddie's Fund offers grants to adoption guarantee shelters for the purchase of new medical equipment. Any adoption guarantee shelter is eligible to apply as long as it is located in the U.S. and employs at least one full-time veterinarian who spends at least 50% of his/her time caring for the animals in their shelter. An adoption guarantee shelter saves all the healthy and treatable animals under their care, with euthanasia reserved only for unhealthy and untreatable animals. An adoption guarantee organization can be an animal shelter, rescue group, foster care organization, or sanctuary. An animal organization does not have to say it is an adoption guarantee organization to qualify for this funding opportunity, but it does have to: (1) save all healthy and treatable animals under its care and make public its commitment to doing so; (2) clearly articulate to its community that it is saving all healthy and treatable animals under its care; (3) use the definitions of healthy and treatable as described in the Asilomar Accords; and (4) agree to publish, at least annually, in the organization's primary publications and on its website the organization's shelter statistics using the Maddie's Fund Animal Statistics Table. Samples of previously funded organizations are located on the website.
Requirements: Proposals should include the description and cost of the medical equipment to be purchased; the number of animals to be cared for as a result of the equipment; a general overview of the shelter's current medical program(s); proof of the organization's tax exempt status; evidence that the shelter meets the full-time veterinarian requirement; and annual shelter statistics from the most recent calendar year using the Animal Statistics Table. Grant size is determined by the impact the grant will have on saving the healthy and treatable shelter dogs and cats in the community. Proposals may be mailed or emailed. There are no deadlines and organizations may apply any time.
Restrictions: Applicants may only submit one medical equipment grant request every three years.
Geographic Focus: All States
Contact: Joey Bloomfield; (510) 337-8988; grants@maddiefund.org
Internet: http://www.maddiesfund.org/Grant_Giving/Medical_Equipment_Grants.html
Sponsor: Maddie's Fund
2223 Santa Clara Avenue, Suite B
Alameda, CA 94501-4416

Madison County Community Foundation - Immediate Need Grants   1227

The Madison County Community Foundation - Immediate Need Grants are available to non-profit agencies who have a proven track record with the Foundation, with an urgent operational need for funding, rather than a program or project.
Requirements: Organizations contact the Program Director and complete a two page application. The application is sent to the grants committee who provide an answer generally within 72 hours.
Geographic Focus: Indiana
Amount of Grant: Up to 2,000 USD
Contact: Tammy Bowman, Program Director; (765) 644-0002; fax (765) 644-3392; tbowman@madisoncf.org
Internet: http://www.madisonccf.org/index.php?submenu=Grants&src=gendocs&ref=Grants&category=Non_Profits
Sponsor: Madison County Community Foundation
33 West 10th Street, Suite 600
Anderson, IN 46015-1056

Maine Women's Fund Economic Security Grants   1228

Recognizing that women's ability to take care of themselves and their families and to contribute to their communities depend upon their ability to obtain financial security, the Maine Women's Fund provides grants to support projects and organizations that build economic security for Maine women and girls. Specifically, the fund invests in organizations that focus in four strategic areas to create systemic change: education and youth development; entrepreneurship and better jobs and wages; financial literacy and asset building; and policy and leadership. Applicants may request general operating support or program/project support. Downloadable guidelines are available from the grant web page. The fund makes the application available to applicants in early December. Completed applications will be reviewed by a group of women selected from the community for their expertise and commitment to social change. Reviewers will evaluate proposals on several factors including alignment with the Maine Women's Fund values, the likelihood of systemic change occurring, the quality of the project implementation and evaluation plan, and the capacity of the organization or group.
Requirements: Nonprofit organizations or groups that demonstrate tax-exempt status under the Internal Revenue Service Code 501(c)3 or groups that submit an application through a fiscal agent with tax-exempt status that agrees to accept funds on its behalf are eligible to apply. Organizations must serve women and girls who reside in Maine. The fund invests in programs and organizations that are focused on creating tangible social change, and not simply service delivery. The fund prefers to support organizations that have limited access to other donors.
Restrictions: Organizations are limited to receiving one grant per year. The fund will not provide over 10% of an organization's annual budget. The fund will not support the following types of entities or activities: projects that discriminate on the basis of ethnicity, race, color, creed, religion, gender or gender identity, national origin, age, disability, marital status, sexual orientation, or veteran's status; individuals; scholarships; capital or endowment; biomedical research; debt reduction; fundraising events; campaigns for political office; organizations that limit or oppose women's right to self determination; or agencies of state or federal government (unless they are part of an eligible community collaborative). Faith-based organizations are eligible to apply; however, projects and services provided by these must not present or incorporate religion in any manner.
Geographic Focus: Maine
Amount of Grant: Up to 15,000 USD
Contact: Sonya Tomlinson; (207) 774-5513; fax (207) 774-5533; grants@mainewomensfund.org or thewomen@mainewomensfund.org
Internet: http://www.mainewomensfund.org/grants/economic_security_initiative/
Sponsor: Maine Women's Fund
565 A Congress Street, Suite 306, P.O. Box 5135
Portland, ME 04101

Manitoba Arts Council Operating Grants For Book Publishers,   1229
Periodical Publishers and Arts Service Organizations

Operating grants support the annual activities of professional Manitoba book publishers, periodicals publishers, and arts service organizations who publish in eligible genres. Publishers present the work of Manitoban and Canadian writers to the public. Service organizations promote writing, books, and magazines to the public as well as provide services to their members. The periodicals publishers grants deadline is April 15; the book publishers grants deadline is December 1; and the Arts Service Organizations grants deadline is May 15.
Requirements: Publishers must have two years of project assessment before applying to the program, and must have been resident in Manitoba at least three years.

Companies that maintain professional industry standards and practices, have published at least four eligible titles in the past two years, and are committed to a continuing and sustained book publishing program may apply. Eligible titles for the book publishers grants must account for 75 percent of the total title production.
Geographic Focus: Canada
Date(s) Application is Due: Apr 15; May 15; Dec 1
Contact: David R. Scott, Associate Director; (204) 945-0645 or (204) 945-2237; fax (204) 945-5925; dscott@artscouncil.mb.ca
Internet: http://artscouncil.mb.ca/2010/02/operating-grants-book-publishers-periodical-publishers-and-arts-service-organizations/
Sponsor: Manitoba Arts Council
525-93 Lombard Avenue
Winnipeg, MB R3B 3B1 Canada

Manitoba Arts Council Operating Grants for Visual Arts Organizations 1230

The Operating Grant Program is available to provide ongoing, partial support to professional, not-for-profit visual arts organizations. An organization that receives support is expected to present and interpret works of art to the general public, participate in the development of Manitoba artists and maintain sound management and financial controls. Guidelines for this program are available through Marian Butler, the Program Consultant.
Requirements: Manitoba visual arts organizations are eligible.
Geographic Focus: All States, Canada
Date(s) Application is Due: Apr 1
Amount of Grant: 2,000 - 20,000 USD
Contact: Marian Butler; (204) 945-0399; mbutler@artscouncil.mb.ca
Internet: http://www.artscouncil.mb.ca/english/vis_grantorg.html
Sponsor: Manitoba Arts Council
525-93 Lombard Avenue
Winnipeg, MB R3B 3B1 Canada

Mann T. Lowry Foundation Grants 1231

Established in Virginia in 1996, the Mann T. Lowry Foundation has specified in primary fields of interest to include: education; health organizations; human services; and social services. Geographic restrictions for giving are primarily in the State of Virginia, and grants come in the form of general operating support. Amounts have varied most recently from $500 to $21,000. Application forms are not required, and there are no identified annual deadlines. Applicants should provide a two- to three-page letter of request, outlining their program and attaching any pertinent brochures or materials.
Geographic Focus: Virginia
Amount of Grant: 500 - 21,000 USD
Samples: Alzheimer's Association, Allen, Virginia, $500 - for general operating support; Joan Grossman Fegely Foundation, Richmond, Virginia, $1,000 - for general operating support; Massey Cancer Center, Richmond, Virginia, $21,000 - for general operating support.
Contact: George R. Hinnant, Director; (804) 643-3512
Sponsor: Mann T. Lowry Foundation
1630 Huguenot Road
Midlothian, VA 23113-2427

Marathon Petroleum Corporation Grants 1232

The Marathon Petroleum Corporation offers grant support within its home-base of Ohio, as well as throughout the states of Illinois, Indiana, Kentucky, Louisiana, Michigan, Texas, and West Virginia. Occasionally, it also gives to national organizations, Its primary purposes are aligned with its core values of health and safety, diversity and inclusion, environmental stewardship and honesty and integrity. With that in mind, special emphasis is also directed toward programs that empower the socially or economically disadvantaged, and provide opportunities for students to reach their full potential. Fields of interest include: the arts, children and youth services, community and economic development, education, the environment, health care, human services, and public affairs. Types of support include: annual campaigns, cause-related marketing, employee matching gifts, general operating support, in-kind donations, and scholarships to individuals.
Geographic Focus: Illinois, Indiana, Kentucky, Louisiana, Michigan, Ohio, Texas, West Virginia
Contact: Bill Conlisk, 419-422-2121; whconlisk@marathonpetroleum.com
Internet: http://www.marathonpetroleum.com/Corporate_Citizenship/
Sponsor: Marathon Petroleum Corporation
539 South Main Street
Findlay, OH 45840-3229

Marcia and Otto Koehler Foundation Grants 1233

Grants are made to support arts and culture, medical, education, and social organizations in San Antonio, Texas. Proposals must demonstrate leadership in effecting positive change; encourage collaborative effort; serve large and diverse sectors of the population; and demonstrate vision, effectiveness, and good fiscal management. Types of support include general operating support, building construction/renovation, and research. Grants are made for one time only. Applicants must send a letter of request for application by March 1 to receive an application.
Requirements: Grants are awarded only to organizations in Bexar County, Texas.
Restrictions: Grants will not be made to individuals or to support other foundations or endowments; salaries; operating deficits; political organizations; or churches, synagogues, or parishes.
Geographic Focus: Texas
Date(s) Application is Due: Jun 1
Amount of Grant: 2,500 - 50,000 USD
Samples: Centro Alameda (San Antonio, TX)—to restore a marquee, canopy, and facade, $30,000; McNay Art Museum (San Antonio, TX)—to sponsor an art exhibit, $50,000.
Contact: Thomas K. Killion, Senior Vice President, Bank of America; (210) 270-5422; fax (210) 270-5520; thomas.k.killion@ustrust.com
Sponsor: Marcia and Otto Koehler Foundation
P.O. Box 121
San Antonio, TX 78291-0121

Mardag Foundation Grants 1234

The Mardag Foundation is committed to making grants to qualified nonprofit organizations in Minnesota that help enhance and improve the quality of life, inspire learning, revitalize communities, and promote access to the arts. The Foundation focuses their grantmaking in these priority areas: improving the lives of at-risk families, children, youth, and young adults; supporting seniors to live independently; building the capacity of arts and humanities organizations to benefit their communities; and supporting community development throughout the St. Paul area. Grants normally support; capital projects, program expansion and special projects of a time-limited nature; start-up costs for promising new programs that demonstrate sound management and clear goals relevant to community needs; support for established agencies that have temporary or transitional needs; funds to match contributions received from other sources or to provide a challenge to raise new contributions. Applicants are encouraged to submit a brief summary of their project prior to preparation of a full proposal to see if the project fits the guidelines and interests of the foundation. The Foundation's grantmaking meetings are in April, August, and November. Generally, full proposals must be received three months prior to a meeting date.
Requirements: Nonprofit 501(c)3 organizations are eligible to apply. Organizations must be in the East Metro area of Dakota, Ramsey, or Washington counties.
Restrictions: The Foundation does not fund: programs exclusively serving Minneapolis and the surrounding West Metro area; scholarships and grants to individuals; ongoing annual operating expenses; sectarian religious programs; medical research; federated campaigns; conservation or environmental programs; events and conferences; programs serving the physically, developmentally or mentally disabled; capital campaigns of private secondary schools; and capital and endowment campaigns of private colleges and universities. The Foundation will review, on their own merits, grant applications received from private secondary schools and private colleges and universities for purposes not excluded in the information above.
Geographic Focus: Minnesota
Date(s) Application is Due: May 1; Aug 1; Dec 31
Amount of Grant: 5,000 - 50,000 USD
Contact: Lisa Hansen, Grants Administration Manager; (651) 224-5463 or (800) 875-6167; lisa.hansen@mnpartners.org
Internet: http://www.mardag.org/apply_for_a_grant/
Sponsor: Mardag Foundation
55 Fifth Street East, Suite 600
St. Paul, MN 55101

Margaret Abell Powell Fund Grants 1235

The Margaret Abell Powell Fund of the William S. Abell Foundation makes grants to support traditional classical theater and classical ballet in the Washington, DC, metropolitan area including the counties of Montgomery, Prince George's, Charles, Calvert, St. Mary's and Arlington; and the city of Alexandria. Support will be given to local organizations producing English language, mainstream theater and classical ballet. Emphasis will be given to organizations which support specific performances, the staging or choreography

of pieces, and the training of young artists. Applications for this program will be accepted for: the underwriting of specific performances; the training of actors, actresses, performers and dancers; and the staging and choreography of specific pieces. Proposals are reviewed only in June and December. Letters of intent to apply are due April 1 and October 1. Deadlines for full proposals are April 15 and October 15. Grants typically do not exceed $25,000.
Requirements: Nonprofit organizations in the District of Columbia and the nearby Maryland counties of Montgomery, Prince George's, Charles, Calvert, and St. Mary's, as well as the city of Arlington, Virginia, are eligible.
Geographic Focus: District of Columbia, Maryland, Virginia
Date(s) Application is Due: Apr 15; Oct 15
Amount of Grant: 5,000 - 40,000 USD
Samples: American Dance Institute, Rockville, Maryland, $25,000 - upport the production of Carmina Burana; Bowen McCauley Dance, Arlington, Virginia, $20,000 - underwrite a new classical ballet; Maryland Youth Ballet, Silver Spring, Maryland, $25,000 - the production of Raymonda, Pas de Dix.
Contact: Janet Miller, Executive Director; (301) 652-2224; fax (301) 652-9173; jmiller@williamsabellfoundation.org or info@williamsabellfoundation.org
Internet: http://www.williamsabellfoundation.org/margaret_abell_powell_fund
Sponsor: William S. Abell Foundation
2 Wisconsin Circle, Suite 890
Chevy Chase, MD 20815

Margaret M. Walker Charitable Foundation Grants 1236

Margaret M. Walker Charitable Foundation was established in Pennsylvania in order to offer support for Christian ministries, relief services organizations, children, women and family services, and food services. Specific fields of interest include: Christian agencies and churches; family services; food distribution; human services; minorities and immigrants; and women's shelters. Types of support include: building and renovation; capital campaigns; equipment; general operating support; and program development. Most recent awards have ranged from $2,000 to $60,000. There are no specific application forms, so interested parties should submit a letter outlining the project and amount of funding requested.
Requirements: 501(c)3 organizations either located in, or serving residents of, Pennsylvania are eligible to apply.
Geographic Focus: Pennsylvania
Amount of Grant: 2,000 - 60,000 USD
Contact: Foundation Administrator; (330) 743-7000
Sponsor: Margaret M. Walker Charitable Foundation
42 McClurg Road
Youngstown, OH 44512

Margaret T. Morris Foundation Grants 1237

The Margaret T. Morris Foundation awards grants, primarily in Arizona, in its areas of interest, including: animal welfare; arts; children and youth, services; education; environment; higher education; homeless service; human services; marine science; medical research and education; mental health and crisis services; museums; performing arts; reproductive health and family planning; and hospices. The Foundation's types of support include: building renovation; capital campaigns; debt reduction; endowments; general operating support; land acquisition; matching and challenge support; and program development. The Board of Directors meets in August, December, and as needed.
Requirements: Applications are not accepted. Applicants should submit a letter of inquiry with their request for funding and a description of the project.
Geographic Focus: Arizona
Contact: Thomas Polk, Trustee; (928) 445-4010
Sponsor: Margaret T. Morris Foundation
P.O. Box 592
Prescott, AZ 86302-0592

Margoes Foundation Grants 1238

The foundation awards grants to California nonprofits in its areas of interest, including cardiac research, rehabilitation of mentally ill patients, and scholarships for minority students and for Asian and African nationals studying in the United States. Types of funding include general operating support, continuing support, program development, fellowships, scholarship funds, research, and matching funds. There are no application forms. Applicants should call or submit a preliminary letter prior to submitting a full proposal.
Requirements: California nonprofits are eligible, with preference given to the San Francisco Bay area.
Restrictions: Grants are not awarded to agencies supported by federated campaigns or to individuals.
Geographic Focus: California

Date(s) Application is Due: Apr 1; Oct 1
Amount of Grant: 10,000 - 20,000 USD
Samples: Community Music Center (San Francisco, CA)—for financial aid, $10,000; U of the Pacific (Stockton, CA)—to increase minority enrollment in the predentistry undergraduate programs, $20,000 over two years; Fred Finch Youth Ctr (Oakland, CA)—for salary support of a part-time counselor for a transitional independent living program for older adolescents and young adults with severe emotional problems, $15,000.
Contact: John Blum; (415) 981-2966; fax (415) 981-5218; margoesfdn@aol.com
Sponsor: Margoes Foundation
57 Post Street, Suite 510
San Francisco, CA 94104

Marie C. and Joseph C. Wilson Foundation Rochester Small Grants 1239

The Marie and Joseph Wilson Foundation strives to improve the quality of life through initiating and supporting projects that measurably demonstrate a means of creating a sense of belonging within the family and community. The Foundation considers 501(c)3 organization requests ranging from $1,000 to $25,000. Grant applications are accepted on an ongoing basis. Foundation board members review applications as they are received. The review committee meets once a month except for July and August. Because the Foundation receives a large number of applications, responses may take up to four months. Prior to the receiving funding, grant recipients are required to sign a grant agreement contract. Written progress reports are required at six months and one year following the date of the grant. Samples of the Foundation's previously funded grants are available online.
Requirements: The Foundation review committee looks for one or more of the following conditions in a proposal: the proposal is a well-planned approach to delivering services; Foundation support would be catalytic to the project's success; the proposal is efficient in its use of funds and expenses are reduced by sharing resources with other agencies or groups; and a collaborative network exists that multiplies the impact of the grant. Applicants may contact the Foundation for a current application form.
Restrictions: Grants are limited to 501(c)3 organizations serving the Rochester, New York area. Grants will not be made to individuals, partisan political organizations, or to support lobbying efforts. Requests for capital projects also will not be considered.
Geographic Focus: New York
Amount of Grant: 1,000 - 25,000 USD
Samples: Association for the Blind and Visually Impaired, Rochester, New York, for a full-time children's programming and recreational coordinator, $25,000; Charles Settlement House, Rochester, New York, Teen Clubs, a neighborhood-based program for teens that reduces violent behavior and teen pregnancy while encouraging community service, $10,000; Horizons at Harley, Rochester, New York, a summer enrichment program that offers academic, cultural, wellness, and recreational activities for children from inner-city Rochester, $24,000.
Contact: Megan Bell; (585) 461-4696; fax (585) 473-5206
Internet: http://www.mcjcwilsonfoundation.org/funding.cfm
Sponsor: Marie C. and Joseph C. Wilson Foundation
160 Allens Creek Road
Rochester, NY 14618-3309

Marilyn Augur Family Foundation Grants 1240

The foundation gives priority to organizations serving basic human needs primarily in the geographical area of Dallas, TX. Basic needs include food, shelter, clothing, health, and education aimed at transforming lives of those living in poverty or in prison. Christian organizations that minister to the needy are of particular interest. The foundation gives emphasis to children's programs. The foundation prefers to support organizations and projects directly rather than supporting fundraising events.
Requirements: Texas nonprofit organizations are eligible.
Restrictions: Generally, the foundation does not give grants in the area of arts and culture.
Geographic Focus: Texas
Amount of Grant: 1,000 - 3,000 USD
Contact: Nancy Roberts, (214) 522-5586; fax (214) 526-0253; maf@waymark.net
Internet: http://fdncenter.org/grantmaker/augur/app.html
Sponsor: Marilyn Augur Family Foundation
4209 McKinney Avenue, Suite 202A
Dallas, TX 75205

Marin Community Foundation Affordable Housing Grants 1241

Marin Community Foundation (MCF) is dedicated to creating housing opportunities in Marin that are affordable and accessible to families and individuals with lower incomes. To support this goal, the Affordable Housing grants fund three strategic areas: increase public support for affordable housing and influence zoning changes that support affordable housing; make investments in affordable housing, both rental properties and owned housing that take advantage of specific market opportunities; and help people at risk of homelessness to remain housed. The grant program manager may be emailed through the grant website.

Requirements: There will not be an open competitive process for these grants. RFPs will be issued to community organizations that are being invited to apply for support under all three strategies. Nonprofit organizations will be invited to submit a Letter of Intent (LOI) in response to a Request for Proposal issued for each of the Strategic Initiatives on the Foundation website. After MCF staff reviews the LOIs, selected applicants will be invited to complete and submit a full proposal. If invited to submit an LOI, nonprofit groups should first register with the Grant Application Center, MCF's online grants application system.

Geographic Focus: California
Contact: Kathleen Harris, Program Director; (415) 44-2549
Internet: http://www.marincf.org/grants-and-loans/grants/strategic-initiatives/increasing-affordable-housing
Sponsor: Marin Community Foundation
5 Hamilton Landing, Suite 200
Novato, CA 94949

Marin Community Foundation Social Justice and Interfaith 1242
Understanding Grants

The Marin Community Foundation Social Justice and Interfaith Understanding Grants are committed to supporting efforts that increase awareness, mobilize communities, and catalyze social change to address social inequities in Marin County. The Foundation defines social justice as equal access to social, political, and economic opportunities and resources. It defines interfaith understanding as communication between and among faith communities that crosses religious lines with an aim to explore common ground in beliefs and values. The Foundation funds two strategies depending on the particular program: 1) to increase community engagement to identify and address social justice issues, and 2) to increase collaboration and dialogue among religious institutions, faith-based communities, and community members. The funding varies by strategy (from $10,000 to $70,000 for strategy 1, and from $10,000 to $50,000 for strategy 2), but both strategies have the same deadline and application process. Each strategy funds staff support and operational costs, with strategy one also funding tech assistance. Organizations should refer to the website for specific information about each strategy.

Requirements: Organizations may apply online for either strategy with the same application process. They are also encouraged to contact the program officer by phone or to email directly through the website.

Restrictions: Strategy 1 does not fund the following: direct social or health services; religious programs that are strictly sectarian; and emergency or capital expenditures, such as computer hardware or software. Strategy 2 does not fund the following: individuals; coalitions that do not have a lead organization; endowments or private foundations; religious organizations that are strictly sectarian; federal, state, or municipal agencies; and political campaigns.

Geographic Focus: California
Date(s) Application is Due: Nov 18
Amount of Grant: 10,000 - 70,000 USD
Contact: Shirin Vakharia, Program Director; (415) 464-2523
Internet: http://www.marincf.org/grants-and-loans/grants/community-grants/social-justice-and-interfaith-understanding
Sponsor: Marin Community Foundation
5 Hamilton Landing, Suite 200
Novato, CA 94949

Marion and Miriam Rose Fund Grants 1243

The Marion and Miriam Rose Fund was established to support childcare facilities serving dependent, neglected, indigent, and emotionally disturbed children, and children in foster care. The Fund was created under the wills of George B. Rose and Marion Rose. The majority of grants from the Fund are one year in duration. Applicants must apply online at the grant website, and are strongly encouraged to do the following before applying: review the downloadable state application procedures for additional helpful information and clarifications; review the downloadable online-application guidelines at the grant website; review the foundation's funding history (link is available from the grant website); review the online application questions in advance; and review

the list of required attachments. These will generally include: a list of board members, financial statements (audited, reviewed, or compiled by independent auditor); an organization summary; a list of other funding sources; an IRS Determination letter; and other required documents. All attachments must be uploaded in the online application as PDF, Word, or Excel files. Most recent awards have ranged from $12,000 to $27,000. The annual application deadline is March 1. Applicants will be notified of grant decisions by June 30.

Requirements: Organizations must be located in, or serve the children of Little Rock, Arkansas.

Restrictions: The Fund will consider requests for general operating support only if the organization's operating budget is less than $1 million. In general, grant requests for individuals, endowment campaigns, or capital projects will not be considered.

Geographic Focus: Arkansas
Date(s) Application is Due: Mar 1
Amount of Grant: 12,000 - 27,000 USD
Samples: Our House, Little Rock, Arkansas, $12,000 - for growing and strengthening programs for homeless and near homeless children (2014); Camp Aldersgate, Little Rock, Arkansas, $12,000 - support of the summer medical camps program (2014); Access Group, Little Rock, Arkansas, $25,000 - support of the Therapeutic Arts Program (2014).
Contact: Robert Fox, Philanthropic Relationship Manager; (214) 209-1370; tx.philanthropic@ustrust.com
Internet: https://www.bankofamerica.com/philanthropic/fn_search.action
Sponsor: Marion and Miriam Rose Fund
901 Main Street, 19th Floor
Dallas, TX 75202-3714

Marion Gardner Jackson Charitable Trust Grants 1244

The Marion Gardner Jackson Charitable Trust was established by Marion Gardner Jackson, the granddaughter of local industrialist, Robert W. Gardner, founder of the Gardner-Denver Company. The Trust funds: the arts and humanities; education; health; religion; and human service organizations. Giving is centered around the Quincy, Illinois, area and its surrounding communities in Adams County. The trust supports capital, program, and operating grants. Grants generally range up to a maximum of $25,000. The application is available at the trust website through Bank of America. The annual deadline for submission is August 31.

Restrictions: For program support grants, the yearly request may not be more than 50% of the program's budget. Organizations can submit one application per year and will not receive more than one award from the trust in any given year. Organizations receiving a multi-year award from the trust that continues into the next grant year are not eligible to apply for an additional grant until the end of the grant cycle. The trust does not support requests from individuals, organizations attempting to influence policy through direct lobbying, or any political campaigns.

Geographic Focus: Illinois
Date(s) Application is Due: Aug 31
Amount of Grant: Up to 25,000 USD
Contact: Debra L. Grand, Philanthropic Relationship Manager; (312) 828-2055; ilgrantmaking@ustrust.com
Internet: https://www.bankofamerica.com/philanthropic/fn_search.action
Sponsor: Marion Gardner Jackson Charitable Trust
231 South LaSalle Street, IL1-231-13-32
Chicago, IL 60604

Marion I. and Henry J. Knott Foundation Discretionary Grants 1245

Founded in 1977, the Marion I. and Henry J. Knott Foundation is a Catholic family foundation committed to honoring its founders' legacy of generosity to strengthen the community within the Archdiocese of Baltimore. Henry J. Knott, the eldest of six boys, grew up in a lively household in the Baltimore area. His father was a hard-working carpenter. Marion Isabel Burk, who was orphaned at the age of eleven, grew up cooking and looking after the children in a small boarding house and received little formal education as a result. Henry and Marion met on a blind date arranged by a good friend in 1926, while Henry was taking classes at Loyola College, and were married in 1928. They went on to build a large family (thirteen children, one lost to cancer) and a thriving construction business. Henry was the first developer in Baltimore to employ the practice of prefabricating wall panels in a factory and then sending them out to construction sites. Projects moved at a blistering pace and eventually led Henry to become the President of Arundel Corporation. Henry and Marion who knew firsthand the challenge of raising a large family always practiced philanthropy. The foundation makes awards in five Program categories: Arts and Humanities; Catholic Activities; Education (Catholic schools, nonsectarian private schools specifically catering to special needs, and private colleges and universities); Health Care; and Human Services. Within the five program categories, the foundation funds within five project categories, including capital expenses, development, new and/or ongoing programs, operating expenses, and technology. In addition to its standard granting program, the Knott Foundation provides a limited number of Discretionary Grants (20-30) throughout the year. These grants, ranging between $500 to $2,500, are designed to increase the Foundation's grant-making options as well as its responsiveness to community needs. Grants are awarded based on the proposed project, the availability of funds, and other current requests for funding. To apply for a discretionary grant, applicants should submit a brief (one page) Letter of Inquiry (LOI) on their organization's letterhead. The LOI should describe the applicant's project or program, detail the applicant's needs, and provide a timeframe for use of the award if granted. In addition to the LOI, the applicant should also submit a 501(c)3 status letter, a project budget if applicable, and a list of the board of directors. Discretionary requests are accepted and awarded on a rolling basis throughout the year. Although not guaranteed, approved funds are usually disbursed within one to two weeks of the discretionary grant's approval date. Interested applicants should visit the website for further details and guidelines.

Requirements: Discretionary grant requests must be in alignment with the foundation's areas of geographic and programmatic giving. Funding is limited to 501(c)3 organizations serving Baltimore City and the following counties in Maryland: Allegheny, Anne Arundel, Baltimore, Carroll, Frederick, Garrett, Harford, Howard, and Washington. Applicants may apply through a fiscal sponsor. The fiscal sponsor must be a 501(c)3 nonprofit organization that has a formal relationship and Memorandum of Understanding (MOU) with the applicant. Selected applicants will need to submit a copy of their most recent IRS 990 and/or audited financials.

Restrictions: The following will not be funded: organizations that have not been in operation for at least one year, scholarships, public education/public sector agencies, pro-choice or reproductive health programs, individuals, annual giving, political activities, one-time only events/seminars/workshops, legal services, environmental activities, medical research, day care centers, endowment funds for arts/humanities, national/local chapters for specific diseases, agencies that redistribute grant funds to other nonprofits, reimbursables or any prior expenses, or government agencies that form 501(c)3 nonprofits to fund public sector projects.

Geographic Focus: Maryland

Amount of Grant: 500 - 2,500 USD

Samples: Museum of Ceramic Art, Baltimore, Maryland, $2,500 - to the after-school Middle School Ceramics Art Program though out Baltimore City; Filbert Street Garden, Baltimore, Maryland, $980 - to suppor their Winter Greens: Student-Supported Agriculture program; Maryland Association of Nonprofits (MANO), Baltimore, Maryland, $5,000 - to support the Leaders Circle's forum on building better relationships between nonprofit executive directors and their board leadership.

Contact: Kathleen McCarthy, Grants Manager; (410) 235-7068; fax (410) 889-2577; knott@knottfoundation.org or info@knottfoundation.org

Internet: http://www.knottfoundation.org/what_we_do/grant_application_process/discretionary_grant_application_process

Sponsor: Marion I. and Henry J. Knott Foundation

3904 Hickory Avenue

Baltimore, MD 21211-1834

Marion I. and Henry J. Knott Foundation Standard Grants   1246

Founded in 1977, the Marion I. and Henry J. Knott Foundation is a Catholic family foundation committed to honoring its founders' legacy of generosity to strengthen the community within the Archdiocese of Baltimore. Henry J. Knott, the eldest of six boys, grew up in a lively household in the Baltimore area. His father was a hard-working carpenter. Marion Isabel Burk, who was orphaned at the age of eleven, grew up cooking and looking after the children in a small boarding house and received little formal education as a result. Henry and Marion met on a blind date arranged by a good friend in 1926, while Henry was taking classes at Loyola College, and were married in 1928. They went on to build a large family (thirteen children, one lost to cancer) and a thriving construction business. Henry was the first developer in Baltimore to employ the practice of prefabricating wall panels in a factory and then sending them out to construction sites. Projects moved at a blistering pace and eventually led Henry to become the President of Arundel Corporation. Henry and Marion who knew firsthand the challenge of raising a large family always practiced philanthropy. The foundation makes both standard and discretionary awards in five Program categories: Arts and Humanities; Catholic Activities; Education (Catholic Schools, Nonsectarian private schools specifically

catering to special needs, and private colleges and universities); Health Care; and Human Services. Within the five program categories, the foundation funds within five project categories, including capital expenses, development, new and/or ongoing programs, operating expenses, and technology. The Knott Foundation uses a two-step online application process for its standard-grants program. Step one requires the submission of an online Letter of Inquiry (LOI) along with a Financial Analysis Form. Applicants whose LOIs are approved will move on to step two which requires online submission of a full proposal. Applicants are given the opportunity to submit a draft of their proposal for comments and feedback prior to their final submission. The review process for the foundation's standard grants program takes approximately four months from the date of the LOI submission until a final funding decision is made. The Knott Foundation accepts standard-grant applications three times per year - February, June and October. LOIs and proposals must be received by 5 p.m. on the applicable deadline date. Complete details, guidelines, and links to the online submission system are available at the grant website.

Requirements: Funding is limited to 501(c)3 organizations serving Baltimore City and the following counties in Maryland: Allegheny, Anne Arundel, Baltimore, Carroll, Frederick, Garrett, Harford, Howard, and Washington. Applicants may apply through a fiscal sponsor. The fiscal sponsor must be a 501(c)3 nonprofit organization that has a formal relationship and Memorandum of Understanding (MOU) with the applicant.

Restrictions: Organizations that are denied funding at the LOI stage of the grant process are eligible to apply again during the next grant cycle; organizations that are denied funding after submitting a full grant proposal must wait one year before reapplying; organizations that receive a grant award must wait two years before reapplying. The following will not be funded: organizations that have not been in operation for at least one year, scholarships, public education/public sector agencies, pro-choice or reproductive health programs, individuals, annual giving, political activities, one-time only events/seminars/workshops, legal services, environmental activities, medical research, day care centers, endowment funds for arts/humanities, national/local chapters for specific diseases, agencies that redistribute grant funds to other nonprofits, reimbursables or any prior expenses, or government agencies that form 501(c)3 nonprofits to fund public sector projects.

Geographic Focus: Maryland

Date(s) Application is Due: Mar 7; Jul 9; Nov 12

Amount of Grant: 35,000 - 45,000 USD

Samples: Pathfinders for Autism, Hunt Valley, Maryland, $32,294 - to support half of the Resource Center and Outreach Coordinator's salary and operating expenses related to expanding the Parent and Professional Training Series; St. Elizabeth School, Baltimore, Maryland, $44,748 - to support the purchase and installation of five new SMART Boards; Big Brothers Big Sisters of the Greater Chesapeake, Baltimore, Maryland, $45,000 - to support salaries for professionals engaged in the mentoring of children facing adversity in Baltimore City.

Contact: Kathleen McCarthy, Grants Manager; (410) 235-7068; fax (410) 889-2577; knott@knottfoundation.org or info@knottfoundation.org

Internet: http://www.knottfoundation.org/what_we_do/grant_application_process

Sponsor: Marion I. and Henry J. Knott Foundation

3904 Hickory Avenue

Baltimore, MD 21211-1834

Marjorie Moore Charitable Foundation Grants   1247

The Marjorie Moore Charitable Foundation was established in 1957 to support and promote quality educational, cultural, human-services, environmental, and health-care programming for underserved populations. Grants from the Moore Foundation made in support of operations or programming are one year in duration. Multi-year grants for long-term capital projects will be considered on a case-by-case basis. Applicants must apply online at the grant website. Applicants are strongly encouraged to do the following before applying: review the downloadable state application procedures for additional helpful information and clarifications; review the downloadable online-application guidelines at the grant website; review the foundation's funding history (link is available from the grant website); review the online application questions in advance; and review the list of required attachments. These will generally include: a list of board members, financial statements (audited, reviewed, or compiled by independent auditor); an organization summary; a list of other funding sources; an IRS Determination letter; and other required documents. All attachments must be uploaded in the online application as PDF, Word, or Excel files. The Marjorie Moore Charitable Foundation has biannual deadlines of June 1 and December 1. Applications must be submitted by 11:59 p.m. on the deadline dates. Applicants will be notified of grant decisions by letter within two to three months after each respective proposal deadline.

Requirements: Applicant organizations must have 501(c)3 tax-exempt status and serve the people of Kensington or Berlin, Connecticut. A breakdown of number/percentage of people served by specific towns is required on the online application. Preference is given to organizations that provide human services or health care programming.

Restrictions: The foundation does not support requests from individuals, organizations attempting to influence policy through direct lobbying, or any political campaigns.

Geographic Focus: Connecticut

Date(s) Application is Due: Jun 1; Dec 1

Contact: Kate Kerchaert; (860) 657-7016; kate.kerchaert@baml.com

Internet: https://www.bankofamerica.com/philanthropic/fn_search.action

Sponsor: Marjorie Moore Charitable Foundation

200 Glastonbury Boulevard, Suite # 200, CT2-545-02-05

Glastonbury, CT 06033-4056

MARPAT Foundation Grants   1248

The foundation supports nonprofit organizations based in or benefiting the greater Washington metropolitan area. Grants are awarded to support organizations that promote the visual and performing arts; encourage family planning; conserve natural resources or advance knowledge of the natural world; promote international understanding; preserve historic resources or advance knowledge of American history and culture, or; expand opportunities in the District of Columbia's Wards 7 and 8 for low-income youth and adults. Grant support includes general operating support, building funds, equipment, programs/projects, and publications. Stage One summary sheets are due by the listed application deadline; full proposals are by invitation.

Requirements: Organizations determined to be tax-exempt under section 501(c)3 of the U.S. Internal Revenue Code of 1986 and which are not private foundations are eligible. Grants will only be made to organizations based in or benefiting the greater Washington metropolitan area.

Restrictions: The foundation does not make grants for medical research, to endowment funds, to individuals, or to organizations based outside the United States.

Geographic Focus: District of Columbia, Maryland, Virginia

Date(s) Application is Due: May 22

Amount of Grant: 5,000 - 50,000 USD

Samples: 2008: GALA (Grupo de Artistas Latino Americanos) - $35,000 to support artistic, education and community engagement programming; Textile Museum - $20,000 for general operating support; International Student House - $20,000 to update electrical service to the building; Earthwatch - $15,000 to support D.C. middle/high school teacher volunteers in ?????eld research; Catholics for a Free Choice - $15,000 to support 'Condoms4Life' and 'Prevention Not Prohibition' initiatives; Jewish Historical Society of Greater Washington $5,000 to support an exhibition about Jewish life in Washington, D.C. and Alexandria during the Civil War

Contact: Joan Koven, Secretary/Treasurer; jkoven@marpatfoundation.org

Internet: http://fdncenter.org/grantmaker/marpat

Sponsor: MARPAT Foundation

P.O. Box 1769

Silver Spring, MD 20915-1769

Mars Foundation Grants   1249

The foundation awards grants to eligible nonprofit organizations primarily within the Washington, DC, metropolitan area, including Virginia, Maryland, and the District of Columbia. Areas of support include arts and culture, animal/wildlife, civic and community, education, environment, health and human services, and historic preservation. Types of support include capital grants, challenge grants, general operating grants, and project grants. Grants are awarded once a year. Requests must be submitted on the foundation's application form.

Requirements: U.S. 501(c)3 nonprofit organizations are eligible.

Geographic Focus: All States

Date(s) Application is Due: Oct 15

Amount of Grant: 1,000 - 100,000 USD

Samples: Colonial Williamsburg (Williamsburg, VA)—for new 17th- and 18th-century costumes for the casts of the Cry Witch! program, $25,000.

Contact: Grants Administrator; (703) 821-4900; fax (703) 448-9678

Internet: http://www.mars.com

Sponsor: Mars Foundation

6885 Elm Street

McLean, VA 22101

Marsh Corporate Grants   1250

The corporate giving program targets nonprofit organizations in corporate communities. Support goes to food banks - financial support and in-kind product donations, and nutrition programs that provide free hot meals for underprivileged children; education and youth programs - operating grants or project support to human service agencies that provide services to people, particularly children, in need in Marsh communities, and projects that directly benefit children, promote the education of children, or encourage the positive development of children; community development - support for operations or projects to community and civic organizations that focus on civic involvement, citizen participation, or positive improvements that benefit the community; arts - cultural and arts organizations that serve broad audiences with programming of the highest quality, and one-time capital grants for arts and cultural facilities; and hometown or neighborhood activities - grass-roots organizations that focus their efforts on improving their immediate community through activities that benefit families in their hometowns or neighborhoods.

Restrictions: Marsh is unable to provide support to for-profit organizations (employee recognition programs, company events, etc.) and third-party organizations.

Geographic Focus: Indiana, Ohio

Contact: Community Relations Manager; (317) 594-2100 or (800) 845-7686; fax (317) 594-2705

Internet: http://www.marsh.net/about/community/marsh-giving/

Sponsor: Marsh Supermarkets

9800 Crosspoint Boulevard

Indianapolis, IN 46256

Mary Black Foundation Active Living Grants   1251

The Mary Black Foundation makes grants to nonprofit organizations in Spartanburg County, South Carolina, region. The Foundation has three applications for active living grants: Programs and Services assist people in becoming more physically active, either for recreation or for transportation; Policies and Places have a direct impact on whether people have the opportunity to be active; and Planning and Capacity Building for organizations that have as part of their core mission to increase active living. Each area of Active Living has different goals and grant submission procedures. The Foundation accepts applications quarterly: March 1, June 1, September 1, and December 1.

Requirements: Nonprofit organizations in South Carolina's Spartanburg County are eligible. Before submitting an application for a grant in Active Living, potential applicants must meet with the Foundation's program staff.

Restrictions: The Foundation does not accept applications from individuals or general fundraising solicitations.

Geographic Focus: South Carolina

Date(s) Application is Due: Mar 1; Jun 1; Sep 1; Dec 1

Amount of Grant: 2,000 - 200,000 USD

Samples: City of Woodruff, Woodruff, South Carolina, $150,000 - to support the Woodruff Greenway Trail; Partners for Active Living, Spartanburg, South Carolina, $75,900 - for the last year of a three-year grant to support a community initiative to increase usage of the 1.9-mile Mary Black Foundation Rail Trail; Spartanburg County School District One, Spartanburg, South Carolina, $198,000 - to support the Inman Trail.

Contact: Amy Page, Grant Consultant; (864) 573-9500; fax (864) 573-5805; apage@maryblackfoundation.org

Internet: http://www.maryblackfoundation.org/active-living/targeted-results

Sponsor: Mary Black Foundation

349 East Main Street, Suite 100

Spartanburg, SC 29302

Mary D. and Walter F. Frear Eleemosynary Trust Grants   1252

Walter Francis Frear was a lawyer and judge in the Kingdom of Hawaii and Republic of Hawaii, and the third Territorial Governor of Hawaii from 1907 to 1913. The Mary D. and Walter F. Frear Eleemosynary Trust was established to sponsor educational projects. Grants are awarded to Hawaii nonprofit organizations in the areas of child welfare and youth, education, social services, music, and the arts. Types of support include building construction and renovation, capital campaigns, conferences and seminars, equipment acquisition, general operating support, matching/challenge grants, program development, and seed grants. There are three annual deadlines specified, and applicants should begin by contacting the Trust administrative office.

Requirements: Grant applications are accepted from qualified tax-exempt charitable organizations in Hawaii.

Restrictions: Grants are not made to individuals, nor for endowments, reserve purposes, deficit financing, or travel.

Geographic Focus: Hawaii
Date(s) Application is Due: Jan 1; Jul 1; Oct 1
Amount of Grant: 5,000 - 25,000 USD
Contact: Paula Boyce, Grants Administrator, c/o Bank of Hawaii; (808) 537-8822; fax (808) 538-4007; pboyce@boh.com
Sponsor: Mary D. and Walter F. Frear Eleemosynary Trust
130 Merchant Street, P.O. Box 3170
Honolulu, HI 96802-3170

Mary E. Bivins Foundation Grants   **1253**
The foundation supports U.S. organizations and distributes funding for religious education, religious welfare, and scholarships. Types of support include building construction/renovation, capital campaigns, conferences and seminars, research, scholarship funds and scholarships to individuals, and seed grants. Applicants should submit a brief letter of inquiry, including program description and organization background, religious preference, and future plans.
Requirements: Christian nonprofits in Texas are eligible.
Geographic Focus: Texas
Amount of Grant: 5,000 - 50,000 USD
Samples: Ozark Christian College (Joplin, MO)—for scholarships, $23,805; Abilene Christian U (Abilene, TX)—for scholarships, $3300.
Contact: Linda Pitner, Program Coordinator; (806) 379-9400; fax (806) 379-9404; linda@bivinsfoundation.org
Internet: http://www.bivinsfoundations.org/grants.php
Sponsor: Mary E. Bivins Foundation
P.O. Box 1727
Amarillo, TX 79105

Mary Flagler Cary Charitable Trust Grants   **1254**
Grants are awarded for general operating support and for program support. The trust considers grant proposals in three areas: for music in New York City (with an emphasis on the performance of contemporary music; and support of music education programs, primarily at community schools of the arts); for the conservation of natural resources (the protection of coastal wetlands, with an emphasis on the Virginia Barrier Islands and South Carolina Coastal Focus Areas, through the support of efforts to provide for the long-term protection of natural resources as a part of regional ecosystems); and for urban environmental programs in New York City (focused on support for community initiatives and to help develop local leadership to work on the environmental problems within low-income neighborhoods of the city). The balance of the trust's grant budget is devoted primarily to support the Mary Flagler Cary Arboretum and its scientific program, the Institute of Ecosystem Studies, in Millbrook, NY. Multiple-year grants may be awarded when appropriate. Initial contact should be by letter outlining the project for which funds are requested; the amount needed; and information on the structure, activities, budget, and staff of the requesting organization. Proposals are accepted at any time.
Requirements: Grants are made to tax-exempt organizations whose programs fall within the trust's interests.
Restrictions: Grants are not made to individuals or for scholarships, fellowships, capital funds, annual campaigns, seed grants, emergency funds, deficit financing, or endowment funds.
Geographic Focus: New York
Amount of Grant: 5,000 - 50,000 USD
Samples: American Symphony Orchestra (New York, NY)—for general support of its concert season at Avery Fisher Hall, $45,000; Uprose (Brooklyn, NY)—support for the Sunset Park Environmental Justice Community Organizing initiative, $20,000; National Audubon Society (New York, NY)—general support of the society's Florida Everglades program, $40,000.
Contact: Administrator; (212) 953-7700; fax (212) 953-7720; info@carytrust.org
Internet: http://www.carytrust.org
Sponsor: Mary Flagler Cary Charitable Trust
122 E 42nd Street, Room 3505
New York, NY 10168

Mary K. Chapman Foundation Grants   **1255**
Mary K. Chapman was born in Oklahoma in 1920. She graduated from the University of Tulsa and worked as a nurse before her marriage to Allen Chapman in 1960. After the death of her husband in 1979, Mary Chapman maintained her own personal charitable giving program. Before her death in 2002, she established The Mary K. Chapman Foundation, a charitable trust founded to perpetuate her own charitable giving program. This foundation was fully funded with a bequest from her estate in 2005. Mary K. Chapman was very interested in supporting education, but as a former nurse and a very

compassionate person, much of her charity was directed to health, medical research, and educating and caring for the less fortunate and disadvantaged. There are two steps in the process of applying for a grant. The first is a Letter of Inquiry from the applicant. This letter is used to determine if the applicant will be invited to take the second step of submitting a formal Grant Proposal.
Requirements: IRS 501(c)3 non-profits are eligible to apply.
Restrictions: Grant requests for the following purposes are not favored: endowments, except as a limited part of a capital project reserved for maintenance of the facility being constructed; deficit financing and debt retirement; projects or programs for which the Chapman Trusts would be the sole source of financial support; travel, conferences, conventions, group meetings, or seminars; camp programs and other seasonal activities; religious programs of religious organizations; project or program planning; start-up ventures are not excluded, but organizations with a proven strategy and results are preferred; purposes normally funded by taxation or governmental agencies; requests made less than nine months from the declination of a previous request by an applicant, or within nine months of the last payment made on a grant made to an applicant; requests for more than one project.
Geographic Focus: Oklahoma
Amount of Grant: Up to 300,000 USD
Samples: Arts and Humanities Council of Tulsa, Tulsa, Oklahoma, $200,000 - Brady District Visual Arts Center capital campaign; Tulsa Zoo Management, Tulsa, Oklahoma, $300,000 - general operating fund; Northeastern Oklahoma A&M College, Miami, Oklahoma, $197,000 - equipment and furnishings for NEO athletic training facility.
Contact: Andie Doyle, Program Officer; (918) 496-7882; fax (918) 496-7887; andie@chapmantrusts.com
Internet: http://www.chapmantrusts.org/grants_programs.php
Sponsor: Mary K. Chapman Foundation
6100 South Yale, Suite 1816
Tulsa, OK 74136

Mary Kay Foundation Domestic Violence Shelter Grants   **1256**
Every October, The Mary Kay Foundation observes National Domestic Violence Awareness Month by awarding grants to deserving women's domestic violence shelters across the United States. During the past year, the Foundation awarded $20,000 grants to more than 150 women's domestic violence shelters across the nation for a total of $3 million. Each year, the Foundation awards a grant to at least one domestic violence shelter in every state. Any remaining funds are distributed based on state population. Grant applications are reviewed by the Domestic Violence Shelter Grant Committee, which makes recommendations to the TMKF Board of Directors. After reviewing these recommendations, the Foundation's Board of Directors selects the final grant recipients. Domestic violence shelter grant applications are available from this Web site or from The Mary Kay Foundation from January to June 30 each year. We announce grant recipients in the fall to coincide with National Domestic Violence Awareness Month in October.
Geographic Focus: All States
Amount of Grant: 20,000 USD
Samples: Abused Women's Aid in Crisis, Inc., Anchorage, Alaska, $20,000; Domestic Violence Services of Greater New Haven (DVS), New Haven, Connecticut, $20,000; Crisis Intervention Service Shelter, Mason City, Iowa, $20,000.
Contact: Lana Rowe, (972) 687-4822; Lana.Rowe@mkcorp.com
Jennifer Cook, (972) 687-5889 or (972) 687-4822; Jennifer.cook@mkcorp.com or MKCares@marykayfoundation.org
Internet: http://www.marykayfoundation.org/Pages/ShelterGrantProgram.aspx
Sponsor: Mary Kay Foundation
P.O. Box 799044
Dallas, TX 75379-9044

Maryland State Arts Council Track 1 General Operating Grants for   **1257**
   Organizations
The Arts Council's Track 1 General Operating Grants support arts organizations in the state whose programming is open to the general public. Arts organizations are defined as those who purpose is producing or presenting the arts through public programs or services. A three year application cycle is offered for these grants (see the online grant guidelines for specific deadlines about the grant cycle). In order to be recommended for the three-year application cycle, the organization must receive consistently favorable reviews. Organizations applying for these grants must have allowable operating expenses of more than $20,000. The minimum grant is $1,000.
Requirements: In order to apply for general operating support, an arts organization must have been both incorporated in Maryland as not-for-profit and received tax exempt status from the U. S. Internal Revenue Service. All arts organizations

must have operated for one full fiscal year at the time of application. All applications are required to be entered through the eGrant system. The Maryland Cultural Data Project (MDCDP) funder report must be submitted as part of the application process and should be attached to the eGrant application. Applicants are encouraged to contact MSAC and speak with a program director before an application is submitted. See the online guidelines with a list of appropriate program director contacts according to artistic categories.

Geographic Focus: Maryland
Date(s) Application is Due: Dec 8
Contact: Program Director; (410) 767-6555
Internet: http://www.msac.org/gfo
Sponsor: Maryland State Arts Council
175 West Ostend Street, Suite E
Baltimore, MD 21230

Mary Owen Borden Foundation Grants 1258

The Mary Owen Borden Foundation Grants support programs that address the needs of economically disadvantaged youth and their families. This includes needs such as health, family planning, education, counseling, childcare, substance abuse, and delinquency. Other areas of interest for the foundation include affordable housing, conservation, environment, and the arts. Grants average $10,000, and the maximum grant is $15,000. In unique circumstances, the Foundation considers a more significant grant for a program having a major impact in their areas of interests.

Requirements: New Jersey nonprofits in Monmouth and Mercer Counties are eligible. Most of the Foundation's grant go to nonprofit entities in Trenton, Asbury Park, and Long Branch.
Geographic Focus: New Jersey
Date(s) Application is Due: Mar 15; Sep 15
Amount of Grant: Up to 15,000 USD
Contact: Quinn McKean, Executive Director; (732) 741-4645; fax (732) 741-2542; qmckean@aol.com
Internet: http://fdncenter.org/grantmaker/borden/guide.html
Sponsor: Mary Owen Borden Foundation
4 Blackpoint Horseshoe
Rumson, NJ 07760

Mary Reinhart Stackhouse Foundation Grants 1259

The Mary Reinhart Stackhouse Foundation was established in 1999 to provide scholarships for golf caddies in New Jersey and to promote preservation of the natural environment in the state of New Jersey. In addition, annual gifts may be awarded to The Conservancy of Southern Florida. Grant requests for general operating support are strongly encouraged. Program support will also be considered. Small, program-related capital expenses may be included in general operating or program requests. The majority of grants from the Stackhouse Foundation are one year in duration; on occasion, multi-year support is awarded. Applicants must apply online at the grant website. Applicants are strongly encouraged to do the following before applying: review the downloadable state application procedures for additional helpful information and clarifications; review the downloadable online-application guidelines at the grant website; review the foundation's funding history (link is available from the grant website); review the online application questions in advance; and review the list of required attachments. These will generally include: a list of board members, financial statements (audited, reviewed, or compiled by independent auditor); an organization summary; a list of other funding sources; an IRS Determination letter; and other required documents. All attachments must be uploaded in the online application as PDF, Word, or Excel files. The application deadline for the Mary Reinhart Stackhouse Foundation is 11:59 p.m. on September 15. Applicants will be notified of grant decisions before December 31.

Requirements: Applicants must have 501(c)3 tax-exempt status.
Restrictions: In general, grant requests for endowment campaigns, capital projects, or scholarly research will not be considered. Grant requests from individuals, organizations attempting to influence policy through direct lobbying, or any political campaigns will not be considered.
Geographic Focus: New Jersey
Date(s) Application is Due: Sep 15
Contact: Ken Goody; (646) 855-0956; kenneth.l.goody@baml.com
Internet: https://www.bankofamerica.com/philanthropic/fn_search.action
Sponsor: Mary Reinhart Stackhouse Foundation
One Bryant Park, NY1-100-28-05
New York, NY 10036

Mary Reynolds Babcock Foundation Grants 1260

The Mary Reynolds Babcock Foundation's priority is to support nonprofits in the Southeastern United States that have track records for helping low-wealth people build assets and transform economic conditions in their communities. The Foundation looks for the most promising work that advances the mission of moving people and places out of poverty, and that aligns with the Foundation's belief in the responsibility and power of individuals to improve their own lives and act collectively to improve their communities. Throughout the region, people who live in low-wealth communities and individuals from the public, private and nonprofit sectors are forming creative and strategic partnerships to advance economic and social justice. The Foundation encourages promising partnerships, and invites groups who are already doing this work and meet the following description to contact them. The Foundation supports grassroots groups and networks in low-wealth communities who are poised to expand their scale of impact. It also supports statewide and regional organizations and networks that are achieving large-scale impact. Applicants should begin by providing an organizational summary (available at the website), followed by a required application form. Currently, the Foundation reports that it has rolling deadlines, although the Board meets only twice each year (June and October).

Requirements: The Mary Reynolds Babcock Foundation invites proposals from local, statewide and regional nonprofits in the Southeastern United States that have track records of helping low-wealth people build assets and transform economic conditions in their communities. Applicants must be located in the southeastern U.S., with emphasis on eastern Alabama, Arkansas, Georgia, Louisiana, Mississippi, North Carolina, South Carolina, Tennessee, north and central Florida, and the Appalachian regions of Kentucky and West Virginia.
Restrictions: No grants are given to individuals, or for capital improvements, direct services (such as food or medical assistance), or for satellite operations of organizations outside the southeast.
Geographic Focus: Alabama, Arkansas, Georgia, Kentucky, Louisiana, Mississippi, North Carolina, South Carolina, Tennessee, Virginia, West Virginia
Amount of Grant: 10,000 - 600,000 USD
Samples: Appalachian Community Enterprises, Cleveland, Georgia, $350,000 - general operations; Anderson Interfaith Ministries, Anderson, South Carolina, $130,000 - general operations; Greater Birmingham Ministries, Birmingham, Alabama, $200,000 - general operations.
Contact: David A. Jackson, Executive Director; (336) 748-9222; fax (336) 777-0095; info@mrbf.org
Internet: http://mrbf.org/program-description
Sponsor: Mary Reynolds Babcock Foundation
2920 Reynolda Road
Winston-Salem, NC 27106-3016

Massachusetts Cultural Council Cultural Investment Portfolio 1261

The primary purpose of MCC's Cultural Investment Portfolio is to strengthen the cultural sector as a whole. State investment in nonprofit arts, humanities, and science organizations yields returns in economic impact and increasing public access, according to the information gathered from the Massachusetts Cultural Data Project. The Cultural Investment Portfolio is not a traditional grant program, but a partnership that will better position the cultural sector as vital components of Massachusetts' economy and the quality of life of our citizens. Providing unrestricted general operating support is a core priority for the Massachusetts Cultural Council (MCC). There are three levels of participation to the Portfolio - Peers, Colleagues, and Partners. Peer grants are designed primarily for organizations new to the MCC operating support funding pool, not fully-cultural organizations, and other groups offering cultural programming who do not meet the requirements for Partners or Colleagues. Colleague grants are available to organizations with a track record of offering public cultural programming in Massachusetts for at least five years, and have received operational support from the MCC for at least four fiscal years. Partner grants are available to given to organizations with a track record of offering public cultural programming in Massachusetts for at least 10 years, and have received operational support from the MCC for at least eight fiscal years since FY1997.

Geographic Focus: Massachusetts
Contact: Cheryl Balukonis, Senior Program Officer; (617) 727-3668, ext. 318 or (800) 232-0960; fax (617) 727-0044; cheryl.balukonis@art.state.ma.us
Charles Coe, Program Officer; (617) 727-3668, ext. 339 or (800) 232-0960; fax (617) 727-0044; charles.coe@art.state.ma.us
Internet: http://www.massculturalcouncil.org/programs/cultural_investment_portfolio.asp
Sponsor: Massachusetts Cultural Council
10 St. James Avenue, 3rd Floor
Boston, MA 02116-3803

MassMutual Foundation for Hartford Grants 1262

Programs are supported in the areas of education, housing, and health. Grants in education support collaborative relationships between the Connecticut Mutual/Hartford Public High School and Connecticut Mutual/Quirk Middle School Alliances; an employee matching gifts contribution program; and scholarship funding earmarked for Hartford Public High School graduates granted directly to the institutions of higher education and training. In the area of health, the foundation gives special consideration to proposals concerned with increasing the efficiency and effectiveness of health care in such areas as health education and disease prevention, alternative modes of health care delivery, and programs for cost containment. In the area of housing, the foundation will give special consideration to contributions relating to the city of Hartford and the Asylum Hill neighborhood in particular. Types of support include general operating support, continuing support, capital campaigns, program development, seed grants, internships, scholarship funds, matching funds, employee matching gifts, and technical assistance. Application address: 1295 State Street, H356, Springfield, MA 01111-0001.
Requirements: Grants are limited to Connecticut tax-exempt organizations.
Restrictions: No support for sectarian groups; political, fraternal, labor, or veterans' organizations; or federated drives outside the local area. No grants to individuals (including direct scholarships), or for endowment funds, deficit financing, emergency funds, publications, land acquisition, fellowships, capital fund drives outside the local area, or goodwill advertising.
Geographic Focus: Connecticut
Amount of Grant: 500 - 300,000 USD
Contact: Ronald Copes, Executive Director; (860) 987-2085
Sponsor: MassMutual Foundation for Hartford
140 Garden Street, H356
Hartford, CT 06154

Mathile Family Foundation Grants 1263

The Mathile Foundation awards grants to eligible Ohio nonprofit organizations in its areas of interest, including Catholic schools, low income and at-risk children to focus on academic excellence; leadership and professional development; faith formation; finance and governance; and student support. With these initiatives, the Foundation hopes to increase the number of low income post secondary graduates. The Foundation also strives to help nonprofit organizations accomplish meaningful change in the lives of those most vulnerable by investing in opportunities for educational, social-emotional, and physical development for children and their families. The Foundation also considers funding for capital and operating expenses. The Foundation considers proposals for grant amounts of $1,000 and higher. Multi-year funding requests may be considered for up to three years. The size of the request should be 10% of the project's budget. Proposal are accepted four times a year, with funding decisions made within 100 days of submission. Proposal forms with a list of additional information required are available at the Foundation website. For first time applicants, a letter of inquiry is recommended. All letters or applications must be submitted online.
Requirements: Organizations who request funds must be tax-exempt under the IRS Code Section 501(c)3. Ohio nonprofit organizations are eligible. Giving primarily is limited to the Dayton area. Organizations outside this area will only be considered under special circumstances.
Restrictions: Funding is not considered for endowment funds; mass funding appeals; sponsorships; advertising for fundraising events tickets; grants or loans to individuals; or political campaigns or activities.
Geographic Focus: Ohio
Date(s) Application is Due: Feb 1; May 1; Aug 1; Nov 1
Amount of Grant: 1,000 - 250,000 USD
Contact: Mary Walsh, Trustee; (937) 264-4600; fax (937) 264-4805; mffinfo@mathilefamilyfoundation.org
Internet: http://mathilefamilyfoundation.org/grantmaking/guidelines
Sponsor: Mathile Family Foundation
P.O Box 13615
Dayton, OH 45413-0615

Matilda R. Wilson Fund Grants 1264

Matilda Rausch Dodge Wilson died on September 19, 1967, leaving most of her wealth to the Matilda R. Wilson Fund, a charitable trust she had established in Detroit in 1944. Today, the Matilda R. Wilson Fund awards grants, primarily in southeast Michigan, in support of the arts, youth agencies, higher education, hospitals, and social services. Types of support include building construction/renovation, endowments, equipment acquisition, general operating support, matching/challenge grants, program development, research, and scholarship funds. There are no application forms; initial approach should be a letter of request. The board considers requests at board meetings in January, April, and September.
Requirements: Michigan tax-exempt organizations are eligible.
Restrictions: Grants or loans are not made to individuals.
Geographic Focus: Michigan
Amount of Grant: 10,000 - 100,000 USD
Contact: David P. Larsen, Grants Administrator; (313) 259-7777; fax (313) 393-7579; roosterveen@bodmanllp.com
Sponsor: Matilda R. Wilson Fund
1901 Saint Antoine Street, 6th Floor
Detroit, MI 48226-2310

Mattel International Grants 1265

The corporation and its foundation award grants to charitable organizations that directly serve children in need. Funding priorities include international organizations or programs that creatively address a defined need directly impacting children in need, and international organizations or programs that align with Mattel's philanthropic priorities, including health—supporting the physical and mental health and well-being of children, and increasing access to health care services for children in need; education—increasing access to education, promoting literacy to children in need, and resources that promote after-school educational achievement; and girls empowerment—promoting self-esteem of girls and increasing access to education, health, and community resources for girls. Types of support include program-specific grants—funding for new programs or expansion of existing programs; and core operating support—support of organizations to sustain their programs. Applications must be submitted online. Applications will not be accepted by fax or mail. Submit questions via email.
Requirements: Organizations must serve children in non-U.S. communities; and must not discriminate against a person or a group on the basis of age, political affiliation, race, national origin, ethnicity, gender, disability, sexual orientation, or religious belief. Pilot projects and new organizations may be considered as long as all eligibility criteria are met; however, preference will be given to organizations that have at least two years of experience. Preference is given to organizations that have an annual operating budget of less than $1 million and are not affiliated with a national organization.
Restrictions: The program does not not fund capital funding for physical property purchase, renovation, or developments; individuals; political parties, candidates, or partisan political organizations; labor organizations, fraternal organizations, athletic clubs, or social clubs; sectarian or denominational religious organizations, except for programs that are available to anyone, broadly promoted, and free from religious orientation; schools and school districts; fundraising events (e.g., dinners, tournaments); advertising or marketing sponsorships; or research overhead and/or indirect costs (including fiscal sponsor fees) that exceed 15 percent of the direct project costs.
Geographic Focus: All States
Amount of Grant: 5,000 - 25,000 USD
Contact: Grants Administrator; (310) 252-2000; fax (310) 252-2180; foundation@mattel.com
Internet: http://corporate.mattel.com/about-us/philanthropy/internationalgrants.aspx
Sponsor: Mattel Children's Foundation
333 Continental Boulevard, M1-1418
El Segundo, CA 90245-5012

Maurice Amado Foundation Grants 1266

For several decades the Foundation primarily supported organizations that served members of the Sephardic Jewish community, promoted knowledge of Sephardic Jewish culture and heritage, and expanded knowledge of the contributions of Sephardic Jews to Jewish life. More recently, the Foundation has awarded grants to a wide array of charitable organizations that reflect the philanthropic interests of the Foundation's directors and advisors.
Requirements: Prospective grantees may call the Foundation's Executive Director to determine if the grant seeker's organizational need fit the Foundation's current grantmaking interests. They may email the Executive Director with the name of the organization, its mission, and for what purpose funding is requested. The letter of inquiry should be no more than one page.
Geographic Focus: All States
Contact: Pam Kaizer, Executive Director; (818) 980-9190; pkaizer@mauriceamadofoundation.org
Internet: http://www.mauriceamadofdn.org
Sponsor: Maurice Amado Foundation
12400 Ventura Boulevard, #809
Studio City, CA 91604

Maurice J. Masserini Charitable Trust Grants 1267

The trust awards one-year grants to eligible San Diego County, California nonprofit organizations in its areas of interest, including children and youth, aging, music, higher education, and marine sciences. Types of support include building construction/renovation, equipment acquisition, program development, research grants, matching grants, development grants, internships, and scholarships.

Requirements: San Diego County, California, 501(c)3 tax-exempt organizations are eligible. Interested organizations should contact the trust with a letter of inquiry prior to submitting a formal proposal.

Geographic Focus: California

Amount of Grant: Up to 25,000 USD

Contact: Robert Roszkos, (213) 253-3235

Sponsor: Maurice J. Masserini Charitable Trust

c/o Wells Fargo Bank N.A.

Philadelphia, PA 19106-2112

Max A. Adler Charitable Foundation Grants 1268

The foundation awards grants to eligible New York nonprofit organizations serving the greater Rochester area in its areas of interest, including arts, children and youth services, Jewish services, health care, higher education, and social services. Types of support include building construction/renovation, capital campaigns, general operating support, and program development. There are no application forms or deadlines.

Requirements: New York 501(c)3 nonprofit organizations serving the greater Rochester area are eligible.

Geographic Focus: New York

Amount of Grant: 1,000 - 25,000 USD

Samples: Nazareth College (Rochester, NY)—for its capital campaign to expand the size of its campus, $50,000.

Contact: David Gray, President; (585) 232-7290; fax (585) 232-7260

Sponsor: Max A. Adler Charitable Foundation

1010 Times Square Building

Rochester, NY 14614

Max and Anna Levinson Foundation Grants 1269

The Levinson Foundation makes grants to nonprofit organizations committed to developing a more just, caring, ecological, and sustainable world. They seek people and organizations that combine idealism, dedication, and genuine concern with rigorous analysis and strategic plans, and that foster a sense of social connection, mutual recognition, and solidarity. Their funding is distributed among three categories: environment, including ecosystem protection and biological diversity, alternative energy and conversion into the oil economy, alternative agriculture and local green development, climate change, and the development of environmental movements; social, including the promotion of a more democratic, equitable, just and rewarding society, world peace, protection of civil and human rights, alternative media, arts and education, community-based economic development, youth leadership, and violence prevention and response; Jewish/Israel—including Jewish culture, religion, and spirituality, Yiddish, building Jewish community in the Diaspora, Jewish organizations for social change, and peace, social, and environmental issues in Israel. There are no deadlines. Grants are awarded in the $15,000 to $25,000 range. Applicants may refer to the website for types of previous support given to organizations.

Requirements: Applicants within the giving criteria may apply, but grantees must submit the online letter of inquiry to see if they are eligible for funding.

Geographic Focus: All States

Amount of Grant: 15,000 - 25,000 USD

Contact: Charlotte Levinson, President; (505) 995-8802; fax (505) 995-8982; info@levinsonfoundation.org

Internet: http://www.levinsonfoundation.org

Sponsor: Max and Anna Levinson Foundation

P.O. Box 6309

Santa Fe, NM 87502-6309

May and Stanley Smith Charitable Trust Grants 1270

Created in 1989, the May and Stanley Smith Charitable Trust supports organizations serving people in the United States, Canada, the United Kingdom, Australia, the Bahamas, and Hong Kong – places that May and Stanley Smith lived in or spent time in during their lifetimes. The trust supports organizations that offer opportunities to children and youth, elders, the disabled and critically ill, and disadvantaged adults and families which enrich the quality of life, promote self-sufficiency, and assist individuals in achieving their highest potential. The trust will fund requests for general-operating, capacity-building, and program support. All grant seekers (including previously-funded organizations) should follow the step-by-step application process laid out at the website to determine eligibility and fit with the trust's funding goals. Eligible organizations whose projects fall within the trust's areas of interest must submit an online Letter of Inquiry (LOI) from the grant website. The trust's staff will review these and invite selected applicants to submit a full proposal. LOIs may be submitted at any time during the year. Processing a grant application from receipt of the LOI to funding notification generally takes between four and six months.

Requirements: The May and Stanley Smith Charitable Trust has a two-stage application process: an online letter of inquiry (LOI) submission followed by an invited proposal submission. Processing a grant application from receipt of the LOI to funding notification generally takes between four and six months. Please note that proposals are accepted by invitation only. Applications are accepted from organizations meeting the Trust's program area priorities and serving individuals living in British Columbia, Canada and the Western United States: Alaska, Arizona, California, Colorado, Hawaii, Idaho, Montana, Nevada, New Mexico, Oregon, Texas, Utah, Washington, and Wyoming. The Trust makes grants to nonprofit organizations that are tax exempt under Section 501(c)3 of the IRS Code and not classified as a private foundation under Section 509(a) of the Code, and to non-U.S. organizations that can demonstrate that they would meet the requirements for such status. Organizations can also submit applications through a sponsoring organization if the sponsor has 501(c)3 status, is not a private foundation under 509(a), and provides written authorization confirming its willingness to act as the fiscal sponsor. The Trust will only accept proposals sent by regular or express mail services that do not require a signature upon delivery.

Restrictions: The trust rarely supports 100% of a project budget, or more than 25 percent of an organization budget, and takes into account award sizes from other foundations. The trust prefers to fund organizations receiving less than 30% of total revenue from government sources. The trust does not fund the following types of organizations or requests: organizations which are not, or would not qualify as, a 501(c)3 public charity; hospitals or hospital foundations; medical clinics or services; scientific or medical research; building funds or capital projects; schools and universities (except those receiving less than 25% of their operating funds from families and those serving a 100% disabled population); endowment funds; individuals; organizations or programs operated by governments; film or media projects; start-up programs or organizations; proselytizing or religious activities that promote specific religious doctrine or that are exclusive and discriminatory; public policy, research, or advocacy; public awareness, education, or information campaigns/programs; debt reduction; conferences or benefit events; projects which carry on propaganda or otherwise attempt to influence legislation; projects which participate or intervene in any political campaign on behalf of or in opposition to any candidate for public office; projects which conduct, directly or indirectly, any voter registration drive; and organizations that pass through funding to an organization or project that would not be eligible for direct funding as described above.

Geographic Focus: All States, Australia, Bahamas, Canada, Hong Kong, United Kingdom

Contact: Dan Gaff, Grants Manager; (415) 332-0166; grantsmanager@adminitrustllc.com or dgaff@adminitrustllc.com

Internet: http://www.adminitrustllc.com/may-and-stanley-smith-charitable-trust/

Sponsor: May and Stanley Smith Charitable Trust

c/o Adminitrust LLC

Corte Madera, CA 94925

Mayer and Morris Kaplan Family Foundation Grants 1271

Grants are available to nonprofit organizations serving inner-city Chicago residents in seven program areas: education, self-help, basic human needs, museums, cultural arts, civic affairs, and Jewish affairs. The foundation considers providing seed money, challenge grants, support for general operations, and special project funding. Agencies awarded multiyear grants are required to submit annual progress reports, including a current audit, board list, and statement of accomplishments prior to the release of precommitted support. The first step that must be followed by all applicants is submission of a two-page summary request letter and budget. If requested by the board, a full proposal will be invited.

Requirements: Illinois nonprofit organizations are eligible.

Restrictions: Grants are generally not given to sectarian institutions; purchase of tickets to testimonial events or goodwill advertising; medical, scientific, or academic research; individuals, films, or funding of meetings; capital and endowment campaigns, building and equipment acquisition, or fund-raising

drives; health care institutions; national health, welfare, education, or cultural organizations; or an institution more than once during the fiscal year.
Geographic Focus: Illinois
Date(s) Application is Due: Jan 15; May 15; Sep 15
Amount of Grant: 5,000 - 120,000 USD
Contact: Jason Heeney; (847) 926-8350; Jheeney@kapfam.com
Sponsor: Mayer and Morris Kaplan Family Foundation
1780 Green Bay Road, Suite 205
Highland Park, IL 60035

MAZON Grants: A Jewish Response to Hunger   **1272**
MAZON's domestic grant program makes awards for general support or special projects in four categories. Advocacy Education/Research grants, ranging from $5000-$20,000, support programs to change public policy or opinion or the operation and administration of federal food assistance programs. Emergency/Direct Food Assistance grants, ranging from $5000-$7000, support food pantries, soup kitchens, and programs providing meals to special-needs populations. Food Bank grants, ranging from $5000-$15,000, are awarded to warehouses that collect and distribute food to nonprofit feeding programs; applicants must demonstrate that they participate in antihunger advocacy and education efforts. Multiservice Organization grants, ranging from $5000-$15,000, support organizations that provide food and a broad array of services to hungry and low-income people. Deadlines listed are for letters of inquiry.
Requirements: U.S. nonprofits that meet program criteria may apply.
Restrictions: MAZON does not make grants to groups that proselytize or place any religious requirements on service; have national name recognition; are principally focused on homelessness; charge individuals for food; or are government entities, professional associations, job training programs, or grantmaking organizations. Capital grants for building projects are not eligible for support. Prepared and perishable food programs are not eligible unless they are in their first two years of operation. MAZON does not fund holiday meal programs.
Geographic Focus: All States
Date(s) Application is Due: May 15; Nov 15
Samples: 28 nonprofit organizations nationwide—for their work to relieve hunger in the United States, $110,500 divided.
Contact: Grants Administrator; (310) 442-0020; fax (310) 442-0030; mazonmail@mazon.org
Internet: http://www.mazon.org/What_We_Fund/Funding_Guidelines/
Sponsor: MAZON: A Jewish Response to Hunger
1990 S Bundy Drive, Suite 260
Los Angeles, CA 90025-5232

McCarthy Family Foundation Grants   **1273**
The McCarthy Family Foundation is a small private foundation established in 1988. Organized as a California public benefit nonprofit corporation, it operates from San Diego, California. The foundation's current program interest areas have been funded throughout its almost two decades history. These funding areas are: K-12 science education; HIV/AIDS research, education and direct services; assistance to homeless persons; and child abuse prevention and services for victims and families. The board will occasionally fund a special project outside these categorical areas and/or for regional, national or international charitable purposes. A small portion of the grantmaking budget is provided for director matching grants to encourage and amplify personal philanthropy by the foundation's board of directors. Proposals will be considered in the above general areas or for special project areas established by the Board. Proposals will only be accepted for programs within San Diego County. Multiple year proposals may be considered but it is not the foundation's intention to provide annual support. It is not normally the foundation's desire to be the sole source of funds for a project. Most grants are expected to be small, $5,000-$15,000, reflecting the foundation's limited budget although there are no fixed minimum or maximum amounts. Grant proposals received by March 15 will be considered for decision/funding in June. Grant proposals received by September 15 will be considered for decision/funding in December.
Requirements: Proposals will only be accepted for programs within San Diego County, California. All applicants should first submit a letter of inquiry, which can be submitted directly from the Foundation's web site. The letter (1-2 pages) must contain a brief statement describing the applicant and the need for funds with enough information for the foundation to determine whether or not the application falls within its program areas. Proposals submitted without an initial letter of inquiry will not be reviewed by the foundation. Applicants should briefly and clearly provide a statement of their needs and the specific request to the foundation, taking into account other possible sources of funding. Letters of inquiry will be acknowledged upon their receipt, but

because the foundation operates without a professional staff, a more detailed response may be delayed. Applicants who receive a favorable response to their initial inquiry will be invited to submit a grant application. The foundation accepts the Common Grant Application of San Diego Grantmakers, which can be downloaded from the Foundation's web site. Five copies of the application (proposal) should be submitted. Only one copy of required attachments need be submitted. The application should be signed by the organization's board chair or the executive director (or equivalent individuals).
Restrictions: The foundation does not consider grants for individuals, scholarship funds, or sectarian religious activities. Normally the foundation does not consider requests for general fundraising drives. It does not make grants intended directly or indirectly to support political candidates or to influence legislation.
Geographic Focus: California
Date(s) Application is Due: Mar 15; Sep 15
Amount of Grant: 500 - 250,000 USD
Contact: Rachel McCarthy Bender, President; (858) 485-0129; mail@mccarthyfamilyfdn.org
Internet: http://www.mccarthyfamilyfdn.org/guide.html
Sponsor: McCarthy Family Foundation
P.O. Box 27389
San Diego, CA 92198-1389

McColl Foundation Grants   **1274**
Established in 1996, the Foundation awards funding in its areas of interest, including: the arts; community and economic development; early childhood education; elementary and secondary education; federated giving programs; health organizations; higher education; and performing arts. Types of support include: annual campaigns, building and renovation, curriculum development, general operations, and scholarship funds. Giving is primarily focused in North Carolina, with an initial approach requesting a Letter of Inquiry. The Board meets twice annually.
Geographic Focus: North Carolina
Amount of Grant: 500 - 25,000 USD
Contact: Jane McColl Lockwood, President; (704) 376-6978
Sponsor: McColl Foundation
P.O. Box 6144
Charlotte, NC 28207-0001

McCune Charitable Foundation Grants   **1275**
The Marshall L. and Perrine D. McCune Charitable Foundation is dedicated to enriching the health, education, environment, and cultural and spiritual life of New Mexicans. The Foundation engages in proactive grantmaking that seeks to foster positive social change. Specifically, the Foundation funds projects that benefit New Mexico in the areas of arts, economic development, education, environment, health, and social services. It is working to stimulate economic diversity, nurture sustainability, and bridge the economic gaps that exist in our communities with the aim of creating wealth for all New Mexicans.
Requirements: Grants can be awarded to qualified 501(c)3 nonprofit organizations, federally recognized Indian tribes, public schools, and governmental agencies. Applications are available online via the Foundation's website.
Restrictions: Grants are not awarded to individuals or to support endowments.
Geographic Focus: New Mexico
Date(s) Application is Due: Sep 30
Amount of Grant: Up to 150,000 USD
Contact: Norty Kalishman, M.D., Program Director; (505) 983-8300; fax (505) 983-7887; mccune@nmmccune.org
Internet: http://www.nmmccune.org/
Sponsor: McCune Charitable Foundation
345 East Alameda Street
Santa Fe, NM 87501

McCune Foundation Civic Grants   **1276**
The McCune Foundation's grants are assigned to one of four program areas, including: education, human services, humanities, and civic. In the area of civic affairs, the Foundation focuses new job growth and generating community wealth, support of core community assets, and quality of life. Community development, public amenities, conservation, and overall regional grants are made in this program area. The civic agenda supports capital projects, research and development, organizational capacity building, and programming with the following strategic priorities: spur investment in Pittsburgh's urban core and metropolitan area; leverage public and private dollars for broad-based support of community assets; revitalize Pittsburgh's neighborhoods by changing blighted market conditions; support broad based community

assets improving the livability of the region; and develop a New Economy in Pittsburgh that will return greater prosperity to the region.

Requirements: The foundation supports 501(c)3 organizations in southwestern Pennsylvania and throughout the country, with emphasis on the Pittsburgh area. This area includes the following counties: Allegheny, Beaver, Butler, Armstrong, Westmoreland, and Washington. To apply, an organization should send a brief (2 to 3 page) initial inquiry, preferably using the Foundation's website. The letter should contain: project overview - describe what the proposed efforts are intended to achieve for the region as well as for the organization; what activities/actions are planned to meet the stated goals; project timeline; resources required - total cost of the project; anticipated income, including private and public funders; amount of funding requested; IRS 501(c)3 determination letter - attach a copy (either scanned via email or hard copy via regular mail); and a copy of the organization's latest audit (either scanned via email or hard copy via regular mail).

Restrictions: Grants are not awarded to individuals or for general operating purposes or loans. Unsolicited proposals from outside the funding area are not accepted.

Geographic Focus: All States

Amount of Grant: 1,000 - 1,000,000 USD

Samples: University of Pittsburgh, Center for Social and Urban Research, Pittsburgh, Pennsylvania, $10,000 - symposium for reducing youth violence; Focus on Renewal Sto-Rox Neighborhood Association, McKees Rocks, Pennsylvania, $175,000 - capacity building; Metro Dallas Homeless Alliance, Dallas, Texas, $300,000 - bridge project.

Contact: Henry S. Beukema, Executive Director; (412) 644-8779; fax (412) 644-8059; info@mccune.org

Internet: http://www.mccune.org/foundation:Website,mccune,grants

Sponsor: McCune Foundation

750 Sixth PPG Place

Pittsburgh, PA 15222

McCune Foundation Education Grants   1277

The McCune Foundation's grants are assigned to one of four program areas, including: education, human services, humanities, and civic. In the area of education, the Foundation promotes excellence in the institutions of higher education, independent elementary and secondary schools, and ancillary education programs (general education). The education program supports capital projects, research and development, financial aid, programming, and endowment to accomplish the following strategic priorities: leverage university research capacity to enhance the region's competitive advantage in economic development; use universities as anchors for community revitalization strategies; increase access to independent schools and higher education; recruit and retain exceptional faculty; and develop and deliver quality enrichment programs for school aged children, particularly with a focus on math, science and reading.

Requirements: The foundation supports 501(c)3 organizations in southwestern Pennsylvania and throughout the country, with emphasis on the Pittsburgh area. This area includes the following counties: Allegheny, Beaver, Butler, Armstrong, Westmoreland, and Washington. To apply, an organization should send a brief (2 to 3 page) initial inquiry, preferably using the Foundation's website. The letter should contain: project overview - describe what the proposed efforts are intended to achieve for the region as well as for the organization; what activities/actions are planned to meet the stated goals; project timeline; resources required - total cost of the project; anticipated income, including private and public funders; amount of funding requested; IRS 501(c)3 determination letter - attach a copy (either scanned via email or hard copy via regular mail); and a copy of the organization's latest audit (either scanned via email or hard copy via regular mail).

Restrictions: Grants are not awarded to individuals or for general operating purposes or loans. Unsolicited proposals from outside the funding area are not accepted.

Geographic Focus: All States

Amount of Grant: 1,000 - 1,000,000 USD

Samples: A Wilson Center for African American Culture, Pittsburgh, Pennsylvania, $10,000 - access and services for artists' programs; Airlift Research Foundation, Sharpsburg, Pennsylvania, $10,000 - leadership excellence program; Pennsylvania Institute for Conservation Education, Elysburg, Pennsylvania, $10,000 - wildlife leadership academy.

Contact: Henry S. Beukema, Executive Director; (412) 644-8779; fax (412) 644-8059; info@mccune.org

Internet: http://www.mccune.org/foundation:Website,mccune,grants

Sponsor: McCune Foundation

750 Sixth PPG Place

Pittsburgh, PA 15222

McCune Foundation Humananities Grants   1278

The McCune Foundation's grants are assigned to one of four program areas, including: education, human services, humanities, and civic. In the area of humanities, the Foundation focuses on culture, preservation, and religion and values. Cultural investments are made from the vantage point of regional economic development and the perspective that a city is more livable with a strong arts and culture sector, and a performance epicenter downtown that attracts patrons and out-of-town visitors. The humanities area supports capital projects, endowment grants, technology, marketing, planning, and programming for the following strategic priorities: promote regional historic and cultural assets; attract new audiences and future generations of residents who appreciate the humanities; contribute to the economic development of the downtown corridor; guard the region's history and religious legacy; and support Christian education through academic institutions.

Requirements: The foundation supports 501(c)3 organizations in southwestern Pennsylvania and throughout the country, with emphasis on the Pittsburgh area. This area includes the following counties: Allegheny, Beaver, Butler, Armstrong, Westmoreland, and Washington. To apply, an organization should send a brief (2 to 3 page) initial inquiry, preferably using the Foundation's website. The letter should contain: project overview - describe what the proposed efforts are intended to achieve for the region as well as for the organization; what activities/actions are planned to meet the stated goals; project timeline; resources required - total cost of the project; anticipated income, including private and public funders; amount of funding requested; IRS 501(c)3 determination letter - attach a copy (either scanned via email or hard copy via regular mail); and a copy of the organization's latest audit (either scanned via email or hard copy via regular mail).

Restrictions: Grants are not awarded to individuals or for general operating purposes or loans. Unsolicited proposals from outside the funding area are not accepted.

Geographic Focus: All States

Amount of Grant: 1,000 - 1,000,000 USD

Samples: National Dance Institute of New Mexico, Albuquerque, New Mexico, $100,000 - general support; Historical Society of Western Pennsylvanie, Pittsburgh, Pennsylvania, $400,000 - operating support; Pittsburgh Arts and Lectures, Pittsburgh, Pennsylvania, $9,665 - lecture on art and life.

Contact: Henry S. Beukema, Executive Director; (412) 644-8779; fax (412) 644-8059; info@mccune.org

Internet: http://www.mccune.org/foundation:Website,mccune,grants

Sponsor: McCune Foundation

750 Sixth PPG Place

Pittsburgh, PA 15222

McCune Foundation Human Services Grants   1279

The McCune Foundation's grants are assigned to one of four program areas, including: education, human services, humanities, and civic. In the area of human services, the Foundation focuses on health, social services, and community improvement. The interdisciplinary approach to grantmaking in this program area works with community-based and regional institutions to address pressing community needs by supporting the critical work of existing programs, as well as new initiatives and programs that seek to find and ameliorate the root causes of community distress and disinvestment. The human services area supports capital projects, research and development, organizational capacity building, and programming with the following strategic priorities: transfer education and research assets into economic opportunities for the region; leverage public and private dollars for broad-based support of community assets; promote self-sufficiency of residents; increase social and economic stability of communities and the region; and test and support effective prevention programs.

Requirements: The foundation supports 501(c)3 organizations in southwestern Pennsylvania and throughout the country, with emphasis on the Pittsburgh area. This area includes the following counties: Allegheny, Beaver, Butler, Armstrong, Westmoreland, and Washington. To apply, an organization should send a brief (2 to 3 page) initial inquiry, preferably using the Foundation's website. The letter should contain: project overview - describe what the proposed efforts are intended to achieve for the region as well as for the organization; what activities/actions are planned to meet the stated goals; project timeline; resources required - total cost of the project; anticipated income, including private and public funders; amount of funding requested; IRS 501(c)3 determination letter - attach a copy (either scanned via email or hard copy via regular mail); and a copy of the organization's latest audit (either scanned via email or hard copy via regular mail).

Restrictions: Grants are not awarded to individuals or for general operating purposes or loans. Unsolicited proposals from outside the funding area are not accepted.

Geographic Focus: All States

Amount of Grant: 1,000 - 1,000,000 USD

Contact: Henry S. Beukema, Executive Director; (412) 644-8779; fax (412) 644-8059; info@mccune.org

Internet: http://www.mccune.org/foundation:Website,mccune,grants

Sponsor: McCune Foundation

750 Sixth PPG Place

Pittsburgh, PA 15222

McGregor Foundation Grants 1280

The program favors grants that address the following priority areas for elders in need: recruitment, education, training, and retention of health care professionals in geriatrics; access to care for underserved populations; promotion of health and wellness; and total quality of life for seniors. The board of directors particularly encourages requests for programs that increase the pool of workers trained in geriatrics, expand access to care for elders in need, or demonstrate effective new methods and approaches. In some instances, the foundation will consider requests for emergency operating support. The foundation will also consider requests for capital projects, with certain restrictions.

Requirements: Tax-exempt nonprofit organizations located within Cuyahoga County, OH, with preference given to communities traditionally served by The A.M. McGregor Home, are eligible. Currently no unsolicited grant applications from organizations outside Cuyahoga County will be accepted.

Restrictions: The foundation discourages capital requests from long-term residential care facilities or requests for debt reduction, annual funds, research, symposia, or endowments. No grants are awarded to individuals.

Geographic Focus: Ohio

Date(s) Application is Due: Mar 1; Sep 1

Samples: Access to the Arts (Cleveland, OH)—for art performances for elderly people in hospitals, nursing homes, and retirement communities, $15,270; Case Western Reserve U (Cleveland, OH)—to support the Gerontological Scholars Program of its Mandel School of Applied Social Sciences during the 2005-06 academic year, $20,000; Ohio Presbyterian Retirement Services (Cleveland, OH)—to implement a program on preventing and managing diabetes, $21,120; Recovery Resources (Cleveland, OH)—to collaborate with Fairhill Center to provide training for staff members caring for elderly people with a history of substance abuse and mental illness, $60,111.

Contact: Susan Althans, Executive Director; (216) 696-7273; fax (216) 621-8198; salthans@fmscleveland.com

Internet: http://mcgregorfoundation.org/guidelines.html

Sponsor: McGregor Foundation

1422 Euclid Avenue, Suite 627

Cleveland, OH 44115-1952

McGregor Fund Grants 1281

The fund makes grants to organizations in the following areas: human services—emphasis on activities in southeastern Michigan addressing emergency needs in housing, food, clothing, and other direct aid; education—early child education and development, colleges and universities in the Detroit metropolitan area, liberal arts colleges and universities in Michigan and Ohio; arts and culture in southeastern Michigan; health care—improving access to primary care for underserved populations in Detroit; and public benefit—civic and community organizations that improve the quality of life in southeastern Michigan. Types of support include project support, operating support, special projects, and capital support. Grant decisions are made by the board of trustees four times annually, in February, May, September, and November. Grant requests may be submitted at any time, but requests may take up to three months for staff review. Application guidelines are available online.

Requirements: Organizations in the metropolitan Detroit, MI area, are eligible. Requests will be considered from organizations located elsewhere for programs or projects that significantly benefit the metropolitan Detroit area (city of Detroit and Wayne, Oakland, and Macomb Counties).

Restrictions: The fund discourages proposals for student scholarships, travel, seminars, conferences, workshops, film or video projects, as well as disease-specific organizations and their local affiliates.

Geographic Focus: Michigan

Amount of Grant: 25,000 - 50,000 USD

Contact: C. David Campbell, President; (313) 963-3495; fax (313) 963-3512; info@mcgregfund.org

Internet: http://www.mcgregorfund.org/guideline.html

Sponsor: McGregor Fund

333 W Fort Street, Suite 2090

Detroit, MI 48226

McKenzie River Gathering Foundation Grants 1282

Grants are awarded to organizations located in Oregon that address peace, social justice, and environmental issues, such as anti-bigotry, domestic violence, homelessness, community-labor coalitions, HIV/AIDS, reproductive rights, ancient forest and watershed protection, and anti-militarism. Types of support include general operating grants, matching grants, program grants, seed money grants, technical assistance, training grants, and travel grants. Interested groups should call the Eugene office which, after prescreening for adherence to MRG's basic criteria, will place prospective groups on a list to receive an application form.

Requirements: Applicant organizations must be located in Oregon, organizing for progressive social change, committed to developing diversity, and have limited access to other funding.

Restrictions: Grants are not awarded to/for social service agencies, schools, health centers, scholarships, cooperatives, individuals, or organizations based outside of Oregon, even if they have an Oregon project.

Geographic Focus: Oregon

Date(s) Application is Due: Feb 25; Sep 2

Amount of Grant: 3,000 - 5,000 USD

Samples: Central Oregon Environmental Ctr (Bend, OR)—for general support, $3000; Latino Coalition (Eugene, OR)—for general support, $3000.

Contact: Anita Rodgers, Program Director; (800) 489-6743 or (503) 234-2338; anita@mrgfoundation.org

Internet: http://www.mrgfoundation.org/html/apply

Sponsor: McKenzie River Gathering Foundation

2705 E Burnside, Suite 210

Portland, OR 97214

McKesson Foundation Grants 1283

The foundation seeks to enhance the health and quality of life in communities where McKesson HBOC operates and its employees live. Emphasis is focused on youth, especially health services for underserved populations, educational enrichment, the environment, recreation, and youth development activities. The foundation also funds emergency services for children and families, and a variety of social, educational and cultural programs. For culture and the arts, support is given primarily to organizations that reach out to youth and other populations that do not have easy access to such programs. Grants are made for specific projects and programs, and general operating support will be considered in some circumstances. Grants are awarded for one to three years. The Foundation does not accept uninvited applications. Initial approach should be to contact the Foundation directly.

Requirements: 501(c)3 tax-exempt organizations are eligible.

Restrictions: Grants are not made to endowment campaigns, individuals or individual scholarships, religious organizations for religious purposes, political causes or campaigns, advertising in charitable publications, research studies or health organizations concentrating on one disease.

Geographic Focus: All States

Amount of Grant: 5,000 - 25,000 USD

Samples: LA Theater Work (CA)—for a project that creates hands-on performing arts and literary workshops aimed at finding a positive outlet for the aggression of 3000 at-risk and incarcerated youths, $7500; Massachusetts Coalition for School-Based Health Ctrs (MA)—to hire a coordinator and to continue providing school-based health care, $125,000 over three years.

Contact: Marcia Argyris, Foundation President; (415) 983-8673 or (415) 983-8300; fax (415) 983-7590; marcia.argyris@mckesson.com or community.relations@mckesson.com

Internet: http://www.mckesson.com/en_us/McKesson.com/About%2BUs/Corporate%2BCitizenship/McKesson%2BFoundation.html

Sponsor: McKesson Foundation

1 Post Street, 32nd Floor

San Francisco, CA 94104-5203

McKnight Foundation Mississippi River Environment Grants 1284

The McKnight Foundation assists nonprofit organizations and public agencies to improve the quality of life for all people, particularly those in need. The goal of the Foundation's Mississippi River Environment Grants is to use their resources to restore the water quality and resilience of the Mississippi River. Three strategies are to: restore and protect floodplains and wetlands in the ten-state Mississippi River corridor; reduce agricultural pollution in four states along the northern half of the river (Minnesota, Wisconsin, Iowa, and Illinois), focusing on farmland and operations with high levels of nitrogen and phosphorus runoff; and achieve cross-boundary and interagency coordination that improves the river's water quality and resilience. Funding is provided for planning, operating, and projects.

Requirements: Applicants must be classified by the Internal Revenue Service as tax-exempt, nonprofit organizations. Applicants are encouraged to call the Foundation to discuss ideas with a Program Officer and to learn more about the Foundation's strategies. If the organization's work fits the Foundation's funding strategies, an initial application may be made on-line, with an email respond from the Foundation within 45 days either to decline funding or to provide instructions to submit a full proposal online.

Restrictions: The following are ineligible: advocacy efforts related to biofuels production; efforts broadly addressing endocrine disruptors; conventional water supply, waste water treatment, storm water conveyance, or flood control facilities; basic research in academic disciplines; scholarships or other types of assistance for individuals; conferences, including attendance or travel, except when related to existing McKnight support; endowments, except in rare cases; activities that have a specific religious purpose; or lobbying prohibited by the Internal Revenue Code.

Geographic Focus: Illinois, Iowa, Minnesota, Wisconsin

Date(s) Application is Due: Feb 1; May 1; Aug 1; Nov 1

Contact: Ron Kroese; (612) 333-4220; rkroese@mcknight.org

Internet: http://www.mcknight.org/environment/river.aspx

Sponsor: McKnight Foundation

710 S Second Street, Suite 400

Minneapolis, MN 55401

McMurry Foundation Grants 1285

The foundation was established to have a significant and beneficial impact on the communities within Wyoming with special emphasis in Natrona County. Areas of interest include education, religion, children and advocacy for children, health and human services, the arts and humanities, and a favorable business environment. The foundation invests in innovative ventures as well as established community programs that have the potential to make a lasting difference. Funds provide seed money to start new programs; general funds to expand or improve services offered by established agencies; and organizational support, such as strategic planning, increasing management capacity, and board development. Priority will be given to promote strengthening the capacity of nonprofit organizations to do their work, leveraging the dollars of the McMurry Foundation, collaboration and efficient use of nonprofit resources, and addressing the causes or prevention of community problems. Application process and guidelines are available online.

Requirements: Wyoming 501(c)3 nonprofit organizations and organizations who have applied and anticipate receiving such status are eligible.

Restrictions: Grants designated to influence legislation or elect public officials are rejected.

Geographic Focus: All States

Date(s) Application is Due: Jan 15; Apr 15; Jul 15; Oct 15

Samples: U of Wyoming (Laramie, WY)—to help renovate the College of Education facility, $250,000.

Contact: Trudi McMurry, Director; (307) 234-4631; trudie@mcmurry.net

Internet: https://online.foundationsource.com/public/home/mcmurryfoundation

Sponsor: McMurry Foundation

P.O. Box 2016

Casper, WY 82602-2016

Mead Johnson Nutritionals Charitable Giving Grants 1286

Mead Johnson Nutritionals considers requests for charitable giving from a broad range of charitable organizations. Requests for charitable giving must be made in connection with a general fund raising effort by the charitable entity, rather than a request directed only to Mead Johnson Nutritionals. In addition, the request for a contribution must come from the organization itself and not from an individual physician, pharmacist, or health care professional who is not an employee of the charity. Applicants should allow at least three months for the processing of a funding request. Grant applications submitted less than three months prior to an event may be rejected due to insufficient time to process the application. Organizations outside the U.S. that wish to request a charitable gift should refer to Mead Johnson contact information within their country or call the charitable giving department at (812) 429-7800.

Requirements: Charitable giving is permitted if the recipient is a tax-exempt organization under Section 501(c)3 of the Internal Revenue Code.

Restrictions: As with grants, charitable giving may not be tied, in any way, to past, present, or future prescribing, purchasing, or recommending (including formulary recommendations) of any product.

Geographic Focus: All States

Contact: Grants Administrator; (812) 429-7831; fax (812) 647-8674; meadjohnson.grants1@bms.com

Internet: http://www.mjn.com/app/iwp/MJN/Content2.do?dm=mj&id=/MJN_Home2/mjnBtnSocialResponsibility2/mjnBtnCharitableGivingApplication&iwpst=B2C&ls=0&csred=1&r=3435833953

Sponsor: Mead Johnson Nutritionals

2400 West Lloyd Expressway

Evansville, IN 47721-0001

MeadWestvaco Foundation Education Grants 1287

The Foundation began as the Mead Corporation Foundation in 1957 and the Westvaco Foundation in 1953, anchored in shared values for community and environmental enrichment. Since merging in 2003, it has offered more than $36 million in support to targeted programs. Adding to this, company employee volunteers have donated over 572,000 hours to more than 3,000 qualified organizations. Across its diverse efforts, the Foundation focuses on three key areas for strategic grants and volunteer initiatives. In the area of Education, it helps to guarantee access to education for people of all ages, including MWV employee families. The Foundation funds specific efforts to ensure tomorrow's workforce is both creative and well-qualified. And it helps to create civic dialogue on issues that matter the most to all people. The Foundation's primary focus is to address important community needs and improve the quality of life in communities where MeadWestvaco operates.

Requirements: Nonprofit 501(c)3 organizations in or serving the following U.S. areas are eligible to apply: Cottonton and Lanett, Alabama; Bentonville, Arkansas; Chino, Corona, and Tecate, California; District of Columbia; Miami and St. Petersburg, Florida; Atlanta, Roswell, Smyrna, and Waynesboro, Georgia; Bartlett, Chicago, Itasca, Lake in the Hills, Schaumburg, and West Chicago, Illinois; Winfield, Kansas; Wickliffe, Kentucky; DeRidder, Louisiana; Minneapolis, Minnesota; Grandview, Missouri; Reno, Nevada; North Brunswick, Rumson, and Tinton Falls, New Jersey; New York, New York; Mebane, North Carolina; Cincinnati and Powell, Ohio; North Charleston and Summerville, South Carolina; Coppell, Evadale, and Silsbee, Texas; Appomattox, Covington, Low Moor, Raphine, and Richmond, Virginia; and Elkins and Rupert, West Virginia. Most areas worldwide are also eligible.

Geographic Focus: Alabama, Arkansas, California, District of Columbia, Florida, Georgia, Illinois, Kansas, Louisiana, Minnesota, Nevada, New Jersey, New York, North Carolina, Ohio, South Carolina, Texas, Virginia, West Virginia, All Countries

Amount of Grant: 100 - 1,500,000 USD

Samples: West Virginia University Foundation, Morgantown, West Virginia, $12,500 - educational support; Virginia Union University, Richmond, Virginia, $100,000 - general operations; Troy State University Foundation, Troy, Alabama, $20,000 - general operations.

Contact: Christine W. Hale, Manager, Contributions Programs; (804) 444-2531; fax (804) 444-1971; foundation@mwv.com

Internet: http://www.mwvfoundation.com/AreasofGiving/index.htm

Sponsor: MeadWestvaco Foundation

501 South 5th Street

Richmond, VA 23219-0501

MeadWestvaco Foundation Environmental Stewardship Grants 1288

The Foundation began as the Mead Corporation Foundation in 1957 and the Westvaco Foundation in 1953, anchored in shared values for community and environmental enrichment. Since merging in 2003, it has offered more than $36 million in support to targeted programs. Adding to this, company employee volunteers have donated over 572,000 hours to more than 3,000 qualified organizations. Across its diverse efforts, the Foundation focuses on three key areas for strategic grants and volunteer initiatives. In the area of Environmental Stewardship, the Foundation feels that the natural environment must be preserved for current and future generations to use and enjoy. To that end, it helps educate through programs, outdoor learning centers and other facilities. Furthermore, it teams with leaders in science and public policy to learn and share more about care for ecosystems and responsible land management. The Foundation's primary focus is to address important community needs and improve the quality of life in communities where MeadWestvaco operates.

Requirements: Nonprofit 501(c)3 organizations in or serving the following U.S. areas are eligible to apply: Cottonton and Lanett, Alabama; Bentonville, Arkansas; Chino, Corona, and Tecate, California; District of Columbia; Miami and St. Petersburg, Florida; Atlanta, Roswell, Smyrna, and Waynesboro, Georgia; Bartlett, Chicago, Itasca, Lake in the Hills, Schaumburg, and West Chicago, Illinois; Winfield, Kansas; Wickliffe, Kentucky; DeRidder, Louisiana; Minneapolis, Minnesota; Grandview, Missouri; Reno, Nevada; North Brunswick, Rumson, and Tinton Falls, New Jersey; New York, New York; Mebane, North Carolina; Cincinnati and Powell, Ohio; North Charleston and Summerville, South Carolina; Coppell, Evadale, and Silsbee, Texas; Appomattox, Covington, Low Moor, Raphine, and Richmond, Virginia; and Elkins and Rupert, West Virginia. Most areas worldwide are also eligible.

Geographic Focus: Alabama, Arkansas, California, District of Columbia, Florida, Georgia, Illinois, Kansas, Louisiana, Minnesota, Nevada, New Jersey, New York, North Carolina, Ohio, South Carolina, Texas, Virginia, West Virginia, All Countries

Amount of Grant: 250 - 1,500,000 USD

Samples: Chicago Horticultural Society, Chicago, Illinois, $2,500 - environmental support; Ruffed Grouse Society, Coraopolis, Pennsylvania, $20,000 - environmental support; Virginia Capital Trail Foundation, Richmond, Virginia, $75,300 - environmental stewardship,.

Contact: Christine W. Hale, Manager, Contributions Programs; (804) 444-2531; fax (804) 444-1971; foundation@mwv.com

Internet: http://www.mwvfoundation.com/AreasofGiving/index.htm

Sponsor: MeadWestvaco Foundation

501 South 5th Street

Richmond, VA 23219-0501

MeadWestvaco Foundation Sustainable Communities Grants   1289

The Foundation began as the Mead Corporation Foundation in 1957 and the Westvaco Foundation in 1953, anchored in shared values for community and environmental enrichment. Since merging in 2003, it has offered more than $36 million in support to targeted programs. Adding to this, company employee volunteers have donated over 572,000 hours to more than 3,000 qualified organizations. Across its diverse efforts, the Foundation focuses on three key areas for strategic grants and volunteer initiatives. In the area of Sustainable Communities, it partners with organizations that help people and families rely on themselves, and offers support to their neighbors. The Foundation's support of central business districts gives communities a strong center around which to grow. And its work with youth programs nurtures tomorrow's community leaders. The Foundation's primary focus is to address important community needs and improve the quality of life in communities where MeadWestvaco operates.

Requirements: Nonprofit 501(c)3 organizations in or serving the following U.S. areas are eligible to apply: Cottonton and Lanett, Alabama; Bentonville, Arkansas; Chino, Corona, and Tecate, California; District of Columbia; Miami and St. Petersburg, Florida; Atlanta, Roswell, Smyrna, and Waynesboro, Georgia; Bartlett, Chicago, Itasca, Lake in the Hills, Schaumburg, and West Chicago, Illinois; Winfield, Kansas; Wickliffe, Kentucky; DeRidder, Louisiana; Minneapolis, Minnesota; Grandview, Missouri; Reno, Nevada; North Brunswick, Rumson, and Tinton Falls, New Jersey; New York, New York; Mebane, North Carolina; Cincinnati and Powell, Ohio; North Charleston and Summerville, South Carolina; Coppell, Evadale, and Silsbee, Texas; Appomattox, Covington, Low Moor, Raphine, and Richmond, Virginia; and Elkins and Rupert, West Virginia. Most areas worldwide are also eligible.

Geographic Focus: Alabama, Arkansas, California, District of Columbia, Florida, Georgia, Illinois, Kansas, Louisiana, Minnesota, Nevada, New Jersey, New York, North Carolina, Ohio, South Carolina, Texas, Virginia, West Virginia, All Countries

Amount of Grant: 250 - 1,500,000 USD

Contact: Christine W. Hale, Manager, Contributions Programs; (804) 444-2531; fax (804) 444-1971; foundation@mwv.com

Internet: http://www.meadwestvaco.com/corporate.nsf/mwvfoundation/applicationsGuidelines

Sponsor: MeadWestvaco Foundation

501 South 5th Street

Richmond, VA 23219-0501

Mead Witter Foundation Grants   1290

Incorporated in Wisconsin in 1951, the Foundation awards grants to nonprofits in company operating locations, primarily in central and northern Wisconsin. Local community programs are funded, focusing on education, including scholarships in higher education and direct contributions to colleges and universities. Grants also are made to support the arts, health care, human services, youth organizations, environmental programs, and Christian and Roman Catholic organizations for nonreligious purposes. Types of support include general operating support, continuing support, annual campaigns, capital campaigns, building construction and renovation, equipment acquisition, endowment funds, professorships, seed grants, scholarship funds, and employee-matching gifts. The board meets twice annually to consider requests. Full proposal is by invitation only.

Requirements: Wisconsin 501(c)3 organizations may apply.

Restrictions: The foundation does not support religious, athletic, or fraternal groups, except when these groups provide needed special services to the community at large; direct grants or scholarships to individuals; community foundations; or flow-through organizations that redispense funds to other charitable causes.

Geographic Focus: Wisconsin

Amount of Grant: 25,000 - 18,000,000 USD

Contact: Cynthia Henke, President; (715) 424-3004; fax (715) 424-1314

Sponsor: Mead Witter Foundation

P.O. Box 39

Wisconsin Rapids, WI 54495-0039

Medina Foundation Grants   1291

The foundation makes grants to a wide range of nonprofits in the Puget Sound area. Grants support several causes: human services—emergency food and housing; education—private entities, grades preschool through 12, and programs in the areas of leadership and management, vocational and alternative schools, and tutoring and mentoring; persons with disabilities—work training and employment opportunities, self-sufficiency; alcohol and drug abuse—education, and treatment. Grants are awarded to fund direct service delivery programs, operating expenses, capital expenses, equipment, emergency funds, seed money grant, and technical assistance. Applications and guidelines are available on the Web site.

Requirements: Organizations operating within the greater Puget Sound region or to projects significantly affecting its residents are eligible. The greater Puget Sound region is defined as the following counties: Clallum, Grays Harbor, Island, Jefferson, King, Kitsap, Mason, Pacific, Pierce, San Juan, Skagit, Snohomish, Thurston, and Whatcom.

Restrictions: Requests will not be accepted from public schools or cultural programs.

Geographic Focus: Washington

Contact: Jennifer Teunon; (206) 652-8783; info@medinafoundation

Internet: http://www.medinafoundation.org/index.php?p=Grants&s=3

Sponsor: Medina Foundation

801 2nd Avenue, Suite 1300

Seattle, WA 98104

Medtronic Foundation HeartRescue Grants   1292

The HeartRescue Grants fund organizations and government agencies that provide community-based education, training, and awareness programs related to sudden cardiac arrest (SCA) and the use of automatic external defibrillators. Working with select partners, efforts are focused on developing an integrated community response to SCA, coordinating education, training and the application of high-tech treatments among the general public, first responders, emergency medical services, and hospitals. Funds may be used for all aspects of a systems-based approach to SCA, including human resources, data collection and measurement tools, training costs at all levels of the system, and technology. If your organization is interested in participating in the program, please submit a letter of inquiry.

Requirements: Nonprofit organizations and government agencies that provide education, training, and awareness programs related to sudden cardiac death, early defibrillation, and early intervention are eligible. Organizations should send a 1-2 page letter of inquiry with detailed information about their organization, their project, their staff, and plans for implementing their program.

Restrictions: The Foundation does not fund the following: Continuing Medical Education (CME) grants; 501(c)3 type 509(a)3 supporting organizations; capital or capital projects; fiscal agents; fundraising events/activities, social events or goodwill advertising; general operating support; general support of educational institutions; greater Twin Cities United Way supported programs; individuals, including scholarships for individuals; lobbying, political or fraternal activities; long-term counseling or personal development; program endowments; purchases of automatic external defibrillators (AEDs); religious groups for religious purposes; private foundations; or research.

Geographic Focus: All States

Amount of Grant: 300,000 - 500,000 USD

Contact: Deb Anderson, Grants Administrator; (763) 514-4000 or (800) 328-2518; fax (763) 505-2648; deb.anderson@medtronic.com

Joan Mellor, HeratRescue Consultant; (763) 514-4000 or (800) 328-2518; fax (763) 505-2648; joan.mellor@medtronic.com

Internet: http://www.medtronic.com/foundation/programs_hr.html

Sponsor: Medtronic Foundation

710 Medtronic Parkway

Minneapolis, MN 55432-5604

Mellon Financial Corporation Foundation Grants 1293

Mellon Bank supports economic development that strengthens communities and initiatives that focus on the needs of low- and moderate-income residents. Current focus is on efforts to attract and develop business and jobs, affordable housing and home ownership, literacy improvement, and technical assistance or capacity building for nonprofit organizations. Types of support include capital grants, program/project grants, matching gifts, technical assistance, and general operating grants. The fund makes grants primarily in its headquarters city of Pittsburgh, as well as in Boston and Philadelphia. Contributions to organizations in other Mellon locations, including outside the United States, are made through corporate donation programs customized to address the needs of specific communities. There are no application deadlines.

Requirements: IRS 501(c)3 organizations in Mellon locations are eligible.

Restrictions: Support is not available for loans or assistance to individuals; ecclesiastical programs of churches or other sectarian organizations; political parties, campaigns, or candidates; or fraternal fraternal organizations. Grants do not support scholarships and fellowships; travel grants, conferences, specialized health campaigns; or endowment funds.

Geographic Focus: All States

Amount of Grant: 5,000 - 20,000 USD

Contact: Program Contact; (412) 234-2732

Internet: http://www.mellon.com/communityaffairs/charitablegiving.html

Sponsor: Mellon Financial Corporation Foundation

One Mellon Center, Suite 1830

Pittsburgh, PA 15258

Memorial Foundation Grants 1294

The Memorial Foundation awards grants to support nonprofit organizations that provide services only to people who live in the area served by Nashville Memorial Hospital. The Foundation also strives to respond to immediate, critical needs that arise in the community. With assistance from the Foundation, organizations including The Salvation Army, The American Red Cross, Second Harvest Food Bank, Nashville Tree Foundation, and YWCA have received funds. Special emphasis is given to organizations that focus on health; youth and children; senior citizens; education; human and social services; community services; and substance abuse (alcohol, drugs, and tobacco). Types of support include capital projects; general operating support; and start-up projects for new initiatives that address important, unmet community needs and that demonstrate potential for ongoing operational support from other sources.

Requirements: An applicant organization must be exempt from federal taxation under Section 501(c)3 of the Internal Revenue Code and not be a private foundation as described in Section 509(a) in order to be eligible.

Restrictions: The Memorial Foundation does not fund grants for the following: individuals; newsletters, magazines; churches and religious organizations for projects that primarily benefit their own members (exception: church-based programs with broad community support and separate financial statements); disease-specific organizations seeking support for national research projects and programs; sponsor special events, productions, telethons, performances, or similar fundraising and advertising activities (exceptions may be given for approved educational videos); legislative lobbying or other political purposes; retire accumulated debt; bricks and mortar capital projects for colleges, universities, and private or public school education; computer labs and related technologies to schools; or multi-year grants for operating funds.

Geographic Focus: Tennessee

Contact: Joyce Douglas; (615) 822-9499; fax (615) 822-7797

Internet: http://www.memfoundation.org

Sponsor: Memorial Foundation

100 Bluegrass Commons Boulevard, Suite 320

Hendersonville, TN 37075

Merck Company Foundation Grants 1295

The foundation advances the company's philanthropic outreach in helping to meet important needs of local and international communities that are consistent with Merck's overall mission to enhance the health and well-being of people around the world. Such needs include improving health care, fostering biomedical and science education; and supporting the arts, social services, and civic, environmental and other charitable organizations.

Requirements: Operating support of health and social service agencies is reserved for Merck communities and generally directed through annual contributions to United Way.

Restrictions: Grants are not made to political, labor, fraternal, or veterans organizations; sectarian groups; or to individuals. Except within foundation programs, grants are not given for elementary/secondary education,

scholarships, fellowships, research, publications, conferences/seminars/symposia, and travel.

Geographic Focus: All States

Samples: Alliance of Community Health Plans (Washington, DC)—to help healthcare groups that use culturally and linguistically appropriate health services demonstrate that those services are financially sound options, $235,000; American National Red Cross (Washington, DC), UNICEF (NY), and several local relief organizations—for relief efforts in South Asia and Africa, $3 million divided; Task Force for Child Survival and Development (Atlanta, GA)—to expand programs to treat people in Africa who are suffering from onchocerciasis, more commonly known as river blindness, as part of the Mectizan Donation Program, $1 million over five years.

Contact: Dr. Shuang Ruy Huang, (908) 423-1000; fax (908) 423-1987

Internet: http://www.merck.com/about/cr/policies_performance/social/philanthropy.html

Sponsor: Merck Company Foundation

P.O. Box 100 (WSIAF-35)

Whitehouse Station, NJ 08889-0100

Merck Family Fund Conserving Ecologically Valuable Land Grants 1296

The primary goals of the Merck Family Fund are to restore and protect the natural environment and ensure a healthy planet for generations to come; and to strengthen the social fabric and the physical landscape of the urban community. In the Conserving Ecologically Valuable Land area, the Fund has determined that natural areas need a combination of land protections and sustainable use policies to ensure clean air, clean water, and sustainability. The geographic focus of this area will be the southeastern United States, with priority given to the Southern Appalachians and the states of Tennessee, North Carolina, Kentucky, South Carolina, Georgia, and Virginia. Specifically, the Fund welcomes proposals that: advocate for and secure public financial resources and commitments to land protection; demonstrate community engagement and certified sustainable management of land particularly concerning forestry and farming; and provide leadership to existing and emerging coalitions that build a multi-stakeholder voice. Upon submitting a letter of inquiry, applicants will be notified of a decision, by email, typically within one week. If invited, full proposals must be submitted through this online application system no later than August 1, at 5:00pm EST for the November decision, and February 1, at 5:00pm for Spring decision.

Requirements: United States tax-exempt organizations in the Southern Appalachians and the states of Tennessee, North Carolina, Kentucky, South Carolina, Georgia, and Virginia are eligible. New and returning requests for support must use the online application system to submit a letter of inquiry prior to a formal application.

Restrictions: The Fund does not support individuals, for-profit organizations, or candidates for political office. The Fund does not generally support: governmental organizations, academic research or books; endowments, debt reduction, annual fund-raising campaigns, capital construction, purchase of equipment, the acquisition of land, or film or video projects.

Geographic Focus: Georgia, Kentucky, North Carolina, South Carolina, Tennessee, Virginia

Date(s) Application is Due: Feb 1; Aug 1

Amount of Grant: 10,000 - 50,000 USD

Samples: American Rivers, Washington, DC, $40,000 - to secure long-term protections for hardwood forests critical to preserving clean water in the Southern Appalachians; Dogwood Alliance, Asheville, North Carolina, $50,000 - to advance forest conservation in the Southeast through the development of viable ecosystem markets, beginning with carbon; Lowcountry Open Land Trust, Charleston, South Carolina, $25,000 - to increase protected lands in the Lowcountry and focus on land that will aid climate adaptation.

Contact: Jenny Russell; (617) 696-3580; fax (617) 696-7262; merck@merckff.org

Internet: http://www.merckff.org/programs.html

Sponsor: Merck Family Fund

303 Adams Street, P.O. Box 870245

Milton Village, MA 02187

Merck Family Fund Making Paper Production Sustainable Grants 1297

The primary goals of the Merck Family Fund are to restore and protect the natural environment and ensure a healthy planet for generations to come; and to strengthen the social fabric and the physical landscape of the urban community. In the area of Making Paper Production Sustainable, the goal is to increase the rates of recycled paper in large paper sectors, reduce sourcing from endangered forests, and maximize clean production. Specifically, the Fund welcomes proposals that: assist major paper users and suppliers to adopt environmentally preferable paper practices; support networks that align paper

production strategies and goals; and provide information to consumers to opt-out of large-scale distributions such as direct mail and catalogs. Upon submitting a letter of inquiry, applicants will be notified of a decision, by email, typically within one week. If invited, full proposals must be submitted through this online application system no later than August 1, at 5:00pm EST for the November decision, and February 1, at 5:00pm for Spring decision.
Requirements: United States tax-exempt organizations are eligible. New and returning requests for support must use the online application system to submit a letter of inquiry prior to a formal application.
Restrictions: The Fund does not support individuals, for-profit organizations, or candidates for political office. The Fund does not generally support: governmental organizations, academic research or books; endowments, debt reduction, annual fund-raising campaigns, capital construction, purchase of equipment, the acquisition of land, or film or video projects.
Geographic Focus: All States
Date(s) Application is Due: Feb 1; Aug 1
Amount of Grant: 10,000 - 75,000 USD
Samples: Canopy, San Francisco, California, $60,000 - to protect forests through environmentally sensitive practices in the print and publishing sectors; Green America, Washington, DC, $30,000 - general support for the Better Paper Project, which works to change the magazine industry's paper practices; Natural Resources Defense Council, New York, New York, $50,000 - to continue protecting key forests in the Cumberland Plateau BioGem.
Contact: Jenny Russell, Executive Director; (617) 696-3580; fax (617) 696-7262; merck@merckff.org
Internet: http://www.merckff.org/programs.html
Sponsor: Merck Family Fund
303 Adams Street, P.O. Box 870245
Milton Village, MA 02187

Merck Family Fund Promoting Energy Efficiency Grants   1298
The primary goals of the Merck Family Fund are to restore and protect the natural environment and ensure a healthy planet for generations to come; and to strengthen the social fabric and the physical landscape of the urban community. In the area of Making Paper Production Sustainable, the goal is to support state and regional policies in the Northeast and Southeast that provide incentives and subsidies for energy efficiency implementation. Specifically, the Fund welcomes proposals that: advocate for residential and commercial standards that result in measurable efficiencies; demonstrate financing models that create affordable capital for retrofits; promote utility-based efficiency programs; and lead state networks that create and implement climate action plans. Upon submitting a letter of inquiry, applicants will be notified of a decision, by email, typically within one week. If invited, full proposals must be submitted through this online application system no later than August 1, at 5:00pm EST for the November decision, and February 1, at 5:00pm for Spring decision.
Requirements: United States tax-exempt organizations are eligible. New and returning requests for support must use the online application system to submit a letter of inquiry prior to a formal application.
Restrictions: The Fund does not support individuals, for-profit organizations, or candidates for political office. The Fund does not generally support: governmental organizations, academic research or books; endowments, debt reduction, annual fund-raising campaigns, capital construction, purchase of equipment, the acquisition of land, or film or video projects.
Geographic Focus: All States
Date(s) Application is Due: Feb 1; Aug 1
Amount of Grant: 10,000 - 100,000 USD
Contact: Jenny Russell, Executive Director; (617) 696-3580; fax (617) 696-7262; merck@merckff.org
Internet: http://www.merckff.org/programs.html
Sponsor: Merck Family Fund
303 Adams Street, P.O. Box 870245
Milton Village, MA 02187

Merck Family Fund Urban Farming and Youth Leadership Grants   1299
The primary goals of the Merck Family Fund are to restore and protect the natural environment and ensure a healthy planet for generations to come; and to strengthen the social fabric and the physical landscape of the urban community. In the area of Urban Farming and Youth Leadership, the Fund will support programs in low-income urban areas in the Northeast that are harnessing the power of young people to create urban farms and local markets. Specifically, the Fund welcomes proposals that: provide high quality leadership development and employment for youth; support highly productive urban farming projects and increase local access to fresh food; and engage residents

in food access and food security issues in the community. Upon submitting a letter of inquiry, applicants will be notified of a decision, by email, typically within one week. If invited, full proposals must be submitted through this online application system no later than August 1, at 5:00pm EST for the November decision, and February 1, at 5:00pm for Spring decision.
Requirements: United States tax-exempt organizations are eligible. Priority will be given to projects that originate in the six New England states, New York, New Jersey and the Delaware Valley region including Philadelphia, Pennsylvania, and Wilmington, Delaware. New and returning requests for support must use the online application system to submit a letter of inquiry prior to a formal application.
Restrictions: The Fund does not support individuals, for-profit organizations, or candidates for political office. The Fund does not generally support: governmental organizations, academic research or books; endowments, debt reduction, annual fund-raising campaigns, capital construction, purchase of equipment, the acquisition of land, or film or video projects.
Geographic Focus: Delaware, Maine, Maryland, Massachusetts, New Hampshire, New Jersey, New York, Pennsylvania, Rhode Island, Vermont
Date(s) Application is Due: Feb 1; Aug 1
Amount of Grant: 3,000 - 50,000 USD
Samples: Capital District Community Gardens, Troy, New York, $26,000 - to increase food access and economic opportunities by providing entrepreneurial training and employment to teens on urban farms; Nuestras Raices, Holyoke, Massachusetts, $50,000 - to convert a vacant lot into an urban garden and train and employ youth in farming, organizing, and entrepreneurship; St. Mary's Nutrition Center, Lewiston, Maine, $40,000 - to increase the sustainability of the Nutrition Center to train and employ young people and grow and distribute food from urban farms.
Contact: Jenny Russell, Executive Director; (617) 696-3580; fax (617) 696-7262; merck@merckff.org
Internet: http://www.merckff.org/programs.html
Sponsor: Merck Family Fund
303 Adams Street, P.O. Box 870245
Milton Village, MA 02187

Merck Family Fund Youth Transforming Urban Communities Grants   1300
The primary goals of the Merck Family Fund are to restore and protect the natural environment and ensure a healthy planet for generations to come; and to strengthen the social fabric and the physical landscape of the urban community. In the area of Youth Transforming Urban Communities, the goals have been to support a cadre of young social justice leaders across the country; to link local campaigns with national movements; and to document the impact of their work on communities and themselves. Upon submitting a letter of inquiry, applicants will be notified of a decision, by email, typically within one week. If invited, full proposals must be submitted through this online application system no later than August 1, at 5:00pm EST for the November decision, and February 1, at 5:00pm for Spring decision.
Requirements: United States tax-exempt organizations are eligible. New and returning requests for support must use the online application system to submit a letter of inquiry prior to a formal application.
Restrictions: The Fund does not support individuals, for-profit organizations, or candidates for political office. The Fund does not generally support: governmental organizations, academic research or books; endowments, debt reduction, annual fund-raising campaigns, capital construction, purchase of equipment, the acquisition of land, or film or video projects.
Geographic Focus: All States
Date(s) Application is Due: Feb 1; Aug 1
Amount of Grant: 10,000 - 45,000 USD
Samples: Campaign for Quality Education, Long Beach, California, $15,000 - to support a youth-led statewide alliance of grassroots, civil rights, policy and research organizations committed to educational equity for all communities served by California's public schools; Hyde Square Task Force, Jamaica Plain, Massachusetts, $45,000 - to empower youth to examine the social, economic, and political forces affecting their lives and act as agents of change in their communities and schools; Padres y Jovenes Unidos, Denver, Colorado, $45,000 - to equip youth members with the tools they need to organize for social, racial, economic, and educational justice.
Contact: Jenny Russell, Executive Director; (617) 696-3580; fax (617) 696-7262; merck@merckff.org
Internet: http://www.merckff.org/programs.html
Sponsor: Merck Family Fund
303 Adams Street, P.O. Box 870245
Milton Village, MA 02187

Mericos Foundation Grants 1301

The Mericos Foundation primarily awards grants to organizations based in California with emphasis on Santa Barbara. Fields of interest include aging; animals/wildlife; environment; arts and arts education; child development; children and youth; elementary and secondary education; higher education; hospitals; medical care; medical research; libraries; and museums (art and natural history). Types of support include building/renovation, equipment, fellowships, general/operating support, matching/challenge support, and program development. Grants are usually initiated by the foundation. Interested organizations should contact the Vice-President to discuss their project.
Requirements: Nonprofit organizations in California are eligible to apply.
Restrictions: Grants are not made to individuals.
Geographic Focus: California
Amount of Grant: 15,000 - 200,000 USD
Samples: Music Academy of the West, Santa Barbara, California, $125,000; Friends of Independent Schools and Better Education, Tacoma, Washington, $25,000; Los Angeles Children's Chorus, Pasadena, California, $25,000.
Contact: Linda Blinkenberg; (626) 441-5188; fax (626) 441-3672
Sponsor: Mericos Foundation
625 South Fair Oaks Avenue, Suite 360
South Pasadena, CA 91030-2630

Meriden Foundation Grants 1302

The foundation awards grants to eligible Connecticut nonprofit organizations in its areas of interest, including arts, children and youth, civic affairs, Christian organizations and churches, health organizations and hospitals, higher education, public libraries, and social services. Types of support include annual campaigns, general operating support, scholarships, and social services delivery. There are no application deadlines. A formal application is required, and the initial approach should be a letter, on organizational letterhead, describing the project and requesting an application.
Requirements: Connecticut nonprofit organizations in the Meriden-Wallingford area are eligible.
Geographic Focus: Connecticut
Amount of Grant: 175 - 10,000 USD
Samples: Best Friends Animal Sanctuary, Kanab, Utah, $3,500 - general operations; Church of the Holy Angels, Meriden, Connecticut, $3,296 - general operations; Franciscan Home Care and Hospice, Meriden, Connecticut, $5,000 - to purchase laptop computers.
Contact: Jeffrey F. Otis, Director; (203) 782-4531; fax (203) 782-4530
Sponsor: Meriden Foundation
123 Bank Street
Waterbury, CT 06702-2205

Merrick Foundation Grants 1303

The Merrick Foundation was established in Texas in 2011 to support charitable programs in the States of Texas and Wyoming. The Foundation's primary fields of interest include: animals and wildlife; community development; economic development; and higher education. Typically, grants are given to support general operating costs. Most recent awards have ranged from $500 to $25,000. Along with a formal application secured from the Foundation office, applicants should submit: a detailed description of the project; amount requested; a copy of the most recent audit; and a copy of the IRS determination letter. There are no specified annual deadlines.
Requirements: 501(c)3 organizations located in, or serving the residents of, the States of Texas or Wyoming are eligible to apply.
Geographic Focus: Texas, Wyoming
Amount of Grant: 500 - 25,000 USD
Contact: Noelle Kilgore, Executive Director; (806) 350-5515
Sponsor: Merrick Foundation
101 SE 11th Avenue, Suite 100
Amarillo, TX 79101

Merrick Foundation Grants 1304

The goal of Merrick Foundation is to improve the quality of life in the Merrick County area of Nebraska by supporting needs that are not being met in the areas of civic, cultural, health, education and social service. Grants are awarded on the condition that grantees attend Merrick Foundation's Annual Meeting on the 4th Monday of November and provide a poster board display demonstrating the goal, progress or completion of their grant project. Proposals from organizations demonstrating broad community support for their proposed programs are given priority consideration. Most recent awards have ranged from $5,800 to $45,000. Grant requests over $10,000 may be required to attend a regular meeting for

explanations and/or clarifications. Grants over $15,000 shall be reviewed in January and June. Deadline dates for submitting applications are due the 10th of each month or the following Monday if the 10th falls on a weekend. Grants are approved every month except December.
Requirements: Only organizations in Merrick County or organizations serving Merrick County residents are eligible to apply.
Restrictions: The Foundation does not make grants to individuals, for religious purposes, or organizations that operate for profit. he Foundation as a general policy gives less consideration to applications from tax-supported institutions, veterans and labor organizations, social clubs and fraternal organizations. A grant cannot be used for political purposes.
Geographic Focus: Nebraska
Date(s) Application is Due: Jan 1; Feb 1; Mar 1; Apr 1; May 1; Jun 1; Jul 1; Aug 1; Sep 1; Oct 1; Nov 1
Amount of Grant: 5,800 - 45,000 USD
Samples: St. Paul's Lutheran Church, Grand Island, Nebraska, $12,000 - community help programs; Merrick County Child Development Center, Central City, Nebraska, $15,000 - general operating costs; Platte Peer Group, Chapman, Nebraska, $45,000 - park development project support.
Contact: Chuck Griffith, Executive Director; (308) 946-3707; merrickfoundation@gmail.com
Internet: http://www.merrick-foundation.org/grants.htm
Sponsor: Merrick Foundation
1532 17th Avenue, P.O. Box 206
Central City, NE 68826

Merrick Foundation Grants 1305

The Merrick Foundation was established in 1948 by Ward S. Merrick, Sr., as a memorial to his father F.W. Merrick and at the request of F.W.'s wife, Elizabeth B. Merrick. The mission of the Foundation is to enhance the quality of life and the improvement of health for Oklahoma residents and their communities, with a primary emphasis on south central Oklahoma. With this goal in mind, the Foundation trustees are committed to furthering the philanthropic vision of Ward S. Merrick, Sr., by awarding grants to charitable organizations that foster independence and achievement, and that stimulate educational, economic, and cultural growth. Primary fields of interest include: the arts; higher education; human services; medical research; and youth services. The majority of awards are given for general operations. Most recent grants have ranged from $500 to $25,000. The grants committee will review all request letters received through the online grant application process and will email instructions on how to complete an application to qualifying charities. Grant applications will be due October 1 each year.
Requirements: The trustees invite proposals from 501(c)3 organizations located in Oklahoma. A letter of request is due by the August 15 deadline, summarizing the project for funding must be submitted through the online grant application process.
Geographic Focus: Oklahoma
Date(s) Application is Due: Oct 1
Amount of Grant: 500 - 25,000 USD
Samples: Arbuckle Life Solutions, Ardmore, Oklahoma, $5,000 - general operation support; CASA of Southern Oklahoma, Oklahoma City, Oklahoma, $10,000 - general operating support; Delta Upsilon Fraternity, Oklahoma City, Oklahoma, $5,000 - general operating support.
Contact: Randy Macon, Executive Director; 405-755-5571; fax (405) 755-0938; fwmerrick@foundationmanagementinc.com
Internet: https://www.foundationmanagementinc.com/foundations/merrick-foundation/
Sponsor: Merrick Foundation
2932 NW 122nd Street, Suite D
Oklahoma City, OK 73120-1955

Merrill Lynch Philanthropic Program Grants 1306

The foundation supports a variety of charitable causes throughout the world, with a focus on education. Through 2005, the foundation has adopted children and youth as its global cause. Programs should meet the educational needs and interests of uderserved children and youth. Programs should support an ethnically diverse population of children and youth; provide direct services from early childhood to postsecondary education, and incorporate one or more of the following elements: academic support, global exchange, community service, internships, cultural enrichment, life skills, digital divide, mentoring, entrepreneurship, scholarships, personal finance, technology skills, GED programs linked with four-year colleges, and workforce preparation. The foundation gives priority to specific programs and projects, rather than general operating support. Preference will be given to requests from the five boroughs of New York City and national organizations that reflect that focus. Requests outside of New York City should be submitted to managers of local branches or offices.

Requirements: Tax-exempt 501(c)3 organizations are eligible.

Restrictions: Grants will not be made to private foundations; individuals; fundraising activities related to individual sponsorships (e.g., walk-a-thons, marathons); seed money for new organizations; political causes, candidates, and campaigns as well as organizations designed specifically for lobbying; religious, fraternal, social, or other membership organizations providing services mainly to their own constituencies; athletic events and sports tournaments (Special Olympics is eligible); and fundraising events (dinners, luncheons).

Geographic Focus: All States

Samples: Sesame Workshop (New York, NY)—for the WorldwideKids program, which will use multimedia tools and resources to educate three- to six-year olds about diverse people and cultures, $5 million; United Nations Assoc of the United States of America (Washington, DC)—to expand to 14 countries the Global Classrooms program, which supports Model United Nations activities in schools, and to develop a curriculum on global development, finance, and trade, $7.5 million.

Contact: Westina Matthews, Vice President, Philanthropic Programs; (212) 236-4319; fax (212) 236-8007; SDimaggio@exchange.ml.com

Internet: http://philanthropy.ml.com

Sponsor: Merrill Lynch and Company Foundation

2 World Financial Center, 5th Floor

New York, NY 10281-6100

Mervin Bovaird Foundation Grants 1307

The foundation awards grants, with a focus on Tulsa, OK, to nonprofit organizations such as churches, homeless shelters, medical centers, nursing homes, parochial schools, religious welfare organizations, the Salvation Army, and youth organizations. Areas of interest include arts, community development, education, environment, health care and health organizations, and social services. Types of support include general operating support, matching, project, and research grants.

Requirements: Nonprofits in and serving the population of Tulsa, Oklahoma, are eligible. Applicants should submit a brief letter of inquiry, including program and organization descriptions.

Geographic Focus: Oklahoma

Date(s) Application is Due: Nov 15

Amount of Grant: Up to 250,000 USD

Contact: R. Casey Cooper, (918) 592-3300; casey.cooper@cmw-law.com

Sponsor: Mervin Bovaird Foundation

401 South Boston Avenue, Suite 3300

Tulsa, OK 74103

Metro Health Foundation Grants 1308

The foundation awards grants in southeastern Michigan in its areas of interest, including children and youth, disabled, elderly, health associations, homeless, and women. Types of support include challenge grants, equipment acquisition, general operating support, project development, scholarship funds, seed grants, and federated giving. Obtain application materials from the office; the board meets in April and October.

Requirements: Nonprofit organizations in the metropolitan tri-county Detroit, MI, area are eligible to apply.

Restrictions: Grants do not support advertising, advocacy organizations, athletic groups, individuals, international organizations, political organizations, special events, benefit dinners, or state or local government agencies.

Geographic Focus: Michigan

Date(s) Application is Due: Feb 1; Aug 1

Amount of Grant: 1,000 - 25,000 USD

Contact: Theresa Sondys, Program Contact; (313) 965-4220; fax (313) 965-3626; metrohealthfdn@aol.com

Sponsor: Metro Health Foundation

333 W Fort Street, Suite 1370

Detroit, MI 48226-3134

Meyer and Pepa Gold Family Foundation Grants 1309

Established in 1986 and formerly known as the Gold Family Foundation, the revamped Meyer and Pepa Gold Family Foundation offers grant support in New Jersey and New York. Its primary fields of interest include the arts, health organizations, and medical research agencies. The are no specified application forms required or annual deadlines. Interested parties should begin by contacting the Foundation directly, offering an overview of their program and budgetary needs. Recent grants, which predominately support general operations, range up to $35,000.

Requirements: Any 501(c)3 located in, or serving the residents of, New Jersey and/or New York are eligible to apply.

Restrictions: No grants are offered to individuals.

Geographic Focus: New Jersey, New York

Amount of Grant: Up to 35,000 USD

Contact: Pepa Gold, Trustee; (732) 229-0569 or (732) 660-1770

Sponsor: Meyer and Pepa Gold Family Foundation

P.O. Box 777

Oakhurst, NJ 07755

Meyer Foundation Economic Security Grants 1310

Eugene Meyer was an investment banker, public servant under seven U.S. presidents, and owner and publisher of the Washington Post. His wife Agnes Ernst Meyer was an accomplished journalist, author, lecturer, and citizen activist. Eugene and Agnes created the Meyer Foundation in 1944. For more than sixty-five years the Meyer Foundation has identified, listened to, and invested in visionary leaders and effective community-based nonprofit organizations that work to create lasting improvements in the lives of low-income people in the Washington, D.C. metropolitan region. The foundation offers program, operating, and capital support in four priority program areas: education, healthy communities, economic security, and a strong nonprofit sector. In the area of economic security, the foundation funds organizations that help low-income adults and families to stabilize their lives, build assets, and achieve financial independence. Examples of types of organizations funded are as follows: comprehensive, multi-service, anti-poverty organizations with the capacity to expand their services; legal-service providers that provide both direct legal services and advocacy; and advocacy organizations and coalitions. Specifically the foundation funds the following types of programming; facilitating access to workforce development; facilitating access to legal services and advocacy in matters of legal status, housing, work supports and public benefits, and employment crises; and facilitating access to money-management education and financial literacy. Letters of Intent (LOIs) may be submitted through the foundation's online application system twice a year, in January and June; exact deadline dates may vary from year to year. Applicants will receive an email confirming receipt of their LOI within two to three weeks of submission and will be notified two months after the LOI deadline whether or not they will be invited to submit a full proposal for the board meetings in April and October. Prospective applicants should visit the foundation's website for detailed funding guidelines and current deadline dates before submitting an LOI.

Requirements: Eligible applicants must be 501(c)3 organizations that are located within and primarily serve the Washington, D.C. region defined by the foundation to include the following geographic areas: Washington, D.C; Montgomery and Prince George's counties in Maryland; Arlington, Fairfax, and Prince William counties in Virginia; and the cities of Alexandria, Falls Church, and Manassas Park, Virginia. The foundation looks for organizations that demonstrate visionary and talented leadership, effectiveness, sustainability, and long-term impact.

Restrictions: The foundation does not fund entrepreneurship, microenterprise, small-business-development projects, government agencies, for-profit businesses, individuals (including scholarships or other forms of emergency financial assistance), scientific or medial research, special events or conferences, or endowments.

Geographic Focus: All States

Amount of Grant: 1,500 - 50,000 USD

Contact: Julie Rogers; (202) 483-8294; fax (202) 328-6850; jrogers@meyerfdn.org

Internet: http://www.meyerfoundation.org/our-programs/grantmaking/economic-security

Sponsor: Meyer Foundation

1250 Connecticut Avenue, Northwest, Suite 800

Washington, D.C. 20036

Meyer Foundation Education Grants 1311

Eugene Meyer was an investment banker, public servant under seven U.S. presidents, and owner and publisher of the Washington Post. His wife Agnes Ernst Meyer was an accomplished journalist, author, lecturer, and citizen activist. Eugene and Agnes created the Meyer Foundation in 1944. For more than sixty-five years the Meyer Foundation has identified, listened to, and invested in visionary leaders and effective community-based nonprofit organizations that work to create lasting improvements in the lives of low-income people in the Washington, D.C. metropolitan region. The foundation offers program, operating, and capital support in four priority program areas: education, healthy communities, economic security, and a strong nonprofit sector. In the area of education, the foundation supports a broad range of work, all designed to ensure that young people graduate from high school, go on to earn post-secondary credentials, and enter the skilled work force. This work includes programming that facilitates the following outcomes: successful transitions for children of low-income families throughout their entire education; multiple pathways for children and youth to enter the skilled work force; and education reform in K-12 public education in the D.C. area. Letters of Intent (LOIs) may be submitted through the foundation's online application system twice a year, in January and June; exact deadline dates may vary from year to year. Applicants will receive an email confirming receipt of their LOI within two to three weeks of submission and will be notified two months after the LOI deadline whether or not they will be invited to submit a full proposal for the board meetings in April and October. Prospective applicants should visit the foundation's website for detailed funding guidelines and current deadline dates before submitting an LOI.

Requirements: Eligible applicants must be 501(c)3 organizations that are located within and primarily serve the Washington, D.C. region defined by the foundation to include the following geographic areas: Washington, D.C; Montgomery and Prince George's counties in Maryland; Arlington, Fairfax, and Prince William counties in Virginia; and the cities of Alexandria, Falls Church, and Manassas Park, Virginia. The foundation looks for organizations that demonstrate visionary and talented leadership, effectiveness, sustainability, and long-term impact.

Restrictions: The foundation does not fund short-term or seasonal programs, individual public or private schools, PTAs, organizations that provide out-of-school programs solely for elementary-school children, government agencies, for-profit businesses, individuals (including scholarships or other forms of financial assistance), scientific or medial research, special events or conferences, or endowments.

Geographic Focus: District of Columbia, Maryland, Virginia

Amount of Grant: 1,500 - 50,000 USD

Samples: Advocates for Justice and Education, Washington, D.C., $50,000—general operating support; Beacon House, Washington, D.C., $25,000—general operating support; DanceMakers, Lanham, Maryland, $20,000—to support the One Step Forward program.

Contact: Julie Rogers; (202) 483-8294; fax (202) 328-6850; jrogers@meyerfdn.org

Internet: http://www.meyerfoundation.org/our-programs/grantmaking/education

Sponsor: Meyer Foundation

1250 Connecticut Avenue, Northwest, Suite 800

Washington, D.C. 20036

Meyer Foundation Healthy Communities Grants 1312

Eugene Meyer was an investment banker, public servant under seven U.S. presidents, and owner and publisher of the Washington Post. His wife Agnes Ernst Meyer was an accomplished journalist, author, lecturer, and citizen activist. Eugene and Agnes created the Meyer Foundation in 1944. For more than sixty-five years the Meyer Foundation has identified, listened to, and invested in visionary leaders and effective community-based nonprofit organizations that work to create lasting improvements in the lives of low-income people in the Washington, D.C. metropolitan region. The foundation offers program, operating, and capital support in four priority program areas: education, healthy communities, economic security, and a strong nonprofit sector. In the area of health, the foundation funds programming that facilitates the following outcomes for low-income people in the Washington, D.C. metropolitan area: access to high-quality primary care that integrates mental and behavioral health care and eliminates health disparities; access to affordable places to live, healthful food to eat, and services that promote health and personal safety; public policies at the state and local level that are aimed at strengthening the safety net, reducing poverty, and improving lives. The foundation funds clinics, social-service organizations, community-organizing groups, and multi-issue research and advocacy groups and gives priority to issues such as homelessness, child abuse, domestic violence, and rape. In the case of service organizations, the foundations gives priority to those who track participant outcomes with quantitative and qualitative measures. Letters of Intent (LOIs) may be submitted through the foundation's online application system twice a year, in January and June; exact deadline dates may vary from year to year. Applicants will receive an email confirming receipt of their LOI within two to three weeks of submission and will be notified two months after the LOI deadline whether or not they will be invited to submit a full proposal for the board meetings in April and October. Prospective applicants should visit the foundation's website for detailed funding guidelines and current deadline dates before submitting an LOI.

Requirements: Eligible applicants must be 501(c)3 organizations that are located within and primarily serve the Washington, D.C. region defined by the foundation to include the following geographic areas: Washington, D.C; Montgomery and Prince George's counties in Maryland; Arlington, Fairfax, and Prince William counties in Virginia; and the cities of Alexandria, Falls Church, and Manassas Park, Virginia. The foundation looks for organizations that demonstrate visionary and talented leadership, effectiveness, sustainability, and long-term impact.

Restrictions: The foundation does not fund medical or scientific research, organizations or programs focused on a single disease or medical condition, capital for construction or development of housing, start-up housing developers, operating support for housing developers, AIDS-related programs (the foundation supports these exclusively through the Washington AIDS Partnership), government agencies, for-profit businesses, individuals (including scholarships or other forms of financial assistance), special events or conferences, or endowments.

Geographic Focus: All States

Amount of Grant: 1,500 - 50,000 USD

Samples: Calvary Women's Services, Washington, D.C., $25,000—general operating support; Anacostia Watershed Society, Bladensburg, Maryland, $30,000—to support general operations over two years; Arlington Free Clinic, Arlington, Virginia, $35,000—to support general operations.

Contact: Julie Rogers, President; (202) 483-8294; fax (202) 328-6850; jrogers@meyerfdn.org

Internet: http://www.meyerfoundation.org/our-programs/grantmaking/healthy-communities

Sponsor: Meyer Foundation

1250 Connecticut Avenue, Northwest, Suite 800

Washington, D.C. 20036

Meyer Foundation Strong Nonprofit Sector Grants 1313

Eugene Meyer was an investment banker, public servant under seven U.S. presidents, and owner and publisher of the Washington Post. His wife Agnes Ernst Meyer was an accomplished journalist, author, lecturer, and citizen activist. Eugene and Agnes created the Meyer Foundation in 1944. For more than sixty-five years the Meyer Foundation has identified, listened to, and invested in visionary leaders and effective community-based nonprofit organizations that work to create lasting improvements in the lives of low-income people in the Washington, D.C. metropolitan region. The foundation offers program, operating, and capital support in four program areas: education, healthy communities, economic security, and a strong nonprofit sector—this final area is intended to strengthen nonprofits' leadership, impact, and sustainability. Retention and attraction of capable staff and board members, an increased ability by the nonprofit sector to document and communicate the impact of their work, recognition of nonprofits by government and business leaders as essential partners in improving the lives of low-income people in the D.C. metropolitan region, financial stability of nonprofits, and increased levels of philanthropy from individual and institutional donors are among the desired outcomes of the foundation's Strong Nonprofit Sector Grants. The foundation will fund the following types of programs and/or organizations: professional-development programs (provided these are designed with input from nonprofit executives) for executive directors, emerging leaders, and boards; efforts to increase individual philanthropy in the region and to help nonprofits become more effective at attracting contributions and other types of support; nationally significant research that highlights the unique challenges and needs of nonprofit executive directors and explores how to create stronger support systems for them; programs to build a nonprofit's communications capacity to better demonstrate their impact; region-wide organizations that strengthen the voice and visibility of the nonprofit sector and enable it to serve in broader community leadership roles; and organizations that encourage grant-makers to work together more effectively to be more responsive to needs of grantees and to serve as champions of the region's nonprofit sector. Letters of Intent (LOIs) may be submitted through the foundation's online application system twice a year, in January and June; exact deadline dates may vary from year to year. Applicants will receive an email confirming receipt of their LOI within two to three weeks of submission and will be notified two months after the LOI deadline whether or not they will be invited to submit a full proposal for the board meetings in April and October. Prospective applicants should visit the foundation's website for detailed funding guidelines and current deadline dates before submitting an LOI. The foundation also addresses the desired outcomes for the Strong Nonprofit Sector program area through its Management Assistance Program (MAP), Benevon grants, and the Exponent Award. Participation in these programs is limited to current grantees.

Requirements: Eligible applicants must be 501(c)3 organizations that are located within and primarily serve the Washington, D.C. region defined by the foundation to include the following geographic areas: Washington, D.C; Montgomery and

Prince George's counties in Maryland; Arlington, Fairfax, and Prince William counties in Virginia; and the cities of Alexandria, Falls Church, and Manassas Park, Virginia. The foundation looks for organizations that demonstrate visionary and talented leadership, effectiveness, sustainability, and long-term impact.

Restrictions: The foundation does not fund the following types of requests and/ or organizations: organizations which provide technology support, hardware, or software for nonprofits; volunteer centers; capacity-building initiatives and organizations that are not region-wide or that serve a small number or a sub-sector of nonprofits (with the exception of initiatives to strengthen the nonprofit sector in Prince George's County, Maryland); government agencies, for-profit businesses, individuals (including scholarships or other forms of financial assistance), scientific or medial research, special events or conferences, or endowments.

Geographic Focus: All States

Amount of Grant: 1,500 - 50,000 USD

Samples: Maryland Association of Nonprofit Organizations, Baltimore, Maryland, $20,000—to support the executive search; Center for Social Impact Communication, Georgetown University, Arlington, Virginia, $50,000—to support a storytelling initiative for Meyer grantees; Grantmakers for Effective Organizations, Washington, D.C., $25,000—to support general operations and 2013 membership dues.

Contact: Julie Rogers; (202) 483-8294; fax (202) 328-6850; jrogers@meyerfdn.org

Internet: http://www.meyerfoundation.org/our-programs/grantmaking/strong-nonprofit-sector

Sponsor: Meyer Foundation

1250 Connecticut Avenue, Northwest, Suite 800

Washington, D.C. 20036

Meyer Memorial Trust Emergency Grants   1314

Emergency Grants are intended for sudden, unanticipated and unavoidable challenges that, if not addressed immediately, could threaten an organization's stability and/or ability to achieve its mission. Examples of emergencies would include: natural disaster; theft or damage to equipment required to operate core programs; or an accident or unexpected occurrence that causes facilities to be inaccessible or programs unable to be operated until the situation is resolved. Emergency proposals can be considered at any program meeting. The application and frequently asked questions are available at the Trust's website.

Requirements: Grants are awarded to 501(c)3 nonprofit organizations in Oregon and Clark County, Washington.

Restrictions: Processing grant requests may take up to 45 days. MMT's Emergency Grants are not intended to address an organization's failure to comply with legal requirements or problems that can be attributed to organizational neglect; failure to plan for likely contingencies, such as the breakdown of aging equipment; or to replace a gradual loss of organizational funding. In addition, the Emergency Grant program cannot be used solely to expedite the standard processing time for a Responsive or Grassroots Grants application.

Geographic Focus: Oregon, Washington

Amount of Grant: 7,500 - 100,000 USD

Samples: Port Orford Public Library Foundation, Curry, Oregon, $25,000 - to provide core support to offset unexpected emergency expenses; Boys and Girls Clubs of Central Oregon, Deschutes, Oregon, $30,000 - to provide support for operations during temporary club relocation; United Community Action Network, Douglas, Oregon, $15,000 - to replace the central phone system that provides information and referral for basic needs service in Douglas County.

Contact: Maddelyn High; (503) 228-5512; maddelyn@mmt.org

Internet: http://www.mmt.org/program/emergency-grants

Sponsor: Meyer Memorial Trust

425 NW 10th Avenue, Suite 400

Portland, OR 97209

Meyer Memorial Trust Grassroots Grants   1315

The Grassroots Grants program is designed to give smaller organizations (often without development departments) an opportunity to compete for grants from MMT. Focus areas include: health and human services; arts and culture; environmental conservation; education; and public affairs. Applications may be submitted at any time but proposals are collected for consideration on the 15th of March, July and October. Grants of $1,000 to $40,000 are made three to four months later: in June, October and February. Grant periods may be one to two years in length. A list of previous funded projects is available at the Trust's website.

Requirements: Grants are awarded to 501(c)3 nonprofit organizations in Oregon and Clark County, Washington. Organizations must apply through the Trust's online application process.

Geographic Focus: Oregon, Washington

Date(s) Application is Due: Mar 15; Jul 15; Oct 15

Amount of Grant: 1,000 - 25,000 USD

Samples: Friends of Latimer Quilt and Textile Center, Tillamook, Oregon, $8,000 - for capital improvements to the exhibition center; Hand 2 Mouth, Portland, Oregon, $20,000 - for infrastructure to support the theater company's artistic quality and expand its reach to smaller rural communities; Redmond Council for Senior Citizens, Redmond, Oregon, $12,000 - for capital repairs to the center.

Contact: Maddelyn High; (503) 228-5512; maddelyn@mmt.org

Internet: http://www.mmt.org/program/grassroots-grants

Sponsor: Meyer Memorial Trust

425 NW 10th Avenue, Suite 400

Portland, OR 97209

Meyer Memorial Trust Responsive Grants   1316

Responsive Grants are awarded in the areas of human services; health; affordable housing; community development; conservation and environment; public affairs; arts and culture; and education. Funding ranges from $40,000 to $300,000, with grants periods from one to three years in length. Responsive grants help support many kinds of projects, including core operating support, building and renovating facilities, and strengthening organizations. There are two stages of consideration before Responsive Grants are awarded. Initial Inquiries are accepted at any time through MMT's online grants application. Applicants that pass initial approval are invited to submit full proposals. The full two-step proposal investigation usually takes five to seven months. Final decisions on Responsive Grants are made by trustees monthly, except in January, April and August. Additional information about the application process, along with the online application, is available at the website.

Requirements: Support is available to 501(c)3 nonprofit organizations in Oregon and Clark County, Washington.

Restrictions: Funding is not available for sectarian or religious organizations for religious purposes, or for animal welfare organizations, or projects that primarily benefit students of a single K-12 school (unless the school is an independent alternative school primarily serving low-income and/or special needs populations). Funding is also not available for individuals or for endowment funds, annual campaigns, general fund drives, special events, sponsorships, direct replacement funding for activities previously supported by federal, state, or local public sources, deficit financing, acquisition of land for conservation purposes (except through Program Related Investments), or hospital capital construction projects (except through Program Related Investments).

Geographic Focus: Oregon, Washington

Amount of Grant: 40,000 - 300,000 USD

Contact: Maddelyn High; (503) 228-5512; maddelyn@mmt.org

Internet: http://www.mmt.org/program/responsive-grants

Sponsor: Meyer Memorial Trust

425 NW 10th Avenue, Suite 400

Portland, OR 97209

Meyer Memorial Trust Special Grants   1317

From time to time, Meyer Memorial Trust issues Requests for Proposals (RFPs) in targeted, short-term programs that address immediate pressing needs in the nonprofit community. Nonprofits may subscribe to their email announcements to be notified when RFPs are issued. A list of previously funded projects is posted on the Trust's website.

Requirements: Grants are awarded to 501(c)3 nonprofit organizations in Oregon and Clark County, Washington.

Geographic Focus: Oregon, Washington

Amount of Grant: Up to 50,000 USD

Contact: Maddelyn High; (503) 228-5512; maddelyn@mmt.org

Internet: http://www.mmt.org/program/rfp

Sponsor: Meyer Memorial Trust

425 NW 10th Avenue, Suite 400

Portland, OR 97209

MGN Family Foundation Grants   1318

The MGN Family Foundation makes grants to qualified 501(c)3 organizations specializing in the following areas: education; health care and medical research; children in need; armed service personnel. Areas of particular interest include: colleges, universities and private schools, examples would be: to fund a chair to provide lecturers in literature, philosophy or the arts, and provide scholarships; hospitals and clinics that specialize in excellent patient care and continuing medical research such as Memorial Sloan-Kettering Cancer Center and the Mayo and Cleveland Clinics are other examples, also under consideration would be hospice organizations that provide palliative care to the dying; organizations that support children in need whether due to emotional, physical abuse, neglect or disadvantaged circumstances. Support can be for basic necessities such as food, shelter, education, medical as well as, spiritual and emotional counseling; in light of recent events, this Foundation would like to offer assistance to our servicemen/ servicewomen and their families through those charities which give support to their unique needs. The examples provided above reflect the true mission and goals of the MGN Foundation. There should be no exclusions due to race or creed, provided all applicants have a strong moral base and core values in the areas of education, health care, welfare of children and service personnel and their families. The Foundation Board meets semi-annually in May and November. Applications are due by April 1st and October 1st. Application form is available online.

Requirements: Qualified 501(c)3 organizations specializing in the following areas: education; health care and medical research; children in need; armed service personnel. To apply, submit seven (7) sets of the following items: Grant application form completed, dated, and signed by the Chief Executive Officer or Chairman of the Board of the organization; list of Board of Directors; Financial Statement (audited if available), for the most recent complete fiscal year; copy of IRS 501(c)3 Determination Letter. If you wish, you may submit your proposal in a narrative format of not more than two pages in addition to the completed application form. Optional materials may be submitted but are not required (such as brochures discussing or depicting the activities of the organization).

Restrictions: Do not staple materials or place them in a bound notebook.
Geographic Focus: All States
Date(s) Application is Due: Apr 1; Oct 1
Amount of Grant: 1,000 - 10,000 USD
Contact: Pamela Nothstein; (843) 937-4614; grantinquiries7@wachovia.com
Internet: https://www.wachovia.com/foundation/v/index.jsp?vgnextoid=6107 8689fb0aa110VgnVCM1000004b0d1872RCRD&vgnextfmt=default
Sponsor: MGN Family Foundation
16 Broad Street (SC1000)
Charleston, SC 29401

MHRC Operating Grants 1319

Grants in aid of research are designed to defray the normal direct costs of research including, among others, personnel costs, supplies and expendable materials, experimental animals, equipment costing less than $C5000, computer costs, and publication costs. Up to five percent of the operating grant may be used for travel related to the investigator's research program. Grants are normally awarded for one year. The council gives priority to new investigators and new projects. The starting date for successful grants is July 1.

Requirements: Normally only investigators holding academic appointments or equivalent in the province of Manitoba are eligible to apply. Investigators who do not hold academic appointments should consult with the council to establish their eligibility before applying.

Restrictions: Individuals holding continuing operating grants from the council are not eligible to apply for other operating grants that would become effective during the tenure of their present grants. Expenditures for student and postdoctoral salaries will not be considered on operating grants.
Geographic Focus: All States, Canada
Amount of Grant: Up to 100,000 CAD
Contact: Contact; (204) 775-1096; fax (204) 786-5401; mhrc@cc.umanitoba.ca
Internet: http://www.umanitoba.ca/academic_support/MHRC/PROGRAMS.HTM#contents
Sponsor: Manitoba Health Research Council
770 Bannatyne Avenue
Winnipeg, MB R3E 0W3 Canada

Michael and Susan Dell Foundation Grants 1320

The Michael and Susan Dell Foundation's primary goal is to support and initiate programs that directly serve the needs of children living in urban poverty. The Foundation focuses on education, health, and family economic stability to help ensure that underprivileged children escape poverty to become healthy, productive adults. Priority is given to initiatives addressing children's health, education and microfinance, as well as initiatives in India and Central Texas that specifically address the needs of children. Grant amounts vary, but generally the Foundation does not fund more than 25% of a project's budget or more than 10% of an organization's total annual operating expenses.

Requirements: Before beginning a formal grant application, organizations must meet basic eligibility requirements for funding, then submit an online grant proposal via the Foundation website. The proposal will be reviewed, then the organization will receive an emailed response to the proposal within six weeks. Organizations are encouraged to review the Foundation's priorities before beginning the proposal.

They are also encouraged to review the master grant list page for more in-depth explanations, including specific instructions for the online grant proposal.

Restrictions: Proposals must be submitted through the Foundation's online form. Proposals by mail are not accepted. In general, the Foundation does not support programs or organizations that fall outside of their key focus areas, nor does it accept proposals to support individuals, medical research projects, event fundraisers or sponsorships, endowments, or lobbying of any kind.
Geographic Focus: Texas, India, South Africa
Contact: Janet Mountain; (512) 732-2765; fax (512) 600-5501; info@msdf.org
Internet: http://www.msdf.org/grants/Grant_Application
Sponsor: Michael and Susan Dell Foundation
P.O. Box 163867
Austin, TX 78716-3867

Michael Reese Health Trust Core Grants 1321

The primary focus of the Michael Reese Health Trust is to improve the health status and well-being of vulnerable populations in the Chicago metropolitan area. The Health Trust is committed to supporting community-based health-related services and education that are effective, accessible, affordable, and culturally competent. It is especially interested in efforts to address the barriers that prevent vulnerable groups from accessing quality health care, and in programs that deliver comprehensive, coordinated services. Each year, the Health Trust awards a small number of Core grants. Core grants are larger, multi-year grants designed to strengthen both program quality and organizational capacity. Organizations approved by Health Trust staff may request up to $100,000 a year for each of three years for a total of up to $300,000.

Requirements: Nonprofit organizations operating in the Chicago metropolitan area are eligible to apply, but preference is given to organizations within the City of Chicago. The applicant must have a 501(c)3 and non-private foundation determination letter from the Internal Revenue Service and be designated as a public charity under section 509(a)1 or 509(a)2, of the Internal Revenue Code. Generally, the Health Trust does not provide grants to 509(a)3 "supporting organizations." Organizations must be non-discriminatory in the hiring of staff and in providing services on the basis of race, religion, gender, sexual orientation, age, national origin or disability. Qualified applicants must have prior approval from Health Trust staff to submit a Core grant request. Contact the Program Officer by phone or by email to discuss how your organization would use a Core grant. Once staff approval has been obtained, the sponsor will send an invitation to submit a Letter of Inquiry for a Core grant through its online application process. The Health Trust awards grants twice a year. The submission deadlines for Letters of Inquiry are June 15 (for grants to run January 1 through December 31) and December 15 (for grants to run July 1 through June 30). If the due date falls on a weekend, they will accept submissions until 5:00pm the following business day. Core grants should focus on the following: quality of services; planning for and supporting staff, volunteers and activities fundamental to the organization's health-related mission; mission-related infrastructure needs; and/or sustainability of the agency and its health services. Use of evidence-based practices or using the Core grant to systematically learn about and implement evidence-based practices is encouraged. Participation in this program requires a willingness to share findings and lessons learned in order to assist other Health Trust grantees and others in the field.

Restrictions: Grants do not support: lobbying, propaganda, or other attempts to influence legislation; sectarian purposes (programs that promote or require a religious doctrine); capital needs, such as buildings, renovations, vehicles, and major equipment; durable medical equipment; fundraising events, including sponsorship, tickets, and advertising; or, debt reduction; individual and scholarship support. In general, the Health Trust does not provide endowment support.
Geographic Focus: Illinois
Date(s) Application is Due: Jun 15; Dec 15
Amount of Grant: Up to 300,000 USD
Contact: Jennifer M. Rosenkranz, (312) 726-1008; fax (312) 726-2797; jrosenkranz@healthtrust.net
Internet: http://www.healthtrust.net/content/how-apply/new-applicants/application-procedures
Sponsor: Michael Reese Health Trust
150 North Wacker Drive, Suite 2320
Chicago, IL 60606

Michael Reese Health Trust Responsive Grants 1322

The primary focus of the Michael Reese Health Trust is to improve the health status and well-being of vulnerable populations in the Chicago metropolitan area. The Health Trust is committed to supporting community-based health-related services and education that are effective, accessible, affordable, and culturally competent. It is especially interested in efforts to address the barriers that prevent vulnerable groups from accessing quality health care, and in programs that deliver comprehensive, coordinated services. Responsive grants generally range from $25,000-$60,000. The Health Trust will entertain requests for program support and general operating and for both one-year and multi-year projects. However, multi-year grants are generally considered for organizations that have received significant prior Health Trust support. Requests may be for continuation or expansion of a current program, or a new program.

Requirements: Nonprofit organizations operating in the Chicago metropolitan area are eligible to apply, but preference is given to organizations within the City of Chicago. The applicant must have a 501(c)3 and non-private foundation determination letter from the Internal Revenue Service and be designated as a public charity under section 509(a)1 or 509(a)2, of the Internal Revenue Code. Generally, the Health Trust does not provide grants to 509(a)3 "supporting organizations." Organizations must be non-discriminatory in the hiring of staff and in providing services on the basis of race, religion, gender, sexual orientation, age, national origin or disability. The Health Trust awards grants twice a year. The submission deadlines for Letters of Inquiry are June 15 (for grants to run January 1 through December 31) and December 15 (for grants to run July 1 through June 30). If the due date falls on a weekend, they will accept submissions until 5:00pm the following business day.

Restrictions: Grants do not support: lobbying, propaganda, or other attempts to influence legislation; sectarian purposes (programs that promote or require a religious doctrine); capital needs, such as buildings, renovations, vehicles, and major equipment; durable medical equipment; fundraising events, including sponsorship, tickets, and advertising; or, debt reduction; individual and scholarship support. In general, the Health Trust does not provide endowment support.

Geographic Focus: Illinois
Date(s) Application is Due: Jun 15; Dec 15
Amount of Grant: 25,000 - 60,000 USD
Contact: Jennifer M. Rosenkranz, Senior Program Officer for Responsive Grants; (312) 726-1008; fax (312) 726-2797; jrosenkranz@healthtrust.net
Internet: http://www.healthtrust.net/content/how-apply/new-applicants/grantmaking-guidelines
Sponsor: Michael Reese Health Trust
150 North Wacker Drive, Suite 2320
Chicago, IL 60606

Michigan Arts Organization Development Program Grants   1323
The program provides funding to small to midsized professional, arts-producing organizations to achieve increased levels of financial support and administrative stability, and to expand delivery of services. The two categories of grants provided are Strategic Planning and Administrative Development. Annual deadline dates may vary; contact program staff for exact dates.

Requirements: Professional arts-producing organizations in Michigan that meet the following criteria may apply development program: have produced or presented in each of the three fiscal years prior to the date of application; have an operating budget under $250,000 at the time of application; have administrative and artistic staff sufficient to satisfy program requirements; and have either an audit or review of financial statements prepared by an independent certified public accountant. Organizations that have successfully completed multiyear business/strategic plans through this program or completed a planning process within the past two years may apply for implementation grants.

Restrictions: No part of the net earnings may benefit a private individual.
Geographic Focus: Michigan
Date(s) Application is Due: May 1
Amount of Grant: 25,000 - 10,000 USD
Contact: Coordinator; (517) 241-4011; fax (517) 241-3979; artsinfo@michigan.gov
Internet: http://www.michigan.gov/hal/0,1607,7-160-18833_18834_18842—,00.html
Sponsor: Michigan Council for Arts and Cultural Affairs
300 N. Washington Square
Lansing, MI 48913

Michigan Local Art Agencies and Service Programs   1324
This program is intended to support those projects that are often unique to local arts agencies, regional, or statewide service providers in their efforts to promote, coordinate, fund, and/or improve the climate for the arts and cultural activities in their communities. Such activities include calendars of events, coordinated booking, regranting, cultural planning, workshops and conferences, board development, technical services, coordinated management, facility operations, etc. Annual deadline dates may vary; contact program staff for exact dates.

Requirements: Eligible to apply are local Michigan arts agencies and regional or statewide service organizations, which are defined as public or private nonprofit councils, commissions, societies, or organizations that, by their charters and operating policies, are publicly accountable to provide financial and/or service support for the arts in the communities that they serve. Applicants must provide a cash match of at least 50 percent of the grant amount requested. The remainder of the match requirement may be in any combination of cash and/or in-kind contributions.

Restrictions: No part of the net earnings may benefit a private individual. Funding may not exceed one-third of a project's total cost. State funds may not be used as a match. The same matching funds may not be utilized in more than one project application.
Geographic Focus: Michigan
Date(s) Application is Due: May 1
Amount of Grant: Up to 40,000 USD
Contact: Program Contact; (517) 241-4011; fax (517) 241-3979
Internet: http://www.michigan.gov/hal/0,1607,7-160-18833_18834_18840—,00.html
Sponsor: Michigan Council for Arts and Cultural Affairs
300 N. Washington Square
Lansing, MI 48913

Microsoft Community Affairs Puget Sound Grants   1325
Microsoft provides direct grants and matching support to a broad range of nonprofit organizations that address community needs in the Puget Sound region. Organizations with missions and work that align with funding areas - human services, arts and culture, civic affairs, work-force development, and K-12 math education - can apply. Human services focus is on assisting people in need to move toward self sufficiency. Arts and culture funding supports visual, literary, and performing arts, as well as cultural organizations such as science and history museums. Civic affairs funding supports organizations and projects that promote civic engagement, voter registration, and public policy education. Workforce development funding provides technology that will transform education, foster local innovation, and enable jobs. Education funding helps to improve middle school student academic performance and participation in math. Types of support include employee matching grants to health and human service organizations, general operating support, and capital grants. Applications for donations of software to Washington State nonprofits are considered on an ongoing basis. Grant proposals from community organizations are accepted throughout the year; proposals are requested by the listed application deadline to coincide with meeting schedules.

Requirements: The corporation contributes cash and software to 501(c)3 nonprofits in the Puget Sound, WA, area.

Restrictions: Ineligible organizations and projects include: individuals; private enterprises (for profit); private educational institutions; hospitals or medical clinics (though hospitals or medical clinics designated as Community Health Center Programs by the U.S. Department of Health are eligible to apply); private foundations; political, religious, or fraternal organizations; amateur or professional sports groups, teams, or events; conferences or symposia; or endowments.
Geographic Focus: Washington
Date(s) Application is Due: Oct 31
Samples: Elderhealth Northwest (Seattle, WA)—to construct low-cost housing units for elderly people, $50,000; Urban Enterprise Ctr (Seattle, WA)—to foster effective dialogues on race and to expand job creation and economic development in the Central and Rainier Valley neighborhoods of Seattle, $25,000; Washington Early Learning Foundation (Seattle, WA)—for a statewide public-awareness campaign on early childhood development, $15,000; Boys and Girls Clubs of King County (Seattle, WA)—for its capital campaign, $175,000.
Contact: Bruce Brooks, Director of Community Affairs; (425) 936-8185; fax (425) 936-7329; upinfo@microsoft.com or giving@microsoft.com
Internet: http://www.microsoft.com/About/CorporateCitizenship/Citizenship/giving/programs/grants.mspx
Sponsor: Microsoft Corporation
One Microsoft Way
Redmond, WA 98052-6399

Miles of Hope Breast Cancer Foundation Grants   1326
The Fund provides programs and support services for women and families in the Hudson Valley, New York, affected by breast cancer. All funds raised for the Foundation are used in the Hudson Valley. The Miles of Hope Breast Cancer Foundation is currently offering grants for projects in the areas of breast health and breast cancer education, outreach, screening, treatment and support projects.

Requirements: Services must be provided in the eight counties served by the Miles of Hope Breast Cancer Foundation, which include: Columbia, Dutchess, Greene, Orange, Putnam, Rockland, Westchester and Ulster.
Restrictions: Project must be specific to breast health and/or breast cancer. Applicants must be a U.S. nonprofit (federally tax-exempt) organization. Nonprofit organizations, known educational institutions (i.e. college or university), government agencies, and Indian tribes are eligible. Equipment costs, if applicable, may not exceed 30% of direct costs and should be used exclusively on this project. Salaries, if requested, are for personnel related to this project only and not the general work of the employee. Funds will not be awarded to capital campaigns
Geographic Focus: New York
Contact: Program Administrator; (845) 527-6884 or (845) 264-2005; info@ milesofhopebcf.org
Internet: http://www.milesofhopebcf.org/funds.html#grants
Sponsor: Miles of Hope Breast Cancer Foundation
P.O. Box 405
La Grangeville, NY 12540

Miller Brewing Corporate Contributions Program Grants   1327
The corporate contributions program funds programs of nonprofit organizations in corporate operating communities. Applicants should call the local Miller community affairs manager to discuss an idea before submitting a proposal. The corporation also supports the Thurgood Marshall Scholarship Fund, which provides four-year merit scholarships to students attending the 44 historically black public colleges and universities, and two-year scholarships to law schools at Texas Southern, North Carolina Central, Southern, and Howard Universities; and ?Adelante! U.S. Education Leadership Fund, which awards scholarships to Hispanic-American students.
Requirements: Nonprofits must be near Miller operating locations, in Irwindale, CA; Albany, GA; Trenton, OH; Eden, NC; Fort Worth, TX; and Milwaukee, WI.
Geographic Focus: California
Amount of Grant: 1,000 - 15,000 USD
Samples: Advocates of Ozaukee (West Bend, WI)—for a round-the-clock crisis line and other services for victims of domestic violence, $15,000; Goodwill Industries of Southeastern Wisconsin (Milwaukee, WI)—to purchase a vehicle for a program that provides elderly people with assistance with errands and shopping, $10,000; America's Second Harvest-Milwaukee (WI)—for a nutrition program for elderly people, $15,000; COA Youth and Family Ctrs (Milwaukee, WI)—for GED programs and job-readiness training and placement services, $15,000.
Contact: Grants Administrator; (414) 931-3110; fax (414) 931-6352
Internet: http://www.millerbrewing.com/inthecommunity/default.asp
Sponsor: Miller Brewing Corporation
3939 W Highland Boulevard
Milwaukee, WI 53201-0482

Millipore Foundation Grants   1328
The foundation supports nonprofit organizations in company operating communities in five main areas: education and research, social services, culture, health care, and public policy. Types of support include general operating support, employee matching gifts, and employee-related scholarships. Applications are accepted throughout the year.
Requirements: 501(c)3 tax-exempt organizations are eligible.
Geographic Focus: All States
Amount of Grant: 2,500 - 5,000 USD
Contact: Charleen Johnson, Executive Director; (978) 715-1268; fax (978) 715-1385; Charleen_Johnson@millipore.com
Internet: http://www.millipore.com/corporate/milliporefoundation.nsf/ foundationhome
Sponsor: Millipore Foundation
290 Concord Road
Billerica, MA 01821-7037

Millstone Foundation Grants   1329
The foundation awards grants to eligible Missouri nonprofit organizations in its areas of interest, including education and higher education, Jewish services, and Israel. Types of support include annual campaigns, continuing support, deficit financing, emergency funds, general operating support, and research grants. There are no application forms or deadlines.
Requirements: Missouri tax-exempt organizations are eligible. Preference is given to requests from Saint Louis.
Geographic Focus: Missouri

Amount of Grant: Up to 100,000,000 USD
Contact: Colleen Millstone, Director; (314) 961-8500
Sponsor: Millstone Foundation
7701 Forsyth Boulevard, Suite 925
Saint Louis, MO 63105-1842

Mimi and Peter Haas Fund Grants   1330
The Mimi and Peter Haas Fund supports early childhood development. Their primary focus is for activities that provide San Francisco's young (ages 2-5), low-income children and their families with access to high-quality early childhood programs that are part of a comprehensive, coordinated system. The Fund recognizes the importance of connecting the work of its direct service grants to the ongoing discussions of public policy and seek specific opportunities to collaborate with organizations to improve early childhood settings. The Fund will also continue trustee-initiated grantmaking to arts, education, public affairs, and health and human services organizations. Applicants should contact the trustee office to begin the application process. There are no particular application forms or deadlines with which to adhere.
Geographic Focus: California
Amount of Grant: Up to USD
Contact: Lynn Merz, Executive Director; (415) 296-9249; fax (415) 296-8842; mphf@mphf.org
Sponsor: Mimi and Peter Haas Fund
201 Filbert Street, 5th Floor
San Francisco, CA 94133-3238

Minneapolis Foundation Community Grants   1331
The foundation awards grants throughout Minnesota. Eligible activities include policy and systems change work in the following areas: affordable housing; economic opportunity; educational achievement; and the health and well-being of children, youth, and families. The foundation also focuses on systems and policy work that addresses the intersection of issues, such as housing and health. Types of support include program/project support, operating support, capital support (limited to the seven-county metro area); and some multiyear grants. Proposals are accepted throughout the year. Guidelines are available online.
Requirements: 501(c)3 nonprofit organizations located in the seven-county metropolitan area of Minneapolis and Saint Paul may apply.
Restrictions: The foundation does not fund individuals, organizations/activities outside of Minnesota, conference registration fees, memberships, direct religious activities, political organizations or candidates, direct fundraising activities, telephone solicitations, courtesy advertising, or financial deficits.
Geographic Focus: Minnesota
Date(s) Application is Due: Mar 15; Sep 15
Contact: Paul Verrette, Senior Grants Administrator; (612) 672-3836; pverrette@mplsfoundation.org
Internet: http://www.mplsfoundation.org/grants/guidelines.htm
Sponsor: Minneapolis Foundation
800 IDS Center, 80 South Eighth Street
Minneapolis, MN 55402

Miranda Lux Foundation Grants   1332
The foundation supports promising proposals for preschool education through community college programs in San Francisco, CA. Areas of interest include vocational education and training, adult basic education, literacy and reading programs, employment services, and children and youth services. Grants are awarded in support of general operating costs, continuing support, equipment, program/project development, seed money, fellowships, internships, scholarship funds, and matching funds. There are no application forms or deadlines. Proposals should be submitted five weeks prior to board meetings, in January, March, June, and September.
Requirements: Grants are awarded in San Francisco, CA.
Restrictions: Support will not be given to individuals or for annual campaigns, emergency funds, deficit financing, building or endowment funds, land acquisition, renovations, research, publications, or loans.
Geographic Focus: California
Amount of Grant: 1,500 - 34,000 USD
Samples: Bay Area Discovery Museum (San Francisco, CA)—for the My Story by the Bay Initiative, $10,000; Arriba Juntos Ctr (San Francisco, CA)—to support the Youth at Work program, $25,000; Youth Assistance Assoc (San Francisco, CA)— for the Auto Technician program, $17,500; YMCA, Embarcadero Branch (San Francisco, CA)—to support an employment readiness training program, $10,000.

Contact: Kenneth Blum, Executive Director; (415) 981-2966; fax (415) 981-5218; admin@mirandalux.org
Internet: http://www.mirandalux.org
Sponsor: Miranda Lux Foundation
57 Post Street, Suite 510
San Francisco, CA 94104-5020

Mississippi Arts Commission Arts-Based Community Development Program Grants 1333

The arts-based community development program responds to the commission's goal to support the development of Mississippi communities through the arts by working to stimulate increased participation in the arts and access to the arts by the entire community; advance community support for arts programs and local understanding of the benefits of the arts to community life; and increase the capacity of Mississippi communities and organizations to use the arts to effect positive community change. The program offers mini-grants, project grants, and operating grants. These grants must be matched dollar for dollar in cash. In addition, as a publicly funded agency, the commission works to ensure that the public at large has access to artistic resources of the state. Services include training seminars and information services, staff consultations, facilitation of board workshops and planning discussions that strengthen the capacities of community arts organizations, and access to national, regional, and statewide information and potential partnerships. Mini-grants and operating grants are paid in two installments: 50 percent as soon as possible following receipt and approval of a properly signed contract, and 50 percent as soon as possible following receipt and approval of the final report. Project grants are also paid in two installments: 75 percent after the contract is signed, and 25 percent after the final report is received. Grantee must submit a final report, which must be postmarked no later than 60 days after the completion of the project or by the deadline date, whichever comes first. Contact program staff for deadlines.
Requirements: Applicants must reside in Mississippi.
Geographic Focus: Mississippi
Amount of Grant: 50 - 25,000 USD
Contact: Beth Batton, Arts-Based Community Development Program Director; (601) 359-6546; bbatton@arts.state.ms
Internet: http://www.arts.state.ms.us/grants_abcd.html
Sponsor: Mississippi Arts Commission
501 North West Street, Suite 1101A
Jackson, MS 39201

Mississippi Arts Commission Arts in Education Program Grants 1334

The goal of the arts in education program is to strengthen education in and through the arts with a focus on promoting sequential, comprehensive arts education in grades K-12 for all students throughout the state. The program offers minigrants, project grants, large-scale project grants, and operating grants, all requiring a dollar-to-dollar match. Mini-grants have quarterly deadlines and are paid in two installments: 50 percent of the grant award as soon as possible following receipt and approval of a properly signed contract, and 50 percent as soon as possible following receipt and approval of the final report. Grantees must submit a final report, which must be postmarked no later than 60 days after the completion of the project or by the deadline date, whichever comes first.
Requirements: Applicants must reside in Mississippi.
Geographic Focus: Mississippi
Amount of Grant: 50 - 25,000 USD
Contact: Wendy Shenefelt, Arts in Education Program Director; (601) 359-6037; wshenefelt@arts.state.ms.us
Internet: http://www.arts.state.ms.us/grants_education.html
Sponsor: Mississippi Arts Commission
501 North West Street, Suite 1101A
Jackson, MS 39201

Missouri Arts Council Community Arts Program Grants 1335

The council assists community arts councils and other local arts coordinating agencies that sponsor programs in more than one art form to provide high-quality arts programs and services to nonmetropolitan areas of the state. To help local arts agencies upgrade their management and sponsorship capabilities, financial assistance is available for projects assistance up to a maximum of 50 percent of the costs of providing programs in the visual arts, music, dance, theater, media, architecture, folk art, arts education, literature, and technical assistance; and salary support for the cost of arts agency administration (funding for part- or full-time salary support is not limited to a specific dollar amount). Assistance is also available to help cover the expenses of an official arts council office. Contact the council for annual deadline dates.
Requirements: Applicants must be nonmetropolitan community arts councils and other local arts coordinating agencies in Missouri, must be nonprofit and tax-exempt, and must be governed by citizen boards. Organizations can request arts agency administration support only in conjunction with project support; funds are not available for arts agency administration only.
Geographic Focus: Missouri
Amount of Grant: 2,000 USD
Contact: Julie Hale, (314) 340-6845 or (866) 407-4752; fax (314) 340-7215; julie.hale@ded.mo.gov
Internet: http://www.missouriartscouncil.org/html/funding.shtml
Sponsor: Missouri Arts Council
815 Olive Street, Suite 16
Saint Louis, MO 63101-1503

Missouri Housing Trust Fund Grants 1336

Grants provide funding to help meet the housing needs of very low-income families and individuals. It provides funding for a variety of eligible activities, including rental housing production, housing and related services for the homeless, and other activities. Grants are awarded for two years. Typically, a Notice of Funding Availability (NOFA) is published during the month of August. The deadline for proposal submission is typically in late October, and recommendations are made to the Commission in January or February. Application forms are available on the Web site.
Requirements: Any Missouri developers or nonprofit organizations involved in housing, community service, or community or economic development may apply. Applicants must demonstrate prior, successful housing experience and have the financial capacity to successfully complete and operate the housing and/or service proposed. Provider of services must have qualified and trained staff, and a successful recording of providing the proposed services.
Geographic Focus: Missouri
Contact: Valori Sanders, (816) 759-7226; vsanders@mhdc.com
Internet: http://www.mhdc.com/housing_trust_fund/index.htm
Sponsor: Missouri Housing Trust Fund
3435 Broadway
Kansas City, MO 64111-2415

Mitsubishi Electric America Foundation Grants 1337

The foundation follows a long tradition of philanthropy by the Mitsubishi Electric America companies. It seeks to contribute to the greater good of society by assisting young Americans with disabilities, through education, technology, and other means, to lead fuller and more productive lives. Requests from all areas of the United States will be considered, though priority will be given to communities where MEA companies are located. A major program emphasis is to advance the independence, productivity, and community inclusion of young people with disabilities. Funding is available for projects and general organizational support. The foundation awards matching grants locally. Concept papers are accepted throughout the year. Invited proposals are due by the listed application deadline. Application and guidelines are available online.
Requirements: Grants are made only to 501(c)3 tax-exempt nonprofits.
Restrictions: The foundation does not support individuals; intermediary organizations; ethnic, fraternal, labor, or political organizations; religious organizations for religious purposes; endowments; the purchase of tickets for fundraising; or advertising, mass mailing, or conference expenses.
Geographic Focus: All States
Date(s) Application is Due: Jul 1
Samples: American Assoc of People with Disabilities (Washington, DC)—for a Congressional internship program that provides internships to college students with disabilities, $222,000 over three years; Easter Seals (Chicago, IL)—for partnerships between six Easter Seals affiliates and local recreation groups that will serve as models for including disabled children and youths in recreational activities, $150,000; Wilderness Inquiry (Minneapolis, MN)—to support inclusive outdoor educational and recreational activities for youths with and without disabilities, in partnership with Girls Scouts and Boy Scouts groups in the Minneapolis-Saint Paul region, and to duplicate those partnerships nationwide, $165,000.
Contact: Program Officer; (703) 276-8240; fax (703) 276-8260
Internet: http://www.meaf.org/apply/priorities.html
Sponsor: Mitsubishi Electric America Foundation
1560 Wilson Boulevard, Suite 1150
Arlington, VA 22209

MLB Tomorrow Fund Grants   1338

The Baseball Tomorrow Grant funds programs, fields, and equipment purchases for youth baseball in the United States and around the world. Grants enable applicants to address needs unique to their communities. The funds may be used to finance a new program, expand or improve an existing program, undertake a new collaborative effort, or obtain facilities or equipment necessary for youth baseball or softball programs. Organizations seeking to implement or improve a youth baseball and/or softball program for youth ages 10 to 16 are encouraged to apply. Grants are awarded on a quarterly basis after a thorough and selective application process which can last from three to six months. The selection process consists of the following steps: letter of inquiry review; application review and evaluation; site visit; and final selection by the Board of Directors. Organizations are encouraged to apply for the grant to fund grant writing for their project, if needed, with information available at the website. The application or letter of inquiry and all supporting materials must be mailed to the MLB New York address.

Requirements: Organizations are encouraged to carefully review the application process before applying. Evaluation criteria are specific to the individual organization's needs, including field lights, travel and and specific instructions and contacts for international applicants. Applicants should also review the frequently asked questions section, application help guide, budget template, and samples of previous grant recipients on the website.

Restrictions: Grants are not a substitute for existing funding or fundraising activities. Grants do not support routine or recurring operating costs or funding for construction or maintenance of buildings.

Geographic Focus: All States, Canada

Date(s) Application is Due: Jan 1; Apr 1; Jul 1; Oct 1

Amount of Grant: 40,000 USD

Contact: Grant Contact; (212) 931-7800; fax (212) 949-5654; btf@mlb.com

Internet: http://mlb.mlb.com/NASApp/mlb/mlb/official_info/community/btf.jsp

Sponsor: Major League Baseball

245 Park Avenue, 31st floor

New York, NY 10167

Modest Needs Non-Profit Grants   1339

The purpose of the grant is to allow small non-profits to appeal directly to the general public for help to afford expenses that will strengthen the programs and services they provide to the communities that they serve. The maximum grant available under this program is $2,500.00, but the foundation will negotiate with the vendor named in the non-profit's documentation to secure the item the organization has requested at the lowest possible price.

Requirements: This grant type is open only to non-profits with gross incomes of at least $50,000.00 but not more than $500,000.00, that file a Form 990-EZ or Form 990, and that have registered with Modest Needs.

Restrictions: Organizations that file Form 990-N 'postcards' are not eligible to apply for this grant. Under this grant type, non-profits may not apply for help to afford fundraising expenses, like the cost to hire a professional fundraiser or the cost to afford some or all of the expenses involved with an annual fundraising dinner.

Geographic Focus: All States

Amount of Grant: Up to 2,500 USD

Contact: Keith Taylor; (212) 463-7042; kptaylor@modestneeds.org

Internet: https://www.modestneeds.org/about-us/grants-types-non-profit.asp

Sponsor: Modest Needs Foundation

115 East 30th Street, FL 1

New York, NY 10016

Molly Bee Fund Grants   1340

The fund awards grants to support nonprofits in its areas of interest, including arts and cultural programs, education, and hospitals. Types of support include general operating support, capital campaigns, building construction/renovation, equipment acquisition, endowment funds, and program-related investments. Giving is primarily in Palm Beach and West Palm Beach, FL, and Cleveland, OH. There are no application forms or deadlines.

Restrictions: Grants are not made to individuals.

Geographic Focus: All States

Amount of Grant: 5,000 - 100,000 USD

Contact: Thomas Allen, (440) 331-8220

Sponsor: Molly Bee Fund

20325 Center Ridge Road, Suite 629

Rocky River, OH 44116

Monfort Family Foundation Grants   1341

The foundation awards general operating grants to Colorado nonprofit organizations in its areas of interest, including education, health and medical research, arts and culture, agriculture, and general charitable giving. Application forms must be obtained.

Requirements: Colorado nonprofits, primarily in Weld County, are eligible.

Restrictions: Grants are not made to individuals.

Geographic Focus: Colorado

Date(s) Application is Due: May 1; Oct 1

Amount of Grant: 5,000 - 100,000 USD

Contact: Dave Evans, Program Contact; (970) 454-1357

Sponsor: Monfort Family Foundation

Box 337300

Greeley, CO 80633

Montana Arts Council Cultural and Aesthetic Project Grants   1342

In 1975, the Montana Legislature set aside a percentage of the Coal Tax to restore murals in the Capitol and support other cultural and aesthetic projects. This unique funding source is a Cultural Trust, with grant money allocated every two years. Grant funds are derived from the interest earned on the Cultural Trust. In 1983, the Legislature established a Cultural and Aesthetic Projects Advisory Committee with 16 members, half appointed by the Montana Arts Council and half by the Montana Historical Society. The committee reviews all grant proposals and makes funding recommendations to the Legislature, which determines who will receive grant funds. Applications must be for cultural and aesthetic projects including, but not limited to, the visual, performing, literary and media arts, history, archaeology, folklore, archives, collections, research, historic preservation and the construction or renovation of cultural facilities. Applications are encouraged for applicants serving rural communities, racial and ethnic groups, people with disabilities, institutionalized populations, youth and the aging.

Requirements: Any person, association, group, or a governmental agency may submit an application for funding. Individuals may apply to special projects using a fiscal agent, which is a 501(c)3 incorporated nonprofit tax-exempt organization that is eligible to apply for Cultural Trust grants. You must contact the Montana Arts Council prior to submitting a grant application if you intend to use a fiscal agent. Proposals must be submitted in one of four categories: (1) Special Projects Requesting $4,500 or Less - organizations that are all-volunteer or employ no more than one half-time person; (2) Special Projects - for the expansion of ongoing programs, adding staff or increasing staff time and for specific cultural and aesthetic activities, services or events of limited duration; (3) Operational Support - for cultural institutions that have been formally organized for at least two years with an ongoing program and with paid professional staff and whose budgets reflect only the cost of continuing their program; (4) Capital Expenditures - for additions to a collection or for acquisition of works of art, artifacts or historical documents, historic preservation, purchase of equipment over $5,000, or the construction or renovation of cultural facilities. For Special Projects $4,500 and Under, Special Projects and Operational Support, each grant dollar is matched with one dollar in cash or in-kind goods and services. For Capital Expenditures, each grant dollar is matched with three dollars in cash or in-kind goods and services. Applications must be received by 5:00 pm of the deadline date.

Restrictions: Hard-copy applications will not be accepted. Applications must be completed online. Funds will not be awarded to support projects created to meet school accreditation standards or other mandated requirements or supplant other funds for current or ongoing programs operated by schools, colleges or universities.

Geographic Focus: Montana

Date(s) Application is Due: Aug 1

Amount of Grant: 2,000 - 15,000 USD

Contact: Kristin Han Burgoyne, (406) 444-6449; kburgoyne@mt.gov

Internet: http://art.mt.gov/orgs/orgs_ca.asp

Sponsor: Montana Arts Council

830 North Warren, First Floor

Helena, MT 59620-2201

Montana Arts Council Organizational Excellence Grants   1343

Grants are awarded every two years to outstanding Montana arts organizations for biennial funding. Eligible to apply are nonprofit organizations that have had 501(c)3 status for at least five years and have at least a half-time paid director. Grant funds may support artistically related expenses, and statewide arts service organizations may apply to support any operational expense. The applicant must match each dollar in grant funds with one dollar in cash. Annual deadline dates may vary; contact program staff for exact dates.

Requirements: Nonprofit organizations and units of government in Montana are eligible to apply.

Restrictions: Grant funds may not be used to fund permanent capital expenditures; purchase equipment, art, or artifacts; establish or develop a cash reserve; establish or add to a permanent endowment; or reduce a deficit.

Geographic Focus: Montana

Amount of Grant: 1,000 - 8,000 USD

Contact: Contact; (406) 444-6430; fax (406) 444-6548; khan@state.mt.us

Internet: http://www.art.state.mt.us/orgs/orgs_excellence.asp

Sponsor: Montana Arts Council

830 North Warren, First Floor

Helena, MT 59620-2201

Montana Community Foundation Grants   1344

The Foundation is committed to improving the lives of Montanans by helping individuals and families achieve their philanthropic goals and by supporting Montana nonprofit organizations. The Foundation has discretionary control over a small number of funds for which the organization maintains competitive grantmaking opportunities for community leaders. Grants range from $5,000 to $50,000.

Restrictions: Unsolicited general grant applications are not accepted, but when there is a competitive grant opportunity the application information is posted on the website.

Geographic Focus: Montana

Samples: Acts of Kindness, Stevensville, Montana, $8,500 - support for Northwest Area Foundation/MCF Horizons Program; American Legion Post 14, Bozeman, Montana, $10,000 - support for new building; and Big Sky Institute for the Advancement of Nonprofits, Helena, Montana, $50,175 - school computers expansion project.

Contact: Cathy Cooney, Program Director; (406) 443-8313, ext. 108; fax (406) 442-0482; ccooney@mtcf.org or info@mtcf.org

Internet: http://www.mtcf.org/receive.html

Sponsor: Montana Community Foundation

101 North Last Chance Gulch, Suite 211

Helena, MT 59601

Montgomery County Community Foundation Grants   1345

The Montgomery County Community Foundation Grants help fund non-profit organizations and agencies in Montgomery County, Indiana. Significant grants have been awarded to organizations such as the Crawfordsville District Public Library, Boys and Girls Club, and the Family Crisis Shelter. Organizations should contact the Foundation for a grant proposal application and other documentation required.

Requirements: A strong proposal will have several or all of the following characteristics: an estimate of who and how many will benefit; show long term potential; address a community problem of some significance for which funding is not covered by the regular budget; present an innovative and practical approach to solve a community problem or project; identify possible future funding, if needed; give evidence of the stability and qualifications of the organization applying; show cooperation within the organization and avoid duplication effort.

Restrictions: The Foundation will usually not fund any of the following: grants to individuals; programs which are religious or sectarian in nature, except when the program is open to the entire community; operating expenses such as salaries and utilities; parades, festivals and sporting events; endowment funds; any propaganda, political or otherwise, attempting to influence legislation or intervene in any political affairs or campaigns; an organization's past debts or existing obligations; or post-event or after-the-fact situations.

Geographic Focus: Indiana

Date(s) Application is Due: May 10

Amount of Grant: Up to 50,000 USD

Samples: Crawfordsville Main Street Program, $48,000 to ensure ongoing growth and fiscal sustainability of Athens of Indiana Arts Studio and Gallery; Animal Welfare League, $17,000 to purchase a pre-owned pickup truck to be used for animal control; Educational Foundation, $20,000 for teacher grants of up to $1,000 each for innovative and imaginative projects that go beyond the normal curriculum; Lew Wallace Preservation Society, $9,500 to produce a Historic Structures Report considered vital for the preservation of significant structures; Boys and Girls Club, $17,000 for operational costs of the After School Program.

Contact: Cheryl Keim, Grant Coordinator; (765) 362-1267; fax (765) 361-0562; cheryl@mccf-in.org

Internet: http://www.mccf-in.org/Granthomenewpage.html

Sponsor: Montgomery County Community Foundation

119 East Main Street

Crawfordsville, IN 47933

MONY Foundation Grants   1346

The foundation awards grants in its areas of interest, including after-school community service and volunteer programs for youth, New York, NY; meeting the essential after-school needs of children and teens at risk, Syracuse, NY; and meeting the essential needs of minority children nationwide (with local MONY sales office). Types of support include employee matching gifts, employee-related scholarships, general operating support, in-kind gifts, matching/challenge support, and program development. Contact headquarters or local office by mail to obtain guidelines.

Restrictions: Grants do not support private foundations; fully participating members of the United Way; religious, fraternal, athletic, social, or veterans' organizations; individuals; capital fund drives; endowments; or deficit financing.

Geographic Focus: All States

Amount of Grant: 1,500 - 10,000 USD

Samples: To be distributed among 19 nonprofit organizations—for awards through the Field Grant Program, which provides fund-raising and financial assistance to groups that offer services to minority children, $95,000.

Contact: Grants Administrator; (212) 708-2468; fax (212) 708-2001; lynn_stekas@mony.com

Internet: http://www.mony.com

Sponsor: MONY Foundation

1740 Broadway, Mail Drop 10-36

New York, NY 10019

Morgan Stanley Foundation Grants   1347

The foundation awards grants to nonprofit organizations in its areas of interest, including education, civic and community development, culture and the arts, and health and welfare. In the area of education, programs are supported that work to strengthen the teaching profession, address adult literacy, and retrain seniors and the disadvantaged. Economic development organizations with innovative programs designed to enhance and broaden the economic stability of communities receive consideration. In the area of health and welfare, applied research, educational programs, and other innovative programs in preventive health care, particularly those targeted to youth and seniors, receive support. Under arts and culture, performing arts and cultural programs in major metropolitan serving areas with outreach potential receive consideration. Types of support include capital campaigns, general operating support, continuing support, employee matching gifts, and in-kind gifts. The foundation prefers to fund project-specific proposals rather than requests for grants to underwrite operating or capital budgets.

Requirements: New York 501(c)3 organizations in company-operating areas are eligible.

Restrictions: Grants do not support United Way member agencies, individuals, endowment or building funds, capital campaigns, deficit financing, equipment acquisition, scholarships, fellowships, special projects, journal advertisements, research, publications, conferences, fund-raising dinners, or benefit events.

Geographic Focus: New York

Amount of Grant: 500 - 25,000 USD

Samples: New York Presbyterian Hospital (New York, NY)—for the capital campaign for the Children's Hospital, $2 million.

Contact: Director of Community Affairs; (212) 259-1235 or (212) 761-4000; fax (212) 259-1253; whatadifference@msdw.com

Internet: http://www.morganstanley.com/about/inside/community.html?page=about

Sponsor: Morgan Stanley Foundation

1601 Broadway, 12th Floor

New York, NY 10019

Moriah Fund Grants   1348

The fund awards grants to nonprofit organizations in its areas of interest, including women's rights, human rights and democracy; community development and education in Israel and Guatemala; and disadvantaged in the United States, with emphasis on housing and family planning. Priority will be given to funding requests for the disadvantaged in Washington, DC. Types of support include continuing support, matching funds, operating budgets, seed money, technical assistance, and program development. Submit a two-page letter of application. The board meets in May and November to consider requests.

Restrictions: Grants do not support political campaigns, private foundations, arts organizations, medical research, or individuals.

Geographic Focus: All States

Date(s) Application is Due: Mar 1; Aug 1

Amount of Grant: 20,000 - 50,000 USD

Samples: Ctr for Community Change (Washington, DC)—for general support, including work on welfare reform and public housing, $70,000;

Washington Regional Assoc of Grantmakers (Washington, DC)—for Community Development Support Collaborative, to revitalize and stabilize low-income, distressed neighborhoods in the District of Columbia, $60,000; Shefa Fund, Tzedek Economic Development Campaign, (Philadelphia, PA)—for matching grant for Local Tzedek Challenge Fund, which facilitates increased investment by Jewish communal organizations in institutions that finance efforts to revitalize low-income communities, $55,000.
Contact: Contact; (202) 783-8488; fax (202) 783-8499; info@moriahfund.org
Internet: http://www.moriahfund.org/grants/index.htm
Sponsor: Moriah Fund
1634 I Street NW, Suite 1000
Washington, D.C. 20006

Morris Stulsaft Foundation Grants   1349

The foundation awards grants to California nonprofits for programs that focus on the needs of homeless children and youth; services for children living in subsidized housing; the needs of children and youth in foster care, especially as they prepare for emancipation; early intervention development programs for children with disabilities; child care for low-income families; and training for child care providers and staff. Types of support include operating budgets, building construction/renovations matching funds, research, special projects, and seed money. There are no application deadlines. Applicant should request an application form. At the full proposal stage, review turn around time is six months.
Requirements: Nonprofits in California counties, including Alameda, Contra Costa, Marin, San Francisco, Santa Clara, and San Mateo, are eligible.
Restrictions: Grants do not support individuals, deficit funding, emergency funding, endowments, fundraising, or special events/benefit dinners.
Geographic Focus: California
Amount of Grant: 5,000 - 15,000 USD
Samples: Dance Palace (CA)—toward dance scholarships for low-income Latino children, $2500; Fort Milky Adventures Rope Course (CA)—to purchase and upgrade equipment for the Ropes Course, $5000; National Junior Tennis League of San Francisco (CA)—to expand summer after-school program for low-income minority children and youth, $7500.
Contact: Contact; (415) 986-7117; fax (415) 986-2521; Stulsaft@aol.com
Internet: http://www.stulsaft.org/approvedgrants.html
Sponsor: Morris Stulsaft Foundation
100 Bush Street, Suite 825
San Francisco, CA 94104-3911

Morton-Kelly Charitable Trust Grants   1350

The trust awards grants to Maine nonprofits in its areas of interest, including historic preservation, arts and culture, education and vocational education, and environment. Types of support include general operating support, continuing support, annual campaigns, capital campaigns, building construction/renovation, endowment funds, equipment acquisition, fellowships, capital campaigns, program development, seed grants, scholarship funds, and research. There are no application forms; submit a letter of request.
Requirements: Maine nonprofit organizations are eligible.
Geographic Focus: All States
Amount of Grant: Up to 209,000 USD
Contact: Program Contact; (207) 775-7271; fax (207) 775-7935
Sponsor: Morton-Kelly Charitable Trust
10 Free Street, Box 4510
Portland, ME 04112

Moses Kimball Fund Grants   1351

The Moses Kimball Fund was established in Massachusetts, in 1925, founded by Helen Kimball, former president of the New England Hospital for Women and Children, in honor of her father. Trustees emphasize grants to organizations which either provide jobs to minorities and disadvantaged members of the Greater Boston community, or links between educational organizations and the needy members of the adjacent communities. Their primary fields of interest include: education; employment services; families; human services; and youth development. Populations served include: children and youth; families; minorities; and the economically disadvantaged. Most recent awards have ranged from $2,000 to $14,000. The annual application deadline for submission is March 1.
Requirements: Fund Trustees accept grant applications between June 1 and March 1 each year. Grant making decisions and distributions are made at the Trustees meeting in April. Any 501(c)3 serving the residents of Massachusetts is eligible to apply.
Geographic Focus: Massachusetts

Date(s) Application is Due: Mar 1
Amount of Grant: 2,000 - 14,000 USD
Samples: Strive Boston Employment, Boston, Massachusetts, $3,000 - general operating support (2014); Tutoring Plus, Cambridge, Massachusetts, $6,000 - general program support (2014); Margaret Fuller Neighborhood Houses, Cambridge, Massachusetts, $6,000 - technology and literacy initiatives (2014).
Contact: Susan Harrington; (617) 523-6531 or (617) 523-6531
Internet: http://www.moseskimballfund.org/
Sponsor: Moses Kimball Fund
230 Congress Street
Boston, MA 02110-2409

Motorola Foundation Grants   1352

Motorola concentrates its giving in the following areas: engineering, technical, science or mathematics programs in K-12 schools or in universities and colleges; programs reaching traditionally under-represented groups in the areas of math, science, engineering and business; programs providing technical assistance, research and statistical information on the state of science and engineering education, or; progams that support the protection and preservation of the environment.
Requirements: All grants are made to 501(c)3 tax-exempt organizations.
Restrictions: Grants may not be made to individuals (scholarships, travel, business loans), religious groups, fraternity or sorority programs, political campaigns, private foundations, benefit events or ads, single disease causes, national health organizations or their local chapters, trade schools, product donations, media projects, capital fund drives, sports sponsorships, or endowment funds.
Geographic Focus: Arizona, California, Florida, Georgia, Illinois, Massachusetts, New Jersey, Pennsylvania, Texas
Amount of Grant: 10,000 - 100,000 USD
Samples: National Ctr for Disability Services, National Business and Disability Council (Albertson, NY)—to develop a publication designed to help employers who hire people with disabilities, $22,540.
Contact: Matthew Blakely, (847) 576-7895; giving@motorola.com
Internet: http://www.motorola.com/content.jsp?globalObjectId=8152
Sponsor: Motorola Foundation
1303 E Algonquin Road
Schaumburg, IL 60196

Motorola Foundation Innovation Generation Collaborative Grants   1353

The Innovation Generation Collaborative Grants Support medium to large-scale STEM education collaborations between two or more non-profit organizations, schools and/or school districts, with joint requests ranging from $150,000 to $500,000. Programming must have nationwide and/or online reach or take place near communities where Motorola has an employee presence: Tempe, Arizona; San Diego, California; Miami, Florida; Chicago, Illinois; Lowell, Massachusetts; New York City and Long Island, New York; Philadelphia, Pennsylvania; or Fort Worth, Texas. Program must demonstrate measurable outcomes & impact on at least 250 primary participants. Grants may be for up to two years of project work starting after June of this year. Grant applications are accepted at the Motorola Foundation website, with a deadline date of April 1st.
Requirements: Any U.S. non-profit organization, school or school district may apply. Programming must have nationwide and/or online reach or take place near communities where Motorola has an employee presence: Tempe, Arizona; San Diego, California; Miami, Florida; Chicago, Illinois; Lowell, Massachusetts; New York City and Long Island, New York; Philadelphia, Pennsylvania; or Fort Worth, Texas. All requests must be partnerships between two or more non-profit organizations or schools. Only prior Motorola Foundation Innovation Generation grant recipients may apply. Organizations will be expected to interact and share program attributes with other grantees through conferences and online forums. Applications must be accompanied by letters of support from each member of the partnership. Funding priority will be placed on partnerships that: focus on a key STEM interest area such as teacher training, girls programming, out-of-school programming or online programs; engage students and teachers in innovative, hands-on activities; teach not only STEM, but also innovative thinking and creative problem-solving skills; focus on girls and underrepresented minorities; engage Motorola employees as volunteers.
Restrictions: Only prior Motorola Foundation Innovation Generation grant recipients may apply.
Geographic Focus: All States
Amount of Grant: 150,000 - 500,000 USD
Samples: Society of Women Engineers, Chicago, IL,—encourages girls in grades K-12 to capture the spirit of innovation and open their eyes and minds to a rewarding profession through a host of events, resources and in-person outreach programs (Out-of-School Programming); Texas Alliance for

Minorities in Engineering (TAME), Austin, TX, TAME Statewide Math and Science Competition engages hundreds of female and underrepresented middle school and high school students from across Texas through individual competition and a Team Design Challenge, encouraging teamwork, leadership, academic achievement and an interest in science and math-related careers. (Out-of—School Programming).
Contact: Matthew Blakely, (847) 576-7895; giving@motorola.com
Internet: http://www.motorola.com/staticfiles/Business/Corporate/US-EN/corporate-responsibility/society/community-investment-education-more-about-innovation-generation-grants.html?globalObjectId=8153
Sponsor: Motorola Foundation
1303 E Algonquin Road
Schaumburg, IL 60196

Motorola Foundation Innovation Generation Grants   1354
The Motorola Foundation's Innovation Generation program equips students with the skills essential to both their lives today and their future success. By making the complex concepts behind math and science real and relevant, students look at their world differently through strengthened problem-solving skills. The Innovation Generation Grants support targeted, innovative STEM education programs for U.S. pre-school through 12th grade students and teachers, with grants ranging from $25,000 to $50,000. Program must: impact at least 100 primary participants, teacher training programs are exempt; demonstrate measurable change in STEM awareness or education. At least 25 percent of total grant dollars will support new programming that has been operating for less than two years and is not simply an expansion of an existing program. At least 15 percent of total grant dollars will support environment-focused programming.
Requirements: Any U.S. non-profit organization, school or school district may apply. Programming must have nationwide and/or online reach or take place near communities where Motorola has an employee presence: Tempe, Arizona; San Diego, California; Miami, Florida; Chicago, Illinois; Lowell, Massachusetts; New York City and Long Island, New York; Philadelphia, Pennsylvania; or Ft. Worth, Texas
Geographic Focus: All States
Date(s) Application is Due: Mar 1
Amount of Grant: 25,000 - 50,000 USD
Samples: Discovery Science Center, Santa Ana, CA.—Future Scientists and Engineers of America develops and instills the thrill and excitement of science, technology, engineering and math through the use of real-world hands-on projects and curricula for 2,000 students grades 4-12 across the nation; National Society of Black Engineers, Alexandria, VA— Summer Engineering Experience for Kids (SEEK) Academy engages hundreds of students across the country in grades 3-8 in team-based, interactive engineering projects designed to increase their aptitude in math and science and their interest in pursuing careers in STEM fields.
Contact: Matthew Blakely, (847) 576-7895; giving@motorola.com
Internet: http://www.motorola.com/staticfiles/Business/Corporate/US-EN/corporate-responsibility/society/community-investment-education-more-about-innovation-generation-grants.html?globalObjectId=8153
Sponsor: Motorola Foundation
1303 E Algonquin Road
Schaumburg, IL 60196

Ms. Foundation for Women Health Grants   1355
The Ms. Foundation for Women supports organizing at grassroots, state and national levels to promote equitable access to health care and education for women and youth. The Foundation delivers strategic funding, technical assistance, and networking support to organizations that are working in their communities and beyond to address the urgent priorities of those most affected by failed health policies, especially low-income women, women of color, immigrant women, women living with HIV/AIDS, and LGBTQ youth. The Foundation strives to build social movements and advance policy and culture change in key areas: reproductive health, rights and justice; sexuality education; and women and AIDS.
Requirements: Applicants must be tax exempt nonprofit organizations. The application process, current deadlines, and previous grant recipients can be found on the Foundation website.
Geographic Focus: All States
Contact: Contact; (212) 742-2300; fax (212) 742-1653; info@ms.foundation.org
Internet: http://ms.foundation.org/our_work/broad-change-areas/womens-health
Sponsor: Ms. Foundation for Women
12 MetroTech Center, 26th Floor
Brooklyn, NY 11201

**Mt. Sinai Health Care Foundation Health of the Urban Community   1356
Grants**
In the tradition of The Mt. Sinai Medical Center, the Foundation is committed to improving the health of Greater Cleveland's most vulnerable individuals and families. To achieve impact in this area, scale is a significant factor. The Foundation seeks to support especially those projects focusing on health promotion and disease prevention that have the potential to access large populations through existing community infrastructure. To optimize impact in large populations, partnering with both public and private funding sources may be appropriate and necessary. Of particular interest are proposals in the areas of health-related early childhood development and health-related aging.
Requirements: 501(c)3 nonprofits serving greater Cleveland, Ohio may submit proposals for grant support. The foundation welcomes and encourages an informal conversation with program staff prior to the submission of a grant request.
Restrictions: In general, the foundation does not support general operating expenses, direct provision of health services, building or equipment expenses, fund-raising events, projects outside of greater Cleveland, endowment funds, lobbying, program advertising, grants for individuals, or scholarships.
Geographic Focus: Ohio
Date(s) Application is Due: Jan 1; Apr 1; Jul 1; Oct 1
Contact: Ann Freimuth; (216) 421-5500; fax (216) 421-5633; aks17@case.edu
Internet: http://www.mtsinaifoundation.org/whatwefund_urbancommunity.html
Sponsor: Mount Sinai Health Care Foundation
11000 Euclid Avenue
Cleveland, OH 44106-1714

Musgrave Foundation Grants   1357
The foundation awards grants to eligible Missouri tax-exempt organizations in its areas of interest, including civic and public affairs, community development, elementary education, secondary education, higher education, and social services. Types of support include annual campaigns, building construction/renovation, capital campaigns, continuing support, equipment acquisition, general operating support, matching grants, and scholarship funds.
Requirements: 501(c)3 tax-exempt organizations and colleges, universities, and schools in Missouri may apply.
Restrictions: Grants are not made to individuals.
Geographic Focus: Missouri
Date(s) Application is Due: May 31
Amount of Grant: 500 - 61,000 USD
Contact: Jerry Redfern, Program Contact; (417) 841-4698 or (417) 882-9090; fax (417) 882-2529; jredfern@musgravefoundation.org
Internet: http://www.musgravefoundation.org
Sponsor: Musgrave Foundation
P.O. Box 10327
Springfield, MO 65804

Myers Family Foundation Grants   1358
The foundation awards grants to nonprofit organizations in its areas of interest, including arts and culture, education, hospitals, family services, and churches. Types of support include capital grants, general operating grants, programs grants, and seed money grants. There are no application deadlines.
Requirements: 501(c)3 nonprofit organizations are eligible. Giving is primarily made in California.
Geographic Focus: All States
Amount of Grant: 25 - 150,000 USD
Contact: William Myers, Trustee; (805) 963-2690
Sponsor: Myers Family Foundation
1114 State Street, Suite 232
Santa Barbara, CA 93101-9650

Naomi and Nehemiah Cohen Foundation Grants   1359
The foundation awards grants primarily for Jewish organizations, especially welfare funds, community services, and educational institutions. Grants also are awarded to Christian nonprofits and to organizations for peace activities. Types of support include annual campaigns, building construction/renovation, capital campaigns, equipment acquisition, general operating support, project support, publications, seed money, and technical assistance. Nonprofits in the District of Columbia receive preference. There are no formal grant procedures or application deadlines. Initial approach should be a letter of inquiry.
Restrictions: Grants are not made to individuals.
Geographic Focus: All States, Israel
Amount of Grant: 1,000 - 50,000 USD

Samples: Jewish Federation of Greater Washington (Rockville, MD)—for the United Jewish Endowment Fund's annual campaign, $4 million; Shefa Fund (Wyndmoor, PA)—to leverage investments from Jewish institutions and individuals for use by community development financial institutions, $360,000; United Jewish Appeal Federation (Rockville, MD)—operating support, $200,000.
Contact: Alison McWilliams; (202) 234-5454; NNCF@erols.com
Sponsor: Naomi and Nehemiah Cohen Foundation
P.O. Box 73708
Washington, D.C. 20056

Narragansett Number One Foundation Grants   1360
Narragansett Number One Foundation (NNOF) is a Maine nonprofit corporation established by Pat and Erwin Wales on September 7, 2001, thirteen days after winning the national Powerball lottery drawing. The Wales formed the Foundation to share their good fortune with others and to encourage other possible donors to help their community and state. Giving is concentrated first on helping the Foundation's neighbors in Buxton, Maine, and surrounding areas. NNOF provides funds for start-up expenses, new or special projects, and general operating support.
Requirements: Nonprofit 501(c)3 organizations in any state, possession of the United States, or political subdivision (a public school, town, city or government agency) if the proposed grant is to be used exclusively for public purposes are eligible to apply. Priority will be given to public charities in the Town of Buxton, Maine and the surrounding areas with focus on schools, fire departments, police departments, parks, recreational facilities, religious organizations, libraries, shelters for children, the homeless and abused persons, museums and shelters for animals. Once the immediate needs of this geographic area in southern Maine are addressed, it is likely that future grants will be made to charities throughout Maine and in other states. Applications should be received by NNOF no earlier than November 1 and no later than April 1 of the following year. Grants will be awarded on or before June 30.
Restrictions: Grants do not support individuals, campaigns to elect candidates to public office, lobbying or propaganda campaigns, or programs or projects that discriminate.
Geographic Focus: Maine
Date(s) Application is Due: Apr 1
Contact: Pat Wales, President
Internet: http://www.nnof.org/apply.htm
Sponsor: Narragansett Number One Foundation
P.O. Box 779
Bar Mills, ME 04004

Natalie W. Furniss Charitable Trust Grants   1361
The Mission of the Furniss Foundation is to promote the humane treatment of animals by providing funding to societies for the prevention of cruelty to animals.
Requirements: Qualifying tax-exempt 501(c)3 organizations operating in the state of New Jersey are eligible to apply. Applications are accepted Ocotber 1 - December 1. Complete the Common Grant Application form available at the Wachovi website to apply for funding.
Restrictions: Grants are not made for political purposes, nor to organizations which discriminate on the basis of race, ethnic origin, sexual or religious preference, age or gender.
Geographic Focus: New Jersey
Date(s) Application is Due: Dec 1
Samples: Oasis Animal Sanctuary, Inc., $4,200—animal sterilization program; Woodford Cedar Run Wildlife Refuge, Inc., $4,5000—winter operating support for wildlife rehab; Society for the Prtevention of Cruelty to Animals, $5,000—humane education in Cumberland Co. School system; Greyhound Friends of New Jersey, Inc., $5,000—broken leg program.
Contact: Wachovia Bank, N.A., Trustee; grantinquiries6@wachovia.com
Internet: https://www.wachovia.com/foundation/v/index.jsp?vgnextoid=6107 8689fb0aa110VgnVCM1000004b0d1872RCRD&vgnextfmt=default
Sponsor: Natalie W. Furniss Foundation
100 North Main Street
Winston Salem, NC 27150

Nathan Cummings Foundation Grants   1362
The Nathan Cummings Foundation is rooted in the Jewish tradition and committed to democratic values and social justice, including fairness, diversity, and community. It seeks to build a socially and economically just society that values nature and protects the ecological balance for future generations; promotes humane health care; and fosters arts and culture that enriches communities. The Foundation's core programs include arts and culture; the environment;

health; interprogram initiatives for social and economic justice; and the Jewish life and values/contemplative practice programs. Basic themes informing the Foundation's approach to grantmaking are: concern for the poor, disadvantaged, and underserved; respect for diversity; promotion of understanding across cultures; and empowerment of communities in need. The Board meets twice a year. Applicants should apply by January 15 to be considered for the spring Board meeting and by August 15 to be considered for the fall Board meeting.
Requirements: Eligible applicants must be 501(c)3 organizations. A two or three page letter of inquiry may be submitted with the following information: basic organizational information; contact person; grant purpose; key personnel; project budget and total organizational budget; amount requested and the length of time for which funds are being requested; and other funding sources. Projects that most closely fit with the Foundation's goals will be invited to submit a complete application.
Restrictions: The following is not funded: individuals; scholarships; sponsorships; capital or endowment campaigns; foreign-based organizations; specific diseases; local synagogues or institutions with local projects; Holocaust related projects; projects with no plans for replication; and general support for Jewish education.
Geographic Focus: All States
Contact: Armanda Famiglietti, Director of Grants Management; (212) 787-7300; fax (212) 787-7377; info@nathancummings.org
Internet: http://www.nathancummings.org/programs/index.html
Sponsor: Nathan Cummings Foundation
475 10th Avenue, 14th Floor
New York, NY 10018

Nathaniel and Elizabeth P. Stevens Foundation Grants   1363
The Foundation awards funding to eligible Massachusetts nonprofit organizations to improve the quality of life in the greater area comprising Lawrence and Merrimack Valley. Funding includes operating support, program support, special projects, renovations, capital and equipment. The Foundation Trustees generally meet monthly, with the exceptions of July and August. Applicants are encouraged to seek other sources of funding while waiting for funding decisions. Awards range from $250 to $30,000.
Requirements: Eligible applicants must be 501(c)3 Massachusetts charitable organizations. Applications will be considered for experimental and demonstration projects, program expansion, evaluation, renovations, new construction projects and capital funding. Grants may be made to a 501(c)3 organization for the benefit of another organization awaiting its own tax-exempt status. A complete proposal should include: most recent annual financial statement (preferably audited); institutional income and expense budget for current fiscal year; detailed program budget for which support is being requested; and starting and completion dates of proposed program and planned cash flow. If an organization's proposal is complete and fits within the guidelines of the Foundation, the applicant organization may be contacted to provide further information. Contact information should be included with the application.
Restrictions: Awards are not made to the following: individuals; national organizations; annual giving campaigns; and state or federal agencies. The Foundation will not consider a proposal from an organization previously funded until a full report of the expenditures of the previous grant has been submitted. The Trustees will not consider more than one application from an agency in the same calendar year except for summer youth programs.
Geographic Focus: Massachusetts
Samples: ABC Masconomet, Topsfield, Massachusetts, $7,500 - operating support; Lazarus House, Lawrence, Massachusetts, $14,000 - food preparation program and renovation; and Youth Development Organization, Lawrence, Massachusetts, $30,000 - operating support.
Contact: Joshua Miner, Executive Director; (978) 688-7211; fax (978) 686-1620; grantprocess@stevensfoundation.com
Sponsor: Nathaniel and Elizabeth P. Stevens Foundation
P.O. Box 111
North Andover, MA 01845

National Starch and Chemical Foundation Grants   1364
The foundation supports nonprofits in company-operating locations in the areas of higher education, children's services, and hospitals. Types of support include general operating support, continuing support, employee-related scholarships, and employee matching gifts. There are no application guidelines. Applicants are asked to submit a written proposal.
Requirements: Nonprofits in company operating areas such as Georgia, Illinois, Indiana, Missouri, North Carolina, New Jersey, Pennsylvania, South Carolina, and Tennessee may apply.

Geographic Focus: Georgia, Illinois, Indiana, Missouri, New Jersey, North Carolina, Pennsylvania, South Carolina, Tennessee
Amount of Grant: 500 - 10,000 USD
Contact: Carmen Ortiz, (908) 685-5201; carmen.ortiz@nstarch.com
Internet: http://news.nationalstarch.com/NewsStory.asp?newsItemId=214
Sponsor: National Starch and Chemical Foundation
10 Finderne Avenue
Bridgewater, NJ 08807

Nationwide Insurance Foundation Grants   1365

The Nationwide Insurance Foundation's mission is to improve the quality of life in communities in which a large number of Nationwide members, associates, agents and their families live and work. The foundation's grants fall into three categories: General Operating Support, Program and/or Project Support, and Capital Support. Funding priorities are then placed into one of four tiers. Tier 1-Emergency and basic needs: the foundation partners with organizations that provide life's necessities. Tier 2-Crisis stabilization: the foundation partners with organizations that provide resources to prevent crises or help pick up the pieces after one occurs. Tier 3-Personal and family empowerment: Nationwide helps at-risk youth and families in poverty situations who need tools and resources to advance their lives by partnering with organizations that assist individuals in becoming productive members of society. Tier 4-Community enrichment: the foundation partners with organizations that contribute to the overall quality of life in a community.
Requirements: In the following communities, the Nationwide Insurance Foundation will consider funding 501(c)3 organizations from all four tiers of funding priorities: Columbus, Ohio; Des Moines, Iowa; Scottsdale, Arizona. In the following communities, only Tiers 1 and 2 of the foundation's funding priorities will be considered: Sacramento, California; Denver, Colorado; Gainesville, Florida; Atlanta (Metro), Georgia; Baltimore, Maryland; Lincoln, Nebraska; Raleigh/Durham, North Carolina; Syracuse, New York; Canton, Ohio; Cleveland, Ohio; Harrisburg, Pennsylvania; Philadelphia (Metro), Pennsylvania; Nashville, Tennessee; Dallas (Metro), Texas; San Antonio, Texas; Lynchburg, Virginia; Richmond, Virginia; Wausau, Wisconsin.
Restrictions: The Nationwide Insurance Foundation generally does not fund national organizations (unless the applicant is a local branch or chapter providing direct services) or organizations located in areas with less than 100 Nationwide associates. Also, the foundation does not fund the following: Organizations that are not tax-exempt under paragraph 501(c)3 of the U.S. Internal Revenue Code; Fund-raising events such as walk-a-thons, telethons or sponsorships; Individuals for any purpose; Athletic events or teams, bands and choirs (including equipment and uniforms); Debt-reduction or retirement campaigns; Research; Public or private primary or secondary schools; Requests to support travel; Groups or organizations that will re-grant the foundation's gifts to other organizations or individuals (except United Way); Endowment campaigns; Veterans, labor, religious or fraternal groups (except when these groups provide needed services to the community at-large); Lobbying activities.
Geographic Focus: Arizona, California, Colorado, Florida, Georgia, Iowa, Maryland, Nebraska, New York, North Carolina, Ohio, Pennsylvania, Tennessee, Texas, Virginia, Wisconsin
Date(s) Application is Due: Sep 1
Amount of Grant: 5,000 - 50,000 USD
Contact: Chad Jester; (614) 249-4310 or (877) 669-6877; corpcit@nationwide.com
Internet: http://www.nationwide.com/about-us/nationwide-foundation.jsp
Sponsor: Nationwide Insurance Foundation
1 Nationwide Plaza, MD 1-22-05
Columbus, OH 43215-2220

NCI Technologies and Software to Support Integrative Cancer Biology Research (SBIR) Grants   1366

This Funding Opportunity Announcement (FOA), issued by the National Cancer Institute (NCI), invites Small Business Innovation Research (SBIR) grant applications from small business concerns (SBCs) that propose the development of commercial software tools, computational/mathematical methods, and technologies that will enable integrative cancer biology research. Integrative cancer biology focuses on understanding cancer as a complex biological system by utilizing both computational and experimental biology to integrate heterogeneous data sources and ultimately to generate predictive computational models of cancer processes. Phase I applications may request up to 2 years of support with total costs of up to $300,000 for the duration of the award (not to exceed $200,000 total costs in any one year). Budgetary requests of Phase II applications will conform to standard SBIR guidelines (up to $750,000 total costs for up to two years).
Requirements: Only United States small business concerns (SBCs) are eligible to submit SBIR applications.

Geographic Focus: All States
Date(s) Application is Due: Apr 5; Aug 5; Dec 5
Amount of Grant: 200,000 - 750,000 USD
Contact: Greg Evans, (301) 594-8807; evansgl@mail.nih.gov
Internet: http://grants.nih.gov/grants/guide/pa-files/PA-09-188.html
Sponsor: National Cancer Institute
31 Center Drive, Building 31, Room 10A19, MSC 2580
Bethesda, MD 20892-2580

Nebraska Arts Council Basic Support Grants   1367

Grants offer general operating support for arts organizations in Nebraska, allowing them to improve and extend the arts services they annually provide to their communities. Grants are awarded to community and volunteer organizations (BSG-C) or discipline-based organizations (BSG-D). Organizations that have been receiving BSG funds may request up to 25 percent more than their most recent BSG award. Organizations that are applying in the BSG category for the first time may request up to $2500. Community and volunteer organizations that do not currently receive funding but are interested in applying must contact NAC staff. Annual deadline dates may vary; contact the council for exact dates.
Requirements: Nebraska nonprofit, tax-exempt organizations that dedicate 51 percent or more of their budget to producing or sponsoring arts events or to providing arts services are eligible. In addition, if applying organizations are not currently participating in a community challenge grant program, they must have done so three years prior to application in this category.
Geographic Focus: Nebraska
Date(s) Application is Due: Mar 1
Contact: Elaine Buescher, Grants Manager; (800) 341-4067 or (402) 595-2122; fax (402) 595-2334; ebuescher@nebraskaartscouncil.org
Internet: http://www.nebraskaartscouncil.org/index_html?page=content/GRANTS/Categories/CatGrants.htm
Sponsor: Nebraska Arts Council
3838 Davenport Street
Omaha, NE 68131-2329

Needmor Fund Grants   1368

The fund awards grants to grassroots, community-based organizations for a range of activities in the areas of justice, political liberty, human services (food, shelter, health care, and safety), and education that enables low- and moderate-income individuals to contribute to society and the opportunity to secure productive work with just wages and benefits. Needmor gives to groups that help people take control of their lives and change the conditions that adversely affect them. Preference will be given to groups that have a highly committed membership, develop leadership from within, can determine solutions to major problems facing their communities, and formulate effective strategic plans. Types of support include general operating budgets, seed money, and technical assistance. Grantees are encouraged to develop alternative means of long-term fundraising to promote self-sufficiency. The January 10 deadline is for applicants located in Alabama, Arizona, southern California, Louisiana, Mississippi, New Mexico, and southern Texas (including San Antonio). The June 30 deadline is for applicants in all other states, and required a pre-application process with a deadline of May 31.
Requirements: Nonprofit community-based organizations may apply.
Restrictions: Grants do not support individuals, capital funds, scholarships, fellowships, deficit financing, replacement of lost government funding, land acquisition, purchase of buildings or equipment, publications, media, films, TV or radio productions, computer projects, or university research. Nonprofits with access to traditional funding sources generally are denied support.
Geographic Focus: Arizona, California, Colorado, New Mexico, Wyoming
Date(s) Application is Due: Jan 10; Jun 30
Amount of Grant: 15,000 - 40,000 USD
Samples: Birmingham Area Interfaith Sponsoring Committee, Birmingham, Alabama, $30,000 - general operations; Mississippi Workers' Center for Human Rights, Greenville, Mississippi, $30,000 - to fight worker mistreatment through community education outreach and the organizing of indigenous worker leadership; Northern Louisiana Interfaith, Baton Rouge, Louisiana, $40,000 - general operations.
Contact: Mary Sobecki, Grants Manager; (419) 255-5560; fax (419) 255-5561; msobecki@needmorfund.org
Internet: http://fdncenter.org/grantmaker/needmor
Sponsor: Needmor Fund
42 South Saint Clair Street
Toledo, OH 43604-8736

NEFA National Dance Project Grants   1369

These grants provide funding for the creation of new dance work that will tour nationally. Funds support a project's development through the time of its premiere, covering costs related to producing the work. Every season, 15 to 20 production grants are awarded. Each awardee also receives a touring grant, to support a tour of the new work.

Requirements: Production grants are awarded to dance projects based on nominations received from presenters, artists, artist managers, and agents.

Restrictions: Artists receiving production grants in any given season are not eligible to apply for production grant support in the following season.

Geographic Focus: Connecticut, Maine, Massachusetts, New Hampshire, Rhode Island, Vermont

Date(s) Application is Due: Apr 1

Amount of Grant: 15,000 - 35,000 USD

Samples: Nineteen contemporary-dance companies—for production grants that support the development of new dance projects, $560,000 divided.

Contact: Contact; (617) 951-0010; fax (617) 951-0016; dance@nefa.org

Internet: http://www.nefa.org/grantprog/ndp/ndp_prod_grant_app.html

Sponsor: New England Foundation for the Arts

145 Tremont Street, 7th Floor

Boston, MA 02111

Nellie Mae Education Foundation District-Level Change Grants   1370

The Nellie Mae Education Foundation District-Level Systems Change Grants support the shift in high school-level education in New England to prepare students to thrive in a global, complex, fast changing society. Grant programs promote student centered models of schooling that offer a path away from a one size fits all approach to a more customized approach to maximize learning for all students. The initiative focuses on three priority areas: developing school and district designs and practices that enable all learners to achieve high standards; creating sustainable policy change to support these new approaches; and generating public will and increasing demand for changes in practice. Examples of allowable activities for funding include: engaging central office, school administrators, and teachers in identifying current initiatives and how they compete with or support a student centered learning frame; surveying student needs and challenges and what motivates them to achieve academically and personally; creating greater building level autonomy and funding streams based on student needs rather than programs; researching feasibility, designing and planning for the appropriate blended learning model including visits to blended learning schools; using technology as an essential tool in learning environments and professional development; or administrator visits from student centered schools. The Foundation will support self-assessment activities, efforts to build, forge or nurture a common vision and mission for the work, and integration of this work with other school/district initiatives. Funds can support purchasing online and hardcopy literacy materials to support complex Common Core State Standards (CCSS) text demands; engaging a team of district stakeholders to conduct an analysis of culture of the system's various dimensions; or administrative visits from student centered schools. Proposal information, including the request for proposal, a list of supplemental materials and instructions, questions to address in the proposal, a list of frequently asked questions and previously funded projects, and an instructional webinar, is located at the Foundation website.

Requirements: The Foundation's activities include both making grants to the public charities it supports and providing services to those organizations. The Foundation operates exclusively to promote the charitable and educational purposes of nonprofit educational organizations, including universities, colleges, secondary schools, elementary schools and other educational organizations that are described in the IRS Code Section 501(c)3.

Restrictions: Funding for this project is concentrated on urban school districts and learning centers in Connecticut, Massachusetts, and Rhode Island. The Foundation does not fund capital campaigns, endowments, scholarships or fellowships, debt reduction or cash reserves, building construction or renovation, and certain indirect costs.

Geographic Focus: Connecticut, Massachusetts, Rhode Island

Date(s) Application is Due: Oct 18

Amount of Grant: 25,000 - 1,000,000 USD

Samples: New England Resource Center for Higher Education, Boston, Massachusetts, Project Compass: a multi-year initiative that supports institutions seeking to systematize changes essential to expanding, sustaining, and integrating rigorous, evidence-based efforts to retain larger numbers of underserved students, $375,000; Sanford School Department, Sanford, Maine, based on the Reinventing Schools Coalition (RISC) model, a model that focuses on a research based approach to student-centered, proficiency based

learning where students demonstrate proficiency at commonly understood and meaningful standards, $1.1 million; Hyde Park Task Force, Youth Organizing Project, Jamaica Plain, Massachusetts, project that focuses on developing 50 urban youth leaders who successfully advocate for themselves and their peers in their communities and schools by engaging in community organizing campaigns, $25,000.

Contact: Stephanie Cheney, Senior Manager, Grants and Special Programs; (781) 348-4240; fax (781) 348-4299; scheney@nmefdn.org

Internet: http://www.nmefoundation.org/grants/district-level-systems-change

Sponsor: Nellie Mae Education Foundation

1250 Hancock Street, Suite 205N

Quincy, MA 02169

Nellie Mae Education Foundation Research & Development Grants   1371

The Nellie Mae Education Foundation Research and Development Grants work to build and deepen understanding of student-centered learning approaches in order to foster more widespread adoption and implementation. Grants focus on three areas: gathering and promoting existing knowledge of student-centered approaches to learning; creating new research to promote student-centered approaches in order to support overall system change, policy change and community engagement; and developing new tools that support student-centered teaching, learning and assessment. Funding opportunities for this grant are posted on the Foundation website when funding is available. A list of frequently asked questions and additional list of previously funded projects are listed on the website.

Requirements: The Foundation's activities include making grants to the public charities it supports and providing services to those organizations. The Foundation operates exclusively to promote the charitable and educational purposes of nonprofit educational organizations, including universities, colleges, secondary schools, elementary schools and other educational organizations that are described in IRS Code Section 501(c)3. Funding is available primarily for the New England area, but the Foundation occasionally supports programs, organizations, research, and conferences outside of the New England area in order to influence policy, and advance knowledge of public opinion toward education.

Restrictions: The Foundation does not fund capital campaigns, endowments, scholarships or fellowships, debt reduction or cash reserves, building construction or renovation, and certain indirect costs.

Geographic Focus: All States

Amount of Grant: 10,000 - 185,000 USD

Samples: Council of the Chief State School Officers (CCSSO), Washington, D.C., develop an evaluation framework and design to assess the work of the Innovation Lab Network (ILN), $30,000; Expeditionary Learning Schools Outward Bound, Amherst, Massachusetts, an important step toward developing a solid understanding of underlying practices of student-centered learning as they are implemented in a highly successful student-centered learning environment in an urban context, $235,000; Boston Day and Evening Academy, Roxbury, Massachusetts, funding for the Academy's website for its Responsive Education Alternatives Laboratory, $18,000.

Contact: Stephanie Cheney, Senior Manager, Grants and Special Programs; (781) 348-4240; fax (781) 348-4299; scheney@nmefdn.org

Internet: http://www.nmefoundation.org/grants/research-development

Sponsor: Nellie Mae Education Foundation

1250 Hancock Street, Suite 205N

Quincy, MA 02169

Nell J. Redfield Foundation Grants   1372

The foundation awards grants to eligible Nevada organizations in its areas of interest, including biomedical research, health care and health organizations, elderly, children with disabilities, education, human services, and religion. Types of support include building construction/renovation, capital campaigns, equipment acquisition, program development, and scholarship funds. Deadlines are at least ten days before a regularly scheduled quarterly meeting of the Board (March, June, September and December). Contact the office to request the application form and guidelines.

Requirements: Nevada nonprofit organizations are eligible with preferences for organizations in northern Nevada.

Geographic Focus: Nevada

Amount of Grant: Up to 100,000 USD

Contact: Gerald C. Smith, Vice President and Secretary; (775) 323-1373; redfieldfoundation@yahoo.com

Sponsor: Nell J. Redfield Foundation

P.O. Box 61

Reno, NV 89502

Nevada Arts Council Partners in Excellence Grants　　1373

Partners in Excellence grants strengthen Nevada's arts infrastructure by funding cultural organizations and institutions throughout the state. The relationship between a state arts agency and its grantees goes beyond a funder-grantee arrangement. Together, NAC and the arts organizations it supports have increased access to and participation in the arts across the state - through quality arts programming, arts education initiatives and cultural leadership. Partners in Excellence Grants (PIE) reflect and enhance this important partnership. Six levels of PIE grants offer funding determined by organizational budget size that supports professional salaries, artistic fees, marketing costs and other expenses consistent with the mission of the grantee. Applicants may apply for $4,000 to $30,000. Applicants may also request funding of up of to $7,500 to support imaginative arts education/learning projects and artist residencies through the PIE Arts Learning Component.

Requirements: Nevada 501(c)3 nonprofit arts/cultural organizations, and public institutions and agencies with designated arts or cultural commissions/agencies can apply. A 1:1 match is required.

Geographic Focus: Nevada

Date(s) Application is Due: May 25

Amount of Grant: 4,000 - 30,000 USD

Contact: Ann Libby, Grants Program Coordinator; (775) 687-7102; fax (775) 687-6688; ann.libby@nevadaculture.org

Internet: http://nac.nevadaculture.org/index.php?option=com_content&view=article&id=1266&Itemid=414

Sponsor: Nevada Arts Council

716 N Carson Street, Suite A

Carson City, NV 89701

Nevada Arts Council Professional Development Grants　　1374

Nevada Arts Council Professional Development grants are designed to promote the continuing education of Nevada's nonprofit arts industry to advance their work and careers through attendance at regional or national conferences, workshops, or seminars for skills training. For artists, educators, board members, and arts administrators, PDG funds cover costs associated with professional development activities on a reimbursement basis. Must demonstrate travel of at least 100 miles round-trip to qualify. Up to $650 for out-of-state activities, up to $500 for in-state opportunities and up to $350 to attend Nevada Arts Council sponsored activities are allowed.

Requirements: 501(c)3 Nevada arts/cultural organizations applying for the first time to the grants program must apply in this category, no matter the age of the organization or its budget size.

Geographic Focus: Nevada

Amount of Grant: Up to 650 USD

Contact: Ann Libby, Grants Program Coordinator; (775) 687-7102; fax (775) 687-6688; ann.libby@nevadaculture.org

Internet: http://nac.nevadaculture.org/index.php?option=com_content&view=article&id=1266&Itemid=414

Sponsor: Nevada Arts Council

716 N Carson Street, Suite A

Carson City, NV 89701

Nevada Arts Council Project Grants　　1375

Nevada Arts Council Project Grants are designed to support activities and projects of non-arts organizations and public institutions that are: integral to the applicant's overall mission and goals; and achieved through community partnerships. Partnerships, including those that involve sectors outside of the arts, are key to the success of activities funded by Project Grants and must be reflected in every application. Eligible activities may include, but are not limited to, performances, ethnic festivals, film series, and visual arts exhibitions. Requests to fund ongoing programming are allowable. Applicants need to supply budget information that reflects the cost of the proposed project only, not a total organization budget.

Requirements: Nevada 501(c)3 nonprofit organizations are eligible.

Geographic Focus: Nevada

Date(s) Application is Due: Mar 25

Amount of Grant: 1,000 - 6,500 USD

Contact: Ann Libby, Grants Program Coordinator; (775) 687-7102; fax (775) 687-6688; ann.libby@nevadaculture.org

Internet: http://nac.nevadaculture.org/index.php?option=com_content&view=article&id=1266&Itemid=414

Sponsor: Nevada Arts Council

716 N Carson Street, Suite A

Carson City, NV 89701

New-Land Foundation Grants　　1376

The foundation supports U.S. nonprofit organizations for programs that emphasize the areas of civil rights, justice, peace, and arms control. The foundation also focuses on the environment, population control, and leadership development in these areas. Types of support include general operating expenses, annual campaigns, seed grants, research, continuing support, internships, matching funds, and programs/projects. The foundation board generally meets in the fall and spring of each year to consider grant requests. Application form and guidelines should be requested in writing.

Restrictions: Individuals are ineligible.

Geographic Focus: All States

Date(s) Application is Due: Feb 1; Aug 1

Amount of Grant: 5,000 - 25,000 USD

Samples: Ms. Foundation for Women (New York, NY)—$60,000; Institute for Policy Studies (Washington, DC)—$40,000; Land and Water Fund of the Rockies (Boulder, CO)—$25,000.

Contact: Program Contact; (212) 479-6162

Sponsor: New-Land Foundation

1114 Avenue of the Americas, 46th Floor

New York, NY 10036-7798

New Covenant Farms Grants　　1377

The Program, established in Idaho in 2000 by the L.M. Davenport Warehouse, provides funding and goods for children and families in both Texas and Mexico. Types of support include: cash; housing; clothing; food; education; and other necessities. There are no specific deadlines, though written applications are required. Applicants should include: name and location; exemption status; what food products and distribution needs are required; and budget.

Geographic Focus: Texas, Mexico

Samples: Rick Caywood Ministries, Crawford, TX, $3,500—food distribution to the poor; Rio Bravo W-4stries, Mission, TX,—home to 65 children in Reynosa Tam, Mexico; Instituto De Magdiel, Matamoros Tam, Mexico—training students for Christian Ministry.

Contact: Lewis M. Davenport III, CEO; (208) 934-5600 or (208) 934-5609

Sponsor: New Covenant Farms

1737 East 1800 South

Gooding, ID 83330-5095

New Earth Foundation Grants　　1378

The New Earth Foundation (NEF) supports nonprofit organizations in the following areas: education, social services, the arts, communication, and the preservation of sacred spaces, among other areas. NEF prefers to fund smaller and newer organizations. Typical grantee organizations are less than 15 years old with annual operating budgets of less than $350,000, including programs and administration. If you are a 501(c)3 organization, or are working under the umbrella of a 501(c)3 organization, you may apply for a grant of between $5,000 and $7,500. If you are working under an umbrella, a clear relationship between that organization and your project must be demonstrated. You must include a letter that shows that the board of directors (not just the staff or chair) agrees that the umbrella organization may act as your funding agent. The letter should address your project's relationship to the organization and be signed by the president/chair.

Requirements: 501(c)3 nonprofit organizations are eligible to apply. To begin the application process submit (electronically) a Letter of Inquiry to the foundation, providing basic information about your organization and about your program/project. After reviewing the Letter of Inquiry, you maybe invited to submit a complete application.

Restrictions: NEF does not fund organizations that: offer mainstream social services or are local organizations that are affiliated with a national organization such as Boys & Girls Clubs, Big Brothers/Big Sisters, Habitat for Humanity, the Cancer Society and other such organizations; are good candidates for governmental funding; are involved in community housing and renovation; have standard forms of after-school programs, outdoor summer camps/expeditions, or gardening programs; are land and building preservation programs; are capital improvement/building projects; are involved in land purchases.

Geographic Focus: All States

Amount of Grant: 5,000 - 7,500 USD

Contact: David Belskis; newearthfoundation@foundationsource.com

Internet: http://www.newearthfoundation.org/application.html

Sponsor: New Earth Foundation

Foundation Source, 55 Walls Drive

Fairfield, CT 06824

New England Biolabs Foundation Grants 1379

The foundation has special program interests in marine conservation, estuary protection, sustainable economic development, sustainable organic agriculture, education in women's health issues (developing countries only), and environmental education for teachers or elementary age students. Additional funding supports local education and art programs. Education and community projects are limited to Boston and the North Shore. International grants are made to small developing countries, with priority given to environmental protection and education projects. Grants provide general operating support. Applicants should make preliminary inquiry by letter, phone, or email. Proposals are accepted online, and the foundation will also accept the NNG common grant application.

Requirements: The foundation makes grants to grassroots organizations, emerging support groups, and other charitable organizations, generally nonprofits with revenue under $3 million. International projects located in Cambodia, Cameroon, the Caribbean (not Haiti, Cuba, the U.S. Virgin Islands, or the Dominican Republic), Central America (not Mexico, Costa Rica, Panama or Belize), Guatemala (funding environmental education projects for students and/or teachers), Ghana (environmental projects only), Tanzania, Madagascar, Papua New Guinea, South America (not Argentina, Brazil, Fr. Guiana, Suriname, Uruguay, Columbia, or Venezuela), Viet Nam, and Zimbabwe will be considered. Under certain provisions, individuals also may be eligible.

Restrictions: Grants are not awarded to support religious activities, specific animal protection, services for the elderly or the disabled, projects normally funded by major agencies, or art projects outside the immediate community. Grants do not support capital endowment or building funds, fellowships, movies or videos, scholarships, or conferences.

Geographic Focus: All States, Algeria, Angola, Argentina, Benin, Bolivia, Botswana, Brazil, Burkina Faso, Burundi, Cameroon, Cape Verde, Central African Republic, Chad, Chile, Colombia, Comoros, Congo, Congo, Democratic Republic of, Cote d' Ivoire (Ivory Coast), Djibouti, Ecuador, Egypt, Equatorial Guinea, Eritrea, Ethiopia, Gabon, Gambia, Ghana, Guinea, Guinea-Bissau, Guyana, Kenya, Lesotho, Liberia, Libya, Madagascar, Malawi, Mali, Mauritania, Mauritius, Morocco, Mozambique, Namibia, Niger, Nigeria, Paraguay, Peru, Rwanda, Sao Tome & Principe, Senegal, Seychelles, Sierra Leone, Somalia, South Africa, Sudan, Swaziland

Date(s) Application is Due: Mar 1; Sep 1

Amount of Grant: 500 - 20,000 USD

Samples: Artcorps (Boston, MA)—to support inner city teens art design in Boston, $20,000; A Woman's Voice—to prevent female circumcision in young girls in Kenya, $5000; Lesson One (Peabody, MA)—for violence prevention programs in elementary schools in Peabody, MA, $7500; Idea Wild (Fort Collins, CO)—to continue a biodiversity and conservation program in Latin America, $5000.

Contact: Martine Kellett; (978) 927-2404; fax (508) 921-1350; kellett@nebf.org

Internet: http://www.nebf.org/application.html

Sponsor: New England Biolabs Foundation

8 Enon Street #2B

Beverly, MA 01915

New England Grassroots Environment Fund Grants 1380

The purpose of the fund is to increase engagement and participation in grassroots environmental initiatives and to build and connect healthy, sustainable communities in New England. Applicants must be working at the grassroots level and must demonstrate a major element of volunteer involvement in their programs. A broad range of activities will be funded, including community needs, computer networking, capacity building, advocacy campaigns, institutional support, conferences, meeting travel, and enhancing partnerships in the region. Types of support include but are not limited to general operating support, equipment acquisition, program development, conferences and seminars, and scholarship funds. The fund has three funding cycles each year. Applications are accepted at any time.

Requirements: 501(c)3 nonprofit, grassroots organizations in Maine, Massachusetts, New Hampshire, Rhode Island, and Vermont are eligible. Grassroots groups are defined as being largely volunteer driven, having no more than two paid full-time staff members, and an annual budget (including projects) of less than $100,000. Proposals may be considered from larger community-based groups for projects at the grassroots level.

Restrictions: Grants do not support lobbying or partisan political purposes.

Geographic Focus: Connecticut, Maine, Massachusetts, New Hampshire, Rhode Island, Vermont

Date(s) Application is Due: Jan 15; May 1; Sep 15

Amount of Grant: 500 - 2,500 USD

Samples: Maine Wolf Coalition (South China, ME)—to purchase a computer, other office equipment, and furniture, $2250; Toxics Action Ctr (Boston,

MA)—to finance scholarships to allow local activists to attend an annual training conference, $175; New Hampshire Council of Churches (Concord, NH)—to hire an intern to set up a network of faith-based environmental groups and congregations, $2500; Saugatucket River Heritage Corridor (Wakefield, RI)—for general operating support, $2500.

Contact: Cheryl King Fischer, Executive Director; (802) 223-4622; fax (802) 229-1734; fischer@grassrootsfund.org

Internet: http://www.grassrootsfund.org/guide_1.html

Sponsor: New England Grassroots Environment Fund

P.O. Box 1057

Montpelier, VT 05601

Newfoundland and Labrador Arts Council Sustaining Grants 1381

The Newfoundland and Labrador Arts Council Sustaining Grants are available to professional arts organizations that further the arts of Newfoundland and Labrador. Grants support administration and project costs. Potential applicants should contact the Program Manger to confirm eligibility before applying.

Requirements: Professional arts organizations must: have the development, production, or promotion of the arts as its primary mandate; be based in Newfoundland and Labrador; have at least half its board and/or membership currently residing in Newfoundland and Labrador for a minimum of 12 consecutive months immediately prior to the time of application; be registered as a not-for-profit organization in the province; have completed two consecutive years of significant operations in keeping with the mandate of the organization; have a formal organizational structure including an active board of directors; employ a professional artistic director/executive director or equivalent; have sound administrative and financial management using typical business accounting and organizational management practices; have a good record of providing local employment; pay artist and professional fees in keeping with established national guidelines; have an annual financial statement prepared (minimum acceptable is a review engagement prepared by an independent professional accountant); offer professional development opportunities for staff and/or membership; demonstrate community outreach through workshops, school visits, fundraising, etc; maintain a minimum annual budget of $50,000 ($20,000 for dance and visual art organizations) for the last two years and the current year; maintain a minimum annual budget of $50,000 ($20,000 for dance and visual art organizations) on all proposed budgets included in the application; and maintain a minimum annual budget of $50,000 ($20,000 for dance and visual art organizations) for the overall organizational budget for each fiscal year in which it receives sustaining program funding.

Restrictions: Applicants funded through this program are not eligible to apply for Professional Project Grants, Professional Festivals Grants, or the Community Arts Grants.

Geographic Focus: Canada

Date(s) Application is Due: Feb 15

Amount of Grant: 15,000 USD

Samples: Artistic Fraud of Newfoundland, St. John's, Newfoundland and Labrador, Canada, $25,000; Wonderbolt Productions, St. John's, Newfoundland and Labrador, Canada, $28,000; and Rising Tide Association, Trinity-Trinity Bay, Newfoundland and Labrador, Canada, $65,000.

Contact: Ken Murphy, Program Manager; (709) 726-2212 or (866) 726-2212; fax (709) 726-0619; kmurphy@nlac.ca

Internet: http://www.nlac.ca/grants/sppao.htm

Sponsor: Newfoundland and Labrador Arts Council

Newman Building, 1 Springdale Street, P.O. Box 98

St Johns, NL A1C 5H5 Canada

Newman W. Benson Foundation Grants 1382

Established in New York in 1990, the Foundation supports both human service programs and religious agencies. Generally, funding comes in the form of operating costs, with giving centered around Bradford and Towanda County, Pennsylvania. A selection of grants are also provided to organizations outside of Pennsylvania. There are no specific application forms or deadlines with which to adhere, and applicants should send a letter of request detailing the program or project, and include both a budget narrative and 501(c)3 letter.

Geographic Focus: All States

Amount of Grant: Up to 12,000 USD

Samples: First United Methodist Church, Towanda, Pennsylvania, $10,200; Wysox Presbyterian Church, Wysox Township, Pennsylvania, $675.

Contact: Newman W. Benson, President; (570) 265-3498

Sponsor: Newman W. Benson Foundation

P.O. Box 430, Lake Wesauking

Towanda, PA 18848-0430

New Prospect Foundation Grants 1383

The foundation awards grants nationally and internationally (Central America and Israel) to support activities directed toward human rights. Nonprofits also are eligible for support of housing improvement, employment, health, welfare, and the economic viability of urban and inner-city neighborhoods. Additional areas of interest are pro-choice activities, health care policy and advocacy, human and civil rights, and public school reform. Types of support include general operating support, continuing support, program development, and seed money. Priority is given to requests from the Chicago metropolitan area. Applications are due six weeks before board meetings in March, June, October, and December.
Requirements: Priority is given to requests from the Chicago metropolitan area.
Restrictions: Grants do not fund the arts, higher education, individuals, capital or endowment requests, basic research, scholarships, fellowships, or loans.
Geographic Focus: Illinois
Amount of Grant: 1,500 - 7,500 USD
Samples: Shefa Fund (Wyndmoor, PA)—to leverage investments from Jewish institutions and individuals for use by community-development financial institutions, $180,000.
Contact: Paul Lehman, Director; (847) 328-2288
Sponsor: New Prospect Foundation
1603 Orrington Avenue, Suite 1880
Evanston, IL 60201

New World Foundation Grants 1384

The foundation supports grassroots organizations that foster citizen engagement and local empowerment in the areas of public education, equal rights and opportunities, public health, community initiatives, and the avoidance of war. Types of support include general operating grants, seed money grants, and technical assistance. To increase the impact small groups can make, the foundation works on providing opportunities for grassroots groups to come together to share experience, expertise, and constituencies. The foundation also aims to connect grassroots organizations with the wider philanthropic sector. Application consists of a brief letter outlining the project needing funding, amount needed, and specifics of the requesting organization. The foundation will advise if more detailed information is needed. Grants are usually awarded for one year and sometimes are renewable. Applications are accepted at any time.
Geographic Focus: All States
Amount of Grant: 5,000 - 25,000 USD
Contact: Grants Administrator; (212) 249-1023; fax (212) 472-0508; info@newwf.org
Internet: http://www.newwf.org/grant_programs/main.html
Sponsor: New World Foundation
666 W End Avenue
New York, NY 10025

New York Foundation Grants 1385

The Foundation supports groups in New York City that are working on problems of urgent concern to residents of disadvantaged communities and neighborhoods. Support is provided to organizations that work in ways that inspire New Yorkers to become more educated and active participants in the overall life of the city. The Foundation places a priority on supporting community organizing and advocacy strategies. While support is given to groups that utilize multiple strategies, including direct service, preference is given to those moving toward incorporating advocacy and organizing. Of particular interest is start-up grants to new, untested programs that have few other sources of support. Interested applicants should send a letter of inquiry outlining the project and the budget.
Requirements: Eligible projects must: involve New York City or a particular neighborhood of the city; address a critical or emerging need, particularly involving youth or the elderly; and articulate how a grant from the Foundation would advance the applicant's work.
Restrictions: The following is not eligible: grants to individuals or to capital campaigns; support of research studies, films, conferences, or publications; requests from outside New York City except from organizations working on statewide issues of concern to youth, the elderly, or the poor; and grants outside of the United States. Letters of inquiry are accepted by mail only, not fax or email.
Geographic Focus: New York
Date(s) Application is Due: Mar 1; Jul 1; Nov 1
Amount of Grant: 40,000 - 50,000 USD
Contact: Maria Mottola, Executive Director; (212) 594-8009
Internet: http://www.nyf.org/how/guidelines
Sponsor: New York Foundation
350 Fifth Avenue, Room 2901
New York, NY 10118

New York Life Foundation Grants 1386

The foundation awards grants to nonprofit organizations in its areas of interest. Periodically, the foundation selects an area of special priority. The current focus, Nurturing the Children, directs the majority of the foundation's resources toward organizations, programs, and services aimed at helping young people. This initiative specifically focuses on safe places to learn and grow; educational enhancement; and mentoring. The foundation has initiated a new grant award program for nonprofit organizations based in New York City. Youth In Action recognizes innovative Nurturing the Children programs that engage youth in planning, coordinating and/or helping to provide services.
Requirements: Nonprofit 501(c)3 organizations may submit grant requests. The foundation funds projects in New York City, where New York Life's Home Office is located. The foundation also considers multi-site projects implemented by national organizations. These projects must serve two or more of the following locations: Atlanta; Cleveland; Clinton/Hunterdon County, New Jersey; Dallas; Kansas City; Minneapolis; New York City; Parsippany/Morris County, New Jersey; Tampa; and Westchester County, New York.
Restrictions: The foundation does not support sectarian or religious organizations or activities; fraternal, social, professional, athletic, or veterans groups; seminars or conferences; preschool, primary, or secondary education; endowments; memorials; basic or applied research; capital campaigns; or fund-raising activities.
Geographic Focus: All States
Date(s) Application is Due: Dec 1
Samples: Coalition for the Homeless (New York, NY)—for its after-school programs at five New York City shelters and its summer camp programs for children living in homeless shelters, $140,000; Harlem Education Activities Fund (New York, NY)—to expand the Summer Quest Program, a six-week summer academic program for middle-school students, $290,750 over three years; New York Historical Society (New York, NY)—for a new educational program that will serve at-risk elementary- and middle-school students in New York, $160,000; Foundation for the National Archives (Washington, DC)—to produce a film and companion book for children as part of the National Archives Experience, an interactive learning program for students and families, and to expand exhibition spaces at the National Archives building, $1.2 million over three years.
Contact: Program Contact; (212) 576-7341; fax (212) 576-6220; NYLFoundation@newyorklife.com
Internet: http://www.newyorklife.com/foundation/index.html
Sponsor: New York Life Foundation
51 Madison Avenue, Room 1600
New York, NY 10010-1655

New York Times Company Foundation Grants 1387

The major areas in which the foundation entertains applications for grants are education, journalism, cultural affairs, community services, and environmental concerns, with the greatest portion going to cultural affairs. Types of support include general operating purposes, scholarship funds, building construction funds, employee matching gifts, seed grants, and programs/projects. Under education, direct grants are given to colleges as well as college associations; scholarship programs are also supported, especially for minorities, as are a number of general programs. Freedom of the press and of all channels of communications is a matter of highest priority to the foundation. The cultural affairs program makes grants to museums, libraries, the performing arts, and for general requests to improve arts-related activities. Foundation support of the disadvantaged is divided among urban, national, and international community services. Grants in the area of environmental concerns are made largely in the New York City area. All grants will be made in localities where there is a New York Times affiliate, or to organizations of national stature in wildlife protection and conservation. Applications may be submitted at any time. The board meets during the first and third quarters to award monies based on the president's recommendations. Giving is primarily in the New York, NY, metropolitan area and in localities served by business units of the company.
Requirements: A brief letter describing the purpose for which funds are requested, including details of other potential sources of support, is sufficient for an application. Proof of tax-exempt status is also required.
Restrictions: Grants are not made to individuals, to sectarian religious institutions and causes, or for drug, alcohol, or health-related purposes.
Geographic Focus: All States
Amount of Grant: 1,000 - 25,000 USD
Contact: Program Contact; (212) 556-1091; fax (212) 556-4450
Internet: http://www.nytco.com/company/foundation/index.html
Sponsor: New York Times Company Foundation
229 W 43rd Street, 2nd Floor
New York, NY 10036

New York Women's Foundation Grants   1388

The foundation's goal is to support women helping low-income girls and women in New York City to achieve sustained economic self-sufficiency and self-reliance. The foundation's specific program areas of interest include community organizing and advocacy, economic security, girls' positive development, violence against women and girls, and women's health and reproductive rights. For the current year, only organizations whose constituencies consist of or who serve a majority of women and/or girls are eligible to apply for general operating support. As part of its grantmaking, the foundation is committed to supporting the efforts of organizations to develop their administrative and programmatic infrastructure. Capacity-building initiatives may be included as part of an organization's proposal for general or program support. The foundation also encourages the collaboration of organizations to increase the efficiency and effectiveness of service delivery and advocacy efforts and welcomes proposals for collaborative activities within its five program areas. Guidelines are available online.

Requirements: Organization/program criteria include: are within the five boroughs of New York City; work in the following issue areas: community organizing and advocacy, economic security, girls' positive development, violence against women and girls, and women's health and reproductive rights; are community-based, led by women (board and staff), and include recognized leaders of their community; are designed specifically for low-income women and girls, particularly women of color, immigrants, lesbians, the elderly, or other underserved populations; strive toward the philosophy of women helping women, an active, consensus-driven form of management; encourage the involvement of program participants in the decision-making; have limited access to ongoing traditional funding sources, i.e., government, foundations, and individual donors; and have been in existence for at least six months.

Restrictions: The foundation does not provide funds to individuals; start a new project (seed money); capital fund projects; endowments; fundraising events; feasibility studies; real estate purchases; public or private schools; colleges or universities; campaigns to elect candidates to public office; programs to promote religious activities; statewide, national, or international organizations; programs that are primarily artistic or cultural; programs located outside the five boroughs of New York City; or programs that do not comply with federal, state, or local equal employment statutes.

Geographic Focus: New York

Date(s) Application is Due: Oct 14

Amount of Grant: 10,000 - 40,000 USD

Contact: Administrator; (212) 414-4342; fax (212) 414-5708; info@nwf.org

Internet: http://www.nywf.org/grant.html

Sponsor: New York Women's Foundation

34 W 22nd Street

New York, NY 10010

NFF Collaboration Support Grants   1389

The intent of the Collaborative Support Program is to promote innovation and advancement in the field of community-based natural resource collaboration, and to support collaborative processes whose work benefits America's National Forests and Grasslands. Grants range up to $5,000 for Capacity grants, and up to $10,000 for Innovation grants. Technical assistance provided includes peer learning, mentoring and coaching opportunities. Examples of grant activities might include: collaborative work on an emerging topic (for example, newly recognized invasive species or private land transfer to public ownership); structured information sharing; new approaches to collaborative stewardship; and multiparty monitoring.

Requirements: Community-based collaborative groups working on stewardship issues on National Forests and Grasslands across the country are eligible to apply.

Geographic Focus: All States

Date(s) Application is Due: Feb 15; Apr 29

Amount of Grant: Up to 10,000 USD

Contact: Adam Liljeblad, Director, Conservation Awards; (406) 542-2805; fax (406) 542-2810; aliljeblad@nationalforests.org

Internet: http://nationalforests.org/conserve/grantprograms

Sponsor: National Forest Foundation

Fort Missoula Road, Building 27, Suite 3

Missoula, MT 59804

NFF Community Assistance Grants   1390

The NFF established the Community Assistance Program (CAP) in 2002 to promote the creation of locally based organizations or groups seeking to resolve natural resource issues through a collaborative, dialogue based process. The program proves support in the form of start-up funds for newly forming (or significantly reorganizing) groups or nonprofit organizations that intend to proactively and inclusively engage local stakeholders in forest management and conservation issues on and around the National Forests and Grasslands. CAP awards provide collaborative groups with start-up grants of $5,000 to $15,000, as well as basic tools and guidance, to enable them to resolve differences and play a more active role in the sustainable management of nearby National Forests, Grasslands and surrounding communities. Organizations applying for funding through CAP will be considered based on need, and will not be required to match the NFF funds. CAP funds can be used for a wide range of tools, including: technical assistance, training, consultants, community outreach, obtaining 501(c)3 status, group facilitation, basic startup and operating costs, materials and equipment, program development, nonprofit management kill building, and communications.

Requirements: In order to qualify for a grant through the CAP, the applicant must be: newly forming or significantly reorganizing collaborative community-based nonprofits or unincorporated groups; engaged in a collaborative process; based in the community in which the collaboration is taking place and be legitimate stakeholders in the collaborative process; working to develop solutions for sustainable management or restoration on and around National Forests and Grasslands that lead to on-the-ground work; specific issues should be related to community-based forest stewardship, recreation, watershed restoration, and/or wildlife habitat; incorporated as a 501(c)3 or utilize a fiscal sponsor organization with that designation; and seeking to build local ecological, social and economic sustainability.

Restrictions: Established organizations, fire safe councils, federal agencies, and state or local governmental entities are not eligible to apply.

Geographic Focus: All States

Date(s) Application is Due: Jan 15; Jul 7

Amount of Grant: 5,000 - 15,000 USD

Contact: Adam Liljeblad, Director, Conservation Awards; (406) 542-2805; fax (406) 542-2810; aliljeblad@nationalforests.org

Internet: http://nationalforests.org/conserve/grantprograms

Sponsor: National Forest Foundation

Fort Missoula Road, Building 27, Suite 3

Missoula, MT 59804

NFF Mid-Capacity Assistance Grants   1391

The primary purpose of the Mid-Capacity Assistance Grants is to assist mid-capacity collaborative organizations whose work benefits America's National Forests and Grasslands in building their organizational capacity. Examples of technical assistance and support include: peer learning, mentoring and coaching opportunities; and development of monitoring/outcome plans in coordination with the Western Collaboration Assistance Network (WestCAN). Grant supported activities may include: strategic planning, support for on-going collaborative process needs, training, and board development.

Requirements: Mid-capacity collaborative, community-based groups working on stewardship issues on National Forests and Grasslands are eligible to apply. Applicants may apply for up to $70,000 for a two-year period.

Geographic Focus: All States

Date(s) Application is Due: Feb 15; Apr 29

Amount of Grant: Up to 70,000 USD

Contact: Adam Liljeblad, Director, Conservation Awards; (406) 542-2805; fax (406) 542-2810; aliljeblad@nationalforests.org

Internet: http://nationalforests.org/conserve/grantprograms/capacitybuilding/ccls

Sponsor: National Forest Foundation

Fort Missoula Road, Building 27, Suite 3

Missoula, MT 59804

NFF Ski Conservation Grants   1392

Through its Ski Conservation Fund, the National Forest Foundation (NFF) has teamed up with ski areas, lodges and resorts located on National Forest lands to raise money for the care of their local National Forest. Funds are raised through voluntary contributions from guests at participating ski areas and lodges throughout the country and are matched with NFF federal funds. These dollars are invested in on-the-ground conservation projects, completed by local nonprofit organizations, on or around the National Forest from which they originate. The projects advance the NFF's on-the-ground, action-oriented approach to wildlife habitat improvement, watershed restoration, community-based forestry programs and forest recreation improvements. Grants can range from $5,000 to $100,000, but typically average $35,000.

Requirements: Nonprofit organizations accomplishing conservation work on a participating National Forest can apply.

Geographic Focus: All States

Amount of Grant: 5,000 - 100,000 USD

Contact: Adam Liljeblad, Director, Conservation Awards; (406) 542-2805; fax (406) 542-2810; aliljeblad@nationalforests.org
Internet: http://nationalforests.org/conserve/grantprograms/ontheground/scf
Sponsor: National Forest Foundation
Fort Missoula Road, Building 27, Suite 3
Missoula, MT 59804

NHSCA Cultural Facilities Grants: Barrier Free Access for All 1393

Cultural Facilities grants will support renovations, maintenance, and purchase of major equipment that supports creating a universal or inclusive environment for the arts where programs, services, and activities are accessible to everyone, including people with and without disabilities. Requests may be made for $1,000 to $8,000. Government agencies, municipalities and towns, county agencies, state agencies, or federal agencies that own a historic cultural facility; or nonprofit organizations that manage publicly owned historic cultural facilities, are encouraged to apply for a Cultural Conservation Grant.
Requirements: At a minimum, grants must be matched on a one-to-one basis. In-kind contributions may comprise one half of the required match and will also be considered by the reviewers as evidence of support and commitment by the community and/or partner organization. Organizations with 501(c)3 tax-exempt status from the IRS and not-for-profit incorporation in the State of New Hampshire may apply, provided that they: own or have a minimum three-year lease on the facility, or demonstrable ability to acquire by deed, or a minimum three-year lease on the proposed facility when it is built or rehabilitated for cultural use; operate or will establish a cultural facility in New Hampshire; have one year of experience in arts programming for the general public prior to the date of application, or have plans for at least one year of arts programming at the facility it plans to operate; must demonstrate that the facility is striving to be in full compliance with the Americans with Disabilities Act (ADA) requirements; have submitted all required reports on past State Arts Council grants; and are in good standing with the N.H. Secretary of State's Office and the N.H. Attorney General's Office.
Restrictions: State Arts Council funds may not be matched by other State Arts Council or National Endowment for the Arts funds.
Geographic Focus: New Hampshire
Date(s) Application is Due: Mar 31
Amount of Grant: 1,000 - 8,000 USD
Contact: Cassandra Erickson Mason, Grants Coordinator; (603) 271-7926 or (603) 271-2789; fax (603) 271-3584; cassandra.mason@dcr.nh.gov
Internet: http://www.nh.gov/nharts/grants/culturalfacilities.htm
Sponsor: New Hampshire State Council on the Arts
19 Pillsbury Street, 1st Floor
Concord, NH 03301

NHSCA Operating Grants 1394

Operating grants are an investment in the cultural infrastructure and creative economy of New Hampshire. The creative economy is made up of artists, not for profit organizations and creative businesses that positively impact quality of life in communities, generate jobs and produce revenue for municipalities, cities and the state. These competitive and matching grants are awarded in two-year cycles to not-for-profit arts and cultural organizations that demonstrate excellence in planning, administration and programming. Grantees are expected to provide high quality arts experiences, activities and services for New Hampshire citizens and ensure that the arts are accessible to all. They are also expected to maintain close and productive relationships with other community organizations and businesses, ensuring that the arts are integral to community infrastructure.
Requirements: Not-for-profit organizations with incorporation in New Hampshire and a 501(c)3 tax-exempt status from the Internal Revenue Service, whose primary mission is to produce, present or serve the arts. In addition, applicant organizations must: have been in continuous operation as a 501(c)3 non-profit arts organization for at least five years prior to application for an Operating Grant; have an independent board of directors that meets at least quarterly; have a paid, full-time arts administrator; have a long-range plan in place that covers the two-year grant period; be fully in compliance with the Americans with Disabilities Act requirements; have submitted all required reports on past State Arts Council grants; and be in good standing with the State Arts Council and NH Attorney General's Office.
Restrictions: Requests are for unrestricted operational funds and may be made for up to $15,000 per year. The request for the first year of the grant period may not exceed 10% of income in the organization's last fiscal year prior to application. Applicants also must be able to leverage other support and project a cash match, excluding federal and state funds, of at least $10 for each $1

requested from the State Arts Council. Applicant organizations must be physically located in New Hampshire, not just incorporated in the state. In general, a college, university, library, or school is not eligible for Operating Grants unless its primary mission is the arts and the majority of its arts activities are open to the general public. Grant awards may not be used for previously incurred debts or deficits. Operating Grant awards may not be used for endowments or capital projects, and recipients are ineligible to receive additional General Project Grants, except for the Traditional Arts Project strand, during the Operating Grant period.
Geographic Focus: New Hampshire
Date(s) Application is Due: Mar 11
Amount of Grant: Up to 15,000 USD
Contact: Cassandra Erickson Mason, Chief Grants Officer; (603) 271-7926 or (603) 271-2789; fax (603) 271-3584; cassandra.mason@dcr.nh.gov
Internet: http://www.nh.gov/nharts/grants/organizations/operating.htm
Sponsor: New Hampshire State Council on the Arts
19 Pillsbury Street, 1st Floor
Concord, NH 03301

Nicholas H. Noyes Jr. Memorial Foundation Grants 1395

The foundation awards grants to eligible Indiana nonprofit organizations in its areas of interest, including arts and culture, education from early childhood through higher education, disadvantaged, museums, social services, health, hospitals, family services, performing arts, and youth. Types of support include general operating support, endowment funds, and scholarship funds.
Requirements: Proposals are welcomed, and encouraged, to be submitted at any time after January 1st for the first funding cycle or after June 1st for the final funding cycle. Submit the following with your proposal: thirteen copies of the complete grant application (available at the foundations website or office) including attachments (i.e. applicable budget(s) as required). You may recreate the application form for ease in completing, but please limit your response to the space provided and use a minimum font of 12. It is also require that you use both sides of the paper i.e. side one is page 1 with page 2 on the flip-side etc; one copy of your organization's 501(c)3 tax determination letter from the IRS; one copy of your organization's most recent audited financial statement for all organizations requesting $25,000 or more.
Restrictions: Organizations may apply only one time in any calendar year. The Foundation does not make grants to individuals. The principle geographic region served by the Noyes Foundation is the greater Indianapolis area. If you intend to request a grant in excess of $50,000, please contact the Foundation's Program Officer before submitting your grant request.
Geographic Focus: Indiana
Date(s) Application is Due: Feb 1; Aug 29
Amount of Grant: Up to 150,000 USD
Contact: Kelly Mills, Executive Administrator; (317) 844-8009; fax (317) 844-8099; kmills@noyesfoundation.org
Internet: http://www.noyesfoundation.org
Sponsor: Nicholas H. Noyes Jr. Memorial Foundation
1950 E Greyhound Pass, #18
Carmel, IN 46033-7730

Nicor Corporate Contributions 1396

Nicor Gas' philanthropy mission is to apply its charitable funds, company expertise and employee volunteer efforts to help fulfill the educational, health, cultural and community needs of the people who reside in our service territory. Its strategic focus is to help educators and those who support the educational system by providing enrichment opportunities that will assist students in achieving their educational goals.
Requirements: Charitable contributions will be made only to eligible organizations that have a current determination letter exempting them from federal tax under Section 501(c)3 of the Internal Revenue Code. Eligible not-for-profit organizations requesting support from Nicor Gas must prepare and submit the required application form (available for downloading at the website) and all required attachments. Requests may be made for the following types of contributions: (a) General Operating - Only one operating gift will be made to an organization during a year. If an organization receives United Way funding, it will not be eligible for a general operating gift, but may be considered for funding an event if Nicor employees are involved. (b) Events - Requests for support of events in the communities Nicor serves and where Nicor Gas employees are involved will be given consideration. (c) Capital Campaigns - Support may be granted for building and remodeling programs of not-for-profit organizations that best advance Nicor Gas' priorities and add value to the communities where Nicor serves. Capital grants are not multi-

year commitments. (d) In-Kind Support - Requests for surplus furniture, equipment or services will be reviewed upon receipt. The response will be based on contribution priorities and availability of the requested gift.

Restrictions: Grants will not be made to: organizations without IRS 501(c)3 designation or equivalent; individuals or foundations; social, athletic, recreational or union groups; endowment or debt reduction drives; churches or religious groups in support of their sacramental or theological functions; organizations with discriminatory practices; political parties, groups or candidates; organizations soliciting advertising space in newspapers or programs; specific schools or foundations supporting specific secondary or primary schools.

Geographic Focus: Illinois

Contact: Julian Brown; (630) 388-2763; jbrown@nicor.com

Internet: http://www.nicor.com/en_us/nicor_inc/nicor_in_the_community/grants_and_donations.htm

Sponsor: Nicor

P.O. Box 3014

Naperville, IL 60566-3014

Nina Mason Pulliam Charitable Trust Grants 1397

The Nina Mason Pulliam Charitable Trust provides grants that focus on the areas of service Nina Pulliam supported during her lifetime: helping people in need; protecting animals and nature; enriching community life. The Trust awards grants for program projects and capital needs, and provides application opportunities three times during the calendar year. The Trust prefers to disperse funds as a one-year grant, but will consider projects of up to three years.

Requirements: Primary consideration is given to 501(c)3 charitable organizations that serve metropolitan Indianapolis and Phoenix. Secondary consideration is given to the states of Indiana and Arizona. National organizations whose programs benefit these priority areas and/or benefit society as a whole are occasionally considered.

Restrictions: Grants are not awarded for international purposes or academic research, Grants are not awarded to individuals, sectarian organizations for religious purposes, or to non-operating private foundations except in extraordinary circumstances.

Geographic Focus: Arizona, Indiana

Date(s) Application is Due: Jan 4; May 4; Sep 4

Samples: Chrysalis Academy of Life and Learning, $75,000 for a residential program to develop self-sufficiency among young men ages 18-24; Indiana Legal Services, to continue a project that helps individuals avoid losing their homes in inner-city Indianapolis neighborhoods because of abusive lending practices, $35,000; Camptown, Inc., to send 100 underprivileged youths on wilderness trips, $28,000; St. Francis Healthcare Foun dation, Inc., $35,000 to hire an additional social worker to serve residents in the Garfield Park area.

Contact: David Hillman, (317) 231-6075; fax (317) 231-9208

Internet: http://www.ninapulliamtrust.org

Sponsor: Nina Mason Pulliam Charitable Trust

135 N Pennsylvania Street, Suite 1200

Indianapolis, IN 46204

NJSCA General Operating Support Grants 1398

General Operating Support (GOS) is awarded to New Jersey based, nonprofit, arts-missioned organizations to help underwrite the expense of their total operation including the expenses of producing and presenting arts events. Receipt of a GOS grant usually carries the commitment of the Council to fund the program over a three-year period, although the funding level will be determined annually. Review and consideration of GOS requests occur only every three years. Applicants must file a Notice of Intent online as well as apply online. Deadline dates may vary; contact the program office for exact dates. Deadlines must be met by eFiling by midnight on the deadline date. The deadline for signed originals and support materials is within two business days of the eDeadline and can be met with either a postmark or actual delivery of the materials to NJSCA offices at 225 West State Street, 4th Floor in Trenton by 5:00 p.m on the deadline date. New Jersey State Council on the Arts is a Division in the New Jersey Department of State and Partner Agency with the National Endowment for the Arts.

Requirements: Applicants must be incorporated in the State of New Jersey as a 501(c)3 organization or be a unit of government; be registered with the New Jersey Charities Registration Bureau; have a clearly articulated mission relating to the arts; have been in existence and actively providing public programs or services for at least the past two years at time of application; have a board of directors empowered to formulate policies and be responsible for the governance and administration of the organization, its programs and finances; demonstrate regional or statewide public impact through the organization's programs or project (regional is defined as serving audiences across a two or more county region of New Jersey). Matching funds are required and must be cash, not in-kind. For each dollar received from the Council, the grantee must show three additional dollars raised and spent, based on operating income. Applicants must apply online and should be advised that the prerequisite pre-registraton process requires up to 72 hours for completion by the system administrator before they can access the system.

Restrictions: Applicants may apply either to the Council or to their County Arts Agency, not both, in a given year. Prospective NJSCA applicants that have been receiving support through their County Arts Agency up to now should attend a scheduled NJSCA grant workshop, work closely with Council staff and their County Arts Agency in filing their Notice of Intent to Apply, and may also want to schedule a meeting early in the process with Council staff. Because the funding periods for the County Arts Agency grants and the State Council grants overlap by six months, applicants should discuss their situation in advance of the Notice of Intent to Apply with the State Council to determine eligibility. K-12 schools and school districts are not eligible to apply, but may be a partner or collaborator on a project with an eligible applicant.

Geographic Focus: New Jersey

Date(s) Application is Due: Feb 23

Contact: Steve Runk; (609) 292-6130; steve.runk@sos.state.nj.us

Internet: http://www.njartscouncil.org/grant.cfm

Sponsor: New Jersey State Council on the Arts

225 West State Street, P.O. Box 306

Trenton, NJ 08625-0306

NNEDVF/Altria Doors of Hope Program 1399

The goal of this initiative is to strengthen the safety net available to survivors of domestic violence through the provision of grant awards that support organizational excellence, innovation, and leadership in the provision of shelter and legal advocacy services. Direct service grants are awarded to domestic violence service providers for shelter services and advocacy/legal services. There is a two stage application process; stage one consists of registration online, which includes key questions that will be used to determine which applicants will be invited to apply for stage two. For the current funding year, grantmaking will be by invitation only. Applicants will be contacted if they are eligible to apply. Additional assistance and information is provided at www.nnedv.org.

Requirements: Eligible organizations must have a primary mission which includes the provision of direct services to survivors of domestic violence; provide shelter and/or legal advocacy services to survivors of domestic violence; be a U.S. based non-profit, non-governmental, tax-exempt organization; have been in operation for a minimum of three years with an organization budget greater than or equal to $250,000; and have nondiscrimination policies that include ethnicity, race, religious creed, national origin, disability, sexual orientation, marital status, age, and gender.

Restrictions: Applications will only be accepted through the online RFP.

Geographic Focus: All States

Amount of Grant: 10,000 - 50,000 USD

Samples: Hmong American Friendship Association (Milwaukee, WI)—to provide group facilitators, education groups in the workplace, and domestic violence training for Hmong elders, $24,000; Susquehanna Valley Women in Transition (Lewisburg, PA)—to implement and teach a curriculum of safe living and violence prevention to group home residents with mental disabilities, $19,000.

Contact: Grants Administrator; (202) 543-5566; fax (202) 543-5626; altriadoorsofhope@nnedv.org

Internet: http://www.altria.com/responsibility/4_9_1_1_2_1_domviolprograms.asp

Sponsor: National Network to End Domestic Violence Fund

660 Pennsylvania Avenue SE, Suite 303

Washington, D.C. 20003

Norcliffe Foundation Grants 1400

The Norcliffe Foundation is a private nonprofit family foundation established in 1952 by Paul Pigott for the purpose of improving the quality of life for all people in the Puget Sound region. The foundation provides grants in the areas of health, education, social services, civic improvement, religion, culture and the arts, the environment, historic preservation and youth programs. Foundation funding types include capital campaigns for building and equipment, certain operating budgets, endowments, challenge/matching grants, land acquisition, new projects, start-up funds, renovation, and research. Requests for publication, videos/films, and website production may be considered as may scholarships, fellowships / chairs, conferences / seminars, social enterprise development, and technical assistance. Multi-year and renewable funding may be considered. Applications are accepted year-round. One copy of a letter proposal and/or common grant application form should be directed to the President in care of the Foundation Manager at the contact information given. An initial phone call is optional. Guidelines, instructions, and a copy of the common grant proposal form are provided at the website. Funding decisions and notification generally occur three to six months after receipt of request.

Requirements: 501(c)3 organizations in the Puget Sound region in and around Seattle, Washington are eligible to apply.

Restrictions: The Norcliffe Foundation does not provide the following types of assistance: deficit financing, emergency funds, grants to individuals, matches to employee-giving, Program-Related Investments / Loans (PRIs), in-kind services, volunteer / loaned executive, and internships. Applicants may only submit one request per year from date of funding or denial. Applicants who have previously received grants of $50,000 or more from the Foundation must wait two years from final payment before submitting a new application.

Geographic Focus: Washington

Amount of Grant: 1,000 - 25,000 USD

Contact: Arline Hefferline, Foundation Manager; (206) 682-4820; fax (206) 682-4821; arline@thenorcliffefoundation.com

Internet: http://www.thenorcliffefoundation.com/

Sponsor: Norcliffe Foundation

999 Third Avenue, Suite 1006

Seattle, WA 98104-4001

Nordson Corporation Foundation Grants 1401

The corporate foundation awards grants to nonprofit organizations in geographic areas where Nordson facilities and employees are located: Cuyahoga and Lorain counties in Ohio; the Greater Atlanta, Georgia area; California, Rhode Island and Southeastern Massachusetts. The foundation provides a source of stable funding for community programs and projects in the areas of education, human welfare, civic, and arts and culture. Educational support is generally limited to improving elementary and secondary schools and certain programs for public and private higher education. Human welfare grants focus on children and youth. The foundation considers other funding areas, including urban affairs, volunteerism, public policy, health and health organizations, and literacy. Grants are awarded for general operating support, continuing support, annual campaigns, capital campaigns, building construction/renovation, equipment acquisition, emergency funds, seed money, scholarship funds, employee matching gifts, and technical assistance. The board meets four times each year. Deadlines vary by state; contact program staff for appropriate deadlines. Application forms are available on the website and may only be submitted online.

Requirements: Private, nonprofit organizations in California, Georgia, Ohio, Rhode Island, and southeastern Massachusetts may apply.

Restrictions: Funding is not provided for organizations whose services are not provided within the foundation's geographic areas of interest; direct grants or scholarships to individuals; organizations not eligible for tax-deductible support; organizations not exempt under Section 501(c)3 of the Internal Revenue Code; political causes, candidates, organizations or campaigns; organizations that discriminate on the basis of race, sex, or religion; or special occasion, goodwill advertising, i.e., journals or dinner programs.

Geographic Focus: California, Georgia, Massachusetts, Ohio, Rhode Island

Date(s) Application is Due: Feb 15; May 15; Aug 15; Nov 15

Amount of Grant: Up to 15,000,000 USD

Samples: Ctr for Leadership in Education (Lorain, OH)—for general operating support, $250,000; Salvation Army of Lorain (Lorain, OH)—for the capital campaign, $50,000; Neighborhood House Assoc of Lorain County (Lorain, OH)—for rejuvenation of the Cityview Ctr, $39,625.

Contact: Cecilia H. Render; (440) 892-1580, ext. 5172; crender@nordson.com

Internet: http://www.nordson.com/Corporate/Community/Foundation

Sponsor: Nordson Corporation Foundation

28601 Clemens Road

Westlake, OH 44145-1119

Norfolk Southern Foundation Grants 1402

The Norfolk Southern Foundation awards grants to nonprofits in the territory served by Norfolk Southern Railway Company. The foundation offers grants in four principal areas: educational programs, primarily at the post-secondary level; community enrichment focusing on cultural and artistic organizations; environmental programs; and health and human services (primarily food banks, homeless programs, and free clinics). Decision are made by December 31 for the following year's discretionary funding program, and applicants are notified early in the following calendar year.

Requirements: Applicants should include the following in their information packet: a valid 501(c)3 or 170(c)1 letter from the IRS; a short request outlining

objectives of the organization, project, and intended use of funds; a listing of the applicant's board of directors; current and potential sources of funding; audited financial statements from the last three years; and the applicant's contact name, phone number, and email address.

Restrictions: Grant requests are only accepted between July 15 and September 30 for funding in the following calendar year. Applications will not be accepted from: organizations not in the NS territory (must be served by Norfolk Southern to be considered); organizations that do not have a 501(c)3 or 170(c)(1) IRS letter; individuals or organizations established to help individuals; religious, fraternal, social or veterans organizations; political or lobbying organizations; public or private elementary and secondary schools; fundraising events, telethons, races or benefits; sports or athletic organizations or activities; community or private foundations, or other organizations that merely redistribute to other eligible organizations aggregated contributions; disease-related organizations and hospitals; mentoring programs; Boys and Girls Scout programs or similar organizations; animal organizations; non-U.S. based charities; and organizations whose programs have national scope

Geographic Focus: Alabama, Connecticut, Delaware, District of Columbia, Florida, Georgia, Illinois, Indiana, Iowa, Kentucky, Louisiana, Maine, Maryland, Massachusetts, Michigan, Mississippi, Missouri, New Hampshire, New Jersey, New York, North Carolina, Ohio, Pennsylvania, Rhode Island, South Carolina, Tennessee, Texas, Vermont, Virginia, West Virginia, Wisconsin

Date(s) Application is Due: Sep 30

Amount of Grant: Up to USD

Contact: Katie Fletcher, Executive Director; (757) 629-2881; fax (757) 629-2361; katie.fletcher@nscorp.com

Internet: http://www.nscorp.com/nscportal/nscorp/Community/NS%20Foundation/

Sponsor: Norfolk Southern Foundation

P.O. Box 3040

Norfolk, VA 23514-3040

Norman Foundation Grants 1403

The Norman Foundation supports efforts that strengthen the ability of communities to determine their own economic, environmental and social well-being, and that help people control those forces that affect their lives. These efforts may: promote economic justice and development through community organizing, coalition building and policy reform efforts; work to prevent the disposal of toxics in communities, and to link environmental issues with economic and social justice; link community-based economic and environmental justice organizing to national and international reform efforts. The following is considered when evaluating grant proposals: does the project arise from the hopes and efforts of those whose survival, well-being and liberation are directly at stake; does it further ethnic, gender and other forms of equity; is it rooted in organized, practical undertakings; and is it likely to achieve systemic change. In pursuing systemic change, the Foundation would hope that: the proposed action may serve as a model; the spread of the model may create institutions that can survive on their own; their establishment and success may generate beneficial adaptations by other political, social and economic institutions and structures. The Foundation provides grants for general support, projects, and collaborative efforts. We also welcome innovative proposals designed to build the capacity of social change organizations working in our areas of interest. Priority is given to organizations with annual budgets of under $1 million.

Requirements: Programs must be 501(c)3 tax-exempt organizations that focused on domestic United States issues. Prospective grantees should initiate the application process by sending a short two or three page letter of inquiry to the Program Director (fax, email or regular mail). There are no set deadlines, and letters of inquiry are reviewed throughout the year. The Foundation only accepts full proposals upon positive response to the letter of inquiry. The letter of inquiry should briefly explain: the scope and significance of the problem to be addressed; the organization's proposed response and (if appropriate) how this strategy builds upon the organization's past work; the specific demonstrable effects the project would have if successful, especially its potential to effect systemic (fundamental, institutional and significant) change; how the project promotes change on a national level and is otherwise related to the foundation's guidelines; the size of the organization's budget. All inquiries will be acknowledged and, if deemed promising, the Foundation will request a full proposal.

Restrictions: The Foundation does not make grants to individuals or universities; or to support conferences, scholarships, research, films, media and arts projects; or to capital funding projects, fundraising drives or direct social service programs, such as shelters or community health programs. The Foundation's grant making is restricted to U.S.-based organizations.

Geographic Focus: All States

Amount of Grant: 5,000 - 30,000 USD
Contact: June Makela; (212) 230-9830; norman@normanfdn.org
Internet: http://www.normanfdn.org/
Sponsor: Norman Foundation
147 East 48th Street
New York, NY 10017

North Carolina Arts Council Folklife Public Program Grants 1404

Public programs support: exhibitions, performances and workshops, publications, and radio and television programs that promote public knowledge and appreciation of the state's traditional arts; or salary assistance to organizations that create a staff position for a professional folklorist. Grant funds also support expenses directly related to the project including production costs, stipends, honoraria, marketing, travel, supplies, telephone, and postage.
Requirements: North Carolina nonprofit organizations are eligible.
Geographic Focus: North Carolina
Date(s) Application is Due: Mar 2
Amount of Grant: Up to 10,000 USD
Contact: Sally Peterson; (919) 807-6507; sally.peterson@ncdcr.gov
Internet: http://www.ncarts.org/grants_programs.cfm?ID=6
Sponsor: North Carolina Arts Council
Department of Cultural Resources, 109 East Jones Street, MSC #4632
Raleigh, NC 27601-2807

North Carolina Arts Council General Support Grants 1405

This category provides funds to arts organizations to support their ongoing artistic and administrative functions. Fundable expenses may include, but are not limited to, salaries, artists fees, production, travel, promotion, postage, telephone, and facility operation. This category is designed to support groups that, over time, have consistently produced strong artistic programs and demonstrated responsible administrative practices. All grant-funded activities must take place between July 1 of the current year and June 30 of the next. Application materials are available on the Web site.
Requirements: North Carolina dance, literary, music, theater, and visual arts organizations may apply. Grants must be matched dollar for dollar from the organization's budget. Organizations not previously funded in this category must contact the council staff to discuss eligibility before submitting applications.
Restrictions: University museums or galleries are not eligible to apply.
Geographic Focus: North Carolina
Date(s) Application is Due: Mar 2
Amount of Grant: 5,000 - 70,000 USD
Contact: Linda Bamford; (919) 807-6502; linda.bamford@ncmail.net
Internet: http://www.ncarts.org/grants_programs.cfm?ID=7
Sponsor: North Carolina Arts Council
Department of Cultural Resources, 109 East Jones Street, MSC #4632
Raleigh, NC 27601-2807

North Carolina Arts Council Outreach Program Grants 1406

The Program has two distinct categories: technical assistance to organizations that have an operating budget of at least $10,000 and that have been producing arts programs for two or more years; and funds to support the ongoing artistic and administrative functions of organizations that have operating budgets of $50,000 or higher and have been producing arts programs for three or more years.
Requirements: North Carolina nonprofit, tax-exempt arts organizations, primarily based in and focused on the African American, Asian American, Hispanic, or Native American communities, may apply. Single-discipline organizations that are not the primary constituents of other council sections are eligible for support, as well as multidisciplinary organizations that serve a wide range of art forms including the performing, visual, and literary arts in their cultures.
Geographic Focus: North Carolina
Date(s) Application is Due: Mar 2
Amount of Grant: 2,500 - 20,000 USD
Contact: Janie Wilson; (919) 807-6508; janie.wilson@ncmail.net
Internet: http://www.ncarts.org/freeform_scrn_template.cfm?ffscrn_id=153
Sponsor: North Carolina Arts Council
Department of Cultural Resources, 109 East Jones Street, MSC #4632
Raleigh, NC 27601-2807

North Carolina Arts Council Statewide Service Organization Grants 1407

This category provides funds to service organizations for projects and programs that serve their members, artists, arts organizations, and the arts community. Funded programs and services may include newsletters, listserv and Web site management, conferences, workshops, classes, consultations, research, resource publications, presentations, and the development and distribution of promotional materials. Grant funds support administrative and program expenses directly related to the proposed programs and services. Grant amounts range from $5,000 - $35,000 and must be matched dollar for dollar by the organization.
Requirements: Organizations that provide programs and services to the arts community on a regional or statewide basis may apply. First-time applicants to this category should consult with staff to determine eligibility.
Geographic Focus: North Carolina
Date(s) Application is Due: Mar 2
Amount of Grant: 5,000 - 35,000 USD
Contact: Jeff Pettus; (919) 807-6513; jeff.pettus@ncmail.net
Internet: http://www.ncarts.org/grants_programs.cfm?ID=18
Sponsor: North Carolina Arts Council
Department of Cultural Resources, 109 East Jones Street, MSC #4632
Raleigh, NC 27601-2807

North Carolina Arts Council Technical Assistance Grants 1408

Funds are provided to organizations to: hire knowledgeable consultants to strengthen an organization's management and programs or conduct planning meetings for a specific project; sponsor workshops or conferences; develop a resource publication; develop a community-wide cultural plan; provide scholarships to send staff members to conferences, workshops or short-term programs (available on a limited basis). Examples of issues consultants may address include, but are not limited to, staff development, community relations, fund-raising, audience development, and financial management. Organizations should contact the council staff before applying in this category.
Requirements: Any North Carolina nonprofit arts organization or organization that provides arts programs, such as schools or community organizations, may apply. Grants must be matched dollar-for-dollar by the applicant, except in cases of demonstrated need.
Geographic Focus: North Carolina
Date(s) Application is Due: Mar 2
Amount of Grant: 2,500 USD
Contact: Janie Wilson; (919) 807-6508; janie.wilson@ncmail.net
Internet: http://www.ncarts.org/freeform_scrn_template.cfm?ffscrn_id=121
Sponsor: North Carolina Arts Council
Department of Cultural Resources, 109 East Jones Street, MSC #4632
Raleigh, NC 27601-2807

North Carolina Arts Council Visual Arts Program Support Grants 1409

The program provides funds to North Carolina nonprofit organizations that: support innovative performing (dance, music, and theater) or visual arts programming and services; provide programs or services to the state's arts community or promote awareness about the arts in the state; advance public discussion and understanding of an artist or art form; and support innovative arts programming for public public television. All grant-funded activities must take place between July 1 of the current year and June 30 of the next. Grant funds support artistic and administrative expenses directly related to the project. Both first-time and experienced applicants are encouraged to contact council staff early in the planning of their grant proposals to receive information on preparing competitive applications and to discuss proposed projects.
Requirements: North Carolina nonprofit organizations that produce literary, performing, or visual arts programs may apply. Statewide service organizations also may apply. Grants must be matched dollar-for-dollar by the organization. Organizations may apply for projects spanning more than one year; applicants must reapply each year for funding of a multiyear project.
Geographic Focus: North Carolina
Date(s) Application is Due: Mar 2
Contact: Jeff Pettus; (919) 807-6513; jeff.pettus@ncmail.net
Internet: http://www.ncarts.org/grants_category.cfm?ID=11&CFID=445783
5&CFTOKEN=61825421&jsessionid=28302898591231777988333
Sponsor: North Carolina Arts Council
Department of Cultural Resources, 109 East Jones Street, MSC #4632
Raleigh, NC 27601-2807

North Carolina Community Development Grants 1410

The foundation supports nonprofit organizations in North Carolina to enrich the quality of life in the state, with special concern for rural regions and Cabarrus County. Grants are awarded primarily for healthcare, higher education, and community service. Other more limited areas of interest are arts, culture, historic preservation, religion, and the environment. Grants generally will be awarded for capital improvements, challenge opportunities, or special purposes rather than for operating purposes. Grant requests are considered on a quarterly basis.

Requirements: IRS 501(c)3 organizations serving North Carolina communities are eligible. Churches and governmental agencies also may apply.

Restrictions: Normally, the foundation does not make multiyear grants or frequent grants to the same organization (except for select, historic relationships); or provide operating funds, start-up funding, or lead gifts. The foundation does not make grants to individuals, to endowment funds, for loans, or for scholarships or fellowships.

Geographic Focus: North Carolina

Date(s) Application is Due: Jan 5; Apr 5; Jul 5; Oct 5

Amount of Grant: 10,000 - 30,000 USD

Samples: Lenoir-Rhyne College (Hickory, NC)—for equipment and technology upgrades, $156,000; Mars Hill College (Mars Hill, NC)—to purchase two boilers and a fire-alarm system, $150,000.

Contact: Frank Davis; (704) 786-8216; fax (704) 785-2051

Internet: http://www.thecannonfoundationinc.org/guidelines.asp

Sponsor: Cannon Foundation

P.O. Box 548

Concord, NC 28026-0548

North Carolina GlaxoSmithKline Foundation Grants 1411

The foundation supports activities primarily in North Carolina that help meet the needs of today's society and future generations by funding programs that emphasize the understanding and application of health, science, and mathematics at all educational and professional levels. Although providing seed funds for new and worthwhile educational programs is the foundation's primary focus, requests for funding of ongoing projects will also receive consideration. Types of support include operating budgets, professorships, and conferences and seminars. Proposals may be submitted for either one-year or multi-year funding with a maximum of five years' duration. The foundation's board of directors meets four times a year to consider and award grants. Completed applications must be received by the listed deadline dates. If the stated deadline falls on a weekend or holiday, the next business day serves as the official deadline. All applicants will be notified of the board's decisions within 15 days of the board meeting.

Requirements: The foundation makes grants only to North Carolina 501(c)3 tax-exempt organizations and institutions or to governmental agencies.

Restrictions: Grants are not made to individuals for construction or restoration projects, or for international programs unless specifically exempted by the board. Funds are not ordinarily provided to programs that benefit a limited geographic region.

Geographic Focus: North Carolina

Date(s) Application is Due: Jan 1; Apr 1; Jul 1; Oct 1

Amount of Grant: 25,000 - 1,000,000 USD

Samples: North Carolina Center for Public Policy Research, $446,000; The Carolina Ballet, Healthier Living Through the Arts, $650,000; Prevent Blindness North Carolina, $100,000.

Contact: Marilyn Foote-Hudson, Executive Director; (919) 483-2140; fax (919) 315-3015; community.partnership@gsk.com

Internet: http://us.gsk.com/html/community/community-grants-foundation.html

Sponsor: North Carolina GlaxoSmithKline Foundation

5 Moore Drive, P.O. Box 13398

Research Triangle Park, NC 27709

North Central Michigan Community Foundation Common Grants 1412

North Central Michigan Community Foundation Common grants are awarded from the Community Needs Fund to non-profits that serve Crawford, Ogemaw, and Oscoda counties. Grants are used to fund programs and projects that benefit this geographical area. Specific funding for programs benefiting health for youth under the age of 18 and senior citizens over the age of 65 is awarded from the Tobacco Settlement Fund in conjunction with Common Grants. Applicants may submit requests up to a maximum of $3,000 per application cycle unless otherwise indicated. Mini-grants up to $300 are available. The annual deadline for application submission is June 30.

Requirements: IRS 501(c)3 nonprofit organizations, schools, churches (for non-sectarian purposes), cities, townships, and other governmental units serving Crawford, Ogemaw, and Oscoda counties are eligible to apply. An organization may apply each year for a grant.

Restrictions: No program may be funded for more than two (2) consecutive grant cycles or two (2) years, whichever is longer. The Foundation will not support the sustained funding of any program. Grants are not given to individuals, except for awards or scholarships from designated donor funds.

Geographic Focus: Michigan

Date(s) Application is Due: Jun 30

Amount of Grant: Up to 3,000 USD

Contact: Barbara Frantz, Executive Director; (989) 354-6881 or (877) 354-6881; fax (989) 356-3319; bfrantz@cfnem.org

Internet: http://www.cfnem.org/NCMCF/Common.aspx

Sponsor: North Central Michigan Community Foundation

P.O. Box 495

Alpena, MI 49707

North Dakota Council on the Arts Community Access Grants 1413

As a community-based grant program, Community Arts Access is designed to benefit nonprofit organizations that present arts programming in small and rural communities in North Dakota. It also supports nonprofit organizations in communities of all sizes whose arts programming makes a deliberate and focused effort to serve a special constituency or an under-served audience in that community. Funds for the program are appropriated by the state of North Dakota. Some of the program goals are to strengthen existing arts organizations and art forms, provide start-up funds for new or emerging arts organizations, and expand new audiences. Examples of supported activities include general operating costs, production costs, honoraria for artistic or technical directors, musical scores/performance rights, printing costs for programs and catalogs, and artist services. Grant requests may not exceed $2,000, and $650 is the minimum request. Applicants are encouraged to submit a notice of intent to apply. While this is not a requirement, it will assist the Council on the Arts in the planning of review panels and other matters.

Requirements: Applicant must be registered as a non-profit organization with the state of North Dakota, or be a community or county government entity. Organizations may form partnerships with state agencies, for-profit businesses, and other entities, but the non-profit organization must be the applicant. A 1:1 match is required. Of this, up to half may be documented in-kind.

Restrictions: Organizations supported through the Institutional Support and Mini-Grant programs, requests for Artists in Residence or LEAP activities, reduction of a deficit, and projects completed at the time of the application are ineligible.

Geographic Focus: North Dakota

Date(s) Application is Due: Apr 1; Nov 1

Amount of Grant: 650 - 2,000 USD

Contact: Amy Schmidt, Public Information Officer; (701) 328-7594; fax (701) 328-7595; amschmid@nd.gov or comserv@nd.gov

Internet: http://www.nd.gov/arts/grants/CAAguidelines.html

Sponsor: North Dakota Council on the Arts

1600 E Century Avenue, Suite 6

Bismarck, ND 58503-0649

North Dakota Council on the Arts Institutional Support Grants 1414

The Institutional Support program is designed to benefit artists, arts organizations, and the general public. The program provides general support for local arts councils and other arts organizations, as well as support for performances, exhibitions, publications, classes, workshops, and special events in all arts disciplines. The program's goals are to assist arts institutions and cultural organizations in improving artistic or administrative standards; encourage arts organizations to attain financial stability by developing a diversified funding base; expand cultural opportunities to new audiences and under-served areas; and increase opportunities for local artists and others to participate in a wide range of arts activities. Examples of funded activities include general operating expenses; honoraria for artistic and technical staff/ services; and production costs for performances, exhibitions, and publications. Letter of intent is due by January 15; application must be received by March 15. Application materials are available on the website.

Requirements: Applicant North Dakota-based organizations must comply with all NDCA general policy guidelines; comply with applicable state and federal laws; submit complete and accurate applications and provide at least 50 percent of the total cash cost of the project; and submit current long-range plans that include goals and measurable objectives for the organization. Applicants whose operating budgets exceed $200,000 must be tax-exempt and submit independent audits for the most recently completed fiscal year. Presentation, production, or service of the arts must be the primary activity of the applicant organization.

Restrictions: The following are ineligible: organizations supported through Access; capital architectural improvements or purchase or long-term rental of equipment or property; benefits or hospitality costs; fellowships, scholarships, or tuition fees; activities restricted to an organization's membership; and proposals which match federal funds with federal funds.

Geographic Focus: North Dakota

Date(s) Application is Due: Mar 15

Amount of Grant: 2,000 - 10,000 USD

Contact: Jan Webb; (701) 328-7592; fax (701) 328-7595; comserv@state.nd.us

Internet: http://www.nd.gov/arts/grants/ISguidelines.html
Sponsor: North Dakota Council on the Arts
1600 E Century Avenue, Suite 6
Bismarck, ND 58503-0649

North Dakota Council on the Arts Presenter Support Grants   1415
Presenter Support is designed to benefit nonprofit organizations that are not eligible for other major grant programs through the North Dakota Council on the Arts, offers financial support for arts events and programming, and supports organizations in communities with a population of 6,000 or more. Goals of the program include: to encourage existing arts organizations to build upon themselves, enhance the artistic quality of their programming, and expand their audience; to promote knowledge and appreciation of the arts in North Dakota's communities; to provide start-up funds or general operating support for new or emerging arts programs; and to provide opportunities for North Dakota artists. Grant requests may not exceed $2,000. Annual deadlines are April 1 and November 1.
Requirements: Applicants are encouraged to submit a notice of intent to apply. While this is not a requirement, it will assist the Council on the Arts in the planning of review panels and other matters.
Restrictions: Applicant must be registered as a 501(c)3 non-profit organization with the state of North Dakota, or be a community or county government entity. Organizations may form partnerships with state agencies, for-profit businesses, and other entities, but the non-profit organization must be the applicant. An applicant must be from a community with a population of 6,000 or more, according to the most recent census available. A 1:1 cash match is required. Requested funds can cover no more than half of the total expenses for the programming.
Geographic Focus: North Dakota
Date(s) Application is Due: Apr 1; Nov 1
Amount of Grant: Up to 2,000 USD
Contact: Amy Schmidt, Public Information Officer; (701) 328-7594; fax (701) 328-7595; amschmid@nd.gov or comserv@nd.gov
Internet: http://www.nd.gov/arts/grants/PRSguidelines.html
Sponsor: North Dakota Council on the Arts
1600 E Century Avenue, Suite 6
Bismarck, ND 58503-0649

North Dakota Council on the Arts Special Project Grants   1416
Grants provide an opportunity for organizations to initiate new projects without delay and to take advantage of possible touring events. The matching funds may be in cash or documented in-kind services and contributions. Examples of supported activities are general operating expenses; honoraria for artistic and technical staff services; and production costs for performances, exhibitions, and publications. Applications will be accepted throughout the year on a funds-available basis. Applications must be submitted no later than four weeks prior to the event. Early application is recommended since grant funds are limited. Special Project grants for a particular fiscal year (July 1 to June 30) may not be submitted after May 31 of that calendar year. Grant requests may not exceed $1,000 or 50 percent of the total project cost, which ever is less, and awards may be less based on review of the application. In-kind match can be up to 25 percent of the total project cost. Application materials are available on the website.
Requirements: Applicant organizations must comply with all NDCA general policy guidelines and be based in North Dakota.
Restrictions: The following are ineligible: organizations supported through Access or Institutional Support; capital architectural improvements or purchase or long-term rental of equipment or property; benefits or hospitality costs; fellowships, scholarships, or tuition fees; activities restricted to an organization's membership; and proposals which match federal funds with federal funds.
Geographic Focus: North Dakota
Amount of Grant: Up to 1,000 USD
Contact: Jan Webb; (701) 328-7592; fax (701) 328-7595; jwebb@state.nd.us
Internet: http://www.nd.gov/arts/grants/SPguidelines.html
Sponsor: North Dakota Council on the Arts
1600 E Century Avenue, Suite 6
Bismarck, ND 58503-0649

Northern Chautauqua Community Foundation Community Grants 1417
The foundation awards grants to nonprofit, tax-exempt organizations located in Northern Chautauqua County, New York. Priority will be given to programs representing innovative and efficient approaches to serving community needs and opportunities, projects that assist citizens whose needs are not met by existing services, projects that expect to test or demonstrate new approaches and techniques in the solutions of community problems, and projects that promote volunteer participation and citizen involvement in the community. Consideration will be given to the potential impact of the request and the number of people who will benefit. Seed grants will be awarded to initiate promising new programs in the foundation's field of interest as well as challenge grants to encourage matching gifts. Except in unusual circumstances, grants are approved for one year at a time. Contact the foundation office for an application.
Requirements: IRS 501(c)3 organizations in Northern Chautauqua County, New York, are eligible.
Restrictions: Areas generally not funded are capital campaigns to establish or add to endowment funds, general operating budgets for existing organizations, publication of books, conferences, or annual fund-raising campaigns.
Geographic Focus: New York
Date(s) Application is Due: Mar 23; Sep 21
Amount of Grant: 12,500 USD
Contact: Diane E. Hannum, Executive Director; (716) 366-4892; fax (716) 366-3905; dhannum@nncfoundation.org or info@nccfoundation.org
Internet: http://www.nccfoundation.org/Grantseekers/ApplyforaGrant/tabid/256/Default.aspx
Sponsor: Northern Chautauqua Community Foundation
212 Lake Shore Drive West
Dunkirk, NY 14048

Northern Trust Company Charitable Trust and Corporate Giving   1418
Contributions from the Charitable Trust support program, general operating, capital, or endowment priorities. Grants usually are confined to programs and agencies that focus on advancing the well-being of disadvantaged women and children, and people with disabilities. Priority is given to programs or agencies that serve the following Chicago neighborhoods: Chatham, Englewood, Humboldt Park, Logan Square, Loop, Washington Park, and West Town. Applications, including all material specified in the checklist must be received in the Community Affairs office before 5:00 pm on the deadline date. Deadlines for requests for funding are determined by area of service, as follows: social welfare—January 13 and August 12, education——May 13; and arts and culture—May 13.
Requirements: Nonprofit organizations in Illinois are eligible. A proposal should include a short cover letter, an operating budget for the current year, a copy of the agency's most recent audited financial statement, a list of members of the agency's governing board, a list of Chicago-based corporate and foundation contributors and amounts each has contributed in the last calendar year, and a letter from the IRS indicating tax-exempt status.
Geographic Focus: Illinois
Date(s) Application is Due: Jan 13; May 13; Aug 12
Amount of Grant: 2,500 - 5,000 USD
Samples: Parents United for Responsible Education (Chicago, IL)—for operating support, $5000; Chicago Reporter (Chicago, IL)—for operating support, $3000.
Contact: Dawn McGovern, Program Contact; (312) 444-4059
Internet: http://www.northerntrust.com/aboutus/community/charitable/index.html
Sponsor: Northern Trust Company
50 S LaSalle Street, Suite L-7
Chicago, IL 60675

Northrop Grumman Foundation Grants   1419
Northrop Grumman's priority is to provide opportunities related to science, technology, engineering and mathematics (STEM) for students and teachers. The foundation supports diverse and sustainable NATIONAL-LEVEL programs that enhance the education experience for students and provide teachers with the training and tools they need to be successful in the classroom.
Requirements: Grant requests must be submitted online via the Foundation's website. Grant requests must include: tax exempt number; non-profit or institution contact name, title, address, phone number, fax number; brief history of the organization, mission statement, goals and objectives; type and scope of services offered, and the geographical area serviced; specific details as to how requested funds would be used; project budget and amount requested; demographic impacted; current operating budget including latest financial statement; list of other corporate funders; list of directors and/or officers, and their affiliations; Northrop Grumman employee sponsor, if applicable (name and phone number); and contact information.
Restrictions: The Foundation will not consider the following requests: individuals; fundraising events such as raffles, walk-a-thons, banquets or dinners; campus student organizations, fraternities, sororities, and honor societies; religious schools or colleges whose primary focus is to promote religious beliefs; athletic

teams, support organizations; advertising or underwriting expenses; capital campaigns; endowments; tuition; choirs, bands, or drill teams.
Geographic Focus: All States
Amount of Grant: 500 - 200,000 USD
Samples: University of Nevada, Las Vegas, Nevada, $30,000 - to purchase computer equipment and software for the Transportation Research Center; California State University at Long Beach, Long Beach, Caliornia, $10,000 - for curriculum development in software engineering.
Contact: Carleen Beste, (888) 478-5478; carleen.beste@ngc.com
Internet: http://www.northropgrumman.com/corporate-responsibility/corporate-citizenship/foundation-grant-guidelines.html
Sponsor: Northrop Grumman Foundation
1840 Century Park E, MS 131/CC
Los Angeles, CA 90067

Northwestern Mutual Foundation Grants 1420
The people of Northwestern Mutual have a long history of community involvement. To carry out its corporate contributions program, Northwestern Mutual created a private foundation, The Northwestern Mutual Foundation. The Northwestern Mutual Foundation focuses its funding in Milwaukee, where the company is headquartered. Therefore, applying for a grant from the Northwestern Mutual Foundation is limited to Milwaukee-area nonprofit organizations with programs centered on Education, Health & Human Services or Arts & Culture.
Requirements: Northwestern Mutual Foundation does not accept unsolicited grant requests. Groups new to the Foundation are asked to submit a written letter of intent, describing the organization, funding request, and provide information about the program for which you are seeking support. The Foundations team will review your letter of intent and, if they are interested in learning more about your project, you will receive an application form. Groups that have an active relationship with the Foundation and currently receive funding are allowed to apply annually for support. Once an organization submits an application, the review process takes about 90 days. The Foundation review's Milwaukee-area grants on a monthly basis.
Restrictions: Milwaukee-area nonprofits are eligible to apply. The Foundation defines the Milwaukee-area as Milwaukee County, with limited programmatic grants in Waukesha, Racine and Ozaukee Counties.
Geographic Focus: Wisconsin
Amount of Grant: 10,000 - 800,000 USD
Samples: Boys and Girls Clubs of Greater Milwaukee, Milwaukee, WI, $800,000; United Performing Arts Fund, Milwaukee, WI, $605,000; Scholarship America, Saint Peter, MN, $205,425;
Contact: Edward J. Zore, President; (414) 271-1444
Internet: http://www.nmfn.com/tn/aboutus—fd_intro
Sponsor: Northwestern Mutual Foundation
720 East Wisconsin Avenue
Milwaukee, WI 53202-4797

Northwest Fund for the Environment Grants 1421
The Northwest Fund for the Environment is designated to be spent promoting change in the uses of natural resources to increase their protection and preservation in the state of Washington. Emphasis is placed on the protection of wild fish, native wildlife, natural forests, wetlands and shorelines, and the preservation of pure and free-flowing waters. Special program areas of interest include aquatic ecosystem protection of freshwater and saltwater; growth management to promote smart growth land use policies and to prevent damage to environmentally sensitive areas; and community response in support of grassroots work that feeds into the fund's goals or supports emergent issues and opportunities not covered by previous funding. The Foundation requires grantees to propose a scope of work lasting up to 16 months, complete the entire 16 month grant period, and submit a final report prior to applying for a new standard grant. Standard grants range from $3,000 to $20,000. The Community Response Fund Grants range from $500 to $3,000. Application deadlines vary according to particular funding requested. Samples of previous funding are available at the website.
Requirements: Applicants must follow the online application process, which includes calling the Foundation to discuss whether it may be eligible for funding. Unsolicited applications or letters of inquiry will not be accepted. Only nonprofit organizations classified as 501(c)3 public charities serving Washington state are eligible. First time applicants may only apply for project support.
Restrictions: The following are not eligible for funding: individuals or for profit organizations; endowments or capital campaigns; debt reduction or loans to organizations; capital projects, such as building acquisition or construction, large equipment purchases or vehicle acquisition; land acquisition; structural

restoration, such as tree planting or culvert removal; purely educational activities (except when an integral part but only one component of your application); organization of, scholarships for, or support of public conferences, as distinct from invited meetings or convening of groups engaged in related efforts; youth group support; production of publications and videos for the general public; web page development; museum displays; art projects, including performances; visual art projects and arts education; partisan political activities; academic scholarships or fellowships; academic research; university overhead costs; or field research (except when an integral part but only one component of your application).
Geographic Focus: Washington
Date(s) Application is Due: Feb 1
Contact: Pam Fujita-Yuhas, Foundation Director; (206) 386-7220; fax (206) 386-7223 (call first); staff@nwfund.org
Internet: http://www.nwfund.org
Sponsor: Northwest Fund for the Environment
1904 Third Avenue, Suite 615
Seattle, WA 98101

Norton Foundation Grants 1422
The Mission of the Norton Foundation, is to make grants designed to meet the needs of children and adolescents in Louisville, Kentucky. The Foundation supports experiential and holistic education that encourages their social, emotional, intellectual, physical and ethical development. The Foundation gives priority to programs that use the arts to achieve this goal. The Foundation also supports social services benefiting children and adolescents which are protective and preventative in nature. Civic projects in Louisville and Jefferson County which enhance the lives of children and adolescents are also considered for funding. The Board of Trustees meets three times per year. Applications must precede the meeting by approximately one month. Deadlines and meeting days fluctuate. Current deadline may be learned by calling or emailing the office. Grant application is available at the Foundation's website.
Requirements: Grants are made to IRS qualified 501(C)3 public charities (but not private foundations) that carry out activities primarily in the greater metropolitan Louisville area.
Restrictions: The Foundation does not make grants to individuals, nor may it designate funds for legislation or support activities that seek to influence the legislative process, except as allowed by the Internal Revenue Code of 1986, as amended.
Geographic Focus: Kentucky
Amount of Grant: 5,000 - 60,000 USD
Samples: Kentucky Museum of Art and Craft, Louisville, KY, $10,000; Waldorf School of Louisville, Louisville, K, $100,000; Healing Place, Louisville, KY, $50,000.
Contact: Lucy Crawford, Executive Director; (502) 893-9549; fax (502) 896-9378; lcrawford@nortonfoundation.com
Internet: http://www.nortonfoundation.com/application.html
Sponsor: Norton Foundation
4350 Brownsboro Road, Suite 133
Louisville, KY 40207-1679

Norwin S. and Elizabeth N. Bean Foundation Grants 1423
The Norwin S. and Elizabeth N. Bean Foundation was established in 1967 as a general purpose foundation to serve the communities of Manchester and Amherst and, consistent with the wishes of the founders, grants are made in the fields of arts and humanities, education, environment, health, human services, and public/society benefit.
Requirements: Applications are accepted from nonprofit 501(c)3 organizations and municipal and public agencies serving the communities of Manchester and Amherst, New Hampshire. Priority consideration is given to organizations operating primarily in those two communities. However, the Foundation will consider applications from statewide or regional organizations which provide a substantial and documented level of service to Manchester and Amherst.
Restrictions: The foundation does not make grants to individuals or provide scholarship aid.
Geographic Focus: New Hampshire
Date(s) Application is Due: Apr 1; Sep 1; Dec 1
Contact: Kathleen Cook, Grant Manager; (603) 493-7257; KCook@BeanFoundation.org
Internet: http://www.beanfoundation.org/grants/bean-foundation-grant/application-criteria.aspx
Sponsor: Norwin S. and Elizabeth N. Bean Foundation
40 Stark Street
Manchester, NH 03301

**NSERC Brockhouse Canada Prize for Interdisciplinary Research in   1424
Science and Engineering Grant**

The Brockhouse Canada Prize for Interdisciplinary Research in Science and Engineering recognizes outstanding Canadian teams of researchers from different disciplines who have combined their expertise to produce achievements of outstanding international significance in the natural sciences and engineering. The prize, accompanied by a team research grant of $250,000, reflects NSERC's commitment to supporting Canadian research through strategic investments in people, discovery and innovation. The grant supports the direct costs of university-based research and/or the enhancement of research facilities. The grant may be distributed in one lump sum or up to five instalments, depending on the needs of the recipients.

Requirements: Research teams nominated for the Brockhouse Canada Prize must have at least two members who are independent researchers, one of whom must hold an NSERC grant. The team can be part of an international effort, but the majority of the nominated team members must be employed at a Canadian university or public or private organization. NSERC recognizes that teams may change between the time of the specific research achievements and the time of nomination. Nominations will be accepted when changes have occurred but only as long as the core of the team remains intact. Contributions must be primarily in the natural sciences and engineering, and of an interdisciplinary and collaborative nature.

Restrictions: Any Canadian citizen may nominate a research team for the Brockhouse Canada Prize. Self nominations will not be accepted. Current NSERC Council members cannot be nominated. Since the prize is for interdisciplinary research, nominators should consult NSERC's Guidelines for the Preparation and Review of Applications in Interdisciplinary Research. Nominators should also consult NSERC's Guidelines for the Preparation and Review of Applications in Engineering and the Applied Sciences. See website for deadline & hyper links to above mentioned guidelines.

Geographic Focus: All States, Canada
Date(s) Application is Due: Jun 1
Amount of Grant: 250,000 USD
Contact: Grants Administrator; (613) 995-5829; fax (613) 992-5337; brockhouse@nserc-crsng.gc.ca
Internet: http://www.nserc-crsng.gc.ca/Prizes-Prix/Brockhouse-Brockhouse/Index-Index_eng.asp
Sponsor: Natural Sciences and Engineering Research Council of Canada
350 Albert Street
Ottawa, ON K1A 1H5 Canada

**NSERC Gerhard Herzberg Canada Gold Medal for Science and   1425
Engineering Grants**

The NSERC Herzberg Medal is awarded annually to an individual who has demonstrated sustained excellence and influence in research, for a body of work conducted in Canada that has substantially advanced the natural sciences or engineering fields. The award is meant to celebrate Canada's most outstanding scientists and engineers and to raise public awareness about the major contributions that Canada's top researchers make to international science and technology, and to bettering people's lives. In addition to the medal, the winner is guaranteed $1 million to use for personal university-based research or to direct in some related way such as the establishment of research scholarships, fellowships or chairs in his or her name at Canadian universities. The monetary award will be distributed over a five-year period.

Requirements: To be eligible, a candidate must be a scientist or engineer from a Canadian university, government lab or private firm. Candidates may be nominated by any individual or group; however, the nominators must be Canadian citizens or permanent residents of Canada. Posthumous or self nominations will not be accepted. Current NSERC Council members are not eligible for nomination.

Restrictions: An individual may win the NSERC Herzberg Medal only once.
Geographic Focus: All States, Canada
Date(s) Application is Due: May 1
Amount of Grant: 1,000,000 USD
Samples: John C. Polanyi, University of Toronto; Chemistry
Contact: Grants Administrator; (613) 995-5829; fax (613) 995-7753; inquiries.herzberg@nserc-crsng.gc.ca
Internet: http://www.nserc-crsng.gc.ca/Prizes-Prix/Herzberg-Herzberg/About-Apropos_eng.asp
Sponsor: Natural Sciences and Engineering Research Council of Canada
350 Albert Street
Ottawa, ON K1A 1H5 Canada

NSERC Michael Smith Awards   1426

The Michael Smith Awards for Science Promotion focus on people and groups who are inspirational in the way they promote science to the general public. The Awards are an opportunity for Canada's science community to recognize, support and encourage outstanding science promoters.

Requirements: Any individual, organization or company within Canada may be nominated for the award. Nominees will have made a successful and sustained effort to encourage public interest in and an understanding of the natural sciences and engineering (including math and technology) outside the formal education system. Science promotion activities with award potential could include activities such as: organizing science camps, fairs, clubs or programs with youth organizations; creating new learning materials; developing science and engineering related co-op programs or job shadowing initiatives; arranging demonstrations, visits and lectures; creating new learning materials;writing books and articles;creating radio or television programs and generating public involvement through multi-media programs.

Geographic Focus: All States, Canada
Date(s) Application is Due: Sep 1
Amount of Grant: 5,000 - 10,000 USD
Contact: Grants Administrator; (613) 996-1417; fax (613) 992-5337; michaelsmithawards@nserc-crsng.gc.ca
Internet: http://www.nserc-crsng.gc.ca/Prizes-Prix/Smith-Smith/Index-Index_eng.asp
Sponsor: Natural Sciences and Engineering Research Council of Canada
350 Albert Street
Ottawa, ON K1A 1H5 Canada

NSF Biological Field Stations and Marine Laboratories Grants   1427

This program supports refurbishment, rehabilitation, enhancement, and construction, including laboratory renovations, at these research resources. Sites are required to have a plan for archiving (in electronic form) and making shareable scientific databases available on the unique data they obtain. Support can be provided for necessary computer equipment, connectivity, and development of these scientific database. Deadline is the first Friday in March each year. NSF 01-59

Requirements: U.S. colleges and universities, free-standing research and education institutions, and U.S. chartered corporations with formally constituted research and education programs at field stations or marine laboratories are eligible to apply.

Geographic Focus: All States
Amount of Grant: Up to 500,000 USD
Contact: Dr. Gerald Selzer; (703) 292-8470; gselzer@nsf.gov
Internet: http://www.nsf.gov/pubs/2001/nsf0159/nsf0159.htm
Sponsor: National Science Foundation
4201 Wilson Boulevard
Arlington, VA 22230

**NSF Partnerships in Astronomy & Astrophysics Research and   1428
Education (PAARE)**

The objective of the program is to enhance diversity in astronomy and astrophysics research and education by stimulating the development of formal, potentially long-term, collaborative research and education relationships between minority-serving colleges and universities and the NSF-supported facilities, projects or faculty members at research institutions (including private observatories). As retention of traditionally underrepresented students is key to the success of this program, a solid mentoring scheme is vital. PAARE awards are expected to help build a foundation for students at an early point in their careers and help these students make the next step in their careers. The partnerships are intended to provide education and mentoring as a form of professional development to help these students succeed long after their work on the PAARE research. Funded activities might include, but are not limited to, the development of collaborative and mutually beneficial astronomy-related research and education projects, support for graduate and undergraduate students and exchanges of faculty and students. Well-prepared high-school students may also participate. Of special interest are activities based on research and education connections between the participants, and designed to increase recruitment, retention and degree attainment by members of groups underrepresented in astronomy and astrophysics research. Proposers are encouraged to contact NSF program staff to discuss the appropriateness of the planned activities.

Requirements: Proposals may only be submitted by minority-serving colleges and universities, including Historically Black Colleges and Universities (HBCUs), Hispanic-serving institutions (HSIs), and Tribally Controlled Colleges (TCCs). Each proposal must be submitted in collaboration with (and may include a

subaward to) one or more NSF-supported facilities, projects or partnering faculty members at research institutions. Colleges and universities eligible to participate in this activity must offer baccalaureate degrees in physics or astronomy and meet at least one of the following criteria: 1) Be designated by the Department of Higher Education in FY 1994 as a Hispanic-serving Institution (HSI) under Title III of the Higher Education Act of 1965, as amended [See 20 USC 1059 (copyright symbol); Public Law 102-325, Section 316, July 22, 1992]. 2) Be designated by the Department of Education as a Historically Black College or University (HBCU) under Title III of the Higher Education Act of 1965, as amended (see 34 CFR 608.2). 3) Be cited as a Tribal College or University in Section 532 of the Equity in Education Land-Grant Status October of 1964; Tribally Controlled Community College Assistance Act of 1978, Public Law 95-471. 4) Be a college or university whose undergraduate enrollment consists of at least 50% one or more ethnic minorities underrepresented in science and engineering in the US, and not a Doctoral/Research University-Extensive institution in the Carnegie classification (for the Carnegie classification see http://www.carnegiefoundation.org/classifications/index.asp?key=785). African American, Hispanic Americans, Native Americans or Native Alaskans and Hawaiian/Pacific islanders are ethnic minorities underrepresented in science and engineering in the US. Partnering institutions or organizations may be any institution or organization eligible for NSF funding that supports a research program in astronomy and astrophysics including AST-funded facilities and also private observatories. Research groups and individual scientists at research institutions are also eligible partners, provided their institution shows evidence of commitment to the proposed program as demonstrated in a letter from the institution describing its support of the partnership. Proposals may include subawards to the partnering institution, provided it has demonstrated a commitment to the activity at least for the duration of the PAARE grant.
Geographic Focus: All States
Date(s) Application is Due: Aug 3
Contact: Tammy Bosler; (703) 292-8248; fax (703) 292-9034; tbosler@nsf.gov
Internet: http://nsf.gov/funding/pgm_summ.jsp?pims_id=501046&org=NSF&sel_org=NSF&from=fund
Sponsor: National Science Foundation
4201 Wilson Boulevard
Arlington, VA 22230

NSS Foundation Hunting Heritage Partnership Grants   1429
The program designed to build a strong partnership between the foundation, the Congressional Sportsmen's Foundation, and state wildlife agencies by providing funding to state wildlife agencies to create greater hunting opportunities and put more hunters in the field. Grants support a range of hunter-related programs—increasing hunter access, hunter retention, hunter recruitment, programs that create more opportunities to hunt, and communications programs geared toward retaining or recruiting hunters. The deadline for submitting proposals normally falls in early spring, and NSSF will notify grant recipients within two months following the deadline. Priority consideration is given to projects that will be completed by March 1st of the year following signing of the official grant documentation. Application materials and instructions are available online.
Requirements: State wildlife agencies are eligible. Eligible projects must address one or more of the following: recruitment of new hunters in the state; retention of current hunters in the state; increased hunter access; and/or communications or outreach geared toward retaining or recruiting hunters.
Restrictions: The following are ineligible: projects including activities other than hunting with a firearm; projects that include the purchase of land; projects that focus specifically on the management of wildlife habitats or ecosystems; projects that focus on the planning of meetings, symposia, conferences, etc; projects that involve building or improving existing structures; or all other projects that are not directly related to the above-stated project eligibility requirements as determined by the foundation.
Geographic Focus: All States
Amount of Grant: Up to 500,000 USD
Samples: Florida Fish and Wildlife Conservation Commission—to help fund a survey and planning efforts for the Summit on the Future of Hunting in Florida, $15,000; Kansas Big Brothers Big Sisters (Wichita, KS)—to expand nationally a mentoring program that teaches youths such outdoor sports as archery, fishing, hunting, and target shooting, $250,000.
Contact: Steve Wagner, (203) 426-1320; swagner@nssf.org or info@nssf.org
Internet: http://www.nssf.org/grants/index.cfm?AoI=generic
Sponsor: National Shooting Sports Foundation
Flintlock Ridge Office Center, 11 Mile Hill Road
Newtown, CT 06470-2359

NYCT Health Services, Systems, and Policies Grants   1430
The Trust supports projects that strengthen preventive health care, improve access to services, promote the efficient use of health resources, and develop the skills and independence of people with special needs. The primary goal of this program is to improve the effectiveness, responsiveness, and equity of health care in New York City. Specifically, the program makes grants: for services, policy research, advocacy, and technical assistance that promote the accessibility of basic health services, especially in minority and immigrant communities; to strengthen health service providers, especially those serving the city's poorest residents; and to promote healthy lifestyles. The grant review process takes from two to six months. Grants range from $5,000 to $100,000; an average grant is around $60,000.
Requirements: Grants are made primarily to nonprofit organizations located in the five boroughs of New York City. Grants for programs outside the area are generally from funds designated for specific charities or have been made at the suggestion of donors.
Restrictions: The trust does not make grants to individuals, offer general or capital funding, endowments, building construction/renovation, deficit financing, films, or religion.
Geographic Focus: New York
Amount of Grant: 5,000 - 100,000 USD
Contact: Joyce M. Bove; (212) 686-0010, ext. 552; fax (212) 534-8528; info@nycommunitytrust.org or grants@nycommunitytrust.org
Internet: http://www.nycommunitytrust.org/ForGrantSeekers/Grantmaking Guidelines/HealthandPeoplewithSpecialNeeds/tabid/207/Default.aspx
Sponsor: New York Community Trust
909 Third Avenue, 22nd Floor
New York, NY 10022

NYFA Artists in the School Community Planning Grants   1431
Planning grants emphasize collaborations between schools, teaching artists, and/or cultural organizations to prepare for first-time Implementation projects or to further develop existing Implementation projects. Planning Grants offer schools the opportunity to assess needs, identify resources, and explore pilot program ideas. Applicants may apply for one year of planning support with the intent to apply for an Implementation grant in the same fiscal year. Funding of Planning grants does not guarantee funding of Implementation grants. The award is not designed to support artist-student contact, though pilot activities are acceptable. Awards are matching grants and range from $500 to $2,000. NYFA contributes up to 50% of total project costs.
Requirements: Schools, school districts, BOCES, Teacher Centers, colleges and universities or on Indian nation land in New York State are eligible to apply. Applicants must provide, through in-kind resources and cash, matching support for artist fees, materials and supplies, teacher release time, teacher compensation and all other project costs. In-kind contributions cannot exceed 1/3 of the applicant's match.
Restrictions: Nonprofit cultural organizations are not eligible to apply. New York State non-profit organizations may work collaboratively with schools and artists; however the school must be the lead organization. Planning Grants can only be used for artist fees and/or artist materials and supplies.
Geographic Focus: New York
Date(s) Application is Due: Nov 5
Amount of Grant: 500 - 2,000 USD
Contact: Susan Ball, Interim Director of Programs; (212) 366-6900, ext. 321; fax (212) 366-1778; sball@nyfa.org or ASC_Plannning@nyfa.org
Internet: http://www.nyfa.org/level3.asp?id=35&fid=2&sid=22
Sponsor: New York Foundation for the Arts
20 Jay Street, 7th Floor
Brooklyn, NY 11201

NYFA Building Up Infrastructure Levels for Dance Grants   1432
The BUILD program sustains New York City dance companies with small- and mid-sized budgets by offering choreographers and their dancers an opportunity to access the financial support necessary to build and maintain infrastructure and longevity. BUILD identifies and awards artistic merit, fosters long-term strategies to develop and sustain organizational health, and strengthens the organizational environment so that time and resources are available to create, conceive, and advance dance companies' artistic missions. BUILD supports, but is not limited to, requests for administrative costs; consultant fees; press and/or booking agent fees; company promotional materials; studio or space rental; and computers/equipment.
Requirements: New York City 501(c)3 tax-exempt organizations (or organizations with a 501(c)3 fiscal sponsor) are eligible to apply under category 1 (have a three-year-average budget between $16,000 and $80,000 per annum; and have performed work at least twice during the past three years) and

category 2 (have a three-year-average budget between $81,000 and $160,000 per annum; and have produced at least three seasons of choreography with one season produced by a presenter other than the company itself). Additionally, BUILD provides stability grants of $1,000 to $2,500.

Restrictions: BUILD will not support requests for production costs associated with the performance of work including costumes, lighting, set design, or music fees; touring or traveling costs; or compensation for dancers, musicians, choreographers, teachers, or accompanists.

Geographic Focus: New York
Date(s) Application is Due: Apr 29
Amount of Grant: 10,000 - 20,000 USD
Contact: Pter Cobb, (212) 366-6900, ext. 212; fax (212) 366-1778; pcobb@nyfa.org
Internet: http://www.nyfa.org/level2.asp?id=78&fid=2
Sponsor: New York Foundation for the Arts
20 Jay Street, 7th Floor
Brooklyn, NY 11201

NYSCA Arts Education: General Operating Support Grants   1433
General Operating Support grants fund an organization's ongoing work, rather than a specific project or program in order to help organizations become more effective in fulfilling their mission, especially in arts education. The Council examines the nature, scope, and quality of an organization's programs and activities, its managerial and fiscal competence, and its public service when considering the provision and level of support.

Requirements: Applicants must register before February 22 to be considered for funding that fiscal year. In addition, applicant's must meet the following conditions: have a primary focus in arts education; have an organizational mission primarily devoted to arts and culture with a prior record of accomplishment in producing or presenting cultural activities; demonstrate fiscal stability as indicated by such factors as a positive Fund Balance, have an absence of substantial and recurring organizational deficits, a realistic and balanced organizational budget, have diverse revenue sources, and strong internal controls; one or more qualified staff; a viable board of directors and officers that exercises oversight and accountability for governance, operations, programming and finances; and must have ongoing programs, exhibitions, productions, or other art and cultural activities that are open to the general public. Applications can be found at the website and must be completed online. First time applicants must contact program staff before registration deadline.

Restrictions: Applicants cannot apply for both General Operating Support and General Program Support. Grants will be no less than $5,000 and shall not exceed 25% of an organization's budget.

Geographic Focus: New York
Date(s) Application is Due: Apr 1
Contact: Kathleen Masterson; (212) 741-2622; kmasterson@nysca.org
Internet: http://www.nysca.org/public/guidelines/arts_education/general_operating.htm
Sponsor: New York State Council on the Arts
300 Park Ave South, 10th Floor
New York, NY 10010

NYSCA Arts Education: Local Capacity Building Grants (Regrants)   1434
Local Capacity Building grants offer support to organizations to administer regrant programs that support arts partnerships between schools and cultural organizations or individual artists. Local Capacity Building programs generally support projects that are small and represent first-time or new forays into arts in education on the part of the school applicants. Each Local Capacity Building program site serves a specific region of the state and is expected to promote the regrant program, coordinate application and panel review processes, and provide ongoing technical assistance and professional development.

Requirements: Applicants must have: a full-time, paid executive director; a designated, qualified staff member (preferably not the executive director) to serve as coordinator of the program; and resources to provide appropriate technical assistance, outreach, and professional development opportunities for constituent schools, artists, and cultural organizations in the service area. First time applicants are required to call program staff before the registration deadline. Applications are at the website and must be submitted online.

Restrictions: NYSCA does not fund: operating expenses of privately owned facilities, such as homes or studios; components of an organization's budget that are not directed toward programs in New York State; and competitions or contests.

Geographic Focus: New York
Date(s) Application is Due: Apr 1
Contact: Kathleen Masterson; (212) 741-2622; kmasterson@nysca.org

Internet: http://www.nysca.org/public/guidelines/arts_education/local_capacity.htm
Sponsor: New York State Council on the Arts
300 Park Ave South, 10th Floor
New York, NY 10010

NYSCA Dance: General Operating Support Grants   1435
General Operating Support grants sponsor an organization's ongoing work, rather than a specific project, in order to help organizations become more effective in fulfilling their mission. The Council examines the nature, scope, and quality of an organization's programs and activities, its managerial and fiscal competence, and its public service when considering the provision and level of support. Support is awarded on a multi-year basis.

Requirements: Applicants must register with the Council before February 22 to be considered for funding. In addition, all applicants must: have a primary focus in dance; have an organizational mission that is primarily devoted to arts and culture with a prior record of accomplishment in producing or presenting cultural activities; demonstrate fiscal stability as indicated by such factors as a positive Fund balance, an absence of substantial and/or recurring organizational deficits, a realistic and balanced organizational budget, diverse revenue sources, and strong internal controls; one or more qualified, salaried administrative staff; a viable board of directors and officers that exercises oversight and accountability for governance, operations, programming and finances; have ongoing programs, exhibitions, productions or other art and cultural activities that are open to the general public; demonstrate significant services or activity in New York State, which is defined as a home season of at least 7 performances within the last three years. Applications can be found at the website and should be submitted online. First-time applicants are required to call staff before the registration deadline.

Restrictions: General Operating Support will be no less than $5,000 and shall not exceed 25% of an organization's budget. Applicants cannot apply for both General Operating Support and General Program Support.

Geographic Focus: New York
Date(s) Application is Due: Apr 1
Contact: Beverly D'Anne, Senior Program Officer; (212) 741-3232 or (212) 741-3331; bdanne@nysca.org or dlim@nysca.org
Internet: http://www.nysca.org/public/guidelines/dance/general_operating.htm
Sponsor: New York State Council on the Arts
300 Park Ave South, 10th Floor
New York, NY 10010

NYSCA Electronic Media and Film: General Operating Support   1436
General Operating Support sponsors an organization's ongoing work, rather than a specific project or program. The Council examines the nature, scope, and quality of an organization's programs and activities, its managerial and fiscal competence, and its public service when considering the provision and level of support. Support is awarded on multi-year basis.

Requirements: Applicants must register with the Council before February 22 to be considered for funding. In addition, applicants must have: a primary focus in Electronic Media and Film; an organizational mission that is primarily devoted to arts and culture with a prior record of accomplishment in producing or presenting cultural activities; demonstrated fiscal stability as indicated by such factors as a positive Fund Balance, an absence of substantial and/or recurring organizational deficits, a realistic and balanced organizational budget, diverse revenue sources, and strong internal controls; one or more qualified, salaried administrative staff; a viable board of directors and officers that exercises oversight and accountability for governance, operations, programming and finances; and ongoing programs, exhibitions, productions or other art and cultural activities that are open to the general public. First-time applicants are required to call staff before the registration deadline.

Restrictions: General Operating Support grants will be no less than $5,000 and shall NOT exceed 25% of the applicant organization's budget. Also, applicants CANNOT apply for both General Operating Support and General Program Support.

Geographic Focus: New York
Date(s) Application is Due: Apr 1
Contact: Karen Helmerson, Senior Program Officer; (212) 741-3003 or (212) 741-7847; khelmerson@nysca.org or fchiu@nysca.org
Internet: http://www.nysca.org/public/guidelines/electronic_media/general_operating.htm
Sponsor: New York State Council on the Arts
300 Park Ave South, 10th Floor
New York, NY 10010

NYSCA Folk Arts: General Operating Support Grants   1437

General Operating Support grants represent an investment by NYSCA in an organization's ongoing work, rather than a specific project or program, in order to help organizations become more effective in fulfilling their mission. The Council examines the nature, scope, and quality of an organization's programs and activities when considering the provision and level of support. Support for this grant is awarded on a multi-year basis.

Requirements: Applicants must register with NYSCA before February 22 to be eligible for funding. An applicant for general operating support must also meet the following conditions: have a primary focus in Folk Arts; have an organizational mission that is primarily devoted to arts and culture with a prior record of accomplishment in producing or presenting cultural activities; demonstrate fiscal stability as indicated by such factors as a positive fund balance, an absence of substantial, recurring organizational deficits, a realistic and balanced organizational budget, diverse revenue sources, and strong controls; one or more qualified, salaried administrative staff; a viable board of directors and officers that exercises oversight and accountability for governance, operations, programming and finances; and must have ongoing programs, exhibitions, productions or other art and cultural activities that are open to the general public. Also, projects must be developed in close consultation and collaboration with the communities and artists whose traditions are to be presented. First time applicants are required to call program staff before the registration deadline. Applications are available at the website and should be submitted online.

Restrictions: Applicants cannot apply for both General Operating Support and General Program Support. Grants will be no less than $5,000 and shall not exceed 25% of an organization's budget. Folk Arts emphasizes support for presentations grounded in the traditional modes of practicing folk art, and not programming involving choreography, theatricality, or stylization that significantly alters traditions. Support is also not available for programming involving artists who appropriate, interpret, or revive the traditions of other communities.

Geographic Focus: New York
Date(s) Application is Due: Apr 1
Contact: Robert Baron, Senior Program Officer; (212) 741-7755 or (212) 741-7143; rbaron@nysca.org or rputnam@nysca.org
Internet: http://www.nysca.org/public/guidelines/folk_arts/general_operating.htm
Sponsor: New York State Council on the Arts
300 Park Ave South, 10th Floor
New York, NY 10010

NYSCA Literature: General Operating Support Grants   1438

General Operating Support grants sponsor an organization's ongoing work, rather than a specific project, in order to help organizations become more effective in fulfilling their mission. The Council examines the nature, scope, and quality of an organization's programs and activities, its managerial and fiscal competence, and its public service when considering the provision and level of support. Support is awarded on a multi-year basis.

Requirements: Applicants must register with the Council before February 22 to be considered for funding. In addition, all applicants must: have a primary focus in Literature; have an organizational mission that is primarily devoted to arts and culture with a prior record of accomplishment in producing or presenting cultural activities; demonstrate fiscal stability as indicated by such factors as a positive Fund balance, an absence of substantial and/or recurring organizational deficits, a realistic and balanced organizational budget, diverse revenue sources, and strong internal controls; one or more qualified, salaried administrative staff; a viable board of directors and officers that exercises oversight and accountability for governance, operations, programming and finances; and have ongoing programs, exhibitions, productions or other art and cultural activities that are open to the general public. Applications can be found at the website and should be submitted online. First-time applicants are required to call staff before the registration deadline.

Restrictions: General Operating Support will be no less than $5,000 and shall not exceed 25% of an organization's budget. Applicants cannot apply for both General Operating Support and General Program Support.

Geographic Focus: New York
Date(s) Application is Due: Apr 1
Contact: Robert Zukerman, Senior Program Officer; (212) 741-7077; rzukerman@nysca.org
Internet: http://www.nysca.org/public/guidelines/literature/general_operating.htm
Sponsor: New York State Council on the Arts
300 Park Ave South, 10th Floor
New York, NY 10010

NYSCA Museum: General Operating Support Grants   1439

General Operating Support grants sponsor an organization's ongoing work, rather than a specific project, in order to help organizations become more effective in fulfilling their mission. The Council examines the nature, scope, and quality of an organization's programs and activities, its managerial and fiscal competence, and its public service when considering the provision and level of support. Support is awarded on a multi-year basis.

Requirements: Applicants must register with the Council before February 22 to be considered for funding. Museums must have been open to the public for a minimum of one year prior to the registration deadline and provide a minimum of 120 days per year. In addition, all applicants must: have a primary focus in Museums; have an organizational mission that is primarily devoted to arts and culture with a prior record of accomplishment in producing or presenting cultural activities; demonstrate fiscal stability as indicated by such factors as a positive Fund balance, an absence of substantial and/or recurring organizational deficits, a realistic and balanced organizational budget, diverse revenue sources, and strong internal controls; one or more qualified, salaried administrative staff; a viable board of directors and officers that exercises oversight and accountability for governance, operations, programming and finances; and have ongoing programs, exhibitions, productions or other art and cultural activities that are open to the general public. Applications can be found at the website and should be submitted online. First-time applicants are required to call staff before the registration deadline.

Restrictions: General Operating Support will be no less than $5,000 and shall not exceed 25% of an organization's budget. Applicants cannot apply for both General Operating Support and General Program Support. Organizations open to the public by appointment only do not meet this requirement.

Geographic Focus: New York
Date(s) Application is Due: Apr 1
Contact: Kristin Herron; (212) 741-7848; kherron@nysca.org
Internet: http://www.nysca.org/public/guidelines/museums/general_operating.htm
Sponsor: New York State Council on the Arts
300 Park Ave South, 10th Floor
New York, NY 10010

NYSCA Music: General Operating Support Grants   1440

General Operating Support grants represent an investment by NYSCA in an organization's ongoing work, rather than a specific project or program, in order to help organizations become more effective in fulfilling their mission. The Council examines the nature, scope, and quality of an organization's programs and activities when considering the provision and level of support. Support for this grant is awarded on a multi-year basis.

Requirements: Applicants must register with NYSCA before February 22 to be eligible for funding. An applicant for general operating support must also meet the following conditions: have a primary focus in Music; have an organizational mission that is primarily devoted to arts and culture with a prior record of accomplishment in producing or presenting cultural activities; demonstrate fiscal stability as indicated by such factors as a positive fund balance, an absence of substantial, recurring organizational deficits, a realistic and balanced organizational budget, diverse revenue sources, and strong controls; one or more qualified, salaried administrative staff; a viable board of directors and officers that exercises oversight and accountability for governance, operations, programming and finances; and must have ongoing programs, exhibitions, productions or other art and cultural activities that are open to the general public. First time applicants are required to call program staff before the registration deadline. Applications are available at the website and should be submitted online.

Restrictions: Applicants cannot apply for both General Operating Support and General Program Support. Grants will be no less than $5,000 and shall not exceed 25% of an organization's budget.

Geographic Focus: New York
Date(s) Application is Due: Apr 1
Contact: Beverly D'Anne; (212) 741-3232; bdanne@nysca.org
Internet: http://www.nysca.org/public/guidelines/music/general_operating.htm
Sponsor: New York State Council on the Arts
300 Park Ave South, 10th Floor
New York, NY 10010

NYSCA Presenting: General Operating Support Grants   1441

General Operating Support grants sponsor an organization's ongoing work, rather than a specific project or program. The Council examines the nature, scope, and quality of an organization's programs and activities, its managerial and fiscal competence, and its public service when considering the provision and level of support.

Requirements: Applicants must register with the Council by February 22 to be considered for funding. Also, an organization must meet the following conditions: a primary focus in presenting; an organizational mission primarily devoted to arts and culture with a prior record of accomplishment in producing or presenting cultural activities; a minimum of ten discrete presentations by ten different professional performing artists; demonstrate fiscal stability as indicated by such factors as a positive Fund balance, an absence of substantial and/or recurring organizational deficits, a realistic and balanced organizational budget, diverse revenue sources and strong internal controls; one or more qualified, salaried administrative staff; a viable board of directors and officers that exercises oversight and accountability for governance, operations, programming and finances; and must have on going programs, exhibitions, productions, or other art and cultural activities that are open to the general public. Applications can be found at the website and must be submitted online. First-time applicants are required to call the Presenting staff before the registration deadline.

Restrictions: Total requested amounts may not exceed 25% of the total project budget and must be more than $5,000. Applicants may not apply for both General Operating Support and General Program Support grants. In addition, the following activities are not eligible: single- and two-day festivals (unless incorporated within a larger presenting season); competitions, contests, talent showcases or parades; poetry readings (unless incorporated within a performance context) or staged readings; magic shows or ventriloquists; lectures, in-school classroom activity, master classes, or workshops; presentations or events that include the presentation of the organization's own work or work of their staff or board members, even when the project includes guest artists; and student work.

Geographic Focus: New York
Date(s) Application is Due: Apr 1
Contact: Leanne Tintori Wells; (212) 741-2227; lwells@nysca.org
Internet: http://www.nysca.org/public/guidelines/presenting/general_operating.htm
Sponsor: New York State Council on the Arts
300 Park Ave South, 10th Floor
New York, NY 10010

NYSCA Special Arts Services: General Operating Support Grants 1442

General Operating Support grants sponsor an organization's ongoing work, rather than a specific project or program. The Council examines the nature, scope, and quality of an organization's programs and activities, its managerial and fiscal competence, and its public service when considering the provision and level of support. This grant specifically helps to ensure the quality, viability, and productivity of artists and institutions within communities of color and other specific cultures. Special Arts Services also welcomes requests from organizations serving the disabled community by offering professionally-directed training in an arts discipline with the goal of more advanced study or career entry.

Requirements: Applicants must register with the Council by February 22 to be considered for funding. Also, an organization must meet the following conditions: a primary focus of providing cultural programs within and for communities of color or other ethnic communities; an organizational mission primarily devoted to arts and culture with a prior record of accomplishment in producing or presenting cultural activities; demonstrate fiscal stability as indicated by such factors as a positive Fund balance, an absence of substantial and/or recurring organizational deficits, a realistic and balanced organizational budget, diverse revenue sources and strong internal controls; one or more qualified, salaried administrative staff; a viable board of directors and officers that exercises oversight and accountability for governance, operations, programming and finances; and must have on going programs, exhibitions, productions, or other art and cultural activities that are open to the general public. Applications can be found at the website and must be submitted online. First-time applicants are required to call the Presenting staff before the registration deadline.

Restrictions: Total requested amounts cannot exceed 25% of the total project budget and will be no less than $5,000. Applicants cannot apply for both General Operating Support and General Program Support. In addition, organizations whose projects are directed toward general audiences or organizations in which artists do not represent those communities previously mentioned are not eligible for support and should consult the guidelines of other areas of support.

Geographic Focus: New York
Date(s) Application is Due: Apr 1
Contact: Robert Baron; (212) 741-7755; rbaron@nysca.org
Internet: http://www.nysca.org/public/guidelines/special_arts_services/general_operating.htm
Sponsor: New York State Council on the Arts
300 Park Ave South, 10th Floor
New York, NY 10010

NYSCA State and Local Partnerships: General Operating Support Grants 1443

General Operating Support grants sponsor an organization's ongoing work, rather than a specific project or program. The Council examines the nature, scope, and quality of an organization's programs and activities, its managerial and fiscal competence, and its public service when considering the provision and level of support. Specifically, State and Local Partnerships grants seek to: strengthen the leadership role of local/regional arts organizations in encouraging local cultural development and increasing resources available for the arts; encourage greater participation in the arts through support of a wide range of local, regional, and statewide programs and services responding to assessed cultural needs and reaching the full diversity of each community served; and enhance the professional capability of multi-arts organizations operating on the local levels and arts service organizations promoting the development of the arts and providing arts services statewide.

Requirements: Applicants must register with the Council by February 22 to be considered for funding. Also, an organization must meet the following conditions: a primary focus of providing local arts and cultural initiatives; an organizational mission primarily devoted to arts and culture with a prior record of accomplishment in producing or presenting cultural activities; demonstrate fiscal stability as indicated by such factors as a positive Fund balance, an absence of substantial and/or recurring organizational deficits, a realistic and balanced organizational budget, diverse revenue sources and strong internal controls; one or more qualified, salaried administrative staff; a viable board of directors and officers that exercises oversight and accountability for governance, operations, programming and finances; and must have on going programs, exhibitions, productions, or other art and cultural activities that are open to the general public. Applications can be found at the website and must be submitted online. First-time applicants are required to call the State and Local Partnerships staff before the registration deadline.

Restrictions: Total requested amounts cannot exceed 25% of the total project budget and will be no less than $5,000. Applicants cannot apply for both General Operating Support and General Program Support.

Geographic Focus: New York
Date(s) Application is Due: Apr 1
Contact: Leanne Tintori Wells; (212) 741-2227; lwells@nysca.org
Internet: http://www.nysca.org/public/guidelines/state_partnerships/general_operating.htm
Sponsor: New York State Council on the Arts
300 Park Ave South, 10th Floor
New York, NY 10010

NYSCA Visual Arts: General Operating Support Grants 1444

General Operating Support grants sponsor an organization's ongoing work, rather than a specific project or program. The Council examines the nature, scope, and quality of an organization's programs and activities, its managerial and fiscal competence, and its public service when considering the provision and level of support. Visual Arts supports a wide range of contemporary art activity for the benefit of the public and the advancement of the field with a goal of assisting New York State artists in their efforts to create and exhibit new work, interpret the work of contemporary visual artists to the public, and encourage dialogue and critical commentary about the visual arts.

Requirements: Applicants must register with the Council by February 22 to be considered for funding. Also, an organization must meet the following conditions: a primary focus in visual arts; an organizational mission primarily devoted to arts and culture with a prior record of accomplishment in producing or presenting cultural activities; demonstrate fiscal stability as indicated by such factors as a positive Fund balance, an absence of substantial and/or recurring organizational deficits, a realistic and balanced organizational budget, diverse revenue sources and strong internal controls; one or more qualified, salaried administrative staff; a viable board of directors and officers that exercises oversight and accountability for governance, operations, programming and finances; and must have on going programs, exhibitions, productions, or other art and cultural activities that are open to the general public. Applications can be found at the website and must be submitted online. First-time applicants are required to call the Visual Arts staff before the registration deadline.

Restrictions: Total requested amounts cannot exceed 25% of the total project budget and will be no less than $5,000. Applicants cannot apply for both General Operating Support and General Program Support. In addition, organizations cannot require or request artists to pay a fee for participation in projects funded by Visual Arts, and commissions on sales of art in projects funded by NYSCA cannot exceed 25% of the sale price. Events such as festivals and open studios are not supported.

Geographic Focus: New York
Date(s) Application is Due: Apr 1
Contact: Karen Helmerson; (212) 741-3003; khelmerson@nysca.org
Internet: http://www.nysca.org/public/guidelines/visual_arts/general_operating.htm
Sponsor: New York State Council on the Arts
300 Park Ave South, 10th Floor
New York, NY 10010

O. Max Gardner Foundation Grants 1445

The O. Max Gardner Foundation was established in North Carolina in 1946, in honor of Oliver Maxwell Gardner. Born in Shelby, North Carolina, Gardner was orphaned as a young child, but went on to to attend North Carolina State University (then known as North Carolina A&M) on a scholarship, where he majored in chemical engineering, was involved in ROTC, played on the football team, managed the baseball team, served as the senior class president, and maintained active membership in the Sigma Nu Fraternity. Gardner returned to Shelby to practice law and married Fay Webb, daughter of prominent politician James L. Webb and niece of Congressman E. Yates Webb. He was elected governor in 1928 and, later, Gardner-Webb University was named for he and his wife. The O. Max Gardner Foundation awards grants in its primary fields of interest, which include: community development; education; human services; and religion. Its geographic area is in and around the community of Shelby, although some grants are given statewide. There is no formal application and no identified annual deadlines. Most recent awards have ranged from $500 to $21,000, with twenty to twenty-five grants approved each year.
Requirements: Although applications are preferred from 501(c)3 organizations serving the residents of Shelby, North Carolina, area, including all of Cleveland County. Some giving is open to other non-profits across the State.
Geographic Focus: North Carolina
Amount of Grant: 500 - 21,000 USD
Samples: Cleveland County Arts, Shelby, North Carolina, $1,500 - general operations; Cleveland County Library System, Shelby, North Carolina, $6,202 - general donation for operations; University of North Carolina, Chapel Hill, North Carolina, $18,000 - general operations.
Contact: John Mull Gardner, President; (704) 487-0755
Sponsor: O. Max Gardner Foundation
P.O. Box 2286
Shelby, NC 28151-0277

Oak Foundation International Human Rights Grants 1446

The foundation awards grants worldwide to address international social and environmental issues, particularly those that have a major impact on the lives of the disadvantaged. In the area of international human rights, the Foundation supports activist organizations involved in documentation, evidence collection, campaigns and strategic litigation that address its priorities. Priorities include: ending impunity for gross human rights violations; freedom from arbitrary detention and torture; supporting and protecting human rights defenders; and broadening human rights constituencies. It also supports those who empower human rights defenders, by improving their physical and digital security and enhancing their effectiveness through a range of technology tools. In this area, the Foundation provides core, project and seed funding in multiyear grants.
Restrictions: Oak does not provide support to individuals, and does not provide funding for scholarships or tuition assistance for undergraduate or postgraduate studies. The Foundation also does not fund religious organizations for religious purposes, election campaigns, or general fund-raising drives.
Geographic Focus: All States, All Countries
Amount of Grant: 25,000 - 2,000,000 USD
Contact: Adrian Arena; ihrp@oakfnd.ch
Internet: http://www.oakfnd.org/node/1299
Sponsor: Oak Foundation
Case Postale 115 58, Avenue Louis Casai
Geneva, Cointrin 1216 Switzerland

OceanFirst Foundation Arts and Cultural Grants 1447

The OceanFirst Foundation concentrates its grantmaking around four core priority areas: health and wellness; housing; improving quality of life; and youth development and education. In addition, grants are made to support emerging community needs and special initiatives consistent with the priorities of the Foundation. The Foundation recognizes that supporting local arts and cultural groups is key to the growth and development of the economy, particularly on the Jersey Shore where tourism is so important to maintaining the health and vitality of communities. OceanFirst is committed to providing critical general operating support grants to organizations that can demonstrate that they are a positive catalyst for bringing people and neighborhoods together while providing enriching arts and cultural opportunities.
Requirements: Arts and Cultural grants are open to nonprofits, cultural outreach organizations, and education foundations with tax-exempt status.
Restrictions: The Foundation, in general, does not fund outside these specific strategic areas or provide support to organizations that cannot demonstrate a significant level of service within the OceanFirst market area. The Foundation cannot provide funding for the following: individuals; research; organizations not exempt under Section 501(c)3 of the Internal Revenue Code; religious congregations; political causes, candidates, organizations or campaigns; organizations whose primary purpose is to influence legislation; or sports leagues and teams.
Geographic Focus: New Jersey
Amount of Grant: 3,500 - 40,000 USD
Contact: Katherine Durante, Executive Director; (732) 341-4676; fax (732) 473-9641; kdurante@oceanfirstfdn.org or info@oceanfirstfdn.org
Internet: http://www.oceanfirstfdn.org/arts-cultural.php
Sponsor: OceanFirst Foundation
1415 Hooper Avenue, Suite 304
Toms River, NJ 08753

OceanFirst Foundation Major Grants 1448

The OceanFirst Foundation concentrates its grantmaking around four core priority areas: health and wellness; housing; improving quality of life; and youth development and education. In addition, grants are made to support emerging community needs and special initiatives consistent with the priorities of the Foundation. Requests for Major Grants are defined as those that are more than $5,000 for program or project support. Such requests must address one of the Foundation's priorities, and applicants must be able to demonstrate a significant impact within the OceanFirst market area. Potential applicants are strongly encouraged to review the application and requirement checklist prior to completing a request to ensure that all qualifications can be met.
Requirements: Organizations may request one major grant per year and if the request is declined, the organization must wait one year before reapplying to the Foundation.
Restrictions: The Foundation, in general, does not fund outside these specific strategic areas or provide support to organizations that cannot demonstrate a significant level of service within the OceanFirst market area. The Foundation cannot provide funding for the following: individuals; research; organizations not exempt under Section 501(c)3 of the Internal Revenue Code; religious congregations; political causes, candidates, organizations or campaigns; organizations whose primary purpose is to influence legislation; or sports leagues and teams.
Geographic Focus: New Jersey
Amount of Grant: 5,000 - 100,000 USD
Contact: Katherine Durante, Executive Director; (732) 341-4676; fax (732) 473-9641; kdurante@oceanfirstfdn.org or info@oceanfirstfdn.org
Internet: http://www.oceanfirstfdn.org/major-grants.php
Sponsor: OceanFirst Foundation
1415 Hooper Avenue, Suite 304
Toms River, NJ 08753

Ohio Arts Council Capacity Building Grants for Organizations and 1449 Communities

Capacity building funds are designed to strengthen Ohio's nonprofit arts and cultural sector by helping applicants improve internal governance and leadership, cultivate strategic community linkages, and develop financial and human resources for long-term stability. Building organizational capacity is a long-term, evolutionary process that organizations must engage in purposefully. The program provides funding for work in three areas of capacity: (1) Organizational Governance and Leadership; (2) Strategic Community Linkages; and, (3) Assets and Resources Development. For other topics appropriate to your organization, contact and discuss with the Program Coordinator. Grants for capacity building generally range from $500 to $5,000. Organizations must show a 1:1 match, half of which may be from allowable, appropriate in-kind donations.
Requirements: All nonprofit arts, cultural and community-based organizations in Ohio that demonstrate a strong commitment to using the arts effectively and authentically in their programming may apply to this program. However, due to limited funding, small, emerging, and mid-sized arts and cultural organizations generally are given priority. Call the OAC before submitting an application. Applications must be received in OLGA (online grant application system) no later than 5 p.m. on the second Friday of any given month. Because effective capacity building activities require careful planning, applications will be accepted only through the second Friday of April (for activities occurring May 15-June 30), except in rare circumstances. Beginning June 1 of each year, applications will be accepted for the next fiscal year.

Restrictions: See the Legal Requirements page of the website for a detailed listing of funding restrictions.
Geographic Focus: Ohio
Amount of Grant: 500 - 5,000 USD
Contact: Katherine Eckstrand; (614) 728-4467 or (614) 466-2613; fax (614) 466-4494; katherine.eckstrand@oac.state.oh.us
Internet: http://www.oac.state.oh.us/grantsprogs/guidelines/CapacityBuilding.asp#top
Sponsor: Ohio Arts Council
30 E. Broad Street, 33rd Floor
Columbus, OH 43215-3414

Ohio Arts Council Sustainability Program Grants　　　　1450

Funding from this program supports organizations that provide essential arts programming to their community and are integral to its cultural legacy. Through direct financial support of ongoing programming by arts, non-arts and cultural organizations, the OAC sustains the vitality of Ohio economically, educationally and culturally. The program allows organizations to plan and conduct ongoing arts programs - either a full year of activities or recurring projects - in both traditional spaces (galleries, concert halls, theaters, museums) and nontraditional venues (hospitals, shopping malls, retirement centers, places of worship). Grants are based on the arts program's budget (see website for formula), not the organization's total budget. Indirect costs may be shown as in-kind but not as part of the cash match. The application deadline is for odd-numbered years only.
Requirements: This funding program provides two-year grants to organizations for annual arts programming or a recurring single project or activity. Repeated events, such as a yearly festival, are eligible. The program supports organizations that offer broad-based arts programming in any discipline (multiarts, performing arts, literature, traditional arts, visual arts) that is produced and presented by nonprofit arts and cultural organizations, other nonprofit or government entities, and colleges or universities that offer arts programming. Applicants to the Sustainability program must have received OAC funds at least twice in the past five years. This previous support must have come from an OAC funding program that evaluated and scored the application through a panel process. First-time applicants to the OAC and organizations with budgets of $25,000 or less should refer to the Arts Access Program. Applicants may be: nonprofit arts and cultural organizations; social service agencies; other nonprofit organizations that provide arts programming; educational organizations that demonstrate a commitment to arts programming in a larger community setting; non-arts organizations such as colleges and universities, government entities and social service organizations may apply to the Sustainability program only for their ongoing arts component or programming.
Restrictions: Please read Legal Requirements and Ohio Arts Council Rules and Grants Process for Organizations before applying to this program. Both documents are available for download at the website.
Geographic Focus: Ohio
Date(s) Application is Due: Feb 1
Contact: Dan Katona, Director of Organizational Services; (614) 995-1662 or (614) 466-2613; fax (614) 466-4494; dan.katona@oac.state.oh.us
Internet: http://www.oac.state.oh.us/grantsprogs/guidelines/Sustainability.asp
Sponsor: Ohio Arts Council
30 E. Broad Street, 33rd Floor
Columbus, OH 43215-3414

Oklahoma City Community Programs and Grants　　　　1451

The community foundation functions to enhance the quality of life in Oklahoma by awarding grants to nonprofits in its areas of interest, including arts and cultural programs, education, health care, health associations, and human services. Types of support include general operating support, continuing support, annual campaigns, building/renovation, equipment, emergency funds, program development, seed grants, fellowships, scholarship funds, research, and matching funds. The grants assist organizations with activities that provide new or expanded services to the community in response to new opportunities and changing circumstances. The community foundation views its role as a partner with other organizations and regards contributions and participation by other individuals and groups as an essential element in grant activities. Especially encouraged are programs and services that are oriented toward the entire population and are not restricted only to those people who live in a particular geographic location or who are members of a particular organization. The foundation encourages nonprofit organizations to cooperate and pool their resources to meet community needs. The use of volunteers as a significant program component is considered favorably as is active participation of the agency's board of directors and a broad base of financial support in the community. Grants are generally made for a specified

time period and are nonrenewable. Applications and guidelines for each program are available on the Web site.
Requirements: 501(c)3 nonprofit organizations serving the greater Oklahoma City area, and programs that benefit persons living in the greater Oklahoma City metropolitan area, are eligible.
Restrictions: Grants are not awarded to individuals or to benefit specific individuals. No faxed or emailed proposals are accepted.
Geographic Focus: Oklahoma
Samples: Arts Council of Oklahoma City (OK)—to support a collaborative summer program of the Oklahoma City Parks and Recreation Department, After School Options, and four local school districts, $20,000; Mesta Park Neighborhood Assoc (OK)—to create a new median strip to reduce the volume of traffic around NW 18th St and N Shartel Boulevard, $10,000; Neighborhood Alliance (OK)—for a computer-resource center, $22,788.
Contact: Manager; (405) 235-5603; fax (405) 235-5612; info@occf.org
Internet: http://www.occf.org/occf/community_programs/index.php
Sponsor: Oklahoma City Community Foundation
P.O. Box 1146
Oklahoma City, OK 73103-1146

Olin Corporation Charitable Trust Grants　　　　1452

The charitable trust supports nonprofits in company-operating areas. Grants focus on three priority categories: education, with a science and technology emphasis; programs that include Olin employees as volunteers and that impact communities in which Olin employees work and live; and conservation, environmental education, and environmental research. Types of support include general operating budgets, continuing support, annual campaigns, seed money, emergency funds, building funds, equipment, land acquisition, special projects, research, publications, conferences and seminars, internships, scholarship funds, employee-related scholarships, fellowships, and employee matching gifts. US-based nonprofits with an international focus are supported primarily through matching gifts. There are no application deadlines. Applicants should submit a letter of request. The board meets in January to consider requests.
Requirements: Support is directed primarily to communities where Olin has a major employee presence.
Restrictions: Grants are not awarded to individuals or for endowments.
Geographic Focus: All States
Amount of Grant: 50 - 50,000 USD
Contact: Program Contact; (314) 480-1400
Internet: http://www.olin.com/about/charitable.asp
Sponsor: Olin Corporation Charitable Trust
190 Carondelet Plaza, Suite 1530
Clayton, MO 63105-3443

Olive Smith Browning Charitable Trust Grants　　　　1453

Established in 1978, the Olive Smith Browning Charitable Trust offers funding to organizations located in the Twin Falls, Idaho, region. Its primary fields of interest include: arts, culture, and humanities; education; the environment; animal welfare; human services; religion; community development; and health care. The annual deadline for application submission is May 31. There are no specified application formats, so applicants should begin by sending their proposal overview directly to the trustee in charge of managing the trust. Most recent grants have ranged from $2,000 to $10,000, with an average of ten awards each year and a total annual giving of $35,000. Grant decisions are generally communicated by July 31 for applications received by the deadline.
Requirements: Applicants should be 501(c)3 organizations either located in, or serving the residents of, Twin Falls, Idaho.
Restrictions: No grants are given to individuals.
Geographic Focus: Idaho
Date(s) Application is Due: May 31
Amount of Grant: 2,000 - 10,000 USD
Contact: Carla Colfack, Trust Officer; (208) 736-1217 or (888) 730-4933
Internet: https://www.wellsfargo.com/privatefoundationgrants/browning
Sponsor: Olive Smith Browning Charitable Trust
P.O. Box 53456, MAC S4101-22G
Phoenix, AZ 85072-3456

Olivia R. Gardner Foundation Grants　　　　1454

The Olivia R. Gardner Foundation was established in Georgia in 2003 as a means of awarding grants in Georgia, Florida, and in some areas of North Carolina. The Foundation's primary fields of interest include: elementary and secondary education; higher education; the arts; and human services. Most recent awards have ranged from $1,000 to $15,000, although much higher amounts are sometimes given to higher education institutions. Between twenty and twenty-five grants are awarded each year. A formal application is required, and can be secured by contacting the Foundation office. There are no identified annual deadlines for submission.

Requirements: Any 501(c)3 organization serving residents of Georgia, Florida, or North Carolina are eligible to apply.

Geographic Focus: Florida, Georgia, North Carolina

Amount of Grant: 1,000 - 65,000 USD

Samples: Vero Beach Museum of Art, Vero Beach, Florida, $2,500 - general operations; Safe Space, Louisburg, North Carolina, $2,500 - general operations; Atlanta Speech School, Atlanta, Georgia, $5,000 - educational support.

Contact: Olivia R. Gardner, President; (404) 355-4747

Sponsor: Olivia R. Gardner Foundation

402 Indies Drive

Vero Beach, FL 32963

OneFamily Foundation Grants   1455

The foundation awards grants to eligible Washington nonprofit organizations working to improve the lives of women living in poverty and at-risk youth, for support services for abused women, and for efforts to end sexual abuse against women and children. Consideration is given to programs that provide training and skills development to low-income women and services providing basic needs such as shelter, counseling, food, and childcare; educational and mentoring projects to help prevent teen pregnancy; job-training programs for youth and school/community-based programs to help low-income youth complete their education; parenting, training, and education programs to help break the cycle of family violence; shelters and services to support abused and neglected children and women; and hands-on programs to encourage philanthropy among children and youth. Grants will support operating expenses, special projects, and minor capital costs necessary to assure the success of a funded project. For general grants, two-page preapplication letters are due on the third Friday in March, July, and November and final proposals are due the second Friday in January, May, and September. Annual deadlines may vary; contact program staff for exact dates.

Requirements: Nonprofit 501(c)3 organizations based in King County, Snohomish County, or the Olympic Peninsula of Washington State are eligible to apply for funding.

Restrictions: Grants are not made to: individuals, scholarships, schools, research, summer camps, athletic events, video or film projects, website development, book publications. No multi-year requests are considered. Groups who have been declined three times are ineligible to reapply.

Geographic Focus: Washington

Amount of Grant: 5,000 - 12,000 USD

Samples: Amara Parenting and Adoption, Seattle, Washington, $12,000 - to foster-adoption the program, training for foster parents, and support for hard-to-place children; First Step Family Support Center, Port Angeles, Washington, $11,154 - Parent-Child Interaction Therapy; Indian Law Resource Center, Helena, Washington. $8,000 - Safe Women/Strong Nations, breaking the cycle of violence against Native women.

Contact: Therese Ogle, Foundation Advisor; (206) 781-3472; fax (206) 784-5987; Oglefounds@aol.com

Internet: http://fdncenter.org/grantmaker/onefamily

Sponsor: OneFamily Foundation

6723 Sycamore Avenue NW

Seattle, WA 98117

Ontario Arts Council Arts Service Organizations Grants   1456

This program supports provincial or national membership-based Arts Service Organizations (ASOs) that provide services and programs to support their members' professional, career or organizational development and promote an awareness of the arts in Ontario. The program provides operating and project support. Potential new applicants must contact the officer well in advance of the deadline to discuss eligibility and to request an application package.

Requirements: To be eligible for this program, arts service organizations must: be not-for-profit (with the exception of book and magazine publishers); be Ontario-based; be led by qualified professional personnel; have been in operation for at least two years; have a demonstrated record of regular, ongoing programming in their communities; have proof of sound financial management; submit verification of financial results of the last completed fiscal year with their applications; and be governed by a board of directors or an advisory body responsible for the organization. ASOs that serve an ethno-racial membership that are not provincial or national in scope, but that may have a provincial or national impact, may also be eligible to apply.

Geographic Focus: All States, Canada

Date(s) Application is Due: Mar 3

Samples: Canadian Music Centre, Toronto, Ontario, Canada, $48,000; CCI - Ontario Presenting Network, Toronto, Ontario, Canada, $55,000; FUSION: The Ontario Clay and Glass Association, Toronto, Ontario, Canada, $32,081; League of Canadian Poets, Toronto, Ontario, Canada, $20,000.

Contact: Lorraine Filyer, Program Officer; (416) 969-7438 or (800) 387-0058, ext. 7438; lfilyer@arts.on.ca

Internet: http://www.arts.on.ca/Page88.aspx

Sponsor: Ontario Arts Council

151 Bloor Street West, 5th Floor

Toronto, ON M5S 1T6 Canada

Ontario Arts Council Choirs and Vocal Groups Grants   1457

This program provides operating support to not-for-profit, professional choral organizations as well as project support to choirs and vocal groups in Ontario to assist them to produce and present art and arts services to the public and to sustain a healthy arts community. There are two types of grants available: operating grants—commit funding to the operating and programming expenses of professional choral organizations that meet the assessment criteria for ongoing support; and project grants—offer assistance toward the professional artistic costs of specific music programming (such as a concert series or individual performances) by choirs or vocal collectives.

Requirements: To be eligible for support, choral organizations must: be not-for-profit (with the exception of book and magazine publishers); be Ontario-based; be led by qualified professional personnel; have been in operation for at least two years; have a demonstrated record of regular, ongoing programming in their communities; have proof of sound financial management; submit verification of financial results of the last completed fiscal year with their applications; and be governed by a board of directors or an advisory body responsible for the organization.

Restrictions: The following are not eligible: choirs that operate under the umbrella of a parent organization that is currently funded through another Ontario Arts Council program (i.e., as part of another choir or orchestra); choirs that are attached to, or affiliated with educational or religious institutions; choirs giving performances exclusively as part of religious worship; tours and exchange programs; or recording projects.

Geographic Focus: All States, Canada

Date(s) Application is Due: Apr 1

Samples: Amabile Choirs of London Canada, London, Ontario, Canada, $18,000; Guelph Youth Singers, Guelph, Ontario, Canada, $12,000; Toronto Children's Chorus, Toronto, Ontario, Canada, $50,000.

Contact: Georgina Braoudakis, Music Officer - French Services; (416) 969-7417 or (800) 387-0058, ext. 7417; gbraoudakis@arts.on.ca

Internet: http://www.arts.on.ca/Page101.aspx

Sponsor: Ontario Arts Council

151 Bloor Street West, 5th Floor

Toronto, ON M5S 1T6 Canada

Ontario Arts Council Community and Multi Arts Organizations Grants   1458

The objective of the program is to provide operating and annual support to Ontario nonprofit, professional community and multi-arts organizations to assist them to produce and present art and arts services to the public and to sustain a healthy arts community. Major goals include: to support growth and sustenance of the arts in Ontario through focused investment in artists and arts organizations; and to fund and encourage opportunities for arts education, public participation, and community involvement in the arts in Ontario. Programming grants commit funding to the programming expenses of professional arts organizations that meet the assessment criteria for ongoing support. There are multi-year and annual grants. Potential new applicants must contact the officer well in advance of the deadline to discuss eligibility and to request an application package. Guidelines are available online.

Requirements: Arts organizations must be nonprofit (with the exception of book and magazine publishers) and Ontario-based; have been in operation for at least two years; have a demonstrated record of regular, ongoing activities in their community; and have proof of sound financial management and be governed by a board of directors or an advisory body responsible for the organization. In addition, to be eligible for OAC operating funding, professional multi-arts festivals must have a year-round infrastructure and artistic leadership.

Restrictions: Art classes are not eligible for funding through this program. In the block grants to book publishers category, ineligible titles are listed in the guidelines.

Geographic Focus: All States, Canada

Date(s) Application is Due: Apr 1

Samples: Art Starts Neighbourhood Cultural Centre, Toronto, Ontario, Canada, $32,000; Atikokan Intergenerational Centre for Arts and Alternatives, Atikokan, Ontario, Canada, $25,400; Workers Arts and Heritage Centre, Hamilton, Ontario, Canada, $15,915.
Contact: Georgina Braoudakis, French Services Director; (416) 969-7417 or (800) 387-0058, ext. 7417; gbraoudakis@arts.on.ca
Internet: http://www.arts.on.ca/Page103.aspx
Sponsor: Ontario Arts Council
151 Bloor Street West, 5th Floor
Toronto, ON M5S 1T6 Canada

Ontario Arts Council Dance Organizations Grants   1459
The Dance Organizations program provides operating support to not-for-profit, professional arts organizations in Ontario to assist them to produce and present dance and dance services to the public in order to sustain a healthy dance community. It supports: excellence in the arts, regional activity, linguistic and cultural diversity and Aboriginal and Franco-Ontarian identity; and arts education, public participation and community involvement in the arts in Ontario.
Requirements: To be eligible for grant funding, arts organizations must: be not-for-profit (with the exception of book and magazine publishers); be Ontario-based; be led by professional personnel; have been in operation for at least two years; have a demonstrated record of regular, ongoing programming in their communities; have proof of sound financial management; submit verification of financial results of the last completed fiscal year with their applications; and be governed by a board of directors or an advisory body responsible for the organization. In addition to the above, in order to apply to the program an applicant must: have produced an annual season or have operated on a continuous basis for at least three years; have an appropriate administrative infrastructure, according to the scope and scale of the organization's mandate; and engage Ontario-resident dance artists.
Restrictions: Ineligible applicants include: membership-based provincial/national dance service organizations; and union or labor organizations that protect or establish economic rights.
Geographic Focus: All States, Canada
Date(s) Application is Due: Mar 17
Samples: Andrea Nann Dreamwalker Dance Company, Toronto, Ontario, Canada, $10,000; Ballet Jorgen Canada, Toronto, Ontario, Canada, $165,000; The Guelph Contemporary Dance Festival, Guelph, Ontario, Canada, $16,245; MOTU.S. O Dance Theatre, Stouffville, Ontario, Canada, $20,000.
Contact: Myles Warren, Dance Officer; (416) 969-7422 or (800) 387-0058, ext. 7422; mwarren@arts.on.ca
Internet: http://www.arts.on.ca/Page123.aspx
Sponsor: Ontario Arts Council
151 Bloor Street West, 5th Floor
Toronto, ON M5S 1T6 Canada

Oppenstein Brothers Foundation Grants   1460
Grants are awarded in the metropolitan area of Kansas, City, Missouri, primarily for social services and early childhood, elementary, secondary, adult-basic, vocational, and higher education; family planning and services; social services and welfare agencies; Jewish welfare organizations; and programs for youth, the handicapped, disadvantaged, mentally ill, homeless, minorities, and elderly. Additional areas of interest include arts/cultural programs, the performing arts, museums, health care and health organizations, and AIDS research. The foundation considers requests for building and renovation, capital campaigns, curriculum development, emergency funds, equipment, general operating support, program development, seed money, technical support, conferences and seminars, consulting services, and matching funds. Application guidelines are available on request. The board meets every other month. Deadlines are generally three weeks prior to board meetings. Notification of award will take place within two to four months.
Requirements: Nonprofit organizations serving the metropolitan area of Kansas City, Missouri are eligible to apply.
Restrictions: The foundation primarily supports 501(c)3 nonprofit organizations serving the metropolitan area of Kansas City, Missouri. Grants are not awarded to support individuals or for annual campaigns.
Geographic Focus: Missouri
Amount of Grant: 5,000 - 15,000 USD
Contact: Beth Radtke, Program Officer; (816) 234-2577
Sponsor: Oppenstein Brothers Foundation
922 Walnut Street, Suite 200
Kansas City, MO 64106-1809

Oprah Winfrey Foundation Grants   1461
The foundation focuses on education and on empowering children, women, and families. Grants are made in a range of interests, including art and community, children and youth, education, health, and social services. Types of support include pilot, program, and operating grants. There are no application deadlines.
Requirements: Nonprofits are eligible, with preference given to Chicago.
Geographic Focus: All States
Amount of Grant: 10,000 - 100,000 USD
Contact: Grants Administrator; (312) 633-1000
Sponsor: Oprah Winfrey Foundation
110 N Carpenter Street
Chicago, IL 60607

Orchard Foundation Grants   1462
The foundation makes grants to eligible New York and New England nonprofit organizations in its areas of interest, including environment (air quality, biodiversity, fresh and coastal waters, forests, toxic substances, and pollution prevention); children, youth, and families (child welfare systems, literacy, and pregnancy prevention); and campaign finance reform. The foundation will occasionally provide seed money, operating support, and start-up capital to smaller home-grown organizations provided that strong local support has been obtained for a project in the form of membership and contributions, and that the entire mission of the organization coincides with a field of interest to the foundation. The listed deadlines are for concept letters.
Requirements: The foundation focuses on Massachusetts, Maine, New Hampshire, New York, Vermont, Connecticut, and Rhode Island. The foundation accepts letters of inquiry from groups in those seven states as well as from national groups with regional offices or projects in the area.
Restrictions: Grants are not made to individuals or for endowments, annual or capital campaigns, religious programs, any religion-affiliated organization, conference participation/travel unrelated to current foundation grant, research efforts unrelated to advocacy interests of the foundation, scholarships, fellowships, building projects, equipment needs, film and video projects, land acquisition, animal hospitals/rehabilitation centers, or groups that focus on specific diseases or conditions. Loans are not made.
Geographic Focus: Connecticut, Maine, Massachusetts, New Hampshire, New York, Rhode Island, Vermont
Date(s) Application is Due: Mar 1; Sep 1
Amount of Grant: 3,000 - 15,000 USD
Samples: New England Forestry Foundation (Groton, MA)—to purchase the largest forestland easement in U.S. history, which will protect 762,192 acres in Maine from development, $35,000.
Contact: Executive Director; (207) 799-0686; orchard@maine.rr.com
Internet: http://home.maine.rr.com/orchard
Sponsor: Orchard Foundation
P.O. Box 2587
Portland, ME 04116

Ordean Foundation Grants   1463
The Foundation, established in 1933, supports organizations involved with alcoholism, children/youth, services, crime/violence prevention, youth, education, family services, food services, health care, homeless, human services, housing/shelter, human services, medical care, rehabilitation, mental health/crisis services, substance abuse, services, YM/YWCAs & YM/YWHAs, aging, disabilities, economically disadvantaged. Grants will be awarded for up to three years. Applications are reviewed on an ongoing basis; the deadline is the 15th of each month.
Requirements: Non-profits in the Duluth and contiguous cities and townships in St. Louis County, Minnesota are eligible. The Foundation accepts the Minnesota Common Grant Application Form.
Restrictions: No support for direct religious purposes, or for political campaigns or lobbying activities. No grants to individuals (directly), or for endowment funds, travel, conferences, seminars or workshops, telephone solicitations, benefits, dinners, research, including biomedical research, deficit financing, national fund raising campaigns, or to supplant government funding.
Geographic Focus: Minnesota
Amount of Grant: 1,000 - 290,000 USD
Contact: Stephen A. Mangan, Executive Director; (218) 726-4785; fax (218) 726-4848; ordean@computerpro.com
Sponsor: Ordean Foundation
501 Ordean Building
Duluth, MN 55802-4725

Oregon Arts Commission Arts Services Grants 1464

Oregon Arts Commission Arts Services grants provide operating support to local and regional art councils or other arts organizations that offer: regular, ongoing arts services to a broad population; programming and services that encourage all people to participate in arts activities; and opportunities that enhance the capacity of artists to contribute to the economic, social and cultural well being of their communities. The most competitive applicants are arts organizations that offer ongoing, sustained high quality artistic programming, outreach programs in the community and opportunities for arts learning. Grant awards range from $3,000 to $50,000, though the majority of grants will range from $5,000 to $25,000. Organizations should submit full applications by May 1 of odd numbered years.

Requirements: Grant requests should be no more than 10% of the applicant's prior year cash budget, and may not exceed $50,000 regardless of the budget size of the applicant. All applicant organizations must: have IRS 501(c)3 federal tax-exempt status; have current corporate, non-profit status in the state of Oregon; have a DUNS number; operate within a mission that describes the arts as the primary purpose of the organization; have been in existence as a 501(c)3 for a minimum of two years; and show at least $150,000 in operating expenses for the past fiscal year and a cash operating budget of at least $150,000 in the current and projected fiscal years.

Restrictions: Arts Services grants will not fund: capital construction; tuition assistance or scholarships for college, university or other formal courses of study; activities that have already been completed; offset of previous operating or project deficits; or events whose primary focus is to raise funds for a non-arts purpose.

Geographic Focus: Oregon

Date(s) Application is Due: May 1

Contact: Brian Wagner, Community Development Coordinator; (503) 986-0083 or (503) 986-0082; fax (503) 986-0260; brian.wagner@oregon.gov

Internet: http://www.oregonartscommission.org/grants/arts-services

Sponsor: Oregon Arts Commission

775 Summer Street NE, Suite 200

Salem, OR 97301-1280

Oregon Arts Commission Operating Support Grants 1465

Oregon Arts Commission Operating Support grants facilitate the activities of and access to Oregon's medium and large not-for-profit arts organizations. The Commission encourages applications for projects that include creation, exhibition, or performance of work created by Oregon artists of demonstrated excellence. Grants are intended for arts groups whose prior year's cash operating revenue totaled at least $150,000. Operating Support grants can range from $2,000 to $50,000. However, the majority of grants will range from $5,000 to $25,000. Full applications from organizations are reviewed by an independent panel on alternating years based on artistic discipline. Organizations will submit applications for: music, dance and multi-disciplinary programs by May 1 of even numbered years; and for theatre, visual arts, and literary programs by May 1 in odd numbered years.

Requirements: Grant requests should be no more than 10% of the applicant's prior year cash budget, and may not exceed $50,000 regardless of the budget size of the applicant. All applicant organizations must: have IRS 501(c)3 federal tax-exempt status; have current corporate, non-profit status in the state of Oregon; have a DUNS number; operate within a mission that describes the arts as the primary purpose of the organization; have been in existence as a 501(c)3 for a minimum of two years; and show at least $150,000 in operating expenses for the past fiscal year and a cash operating budget of at least $150,000 in the current and projected fiscal years.

Restrictions: Operating Support grants will not fund: capital construction; tuition assistance or scholarships for college, university or other formal courses of study; activities that have already been completed; offset of previous operating or project deficits; or events whose primary focus is to raise funds for a non-arts purpose.

Geographic Focus: Oregon

Date(s) Application is Due: May 1

Contact: David Huff; (503) 986-0086 or (503) 986-0082; fax (503) 986-0260; david.huff@oregon.gov or oregon.artscomm@state.or.us

Internet: http://www.oregonartscommission.org/grants/operating-support

Sponsor: Oregon Arts Commission

775 Summer Street NE, Suite 200

Salem, OR 97301-1280

Oregon Arts Commission Small Operating Support Grants 1466

The Oregon Arts Commission has established a program to provide operating support for organizations with an annual operating budget of less than $150,000, which are locally-based. The program is in keeping with the Commission's ongoing effort to streamline and simplify the grant application and review process with the goal of making it easier and less time consuming for organizations apply for operating support. Operating Support grants support the core operation of small not-for-profit arts organizations. Eligible applicants are arts organizations that offer ongoing, sustained, artistic programming and outreach programs in the community. Awards will generally range between $1,000 and $3,000. The annual application deadline is September 16.

Requirements: All applicant organizations must: have IRS 501(c)3 federal tax-exempt status; have current corporate, non-profit status in the state of Oregon; have a DUNS number; operate within a mission that describes the arts as the primary purpose of the organization; have been in existence as a 501(c)3 for a minimum of two years; and show at least $150,000 in operating expenses for the past fiscal year and a cash operating budget of at least $150,000 in the current and projected fiscal years.

Restrictions: Small Operating Support grants will not fund: capital construction; tuition assistance or scholarships for college, university or other formal courses of study; activities that have already been completed; offset of previous operating or project deficits; schools and institutions of higher learning; or preservation of a single artist's work.

Geographic Focus: All States

Date(s) Application is Due: Sep 16

Amount of Grant: 1,000 - 3,000 USD

Contact: Brian Wagner, Community Development Coordinator; (503) 986-0083 or (503) 986-0082; fax (503) 986-0260; brian.wagner@oregon.gov or oregon.artscomm@state.or.us

Internet: http://www.oregonartscommission.org/grants/small-operating-grants

Sponsor: Oregon Arts Commission

775 Summer Street NE, Suite 200

Salem, OR 97301-1280

Ottinger-Sprong Charitable Foundation Scholarships 1467

Established in Indiana in 2002, the Ottinger-Sprong Charitable Foundation provides scholarships to graduates of Zionsville Community High School, in Zionsville, Iindiana, attending a state accredited college, university, or technical/vocational institute. Applications are required, and should include a detailed description of the individual need and amount of funding requested. The annual deadline is March 21, and applicants should use a letter of inquiry as their initial approach.

Geographic Focus: All States, Indiana

Date(s) Application is Due: Mar 21

Amount of Grant: 500 - 2,000 USD

Contact: Candace E. Buckmaster, (317) 873-5669 or (317) 769-5619

Sponsor: Ottinger-Sprong Charitable Foundation

P.O. Box 13

Zionsville, IN 46077-0013

Ottinger Foundation Grants 1468

The Ottinger Foundation is a private family foundation that funds non-profit organizations that promote innovative policies and citizen activism to build a movement for change. It supports organizations that address structural or root causes of social problems and focus on systemic social change rather than direct services. Organizations and projects funded by the Ottinger Foundation include a sound strategic vision, a concrete action plan, and strong components of advocacy and grassroots organizing. Projects must have national significance. The Foundation also favor organizations that are involved in coalition building as well as building leadership and organizational infrastructure. The Foundation continues its program area focusing on economic security issues and is only accepting proposals in the form of a brief letter of intent in this area. Grants generally range from $10,000 to $50,000.

Requirements: IRS 501(c)3 tax-exempt organizations may apply. Due to the large number of proposals received, initial letters of inquiry are discouraged and will not receive a response. email proposals will also not be accepted.

Restrictions: The foundation does not make grants to organizations that traditionally enjoy popular support, such as universities, museums, hospitals, or schools. The foundation does not support individuals, academic research, film or video projects, the construction or restoration of buildings, conferences, books, or local programs that do not have national significance.

Geographic Focus: All States

Amount of Grant: 10,000 - 50,000 USD

Contact: Michele Lord; (212) 764-1508; info@ottingerfoundation.org

Internet: http://www.ottingerfoundation.org/guidelines.html

Sponsor: Ottinger Foundation

80 Broad Street, 17th Floor

New York, NY 10004

Otto Bremer Foundation Grants   1469

The foundation concentrates its grantmaking activity in communities served by Bremer-affiliated banks and provides financial assistance to nonprofit organizations whose work contributes to the well-being of these towns. The foundation looks to support programs that promote civil and political rights, including freedom of assembly, speech, and religion; economic and social rights, including the right to education, food, health care, and shelter; and cultural and environmental rights, including the right to live in a clean environment and participate in the cultural and political events of one's community. Types of support include program development, operating support, capital (including building and equipment), matching or challenge grants, and internships. Applications are accepted throughout the year. Most grants are given for a one-year period, although some multiyear grants are awarded. The foundation encourages initial telephone or written inquiries concerning its interest in a particular project. Applicants are also encouraged to contact foundation staff for assistance in the development of a proposal.

Requirements: Private nonprofit or public 501(c)3 tax-exempt organizations whose beneficiaries are residents of Minnesota, North Dakota, or Wisconsin with priority given to those communities or regions served by Bremer affiliates.

Restrictions: Requests for the following types of projects are discouraged: annual fund drives; benefit events; camps; commercial and business development; K-12 education; medical research; sporting activities; building endowments other than for the development of community foundations; capital requests for hospitals and nursing homes; theatrical productions, including motion pictures, books, and other artistic or media projects; municipal and government services; or historical preservation, museums, and interpretive centers.

Geographic Focus: Minnesota, North Dakota, Wisconsin

Amount of Grant: 552 - 259,235 USD

Contact: Danielle Cheslog, Grants Manager; (651) 312-3717 or (651) 227-8036; fax (651) 312-3665; danielle@ottobremer.org or obf@ottobremer.org

Sponsor: Otto Bremer Foundation

445 Minnesota Stret, Suite 2250

Saint Paul, MN 55101-2107

Overbrook Foundation Grants   1470

The foundation strives to improve the lives of people by supporting projects that protect human and civil rights, advance the self-sufficiency and well being of individuals and their communities, and conserve the natural environment. The foundation's environment program supports organizations working to develop better consumption and production habits in the United States and in Latin America (currently Brazil, Mexico and Ecuador only). In Latin America the primary objective is to conserve the planet's dwindling biodiversity. The foundation's human and civil rights program is multifaceted and provides support to the following: reproductive health rights; domestic criminal system reform efforts; lesbian, gay, bisexual, and transgender rights; gun violence prevention and international human rights. An emphasis is placed on work that protects the rights of children and women. The foundation supports projects both domestically and internationally (with a particular focus in Latin America and South Africa). Generally speaking, the foundation's domestic programs support policy development, advocacy, coalition building, research, legal and other strategies likely to impact large classes of people or shape issues important to the foundation's mission. In its international funding, the foundation also supports organizations providing direct services. The first step in the application process is to Submit a letter of inquiry; full application is by invitation. Guidelines are available online.

Requirements: 501(c)3 tax-exempt organizations are eligible.

Restrictions: The foundation does not make grants to individuals and rarely for endowments, building campaigns, deficit financing, or religious purposes. Grant funds may not be used to participate in or intervene in any political campaign on behalf of or in opposition to any candidate for public office or to conduct, directly or indirectly, any voter registration drive (within 4945(d)2 of the IRS code). Grants are not made for debt reduction. Funding for conferences, publications, and media is limited to projects directly related to priorities in the foundation's program areas.

Geographic Focus: All States

Samples: Rainforest Alliance (New York, NY)—for efforts to ensure the conservation of biological diversity within the tourism industry in Ecuador, $70,000; Gender Public Advocacy Coalition (Washington, DC)—for operating or program support, $40,000; National Public Radio (Washington, DC)—to support coverage of environmental issues on its news program, $50,000; Educational Fund to Stop Gun Violence (Washington, DC)—for its work to spur congressional legislation designed to curb gun-related violence, $50,000.

Contact: Grants Administrator; (212) 661-8710; fax (212) 661-8664; apply@overbrookfoundation.org

Internet: http://www.overbrook.org

Sponsor: Overbrook Foundation

122 E 42nd Street, Suite 2500

New York, NY 10168

Owens Corning Foundation Grants   1471

The Owens Corning Foundation's giving programs are made directly to non-profit organizations that most effectively provide direct service on behalf of disadvantaged children and families in the following areas: affordable housing; K-16 education; federated giving programs; arts and culture; and civic betterment. Funding emphasis is given to projects and organizations that promote diversity and social welfare, serve a broad sector of the community, and have a proven record of success.

Requirements: Applications are not accepted and there are no specific deadlines. Request for contributions (both financial and in-kind) must be made in writing on agency letterhead and include the following: description of the mission and work of the organization, including the audience and community the organization it serves; an outline of the specific request and a statement explaining how it accomplishes and measures the organization's goals; a description of the organization's anticipated outcome and benefits resulting from this grant; the amount requested; an outline of services or promotional opportunities available to the Owens Corning Foundation for contribution; proof of tax exempt status or tax exempt number; and other funding commitments to project.

Restrictions: In general, funding is not considered for the following organizations or types of activities: religious, political or discriminatory organizations; travel funds of any kind; capital campaigns and ongoing operations support; grants to individuals; special events such as conferences and sports competitions; organizations or projects in countries where the U.S. government restricts business dealings; or agencies that receive United Way support to the degree which we are already contributing. Giving is on a national basis in areas of company operations, with emphasis on Ohio.

Geographic Focus: All States

Contact: Simone Hayes, President; (419) 248-8000; fax (419) 325-3031; OCFoundation@owenscorning.com

Internet: http://sustainability.owenscorning.com/contents/community-alliances/oc-foundation/

Sponsor: Owens Corning Foundation

1 Owens Corning Parkway

Toledo, OH 43659

Owens Foundation Grants   1472

The Owens Foundation, established in 1985, supports organizations involved with housing/shelter; development; human services; secondary school/education; economically disadvantaged; homelessness. Giving is primarily in Chicago, IL. area. There are no specific deadlines with which to adhere. Contact the Foundation for further application information and guidelines.

Requirements: Must be a non-profit in Chicago, IL.

Restrictions: No grants to individuals directly, or for capital campaigns, building funds, or raffles.

Geographic Focus: Illinois

Amount of Grant: 10,000 - 300,000 USD

Samples: CARA Program, Chicago, IL, $372,500 - helps homeless and at-risk individuals transform their lives through comprehensive training, permanent job placement and critical support services; The Emergency Fund, Chicago, IL, $264,600 - provides emergency funding into the hands of church and lay organizations located in very poor Chicago neighborhoods. Funds used to avoid homelessness and to provide access to long term self-sufficiency solutions;

Contact: Mary M. Owens, President; (708) 361-8845

Sponsor: Owens Foundation

7804 College Drive, Suite 3SW

Palos Heights, IL 60463-1473

Pacers Foundation Be Drug-Free Grants   1473

The foremost priority of the Pacers Foundation is to help Indiana's youth through the nonprofit organizations that serve them. The foundation's areas of interest are youth programs that address childhood obesity, keep kids in school, prevent and treat adolescent and teenage alcohol/drug abuse, encourage tolerance and prevent bullying, and that help girls build self-esteem during the crucial preteen and teenage years. The foundation's Be Drug-Free grants support the efforts of Indiana groups that help young substance abusers to achieve and maintain their sobriety, help youth who are at serious risk of substance abuse to stay drug and alcohol free, and that educate high-risk youth about the potential consequences of drug and/or alcohol abuse (chronic dependence and links to criminal behavior, high-risk sexual activity, etc.). Substance abuse treatment programs, substance abuse education programs, counseling programs, after-school programs that focus on creating positive alternatives to "the streets," and other similarly focused groups should consider applying. Other types of organizations focused on youth substance abuse may also apply. Grants are one year in length and range from $5,000 - $20,000. Organizations that achieve the results set forth in their applications may apply for continued support in subsequent years. A link to application guidelines and forms is provided at the grant website.

Requirements: 501(c)3 tax-exempt organizations are eligible.

Restrictions: Pacers Foundation does not provide support for: individuals, emergency funds, political candidates or parties, fundraisers, or corporate memberships. Requests to support fundraisers are reviewed by Pacers Sports & Entertainment, not Pacers Foundation. These requests should be directed to Marilynn Wernke, Pacers Sports & Entertainment, at the sponsor address given. Although the foundation will occasionally support efforts of national significance or efforts outside of the state, it remains primarily committed to its hometown of Indianapolis and its home state of Indiana.

Geographic Focus: All States

Date(s) Application is Due: Dec 30

Amount of Grant: 5,000 - 20,000 USD

Samples: Brookside Community Youth Services, Indianapolis, Indiana; Noble County Pride, Albion, Indiana; Hope Academy, Indianapolis, Indiana.

Contact: Rick Fuson, Chairperson; (317) 917-2864; fax (317) 917-2599; foundation@pacers.com

Internet: http://www.pacersfoundation.org/grants.php

Sponsor: Pacers Foundation

125 S Pennsylvania Street

Indianapolis, IN 46204

Pacers Foundation Be Educated Grants 1474

The foremost priority of the Pacers Foundation is to help Indiana's youth through the nonprofit organizations that serve them. The foundation's areas of interest are youth programs that address childhood obesity, keep kids in school, prevent and treat adolescent and teenage alcohol/drug abuse, encourage tolerance and prevent bullying, and that help girls build self-esteem during the crucial preteen and teenage years. The foundation's Be Educated grants support the efforts of Indiana groups that help struggling students to stay in school and out-of-school youth to re-engage in learning. Mentoring and/or tutoring programs, alternative schools, and after-school programs with an emphasis on learning should consider applying. Other types of organizations with a focus on youth education may also apply. Grants are one year in length and range from $5,000 - $20,000. Organizations that achieve the results set forth in their applications may apply for continued support in subsequent years. A link to application guidelines and forms is provided at the grant website.

Requirements: 501(c)3 tax-exempt organizations are eligible.

Restrictions: Pacers Foundation does not provide support for: individuals, emergency funds, political candidates or parties, fundraisers, or corporate memberships. Requests to support fundraisers are reviewed by Pacers Sports & Entertainment, not Pacers Foundation. These requests should be directed to Marilynn Wernke, Pacers Sports & Entertainment, at the sponsor address given. Although the foundation will occasionally support efforts of national significance or efforts outside of the state, it remains primarily committed to its hometown of Indianapolis and its home state of Indiana.

Geographic Focus: All States

Date(s) Application is Due: Sep 30

Amount of Grant: 5,000 - 20,000 USD

Contact: Rick Fuson, Chairperson; (317) 917-2864; fax (317) 917-2599; foundation@pacers.com

Internet: http://www.pacersfoundation.org/grants.php

Sponsor: Pacers Foundation

125 S Pennsylvania Street

Indianapolis, IN 46204

Pacers Foundation Be Healthy and Fit Grants 1475

The foremost priority of the Pacers Foundation is to help Indiana's youth through the nonprofit organizations that serve them. The foundation's areas of interest are youth programs that address childhood obesity, keep kids in school, prevent and treat adolescent and teenage alcohol/drug abuse, encourage tolerance and prevent bullying, and that help girls build self-esteem during the crucial preteen and teenage years. The foundation's Be Healthy and Fit grants support the efforts of Indiana groups that help overweight and obese youth

and/or those who are at serious risk of becoming overweight to make healthier choices with respect to diet and exercise and to cope with the psychosocial effects of, and the stigma associated with, being overweight or obese; and that help educate schools and families about the root causes of obesity and the importance of nutrition and exercise in preventing and fighting obesity. School-based programs, health centers (including mental health programs focused on the psychosocial effects of childhood obesity), organizations focused on fighting and/or treating obesity, and groups focused on educating others about obesity should consider applying. Grants are one year in length and range from $5,000 - $20,000. Organizations that achieve the results set forth in their applications may apply for continued support in subsequent years. A link to application guidelines and forms is provided at the grant website.

Requirements: 501(c)3 tax-exempt organizations are eligible.

Restrictions: Pacers Foundation does not provide support for: individuals, emergency funds, political candidates or parties, fundraisers, or corporate memberships. Requests to support fundraisers are reviewed by Pacers Sports & Entertainment, not Pacers Foundation. These requests should be directed to Marilynn Wernke, Pacers Sports & Entertainment, at the sponsor address given. Although the foundation will occasionally support efforts of national significance or efforts outside of the state, it remains primarily committed to its hometown of Indianapolis and its home state of Indiana.

Geographic Focus: All States

Date(s) Application is Due: Jun 30

Amount of Grant: 5,000 - 20,000 USD

Samples: Boys and Girls Clubs of Indianapolis, Indianapolis, Indiana; Stepping Stones, Indianapolis, Indiana; Community Harvest Food Bank, Fort Wayne, Indiana.

Contact: Rick Fuson, Chairperson; (317) 917-2864; fax (317) 917-2599; foundation@pacers.com

Internet: http://www.pacersfoundation.org/grants.php

Sponsor: Pacers Foundation

125 S Pennsylvania Street

Indianapolis, IN 46204

Pacers Foundation Be Tolerant Grants 1476

The foremost priority of the Pacers Foundation is to help Indiana's youth through the nonprofit organizations that serve them. The foundation's areas of interest are youth programs that address childhood obesity, keep kids in school, prevent and treat adolescent and teenage alcohol/drug abuse, encourage tolerance and prevent bullying, and that help girls build self-esteem during the crucial preteen and teenage years. The foundation's Be Tolerant grants support the efforts of Indiana groups that teach tolerance and respect for diversity; that focus on breaking down racial, ethnic, religious and other barriers by bringing youth from "all walks of life" together and exposing youth to cultures and "ways of life" other than their own; and that carry out anti-bullying and anti-stigma programs. School-based programs, faith-based programs, and other non-profit organizations focused on teaching tolerance should consider applying. Grants are one year in length and range from $5,000 - $20,000. Organizations that achieve the results set forth in their applications may apply for continued support in subsequent years. A link to application guidelines and forms is provided at the grant website.

Requirements: 501(c)3 tax-exempt organizations are eligible.

Restrictions: Pacers Foundation does not provide support for: individuals, emergency funds, political candidates or parties, fundraisers, or corporate memberships. Requests to support fundraisers are reviewed by Pacers Sports & Entertainment, not Pacers Foundation. These requests should be directed to Marilynn Wernke, Pacers Sports & Entertainment, at the sponsor address given. Although the foundation will occasionally support efforts of national significance or efforts outside of the state, it remains primarily committed to its hometown of Indianapolis and its home state of Indiana.

Geographic Focus: All States

Date(s) Application is Due: Mar 30

Amount of Grant: 5,000 - 20,000 USD

Samples: Storytelling Arts of Indiana, Indianapolis, Indiana; Homestead High School Spartan Mentor Program, Fort Wayne, Indiana; Mental Health Association of Michiana, Goshen, Indiana.

Contact: Rick Fuson, Chairperson; (317) 917-2864; fax (317) 917-2599; foundation@pacers.com

Internet: http://www.pacersfoundation.org/grants.php

Sponsor: Pacers Foundation

125 S Pennsylvania Street

Indianapolis, IN 46204

Pacers Foundation Indiana Fever's Be Younique Fund Grants 1477

The foremost priority of the Pacers Foundation is to help Indiana's youth through the nonprofit organizations that serve them. The foundation's areas of interest are youth programs that address childhood obesity, keep kids in school, prevent and treat adolescent and teenage alcohol/drug abuse, encourage tolerance and prevent bullying, and that help girls build self-esteem during the crucial preteen and teenage years. The Indiana Fever's Be Younique Fund grants support the efforts of Indiana groups that help girls build self-esteem; that promote positive body imagery; and that educate girls about dating violence and/or provide services to those who have experienced such violence. School-based programs and other non-profit organizations focused on empowering girls should consider applying. Grants are one year in length and range from $5,000 - $20,000. Organizations that achieve the results set forth in their applications may apply for continued support in subsequent years. A link to application guidelines and forms is provided at the grant website.

Requirements: 501(c)3 tax-exempt organizations are eligible.

Restrictions: Pacers Foundation does not provide support for: individuals; emergency funds, political candidates or parties, fundraisers, or corporate memberships. Requests to support fundraisers are reviewed by Pacers Sports & Entertainment, not Pacers Foundation. These requests should be directed to Marilynn Wernke, Pacers Sports & Entertainment, at the sponsor address given. Although the foundation will occasionally support efforts of national significance or efforts outside of the state, it remains primarily committed to its hometown of Indianapolis and its home state of Indiana.

Geographic Focus: All States

Date(s) Application is Due: Mar 30

Contact: Rick Fuson, Chairperson; (317) 917-2864; fax (317) 917-2599; foundation@pacers.com

Internet: http://www.pacersfoundation.org/grants.php

Sponsor: Pacers Foundation

125 S Pennsylvania Street

Indianapolis, IN 46204

PacifiCare Foundation Grants 1478

The foundation's mission is to improve the quality of life for residents of areas where PacifiCare Health Systems does business. The foundation's focus areas are: child/youth, including child care, youth activity programs, at-risk youth, and counseling programs; education, including school programs that promote self-esteem, encourage academic achievement and the development of specific skills, literacy programs, training programs, and programs that improve the effectiveness of the educational system; health, including prevention, health education, access to health care, and improved quality of health care of targeted populations; human/social services, including housing, shelters, education, protection, community development, crime prevention, food, transportation, and other social services for targeted populations; and senior, including social services, nutrition, education, volunteer, and and adult day care. Preference will be given to proposals for specific projects. Requests for operating costs will be considered if the request is very specific and clearly defined. Seed grant requests also receive consideration. Organizations funded by the foundation are welcome to reapply annually. Application forms are available on the foundation's website.

Requirements: IRS 501(c)3 nonprofit organizations serving residents of PacifiCare regions in Arizona, California, Colorado, Nevada, Oklahoma, Oregon, Texas, and Washington are eligible. The proposal must include two copies of the following: application form; checklist form; cover letter accompanying the proposal, signed by either the CEO or appointee of the organization, summarizing the proposed project, the problem addressed, the amount requested, and the name and phone number of the contact person; the written proposal, which should not exceed 2-5 pages in length and should include background information, description of the problem, need or issue being addressed, and a complete description of the proposed project; most recent audited financial statement and 990; current operating budget and line item budget for the specific project; list of major funders and amounts; list of board of directors; and one paragraph summary of previous support from the PacifiCare Foundation.

Restrictions: The foundation will not consider grants for arts/cultural programs, associations, annual campaigns, associations (professional/technical), capital campaigns, challenge/matching grants, hosting/supporting conferences, individual support, private foundations, programs that promote religious doctrine, research, scholarships, or sponsorship of special events.

Geographic Focus: Arizona, California, Colorado, Nevada, Oklahoma, Oregon, Texas, Washington

Date(s) Application is Due: Jan 1; Jul 1

Amount of Grant: 2,000 - 10,000 USD

Samples: Casa de Esperanza, Green Valley, Arizona, $10,000 - to provide inter-generational community programming for children and the elderly; Escape Family Resource Center, Houston, Texas, $10,000 - for a school-based child abuse prevention and family support program.

Contact: Riva Gebel, Director; (714) 825-5233

Internet: http://www.pacificare.com/vgn/images/portal/cit_60701/127503Guidelines_for_Charitable_Giving.pdf

Sponsor: PacifiCare Foundation

P.O. Box 25186, MS LC03-159

Santa Ana, CA 92799

Pacific Life Foundation Grants 1479

Pacific Life has long recognized the importance of helping communities where their employees reside and work and has a record of community involvement that spans the history of the company. The Foundation accepts proposals from agencies seeking funds for programs and projects in the areas of health and human services; education; arts and culture; and civic, community, and environment. Grant proposals are generally accepted from July 15 through August 15. See the Foundation's website to verify deadlines.

Requirements: Funding is made primarily in areas with large concentrations of Pacific Life employees: generally, the greater Orange County, California, area and other areas, such as Omaha, Nebraska. Ideally, agencies should serve a large area, usually including more than one city or community. Some California statewide and national organizations also receive support. General grants range from $5,000 to $10,000 for a one-year period of funding and are given to support programs, operating expenses, or collaborative programs with other agencies. Capital grants range from $10,000 to $100,000 and are paid over multiple years. Capital grants are generally given to an agency with an organized campaign already under way to raise substantial funds. More than fifty percent of the campaign goal (excluding in-kind donations, anonymous gifts and loans) must be pledged prior to consideration by the Foundation.

Restrictions: The following is not funded: individuals; political parties, candidates, or partisan political organizations; labor organizations, fraternal organizations, athletic clubs, or social clubs; K-12 schools, school districts, or school foundations; sectarian or denominational religious organizations, except for programs that are broadly promoted, available to anyone, and free from religious orientation; fundraising events; sports leagues or teams; and advertising sponsorship or conference underwriting/sponsorship.

Geographic Focus: All States

Samples: Aquarium of the Pacific, Long Beach, California, $258,503 - civic, community and environment support; Greater Santa Ana Vitality Foundation, Santa Ana, California, $10,000 - education; and Southern California Public Radio, Pasadena, California, $40,000 - arts and culture.

Contact: Brenda Hardwig, Program Contact; (949) 219-3787; PLFoundation@PacificLife.com

Internet: http://www.pacificlife.com/About+Pacific+Life/Foundation+or+Community

Sponsor: Pacific Life Foundation

700 Newport Center Drive

Newport Beach, CA 92660

Pajaro Valley Community Health Health Trust Insurance/Coverage 1480 & Education on Using the System Grants

The Trust provides grants for projects that advance our mission to improve the health and quality of life for all people of the greater Pajaro Valley. The primary goals of the Health Insurance/Coverage & Education on Using the System Initiative are to increase the number of Pajaro Valley residents with health insurance, increase residents understanding and appropriate use of a medical home (family practitioner), and decrease inappropriate use of the emergency department. The Trust will support programs that increase the number of Pajaro Valley residents that have health insurance, as well as programs that improve access to health care for our community's more vulnerable populations. Additionally, the Trust will look at community-wide solutions to these issues.

Requirements: Applicant organizations must provide or plan to provide programs/services benefiting the health of residents in the Trust's primary geographic service area. Communities within this service area include Watsonville, Pajaro, Freedom, and Aromas. The home office of the applicant organization need not be located in the Pajaro Valley, but the applicant organization must demonstrate that it provides or plans to provide services that directly benefit residents of the Pajaro Valley. The applicant organization must be a nonprofit, 501(c)3 tax-exempt organization; a school-based health program; or have a 501(c)3, tax-exempt organization as a fiscal sponsor.

Restrictions: In general, the Trust's Board of Directors prefers not to fund programs or projects administered by a city, county, state, or federal government with the exception of school-based health programs. In general, the Trust does not give grants to: projects that do not substantially benefit residents of the Pajaro Valley; projects and proposals unrelated to the Trust's mission, eligibility requirements, and current strategic plan funding priorities and objectives; individuals, with the exception of the Trust's scholarship programs; religious organizations for secular purposes; endowments, building campaigns, annual fund appeals, fundraising events, or celebrations; or commercial ventures.

Geographic Focus: California

Samples: La Manzana Community Resources, La Manzana, California, $12,000 - to assist low-income families in accessing public health benefits; Healthy Kids of Santa Cruz County, Santa Cruz, California, $15,000 - to provide access to health insurance to children in the Pajaro Valley who have incomes at or below 300% of the federal poverty level; Santa Cruz Community Counseling Center, Santa Cruz, $5,000 - to launch a health literacy campaign focusing on low-income families with children birth to five years old.

Contact: Raquel Ramirez Ruiz, Director of Programs; (831) 763-6456 or (831) 761-5639; fax (831) 763-6084; info@pvhealthtrust.org or raquel_dhc@pvhealthtrust.org

Internet: http://www.pvhealthtrust.org/grants_core.html

Sponsor: Pajaro Valley Community Health Trust

85 Nielson Street

Watsonville, CA 95076

Pajaro Valley Community Health Trust Diabetes and Contributing Factors Grants 1481

The Trust provides grants for projects that advance our mission to improve the health and quality of life for all people of the greater Pajaro Valley. The primary goals of the Diabetes and Contributing Factors Initiative are to reduce the risk factors associated with diabetes, reduce complications related to diabetes, and decrease the prevalence of childhood and adult obesity in the Pajaro Valley. The Trust will mobilize communities in the tri-county area to prevent the increase of type-2 diabetes in youth and young adult populations; teach diabetes self-management, and provide medical nutrition therapy to people living with diabetes thereby preventing the life-threatening complications associated with diabetes. Further, the Trust will promote "best practices" in clinical management of diabetes throughout the region. The Trust will seek to minimize factors that contribute to diabetes, including obesity, poor nutrition, and lack of physical activity.

Requirements: Applicant organizations must provide or plan to provide programs/services benefiting the health of residents in the Trust's primary geographic service area. Communities within this service area include Watsonville, Pajaro, Freedom, and Aromas. The home office of the applicant organization need not be located in the Pajaro Valley, but the applicant organization must demonstrate that it provides or plans to provide services that directly benefit residents of the Pajaro Valley. The applicant organization must be a nonprofit, 501(c)3 tax-exempt organization; a school-based health program; or have a 501(c)3, tax-exempt organization as a fiscal sponsor.

Restrictions: In general, the Trust's Board of Directors prefers not to fund programs or projects administered by a city, county, state, or federal government with the exception of school-based health programs. In general, the Trust does not give grants to: projects that do not substantially benefit residents of the Pajaro Valley; projects and proposals unrelated to the Trust's mission, eligibility requirements, and current strategic plan funding priorities and objectives; individuals, with the exception of the Trust's scholarship programs; religious organizations for secular purposes; endowments, building campaigns, annual fund appeals, fundraising events, or celebrations; or commercial ventures.

Geographic Focus: California

Amount of Grant: 5,000 - 30,000 USD

Samples: Community Action Board of Santa Cruz County, Santa Cruz, California, $10,000 - to support the REAL for Diabetes Prevention project; Ecology Action, Willits, California, $9,000 - to support the Boltage program, a daily student biking and walking tracking program; Mesa Verde Gardens, Mesa Verde, California, $15,000 - to support the start-up of a second Community Garden.

Contact: Raquel Ramirez Ruiz, Director of Programs; (831) 763-6456 or (831) 761-5639; fax (831) 763-6084; info@pvhealthtrust.org or raquel_dhc@pvhealthtrust.org

Internet: http://www.pvhealthtrust.org/grants_core.html

Sponsor: Pajaro Valley Community Health Trust

85 Nielson Street

Watsonville, CA 95076

Pajaro Valley Community Health Trust Oral Health: Prevention & Access Grants 1482

The Trust provides grants for projects that advance our mission to improve the health and quality of life for all people of the greater Pajaro Valley. The primary goals of the Oral Health Initiative are to reduce the risk factors associated with oral health disease, increase the number of Pajaro Valley residents with ready access to comprehensive dental care, and decrease the prevalence of dental disease among residents of the Pajaro Valley. The Trust's goals include improving access to dental treatment and preventing dental disease. Through this initiative, the Trust will look at systematic issues facing oral health care, particularly in the areas of prevention and access to care, and work with others in the community to remove these barriers.

Requirements: Applicant organizations must provide or plan to provide programs/services benefiting the health of residents in the Trust's primary geographic service area. Communities within this service area include Watsonville, Pajaro, Freedom, and Aromas. The home office of the applicant organization need not be located in the Pajaro Valley, but the applicant organization must demonstrate that it provides or plans to provide services that directly benefit residents of the Pajaro Valley. The applicant organization must be a nonprofit, 501(c)3 tax-exempt organization; a school-based health program; or have a 501(c)3, tax-exempt organization as a fiscal sponsor.

Restrictions: In general, the Trust's Board of Directors prefers not to fund programs or projects administered by a city, county, state, or federal government with the exception of school-based health programs. In general, the Trust does not give grants to: projects that do not substantially benefit residents of the Pajaro Valley; projects and proposals unrelated to the Trust's mission, eligibility requirements, and current strategic plan funding priorities and objectives; individuals, with the exception of the Trust's scholarship programs; religious organizations for secular purposes; endowments, building campaigns, annual fund appeals, fundraising events, or celebrations; or commercial ventures.

Geographic Focus: California

Amount of Grant: 5,000 - 30,000 USD

Contact: Raquel Ramirez Ruiz; (831) 763-6456 or (831) 761-5639; fax (831) 763-6084; info@pvhealthtrust.org or raquel_dhc@pvhealthtrust.org

Internet: http://www.pvhealthtrust.org/grants_core.html

Sponsor: Pajaro Valley Community Health Trust

85 Nielson Street

Watsonville, CA 95076

Palmer Foundation Grants 1483

The Palmer Foundation was founded by Rogers Palmer and his wife, Mary, in 1990. Today, the Foundation considers proposals that empower young people up to the age of 25. General categories include arts and culture, education, health, and human services. In making awards, the foundation places the highest priority on applications that demonstrate a level of cooperation with other organizations, including leveraging financial and in-kind support from other groups; clearly avoids duplication of existing services; where applicable, demonstrates potential for continued funding from internal or other sources after the grant period; and offer challenge grants in order to stimulate support of the project by other organizations or individuals. The board will review Letters of Intent each month through the listed deadlines; full proposals are by invitation. Letters of intent may be submitted online. Guidelines are available online.

Requirements: 501(c)3 tax-exempt organizations are eligible. The foundation's geographical region is usually limited to the Mid West states, the Mid Atlantic states. Guatemala, and El Salvador.

Restrictions: The foundation does not usually support the following types of activities: grants to individuals or scholarships; endowment drives or capital campaigns; general operating expenses for an existing project, except to support an innovative program during the initial years of operation; grants for political activities, sectarian religious purposes, or individual medical or scientific research projects; or repeated funding to the same program or organization for the same purposes on an annual or ongoing basis.

Geographic Focus: All States

Samples: Art Institute and Gallery, Salisbury, Maryland - general operating support; Carolina Philharmonic, Pinehurst, North Carolina - to bring Carnegie Hall's Link-up educational program to the elementary school children of Moore County; Crohn's and Colitis Foundation of America, New York, New York - support basic and clinical research as well as educational and support programs designed for patients, caregivers, and health-care professionals.

Contact: Charlly Enroth; (202) 595-1020; admin@thepalmerfoundation.org

Internet: http://www.thepalmerfoundation.org

Sponsor: Palmer Foundation

1201 Connecticut Avenue, NW, Suite 300

Washington, D.C. 20036

Parker Foundation (California) Grants 1484

The Parker Foundation was founded for charitable purposes leading to the betterment of life for all people of San Diego County, California. Areas of grant support include culture (visual arts, performing arts, museums/zoos), adult and youth services, medical, education, community activities, and environmental. Initial grant proposals must be submitted in writing. The format can be found on the website. Generally proposals are considered at the next Board meeting, which is generally monthly. Meeting dates can be found on the website under Board Schedule.

Requirements: Applicants must be 501(c)3 organizations.

Restrictions: While occasional grant support is given to religious organizations, those grants are only made for direct support to nonsectarian educational or service projects.

Geographic Focus: California

Samples: San Diego Opera Association, San Diego, California, $75,000 - to purchase pARTicipate software to enhance social networking capabilities; San Diego Air & Space Museum, San Diego, California, $35,000 - for high density shelving for film archives; and Escondido Children's Museum, Escondido, California, $20,000 - for operating expenses to support programs and exhibitions.

Contact: Program Contact; (760) 720-0630; fax (760) 420-1239

Internet: http://www.TheParkerFoundation.org

Sponsor: Parker Foundation: California

2604-B El Camino Real, Suite 244

Carlsbad, CA 92008

Park Foundation Grants 1485

The foundation awards grants to nonprofit organizations in central New York and areas in the U.S. Southeast. Areas of interest include education and higher education, animal welfare, environment, television, and general charitable giving. Types of support include general operating support, program development, professorships, seed money, fellowships, scholarship funds, research grants, and matching funds. There are no application deadlines. The board meets in March, June, August, October, and December. Obtain application forms.

Requirements: 501(c)3 nonprofits in he eastern US, primarily in central NY, Washington, DC, and North Carolina are eligible.

Restrictions: For-profit organizations and individuals are not eligible.

Geographic Focus: All States

Amount of Grant: 5,000 - 100,000 USD

Samples: North Carolina State University (Raleigh, NC)—for Park Scholarships, $647,710; Beach Preservation Assoc of Pine Knoll Shores (Atlantic Beach, NC)—for general operating support, $150,000; North Carolina State U (Raleigh, NC)—for the Park Scholarship program, $226,018.

Contact: Linda Madeo; (607) 272-9124; fax (607) 272-6057

Sponsor: Park Foundation

P.O. Box 550

Ithaca, NY 14851

Partnership Enhancement Program (PEP) Grants 1486

The mission of the National Tree Trust continues through the Arbor Day Foundation, a nonprofit, environmental education organization with a mission of inspiring people to plant, nurture, and celebrate trees. The Partnership Enhancement Program (PEP) makes dollar-for-dollar matching monetary grants to qualifying nonprofits involved in a wide range of tree-related projects. Grants are made in four categories: tree planting and maintenance; education and training; overhead and administration; and national and regional programs. Applications for projects usually become available in June.

Requirements: To be eligible, the applying organization must: be a currently certified 501(c)3 nonprofit organization located within the United States; have been in existence for a minimum of two years; demonstrate that tree planting, maintenance, and education are components of the organization; and be volunteer based.

Geographic Focus: All States

Amount of Grant: Up to 25,000 USD

Contact: Mark Derowitsch, Public Relations Manager; (888) 448-7337; mderowitsch@arborday.org

Internet: http://www.arborday.org/generalinfo/

Sponsor: Arbor Day Foundation

100 Arbor Avenue

Nebraska City, NE 68410

Patricia Price Peterson Foundation Grants 1487

Established in 1964, the foundation awards grants to eligible California 501(c)3 nonprofit organizations and Central American countries in its areas of interest, including environmental protection and conservation (including agricultural university scholarships, orphanages, environmental education, community development, and nature reserve-conservation), science education, and federated giving. Types of support include program grants and general operating grants. Funding can be used for emergency programs, equipment, general operations, land acquisition, management development, capacity building, professorships, program development, scholarship funds, or seed money. The application deadline is in early May; call for the specific date. the applicant's initial approach should be via email, followed by the submission of a written application. Final proposals should be submitted in Spanish.

Requirements: California nonprofit organizations serving the San Francisco Bay area or Central American organizations are eligible to apply.

Geographic Focus: California, Belize, Costa Rica, Cuba, El Salvador, Guatemala, Honduras, Jamaica, Mexico, Nicaragua, Panama

Contact: Stephen W. Bennett, President; (831) 684-0958; fax (415) 622-5388; epeterson@aureos.co.cr or neyastv@aol.com

Sponsor: Patricia Price Peterson Foundation

17 Aqua View Drive

Selva Beach, CA 95076-1625

Patrick and Aimee Butler Family Foundation Community Arts and 1488 Humanities Grants

The Butler Family Foundation makes grants through Community Grants, the Foundation Initiative Fund, and Special Projects programs. Community Grants are competitive and primarily support the Twin Cities metropolitan area of St. Paul and Minneapolis. The Foundation has an interest in making the arts and cultural programs accessible to all communities in the Twin Cities region. Funding will be granted to organizations that emphasize artistic quality, reflect the diversity of the community, and demonstrate stable programming, within the following areas: Historical Societies, primarily in Ramsey County, Minnesota; Humanities programs or organizations; Museums, and Music Education. The Foundation is most likely to make general operating or program support grants.

Requirements: Minnesota 501(c)3 nonprofits are eligible to apply.

Restrictions: The Butler Family Foundation does not make grants to organizations through fiscal agents. The Foundation does not make loans or grants to individuals. No grants are made outside of the United States. The Foundation does not fund criminal justice, economic development or education, work or vocational programs, films or videos, health care, hospitals, medical research, elementary or secondary education, and music or dance.

Geographic Focus: Minnesota

Date(s) Application is Due: Feb 7; Jun 6

Amount of Grant: 5,000 - 30,000 USD

Contact: Kerrie Blevins, Foundation Director; (651) 222-2565; fax (651) 222-2566; kerrieb@butlerfamilyfoundation.org

Internet: http://www.butlerfamilyfoundation.org/guidelines2011.html

Sponsor: Patrick and Aimee Butler Family Foundation

332 Minnesota Street, Suite E-1420

Saint Paul, MN 55101-1369

Patrick and Aimee Butler Family Foundation Community 1489 Environment Grants

The Butler Family Foundation makes grants through Community Grants, the Foundation Initiative Fund, and Special Projects programs. Community Grants are competitive and primarily support the entire State of Minnesota. The Foundation seeks to preserve and promote stewardship of the natural environment for present and future generations. Funding will be granted to programs that positively impact environmental quality and encourage citizen participation in environmental issues. Granting will be limited to organizations and programs operating in Minnesota, whose primary mission is to address one of these issues: Water Quality of the Upper Mississippi Watershed; Environmental Education (with a preference for programs providing in-depth learning experiences); Land Preservation and Use. The Foundation is most likely to make general operating or program support grants.

Requirements: Minnesota 501(c)3 nonprofits are eligible to apply.

Restrictions: The Butler Family Foundation does not make grants to organizations through fiscal agents. The Foundation does not make loans or grants to individuals. No grants are made outside of the United States. The Foundation does not fund criminal justice, economic development or

education, work or vocational programs, films or videos, health care, hospitals, medical research, elementary or secondary education, and music or dance.
Geographic Focus: Minnesota
Date(s) Application is Due: Feb 7; Jun 6
Amount of Grant: 5,000 - 30,000 USD
Contact: Kerrie Blevins, Foundation Director; (651) 222-2565; fax (651) 222-2566; kerrieb@butlerfamilyfoundation.org
Internet: http://www.butlerfamilyfoundation.org/guidelines2011.html
Sponsor: Patrick and Aimee Butler Family Foundation
332 Minnesota Street, Suite E-1420
Saint Paul, MN 55101-1369

Patrick and Aimee Butler Family Foundation Community Human   1490
   Services Grants

The Butler Family Foundation makes grants through Community Grants, the Foundation Initiative Fund, and Special Projects programs. Community Grants are competitive and primarily support the Twin Cities metropolitan area of St. Paul and Minneapolis. The Foundation has a special concern for the condition of women and children in society, particularly those living in poverty. The Foundation seeks to foster a supportive environment for all families to ensure children's healthy development. Priority will be given to enhance the ability of individuals and families to break dependencies and achieve self-reliance in the following areas: Abuse - including domestic and family violence, pornography, and prostitution; Chemical dependency; Affordable housing - including housing and services for homeless youth; Children and Families - with an emphasis on early childhood development and parenting education. Strategies that offer both practical help to those in need and advocate for systems change will be favored. The Foundation is most likely to make general operating or program support grants.
Requirements: Minnesota 501(c)3 nonprofits are eligible to apply.
Restrictions: The Butler Family Foundation does not make grants to organizations through fiscal agents. The Foundation does not make loans or grants to individuals. No grants are made outside of the United States. The Foundation does not fund criminal justice, economic development or education, work or vocational programs, films or videos, health care, hospitals, medical research, elementary or secondary education, and music or dance.
Geographic Focus: Minnesota
Date(s) Application is Due: Feb 7; Jun 6
Amount of Grant: 5,000 - 30,000 USD
Contact: Kerrie Blevins, Foundation Director; (651) 222-2565; fax (651) 222-2566; kerrieb@butlerfamilyfoundation.org
Internet: http://www.butlerfamilyfoundation.org/guidelines2011.html
Sponsor: Patrick and Aimee Butler Family Foundation
332 Minnesota Street, Suite E-1420
Saint Paul, MN 55101-1369

Patrick and Aimee Butler Family Foundation Community   1491
   Philanthropy & the Non-Profit Management Grants

The Butler Family Foundation makes grants through Community Grants, the Foundation Initiative Fund, and Special Projects programs. Community Grants are competitive and primarily support the Twin Cities metropolitan area of St. Paul and Minneapolis. Through its Philanthropy and Non-Profit Management program, the Foundation seeks to foster a vital non-profit sector by supporting regranting through community funds committed to social change; and by supporting intermediary organizations that enhance the management capacity of non-profit organizations. The Foundation is most likely to make general operating or program support grants.
Requirements: Minnesota 501(c)3 nonprofits are eligible to apply.
Restrictions: The Butler Family Foundation does not make grants to organizations through fiscal agents. The Foundation does not make loans or grants to individuals. No grants are made outside of the United States. The Foundation does not fund criminal justice, economic development or education, work or vocational programs, films or videos, health care, hospitals, medical research, elementary or secondary education, and music or dance.
Geographic Focus: Minnesota
Date(s) Application is Due: Feb 7; Jun 6
Amount of Grant: 5,000 - 30,000 USD
Contact: Kerrie Blevins, Foundation Director; (651) 222-2565; fax (651) 222-2566; kerrieb@butlerfamilyfoundation.org
Internet: http://www.butlerfamilyfoundation.org/guidelines2011.html
Sponsor: Patrick and Aimee Butler Family Foundation
332 Minnesota Street, Suite E-1420
Saint Paul, MN 55101-1369

Patrick and Anna M. Cudahy Fund Grants   1492

The Patrick and Anna Cudahy Fund is a general purpose foundation which primarily supports organizations in Wisconsin and the metropolitan Chicago area. The principal areas of interest are social service, youth, and education with some giving for the arts, and other areas. Some support is also given for local and national programs concerned with public interest and environmental issues. A few grants are given for international programs but only to those which are represented by a United States based organization.
Requirements: Nonprofits organizations in Wisconsin and the metropolitan Chicago area are eligible. See Foundations website for additional guidelines and application form: http://www.cudahyfund.org/Guideliines.htm
Restrictions: Organizations may submit only one proposal during any calendar year. Requests are not considered for: organizations and projects primarily serving a local constituency outside of Wisconsin and the Chicago metropolitan area; organizations outside the United States who are not represented by a United States based 501 [c]3 organization; grants to individuals; loans or endowments.
Geographic Focus: Illinois, Wisconsin
Date(s) Application is Due: Jan 5; Apr 5; Jul 5; Oct 5
Amount of Grant: 5,000 - 25,000 USD
Samples: Angel of Hope Clinic, Milwaukee, WI, $10,000 - Angel of Hope Clinic; DePaul University College of Law Chicago,IL, $22,000 - Summer Programs; Helen Bader Institute, Milwaukee, WI, $10,000 - Scholarships;
Contact: Janet S. Cudahy, President; (847) 866-0760; fax (847) 475-0679
Internet: http://www.cudahyfund.org/Guideliines.htm
Sponsor: 1609 Sherman Avenue, #207
Evanston, IL 60201

Patrick John Bennett, Jr. Memorial Foundation Grants   1493

The Patrick John Bennett, Jr. Memorial Foundation, which was established in Maryland in 2004, offers support primarily to assist the disabled with specific educational needs throughout Maryland and Pennsylvania. Therefore, its major fields of interest are education and human services. A specific application form is required, and can be secured from the Foundation officer. This application should include a detailed description of the project, along with the amount of funding needed. There are no annual deadlines. Most recently, grants have ranged from $250 to $2,000.
Geographic Focus: Maryland, Pennsylvania
Amount of Grant: 250 - 2,000 USD
Samples: Katie and Will Brady Foundation, Chase, Maryland, $250 - operating support; St. Josephs School, Cockeysville, Maryland, $2,000 - scholarship fund.
Contact: Deborah Bennett, Trustee; (410) 971-3302 or (410) 527-0207
Sponsor: Patrick John Bennett, Jr. Memorial Foundation
11508 Hunters Run Drive
Cockeysville, MD 21030

Paul and Edith Babson Foundation Grants   1494

The focus of the Foundation is to provide opportunities for the people of Greater Boston. Grants are awarded for specific types of activities in the following areas: entrepreneurship and economic development (programs focused on providing and encouraging youth and community entrepreneurship education, community economic development, job training for youth, and urban youth business and enterprise initiatives); culture, education and leadership development (programs focused on education and leadership development opportunities for young people through team sports, art, dance, music and theater); and environment and community building (programs focused on community building through urban community gardens and urban greenspace initiatives).
Requirements: IRS 501(c)3 tax-exempt organizations in the Greater Boston, Massachusetts, area are eligible. Applicants must telephone or email prior to applying, and then a preliminary letter may be sent. After review the Board may request a full proposal.
Restrictions: Only one preliminary letter may be submitted in a 12-month period. The following is ineligible: support for specific individuals, scholarships, films, videos, conferences, fundraising or donor cultivation events.
Geographic Focus: Massachusetts
Date(s) Application is Due: Feb 6; Sep 9
Amount of Grant: 5,000 - 40,000 USD
Contact: Elizabeth Nichols, Program Officer; (617) 523-8368; fax (617) 523-8949; pebabsonfdn@babsonfoundations.org
Internet: http://www.babsonfoundations.org/peguidelines.htm
Sponsor: Paul and Edith Babson Foundation
50 Congress Street
Boston, MA 02109-4017

Paul and Mary Haas Foundation Contributions and Student Scholarships 1495

Grants are given to tax-exempt organizations in six areas: civic and charitable, education (including adult basic education, adult/family literacy training, curriculum development, and vocational programs), health, religion, the arts, and college scholarships. Funding is generally seed money for innovative services in the Corpus Christi, TX, area. Creative, innovative, and exploratory projects are encouraged, with less interest in building projects and areas covered by normal budgets. Additional types of support include general operating support, equipment acquisition, program development, conferences and seminars, and scholarship funds and scholarships to individuals. Requests for support are normally reviewed on a year-round basis in the order in which they are received. All grants are made for one year and are not automatically renewed. Applications for scholarships are due in August at the beginning of senior high school year; application for other grants are accepted at any time.
Requirements: Grants are made to Texas organizations with 501(c)3 status. Initial inquiries should be made in the form of a one- to two-page written proposal.
Geographic Focus: Texas
Amount of Grant: 35 - 250,000 USD
Contact: Karen Wesson; (361) 887-6955; fax (361) 883-5992; haasfdn@aol.com
Sponsor: Paul and Mary Haas Foundation
P.O. Box 2928
Corpus Christi, TX 78403

Paul E. and Klare N. Reinhold Foundation Grants 1496

The foundation makes grants in Clay County, Florida, for projects in health, religion, children and youth, music appreciation and education, art appreciation and education, and public improvement. Types of support include building construction/renovation, capital campaigns, emergency funds, equipment, land acquisition, matching/challenge grants, operating grants, and seed money grants. Details are available on the Web site.
Requirements: 501(c)3 organizations in Florida's Clay County are eligible.
Restrictions: Grants do not support advertising for fund-raising campaigns, tickets, debt reduction, endowments, attempts to influence legislation, or basic operating costs.
Geographic Focus: Florida
Amount of Grant: Up to 10,000 USD
Samples: Clay County Habitat For Humanity, Inc (FL)—to supplement a Capacity Building Grant to help pay the Executive Director's salary, $20,000; Alzheimer's Assoc (FL)—to support Caregiver Education By enhancing the resource library, $3000; Christ Episcopal Church Building Fund (FL)—dedication of family/gathering room in honor of Thomas E. Camp, III, $50,000; Keystone Heights Elementary School (FL)—for additional supplies for Project Playground, $500.
Contact: Contact; (904) 269-5857; fax (904) 269-8382; lhoke@reinhold.net
Internet: http://www.reinhold.org/html/guidelines.htm
Sponsor: Paul E. and Klare N. Reinhold Foundation
1845 Town Center Boulevard, Suite 105
Orange Park, FL 32003

Pauline E. Fitzpatrick Charitable Trust 1497

The Pauline E. Fitzpatrick Charitable Trust was established in Connecticut in 1991 with a primary purpose of supporting aged citizens of Norwalk, Connecticut. The Trust's major fields of interest include: Catholic agencies and churches, as well as other religious groups supporting human services for the aged. Funding comes in the form of general operating support. There are no specified application forms or annual deadlines, and interested partied should contact the Trust office directly. Typical grants range from $1,000 to $2,500.
Requirements: 505(c)3 organizations supporting the aged in Norwalk, Connecticut, are eligible to apply.
Geographic Focus: Connecticut
Amount of Grant: 1,000 - 2,500 USD
Contact: John B. Devine, (203) 838-0665 or (203) 327-3112
Sponsor: Pauline E. Fitzpatrick Charitable Trust
P.O. Box 411
Norwalk, CT 06852-0411

Paul Rapoport Foundation Grants 1498

The Paul Rapoport Foundation was established in 1987 with funds from the estate of Paul Rapoport, a founder of both New York City's LGBT Community Services Center and GMHC. For its final years of grantmaking the Foundation's focus will be on three populations of low or no income: transgender communities of color; LGTBQ youth of color, ages 24 and under; and LGTB seniors of color aged 60 and over. The Foundation will also consider funding programs of organizations not focused exclusively on the LGTB community if the number of LGTBQ clients of color served by the program is at least 50%. The foundation awards grants to nonprofits in the metropolitan area of New York, New York. Types of support include general operating support, continuing support, building construction and renovation, program development, conferences and seminars, publications, seed money, technical assistance, and matching funds. There are no application forms. The board meets in February, June, and October to consider requests. Grants of $50,000 and higher, per year are awarded.
Requirements: The Foundation funds only non-profit, charitable organizations as defined by the Internal Revenue Service Code Section 509(a). The Foundation funds primarily within the five boroughs of New York City, as well as on Long Island, in Westchester and nearby New Jersey. It will only fund national organizations when they request funding for programs specific to the New York metropolitan area.
Restrictions: The Foundation will no longer support start-up organizations. The Foundation does not support medical research, cultural and artistic activities, major building campaigns, endowments, grants or scholar-ships to individuals or to other foundations. The Foundation does not make grants for purposes of influencing elections or legislation, or for any other activity that may jeopardize the Foundation's tax-exempt status.
Geographic Focus: New York
Date(s) Application is Due: Feb 1; Jun 1; Oct 1
Contact: Jane D. Schwartz; (212) 888-6578; fax (212) 980-0867
Ona M. Winet, Program Director; (212) 888-6578; fax (212) 980-0867
Internet: http://www.paulrapoportfoundation.org/guide.html
Sponsor: Paul Rapoport Foundation
220 E 60th Street, Suite 3H
New York, NY 10022

PDF Community Organizing Grants 1499

Peace Development Fund awards Community Organizing Grants to any organization in the United States, Haiti and/or Mexico that fit into PDF's guidelines. Specifically, this award sponsors organizations that focus on social justice, organizing to shift powers, working to build a movement, dismantling oppression, and creating new structures in these geographical areas.
Requirements: Applications are available at PDF's website and must be emailed to grants@peacefund.org by 5:00 pm Pacific Standard Time on the due date. This grant is highly competitive and the Fund will only award grants to organizations that align with PDF's guidelines.
Restrictions: PDF will not fund programs outside the U.S., Mexico or Haiti unless specified for a special initiative or Donor Advised fund. Also, PDF will not fund: individuals and/or organizations with strong leadership from only one person; conferences and other one-time events; audio-visual productions and distribution, including TV, radio, publications, films, etc; research that is NOT directly linked to an organizing strategy; academic institutions or scholarships; other grant-making organizations; or organizations with large budgets ($300,000 or more) or who have access to other sources of funding.
Geographic Focus: All States, Puerto Rico, Haiti, Mexico, Virgin Islands (U.S.)
Date(s) Application is Due: May 20
Amount of Grant: 2,000 - 5,000 USD
Contact: Kazu Haga, Program Coordinator; (415) 642-0900 or (415) 205-6776; fax (415) 642-8200; kazu@peacefund.org or grants@peacefund.org
Internet: http://www.peacedevelopmentfund.org/page/commorg
Sponsor: Peace Development Fund
44 N Prospect Street, P.O. Box 1280
Amherst, MA 01004

Peacock Foundation Grants 1500

Established by Henry B. Peacock, Jr. in 1947, the mission of Peacock Foundation, Inc. is to enhance and promote the good health and well being of children, families, and underprivileged persons in Southeast Florida, through contributions, gifts, and grants to eligible nonprofit organizations. The priorities of Peacock Foundation, Inc. include: making grants to human services providers that promote youth development, assist abused or neglected children, women, and the elderly, and seek to reduce abuse, prevent homelessness, and end hunger in our community; supporting educational programs in the arts and the environment, as well as special education for disabled persons; contributing to medical research, health care organizations, and hospitals.
Requirements: All applicants must be IRS recognized 501(c)3 public charities classified as not a private foundation, registered with the Department of Agriculture to solicit funds in Florida, when applicable, and located in and/or

of significant benefit to residents to the Southeast Florida counties of Miami-Dade, Broward, or Monroe. In order for a proposal to be considered for funding, the applicant first must send a brief letter of inquiry. See Foundations website for letter of inquiry guidelines: http://www.peacockfoundationinc.org/review_progress.html.
Restrictions: Peacock Foundation, Inc. does not fund: capital campaigns, construction, or renovation projects; deficit financing or debt reduction; conferences or festivals; fundraising events or advertising; special events or athletic events; individuals; lobbying to influence legislation; religious organizations, unless engaged in a significant project benefiting the entire community.
Geographic Focus: Florida
Contact: Joelle Allen, Executive Director; (305) 373-1386
Internet: http://www.peacockfoundationinc.org/eligibility.html
Sponsor: Peacock Foundation
100 SE Second Street, Suite 2370
Miami, FL 33131

Pentair Foundation Education and Community Grants   1501
The Pentair Foundation focuses awards in two focus areas: education and community projects. Educational projects should focus on: supporting science and math education; providing "school-to-work" initiatives that prepare a student for the professional world; projects that offer alternative education; and programs that support art education. Community programs should focus on: water quality education, conservation and action; assistance to individuals in achieving self-sufficiency; entrepreneurial opportunities; opportunities for youth to gain life skills; services for youth in crisis; access to health care services; and assistance, education and rehabilitation services for those suffering from mental and/or physical disabilities and life-threatening illness.
Requirements: Nonprofit organizations, including schools and school districts, in communities where Pentair has a presence may apply. Application must be completed online and is located at the Foundation's website.
Restrictions: The foundation does not support individuals; political, lobbying, or fraternal activities; religious groups for religious purposes; medical research by individuals; scholarships to individuals; fundraising events, sponsorships, or advertising support; travel or tour expenses; conferences, seminars, workshops, or symposiums; athletic or sports-related organizations; non 501(c)3 organizations or those operating under a fiscal agent.
Geographic Focus: Wisconsin
Date(s) Application is Due: Mar 1; Jun 1; Oct 1
Amount of Grant: 2,000 - 50,000 USD
Samples: Casa Pacifica Centers for Children and Families, Camarillo, California, $15,654- project support; Center for Excellence in Education, McLean, Virginia, $2,268- general operating support
Contact: Susan Carter; (763) 656-5237; susan.carter@pentair.com
Internet: http://www.pentair.com/About_pentair_foundation.aspx
Sponsor: Pentair Foundation
5500 Wayzata Boulevard, Suite 800
Minneapolis, MN 55416

Percy B. Ferebee Endowment Grants   1502
Grants from the Percy B. Ferebee Endowment are awarded to support charitable, scientific and literary projects, and in particular, governmental and civic projects designed to further the cultural, social, economic and physical well-being of residents of Cherokee, Clay, Graham, Jackson, Macon and Swain Counties of North Carolina and the Cherokee Indian Reservation. Grants are also awarded in the form of scholarships to assist worthy and talented young men and women who reside in said counties in pursuing their college/university degree education within the state of North Carolina. The deadline for the submission of a grant application is September 30. The deadline for scholarship applications is January 31. Application forms are available online. Applicants will receive notice acknowledging receipt of the grant request, and subsequently be notified of the grant declination or approval.
Requirements: 501(c)3 non-profits in the Cherokee, Clay, Graham, Jackson, Macon and Swain Counties of North Carolina are eligible to apply for grants. Proposals should be submitted in the following format: completed Common Grant Application Form; an original Proposal Statement; an audited financial report and a current year operating budget; a copy of your official IRS Letter with your tax determination; a listing of your Board of Directors. Proposal Statements (second item in the above Format) should answer these questions: what are the objectives and expected outcomes of this program/project/request; what strategies will be used to accomplish your objective; what is the timeline for completion; if this is part of an on-going program, how long has it been in operation; what criteria will you use to measure success; if the request is not

fully funded, what other sources can you engage; an Itemized budget should be included; please describe any collaborative ventures. Prior to the distribution of funds, all approved grantees must sign and return a Grant Agreement Form, stating that the funds will be used for the purpose intended. Progress reports and Completion reports must also be filed as required for your specific grant. All current grantees must be in good standing with required documentation prior to submitting new proposals to any foundation. Scholarship recipients must be a resident of these areas and must attend a college or university in the state of North Carolina. Contact the Foundation for additional application requirements.
Restrictions: Grants are not made for political purposes, nor to organizations which discriminate on the basis of race, ethnic origin, sexual or religious preference, age or gender.
Geographic Focus: North Carolina
Date(s) Application is Due: Jan 31; Sep 30
Amount of Grant: 3,000 - 15,000 USD
Samples: Nantahala Regional Library, $15,000—general operating support; Macon County Historical Society, $7,500—general operating expenses; Reach, Inc. Resources Education Assistance Counseling & Housing, $4,000—general operating support.
Contact: Wachovia Bank, N.A., Trustee; grantinquiries6@wachovia.com
Internet: https://www.wachovia.com/foundation/v/index.jsp?vgnextoid=5d68 52199c0aa110VgnVCM1000004b0d1872RCRD&vgnextfmt=default
Sponsor: Percy B. Ferebee Endowment
Wachovia Bank, NC6732, 100 North Main Street
Winston Salem, NC 27150

Perkin Fund Grants   1503
The Perkin Fund supports projects and programs in the fields of astronomy, medicine, and scientific research, as well as limited giving to leading organizations in the arts, education, and social services. Most grants are awarded to well-established institutions. However, small and medium-sized institutions doing significant work in the fields of interest also are encouraged to apply. Deadlines are March 15 and September 15, with board meetings in May and November. Final notification of funding is usually two to four weeks.
Requirements: U.S. nonprofit institutions and organizations are eligible. Applicants should submit a letter with a detailed description of their project, the amount of funding requested, and a copy of their IRS determination letter.
Restrictions: The Fund does not grant to individuals or institutions outside the United States. Funding is limited to Connecticut, Massachusetts, and New York.
Geographic Focus: Connecticut, Massachusetts, New York
Date(s) Application is Due: Mar 15; Sep 15
Amount of Grant: 20,000 - 100,000 USD
Contact: Winifred Gray; (978) 468-2266; theperkinfund@verizon.net
Sponsor: Perkin Fund
176 Bay Road, P.O. Box 2220
South Hamilton, MA 01982-2232

Perl 6 Microgrants   1504
The program was established by a donation from Best Practical Solutions to help support Perl 6 development. Grants of $500 will be awarded to a range of Perl 6-related projects over the life of the grant program. Proposals will be accepted on a rolling schedule.
Requirements: Accepted grants might be for coding, documentation, testing or even writing articles about Perl 6. The program isn't tied to any one implementation of Perl 6 — they are interested in seeing proposals related to Pugs, Perl 6 on Parrot, Perl 6 on Perl 5 or any other Perl 6 implementation, and in general, projects that can be completed in 4-6 calendar weeks. To submit a grant proposal, send an email to perl6- microgrants@perl.org with the following information: a) A two to three paragraph summary of the work you intend to do; b) A quick bio; c) A brief description of what 'success' will mean for your project (How will we know you're done?); d) Where (if anywhere) you've discussed your project in the past; e) Where you'll be blogging about your progress. (Twice-weekly blog posts are a requirement for getting your grant money.)
Geographic Focus: All States
Amount of Grant: 500 USD
Contact: Jesse Vincent, Grant Manager; jesse@bestpractical.com
Internet: http://www.perlfoundation.org/patrick_michaud_awarded_perl_6_development_grant_as_a_joint_initiative_by_the_perl_foundation_and_mozilla_foundation
Sponsor: Perl Foundation
6832 Mulderstraat
Grand Ledge, MI 48837

Perl Foundation Grants 1505

The Perl Foundation (TPF) is dedicated to the advancement of the Perl programming language through open discussion, collaboration, design, and code.

Requirements: Projects do not have to be large, complex, or lengthy. If you have a good idea and the means and ability to accomplish it, the project will be considered. As a general rule, a properly formatted grant proposal is more likely to be approved if it meets the following criteria: it has widespread benefit to the Perl community or a large segment of it; you can convince TPF that you can accomplish your goals; and, the project can be accomplished in the published funding range ($500 - $3,000). To submit a proposal see the guidelines at http://www.perlfoundation.org/how_to_write_a_proposal and TPF rules of operation at http://www.perlfoundation.org/rules_of_operation. Then send your proposal to tpf-proposals@perl-foundation.org. Note that proposals should be properly formatted accordingly with the required P.O.D template.

Geographic Focus: All States
Date(s) Application is Due: May 31
Amount of Grant: 500 - 3,000 USD
Samples: Improving learn.perl.org, by Eric Wilhelm and Tina Connolly; Web. pm - a lightweight web framework for Perl 6, by Ilya Belikin, Carl Masak and Stephen Weeks
Contact: Richard Dice, President; rdice@perlfoundation.org
Internet: http://news.perlfoundation.org/2009/04/2009q2_call_for_grant_proposal.html
Sponsor: Perl Foundation
6832 Mulderstraat
Grand Ledge, MI 48837

Perpetual Trust for Charitable Giving Grants 1506

The Perpetual Trust for Charitable Giving was established in 1957 to support and promote quality educational, human-services, and health-care programming for underserved populations. Special consideration is given to medical aid and medical research organizations, as well as to institutions of higher learning. Grant requests for general operating support are strongly encouraged. Program support will also be considered. Small, program-related capital expenses may be included in general operating or program requests. To better support the capacity of nonprofit organizations, multi-year funding requests are strongly encouraged. Applicants must apply online at the grant website. Applicants are strongly encouraged to do the following before applying: review the downloadable state application procedures for additional helpful information and clarifications; review the downloadable online-application guidelines at the grant website; review the trust's funding history (link is available from the grant website); review the online application questions in advance; and review the list of required attachments. These will generally include: a list of board members, financial statements (audited, reviewed, or compiled by independent auditor); an organization summary; a list of other funding sources; an IRS Determination letter; and other required documents. All attachments must be uploaded in the online application as PDF, Word, or Excel files. The application deadline for the Perpetual Trust is 11:59 p.m. on September 1. Applicants will be notified of grant decisions before November 30.

Restrictions: The trust does not support requests from individuals, organizations attempting to influence policy through direct lobbying, or any political campaigns.
Geographic Focus: Massachusetts
Date(s) Application is Due: Sep 1
Samples: Forsyth Institute's Forsyth Dental Infirmary for Children, Boston, Massachusetts, $60,000, ForsythKids Program; Bridge Over Troubled Waters, Boston, Massachusetts, $30,000, general operating support; Codman Academy Foundation, Dorchester, Massachusetts, $25,000, general operating support.
Contact: Miki C. Akimoto; (866) 778-6859; miki.akimoto@baml.com
Internet: https://www.bankofamerica.com/philanthropic/fn_search.action
Sponsor: Perpetual Trust for Charitable Giving
225 Franklin Street, 4th Floor, MA1-225-04-02
Boston, MA 02110

Peter Kiewit Foundation General Grants 1507

The foundation supports nonprofits and individuals in designated geographic areas for arts and cultural programs, higher and other education, health care, human services, youth services, rural development, community development, and government/public administration. In the general purpose grants program, there are no limitations on the size or duration of the grants that may be requested. Any applicant may submit a total of up to two applications, for two separate projects, in any 12 month period. All Peter Kiewit Foundation grants are awarded on a matching funds basis.

Requirements: Grant application guidelines and application forms are required to submit a funding request and these materials are available through the Foundation office only. Potential applicants should contact the Foundation to establish an organization's eligibility to apply and to discuss the proposed project. Nonprofit 501(c)3 organizations in Rancho Mirage, California; western Iowa; Nebraska; and Sheridan, Wyoming are eligible for a maximum of 50% of the total project cost. Units of government (tax supported) in Rancho Mirage, California; western Iowa; Nebraska; and Sheridan, Wyoming may apply for a maximum of 25% of the total project cost.
Restrictions: Grants are not awarded to support elementary or secondary schools, churches, or religious groups. Grants are not awarded to individuals (except for scholarships), or for endowment funds or annual campaigns.
Geographic Focus: California, Iowa, Nebraska, Wyoming
Date(s) Application is Due: Jan 15; Apr 15; Jul 15; Oct 15
Amount of Grant: 10,000 - 500,000 USD
Samples: Camp Fire USA, Omaha, Nebraska, $40,000 - program support; Bemis Center for Contemporary Arts, Omaha, Nebraska, $450,000 - capital improvements; Fremont Opera House, Fremont, Nebraska, $75,000 - capital improvements.
Contact: Lynn Wallin Ziegenbein; (402) 344-7890; fax (402) 344-8099
Internet: http://www.peterkiewitfoundation.org/page.aspx?id=13&pid=3
Sponsor: Peter Kiewit Foundation
8805 Indian Hills Drive, Suite 225
Omaha, NE 68114-4096

Peter Kiewit Foundation Small Grants 1508

The foundation supports nonprofits and individuals in designated geographic areas for arts and cultural programs, higher and other education, health care, human services, youth services, rural development, community development, and government/public administration. The small grants program allows the Trustees to assist a large number of worthy organizations with a broad array of small projects which are limited in scope but significant for the organization. Small grants are rarely awarded to large organizations. Small grants range in size from $500 to $10,000. The Trustees created this category of grants to support small, defined projects; not to contribute small amounts to much larger budgets.

Requirements: Grant application guidelines and application forms are required to submit a funding request and these materials are available through the Foundation office only. Potential applicants should contact the Foundation to establish an organization's eligibility to apply and to discuss the proposed project. Nonprofit 501(c)3 organizations in Rancho Mirage, California; western Iowa; Nebraska; and Sheridan, Wyoming are eligible for a maximum of 50% of the total project cost. Units of government (tax supported) in Rancho Mirage, California; western Iowa; Nebraska; and Sheridan, Wyoming may apply for a maximum of 25% of the total project cost.
Restrictions: Grants are not awarded to support elementary or secondary schools, churches, or religious groups. Grants are not awarded to individuals (except for scholarships), or for endowment funds or annual campaigns.
Geographic Focus: California, Iowa, Nebraska, Wyoming
Date(s) Application is Due: Jan 15; Apr 15; Jul 15; Oct 15
Amount of Grant: 500 - 10,000 USD
Samples: Bone Creek Art Museum, David City, Nebraska, $10,000 - program support; Brownsville Fine Arts Association, Brownsville, Nebraska, $5,000 - program support; Joslyn Art Museum, Omaha, Nebraska, $8,500 - program support.
Contact: Lynn Wallin Ziegenbein; (402) 344-7890; fax (402) 344-8099
Internet: http://www.peterkiewitfoundation.org/page.aspx?id=14&pid=3
Sponsor: Peter Kiewit Foundation
8805 Indian Hills Drive, Suite 225
Omaha, NE 68114-4096

Pew Charitable Trusts Arts and Culture Grants 1509

The Pew Charitable Trusts supports a broad spectrum of institutions, artists, projects, and cultural marketing initiatives. The Trusts also helps cultural organizations take advantage of technical assistance and professional development opportunities, which has proven to be an effective means of extending the impact of its investments. Pew's objectives in supporting arts and culture are twofold: to nurture artistic excellence and to expand public participation. its efforts have been successful in Philadelphia, where a thriving arts environment has helped raise the city's profile on the world stage and infused new life and energy into the region.

Requirements: Grants are made only to 501(c)3 tax-exempt organizations that are not private foundations.
Restrictions: Grants are not made to individuals or for endowments, capital campaigns, unsolicited construction requests, debt reduction, or scholarships or fellowships that are not part of a program initiated by the Trusts.

Geographic Focus: All States
Contact: Susan A. Magill, Managing Director; (202) 552-2129 or (202) 552-2000; fax (202) 552-2299; smagill@pewtrusts.org or info@pewtrusts.com
Internet: http://www.pewtrusts.org/our_work_category.aspx?id=18
Sponsor: Pew Charitable Trusts
2005 Market Street, Suite 1700
Philadelphia, PA 19103-7077

Pew Philadelphia Cultural Leadership Program Grants 1510

The goal of The Philadelphia Cultural Leadership Program (PCLP) is to stimulate leadership and best practices within the cultural community by providing multiyear operating support to organizations that meet high standards of programmatic, fiscal, and management performance. All PCLP grants are for three years, and the use of the funds is unrestricted. Guidelines for renewing organizations and for new applicants are available online. Deadlines are September 6 for renewing organizations and September 27 for new applicants.
Requirements: 501(c)3 nonprofits operating in Bucks, Chester, Delaware, Montgomery, or Philadelphia Counties; have a minimum of $150,000 of annual operating revenue as evidenced by the organization's most recent audit; possess a board-approved strategic plan that extends through the proposed three-year grant period that is in active use by board, staff, and volunteers; be professionally managed with at least one full-time, paid professional staff member; provide programming that is available to the general public; attract a substantial local constituency; and show no working capital deficit in the most recent audited fiscal year.
Restrictions: Requests will not be considered for endowments; debt reduction; support for general operations or core programs of organizations outside the Philadelphia five-county area; museum, collection or library acquisitions; computer or multimedia hardware or software, except as part of trusts-initiated programs; grants made directly to individual artists, except as part of trusts-initiated programs; individual commissions, exhibitions, performing arts productions, or television or radio broadcasts, except as part of trusts-initiated programs; cultural exchange activities, except as part of trusts-initiated programs; arts education projects, except as part of the Philadelphia Cultural Leadership Program or other artistic initiatives; conferences or symposia, except as part of trusts-initiated programs; media and technology projects, except those that forward specific culture program interests and priorities; and programs originating outside the United States of America.
Geographic Focus: All States
Samples: Greater Philadelphia Cultural Alliance (PA)—for marketing efforts associated with its Campaign for Culture, including an online events calendar and an email program that offers half-price tickets, $2 million over three years; U of Pennsylvania, Museum of Anthropology and Archaeology (PA)—for general operating support, $608,000 over three years; U of Pennsylvania, Morris Arboretum (PA)—for general operating support, $284,000 over three years.
Contact: Marian Godfrey, Culture Program Director; (215) 575-4870; fax (215) 575-4939; culturemail@pewtrusts.org
Internet: http://www.pewtrusts.com/grants/index.cfm
Sponsor: Pew Charitable Trusts
2005 Market Street, Suite 1700
Philadelphia, PA 19103-7077

Phelps County Community Foundation Grants 1511

The Phelps County Community Foundation's grants program provides a means by which not-for-profit charitable organizations may secure financial assistance for projects and programs which will enhance the quality of life for residents of Phelps County, Nebraska. The foundation awards grants in the areas of education, culture, human services, health and recreation, and community. Priority is given to seed grants to initiate promising new projects or programs, programs representing innovative and efficient approaches to serving community needs and opportunities, challenge grants, organizations that work cooperatively with other community agencies, projects or programs where a moderate amount of grant money can effect a significant result, and projects or programs that enlist volunteer participation and citizen involvement. Types of support include general operating grants, continuing support grants, building construction/renovation, equipment acquisition, program development, publication, seed money, scholarship funds, and matching grants. Applicants must have a plan for future funding and support from other sources.
Requirements: Grants are made to 501(c)3 nonprofit organizations in Phelps County, Nebraska, and sometimes to governmental agencies for capital expenditures and/or capital improvements within Phelps County.
Restrictions: Grants are not made to individuals, to support political activities, to support operating expenses of well-established organizations or public service agencies, to establish new endowment funds, for travel or related expenses for individuals or groups, for operating support of governmental agencies, to religious groups for religious purposes, to profit-making enterprises, or to agencies serving a populace outside of Phelps County. In addition, grants are not made to support annual fund drives or to eliminate previously incurred deficits.
Geographic Focus: Nebraska
Date(s) Application is Due: Apr 1; Oct 1
Amount of Grant: Up to 25,000 USD
Samples: American Legion Baseball, Holdrege, Nebraska, $22,000 - new concession stand; Bertrand Nursing Home, Bertrand, Nebraska, $7,632 - operating expenses.
Contact: Vickie Klein, Executive Director; (308) 995-6847; fax (308) 995-2146; vlpccf@phelpsfoundation.org
Internet: http://www.phelpsfoundation.org/grants.html
Sponsor: Phelps County Community Foundation
504 4th Avenue
Holdrege, NE 68949

Philadelphia Foundation General Operating Support Grants 1512

General Operating Support Grants are funds that are unrestricted for use by high-performing nonprofit organizations. These funds may be used for all mission-related activities, including contributions to capital campaigns and endowments. Nonprofits that meet the basic eligibility requirements are asked to complete the General Operating Support Full Application, which includes a self-selection exercise to determine the organizational life cycle stage. The Foundation does not have application deadlines and accepts General Operating Support applications at any time.
Requirements: IRS 501(c)3 tax-exempt organizations located in Bucks, Chester, Delaware, Montgomery, and Philadelphia Counties of Pennsylvania are eligible.
Restrictions: Grants are rarely made to affiliates of national or international organizations, government agencies, organizations not located in Southeastern Pennsylvania, organizations with budgets of more than $1.5 million, private schools, or umbrella-funding organizations.
Geographic Focus: Pennsylvania
Contact: Libby Walsh, Program Associate; (215) 563-6417; fax (215) 563-6882; lwalsh@philafound.org or oeapplications@philafound.org
Internet: https://www.philafound.org/ForNonprofits/DiscretionaryGrantmaking/GeneralOperatingSupport/tabid/243/Default.aspx
Sponsor: Philadelphia Foundation
1234 Market Street, Suite 1800
Philadelphia, PA 19107

Phil Hardin Foundation Grants 1513

The Phil Hardin Foundation targets its funding to education in the State of Mississippi. Specific priorities are to strengthen the capacity of communities to nurture and educate young children; the capacity of higher education institutions to renew communities and their economies; the capacity of communities for locally initiated educational improvement and economic development; and state- and local-level policy and leadership initiatives that fit with foundation goals. Types of support include general operating support, continuing support, building construction/renovation, equipment acquisition, endowment funds, program development, conferences and seminars, professorships, publication, seed grants, fellowships, scholarship funds, research, and matching funds. The foundation also operates four K-12 fellowship programs. Deadlines vary between programs; contact program staff for specific fellowship deadlines.
Requirements: Applicants must either be based in Mississippi or the project must benefit Mississippi, depending on the program. Contact program staff for eligibility.
Geographic Focus: Mississippi
Amount of Grant: Up to 1,000,000 USD
Samples: Covington County Vocational Technical Center, Collins, Mississippi, $2,000 - support of the Click, Click, Boom program (2014); Meridian Public School District, Meridian, Mississippi, $100,000 - recruitment, retention and incentive program for highly-effective educators (2014); Trinity Dyslexia Education Center, Meridian, Mississippi, $15,000 - general operating costs (2014).
Contact: Lloyd Gray, (601) 483-4282; fax (601) 483-5665; info@philhardin.org
Internet: http://www.philhardin.org/application-and-instructions.cfm
Sponsor: Phil Hardin Foundation
2750 North Park Drive
Meridian, MS 39305

Philip L. Graham Fund Arts and Humanities Grants 1514

The Philip L. Graham Fund awards Arts and Humanities grants to organizations in the Washington, D.C., metropolitan area, including Maryland and Virginia. From its earliest days, the Fund has supported both large and small arts organizations in and around Washington, D.C. Many of the city's largest and most innovative theater companies, museums, dance companies, and arts education programs can trace their earliest funding back to the Graham Fund. The Fund remains committed to supporting longstanding organizations devoted to bringing high-quality and unique programs to the community and to seeking out new organizations bringing fresh ideas and offerings to the metropolitan area. Interested partied must submit a Letter of Inquiry (LOI) online prior to each submission deadline. The annual LOI deadlines are March 16, June 29, and December 2. Recent awards have ranged from $10,000 to $150,000.
Requirements: Applicants are required to submit a letter of inquiry through the Fund's online application system before one of three deadline dates. Organizations must be a tax-exempt 501(c)3 organization to apply and located within the greater Washington D.C. metropolitan area.
Restrictions: Proposals for the following purposes are not considered: advocacy or litigation; research; endowments; special events, conferences workshops or seminars; travel expenses; annual giving campaigns, benefits or sponsorships; courtesy advertising; and production of films or publications. Also, independent schools, institutions of post-secondary education, national or international organizations, and hospitals are not eligible to apply. Grants are also not made to: individuals; religious, political or lobbying activities; to membership organizations; or to any organization that has received a grant from the Fund within the previous thirty-six months.
Geographic Focus: District of Columbia, Maryland, Virginia
Amount of Grant: 5,000 - 150,000 USD
Samples: CityDance, Washington, D.C., $25,000 - fund IT infrastructure upgrades needed to support programmatic and organizational growth (2014); GALA Hispanic Theatre, Washington, D.C., $40,000 - support upgrades to Gala's sound technology, intercom system, and computer technology; Project Create, Washington, D.C., $30,000 - support the renovation of new program space for visual and performing arts Education programming for children, youth and families east of the Anacostia River (2014).
Contact: Eileen F. Daly, President; (202) 334-6640; fax (202) 334-4498; plgfund@ghco.com
Internet: http://www.plgrahamfund.org/content/interest-areas/arts-humanities
Sponsor: Philip L. Graham Fund
1300 North 17th Street, Suite 1700
Arlington, VA 22209

Philip L. Graham Fund Community Endeavors Grants 1515

The Philip L. Graham Fund awards Community Endeavors grants to organizations in the Washington, D.C., metropolitan area, including Maryland and Virginia. Recognizing the importance of Washington, D.C., to the nation and the world, the Fund considers requests from institutions that tell the stories of our country's history, values, accomplishments and those that strengthen the greater metropolitan community as a whole. These include support for a broad spectrum of organizations, such as institutions of national significance located in the metropolitan area, improvement of local parks and playgrounds, and efforts to help the community through programs that strengthen families and neighborhoods. Interested partied must submit a Letter of Inquiry (LOI) online prior to each submission deadline. The annual LOI deadlines are March 16, June 29, and December 2. Recent awards have ranged from $20,000 to $150,000.
Requirements: Applicants are required to submit a letter of inquiry through the Fund's online application system before one of three deadline dates. Organizations must be a tax-exempt 501(c)3 organization to apply and located within the greater Washington D.C. metropolitan area.
Restrictions: Proposals for the following purposes are not considered: advocacy or litigation; research; endowments; special events, conferences workshops or seminars; travel expenses; annual giving campaigns, benefits or sponsorships; courtesy advertising; and production of films or publications. Also, independent schools, institutions of post-secondary education, national or international organizations, and hospitals are not eligible to apply. Grants are also not made to: individuals; religious, political or lobbying activities; to membership organizations; or to any organization that has received a grant from the Fund within the previous thirty-six months.
Geographic Focus: District of Columbia, Maryland, Virginia
Amount of Grant: 20,000 - 150,000 USD
Samples: Trust for the National Mall, Washington, D.C., $150,000 - support the restoration of Constitution Gardens on the National Mall; Friends of Fort

Dupont Ice Arena, Washington, D.C., $25,000 - support the purchase of off-the-ice infrastructure upgrades for KOI PLU.S. team building, academic enrichment, skating instruction, and physical training activities; President Lincoln's Cottage, Washington, D.C., $25,000 - office and technology upgrades.
Contact: Eileen F. Daly; (202) 334-6640; plgfund@ghco.com
Internet: http://www.plgrahamfund.org/content/interest-areas/community-endeavors
Sponsor: Philip L. Graham Fund
1300 North 17th Street, Suite 1700
Arlington, VA 22209

Philip L. Graham Fund Health and Human Services Grants 1516

The Philip L. Graham Fund awards Health and Human Services grants to organizations in the Washington, D.C., metropolitan area, including Maryland and Virginia. The Health and Human Services segment of the Fund's giving portfolio focuses on organizations serving those in greatest need in the community. Organizations providing shelter, food, medical care, and counseling to low income members of our community remain a high priority for the Fund. Interested partied must submit a Letter of Inquiry (LOI) online prior to each submission deadline. The annual LOI deadlines are March 16, June 29, and December 2. Recent awards have ranged from $10,000 to $200,000.
Requirements: Applicants are required to submit a letter of inquiry through the Fund's online application system before one of three deadline dates. Organizations must be a tax-exempt 501(c)3 organization to apply and located within the greater Washington D.C. metropolitan area.
Restrictions: The Fund does not accept proposals from hospitals. Proposals for the following purposes are not considered: advocacy or litigation; research; endowments; special events, conferences workshops or seminars; travel expenses; annual giving campaigns, benefits or sponsorships; courtesy advertising; and production of films or publications. Also, independent schools, institutions of post-secondary education, national or international organizations, and hospitals are not eligible to apply. Grants are also not made to: individuals; religious, political or lobbying activities; to membership organizations; or to any organization that has received a grant from the Fund within the previous thirty-six months.
Geographic Focus: District of Columbia, Maryland, Virginia
Amount of Grant: 10,000 - 200,000 USD
Samples: HomeAid Northern Virginia, Chantilly, Virginia, $35,000 - support the Shelter Care Program which delivers professional pro bono construction management, labor and materials to complete renovations of homeless shelters and transitional housing facilities (2014); D.C. Children's Advocacy Center, Washington, D.C., $75,000 - support the build out of an on-site medical clinic to provide medical attention, gather forensic data and better serve Safe Shores clients; AG Bell Association for the Deaf and Hard of Hearing, Washington, D.C., $40,000 - purchase new servers necessary to expand the AG Bell's Listening and Spoken Language Knowledge Center.
Contact: Eileen F. Daly, President; (202) 334-6640; fax (202) 334-4498; plgfund@ghco.com
Internet: http://www.plgrahamfund.org/content/interest-areas/health-human-services
Sponsor: Philip L. Graham Fund
1300 North 17th Street, Suite 1700
Arlington, VA 22209

Philip L. Graham Fund Journalism and Communications Grants 1517

The Philip L. Graham Fund awards Journalism and Communications grants to organizations in the Washington, D.C., metropolitan area, including Maryland and Virginia. In recognition of the Fund's origins and strong belief in the important role effective journalism plays in our world, grants are occasionally awarded to organizations working to advance broad professional goals in the field of journalism. The Fund considers requests from organizations with focused efforts within the United States and prefers to fund one-time capital expense requests rather than general operating or program support. Organizations from outside the Washington metropolitan area, focused on the advancement of journalism, are welcome to apply. Interested partied must submit a Letter of Inquiry (LOI) online prior to each submission deadline. The annual LOI deadlines are March 16, June 29, and December 2. Recent awards have ranged from $15,000 to $250,000.
Requirements: Applicants are required to submit a letter of inquiry through the Fund's online application system before one of three deadline dates. Organizations must be a tax-exempt 501(c)3 organization to apply.
Restrictions: Proposals for the following purposes are not considered: advocacy or litigation; research; endowments; special events, conferences workshops or seminars; travel expenses; annual giving campaigns, benefits or sponsorships; courtesy advertising; and production of films or publications.

Also, independent schools, institutions of post-secondary education, national or international organizations, and hospitals are not eligible to apply. Grants are also not made to: individuals; religious, political or lobbying activities; to membership organizations; or to any organization that has received a grant from the Fund within the previous thirty-six months.

Geographic Focus: All States

Amount of Grant: 15,000 - 250,000 USD

Samples: Philip Merrill College of Journalism, College Park, Maryland, $250,000 - support the new Shirley Povich Center for Sports Journalism; Committee to Protect Journalists, New York, New York, $30,000 - support upgrades to CPJ's Information and Communications Technology infrastructure; International Center for Journalists, Washington, D.C., $50,000 - equipment and technology needed to expand ICFJ's digital journalism training to participants around the globe.

Contact: Eileen F. Daly, President; (202) 334-6640; fax (202) 334-4498; plgfund@ghco.com

Internet: http://www.plgrahamfund.org/content/interest-areas/journalism-communications

Sponsor: Philip L. Graham Fund

1300 North 17th Street, Suite 1700

Arlington, VA 22209

Phoenix Suns Charities Grants   1518

Ranging in size from $1,000 to $10,000, Phoenix Suns Charities Program Grants are intended for Arizona non-profit organization whose programs and activities focus on helping children and families maximize their potential. The foundation's largest annual gift, the Playmaker Award, is a one-time $100,000 grant which can be used for capital or programs, or a combination of both. For this grant, Suns Charities looks favorably on collaborative ideas and naming or branding opportunities.

Requirements: Applications and supporting documents must be submitted electronically through ZoomGrants at the Suns website. Organizations must consider the prerequisites, answer all questions and carefully follow directions. Applications are available in November, evaluated by Suns board members in April and May, with funding in June.

Geographic Focus: Arizona

Date(s) Application is Due: Apr 1

Amount of Grant: 1,000 - 10,000 USD

Contact: Kathryn Pidgeon, Executive Director; (602) 379-7948; fax (602) 379-7990; kpidgeon@suns.com

Internet: http://www.nba.com/suns/charities.html

Sponsor: Phoenix Suns

201 East Jefferson Street

Phoenix, AZ 85004

Phoenixville Community Health Foundation Grants   1519

The foundation operates in Pennsylvania and seeks to become the champion of community health. Categories of funding include personal health, including physical/behavioral health of children, youth, adults, senior citizens, and those at risk for abuse, neglect, or violence; and community health, including environmental and civic health of the community-at-large and the promotion of educational opportunities for individuals aspiring to be in the health field. Requests must demonstrate that the program/organization is addressing a community need and not duplicating existing efforts. Types of support include program support, general operations, capital projects, and equipment acquisition. Both single- and multiyear initiatives are considered. Applicants should discuss their funding interest with foundation staff; a grant request packet will be given if the proposed initiative fits within foundation guidelines. The board meets bimonthly.

Requirements: Pennsylvania 501(c)3 tax-exempt organizations serving Chester and Montgomery Counties are eligible.

Restrictions: Grants are not awarded for direct scholarship support to individuals; purchases of tickets or advertising for benefit purposes; coverage of continuing operating deficits; document publication; pass-through grant support through a third party (except United Way); and fraternal organizations, political parties or candidates, veterans, labor or local civic groups, or groups engaged in influencing legislation.

Geographic Focus: Pennsylvania

Samples: Montgomery County Dept of Economic and Workforce Development (Norristown, PA)—to expand its CareerLink Employment Program to the Phoenixville Library, $30,800; Chester County Futures (West Chester, PA)—to establish a mentor program to help at-risk youths with the potential to attend college, $15,000; Phoenixville Area Police Athletic League (PA)—for

program support, $10,000; Phoenixville Area Economic Development Corp (PA)—for general operating support, $35,000.

Contact: Carol Poinier, Grants, Operations Manager; (610) 917-9890; fax (610) 917-9861; pchf1@juno.com

Internet: http://www.pchf1.org/gmakeover.html

Sponsor: Phoenixville Community Health Foundation

1260 Valley Forge Road, Suite 102

Phoenixville, PA 19460

Piedmont Health Foundation Grants   1520

The Piedmont Health Care Foundation was established in 1985 through the sale of the first HMO in Greenville County, South Carolina. During the past 25 years, the foundation has invested more than $3.4 million in dozens of nonprofit organizations in the Greenville, South Carolina area. The Piedmont Health Care Foundation has played an important role in catalyzing and providing seed funding to critical projects, and it has provided operating and programmatic funds needed by local health-service organizations. In looking ahead, the foundation recognizes that much of what makes a healthy community takes place outside of the health-care system. So for its 25th anniversary, the foundation decided to change its name to the Piedmont Health Foundation. The foundation currently focuses on the area of policy, system, and environmental change to reduce childhood obesity rates. Applications are accepted on a quarterly basis. Downloadable guidelines and editable forms are provided at the foundation website. Applicants should email their completed forms to the address given by midnight of the deadline date.

Requirements: Nonprofits that serve Greenville County are eligible to apply.

Geographic Focus: South Carolina

Date(s) Application is Due: Jan 31; Apr 10; Jul 10; Oct 10

Amount of Grant: 1,000 - 15,000 USD

Contact: Katy Smith, Executive Director; (864) 370-0212; fax (864) 370-0212; katypughsmith@bellsouth.net or katysmith@piedmonthealthfoundation.org

Internet: http://www.phcfdn.org/grantmaking.php

Sponsor: Piedmont Health Foundation

P.O. Box 9303

Greenville, SC 29604

Piedmont Natural Gas Foundation Health and Human Services   1521
Grants

Piedmont Natural Gas Foundation's Health and Human Services grant focuses funding toward: organizations providing outreach services to community members with basic needs, including shelter, food and clothing; substance abuse or mental illness; organizations providing services or programs for a range of human service needs including youth engagement and mentoring, special needs and disability assistance, substance abuse or mental illnesses, transitional housing and situational homelessness support, and gang violence prevention; organizations providing emergency/disaster relief; increased access to critical healthcare services and comprehensive medical treatment including preventative care, prescription medication, medical exams, screenings, immunizations and dental care; and increased access to mental health services.

Requirements: Organizations must be a 501(c)3 non-profit organization or a qualified government entity. All grant requests must be submitted through Piedmont's online grant application form located at Piedmont's website.

Restrictions: Piedmont Natural Gas Foundation will not fund: religious, fraternal, political or athletic groups; four-year colleges and universities; private foundations; or social or veterans' organizations. In addition to these restrictions, contributions will generally not be made to or for: individuals; pre-college level private schools, except through the Employee Matching Gifts program; travel and conferences; third-party professional fundraising organizations; controversial social causes; religious organizations with programs limited to or expressly for their membership only; athletic events and programs; agencies already receiving Piedmont support through United Way or a united arts drive, with the exception of an approved capital campaign; or any proposal outside of the geographic area where Piedmont Natural Gas does business.

Geographic Focus: North Carolina, South Carolina, Tennessee

Amount of Grant: 500 - 30,000 USD

Contact: George Baldwin, President; (704) 731-4063; fax (704) 731-4086; george.baldwin@piedmontng.com

Internet: http://www.piedmontng.com/ourcommunity/ourfoundation.aspx#guidelines

Sponsor: Piedmont Natural Gas Foundation

4720 Piedmont Row Drive

Charlotte, NC 28210

Pinellas County Grants 1522

The Pinellas Community Foundation was established in 1969, it distributes grants twice annually to a wide variety of non-profit agencies, organizations and programs that enhance and support the quality of life in Pinellas County, Florida. Areas of interest are: art, culture, health care, environment, community development, employment opportunities, the underserved, and social services. *Requirements:* Eligibility: a non-profit, 501(c)3; be headquartered in Pinellas County; provide social services to people in Pinellas County; not have a large endowment or fund raising staff; provide recent audited financial statements. For Grant Applications call Pinellas Community Foundation: (727)531-0058. *Geographic Focus:* Florida
Date(s) Application is Due: Jun 15; Oct 1
Contact: Julie Scales; (727) 531-0058; fax (727) 531-0053; info@pinellasccf.org
Internet: http://www.pinellasccf.org/pinellas-community-foundation-pcf-clearwater-fl-our-grants-programs.htm
Sponsor: Pinellas County Community Foundation
5200 East Bay Drive, Suite 202
Clearwater, FL 33764

Pinkerton Foundation Grants 1523

The Pinkerton Foundation is an independent grantmaking foundation established in 1966 by Robert Allan Pinkerton with the broad directive to reduce the incidence of crime and to prevent juvenile delinquency. The Foundation's principal program interests are focused on economically disadvantaged children, youth and families, and severely learning disabled children and adults of borderline intelligence. The Foundation supports efforts to strengthen and expand community-based programs for children, youth and families in New York City. The Foundation also occasionally funds research, demonstration and evaluation projects in its principal program areas. While grants for direct service projects are usually limited to New York City, those with potential for national impact or replication may go beyond this geographic limitation. The Foundation's Board of Directors have two grantmaking meetings per year, in May and in December. Letters of inquiry are welcome throughout the year. Additional guidelines are available at the Foundation's website.
Requirements: Grants are awarded primarily to New York City 501(c)3 nonprofit public charitable organizations.
Restrictions: The foundation does not grant requests for emergencies, medical research, direct provision of health care, religious education, conferences, publications, or capital projects.
Geographic Focus: All States
Date(s) Application is Due: Feb 1; Sep 1
Amount of Grant: 25,000 - 250,000 USD
Samples: Reel Works Teen Filmmaking, Brooklyn, NY, $35,000—operating support for filmmaking program that serves up to 180 high school students; Madison Square Boys & Girls Club (New York, NY) $250,000—for after school and summer program operations at Madison's clubhouses; New York Cares, Inc., New York, NY, $20,000—in support of their SAT Prep Program.
Contact: Joan Colello, Executive Director; (212) 332-3385; fax (212) 332-3399; pinkfdn@pinkertonfdn.org
Internet: http://fdncenter.org/grantmaker/pinkerton
Sponsor: Pinkerton Foundation
610 Fifth Avenue, Suite 316
New York, NY 10020

Pinnacle Entertainment Foundation Grants 1524

The Pinnacle Entertainment Foundation awards grants in its primary fields of interest, including: the arts; children and youth services; food banks; community foundations; health care; patient services; higher education; hospitals; the humanities; performing arts; and recreation programs. Types of support include: general operating funds; program development; scholarship funds; and sponsorships. Applications are limited to two per calendar year, per organization. An online application form is required, and should include: plans for acknowledgement; a detailed description of project and amount of funding requested; a brief history of organization and description of its mission; contact information; and a copy of the IRS Determination Letter.
Requirements: 501(c)3 organizations serving the residents of Louisiana or Nevada are eligible to apply.
Restrictions: The Foundation does not support: organizations that are not 501(c)3 entities; political causes, candidates, organizations or campaigns; organizations whose primary purpose is to influence legislation; organizations that discriminate on the basis of age, color, disability, disabled veteran status, gender, race, religion, national origin, marital status, sexual orientation or military service; administrative expenses or programs with administrative

expenses in excess of 15%; capital project funding; purchase of uniforms or trips for school-related organizations and booster clubs, youth athletics or amateur sports teams; activities whose sole purpose is promotion or support of a specific religion, denomination or religious institution; fraternal, alumni, trade, professional or social organizations; individuals; medical fundraisers; political or partisan organizations or candidates; or study or travel grants (scholarships, stipends, writing allowances).
Geographic Focus: Louisiana, Nevada
Amount of Grant: 5,000 - 60,000 USD
Samples: McNeese State University Foundation, Lake Charles, Louisiana, $60,000 - general operating funds; West Jefferson Hospital Foundation, Marrero, Louisiana, $50,000 - general operating funds; University of Nevada Las Vegas Foundation, Las Vegas, Nevada, $12,500 - general operating funds.
Contact: Shelly Peterson, (702) 541-7777 or (818) 710-2719
Internet: https://www.pnkinc.com/pinnacle-entertainment-foundation/
Sponsor: Pinnacle Entertainment Foundation
8918 Spanish Ridge Avenue
Las Vegas, NV 89148-1302

Pioneer Hi-Bred Community Grants 1525

The international corporation supports community-based projects in the areas of agriculture, education, farm safety, and the environment. Priority consideration is given to projects located in Pioneer facility communities or rural agricultural regions and to organizations with active Pioneer management/employee participation and company-related expertise and interest. Types of support include capital grants, general operating grants, program development grants, and seed money grants. The company accepts proposals from nonprofit organizations nationwide but favors programs in its operating communities. Pioneer prefers to make direct contributions to organizations, rather than sponsorships, ticket or table purchases. This allows more funding to go directly toward the non-profit organization; however, we are willing to consider sponsorships when Pioneer employees are actively involved with the organization. The employee must present the request to Community Investment at least one month in advance. Due to the number of non-profit events held annually, there is a $1,000 maximum contribution level per event per year. The company favors proposals that demonstrate cooperation with other community-based programs, broad-based funding, community need, and positive results. Grant proposals are reviewed on a quarterly basis.
Requirements: Nonprofit organizations are eligible. All requests should be directed to the Pioneer Hi-Bred office within the local area. Otherwise, send to the contact listed. Pioneer does not respond favorably to verbal requests.
Restrictions: Grants are not made to individuals, religious or political organizations that promote a particular doctrine, elected officials, company marketing or advertising, or organizations where there is a conflict of interest with Pioneer Hi-Bred.
Geographic Focus: All States
Amount of Grant: Up to 5,000 USD
Contact: Grants Administrator; (800) 247-6803, ext. 3915; fax (515) 334-4415; community.investment@pioneer.com
Internet: http://www.pioneer.com/web/site/portal/menuitem.bb020a6d93d9d318bc0c0a03d10093a0/
Sponsor: Pioneer Hi-Bred International
6900 NW 62nd Avenue, P.O. Box 246
Johnston, IA 50131

Piper Jaffray Foundation Communities Giving Grants 1526

The foundation supports organizations and programs that enhance the lives of people living and working in communities in which the company has offices. Of primary interest is support for organizations that increase opportunities for individuals to improve their lives and help themselves. Highest priority is given to family stability programs (including housing, family violence, responsible parenting), early childhood development, job training/career development, youth development, and adult education services. The foundation will also consider requests from organizations that work to increase citizen understanding or involvement in civic affairs or that enhance the artistic and cultural life of the community. Requests for general operating support from proven nonprofit organizations will be considered. Requests for project and capital support will be considered on a very selective basis. Support for higher education and K-12 public and private schools is provided primarily through the company gift-matching program. Contact the foundation for deadline dates.
Requirements: IRS 501(c)3 organizations located in the Minneapolis/Saint Paul metropolitan area should submit requests directly to the foundation. Organizations located outside the Minneapolis/Saint Paul metropolitan area

should submit requests to the nearest Piper Jaffray office for forwarding to the foundation. Offices are located in communities in Arizona, California, Colorado, Idaho, Illinois, Iowa, Kansas, Kentucky, Minnesota, Missouri, Montana, Nebraska, Nevada, North Dakota, Ohio, Oregon, South Dakota, Tennessee, Utah, Washington, Wisconsin, and Wyoming.

Restrictions: Requests will not be considered from newly formed nonprofit organizations; individuals; teams; religious, political, veterans, or fraternal organizations; or organizations working to treat or eliminate specific diseases. Support is not available for basic or applied research, travel, event sponsorship, benefits or tickets, or to eliminate an organization's operating deficit.

Geographic Focus: Arizona, Arkansas, California, Colorado, Idaho, Illinois, Iowa, Kansas, Kentucky, Minnesota, Missouri, Montana, Nebraska, Nevada, North Dakota, Ohio, Oregon, South Dakota, Tennessee, Utah, Washington, Wisconsin, Wyoming

Date(s) Application is Due: Mar 18

Amount of Grant: 1,000 - 5,000 USD

Contact: Connie McCuskey, Vice President; (612) 303-1309; fax (612) 342-6085; communityrelations@pjc.com

Internet: http://www.piperjaffray.com/2col_largeright.aspx?id=127

Sponsor: Piper Jaffray Foundation

800 Nicollet Mall, Suite 800

Minneapolis, MN 55402

Piper Trust Arts and Culture Grants   1527

The Piper Trust's grantmaking focuses on Virginia Galvin Piper's commitment to improving the quality of life for residents of Maricopa County. Piper Trust's particular interest lies with projects that benefit young children, adolescents and older adults in Maricopa County. The Trust makes grants to faith-based organizations that serve these target populations in a manner consistent with program guidelines. For Arts and Culture grants, the trust is focused on improved business and financial operations; collaborations for greater effectiveness and efficiencies; and, revenue generation, cost reduction, and mergers.

Requirements: Piper Trust makes grants to actively operating Section 501(c)3 organizations in Maricopa County. These organizations must have been in operation for at least three years from the effective date of their IRS ruling. Special rules apply to private foundations and 509(a)3 (Type III) organizations. There are no deadlines on initial proposals, and letters of inquiry throughout the year are reviewed throughout the year. If the Trust asks for a full proposal, its disposition depends on its completeness and the meeting schedule of the Piper trustees. Virginia G. Piper Charitable Trust requires all arts and culture grantees to participate in the Arizona Cultural Data Project (Arizona CDP). The Arizona CDP is a powerful online management tool designed to strengthen arts and cultural organizations by providing an amazing array of reports designed to increase management capacity, inform decision-making, and document the economic value of the arts.

Restrictions: Individuals are not eligible.

Geographic Focus: Arizona

Amount of Grant: Up to 350,000 USD

Contact: Ellen Solowey; (480) 556-7133; esolowey@pipertrust.org

Internet: http://pipertrust.org/our-grants/arts-culture/

Sponsor: Virginia G. Piper Charitable Trust

1202 East Missouri Avenue

Phoenix, AZ 85014

Piper Trust Children Grants   1528

The Piper Trust's grantmaking focuses on Virginia Galvin Piper's commitment to improving the quality of life for residents of Maricopa County. Piper Trust's particular interest lies with projects that benefit young children, adolescents and older adults in Maricopa County. The Trust makes grants to faith-based organizations that serve these target populations in a manner consistent with program guidelines. For Children grants, the trust is focused on improved parent and caregiver child-rearing know-how; assistance for children without resources or with special needs; enhanced child care practices and after school care; and, integrated early childhood policies and practices.

Requirements: Piper Trust makes grants to actively operating Section 501(c)3 organizations in Maricopa County. These organizations must have been in operation for at least three years from the effective date of their IRS ruling. Special rules apply to private foundations and 509(a)3 (Type III) organizations. There are no deadlines on initial proposals, and letters of inquiry throughout the year are reviewed throughout the year. If the Trust asks for a full proposal, its disposition depends on its completeness and the meeting schedule of the Piper trustees.

Geographic Focus: Arizona

Contact: Terri Leon, Program Officer; (480) 556-7121; tleon@pipertrust.org

Internet: http://pipertrust.org/our-grants/children/

Sponsor: Virginia G. Piper Charitable Trust

1202 East Missouri Avenue

Phoenix, AZ 85014

Piper Trust Education Grants   1529

The Piper Trust's grantmaking focuses on Virginia Galvin Piper's commitment to improving the quality of life for residents of Maricopa County. Piper Trust's particular interest lies with projects that benefit young children, adolescents and older adults in Maricopa County. The Trust makes grants to faith-based organizations that serve these target populations in a manner consistent with program guidelines. For Education grants, the trust is most interested in proposals that address improved early learning environments, academic enhancements for youth, and engagement of older adults in learning.

Requirements: Piper Trust makes grants to actively operating Section 501(c)3 organizations in Maricopa County. These organizations must have been in operation for at least three years from the effective date of their IRS ruling. Special rules apply to private foundations and 509(a)3 (Type III) organizations. There are no deadlines on initial proposals, and letters of inquiry throughout the year are reviewed throughout the year. If the Trust asks for a full proposal, its disposition depends on its completeness and the meeting schedule of the Piper trustees.

Geographic Focus: Arizona

Contact: Terri Leon, Program Officer; (480) 556-7121; tleon@pipertrust.org

Sponsor: Virginia G. Piper Charitable Trust

1202 East Missouri Avenue

Phoenix, AZ 85014

Playboy Foundation Grants   1530

The Playboy Foundation seeks to foster social change by confining its grants and other support to projects of national impact and scope involved in fostering open communication about, and research into, human sexuality, reproductive health and rights; protecting and fostering civil rights and civil liberties in the United States for all people, including women, people affected and impacted by HIV/AIDS, gays and lesbians, racial minorities, the poor and the disadvantaged; and eliminating censorship and protecting freedom of expression and First Amendment rights. The Foundation does not accept unsolicited proposals, but welcomes letters of inquiry via post for the areas of interest noted above. Grants awarded by the Foundation are typically up to $10,000.

Restrictions: The foundation will not consider religious programs, individual needs, capital campaigns, endowments, scholarships, or fellowships; social services, including residential care, clinics, treatment, or recreation programs; national health, welfare, educational, or cultural organizations, or their state affiliates; or government agencies or projects.

Geographic Focus: All States

Amount of Grant: 5,000 - 10,000 USD

Contact: Executive Director; (312) 373-2437 or (312) 751-8000; fax (312) 751-2818; giving@playboy.com

Internet: http://www.playboyenterprises.com/foundation

Sponsor: Playboy Foundation

680 North Lake Shore Drive

Chicago, IL 60611

PMI Foundation Grants   1531

The PMI Foundation awards grants nationally, with emphasis on California, to a wide range of organizations with the goal of expanding homeownership. The foundation also contributes generously to deserving causes and charities in the areas of arts and culture, health and human services, education, civic organizations, and community development. Application guidelines are available for download from the PMI website. There are no application deadlines. Check with foundation staff to verify whether they are currently accepting applications.

Requirements: 501(c)3 organizations are eligible. Requests must target the disadvantaged, the poor, and distressed populations. Requests must either focus on increasing affordable housing opportunities or directly contribute to the quality of life in under-served communities.

Restrictions: The PMI Foundation does not accept requests for the following purposes: individuals; fraternal, veteran, labor, athletic or religious organizations serving a limited constituency; political or lobbying organizations, or those supporting the candidacy of a particular individual; travel funds; and films, videotapes or audio productions.

Geographic Focus: All States

Amount of Grant: 200 - 200,000 USD

Samples: Habitat for Humanity (East Bay), Oakland, California, $25,000; Animal Rescue Foundation, Walnut Creek, California, $2,500; Consumer Credit Counseling Services, San Francisco, California, $35,000.
Contact: Laura Kinney, Foundation Grant Administrator; (925) 658-6562
Internet: http://www.pmifoundation.org/index.html
Sponsor: PMI Foundation
3003 Oak Road
Walnut Creek, CA 94597-2098

Polk Bros. Foundation Grants 1532

The primary focus of the Foundation is programs that work with populations of need, particularly children, youth, and families in underserved Chicago communities. Very few awards are made to organizations located outside the city of Chicago. Grants are made for both new and ongoing initiatives in four program areas: social service, education, culture and health care. In all areas, proposals should address increased access to services and improvement of the quality of life for area residents. Grants are seldom made for capital support.
Requirements: Illinois 501(c)3 nonprofit organizations are eligible. Preference is given to requests from Chicago. An organization that has not previously received a grant from the Foundation should first call the Foundation office or complete the pre-application form available on the Foundation website. The Foundation will then mail an application form or contact the organization with further questions.
Restrictions: The Polk Bros. Foundation will not support: organizations that devote a substantial portion of their activities to attempting to influence legislation or to participating in campaigns on behalf of candidates for public office; religious institutions seeking support for programs whose participants are restricted by religious affiliation or whose services promote a particular creed; purchase of dinner or raffle tickets or advertising in dinner programs; medical, scientific, or academic research; grants to individuals; tax-generating entities (municipalities, school districts, etc.) for services within their normal responsibilities. The Foundation will not consider more than one request from an organization or its affiliates in a 12-month period, nor will it generally fund more than eight percent of an organization's operating budget.
Geographic Focus: Illinois
Amount of Grant: Up to 15,000 USD
Samples: Chicago High School for the Arts, $750,000 - general operating; Advocate Illinois Masonic Medical Center, $90,000 - school-based health centers at Amundsen and Lake View High Schools; Albany Park Theater Project, $80,000 - youth development through theater program; America Scores Chicago, $25,000 - salary support for the education and soccer directors;
Contact: Suzanne Doombos Kerbow, Assistant Director; (312) 527-4684; fax (312) 527-4681; questions@polkbrosfdn.org
Internet: http://www.polkbrosfdn.org/guidelines.htm
Sponsor: Polk Brothers Foundation
20 West Kinzie Street, Suite 1110
Chicago, IL 60611

Pollock Foundation Grants 1533

The foundation awards grants to Texas nonprofit organizations in its areas of interest, including cultural programs, dental education and schools, health care and health organizations, Jewish organizations and temples, libraries and library science, nursing, public health education and schools, social services, and youth development. Grants support program develoment and general operating expenses. There are no application deadlines. Contact the office for application materials.
Requirements: Texas nonprofits are eligible. Preference is given to requests from Dallas.
Geographic Focus: Texas
Amount of Grant: 1,000 - 300,000 USD
Contact: Robert Pollock, Trustee; (214) 871-7155; fax (214) 871-8158
Sponsor: Pollock Foundation
2626 Howell Street, Suite 895
Dallas, TX 75204

Porter County Community Foundation Professional Development 1534
Grants

The Porter County Community Foundation offers Professional Development Grants to support consulting work for nonprofit organizations or attendance at continuing education programs identified by nonprofit organizations that meet their individual needs and schedules. These grants can be used to cover consulting time, conference registration fees or college tuition fees. Nonprofit organizations may receive up to $1,500 per year, and each organization is limited to two grants per calendar year. The maximum grant amount for

the use of a consultant is $1,500 and the maximum grant amount for the attendance of a conference or training is $750 per registration.
Requirements: In applying for a grant to hire a consultant, the applicant should submit a letter describing the consultant's mission, company, and credentials. In applying for grants to attend conferences, there are several items to be addressed in a numbered narrative that does not exceed two pages. Applicant should consult the website for the detailed information requested in a specific format.
Restrictions: Because funding is limited, grants cannot cover travel expenses, lodging costs, meals, books or supplies.
Geographic Focus: Indiana
Amount of Grant: 1,500 USD
Contact: Brenda A. Sheetz, Program Administrator; (219) 465-0294; fax (219) 464-2733; bsheetz@portercountyfoundation.org
Internet: http://www.portercountyfoundation.org/grantprograms.html
Sponsor: Porter County Community Foundation
57 South Franklin Street, Suite 207, P.O. Box 302
Valparaiso, IN 46384

Porter County Health and Wellness Grant 1535

The Porter County Health and Wellness Fund awards grants to nonprofit organizations that promote, support, and/or advance health care in Porter County. Funding priorities include: increasing health care access for the underserved; improving and promoting healthy lifestyles for youth; and improving the nonprofit's operational capabilities to provide health care services. The maximum grant amount is $25,000.
Requirements: In addition to the application, all grant application packets must include the following information: a grant request cover page; a grant narrative; a project budget; a current operating budget and financial statement; the names and principal occupations of the organization's Board of Directors; the organization's grant application approval by their Board of Directors; and a copy of the organization's 501(c)3 tax exemption ruling.
Restrictions: Grants will not be made to: individuals; membership contributions; event sponsorships; programs that are sectarian or religious in nature; political organizations or candidates; contributions to endowment campaigns; campaigns to reduce previously incurred debt; and programs already completed.
Geographic Focus: Indiana
Date(s) Application is Due: Jun 15
Amount of Grant: 25,000 USD
Contact: Brenda Sheetz, Health/Wellness Fund Contact; (219) 465-0294; fax (219) 464-2733; bsheetz@portercountyfoundation.org
Internet: http://www.portercountyfoundation.org/grantprograms.html
Sponsor: Porter County Community Foundation
57 South Franklin Street, Suite 207, P.O. Box 302
Valparaiso, IN 46384

Portland Foundation Grants 1536

The Portland Foundation Community Grants are particularly interested in proposals for start-up costs for new programs; one-time projects or needs; and capital needs beyond an applicant's capabilities and means. In addition, limited funding is available in the following areas: emergency service agencies; programs that benefit the elderly of Jay County; needy families; libraries; historical facilities; care and prevention of cruelty to animals; handicapped children; and education of sensory impaired children. The Foundation funds twice yearly in the summer and winter. Both applications are available on the website.
Requirements: The grant application is available on the Foundation website, and must be sent electronically. Ten complete proposal packages are then mailed to the Foundation and must include: a completed, computer-generated application (typed or handwritten applications cannot be accepted); copy of the 501(c)3 IRS determination letter; the organization's most recent financial statements; current budget reflecting year-to-date income and expenses; purchase estimates and/or project bids, if applicable; phone number where contact person can be reached; requested signatures; completed Counterterrorism Compliance form; and an explanation of why any of the above is not included.
Restrictions: The Foundation will not normally consider grants for the following purposes: individuals other than scholarships; organizations for religious or sectarian purposes; make-up of operating deficits, post-event or after-the-fact situations; endowment campaigns; or for any propaganda, political or otherwise, attempting to influence legislation or intervene in any political affairs or campaigns. The Foundation is reluctant to approve grants for the purpose of maintaining an on-going operating budget or for multi-year grants requests. However, exceptions to this may be made at the discretion of the Foundation.
Geographic Focus: Indiana

Date(s) Application is Due: Jan 6; Jul 6
Amount of Grant: 1,000 - 25,000 USD
Samples: Jay Community Center, purchase of equipment for senior citizen fitness classes, $2,000; Dunkirk Beautification Committee, underwrite three concerts in the Webster Park Depot Concert Series, $1,450; Jay County 4th of July Committee, operating support of the 4th of July celebration activities, $4,500.
Contact: Douglas Inman, Executive Director; (260) 726-4260; fax (260) 726-4273; tpf@portlandfoundation.org
Internet: http://www.portlandfoundation.org/winter-grants-scholarships
Sponsor: Portland Foundation
112 East Main Street
Portland, IN 47371

Powell Family Foundation Grants   1537
The foundation awards grants to nonprofits in the Kansas City area for support of programs in the areas of environment, civic affairs, and youth. Types of support include general operating support, continuing support, annual campaigns, capital campaigns, equipment acquisition, and program/project development. There are no application forms. Letters of intent must be received 30 days preceding board meetings. The foundation prefers written inquiries and will send guidelines if the project meets foundation criteria.
Requirements: Nonprofits in, or serving the residents of, Missouri are eligible.
Restrictions: The foundation does not support welfare or social services programs.
Geographic Focus: Missouri
Amount of Grant: 2,500 - 25,000 USD
Contact: George Powell, Jr., President; (913) 236-0003; fax (913) 262-0058
Sponsor: Powell Family Foundation
4350 Shawnee Mission Parkway, Suite 280
Fairway, KS 66205-2528

Powell Foundation Grants   1538
The purpose of the Powell Foundation is to distribute funds for public charitable purposes, principally for the support, encouragement and assistance to education, health, conservation, and the arts with a direct impact within the Foundation's geographic zone of interest The Foundation places priority on organizations and programs that serve residents in Harris, Travis and Walker counties, Texas, principally in the fields of education, the arts, health and conservation. The Foundation's current emphasis is in the field of public education in the broadest sense. Other areas of interest continue to be community service projects focused on the needs of children, the disadvantaged, the urban environment, and the visual and performing arts, especially in the Greater Houston, Texas area. The Foundation operates on a calendar year and its Board meets twice a year in the spring and in the fall. Submission of proposals is required at least two months prior to a meeting for consideration at that meeting. To allow for optimum consideration and due diligence, those seeking grants are encouraged to apply to the foundation on an ongoing basis. Grants that do not make the deadline for one meeting will be carried forward to the next meeting. Each request must be in writing and should be accompanied by the proposal summary and the required list of attachments. See the foundation's website for additional guidelines.
Requirements: Texas IRS 501(c)3 tax-exempt organizations serving Harris, Walker, and Travis counties are eligible to apply.
Restrictions: Normally, the Foundation will not support: requests for building funds or grant commitments extending into successive calendar years; grants to religious organizations for religious purposes; fund raising events or advertising; grants to other private foundations; grants to cover past operating deficits or debt retirement; grants for support to individuals; grants that impose the exercise of responsibility upon the Foundation. For example: private operating foundations or certain supporting organizations.
Geographic Focus: Texas
Amount of Grant: 1,000 - 20,000 USD
Samples: Alley Theatre, Houston, Texas - educational outreach support; Travis Audubon Society, Houston, Texas - operational support; Great Expectations Foundation, Tahlequah, Oklahoma - professional development and mentoring for teachers.
Contact: Caroline J. Sabin, Executive Director; (713) 523-7557; fax (713) 523-7553; info@powellfoundation.org
Internet: http://www.powellfoundation.org/powellguide.htm
Sponsor: Powell Foundation of Houston
2121 San Felipe, Suite 110
Houston, TX 77019-5600

Powell Foundation Grants   1539
Established in Tennessee in 2000, the Powell Foundation's primary fields of interest include boy scouts, children and youth programs, Christian agencies and churches, health care, higher education, housing, and volunteer services. There are no specific application formats or deadlines with which to adhere, and applicants should submit a detailed description of their project, along with the amount of funding requested. The average range of funding is $7,500 to $25,000.
Geographic Focus: Tennessee
Amount of Grant: 7,500 - 25,000 USD
Samples: University of Tennessee, Knoxville, Tennessee, $7,500 - support of the veterinary school; East Tennessee State University Foundation, Johnson City, Tennessee, $24,000 - Powell Choral Music Scholars Endowment; Story Telling Association, Johnson City, Tennessee, $20,000 - gift to the local Story Telling Association.
Contact: James J. Powell, Chairperson; (423) 282-0111; fax (423) 282-1541
Sponsor: Powell Foundation of Tennessee
3622 Bristol Highway
Johnson City, TN 37601-1324

PPG Industries Foundation Grants   1540
Funding requests for a variety of project proposals that advance the foundation's interests are eligible for consideration. These may include capital projects, operating grants and special projects. In general, the foundation gives priority to applications from organizations dedicated to enhancing the welfare of communities in which PPG is a resident. Each grant application is reviewed with regard to the: compatibility of the applicant's goals with the foundation's priorities and available resources; financial needs of the organization; past practices of the foundation with respect to that organization; capability and reputation of the applicant; funds available to the applicant from other sources; extent to which the work of the applicant duplicates that of other organizations; public scope and impact of the applicant's proposal; and the interest of other corporate foundations with respect to the applicant. Historically the foundation has supported nonprofits in the areas of human services, health and safety, civic and community affairs, education, and cultural and arts. Requests for funding are accepted year-round. Determinations are made by the foundation's screening committee and board of directors.
Requirements: Applicants must use PPG's online grant making system to apply. The link is on the website. PPG Industries Foundation will review applications on a regular basis and will contact all grantseekers with proposals of interest. Organizations located in the Pittsburgh area and organizations of national scope should direct any questions to the executive director of the foundation. Organizations serving communities where PPG facilities are located should direct any questions to the local PPG Industries Foundation agent in their area. A list of these may be found at the PPG Foundation website under the Foundation Governance link.
Restrictions: The foundation will not award grants for: advertising or sponsorships; endowments; political or religious purposes; projects which would directly benefit PPG Industries, Inc; or special events and telephone solicitations. Operating grants are not made to United Way agencies.
Geographic Focus: All States, Pennsylvania
Samples: YMCA of Metropolitan Milwaukee, South Shore Center, Milwaukee, Wisconsin, $3,000 - funding supports SPLASH swimming program for second-graders; Carlisle Regional Performing Arts Center, location unspecified, $3,000 - funding supports maintenance, technology upgrade costs; Robert Morris University, Moon Township, Pennsylvania, $350,000 - funding supports renovation of the Career and Leadership Development Center.
Contact: Sue Sloan; (412) 434-2453; fax (412) 434-4666; foundation@ppg.com
Internet: http://www.ppg.com/en/ppgfoundation/Pages/Grant_Policies.aspx
Sponsor: PPG Industries Foundation
One PPG Place
Pittsburgh, PA 15272

Price Chopper's Golub Foundation Grants   1541
Price Chopper's Golub Foundation provides financial support to eligible charitable organizations with a current 501(c)3 tax exempt status. Contributions are made through planned, continued giving programs in the areas of health and human services, arts, culture, education, and youth activities, within Price Chopper marketing areas. To be considered for funding, mail a written request, on letterhead for the organization seeking the donation, six to eight weeks prior to needed support or response deadlines. The Foundation reviews capital campaign requests quarterly, so please allow three to four months for a response.
Requirements: The Foundation's six state marketing area includes a specific mile radius around its stores in New York (Albany, Broome, Cayuga, Chenango, Clinton, Columbia, Cortland, Delaware, Dutchess, Essex, Franklin, Fulton, Greene, Hamilton, Herkimer, Jefferson, Lewis, Madison, Montgomery,

Oneida, Onondaga, Orange, Oswego, Otsego, Rensselaer, St. Lawrence, Saratoga, Schenectady, Schoharie, Sullivan, Tioga, Tompkins, Ulster, Warren, and Washington counties), Massachusetts (Berkshire, Hampden, Hampshire, Middlesex, and Worcester counties), Vermont (Addison, Bennington, Caledonia, Chittenden, Essex, Franklin, Grand Isle, Lamoille, Orange, Orleans, Rutland, Washington, Windham, and Windsor counties), Pennsylvania (Lackawanna, Luzerne, Pike, Susquehanna, Wayne, and Wyoming counties), Connecticut (Hartford, Litchfield, New Haven, Tolland, and Windham counties) and New Hampshire (Cheshire, Grafton, and Sullivan counties).

Restrictions: The Foundation does not support: individuals; annual meetings; endowments; film and video projects; program advertising; funding for travel; organizations or events outside of its marketing area; events to raise funds for groups outside of its local community; conferences, conventions, or symposiums; publishing; operating expenses; scholarship programs outside of its own; or capital campaigns of national, religious or political organizations.

Geographic Focus: Connecticut, Massachusetts, New Hampshire, New York, Pennsylvania, Vermont

Contact: Deborah Tanski; (518) 356-9450 or (518) 379-1270; fax (518) 374-4259

Internet: http://www.pricechopper.com/GolubFoundation/GolubFoundation_S.las

Sponsor: Price Chopper's Golub Foundation

P.O. Box 1074

Schenectady, NY 12301

Price Family Charitable Fund Grants   1542

Established in 1983, the Price Family Charitable Fund serves the San Diego, Carlsbad and, San Marcos, California region. The foundation is interested in supporting the economically disadvantaged, giving primarily for education and philanthropy purposes. The types of support include: annual campaigns; fellowships; program evaluation; scholarship funds; scholarships to individuals and; general operating support. There's no formal application to submit. Potential grantees much first submit a letter of Inquiry including: project goals, objectives and expected results (maximum of one page); project narrative (maximum of five pages); project budget (maximum of one page); a list of grants, if any, received by organization in the last 12 months for this program/project (sources and amounts); a list of the organization's current board of directors, including each member's name, profession, and office help on the board, if any.

Requirements: Non-profit organizations with 501(c)3 status or governmental units such as public schools or city departments in are available for funding. The Foundation gives primarily in the following region of: San Diego; Carlsbad; San Marcos, California.

Restrictions: Grants are not made: to organizations whose primary purpose is religious, or for propagandizing, influencing legislation and/or elections, promoting voting registration, for political candidates, political campaigns or organizations engaged in political activities; or to federal appeals or to organizations the collect funds for redistribution to other non-profit groups. Unsolicited requests for funds are not accepted.

Geographic Focus: California

Samples: George G. Glenner Alzheimer's Family Centers, Inc., San Diego, CA, $33,000—Dementia Care Training & Public Scholarships; Episcopal Community Services, San Diego, CA, $60,000—general support; A Reason to Survive, San Diego, CA, $100,000—capacity building.

Contact: Terry Malavenda, (858) 551-2330

Sponsor: Price Family Charitable Fund

7979 Ivanhoe Avenue, Suite 520

La Jolla, CA 92037-4513

Price Gilbert, Jr. Charitable Fund Grants   1543

The Price Gilbert, Jr. Charitable Fund was established under the will of Price Gilbert, Jr. in 1973. During his life, Gilbert made bequests to the Georgia Tech Foundation with preference for the Price Gilbert Memorial Library, the Atlanta Speech School, the University of Georgia Foundation for the Gilbert Infirmary, and Northside Methodist Church. The remainder of his estate funded the Price Gilbert, Jr. Charitable Fund. Wells Fargo Bank serves as Trustee to a portion of this successor fund. The purpose of the Price Gilbert, Jr. Charitable Fund is to distribute to such charitable and/or educational institutions in the Atlanta area as selected by said Trustee as are recognized by the Internal Revenue Service.

Requirements: All grants are made to qualified 501(c)3 organizations in the Atlanta area, taking into consideration the charitable intent of Mr. Gilbert. Consideration will be given to the Georgia Tech Foundation and the Atlanta Speech School in grantmaking decisions. Proposals should be submitted in the following format: completed Common Grant Application Form; an original Proposal Statement; an audited financial report and a current year operating

budget; a copy of your official IRS Letter with your tax determination; a listing of your Board of Directors. Proposal Statements (second item in the above Format) should answer these questions: what are the objectives and expected outcomes of this program/project/request; what strategies will be used to accomplish your objective; what is the timeline for completion; if this is part of an on-going program, how long has it been in operation; what criteria will you use to measure success; if the request is not fully funded, what other sources can you engage; an Itemized budget should be included; please describe any collaborative ventures. Prior to the distribution of funds, all approved grantees must sign and return a Grant Agreement Form, stating that the funds will be used for the purpose intended. Progress reports and Completion reports must also be filed as required for your specific grant. All current grantees must be in good standing with required documentation prior to submitting new proposals to any foundation.

Restrictions: Grants are not made for political purposes, nor to organizations which discriminate on the basis of race, ethnic origin, sexual or religious preference, age or gender.

Geographic Focus: Georgia

Date(s) Application is Due: Aug 1

Amount of Grant: 2,000 - 100,000 USD

Samples: Youth Communication, Metro Atlanta, Inc., $10,000— equipment capital campaign; Metropolitan Atlanta Arts and Culture Coalition, $50,000—arts and culture funding; English for Successful Living, Inc., $2,100—database management system.

Contact: Joyce Yamaato, Wells Fargo Trustee; (888) 234-1999; fax (877) 746-5889; grantadministration@ wellsfargo.com

Internet: https://www.wachovia.com/foundation/v/index.jsp?vgnextoid=13d852199c0aa110VgnVCM1000004b0d1872RCRD&vgnextfmt=default

Sponsor: Price Gilbert, Jr. Charitable Fund

3280 Peachtree Road NE, Suite 400

Atlanta, GA 30305

Priddy Foundation Operating Grants   1544

The Priddy Foundation is a general purpose foundation, interested primarily in programs that have the potential for lasting and favorable impact on individuals and organizations. Considerations for funding include the geographic area served by the project, the individuals and groups served, the problem being addressed, the availability of existing resources and the degree of need. Although the Foundation is wary of fostering annual budget dependency on the part of a grantee agency, its board recognizes that there are circumstances in which a grant for general operating purposes might be critical to an organization's success or viability. Such grants would be for a limited period of time. Among other conditions which might be imposed, based on a specific organization's application, a grantee organization will be required to present a practicable plan to achieve self-sufficiency without additional foundation funding. During the term of the grant the grantee organization might also be required to enter into a formal consulting arrangement with a Center for Non-profit Management, or a similar organization, also with the objective of becoming self-sufficient. Deadlines for preliminary applications are February 1 and August 1, while final applications are due March 1 and September 1.

Requirements: 501(c)3 Texas and Oklahoma nonprofit organizations are eligible. The foundation considers grant applications from organizations in the Wichita Falls, Texas area. In Texas, this includes the following counties: Archer, Baylor, Childress, Clay, Cottle, Foard, Hardeman, Haskell, Jack, King, Knox, Montague, Stonewall, Throckmorton, Wichita, Wilbarger, Wise, and Young. In Oklahoma, it includes the following counties: Comanche, Cotton, Jackson, Jefferson, Stephens, and Tillman.

Restrictions: The Priddy Foundation does not normally make grants for the following purposes: operating deficits; endowments; debt retirement; organizations that make grants to others; charities operated by service clubs; a request for capital funds for a project previously supported; any grant that would tend to obligate the foundation to future funding; fund raising programs and events; grants that impose expenditure responsibility on the foundation; grants to individuals, including individual scholarship awards; start-up funding for new organizations; individual public elementary or secondary schools (K-12); religious institutions except for non-sectarian, human service programs offered on a non-discriminatory basis; basic or applied research; media productions or publications; school trips; conferences or other educational events except through an organizational development grant; or direct grants to volunteer fire departments.

Geographic Focus: Oklahoma, Texas

Date(s) Application is Due: Mar 1; Sep 1

Amount of Grant: 20,000 - 120,000 USD

Samples: Communities In Schools, Wichita Falls, Texas, $120,00 - program operations; Wichita Falls Alliance for the Mentally Ill, Wichita Falls, Texas,

$20,000 - operating support; Wichita-Archer-Clay Christian Womens Job Corps, Wichita Falls, Texas, $30,000 - operating support.
Contact: Debbie C. White, Grants Director; (940) 723-8720; fax (940) 723-8656; debbiecw@priddyfdn.org
Internet: https://priddyfdn.org/policy/
Sponsor: Priddy Foundation
807 Eighth Street, Suite 1010
Wichita Falls, TX 76301-3310

Prince Charitable Trusts Chicago Grants   1545

The trusts awards grants to eligible Chicago nonprofit organizations in its areas of interest: arts and culture, education, environment, health, and social services.
Requirements: The Trusts Chicago program only funds organizations within the city limits of Chicago (with the exception of grants made through the MacArthur Fund for Arts and Culture at Prince). The Trusts make grants only to charitable organizations that are exempt from federal income tax under Section 501(c)3 of the Internal Revenue Code and are classified as public charities under Sections 509(a)(1) or 509(a)(2). All grant applications must include a Prince Charitable Trusts cover sheet, see the Trusts website, http://foundationcenter.org/grantmaker/prince/chi_app.html for proper form and additional guidelines.
Restrictions: The Trusts do not fund projects that promote or proselytize any religion. While the Trusts do fund the projects of faith-based organizations, those projects must be secular in nature. The Trusts do not fund organizations that discriminate on the basis of ethnicity, race, color, creed, religion, gender, national origin, age, disability, marital status, sexual orientation, gender identity, or any veteran's status.
Geographic Focus: Illinois
Date(s) Application is Due: Jan 13; May 1; Jun 1
Contact: Sharon Robison, Grants Manager; (312) 419-8700; fax (312) 419-8558; srobison@prince-trusts.org
Internet: http://www.fdncenter.org/grantmaker/prince/chicago.html
Sponsor: Prince Charitable Trusts
303 West Madison Street, Suite 1900
Chicago, IL 60606

Prince Charitable Trusts District of Columbia Grants   1546

The trusts awards grants to eligible Washington D.C. nonprofit organizations in its areas of interest: arts and culture, community, environment, health, emergency services, youth and provide a limited number of capital grants each year.
Requirements: The Trusts make grants only to charitable organizations that are exempt from federal income tax under Section 501(c)3 of the Internal Revenue Code and are classified as public charities under Sections 509(a)(1) or 509(a)(2). Electronic proposals are preferred. Attachments may be mailed separately. Proposals should include the Prince Charitable Trust Grant Application Cover Sheet and the Common Grant Application Format of Washington Grantmakers. These forms and additional guidelines may be obtained at the Trusts website, http://foundationcenter.org/grantmaker/prince/dc_app.html.
Restrictions: The Trusts do not make grants to individuals, nor does it fund projects that promote or proselytize any religion. While the Trusts do fund the projects of faith-based organizations, those projects must be secular in nature.
Geographic Focus: District of Columbia
Date(s) Application is Due: Feb 1; Aug 10; Sep 1
Amount of Grant: 10,000 - 30,000 USD
Contact: Kristin Pauly, Managing Director; (202) 728-0646; fax (202) 466-4726; kpauly@princetrusts.org
Internet: http://www.fdncenter.org/grantmaker/prince/dc_interest.html
Sponsor: Prince Charitable Trusts
816 Connecticut Avenue NW
Washington, D.C. 20006

Prince Charitable Trusts Rhode Island Grants   1547

The trusts awards grants to eligible Rhode Island nonprofit organizations in its areas of interest: arts and culture, environment and social services. In Rhode Island, the Trusts support programs that improve the quality of life for residents of the city of Newport and Aquidneck Island. Generally, the Trusts only support programs that are regional or statewide when these programs have a direct or indirect impact on Newport or Aquidneck Island.
Requirements: The Trusts make grants only to charitable organizations that are exempt from federal income tax under Section 501(c)3 of the Internal Revenue Code and are classified as public charities under Sections 509(a)(1) or 509(a)(2). All grant applications must include a Prince Charitable Trusts cover sheet, see the Trusts website, http://foundationcenter.org/grantmaker/prince/ri_app.html for proper form and additional guidelines.

Restrictions: The Trusts do not fund organizations that discriminate on the basis of ethnicity, race, color, creed, religion, gender, national origin, age, disability, marital status, sexual orientation, gender identity, or any veteran's status. The Trusts do not fund projects that promote or proselytize any religion. While the Trusts do fund the projects of faith-based organizations, those projects must be secular in nature. The Trusts also do not make grants to individuals.
Geographic Focus: Rhode Island
Date(s) Application is Due: Jun 1
Contact: Sharon Robison, Grants Manager; (312) 419-8700; fax (312) 419-8558; srobison@prince-trusts.org
Internet: http://fdncenter.org/grantmaker/prince/ri.html
Sponsor: Prince Charitable Trusts
303 West Madison Street, Suite 1900
Chicago, IL 60606

Principal Financial Group Foundation Grants   1548

The foundation addresses concerns in the areas of health and human services, education, arts and culture, environment, and recreation and tourism. The primary objective is to support, through charitable contributions, selected nonprofit organizations primarily located in the greater Des Moines, IA, area. The foundation also will consider requests from organizations located in areas where the corporation has offices, including Des Moines, Mason City and Cedar Falls, IA; Grand Island, NE; Spokane, WA; Wilmington, DE; Appleton, WI; and Phoenix, AZ. The objectives, priorities, and programs seek to reflect the needs and concerns of communities in which the corporation operates. Support is given for annual campaigns, building funds, capital campaigns, continuing support, employee matching gifts, in-kind gifts, performances and exhibitions, conferences and workshops, adult basic education, vocational programs, operating budgets, internships, demonstration grants, matching grants, and seed grants. Contribution requests are considered on a quarterly basis, in accordance with the following schedule: health and human services, March 1; education, June 1; arts and culture, September 1; and environment, recreation, and tourism, December 1.
Requirements: 501(c)3 tax-exempt organizations in company operating locations may apply.
Restrictions: Proposals for athletic groups, conferences, endowments, fellowships, festivals, fraternal organizations, health care facility fund drives, libraries, or religious groups are denied.
Geographic Focus: Delaware, Iowa, Nebraska, Washington
Date(s) Application is Due: Mar 1; Jun 1; Sep 1; Dec 1
Amount of Grant: 1,000 - 50,000 USD
Contact: Laura Sauser; (515) 247-7227; fax (515) 246-5475
Internet: http://www.principal.com/about/giving/grant.htm
Sponsor: Principal Financial Group Foundation
711 High Street
Des Moines, IA 50392-0150

Procter and Gamble Fund Grants   1549

The fund supports nonprofit organizations in company-operating locations in the areas of education, health and social services, civic projects, cultural organizations, disaster relief, and environmental efforts. Grants are awarded to education initiatives in local communities, such as teacher training efforts, with a focus on economic teaching; and other efforts by public policy, research, and economic education organizations. Employee voluntarism is prevalent in many K-12 initiatives. Most health and human services funding supports the United Way. The Salvation Army, Red Cross, hospitals, food banks, and other social service organizations receive support. Community support is awarded through grants that bolster economic growth and enrichment, including support for a youth jobs program, libraries, zoos, and local chambers of commerce. Support is awarded to a variety of arts organizations, including theater, dance, music, and visual arts. Major environmental groups also receive support. Grant Application Cycles are July 1 through September 30 and December 1 through February 28, grant requests are only accepted during those times.
Requirements: 501(c)3 organizations in communities where Procter and Gamble Company manufacturing plants are located are eligible.
Geographic Focus: All States
Amount of Grant: Up to 25,000,000 USD
Contact: Brenda Ratliff; (513) 945-8454; pgfund.im@pg.com
Internet: http://www.pg.com/company/our_commitment/grant_application_guidelines.shtml
Sponsor: Procter and Gamble Fund
P.O. Box 599
Cincinnati, OH 45201

Prospect Hill Foundation Grants 1550

The foundation's national giving focuses on environmental conservation, especially in the Northeast and in Latin America; nuclear weapons control; and population growth/control in relation to natural resources, food supply, and opportunity to live a quality life. Types of support include matching funds, operating budgets, seed grants, and projects/programs. Preference goes to proposals for projects rather than for general support. Grant requests may be submitted year-round. Information and guidelines are available online.

Requirements: Giving is primarily in the northeastern United States, including New York and Rhode Island. Social service grants are limited to New York groups.

Restrictions: The foundation does not consider grants to individuals nor for basic research, sectarian religious activities, or organizations that lack tax exemption under United States law.

Geographic Focus: All States

Amount of Grant: 10,000 - 25,000 USD

Samples: Bulletin of the Atomic Scientists (Chicago, IL)—to enhance coverage of international and security issues in the Bulletin of the Atomic Scientists, $15,000; San Miguel-CASA (Guanajuato, Mexico)—toward the Professional Midwifery School, $35,000; Cunningham Dance Foundation (New York, NY)—for general support, $25,000; Fifth Avenue Presbyterian Church (New York, NY)—toward the capital campaign, $50,000.

Contact: Laura Callanan; (212) 370-1165; fax (212) 599-6282

Internet: http://fdncenter.org/grantmaker/prospecthill

Sponsor: Prospect Hill Foundation

99 Park Avenue, Suite 2220

New York, NY 10016-1601

Proteus Fund Grants 1551

Proteus Fund is a foundation committed to advancing justice through democracy, human rights and peace. Proteus Fund collaborative grant making initiatives work on some of the most cutting edge issues of our time. Each initiative is uniquely structured and focused to achieve the goals of its funding partners and led by experienced program staff. Proteus Fund works to connect this work to other social movements and resources while providing a full compliment of services to support the work, including partnership development, marketing, grants and financial management and administrative support.

Geographic Focus: All States

Contact: Beery Adams Jimenez; (413) 256-0349; info@proteusfund.org

Internet: http://www.proteusfund.org/initiatives

Sponsor: Proteus Fund

101 University Drive, Suite A2

Amherst, MA 01002

Prudential Foundation Arts and Culture Grants 1552

The Prudential Foundation's areas of interest are ready-to-learn programs, ready-to-work programs, and ready-to-live programs. In order to promote sustainable communities and improve social outcomes for community residents, the Foundation focuses its strategy in the following Arts and Culture areas: arts as an economic engine and as a quality-of-life issue to ensure that residents have access to quality arts programs; and capacity building activities for nonprofit organizations to ensure their sustainability and growth. Types of support include operating support, continuing support, annual campaigns, seed money, matching funds and employee matching gifts, consulting services, technical assistance, employee-related scholarships, research, capital campaigns, conferences and seminars, and projects/programs. Results the Foundation seeks from their investments include: successful contributions by arts and culture organizations to the economic development and vitality of the community they serve; increased quality and diversity of artistic creations that reflect emerging ethnic and historically underserved populations; and underserved community members that increase their participation or experiences of the arts. Funds are targeted to areas where Prudential has a strong presence. Applicant should make initial contact with a brief letter to determine whether a more detailed proposal would be acceptable.

Requirements: The Prudential Foundation supports nonprofit, charitable organizations, and programs whose mission and operations are broad and non-discriminatory. The Foundation focuses its resources to support organizations whose activities address social needs or benefit underserved groups and communities. The Foundation funds programs in Newark, New Jersey; Hartford, Connecticut; Los Angeles, California; Chicago, Illinois; Phoenix, Arizona; Jacksonville, Florida; Dubuque, Iowa; Minneapolis, Minnesota; Philadelphia and Scranton, Pennsylvania; and Houston and Dallas, Texas.

Restrictions: The Foundation does not fund organizations that are not tax-exempt under paragraph 501(c)3 of the U.S. Internal Revenue Code; labor, religious,

political, lobbying, or fraternal groups—except when these groups provide needed services to the community at large; direct grants or scholarships to individuals; support for single-disease health groups; or good will advertising.

Geographic Focus: Arizona, California, Connecticut, Florida, Georgia, Illinois, Iowa, Minnesota, New Jersey, New York, Pennsylvania, Texas

Amount of Grant: Up to 1,000,000 USD

Contact: Lata Reddy, Director of Programs and Operations; (973) 802-4791; community.resources@prudential.com

Internet: http://www.prudential.com/view/page/public/12373

Sponsor: Prudential Foundation

751 Broad Street, 15th Floor

Newark, NJ 07102-3777

Prudential Foundation Economic Development Grants 1553

The Prudential Foundation's areas of interest are ready-to-learn programs, ready-to-work programs, and ready-to-live programs. In order to promote sustainable communities and improve social outcomes for community residents, the Foundation focuses its strategy in the following economic development areas: workforce development programs to train and place individuals in high-demand occupations; business development opportunities to create and grow businesses; and community revitalization initiatives to strengthen community development corporations (CDCs). Types of support include operating support, continuing support, annual campaigns, seed money, matching funds and employee matching gifts, consulting services, technical assistance, employee-related scholarships, research, capital campaigns, conferences and seminars, and projects/programs. The Foundation is especially interested in proposals that anticipate and address potential major problems. Funds are targeted to areas where Prudential has a strong presence. Applicant should make initial contact with a brief letter to determine whether a more detailed proposal would be acceptable.

Requirements: The Prudential Foundation supports nonprofit, charitable organizations, and programs whose mission and operations are broad and non-discriminatory. The Foundation focuses its resources to support organizations whose activities address social needs or benefit underserved groups and communities. Funding locations include Newark, New Jersey, and surrounding communities; Los Angeles, California; Jacksonville, Florida; Chicago, Illinois; Dubuque, Iowa; Phoenix, Arizona; New York, New York; Minneapolis, Minnesota; Philadelphia and Scranton, Pennsylvania; New Orleans, Louisiana; Houston and Dallas, Texas. Third priority are national programs that can be implemented or replicated in the above cities.

Restrictions: The Foundation does not fund: organizations that are not tax-exempt under paragraph 501(c)3 of the U.S. Internal Revenue Code; labor, religious, political, lobbying, or fraternal groups—except when these groups provide needed services to the community at large; direct grants or scholarships to individuals; support for single-disease health groups; or good will advertising.

Geographic Focus: Arizona, California, Connecticut, Florida, Georgia, Iowa, Louisiana, Minnesota, New Jersey, New York, Pennsylvania, Texas

Amount of Grant: Up to 1,000,000 USD

Contact: Lata Reddy, Director of Programs and Operations; (973) 802-4791; community.resources@prudential.com

Internet: http://www.prudential.com/view/page/public/12373

Sponsor: Prudential Foundation

751 Broad Street, 15th Floor

Newark, NJ 07102-3777

Prudential Foundation Education Grants 1554

The Prudential Foundation's areas of interest are ready-to-learn programs, ready-to-work programs, and ready-to-live programs. In order to promote sustainable communities and improve social outcomes for community residents, the Foundation focuses its strategy in the following educational areas: education leadership to support reform in public education by increasing the capacity of educators, parents, and community residents to implement public school reform; and youth development to build skills and competencies needed for young people to be productive citizens (this includes expanding arts education opportunities and supporting effective out-of-school-time programs for young people). Finally, the Foundation also funds organizations whose efforts influence policy that adapts promising practices and evidence-based approaches to instruction and learning in schools. Types of support include operating support, continuing support, annual campaigns, seed money, matching funds and employee matching gifts, consulting services, technical assistance, employee-related scholarships, research, capital campaigns, conferences and seminars, and projects/programs. The Foundation is especially interested in proposals that anticipate and address potential major problems. Funds are targeted to areas where Prudential has a strong presence. Applicant should make initial contact with a brief letter to determine whether a more detailed proposal would be acceptable.

Requirements: The Prudential Foundation supports nonprofit, charitable organizations, and programs whose mission and operations are broad and non-discriminatory. The Foundation focuses its resources to support organizations whose activities address social needs or benefit underserved groups and communities. Priority in order of preference goes to programs in Newark, New Jersey, and surrounding communities; Los Angeles, California; Hartford, Connecticut; New York, New York; Chicago, Illinois; Jacksonville, Florida; Atlanta, Georgia; Minneapolis, Minnesota; Philadelphia and Scranton, Pennsylvania; Houston and Dallas, Texas; Dubuque, Iowa; Phoenix, Arizona; and New Orleans, Louisiana.

Restrictions: The Foundation does not fund: organizations that are not tax-exempt under paragraph 501(c)3 of the U.S. Internal Revenue Code; labor, religious, political, lobbying, or fraternal groups—except when these groups provide needed services to the community at large; direct grants or scholarships to individuals; support for single-disease health groups; or good will advertising.

Geographic Focus: Arizona, California, Connecticut, Florida, Georgia, Illinois, Iowa, Louisiana, Minnesota, New Jersey, New York, Pennsylvania, Texas

Amount of Grant: Up to 1,000,000 USD

Contact: Lata Reddy, Director of Programs and Operations; (973) 802-4791; community.resources@prudential.com

Internet: http://www.prudential.com/view/page/public/12373

Sponsor: Prudential Foundation

751 Broad Street, 15th Floor

Newark, NJ 07102-3777

Public Welfare Foundation Grants 1555

Grants are awarded primarily to grassroots organizations in the United States and abroad, with emphasis on the environment, disadvantaged elderly and youth, population and reproductive health, economic development, welfare reform, health, human rights and global security, criminal justice, and community development. Programs must serve low-income populations, with preference to short-term needs. Types of support include matching funds, operating budgets, seed money, continuing support, and special projects. Grant guidelines are available upon request. Proposal with cover letter should be addressed to the Steering Committee at the address listed.

Requirements: Nonprofit organizations and, in certain cases, organizations without 501(c)3 status, may apply for grant support. Eligible exceptions are listed in the guidelines (available upon request).

Restrictions: Grants will not be made to individuals or for religious purposes, building funds, capital improvements, endowments, scholarships, graduate work, foreign study, conferences, seminars, publications, research, workshops, consulting services, annual campaigns, or deficit financing.

Geographic Focus: All States

Amount of Grant: 25,000 - 50,000 USD

Samples: Fair Housing Agency of Alabama (Mobile, AL)—to provide temporary and long-term housing and other support to people in Mobile, AL, left homeless by Hurricane Katrina, $10,000; Louisiana Bucket Brigade (Baton Rouge, LA)—to train people to monitor environmental pollution in their neighborhoods, $25,000; Share Foundation (San Francisco, CA)—to provide relief and support for reconstruction efforts in El Salvador following Hurricane Stan, $25,000; Environmental Support Ctr (Washington, DC)—to provide small grants to environmental justice groups in the Gulf Coast region that are struggling to reestablish their programs in the wake of recent hurricanes, $75,000.

Contact: Grants Administrator; (202) 965-1800; fax (202) 265-8851; reviewcommittee@publicwelfare.org

Internet: http://www.publicwelfare.org/about/about.asp

Sponsor: Public Welfare Foundation

1200 U Street NW

Washington, D.C. 20009

Puerto Rico Community Foundation Grants 1556

The Foundation wishes to develop the capacities of communities in Puerto Rico so that they may achieve social transformation and economic self-sufficiency, by stimulating investment in communities and maximizing the impact and yield of each contribution. Grants are awarded in the areas of: education; community development; financial development; development of social interest housing; and philanthropy. Types of support include: general operating support; emergency funds; conferences and seminars; professorships; publications; research; technical assistance; consulting services; and matching funds. There are no application deadlines; the board meets in March, June, September, and December to consider requests.

Requirements: Organizations applying for grants must comply with the conditions below in order to demonstrate eligibility: be duly incorporated and registered as a nonprofit organization, according to the laws of the Commonwealth of Puerto Rico; be located and offer services in Puerto Rico. Present a copy of the following documents: certificate of good standing from the State Department; certificate from the Treasury Department; statement of organization's total budget for the year for which funds are solicited; financial statements; list of current members of Board of Directors. Should include each member's address and phone number; resume or curriculum vitae of the Project Director.

Restrictions: The foundation does not make grants to support individuals, annual campaigns, seed money, endowments, deficit financing, scholarships, or building funds.

Geographic Focus: Puerto Rico

Amount of Grant: 1,000 - 40,000 USD

Contact: Administrator; (787) 721-1037; fax (787) 721-1673; fcpr@fcpr.org

Internet: http://www.fcpr.org/

Sponsor: Puerto Rico Community Foundation

P.O. Box 70362

San Juan, PR 00936-8362

Puerto Rico

Pulido Walker Foundation 1557

Established in 1996, the Pulido Walker Foundation offers grant support throughout California and South Carolina (though awards are occasionally given in other states). Its primary fields of interest include: the arts; general education; health and health care organizations; higher education; and a variety of human services. Typically, awards are given for general operating support. A formal application should be secured from the Foundation office, though no annual application deadlines have been identified. Most recent grants have ranged from $100 to $10,000.

Requirements: 501(c)3 organizations either located in, or serving residents of, California and South Carolina are eligible to apply.

Geographic Focus: California, South Carolina

Amount of Grant: 100 - 10,000 USD

Samples: American Diabetes Association, San Diego, California, $1,000 - general operating support; Classics for Kids Foundation, Holliston, Massachusetts, $10,000 - general operating support; Ranch Santa Fe, California, $1,000 - general operating support.

Contact: Donna J. Walker, President; (858) 756-6150 or (858) 558-9200

Sponsor: Pulido Walker Foundation

P.O. Box 1334

Rancho Santa Fe, CA 92067-1334

Putnam County Community Foundation Grants 1558

The Putnam County Community Foundation is a nonprofit public charity established to administer funds, award grants and provide leadership, enriching the quality of life and strengthening community in Putnam County. The Foundation makes grants to qualified non-profit organizations seeking to make a difference in Putnam County and its residents. Grants are made in the following areas: animal welfare; arts and culture; civic and community; economic development; education; environment; health and human services; recreation; and youth. The application and samples of previously funded grants are available at the website.

Requirements: To be considered for funding, organizations must first submit a preliminary grant application form. The Grants Committee will review all preliminary applications to determine who will be invited to submit a full grant application.

Restrictions: Funding is not allowed for the following: individuals; ongoing operational expenses, i.e. salaries, rent, and utilities; projects that do not serve Putnam County citizens; projects normally fully funded by units of government; programs to build or fund an endowment; religious activities or programs that appear to serve one denomination and not the community at large; political organizations or campaigns; national and state-wide fund raising projects; for-profit companies; or projects requesting retroactive funding.

Geographic Focus: Indiana

Date(s) Application is Due: Feb 1; Mar 9; Aug 1; Sep 9

Contact: M. Elaine Peck, Executive Director; (765) 653-4978; fax (765) 653-6385; epeck@pcfoundation.org or info@pcfoundation.org

Internet: http://www.pcfoundation.org/grant_what_we_fund.html

Sponsor: Putnam County Community Foundation

2 South Jackson Street, P.O. Box 514

Greencastle, IN 46135

Putnam Foundation Grants 1559

The foundation, established in 1952, awards grants to eligible New Hampshire nonprofit organizations in its areas of interest, including civic and public affairs, cultural programs, ecology and environmental protection, education, historic preservation, public affairs and government, and youth programs. Types of support include capital campaigns (including endowments), general operating grants, and project grants. There are no application deadlines or forms.

Requirements: New Hampshire nonprofit organizations serving the Monadnock region are eligible.

Geographic Focus: New Hampshire

Amount of Grant: 30,000 - 500,000 USD

Samples: Keene State College, Keene, NH, $500,000—for distinguished chair in chemistry; Historic Harrisville, Harrisville, NH, $100,000—for second of three payment pledge; Apple Hill Center for Chamber Music, Sullivan, NH, $50,000—for grant to support a Playing for Peace tour.

Contact: Rosamond P. Delori; (603) 352-2448; fax (603) 355-9954

Sponsor: Putnam Foundation

20 Central Square, 2nd Floor, P.O. Box 323

Keene, NH 03431-0323

Quixote Foundation Grants 1560

The foundation awards grants in its areas of interest, including restoring democracy in the United States through voter engagement and voter-verified paper ballots; safeguarding the world's natural environment through science, conservation, and advocacy; promoting sustainable energy use and technologies; and protecting civil liberties and reproductive rights in the United States. Support takes the form of operating and program grants, technical assistance, research, convening, and activism. Grants do not support endowment or capital purposes. Proposals are by invitation only. Currently letters of inquiry are accepted in the following areas: developing effective message strategies to safeguard the world's natural environment and reforming media coverage and promoting public awareness of economic inequality. Unless you are a current grant recipient, please do not telephone or email the foundation with project briefings or requests for meetings. Guidelines are available online.

Restrictions: Letters of request may not be submitted before November 15.

Geographic Focus: All States

Contact: Program Contact; (206) 783-5554; fax (206) 783-1815; lenore@quixotefoundation.org

Internet: http://www.iinet.com/~quixoteman/index.htm

Sponsor: Quixote Foundation

5703 20th Avenue NW

Seattle, WA 98107

R.C. Baker Foundation Grants 1561

The foundation makes grants to U.S. nonprofit organizations for projects and programs that support social services for youth and the elderly, crime prevention, education, religion (Christian, Episcopal, Friends, Jewish, Methodist, and Presbyterian), scientific research, culture, and health. Support will be provided for fellowships and scholarships, general operating grants, challenge/matching grants, emergency funds, building funds, equipment, continuing support, annual campaigns, capital campaigns, renovation projects, and special projects. Submit cover letter with proposal. The board meets in June and November to consider requests.

Requirements: Nonprofit organizations are eligible. $25,000 to

Restrictions: Anaheim Memorial Medical Center, Anaheim, CA - $40,000; Harvey Mudd College, Claremont, CA - $25,000;

Date(s) Application is Due: May 1; Oct 1

Amount of Grant: 1,000 - 280,000 USD

Samples: Anaheim Memorial Medical Center, Anaheim, CA - $40,000; Harvey Mudd College, Claremont, CA - $25,000;

Contact: Frank Scott, Chairman; (714) 750-8987

Sponsor: R.C. Baker Foundation

P.O. Box 6150

Orange, CA 92863-6150

R.T. Vanderbilt Trust Grants 1562

The trust awards grants in its areas of interest, including the arts, education, environmental programs, health care, historic preservation and societies, hospitals, and human services. Types of support include building construction/renovation, endowments, general operating support, and program development. The board meets in April, June, September, and December.

Requirements: There are no applications to submit. Proposals should be submitted in writing.

Restrictions: Applications are not accepted. Gives primarily to Connecticut, with some giving in Maine and New York. The trust does not give grants to individuals.

Geographic Focus: Connecticut, Maine, New York

Amount of Grant: Up to USD

Samples: The Historical Society of the Town of Greenwich, Cos Cob, Connecticut - $70,000; Music for Youth, Westport, Connecticut - $20,000; Metropolitan Museum of Art, New York, New York - $15,000

Contact: Gloria Kallas; (908) 598-3582; fax (336) 732-2024/(336) 747-8722

Sponsor: R.T. Vanderbilt Trust

1525 West WT Harris Boulevard

Charlotte, NC 28288-5709

RadioShack StreetSentz Community Grants 1563

The grant program is designed to offer answers—answers that bring community impact through programs or projects conducted by local nonprofit organizations. The program currently focuses on two areas: prevention of family violence/abuse, and/or child abduction. Guidelines are available online.

Requirements: 501(c)3 tax-exempt organizations and municipalities, including local police departments, are eligible. Applicant organization must offer solutions to help prevent family violence/abuse and/or child abduction; and directly impact or benefit, through programs and/or services, a RadioShack community.

Restrictions: Grants cannot be considered for individuals; endowments or private foundations that are themselves grant-making organizations; construction or major renovation projects; to fund advertising or marketing programs; fundraising events and sponsorships (i.e., golf tournaments, dinners, auctions); multiyear grants; religious, political, and fraternal organizations; or trips, sporting events, tours, and transportation.

Geographic Focus: All States

Date(s) Application is Due: Mar 15; Jun 15; Sep 15; Dec 15

Amount of Grant: Up to 500 USD

Contact: Community Relations Manager; (817) 415-3699; fax (817) 415-0939; corporate.citizenship@radioshack.com

Internet: http://www.radioshackcorporation.com/cc/contributions.html

Sponsor: RadioShack Corporation

200 RadioShack Circle, MS CF3-323

Fort Worth, TX 76102-1964

Ralph and Virginia Mullin Foundation Grants 1564

The foundation provides small grants to animal welfare and shelter organizations. The foundation also gives a few gifts annually to organizations that are working to become incorporated and obtain 501(c)3 status. Those grant recipients must use funds for costs directly related to achieving these goals.

Requirements: The foundation currently does not have a website. Contact the sponsor by mail or email for any additional guidelines or questions.

Geographic Focus: All States

Date(s) Application is Due: Sep 30

Amount of Grant: Up to 2,000 USD

Contact: Rob Rauh, (520) 881-6607; fax (520) 881-6775; rob@hrtucson.com

Sponsor: Ralph and Virginia Mullin Foundation

2401 E Speedway Boulevard

Tucson, AZ 85719

Ralphs Food 4 Less Foundation Grants 1565

The foundation supports nonprofits primarily in areas of company operations in southern California, from Santa Barbara to San Diego, for programs and activities to improve the well-being of youth through education, recreation, and health-related programs; expand cultural awareness and appreciation of the arts; strengthen neighborhoods; and assist communities in the aftermath of local disasters. Types of support include special projects and general operating expenses. There are no application deadlines. Applicants should submit a letter of application.

Requirements: To be eligible, your organization must be: a 501(3) tax exempt nonprofit; located in Southern California; working in one of the focus areas. Requests for funding must arrive eight (8) weeks prior to the event date or date of need.

Restrictions: Funding is not available to: individuals; capital campaigns; travel expenses; projects of sectarian or religious organizations whose principal benefit is for their own members or adherents; organizations that discriminate on the basis of sex, race, religion, sexual orientation or national origin; third party giving.

Geographic Focus: California

Samples: Los Angeles Rescue Mission, Los Angeles, CA - $10,000; Community Environmental Council, Santa Barbara, CA - to support its annual Earth Day Festival $1,250; The Museum of Tolerance (MOT), Los Angeles, CA - to fund the MOT's student programs $10,000;

Contact: Michelle Williams; (310) 884-6205 or (310) 900-3522
Internet: http://www.ralphs.com/corpnewsinfo_charitablegiving_art5.htm
Sponsor: Ralph's-Food 4 Less Foundation
P.O. Box 54143
Los Angeles, CA 90054

Raskob Foundation for Catholic Activities Grants   1566
The Raskob Foundation is an independent private Catholic family foundation
that makes grants worldwide for projects and programs associated with the
Catholic Church. Grants support elementary and secondary education,
community action and development, missionary activities, ministries (including
youth and parish), health care, social concerns, AIDS victims, finance and
development, and relief services. Types of support include operating budgets,
seed money, emergency funds, equipment, land acquisition, conferences and
seminars, program-related investments, renovation projects, special projects,
and matching funds. Deadlines are June 8 and August 8 for the fall meeting;
and December 8 and February 8 for the spring meeting.
Requirements: Roman Catholic organizations listed in the Kenedy Directory of Official
Catholic Organizations may apply. Organizations should refer to the application
guidelines for specific instruction on how to apply and information to submit.
Restrictions: The Foundation does not accept applications for the following
purposes: tuition, scholarships or fellowships; reduction of debt; endowment
funds; grants made by other grantmaking organizations; individual scholarly
research; lobbying or legislation; or projects completed prior to our board
meetings (mid-May and late November).
Geographic Focus: All States, All Countries
Amount of Grant: 5,000 - 15,000 USD
Contact: Maureen Horner; (302) 655-4440; fax (302) 655-3223; info@rfca.org
Internet: http://www.rfca.org/en/Grantmaking/tabid/63/Default.aspx
Sponsor: Raskob Foundation for Catholic Activities
P.O. Box 4019
Wilmington, DE 19807

Rathmann Family Foundation Grants   1567
The foundation's main funding areas are education, with priority given to science
and math; the arts; children and youth health organizations; and preservation of
the environment. Types of support include general operating support, continuing
support, capital campaigns, equipment acquisition, endowment funds, program
development, conferences and seminars, seed grants, curriculum development,
fellowships, internships, scholarship funds, research, and matching funds. There
are no specific deadlines or application forms, and interested parties should
begin by contacting the Foundation directly.
Requirements: Grants are awarded to organizations in the San Francisco Bay, California
area; the Annapolis, Maryland area; the Seattle, Washington area; the Philadelphia,
Pennsylvania area: and metropolitan Minneapolis/Saint Paul, Minnesota.
Restrictions: Grants are not awarded to/for private foundations; religious organizations
for religious activities; civil rights; social action; advocacy organizations; fraternal
groups; political purposes; mental health counseling; individuals; or fundraisers,
media events, public relations, annual appeals, or propaganda.
Geographic Focus: California, Maryland, Minnesota, Pennsylvania, Washington
Amount of Grant: 1,000 - 100,000 USD
Contact: Rick Rathmann, (410) 349-2376; fax (410) 349-2377
Sponsor: Rathmann Family Foundation
1290 Bay Dale Drive, P.O. Box 352
Arnold, MD 21012

Rayonier Foundation Grants   1568
The foundation awards grants to eligible nonprofit organizations in its areas of
interest, including children and youth, community development, disadvantaged
(economically), education, engineering, environmental programs, families,
health care and hospitals, libraries, minorities, performing arts, recreation
science, social services, technology, and volunteerism. Types of support include
annual campaigns, building construction/renovation, continuing support,
employee matching gifts, employee-related scholarships, endowments,
equipment acquisition, general operating support, matching/challenge grants,
performing arts, program development, recreation, science, research grants,
scholarship funds, and seed grants.
Requirements: Nonprofits in Florida, Georgia, and Washington are eligible.
Geographic Focus: Florida, Georgia, Washington
Amount of Grant: 250 - 25,000 USD
Samples: United Way of Clallam County, Port Angeles, WA - $4,243; Florida
Community College at Jacksonville Foundation, Jacksonville, FL - $25,000;
University of Virginia, Charlottesville, VA - $7,500;

Contact: Charles H. Hood; (904) 357-9100; info@rayonier.com
Sponsor: Rayonier Foundation
50 North Laura Street, Stuite 1900
Jacksonville, FL 32202

RBC Dain Rauscher Foundation Grants   1569
The foundation awards grants to youth education efforts, social services programs,
and the arts. In youth education, K-12 programs that serve students of color or
disadvantaged children, and programs that help children understand the country's
economic system are funded. The emphasis in social services giving is programs
that foster economic independence and self-sufficiency and that help families.
Types of support include general operating support, continuing support, annual
campaigns, building construction/renovation, seed grants, and matching gifts.
Requirements: Organizations in Arizona, California, Illinois, Iowa, Kansas,
Louisiana, Minnesota, Montana, Nebraska, North Dakota, Oklahoma, Oregon,
South Dakota, Texas, Utah, Washington, and Wyoming are eligible.
Geographic Focus: Arizona, California, Illinois, Iowa, Kansas, Louisiana,
Minnesota, Montana, Nebraska, North Dakota, Oklahoma, Oregon, South
Dakota, Texas, Utah, Washington, Wyoming
Amount of Grant: Up to 20,000 USD
Contact: Sherry Koster, Program Manager; (612) 371-2765 or (612) 371-2936;
fax (612) 371-7933; sherry.koster@rbcdain.com
Internet: http://www.rbcwm-usa.com/DRP_1.0/Public_Site/Common_
Pages/DRP_1.0VSectionIndex/1,73394,4-3-2-0,00.html
Sponsor: RBC Dain Rauscher Foundation
60 South 6th Street, P2
Minneapolis, MN 55402-4422

RCF General Community Grants   1570
Six times a year, the Richland County Foundation awards General
Community Grants to nonprofit organizations through a competitive process.
In doing so, the Foundation looks to partner with nonprofit organizations to
respond to current community needs in the following areas: education; health
services; arts and culture; community services; children, youth and families;
human services; environment; and employment and economic development.
Application deadlines are 5:00 p.m. on the first Friday of January, March,
May, July, September, and November. Applications must be at the Foundation
Office by 5:00 p.m. on the due date to meet the deadline. Final decisions on
all grant applications are made by the Board of Trustees approximately 6 – 8
weeks following the grant deadline.
Requirements: 501(c)3 public charities, government entities, schools, and
nonprofit medical facilities serving residents of Richland County are eligible
to apply. The application procedure should begin with a telephone call to
the Program Officer to schedule an initial meeting to discuss the project.
The Foundation typically looks for several of the following key elements in
submitted applications: a one-time grant, especially for a pilot project which
can serve as a model or be replicated; a project in which the Foundation is
a funding partner, rather than the sole funder; a project or program which
promotes volunteer involvement; an organization which can demonstrate the
ability to sustain the project in the future when Foundation grant dollars
end; projects or programs which are a collaborative effort(s) among nonprofit
organizations in the community which eliminate duplication of services; a
project which is likely to make a clear difference in the quality of life of a
substantial number of people; an organization which is proposing a practical
approach to a solution of a current community problem; a project or program
which is focusing on prevention; and a worthy community project for which
a grant from the Foundation will most likely leverage additional financial
support. Applicants who have a program or project that meets these criteria are
encouraged to contact the Foundation to discuss submitting an application.
Restrictions: Community grants are awarded from endowed, unrestricted and
field of interest funds. Richland County Foundation typically does not provide
funding from unrestricted funds for the following: sectarian activities of religious
organizations; operating expenses for annual drives or to eliminate debt; medical,
scientific or academic research; individuals other than for college scholarships;
travel to or in support of conferences, or travel for groups such as bands, sports
teams and classes (unless through special grant programs such as Summertime Kids
or the Teacher Assistance Program); capital improvements to building and property
not owned by the organization or covered by a long term lease; computer systems;
projects that taxpayers support or expected to support; and political issues.
Geographic Focus: Ohio
Samples: Ashland University, Ashland, Ohio, $250,000 - this grant is part of
a $15.5 million campaign to build a College of Nursing facility in Richland
County; Richland Community Development Group, Mansfield, Ohio,

$50,000 - this supports phase two of a pilot project to coordinate a county-wide collaborative effort for both economic and community development.
Contact: Bradford Groves, President; (419) 525-3020; fax (419) 525-1590; bgroves@rcfoundation.org
Internet: http://www.richlandcountyfoundation.org/grant-information/types-of-grants/community
Sponsor: Richland County Foundation
24 West Third Street, Suite 100
Mansfield, OH 44902-1209

Regional Arts and Cultural Council General Support Grants 1571

RACC supports the region's vital arts and culture community through a variety of grant programs. The General Support Grants Program aims to provide general financial support to arts organizations in Multnomah, Washington, and Clackamas Counties, based on their artistic excellence, proven service to the community, administrative and fiscal competence and RACC grant compliance. The General Support Grants Program seeks to fund arts organizations and provide a wide range of high quality arts programming made available to the public. The General Support application process is bi-annual. General Support grants are for arts organizations with eligible expenses between $80,000 and $500,000.
Requirements: Some of the basic eligibility requirements for General Support are: be an arts organization; have IRS 501(c)3 tax status; have been in existence for a minimum of three years or be the result of merging organizations with at least a three-year history each; have minimum eligible income of $80,000; have at least one paid professional administrative staff; and have continuous administration throughout the year. The General Support Grant program provides financial support to Multnomah, Washington and Clackamas County not-for-profit organizations and individual artists.
Geographic Focus: Oregon
Amount of Grant: 6,000 - 150,000 USD
Contact: Tonisha Toler, Grants & Outreach Coordinator; (503) 823-5866 or (503) 823-5111; fax (503) 823-5432; ttoler@racc.org
Internet: http://www.racc.org/grants/general-support-grants
Sponsor: Regional Arts and Cultural Council
108 NW 9th Avenue, Suite 300
Portland, OR 97209-3318

Regional Arts and Cultural Council Opportunity Grants 1572

The Opportunity Grant Program is funded by the City of Portland and is designed to provide grants to Portland-based nonprofit arts and cultural organizations to help meet special opportunities or assist organizations with emergencies that arise during the year and that are not part of the applicant's annual budget or regular programming. There will be multiple cycles of this grant throughout the fiscal year. It is meant to supplement but not be a substitute for any other existing RACC grant.
Requirements: Portland-based nonprofit arts and culture organizations are eligible to apply for the Opportunity Grant provided that they meet all the following requirements: is a nonprofit arts and culture organization that regularly presents arts and/or cultural events or arts projects; has current tax-exempt status under Section 501(c)3 of the Internal Revenue Service and regularly produces financial statements; is headquartered and has a physical address in the City of Portland; provides arts and culture programs and events that are advertised and open to the public; and is current on all RACC grant agreements and has submitted final reports for all completed RACC grants.
Restrictions: Applicants receiving funds from this program will not be eligible to apply again for a period of 24 months from the date of the final report submission to RACC.
Geographic Focus: Oregon
Date(s) Application is Due: Sep 7
Contact: Tonisha Toler, Grants & Outreach Coordinator; (503) 823-5866 or (503) 823-5111; fax (503) 823-5432; ttoler@racc.org
Internet: http://www.racc.org/grants/opportunity-grants
Sponsor: Regional Arts and Cultural Council
108 NW 9th Avenue, Suite 300
Portland, OR 97209-3318

Reinberger Foundation Grants 1573

Clarence T. Reinberger was born in 1894 on Cleveland's west side, and began his business career in the 1920's as a pioneer in the automobile replacement parts field. Starting as a clerk in the Cleveland retail store of the National Automotive Parts Association's (NAPA) Automotive Parts Company, he became president of that company in 1948. In the 1960's the Automotive Parts Company merged with the Genuine Parts Company of Atlanta. Mr. Reinberger held the position of Chairman of the Board of Genuine Parts Company until his death in 1968. Louise Fischer Reinberger was born in Germany. After graduation from high school in the United States, she was employed by the Halle Brothers Company, a large Cleveland department store. The Reinberger Foundation was established by Mr. and Mrs. Reinberger in 1966. Mr. Reinberger left a substantial bequest to the Foundation at his death in 1968. Upon Mrs. Reinberger's death in 1984, the major portion of her estate was also bequeathed to the Foundation. Although the Reinbergers had no children, the foundation continues to be managed by several generations of Mr. Reinberger's family. Since its inception, the foundation has distributed over $91,000,000 to the non-profit community. The foundation divides its support among the following program areas: Arts, Culture, and Humanities; Education; Human Service - Health; and Human Service - Other. Categories supported under Arts, Culture and Humanities include museums, visual arts, performing arts, media and communication, arts education, zoos, and public recreation. Categories supported under Education include K-12 schools, early childhood education, adult education/literacy, libraries, and workforce development. Categories supported under Human Service - Health include hospitals and clinics, substance abuse prevention/treatment, medical and disease research, disease prevention, and speech and hearing. Categories supported under Human Service - Other include children and youth services, residential and home care, emergency food programs, youth development, domestic violence, and temporary housing/homeless shelters. Letters of Inquiry for grants of any type may be submitted according to the following program-area schedule: Education - March 1; Human Service (Health) - June 1; Human Service (Other) - September 1; and Arts, Culture, and Humanities - December 1. Letters of Inquiry may either be sent by U.S. Mail or emailed and are due in the foundation office by the deadline date. Full proposals are accepted only at the request of the foundation.
Requirements: Applicants must be 501(c)3 organizations. Preferential consideration is given to organizations serving Northeast Ohio, or the greater-Columbus area.
Restrictions: No loans are made, nor are grants given to individuals. The Reinberger Foundation does not make more than one grant to a particular organization during a given calendar year, nor will new proposals be considered until existing multi-year commitments have been paid.
Geographic Focus: Ohio
Date(s) Application is Due: Mar 1; Jun 1; Sep 1; Dec 1
Contact: Karen R. Hooser, President; (216) 292-2790; fax (216) 292-4466; info@reinbergerfoundation.org
Internet: http://reinbergerfoundation.org/apply.html
Sponsor: Reinberger Foundation
30000 Chagrin Boulevard #300
Cleveland, OH 44122

Reneau Alline Charitable Trust Grants 1574

The Reneau Alline Charitable Trust was established in Kentucky in 1998, offering support for community development, economic development, and education at all levels. Funding is primarily centered around the community of Glasgow and the greater Barren County region. The primary type of support is dedicated to general operations, and grants typically range from $2,500 to $30,000. The annual deadline is September 30. Along with the formal application, interested parties should provide: a copy of IRS Determination Letter; and a list of current board of directors, trustees, officers and other key people and their affiliations.
Restrictions: Grants are never awarded to individuals.
Geographic Focus: Kentucky
Date(s) Application is Due: Sep 30
Amount of Grant: 2,500 - 30,000 USD
Contact: Trustee; (270) 782-4477 or (270) 782-4471
Sponsor: Reneau Alline Charitable Trust
P.O. Box 2907
Wilson, NC 27894-2907

RESIST Arthur Raymond Cohen Memorial Fund Grants 1575

RESIST, founded in 1967, was originally formed to oppose the war in Vietnam and to support draft resistance. By the 1970s, RESIST expanded its scope dramatically by making the connection between the unequal distribution of power and money at home, and a system of U.S. domination abroad. The Arthur Raymond Cohen Memorial Fund Grant is designed to support the causes to which Arthur Cohen (1918-1986) was committed: opposition to the arms race, the cold war, and American intervention abroad; and support for civil liberties, the fight against racism; and the struggle of workers and unions at home.
Restrictions: RESIST does not fund: organizations with annual budgets over $150,000; individuals; groups that primarily provide direct services

(to individuals, families or communities) that are not part of progressive organizing activities; research, litigation or legal organizations unless they are directly connected to progressive organizing campaigns; organizations located outside the United States; the development or production of films, videos or radio projects; media or cultural organizations not directly connected to progressive organizing campaigns; organizations with access to traditional sources of funding; or other foundations or grant giving organizations.

Geographic Focus: All States

Date(s) Application is Due: Feb 4; Apr 1; Jun 3; Aug 5; Sep 30; Dec 3

Contact: Robin Carton; (617) 623-5110; robin@resistinc.org

Internet: http://www.resistinc.org/node/1528

Sponsor: RESIST

259 Elm Street

Somerville, MA 02144

RESIST Freda Friedman Salzman Memorial Fund Grants   1576

RESIST, founded in 1967, was originally formed to oppose the war in Vietnam and to support draft resistance. By the 1970s, RESIST expanded its scope dramatically by making the connection between the unequal distribution of power and money at home, and a system of U.S. domination abroad. The Freda Friedman Salzman Memorial Fund is dedicated to the purpose of supporting organized resistance to the institutions and practices that rob people of their dignity as full human beings, giving a high priority to the efforts of Native American peoples to resist cultural as well as actual genocide.

Restrictions: RESIST does not fund: organizations with annual budgets over $150,000; individuals; groups that primarily provide direct services (to individuals, families or communities) that are not part of progressive organizing activities; research, litigation or legal organizations unless they are directly connected to progressive organizing campaigns; organizations located outside the United States; the development or production of films, videos or radio projects; media or cultural organizations not directly connected to progressive organizing campaigns; organizations with access to traditional sources of funding; or other foundations or grant giving organizations.

Geographic Focus: All States

Date(s) Application is Due: Feb 4; Apr 1; Jun 3; Aug 5; Sep 30; Dec 3

Contact: Robin Carton; (617) 623-5110; robin@resistinc.org

Internet: http://www.resistinc.org/node/1528

Sponsor: RESIST

259 Elm Street

Somerville, MA 02144

RESIST General Support Grants   1577

RESIST, founded in 1967, was originally formed to oppose the war in Vietnam and to support draft resistance. By the 1970s, RESIST expanded its scope dramatically by making the connection between the unequal distribution of power and money at home, and a system of U.S. domination abroad. Organizations with an annual budget of $150,000 or less may apply for a one-year grant with the maximum amount requested not to exceed $3,000. RESIST provides funds for general support as a means of enabling grantees to build infrastructure and capacity while engaged in on-going social justice activism. Up to $4,000 is given for general support as a means of building infrastructure and capacity while engaged in on-going social justice activism.

Requirements: Organizations with a budget of approximately $125,000 or less may apply for a one-year grant.

Restrictions: RESIST does not fund: organizations with annual budgets over $150,000; individuals; groups that primarily provide direct services (to individuals, families or communities) that are not part of progressive organizing activities; research, litigation or legal organizations unless they are directly connected to progressive organizing campaigns; organizations located outside the United States; the development or production of films, videos or radio projects; media or cultural organizations not directly connected to progressive organizing campaigns; organizations with access to traditional sources of funding; or other foundations or grant giving organizations.

Geographic Focus: All States

Date(s) Application is Due: Feb 4; Apr 1; Jun 3; Aug 5; Sep 30; Dec 3

Amount of Grant: 500 - 4,000 USD

Contact: Robin Carton; (617) 623-5110; robin@resistinc.org

Internet: http://www.resistinc.org

Sponsor: RESIST

259 Elm Street

Somerville, MA 02144

RESIST Hell Yes! Award   1578

RESIST, founded in 1967, was originally formed to oppose the war in Vietnam and to support draft resistance. By the 1970s, RESIST expanded its scope dramatically by making the connection between the unequal distribution of power and money at home, and a system of U.S. domination abroad. To honor the moral clarity, courage and political commitment of its founders, RESIST created a new tribute grant in 2008: the Hell Yes! Award. This grant recognizes inspiring, radical activism that cuts to the heart of RESIST's mission to challenge illegitimate authority.

Restrictions: RESIST does not fund: organizations with annual budgets over $150,000; individuals; groups that primarily provide direct services (to individuals, families or communities) that are not part of progressive organizing activities; research, litigation or legal organizations unless they are directly connected to progressive organizing campaigns; organizations located outside the United States; the development or production of films, videos or radio projects; media or cultural organizations not directly connected to progressive organizing campaigns; organizations with access to traditional sources of funding; or other foundations or grant giving organizations.

Geographic Focus: All States

Date(s) Application is Due: Feb 4; Apr 1; Jun 3; Aug 5; Sep 30; Dec 3

Contact: Robin Carton; (617) 623-5110; robin@resistinc.org

Internet: http://www.resistinc.org/node/1528

Sponsor: RESIST

259 Elm Street

Somerville, MA 02144

RESIST Ken Hale Tribute Grants   1579

RESIST, founded in 1967, was originally formed to oppose the war in Vietnam and to support draft resistance. By the 1970s, RESIST expanded its scope dramatically by making the connection between the unequal distribution of power and money at home, and a system of U.S. domination abroad. The Ken Hale Tribute Grant is given in memory of the life and work of Ken Hale (1934-2001), one of the world's foremost linguists, a RESIST founder and a passionate activist for justice. This grant is given to support organizations which ensure that the voices of those most affected are given primacy in the struggle to protect and expand civil, cultural and political rights.

Restrictions: RESIST does not fund: organizations with annual budgets over $150,000; individuals; groups that primarily provide direct services (to individuals, families or communities) that are not part of progressive organizing activities; research, litigation or legal organizations unless they are directly connected to progressive organizing campaigns; organizations located outside the United States; the development or production of films, videos or radio projects; media or cultural organizations not directly connected to progressive organizing campaigns; organizations with access to traditional sources of funding; or other foundations or grant giving organizations.

Geographic Focus: All States

Date(s) Application is Due: Feb 4; Apr 1; Jun 3; Aug 5; Sep 30; Dec 3

Contact: Robin Carton; (617) 623-5110; robin@resistinc.org

Internet: http://www.resistinc.org/node/1528

Sponsor: RESIST

259 Elm Street

Somerville, MA 02144

RESIST Leslie D'Cora Holmes Memorial Fund Grants   1580

RESIST, founded in 1967, was originally formed to oppose the war in Vietnam and to support draft resistance. By the 1970s, RESIST expanded its scope dramatically by making the connection between the unequal distribution of power and money at home, and a system of U.S. domination abroad. The Leslie D'Cora Holmes Memorial Fund Grant was established in 1999 to honor the life's work and legacy of Leslie D'Cora Holmes. This fund supports activities and organizations that embody the characteristics, values, and principles that reflect her spirit-filled mission, including: empowerment for communities and individuals; self-determination through education and community organizing; harmonization of diverse communities of interest; actualization and recognition of individual potential; courage of conviction; and pride in culture, community and self.

Restrictions: RESIST does not fund: organizations with annual budgets over $150,000; individuals; groups that primarily provide direct services (to individuals, families or communities) that are not part of progressive organizing activities; research, litigation or legal organizations unless they are directly connected to progressive organizing campaigns; organizations located outside the United States; the development or production of films, videos or radio projects; media or cultural organizations not directly connected

to progressive organizing campaigns; organizations with access to traditional sources of funding; or other foundations or grant giving organizations.
Geographic Focus: All States
Date(s) Application is Due: Feb 4; Apr 1; Jun 3; Aug 5; Sep 30; Dec 3
Contact: Robin Carton; (617) 623-5110; robin@resistinc.org
Internet: http://www.resistinc.org/node/1528
Sponsor: RESIST
259 Elm Street
Somerville, MA 02144

RESIST Mike Riegle Tribute Grants 1581

RESIST, founded in 1967, was originally formed to oppose the war in Vietnam and to support draft resistance. By the 1970s, RESIST expanded its scope dramatically by making the connection between the unequal distribution of power and money at home, and a system of U.S. domination abroad. The Mike Riegle Tribute Grant is given in memory of the life and work of Boston activist Mike Riegle, a supporter of prisoners' rights, gay and lesbian liberation, and the radical movement for justice.
Restrictions: RESIST does not fund: organizations with annual budgets over $150,000; individuals; groups that primarily provide direct services (to individuals, families or communities) that are not part of progressive organizing activities; research, litigation or legal organizations unless they are directly connected to progressive organizing campaigns; organizations located outside the United States; the development or production of films, videos or radio projects; media or cultural organizations not directly connected to progressive organizing campaigns; organizations with access to traditional sources of funding; or other foundations or grant giving organizations.
Geographic Focus: All States
Date(s) Application is Due: Feb 4; Apr 1; Jun 3; Aug 5; Sep 30; Dec 3
Contact: Robin Carton; (617) 623-5110; robin@resistinc.org
Internet: http://www.resistinc.org/node/1528
Sponsor: RESIST
259 Elm Street
Somerville, MA 02144

RESIST Multi-Year Grants 1582

RESIST, founded in 1967, was originally formed to oppose the war in Vietnam and to support draft resistance. By the 1970s, RESIST expanded its scope dramatically by making the connection between the unequal distribution of power and money at home, and a system of U.S. domination abroad. Grantees who have been funded by RESIST at least two times during the preceding five years may apply for a multi-year grant. Of the two prior grant awards, the most recent must have been for the full amount given out during that cycle. Multi-year grants will cover a three year period and are designed to provide general support to eligible grantee organizations.
Requirements: All multi-year applicants must: submit answers to the Multi-Year Grant Questionnaire; and be currently eligible to receive grant awards under RESIST's Funding Guidelines. All applicants must provide specific, measurable objectives as part of their proposal. These objectives should demonstrate the capacity to plan at least one to three years ahead. In addition, groups must submit evidence of their past performance, examples of which might include prior Progress or Annual Reports, with their proposal.
Restrictions: RESIST does not fund: organizations with annual budgets over $150,000; individuals; groups that primarily provide direct services (to individuals, families or communities) that are not part of progressive organizing activities; research, litigation or legal organizations unless they are directly connected to progressive organizing campaigns; organizations located outside the United States; the development or production of films, videos or radio projects; media or cultural organizations not directly connected to progressive organizing campaigns; organizations with access to traditional sources of funding; or other foundations or grant giving organizations.
Geographic Focus: All States
Date(s) Application is Due: Feb 4; Apr 1; Jun 3; Aug 5; Sep 30; Dec 3
Contact: Robin Carton; (617) 623-5110; robin@resistinc.org
Internet: http://www.resistinc.org/node/1527
Sponsor: RESIST
259 Elm Street
Somerville, MA 02144

RESIST Sharon Kurtz Memorial Fund Grants 1583

RESIST, founded in 1967, was originally formed to oppose the war in Vietnam and to support draft resistance. By the 1970s, RESIST expanded its scope dramatically by making the connection between the unequal distribution of

power and money at home, and a system of U.S. domination abroad. In 2008, the friends and family of Sharon Kurtz chose RESIST as the home of a new fund in her name. The Sharon Kurtz Memorial Fund commemorates the life of Sharon Kurtz, a community organizer who dedicated her life to making the world a more just and humane place.
Restrictions: RESIST does not fund: organizations with annual budgets over $150,000; individuals; groups that primarily provide direct services (to individuals, families or communities) that are not part of progressive organizing activities; research, litigation or legal organizations unless they are directly connected to progressive organizing campaigns; organizations located outside the United States; the development or production of films, videos or radio projects; media or cultural organizations not directly connected to progressive organizing campaigns; organizations with access to traditional sources of funding; or other foundations or grant giving organizations.
Geographic Focus: All States
Date(s) Application is Due: Feb 4; Apr 1; Jun 3; Aug 5; Sep 30; Dec 3
Contact: Robin Carton; (617) 623-5110; robin@resistinc.org
Internet: http://www.resistinc.org/node/1528
Sponsor: RESIST
259 Elm Street
Somerville, MA 02144

Reynolds Family Foundation Grants 1584

The Foundation, established in California in support of its residents, is primarily aimed at supporting educational programs, human services, and international affairs. Funding most often comes in the form of general operating support. Although there are no specific grant applications required, applicants should contact the Foundation initially by either letter or telephone, followed by a detailed letter of application outlining the project and amount of funding requested.
Geographic Focus: California
Amount of Grant: 500 - 3,000 USD
Samples: Angel Kiss Foundation, Reno, Nevada, $300,; Saint Johns Health Center Foundation, Santa. Monica, California, $3,000.
Contact: Paula M. Golden, President; (310) 600-0598 or (310) 829-8433; fax (310) 556-7986; paula@paulagolden.net
Internet: http://paulagolden.net/about_us
Sponsor: Reynolds Family Foundation
2132 Century Park Lane, #209
Los Angeles, CA 90067-3312

Rhode Island Foundation Grants 1585

The foundation seeks to promote philanthropic activities that will improve the living conditions and well-being of the inhabitants of Rhode Island. Grants for capital and operating purposes principally to agencies working in the fields of education, health care, the arts and cultural affairs, youth, the aged, social services, urban affairs, historic preservation, and the environment.
Requirements: Rhode Island nonprofits organizations may apply. See Foundations website for additional guidelines.
Restrictions: The foundation does not make grants for endowments, research, religious groups for religious purposes, hospital equipment, capital needs of health organizations, or to educational institutions for general operating expenses.
Geographic Focus: Rhode Island
Samples: Ocean State Action Fund, Cranston, RI, $50,000 - for continued funding for grassroots organizing, coalition work, and public communications in support of affordable, quality health care for all Rhode Islanders; Community Housing Land Trust of Rhode Island, Providence, RI, $50,000 - for new program targeting foreclosed properties or those close to being foreclosed upon; Sakonnet Preservation Association, Little Compton, RI, $25,000 - for three-community partnership to preserve drinking water quality and open space in Newport County;
Contact: Owen Heleen, Vice President for Grant Programs; (401) 427-4009 or (401) 274-4564; fax (401) 331-8085; oheleen@rifoundation.org
Internet: http://www.rifoundation.org/Nonprofits/GrantOpportunities/tabid/175/Default.aspx
Sponsor: Rhode Island Foundation
1 Union Station
Providence, RI 02903

Rice Foundation Grants 1586

The foundation awards grants to Illinois nonprofit organizations in its areas of interest, including civic affairs, higher education, hospitals, libraries, medical education, and youth programs. Project and operating support are available. There are no application forms or deadlines.

Requirements: Applicants should submit a proposal with directly to the Foundation including the following: statement of problem project will address; copy of IRS Determination Letter; brief history of organization and description of its mission; detailed description of project and amount of funding requested.
Geographic Focus: Illinois
Amount of Grant: 25,000 - 1,000,000 USD
Samples: John G. Shedd Aquarium, Chicago, IL $1,000,000 - for general support; Northwestern University, Evanston, IL $386,700 - for general support; Big Shoulders Fund, Chicago, IL $30,000 - for general support;
Contact: Peter Nolan, President; (847) 581-9999
Sponsor: Daniel F. and Ada L. Rice Foundation
8600 Gross Point Road
Skokie, IL 60077-2151

Richard and Helen DeVos Foundation Grants 1587

The foundation supports nonprofit organizations primarily in western Michigan and central Florida in its areas of interest, including religious agencies and churches and education and outreach, social services, the arts, public policy, and health care. Types of support include general operating support, continuing support, annual campaigns, capital campaigns, building construction/ renovation, program development, seed grants, and matching funds.
Requirements: Application forms are not required. Applicants should submit the following: copy of IRS Determination Letter; copy of current year's organizational budget and/or project budget. The Board meets every 3 months, submit your proposal two weeks prior to the review (contact Foundation for deadline dates). Mail applications to: 126 Ottawa Avenue, N.W., Suite 500, Grand Rapids, MI 49503
Restrictions: No grants to individuals.
Geographic Focus: Florida, Michigan
Amount of Grant: 300 - 5,000,000 USD
Contact: Ginny Vander Hart, Foundation Director; (616) 643-4700; fax (616) 774-0116; virginiav@rdvcorp.com
Sponsor: Richard and Helen DeVos Foundation Grants
P.O. Box 230257
Grand Rapids, MI 49523-0257

Richard and Rhoda Goldman Fund Grants 1588

The fund is interested in supporting programs that will have a significant positive impact in an array of fields, including culture, the environment, population, Jewish affairs, violence prevention, children and youth, the elderly, and social and human services. Types of support include general operating support, continuing support, capital campaigns, program development, and seed money. Funds will be allocated primarily in the San Francisco Bay area of California and to organizations benefiting this area. There are no application deadlines.
Requirements: Nonprofit organizations serving primarily the San Francisco Bay area of California are eligible.
Restrictions: The fund does not accept applications for research or award grants or scholarships for individuals, conferences, documentary films, or fund-raisers. Unsolicited proposals for support of arts organizations or institutions of primary, secondary, or higher education will not be accepted.
Geographic Focus: California
Amount of Grant: 1,000 - 500,000 USD
Samples: San Francisco Beautification (CA)—for efforts to increase green schoolyards, $10,000; American Jewish Joint Distribution Committee (New York, NY)—for relief efforts following the earthquake and tsunamis that struck Southeast Asia in 2004, $30,000; United States Public Interest Research Group Education Fund (Washington, DC)—for efforts to increase attention to the role of hard money in federal political campaigns, $20,000; Community Awareness and Treatment Services (San Francisco, CA)—for support of this 24-hour shelter and transitional-housing program for women, $25,000.
Contact: Sam Salkin, Executive Director; (415) 345-6300; fax (415) 345-9686; info@goldmanfund.org
Internet: http://www.goldmanfund.org
Sponsor: Richard and Rhoda Goldman Fund
211 Lincoln Boulevard, P.O. Box 29924
San Francisco, CA 94129

Richard and Susan Smith Family Foundation Grants 1589

The foundation awards grants to Massachusetts nonprofit organizations in its areas of interest, including arts and culture, children and youth, disadvantaged (economically), education (early childhood, elementary, and higher), minorities, biomedical research, health care and social services delivery. Types of support include annual campaigns, building construction/ renovation, capital campaigns, curriculum development, general operating grants, program/project support, seed grants, and service delivery programs. There are no application forms.
Requirements: Massachusetts nonprofit organizations serving the greater Boston area are eligible.
Restrictions: Grants do not support political activities; religious activities; individuals; or requests for deficit financing or endowment funds.
Geographic Focus: Massachusetts
Date(s) Application is Due: Mar 15; Aug 15
Amount of Grant: 5,000 - 238,000 USD
Samples: Compassionate Care ALS, West Falmouth, MA $25,000 - for the purchase of a cargo van to transport adaptive equipment to and from patient homes; United Teen Equality Center, Lowell, MA $944,780 - funding provides violence prevention, youth development, education and community organizing programs for the youth center, the grant is payable over 5 years;
Contact: David Ford, Executive Director; (617) 278-5200; fax (617) 278-5250; dford@smithfamilyfoundation.net
Internet: http://www.smithfamilyfoundation.net
Sponsor: Richard and Susan Smith Family Foundation
1280 Boylston Street, Suite 100
Chestnut Hill, MA 02467

Richard D. Bass Foundation Grants 1590

The Richard D. Bass Foundation's area of interest include: arts/cultural-programs, including music and dance companies; Catholic/Protestant agencies & churches; community/economic development; education; health organizations, association. The type of support available include: annual campaigns; building/ renovation; capital campaigns; general/operating support. Giving primarily in the metropolitan Dallas, Texas area. Grants range from $500 - $15,000. Application deadlines are March 31 and September 30 annually.
Requirements: IRS 501(c)3 nonprofit organizations are available to apply. The Foundations gives primarily to the Dallas, Texas region of the United States but funding is not limited to Texas. Grant proposals are available through out the U.S., contact the Foundation directly before submitting a proposal to access the likely hood of funding for your project. There is no application form required when applying for funding. Submit the proposal with one copy of the organizations IRS Determination Letter.
Restrictions: Funding is not available for: private foundations; individuals.
Geographic Focus: All States
Date(s) Application is Due: Mar 31; Sep 30
Amount of Grant: 500 - 10,000 USD
Contact: Barbara B. Moroney, Treasurer; (214) 351-6994
Sponsor: Richard D. Bass Foundation
4516 Wildwood Road
Dallas, TX 75209-1926

Richard F. and Janice F. Weaver Educational Trust Grants 1591

The Richard F. and Janice F. Weaver Educational Trust was established in Kentucky with the primary purpose of supporting higher education institutions in Kentucky. Support typically comes in the form of funding for general operating costs. Since no formal application is required, interested parties should send a letter of request to the Trust officer. There are no annual deadlines, and typical grant amounts are up to $1,000.
Requirements: Colleges and Universities in Kentucky are eligible to apply.
Geographic Focus: Kentucky
Amount of Grant: Up to 1,000 USD
Contact: Richard F. Weaver, Chief Executive Officer; (270) 753-2899
Sponsor: Richard F. and Janice F. Weaver Educational Trust
1608 Sycamore Street
Murray, KY 42071

Richard H. Driehaus Foundation Grants 1592

The Richard H. Driehaus Foundation, founded in 1983 and as a family foundation in 1992, benefits individuals and communities primarily by supporting the preservation and enhancement of the built and natural environments through historic preservation, encouragement of quality architectural and landscape design, and conserving open space. The Foundation also supports the performing and visual arts and makes grants to organizations that provide opportunities for working families who remain poor. The foundation currently provides funding in the areas of the Built Environment, Economic Opportunity for the Working Poor, Government Accountability/Investigative Reporting, Small Museums and Cultural Centers. The Foundation accepts no unsolicited proposals, but welcomes letters of inquiry and phone calls. Proposals are encouraged from companies that emphasize presentation instead of education or community outreach. Guidelines and application information are available online.

Requirements: Dance and theater companies in the Chicago metropolitan area that have produced at least one show in the Chicago area and that have annual operating budgets of less than $100,000 are eligible.

Restrictions: The Foundation tends not to fund large organizations with multi-million dollar budgets; arts education or arts outreach; community theater and community dance; public, private or parochial education; or health care.

Geographic Focus: Illinois

Date(s) Application is Due: Mar 1; Jul 1; Nov 1

Amount of Grant: 5,000 - 50,000 USD

Samples: Arts & Business Council of Chicago, Illinois, $30,000 - a two-year grant for operating support; Arts Work Fund for Organizational Development, Chicago, Illinois, $30,000 - operating support; DuSable Museum of African American History, Chicago, Illinois, $20,000 - for an exhibit on "Geoffrey and Carmen: A memoir in four movements."

Contact: Sonia Fischer, Executive Director; (312) 641-5772; fax (312) 641-5736; sunnyfischer@driehausfoundation.org

Internet: http://www.driehausfoundation.org

Sponsor: Richard H. Driehaus Foundation

333 North Michigan Avenue, Suite 510

Chicago, IL 60601

Richard H. Driehaus Foundation MacArthur Fund for Arts & Culture 1593

The fund will make multiyear, general operating support grants to organizations that have budgets of $500,000 or less and that reside in, and serve, the Chicago metropolitan area (the counties of Cook, DuPage, Lake, McHenry, Kane, and Will). Most grants will be in the range of $5,000 to $15,000. Most of the grants will be for general operating support. The deadline for receipt of proposals from performing arts organizations (music, theater and dance groups) is 5 p.m. on March 1. The deadline for receipt of proposals from all other groups: literary arts, visual and media arts, interdisciplinary arts, special projects, museums as well as service, policy or advocacy groups is 5 p.m. on June 1. Letters of inquiry must be: received by the listed deadline date; limited to five pages; the first four pages should include a brief description of your organization and your request; the final page should be a summary of your organization's budgets for this year. Full proposals are by invitation only.

Requirements: The following arts and culture organizations may apply: performing arts; visual and media arts; literary arts; interdisciplinary arts; special projects; museums, and service, policy or advocacy groups.

Restrictions: This program is not intended for arts education programs. Nor is it intended, for professional theater and dance companies with operating budgets of less than $150,000; those companies should visit the MacArthur Foundation website to review the guidelines for the Small Theater and Dance Group Funding Program.

Geographic Focus: Illinois

Date(s) Application is Due: Mar 1; Jun 1

Amount of Grant: 5,000 - 15,000 USD

Samples: Fear No Arts, Chicago, IL, $8,500—matching grant for the production of a 30-minute program for WTTW that will take viewers into the studios of Chicago artists; I Am Chicago, Chicago, Il, $5,000—for a photo project that will document the appearance of typical Chicago residents around the city.

Contact: Richard Cahan, Program Oficer; (312) 641-5772 or (847) 722-9244; fax (312) 641-5736; RichardCahan@aol.com

Internet: http://www.driehausfoundation.org/support

Sponsor: Richard H. Driehaus Foundation

333 North Michigan Avenue, Suite 510

Chicago, IL 60601

Richard H. Driehaus Foundation Small Theater and Dance Grants 1594

The Richard H. Driehaus Foundation, founded in 1983 and as a family foundation in 1992, benefits individuals and communities primarily by supporting the preservation and enhancement of the built and natural environments through historic preservation, encouragement of quality architectural and landscape design, and conserving open space. This program addresses the needs of small theater and dance companies in the Chicago area. Companies that emphasize professional presentation instead of education or community outreach are encouraged to apply. Use of grants may be unrestricted.

Requirements: Dance and theater companies that reside in the Chicago metropolitan area, have produced at least one show in the Chicago area, and have annual operating budgets of less than $150,000 are eligible.

Geographic Focus: Illinois

Date(s) Application is Due: Apr 25; Sep 12

Amount of Grant: 2,500 - 10,000 USD

Contact: Peter Handler, Program Officer; (312) 641-5772; fax (312) 641-5736; peterhandler@driehausfoundation.org

Internet: http://www.driehausfoundation.org/support

Sponsor: Richard H. Driehaus Foundation

333 North Michigan Avenue, Suite 510

Chicago, IL 60601

Richard King Mellon Foundation Grants 1595

On a national basis, the foundation makes grants to acquire and preserve key tracts of land in danger of being lost to urban growth and environmentally insensitive development. Mellon gives to nonprofits in Pittsburgh and throughout southwestern Pennsylvania to improve human services, education, medical care, civic affairs, and cultural activities. Types of support include capital grants, challenge/matching grants, general operating grants, project grants, and seed money grants. Application and guidelines are available online.

Requirements: Projects originating in Pittsburgh and southwestern Pennsylvania are given special priority.

Restrictions: The Foundation gives priority to projects and programs that have clearly defined outcomes and an evaluation component. It does not consider requests on behalf of individuals, or from outside the Untied States. The Foundation does not encourage requests from outside Pennsylvania.

Geographic Focus: Pennsylvania

Samples: Saint Vincent College (LaTrobe, PA)—for a business and conference center, $5 million; Westminster College (New Wilmington, PA)—to renovate an academic and administration building, $300,000; Carnegie Museums of Pittsburgh (PA)—to renovate and expand dinosaur exhibits at the Carnegie Museum of Natural History, $3 million; Direct Relief International (Santa Barbara, CA)—to assist tsunami-relief efforts, $500,000.

Contact: Michael Watson; (412) 392-2800; fax (412) 392-2837

Internet: http://foundationcenter.org/grantmaker/rkmellon/

Sponsor: Richard King Mellon Foundation

500 Grant Street, Suite 4106

Pittsburgh, PA 15219-2502

Richard M. Fairbanks Foundation Grants 1596

The Richard M. Fairbanks Foundation, Inc. was established in 1986 by Richard M. Fairbanks, founder and owner of Fairbanks Communications. An independent private foundation granting funds to qualifying nonprofit organizations, programs, and projects in the greater Indianapolis, Indiana area. Exceptions to this geographic limitation are normally made only for organizations historically supported by the Fairbanks family or for national disasters. If you are interested in learning if your organization and project/program matches the Richard M. Fairbanks Foundation's areas of interest and funding guidelines, you may contact the foundation by telephone, email or brief written letter of inquiry. Please note that the Fairbanks Foundation does not accept unsolicited proposals.

Requirements: The Foundation: makes grants only to tax exempt public charities as defined in Sections 501(c)3 & 509(a)(1)(2)(3) of the Internal Revenue Code, except as prohibited for 509(a)(3) Type III organizations; will not consider requests for loans and grants to individuals; does not make grants or give support to conferences, seminars, media events, or workshops unless they are an integral part of a broader program; ordinarily considers grant requests only from organizations located in Greater Indianapolis, Indiana.

Geographic Focus: Indiana

Contact: Claire Fiddian-Green, Grants Officer; (317) 663-4189 or (317) 846-7111; fax (317) 844-0167; Fiddiangreen@rmfairbanksfoundation.org

Internet: http://www.rmfairbanksfoundation.org/default.asp?p=3

Sponsor: Richard M. Fairbanks Foundation

9292 North Meridian Street, Suite 304

Indianapolis, IN 46260

Rich Foundation Grants 1597

The foundation awards grants to nonprofit organizations in Atlanta, GA, to support community funds, performing arts, cultural programs, higher education, social services, homeless, youth, hospitals, heart disease, theater, and AIDS. Types of support include annual campaigns, building funds, continuing support, equipment acquisition, operating budgets, technical assistance, and research. Contact the office for application forms. The board meets quarterly to review requests.

Requirements: Nonprofit organizations in the Atlanta, GA, area are eligible for grant support.

Geographic Focus: Georgia
Date(s) Application is Due: Mar 15; Jun 15; Sep 15; Dec 15
Amount of Grant: 5,000 - 100,000 USD
Contact: Anne Poland Berg, Grant Consultant; (404) 262-2266
Sponsor: Rich Foundation
11 Piedmont Center, Suite 204
Atlanta, GA 30305

Richland County Bank Grants 1598

The Richland County Bank has had a long tradition of community involvement, dedication and volunteerism. The Bank is committed to supporting the community in which it serves. In addition to monetary contributions, the bank encourages its employees to take an active role in our community. As a corporate sponsor, we support various organizations in Richland and surrounding counties, including: Vernon, Crawford, Grant, Iowa, and Sauk counties. Areas of interest include: health care; higher education; agricultural agencies; community development; children and youth programs; and scholarship funds.
Requirements: Applicants must be 501(c)3 organizations serving the Wisconsin counties of Richland, Vernon, Crawford, Grant, Iowa, or Sauk.
Geographic Focus: Wisconsin
Contact: Gail Surrem, Vice President; (608) 647-6306
Internet: http://www.richlandcountybank.com/aboutInvolvement.cfm
Sponsor: Richland County Bank
195 West Court Street
Richland Center, WI 53581

Righteous Persons Foundation Grants 1599

The foundation, established by Steven Spielberg, makes grants nationally for projects to revitalize Jewish life, help young people learn about Judaism, and promote tolerance among people of all faiths and ethnicities. Many of the awards are for projects that explore new ideas and opportunities with a special emphasis on young people and that include many projects that may have otherwise had a difficult time obtaining funding. Projects that are national in scope or can serve as models for other communities will receive preference.
Requirements: U.S. 501(c)3 nonprofits are eligible.
Restrictions: Grants are not awarded to support endowments, capital campaigns, building funds, university faculty chairs, individual synagogues or day schools, research, or the publication of books or magazines.
Geographic Focus: All States
Amount of Grant: 5,000 - 400,000 USD
Samples: Raoul Wallenberg Committee of the United States (New York, NY)—to help bring its A Study of Heroes curriculum to additional U.S. schools and communities, $20,000 matching grant over two years; Anti-Defamation League (Los Angeles, CA)—for its Stop the Hate Program, $50,000 matching grant; Clark U (Worcester, MA)—to support a doctoral fellow in its program on the history of the Holocaust, $60,000; Jewish Television Network (Los Angeles, CA)—to produce a television program on Jewish art and culture, $50,000.
Contact: Rachel Levin, Program Officer; (310) 314-8393; fax (310) 314-8396
Sponsor: Righteous Persons Foundation
2800 28th Street, Suite 105
Santa Monica, CA 90405

RISCA General Operating Support Grants 1600

Rhode Island State Council of the Arts (RISCA) awards General Operating Support (GOS) to Rhode Island's major arts presenting and producing institutions. Interested applicants who meet the eligibility requirements below should contact RISCA's organization support program coordinator for more information.
Requirements: Organizations are eligible for General Operating Support if, at the time of application, they: are a nonprofit corporation, incorporated in and conducting business in the State of Rhode Island; have 501(c)3 tax exempt status; have a primary mission that is clearly arts or arts-related; have a record of receiving grant support for at least the past three consecutive years from the Rhode Island State Council on the Arts; can provide a planning document, approved by their board of directors, which addresses artistic and administrative issues; have an operating budget in excess of $50,000 at the time of application, as shown by an certified independent audit, review, or accountant's compilation; and perform or exhibit work in a space that is physically accessible to people with disabilities, as required by law. Applicants must be governed by a revolving board of directors, trustees or an advisory board drawn from the community at large and shown to be actively involved in the activities of the organization. Organizations with budgets of $100,000 or less must have at least one part-time (minimum of 20 hours per week),

year-round, paid staff member who is responsible for the oversight of the organization. Organizations with budgets from $100,000 to $1,000,000 must have both a paid professional business manager and a paid artistic director (or individuals with these functions if titles differ). The minimum combined hours for these two jobs must equal one and one-half full time positions. Organizations with budgets greater than $1,000,000 must have both a full-time, paid business manager and full-time, paid artistic director.
Geographic Focus: Rhode Island
Samples: Rhode Island School of Design, Providence, Rhode Island, $87,550; Rhode Island Philharmonic Orchestra & Music School, East Providence, Rhode Island, $89,471; South County Center for the Arts, West Kingston, Rhode Island, $9,256
Contact: Randall Rosenbaum, Executive Director; (401) 222-3883; fax (401) 222-3018; randy@arts.ri.gov
Internet: http://www.arts.ri.gov/grants/gos.php
Sponsor: Rhode Island State Council on the Arts
One Capitol Hill, Third Floor
Providence, RI 02908

Robbins-de Beaumont Foundation Grants 1601

Established in Massachusetts in 1992, the Robbins-de Beaumont Foundation offers funding nationally, and seeks nonprofit organizations whose goals are helping people reach their full potential as contributing members of their family, neighborhoods, and society at large. Limited funds are available for unsolicited grants for new, innovative projects which address identified needs of the community served and have relatively modest operating budgets. The foundation also has an interest in the education of children and adults in the areas of parenting, volunteerism, employment and life skills, preservation of the environment, the performing and visual arts, and substance abuse. A formal proposal is by invitation only, after review of initial concept paper. The concept paper should not exceed two pages. If given a go-ahead, the formal application consists of: program description; population served; budgetary needs; and how project will be sustained once the grant maker support is completed. The annual deadline for the concept paper is March 1, with full proposals due by June 30. Most recent awards have ranged from $5,000 to $30,000.
Restrictions: No support is offered to organizations whose primary focus is mental health, medical training, physical and mental disabilities, special programs, or for organizations whose annual operating budget exceeds $1,000,000, or which have been in existence for over ten years. No grants are given to individuals, or for capital campaigns, debt reduction or cash reserves, endowments, multi-year pledges, seed money, or start up costs.
Geographic Focus: All States
Date(s) Application is Due: Jun 30
Amount of Grant: 5,000 - 30,000 USD
Samples: Berkshire Children and Families, Pittsfield, Massachusetts, $10,000 - general operating support; Bikes Not Bombs, Jamaica Plain, Massachusetts, $20,000 - general operating support; Center for Whole Communities, Waitsfield, Vermont, $5,000 - general operating support.
Contact: John K. Graham, (617) 338-2445 or (617) 338-2800; fax (617) 338-2880; jgraham@sandw.com
Sponsor: Robbins-de Beaumont Foundation
1 Post Office Square
Boston, MA 02109-2106

Robbins Charitable Foundation Grants 1602

The Robbins Charitable Foundation, based in Brookline, Massachusetts, provides support throughout the State of Massachusetts in its primary fields of interest. These interest areas include: arts and culture; the environment; health organizations; and religious welfare programs. Typically, awards are given for general operations, and most recent grants have ranged from $50 to $800. There is no formal application required, and no specified annual deadlines for submission. Interested parties should begin by contacting the Foundation office directly.
Requirements: 501(c)3 organizations in the State of Massachusetts are eligible.
Restrictions: No grants are given directly to individuals.
Geographic Focus: Massachusetts
Amount of Grant: 50 - 800 USD
Samples: Dana Farber Jimmy Fund, Brookline, Massachusetts, $320 - general operating support (2014); Perkins Institute for the Blind, Watertown, Massachusetts, $200 - general operating support (2014); Museum of Fine Arts, Boston, Massachusetts, $500 - general operating support (2014).
Contact: Phillis Robbins, Trustee; (617) 566-4919
Sponsor: Robbins Charitable Foundation
77 Marion Street
Brookline, MA 02246

Robbins Family Charitable Foundation Grants 1603

The Robbins Family Charitable Foundation, based in Omaha, Nebraska, provides grant support for local non-profit organizations. The Foundation's primary fields of interest include: children and youth services; community development; families; K-12 education; neighborhood development; religious programs; and emergency services. Funding is typically provided for general operating costs, with most recent awards ranging from $1,500 to $12,500. Though there are no identified annual submission deadlines, a formal application is required. Interested parties should begin by contacting the Foundation office directly.

Requirements: 501(c)3 organizations either located in, or serving residents of, Omaha, Nebraska, are eligible to apply.

Geographic Focus: Nebraska

Amount of Grant: 1,500 - 12,500 USD

Samples: World Herald Goodfellows Charities, Omaha, Nebraska, $10,000 - general operations (2014); Nebraska Lutheran Outdoor Ministries, Omaha, Nebraska, $8,500 - general operations (2014); Abide Network, Omaha, Nebraska, $2,500 - general operations (2014).

Contact: Leslie J. Robbins, Jr.; (402) 333-7058; lesrobbins@cox.net

Sponsor: Robbins Family Charitable Foundation

18025 Oak Street

Omaha, NE 68130-6037

Robert and Polly Dunn Foundation Grants 1604

The foundation awards grants in the U.S. Southeast, with emphasis on the Atlanta, GA, area, for projects in the area of youth, child development, and higher education. Types of support include capital campaigns, general operating support, and scholarship funds. There are no application forms. The board meets in June and December to consider requests.

Restrictions: Grants do not support individuals and not awarded to support endowment funds, loans, or program-related investments

Geographic Focus: Georgia

Date(s) Application is Due: Apr 30; Sep 30

Amount of Grant: Up to 587,925 USD

Contact: Karen Wilbanks; (404) 816-2883; fax (404) 816-2883

Sponsor: Robert and Polly Dunn Foundation

P.O. Box 723194

Atlanta, GA 31139

Robert G. Cabell III and Maude Morgan Cabell Foundation Grants 1605

The Robert G. Cabell III and Maude Morgan Cabell Foundation supports capital projects of Virginia nonprofit organizations in the areas of arts and culture, community development, higher education, historic preservation, the arts and culture, religion (Christian, Episcopal, Protestant, and Roman Catholic), social services, and community welfare. Preference will be given to the Richmond, Virginia, area. There are no application forms. Applicants may submit a written proposal that includes a brief description of the overall mission of the organization, a brief description of how the specific project supports the overall mission, a project budget, the level and type of support for the project from the local area, applicant's current operating budget and most recent budget, list of governing board and its officers, evidence of 501(c)3 status, and cover letter. Proposals are considered at grant review meetings each spring and fall.

Requirements: Virginia 501(c)3 tax-exempt organizations that are not classified as private foundations or private operating foundations are eligible.

Restrictions: The Foundation does not make grants to individuals, primary or secondary schools, or state-supported organizations; nor will grants be made for debt reduction, endowments (except for faculty development), general operating expenses, research, or scholarships.

Geographic Focus: District of Columbia, Maryland, Virginia

Date(s) Application is Due: Mar 1; Sep 1

Amount of Grant: 25,000 - 500,000 USD

Contact: Jill A. McCormick, Executive Director; (804) 780-2050; fax (804) 780-2198; cabell.foundation@gmail.com

Sponsor: Robert G. Cabell III and Maude Morgan Cabell Foundation

901 E Cary Street, Suite 1402

Richmond, VA 23219-4037

Robert Lee Adams Foundation Grants 1606

Established in 1993, the Robert Lee Adams Foundation offers general operating support funding throughout the State of California, though its region of concentration is the Los Angeles metropolitan area. The Foundation's primary fields of interest have been youth camps and human services. Applications are required and accepted at any time, though interested parties should first contact the office with a one- to two-page letter of interest delineating the need and budgetary desires.

Geographic Focus: California

Contact: Julian Eli Capata, Trustee; (213) 739-2022

Sponsor: Robert Lee Adams Foundation

3580 Wilshire Boulevard, 10th Floor

Los Angeles, CA 90010-2543

Robert Lee Blaffer Foundation Grants 1607

Established in Indiana in 2001, the Robert Lee Blaffer Foundation offers support primarily in the State of Indiana. The Foundations primary fields of interest include: education; operating support for community charities; and human services. There is no specific application form, and organizations interested in applying should contact the office directly. Final submissions should be in the form of a letter which includes: name and description of the requesting organization; and purpose of the grant; budget detail. The annual deadline is March 31

Geographic Focus: Indiana

Date(s) Application is Due: Mar 31

Amount of Grant: Up to 25,000 USD

Samples: New Harmony Foundation, New Harmony, Indiana, $23,800 - general operating expenses; Ribeyre Gymnasium Restoration, New Harmony, Indiana, $14,000 - general operating expenses; Evansville Philharmonic Orchestra, Evansville, Indiana, $9,897 - general operating expenses.

Contact: Gary Gerard, Secretary; (812) 682-3631

Sponsor: Robert Lee Blaffer Foundation

P.O. Box 399

New Harmony, IN 47631-0399

Robert R. Meyer Foundation Grants 1608

The Robert R. Meyer Foundation is a private foundation established in 1949 by Mr. Robert R. Meyer and further funded by bequests from the wills of Robert R. Meyer and John Meyer. Mr. Meyer desired that assets from his foundation be used to address needs in Birmingham and its vicinity. The foundation has made awards in the areas of arts and culture, education, environment, health, human services, and public/society benefit. The foundation meets twice a year in the spring and fall to review proposals. Applicants should contact the Trustee for application forms and guidelines.

Requirements: Giving is limited to 501(c)3 organizations in the metropolitan Birmingham, Alabama area. All applicant organizations are encouraged (but not required) to join the Alabama Association of Nonprofits.

Geographic Focus: Alabama

Date(s) Application is Due: Mar 1; Sep 1

Amount of Grant: 5,000 - 100,000 USD

Samples: A+ College Ready, Birmingham, Alabama, $50,000—to increase participation and performance of high school students in rigorous, college-level advancement placement courses in math, science, and English; Alabama Ballet, Birmingham, Alabama, $25,000—to help fund a new full-length ballet, Alice in Wonderland, in collaboration with the Alabama Symphony; Alabama Ear Institute, Mountain Brook, Alabama, $12,000—to help fund the Auditory-Verbal Mentoring Program.

Contact: Carla B. Gale, Vice President and Trust Officer; (205) 326-5382

Sponsor: Robert R. Meyer Foundation

P.O. Box 11647

Birmingham, AL 35202-1647

Robert W. Deutsch Foundation Grants 1609

The foundation provides support to technology programs in institutions of higher education in Maryland. Types of support include: continuing support, curriculum development, fellowships, general operating support, internship funds, organizational development, program development, research, and seed grants. There are no application deadlines or forms; submit initial inquiries by email or postal mail.

Restrictions: No support for religious or political organizations.

Geographic Focus: Maryland

Amount of Grant: 5,000 - 210,000 USD

Samples: University of Maryland-College Park, College Park, MD. $250,000 - For nanotechnology research, payable over 1 year.

Contact: Jane Brown, Executive Director; (410) 252-9244; fax (410) 252-0997; rdeutsch@rwd.com

Sponsor: Robert W. Deutsch Foundation

5521 Research Park Drive

Baltimore, MD 21228-4664

Robin Hood Foundation Grants 1610

The foundation's mission is to end poverty in New York City. Robin Hood makes grants to poverty-fighting organizations that are direct service providers operating in the five boroughs of New York City and has a continuing commitment to community-based programs and strong leaders in the city's poorest neighborhoods. First time grant requests are generally in the area of $100,000 to $200,000. Robin Hood will consider requests for a variety of purposes, including specific programs, salaries or start-up costs. Capital, renovation and general operating funds are given only to those groups already receiving Robin Hood support.

Requirements: Robin Hood seeks to fund 501(c)3 tax-exempt nonprofits in New York City with the following characteristics: proven track record; bold idea that is feasible; clear sense of mission and the steps needed to accomplish that mission; strong, committed leadership; existing evaluation procedures or willingness to evaluate programs and measure outcomes; commitment to, and knowledge of, the population served; high quality, dedicated staff; financial stability; and, respect or standing in its community and relationships with other organizations in the community. Applications are accepted year-round, and grant decisions will be made on a quarterly basis although decisions may take up to one year. Contact the Grants Manager before completing an application.

Restrictions: Programs that do not wish to evaluate the outcomes of their efforts should not apply to Robin Hood for funds. In general, Robin Hood does not make grants to technical assistance providers, other funders, or individuals. Robin Hood does not give grants to distribute propaganda, to attempt to influence legislation or the outcome of any public election or to engage in any activity that is not exclusively charitable, scientific or educational. Robin Hood will not support organizations that discriminate against people seeking either services or employment based on race, sex, religion, age, sexual orientation or physical disability.

Geographic Focus: New York

Amount of Grant: Up to 200,000 USD

Contact: Karen Moody, Grants Manager; (212) 227-6601; fax (212) 227-6698; grants@robinhood.org

Internet: https://www.robinhood.org/programs/get-funding

Sponsor: Robin Hood Foundation

826 Broadway, 9th Floor

New York, NY 10003

Robins Foundation Grants 1611

The foundation awards grants to nonprofit organizations in the Richmond, VA, area. Areas of interest include general grants—including cultural, charitable, scientific, environmental, and educational programs, and at-risk youth; and early childhood/quality improvement grants— for organizations that devote a major portion of their resources to young children and their families. The goal is to help improve the quality of services by providing funding for accreditation, staff training, facilities improvements, and similar initiatives. The foundation seeks projects that meet well-defined community needs, use effective approaches that build on proven programs, develop models with potential for wider application, foster self-reliance and/or end dependency, and focus on prevention as well as treatment. Types of support include capital grants and endowments.

Requirements: 501(c)3 organizations based in Virginia are eligible. Organizations based in Virginia that have or support programs outside Virginia or the United States also are eligible.

Restrictions: In general, the foundation does not make grants to support annual operating funds or budgets, special events or fundraising benefits, or religious purposes unless they are otherwise compatible with the objectives of the foundation.

Geographic Focus: Virginia

Amount of Grant: 10,000 - 100,000 USD

Contact: William Roberts Jr., Executive Director; (804) 697-6917; fax (804) 697-6797; wlrjr@robins-foundation.org

Internet: http://www.robins-foundation.org

Sponsor: Robins Foundation

Capitol Station, P.O. Box 1124

Richmond, VA 23218-1124

Rochester Area Community Foundation Grants 1612

The foundation seeks to improve the quality of life in the community and awards grants in the areas of child development, education, the environment, arts and cultural programs, health services, community development, and social services and general charitable giving. Types of support include general operating support, building construction/renovation, equipment acquisition, program development, conferences and seminars, publication, seed grants, scholarship funds, technical assistance, consulting services, and scholarships to individuals. There are no application deadlines. The board meets in January, February, March, May, June, July, October, and November.

Requirements: Nonprofits in Monroe, Livingston, Ontario, Orleans, Genessee, and Wayne Counties, NY, are eligible.

Restrictions: Grants do not support partisan political organizations or religious projects, individuals, annual campaigns, deficit financing, land acquisition, endowments, or emergency funds.

Geographic Focus: New York

Samples: Heritage Christian Services, $5,000—to support the annual Sheep Shearing Festival at Springdale Farm; Step by Step of Rochester, $12,000—to support the merger of Step by Step and Samaritan Women. Both organizations provide support to incarcerated women and their children; Arts & Cultural Council for Greater Rochester, $42,500—for Community Arts Grants, which are administered by the Arts & Cultural Council, have a capacity-building focus, and are aimed at smaller arts organizations; Lifespan of Greater Rochester, $10,000—for a financial management program which trains volunteers to provide in-home assistance with bill paying, budgeting, government benefits (such as Medicare and Medicaid), and other financial tasks for physically and/or mentally frail older adults.

Contact: Marlene Cole; (585) 341-4333; fax (585) 271-4292; mcole@racf.org

Internet: http://www.racf.org/page10000903.cfm

Sponsor: Rochester Area Community Foundation

500 East Avenue

Rochester, NY 14607-1912

Rockefeller Brothers Fund Charles E. Culpeper Arts and Culture 1613
Grants in New York City

The Fund seeks to foster an environment in which artists and the creative process can flourish by supporting organizations that assist individual artists and the creative process, provide infrastructure to sustain the artistic life, and offer additional opportunities to artists for developing skills complementary to their creative talents. In addition, the Fund seeks to sustain and advance small and mid-size cultural organizations, particularly those that are community based and/or culturally specific through the following strategies: supporting core operations by providing non-renewable, two-year capacity-building grants of up to $50,000 per year; strengthening long-term financial viability by providing endowment grants and cash reserve grants of up to $250,000 to cultural and arts organizations that demonstrate the potential for long-term leadership and excellence in the presentation of creative work to the broadest possible audiences; enhancing institutional leadership through competitive awards to arts and cultural organizations for innovative, team-based leadership conferences designed to strengthen long-range organizational management and governance; and offering grants of up to $15,000 to cover the costs of the leadership conference, including the participation of professional consultants, advisors, or facilitators (following completion of a leadership conference, the Fund may make an additional award of up to $25,000 to support the participating organization's efforts to implement some aspects of what was learned through the conference.

Requirements: A prospective grantee must be located in New York City, and must be either a tax-exempt organization or an organization seeking support for a project that would qualify as educational or charitable.

Restrictions: The fund does not make grants to individuals, nor does it as a general rule support research, graduate study, or the writing of books or dissertations by individuals.

Geographic Focus: New York

Amount of Grant: Up to 250,000 USD

Contact: Ben Rodriguez-Cubenas; (212) 812-4200; info@rbf.org

Internet: http://www.rbf.org/programs/

Sponsor: Rockefeller Brothers Fund

437 Madison Avenue, 37th Floor

New York, NY 10022-7001

Rockefeller Brothers Fund Democratic Practice Grants 1614

The Fund's Democratic Practice program has two parts: the health of democracy in the United States and the strength of democracy in global governance. Each focus has two distinct goals. Based on a careful assessment of local needs and priorities, the Fund may also pursue one or more of these goals in a limited number of its pivotal places. Recognizing that there is no single model of effective democratic practice, the Fund emphasizes flexibility and adaptability to different contexts in these pivotal places.

Requirements: A prospective grantee in the United States or foreign counterpart must be either a tax-exempt organization or an organization seeking support for a project that would qualify as educational or charitable.

Restrictions: The fund does not make grants to individuals, nor does it as a general rule support research, graduate study, or the writing of books or dissertations by individuals.

Geographic Focus: All States
Amount of Grant: 25,000 - 300,000 USD
Contact: Benjamin R. Shute; (212) 812-4200; fax (212) 812-4299; info@rbf.org
Internet: http://www.rbf.org/programs/
Sponsor: Rockefeller Brothers Fund
437 Madison Avenue, 37th Floor
New York, NY 10022-7001

Rockefeller Brothers Fund Sustainable Development Grants 1615

The Fund's sustainable development grant making endeavors to address global challenges by supporting environmental stewardship that is ecologically based, economically sound, socially just, culturally appropriate, and consistent with intergenerational equity. The Fund encourages government, business, and civil society to work collaboratively on environmental conservation and to make it an integral part of all development planning and activity. Recognizing the global nature of many environmental problems, the Fund also promotes international cooperation in addressing these challenges. Some of the Fund's sustainable development strategies are pursued at the global level, while others are pursued primarily in North America. The Russian Far East is the focus of a modest program of grant making. Major goals include: combating global warming; protecting ecosystems; and conserving biodiversity. In all regions where the RBF is engaged in sustainable development grant making, it monitors the social and environmental effects of development programs and fiscal policies that are associated with global economic integration and seeks to integrate activities across geographic areas to promote maximum impact.
Requirements: A prospective grantee in the United States or foreign counterpart must be either a tax-exempt organization or an organization seeking support for a project that would qualify as educational or charitable.
Restrictions: The fund does not make grants to individuals, nor does it as a general rule support research, graduate study, or the writing of books or dissertations by individuals.
Geographic Focus: All States
Amount of Grant: 25,000 - 300,000 USD
Contact: Michael Northrop; (212) 812-4200; fax (212) 812-4299; info@rbf.org
Internet: http://www.rbf.org/programs/
Sponsor: Rockefeller Brothers Fund
437 Madison Avenue, 37th Floor
New York, NY 10022-7001

Rockwell International Corporate Trust Grants 1616

Grants are awarded in the areas of education and youth development, with emphasis in math, science, and engineering; and culture and the arts, with emphasis on youth educational programs. Rockwell also contributes to health, human services, and civic organizations and also gives special consideration to qualifying organizations in which employees are involved as volunteers. Types of support include capital grants, challenge/matching grants, conferences and seminars, development grants, endowments, research grants, scholarship funds, and general operating grants. Awards include single-year, multiple-year, and provisional continuing support of specific programs. Applicants should submit full, detailed proposals. Proposals are accepted at any time. At the Web site, click on About Us, then Corporate Citizenship, and then Rockwell Automation Corporation Trust.
Restrictions: Organizations are not eligible if they have not received a permanent, tax-exempt ruling determination from the federal government; if they cannot provide current full, certified, audited financial statements; or if they are private foundations. Funding will not be considered for the following purposes: general endowments, deficit reduction, grants to individuals, federated campaigns, organizations or projects outside the United States, religious organizations for religious purposes, or fraternal or social organizations.
Geographic Focus: All States
Amount of Grant: 1,000 - 50,000 USD
Contact: General Information; (562) 797-3311
Internet: http://www.rockwell.com
Sponsor: Rockwell International Corporate Trust
1201 S Second Street
Milwaukee, WI 53204

Roger L. and Agnes C. Dell Charitable Trust II Grants 1617

The trust's major purpose is to assist education, the arts, and human service programs. The trust awards grants to eligible Minnesota nonprofit organizations in its areas of interest, including arts and culture, education, human services, Jewish agencies and temples, YMCAs, YWCAs, youth, and service programs. Types of support include funding for general operations and for specific project proposals.

Requirements: Minnesota 501(c)3 tax-exempt organizations in Fergus Falls and the surrounding area are eligible.
Restrictions: Individuals are not eligible for grants.
Geographic Focus: Minnesota
Date(s) Application is Due: Jun 15; Oct 15
Amount of Grant: 100 - 50,000 USD
Contact: Richard C. Hefte, Trust Manager; (218) 998-3355; fax (218) 736-3950; dell@prtel.com
Sponsor: Roger L. and Agnes C. Dell Charitable Trust II
110 North Mill Street
Fergus Falls, MN 56537

Rogers Family Foundation Grants 1618

The Rogers Family Foundation funds nonprofit organizations that provide educational, medical, artistic, and religious services within Massachusetts' Merrimack Valley and North Shore and southeastern New Hampshire. See website for specific areas served.
Requirements: Applicants must be tax exempt under section 501(c)3 of the Internal Revenue Code and classified as "not a private foundation" under Section 509(a) of the Code. All applications are submitted on-line. The online application follows the Common Proposal designed and published by Associated Grant Makers, Inc. See website for detailed online application and instructions.
Restrictions: Traditionally the Foundation awards grants to organizations located in Massachusetts' Merrimack Valley and North Shore and southeastern New Hampshire. From time to time grants may be made outside of this normal geographic area.
Geographic Focus: Massachusetts, New Hampshire
Date(s) Application is Due: Mar 1; Sep 1
Amount of Grant: 25,000 USD
Contact: Susan Haff, (617) 426-7080; fax (617) 426-7087
Internet: http://www.rogersfamilyfoundation.com/app/
Sponsor: Rogers Family Foundation
c/o GMA Foundations
Boston, MA 02110

Rollins-Luetkemeyer Foundation Grants 1619

The Foundation awards grants to eligible Maryland nonprofit organizations in its areas of interest, including education (early childhood, elementary school, and higher education), health care and health organizations, historic preservation/societies, and social services. Types of support include annual campaigns, building construction/renovation, general operating support, and project support.
Requirements: Applications are not required. Letters of intent are accepted at any time.
Restrictions: Maryland nonprofit organizations, with preference given to the Baltimore area, are eligible. No grants to individuals.
Geographic Focus: Maryland
Amount of Grant: 2,000 - 2,000,000 USD
Contact: John A. Luetkemeyer, Jr., President; (443) 921-4358
Sponsor: Rollins-Luetkemeyer Foundation
1427 Clarkview Road, Suite 500
Baltimore, MD 21209

Roney-Fitzpatrick Foundation Grants 1620

The Roney-Fitzpatrick Foundation was established to offer support in the central region of New Jersey (although grants are sometimes given throughout the United States). Its primary fields of interest include both education and human service programs. Types of funding are limited to general operating costs. There are no specified application formats or annual deadlines, and interested parties should begin by contacting the grant office with a letter describing the program and financial need. Recent funding amounts have ranged from $300 to $6,000.
Requirements: Nonprofit organizations throughout the United States are eligible to apply, although emphasis is on central New Jersey.
Restrictions: Foundation grants are not given to individuals.
Geographic Focus: All States
Amount of Grant: 4,600 - 200,000 USD
Samples: University of Miami, School of Business, Coral Gables, Florida, $6,000 - general operating costs; SPCA of Monterey County, Salinas, California, $2,500 - general operating costs; Madeira School, McLean, Virginia, $500 - general operating costs.
Contact: Edwin J. Fitzpatrick, Trustee; (212) 922-8189
Sponsor: Roney-Fitzpatrick Foundation
P.O. Box 185
Pittsburgh, PA 15230-0185

RosaMary Foundation Grants 1621

The foundation supports grantseekers within the greater New Orleans area. Highest priority is given to grants in the following categories: education, with emphasis on private institutions; human service organizations; arts, both performing and applied; community development activities; and governmental oversight activities. Types of support include capital, program, and short-term operating grants. Guidelines are available online.
Requirements: Nonprofit organizations serving the greater New Orleans, LA, area may submit grant proposals.
Restrictions: Grants are not awarded to support ticket purchases or to back fund-raising events.
Geographic Focus: Louisiana
Date(s) Application is Due: Feb 1; Sep 1
Amount of Grant: 5,000 - 150,000 USD
Contact: Toni Myers, Executive Administrator; (504) 895-1984; fax (504) 895-1988; info@rosamary.org
Internet: http://www.rosamary.org
Sponsor: RosaMary Foundation
P.O. Box 13218
New Orleans, LA 70185

Rose Community Foundation Aging Grants 1622

In its Aging program area, Rose Community Foundation promotes change in how communities organize care and support for both seniors and caregivers, with particular attention to the needs of low- and moderate-income seniors. In addition to funding community-based programs, the Foundation plays a leadership role in strengthening the existing network of aging resources, including initiatives that bring together community and government partners to address key issues in aging. The Foundation is especially interested in projects that address the following priorities: direct in-home and community-based services; transportation; and end-of-life care.
Requirements: Colorado 501(c)3 tax-exempt organizations serving the residents of Adams, Arapahoe, Boulder, Denver, Douglas, and Jefferson Counties are eligible.
Geographic Focus: Colorado
Contact: Therese Ellery, Senior Program Officer; (303) 398-7413 or (303) 398-7400; fax (303) 398-7430; tellery@rcfdenver.org
Internet: http://www.rcfdenver.org/programs_aging.htm
Sponsor: Rose Community Foundation
600 South Cherry Street, Suite 1200
Denver, CO 80246-1712

Rose Community Foundation Education Grants 1623

The Foundation's grantmaking in education reflects the principle that school programs, policies and practices should ensure the highest possible quality teaching in a community's classrooms. While the Foundation focuses its resources on efforts that lead to improved student achievement, it places greatest emphasis on two priorities in prekindergarten through grade 12. The first is quality teaching. Research consistently shows that more than any other factor in school, the quality of a student's teacher has the greatest impact on his or her performance. As a result, Rose Community Foundation values efforts to recruit, develop and retain great educators. The second priority is systemic change in individual schools and in public education. While the root causes of low student performance are many, schools and school districts do not always have the systems in place to advance learning and close persistent learning gaps between high-achieving and low-achieving students.
Requirements: Colorado 501(c)3 tax-exempt organizations serving the students of Adams, Arapahoe, Boulder, Denver, Douglas, and Jefferson Counties are eligible.
Geographic Focus: Colorado
Contact: Janet Lopez, Education Program Officer; (303) 398-7415 or (303) 398-7400; fax (303) 398-7430; jlopez@rcfdenver.org
Internet: http://www.rcfdenver.org/programs_education.htm
Sponsor: Rose Community Foundation
600 South Cherry Street, Suite 1200
Denver, CO 80246-1712

Rose Foundation For Communities and the Environment Consumer 1624
Privacy Rights Grants

The Rose Foundation supports grassroots initiatives to inspire community action to protect the environment, consumers and public health. The purpose of the Consumer Privacy Rights Fund is to support projects that relate to the preservation or promotion of privacy rights of California consumers or residents, among others. This includes, but is not limited to, grants to strengthen the organizational capacity of groups whose core mission is privacy rights.

Requirements: The applicant must demonstrate that it has the experience and expertise to promote the goals of the fund, and the capability to carry out the proposed project. The applicant must have 501(c)3 non-profit status, or a fiscal sponsor. Funds may not be used for litigation or lobbying purposes. All applicants must submit a letter of inquiry (2-pages maximum) before submitting a full proposal. Letters of inquiry are due August 31. This allows the Foundation to determine if the project will fit within the guidelines of any currently-available restitution fund. Letters of inquiry may be sent by either regular mail or email. Letters should be addressed to Karla James, Managing Director. Rose Foundation staff will contact you either by phone or email within one week of receiving your letter. At that time, the Foundation will either invite a proposal, or decline a proposal. If invited to, submit a full proposal which explains your project in detail. Full proposals are due on October 1.
Geographic Focus: California
Date(s) Application is Due: Aug 31; Oct 1
Contact: Tim Little; (510) 658-0702; fax (510) 658-0732; tlittle@rosefdn.org
Internet: http://rosefdn.org/article.php?list=type&type=76
Sponsor: Rose Foundation For Communities and the Environment
6008 College Avenue, Suite 10
Oakland, CA 94618

Rose Foundation For Communities and the Environment Northern 1625
California Environmental Grassroots Grants

The Rose Foundation supports grassroots initiatives to inspire community action to protect the environment, consumers and public health. The Grassroots Fund supports small groups throughout greater northern California that are tackling tough environmental problems including toxic pollution, urban sprawl, environmental degradation of rivers, wild places, as well as the communities health. Most grant are for a one year period. Grassroots Fund grantees are also eligible to receive up to $200 of training scholarships per year. The scholarships cover 80% of the registration cost of training. Grantees traveling more than 75 miles round trip will also receive a travel stipend. See Foundations website for further guidelines.
Requirements: To be eligible for a grassroots grant, the applicant must meet the following criteria: geographic scope - project impact must be in Northern California (includes the entire Sierra Nevada Mountains, Bay Area, Central Valley, Central Coast, and North Coast); organization size - annual income or expenses of $100,000 or less; issues supported - include, but are not limited to; environmental health and justice, land management and urban sprawl, habitat and wilderness protection, sustainable forestry, water resources, agriculture, sustainability, and pollution; strategies supported - general support for organizations with an environmental mission, or project support for strategies such as community-based advocacy, technical assistance, litigation, restoration projects, organizing expenses, grassroots campaigns, and environmental education; tax status - applicants may be a nonprofit, be fiscally sponsored by another nonprofit, or ask for fiscal sponsorship from the fund. An application form is available for download on the Foundations website. Mail application in by deadline, emailed or faxed applications will not be accepted.
Restrictions: Not eligible for support: capital campaigns, annual fundraising appeals, government agencies, colleges or universities and individuals.
Geographic Focus: California
Date(s) Application is Due: Feb 1; May 1; Aug 1; Nov 1
Amount of Grant: Up to 5,000 USD
Contact: Tim Little; (510) 658-0702; fax (510) 658-0732; tlittle@rosefdn.org
Internet: http://rosefdn.org/article.php?list=type&type=36
Sponsor: Rose Foundation For Communities and the Environment
6008 College Avenue, Suite 10
Oakland, CA 94618

Rose Foundation For Communities and the Environment Southeast 1626
Madera County Responsible Growth Grants

The Rose Foundation supports grassroots initiatives to inspire community action to protect the environment, consumers and public health. The Southeast Madera County Responsible Growth Fund was created to advocate for responsible growth in Madera County through adherence to California land use laws and Madera County General Plan policies, to promote comprehensive and integrated planning, and to ensure full compliance with the requirements of the California Environmental Quality Act, within, or pertaining to, the southeastern portion of Madera County. This Target Area is bounded on the West by State Route 99, on the North by SR 145 and on the East and South by the Millerton Reservoir and the San Joaquin River.
Requirements: Eligible applicants include governmental, public agency, quasi-governmental, or non-profit entities qualified pursuant to the requirements of the California Franchise Tax Board and the Internal Revenue Code whose

purposes include advocating for or engaging in comprehensive planning within, or for the benefit of, Madera County. Initial contact should be through a Letter of Inquiry, no more than three pages concisely describing each of the following: proposed project; project goals; explain your strategy and why this project is important; time frame; funding need; other anticipated sources of support; and a brief description of the organization requesting funds. If invited to submit a full proposal include the following: 1 page cover sheet consisting of: applicant's name, address, telephone number and website; primary contact person's name, address, telephone number, and email; amount of funds requested; EIN number; 1 - 2 paragraph short description of the proposed project; proposed start date for the project; specific statement of authorization of the application by the applicant's executive officer, including executive officer's signature. Narrative project description, not more than 5 pages long. The narrative description should describe the applicant, proposed project, overall strategic considerations, specific project workplan, key deliverables, and any other factors for consideration, such as urgency of need for support. Required Attachments: project budget; identification of other potential sources of project funding; organizational budget for the current year; balance sheet and profit/loss statement for the most recently completed year; description of lead project staff; Board of directors roster; timetable of activities; description of how the applicant will evaluate progress and any key metrics that will be used to measure performance towards grant objectives; IRS 501(c)3 determination letter or other acceptable documentation of nonprofit purpose or fiscal sponsorship. Optional Attachments: press clippings or other material describing the organization and key past accomplishments (limit 3); Letters of Reference (limit 3); submit the original application, plus 5 copies, by U.S. mail or delivery service to the Foundation.

Geographic Focus: California
Amount of Grant: 12,000 - 100,000 USD
Contact: Tim Little; (510) 658-0702; fax (510) 658-0732; tlittle@rosefdn.org
Internet: http://rosefdn.org/article.php?list=type&type=114
Sponsor: Rose Foundation For Communities and the Environment
6008 College Avenue, Suite 10
Oakland, CA 94618

Rose Hills Foundation Grants 1627

The Rose Hills Foundation accepts and processes applications for grants throughout the year with the expectation of grant distributions every six months. Depending on timing, requests are reviewed at six annual Board Meetings. At times, there may be an approximate wait of up to six months prior to a request being reviewed. Grants range from $5,000 to million dollar commitments. Foundation directors may opt to grant less than the amount requested, depending upon resources available, or spread payments over more than one year.

Requirements: Preferential attention is given to organizations that exhibit the following criteria: a history of achievement, good management, and a stable financial condition; self-sustaining programs that are unlikely to depend on future Foundation funding; significant programs that make a measurable impact; funding that is matched or multiplied by other sources; projects or programs that benefit people of southern California; and programs that reach the greatest number of people at the most reasonable cost. Organizations should send a two page letter of introduction (LOI) addressed to the Foundation's President. Initial correspondence should include the following information: brief purpose and history of organization; brief outline of program/project for which funds are being sought; program/project budget; specific amount being requested from Foundation; geographic area, demographics of population, and the number of individuals served annually; list of Board of Directors; current operating budget and most recent audited financials (if not available, please provide most recent financial statement); copy of IRS determination letter; and a detailed funding history.

Restrictions: Funding is not available for propagandizing, influencing legislation and/ or elections or promoting voter registration; political candidates, political campaigns or organizations engaging in political activities; programs which promote religious doctrine; individuals (except as permitted by the IRS); governmental agencies; or endowments.

Geographic Focus: California
Amount of Grant: 5,000 - 1,000,000 USD
Contact: Victoria Rogers, President; (626) 696-2220; fax (626) 696-2210; vbrogers@rosehillsfoundation.org
Internet: http://www.rosehillsfoundation.org/AppProcedures.htm
Sponsor: Rose Hills Foundation
225 South Lake Avenue, Suite 1250
Pasadena, CA 91101

Roy A. Hunt Foundation Grants 1628

The foundation awards general grants in the areas of arts and culture; education; environmental conservation; health; human services; international affairs, development, and peace; public/safety benefit; and religion. Most grants are awarded for general operating support. The foundation also funds special initiatives in the areas of community development, environment, and youth violence prevention. Special initiative grants are administered according to specific guidelines and have earlier application deadlines. Guidelines for both categories are available online. First-time applicants are advised to submit a preliminary letter of inquiry. Proposals for general grants from previously funded organizations are considered only in November and do not require a preliminary letter of inquiry. Deadlines are April 15 and September 15 for general grants; and March 1 and August 1 for special initiatives.

Requirements: Tax-exempt organizations are eligible.
Geographic Focus: Massachusetts, Pennsylvania
Amount of Grant: 100 - 25,000 USD
Contact: Administrator; (412) 281-8734; fax (412) 255-0522; info@rahuntfdn.org
Internet: http://www.rahuntfdn.org/programs.shtml
Sponsor: Roy A. Hunt Foundation
1 Bigelow Square, Suite 630
Pittsburgh, PA 15219-3030

Roy and Christine Sturgis Charitable Trust Grants 1629

The Roy and Christine Sturgis Charitable Trust was established in 1981 to support and promote quality educational, cultural, human-services, and health-care programming for all people. Roy Sturgis was one of ten children of an Arkansas farmer and homemaker. He dropped out of school after the tenth grade to join the Navy during World War I. Sturgis returned to his family home in southern Arkansas after the war and went to work in the local sawmills. In 1933, he married Texas native Christine Johns. They became very successful in the timber, lumber, and sawmill industries in Arkansas, owned other prosperous business enterprises, and had notable success managing their investments. The Sturgis' spent most of their lives in Arkansas and Dallas, Texas. They did not have children, but were particularly interested in educational opportunities for young people. In addition, they supported organizations working in the areas of health, social services, and the arts. The Sturgis Charitable Trust encourages requests for the following types of grants: capital, project-related, medical research, and endowment campaign. Funding for start-up programs and limited general-operating requests will also be considered. Approximately 65% of the trust's annual distributions are made within the state of Arkansas. The remaining 35% of grants are distributed within the state of Texas with strong preference given to organizations located in the Dallas area. The majority of grants from the Sturgis Charitable Trust are one year in duration; on occasion, multi-year support is awarded. Applicants should apply online at the grant website, and are strongly encouraged to do the following before applying: review the downloadable state application procedures for additional helpful information and clarifications; review the downloadable online-application guidelines at the grant website; review the trust's funding history (link is available from the grant website); review the online application questions in advance; and review the list of required attachments. These will generally include: a list of board members, financial statements (audited, reviewed, or compiled by independent auditor); an organization summary; a list of other funding sources; an IRS Determination letter; and other required documents. All attachments must be uploaded in the online application as PDF, Word, or Excel files. Most recent awards have ranged from $150,000 to $200,000. The annual application deadline is March 1.

Requirements: 501(c)3 nonprofits in Texas and Arkansas are eligible.
Restrictions: Former grantees must skip a year before submitting a subsequent application. The trust does not support requests from individuals, organizations attempting to influence policy through direct lobbying, or any political campaigns.
Geographic Focus: Arkansas, Texas
Date(s) Application is Due: Mar 1
Amount of Grant: 150,000 - 200,000 USD
Samples: University of Arkansas, Little Rock, Arkansas, $200,000 - support of an endowed professorship at the Nanotechnology and Educational Center (2014); City of Little Rock, Little Rock, Arkansas, $150,000 - support of the Stone Bridge at William J. Clinton Presidential Library Center and Park (2014).
Contact: Robert Fox, Senior Philanthropic Relationship Manager; (214) 209-1965 or (214) 209-1370; tx.philanthropic@ustrust.com
Internet: https://www.bankofamerica.com/philanthropic/fn_search.action
Sponsor: Roy and Christine Sturgis Charitable Trust
901 Main Street, 19th Floor
Dallas, TX 75202-3714

Roy J. Carver Charitable Trust Public Library Grants   **1630**

The Trust offers directed support for the establishment, expansion and enhancement of community-based library facilities and services. Grants of up to $60,000 are generally awarded for construction, renovation and/or furnishings and equipment needs, including technology-based initiatives that link libraries across multiple sites. Projects emphasizing library patronage among youth are especially encouraged.

Requirements: Grants are made to 501(c)3 tax-exempt public libraries in Iowa and western Illinois.

Restrictions: The Trust does not provide grants specifically targeted to making libraries handicapped accessible. In addition, the Trust has traditionally avoided awarding grants to support the creation of Iowa Communications Network (ICN) classrooms within new or existing library facilities. Also, the Trust does not provide funding for joint school/community library projects or facilities. Once a facility has successfully secured a grant award from the Carver Trust, no additional applications for funding will be considered for a period of at least five years.

Geographic Focus: Illinois, Iowa

Amount of Grant: Up to 60,000 USD

Contact: Dr. Troy Ross, Executive Administrator; (563) 263-4010; fax (563) 263-1547; info@carvertrust.org

Internet: https://www.carvertrust.org/index.php?page=45

Sponsor: Roy J. Carver Charitable Trust

202 Iowa Avenue

Muscatine, IA 52761-3733

RRF General Program Grants   **1631**

The program funds service, education, research, and advocacy projects. The foundation is particularly interested in innovative projects that have the potential to change practice, policy, or delivery systems. The foundation's programs seek to improve the availability and quality of community-based and institutional long-term care programs; expand opportunities for older persons to play meaningful roles in society; support selected basic, applied, and policy research into the causes and solutions of significant problems of the aged; and increase the number of professionals and paraprofessionals adequately prepared to serve the elderly. Proposals fall into three general categories: research, model projects and service, and education and training. Guidelines are available online.

Requirements: Direct service projects that seek to improve the availability and quality of community-based and institutional long-term care programs; expand opportunities for older persons to play meaningful roles in society; support selected applied and policy research into the causes and solutions of significant problems of the aged; increase the number of professionals and paraprofessionals adequately prepared to serve the elderly.

Restrictions: The foundation will only consider proposals from applicants in Illinois, Indiana, Iowa, Kentucky, Missouri, Wisconsin, and Florida. Priority is given to nonprofit organizations serving the Chicago metropolitan area.

Geographic Focus: Florida, Illinois, Indiana, Iowa, Kentucky, Missouri, Wisconsin

Date(s) Application is Due: Feb 1; May 1; Aug 1

Amount of Grant: Up to 15,000,000 USD

Contact: Marilyn Hennessy; (773) 714-8080; fax (773) 714-8089; info@rrf.org

Internet: http://www.rrf.org/generalProgram.htm

Sponsor: Retirement Research Foundation

8765 W Higgins Road, Suite 430

Chicago, IL 60631-4170

RRF Organizational Capacity Building Grants   **1632**

The foundation provides grants for capacity-building activities that will help a nonprofit organization improve its management or governance to better serve the elderly. The following are examples of activities that will be supported but are not meant to exclude other ideas: planning (strategic, business, and financial plans) to steer an organization through changes; organizational assessments to identify problem areas that need to be strengthened; evaluation to develop outcome measures and determine progress in order to strengthen accountability to constituents and funding sources; public relations, communications, and marketing to increase awareness and utilization of services; financial management and resource development to improve financial systems, explore revenue options, and develop a stronger funding base; human resources management to enhance professional development, do team building, and improve the working environment; information systems management to identify and incorporate technology to improve efficiency; restructuring and building relations among organizations to strengthen service delivery, reduce costs, share resources, develop joint evaluations, or achieve other benefits;

and board assessment, recruitment, training and structuring to strengthen the governance of the organization. All organizations that receive a grant are eligible for additional funding over the course of the grant, to be used flexibly for technical assistance opportunities that arise during the course of the grant. These may include seminars, workshops, short-term courses, publications, or other training opportunities related to organizational capacity building.

Requirements: For an organization to be eligible, it must meet the following criteria: be a nonprofit organization, but not a unit of government; be located in Cook, DuPage Kane, Kendall, Lake, or McHenry County, IL; provide services to the elderly; and intentionally give a high priority to the elderly.

Restrictions: The foundation will not fund building, renovation or capital improvements; emergency needs; deficits; or one-time events that do not build long-term capacity, i.e. fundraising events or one-time conferences.

Geographic Focus: Illinois

Date(s) Application is Due: Feb 1; May 1; Aug 1

Amount of Grant: 30,000 - 75,000 USD

Contact: Mary O'Donnell, Coordinator; (773) 714-8080; info@rrf.org

Internet: http://www.rrf.org/organizationalCapacityBuildingProgram.htm

Sponsor: Retirement Research Foundation

8765 W Higgins Road, Suite 430

Chicago, IL 60631-4170

Rucker-Donnell Foundation Grants   **1633**

The Foundation, established in 2001, is involved with the support of community expansion and development throughout the Murfreesboro, Tennessee, region. It would appear that, in the past, the Foundation's primary fields of interest include: community development/expansion, the arts, and the environment. Specific support is given for general operations. There are no particular deadlines or guidelines, and potential applicants should contact the office before proceeding.

Geographic Focus: Tennessee

Contact: Rick G. Mansfield, Trustee; (615) 890-5700

Internet: http://ruckerdonnellfoundation.org/templates/System/default.asp?id=37512

Sponsor: Rucker-Donnell Foundation

110 S Maple Street

Murfreesboro, TN 37130-3530

Russell Berrie Foundation Grants   **1634**

The foundation supports nonprofit organizations primarily in Israel and the New York and New Jersey metropolitan areas. Grants are awarded for education (colleges and universities, Jewish education, divinity schools, parochial elementary and secondary schools, and religious higher education), health care (hospitals and respite homes), international programs (development programs, ministries, and missions), religious organizations (religious welfare, synagogues, and temples), social issues, and youth welfare. Types of support include capital support and general operating support. Applicants should submit a brief letter of inquiry and include a description of the program and the organization, including a financial statement. There are no application deadlines.

Requirements: Christian, Jewish, and Roman Catholic organizations in New York, New Jersey, and Israel are eligible.

Geographic Focus: New Jersey, New York, Israel

Amount of Grant: 5,000 - 20,000 USD

Samples: Pave the Way Foundation (New York, NY)—for unrestricted support of this organization that promotes good will and reconciliation between different religions, $100,000; American Technion Society (New York, NY)—to establish a nanotechnology institute at the Technion-Israel Institute of Technology, in Haifa, $26 million.

Contact: Susan Strunk, Administrative Director; (201) 928-1880

Internet: http://www.russberrie.com/foundation.html

Sponsor: Russell Berrie Foundation

300 Frank Burr Boulevard, Building E, 7th Floor

Teaneck, NJ 07666-6704

Russell Family Foundation Environmental Sustainability Grants   **1635**

The foundation is committed to improving protection of the environment in western Washington, with an emphasis on the waters of Puget Sound. The foundation focuses its grantmaking in this program on Puget Sound, Environmental Education and Green Business and supports systemic and community-centered strategies that encourage collaboration across sectors and, where possible, leverage other support, build partnerships and reach new audiences. Though not a requirement for funding, they welcome projects that effectively address and connect several of the above-mentioned areas of interest.

Requirements: A Letter of Inquiry is required prior to any formal application. If the foundation is interested in considering a grant request, they will ask for a more detailed proposal. Full proposals are accepted by invitation only.
Restrictions: Requests are accepted from 501(c)3 organizations. Nonprofit entities such as public schools and school districts also may apply. Organizations must be located in and/or provide services within the Puget Sound region. The region includes 12 counties: Clallam, Jefferson, Kitsap, Mason, Thurston, Pierce, King, Snohomish, Skagit, Whatcom, Island, and San Juan.
Geographic Focus: Washington
Date(s) Application is Due: Jan 8; Jul 16
Amount of Grant: 1,000 - 35,000 USD
Contact: Grant Administrator; info@trff.org
Internet: http://www.trff.org/grant_programs/env_education.asp
Sponsor: Russell Family Foundation
P.O. Box 2567
Gig Harbor, WA 98335

Ruth Anderson Foundation Grants 1636

The Ruth Anderson Foundation awards grants to Florida nonprofit organizations in Dade County. The Foundation's funding interests include AIDS research; children and youth services; homeless/housing shelters; human services; and substance abuse services. There are no application forms or deadlines. The initial approach should consist of a brief exploratory letter; full proposals will be by invitation only. The board meets throughout the year to consider requests for funding.
Requirements: Miami Dade County 501(c)3 organizations are eligible.
Restrictions: Grants are not awarded to individuals. Funding is limited to the Miami area.
Geographic Focus: Florida
Amount of Grant: 1,000 - 10,000 USD
Contact: Funding Contact; (305) 789-4929
Sponsor: Ruth Anderson Foundation
1525 W. W.T. Harris Boulevard, D1114-044
Charlotte, NC 28288-1161

Ruth and Vernon Taylor Foundation Grants 1637

The foundation awards grants to nonprofit organizations in the areas of arts and humanities, civic and public affairs, secondary schools, higher education, environment, hospitals, human services, health, youth services, and social services. Types of support include general operating support, building construction and renovation, endowment funds, and research. The foundation suggests that initial contact be made in writing, since unsolicited requests for funds are not accepted. The Board meets in May and September.
Requirements: Organizations located in Colorado, Illinois, Montana, New Jersey, New York, Pennsylvania, Texas, or Wyoming are eligible.
Restrictions: Grants are not awarded to individuals.
Geographic Focus: Colorado, Illinois, Montana, New Jersey, New York, Pennsylvania, Texas, Wyoming
Amount of Grant: 1,000 - 20,000 USD
Contact: Douglas Taylor, Trustee; (303) 893-5284; fax (303)893-8263
Sponsor: Ruth and Vernon Taylor Foundation
518 17th Street, Suite 1670
Denver, CO 80202

Ruth Eleanor Bamberger and John Ernest Bamberger Memorial 1638
Foundation Grants

The Foundation is dedicated to fulfilling the Founders' desires to help people reach their individual potential. The Foundation assists people of all ages, but especially children and young people through educational opportunities and scholarships, supporting crisis care and protective services, dental aid, after school programs, etc.
Requirements: Only residents of Utah may apply.
Restrictions: Grants and scholarships are given only to organizations, not to individuals personally.
Geographic Focus: Utah
Date(s) Application is Due: Mar 16; Sep 28
Amount of Grant: 1,000 - 20,000 USD
Contact: Eleanor Roser, Treasurer; (801) 364-2045; bambergermemfdn@ qwestoffice.net
Internet: http://www.ruthandjohnbambergermemorialfdn.org/
Sponsor: Ruth Eleanor Bamberger and John Ernest Bamberger Memorial Foundation
136 S Main, Suite 418
Salt Lake City, UT 84101-1690

Ruth H. and Warren A. Ellsworth Foundation Grants 1639

The foundation awards grants to nonprofits in Massachusetts in support of the arts, children and youth, community development, education and higher education, and health care and hospitals. Types of support include general operating support, continuing support, annual campaigns, building construction/renovation, equipment acquisition, emergency funds, and seed grants. There are no application forms.
Requirements: Nonprofits in the Worcester, MA, area are eligible.
Restrictions: Grants are not awarded to individuals or for endowment funds, scholarships, fellowships, research, publications, conferences, matching gifts, or loans.
Geographic Focus: Massachusetts
Amount of Grant: 500 - 100,000 USD
Samples: Bancroft School, Worcester, MA, $125,000; UMass Memorial Foundation, Worcester, MA, $50,000;
Contact: Sumner Tilton Jr., Trustee; (508) 798-8621
Sponsor: Ruth H. and Warren A. Ellsworth Foundation
370 Main Street, 12th Floor, Suite 1250
Worcester, MA 01608-1723

Ruth Mott Foundation Grants 1640

The community is invited to submit grant requests for the program areas of arts—culture, music, theater, dance, media, graphics, photography, storytelling, and crafts; beautification—enhance neighborhoods and quality of life in the greater Flint area; and health promotion—healthy and active lifestyles and environments such as physical activity, proper nutrition, responsible sexual behavior, and overall well-being. Types of support include special projects, capacity building (planning, technical assistance, and resource development), evaluation, and general purposes. Priority is given to requests that bring diverse segments of the community together to share ideas and common interests and to respectfully address and resolve differences; enable the engagement of citizens in civic life, community service and leadership; ensure that all stakeholders are informed and involved in decisions affecting them; promote life-long learning and involvement; share and celebrate community members' unique talents, histories, cultures, and contributions; and benefit low-income segments of the community and reduce social, economic, and racial disparities. Concept papers may be submitted at any time throughout the year; full proposals are by invitation.
Requirements: Michigan nonprofit organizations are eligible. Preference is given to requests from Flint, MI.
Geographic Focus: All States
Amount of Grant: Up to 65,000,000 USD
Contact: Grants Administrator; (810) 233-0170
Internet: http://www.ruthmottfoundation.org
Sponsor: Ruth Mott Foundation
111 E Court Street, Suite 3C
Flint, MI 48502-1649

RWJF Partners Investing in Nursing's Future Grants 1641

The Partners Investing in Nursing's Future Grants program is a collaborative initiative of the Robert Wood Johnson Foundation (RWJF) and the Northwest Health Foundation (NWHF), with the intention of addressing nursing issues at the community level through funding partnerships with local and regional foundations. Up to ten awards of up to $250,000 each will be made for projects lasting up to 24 months. Local foundations, with other partners (such as state workforce investment boards, hospital and long-term-care associations, foundations and other funding sources) will match these awards with at least $1 for every $2 provided by the program. Funding will be commensurate with the size and scope of the proposed activity and the foundation's experience with nursing issues. Funding is not intended to support the continuation of ongoing projects, but it may support new programs led by foundations that are already working in the field of nursing.
Requirements: Eligible institutions include local or regional private, family or community foundations and public charities. Eligible foundations are those classified as tax-exempt under Section 501(c)3 as a public charity or private foundation, a nonexempt charitable trust treated as a private foundation under Section 4947(a)(1), or organizations that claim status as private operating foundations under Section 4942(j)3 or 4942(j)5 of the Internal Revenue Code. Government entities, corporate grant-makers and others may participate as part of funding collaboratives; however, they may not serve as the applicant institution. All proposals to this program must address one or more of these topics: Diversity; Educational Infrastructure and Faculty Development; Public Health; Long-Term Care; and/or Mid-Level Management. Proposals for planning as well as implementation projects will be considered.

Geographic Focus: All States
Amount of Grant: Up to 250,000 USD
Contact: Renee' Jensen Reinhardt, Program Officer; (971) 230-0093; fax (503) 220-1335; renee@nwhf.org or info@PartnersInNursing.org
Internet: http://www.partnersinnursing.org/
Sponsor: Robert Wood Johnson Foundation
Route 1 and College Road East, P.O. Box 2316
Princeton, NJ 08543-2316

Ryder System Charitable Foundation Grants 1642

The Ryder System Charitable Foundation was established in 1984 in Florida. The Foundation supports zoological societies and organizations involved with arts and culture, education, animal welfare, health, cystic fibrosis, and human services. Giving is limited to Los Angeles, CA, southern FL, Atlanta, GA, St. Louis, MO, Cincinnati, OH, and Dallas, TX.
Requirements: Organizations in California, Florida, Georgia, Missouri, Ohio, and Texas are eligible to apply. There is no application form, Applicants should submit the following: brief history of organization and description of its mission; copy of most recent annual report/audited financial statement/990; explanation of why grantmaker is considered an appropriate donor for project; listing of board of directors, trustees, officers and other key people and their affiliations; detailed description of project and amount of funding requested; copy of IRS Determination Letter.
Geographic Focus: California, Florida, Georgia, Missouri, Ohio, Texas
Amount of Grant: 100 - 100,000 USD
Samples: Scholarship America, Saint Peter, MN, $10,000;
Contact: Grants Administrator c/o Corp. Tax; (305) 500-3031; fax (305) 500-4579; foundation@ryder.com
Sponsor: Ryder System Charitable Foundation
11690 NW 105th Street
Miami, FL 33178-1103

S. D. Bechtel, Jr. Foundation / Stephen Bechtel Fund Character and 1643 Citizenship Development Grants

The Foundation/Fund believe that all people are capable of making positive choices and ethical decisions, and of becoming active citizens. For young people, it is critical that they are provided with consistent and sound mentoring, and the encouragement to participate in new learning opportunities to realize their full potential and become responsible and active citizens. The directors have a strong interest in programs for young people that build character and programs for the broader public that advance an understanding of, and commitment to, the practice of citizenship. The Foundation/Fund support organizations working to achieve the following objectives: increasing opportunities for youth in the San Francisco Bay Area to interact with exemplary role models and participate in a variety of worthwhile learning opportunities so that they are able to develop a framework for ethical living; and advancing a vibrant and productive national conversation about why active citizenship matters and how Americans can cultivate and sustain these values.
Requirements: The primary geographic focus of the Foundation/Fund is the San Francisco Bay area. The Foundation/Fund: support non-profit organizations providing quality programs in science, technology, engineering and math (STEM) education, environment, environmental education, character and citizenship development and preventive healthcare and selected research; provide capital support; provide operational support; and provide project support.
Restrictions: The Foundation/Fund do not provide endowment funding, international grants, or grants for individuals.
Geographic Focus: California
Date(s) Application is Due: Oct 1
Amount of Grant: 5,000 - 25,000 USD
Contact: Program Coordinator; (415) 284-8675; fax (415) 284-8571; sdbjr@sdbjrfoundation.org
Internet: http://www.sdbjrfoundation.org/program_areas.htm#Char_citiz
Sponsor: S. D. Bechtel, Jr. Foundation / Stephen Bechtel Fund
P.O. Box 193809
San Francisco, CA 94119-3809

S. D. Bechtel, Jr. Foundation/Stephen Bechtel Fund Environmental 1644 Education Grants

The Foundations believe that environmental education is vital to the development of a knowledgeable, skilled, and responsible California population that takes individual and collective actions to protect and improve the environment, human health, and economic prosperity. The Directors have a particular interest in supporting environmental education in order to further the goals of the STEM education, environment, character and citizenship development, and preventive healthcare program areas by improving access to high-quality programs and engaging all Californians in environmental learning and behavior. The Foundation supports organizations working to achieve the following objectives: building the research base to advance environmental education teaching and learning; expanding support for environmental education and promote environmental behavior; inspiring personal connections to the natural world and interest in STEM learning by strengthening systems that serve students in the San Francisco Bay Area; and encouraging local stewardship and develop new environmental leaders from urban communities in the San Francisco Bay Area.
Requirements: The primary geographic focus of the Foundation/Fund is the San Francisco Bay area. The Foundation/Fund: support non-profit organizations providing quality programs in science, technology, engineering and math (STEM) education, environment, environmental education, character and citizenship development and preventive healthcare and selected research; provide capital support; provide operational support; and provide project support.
Restrictions: The Foundation/Fund do not provide endowment funding, international grants, or grants for individuals.
Geographic Focus: California
Date(s) Application is Due: Oct 1
Amount of Grant: 5,000 - 25,000 USD
Contact: Coordinator; (415) 284-8675; sdbjr@sdbjrfoundation.org
Internet: http://www.sdbjrfoundation.org/program_areas.htm#enviro_ed
Sponsor: S. D. Bechtel, Jr. Foundation / Stephen Bechtel Fund
P.O. Box 193809
San Francisco, CA 94119-3809

S. D. Bechtel, Jr. Foundation / Stephen Bechtel Fund Environment 1645 Grants

The Foundation/Fund believe that the sustainable management of natural resources is vital to California's quality of life and economic well-being. The directors have a particular interest in supporting well-managed organizations and networks that promote lasting environmental benefits for California. The Foundation/Fund support organizations working to achieve the following objectives: advance the institutions and infrastructure necessary for California to manage its water resources to support a healthy economy while protecting public health, safety and critical ecosystem services; protect and enhance the network of lands, waters, and organizations sustaining the migratory birds of the Pacific Flyway; secure sustained investment in parks and build capacity of park managers and park supporting organizations; and support selected science and policy research to illuminate the path to a more secure and sustainable energy future.
Requirements: The primary geographic focus of the Foundation/Fund is the San Francisco Bay area. The Foundation/Fund: support non-profit organizations providing quality programs in science, technology, engineering and math (STEM) education, environment, environmental education, character and citizenship development and preventive healthcare and selected research; provide capital support; provide operational support; and provide project support.
Restrictions: The Foundation/Fund do not provide endowment funding, international grants, or grants for individuals.
Geographic Focus: California
Date(s) Application is Due: Oct 1
Amount of Grant: 5,000 - 25,000 USD
Contact: Coordinator; (415) 284-8675; sdbjr@sdbjrfoundation.org
Internet: http://www.sdbjrfoundation.org/program_areas.htm
Sponsor: S. D. Bechtel, Jr. Foundation / Stephen Bechtel Fund
P.O. Box 193809
San Francisco, CA 94119-3809

S. D. Bechtel, Jr. Foundation / Stephen Bechtel Fund Preventive 1646 Healthcare and Selected Research Grants

The Foundation?fund believe that access to quality care, preventive health care and research programs can help individuals of all ages increase life expectancy and improve their quality of life. The directors have a particular interest in promoting nutritional health, fitness, and wellness in order to increase positive health outcomes. The Foundation/Fund support organizations working to achieve the following objectives: enabling San Francisco Bay Area community clinics and school-based health centers to improve the quality and delivery of medical care; enhancing and expand school-based efforts in the San Francisco Bay Area that improve the nutritional health and fitness of children; and advancing research related to Alzheimer's, aging, nutrition or other Board-determined specific research initiatives.

Requirements: The primary geographic focus of the Foundation/Fund is the San Francisco Bay area. The Foundation/Fund: support non-profit organizations providing quality programs in science, technology, engineering and math (STEM) education, environment, environmental education, character and citizenship development and preventive healthcare and selected research; provide capital support; provide operational support; and provide project support.

Restrictions: The Foundation/Fund do not provide endowment funding, international grants, or grants for individuals.

Geographic Focus: California

Date(s) Application is Due: Oct 1

Amount of Grant: 5,000 - 25,000 USD

Contact: Coordinator; (415) 284-8675; sdbjr@sdbjrfoundation.org

Internet: http://www.sdbjrfoundation.org/program_areas.htm#health

Sponsor: S. D. Bechtel, Jr. Foundation / Stephen Bechtel Fund

P.O. Box 193809

San Francisco, CA 94119-3809

S. D. Bechtel, Jr. Foundation / Stephen Bechtel Fund Science, Technology, Engineering and Math Education Grants 1647

The Foundation/Fund believe that America's strength in the STEM fields enables its capacity to compete globally, enhances its opportunities for innovation, and leads to economic prosperity and a better quality of life for society as a whole. The directors have a particular interest in supporting science, technology, engineering, and math education in order to foster a robust and competitive workforce and to develop a STEM-literate populace that understands and appreciates the contributions made by engineering and science to society's welfare. The Foundation/Fund support organizations to achieve the following objectives: engaging students at an early age (K-8) in STEM learning both in-school and out-of-school, particularly in the San Francisco Bay Area; enable and strengthen STEM pathways at key transition points along California's K-14 public educational system; developing regional and state infrastructure, capacity and networks to advance STEM teaching and learning in California; and supporting public awareness and advocacy efforts to build demand for STEM education.

Requirements: The primary geographic focus of the Foundation/Fund is the San Francisco Bay area. The Foundation/Fund do: support non-profit organizations providing quality programs in science, technology, engineering and math (STEM) education, environment, environmental education, character and citizenship development and preventive healthcare and selected research; provide capital support; provide operational support; and provide project support.

Restrictions: The Foundation does not provide endowment funding, international grants, or grants for individuals.

Geographic Focus: California

Date(s) Application is Due: Oct 1

Amount of Grant: 5,000 - 25,000 USD

Contact: Coordinator; (415) 284-8675; sdbjr@sdbjrfoundation.org

Internet: http://www.sdbjrfoundation.org/program_areas.htm

Sponsor: S. D. Bechtel, Jr. Foundation / Stephen Bechtel Fund

P.O. Box 193809

San Francisco, CA 94119-3809

S.H. Cowell Foundation Grants 1648

The foundation awards grants for a wide variety of causes to nonprofit organizations in northern California. Projects of interest include those that support children, youth, and families; education; housing; alcohol abuse prevention; religious organizations, education, and welfare; school-to-work employment training; population and environment; family planning; and conventional arms control. Applicants are encouraged to obtain most of their operating and project funding from other sources. Matching and challenge grants will be awarded under appropriate circumstances. The foundation prefers to award grants for one-time capital needs or for specific projects that are time-definite in nature and likely to become self-sufficient within several years. The application process should begin with a phone call. If interested, the foundation will request a short letter and then a formal proposal.

Requirements: Grants are made only to 501(c)3 tax-exempt organizations primarily in northern California.

Restrictions: The foundation does not normally make grants to individuals, for start-up of new organizations, for academic or other research, for general support, for annual fund-raising, to governmental agencies, to churches for religious support, to hospitals for medical research or treatment, for conferences, for media projects, or for political lobbying.

Geographic Focus: California

Amount of Grant: Up to 500,000 USD

Samples: Adventure Risk Challenge, Truckee, CA, $25,000 - to launch year-round expansion of the Adventure Risk Challenge (ARC) summer program; Boys & Girls Clubs of the North Valley Chico, CA, $500,000 - to launch a Boys & Girls Club in South Oroville; East Bay Asian Local Development Corporation Oakland, CA, $375,000 - to complete the budget to install a park at Lion Creek Crossings;

Contact: Susan Vandiver; (415) 397-0285; fax (415) 986-6786; info@shcowell.org

Internet: http://www.shcowell.org/grant/grant.php

Sponsor: S.H. Cowell Foundation

120 Montgomery Street, Suite 2570

San Francisco, CA 94104

S. Livingston Mather Charitable Trust Grants 1649

The S. Livingston Mather Charitable Trust was established in 1953 in Ohio by Cleveland-Cliffs vice-president Samuel Livingston Mather. The Trust's primary areas of interest include cultural programs, education, child welfare, and social services. Support is also available for youth programs, the environment, and natural resources. Giving is primarily restricted to the northeastern Ohio area. Applicants should contact the Trust prior to submitting an application.

Requirements: Unsolicited requests for funds not accepted, contact the Trust before sending a proposal.

Restrictions: No support is available for: endowments; science; medical research programs; in areas appropriately supported by the government and/or the United Way; individuals; or deficit financing.

Geographic Focus: Ohio

Amount of Grant: 100 - 100,000 USD

Samples: Cleveland Museum of Art, Cleveland, OH, $20,000; Cuyahoga Valley Countryside Conservancy, Peninsula, OH, $7,500.

Contact: Janet W. Havener; (215) 419-6000

Sponsor: S. Livingston Mather Charitable Trust

1 Corporate Exchange, 25825 Science Park Drive, Suite 110

Beachwood, OH 44122

S. Mark Taper Foundation Grants 1650

The S. Mark Taper Foundation, founded in 1989, is a private family foundation dedicated to enhancing the quality of people's lives by supporting nonprofit organizations and their work in the Los Angeles, Long Beach, Santa Ana, California communities. Areas of interest are broad and include but are not limited to education, the environment, independent living for the disabled, abused women, immigrant health care, children, hunger, housing, AIDS, teenage pregnancy prevention, job creation and economic revitalization, individuals with visual impairments, and the arts. Types of support include capital grants, challenge/matching grants, general operating grants, research grants, program/project grants, seed money grants, and scholarships. Grants are made generally for one year.

Requirements: 501(c)3 nonprofit organizations in California are eligible for grant support. Application forms are required therefore your initial approach should be a Letter of Inquiry containing one copy of the proposal and the following: brief history of organization and description of its mission; copy of most recent annual report/audited financial statement/990; detailed description of project and amount of funding requested; list of source(s) of last three years of funding for the specific project (if any) and, the organization.

Geographic Focus: California

Date(s) Application is Due: Dec 1

Amount of Grant: 5,000 - 500,000 USD

Samples: Korean Health Education Information and Research Center, Los Angeles, CA - $500,000; Santa Clarita Child and Family Development Center, Santa Clarita, CA - $100,000; Los Angeles Unified School District Education Foundation, Los Angeles, CA - $200,000;

Contact: Raymond Reister, Executive Director; (310) 476-5413; fax (310) 471-4993; rreisler@smtfoundation.org or info@smtfoundation.org

Internet: http://www.smtfoundation.org/

Sponsor: S. Mark Taper Foundation

12011 San Vicente Boulevard, Suite 400

Los Angeles, CA 90049

S. Spencer Scott Fund Grants 1651

Established in New York in 1949, the S. Spencer Scott Fund serves the residents of Connecticut, Rhode Island, New York, Vermont, Maine, Maryland, New Hampshire, Pennsylvania, and Massachusetts. Its primary fields of interest include the arts, museums, education, and religion. There are no particular application forms or annual deadlines, and applicants are advised to contact the Fund directly. Funding general is given for general operations, and amounts range from $250 to $5,000.

Requirements: Any 501(c)3 organization serving the residents of Connecticut, Rhode Island, New York, Vermont, Maryland, Maine, New Hampshire, Pennsylvania, and Massachusetts are eligible to apply.
Geographic Focus: Connecticut, Maine, Maryland, Massachusetts, New Hampshire, New York, Pennsylvania, Rhode Island, Vermont
Amount of Grant: 250 - 5,000 USD
Contact: Suzette Hearn, Treasurer; (212) 286-2600
Sponsor: S. Spencer Scott Fund
60 E. 42nd Street, Suite 3600
New York, NY 10165-0006

Sabina Dolan and Gladys Saulsbury Foundation Grants   1652
The Sabina Dolan and Gladys Saulsbury Foundation was established in New Haven, Connecticut, to support needy children who wish to attend summer camp. Its primary fields of interest are education and human services. Types of grant support include: general operations for human services agencies; and awards given to individuals. Amounts generally range from $100 to $2,000. There are no specified annual application deadlines, though a formal application is required. Interested parties should contact the Foundation directly.
Geographic Focus: Connecticut
Amount of Grant: 100 - 2,000 USD
Contact: Edward J. Dolan, President; (203) 787-3513 or (203) 789-1605
Sponsor: Sabina Dolan and Gladys Saulsbury Foundation
400 Orange Street
New Haven, CT 06511-6405

Sage Foundation Grants   1653
The foundation awards grants nationwide, with emphasis on the Midwest, to nonprofit organizations in support of higher education, legal education, and secondary education; seniors; hospitals; disabled; Catholic giving and welfare; youth; child welfare; social services; and cultural programs. Types of support include annual campaigns, building construction/renovation, capital campaigns, challenge grants, endowments, equipment acquisition, general operating grants, multi-year support, project development, research, and scholarship funds. There are no application deadlines or forms; submit a letter of inquiry. The board meets quarterly.
Geographic Focus: All States
Amount of Grant: 1,000 - 250,000 USD
Contact: Melissa Sage Fadim; (810) 227-7660 or (212) 737-7311
Sponsor: Sage Foundation
P.O. Box 1919
Brighton, MI 48116

Saint Ann Legacy Grants   1654
The Sisters of Charity of St. Augustine formed the Saint Ann Foundation in 1973 with an endowment from the sale of the Saint Ann Hospital, a maternity hospital that served Cleveland's women and babies for 100 years. The Saint Ann Legacy Grant program recognizes the Saint Ann Foundation's vision to be a resource for ministries of women religious, particularly those that improve the lives of women and children. The Sisters of Charity Foundation of Cleveland awards grants to support the ministries of women religious as as they work to meet the needs of God's people. Grants may be awarded to ministries of women religious in Northeast Ohio, defined as the Dioceses of Cleveland and Youngstown.
Requirements: Organizations must have a tax-exempt status as nonprofit organizations, as identified by the Internal Revenue Service Code. Ministries of women religious include those that are sponsored or led by Catholic Sisters or programs at other organizations where women religious are significantly involved.
Restrictions: Grants are not made to individuals.
Geographic Focus: Ohio
Date(s) Application is Due: Jun 16
Amount of Grant: 20,000 USD
Contact: Erin McIntyre, Program Officer, Religious Communities; (216) 241-9300 ext. 232; fax (216) 241-9345; emcintyre@socfcleveland.org
Internet: http://www.socfcleveland.org/our-focus-areas/religious-communities/saint-ann-legacy-grants/
Sponsor: Sisters of Charity Foundation of Cleveland
The Halle Building, 1228 Euclid Avenue, Suite 330
Cleveland, OH 44115-1834

Saint Louis Rams Foundation Community Donations   1655
The foundation supports nonprofits that help inspire positive change for youth in the Saint Louis area. Programs that impact youth in the general fields of education, literacy, health, and recreation will be considered. Annually, the Rams provide to charitable groups more than 3,500 items, helping recipient organizations raise thousands of dollars through raffles, auctions and other fundraising endeavors. Other types of financial support include program development grants and general operating grants. The foundation does not accept unsolicited requests, but initial information may be sent for the office to keep on file for future opportunities.
Requirements: Nonprofits in the metropolitan Saint Louis, Missouri, area, including southern Illinois and eastern Missouri, are eligible. Preference is given to organizations that partner with other local nonprofits and offer creative approaches for more than grants (i.e., personnel involvement or in-kind support) and ways the Rams can participate.
Restrictions: The Rams do not provide monetary contributions or merchandise donations for the following: businesses, retail and otherwise; capital campaigns/start-up funding for new businesses; on-line auctions; chamber of commerce/city/neighborhood festivals such as homecoming celebrations and carnivals that do not directly benefit a charitable organization; class reunions; family reunions; pageant contestants (beauty and otherwise); student ambassador/exchange programs; or non-charity events and organizations such as company picnics, employee golf tournaments, employee recognition/incentive programs, card clubs, car shows, "poker runs", and organized adult leisure sports teams.
Geographic Focus: Missouri
Date(s) Application is Due: Jan 1; Jul 1
Contact: Coordinator; (314) 516-8788 or (314) 982-7267; fax (314) 770-0392
Internet: http://www.stlouisrams.com/community/donations.html
Sponsor: Saint Louis Rams Foundation
1 Rams Way
Saint Louis, MO 63045

Saint Paul Companies Foundation Grants   1656
Saint Paul Companies is dedicated to strengthening the communities in which its employees live and work. Grants are considered for programs that fall under one or more of the following focus areas: enrich lives and celebrate diversity through arts and culture; revitalize communities; and educate underserved populations to create social and economic opportunities. Grants are made for operating,support, program/project support, capital support, start-up funding, and transitional support. Grantmaking is restricted to the Twin Cities (primarily Saint Paul), the Baltimore area, the United Kingdom, and selected locations where the corporation has a significant business presence. An organization seeking funds for new programs should begin the application process by submitting a one-page letter describing the request. The foundation no longer accepts paper applications; all applications must be made online. Application guidelines at the Travelers website.
Geographic Focus: Minnesota, United Kingdom
Date(s) Application is Due: Sep 1
Amount of Grant: 15,000 - 250,000 USD
Contact: Ronald McKinley; (651) 310-2623 or (800) 328-2189
Internet: http://www.travelers.com/corporate-info/about/community/foundation.aspx
Sponsor: Saint Paul Companies
385 Washington Street
Saint Paul, MN 55102-1396

Saint Paul Foundation Grants   1657
The community foundation serves the greater Saint Paul, Minnesota, area and makes grants to support educational (including adult basic education and literacy programs), charitable, or cultural programs/projects that benefit residents of Ramsey, Washington, and Dakota Counties. The foundation's grantmaking vehicles include project/program, start-up costs, general operating support, capital projects, and matching funds. Support will ordinarily not exceed three years. There are no application deadlines; however, full proposals must be received approximately three and one-half months prior to the meeting date. The board meets in April, August, and December.
Requirements: Minnesota 501(c)3 tax-exempt organizations are eligible.
Restrictions: The foundation will not consider requests for ongoing annual operating expenses; sectarian religious programs; grants to individuals; capital projects located outside Ramsey, Dakota, and Washington Counties; or programs not serving residents of Ramsey, Dakota, and Washington Counties.
Geographic Focus: Minnesota
Contact: John G. Couchman, Vice-President; (651) 224-5463; fax (651) 224-8123; jgc@saintpaulfoundation.org or inbox@saintpaulfoundation.org
Internet: http://www.saintpaulfoundation.org/grants/apply_for_a_foundation_grant/
Sponsor: Saint Paul Foundation
55 Fifth Street E, Suite 600
Saint Paul, MN 55101-1797

Saint Paul Travelers Foundation Grants 1658

Saint Paul Travelers partners with employees, communities, and business partners to help build a civil society by investing in people and institutions for long-term success. The foundation supports initiatives that: revitalize communities; educate underserved populations to create social and economic opportunities; and enrich lives and celebrate diversity through arts and culture. Contributions will be designated for operating support, program/project support, capital support, start-up funding, or transitional support. The foundation will accept online grant applications at any time during the year. Guidelines are available online.

Requirements: Grantmaking will be restricted to nonprofit organizations in the Twin Cities (primarily Saint Paul), the Baltimore area, the United Kingdom, and selected locations where Saint Paul Travelers has a significant business presence. National organizations may receive support for specific initiatives that fit within the foundation's funding priorities.

Restrictions: Contributions will not be used for organizations that discriminate on the basis of race, gender, religion, culture, age, physical disability, sexual orientation, or status as a military veteran; sectarian religious organizations, unless it can be shown that the organization is seeking charitable funds in the direct interest of the whole community; veterans' and fraternal organizations; political or lobbying organizations; benefits, fundraisers, walk-a-thons, telethons, galas, or other revenue-generating events; advertising; scholarships to individuals; health or disease-specific organizations, health care or other emergency assistance for individuals, or hospitals and other health services generally supported by third-party reimbursement mechanisms; replacement of government funding; start-up, capital, or operations of public or charter schools; human services such as counseling, chemical abuse, or family programs; environmental programs; special events, except when the event is a key strategy in a continuum of efforts to achieve community goals in the foundation's priority areas; or nonacademic job placement programs.

Geographic Focus: All States
Date(s) Application is Due: Sep 15
Samples: Approximately 100 nonprofit groups in Minneapolis-Saint Paul, and Hartford, CT (MN, CT)—to support work in the areas of arts and culture, community development, and education, $2.619 million divided; Nonprofit groups in Minneapolis-Saint Paul, MN; Hartford, CT; and elsewhere—for support of arts and cultural organizations, in conjunction with the Saint Paul Travelers Foundation and the Saint Paul Travelers Connecticut Foundation, $1,871,750 distributed.
Contact: Grants Administrator; (651) 310-7911
Internet: http://www.stpaultravelers.com/about/community/stpaul/index.html
Sponsor: Saint Paul Travelers Foundation
385 Washington Street
Saint Paul, MN 55102

Salem Foundation Grants 1659

The primary purpose of the Foundation is support of higher education, cultural activities, health services, hospital building funds, and Christian giving. Its fields of interest include: arts; Christian agencies and churches; the disabled; education (secondary and higher); the environment; family services; federated giving programs; health care (particularly heart and circulatory disease research); hospitals; human services; museums; and Protestant federated giving programs. Types of support include: annual campaigns, building/renovation projects, capital campaigns, general operating support, and program development. There is no formal application process and no deadlines. Please contact via letter.

Restrictions: Giving primarily in Florida, Maine and Minnesota. No grants to individuals.
Geographic Focus: Florida, Maine, Minnesota
Amount of Grant: Up to 10,000 USD
Contact: Robert S. Parish, President; (952) 476-6292
Sponsor: Salem Foundation
2181 Springwood Road
Wayzata, MN 55391-2254

Salt River Project Environmental Quality Grants 1660

Salt River Project (SRP) is an energy/utilities company serving electric customers and water shareholders in the Phoenix metropolitan area. SRP provides funding to nonprofit organizations that address critical needs within its service communities. SRP believes in stewardship of Arizona's natural resources and protecting the water and air quality of Arizona. Environmental Quality Grants focus on improving the environmental quality of neighborhoods and supporting programs that promote the awareness and understanding of technical environmental issues.

Requirements: Eligible applicants must be 501(c)3 nonprofit, organizations within SRP's service area. SRP's service area is central Arizona and includes the following cities and towns: Phoenix, Mesa, Tempe, Paradise Valley, Fountain Hills, Scottsdale, Apache Junction, Peoria, Queen Creek, Avondale, Chandler, Gilbert, Glendale, Guadalupe, and Tolleson. There are no specific grant deadlines. Requests are reviewed in an on-going process which typically takes eight weeks.

Restrictions: The following are ineligible: individuals, including support for specific students, researchers, travel expenses, conference fees; organizations that discriminate on the basis of race, creed, color, sex, or national origin; endowment programs; medical research projects or medical procedures for individuals; professional schools of art, academic art programs, individual high school or college performing groups; political or lobbying groups or campaigns; fraternal organizations, veterans' organizations, professional associations, and similar membership groups; public or commercial broadcasting programs; religious activities or church-sponsored programs limited to church membership; and debt-reduction campaigns. SRP does not donate services, including water or electricity, or equipment for which a fee is normally charged.

Geographic Focus: Arizona
Contact: Corporate Contributions Administrator; (602) 236-5900
Internet: http://www.srpnet.com/community/contributions/guidelines.aspx
Sponsor: Salt River Project
1521 North Project Drive
Tempe, AZ 85281-1298

Samuel Freeman Charitable Trust Grants 1661

The trust has broad funding interests in supporting U.S. charitable, scientific, literary, and education programs. The trust awards grants to support cancer research and treatment; the preservation, exhibition, and operation of historical railway equipment; and secondary schools and universities. Types of support include general operating support, continuing support, annual campaigns, and seed money. There are no application deadlines; proposals are reviewed throughout the year.

Requirements: U.S. nonprofit organizations may apply.
Geographic Focus: All States
Amount of Grant: 1,000 - 150,000 USD
Contact: Linda Franciscovich, (212) 852-3683; fax (212) 852-3377
Sponsor: Samuel Freeman Charitable Trust
114 W 47th Street
New York, NY 10036-1532

Samueli Foundation Jewish Cultures and Values Grants 1662

The Samueli Foundation considers grants to agencies, primarily in Orange County, California, that serve the community, and whose programs meet the guidelines listed. Grants are usually approved for a defined period of time, but may be paid over a multi-year period. In the area of Jewish Cultures and Values, its goals are to: support Jewish education, spirituality, heritage and community identity; and sponsor programs that promote tolerance and diversity and combat Anti-Semitism in the community. The Foundation has a two-phase application process, the first of which is a Letter of Inquiry. If there is interest upon review of the Letter, the Foundation will contact applicants for further information and may request submission of a formal application for funding consideration.

Requirements: 501(c)3 tax-exempt organizations throughout the U.S. are eligible to apply.
Restrictions: The foundation does not fund umbrella fund raising organizations, political campaigns, or grants to individuals.
Geographic Focus: All States
Amount of Grant: 1,000 - 50,000 USD
Contact: Gerald R. Solomon, Executive Director; (949) 760-4400; fax (949) 759-5707; Info@samueli.org
Internet: http://www.samueli.org/JewishCulturesandValues.aspx
Sponsor: Samueli Foundation
2101 East Coast Highway, 3rd Floor
Corona del Mar, CA 92625

Samuel Rubin Foundation Grants 1663

The Rubin Foundation is dedicated to the pursuit of peace and justice and the search for an equitable reallocation of the world's resources and believes these objectives can be achieved only through the fullest implementation of social, economic, political, civil, and cultural rights for all the world's people. Grants are awarded to support projects that reach toward the solutions to bring about this state. Types of support include general operating support and seed money. Applications should be in the form of a letter and include a budget and tax determination letter. The Board of Directors normally meets three times a year.

Application deadlines are the first Friday in January, September, and May. Applicants are notified of the Foundation's decision within a week of its meeting. Faxed or emailed applications will not be accepted, nor will phone solicitations.

Restrictions: Funds are not granted to individuals or for buildings, endowments, or scholarships.

Geographic Focus: All States

Amount of Grant: 5,000 - 10,000 USD

Contact: Lauranne Jones, Grants Administrator; (212) 697-8945; fax (212) 682-0886; joneslauranne@gmail.com

Internet: http://www.samuelrubinfoundation.org/guidelines.html

Sponsor: Samuel Rubin Foundation

777 United Nations Plaza

New York, NY 10017-3521

Samuel S. Fels Fund Grants 1664

Since the Fels Fund has a small budget - approximately $2.5 million in the next few years - it could not possibly provide ongoing operating support to hundreds of organizations. Instead, the Fund tries to make grants at critical junctures. Critical junctures are points in an organization's life when there is a need to change methodologies. This could mean growing, shrinking, trying a new type of programming, experimenting with staffing, piloting a project that might support itself eventually, opening a satellite, seeking new accreditation, retraining staff or board or rethinking the physical plant. The fund supports activities or projects in the fields of education, the arts, and community services, which are intended to improve the quality of life in Philadelphia, Pennsylvania. Applicant organizations also must be located in Philadelphia. Types of support include general operating support, continuing support, program development, seed funding, curriculum development, internships, matching funds, and technical assistance. Grants at Fels range in size from $3,000 to $30,000. Occasionally, the Fund will make a larger grant in an exceptional situation. Applications are accepted at any time (with the exception of Arts and Humanities projects which are due by 5 p.m. on January 15th or May 15th).

Requirements: Philadelphia nonprofits may apply.

Restrictions: Grants are not awarded to support multi-year projects, umbrella-funding groups, scholarships, travel, research, capital funds, major equipment, endowments, deficit financing, ticket purchases, ads, fund-raising events, or emergency aid.

Geographic Focus: Pennsylvania

Amount of Grant: 3,000 - 30,000 USD

Samples: 11th Hour Theatre Company, Philadelphia, Pennsylvania, $3,000 - General support; 1812 Productions, Philadelphia, Pennsylvania, $5,000 - General support; Community Women's Education Project, Philadelphia, Pennsylvania, $15,000 - Capacity building.

Contact: Helen Cunningham, Executive Director; (215) 731-9455; fax (215) 731-9457; helenc@samfels.org

Internet: http://www.samfels.org/apps.html

Sponsor: Samuel S. Fels Fund

1616 Walnut Street, Suite 800

Philadelphia, PA 19103-5313

Samuel S. Johnson Foundation Grants 1665

The Samuel S. Johnson Foundation was incorporated in 1948 and supports organizations primarily in the Oregon and Clark County, Washington, region. The Foundation gives to: formal education programs leading to an R.N. status or baccalaureate or higher college/university degree in nursing; vocational education programs targeting high school drop-outs and high school grads who are not able to pursue junior college or higher formal education and which offer them job-specific technical training, mentoring or coaching; emergency food assistance programs; rural mobile health screening/care projects benefiting the uninsured medically needy; environmental programs, coastal & marine ecosystems, sustainable agriculture and communities. Most recent awards have range from $500 to $26,000. Though there are no specified deadlines, the board meets in July and November to make grant making decisions.

Requirements: Grants are awarded to non-profit organizations in Oregon and Clark County, Washington. Contact the Foundation for current focus and guidelines with a phone call before submitting a proposal. No Application form is required, however you must include the following in your proposal: copy of IRS Determination Letter; brief history of organization and description of its mission; copy of most recent annual report/audited financial statement/990; listing of board of directors, trustees, officers and other key people and their affiliations; detailed description of project and amount of funding requested; contact person; copy of current year's organizational budget and/or project budget; listing of additional sources and amount of support. Include one copy of the proposal. The board meets twice a year, in May and October, with no

deadline date for the submitting of proposals. If your proposal is accepted, you will receive notification within 2 - 3 weeks after the board meets.

Restrictions: No support for foreign organizations. No grants or scholarships to individuals, or for leadership training or staff development, campaigns to retire debt, annual campaigns, deficit financing, construction, sole underwriting of major proposals or projects, demolition or endowments.

Geographic Focus: Oregon, Washington

Amount of Grant: 500 - 26,000 USD

Samples: Volunteers of America in Oregon, Portland, Oregon, $2,500 - general operations (2014); Tollamook County Women's Resource Center, Tillamook, Oregon, $5,000 - matching challenge grant (2014); Junior ROTC Army Madras High School, Madras, Oregon, $1,000 - volunteer mentoring program (2014).

Contact: Mary A. Krenowicz; (541) 548-8104; mary@tssjf.org

Sponsor: Samuel S. Johnson Foundation

P.O. Box 356

Redmond, OR 97756-0079

San Antonio Area Foundation Grants 1666

Grants are usually awarded in the areas of health care and biomedical research, community and social services, arts and culture, education (early childhood education, higher education, medical schools, nursing schools, adult basic education and literacy), and animal services. Types of support include operating budgets, continuing support, annual campaigns, seed grants, emergency funds, equipment acquisition, matching funds, scholarship funds, research, lectureships, professorships, and building renovations. Applicants must submit a letter of intent to apply; if the letter is approved, the foundation will send a request for a proposal to the applicant. The foundation only reviews full proposals from applicants whose letters of intent have been approved. If asked to submit a proposal, the applicant will be sent an application package with a letter of notification in early February.

Requirements: Grants are made to organizations in the San Antonio, Texas, area.

Geographic Focus: Texas

Date(s) Application is Due: Nov 15

Amount of Grant: 250 - 250,000 USD

Samples: San Antonio Symphony (TX)—for the Young People's Concert series, $25,000; Southwest Foundation for Biomedical Research (San Antonio, TX)—to purchase equipment, $15,000.

Contact: Lydia R. Saldana, Program Officer; (210) 228-3753 or (210) 225-2243; fax (210) 225-1980; lsaldana@saafdn.org or info@saafdn.org

Internet: http://www.saafdn.org/NetCommunity/Page.aspx?pid=254

Sponsor: San Antonio Area Foundation

110 Broadway Street, Suite 230

San Antonio, TX 78205-1948

San Diego Foundation Arts & Culture Grants 1667

The Foundation's grant-making process in the area of arts and culture will distribute funds to organizations working collaboratively to create innovative new works and/or processes. It anticipates making six to eight high-impact grants in the community in this grant cycle, with grants between $10,000 and $50,000. This Art Works for San Diego program supports projects that can achieve the following results: provide San Diego residents and visitors with high quality arts and culture experiences; incorporate arts and culture into community problem solving; enable people to come together and connect with each other; build bridges between the arts and culture community and the community at large; and increase cultural patronage including hands-on involvement, audience participation and philanthropy.

Requirements: To be eligible, organizations must be providing services in San Diego County. The organizations must have a 501(c)3 IRS tax exempt status. An organization may serve as a fiscal sponsor for a charitable organization that does not have a 501(c)3 status if a cooperative relationship between the two can clearly be demonstrated. The fiscal sponsor must be willing to administer the grant if awarded.

Restrictions: Generally, the Foundation does not make grants for: organizations that have previously received funding from the Foundation but have not submitted required final reports; major building/capital campaigns; scholarships; endowments; for-profit organizations; projects that promote religious doctrine; individuals; organizations outside San Diego County; marketing and/or promotional materials (annual reports, brochures, video productions); re-granting dollars to other nonprofit organizations or individuals; short-term, annual or one time events, including festivals, performances and conferences; travel outside of the San Diego region, or; existing obligations or debt.

Geographic Focus: California

Date(s) Application is Due: Jan 16
Contact: Kerri Favela, (619) 235-2300, ext. 1329; kerri@sdfoundation.org
Internet: http://www.sdfoundation.org/communityimpact/cycle2006.html#ac
Sponsor: San Diego Foundation
2508 Historic Decatur Road, Suite 200
San Diego, CA 92106

San Diego Foundation Civil Society Grants   **1668**
The San Diego Foundation's Civil Society Working Group was established with the mission to foster civic engagement in community problem solving leading to an improved quality of life for all residents. The San Diego region requires a shared vision to enable effective and inclusive dialogue for the purpose of planning for balanced and equitable future growth. The goal of this initiative is to establish a framework to address the need for housing across the San Diego region resulting in livable communities with choices for all. Preference will be given to applicants with strategic partnerships that demonstrate the experience, skills, and capacity to achieve stated results and commit to sharing best practices and lessons learned to advance initiative goals. Applicants are encouraged to apply for grants generally between $25,000 and $50,000.
Requirements: To be eligible, organizations must be providing services in San Diego County. The organizations must have a 501(c)3 IRS tax exempt status. An organization may serve as a fiscal sponsor for a charitable organization that does not have a 501(c)3 status if a cooperative relationship between the two can clearly be demonstrated. The fiscal sponsor must be willing to administer the grant if awarded.
Restrictions: Generally, the Foundation does not make grants for: organizations that have previously received funding from the Foundation but have not submitted required final reports; major building/capital campaigns; scholarships; endowments; for-profit organizations; projects that promote religious doctrine; individuals; organizations outside San Diego County; marketing and/or promotional materials (annual reports, brochures, video productions); re-granting dollars to other nonprofit organizations or individuals; short-term, annual or one time events, including festivals, performances and conferences; travel outside of the San Diego region, or; existing obligations or debt.
Geographic Focus: California
Date(s) Application is Due: Jan 16
Amount of Grant: 25,000 - 50,000 USD
Contact: Shelley Lyford, Research & Development Manager; (619) 235-2300; Shelley@sdfoundation.org
Internet: http://www.sdfoundation.org/communityimpact/cycle2006.html#ac
Sponsor: San Diego Foundation
2508 Historic Decatur Road, Suite 200
San Diego, CA 92106

San Diego Women's Foundation Grants   **1669**
The San Diego Women's Foundation (SDWF) strengthens and improves women's capacities to engage in significant philanthropy in the San Diego region. The foundation chooses one focus area of grant making each year. Its primary focus areas include: education, arts and culture, environment, employment and economic development, civil society, and health and human services. Check the web site each September for that year's focus guidelines.
Requirements: Only 501(c)3 organization within San Diego County should apply.
Geographic Focus: California
Date(s) Application is Due: Dec 6
Amount of Grant: 25,000 USD
Samples: AjA Project in Community Heights, $40,000; Eveoke Dance Theater: Young Artists Program, $28,000; La Jolla Playhouse: Enriching Children's Lives Through Theater, $17,000.
Contact: Tracy Johnson, Director; (619) 814-1374 or (619) 235-2300; fax (619) 239-1710; tracy@sdfoundation.org
Internet: http://www.sdwomensfoundation.org/
Sponsor: San Diego Women's Foundation
2508 Historic Decatur Road, Suite 200
San Diego, CA 92106

Sands Foundation Grants   **1670**
The Venetian Foundation (now the Sands Foundation) was formed December 7, 2000, by the Venetian Casino Resort. Today, the Las Vegas Sands Corporation's primary philanthropic initiative is pursued through Sands Foundation, a non-profit 501(c)3 organization. Sands Foundation pursues a mission of supporting charitable organizations and endeavors that concentrate on assisting youth, promoting health, and expanding educational opportunities within

the local communities. The Foundation also supports causes that empower minority communities and improve underprivileged areas, as well as other valuable charitable and philanthropic activities permitted under relevant tax-exempt laws. Sands Foundation pursues a mission of supporting charitable organizations and endeavors that concentrate on assisting youth, promoting health, and expanding educational opportunities within our local communities. The Foundation also supports causes that empower minority communities and improve underprivileged areas, as well as other valuable charitable and philanthropic activities permitted under relevant tax-exempt laws. Charitable requests along with supporting documents may either be faxed or mailed.
Requirements: All charitable requests must be submitted in writing. Written requests should include the following: agency/organization information (brochures, information packet, list of the board of directors, history, background, or other helpful information); 501(c)3 tax identification number; contact person; mailing address and telephone number; overview of project or event at hand; date, time, location for event requests; purpose of request; very specific information about the amount/item(s) requested; and target population which will benefit from support.
Geographic Focus: Nevada, Pennsylvania, Macau, Singapore
Amount of Grant: 5,000 - 100,000 USD
Samples: Keep Memory Alive, Las Vegas, Nevada, $25,000; Landmark Media Enterprises, Norfolk, Virginia, $37,500; Emeril Lagasse Foundation, New Orleans, Louisiana, $5,000.
Contact: Community Development Department; (702) 607-1677; fax (702) 607-1044; foundation@venetian.com
Internet: http://www.lasvegassands.com/LasVegasSands/Sands_Foundation/Donation_Request.aspx
Sponsor: Sands Foundation
3355 Las Vegas Boulevard South
Las Vegas, NV 89109-8941

Sands Memorial Foundation Grants   **1671**
The foundation awards grants to Montana nonprofits in the area of companion animal protection and care, including spay/neuter programs and cruelty-prevention programs. Types of support include general operating support, continuing support, building construction/renovation, equipment acquisition, emergency funds, and seed grants. Application forms are required.
Requirements: Montana nonprofit organizations may apply.
Restrictions: Individuals are ineligible.
Geographic Focus: Montana
Date(s) Application is Due: Oct 30
Contact: Cynthia Bryson; (406) 265-4271; smf@hi-line.net
Sponsor: Sands Memorial Foundation
P.O. Box 1450
Havre, MT 59501-1450

Sands Point Fund Grants   **1672**
Established by Howard and Roslyn Zuckerman in Monsey, New York, in 2007, the Sands Point Fund is primarily interested in offering support to educational programs and Jewish agencies/synagogues. Amounts range up to a maximum of $2,500. There are no specific guidelines, application formats, or deadlines with which to adhere, and applicants should begin by contacting the Trust directly.
Geographic Focus: New York
Amount of Grant: Up to 2,500 USD
Samples: Ohr Somayach Educational Program, Monsey, New York, $2,500; Mesivta Tifereth Jerusalem Project, New York, New York, $2,500.
Contact: Howard Zuckerman, Trustee; (212) 972-3600
Sponsor: Sands Point Fund
6 Sand Point Road
Monsey, NY 10952-2110

Sandy Hill Foundation Grants   **1673**
The Sandy Hill Foundation offers awards to eligible nonprofit organizations in the areas of education, health care, and social services. The foundation gives primarily to the arts and culture, higher education, hospitals, health associations, social services, and federated giving programs. Their areas of interest include the arts; child and youth services; community and economic development; health organizations and associations; higher education; hospitals; human services; Protestant agencies and churches; recreation camps; and United Way and Federated Giving Programs. It also offers college scholarships for designated local area schools.
Requirements: There is no application or specific deadline for nonprofit giving. See contact information for current scholarship application due April 1.

Restrictions: The foundation gives primarily to the greater Hudson Falls, NY area. No grants are given to individuals.
Geographic Focus: New York
Date(s) Application is Due: Apr 1
Amount of Grant: Up to USD
Samples: Glens Falls Hospital Foundation, Glens Falls, New York - $65,000; World Awareness Childrens Museum, Glens Falls, New York - $22,500
Contact: Nancy Juckett Brown, Trustee; (518) 791-3490
Sponsor: Sandy Hill Foundation
P.O. Box 30
Hudson Falls, NY 12839-0030

Santa Barbara Foundation Strategy Grants - Core Support   1674
As the community foundation for all of Santa Barbara county, the foundation funds a wide range of initiatives and projects that address community needs, strengthen the nonprofit sector, develop community leadership, and encourage collaboration. Strategy Grants are distributed annually and aim to help nonprofit organizations fulfill their important missions so that community needs and affect positive change can be addressed. Core Support Grants are available to nonprofit organizations looking to sustain their organizational infrastructure. Core support is defined as unrestricted funding that enables an organization to carry out its mission. A Core Support Grant can be used to underwrite administrative infrastructure and/or to maintain core programs and essential staff. The foundation's philanthropic purpose for offering core support at this time is to maintain organizations that provide safety net services for the poor and underserved members of our community, and to support increased demand for services whether due to sustained need and/or significant reductions in funding that impact the delivery of core programs and services.
Requirements: The foundation provides grants to nonprofit organizations serving Santa Barbara County. Organizations must have 501(c)3 tax-exempt status or operate under a fiscal agent. Organizations may submit one Strategy Grant application (Core Support, Capital, or Innovation), as well as be part of one or more Collaborative Strategy Grant applications. The organization must be addressing issues of hunger or shelter, or providing primary or behavioral health care for vulnerable populations. The organization must demonstrate increasing demand for services and/or significant reductions in funding over the past three years. Priority for Core Support Grants will be given to organizations that are providing direct services to address hunger, shelter, and primary and/or behavioral health care; are established, well-managed, financially viable, and operate effective programs that primarily serve the needs of poor and underserved communities; and, have developed short- and long-term strategies for addressing identified organizational needs. Applications must be received by the foundation by 5:00 pm of the deadline date.
Restrictions: The foundation does not make grants for the following purposes or activities: debt; endowment; fundraising events; individuals; religious organizations for religious purposes; government entities (including schools) for basic services or capital needs; projects that discriminate on the basis of ethnicity, race, color, creed, religion, gender, national origin, age, disability, marital status, sexual orientation, gender identity, gender expression, or any veteran status; or, activities that occurred prior to the beginning date of the grant.
Geographic Focus: California
Amount of Grant: Up to 50,000 USD
Contact: Jack Azar; (805) 963-1873; fax (805) 966-2345; jazar@sbfoundation.org
Internet: http://www.sbfoundation.org/page.aspx?pid=778
Sponsor: Santa Barbara Foundation
1111 Chapala Street, Suite 200
Santa Barbara, CA 93101

**Santa Barbara Foundation Towbes Fund for the Performing Arts   1675
Grants**
The Towbes Fund for the Performing Arts, a field of interest fund of the Santa Barbara Foundation, has been created to support performing arts organizations and programs primarily serving Santa Barbara County. Grants will be made two to three times per calendar year from a pool of qualified performing arts organizations and are awarded based on a process of research, due diligence, and evaluation by an internal grant committee consisting of senior level foundation staff. Funds may be used for general operating support or for a specific program, project, or initiative. Award amounts generally range from $2,000 to $50,000 and are commensurate to organizational size and scale of work.
Requirements: The foundation provides grants to nonprofit organizations serving Santa Barbara County. Organizations must have 501(c)3 tax-exempt status or operate under a fiscal agent. Grant selection will be based on alignment with the donor's interest and history of giving in the performing arts as well as

foundation initiatives. To be included in the pool of qualified organizations for funding consideration, organizations must provide the following to the foundation: Qualification letter (two page maximum) that includes organizational mission statement or purpose, description of organization and program offerings (performances, outreach and education, numbers served, demographics, etc.), and highlight of a specific program, initiative, or campaign you would like considered for funding; Annual operating budget and balance sheet; and, Board roster. Qualification materials can be submitted at any time in the calendar year.
Restrictions: The foundation does not make grants for the following purposes or activities: debt; endowment; fundraising events; individuals; religious organizations for religious purposes; government entities (including schools) for basic services or capital needs; projects that discriminate on the basis of ethnicity, race, color, creed, religion, gender, national origin, age, disability, marital status, sexual orientation, gender identity, gender expression, or any veteran status; or, activities that occurred prior to the beginning date of the grant.
Geographic Focus: California
Amount of Grant: 2,000 - 50,000 USD
Contact: Jack Azar, Grants Associate; (805) 963-1873; fax (805) 966-2345; jazar@sbfoundation.org
Internet: http://www.sbfoundation.org/page.aspx?pid=906
Sponsor: Santa Barbara Foundation
1111 Chapala Street, Suite 200
Santa Barbara, CA 93101

Santa Fe Community Foundation root2fruit Santa Fe   1676
SFCF root2fruit provides resources for local, small organizations to build their capacity to thrive and succeed. The program provides funding, mentoring and peer partnerships to grantees. Three organizations will be selected per year to receive up to $10,000 per year for three years. Project-specific proposals will not be funded within this program.
Requirements: Organizations must be located in the County of Santa Fe and/or provide a significant amount of their services to Santa Fe residents. This is an initiative for smaller organizations with annual operating budgets of approximately $150,000 or smaller. Contact the Foundation and discuss your ideas prior to submitting a proposal.
Restrictions: The foundation does not award grants for religious purposes, capital campaigns or endowments, scholarships, or individuals.
Geographic Focus: New Mexico
Date(s) Application is Due: Aug 20
Amount of Grant: Up to 30,000 USD
Contact: Katie Dry; (505) 988-9715 x 7016; kdry@santafecf.org
Internet: http://www.santafecf.org/nonprofits/grantseekers/root2fruit
Sponsor: Santa Fe Community Foundation
501 Halona Street
Santa Fe, NM 87505

Santa Fe Community Foundation Seasonal Grants-Fall Cycle   1677
Through its outreach to nonprofits, donors and community leaders, the Foundation organizes its annual grants cycle into a two-season grants program. Each season (Spring and Fall) focuses on its own specific goals and strategies. The Foundation is devoted to building healthy and vital communities in the region where: racial, cultural or economic differences do not limit access to health, education or employment; diverse audiences enjoy the many arts and cultural heritages of our region; and, all sectors of its community take responsibility for ensuring a healthy environment. The areas of interest for the Fall Cycle are Arts, Animal Welfare, and Health and Human Services. For Arts proposals, projects should: increase public engagement in the arts; and, support public policy, community organizing or public information to strengthen the arts segment of the creative economy locally. For Health and Human Services proposals, projects should: improve the health of underserved residents of the Santa Fe region; improve access to affordable healthy food; strengthen the delivery of homelessness services; improve safety for children, women, families, sexual minorities and the elderly; and/or, support public policy, civic engagement, community organizing or public information to improve the health and well-being of local residents. For Animal Welfare proposals, the Foundation has approximately $25,000 available for animal welfare-related grants, and will include summaries of all animal welfare proposals (that meet basic due diligence) in the 'Giving Together' catalogue that accompanies the Fall Community Grant Cycle. The Giving Together catalogue is then shared with the Foundation's fundholders who are invited to make grants toward any proposal in the catalogue.

Requirements: Applications will be accepted from organizations that: are located in or serve the people of Santa Fe, Rio Arriba, Taos, Los Alamos, San Miguel or Mora Counties; are tax-exempt under Section 501(c)3 of the Internal Revenue Code or are a public or governmental agency or a federally recognized tribe in the state of New Mexico, or that have a fiscal sponsor; employ staff and provide services without discrimination on the basis of race, religion, sex, age, national origin, disability, or sexual orientation; and, are at least three years old. Each nonprofit entity may only apply for funding once per year. All grants will be $5,000, $10,000 or $15,000, depending on your annual budget. For organizations whose annual budget is under $150,000, you may apply for a $5,000 grant; for organizations whose annual budget is between $150,000 and $500,000, you may apply for a $10,000 grant; for organizations with an annual budget over $500,000, you may apply for a $15,000 grant. Grant applications will be accepted online only. Applications must be received by 5:00 pm of the deadline date.

Restrictions: The foundation does not award grants for religious purposes, capital campaigns or endowments, scholarships, or individuals. Organizations that received a community grant from SFCF in the last calendar year are not eligible to apply for a community grant in the current calendar year.

Geographic Focus: New Mexico
Date(s) Application is Due: Aug 26
Amount of Grant: 5,000 - 15,000 USD
Contact: Christa Coggins; (505) 988-9715 x 7002; ccoggins@santafecf.org
Internet: http://www.santafecf.org/nonprofits/grantseekers/general-grant-information
Sponsor: Santa Fe Community Foundation
501 Halona Street
Santa Fe, NM 87505

Santa Fe Community Foundation Seasonal Grants-Spring Cycle   1678
Through its outreach to nonprofits, donors and community leaders, the Foundation organizes its annual grants cycle into a two-season grants program. Each season (Spring and Fall) focuses on its own specific goals and strategies. The Foundation is devoted to building healthy and vital communities in the region where: racial, cultural or economic differences do not limit access to health, education or employment; diverse audiences enjoy the many arts and cultural heritages of our region; and, all sectors of its community take responsibility for ensuring a healthy environment. The areas of interest for the Spring Cycle are Economic Opportunity, Education and Environment. For Economic Opportunity proposals, the projects should: increase the number of low-income individuals who have achieved stable housing; measurably improve the outcomes of and access to job training programs and the income of low- wage earners; assist low-income families and individuals to save for and invest in future economic success through education, achieving affordable and sustainable housing, and building entrepreneurial skills and activities; and/or support public policy, civic engagement, community organizing or public information to improve economic opportunity. For Education (Closing the Educational Achievement Gap) proposals, projects should: increase the number of low-income children who are prepared for academic success in school through an investment in all learning experiences, parent involvement, and extended time spent learning; increase the number of low-income students who access post-secondary education ready to succeed through an investment in student preparation, college access, and coordination of providers; and/or support public policy, civic engagement, community organizing or public information to improve education. For Environment proposals, projects should: strengthen infrastructure for local food production and availability; support programs supporting sustainable agriculture; increase number of youth and adults engaged in agricultural and ecological restoration; expand support for groups engaged in advocacy and policy development for regional resource management, including land, air and water; and/or support promotion of and advocacy for local, renewable energy.

Requirements: Applications will be accepted from organizations that: are located in or serve the people of Santa Fe, Rio Arriba, Taos, Los Alamos, San Miguel or Mora Counties; are tax-exempt under Section 501(c)3 of the Internal Revenue Code or are a public or governmental agency or a federally recognized tribe in the state of New Mexico, or that have a fiscal sponsor; employ staff and provide services without discrimination on the basis of race, religion, sex, age, national origin, disability, or sexual orientation; and, are at least three years old. Each nonprofit entity may only apply for funding once per year. All grants will be $5,000, $10,000 or $15,000, depending on your annual budget. For organizations whose annual budget is under $150,000, you may apply for a $5,000 grant; for organizations whose annual budget is between $150,000 and $500,000, you may apply for a $10,000 grant; for organizations with an annual budget over $500,000, you may apply for a $15,000 grant. Grant applications will be accepted online only. Applications must be received by 5:00 pm of the deadline date.

Restrictions: The foundation does not award grants for religious purposes, capital campaigns or endowments, scholarships, or individuals. Organizations that received a community grant from SFCF in the last calendar year are not eligible to apply for a community grant in the current calendar year.

Geographic Focus: New Mexico
Date(s) Application is Due: Mar 3
Amount of Grant: 5,000 - 15,000 USD
Contact: Christa Coggins; (505) 988-9715 x 7002; ccoggins@santafecf.org
Internet: http://www.santafecf.org/nonprofits/grantseekers/general-grant-information
Sponsor: Santa Fe Community Foundation
501 Halona Street
Santa Fe, NM 87505

Santa Fe Community Foundation Special and Urgent Needs Grants   1679
The Foundation created the Special and Urgent Needs (SUN) grants to address the short-term needs of nonprofits. With a relatively small amount of funding, SUN grants help an organization take advantage of an unbudgeted, unforeseen, and time-sensitive opportunity or emergency that will enhance or preserve the ability of the organization to meet its mission. There is no deadline - you may apply anytime. Only electronic applications are accepted. Decisions are made within 14 days of receiving application. Grants funds awarded will be up to $2,500.

Requirements: Applications will be accepted from organizations that are located in and serve the people of Santa Fe, Rio Arriba, Taos, Los Alamos, San Miguel or Mora Counties. Organizations must be tax-exempt under Section 501(c)3 of the Internal Revenue Code or be a public agency in the state of New Mexico. Nonprofit organizations or community groups who do not have 501(c)3 status may apply for grant awards if another tax-exempt organization acts as a fiscal sponsor. Applicants must employ staff and provide services without discrimination on the basis of race, religion, sex, age, national origin, disability, or sexual orientation.

Restrictions: The Foundation will not generally make SUN grants for: organizations with an operating budget larger than $1.5 million; independent/private schools; endowments; capital campaigns (except for initial planning expenses); religious purposes; individuals; debts; equipment (unless it is an integral part of an otherwise eligible project); and SFCF does not fund work that has already been completed. SFCF also cannot consider applications for budget deficits or shortfalls.

Geographic Focus: New Mexico
Amount of Grant: Up to 2,500 USD
Contact: Christa Coggins; (505) 988-9715 x 7002; ccoggins@santafecf.org
Internet: http://www.santafecf.org/nonprofits/grantseekers/SUN-grants
Sponsor: Santa Fe Community Foundation
501 Halona Street
Santa Fe, NM 87505

Santa Maria Foundation Grants   1680
Established in New York in 1978, the foundation awards grants primarily to Catholic organizations to provide spiritual and religious renewal shelters for the homeless and unwed mothers. Types of support include continuing support and general operating grants. There are no application forms or deadlines with which to adhere. Initial approach should be by letter.

Geographic Focus: All States
Date(s) Application is Due: Sep 1
Amount of Grant: Up to 400,000 USD
Contact: Patrick P. Grace, President and Director; (914) 395-1830
Sponsor: Santa Maria Foundation
19 Mountain Avenue
Mount Kisco, NY 10549-1321

Sapelo Foundation Environmental Protection Grants   1681
The Sapelo Foundation is a private family foundation focusing its funding within the State of Georgia. The Foundation is particularly interested in projects that involve multiple groups that work cooperatively toward common goals, accomplish systemic reform, and have a statewide impact. In addition, the Foundation gives special attention to low-resource regions in the state and innovative, community-based projects within the Foundation's focus areas. The Foundation believes that the preservation of Georgia's finite natural resources benefits all species of life and is essential to their health and long-term survival. Currently, the Foundation's primary focus is a strategic campaign addressing water resource management and policy in Georgia. The Foundation was instrumental in the creation of the Georgia Water Coalition and its active

members currently receive priority for funding. Grants range from $1,000 to $60,000, and the average award is between $5,000 and $25,000.

Requirements: Georgia 501(c)3 nonprofit organizations are eligible.

Restrictions: The Foundation does not give priority to: academic research; land acquisition; environmental education centers and nature centers; wildlife parks or animal rehabilitation center; or museums. The Foundation does not support projects operating solely within the Metro Atlanta Area. The Foundation does not fund the following: brick-and-mortar, building projects or renovations, including construction materials and labor costs; endowment funds; fraternal groups or civic clubs; health care initiatives or medical research; individuals; national or regional organizations, unless their programs specifically benefit Georgia and all funds are spent within the state; organizations that are not tax-exempt; or payment of debts.

Geographic Focus: Georgia

Date(s) Application is Due: Mar 1; Sep 1

Amount of Grant: 1,000 - 60,000 USD

Contact: Phyllis Bowen, Executive Director; (912) 265-0520; fax (912) 254-1888; info@sapelofoundation.org or sapelofoundation@mindspring.com

Internet: http://www.sapelofoundation.org/index.html

Sponsor: Sapelo Foundation

1712 Ellis Street, 2nd Floor

Brunswick, GA 31520

Sapelo Foundation Social Justice Grants   1682

The Sapelo Foundation is a private family foundation focusing its funding within the State of Georgia. The Foundation is particularly interested in projects that involve multiple groups that work cooperatively toward common goals, accomplish systemic reform, and have a statewide impact. In addition, the Foundation gives special attention to low-resource regions in the state and innovative, community-based projects within the Foundation's focus areas. The Foundation believes that the development of sound public policy is crucial to effective government and the empowerment of the citizenry. Therefore, it is the aim of the Foundation to strengthen representative democracy in Georgia through efforts that educate the public about government institutions and policies, promote civic engagement and responsibility, and monitor government performance. Currently, the Foundation's primary focus is a strategic campaign advocating for fairness for children in the state's justice system. Grants range from $1,000 to $60,000, and the average award is between $5,000 and $25,000.

Requirements: Georgia 501(c)3 nonprofit organizations are eligible.

Restrictions: The Foundation does not give priority to: academic research; local government entities; human services programs; criminal justice programs designed to rehabilitate and/or punish individuals; senior citizen's programs; after-school mentoring/tutoring programs; single-site day care facilities; homeless shelters or programs; affordable housing; or programs serving the physically or developmentally disabled. The Foundation does not support projects operating solely within the Metro Atlanta Area. The Foundation does not fund the following: brick-and-mortar, building projects or renovations, including construction materials and labor costs; endowment funds; fraternal groups or civic clubs; health care initiatives or medical research; individuals; national or regional organizations, unless their programs specifically benefit Georgia and all funds are spent within the state; organizations that are not tax-exempt; or payment of debts.

Geographic Focus: Georgia

Date(s) Application is Due: Mar 1; Sep 1

Amount of Grant: 1,000 - 60,000 USD

Contact: Phyllis Bowen, Executive Director; (912) 265-0520; fax (912) 254-1888; info@sapelofoundation.org or sapelofoundation@mindspring.com

Internet: http://www.sapelofoundation.org/index.html

Sponsor: Sapelo Foundation

1712 Ellis Street, 2nd Floor

Brunswick, GA 31520

Sarah Scaife Foundation Grants   1683

Approximately 80 percent of the annual grants are made to public policy programs that address major domestic and international issues. There are no geographic restrictions. Other grants are made in the fields of education and culture, health and medicine, scientific research, public affairs, and recreation and equipment in all geographic areas, but primarily in western Pennsylvania. Types of support include general operating support, continuing support, program development, conferences and seminars, publication, seed grants, fellowships, research, and matching funds. Applications are accepted at any time. Foundation staff considers requests in February, May, September, and November.

Restrictions: Grants are not made to individuals or to national organizations for general fund-raising purposes.

Geographic Focus: All States

Amount of Grant: 25,000 - 200,000 USD

Samples: U of Pittsburgh (Pittsburgh, PA)—to construct facilities for the planned Pittsburgh Institute for Neurodegenerative Diseases, $5.4 million.

Contact: Michael Gleba, Vice President of Programs; (412) 392-2900

Internet: http://www.scaife.com/sarah.html

Sponsor: Sarah Scaife Foundation

1 Oxford Center, 301 Grant Street, Suite 3900

Pittsburgh, PA 15219

Sara Lee Foundation Grants   1684

The foundation's cash grants program concentrates on the Chicago metropolitan area. Special interests include organizations that serve the disadvantaged with emphasis on programs concerning hunger and homelessness, job placement, housing, and women's issues; education, including child development education, adult basic education, and literacy skills; and arts and cultural institutions including libraries. The foundation also funds a scholarship program and youth ambassador program for employees of the Sara Lee Corporation and its subsidiaries. Additional types of support include employee matching gifts, special projects, operating budgets, annual campaigns, and continuing support. The annual leadership awards recognize and support nonprofit organizations that demonstrate innovative leadership in improving life for the disadvantaged in communities where Sara Lee Corporation divisions have facilities; two to four awards are presented each year. Leadership awards are not restricted to Illinois nonprofits. Annual deadline may vary; contact program officer for exact date.

Requirements: IRS 501(c)3 nonprofit organizations in Illinois that have been in existence for at least two years at the time of application and that are located in a community where a Sara Lee Corporation division has facilities are eligible.

Restrictions: Grants do not support individuals; organizations with a limited constituency, such as fraternities or veterans groups; organizations that limit their services to members of one religious group, or those whose services propagate religious faith or creed, including churches, seminaries, bible colleges, and theological institutions; political organizations or those having the primary purpose of influencing legislation or promoting a particular ideological point of view; elementary and secondary schools, either private or public; units of government or quasi-governmental agencies; or hospitals and health organizations concentrating their research and/or treatment in one area of human disease.

Geographic Focus: Illinois

Date(s) Application is Due: Jan 10; Jul 10

Amount of Grant: Up to 15,000 USD

Contact: Robin Tryloff; (312) 558-8448; fax (312) 419-3192

Internet: http://www.saraleefoundation.org/funding/focus.cfm

Sponsor: Sara Lee Foundation

3 First National Plaza

Chicago, IL 60602-4260

Sartain Lanier Family Foundation Grants   1685

The Sartain Lanier Family Foundation awards grants to Georgia nonprofits in support of education, health and human services, arts, environment, and community development, with the majority of new grantmaking in the area of education. Types of support include building and renovation; capital campaigns; endowments; general operating support; program development; and program-related investments and loans. The foundation's board meets in May and November of each year to consider grant requests, which will be by invitation only. Interested applicants should provide an organizational overview for consideration purposes. Prior to submitting a full proposal, interested parties should submit a letter limited to two pages summarizing the request. The letter should include a brief description of the organization and its purpose, the project for which funding is requested, the total cost of the project, and the amount being requested.

Requirements: Nonprofit organizations in the southeastern United States are eligible to apply if invited to do so; however, the majority of recipients are located in Georgia and specifically the Atlanta metro area.

Restrictions: The foundation does not make grants for individuals; churches or religious organizations for projects that primarily benefit their own members; partisan political purposes; tickets to charitable events or dinners, or to sponsor special events or fundraisers.

Geographic Focus: Georgia

Contact: Patricia E. Lummus, Associate Director; (404) 564-1259; fax (404) 564-1251; plummus@lanierfamilyfoundation.org

Internet: http://lanierfamilyfoundation.org/funding-priorities/

Sponsor: Sartain Lanier Family Foundation

25 Puritan Mill, 950 Lowery Boulevard NW

Atlanta, GA 30318

Schering-Plough Foundation Community Initiatives Grants 1686

The Schering-Plough Foundation, a non-profit membership corporation established in 1955, is dedicated to working with the citizens of our communities to help them realize their full potential and enhance their quality of life. Support for community development takes many forms and allows the Foundation to reach out to numerous, highly diverse groups within its communities. The Foundation continues to support organizations that promote culture and the arts, environmental issues, legal services, etc. and are always seeking out new and innovative ways to serve the citizens of its communities.

Requirements: The Foundation considers requests from tax-exempt, 501(c)3 non-profit organizations located in the United States, or its possessions, whose goals and activities fall within its stated objectives and areas of interest. All requests for funding must be made online. National organizations are eligible to apply.

Restrictions: Grants are not made to individuals.

Geographic Focus: All States

Amount of Grant: 5,000 - 200,000 USD

Contact: Christine Fahey; (908) 298-7232; fax (908) 298-7349

Internet: http://www.schering-plough.com/company/foundation.aspx

Sponsor: Schering-Plough Foundation

2000 Galloping Hill Road

Kennilworth, NJ 07033-0530

Scherman Foundation Grants 1687

The main areas of interest for the foundation are the environment, peace and security, reproductive rights and services, human rights and liberties, the arts, and social welfare. Priority is given to organizations in New York City in the areas of the arts and social welfare. Requests for support should be made in a brief letter addressed to the President (Mike Pratt) outlining the purpose for the funds being sought; program description; budget; list of directors and staff; audited financial statement; sources of support; and evidence of tax status. The board meets four times a year to consider applications.

Requirements: Organizations must be tax-exempt 501(c)3. Requests for support may be submitted online at submissions@scherman.org, clearly marked as PROP.O.SAL in the subject line.

Restrictions: The foundation does not accept applications through fax. Funding is not given to: individuals; colleges, universities, or professional schools; medical, science, or engineering research; capital campaigns; conferences; or specific media or arts productions. Do not submit video or audio cassettes or CD's, unless requested to do so.

Geographic Focus: All States, New York

Amount of Grant: 1,000 - 60,000 USD

Samples: Center for Community Change, Washington, D.C., $50,000; Green Guerillas, New York, New York, $25,000

Contact: Mike Pratt; (212) 832-3086; fax (212) 838-0154; mpratt@scherman.org

Internet: http://www.scherman.org/html2/approc.html

Sponsor: Scherman Foundation

16 East 52nd Street, Suite 601

New York, NY 10022-5306

Scheumann Foundation Grants 1688

Established in Indiana in 2002, the Scheumann Foundation offers grants in support of youth services, recreation, camps, and housing development within the State of Indiana. There are no specific application forms or annual deadlines. With that in mind, applicants should forward a two- to three-page letter of application outlining their program and budgetary needs. Most recent awards have ranged from $500 to $400,000.

Requirements: Giving is restricted to non-profit programs serving youth and families within Indiana.

Geographic Focus: Indiana

Amount of Grant: 500 - 400,000 USD

Contact: John B. Scheumann, President; (765) 742-0300

Sponsor: Scheumann Foundation

P.O. Box 811

Lafayette, IN 47902-0811

Schlessman Family Foundation Grants 1689

The foundation awards grants to Colorado nonprofits in its areas of interest: education, disadvantaged youth programs and services, elderly/senior programs, special needs groups, and established cultural institutions (such as museums, libraries and zoos). Performing arts grants are available but are very limited.

Requirements: Grants are limited to Colorado charities, primarily greater metro-Denver organizations. The Foundation accepts, but does not require, the Colorado Common Grant Application. All requests must be in writing

and discourages lengthy proposals with multiple attachments. If additional information is required, you will be contacted. Proposals are accepted throughout the year, however they must be postmarked on or before the deadline date if they are to be considered in time for the once-a-year distributions on March 31.

Restrictions: The following are ineligible: individuals, start-ups, support for benefits or conferences, public/private/charter schools.

Geographic Focus: Colorado

Date(s) Application is Due: Dec 31

Contact: Patricia Middendorf, (303) 831-5683; fax (303) 831-5676; contact@schlessmanfoundation.org

Internet: http://www.schlessmanfoundation.org

Sponsor: Schlessman Family Foundation

1555 Blake Street, Suite 400

Denver, CO 80202

Schramm Foundation Grants 1690

The foundation awards grants to Colorado nonprofit organizations in its areas of interest, including arts and culture, civic affairs, community development, education (elementary, secondary, and higher), health care, housing, humanities, medical research, science, social services delivery, technology, women's issues, and youth. Types of support include building construction/renovation, continuing support, equipment acquisition, general operating support, matching/challenge grants, program development, and scholarship funds. Applications are accepted from July 1 through August 31 (postmarked).

Requirements: Colorado 501(c)3 nonprofit organizations are eligible. Preference is given to requests from the Denver area. Applications must clearly express the reason(s) for the request, attach financial statements and copy of exemption letter.

Restrictions: Grants do not support advertising, advocacy organizations, individuals, international organizations, political organizations, religious organizations, school districts, special events, or veterans organizations.

Geographic Focus: Colorado

Date(s) Application is Due: Aug 31

Amount of Grant: 500 USD

Contact: Gary Kring, President; (303) 861-8291

Sponsor: Schramm Foundation

800 Grant Street, Suite 330

Denver, CO 80203-2944

Schumann Fund for New Jersey Grants 1691

The Schumann Fund for New Jersey is a tax exempt, private foundation, incorporated as a corporation not for pecuniary profit under the laws of the State of New Jersey. Schumann Fund program priorities fall into four categories: Early Childhood Development; Environmental Protection; Essex County; and Public Policy.

Requirements: There is no standard application form to be used in presenting a request to the Schumann Fund for New Jersey, but organizations may use the New York/New Jersey Common Application Form if they choose. The Foundation asks that a written proposal be submitted which includes a clear description of the purpose of the grant, the need or problem that will be addressed, the work to be undertaken, the staffing plan for project implementation, any collaborative efforts underway or contemplated, and the means of evaluating progress. The proposal must include the following items: a copy of the organization's latest audited financial statement; current organizational and project budgets identifying all sources of revenue and categories and amounts of expenditures; brief resumes of key organization and project staff; the project time frame and projected sources of future funding; a list of the organization's board of directors; Internal Revenue Service documents confirming the organization's status as a 501(C)3 organization. The Schumann Fund Board of Trustees meets quarterly.

Restrictions: In general, the Schumann Fund for New Jersey does not accept applications for capital campaigns, annual giving, endowment, direct support of individuals, or local programs in counties other than Essex. Projects in the arts, health care, and housing development normally fall outside the fund's priority areas.

Geographic Focus: New Jersey

Date(s) Application is Due: Jan 15; Apr 15; Jul 15; Oct 15

Amount of Grant: 15,000 - 100,000 USD

Samples: New Jersey Association of Child Care Resource and Referral Agencies, Trenton, New Jersey, $15,000 - for using new data to develop an advocacy agenda to improve family child care; Rutgers, the State University of New Jersey, Camden, New Jersey, $80,000 - for campaign for Children's Literacy, comprehensive effort that provides professional development and certification to early childhood teachers, monthly seminars for parents, and library outreach initiative to encourage parents to read to their children.

Contact: Barbara Reisman; (973) 509-9883; fax (973) 509-1149
Internet: http://foundationcenter.org/grantmaker/schumann/program_guidelines.html
Sponsor: Schumann Fund for New Jersey
21 Van Vleck Street
Montclair, NJ 07042

Scott B. and Annie P. Appleby Charitable Trust Grants   1692

The trust supports programs and projects of nonprofit organizations in the categories of higher education, cultural programs, and child welfare. Types of support include general operating support, continuing support, capital campaigns, building construction and renovation, research, and scholarship funds. An application form is required, although there are no specified deadlines. Most recent awards have ranged from $1,000 to $100,000.
Requirements: The foundation awards grants to nonprofit organizations in the United States. There are no deadlines. Interested applicants are encouraged to submit a letter describing the intent and purpose of the organization with a specific proposal for allocation of funds.
Geographic Focus: All States
Amount of Grant: 1,000 - 100,000 USD
Samples: Asheville Art Museum, Asheville, North Carolina, $100,000 - general operations; Medical Foundation of North Carolina, Chapel Hill, North Carolina, $25,000 - general operations; Regents of the University of California, Oakland, California, $40,000 - general operations.
Contact: Benjamin N. Colby, Co-Trustee; (941) 329-2628; bncolby@uci.edu
Sponsor: Scott B. and Annie P. Appleby Charitable Trust
c/o The Northern Trust Company
Sarasota, FL 34236

Seattle Foundation Annual Neighborhoods & Communities Grants   1693

The Foundation's Neighborhoods & Communities Annual Grants Program will prioritize organizations or programs that are aligned with one or both of the following funding strategies: support organizations or programs that increase civic engagement, develop local leadership, or encourage community organizing and advocacy; or support organizations or programs that build relationships and trust within and across communities (geographic and non-geographic). Some project examples include: local community spaces or events that provide programming and opportunities for people to meet and build relationships; programs or organizations that work to increase interfaith, intergenerational or cross-cultural understanding; and neighborhood or cultural groups that bring people together to share resources and build social networks. The Foundation's Annual Grants Program typically provides general operating support grants, but may also award program/project funding when the overall organization's work does not align with the specific strategies. Capital campaign funding is also awarded in some cases, but is not a priority for the Foundation.
Requirements: To qualify for a grant from the Foundation's Grantmaking program, an organization must: be a 501(c)3 tax-exempt nonprofit organization; serve residents of King County, Washington; and provide programming in neighborhood and community funding needs that align with one or both of the Foundation's two strategies.
Restrictions: Capital campaign funding requests are typically considered a low priority. Organizations that have an annual operating budget less than $100,000 as reflected in the most recently filed IRS Form 990 are considered a lower priority for the Annual Grants Program, but may be eligible for Neighbor to Neighbor funding, which focuses on the White Center, South Seattle and Kent neighborhoods. Multi-year grants are not currently considered. Grants are not made to individuals or to religious organizations for religious purposes. Grants will not be awarded for: endowment; funding of conferences or seminars; operating expenses for public or private elementary and secondary schools, colleges and universities; fundraising events such as walk-a-thons, tournaments, auctions and general fundraising solicitations; or the production of books, films, or videos.
Geographic Focus: Washington
Date(s) Application is Due: Jan 15
Amount of Grant: 15,000 - 50,000 USD
Contact: Ceil Erickson, Grantmaking Director; (206) 515-2131 or (206) 515-2109; fax (206) 622-7673; grantmaking@seattlefoundation.org or c.erickson@seattlefoundation.org
Internet: http://www.seattlefoundation.org/nonprofits/grantmaking/communities/Pages/NeighborhoodsCommunities.aspx
Sponsor: Seattle Foundation
1200 Fifth Avenue, Suite 1300
Seattle, WA 98101-3151

Seattle Foundation Arts and Culture Grants   1694

The Seattle Foundation believes that the arts play a crucial role in the health of the community. The Foundation awards grants to nonprofits in all fields that improve the quality of life for King County residents, and is currently looking to fund organizations working to make significant progress towards the following three arts and culture strategies: broaden community engagement in the arts; support a continuum of arts education for students; and preserve and fully utilize arts space. The Foundation awards grants to provide general support to organizations. The next deadline for Arts and Culture is February 1.
Requirements: To qualify for a grant from the Foundation's Grantmaking program, an organization must: be a 501(c)3 tax-exempt nonprofit organization; serve residents of King County, Washington; and provide programming in arts and culture that aligns with one of the Foundation's three strategies.
Restrictions: Grants are not made to individuals or to religious organizations for religious purposes. Grants will not be awarded for: endowment; funding of conferences or seminars; operating expenses for public or private elementary and secondary schools, colleges and universities; fundraising events such as walk-a-thons, tournaments, auctions and general fundraising solicitations; or the production of books, films, or videos.
Geographic Focus: Washington
Date(s) Application is Due: Feb 1
Amount of Grant: 10,000 - 25,000 USD
Contact: Ceil Erickson, Grantmaking Director; (206) 515-2131 or (206) 515-2109; fax (206) 622-7673; grantmaking@seattlefoundation.org or c.erickson@seattlefoundation.org
Internet: http://www.seattlefoundation.org/nonprofits/grantmaking/artsandculture/Pages/GrantmakingforArtsCulture.aspx
Sponsor: Seattle Foundation
1200 Fifth Avenue, Suite 1300
Seattle, WA 98101-3151

Seattle Foundation Benjamin N. Phillips Memorial Fund Grants   1695

The Benjamin N. Phillips Memorial Fund was established by the estate of Joy Phillips to honor her late husband in 2006 as an area of interest fund of The Seattle Foundation. The goal of the Fund is to make grants to organizations improving the lives of Clallam County, Washington, residents. The Benjamin N. Phillips Memorial Fund is interested in supporting organizations that have: a mission statement that clearly defines the organization's purpose and reflects its understanding of the communities they serve; a clear articulation of why it believed what it is doing is important and that it will be effective and produce desired results; clearly defined priorities, goals and measurable outcomes; experienced and highly qualified staff and volunteer leadership; a skilled governing board whose knowledge includes management, fundraising and the community served; a funding plan appropriate to agency size and developmental state-guiding development efforts; sound financial management practices; support in the community and constituent involvement; and proven ability to mobilize financial and in-kind support, including volunteers. Grants are predominately made for one year, with no implied renewal funding. However, a two-year grant will be considered if a case is made for why funding is required for a longer period. An example of this exception is a planning or capacity-building process occurring over a two-year period of time. Approximately $250,000 will be distributed annually, with grants ranging in size from $1,000 to $25,000; the average grant size is $11,000.
Requirements: To qualify for a grant from the Foundation, an organization must: be a 501(c)3 tax-exempt nonprofit organization serving residents of Clallam County, Washington.
Geographic Focus: Washington
Date(s) Application is Due: Jul 1
Amount of Grant: 1,000 - 25,000 USD
Samples: Compassion and Choices of Washington, Seattle, Washington, $10,000 - support two years of added outreach, partnership development and fund development activities in Clallam County; First Book of Clallam County, Seattle, Washington, $1,000 - to support the purchase of books for low-income children; Juan de Fuca Festival of the Arts, Port Angeles, Washington, $8,000 - support sponsorship of Baka Beyond workshops and concerts.
Contact: Ceil Erickson, Grantmaking Director; (206) 515-2131 or (206) 515-2109; fax (206) 622-7673; c.erickson@seattlefoundation.org or phillips@seattlefoundation.org
Internet: http://www.seattlefoundation.org/nonprofits/phillips/Pages/benjaminphillipsmemorialfund.aspx
Sponsor: Seattle Foundation
1200 Fifth Avenue, Suite 1300
Seattle, WA 98101-3151

Seattle Foundation Economy Grants 1696

The security of the King County, Washington, region depends on its economy. The Foundation believes that a strong economy is the essential engine that fuels all other elements of a healthy community. The Foundation awards grants to nonprofits in all fields that improve the quality of life for King County residents. The Foundation is currently looking to provide funding to scale up innovative programs or project with proven success in the following three strategies: supporting education and training for low-income adults, particularly organizations that demonstrate a link to career pathways and living wage employment for participants; improving financial stability for individuals; and increasing access to resources for underserved businesses. Funding will be unrestricted and is intended to help build the capacity to expand proven innovative programs or projects. Proposals must demonstrate cultural competency and stakeholder engagement. Grant awards will likely range from $20,000 to $50,000. All proposals and back-up materials must be received at the Foundation by 5:00 p.m. on May 1.

Requirements: To qualify for a grant: the applicant must be a 501(c)3 tax-exempt nonprofit organization or be sponsored by a tax-exempt nonprofit organization; the applicant must serve residents of King County; the applicant's' mission and core services must align with one or more of our three strategies in the economy element; and the applicant's projects/programs must demonstrate a track record of success (new program or pilots are not eligible).

Geographic Focus: Washington
Date(s) Application is Due: May 1
Amount of Grant: 20,000 - 50,000 USD
Contact: Ceil Erickson, Grantmaking Director; (206) 515-2131 or (206) 515-2109; fax (206) 622-7673; grantmaking@seattlefoundation.org or c.erickson@seattlefoundation.org
Internet: http://www.seattlefoundation.org/nonprofits/grantmaking/economy/Pages/Economy.aspx
Sponsor: Seattle Foundation
1200 Fifth Avenue, Suite 1300
Seattle, WA 98101-3151

Seattle Foundation Health and Wellness Grants 1697

The Seattle Foundation is committed to fostering health and wellness for people throughout the King County, Washington, region. The Foundation awards grants to nonprofits in all fields that improve the quality of life for county residents, and is focused on making sure that everyone in the county has access to quality care, including physical and dental health, cognitive, emotional, and mental health. Goals within the Health and Wellness element are to: improve access to: basic healthcare, especially services and treatment for those who are low-income, uninsured and/or underinsured; support efforts designed to reduce and/or eliminate disparities in health status due to poverty and/or race; foster efforts to strengthen the ability and capacity of providers to deliver quality services; and support efforts that protect the safety net for the vulnerable in our community through case management, treatment, and counseling services. The fields of interest and populations captured in this element include: healthcare, dental care, mental health, domestic violence, developmentally disabled, physically disabled, seniors, and birth to three programs, substance abuse programs and child welfare programs. The deadline for Health and Wellness is May 1.

Requirements: To qualify for a grant from the Seattle Foundation's Grantmaking Program, an organization must: be a 501(c)3 tax-exempt nonprofit organization; serve residents of King County; and provide programming in Health and Wellness that aligns with one of our three strategies.

Restrictions: The Foundation does not support disease-specific organizations and does not support health research projects. Multi-year grants are not considered.

Geographic Focus: Washington
Date(s) Application is Due: May 1
Amount of Grant: 15,000 - 50,000 USD
Contact: Ceil Erickson, Grantmaking Director; (206) 515-2131 or (206) 515-2109; fax (206) 622-7673; grantmaking@seattlefoundation.org or c.erickson@seattlefoundation.org
Internet: http://www.seattlefoundation.org/nonprofits/grantmaking/healthwellness/Pages/HealthWellness.aspx
Sponsor: Seattle Foundation
1200 Fifth Avenue, Suite 1300
Seattle, WA 98101-3151

Seattle Foundation Medical Funds Grants 1698

The Seattle Foundation administers the Medical Funds program to support medical research of potential benefit to the community and to address specific healthcare needs. In the area of medical research, grants are available in the fields of cancer, cardio-pulmonary disease, multiple sclerosis and diabetes. Special consideration will be given to research projects related to immunology, oncology, neurology, molecular biology and genetics. Grants will also be given to requests for specific equipment. Grants are also available to organizations that are administering projects addressing the healthcare needs of low-income children. In this area, grants will be given to requests for specific equipment and support for capital campaigns or facility renovation projects. A total amount of $200,000 is available for grants annually in this entire program. Typically no more than $50,000 is disbursed to any one organization.

Requirements: Preference will be given to organizations/institutions with the capacity to disseminate research findings and who receive regular support from other recognized funding sources (including the federal government).

Restrictions: These funds are not to be used for patient care. Research activities can include patient care, but the primary purpose of these grants is to support the purchase of equipment used in medical research.

Geographic Focus: Washington
Contact: Ceil Erickson, Grantmaking Director; (206) 515-2131 or (206) 515-2109; fax (206) 622-7673; grantmaking@seattlefoundation.org or c.erickson@seattlefoundation.org
Internet: http://www.seattlefoundation.org/nonprofits/medicalfunds/Pages/MedicalFunds.aspx
Sponsor: Seattle Foundation
1200 Fifth Avenue, Suite 1300
Seattle, WA 98101-3151

Seattle Foundation Neighbor to Neighbor Small Grants 1699

Neighbor to Neighbor, the Seattle Foundation's Small Grants program will prioritize organizations or programs that are aligned with one or both of the following funding strategies: organizations or programs that increase civic engagement, develop local leadership, or encourage community organizing and advocacy; or organizations or programs that build relationships and trust within and across communities (geographic and non-geographic). The quarterly deadlines for submitting applications are January 15, April 15, July 15 and October 15.

Requirements: To qualify for the Neighbor to Neighbor Small Grants program, an applicant must: be a 501(c)3 tax-exempt nonprofit organization, or be fiscally sponsored by one; have a small budget (generally under $100,000); and have a presence in South Seattle, White Center or Kent, and engage diverse, low-income community members to address disparities in these neighborhoods (South Seattle is defined as areas south of Interstate 90, west of Lake Washington, and north of Seattle's southern border; White Center is defined as the unincorporated area between the cities of Burien and Seattle).

Geographic Focus: Washington
Date(s) Application is Due: Jan 15; Apr 15; Jul 15; Oct 15
Amount of Grant: Up to 15,000 USD
Contact: Ceil Erickson, Grantmaking Director; (206) 515-2131 or (206) 515-2109; fax (206) 622-7673; grantmaking@seattlefoundation.org or c.erickson@seattlefoundation.org
Internet: http://www.seattlefoundation.org/nonprofits/neighbortoneighbor/Pages/Neighbor2NeighborFund.aspx
Sponsor: Seattle Foundation
1200 Fifth Avenue, Suite 1300
Seattle, WA 98101-3151

SecurianFoundation Grants 1700

The program mission is to enhance the quality of life and vitality of the communities in which it does business. Areas of priority include economic independence—programs that promote economic independence, including job-training and -placement services, work readiness, and career development programs for unemployed/underemployed and disadvantaged individuals; higher education—support to private colleges and universities (and tax-supported colleges and universities under certain conditions), with priority given to math, economics, and business and youth development intervention programs that encourage the pursuit of higher education; human services and special community needs—major operating support to the United Way and to non-United Way human services organizations that are demonstrating a service in an area of unmet need; and the arts—major arts and cultural organizations that provide services to a broad audience and stimulate the cultural vitality of the community. The company also has an employee matching gifts program for K-12 and higher education, vocational and specialized schools, hospitals, and arts and cultural organizations.

Requirements: IRS 501(c)3 nonprofit organizations primarily in the twin cities of Saint Paul and Minneapolis, MN, where the company and foundation are headquartered, are eligible.

Restrictions: Grants are not awarded to individuals or for benefits, trips, tours, political activities, or religious services/groups.
Geographic Focus: Minnesota
Date(s) Application is Due: Feb 15; May 15; Aug 15; Nov 15
Amount of Grant: 1,000 - 50,000 USD
Samples: United Way, Greater Twin Cities, (Minneapolis, MN)—for annual support, $355,000; University of Minnesota (Minneapolis, MN)—for leadership course and speaker series, $200,000.
Contact: Lori Koutsky, Manager; (651) 665-3501; fax (651) 665-3551; Lori. Koutsky@minnesotamutual.com
Internet: http://www.securian.com/About/giveguide.asp
Sponsor: Securian Foundation
400 Robert Street N
Saint Paul, MN 55101-2098

Sensient Technologies Foundation Grants   1701
The foundation supports organizations involved with arts and culture; children/youth, services; community/economic development; education; education, fund raising/fund distribution; education, research; family services; food services; general charitable giving; health care; higher education; homeless, human services; hospitals (general); human services; medical research, institute; mental health/crisis services; nutrition; performing arts; residential/custodial care, hospices; United Ways and Federated Giving Programs; Urban/community development; and voluntarism promotion. The foundation's types of support include: annual campaigns; capital campaigns; emergency funds; endowments; general operating support; matching/challenge support; program development; research; and scholarship funds.
Requirements: An application form is not required. Submit a letter of inquiry as an initial approach. The advisory board meets in January and June/July or as needed, with deadline for proposal review one month prior to board meetings.
Restrictions: The foundation gives primarily to its areas of interest in Indianapolis, Indiana; St. Louis, Missouri; and Milwaukee, Wisconsin. It does not support sectarian religious, fraternal, or partisan political organizations. It does not give grants to individuals.
Geographic Focus: Indiana, Missouri, Wisconsin
Contact: Douglas L. Arnold, (414) 271-6755; fax (414) 347-4783
Sponsor: Sensient Technologies Foundation
777 E Wisconsin Avenue
Milwaukee, WI 53202-5304

Seventh Generation Fund Grants   1702
The fund works directly with grassroots Native American communities and traditional indigenous societies throughout the Americas in support of Native peoples' community organizing, issue advocacy, economic renewal, cultural revitalization, environmental justice, and related restorative development efforts. Grants support projects in the areas of arts and cultural expression, environmental health and justice, indigenous people of the Americas, sacred Earth, and sustainable communities. Types of support include small grants—seed money, general operating support; technical assistance grants—training and capacity building; and mini grants—community-based projects. Application and guidelines are available online.
Requirements: 501(c)3 (and organizations with 501(c)3 fiscal sponsors) focused in the Native American community are eligible. Mini-grant applicants need not have 501(c)3 status.
Geographic Focus: All States
Date(s) Application is Due: Mar 1; Jun 1; Sep 1; Dec 1
Amount of Grant: 50 - 10,000 USD
Contact: Elaine Quitiquit; (707) 825-7640; eq7gen@pacbell.net
Internet: http://www.7genfund.org/we_help.html
Sponsor: Seventh Generation Fund
P.O. Box 4569
Arcata, CA 95518

Seybert Institution for Poor Boys and Girls Grants   1703
The charitable foundation supports nonprofit organizations providing services for disadvantaged youth in Philadelphia. The foundation is interested in projects for abused, deprived children and youth counseling services. The institute also supports special projects that encourage disadvantaged children in Philadelphia public elementary schools to develop leadership and academic skills. Generally grants range up to $7,500 and are made on a one-year basis. Recipients must provide a detailed narrative and financial report on how the funds were spent. The deadline for requests for after school and summer programs is March 17. The deadlines for other grant requests are January 2 and October 1.

Requirements: IRS 501(c)3 tax-exempt nonprofit organizations operating to benefit poor boys and girls in Philadelphia, PA, are eligible.
Geographic Focus: Pennsylvania
Date(s) Application is Due: Jan 2; Mar 17; Oct 1
Amount of Grant: Up to 7,500 USD
Contact: Judith L. Bardes; (610) 828-8145; fax (610) 834-8175; judy1@aol.com
Internet: http://www.grants-info.org/seybert/guidelines.htm
Sponsor: Adam and Maria Sarah Seybert Institution for Poor Boys and Girls
P.O. Box 540
Plymouth Meeting, PA 19462-0540

Shared Earth Foundation Grants   1704
The foundation is committed to the tenet that all creatures have an enduring claim to sustainable space on this planet. The foundation will fund organizations that promote protection and restoration of habitat for the broadest possible biodiversity, that foster respect for other species and individual creatures, that work to limit detrimental human impact on the planet, and that further the inherent right of all creatures to share the Earth. The foundation looks to fund primarily, though not exclusively, small organizations. It will provide administrative as well as project funds, with possibility for renewal or continuation, in the United States and abroad, to groups working in the natural and political worlds. The Foundation will fund a few applications for projects only, in the $5,000 to $10,000 range. The Foundation will acknowledge the request within one month, and respond within two months with a request for a full proposal, or declination. The Foundation will make grant decisions by December 15 of each year.
Restrictions: The Foundation will not fund individuals, scholarships, fellowships, or financial aid to students.
Geographic Focus: All States
Date(s) Application is Due: Dec 1
Amount of Grant: 5,000 - 10,000 USD
Samples: Alliance for International Reforestation, DeLand, Florida, $15,000.00 - to continue programs of tree-planting and efficient stove construction for the indigenous people of Guatemala's Altiplano; ecoAmerica, Washington, DC, $5,000 - general operations; Northern Jaguar Project, Tucson, Arizona, $25,000 - to protect, enhance and enlarge the Jaguar habitat in this northern Mexico state.
Contact: Caroline D. Gabel; (410) 778-6868; sharedearth@aol.com
Internet: http://www.sharedearth.org
Sponsor: Shared Earth Foundation
113 Hoffman Lane
Chestertown, MD 21620

Shubert Foundation Grants   1705
The grants build and perpetuate the live performing arts, particularly the professional theater, in the United States by supporting theatrical organizations, dance companies, and arts-related institutions that maintain and support the theater. Professional resident theaters are major recipients of financial support. Artistic achievement, administrative strength, and fiscal stability are factored into each evaluation, as is the company's development of new work and other significant contributions to the field of professional theater in the United States. Applications from dance companies will be accorded consideration in the same manner and under the same criteria as theater companies. Support is also provided for nonperforming arts-related organizations, such as those that coordinate and/or assist in the development of the performing arts. A limited number of grants are made to graduate drama departments of private universities. These departments are evaluated principally in terms of their ability to train and develop theater artists. A limited number of human services grants are made to exceptional institutions that are dedicated to improving the quality of life, both in and beyond their own communities. Applications are October 17, for dance, arts related, education, and human services applications; and December 1, for theater applications. Application and guidelines are available online.
Requirements: Tax-exempt 501(c)3 organizations may apply for grant support.
Restrictions: Grants are not awarded to individuals or for capital or endowment funds, seed money, research, conduit organizations, renovation projects, audience development, productions for specialized audiences, scholarships, fellowships, or matching gifts.
Geographic Focus: All States
Date(s) Application is Due: Oct 17; Dec 1
Amount of Grant: 5,000 - 35,000 USD
Contact: Vicki Reiss; (212) 944-3777; fax (212) 944-3707
Internet: http://www.shubertfoundation.org/grantprograms/default.asp
Sponsor: Shubert Foundation
234 W 44th Street
New York, NY 10036

Sidgmore Family Foundation Grants   1706

The Sidgmore Family Foundation honors the legacy of John W. Sidgmore by taking a proactive approach to helping others succeed. The Foundation desires to use its resources to find creative and innovative solutions so that people may achieve their full potential and become responsible, healthy and productive members of society. In recognition that an impoverished environment limits the possibilities for people to develop and thrive, the Sidgmore Family Foundation is particularly interested in funding organizations that: improve the quality of education and teacher training; further the advancement of knowledge in the field of medicine with a special emphasis on hearing and cardiology; utilize entrepreneurial skills to explore and develop creative, scalable, and sustainable solutions to critical social problems; and, provide support and services to those in need in the Washington D.C. area. Grants are awarded to organizations that have a clear, replicable plan for success, measured sustainable results, and high approval ratings from charity evaluator organizations, such as Charity Navigator. The Foundation also awards multi-year grants that can sustain a program or project.

Requirements: Nonprofit 501(c)3 organizations are eligible. Preference is given to organizations that serve residents in the Washington, D.C. metropolitan area, Maryland, and Virginia. Applicants must begin the process with an initial Letter of Inquiry (LOI). LOIs will receive a response if the Foundation wishes to receive a proposal from your organization.

Restrictions: The Sidgmore Family Foundation does not make grants to individuals, national health organizations, government agencies, or political and public policy advocacy groups.

Geographic Focus: All States

Contact: M. Gelbwaks, Director; (516) 541-2713; SidgmoreFound@aol.com

Internet: http://www.sidgmorefoundation.com/#application_process

Sponsor: Sidgmore Family Foundation

71 Leewater Avenue

Massapequa, NY 11758

Sid W. Richardson Foundation Grants   1707

Grants are provided to tax-exempt organizations in Texas in the areas of education (museums, learning centers, day schools, K-12 schools, higher education institutions, and business and economic education), health (medical schools, organ donor registries, hospitals, disease prevention, health science centers, and nursing associations), arts (arts councils, visual and performing arts festivals, museums, ballet, symphony orchestra, and arts education programs), and human services (boys' and girls' clubs, united funds, the elderly, crime prevention, the disabled, housing opportunities, food programs, and drug and alcohol abuse prevention). Types of support include operating budgets, seed grants, building construction funds, equipment acquisition, endowment funds, research, publications, conferences and seminars, matching funds, continuing support, and projects/programs. Award amounts vary depending on proposed projects. Applications must be received no later than January 15.

Requirements: Grant requests will be considered only from tax-exempt organizations described in Section 501(c)3 of the Internal Revenue Code of 1986 and classified as other than a private foundation within the meaning of Section 509(a) of the Code, or from a qualified public entity described in Section 170 of the Code.

Restrictions: Grants are not made to individuals, or for the support of school trips, testimonial dinners, fundraisers, or marketing events. An organization is limited to one application per calendar year.

Geographic Focus: Texas

Date(s) Application is Due: Jan 15

Amount of Grant: 10,000 - 100,000 USD

Contact: Carolyn Johns, (817) 336-0494; fax (817) 332-2176; cjohns@sidrichardson.org or info@sidrichardson.org

Internet: http://www.sidrichardson.org/grants/

Sponsor: Sid W. Richardson Foundation

309 Main Street

Fort Worth, TX 76102

Silicon Valley Community Foundation Opportunity Grants   1708

The Silicon Valley Community Foundation makes strategic grants from its discretionary funds. For the past five years it has prioritized solving grant making strategies to meet the most pressing needs in the region. The Foundation will set aside a pool of dollars in its Community Opportunity Fund to respond to safety-net needs and emerging new ideas, specifically the critical needs of food and shelter. The Foundation will award grants for continuation and expansion of services and will consider related general operating support under the Community Opportunity Fund. Each successful applicant will receive a grant in the range of $25,000 to $75,000 for a minimum of one year.

Requirements: San Mateo and Santa Clara County-serving organizations are eligible. Organizations headquartered outside the two-county region must demonstrate significant service to the area. Organizations with a 501(c)3 designation or those that have a fiscal sponsor with a 501(c)3 designation, public institutions or other entities that have a designated charitable purpose are also eligible.

Restrictions: Ineligible requests include organizations that provide services linked to one of the other four grantmaking strategy areas defined by the community foundation (e.g., immigrant integration, economic security, regional planning and education) or sponsorship requests for fundraising events.

Geographic Focus: California

Date(s) Application is Due: Oct 31

Amount of Grant: 25,000 - 75,000 USD

Contact: Manuel Santamaria, Vice President, Strategic Initiatives and Grantmaking; (650) 450-5400; fax (650) 450-5401; mjsantamaria@siliconvalleycf.org

Internet: http://www.siliconvalleycf.org/content/community-opportunity-fund

Sponsor: Silicon Valley Community Foundation

2440 West El Camino Real, Suite 300

Mountain View, CA 94040

Simmons Foundation Grants   1709

The foundation awards grants to Maine nonprofits in its areas of interest, including arts, higher education, family services, health care, food services, health organizations, human services, children and youth, services and women. Types of support include general operating support, building construction/renovation, equipment acquisition, and scholarship funds.

Requirements: There are no application forms or deadlines however your initial approach should be in the form of a letter. Applicants should submit the following: detailed description of project and amount of funding requested; brief history of organization and description of its mission; descriptive literature about organization; copy of IRS Determination Letter.

Geographic Focus: Maine

Contact: Suzanne McGuffey, Treasurer; (207) 774-2635

Sponsor: Simmons Foundation

1 Canal Plaza

Portland, ME 04101-4098

Sioux Falls Area Community Foundation Community Fund Grants   1710

The purpose of the Sioux Falls Area Foundation (SFACF)'s unrestricted grantmaking program is to provide support across a wide spectrum of charitable needs and interests. Grantmaking categories include Arts and Humanities (e.g., theatre, music, arts, dance, cultural development, historic preservation, library programs, and museums); Community Affairs and Development (e.g., citizen participation, public use of parks and recreation, administration of justice, economic development, employment, and training); Education (e.g., lifelong-learning activities in formal educational settings, support of educational facilities and systems, and scholarships); Environment (e.g., protection of natural areas, conservation of energy, prevention and elimination of pollution or hazardous waste, wildlife protection, and water quality); Health (e.g., improvement of healthcare, prevention of substance abuse; support of mental-health needs, and medical research); Human Services (e.g., assistance to families, youth, the elderly, disabled, special groups, social service providers, and those who stand in need); and Religion (e.g., support for churches, religious institutions, and religion programs). SFACF offers two grant programs from its unrestricted funds: Spot Grants for projects up to $3,000 and Community Fund Grants for projects over $3,000. The majority of Community Fund Grants are made in the range of $5,000 - $10,000. Proposals for Community Fund Grants must be submitted using a standard application form (available from the SFACF office or downloadable from the website). Applications are accepted anytime and will be reviewed by the Grants Committee at their next scheduled meeting. Meetings take place six times a year: January, March, May, July, September, and November (a schedule is posted at the SFACF website).

Requirements: Nonprofit organizations serving residents in the Sioux Falls, South Dakota area (Minnehaha, Lincoln, McCook, and Turner counties) are eligible to apply. SFACF considers grant requests for programs that require start-up funds to address important community needs or opportunities, expansion of programs that meet important community needs or opportunities, assistance to organizations weathering unforeseen or unusual financial crises; programs that increase an organization's capacity to advance its mission more efficiently or effectively; and programs or studies that inform the community's understanding of needs or opportunities. Requests are evaluated by the following criteria: comparative benefit to the community; the organization's capacity to achieve the stated objectives; the amount of support requested versus the number of people benefited; a well-planned approach to achieving stated objectives; a reasonable expectation that the program can be sustained over time (where applicable); the organization's history of working collaboratively to address community needs and opportunities; and when applicable, the organization's past SFACF grant performance.

Restrictions: SFACF does not consider grant requests for individuals, national fundraising efforts, political advocacy, and sectarian religious programs. The following types of requests are discouraged: large capital improvements or construction drives; ongoing operational support; reduction or elimination of organizational deficits; reimbursement of expenses undertaken prior to submission of a grant application; computer hardware and software, unless these are the focus of a new or enhanced program; public art for which approval and placement has not yet been secured; and multi-year requests.

Geographic Focus: South Dakota

Date(s) Application is Due: Jan 1; Mar 1; May 1; Jul 1; Sep 1; Nov 1

Samples: Horsepower, Rapid City, South Dakota, $10,000 - to provide therapeutic riding sessions for children who have physical or cognitive challenges and who come from low-income families; Hope Haven International Ministries, Sioux Falls, South Dakota, $7,990 - to provide South Dakota State Penitentiary inmates and volunteers with the proper tools to repair and refurbish wheelchairs to be sent overseas to help those in need; Helpline Center, Sioux Falls, South Dakota, $4,000 - to purchase new volunteer management software for the agency's website.

Contact: Candy Hanson, President; (605) 336-7055 ext. 12; fax (605) 336-0038; chanson@sfacf.org

Internet: http://www.sfacf.org/AboutGrants.aspx

Sponsor: Sioux Falls Area Community Foundation

300 N Philips Avenue, Suite 102

Sioux Falls, SD 57104-6035

Sioux Falls Area Community Foundation Spot Grants   1711

The purpose of the Sioux Falls Area Foundation (SFACF)'s unrestricted grantmaking program is to provide support across a wide spectrum of charitable needs and interests. Grantmaking categories include Arts and Humanities (e.g., theatre, music, arts, dance, cultural development, historic preservation, library programs, and museums); Community Affairs and Development (e.g., citizen participation, public use of parks and recreation, administration of justice, economic development, employment, and training); Education (e.g., lifelong-learning activities in formal educational settings, support of educational facilities and systems, and scholarships); Environment (e.g., protection of natural areas, conservation of energy, prevention and elimination of pollution or hazardous waste, wildlife protection, and water quality); Health (e.g., improvement of healthcare, prevention of substance abuse; support of mental-health needs, and medical research); Human Services (e.g., assistance to families, youth, the elderly, disabled, special groups, social service providers, and those who stand in need); and Religion (e.g., support for churches, religious institutions, and religion programs). SFACF offers two grant programs from its unrestricted funds: Community Fund Grants for projects over $3,000 and Spot Grants for projects up to $3,000. Spot Grant proposals may be submitted at any time and do not require SFACF's standard application form. Applicants should include the following components in their requests: a typed summary of their program in two pages or fewer; signatures of the organization's executive director and board chair; a board of directors roster; a copy of the organization's IRS tax determination letter; and a project budget. In most cases, SFACF will review and respond to Spot Grant requests within two weeks of receipt. SFACF has provided complete guidelines and an informative FAQ at their website.

Requirements: Nonprofit organizations serving residents in the Sioux Falls, South Dakota area (Minnehaha, Lincoln, McCook, and Turner counties) are eligible to apply. SFACF considers grant requests for programs that require start-up funds to address important community needs or opportunities, expansion of programs that meet important community needs or opportunities, assistance to organizations weathering unforeseen or unusual financial crises; programs that increase an organization's capacity to advance its mission more efficiently or effectively; and programs or studies that inform the community's understanding of needs or opportunities. Requests are evaluated by the following criteria: comparative benefit to the community; the organization's capacity to achieve the stated objectives; the amount of support requested versus the number of people benefited; a well-planned approach to achieving stated objectives; a reasonable expectation that the program can be sustained over time (where applicable); the organization's history of working collaboratively to address community needs and opportunities; and when applicable, the organization's past SFACF grant performance.

Restrictions: SFACF does not consider grant requests for individuals, national fundraising efforts, political advocacy, and sectarian religious programs. The

following types of requests are discouraged: large capital improvements or construction drives; ongoing operational support; reduction or elimination of organizational deficits; reimbursement of expenses undertaken prior to submission of a grant application; computer hardware and software, unless these are the focus of a new or enhanced program; public art for which approval and placement has not yet been secured; and multi-year requests.

Geographic Focus: South Dakota

Amount of Grant: Up to 3,000 USD

Samples: Hawthorne Elementary School, Sioux Falls, South Dakota, $1,000 - to provide students with milk as part of the school's mid-morning snack program; Here4Youth, Sioux Falls, South Dakota, $2,481 - to improve efficiency and donor and volunteer relations with the purchase of donor management software; Hillcrest Baptist Church, Sioux Falls, South Dakota, $900 - to provide opportunity for children in the Whittier neighborhood to learn teamwork and good sportsmanship through participation in the Meldrum Soccer League.

Contact: Candy Hanson, President; (605) 336-7055 ext. 12; fax (605) 336-0038; chanson@sfacf.org

Internet: http://www.sfacf.org/sfacf/aboutgrants.aspx

Sponsor: Sioux Falls Area Community Foundation

300 N Philips Avenue, Suite 102

Sioux Falls, SD 57104-6035

Sister Fund Grants for Women's Organizations   1712

The Sister Fund is a private foundation that supports and gives voice from a faith based perspective to the marginalized, especially women working for healing in the world. The Sister Fund believes that women can transform faith, and faith can transform feminism. It funds this kind of transformation in a variety of contexts. They are committed to woman-centered philanthropy and the empowerment of faith-based women, because the Fund believes the energy of love heals. The Sister Fund provides grants, technical support, communication tools and networking opportunities in a variety of forms. Some of the activities they support are: naming and validating both historical and contemporary examples of faith-fueled feminism; building bridges between faith-based and secular women; bolstering women's leadership in all sectors of society, especially faith-based institutions; fostering the emergence of young women's voices in leadership spheres; decreasing domestic violence; supporting the rights of incarcerated women; and empowering women economically. The Fund does not accept or respond to unsolicited requests for funding. Contact the Fund for further information.

Requirements: Nonprofit organizations are eligible to apply.

Geographic Focus: All States

Contact: Sunita Mehta, Director of Grants and Programs; (212) 260-4446; fax (212) 260-4633; info@sisterfund.org

Internet: http://www.sisterfund.org/

Sponsor: Sister Fund

79 Fifth Avenue, 4th Floor

New York, NY 10003

Sisters of Charity Foundation of Canton Grants   1713

The Sisters of Charity Foundation of Canton's initiatives focus on health, education, and social services. The Foundation strives to fund innovative, effective programs within these areas that exemplify its mission and guiding principles. In its attempts to address the root causes of poverty and to reach out to youth and families, the Foundation focuses its resources on programs designed to make a measurable impact in one or more of the following areas: the needs of the poor and underserved; enhancing organizational capacity; innovative ways of supporting children and families; and health care access.

Requirements: The Foundations primary service area is Stark County. However, proposals will be considered from the surrounding counties including Carroll, Holmes, Tuscarawas, and Wayne. The programs and services of the organization requesting funding must be consistent with the Foundation's Mission and Guiding Principles. The applicant must be a 501(c)3 nonprofit organization and the request must be in compliance with local, state, and federal laws. Organizations must first complete the two-page concept form at the Foundation website that explains the purpose of the organization's request. Foundation representatives will review and respond to concept forms within two weeks, when organizations may be invited to submit a proposal.

Restrictions: The Foundation generally does not fund requests for the following, unless it can be demonstrated that program services will have a significant effect on the root causes of poverty: debt reduction; annual appeals or membership drives; general endowments; or grants to individuals.

Geographic Focus: Ohio

Contact: Anne Savastano, Grants Manager; (330) 454-5800; fax (330) 454-5909; asavastano@sfcanton.org
Internet: http://www.scfcanton.org/grantguidlines.html
Sponsor: Sisters of Charity Foundation of Canton
400 Market Avenue North, Suite 300
Canton, OH 44702-1556

Sisters of Charity Foundation of Cleveland Good Samaritan Grants   1714

The Sisters of Charity Foundation of Cleveland provides support each year to organizations meeting the basic needs such as food, clothing, shelter, and transportation of those living in poverty in Cuyahoga County. The Good Samaritan Grants are intended for programs that provide direct goods and services for individuals living in poverty. To celebrate the foundation's 15th anniversary, the foundation has increased the Good Samaritan funding to establish a unique transportation project this year called Ride Your Way. Grant funds may be used for program support, operating support, program-related capital support, planning, or capacity building. Grant periods will vary depending upon the particular grant. Most grants are for one year. Grant periods for planning may be shorter, and multi-year grants are possible.
Requirements: Organizations must be tax-exempt, nonprofit organizations that primarily serve the Cuyahoga County region.
Restrictions: The Foundation does not make grants to support endowments, fundraising campaigns (including annual appeals), membership drives, debt retirement, and individual scholarships. Further, the Foundation does not make grants to individuals.
Geographic Focus: Ohio
Date(s) Application is Due: Jun 2
Amount of Grant: Up to 10,000 USD
Contact: Ursula Craig, Grants Coordinator; (216) 241-9300; fax (216) 241-9345; ucraig@socfdncleveland.org
Internet: http://www.socfdncleveland.org/RespondingToOurCommunity/GoodSamaritanGrantProgram/tabid/148/Default.aspx
Sponsor: Sisters of Charity Foundation of Cleveland
The Halle Building, 1228 Euclid Avenue, Suite 330
Cleveland, OH 44115-1834

Sisters of Charity Foundation of Cleveland Reducing Health and   1715
Educational Disparities in the Central Neighborhood Grants

The Sisters of Charity Foundation of Cleveland is committed to helping families and individuals overcome the challenges of poverty. In this grant opportunity the Foundation focuses on health, housing and education as key components to building stronger families and stable neighborhoods. The Foundation seeks to reduce both health and educational disparities in Cuyahoga County. Grant funds may be used for program support, operating support, program-related capital support, planning, or capacity building. Grant periods will vary depending upon the particular grant. Most grants are for one year. Grant periods for planning may be shorter, and multi-year grants are possible.
Requirements: Applicants must be 501(c)3 organizations or governmental units or agencies (such as schools) that primarily serve the Cuyahoga County region.
Restrictions: The Foundation does not make grants to support endowments, fundraising campaigns (including annual appeals), membership drives, debt retirement, and individual scholarships. Further, the Foundation does not make grants to individuals.
Geographic Focus: Ohio
Date(s) Application is Due: Apr 7
Amount of Grant: 40,000 - 150,000 USD
Contact: Ursula Craig, Grants Coordinator; (216) 241-9300; fax (216) 241-9345; ucraig@socfdncleveland.org
Internet: http://www.socfdncleveland.org/sistersofcharity/OurFocusAreas/HealthDisparities/HealthintheCentralNeighborhood/tabid/344/Default.aspx
Sponsor: Sisters of Charity Foundation of Cleveland
The Halle Building, 1228 Euclid Avenue, Suite 330
Cleveland, OH 44115-1834

Sisters of Mercy of North Carolina Foundation Grants   1716

The foundation provides grants to tax-exempt health care, educational, and social service organizations that assist women, children, the elderly, and the poor to improve the quality of their lives. Types of support include start-up grants for new organizations or programs, ongoing operating expenses for individual organizations, program or project expenses, building renovation, and equipment acquisition. Preference will be given to organizations whose efforts are collaborative, ecumenical, and multicultural. Particular attention

will be given to organizations that serve the unserved or underserved. Annual deadline dates may vary; contact program staff for exact dates.
Requirements: Tax-exempt health care, education, and social service organizations in North and South Carolina are eligible to apply.
Restrictions: The foundation does not ordinarily support projects, programs, or organizations that serve a limited audience; biomedical or clinical research; units of the federal government; political activities; publication of newsletters, magazines, books and the production of videos; conferences and travel; endowment funds; capital fundraising campaigns; annual giving campaigns; or social events or similar fundraising activities.
Geographic Focus: North Carolina, South Carolina
Date(s) Application is Due: Apr 1; Aug 1; Dec 1
Amount of Grant: 25,000 - 150,000 USD
Contact: Administrator; (704) 366-0087; contact@somncfdn.org
Internet: http://www.somncfdn.org/grantseekers.html
Sponsor: Sisters of Mercy of North Carolina Foundation
2115 Rexford Road, Suite 401
Charlotte, NC 28211

Sisters of St. Joseph Healthcare Foundation Grants   1717

The Sisters of St. Joseph Healthcare Foundation is a non-profit, public benefit corporation, which addresses the needs of the working and indigent poor in: Southern California; San Francisco Bay Area; Humboldt County; Fresno County. The Sisters of St. Joseph Healthcare Foundation funds programs which directly serve the needs of the underserved, especially families and children at risk. The Foundation sponsors or supports long-term efforts which are closely identified with the Sisters of St. Joseph of Orange and their mission of bringing unity and healing where divisiveness and oppression exist. The foundation supports the concept of Healthy Communities and desire to fund programs and organizations that: provide direct health-related services; support and transform the individual, social, economic, institutional, and cultural aspects of communities; provide change within larger societal systems to benefit low-income and at-risk populations; and develop the leadership and capacity for self-determination of those served by our funding. The Sisters of St. Joseph Healthcare Foundation is particularly interested in proposals which fall into these funding categories: mental health services; health services; homeless services; violence prevention.
Requirements: Southern California, Humbolt County, Fresno County and San Francisco bay area nonprofits are eligible.
Restrictions: The Foundation does not fund direct support to individuals, annual fund drives, or capital campaigns.
Geographic Focus: California
Amount of Grant: 1,000 - 50,000 USD
Samples: Access OC, Irvine, CA $50,000 - to improve access to specialty care for the safety net population; Boys & Girls Clubs, Garden Grove, CA $30,000 - to fund transportation to improve access to healthcare for low-income families; Casa Teresa, Orange, CA $40,000 - to assist homeless pregnant women with services to help them move from a low-income situation to self-sufficiency;
Contact: Sister Regina Fox, Program Director; (714) 633-8121, ext. 7109; rfox@csjorange.org
Sponsor: Sisters of St. Joseph Healthcare Foundation
440 South Batavia Street
Orange, CA 92868-3998

Skaggs Foundation Grants   1718

The Skaggs Foundation was established in 1962 in California, and currently provides funding in Alaska. The foundations area of interest include: animals/wildlife; preservation/protection; children services; special education; environmental education; environment; natural resources; marine science. Types of support available with these funds include: continuing support; endowments; equipment; general/operating support; internship funds; land acquisition; matching/challenge support; program evaluation; research; technical assistance.
Requirements: Nonprofit organizations are eligible, preference is given to requests from Alaska. The initial approach should be a one or two page letter of inquiry. There is no formal application form. Applicants should submit the following: copy of IRS Determination Letter; copy of current year's organizational budget and/or project budget; one copy of the proposal.
Restrictions: No grants to individuals.
Geographic Focus: Alaska
Date(s) Application is Due: May 1; Oct 1
Contact: Samuel D. Skaggs Jr., President; (907) 463-4843
Sponsor: Skaggs Foundation
P.O. Box 20510
Juneau, AK 99802-0510

Skillman Foundation Good Neighborhoods Grants 1719

The Good Neighborhoods program encourages the creation of safe, healthy, and vibrant neighborhoods where children with the support of caring adults, programs, and experiences can develop fully. Launched in January 2006, the program provides full-scale support to six Detroit neighborhoods where more than 65,000 children live, roughly 30% of the city's child population. Half of the children in these neighborhoods live in poverty. This program encourages the creation of safe, healthy and vibrant neighborhoods where children, with support of caring adults, programs and experiences, can develop fully. The six neighborhoods are: Brightmoor; Cody/Rouge; Northend (also known as Central); Osborn; Chadsey/Condon, in Southwest Detroit; and Vernor, in Southwest Detroit. The goal of the Good Neighborhoods program is to ensure that children experience safe, healthy and high-quality environments where they can thrive: neighborhoods with resources, opportunities and assets for children to develop fully and pursue prosperity.

Requirements: The applicant organizations must be tax exempt and may not be a 509(a) private foundation. The foundation's primary geographic area of focus is the Detroit metropolitan area.

Restrictions: The foundation does not award grants directly to individuals or provide loans of any kind; nor does it support sectarian religious activities, political lobbying, political advocacy, legislative activities, endowments, annual fund drives, basic research, or support of past operating deficits.

Geographic Focus: Michigan
Amount of Grant: 10,000 - 2,000,000 USD
Contact: Tonya Allen, Vice President of Programs; (313) 393-1185; fax (313) 393-1187; info@skillman.org
Internet: http://www.skillman.org/good-neighborhoods/
Sponsor: Skillman Foundation
100 Talon Centre Drive, Suite 100
Detroit, MI 48207

SOBP A.E. Bennett Research Award 1720

The Society of Biological Psychiatry offers an annual award of $2,000 each in basic science and in clinical science for the purpose of stimulating international research in biological psychiatry by young investigators. Candidates must be actively engaged in the research for which the award is sought. Applicants need only write a brief description of their research, submit 2-3 published or submitted papers and arrange for two letters of support (at least one of the letters needs to be from a member of the Society). Although the research is not to be judged in comparison with the work of the more senior investigators, special consideration will be given to the originality of the approach and independence of thought evident in the submission. Nominations should be submitted on-line on or before November 29.

Requirements: Submissions are welcomed from laboratory researchers in any country who have not passed their 45th birthday or have not been engaged in research for greater than 10 years following award of their terminal degree or the end of formal clinical/fellowship training, whichever is later by deadline date; candidates need not be current members of the society.

Geographic Focus: Wisconsin
Date(s) Application is Due: Feb 1; Mar 15; Aug 1; Sep 13; Sep 15; Nov 29
Amount of Grant: 2,000 USD
Contact: Executive Director; (904) 953-2842; fax (904) 953-7117; maggie@mayo.edu or sobp@sobp.org
Internet: http://www.sobp.org/i4a/pages/index.cfm?pageID=3379
Sponsor: Society of Biological Psychiatry
4500 San Pablo Road, Birdsall 310
Jacksonville, FL 32224

SOCFOC Catholic Ministries Grants 1721

The Sisters of Charity Foundation of Cleveland belongs to a community of Catholic health and social service organizations inspired to service by the healing ministry of Jesus Christ. As a supporting foundation to the congregation of the Sisters of Charity of St. Augustine, the Foundation gives priority to the ministries of the Sisters of Charity Health System. A limited amount of remaining funds may be available to other Catholic ministries in health and human services in Cuyahoga County. Funding is limited to Invited Proposals.

Requirements: Each proposal to the Foundation must include a completed application form, proposal narrative, budget, and Budget Narrative. The application form and guidelines for the proposal narrative may be found on this website under the specific program area. Eligible organizations are 501(c)3 organizations or governmental agencies or units.

Restrictions: The Foundation does not make grants to individuals.
Geographic Focus: Ohio
Amount of Grant: 10,000 - 150,000 USD
Samples: Secretariat for Parish Life & Development, OH, $10,000;2008; St. Vincent Charity Hospital, OH, $151,600;2008;
Contact: Lynn Berner, Program Officer; (216) 241-9300; fax (216) 241-9345; lberner@socfdncleveland.org
Internet: http://www.socfdncleveland.org/RespondingToOurCommunity/CatholicMinistries/tabid/313/Default.aspx
Sponsor: Sisters of Charity Foundation of Cleveland
The Halle Building, 1228 Euclid Avenue, Suite 330
Cleveland, OH 44115-1834

Social Justice Fund Northwest Economic Justice Giving Project 1722
Grants

Social Justice Fund Northwest is a public membership foundation that supports organizations working for structural change, to improve the lives of people most affected by political, economic and social inequities. Economic Justice Giving Project grants are one-year awards of up to $10,000 each to support social change in Idaho, Montana, Oregon, Washington and Wyoming, specifically focused on economic justice issues. Such issues are defined broadly to include work that addresses the root causes of economic inequity using community led solutions to build power among its members (ie. workers, families, faith communities etc.) to advocate for and create thriving communities. Examples of this activity include, but are not limited to: worker and consumer protections, transportation access, healthcare solutions, affordable housing, tax policy, and impacts of the wealth divide on low income, people of color, immigrants, disability and LGBTQ populations.

Requirements: To be eligible for any Social Justice Fund grant program, an organization must: be a nonprofit organization with 501(c)3 or 501(c)4 status as determined by the IRS, or be a federally recognized American Indian tribal government or agency; be led by people who are most directly affected by the problems that the organization or project is addressing; carry out most of its work in Idaho, Montana, Oregon, Washington, and/or Wyoming; and satisfy evaluation requirements for all previous Social Justice Fund grants.

Geographic Focus: Idaho, Montana, Oregon, Washington, Wyoming
Date(s) Application is Due: Jun 8
Amount of Grant: 10,000 USD
Contact: Kylie Gursky, Project Manager; (206) 624-4081; fax (206) 382-2640; kylie@socialjusticefund.org
Internet: http://www.socialjusticefund.org/apply-grant
Sponsor: Social Justice Fund Northwest
1904 Third Avenue, Suite 806
Seattle, WA 98101

Social Justice Fund Northwest Environmental Justice Giving Project 1723
Grants

Social Justice Fund Northwest is a public membership foundation that supports organizations working for structural change, to improve the lives of people most affected by political, economic and social inequities. Environmental Justice Giving Project grants are one-year grants of up to $10,000 each to support social change in Idaho, Montana, Oregon, Washington and Wyoming specifically working for environmental justice. Grants are defined in the environmental justice movement as the spaces where we live, work, learn, play, pray, and heal. For the purpose of this grant, environmental justice organizations: strive for equitable access to a clean and healthy environment; work for sustainability, including racial and economic justice; and are community-based and led by the people who are most disproportionally affected by environmental justice issues. Some examples are: safe and healthy housing, workplaces, and schools; transportation; access to healthy food; air, water, soil, light, and noise pollution; health care; waste disposal; distribution of natural resources and the benefits of a green economy; preservation and restoration of wildlife and wildlands; and climate change. This granting committee is open to considering other environmental justice issues not identified here, particularly as they relate to the fundamental rights to air, water, land, and food.

Requirements: To be eligible for any Social Justice Fund grant program, an organization must: be a nonprofit organization with 501(c)3 or 501(c)4 status as determined by the IRS, or be a federally recognized American Indian tribal government or agency; be led by people who are most directly affected by the problems that the organization or project is addressing; carry out most of its work in Idaho, Montana, Oregon, Washington, and/or Wyoming; and satisfy evaluation requirements for all previous Social Justice Fund grants. The committee welcomes applications from people with all levels of English fluency and formal education; therefore, grammatical and spelling errors will not negatively impact scores. In addition, small and/or new organizations are

encouraged to apply. If your organization does not have tax-exempt status or sponsorship, but might otherwise be a good fit for this grant, contact Social Justice Fund staff so that they can assist you with your eligibility.
Geographic Focus: Idaho, Montana, Oregon, Washington, Wyoming
Date(s) Application is Due: Jun 8
Amount of Grant: Up to 10,000 USD
Contact: Mijo Lee, Project Manager; (206) 624-4081; fax (206) 382-2640; mijo@socialjusticefund.org or generalgrant@socialjusticefund.org
Elsa Batres-Boni, Project Manager; (206) 624-4081; fax (206) 382-2640; elsa@socialjusticefund.org or generalgrant@socialjusticefund.org
Internet: http://www.socialjusticefund.org/apply-grant
Sponsor: Social Justice Fund Northwest
1904 Third Avenue, Suite 806
Seattle, WA 98101

Social Justice Fund Northwest General Grants 1724

Social Justice Fund Northwest is a public membership foundation that supports organizations working for structural change, to improve the lives of people most affected by political, economic and social inequities. General Grants are one-year grants of up to $10,000 each to support social change in Idaho, Montana, Oregon, Washington and Wyoming. These grants may be for general support or for specific projects.
Requirements: To be eligible for any Social Justice Fund grant program, an organization must: be a nonprofit organization with 501(c)3 or 501(c)4 status as determined by the IRS, or be a federally recognized American Indian tribal government or agency; be led by people who are most directly affected by the problems that the organization or project is addressing; carry out most of its work in Idaho, Montana, Oregon, Washington, and/or Wyoming; and satisfy evaluation requirements for all previous Social Justice Fund grants. The committee welcomes applications from people with all levels of English fluency and formal education; therefore, grammatical and spelling errors will not negatively impact scores. In addition, small and/or new organizations are encouraged to apply. If your organization does not have tax-exempt status or sponsorship, but might otherwise be a good fit for this grant, contact Social Justice Fund staff so that they can assist you with your eligibility.
Geographic Focus: Idaho, Montana, Oregon, Washington, Wyoming
Date(s) Application is Due: Jul 13
Amount of Grant: Up to 10,000 USD
Contact: Kylie Gursky, Project Manager; (206) 624-4081; fax (206) 382-2640; kylie@socialjusticefund.org or generalgrant@socialjusticefund.org
Elsa Batres-Boni, Project Manager; (206) 624-4081; fax (206) 382-2640; elsa@socialjusticefund.org or generalgrant@socialjusticefund.org
Internet: http://www.socialjusticefund.org/apply-grant
Sponsor: Social Justice Fund Northwest
1904 Third Avenue, Suite 806
Seattle, WA 98101

Social Justice Fund Northwest Montana Giving Project Grants 1725

Social Justice Fund Northwest is a public membership foundation that supports organizations working for structural change, to improve the lives of people most affected by political, economic and social inequities. The Montana Giving Project is a diverse group of people who have committed to building community together, learning about a multi-issue movement for justice, and working together to fund strategic, inspiring, and under-resourced community organizing in Montana. Montana Giving Project grants are one-year grants of up to $10,000 each to support community organizing for social change in Montana only. These grants may be for general support or for specific projects.
Requirements: To be eligible for this Social Justice Fund grant program, an organization must: be a nonprofit organization with 501(c)3 or 501(c)4 status as determined by the IRS, or be a federally recognized American Indian tribal government or agency; be led by people who are most directly affected by the problems that the organization or project is addressing; carry out most of its work in Montana; and satisfy evaluation requirements for all previous Social Justice Fund grants.
Geographic Focus: Montana
Date(s) Application is Due: Jun 29
Amount of Grant: Up to 10,000 USD
Contact: Kylie Gursky, Project Manager; (206) 624-4081; fax (206) 382-2640; kylie@socialjusticefund.org or mtgp@socialjusticefund.org
Internet: http://www.socialjusticefund.org/apply-grant
Sponsor: Social Justice Fund Northwest
1904 Third Avenue, Suite 806
Seattle, WA 98101

Solo Cup Foundation Grants 1726

The foundation awards grants to Illinois nonprofit organizations in its areas of interest, including higher education, health, social services, and Christian organizations and churches. Types of support include capital campaigns, general operating support, and scholarship funds. There are no application deadlines or forms.
Requirements: Illinois nonprofit organizations are eligible.
Geographic Focus: Illinois
Amount of Grant: 5,000 - 85,000 USD
Contact: Robert M. Korzenski, President and CEO; (847) 831-4800; fax (847) 579-3245; info@solocup.com
Sponsor: Solo Cup Foundation
1700 Old Deerfield Road
Highland Park, IL 60035

Sony Corporation of America Corporate Philanthropy Grants 1727

Sony Corporation of America consists of three operating companies as well as the corporate headquarters, which is based in New York City: Sony Electronics, Inc. (headquarters in San Diego, California); Sony Pictures Entertainment, Inc. (headquarters in Culver City, California); and Sony Music Entertainment, Inc. (headquarters in New York City). Each company, as well as the overall corporation, has its own philanthropic priorities and resources (e.g. grants, product donations, and recordings and screenings) that benefit a multitude of causes. Taken together the corporation's areas of interest cover arts and culture; health and human services; civic and community outreach, education; the environment; disaster response; and volunteerism. The core of Sony's various corporate philanthropy programs are their contributions to the communities in which Sony employees work and live; however, the corporation and subsidiaries contribute to national nonprofits as well. In the past, types of support have included general operating budgets, continuing support, annual campaigns, seed grants, building construction, equipment acquisition, endowment funds, employee matching gifts, internships, and employee-related scholarships. Sony Corporation of America and its subsidiaries welcome requests for support throughout the year. There is no grant application form. Requests must be submitted in writing to the corporation or its operating companies. Contact information is given on this page and at the website. Guidelines for what to include in the application as well as more information on types of programs the corporation and/or its subsidiaries have supported are available at the grant website. Notification of grant-request approval or rejection will be made in writing within one month of receipt of all proposed materials.
Requirements: U.S. nonprofits, including schools and school districts, are eligible.
Restrictions: The corporation does not consider multi-year requests for support. The following types of organizations will not be funded: organizations that discriminate on the basis of race, color, creed, gender, religion, age, national origin, or sexual orientation; partisan political organizations, committees, or candidates and public office holders; religious organizations in support of their sacramental or theological functions; labor unions; endowment or capital campaigns of national origin; organizations whose prime purpose is to influence legislation; testimonial dinners in general; for-profit publications or organizations seeking advertisements or promotional support; individuals seeking self-advancement; foreign or non-U.S.-based organizations; and organizations whose mission is outside of the U.S.
Geographic Focus: All States
Amount of Grant: 1,000 - 100,000 USD
Contact: Janice Pober, Senior Vice President; (310) 244-7737
Internet: http://www.sony.com/SCA/philanthropy/guidelines.shtml
Sponsor: Sony Corporation of America
550 Madison Avenue, 33rd Floor
New York, NY 10022-3211

Sophia Romero Trust Grants 1728

The Sophia Romero Trust was established in 1948 to support and promote quality human-services and health-care programming for underserved elders living in Bristol County, Massachusetts. Special consideration will be given to organizations that serve older women living in Bristol County, Massachusetts. Grant requests for general operating support or program support are strongly encouraged. The majority of grants from the Romero Trust are one year in duration. Applicants must apply online at the grant website. Applicants are strongly encouraged to do the following before applying: review the downloadable state application procedures for additional helpful information and clarifications; review the downloadable online-application guidelines at the grant website; review the trust's funding history (link is available from the grant website); review the online application questions in advance; and review the list of required attachments. These will generally include: a list of board

members, financial statements (audited, reviewed, or compiled by independent auditor); an organization summary; a list of other funding sources; an IRS Determination letter; and other required documents. All attachments must be uploaded in the online application as PDF, Word, or Excel files. The application deadline for the Sophia Romero Trust is 11:59 p.m. on February 1. Applicants will be notified of grant decisions before April 30.
Requirements: Applicants must have 501(c)3 tax-exempt status and serve the residents of Bristol County, Massachusetts.
Restrictions: The fund does not support requests from individuals, organizations attempting to influence policy through direct lobbying, or any political campaigns.
Geographic Focus: Massachusetts
Date(s) Application is Due: Feb 1
Contact: Emma Greene; (617) 434-0329; emma.m.greene@baml.com
Internet: https://www.bankofamerica.com/philanthropic/fn_search.action
Sponsor: Sophia Romero Trust
225 Franklin Street, 4th Floor, MA1-225-04-02
Boston, MA 02110

Sorenson Legacy Foundation Grants 1729
The foundation has a broad spectrum of philanthropic interests and supports endeavors that: encourage and support the long-term preservation and enhancement of the quality of life of all humankind, especially of families and children; assist the disenfranchised of society, such as but not limited to, abused spouses and children, in order that they receive the full benefits of membership in society and fulfill their potential as human beings; promote medical research and the development of innovative medical technologies for saving lives and alleviating pain and suffering; promote the development of the arts, including art education in schools, assistance of promising young artists, and support of performing arts organizations; promote community development and security, adequate and affordable housing, and education and job training; promote law and order generally and provide youth with alternatives to gangs, crime and socially nonproductive behavior; protect and enhance the environment, preserve wild and open spaces, and promote development of parks and green spaces; promote the development of science, culture and recreation; promote world peace and unity through a greater understanding, tolerance and harmony among religious, national and ethnic groups; advance the programs at private and state universities and colleges that are consistent with the foundation's charter; and, advance the mission of the Church of Jesus Christ of Latter-day Saints in all its places.
Geographic Focus: All States
Contact: Executive Director, (801) 461-9700; (801) 461-9722
Internet: http://www.sorensoncompanies.com/giving_back.html
Sponsor: Sorenson Foundation
2511 South West Temple Street
Salt Lake City, UT 84115

Sosland Foundation Grants 1730
The foundation awards grants to nonprofit organizations in the metropolitan bistate Kansas City area. Areas of interest include arts and culture, higher education, health care, Jewish services, and social services. Types of support include program development, building construction/renovation, equipment acquisition, development grants, endowments, general operating grants, and matching gifts. There are no application forms or deadlines. Applicants should send a letter including a description of the program and the organization, a list of board and staff, and proof of tax-exempt status.
Requirements: Metro bistate Kansas City 501(c)3 nonprofits are eligible.
Restrictions: Individuals and publications or conferences are ineligible.
Geographic Focus: Kansas, Missouri
Contact: Program Contact; (816) 756-1000; fax (816) 756-0494
Internet: http://www.soslandfoundation.org
Sponsor: Sosland Foundation
4800 Main Street, Suite 100
Kansas City, MO 64112

South Carolina Arts Commission Annual Operating Support for 1731 Organizations Grants
This program provides twelve-month operational support to SC arts organizations with primary missions involving these artistic functions: Producing, Service, Presenting, Education. Support is broad in scope and can be used for a variety of arts programs, salaries, artist fees, supplies, and other operating expenses at the discretion of the organization within the eligibility and legal requirements defined in these guidelines. There is no pre-set funding range. Awards will be based on organizational budgets, application reviews, and the availability of funds.

Requirements: Organizations requesting Annual Operating Support must have completed one fiscal year of programming in order to be eligible to apply. Applicant must be a SC organization with primary mission focused on the arts (or an organization that serves as the primary arts provider in its community). Applicant must also be (1) a charitable organization currently registered with the Office of the Secretary of State that has its own federal tax exempt status with the Internal Revenue Service; or, (2) a charitable organization currently registered with the Office of the Secretary of State applying through a tax exempt fiscal agent organization; or, (3) a unit of local government. Applicant must have a valid DUNS number. A minimum of 2:1 cash match is required. No in-kind expenses are allowed as part of applicant's match in this category. Applications must be submitted via the Online SC Arts Resources (OSCAR) application process by 5:00 PM on the posted deadline date. NOTE: This grant requires a filing fee of $15.00, payable by check made out to South Carolina Arts Commission OR online credit card payment.
Restrictions: No in-kind expenses are allowed as part of applicant's match in this category. Payment will be on a reimbursement basis only. Organizations requesting Annual Operating Support may not apply for Long Term or Quarterly Support (except for requests for staff professional development under Quarterly Support grants).
Geographic Focus: South Carolina
Date(s) Application is Due: Feb 15
Contact: Rusty Sox, Coordinator; (803) 734-8696; rsox@arts.sc.gov
Internet: http://www.southcarolinaarts.com/grants/organizations/annual.shtml
Sponsor: South Carolina Arts Commission
1800 Gervais Street
Columbia, SC 29201

South Carolina Arts Commission Incentive Grants for Employer 1732 Sponsored Benefits (ESB)
Many arts organizations are facing difficulties recruiting and retaining qualified staff because they lack the capacity to compete with larger organizations when it comes to benefits packages. Competitive salaries or bonuses are no longer enough to recruit and retain staff. Today's market requires an attractive package which includes employer sponsored benefits which are a direct cost to the organization. The bottom line for many organizations looking to build organizational capacity through staff recruitment and retention is whether or not the organization is able to afford basic health insurance coverage as an employee benefit. And, for organizations that do offer benefits, there is need to control the costs. In an effort to assist organizations, SCAC is offering a grant program to encourage employer sponsored benefits.
Requirements: Applicant must be a SC organization with primary mission focused on the arts (or an organization that serves as the primary arts provider in its community). Applicant must also be: (1) a charitable organization currently registered with the Office of the Secretary of State that has its own federal tax exempt status with the Internal Revenue Service; (2) a charitable organization currently registered with the Office of the Secretary of State applying through a tax exempt fiscal agent organization; or, (3) a unit of local government with primary mission focused on the arts. This program requires a match: 1:1 - up to 50% of benefits for year 1; 2:1 - up to 33% of benefits for year 2.
Restrictions: Applicant may not be a unit of state or federal government, college, university, or K-12 public or private school. Funds may not be used for employee bonuses or salary increases. Payment will be on an expense reimbursement basis only.
Geographic Focus: South Carolina
Amount of Grant: Up to 2,000 USD
Contact: Rusty Sox, Coordinator; (803) 734-8696; rsox@arts.sc.gov
Internet: http://www.southcarolinaarts.com/grants/organizations/benefits.shtml
Sponsor: South Carolina Arts Commission
1800 Gervais Street
Columbia, SC 29201

South Carolina Arts Commission Leadership and Organizational 1733 Development Grants
The program was established to support arts leaders' (professional administrators and board members) acquisition of skills and practical tools which hone their ability to lead, develop, and sustain the overall health and vitality of South Carolina's arts organizations. Funding is targeted to professional arts administrators and board members of arts organizations. Grantees will identify a set of critical individual or operational capacity-building issues toward which the funds will be used. For the purpose of this initiative, capacity-building is defined as activities that either strengthen individual ability to lead or improve organizational functioning and sustainability. Leadership Development

funding includes: costs for individuals to receive professional development; costs involved in coordinating and/or conducting professionally facilitated learning for individuals or groups across position or discipline. Organizational Development funding includes: costs for professional consultant/consulting firms providing services in areas such as fundraising, financial management, marketing, executive transition, public relations, board development, strategic planning, program development, technology, etc; costs involved with coordinating and/or conducting professionally facilitated learning for individuals or groups across position or discipline.

Requirements: Before applying, you are strongly advised to discuss the project with your county coordinator to determine whether your project meets the guidelines. Applicants must: (1) be a nonprofit, charitable arts organization that is currently registered with the Office of the Secretary of State of South Carolina, and that either has its own federal tax-exempt status with the IRS or applies through a fiscal agent; (2) have the production or presentation of arts events or service to the arts as its primary organizational mission; OR be the primary provider of general, multidisciplinary arts programs and/or services within a particular community or region; and, (3) have completed at least one full fiscal year in operation prior to application. Applications must be received at least six weeks before the start of the project or activity. Projects must be completed by June 30. Applications received after May 15 must be for projects beginning after July 1. A 1:1 match is required - 50% of the applicant's match must be cash.

Restrictions: Applicants may not be a unit of SC State government. Individual artists are not eligible to apply to this program. Applicants may submit only one application per project per year. This category is not intended to fund annual or recurring projects. However, organizations/individuals previously funded under this category and intending to apply for funds to support the same or a similar project must demonstrate how receiving additional funds will substantially improve organizational functioning and sustainability or strengthen an individual's ability to lead the organization. Payment will be on an expense reimbursement basis only.

Geographic Focus: South Carolina
Amount of Grant: Up to 2,000 USD
Contact: Joy Young, Program Director; (803) 734-8203; jyoung@arts.sc.gov
Internet: http://www.southcarolinaarts.com/grants/organizations/leadershiporgdev.shtml
Sponsor: South Carolina Arts Commission
1800 Gervais Street
Columbia, SC 29201

Southwest Florida Community Foundation Arts & Attractions Grants 1734

The program was established to use existing resources in Lee County to assist arts and attractions agencies, especially to encourage repeat visits, strengthen a need in the arts, provide the financial foundation that will encourage additional and create greater resources for growth, and partner with motivated professionals to maximize the expenditure and ensure a quality return on investments. Two types of grants will be offered: Marketing & Visitor Enhancement Grants and Basic Operating Grants.

Requirements: Marketing and Visitor Enhancement Grants: All Tourist Development Council funds will be granted to this grant category. Only Lee County 501(c)3 agencies will be eligible. Basic Operating Grants: These grants provide unrestricted funds for the general administration, operations and programs of arts and attractions organizations located in Lee County. These grants can be allocated for capital improvement purchases. Guidelines and the required application can be found at the sponsor's website.

Geographic Focus: Florida
Date(s) Application is Due: Jun 12
Amount of Grant: Up to 25,000 USD
Contact: Carol McLaughlin, Chief Program Officer; (239) 274-5900, ext. 225; fax (239) 274-5930; cmclaughlin@floridacommunity.com
Internet: http://www.floridacommunity.com/grantseekers/applications/
Sponsor: Southwest Florida Community Foundation
8260 College Parkway, Suite 101
Fort Myers, FL 33919

Southwest Gas Corporation Foundation Grants 1735

The corporate foundation supports nonprofit organizations in its service communities. General support grants and employee matching gifts are made in the areas of education (universities, colleges, and literacy programs) and social services (United Way organizations, youth groups, community service, and volunteer organizations). Additional areas of interest are arts/culture and health. Types of support include general operating grants, projects

grants, conferences and seminars, building construction/renovation, capital campaigns, emergency funds, employee matching gifts, research grants, donated equipment, and in-kind services. In southern Arizona, contact Marty Looney, P.O. Box 26500, Tucson, AZ 85726-6500; (520) 794-6416.

Requirements: Nonprofit organizations in Arizona; San Bernardino County, CA; and Nevada may apply.
Geographic Focus: Arizona, California, Nevada
Amount of Grant: Up to 620,567 USD
Samples: Phoenix Art Museum (Phoenix, AZ)—for general support, $3000; Boys and Girls Clubs (Tucson, AZ)—for general support, $1000; Community Food Bank (Phoenix, AZ)—for general support, $3500.
Contact: Suzanne Farinas, (702) 876-7247; fax (702) 876-7037
Internet: http://www.swgas.com
Sponsor: Southwest Gas Corporation
P.O. Box 98510
Las Vegas, NV 89193-8510

Speckhard-Knight Charitable Foundation Grants 1736

The foundation is dedicated to improving the quality of life in Jackson and Washtenaw counties in Michigan, and aiding environmental efforts in the third world. Grants support nonprofit organizations that work in the areas of adoption, foster care, at-risk families, and the environment. Types of support include start-up grants, salaries, and operating support. To apply for a grant, download and print out the Common Grant Application Form from the Council of Michigan Foundations.

Requirements: Michigan nonprofit organizations serving Jackson and Washtenaw Counties are eligible.
Restrictions: Grants do not support construction costs.
Geographic Focus: Michigan
Date(s) Application is Due: Mar 20; Jun 6; Oct 17
Amount of Grant: 2,000 - 20,000 USD
Contact: Gerald Knight, (734) 761-8752 or (734) 355-9926; fax (734) 827-0091; zmjk@comcast.net
Internet: http://www.skcf.org
Sponsor: Speckhard-Knight Charitable Foundation
771 Bogey Court
Ann Arbor, MI 48103

Sport Manitoba Women to Watch Grants 1737

A major initiative is the Women to Watch Grant Program. Working in partnership with Provincial Sport Organizations and Coaching Manitoba, Sport Manitoba provides a monthly grant of $500 to a female athlete, team, official or volunteer to assist them in enhancing their women in sport career. A $500 monthly grant is also awarded to a female coach to assist them in further developing the skills necessary to attain a higher level of coaching or increased level of coaching experience. Grants may be used to offset costs such as training, travel, certification, sport equipment, competitions/tournaments, camps, leadership development, professional development and child care costs related to future development in their sport.

Requirements: Applicants must be female and a member of their provincial sport organization in good standing as an athlete, coach, official or in a leadership position either as a volunteer or paid staff. The application must be endorsed by the PSO with a commitment to matching the $250 grant from Sport Manitoba/Coaching Manitoba.
Geographic Focus: All States, Canada
Date(s) Application is Due: Mar 15; Jul 15; Nov 30
Amount of Grant: 1,000 USD
Contact: Shawnee Scatliff, Program Coordinator; (204) 885-7400; fax (204) 925-5916; sscatliff@mts.net
Internet: http://sportmanitoba.ca/programs/womensport.php
Sponsor: Sport Manitoba
200 Main Street
Winnipeg, MB R3C 4M2 Canada

Sprague Foundation Grants 1738

Grants are made to hospitals, arts and cultural organizations, civic and community affairs, educational institutions, and health and human service organizations and charities located in New York and Massachusetts. Types of support include general operating support, matching and challenge funds, and program development. The initial approach should be a letter requesting the foundation's guidelines. Grants are awarded at the June and December board meetings.

Requirements: Only residents of New York and Massachusetts may apply.
Restrictions: No grants are provided to individuals, for building funds, or for loans.

Geographic Focus: Massachusetts, New York
Date(s) Application is Due: Apr 15; Oct 1
Amount of Grant: 1,000 - 55,000 USD
Contact: Linda Franciscovich, (212) 852-3377
Sponsor: Seth Sprague Educational and Charitable Foundation
114 W 47th Street
New York, NY 10036-1532

Springs Close Foundation Grants 1739

Since it was chartered in 1942, the Springs Close Foundation has contributed over $85 million to a wide variety of charitable and educational causes designed to improve the quality of life and well-being of the people in Chester, Lancaster and York Counties. Support includes, but is not limited to, food, shelter and medical assistance. This temporary change in focus is in response to high levels of unemployment and economic distress in the Foundation's service areas. The Foundation also makes occasional statewide grants in South Carolina. There are three major areas of program interest: Recreation and Environment, Public Education and Early Childhood Development, Community Service and Health
Requirements: Grants are made only to organizations that are tax-exempt under Section 501(c)3 of the Internal Revenue Code. No grants are made to individuals.
Restrictions: The Foundation will only consider grant requests from eligible nonprofit organizations that can effectively deliver emergency and basic support to citizens in Chester and Lancaster counties and a portion of York County.
Geographic Focus: South Carolina
Date(s) Application is Due: Mar 1; Oct 1
Amount of Grant: 5,000 - 50,000 USD
Contact: Angela McCrae, President; (803) 548-2002; fax (803) 548-1797
Internet: http://www.thespringsclosefoundation.org/grants.htm
Sponsor: Springs Close Foundation
1826 Second Baxter Crossing
Fort Mill, SC 29708

Sprint Foundation Grants 1740

The foundation's charitable giving program emphasizes support of nonprofit local and regional organizations in those communities in which the corporation has a major presence. The foundation focuses its contributions in four major areas of interest. Education—programs that increase and improve student achievement, family engagement and professional development for educators; K-12 education; and higher education through its Matching Gift program, as well as through partnerships with the United Negro College Fund, the Hispanic College Fund, and targeted MBA programs and undergraduate institutions to provide financial assistance and employment opportunities for students pursuing degrees in business and technology-related fields. Unsolicited scholarship requests will not be considered for funding. Arts and Culture—visual and performing arts organizations, theater, symphonies, museums, and other cultural organizations and activities that contribute to a thriving and diverse community. Youth Development—mentoring programs, minority youth endeavors, broad-scale community youth activities focused on building leadership and social skills, and programs that support business and economic education for youth. Community Development—regional initiatives that contribute to a strong civic infrastructure and a vibrant, healthy community; and, on a national level, the foundation matches funds raised for its national food drive and United Way pledges made by Sprint employees who participate in the corporation's national campaign. Types of support include general operating support, continuing support, annual campaigns, capital campaigns, program development, and employee matching gifts. The foundation accepts proposals throughout the year.
Requirements: 501(c)3 organizations in Atlanta, Boston, Chicago, Dallas, Kansas City, Las Vegas, Los Angeles, New York City, Orlando, San Francisco and the District of Columbia are eligible; however, these areas are subject to change. Support of national organizations with a broad sphere of interests will be considered on a case-by-case basis. The foundation's geographic focus is primarily domestic.
Restrictions: Organizations generally excluded from the foundation's grantmaking activities include political, religious, fraternal, labor, and veterans organizations; hospitals; and neighborhood associations. No grants are made to individuals.
Geographic Focus: All States
Amount of Grant: Up to 52,000,000 USD
Contact: David Thomas; (913) 624-3343; fax (913) 624-3490
Internet: http://www.sprint.com/community/sprint_foundation/index.html
Sponsor: Sprint Foundation
2330 Shawnee Mission Parkway
Westwood, KS 66205

Square D Foundation Grants 1741

The foundation makes donations for operating support, capital development needs, and special projects to nonprofit organizations in the areas of education, social welfare, arts and cultural and civic affairs, and health. Each year the foundation supports United Way in communities where the company and its domestic subsidiaries have significant operations. Donations are not normally made to organizations already receiving support through United Way. Support of higher education is achieved through scholarships, endowments for faculty and acquisition or expansion of equipment or facilities, unrestricted operating support, and the matching gift program. Submit letters of application between June and August.
Requirements: Giving primarily to 501(c)3 tax-exempt organizations in areas of company operations, with emphasis on: Illinois; Indiana; Iowa; Kentucky; Missouri; Nebraska; North Carolina; Ohio; South Carolina; Tennessee; and Wisconsin. Restrictions: Grants are not made to religious organizations for religious purposes, political groups and organizations, labor unions and organizations, organizations making requests by telephone, organizations listed by the U.S. attorney general as subversive, or to individuals.
Geographic Focus: Illinois, Indiana, Iowa, Kentucky, Nebraska, North Carolina, Tennessee, Texas, Wisconsin
Date(s) Application is Due: Aug 31
Amount of Grant: Up to 27,000,000 USD
Contact: Harry Wilson, Secretary; (847) 397-2600
Internet: http://www.squared.com
Sponsor: Square D Foundation
1415 South Roselle Road
Palatine, IL 60067

SSA Work Incentives Planning and Assistance (WIPA) Projects 1742

The overall goal of the Work Incentives Planning and Assistance (WIPA) Program is to better enable SSA's beneficiaries with disabilities to make informed choices about work. The major purpose of these projects is to disseminate accurate information to beneficiaries with disabilities (including transition-to-work aged youth) about work incentives programs and issues related to such programs, to enable them to make informed choices about working and whether or when to assign their Ticket to Work, as well as how available work incentives can facilitate their transition into the workforce. Subject to the availability of funds, SSA anticipates minimum awards of $100,000 for individual state WIPA projects (minimum awards for territories will remain at $50,000) and a maximum of $300,000 will be available to fund specific WIPA projects annually. Awardees are required to contribute a non-Federal match of project costs of at least 5% of the total project cost. The non-Federal share may be cash or in-kind (property or services). Awards made under this announcement may be renewed annually through FY 2009. A cooperative agreement may be awarded to any State or local government (excluding any State administering the State Medicaid program), public or private organization, or nonprofit or for-profit organization (for profit organizations may apply with the understanding that no cooperative agreement funds may be paid as profit to any awardee), as well as Native American tribal organizations that the Commissioner determines is qualified to provide work incentives planning, assistance and outreach services to all SSDI and SSI beneficiaries with disabilities, within the targeted geographic area. The deadline is July 1, with Letters of Intent due by May 30.
Requirements: States, local governments, the District of Columbia, Puerto Rico, U.S. territories, and nonprofit and for-profit organizations are eligible to apply.
Geographic Focus: All States
Date(s) Application is Due: Jul 1
Amount of Grant: 50,000 - 300,000 USD
Contact: Regina Bowden, Project Officer, Office of Employment Support Programs; (410) 965-7145 or (800) 772-1213; regina.bowden@ssa.gov
Internet: http://www.socialsecurity.gov/work/ServiceProviders/wipafactsheet.html
Sponsor: Social Security Administration
6401 Security Boulevard, 107 Altmeyer Building
Baltimore, MD 21235-6401

St. Joseph Community Health Foundation Improving Healthcare 1743
Access Grants

The St. Joseph Community Health Foundation was established in 1998 when the Poor Handmaids of Jesus Christ sold the St. Joseph Medical Center and reorganized the St. Joseph Community Health Foundation with a significant share of the proceeds. Proceeds from the Foundation's endowment are redistributed as grants typically ranging from $5,000 to $35,000 to advance programs, projects and partnerships that improve the access to quality health care and the health of the poor and powerless of Allen County, Indiana. Typically, only programs that can demonstrate that greater than 51 percent of their clients are very low income with health issues are considered for these grants. The Foundation also considers these values of the Poor Handmaids as a part of its grant review process: respecting and valuing each person; standing with the poor and powerless; using our talents and resources to respond to the emerging needs of society; nurturing leadership in our efforts to bring peace to the world. The Foundation will consider requests for program support, operations, seed monies, program-related equipment, staff continuing education, technical assistance, and matching funds. The Foundation will commit support on an annual basis only. Additional funding will be contingent upon program performance.

Requirements: Applicants should have a demonstrated history of serving poor and powerless populations with medical, dental, mental, and/or spiritual health care and wellness services. Applicants should be not-for-profit entities classified as 501(C)(3) by the Internal Revenue Service. Partnerships between not-for-profits are encouraged. The proposed grant must be operated for the benefit of residents of Allen County, Indiana.

Restrictions: Grant applications will not be accepted for building projects, elimination of deficits, support of political activities, individuals, or projects already completed.

Geographic Focus: Indiana
Date(s) Application is Due: Mar 1; Sep 1
Amount of Grant: 5,000 - 35,000 USD
Contact: Meg Distler, Executive Director; (260) 969-2001, ext. 201; fax (260) 969-2004; mdistler@sjchf.org
Internet: http://www.stjosephhealthfdn.org/index.php?option=com_content&view=article&id=79&Itemid=70
Sponsor: St. Joseph Community Health Foundation
2826 South Calhoun Street
Fort Wayne, IN 46807

Stackner Family Foundation Grants 1744

The foundation awards grants concentrated in the Milwaukee metropolitan area for building programs and equipment acquisition, medical research, programs at all levels of education, social welfare, child welfare, and programs that assist the physically disabled. Additional categories of support include general operating support, continuing support, annual campaigns, capital campaigns, and program development. The board meets each year in January, April, July, and October. Application forms are not required.

Requirements: Nonprofit organizations in the greater Milwaukee, WI, area may request grant support.

Geographic Focus: Wisconsin
Date(s) Application is Due: Mar 15; Jun 15; Sep 15; Dec 15
Amount of Grant: 25 - 25,000 USD
Contact: Paul Tillman, (414) 646-5409; Stackner@MSH.com
Sponsor: Stackner Family Foundation
411 E Wisconsin Avenue
Milwaukee, WI 53202-4497

Stan and Sandy Checketts Foundation 1745

Established by Stan and Sandy Checketts in 1998, the Foundation's primary focus is on human services and helping individuals defray medical expenses. Primary fields of interest include: children and youth programs, health care, housing and shelter programs, human services, and recreation. Types of support are general operating funds and grants to individuals. Applicants should submit a detailed description of the project, along with the amount of funding requested. There are no deadlines, and the primary geographic focus is Utah.

Geographic Focus: Utah
Contact: Stan Checketts, President; (435) 752-1987; fax (435) 752-1948
Sponsor: Stan and Sandy Checketts Foundation
350 West 2500 North
Logan, UT 84341-1734

Starr Foundation Grants 1746

The foundation awards grants to nonprofit organizations in the areas of education, medicine and health care, human needs, public policy, and culture. Education grants support scholarships for deserving students, groups that offer need-based financial aid, and international-exchange programs. Human needs grants support food programs for the poor, job training, literacy, adequate housing, and programs for the disabled. Medicine and health care grants include capital grants to hospitals, significant research grants, and grants to assist in the provision of health care to underserved communities. Public policy grants support international relations and democratic institutions around the world. Culture grants go to exchange programs and provide services to the elderly and/or disabled. The foundation rarely funds local charities outside of New York City but may fund national organizations that serve communities outside of New York. Types of support include multiyear grants, general operating grants, and capacity-building grants. There are no application deadlines. The board meets throughout the year.

Geographic Focus: All States
Amount of Grant: Up to 70,000,000 USD
Samples: World Trade Ctr Memorial Foundation (New York, NY)—to build the World Trade Center Memorial and a museum to remember the September 11, 2001, and February 26, 1993, terrorist attacks, $25 million; Johns Hopkins U (Baltimore, MD)—to endow a professorship and support other needs at the South Asia Studies program of the university's Nitze School of Advanced International Studies, $3 million; Dickinson College (Carlisle, PA)—to augment a scholarship endowment, $1 million; For relief efforts in South Asia and Africa—$2.5 million distributed.
Contact: Florence Davis, President; (212) 770-6882; florence.davis@starrfdn.org or grants@starrfoundation.org
Internet: http://fdncenter.org/grantmaker/starr
Sponsor: Starr Foundation
70 Pine Street, 14th Floor
New York, NY 10270

State Farm Companies Strong Neighborhoods Grants 1747

State Farm is committed to helping maintain the vibrancy and culture of neighborhoods in various communities throughout the U.S. and Canada. They demonstrate this commitment by supporting nonprofit organization programs that: make housing affordable; promote first-time homeownership; eliminate barriers to homeownership; educate homebuyers about insurance, loss mitigation, and homeownership; foster sustainable communities, and; rehabilitate neighborhoods or communities.

Restrictions: The company does not fund: organizations that are not a governmental entity, a stable nonprofit 501(c)3 organization with a diverse funding base, an educational institution, or a Canadian charitable organization; individuals seeking personal help or scholarships; religious programs; politically partisan programs, or; organizations outside the U.S. and Canada.

Geographic Focus: All States
Contact: Strong Neighborhoods Grants Coordinator; (309) 766-2161; fax (309) 766-2314; home.sf-foundation.494b00@statefarm.co
Internet: http://www.statefarm.com/about/part_spos/grants/cogrants.asp
Sponsor: State Farm Insurance Company
1 State Farm Plaza, B-4
Bloomington, IL 61710-0001

State Strategies Fund Grants 1748

The program supports state-based strategies to increase civic participation in political life, empower disadvantaged constituencies, and promote political reform. Areas of interest include campaign finance reform, fair tax policy, affordable health care, and the environment. Permanent state-based coalitions that have a long-term strategy for uniting diverse constituencies with a grassroots base and that have a common vision and policy agenda for economic and social justice receive grants. The grant program supports organizations with the following goals: to build strong and effective relationships and collaboration among diverse groups; to integrate a broad array of issues into a common progressive agenda; to develop the collective power of constituents to implement this common agenda; to increase the capacity of underrepresented constituencies to have greater impact on public policy and governance at the state level; to enhance the capacity of grassroots organizations to mobilize their members; and to develop new public leaders representing and accountable to disadvantaged constituencies. Applications should be submitted by email. Attachments and/or mailed applications must be postmarked by the listed application deadline.

Geographic Focus: All States
Date(s) Application is Due: Aug 25
Samples: Alabama Organizing Project (AL)—to support Greater Birmingham Ministries, $35,000; Citizen Action Illinois (IL)—to support the Public Action Foundation, $40,000; New York Community Leadership Institute (NY)—$30,000; Wisconsin Citizen Action (WI)—$50,000.
Contact: Amy Clough, Grants Manager; (413) 256-0349, ext. 12; fax (413) 256-3536; aclough@proteusfund.org
Internet: http://www.proteusfund.org/grantmaking/ssf
Sponsor: State Strategies Fund
264 N Pleasant Street
Amherst, MA 01002

State Street Foundation Grants   1749

The foundation focuses grantmaking worldwide on three areas: neighborhood revitalization, education and job training and development, and youth programs. Of special interest are projects that strengthen organizations' capacity to address community needs. In addition, the foundation provides funding for health and human needs and civic improvement projects that support its areas of focus. Types of support include annual campaigns, employee matching gifts, general operating budgets, matching funds, special projects, affordable housing rehabilitation projects, and technical assistance to achieve nonprofit performance improvement. Creative partnerships are encouraged between the public and private sectors. Contact the office for proposal guidelines.

Requirements: 501(c)3 organizations that are not private foundations and are located in Alameda, Los Angeles, and San Francisco, CA; Connecticut; Florida; Atlanta, GA; Illinois; Boston and the Cape Cod, MA, area; Saint Louis and Kansas City, MO; New Hampshire; New Jersey; and New York are eligible.

Restrictions: The foundation does not make grants for scholarships or fellowships; research projects; emergency cash flow, deficit spending, or debt liquidation situations; seed money/start-up programs; trips, tours, and transportation expenses; or films or videos.

Geographic Focus: California, Connecticut, Florida, Georgia, Illinois, Massachusetts, Missouri, New Hampshire, New Jersey, New York

Amount of Grant: 3,000 - 25,000 USD

Samples: Volunteer Florida Foundation (Tallahassee, FL)—for the Hurricane Charley Disaster Relief Fund, $150,000.

Contact: Grants Administrator; (617) 664-1937; gabowman@statestreet.com

Internet: http://www.statestreet.com/company/community_affairs/global_philanthropy/overview.html

Sponsor: State Street Foundation

225 Franklin Street, 12th Floor

Boston, MA 02110

Staunton Farm Foundation Grants   1750

The Staunton Farm Foundation is a family foundation established in 1937 in accordance with the wishes of Matilda Staunton Craig, who wanted her estate to be used to benefit people with mental illness. The Foundation awards grants in the field of mental health in southwestern Pennsylvania. Projects that represent new and different approaches for organizations and ultimately affect patient care are encouraged. Support may be for more than one year, but the project must become self-sustaining following the grant period. Applicants should submit a letter of intent; full proposals are by invitation.

Requirements: Nonprofit organizations in the 10-county area in southwestern Pennsylvania including Washington, Greene, Fayette, Westmoreland, Armstrong, Butler, Lawrence, Beaver, Indiana, and Allegheny are eligible.

Geographic Focus: Pennsylvania

Date(s) Application is Due: Jun 1; Dec 1

Contact: Joni S. Schwager, Executive Director; (412) 281-8020; fax (412) 232-3115; jschwager@stauntonfarm.org

Internet: http://www.stauntonfarm.org

Sponsor: Staunton Farm Foundation

650 Smithfield Street, Suite 210

Pittsburgh, PA 15222

Steelcase Foundation Grants   1751

The foundation make grants to nonprofit organizations, projects, and programs in corporate communities. Grants are awarded in the areas of human service, health, education, community development, the arts, and the environment. Preference is given to programs designed to improve the quality life for disadvantaged, disabled, young, and elderly people. Matching gifts are made to educational, arts, and environment programs supported by Steelcase employees, retirees, and directors. To obtain a grant application, send a letter on letterhead, signed by the organization's chief executive officer. Include the following items in the letter: description of the organization or project; expected results of the project; amount of grant funds requested; and a copy of 501(c)3 nonprofit certification. Guidelines are available online.

Requirements: The foundation makes grants to IRS-certified nonprofit organizations in areas where Steelcase manufacturing plants are located (Grand Rapids, MI; Fletcher, NC; City of Industry, CA; Athens, AL; Toronto, Canada; and Tijuana, Mexico.)

Restrictions: The foundation does not provide grants to individuals or to organizations that discriminate on the basis of race, religion, sex, disability, or national origin; have received a Steelcase foundation grant within the past 12 months; request support for a conference or seminar; or request support for religious programs (nonsectarian programs for humanitarian purposes are eligible for consideration.)

Geographic Focus: Alabama, California, Michigan, Canada, Mexico

Amount of Grant: 2,000 - 673,000 USD

Contact: Director; (616) 475-2009; fax (616) 475-2200; sbroman@steelcase.com

Internet: http://www.steelcase.com/na/ourcompany.aspx?f=10042&c=10022

Sponsor: Steelcase Foundation

P.O. Box 1967, CH4E

Grand Rapids, MI 49501

Steele-Reese Foundation Grants   1752

The foundation's available income is divided equally for grants to operating charities in southern Appalachia (particularly Kentucky) and in the Northwest (particularly Idaho). In both areas the funds are devoted to education, health, welfare, and the humanities. Types of support include general operating support, equipment, endowment funds, matching funds, professorships, scholarship funds, and capital campaigns. The foundation gives preference to projects that have, among others, the following characteristics: rural, modest in ambition, narrow in function, unglamorous, based on experience, enjoying community financial support, and essential rather than merely desirable. While the foundation considers southern Kentucky and Idaho to be its territories of primary concern, it makes grants to organizations operating throughout southern Appalachia and in Oregon, Montana, and Wyoming.

Requirements: Applicant should submit a letter requesting guidelines. Only residents of Georgia, Idaho, Kentucky, Montana, North Carolina, Texas, and Wyoming are eligible to apply. Personal and telephone inquiries are not encouraged.

Restrictions: The foundation does not make grants to individuals, to community chest or similar drives, for conferences or workshops, for efforts to influence elections or legislation, for planning purposes or experimental projects, for emergencies, or for permanent support except for occasional endowment grants to organizations where stability is critically important.

Geographic Focus: Georgia, Idaho, Kentucky, Montana, North Carolina, Texas, Wyoming

Date(s) Application is Due: Mar 1

Amount of Grant: 10,000 - 50,000 USD

Samples: Frontier Nursing Service, Wendover, KY, $40,000 - to purchase a new phone system for the Mary Breckenridge Hospital; Mountain Home Montana, Missoula, MT, $28,000 - salary support for the director of a teen-mother residency program; West Central Highlands Resource Conservation and Development Council, Emmett, ID, $10,000 - for upgrades and renovations of the Indian Valley Community Hall.

Contact: Charles U. Buice, (212) 505-2696; charlesbuice@hotmail.com

Internet: http://www.steele-reese.org/what.html

Sponsor: Steele-Reese Foundation

32 Washington Square West

New York, NY 10011

Stella and Charles Guttman Foundation Grants   1753

The majority of grants are made to organizations providing services to people in the New York City metropolitan area. Beginning in 2014, the Stella and Charles Guttman Foundation intends to direct a substantial portion of its grantmaking to programs that serve low income infants, toddlers and preschoolers as they transition to kindergarten. Special emphasis will be placed on programs that improve quality, expand services and create a strong continuum of care for children ages 0 to 3 in high-need neighborhoods. Systemic investments in early childhood programs may include the expansion of evidence-based home visiting programs, infant health and mental health programs and professional development for center-based teachers, as well as home-based caregivers. The Foundation is also committed to fund programs in neighborhoods with high levels of poverty and a large concentration of public housing. In addition to early childhood programs, the Foundation will support programs that work to build a network of education, health and social services for children from birth through college graduation.

Requirements: Charitable 501(c)3 or 170(b)1 organizations are eligible with a strong emphasis on New York City and Israel.

Restrictions: The foundation does not make grants directly to individuals or to organizations not qualified as charitable, for foreign travel or study, to initiate or defend public interest litigation, to support anti-vivisectionist causes, or to religious organizations for religious observances.

Geographic Focus: New York

Amount of Grant: 25,000 - 100,000 USD

Samples: Citizens' Committee for Children of New York, New York, New York, $50,000 - support of educational, policy and advocacy initiatives focused on early childhood education; Good Shepherd Services, Brooklyn, New York, $50,000 - support of the Bronx Opportunity Network, a collaboration of

seven community-based organizations; Henry Street Settlement, New York, New York, $100,000 - support of the Henry Street capital campaign and the renovation of the Charles and Stella Guttman Building.
Contact: Elizabeth Olofson, Executive Director; (212) 371-7082; fax (212) 371-8936; eolofson@guttmanfoundation.org
Internet: http://www.guttmanfoundation.org
Sponsor: Stella and Charles Guttman Foundation
122 East 42nd Street, Suite 2010
New York, NY 10168

Stella B. Gross Charitable Trust Grants   **1754**
The charitable trust supports Santa Clara County, CA, tax-exempt charitable organizations in its areas of interest, including arts and culture, child development, education and higher education, hospitals and health care organizations, medical research, human services, Roman Catholic federated giving programs, and government/public administration. Programs should be unique, have measurable outcome objectives, and organizations should have a plan to sustain the program. Types of support include general operating support, continuing support, program development, and seed money grants.
Requirements: Santa Clara County, CA, nonprofits may apply.
Geographic Focus: California
Date(s) Application is Due: May 31; Nov 30
Amount of Grant: 1,000 - 23,000 USD
Samples: Fremont Union High School District (Fremont, CA)—for the teen parenting program, $4000; Catholic Charities, Diocese of San Jose (San Jose, CA)—general support, $10,000.
Contact: Fatima Mendoza, Trust Associate; (800) 232-2430 or (408) 947-5160; fmendoza@bankofthewest.com
Sponsor: Stella B. Gross Charitable Trust
P.O. Box 1121
San Jose, CA 95108

Sterling-Turner Charitable Foundation Grants   **1755**
The charitable foundation awards grants to Texas organizations, primarily for higher and secondary education, adult basic education and literacy, social services, youth, the elderly, fine and performing arts groups and other cultural programs, church support and religious programs (Catholic, Jewish, and Protestant), hospitals and health services, hospices, research, conservation, and civic and urban affairs. Grants are awarded for general operating support, annual campaigns, capital campaigns, continuing support, building construction/renovation, equipment acquisition, endowment funds, program and project development, conferences and seminars, curriculum development, fellowships, scholarship funds, research, and matching funds. The board meets in April.
Requirements: Nonprofit Texas organizations in the following counties are eligible to apply: Fort Bend, Harris, Kerr, Tom Green, and Travis. Only those 501(c)3 organizations with offices located within the counties being considered within the State of Texas may submit and all funds must be managed, used and services provided within those counties in the State of Texas. All funds must be used within the requesting county. If the organization is a 509(a)3, there is a template for a required letter of explanation as to why your organization falls under the category that must be submitted for consideration. All documents must be received by 5:00 pm of the deadline date.
Restrictions: Individuals are ineligible.
Geographic Focus: Texas
Date(s) Application is Due: Mar 1
Amount of Grant: 5,000 - 25,000 USD
Contact: Patricia Stilley, Executive Director; (713) 237-1117; fax (713) 223-4638; pstilley@stfdn.org or jarnold@sterlingturnerfoundation.org
Internet: http://sterlingturnerfoundation.org/information_and_instructions.htm
Sponsor: Sterling-Turner Charitable Foundation
5850 San Felipe Street, Suite 125
Houston, TX 77057-3292

Sterling and Shelli Gardner Foundation Grants   **1756**
The Sterling and Shelli Gardner Foundation was established by co-founders and operators of "Stampin' Up!", a multi-million dollar catalog-based business, in Utah in 2002. The Foundation's major fields of interest include: community and economic development; education; and human services. With a geographic focus throughout the State of Utah, applicants should request a formal application from the Foundation office. The Foundation awards between thirty and forty grants each year, and amounts have recently ranged from $500 to $40,000. Most often, these awards are unrestricted contributions applied toward general operating costs. There are no specified annual deadlines, and applications are taken on a rolling basis.
Requirements: Any 501(c)3 organization serving residents of Utah are eligible.
Geographic Focus: Utah
Amount of Grant: 500 - 40,000 USD
Samples: Ability Found, Salt Lake City, Utah, $5,000 - general operating support for disabled individuals; Friday's Kids Respite, Orem, Utah, $2,500 - general operations; Courage Reins, Highland, Utah, $35,000 - general operations.
Contact: Megan White, Administrator; (801) 717-6789
Sponsor: Sterling and Shelli Gardner Foundation
610 W. Westfield Road
Alpine, UT 84004-1501

Stern Family Foundation Grants   **1757**
The Stern Family Foundation was established in New Jersey in 1999 with the expressed commitment to provide support for education at all levels, as well as for Jewish agencies and synagogues. Giving is primarily centered in the states of New Jersey and New York. There are no specified deadline for submission, and a formal application is not required. Interested parties should, therefore, begin by forwarding a letter of application, which includes program information, amount of request, a budget detail, and proof of 501(c)3 status. Most recently, awards have ranged from $7,500 to as much as $75,000.
Geographic Focus: New Jersey, New York
Amount of Grant: 7,500 - 75,000 USD
Samples: Yeshiva University, New York, New York, $75,560 - general operations and religion; American Friends of the Kiev Jewish Community, New York, New York, $47,966 - general educational fund; American Friends of Yeshivat Hessder Sderot, Great Neck, New York, $22,000 - general fund.
Contact: Ronald Stern, Trustee; (212) 302-3400; fax (212) 764-3269
Sponsor: Stern Family Foundation
514 Maitland Avenue
Teaneck, NJ 07666-2918

Steven B. Achelis Foundation Grants   **1758**
Steven B. Achelis is the founder, owner, and president of EQUIS International. His company is a leading provider of investment analysis, portfolio management, and stock market data collection software. Established in 1990 in Utah, the Steve B. Achelis Foundation is a small private foundation with limited resources. Typical grants range between $500 and $6,000 with an average grant of $2,000. Total annual grants are approximately $50,000. Applicants should include: a description of the services provided; a copy of the applicant's 501(c)3 IRS ruling letter; and a breakdown of revenue sources and expenditures. Though giving is aimed primarily in Salt Lake City, the foundation also offers awards nationwide. There are no specified annual deadlines.
Geographic Focus: All States
Amount of Grant: 500 - 6,000 USD
Samples: Global Education Fund, Boulder, Colorado, $4,000 - general operating support (2014); Nature Conservancy of Utah, Salt Lake City, Utah, $3,000 - general operating support (2014); Bay Area Gardeners, Redwood City, California, $4,000 - general operating support (2014).
Contact: Steven B. Achelis, Trustee; (801) 560-5733 or (801) 972-4800; fax (801) 272-1148; info@eMedic.com or steve@rescuerigger.com
Internet: http://stevesfoundation.org/guidelines.htm
Sponsor: Steven B. Achelis Foundation
6154 Oak Canyon Drive, P.O. Box 71342
Salt Lake City, UT 84121-6344

Steve Young Family Foundation Grants   **1759**
The major fields of interest of the foundation include philanthropy, voluntarism, and recreation programs. Areas of most recent giving has concentrated its efforts on assisting children in need, focusing on family togetherness and welfare, as well as major health issues. The foundation's geographic focus is of a national scope.
Restrictions: 501(c)3 organizations that have a national appeal.
Geographic Focus: All States
Samples: $10,000, Twin Towers Orphan Fund, Bakersfield, CA; National Brain Tumor Foundation, San Francisco, CA;
Contact: Jon Steven Young, (800) 994-3837
Sponsor: Steve Young Family Foundation
559 W 500th Street South
Bountiful, UT 84010

Stewart Huston Charitable Trust Grants   1760

The purpose of the Trust is to provide funds, technical assistance and collaboration on behalf of non-profit organizations engaged exclusively in religious, charitable or educational work; to extend opportunities to deserving needy persons. Giving primarily in the Savannah, GA, area and Coatesville, PA.

Requirements: 501(c)3 nonprofit organizations are eligible.

Restrictions: Grants are not awarded for scholarship support to individuals, endowment purposes, purchases of tickets or advertising for benefit purposes, coverage of continuing operating deficits, or document publication costs. Support is not provided to intermediate or pass-through organizations (other than United Way) that in turn allocate funds to beneficiaries or to fraternal organizations, political parties or candidates, veterans, labor or local civic groups, volunteer fire companies, or groups engaged in influencing legislation.

Geographic Focus: Georgia, Pennsylvania

Date(s) Application is Due: Jan 15; Mar 1; Sep 1

Amount of Grant: 1,000 - 15,000 USD

Samples: Graystone Society, Coatesville, PA, $325,000 - for building support; Grace United Methodist Church, Savannah, GA, $20,000 - for sponsorships; University of Pennsylvania Health System, Philadelphia, PA, $20,000 - for general support;

Contact: Scott Huston, Program Director; (610) 384-2666; fax (610) 384-3396; admin@stewarthuston.org

Internet: http://www.stewarthuston.org

Sponsor: Stewart Huston Charitable Trust

50 South First Avenue

Coatesville, PA 19320

Straits Area Community Foundation Common Grants   1761

The Straits Area Community Foundation (SACF) serves Cheboygan County and Mackinaw City. The Foundation's Common grants for any type of program or project (not including religious programs) through an eligible nonprofit will be considered for funding. Preference may be given to programs that fall within the following areas: basic human needs; drug use prevention; programs promoting community service, volunteerism or community education; access to health care; and community advancement opportunities. A Grant Screening Committee comprised of members from the SACF service area makes all allocation recommendations. The maximum amount for this category of funding is $1,000, with Mini-Grants up to $300 available. The annual grant submission postmark deadline is January 1.

Requirements: IRS 501(c)3 nonprofit organizations, schools, churches (for non-sectarian purposes), cities, townships, and other governmental units serving Cheboygan County or Mackinaw City are eligible to apply. An organization may apply each year for a grant.

Restrictions: No program may be funded for more than two (2) consecutive grant cycles or two (2) years, whichever is longer. The Foundation will not support the sustained funding of any program. Grants are not given to individuals, except for awards or scholarships from designated donor funds.

Geographic Focus: Michigan

Date(s) Application is Due: Jan 1

Amount of Grant: Up to 1,000 USD

Samples: Cheboygan Compassionate Ministries, Cheboygan, Michigan, $1,000 - Back to School Giveaway Event (2014); Inland Lakes Schools, Indian River, Michigan, $1,000 - Helping Kids Grow Strong program (2014); Mackinaw Area Historical Society, Mackinaw City, Michigan, $1,000 - Booklet Diary of Mary Anderson (2014).

Contact: Barbara Frantz, Executive Director; (989) 354-6881 or (877) 354-6881; fax (989) 356-3319; bfrantz@cfnem.org

Internet: http://www.cfnem.org/SACF/Common.aspx

Sponsor: Straits Area Community Foundation

P.O. Box 495

Alpena, MI 49707

Strake Foundation Grants   1762

The Foundation supports hospitals, schools, colleges, and Catholic charities, as well as projects focusing in adult basic education and literacy, museums, and arts and culture. Support is considered for operating budgets, capital campaigns, special projects, research, matching funds and general purposes.

Requirements: Awards are made to 501(c)3 organizations located only in the United States, primarily in Texas. Organizations may submit only one request per calendar year. There are no set amounts for requests, however awards generally range between $2,000 and $20,000 with a few exceptions as high as $50,000.

Restrictions: Awards are not made to support individuals, nor for deficit financing, consulting services, technical assistance, publications, or loans.

Geographic Focus: All States

Samples: Corporation for Educational Radio and Television, New York, NY, $2,500–to support the 'Black American Conservatism' companion website; El Centro de Corazon, Houston, TX, $$7,500–operating support; Fund for American Studies, Washington, DC, $5,000–scholarship support.

Contact: George Strake, Jr.; (713) 216-2400; foundation@strake.org

Sponsor: Strake Foundation

712 Main Street, Suite 3300

Houston, TX 77002

Stranahan Foundation Grants   1763

The Stranahan Foundation was created in 1944 by brothers Frank D. and Robert A. Stranahan, founders of the Champion Spark Plug Company in Toledo, Ohio. The purpose of the foundation is to assist individuals and groups in their efforts to become more self-sufficient and contribute to the improvement of society and the environment. The foundation supports a multitude of important programs that fit within five priority areas of interest: Human Services, Ecological Well-Being, Arts & Culture, Education, and Mental & Physical Health. Grant funds may be used for start up support for a new program, operating support, expansion or capacity building, or capital support.

Requirements: Nonprofit organizations with 501(c)3 tax-exempt status are eligible to apply. While the foundation awards funds nationwide, its focus is on the Toledo, Ohio area. All applicants must, as a first step, submit a letter of inquiry to the Stranahan Foundation. Full proposals are by invitation only and may only be submitted by organizations that are invited to apply after their letter of inquiry has been accepted and reviewed. The Foundation will contact those organizations invited to submit a full proposal and notify those that are not eligible to apply. Instructions and forms for letters of inquiry and full grant proposals can be found on the website.

Restrictions: The Stranahan Foundation does not normally consider proposals for funding in the following areas: personal businesses; reduction or elimination of deficits; projects that are located outside of the United States; endowment fund campaigns; government sponsored or controlled projects; or individuals. Additionally, the foundation will not support organizations that discriminate in the leadership, staffing or service provision on the basis of age, gender, race, ethnicity, sexual orientation, disability, national origin, political affiliation or religious beliefs.

Geographic Focus: All States

Date(s) Application is Due: Jul 1

Amount of Grant: 1,000 USD

Contact: Pam Roberts, Grants Manager; (419) 882-5575; fax (419) 882-2072; proberts@stranahanfoundation.org

Internet: http://www.stranahanfoundation.org/index.php?src=gendocs&ref=GrantmakingPriorities&category=Main

Sponsor: Stranahan Foundation

4169 Holland-Sylvania Road, #201

Toledo, OH 43623

Streisand Foundation Grants   1764

The foundation awards grants for national programs affecting women and at-risk youth. Areas of support include programs for children and youth, with a focus on the economically disadvantaged; civil rights, with emphasis on race relations between African Americans and Jews; AIDS research, advocacy, service, and litigation; nuclear disarmament; and environmental preservation. Types of support include general operating grants, technical assistance, and project-specific support. Applicants are asked to submit one- to two-page letters of inquiry along with a copy of the 501(c)3 determination letter. Applications are accepted between September 1 and the listed deadline. Guidelines are available online.

Requirements: 501(c)3 nonprofits and California projects in the Los Angeles area are eligible.

Restrictions: Grants are not made to individuals nor do they support start-up organizations, endowments, or capital campaigns.

Geographic Focus: All States

Date(s) Application is Due: Dec 1

Amount of Grant: 10,000 - 20,000 USD

Contact: Contact; (310) 535-3767; fax (310) 314-8396; stfnd@aol.com

Internet: http://www.barbrastreisand.com/bio_streisand_foundation.html

Sponsor: Streisand Foundation

2800 28th Street, Suite 105

Santa Monica, CA 90405

Strengthening Families - Strengthening Communities Grants   1765

The foundation is committed to improving the quality of life for residents of metropolitan Richmond. Competitive grantmaking focuses on building or enhancing the resources of the charitable sector to address: basic human needs for children and families who are impoverished; child and youth development, with an emphasis on young people who are at moderate or high risk of experiencing problems in school, in their social interactions, or with lifestyle choices; community development that promotes affordable housing and safe neighborhoods; opportunities to broadly enrich family and community life; and collaborative models of service, volunteerism, and community leadership development. Generally, projects undertaken in collaboration with other nonprofits receive a higher priority. These may include requests that address unmet or emerging community needs or allow for program expansion or enhancement. Collaboratives that include current recipient organizations or that minimize duplication of services will be considered. The foundation will give preference to those organizations that seek to develop or enhance their work through a cohesive regional strategy. Guidelines are available online.

Requirements: Proposals will be accepted from charitable organizations that serve the residents of metropolitan Richmond and Central Virginia. Generally, projects undertaken in collaboration with other nonprofits receive a higher priority. These may include requests that address unmet or emerging community needs or allow for program expansion or enhancement. Collaboratives that include current recipient organizations or that minimize duplication of services will be considered. The foundation will give preference to those organizations that seek to develop or enhance their work through a cohesive regional strategy.

Geographic Focus: Virginia

Date(s) Application is Due: May 5; Nov 5

Amount of Grant: 5,000 - 100,000 USD

Samples: Daily Planet, Inc (VA)—to provide operating support for the Health Care Clinic, which serves homeless men and women, $25,000; Richmond SCORE (VA)—to equip the agency, whose retired business owners and managers volunteer to provide assistance to nonprofit and for-profit organizations, with technology to track and evaluate its work, $10,000; ElderHomes Corp (VA)—to provide program support for the Volunteer Services Program, which provides home repairs for low-income elderly and/or disabled, $35,000; Assisting Families of Inmates, Inc (VA)—to support the Milk and Cookies Children's Program, designed to address the physical, emotional, and social needs of children with incarcerated parents and their caregivers, $15,000.

Contact: Susan Hallett, Program Officer; (804) 330-7400; fax (804) 330-5992; shallett@tcfrichmond.org

Internet: http://www.tcfrichmond.org/page2954.cfm#CF

Sponsor: Community Foundation Serving Richmond and Central Virginia

7501 Boulders View Drive, Suite 110

Richmond, VA 23225

Strowd Roses Grants 1766

Strowd Roses, Inc. is a private charitable foundation which was established in 2001 under the will of Mrs. Irene Harrison Strowd of Chapel Hill, North Carolina. The Board of Directors of Strowd Roses, Inc. makes grants to qualified tax-exempt charitable, educational, religious and public organizations that are based in Chapel Hill or Carrboro, or are devoted primarily to benefiting the citizens of those communities. Grants may also be made to individuals engaged in projects designed to enhance the Chapel Hill/Carrboro community. Grants may, at the Board's discretion, include support for operating as well as capital expenditures, seed money and matching grants. Grants to individuals may be used for scholarships or fellowships; to produce a report or similar product; or to improve or enhance a literary, artistic, musical, scientific, teaching or similar capacity, skill or talent which will be used to benefit the life of the community. Particular consideration is given to those projects and purposes which further the interests of Mr. and Mrs. Strowd, including the welfare of children and youth, the enhancement of the environment, and the promotion of a sense of civic duty.

Requirements: Applicants should submit the appropriate application form (see foundations website), along with a proposed budget and evidence of their tax-exempt status (IRS determination letter or comparable documentation) to: Board of Directors, Strowd Roses, Inc., P.O. Box 3558, Chapel Hill, NC, 27515-3558.

Geographic Focus: North Carolina

Date(s) Application is Due: Jan 31; Apr 30; Jul 31; Oct 31

Amount of Grant: 10,000 USD

Contact: Jennifer Boger, Grant Coordinator; (919) 929-1984; fax (919) 929-1990; jboger@strowdroses.org

Internet: http://www.strowdroses.org/grantApp.htm

Sponsor: Strowd Roses

P.O. Box 3558

Chapel Hill, NC 27515-3558

Stuart Foundation Grants 1767

The foundation's mission is to help children and youth in California and the state of Washington become capable, responsible citizens. Areas of interest include strengthening communities that serve families (community building, service integration, institutional and community partnerships, professional development, and technical assistance), strengthening the child welfare system (permanency, supportive services for youth, comprehensive assessment and services, prevention, or volunteering), strengthening public schools (teacher development, public policy, early learning, systemic school reform, and other opportunities), and policy analysis and advocacy. The foundation is interested in funding programs that promote collaboration and integrated services to improve children's outcomes. Grants also include assistance with community engagement, conflict resolution, research, technology, and training. Types of support include seed money, operating support, and special projects. Programs receive funding each year; renewal is subject to board and staff decisions. Obtain a guidelines brochure from the office.

Requirements: The foundation supports programs serving California and Washington.

Restrictions: The foundation does not make grants to support political activities, endowments, building campaigns, fundraising events, material acquisition, or operating funds.

Geographic Focus: California, Washington

Date(s) Application is Due: Mar 1; Jun 1; Sep 1; Dec 1

Amount of Grant: 5,000 - 100,000 USD

Samples: Washington Education Foundation (Issaquah, WA)—for the Foster Care to College Partnership, which seeks to expand access to college for children in Washington State who are in foster care, $234,751; Partnership for Learning (Seattle, WA)—for its efforts to increase public understanding of, and support for, standards-based education reforms in Washington State, $100,000; Parent Services Project (San Rafael, CA)—for an institute that works to build the leadership skills of parents in Marin County, CA, $25,000; Foundation Consortium/San Francisco Foundation Community Initiative Funds (San Francisco, CA)—for general support as this organization ceases operations, documents its work, and transitions its projects to other entities, $160,000.

Contact: Stephanie Titus; (415) 393-1551; fax (415) 393-1552

Internet: http://www.stuartfoundation.org/how.html

Sponsor: Stuart Foundation

50 California Street, Suite 3350

San Francisco, CA 94111-4735

Sulzberger Foundation Grants 1768

The foundation awards grants to eligible nonprofit organizations in its areas of interest, including arts and culture, education, environmental protection and natural resource conservation, hospitals, and social services delivery. Types of support include annual campaigns, building construction/renovation, endowments, general operating support, multiyear grants, programs and projects, and scholarship funds. There are no application forms or deadlines. Preference is given to requests from New York City and Chatanooga.

Restrictions: Individuals are not eligible.

Geographic Focus: All States

Amount of Grant: 100 - 255,000 USD

Samples: New York Times Company Foundation (New York, NY)—for the Neediest Cases Fund, $100,000.

Contact: Marian Heiskell, President; (212) 556-1400

Sponsor: Sulzberger Foundation

229 W 43rd Street, Suite 1031

New York, NY 10036

Sunflower Foundation Capacity Building Grants 1769

The Foundation funds two types of Capacity Building grants: Assessment (grant limit is based on scope of work) —the first step of any effort to build capacity within an organization is an assessment of present capacity to identify what is working well and what needs to be strengthened (the Foundation will fund technical assistance, consulting, and other expenses related to conducting a formal assessment of current organizational capacity); and Implementation ($20,000 grant limit)—the Foundation will fund the implementation of capacity building strategies. Allowable expenses typically include such items as technical assistance/consulting, technology (hardware and/or software), limited equipment (e.g. telephone systems), training and assessment/evaluation.

Requirements: Proposals are invited from private nonprofit or public organizations that have a mission to improve health status or access to quality, affordable health care for Kansans.

Restrictions: The foundation will not fund ongoing general operating expenses or existing deficits; capital, endowment or specific fund-raising campaigns; fund raising events; routine continuing education; travel to conferences not directly related to the project; programs that are not Kansas-based; programs that require additional staff but demonstrate no clear means of sustainability after foundation funding; individual medical care or support; medical equipment; capital equipment (except for allowable technology); political purposes; or support of organizations that practice discrimination. Additional exclusions include: program expenses; existing staff salaries/benefits; Electronic Medical Records (EMR) technology; medical equipment; capital equipment (except for allowable technology); routine continuing education; and travel to conferences not directly related to the project.
Geographic Focus: Kansas
Date(s) Application is Due: Jun 19
Amount of Grant: Up to 20,000 USD
Contact: Grants Administrator; (785) 232-3000 or (866) 232-3020; info@sunflowerfoundation.org
Internet: http://www.sunflowerfoundation.org/flash/request.html
Sponsor: Sunflower Foundation: Health Care for Kansans
1200 SW Executive Drive, Suite 100
Topeka, KS 66615-3850

SuperValu Foundation Grants   1770
Super Valu Stores is a wholesale food supplier. Super Valu does all of its giving directly, some through its headquarters and some through certain local plants which have their own funds. Broad areas of interest are those concerned with education and hunger. The company focuses giving in five categories, hunger relief, product and financial donations to comprehensive hunger relief organizations and non-profit food distribution centers, education, K-12 and post-secondary educational programs with a special interest in leadership development, school-to-work readiness, and after-school programs for children, workforce development, job training and self-sufficiency programs for minority, physically challenged, disabled and disadvantaged persons, fine arts, arts education programs in the corporate headquarters community, and social services, which are generally addressed through significant grants allocated to the United Way in the corporate headquarters communities.
Requirements: Organizations must be tax-exempt under Section 501(c)3 of the Internal Revenue Code.
Restrictions: Grants generally do not support: individuals; travel or research expenses; fees for participation in competitive programs; organizations that receive more than 30 percent of their funding from the United Way; capital campaigns; veteran, fraternal or labor organizations; lobbying, political, or religious programs; or organizations that are not tax-exempt under section 501(c)3 of the IRS tax code.
Geographic Focus: All States
Date(s) Application is Due: Feb 15; May 15; Aug 15; Nov 15
Amount of Grant: 250 - 300,000 USD
Contact: Jesse Benson, Director; (864) 597-4403; fax (612) 828-8955
Internet: http://www.supervalu.com/community/comm_application.html
Sponsor: SuperValu Foundation
P.O. Box 990
Minneapolis, MN 55440

Surdna Foundation Arts Teachers Fellowships   1771
The Surdna Foundation announces the annual national initiative to support the artistic revitalization of outstanding arts teachers in public arts high schools. Surdna recognizes that arts teachers often lack the time and resources to reconnect with other arts professionals and with the artistic processes they teach. Through the Surdna Arts Teachers Fellowship Program (SATF), Fellows design individualized courses of study that provide both immersion in their own creative work and the opportunity to interact with other professional artists in their fields. Surdna believes that this approach to professional development will enhance the effectiveness of arts teachers and will directly benefit the young people they teach. All permanently assigned full- and part-time arts faculty in public arts high schools are eligible. Twenty awards of $5,500 each, with a complementary grant of $1,500 to the Fellow's school to support post-fellowship activities, will be made. The fellowship award may be used to defray the costs of tuition and other fees, room and board, travel, purchase of materials and/or equipment for personal art-making, childcare, and other relevant expenses.
Requirements: All permanently assigned full- and part-time arts faculty in public arts high schools are eligible. Applicants must be minimally in their fifth year of teaching arts in high school, and plan to continue as an arts teacher in their public arts high school during the upcoming school year.
Geographic Focus: All States

Date(s) Application is Due: Feb 10
Amount of Grant: Up to 6,500 USD
Contact: Kimberly Bartosik, SATF Program Director; (212) 557-0010, ext. 256; fax (212) 557-0003; artsfellowship@surdna.org
Internet: http://www.surdna.org/what-we-fund/thriving-cultures/109.html
Sponsor: Surdna Foundation
330 Madison Avenue, 30th Floor
New York, NY 10017-5001

Surdna Foundation Sustainable Environments Grants   1772
The Surdna Foundation seeks to create just and sustainable communities where consumption and conservation are balanced and innovative solutions to environmental problems improve people's lives. It works from a sustainable development perspective to demonstrate that a healthy environment is the backbone of a healthy economy and a democratic society. The Foundation funds three key related priority areas - Climate Change, Green Economy, and Transportation and Smart Growth - that aim to transform how Americans work, consume, and move. Together these will help make the theory of a carbon free society into a practical and achievable reality for communities across the United States. The Surdna Foundation accepts applications on an ongoing basis. However, grants are approved three times per year: in February, May and September. Applicants should use the online letter of inquiry to apply for funding.
Requirements: 501(c)3 organizations may apply. The foundation urges applicants to send two-to three-page letters of intent before sending proposals. IRS nonprofit status certification, recent audited financial statements, and project budget should also be included.
Restrictions: Generally, the Surdna Foundation does not support: programs addressing toxics, hazardous waste, land and habitat conservation; animal welfare, biodiversity and ocean management; individuals; or academic fellowships.
Geographic Focus: All States
Amount of Grant: 15,000 - 1,000,000 USD
Contact: Edward Skloot, Executive Director; (212) 557-0010; fax (212) 557-0003; grants@surdna.org or executivedirector@surdna.org
Internet: http://www.surdna.org/what-we-fund/sustainable-environments.html
Sponsor: Surdna Foundation
330 Madison Avenue, 30th Floor
New York, NY 10017-5001

Susan Mott Webb Charitable Trust Grants   1773
The trust awards grants to eligible Alabama nonprofit organizations in its areas of interest, including the arts, civic and public affairs, animals/wildlife, community development, education, health care, religion, social services, youth programs and homelessness. Types of support include annual campaigns, building construction/renovation, capital campaigns, continuing support, curriculum development, emergency funds, endowments, equipment, general/operating support, internship funds, program development, publication, and technical assistance. Contact the Foundation for further application information and guidelines.
Requirements: Giving limited to the greater Birmingham, AL, area.
Restrictions: Grants do not support advertising, individuals, international organizations, or political organizations.
Geographic Focus: Alabama
Date(s) Application is Due: Apr 1; Oct 1
Amount of Grant: 2,000 - 100,000 USD
Samples: Alabama Symphonic Association, Birmingham, AL, $40,000; Crisis Resource Center of Southeast Kansas, Pittsburg, KS, $25,000;
Contact: Laura Wainwright, Vice President, c/o Regions Bank; (205) 801-0380; fax (205) 581-7433; laura.wainwright@regions.com
Sponsor: Susan Mott Webb Charitable Trust
P.O. Box 11426
Birmingham, AL 35202-1426

Susan Vaughan Foundation Grants   1774
The Susan Vaughan Foundation established in 1952, supports non-profits involved with: education, particularly to a library; arts; environment, natural resources; higher education; human services. The Foundation gives primarily in Houston and Austin Texas area with support in the form of: annual campaigns; building/renovation; capital campaigns; general/operating support; matching/challenge support.
Requirements: There is no formal application form required, applicant must be a non-profit in the Houston and Austin, Texas region. Initial contact should be made through a Letter of Inquiry.
Geographic Focus: Texas
Amount of Grant: 2,500 - 630,000 USD

Samples: Clayton Library Friends, Houston, TX, $630,000; Houston Downtown Park Conservancy, Houston, TX, $50,000; Trees for Houston, Houston, TX, $30,000;
Contact: Jennifer Grosvenor, Grant Coordinator c/o Legacy Trust Co; (713) 651-8980; jgrosvenor@legacytrust.com
Sponsor: Susan Vaughan Foundation
600 Jefferson Street, Suite 300
Houston, TX 77002-7377

SVP Early Childhood Development and Parenting Grants   1775
The foundation has established education and children's issues as grantmaking priorities and awards grants to Puget Sound nonprofits to support positive outcomes for children (prenatal through 18 years old). There are two grant cycles: a fall children's grant cycle and a spring education grant cycle. Types of support include curriculum development/teacher training, institutional development, education programs, general operating support, materials/equipment acquisition, seed grants, service delivery programs, and technical assistance. Letters of inquiry are invited. The letter of inquiry should not exceed two pages in length and have no attachments, with the following information: one paragraph summarizing the organization's mission, history, and goals; a summary of goals and specific activities to be supported by the grant (include population served); a description of how success will be measured; a description of how SVP volunteer or professional services will be used; and budget figures, including the amount requested, the total budget for the project, and the organization's operating budget for the current year. Letters of inquiry may be sent by fax, email as a Word attachment, and mail. Full proposals will be invited.
Requirements: Programs must serve King County in Washington. Applicants must be classified as nonprofit 501(c)3 public charities or public schools or school districts qualifying under section 170(c) of the IRS code.
Restrictions: The foundation does not consider requests from individuals, organizations that discriminate, religious organizations for sectarian purposes, sports teams, and political or lobbying organizations. The foundation does not consider requests for auctions or fund-raising events, debt reduction, endowment funds or capital campaigns, litigation or legal expenses, land acquisition, productions, or performances.
Geographic Focus: Washington
Date(s) Application is Due: Dec 2
Amount of Grant: 40,000 USD
Samples: Kimball Elementary School (WA)—to continue funding for the counselor and coordinator positions as well as start-up funds for an extended learning program, $45,000; Youth Eastside Services (WA)—to hire program evaluation and research staff, a parenting volunteer coordinator, and to network the YES agency, $60,000.
Contact: Paul Shoemaker, Executive Director; (206) 374-8757; fax (206) 728-0552; paulshoe@svpseattle.org or info@svpseattle.org
Internet: http://www.svpseattle.org/grant_guidelines/early_childhood.htm
Sponsor: Social Venture Partners
1601 Second Avenue, Suite 605
Seattle, WA 98101-1541

Swaim-Gause-Rucker Foundation Grants   1776
The Foundation, established in May of 1979, offers general charitable giving throughout the Mart, Texas, region. Funding comes in the form of gifts, grants, and general loans that support 501(c)3 organizations' general operations and new projects. There are no specific application forms or deadlines with which to adhere. Applicants seeking support should submit: a copy of their IRS determination letter; a detailed description of the project; and a budgeted amount of funding requested.
Geographic Focus: Texas
Contact: Wells Fargo Private Client Services; (254) 714-6160
Sponsor: Swaim-Gause-Rucker Foundation
P.O. Box 2626
Waco, TX 76702-2626

Swindells Charitable Foundation   1777
The Swindells Charitable Foundation was established in 1933 to support and promote quality health and human-services programming for underserved children and adults. The Swindells Charitable Foundation also makes grants to public charitable hospitals. Preference is given to organizations that serve sick or economically disadvantaged children or older adults. Special consideration is given to organizations that provide for the "basic human needs" of individuals. Grants from the Swindells Charitable Foundation are one year in duration. Applicants must apply online at the grant website.

Applicants are strongly encouraged to do the following before applying: review the downloadable state application procedures for additional helpful information and clarifications; review the downloadable online-application guidelines at the grant website; review the foundation's funding history (link is available from the grant website); review the online application questions in advance; and review the list of required attachments. These will generally include: a list of board members, financial statements (audited, reviewed, or compiled by independent auditor); an organization summary; a list of other funding sources; an IRS Determination letter; and other required documents. All attachments must be uploaded in the online application as PDF, Word, or Excel files. The Swindells Charitable Foundation has biannual deadlines of February 1 and August 1. Applications are by 11:59 p.m. on the deadline dates. Applicants will be notified of grant decisions by letter within two to three months after each respective proposal deadline.
Requirements: Applicants must have 501(c)3 tax-exempt status.
Restrictions: Applicants will not be awarded a grant for more than three consecutive years. The trust does not support requests from individuals, organizations attempting to influence policy through direct lobbying, or any political campaigns. Capital requests will not be considered.
Geographic Focus: Connecticut
Date(s) Application is Due: Feb 1; Aug 1
Samples: Mercy Housing and Shelter Corporation, Hartford, Connecticut, $4,000, to cover portion of anticipated budgetary shortfall; Plymouth Community Food Pantry, Terryville, Connecticut, $3,000, general operations; Christian Fellowship Center, Bristol, Connecticut, $3,000, general program support.
Contact: Kate Kerchaert; (860) 657-7016; kate.kerchaert@baml.com
Internet: https://www.bankofamerica.com/philanthropic/fn_search.action
Sponsor: Swindells Charitable Foundation
200 Glastonbury Boulevard, Suite # 200, CT2-545-02-05
Glastonbury, CT 06033-4056

T. James Kavanagh Foundation Grants   1778
A large percentage of funding supports the Catholic church and religious associations, along with support for U.S. Roman Catholic schools, with emphasis on Pennsylvania and southern New Jersey. The foundation also makes music awards. Types of support include annual campaigns, continuing support, equipment, general operating support, program development, research, and scholarship funds. Proposals should be submitted preferably by the end of February, July, or October. The board meets in March, August, and November to consider requests.
Requirements: Giving is strictly limited to the US, with emphasis on southern NJ and PA. Any Roman Catholic affiliate, church, school, college, or hospital will be considered.
Restrictions: Grants will not be awarded outside of the United States, not even to U.S. missions or to help their agencies abroad. No funding will be given for individuals; endowment funds; seed money; deficit financing; land acquisition; publications; conferences; scholarships or fellowships; matching gifts; or loans.
Geographic Focus: All States
Amount of Grant: 2,000 - 10,000 USD
Samples: Saint Joseph's R.C. School (Sharon, PA)—for the learning assistance program, $10,000; Opera Company of Philadelphia (Philadelphia, PA)—$10,000; Merion Mercy Academy (Merion Station, PA)—$5000.
Contact: Thomas Kavanagh, Trustee; (610) 356-4606
Sponsor: T. James Kavanagh Foundation
234 E State Street
Sharon, PA 16146

T.L.L. Temple Foundation Grants   1779
The T.L.L. Temple Foundation was established in 1962 by Georgie Temple Munz in honor of her father, Thomas Lewis Latané Temple, an East Texas lumberman and founder of Southern Pine Lumber Company, which later became Temple Industries. It was her wish to create a charitable foundation that would operate primarily to improve the quality of life for the inhabitants of Deep East Texas. The foundation supports organizations devoted to programs in the areas in education, public health, public affairs, human services, arts and culture, and the environment. Since its inception, the T.L.L. Temple Foundation has been committed to supporting environmental initiatives devoted to the conservation of forest lands and river systems, and the preservation of native plant and wildlife species—to protect and ensure the perpetuity of these significant natural resources.
Requirements: The foundation primarily makes grants to projects located and/or to be operated in the area constituting the East Texas pine timber belt and Miller County, Arkansas in which T.L.L. Temple founded and operated

his timber production and manufacturing enterprises. Governmental units exempt under the IRS code and 501(c)3 nonprofit organizations (not classified as a private foundation) are eligible to apply. There are no specific deadlines.
Restrictions: Grants do not support private foundations. Grants are not made to individuals for scholarships, research or other purposes.
Geographic Focus: Arkansas, Texas
Contact: Millard F. Zeagler; (936) 634-3900; fax (936) 639-5199
Sponsor: T.L.L. Temple Foundation
204 Champions Drive
Lufkin, TX 75901-7321

T. Raymond Gregory Family Foundation Grants   1780
The Foundation, established in 1991, is supported by Gregory Galvanizing & Metal Processing and Gregory Industries. Offering general operating support primarily in the Canton, Ohio, Region, the Foundation supports service clubs and organizations involved with nursing education and human services. Fields of interest include: child and youth services; community development; service clubs; family and human services; nursing school programs; and service delivery programs. A formal application is not required, and an applicant should contact the Foundation initially with a letter of inquiry. There are no specific deadlines.
Geographic Focus: Ohio
Amount of Grant: 1,800 - 12,000 USD
Samples: Aultman College of Nursing, Canton, OH, $17,320; Pathway Caring for Children, Canton, OH, $12,000; Pegasus Farm & Equestrian Center for the Disabled, Canton, OH, $1,000.
Contact: T. Raymond Gregory, (330) 477-4800; fax (330) 453-9691
Sponsor: T. Raymond Gregory Family Foundation
1723 Cleveland Avenue SE
Canton, OH 44707

T. Rowe Price Associates Foundation Grants   1781
T. Rowe Price has a long tradition of philanthropy and investment in the communities where our associates live and work. Central to this tradition is the T. Rowe Price Foundation. Launched in 1981, the Foundation provides direct grants to U.S.-based nonprofit organizations that enhance community life through education, arts and culture, human services, and civic and community initiatives. Globally, nonprofit organizations receive support from the Foundation's associates through a Matching Gift Program. The Foundation's history of giving in its communities is strong—and consistent with the firm's goals and values.
Requirements: Although not limited to, giving is primarily made in the metropolitan Baltimore, Maryland, area.
Restrictions: No support provided for religious or political organizations; hospitals or health care providers; recreational sports leagues and sports related fundraisers; private foundations; or grants to individuals.
Geographic Focus: Maryland
Amount of Grant: 25 - 275,000 USD
Contact: Christine Stein; (410) 345-3603; fax (410) 345-2848
Internet: http://corporate.troweprice.com/ccw/home/ourCompany/aboutUs/communityInvolvement.do
Sponsor: T. Rowe Price Associates Foundation
100 E Pratt Street, 8th Floor
Baltimore, MD 21202

T. Spencer Shore Foundation Grants   1782
The T. Spencer Shore Foundation offers financial support in the New England region, as well as New York and Ohio. Its primary fields of interest is funding for higher education, religion, and heath care. Grants are given for general operating support only. A specific application form is required, though there are no annual deadlines. Applicants should contact the office for further instructions. Amounts range from $500 to $3,000.
Requirements: Any college or university in Massachusetts, New Hampshire, Connecticut, Vermont, Rhode Island, Maine, Ohio, or New York are eligible to apply.
Geographic Focus: Connecticut, Maine, Massachusetts, New Hampshire, New York, Ohio, Rhode Island, Vermont
Amount of Grant: 500 - 3,000 USD
Samples: Carver Center, New York, New York, $1,000 - general operations; Rye Presbyterian Church, Rye, New York, $3,000 - general operations; Wellesley College, Wellesley, Massachusetts, $1,000 - general operations.
Contact: Thomas S. Shore, Jr., Trustee; (207) 967-0129
Sponsor: T. Spencer Shore Foundation
P.O. Box 629
Kennebunkport, ME 04046-0629

TAC Arts Projects Grants   1783
The Tennessee Arts Commission (TAC) Arts Project Support (APS) grants supply funding to organizations which are located in urban areas of Tennessee and which provide a wide variety of public-value arts projects and programs such as: projects that involve and promote professional Tennessee artists; visiting artists conducting master classes; specific aspects of workshops, festivals, and conferences; public performances, productions, and exhibitions produced by the applicant; exhibitions of art by Tennessee artists and artists from outside Tennessee; promotion, publicity, and newsletters; administrative and artistic staff support; research and documentation as part of an arts project or program development; consultancies and residencies for administrative and artistic activities; the development of long-range planning documents; touring projects that bring professional performers to communities across the state; improved program accessibility for underserved constituencies, e.g., children, people living in rural communities or isolated settings, people with disabilities, people of color and senior citizens; art in public places (additional information available from the Director of Visual Arts); extensions of literary projects, journals with continuing publication or juried anthologies; apprenticeship programs; computer software/training; technical/production support; and technical assistance projects. APS grant amounts range from $500 to $7,000 for non-arts organizations and $500 to $9,000 for arts-focused groups. Arts organizations serving a statewide audience may apply for up to $10,000. Applicants should contact the Tennessee Arts Commission to verify current submission dates and requirements.
Requirements: The following entities are eligible to apply for APS grants: 501(c)3 not-for-profit organizations in urban areas of and chartered in Tennessee; and Tennessee colleges and universities who meet the tax-exempt requirements just described for not-for-profit organizations. Entities bordering Tennessee (and serving urban areas in Tennessee) are also eligible to apply if they meet the criteria described for instate applicants. First time applicants must contact the TAC prior to submitting an application to verify eligibility. All first time 501(c)3 applicants must provide the TAC with copies of all of the basic nonprofit status documentation, which includes a copy of the organization's Tennessee State Charter, the IRS 501(c)3 Determination Letter and a recent copy of the by-laws of the organization. Proposed projects must involve one or more TAC recognized classical art forms, including visual art, crafts, media, music, theater, dance, folk and ethnic art, or literary arts. Applicants who apply in more than one TAC grant category in a single fiscal year must submit entirely unrelated projects for each proposal. All APS applicants must submit an online eGRANT application by January 18 at 4:30 pm. The link to the eGRANT form is available at the grant website. Additionally, hard copies and required supporting documents described in the guidelines at the grant website must be mailed or hand-delivered to the TAC by Jan 18 at 4:30 pm to complete the application process. Applications must contain a clear, single- project focus. Requested funds should be listed under one expense category on the budget page (and should correspond with the Activity Code indicated on the application). Grant funds must be matched one-to-one (1:1). A project may start no earlier than July 1 and must end no later than June 15. For more requirements, applicants should read the guidelines at the grant website. Additionally applicants should read the legal requirements page at http://www.tn.gov/arts/legal.htm.
Restrictions: An APS application may be submitted only by an organization chartered in Tennessee and located in an urban county (for a list of TAC's urban and rural designations, see the downloadable guidelines at the grant website). K-12 schools are not eligible to apply. Colleges and universities are eligible only for activities that clearly serve the needs of surrounding communities or the state and are designed to involve a broad audience. Activities that are credit-producing or are oriented primarily to students and the academic community are not eligible. An eligible organization may submit only one APS application for the current fiscal year. APS applicants may not apply for a Partnership Support, Cultural Education Partnership or Major Cultural Institution grant. Additional restrictions on funding are listed on the legal requirements page at http://www.tn.gov/arts/legal.htm.
Geographic Focus: Alabama, Arkansas, Georgia, Kentucky, Mississippi, Missouri, North Carolina, Tennessee, Virginia
Date(s) Application is Due: Jan 18
Amount of Grant: 500 - 10,000 USD
Contact: Kim Leavitt; (615) 532-5934; kim.leavitt@tn.gov
Internet: http://www.tn.gov/arts/grant_categories.htm
Sponsor: Tennessee Arts Commission
401 Charlotte Avenue, Citizens Plaza Building
Nashville, TN 37243-0780

TAC Cultural Education Partnership 1784

The Cultural Education Partnership (CEP) category offers general, non-project support to well-established, free-standing 501(c)3 college/university level arts educational institutions. Only academic institutions which have as their mission training and/or accreditation in one or more arts disciplines and represent the highest level of quality art education and administration are eligible in this category. CEP applicants must also have an annual cash operating income (excluding in-kind contributions) of at least $1 million per year. The maximum grant amount is 10 percent of the total operating expenses of the most recently completed, audited year, up to $60,000. The total cash operating expenses (less any capital expenditures, loan payments or penalties, endowment funds, cash reserves, furniture or fixtures exceeding $2,500.00) will be determined by adding together the personnel, outside fees and services, space rental, travel, marketing, and remaining operating expenses. Annual deadline dates may vary; contact Tennessee Arts Commission (TAC) staff or check the TAC website for exact dates.

Requirements: Applicants must read the legal requirements section at the TAC website (under the Grants tab) for further requirements before making application. In addition to satisfying all "General Requirements," eligible applicants must be a freestanding academic arts institution which has as its mission training and/or accreditation in one or more arts disciplines and which demonstrates significant community involvement in the grant application. Applicants must also comply with all of the following conditions to qualify in the CEP category: have one or more full time and adequately compensated personnel (president, academic dean, teaching staff, and other administrative staff); have existed as an academic arts institution for a minimum of five (5) years prior to the date of application; be an accredited institution or recognized nationally for the quality of specialized training or academic instruction offered; have received, for three (3) of the past five (5) years, funding from the TAC through the Arts Access, Arts Project Support, Rural Arts Project Support, Partnership Support, or Major Cultural Institution grants; demonstrate proof of arts advocacy; demonstrate ongoing fiscal responsibility through an audit conducted externally by a certified public accountant for its most recently completed fiscal year; use an accrual accounting system; and have evidence of significant service to the community (because of public dollars awarded by the TAC). Public service is defined as programming and activities that add value to the community being served by the applicant institution. These activities can be, but are not exclusive to: providing needed services to under-served populations; neighborhood outreach classes and workshops; and concerts, performances, and exhibitions that are of interest to the community. Institutions must submit an audit of their most recently completed fiscal year at the time of application. If a more recent audit is in process, applicants may include a letter from the institution's CPA explaining when it will be completed and available. However, no audits will be accepted after March 1, 2011. First time applicants must include an audit of their most recently completed fiscal year at the time of application. All CEP applicants must submit an online eGRANT application (the link to which can be found at the grant website) by 4:30 p.m. (CST) on the due date. In addition, the correct number of printed eGrant applications along with any required documents must be postmarked or hand-delivered to the TAC by 4:30 p.m. (CST) on the due date. Applicants who apply every year are reviewed every third year by an out-of-state reviewer with knowledge of academic arts institutions. Organizations being reviewed must submit 8 (eight) printed sets of applications and accompanying documents. Organizations not being reviewed submit only 3 (three) printed sets.

Restrictions: CEP funds may not be used for: capital improvements (building or construction); elimination of an accumulated debt; planned fundraising activities; projects that have implicit religious content, express a particular religious view or advance a religious purpose; "seed money" for starting new organizations; out-of-state travel expenses; any type of endowment campaign or program; insurance premiums; office space rental; janitorial service and general physical plant maintenance; food and hospitality; vanity publications; scholarly arts-related research and writing; cash awards; legal fees; and payments to members of the organization's board. Previous applicants who fail to meet the $1 million base operating figure will have a one-year "grace period" before losing eligibility in the CEP category; however, the applicants must maintain the $1 million base operating figure for a minimum of two consecutive years before another request for a one year grace period may be made. The TAC will not make grants to an organization with a standing deficit unless a plan to reduce that deficit is submitted with the application.

Geographic Focus: Tennessee
Date(s) Application is Due: Jan 4
Amount of Grant: Up to 60,000 USD

Contact: Rod Reiner, Deputy Director; (615) 741-2093; fax (615) 741-8559; rod.reiner@tn.gov
Internet: http://www.tn.gov/arts/grant_categories.htm
Sponsor: Tennessee Arts Commission
401 Charlotte Avenue, Citizens Plaza Building
Nashville, TN 37243-0780

TAC Major Cultural Institutions Grants 1785

The major cultural institution (MCI) grants from the Tennessee Arts Commission (TAC) offer general, nonproject-oriented support to those well-established Tennessee arts organizations that represent the highest level of quality programming and administration and have annual operating incomes (excluding in-kind contributions) of $1 million per year. The maximum grant amount is 10 percent of the total operating expenses of the most recently completed, audited year, up to $100,000. The total cash operating expenses will be determined by adding together the personnel, outside fees and services, space rental, travel, marketing, and remaining operating expenses. Annual deadline dates may vary; contact program staff for exact dates.

Requirements: The following presentations of requirements and restrictions are not all-inclusive. Before applying for a grant, applicants are responsible for reading TAC's Legal Requirements found on the web site at: http://www.arts.state.tn.us/legal.htm. An applicant must be a 501(c)3 organization with an artistic mission chartered in the state of Tennessee; be either a single-entity agency responsible for its own programming and primarily dedicated to one art discipline, or an arts council which serves a broad population and interacts with local arts organizations; have existed as an arts institution or arts council for a minimum of five (5) years prior to the date of application; have received funding from the TAC Arts Access, Arts Project Support, Rural Arts Project Support, or Partnership/General Operating Support grants for three (3) of the past five (5) years; have a full-time, paid professional business staff and/or full-time paid artistic director; have a demonstrated commitment to compensate (in salaries, wages, fees, and/or benefits) the administrative, artistic, and technical/production personnel whose services contribute directly to the organization applying for matching funds; have a significant amount of year-round public activity; and demonstrate ongoing fiscal responsibility through an audit conducted externally by a certified public accountant for its most recently completed fiscal year. Applicants should use an accrual accounting system. Organizations must submit an audit of their most recently completed fiscal year at the time of application. If a more recent audit is in process, include a letter from the organization's CPA explaining when the audit will be completed and available. However, the most recent audit must be submitted no later than March 1. Under no circumstances will a MCI grant contract be issued without receipt of the grantee's audit covering the required time period. First time applicants must include an audit at the time of application. All MCI applicants must submit an online eGRANT application (the link to which can be found at the grant website) by 4:30 p.m. (CST) on the due date. In addition, applicants must print the required number of copies of the completed eGRANT application, attach the required accompanying documents to each copy and mail or hand carry these sets to the TAC by 4:30 p.m. (CST) on the due date. Applicant organizations are reviewed every other year by out-of-state evaluators. Organizations must submit a completed application with the required attachments every year. Organizations being reviewed must submit 8 (eight) sets. Organizations not being reviewed submit only 3 (three) sets.

Restrictions: MCI funds may not be used for capital expenditures; loan payments or penalties; endowment funds; cash reserves; furniture or fixtures exceeding $2,500; out-of-state travel expenses; or in-school, curriculum-based projects. Previous applicants who fail to meet the $1 million base operating figure will have a one-year "grace period" before losing eligibility in the MCI category; however, the applicants must maintain the $1 million base operating figure for a minimum of two consecutive years before another request for a one year grace period may be made. Freestanding academic institutions, which have as their mission training and accreditation in one or more arts disciplines, are not eligible in this category. (These organizations currently include: Arrowmont School of Arts and Crafts, Memphis College of Art, O'More College of Design, and Watkins College of Art and Design.) These and eligible organizations may submit an application under TAC's Cultural Education Partnership grant category.

Geographic Focus: Tennessee
Date(s) Application is Due: Jan 4
Amount of Grant: Up to 100,000 USD
Samples: Memphis Orchestral Society, Inc., Memphis, Tennessee, $79,800; Memphis Arts Council, Memphis, Tennessee, $71,300

Contact: Diane Williams, Director of Grants Management; (615) 741-6395; fax (615) 741-8559; diane.williams@tn.gov
Internet: http://www.tn.gov/arts/grant_categories.htm
Sponsor: Tennessee Arts Commission
401 Charlotte Avenue, Citizens Plaza Building
Nashville, TN 37243-0780

TAC Partnership Support Grants   1786
The Partnership Support (PS) grants provide annual general (non-project) support toward ongoing administrative costs to established Tennessee arts organizations. An organization may receive up to 12 percent of its total cash operating expenses in its most recently completed and audited fiscal year. An organization's total day-to-day operating expenses will be determined by adding together personnel, outside fees and services, space rental, travel, marketing, and remaining operating expenses as verified within the submitted audit. The applicant may request no more than $40,000. The actual amount of an applicant organization's grant for PS will depend upon its rating in the review process and upon the total amount of funds available to the Tennessee Arts Commission (TAC). Renewing applicant organizations are reviewed every other year by a peer advisory panel. New applicants must be reviewed for two consecutive years by a peer advisory panel before they may begin the review rotation process. The staff of the TAC will contact all current PS applicants and inform them of the review schedule. Annual application deadline dates vary; contact program staff for exact dates. First time applicants in the PS category MUST consult with TAC staff before applying.
Requirements: An applicant must be a free-standing 501(c)3 arts group independent of any other organization and chartered in the state of Tennessee; be an established arts organization responsible for its own programming; have a mission statement that is solely arts-focused; and be either a single-entity group dedicated to one arts discipline or a cross-disciplinary group such as an arts council, arts festival, or arts center. Additionally an applicant must comply with all of the following conditions: that the organization has received previous funding from TAC for three (3) of the past five (5) years through TAC's Arts Access, Arts Project Support or Rural Arts Project Support grants; that the organization has year-round paid professional managerial leadership; that the organization directly employs at least one (1) full-time paid administrator (as opposed to using a subsidiary) and that any other full or part time staff are directly employed as well; that the organization demonstrates ongoing fiscal responsibility through a single entity audit conducted externally by a Certified Public Accountant (CPA) for its most recently completed fiscal year; and that the organization has a board-approved long-range plan covering at least the current fiscal year and the next fiscal year. All these conditions must be met at time of application. Please note that in general "full-time" means an employee is paid for approximately 40 hours of work per week and the salary is his or her primary source of income. Arts organizations in neighboring states which are located within five (5) miles of the Tennessee state border, significantly serve Tennesseans and meet all eligibility requirements may also apply for a PS grant. For additional requirements, applicants should review http://www.tn.gov/arts/legal.htm at the TAC website. All PS applicants must submit an online eGRANT application by 4:30 p.m. (CST) on the due date. The link to the eGRANT is available at the grant website. In addition, applicants MUST print the required number of copies of the completed eGRANT application to submit by mail along with all required accompanying documents. The printed applications and documents must also be postmarked or hand-delivered to the TAC by 4:30 p.m. (CST) on the due date. Organizations must complete a full application every year and include required accompanying documents; however, organizations being reviewed must submit sixteen (16) sets while organizations not being reviewed submit only three. Organizations with budgets over $100,000 annually should use an accrual accounting system. Organizations with annual budgets under $100,000 may use a cash accounting system and may submit a one-year audit and management letter every two years, e.g., for Fiscal Year 2012, an audit for either the organization's Fiscal Year 2009 or 2010. Failure to submit a single entity audit by the time of application requires a letter by the organization's CPA explaining why the audit is unavailable and when it will be completed.
Restrictions: Most PS recipients are organizations operating with an annual budget below $1 million. However, the category is open to arts organizations with budgets in excess of this level, but who do not qualify for TAC's Major Cultural Institution (MCI) or Cultural Education Partnership (CEP) grant categories (see guidelines for these categories at the TAC website for further information). Capital expenses, cash reserves, endowment funds, loan repayments or penalties, in-kind, depreciation, bank fees or furniture and fixture expenditures exceeding $2,500 are not allowable as operating expenses.

Colleges, universities, and government units are not eligible for PS unless the unit is an official arts agency. An applicant's audit must be submitted by the date of the application's scheduled panel review and cannot be submitted as a subsidiary of another organization. If the required audit is NOT submitted by that date, the applicant's eligible funding request will be established using the organization's operating expenses from their most recent audit on file at the TAC. Under no circumstances will a PS grant contract be issued without receipt of the grantee's audit covering the required time frame.
Geographic Focus: Alabama, Arkansas, Georgia, Kentucky, Mississippi, Missouri, North Carolina, Tennessee, Virginia
Date(s) Application is Due: Jan 18
Amount of Grant: Up to 40,000 USD
Samples: Children's Museum of Oak Ridge, Anderson, Tennessee, $28,800; Tullahoma Fine Arts Center, Inc., Tullahoma, Tennessee, $5,000; Tennessee Philharmonic Symphony Orchestra, Murfreesboro, Tennessee, $9,800
Contact: Rod Reiner, Deputy Director, Arts Program Division; (615) 741-2093; fax (615) 741-8559; rod.reiner@tn.gov
Internet: http://www.tn.gov/arts/grant_categories.htm
Sponsor: Tennessee Arts Commission
401 Charlotte Avenue, Citizens Plaza Building
Nashville, TN 37243-0780

TAC Rural Arts Project Support Grants   1787
The Tennessee Arts Commission (TAC) Rural Arts Project Support (RAPS) grants supply funding to organizations which are located in rural areas of Tennessee and which provide a wide variety of public-value arts projects and programs such as: projects that involve and promote professional Tennessee artists; visiting artists conducting master classes; specific aspects of workshops, festivals, and conferences; public performances, productions, and exhibitions produced by the applicant; exhibitions of art by Tennessee artists and artists from outside Tennessee; promotion, publicity, and newsletters; administrative and artistic staff support; research and documentation as part of an arts project or program development; consultancies and residencies for administrative and artistic activities; the development of long-range planning documents; touring projects that bring professional performers to communities across the state; improved program accessibility for underserved constituencies, e.g., children, people living in rural communities or isolated settings, people with disabilities, people of color and senior citizens; art in public places (additional information available from the Director of Visual Arts); extensions of literary projects, journals with continuing publication or juried anthologies; apprenticeship programs; computer software/training; technical/production support; and technical assistance projects. RAPS grant amounts range from $500 to $7,000 for non-arts organizations and $500 to $9,000 for arts-focused groups. Applicants should contact the Tennessee Arts Commission to verify current submission dates and requirements.
Requirements: The following entities are eligible to apply for RAPS grants: 501(c)3 not-for-profit organizations in rural areas of and chartered in Tennessee; and Tennessee colleges and universities who meet the tax-exempt requirements just described for not-for-profit organizations. Entities bordering Tennessee (and serving rural areas in Tennessee) are also eligible to apply if they meet the criteria described for instate applicants. First time applicants must contact the TAC prior to submitting an application to verify eligibility. All first time 501(c)3 applicants must provide the TAC with copies of all of the basic nonprofit status documentation, which includes a copy of the organization's Tennessee State Charter, the IRS 501(c)3 Determination Letter and a recent copy of the by-laws of the organization. Proposed projects must involve one or more TAC recognized classical art forms, including visual art, crafts, media, music, theater, dance, folk and ethnic art, or literary arts. Applicants who apply in more than one TAC grant category in a single fiscal year must submit entirely unrelated projects for each proposal. All RAPS applicants must submit an online eGRANT application by January 18 at 4:30 pm. The link to the eGRANT form is available at the grant website. Additionally, hard copies and required supporting documents described in the guidelines at the grant website must be mailed or hand-delivered to the TAC by Jan 18 at 4:30 pm to complete the application process. Applications must contain a clear, single- project focus. Requested funds should be listed under one expense category on the budget page (and should correspond with the Activity Code indicated on the application). Grant funds must be matched one-to-one (1:1). A project may start no earlier than July 1 and must end no later than June 15. For more requirements, applicants should read the guidelines at the grant website. Additionally applicants should read the legal requirements page at http://www.tn.gov/arts/legal.htm.
Restrictions: A RAPS application may be submitted only by an organization chartered in Tennessee and located in a rural county (for a list of TAC's urban

and rural designations, see the downloadable guidelines at the grant website). K-12 schools are not eligible to apply. Colleges and universities are eligible only for activities that clearly serve the needs of surrounding communities or the state and are designed to involve a broad audience. Activities that are credit-producing or are oriented primarily to students and the academic community are not eligible. An eligible organization may submit only one RAPS application for the current fiscal year. RAPS applicants may not apply for a Partnership Support, Cultural Education Partnership or Major Cultural Institution grant. Additional restrictions on funding are listed on the legal requirements page at http://www.tn.gov/arts/legal.htm.
Geographic Focus: Alabama, Arkansas, Georgia, Kentucky, Mississippi, Missouri, North Carolina, Tennessee, Virginia
Date(s) Application is Due: Jan 18
Amount of Grant: 500 - 9,000 USD
Contact: Rich Boyd, Executive Director; (615) 532-9797; fax (615) 741-8559; rich.boyd@tn.gov
Internet: http://www.tn.gov/arts/grant_categories.htm
Sponsor: Tennessee Arts Commission
401 Charlotte Avenue, Citizens Plaza Building
Nashville, TN 37243-0780

Target Foundation Grants 1788
The foundation welcomes applications from nonprofit organizations in the Minneapolis/Saint Paul metropolitan area. Types of support include operating, project, and capital grants. The foundation is specifically interested in partnering with arts and cultural institutions to make special exhibitions, performances, and events visible and accessible to the community; and supporting direct service organizations that sustain the basic shelter, food, and clothing needs of individuals or families at risk. Proposals are accepted throughout the year; the preferred submission time is February through November. Organizations that fit foundation guidelines may apply for funding by submitting a grant request via U.S. postal mail.
Requirements: 501(c)3 nonprofit organizations in the Minneapolis/Saint Paul metropolitan area are eligible.
Restrictions: The foundation does not make grants to individuals or to religious groups for religious purposes; usually support national ceremonies, memorials, conferences, fundraising dinners, testimonials, or other similar events; usually support health, recreation, therapeutic programs; living subsidies; or care of disabled persons.
Geographic Focus: Minnesota
Date(s) Application is Due: Oct 1
Amount of Grant: 10,000 - 50,000 USD
Contact: Bridget McGinnis, Grants Administrator; (612) 696-6098; fax (612) 696-5088; guidelines@target.com
Internet: http://sites.target.com/site/en/corporate/page.jsp?contentId=PRD03-001819
Sponsor: Target Foundation
1000 Nicollet Mall, TPS-3080
Minneapolis, MN 55403

Taubman Endowment for the Arts 1789
The endowment was formed to support the arts through grants awards. Grants are awarded primarily in Detroit, MI. Applications are accepted at any time.
Restrictions: Grants are not made to individuals.
Geographic Focus: Michigan
Samples: Smithsonian Institute (Washington, DC)—for general operating support, $12,000; Detroit Symphony Orchestra Hall (Detroit, MI)—for general operating support, $2000.
Contact: Fred Henshaw; (248) 258-7207; fax (248) 258-7476
Sponsor: Taubman Endowment for the Arts
200 E Long Lake Road, Suite 300
Bloomfield Hills, MI 48304

Ted Arison Family Foundation Grants 1790
The foundation awards general support grants to foreign and United States-based nonprofits in its areas of interest, including: health; education; children and youth; culture, art and sports; populations in distress; disabilities; and research. Preference will be given to support for Middle East relations and Jewish organizations. Lesser consideration will be given to U.S. based nonprofits with an international focus. An applicant should submit a brief proposal that describes the organization, amount requested, purpose of request, recently audited financial statement, and proof of tax exemption. There are no application deadlines.
Geographic Focus: All States, Israel
Amount of Grant: 10,000 - 100,000 USD

Contact: Jason Arison; +972-3-6073100; fax +972-3-6073101; info@arison.co.il
Internet: http://www.arison.co.il/group/en/Content.aspx?PageName=The+Ted+Arison+Family+Foundation+
Sponsor: Ted Arison Family Foundation
Golda Center, 23 Shaul Hamelech Boulevard
Tel Aviv, FL 64367 Israel

TE Foundation Grants 1791
The foundation provides grants to nonprofit organizations in geographic areas where Tyco Electronics has a significant employee population and for specific projects or programs in broad categories, including education (with an emphasis on math and science), community impact, and arts and culture. In addition to a matching gifts program for employee contributions to accredited high schools, colleges, and universities, the foundation makes direct grants for programs that address a business or community concern of Tyco Electronics. Organizations that support pre-college math and science education receive special attention. Agencies that promote personal growth, career opportunities, and economic self-sufficiency are encouraged to apply, as are local chapters of health- and civic-related organizations. Special attention is given to community-wide arts organizations that solicit and allocate funds for a number of arts groups and institutions. Local public television and radio stations are encouraged to apply for funding of specific education initiatives. Capital campaigns of significant arts and cultural organizations serving communities in which the corporation has a major presence also will receive consideration. Grants also are awarded to support general operations, program development, and employee matching gifts. Applications are accepted throughout the year but are considered on the listed application deadlines.
Requirements: The TE Foundation limits grants to U.S. organizations that qualify as nonprofit under Section 501(c)3 of the Internal Revenue Code. Requests receive preferential review if the organization is supported by TE employees as volunteers.
Restrictions: The foundation generally will not support organizations in geographic areas where Tyco Electronics has few or no employees; individuals, private foundations, national organizations, or service clubs; fraternal, social, labor or trade organizations; organizations that discriminate on the basis of race, religion, color, national origin, physical or mental conditions, veteran or marital status, age, or sex; churches or religious organizations, with the exception of nondenominational programs sponsored by a church or religious group such as a food bank, youth center or non-sectarian education programs; political campaigns; loans or investments; or programs that pose a potential conflict of interest.
Geographic Focus: California, Massachusetts, Michigan, North Carolina, Pennsylvania, South Carolina, Texas, Virginia
Date(s) Application is Due: Mar 15; Jun 15; Sep 15; Dec 15
Amount of Grant: 250 - 25,000 USD
Contact: Mary Rakoczy, (717) 592-4869; fax (717) 592-4022; TEfoundation@te.com
Internet: http://www.te.com/en/about-te/responsibility/community.html
Sponsor: Tyco Electronics Foundation
c/o TE Corporation
Harrisburg, PA 17105-3608

Telluride Foundation Community Grants 1792
The foundation offers an annual granting cycle for nonprofit organizations that serve people living and/or working in Colorado's San Miguel County. The foundation awards grants to local nonprofit organizations involved in the arts, education, athletics, childcare, land conservation, environmental, minority programs, and other community-based efforts. Additionally, the foundation provides local nonprofits with technical assistance, such as training seminars, grant writing and consulting and capacity building services. Foundation grants are awarded once a year, at the end of December, with grant awards being distributed the following year. Grants will fall generally in the range of $500 and above, depending on the amount available for distribution.
Requirements: The Telluride Foundation will consider grant applications from 501(c)3 organizations meeting the following eligibility requirements: conduct activities and programs consistent with the Foundation's mission; serve people living or working in San Miguel County (primary emphasis of grant making is to organizations based in San Miguel, Ouray and west Montrose counties—all other organizations must document a strong case to meet "serving people that live and/or work in San Miguel County."). Applicants without 501(c)3 status, but which have applied to the IRS for such status, may apply. Applicants without 501(c)3 status, but which are operating under an organization qualified as a 501(c)3 organization, may apply separately if they have their own advisory board and have the written consent of the qualified organization.
Restrictions: Grants will not be awarded for building/renovation; equipment that could be capitalized on a financial statement; capital campaigns; debt reduction

or retiring past operating deficits; fellowships or other grants to individuals; loans; non-educational publications; litigation; political campaigns; operating support for organizations that conduct lobbying or political action campaigns, economic development, endowment funds, religious organizations for religious purposes, graduate and post-graduate research, or candidates for political office.

Geographic Focus: Colorado
Date(s) Application is Due: Oct 28
Amount of Grant: 500 USD
Contact: April Montgomery, Programs Director; (970) 728-8717; fax (970) 728-9007; april@telluridefoundation.org
Internet: http://www.telluridefoundation.org/index.php?page=community-grants
Sponsor: Telluride Foundation
220 E. Colorado Avenue, Suite 106
Telluride, CO 81435

Telluride Foundation Emergency/Out of Cycle Grants　　　**1793**
The Telluride Foundation Board of Directors recognizes that there will be times when its annual grant cycle does not work for all organizations and their needs. Out-of-cycle grants are requests that fall out of the Foundation's annual cycle of granting. Because of timing issues or emergencies that arise, not all organizations can fit their request into the regular October to December cycle. Out-of-cycle grants are not intended to be a catch-all for organizations that fail to anticipate the October-December cycle or to meet a budget crises, which occur from poor financial planning. The grants are intended to address needs that arise through external or uncontrollable emergencies and that present a compelling story of an unmet and necessary need.
Requirements: The Telluride Foundation will consider grant applications from 501(c)3 organizations meeting the following eligibility requirements: conduct activities and programs consistent with the Foundation's mission; serve people living or working in San Miguel County (primary emphasis of grant making is to organizations based in San Miguel, Ouray and west Montrose counties—all other organizations must document a strong case to meet "serving people that live and/or work in San Miguel County."). Only two types of needs will be considered: Timing-needs which arise because of timing issues on the part of the organization; and, Human Emergencies. Needs which do not fall into one of these two narrow categories will be considered and the request must be for a project or program described under "Types of Support" in the regular grant guidelines.
Restrictions: Grants will not be awarded for building/renovation; equipment that could be capitalized on a financial statement; capital campaigns; debt reduction or retiring past operating deficits; fellowships or other grants to individuals; loans; non-educational publications; litigation; political campaigns; operating support for organizations that conduct lobbying or political action campaigns, economic development, endowment funds, religious organizations for religious purposes, graduate and post-graduate research, or candidates for political office.
Geographic Focus: Colorado
Contact: April Montgomery, Programs Director; (970) 728-8717; fax (970) 728-9007; april@telluridefoundation.org
Internet: http://www.telluridefoundation.org/index.php?page=emergency-out-of-cycle-grants
Sponsor: Telluride Foundation
220 E. Colorado Avenue, Suite 106
Telluride, CO 81435

Telluride Foundation Technical Assistance Grants　　　**1794**
The Telluride Foundation offers local nonprofits with the option of applying for a Technical Assistance Grant. The grants provide an easy, effective way for nonprofit organizations to improve their operational efficiency through a proven, turnkey program for assessing and addressing individual organization's needs. The objective is to provide the nonprofit a professional third part assessment of their current needs then a professional nonprofit consultant to assist through the solution process. The assessment may identify the need for an updated business plan, strategic plan, marketing plan, Board of Directors development, etc. The consultant will assist the organizations staff and Board through the development of the plan. The Assessment will be conducted by the Community Resource Center or a consultant choosen by the nonprofit, if approved by the Telluride Foundation, and will be shared with the Telluride Foundation. The Telluride Foundation will pay for the assessment and will fund part or the entire consultant fees. If selected for a TA, the non-profit will not be eligible for future funding from the Telluride Foundation until they have completed the TA process.
Requirements: The Telluride Foundation will consider grant applications from 501(c)3 organizations meeting the following eligibility requirements: conduct activities and programs consistent with the Foundation's mission; serve people living or working in San Miguel County (primary emphasis of grant making is

to organizations based in San Miguel, Ouray and west Montrose counties—all other organizations must document a strong case to meet "serving people that live or work in San Miguel County."). Applicants without 501(c)3 status, but which have applied to the IRS for such status, may apply. Applicants without 501(c)3 status, but which are operating under an organization qualified as a 501(c)3 organization, may apply separately if they have their own advisory board and have the written consent of the qualified organization. A request for a Technical Assistance Grant may be included in a Community Grant application requesting project or general operating funds or a nonprofit may only request Technical Assitance Funds using the Community Grant application.
Restrictions: Grants will not be awarded for building/renovation; equipment that could be capitalized on a financial statement; capital campaigns; debt reduction or retiring past operating deficits; fellowships or other grants to individuals; loans; non-educational publications; litigation; political campaigns; operating support for organizations that conduct lobbying or political action campaigns, economic development, endowment funds, religious organizations for religious purposes, graduate and post-graduate research, or candidates for political office.
Geographic Focus: Colorado
Date(s) Application is Due: Oct 28
Contact: April Montogomery, Programs Director; (970) 728-8717; fax (970) 728-9007; april@telluridefoundation.org
Internet: http://www.telluridefoundation.org/index.php?page=technical-assistance-grants
Sponsor: Telluride Foundation
220 E. Colorado Avenue, Suite 106
Telluride, CO 81435

Temple-Inland Foundation Grants　　　**1795**
The foundation makes grants to IRS 501(c)3 tax-exempt organizations located in geographic operating areas of Temple-Inland Inc's subsidiary companies. Areas of interest include services for children and youth, Christian churches and organizations, education at all levels, health care and organizations, human services, and arts and culture. Types of support include general operating support, research, employee matching gifts, and employee-related scholarships. Requests should be received two weeks prior to quarterly board meetings. Submit a written request for guidelines and specific application deadlines. The listed deadline date is for scholarships.
Restrictions: Ineligible applicants include fraternal, veterans, political, local social, and service organizations.
Geographic Focus: All States
Date(s) Application is Due: Mar 15
Amount of Grant: 1,000 - 30,000 USD
Contact: Richard Warner, (936) 829-1721; fax (936) 829-7727
Internet: http://www.templeinland.com
Sponsor: Temple-Inland Foundation
1300 S Mopac
Austin, TX 78749

Temple Hoyne Buell Foundation Grants　　　**1796**
The foundation awards grants to nonprofits in Colorado for programs that help underserved children in three areas: early childhood education and development (preschools, home visitation, service provider's professional development, parenting skills, and literacy); social and emotional development of children (mentoring, intergenerational, and after-school activities); and family stability for children (teen pregnancy prevention, counseling services, and family centers). Types of support include operating budgets, continuing support, equipment acquisition, curriculum development, scholarship funds, technical assistance, program development, and matching funds. Contact the office for application materials. Applications are due the 1st business day of January, May, and September.
Requirements: Nonprofit organizations in Colorado may apply.
Restrictions: Grants do not support advertising, athletic groups, individuals, international organizations, religious or political projects, special events, past operating deficits, debt retirement, litigation, medical programs, multiyear awards, testimonial events, annual campaigns, endowments, membership drives, or conferences.
Geographic Focus: Colorado
Date(s) Application is Due: Jan 2; May 1; Sep 1
Amount of Grant: 10,000 - 50,000 USD
Contact: Susan Steele; (303) 744-1688; info@buellfoundation.org
Internet: http://www.buellfoundation.org/granttypes.htm
Sponsor: Temple Hoyne Buell Foundation
1666 S University Boulevard, Suite B
Denver, CO 80210

Texas Commission on the Arts Arts Respond Project Grants 1797

This program provides project assistance grants on a short-term basis and may include administrative costs directly related to the project. Projects must address one of the following priority areas: education, health and human services, economic development, public safety, criminal justice, natural resources, or agriculture. Organizations that are eligible are: Arts Organizations, Established Arts Organizations, Minority Arts Organizations, Rural Arts Providers.

Requirements: To be eligible for TCA grants, an organization must: be a tax-exempt nonprofit organization as designated by the Internal Revenue Service and/or must be an entity of government; be incorporated in Texas; have fulfilled all its outstanding contractual obligations to the State of Texas (i.e. student loans, child support, taxes, etc.); and comply with regulations pertaining to federal grant recipients including Title VI of the Civil Rights Act of 1964, Section 504 of the Rehabilitation Act of 1973, the Age Discrimination Act of 1975, the Education Amendments of 1972, the Americans with Disabilities Act of 1990, and the Drug Free Workplace Act of 1988.

Geographic Focus: Texas
Amount of Grant: Up to 45,000 USD
Contact: Director of Programs; (512) 463-5535 or (800) 252-9415; fax (512) 475-2699; front.desk@arts.state.tx.us
Internet: http://www.arts.state.tx.us/index.php?option=com_wrapper&view =wrapper&Itemid=86
Sponsor: Texas Commission on the Arts
P.O. Box 13406
Austin, TX 78711-3406

Texas Commission on the Arts Create-5 Program Grants 1798

The intent of this grant is to advance the creative economy of Texas by investing in arts organizations. This program provides multi-year operational support. Applicants write their grant for a one year period, and if funded, will provide an update for the second year. Depending on the availability of funds, the organization's award amount will be the same for two fiscal years. New organizations may only apply in odd numbered years.

Requirements: To be eligible for TCA grants, an organization must: Be a tax-exempt nonprofit organization as designated by the Internal Revenue Service and/or must be an entity of government Be incorporated in Texas Have fulfilled all its outstanding contractual obligations to the State of Texas (i.e. student loans, child support, taxes, etc.) Comply with regulations pertaining to federal grant recipients including Title VI of the Civil Rights Act of 1964, Section 504 of the Rehabilitation Act of 1973, the Age Discrimination Act of 1975, the Education Amendments of 1972, the Americans with Disabilities Act of 1990, and the Drug Free Workplace Act of 1988.

Geographic Focus: Texas
Date(s) Application is Due: Mar 15
Amount of Grant: 3,000 - 50,000 USD
Contact: Director of Programs; (512) 463-5535 or (800) 252-9415; fax (512) 475-2699; front.desk@arts.state.tx.us
Internet: http://www.arts.state.tx.us/index.php?option=com_wrapper&view =wrapper&Itemid=86
Sponsor: Texas Commission on the Arts
P.O. Box 13406
Austin, TX 78711-3406

Textron Corporate Contributions Grants 1799

Textron Inc. was founded in 1923 as a small textile company and has since become one of the world's best known multi-industry companies. Textron focuses philanthropic giving in the following areas: workforce development and education; healthy families/vibrant communities; and sponsorships. In the area of workforce development and education, the company focuses on job-training and employment development (eg., school-to-work, welfare-to-work, job-training for underserved-audiences, literacy, and English-as a-Second-Language programs). In the area of healthy families/vibrant communities, the company focuses on arts and culture (with emphasis on outreach programs that enhance learning and target low- and moderate-income individuals), community revitalization (eg., affordable housing and economic development in low-income areas), and health and human-service organizations (eg., food pantries, homeless shelters, and services for low-income residents). In the area of sponsorships, the company encourages volunteerism and sponsors worthwhile events that benefit the communities where employees live and work. Textron's grant history has included funding of general-operating costs, capital campaigns, building construction/renovation, equipment acquisition, program development, conferences and seminars, publication, seed money, fellowships, scholarship funds, research, technical assistance, consulting

services, and matching funds. Downloadable guidelines (PDF) and application (Word document) are available online. The completed application and required accompanying documentation must be received via mail by the deadline date.

Requirements: Textron targets its giving to nonprofit agencies located in its headquarters state of Rhode Island and those locations where the company has divisional operations. Organizations outside of Rhode Island should contact the Textron company in their area; a listing of Textron businesses along with their contact information can be accessed by clicking the "Contact Us" link at the Textron website.

Restrictions: Textron will review only one request per organization during a 12-month period. Contributions will not be made to the following types of organizations: organizations without 501(c)3 status as defined by the Internal Revenue Service; individuals; political, fraternal or veterans organizations; religious institutions when the grant would support sectarian activities; and organizations that discriminate by race, creed, gender, ethnicity, sexual orientation, disability, age or any other basis prohibited by law.

Geographic Focus: Georgia, Illinois, Kansas, Louisiana, Maryland, Massachusetts, New York, North Carolina, Pennsylvania, Rhode Island, Texas, Germany, Great Britain
Date(s) Application is Due: Mar 1; Sep 1
Samples: The Providence Center, Providence, Rhode Island, $10,000 - to provide training opportunities in receptionist, production, driver, and computer vocations.
Contact: Karen Warfield; (401) 421-2800; fax (401) 457-2225
Internet: http://www.textron.com/about/commitment/corp-giving/
Sponsor: Textron Charitable Trust
40 Westminster Street
Providence, RI 02903

Thelma Doelger Charitable Trust Grants 1800

Established in California in 1995, the Thelma Doelger Charitable Trust awards grants in the San Francisco Bay. Giving is primarily aimed at animal welfare, social services, medical centers, and children and youth services. The Trust's major fields of interest include: aging centers and services; animal welfare; boys and girls clubs; children and youth services; higher education; hospitals; human services; museums; and zoos. Grants typically take the form of general purposes and support of operating budgets. Most recently, awards have ranged from $3,000 to $50,000. Though a formal application is required, there are no annual submission deadlines. The initial approach should be by letter or telephone, requesting the application.

Requirements: Nonprofit organizations in the San Francisco Bay area of northern California may submit grant requests.
Restrictions: Individuals are not eligible.
Geographic Focus: California
Amount of Grant: 3,000 - 50,000 USD
Samples: Seton Medical Center, Daly City, California, $35,000 - general operating costs; Marin Humane Society, Novato, California, $50,000 - general operating costs; Curi Odyssey (formerly Coyote Point Museum), San Mateo, California, $50,000 - general operating costs.
Contact: D. Eugene Richard, Trustee; (650) 755-2333
Sponsor: Thelma Doelger Charitable Trust
950 Daly Boulevard, Suite 300
Daly City, CA 94015-3004

The Ray Charles Foundation Grants 1801

Although musician Ray Charles was blind since the age of seven, he always maintained that blindness was not a handicap, but rather that the inability to hear music constituted the truer loss. Because of this philosophy, he began making contributions to the field of hearing impairment and often anonymously contributed to cochlear implants for individuals who couldn't afford such surgeries. In 1986, Mr. Charles founded "The Robinson Foundation for Hearing Disorders" which was later renamed "The Ray Charles Foundation." Convinced of the tremendous need of education for youth, Mr. Charles also directed the foundation to make donations and support institutions and organizations for educational purposes. Over the past 23 years, the Ray Charles Foundation has provided financial donations to various institutions involved in the areas of hearing disorders as well as education. The foundation prefers to fund programs and projects that show promise of strengthening the community beyond the grant period and that offer maximum community impact to achieve long-term results. Types of funding the foundation provides are for capital, program, and core support. Capital funding is available for land, facility, and equipment purchases and renovations or new construction. Renovation and construction projects will be invited only for organizations that have already raised a substantial amount of their fundraising goal. The project must either be in construction or have a firm construction start date. Program funding is available for both new and expansion projects. While these must evidence a viable fundraising and sustainability plan, requests for program development or enhancement activiies will still be considered. Core support funding is available for established and well-managed organizations and programs. Communication with Foundation Directors is discouraged. Applicants to the Ray Charles Foundation should simply fill out and submit the foundation's Grant Application Packet via a mail carrier to the address given. Guidelines, instructions, and links to form are given at the website. Applications are accepted continually throughout the year.

Requirements: 501(c)3 organizations that have been in existence for at least three years and that are incorporated and delivering services to the United States are eligible to apply. Programs must advance the mission of the Foundation in the following program categories: Education, Hearing Disorders, and Culture and the Arts. Educational programs eligible for funding include, but are not limited to, after-school programs and academic activities aimed at college preparation for underprivileged youth, and academic/therapy services for youth who are blind and/or deaf. Hearing Disorder programs eligible for funding include research and treatment in the area of hearing disorders and educational programs and resources for youth with hearing disorders. Culture and Arts programs eligible for funding include institutions and museums whose mission it is to provide musical and cultural education and access to underprivileged and disadvantaged youth.

Restrictions: The Foundation does not fund organizations and programs outside of the United States. Most grants will be limited to one year in duration. Multi-year funding will be considered on an exceptional case by case basis. The Foundation generally does not approve grants to organizations on a continuing annual basis. If an agency applies for a 'one year grant' more than three years in a row, they will be declined and asked to wait at least two years before applying again. More obligations and responsibilities of grant recipients are listed at the website.

Geographic Focus: All States
Contact: Grant Coordinator; (323) 737-8000; fax (323) 737-0148; info@ theraycharlesfoundation.org
Internet: http://www.theraycharlesfoundation.org/GrantQualifications.html
Sponsor: Ray Charles Foundation
2107 W. Washington Boulevard
Los Angeles, CA 90018

Third Wave Foundation Lela Breitbart Memorial Fund Grants   1802

Third Wave Foundation will use this endowed fund to offer an annual grant of $3,000 in memory of Lela Breitbart to innovative organizations working on issues of reproductive justice around the country. This grant will be given to programs that are developed and led by women and transgender people between the ages of 15 and 30, with an emphasis on supporting and strengthening young women, transgender youth and their allies working for gender, racial, social, and economic justice.

Requirements: Applicant organizations and/or programs must be based in the United States.
Geographic Focus: All States
Amount of Grant: 3,000 USD
Contact: Program Director; (212) 228-8311; fax (212) 780-9181; info@ thirdwavefoundation.org
Internet: http://www.thirdwavefoundation.org/grant-making/breitbart
Sponsor: Third Wave Foundation
25 East 21st Street
New York, NY 10010

Third Wave Foundation Organizing and Advocacy Grants   1803

Third Wave is a feminist, activist foundation that works nationally to support young women and transgender youth ages 15 to 30. Through strategic grantmaking, leadership development, and philanthropic advocacy, it supports groups and individuals working towards gender, racial, economic, and social justice. The Organizing and Advocacy (O&A) Fund supports work that challenges sexism, racism, homophobia, transphobia, economic injustice, and other forms of oppression in interesting ways. Grants are provided for both specific projects and general operating support.

Requirements: Applicant organizations and/or programs must be based in the United States.
Geographic Focus: All States
Date(s) Application is Due: Apr 1; Oct 1
Amount of Grant: 1,000 - 10,000 USD
Contact: Monique Mehta, Executive Director; (212) 228-8311; fax (212) 780-9181; info@thirdwavefoundation.org

Internet: http://www.thirdwavefoundation.org/grant-making/organizing-and-advocacy
Sponsor: Third Wave Foundation
25 East 21st Street
New York, NY 10010

Third Wave Foundation Reproductive Health and Justice Grants   1804

The foundation supports work, organizing, and activism that exists to challenge sexism, racism, homophobia, economic injustice, and other forms of oppression. The Reproductive Health and Justice Initiative is grounded in the view that reproductive rights are a fundamental human right, and that these rights cannot be fully expressed or enjoyed unless people have access to the means to fulfill them. The initiative works to help build solidarity and movement between young people, particularly young women of color and transgender youth, who have been overlooked, unheard, or tokenized within the larger movement. Proposed projects should benefit, focus on, and be developed and led by women between the ages of 15 and 30, with an emphasis on low-income women, differently abled women, women of color, and lesbian and bisexual women. Grants are made for project support and for general operating support. One grant proposal per organization will be accepted each year.

Requirements: Applicant organizations and/or programs must be based in the United States.
Geographic Focus: All States
Date(s) Application is Due: Apr 1; Oct 1
Amount of Grant: 1,000 - 10,000 USD
Contact: Monique Mehta, Executive Director; (212) 228-8311; fax (212) 780-9181; info@thirdwavefoundation.org
Internet: http://www.thirdwavefoundation.org/grant-making/reproductive-health-and-justice
Sponsor: Third Wave Foundation
25 East 21st Street
New York, NY 10010

Thomas and Agnes Carvel Foundation Grants   1805

This foundation awards support for general charitable purposes as well as for nutrition research and youth programs to nonprofit organizations in the tri-state area comprising New York, New Jersey, and Connecticut. Types of support include general operations grants, capital grants, grants in aid, program/project grants, matching gifts, and research grants. Application should be by letter and should outline the project, budget, and staffing of the project for which funding is being requested.

Requirements: IRS 501(c)3 organizations in New York, New Jersey, and Connecticut are eligible.
Restrictions: Grants are not made to individuals.
Geographic Focus: Connecticut, New Jersey, New York
Date(s) Application is Due: Oct 1
Amount of Grant: 2,000 - 200,000 USD
Samples: Seton Hall (South Orange, NJ)—to provide full scholarships to 10 high-school students from Newark, NJ, who commit to a year of volunteer service in Newark upon graduation, $50,000.
Contact: Ann McHugh, Vice President; (914) 793-7300
Sponsor: Thomas and Agnes Carvel Foundation
35 E Grassy Sprain Road
Yonkers, NY 10710

Thomas and Dorothy Leavey Foundation Grants   1806

Thomas Leavey and partner John C. Tyler began the Farmer's Insurance Company in 1928. The foundation was begun in 1952 by Leavey and his wife, Dorothy. Thomas Leavey died in 1980 and Dorothy actively led the foundation until her death in 1998. Giving primarily in southern California, the Foundation offers support for: hospitals, medical research, higher and secondary education, Catholic church groups; and provides scholarships to children of employees of Farmers Group.

Requirements: The foundation gives primarily in southern California.
Geographic Focus: California
Amount of Grant: 10,000 - 2,000,000 USD
Samples: Childrens Museum of Los Angeles, Lake View Terrace, CA, $250,000; Santa Clara University, Santa Clara, CA, $2,000,000; Orthopaedic Hospital, Los Angeles, CA, $100,000.
Contact: Kathleen Leavey McCarthy, Chair; (310) 551-9936
Sponsor: Thomas and Dorothy Leavey Foundation
10100 Santa Monica Boulevard, Suite 610
Los Angeles, CA 90067-4110

Thomas Austin Finch, Sr. Foundation Grants 1807

The purpose of the Finch Foundation is the improvement of the mental, moral and physical well-being of the inhabitants of Thomasville, North Carolina, with emphasis on improving education, improving health related facilities and attracting new business to the community. However, grants are made for a wide variety of charitable causes throughout the greater Thomasville area. In general, grants are awarded for seed money, matching funds and general purposes. Primary consideration is given to projects of a non-recurring nature or to start up funding of limited duration. The foundation meets twice a year to review grant requests. Requests must be submitted by February 15th for the Spring Meeting and October 15th for the Fall Meeting. Application forms are available online. Applicants will receive notice acknowledging receipt of the grant request, and subsequently be notified of the grant declination or approval.

Requirements: Eligible applicants are IRS 501(c)3 non-profit organizations located within the corporate limits of the City of Thomasville, North Carolina or, organizations where the benefits of the grant will inure primarily to the residents of Thomasville. Proposals should be submitted in the following format: completed Common Grant Application Form; an original Proposal Statement; an audited financial report and a current year operating budget; a copy of your official IRS Letter with your tax determination; a listing of your Board of Directors. Proposal Statements (second item in the above Format) should answer these questions: what are the objectives and expected outcomes of this program/project/request; what strategies will be used to accomplish your objective; what is the timeline for completion; if this is part of an on-going program, how long has it been in operation; what criteria will you use to measure success; if the request is not fully funded, what other sources can you engage; an Itemized budget should be included; please describe any collaborative ventures. Prior to the distribution of funds, all approved grantees must sign and return a Grant Agreement Form, stating that the funds will be used for the purpose intended. Progress reports and Completion reports must also be filed as required for your specific grant. All current grantees must be in good standing with required documentation prior to submitting new proposals to any foundation.

Restrictions: Grants are generally not made for typical operational or maintenance-oriented purposes, political purposes, nor to organizations which discriminate on the basis of race, ethnic origin, sexual or religious preference, age or gender.

Geographic Focus: North Carolina

Date(s) Application is Due: Feb 15; Oct 15

Amount of Grant: 1,500 - 100,000 USD

Samples: Memorial United Methodist Church, $30,000—general operating funds; Hospice of Davidson County, Inc., $60,000—construction of inpatient facility; Thomasville City Schools, $24,400—active classroom project.

Contact: Wachovia Bank, N.A., Trustee; grantinquiries6@wachovia.com

Sponsor: Thomas Austin Finch, Sr. Foundation

Wachovia Bank, NC6732, 100 North Main Street

Winston Salem, NC 27150

Thomas B. and Elizabeth M. Sheridan Foundation Grants 1808

The foundation awards grants to 501(c)3 organizations in the Greater Baltimore area with an emphasis on private secondary schools and cultural arts.

Requirements: Nonprofit organizations in the Greater Baltimore area are eligible. Applications should send a letter of inquiry prior to submitting a proposal. There are no deadlines—applications are reviewed as received.

Restrictions: Grants are not awarded to individuals, for employee matching gifts, or for loans.

Geographic Focus: District of Columbia, Maryland, Virginia

Amount of Grant: 500 USD

Contact: John Sinclair; (410) 771-0475; jbs@sheridanfoundation.org

Sponsor: Thomas B. and Elizabeth M. Sheridan Foundation

11350 McCormick Road, Executive Plaza II, Suite 704

Hunt Valley, MD 21031

Thomas C. Ackerman Foundation Grants 1809

The Thomas C. Ackerman Foundation was founded in 1991. By Spring, 1992, substantial assets had been received from the Thomas C. Ackerman Trust, funded as a result of Thomas Ackerman's death on February 13, 1991; the Board of Directors was fully constituted; and the guidelines and objectives for grant making were adopted. The Foundation's areas of interest include: arts and culture; education; and health and human services. To be considered for a grant from the Foundation, an organization must initially submit a Letter of Intent online. Directions for completing the grant application will be provided to an organization, if it is invited to submit one. Awards generally range from $1,000 to $40,000.

Requirements: California nonprofits, primarily in San Diego County, are eligible to apply.

Restrictions: It is a policy of the Foundation not to provide continuous support for any project to the extent that the project becomes dependent upon the Foundation for its continued existence. The Foundation may make multi-year commitments on occasion. Grants are not made to individuals. Generally, the Foundation does not support conferences or symposia. While occasional grant support is given to religious organizations, those grants are made for direct support of nonsectarian educational or service projects and not for projects which are of primary benefit to members of a particular religion or belief or which primarily promote a particular religion or belief. The Foundation will not consider grants relating to human medical or biomedical research.

Geographic Focus: California

Amount of Grant: 1,000 - 40,000 USD

Samples: San Diego Public Library, San Diego, California, $35,000 - community development; San Diego Food Bank, San Diego, California, $15,000 - in support of the Food 4 Kids program; Elementary Institute of Science, San Diego, California, $5,000 - educational expansion.

Contact: Lynne Newman, Administrator; (619) 741-0113; info@AckermanFoundation.org

Internet: http://www.ackermanfoundation.org/

Sponsor: Thomas C. Ackerman Foundation

3755 Avocado Boulevard, #518

La Mesa, CA 91941-7301

Thomas Sill Foundation Grants 1810

Mr. Sill lived his entire life in Winnipeg and practiced as a chartered accountant for many years. He was an astute investor who built a fortune which became the basis for the Thomas Sill Foundation. The foundation provides encouragement and financial support to qualifying Manitoba organizations that strive to improve the quality of life in the province. The foundation awards grants in the following areas of interest: Responses to Community (agencies addressing poverty, women's shelters, qualifying daycares, mentally and physically challenged people, and community well-being); Health (eye care, palliative care, mental illness); Education (students at risk, including adults); Arts and Culture; Heritage (museums, architecture, projects); and, Environment (water issues). Grants awarded may be capital, operating or project in nature.

Requirements: Registered charities may obtain an application form by phoning the foundation office, at which time a preliminary discussion will determine eligibility. There are no deadlines by which applications must be submitted. Applicants should allow four months, from the submission of a request, to receive a response.

Restrictions: Successful applicants must wait two years before submitting another request.

Geographic Focus: Canada

Amount of Grant: 1,000 - 50,000 CAD

Contact: Hugh Arklie; (204) 947-3782; fax (204) 956-4702; hugha@tomsill.ca

Internet: http://thomassillfoundation.com/guidelines/

Sponsor: Thomas Sill Foundation

206-1661 Portage Avenue

Winnipeg, MB R3J 3T7 Canada

Thomas Thompson Trust Grants 1811

The Thompson Trust limits its distribution of funds to organizations located in Windham County, Vermont, (primarily the Town of Brattleboro) or in Dutchess County, New York (primarily the Town of Rhinebeck) which predominately serve residents located in those areas. The Will of Thomas Thompson was executed in 1867 and defined his charitable purposes rather narrowly as was the practice with 19th Century philanthropy. By successive court decrees in the 20th Century, the Trustees are now authorized to make grants to charitable organizations whose work and purposes promote health, education or the general social or civic betterment in the stated geographical areas; but the Trustees will continue to place particular emphasis on healthcare and other social services. The Trustees generally meet on the fourth Thursday in January, April, July and October. Applications are due by the first day of the month of the meeting.

Requirements: Organizations must have operated for three consecutive years before applying and be located in Windham County, VT, with preference given to Brattleboro; or Duchess County, New York, with preference given to Rhinebeck.

Restrictions: Grants are not made for general operating support, seed money, endowment purposes, or loans.

Geographic Focus: New York, Vermont

Date(s) Application is Due: Jan 1; Apr 1; Jul 1; Oct 1

Amount of Grant: 1,000 - 20,000 USD

Contact: Susan T. Monahan, Program Contact; (617) 951-1108; fax (617) 542-7437; smonahan@rackemann.com
Internet: http://www.cybergrants.com/thompson/grant.html
Sponsor: Thomas Thompson Trust
160 Federal Street, 13th Floor
Boston, MA 02110-1700

Thomas W. Bradley Foundation Grants 1812

Established in 1976 in Maryland, the Thomas W. Bradley Foundation offer grants in the greater metropolitan Baltimore, Maryland, area. Funding is limited to organizations which work with or benefit mentally or physically handicapped children. Primary fields of interest include: children, children's services, and the developmentally disabled. Funding comes in the form of general operating support. Application forms are required, and applicants should submit the following: name, address and phone number of organization; copy of IRS Determination Letter; a brief history of the organization and description of its mission; a listing of board of directors, trustees, officers and other key people and their affiliations; a detailed description of project and amount of funding requested; and a copy of the current year's organizational budget and project budget. There are no specific deadlines with which to adhere.
Requirements: Only 501(c)3 organizations that serve the residents of Maryland should apply, and the Foundation gives preference in the Baltimore metropolitan area.
Restrictions: No grants, scholarships, fellowships, prizes, or similar benefits are made to individuals.
Geographic Focus: Maryland
Amount of Grant: 3,000 - 6,000 USD
Samples: Muscular Dystrophy Association, Baltimore, Maryland, $5,000 - general operating support; Sheppard Pratt Health Center, Baltimore, Maryland, $5,000 - for general operations; Maryland School for the Blind, Baltimore, Maryland, $5,000 - general operating support.
Contact: Robert L. Pierson; (410) 821-3006; fax (410) 821-3007; info
Sponsor: Thomas W. Bradley Foundation
305 W. Chesapeake Avenue, Suite 308
Towson, MD 21204-4440

Thomas W. Briggs Foundation Grants 1813

The Foundation provides gifts that help serve the needs of thousands in the Memphis area. The focus of the funding includes youth projects and programs, education, social services, arts and cultural organizations and civic organizations that promote quality of life. Although some grants are multi-year pledges, many fall in the one-year $5,000 to $25,000 range.
Requirements: Applicants are asked to submit a proposal letter of not more than two pages, giving a brief history of the organization, stating goals and services provided and a list of present sources of funding. Tennessee nonprofit organizations are eligible to apply.
Restrictions: The Foundation does not support public and private schools, churches and synagogues, nationally affiliated organizations and seminars as well as special events. New applicants are required to set up an appointment before applying for a grant.
Geographic Focus: Tennessee
Date(s) Application is Due: Feb 1; Aug 1
Amount of Grant: 5,000 - 25,000 USD
Samples: Agape, Nashville, TN, $10,000—program support; Fire Museum of Memphis, Memphis, TN, $10,000—program support; Memphis Literacy Council, Memphis, TN, $10,000—program support.
Contact: Joanne Tilley; (901) 680-0276; fax (901) 767-1135
Internet: http://www.thomaswbriggsfoundation.com/funding.html
Sponsor: Thomas W. Briggs Foundation
6075 Poplar Avenue, Suite 330
Memphis, TN 38119

Thompson Charitable Foundation Grants 1814

Established in 1987, the Foundation supports organizations involved with education, Christian organizations, Autism research, health, human services, youth, including funding for capital and building improvements for human service organizations and educational institutions. Giving is limited to Bell, Clay, Laurel, and Leslie counties, Kentucky; Anderson, Blount, Knox, and Scott counties, Tennessee; and Buchanan and Tazewell counties, Virginia.
Requirements: Nonprofits operating in Bell, Clay, Laurel, and Leslie counties, Kentucky; Anderson, Blount, Knox, and Scott counties, Tennessee; and Buchanan and Tazewell counties, Virginia are eligible to apply. Initial contact should be a letter, no more then 2 pages long. The letter should include: a

statement of the problem, the project will address; a detailed description of project, and amount of funding requested.
Restrictions: No support for religious or political organizations, budget deficits or endowments.
Geographic Focus: Kentucky, Tennessee, Virginia
Date(s) Application is Due: Mar 31; Sep 1
Amount of Grant: 2,000 - 500,000 USD
Contact: Debbie Black; (865) 588-0491; fax (865) 588-4496; debbie@cf.org
Sponsor: Thompson Charitable Foundation
800 South Gay Street, Suite 2021
Knoxville, TN 37929-9710

Thompson Foundation Grants 1815

With $3,500 in savings, Bob and Ellen Thompson - along with Thompson's uncle, Wilford McCully - started the Thompson-McCully Company, a contract road paving company, in 1959. The Thompson Foundation's mission is to help low-income people rise out of poverty and become self-sufficient. The foundation awards grants to eligible Michigan nonprofit organizations that support economically disadvantaged residents and help them rise out of poverty. Types of support include emergency funds, general operating grants, program development, scholarship funds, and seed grants. There are no application forms. The board meets in February, April, June, August, October, and December.
Requirements: Although the Foundation serves a seven-county region (Wayne, Oakland, Macomb, St. Clair, Livingston, Washtenaw, and Monroe), the vast majority of its funds are used to serve those who live in Detroit, Highland Park and Hamtramck.
Geographic Focus: Michigan
Contact: John Ziraldo, Executive Director; (734) 453-6412; fax (734) 453-6475; cebejer@thompsonfdn.org
Internet: http://www.thompsonfdn.org/
Sponsor: Thompson Foundation
P.O. Box 6349
Plymouth, MI 48170

Thorman Boyle Foundation Grants 1816

The Thorman Boyle Foundation was established in California in 2000, with its primary fields of interested designated as: the arts; human services; and youth development. There are no formal application materials required, and interested parties should forward a letter of application stating their organization's purpose, as well as overall budgetary needs. Most recently, grant awards have ranged from $100 to a maximum of $2,000. No annual deadlines for submission have been identified.
Requirements: Though giving is primarily limited to 501(c)3 organizations either located in, or serving the residents of, California, the Foundation has, on occasion, awarded grants outside of this region.
Geographic Focus: All States
Amount of Grant: 100 - 2,000 USD
Contact: Mary E. Boyle, President; (650) 856-7445 or (650) 799-4300
Sponsor: Thorman Boyle Foundation
P.O. Box 2757
Cupertino, CA 95015

Thornton Foundation Grants 1817

The foundation awards grants to Calilfornia nonprofit organizations in its areas of interest, including arts/ and culture and higher/secondary education. Types of support include annual campaigns, building construction/renovation, continuing support, endowment funds, and research. There are no application deadlines.
Requirements: California nonprofit organizations are eligible.
Geographic Focus: California
Amount of Grant: 1,000 - 200,000 USD
Contact: Charles Thornton Jr., President; (213) 629-3867
Sponsor: Thornton Foundation
523 W Sixth Street, Suite 636
Los Angeles, CA 90014

Three Guineas Fund Grants 1818

In 2009, Three Guineas Fund restructured as a private foundation. The fund makes grants in education and the environment consistent with the foundation's bylaws, while keeping its core commitment to women and girls. Currently, the fund welcomes projects that create access to opportunity for women and girls, especially in education and the economy. Grantmaking includes projects that advance and support girls and women in the areas of entrepreneurship; science, math, and technology; leadership; sports; access to education and the economy;

and dissemination and distribution of strategies, research, or documentation of women's and girls' issues. Types of support include start-up projects and general operating grants for established programs. The fund is open to multi-year grants. Submit a letter of inquiry; full proposals are by request only.

Requirements: 501(c)3 tax-exempt organizations and organizations with a fiscal agent with that status are eligible.

Restrictions: The fund does not make grants to support direct service projects, unless they are of strategic interest as potentially scalable models; scholarship programs; film production; fundraising events; conferences; or individuals.

Geographic Focus: All States

Date(s) Application is Due: Jun 15

Contact: Administrator; (415) 348-1581; fax (415) 348-1584; info@3gf.org

Internet: http://www.3gf.org/index.html

Sponsor: Three Guineas Fund

153 Upper Terrace

San Francisco, CA 94117

Tides Foundation Grants 1819

The foundation actively promotes change toward a healthy society and channels its grantmaking to the following issue areas: arts, culture and alternative media; civic participation; death penalty abolishment; drug policy reform; economic development; economic and racial justice; environmental justice; gay, lesbian, bisexual, and transgender issues; HIV/AIDS; Native communities; peace strategies; women's empowerment and reproductive health; youth development and organizing; and violence prevention. The foundation prefers to fund creative, effective solutions to problems.

Requirements: Nonprofit organizations are eligible. Preference is given to nonprofits engaged in grassroots organizing.

Restrictions: Tides does not accept requests from universities, schools, individuals, or corporations; nor for capital campaigns, endowments, or film production.

Geographic Focus: All States

Amount of Grant: 1,000 - 7,000,000 USD

Samples: American Public Media (Saint Paul, MN)—to provide news coverage focused on global sustainability and the economy, $2.1 million.

Contact: Idelise Malave, Executive Director; (415) 561-6366; fax (415) 561-6401; imalave@tides.org

Internet: http://www.tidesfoundation.org/index_tf.cfm

Sponsor: Tides Foundation

P.O. Box 29903

San Francisco, CA 94129-0903

Todd Brock Family Foundation Grants 1820

Established in Texas in 2007, the Todd Brock Family Foundation offers support for educational programs, children, athletics, research, and community projects, as well Protestant agencies and churches. A formal application is required, and applicants should forward the entire proposal to the office. The Foundation rarely offers funding outside of Texas. There are no deadlines for submitting a completed proposal, and grants have most recently ranged from $300 to $250,000.

Geographic Focus: Texas

Samples: Memorial High School Boosters, Houston, Texas. $1,000 - funding for annual gold tournament; Legacy Christian Academy, Beaumont, Texas, $250,000 - for general operations; Yellowstone Academy, Houston, Texas, $25,000 - support for low-income children and families.

Contact: Todd O. Brock, President; (409) 833-6226; fax (409) 832-3019

Sponsor: Todd Brock Family Foundation

1670 E Cardinal Drive, P.O. Box 306

Beaumont, TX 77704-0306

Topeka Community Foundation Grants 1821

The foundation awards grants to Kansas nonprofits in its areas of interest, including arts and culture, early childhood education, education, environment, substance abuse services, children and youth services, family services, community development, and public affairs. Types of support include general operating support, continuing support, annual campaigns, capital campaigns, building construction/renovation, emergency funds, program development, seed money, scholarship funds and scholarships to individuals, and matching funds. The board meets bimonthly to consider requests.

Requirements: Grants are awarded to Topeka and Shawnee County, KS, nonprofit organizations.

Restrictions: Grants are not awarded to religious organizations for religious purposes or for scientific, medical, or academic research.

Geographic Focus: Kansas

Contact: Roger K. Viola, President; (785) 272-4804; fax (785) 272-4644; viola@topekacommunityfoundation.org

Internet: http://www.topekacommunityfoundation.org/page31525.cfm

Sponsor: Topeka Community Foundation

5431 SW 29th Street, Suite 300

Topeka, KS 66614

Town Creek Foundation Grants 1822

The foundation awards grants in four general areas: preservation and enhancement of the nation's environment and the monitoring of federal, state, and local officials and bodies responsible for the enforcement of legislation enacted to protect the environment; the dissemination, via public radio and television, of news and commentary; the search for ways to secure a peaceful and democratic society, supporting projects that challenge and redirect the military economy, reduce the risk of war, and promote a government responsive and accountable to its citizens; and the improvement of the quality of life and the opportunity for advancement for the people of Talbot County, MD, where such opportunities have been adversely affected by economic and social conditions. Types of support include continuing support, operating support, program development, seed money, and matching funds. The foundation will consider proposals at any time during the year. The foundation can be reached, customarily, on Mondays and Wednesdays.

Requirements: IRS 501(c)3 tax-exempt organizations are eligible. Social service grants are limited to nonprofits in Talbot County, Maryland.

Restrictions: The Foundation does not provide grants for the following: programs or organizations outside of the United States; individuals; primary and secondary schools; colleges or universities, except when some aspect of their work is an integral part of a program supported by the Foundation; hospitals or health care institutions; ministry or religious programs; endowment, capital or building fund campaigns, or the purchase of land and/or buildings; research or scholarship programs; conferences not part of a program supported by the Foundation; publication of books and periodicals; or visual or performing arts projects.

Geographic Focus: All States

Amount of Grant: 10,000 - 250,000 USD

Samples: American Rivers, Durham, North Carolina, $50,000 - renewal of "The Chesapeake Federal Policy Project"; Living on Earth / World Media Foundation, Somerville, Massachusetts, $125,000 - to produce, broadcast and distribute programming focusing on past, present and future efforts to restore the Chesapeake Bay; Wicomico Environmental Trust, Salisbury, Maryland, $50,000 - general support to continue to develop into a strong, sustainable organization that will have an effective, long-term impact on increasing public awareness of and advocacy for environmental protection of the natural resources of Wicomico County.

Contact: Stuart Alan Clarke, Executive Director; (410) 763-8171; fax (410) 763-8172; info@towncreekfdn.org or sclarke@towncreekfdn.org

Internet: http://www.towncreekfdn.org/tcfsite/tguides.html

Sponsor: Town Creek Foundation

121 N. West Street

Easton, MD 21601

Toyota Motor North America of New York Grants 1823

Toyota Motor North America offers grant funding nationally, focusing on three primary areas: the environment, safety, and education. National programs in these areas must have a broad reach by impacting several major U.S. cities, communities or groups. In the local New York City area, Toyota also focuses on those three major areas, and provides other local assistance as well, including arts and culture, civic and community, health and human services and leadership development. Toyota prefers to support programs, rather than sponsor events. Organizations must apply for each new grant requested, and subsequent funding is contingent upon evaluation of previous activities. The geographic scope is the continental U.S. for programs national in scope and the New York City area for community-based programs. Only online applications are accepted.

Requirements: Applicant organizations must have 501(c)3 tax-exempt status, be located within or serve population(s) either on a national scope or specifically in the New York City area, and present a proposal that satisfies the mission, guidelines and limitations of the corporation.

Restrictions: Toyota Motor North America of New York does not make grants for publications, lobbying activities, advertising, capital campaigns or endowments. Individuals are ineligible to apply. Toyota will not make grants to the following types of organizations: those not recognized as 501(c)3 by the Internal Revenue Service; those that practice discrimination by race, creed, color, sex, age or national origin; those that serve only their own memberships, such as fraternal organizations, labor organizations or religious groups; or political parties or candidates.

Geographic Focus: All States
Amount of Grant: 50,000 - 200,000 USD
Contact: Grants Administrator; (212) 223-0303; fax (212) 759-7670
Internet: http://www.toyota.com/about/philanthropy/guidelines/index.html
Sponsor: Toyota Motor North America
601 Lexington Avenue, 49th Floor
New York, NY 10022

TSYSF Team Grants   **1824**
Teemu Selänne, nicknamed "The Finnish Flash," is a Finnish professional ice
hockey winger. An offensive player known for his skill and speed, Selänne
has led the NHL in goal-scoring three times and has been named to the
league's First All-Star Team on two occasions. He has won the Stanley Cup
once with the Ducks in 2007. The Teemu Selänne Youth Sports Foundation
(TSYSF) provides financial, educational and inspirational opportunities for
children and their families through structured sports programs. Team grants
are available for youth athletic teams.
Requirements: The required grant application form must be filled out (available
at website) and submitted with copies of: documentation of any scholarships,
grants or fundraising revenues received by team and/or players and/or
projected revenue if not yet received; confirmed team travel schedule; and a
return envelope for the foundation's decision. Organizations with multiple
teams may submit just one application instead of one for each team within the
organization. There are no specific deadlines. Scholarship applications take a
minimum of eight weeks before the Board makes a decision.
Geographic Focus: All States
Contact: Administrator, (949) 544-3110; fax (949) 309-3845; info@tsysf.org
Internet: http://tsysf.org/tsysf-grant-scholarship-application/
Sponsor: Teemu Selänne Youth Sports Foundation
22431 Antonio Parkway, Suite B160-800
Rancho Santa Margarita, CA 92688

Turner B. Bunn, Jr. and Catherine E. Bunn Foundation Grants   **1825**
The Foundation, established in North Carolina in 2000, gives primarily to
children and youth services, Christian agencies and churches, educational
programs, and human services supporting residents of North Carolina. An
application form is not required, and applicants should submit the following:
brief history of organization and description of its mission; copy of IRS
Determination Letter; and a detailed description of project and amount of
funding requested. There are no annual deadlines, and applicants should
submit the entire proposal via mail.
Geographic Focus: North Carolina
Samples: Barton College Scholarship Fund, Wilson, North Carolina, $8,600;
Boys and Girls Club of Coastal Carolina, Morehead City, North Carolina,
$3,800; Hope Station Renovation, Wilson, North Carolina
Contact: Turner B. Bunn III; (252) 243-3136; tbb3@nc.rr.com
Sponsor: Turner B. Bunn, Jr. and Catherine E. Bunn Foundation
P.O. Box 3299
Wilson, NC 27895-3299

TWS Foundation Grants   **1826**
The foundation awards grants to eligible nonprofit organizations in its areas of
interest, including community development, arts, health care, public policy,
research, and human services. Types of support include general operating
support and scholarship funds. There are no application forms or deadlines.
Requirements: Nonprofit organizations, primarily in Connecticut, New York,
Rhode Island, and Texas, are eligible.
Geographic Focus: Connecticut, New York, Rhode Island, Texas
Amount of Grant: 100 - 230,000 USD
Samples: National Center for Policy Analysis (Dallas, TX)—$200,000;
Westerly Hospital Foundation (Westerly, RI)—$100,000; Philharmonic-
Symphony Society of New York (New York, NY)—$10,000.
Contact: Thomas Smith, Trustee
Sponsor: TWS Foundation
323 Railroad Avenue
Greenwich, CT 06830-6306

U.S. Bank Foundation Grants   **1827**
The Foundation contributes to the strength and vitality of communities
through charitable contributions. They seek to build strong partnerships
and lasting value in communities by supporting organizations that improve
the educational and economic opportunities of low- and moderate-income
individuals and families and enhance the cultural and artistic life of

communities. Funding priorities include: economic opportunity (including
affordable housing, self-sufficiency and economic development); education;
culture and artistic enrichment; and human services. Support is provided for
unrestricted general operating support, program support, capital support,
contributions of equipment and property. Application deadlines vary by state.
See website for states deadlines and state contacts.
Requirements: Applicants must be 501(c)3 not for profit organizations and
located in a community with a U.S. Bank office.
Restrictions: The Foundation will not provide funding for: organizations that are
501(c)3 not for profits; fraternal organizations, merchant associations, chamber
memberships or programs, or 501(c)4 or 6 organizations; section 509(a)3 supporting
organizations; fundraising events or sponsorships; "pass through" organizations
or private foundations; organizations outside U.S. Bancorp communities;
programs operated by religious organizations for religious purposes; political
organizations or organizations designed primarily to lobby; individuals; travel
and related expenses; endowment campaigns; deficit reduction; organizations
receiving primary funding from United Way; and organizations whose practices
are not in keeping with the company's equal opportunity policy.
Geographic Focus: Arizona, Arkansas, California, Colorado, Idaho, Illinois,
Iowa, Kansas, Kentucky, Minnesota, Missouri, Montana, Nebraska, Nevada,
New Mexico, North Dakota, Ohio, Oregon, South Dakota, Tennessee, Utah,
Washington, Wisconsin, Wyoming
Contact: Grants Administator; 612-659-2000
Internet: http://www.usbank.com/cgi_w/cfm/about/community_relations/
grant_guidelines.cfm
Sponsor: U.S. Bank Foundation
800 Nicollet Mall, 23rd Floor
Minneapolis, MN 55402

U.S. Department of Education American Overseas Research Centers 1828
This program provides grants to establish or operate overseas research centers
that promote postgraduate research, exchanges, and area studies. Grants may be
used to pay for all or a portion of the cost of establishing or operating a center or
program. Costs may include faculty and staff stipends and salaries; faculty, staff,
and student travel; operation and maintenance of overseas facilities; teaching
and research materials; the acquisition, maintenance, and preservation of library
collections; travel for visiting scholars and faculty members who are teaching or
conducting research; preparation for and management of conferences; and the
publication and dissemination of material for the scholars and general public.
Requirements: Eligible Applicants are Consortia of institutions of higher
education that: receive more than 50 percent of their funding from public
or private U.S. sources; have a permanent presence in the country in which
the center is located; and, are tax-exempt nonprofit organizations described
in Section 501(c)3 of the Internal Revenue Code. Note: Competitions for
funding are held every four years. The most recent competition: FY 2007.
Geographic Focus: All States
Date(s) Application is Due: Mar 15
Amount of Grant: 80,000 - 100,000 USD
Contact: Cheryl Gibbs, (202) 502-7634; cheryl.gibbs@ed.gov
Internet: http://www.ed.gov/programs/iegpsaorc/index.html
Sponsor: U.S. Department of Education
1990 K Street NW, 6th Floor
Washington, D.C. 20006-8521

Unilever US Grants   **1829**
The foundation awards grants to nonprofit organizations nationwide
in company-operating locations in the areas of civic affairs, education,
environment, health care, and social services. Capital grants are awarded
only to hospitals in plant communities. Types of support include general
operating grants and matching gifts. Applicants must submit a written
proposal; proposals are accepted throughout the year.
Requirements: 501(c)3 nonprofit organizations in company-operating areas
are eligible to apply.
Restrictions: Grants do not support religious, labor, political, or veterans'
organizations; individuals (except for employee-related scholarships); goodwill
advertising, fundraising events, or capital campaigns; or loans.
Geographic Focus: All States
Amount of Grant: 500 - 200,000 USD
Contact: Grants Administrator; (212) 894-2236; fax (212) 318-3600
Internet: http://www.unilever.com
Sponsor: Unilever United States Foundation
700 Sylvan Avenue
Englewood Cliffs, NJ 07632

Union Bank, N.A. Foundation Grants 1830

As part of its ten-year community committment, Union Bank has pledged to annually distribute at least two percent of its annual after-tax net profit to help meet the needs of the communities it serves, a commitment that has resulted in donations exceeding $72 million dollars during the first six years. The two-percent charitable commitment is achieved through contributions and sponsorships made directly by the bank and through grants and investments made by the Union Bank Foundation, a nonprofit public-benefit corporation which serves as an agent for the bank. Because of its belief that the long-term success of the Union Bank business-model is dependent upon the existence of healthy communities, Union Bank Foundation focuses its philanthropy on building innovative initiatives and partnerships to cultivate healthy communities, which it identifies as possessing the following characteristics: stable families with high rates of home ownership; availability of affordable housing; livable-wage job opportunities; accessible public transportation; convenient access to professional services (e.g., doctors, lawyers, and accountants); adequate public services (e.g., police, fire, and sanitation); safe public places to relax and recreate (e.g., parks, libraries, theaters); clean air and water supplies; a high level of civic engagement; a community constituency possessing diverse income levels; well-funded public schools; successful small business owners who live in the community; a variety of retail shops and restaurants; and traditional financial institutions providing access to capital in or adjacent to the community. With an eye toward being an agent of positive change in Union Bank communities, the foundation focuses on the following strategic program areas (targeting resources especially to benefit low- to moderate-income populations): Affordable Housing; Community Economic Development; Education; and Environment. In the area of Affordable Housing, the foundation focuses on for-sale housing, rental housing, special-needs housing, senior housing, transitional-living facilities, emergency/homeless shelters, youth housing, self-help housing, farm-worker housing, pre-development funding to nonprofit developers, and capacity building for nonprofit housing organizations. In the area of Community Economic Development area, the foundation focuses on small business development, individual development, and neighborhood development. Small business development includes micro-enterprise development and support, technical assistance/entrepreneurial training, organizations that promote access to capital for business or farms meeting Small Business Administration criteria, and job creation. Individual development includes job training/apprenticeship, welfare-to-work programs, wealth-accumulation/asset-building programs, life-skills training, financial-literacy/credit-counseling programs, mortgage credit counseling, business education, and intervention/prevention programs for at-risk youth. Neighborhood Development includes gang prevention/gang intervention programs, crime prevention, dispute resolution/mediation/violence prevention, reduction of liquor outlets, improved quality of food in local markets, childcare and daycare programs, drug- and alcohol-rehabilitation programs, independent living programs, organizational capacity building and funding for operating/administrative expenses, and community organizing to engage, inform and empower citizenry. In the area of Education, the foundation focuses on scholarship programs, tutoring programs, general education degree (GED) preparation, English as a second language (ESL) programs, computer education, support for the teaching profession, teacher training, literacy programs, parent education, visual- and performing-arts-organizations outreach programs, enrichment programs, and capacity-building. In the area of Environment the foundation focuses on brown-field remediation, science and education relevant to green building, energy upgrade and conservation, rehabilitation and cleanup, coastal/creek- and reserve-cleanup and preservation, urban green-space projects, environmental education, aquariums and museums, ecology and recycling centers, and state parks, nature centers, conservancy centers, botanical gardens, and wildlife centers. The Union Bank Foundation prefers program grants, but will consider requests for core operating support and/or capacity-building grants to support exceptional work within its strategic funding categories. The foundation considers applications at its bimonthly board meetings. Applications are accepted via an online application system accessible from the foundation website. Applicants must choose from three categories when they apply. These are requests for $1,000 or less, requests for $1001 to $25,000, and requests for over $25,000. Prospective applicants should review the foundation's application guidelines and instructions, which are available at the foundation website. Questions may be directed to the foundation officers listed on this page.

Requirements: 501(c)3 nonprofits in company-operating areas in California and the Pacific Northwest are eligible (e.g., San Diego, San Francisco, Los Angeles, Anaheim, Berkeley, Del Mar, Fresno, Irvine, Mission Grove, Pasadena, Sacramento, Salinas, San Jose, Santa Ana, and Torrance, California). A branch locator is available at the sponsor website.

Restrictions: The foundation does not support the following requests from the following entities or for the following items: individuals; veterans, military, fraternal, or professional organizations; political organizations or programs; service club activities; other intermediary foundations (i.e., foundations which, in turn, make grants to other charities); churches or religious groups (except separately incorporated community development corporations); educational institution operating funds; and individual elementary or secondary schools.

Geographic Focus: California, Oregon, Washington
Amount of Grant: 5,000 - 25,000 USD
Contact: J.R. Raines, Assistant Vice President; (619) 230-3105; charitablegiving@unionbank.com
Internet: https://www.unionbank.com/global/about/corporate-social-responsibility/foundation/foundation-grants.jsp
Sponsor: Union Bank Foundation
P.O. Box 45174
San Francisco, CA 94145-0174

Union Carbide Foundation Grants 1831

The foundation supports nonprofits in areas of company operations, including Danbury, CT; Kanawha Valley, WV; central New Jersey; Taft, LA; and Texas City and Seadrift, TX. Grants also are awarded outside of the United States. The majority of grant supports goes for restructuring elementary and secondary education: developing math and science programs, advancing technology through research, preparing women and minorities for technical careers, and environmental protection. Additional areas of consideration include health and social services, civic affairs, the environment, and higher education. Grants are awarded for general operations, emergency funds, in-kind gifts, and programs/projects. The board meets in the spring and fall to consider grant proposals.

Requirements: Nonprofits in company-operating areas in Connecticut, West Virginia, New Jersey, Louisiana, and Texas may apply.
Geographic Focus: Connecticut, Louisiana, New Jersey, Texas, West Virginia
Amount of Grant: 5,000 - 45,000 USD
Contact: Grants Administrator; (203) 794-2000
Internet: http://www.dow.com/facilities/namerica/texops/community/grants.htm
Sponsor: Union Carbide Foundation
39 Old Ridgebury Road, L-4
Danbury, CT 06817-0001

Union Pacific Foundation Community and Civic Grants 1832

The Foundation has a strong interest in promoting organizational effectiveness among nonprofits. To that end, this Foundation dedicates the majority of their grants to help nonprofit organizations build their capacity, increase their impact, and operate more efficiently and effectively. Grants are made primarily to proposals in the areas of community and civic, and health and human services. The community and civic grants category focuses on assisting community-based organizations and related activities that improve and enrich the general quality of life in the community. This category includes organizations such as aquariums, botanical gardens, children's museums, history/science museums, public libraries, public television and radio, and zoos.

Requirements: The Foundation will accept only online applications; printed copies of the application are not available and will not be accepted. Grants are made to institutions located in communities served by Union Pacific Corporation and its operating company Union Pacific Railroad Company.

Restrictions: The Foundation will not consider a request from or for: individuals; organizations/projects/programs that do not fit within the Foundation's funding priorities; organizations without a Section 501(c)3 public charity determination letter from the Internal Revenue Service; organizations that channel grant funds to third parties; organizations whose dominant purpose is to influence legislation or participate/intervene in political campaigns on behalf of or against any candidate for public office; organization/projects/programs for which the Foundation is asked to serve as the sole funder; organizations that already have an active multi-year Union Pacific Foundation grant; religious organizations for non-secular programs (i.e. programs which promote religious doctrine); organizational deficits; local affiliates of national health/disease-specific organizations; non-U.S.-based charities; organizations whose program activities are mainly international; elementary or secondary schools; athletic programs or events; donations of railroad equipment; conventions, conferences or seminars; fellowships or research; loans; labor organizations; or organizations whose programs have a national scope.

Geographic Focus: Arizona, Arkansas, California, Colorado, Idaho, Illinois, Iowa, Kansas, Louisiana, Minnesota, Missouri, Montana, Nebraska, Nevada,

New Mexico, Oklahoma, Oregon, Tennessee, Texas, Utah, Washington, Wisconsin, Wyoming
Date(s) Application is Due: Aug 15
Contact: Darlynn Myers; (402) 271-5600; fax (402) 501-2291; upf@up.com
Internet: http://www.up.com/found/grants.shtml
Sponsor: Union Pacific Foundation
1400 Douglas Street, Stop 1560
Omaha, NE 68179

Union Pacific Foundation Health and Human Services Grants 1833

The Foundation has a strong interest in promoting organizational effectiveness among nonprofits. To that end, this foundation dedicates the majority of their grants to help nonprofit organizations build their capacity, increase their impact, and operate more efficiently and effectively. Grants are made primarily to proposals in the areas of community and civic, and health and human services. The health and human services category assists organizations dedicated to improving the level of health care or providing human services in the community. Types of support include general operating support, continuing support, capital campaigns, building construction and renovation, curriculum development, equipment acquisition, program development, and matching funds.
Requirements: The Foundation will accept only online applications; printed copies of the application are not available and will not be accepted. Grants are made to institutions located in communities served by Union Pacific Corporation and its operating company Union Pacific Railroad Company.
Restrictions: The Foundation generally will not consider a request from or for: individuals; organizations/projects/programs that do not fit within the Foundation's funding priorities; organizations without a Section 501(c)3 public charity determination letter from the Internal Revenue Service; organizations that channel grant funds to third parties; organizations whose dominant purpose is to influence legislation or participate/intervene in political campaigns on behalf of or against any candidate for public office; organization/projects/programs for which the Foundation is asked to serve as the sole funder; organizations that already have an active multi-year Union Pacific Foundation grant; religious organizations for non-secular programs; organizational deficits; local affiliates of national health/disease-specific organizations; non U.S.-based charities; organizations whose program activities are mainly international; elementary or secondary schools; athletic programs or events; donations of railroad equipment; conventions, conferences or seminars; fellowships or research; loans; labor organizations; or organizations whose programs have a national scope.
Geographic Focus: Arizona, Arkansas, California, Colorado, Idaho, Iowa, Kansas, Louisiana, Minnesota, Missouri, Montana, Nebraska, Nevada, New Mexico, Oklahoma, Oregon, Tennessee, Texas, Utah, Washington, Wisconsin, Wyoming
Date(s) Application is Due: Aug 15
Contact: Darlynn Myers; (402) 271-5600; fax (402) 501-2291; upf@up.com
Internet: http://www.up.com/found/grants.shtml
Sponsor: Union Pacific Foundation
1400 Douglas Street, Stop 1560
Omaha, NE 68179

Union Square Award for Social Justice 1834

Recipients of the the Union Square Award have changed public policies, litigated landmark cases, created innovative models of service, and built important community institutions. Award recipients address concerns and build organizations that bring diverse communities into public discourse. Specifically, the Union Square Award supports work in the following areas: homelessness and hunger; HIV/AIDS prevention, education, and treatment; family and community development; youth leadership and organizing; economic self-sufficiency; and conflict resolution. The Award identifies organizations that have not yet received substantial funding and public recognition. It consists of a general operating support grant of $50,000, comprehensive technical assistance, and the opportunity to apply for re-grants to help build long-term organizational sustainability and community engagement.
Requirements: Candidates for the Award are identified through a nominations process. Nominations are reviewed throughout the year and may be submitted by anyone familiar with the organization's contributions and accomplishments. Submissions must describe the nominee's work and outline why the organization should be considered for an Award. Nominations may be made through the online form and are accepted online, by mail, or fax.
Restrictions: Only organizations in the New York City area are eligible for nomination.
Geographic Focus: New York

Amount of Grant: 50,000 USD
Contact: Denise Beek; (212) 213 6140; fax (212) 213-6372
Internet: http://www.unionsquareawards.org/awards-program
Sponsor: Union Square Awards
9 East 38th Street, 2nd floor
New York, NY 10016

United Technologies Corporation Grants 1835

United Technologies Corporation (UTC) grant-making is centered on the geographic regions where its employees live and work. Additionally the corporation focuses its grants on the following four areas of interest: supporting vibrant communities, building sustainable cities, advancing STEM education, and investing in emerging markets. A more detailed description of each area follows. UTC supports vibrant communities by supporting community revitalization initiatives, health and human service programs, and arts and culture. UTC defines sustainable cities as those that are safe and energy efficient to protect people, assets, and natural resources. In support of sustainable cities, UTC focuses on sustainable building practices, urban green space, and preservation of natural habitats to offset green-house gas emissions. To advance science, technology, engineering, and mathematics (STEM) education and to develop the next generation of engineers and scientists, UTC targets programs that include employee volunteerism to spark students' interest and inspire innovation, especially in minorities and women. As it invests in emerging markets, UTC seeks to lay a foundation for responsible citizenship from the inception of business expansion by supporting communities through employee engagement in China and India. Grant seekers have the option of applying either to UTC corporate headquarters or to a UTC business unit (Pratt & Whitney, Otis, Carrier, Sikorsky, UTC Fire & Security, and Hamilton Sundstrand). Either way, application is made online at the grant website given. Grant applications are accepted between January 1 and June 30 each year. Awardees will receive notification within one quarter of their application submission (or in the case of a UTC-business-unit application, in the first quarter of the calendar year in which funding will occur).
Requirements: 501(c)3 organizations in the U.S. and equivalent nonprofit organizations in the corporation's emerging markets are eligible.
Restrictions: Non-profit organizations may apply only once a year and to only one UTC business - either Corporate Headquarters or one of the UTC business units (see description section). UTC will not fund individuals, religious activities or organizations, municipalities, alumni groups (unless the award is distributed to the eligible higher education institution), booster clubs, sororities or fraternities, political groups, organizations engaged in or advocating illegal action, or any organization determined by UTC to have a conflict of interest. Additionally the corporation will not support fees for publication or merchandise.
Geographic Focus: All States, All Countries
Date(s) Application is Due: Jun 30
Contact: Andrew Olivastro, Manager, Community Affairs; (860) 728-7000; fax (860) 728-7041; contribu@corphq.utc.com
Internet: http://www.utc.com/Corporate+Responsibility/Community/Apply+for+a+grant
Sponsor: United Technologies Corporation
United Technologies Building
Hartford, CT 06101

Until There's a Cure Foundation Grants 1836

The foundation supports HIV/AIDS organizations throughout the United States. Grants focus on four priorities: care and services to meet the immediate needs of people living with HIV/AIDS, prevention education, vaccine development and research, and policy development and research. Types of support include capital campaigns, equipment acquisition, program development, and general operating support.
Requirements: 501(c)3 nonprofit U.S. organizations are eligible.
Restrictions: The foundation does not make grants for: for walk-a-thons, tournaments, or special events; to organizations with religious affiliations, unless the program is open to the entire community without regard to religious beliefs; for costs already incurred by an organization; or to fund general administration expenses of an organization rather than for specific projects and programs
Geographic Focus: All States
Date(s) Application is Due: Apr 29
Amount of Grant: 1,000 - 40,000 USD
Samples: AIDS Service Agency of North Carolina (NC)—$9000; AIDS Task Force Greater Cleveland (Cleveland, OH)—$41,818; AIDS Walk Atlanta (Atlanta, GA)—$15,000; Wisconsin AIDS Fund (WI)—$40,000.

Contact: Grants Administrator; (800) 888-6845 or (650) 332-3200; fax (650) 332-3210; grants@utac.org
Internet: http://www.utac.org
Sponsor: Until There's a Cure Foundation
560 Mountain Home Road
Redwood City, CA 94062

UPS Foundation Nonprofit Effectiveness Grants 1837

Since the launch of its Volunteer Impact Initiative in 1999, the UPS Foundation has focused on helping nonprofit organizations operate more effectively and efficiently. Widely regarded as a well-run company, UPS provides non-profits a variety of management and operational expertise in areas such as human resources management, technology, and other knowledge resources. This provides a robust hands on component that supports the foundation's philanthropy. It's the perfect example of taking the core assets of the corporation and applying them in a way that helps the independent sector address society's many challenges. Most nonprofit agencies face daunting tasks in raising funds, analyzing needs, managing volunteers and measuring results. With its employees and families volunteering more than 1.2 million hours of their time each year, UPS understands these challenges first hand. Helping nonprofit agencies more effectively manage them can further the impact of the services they provide to local communities. The UPS Foundation is currently focusing its resources on such areas as volunteer management, leadership development, social enterprise, and capacity building through new technology.
Requirements: IRS 501(c)3 tax-exempt organizations are eligible to apply.
Restrictions: The foundation does not award grants to individuals, religious organizations or theological functions, or church-sponsored programs limited to church members. Grants supporting capital campaigns, endowments, or operating expenses are seldom approved.
Geographic Focus: All States
Amount of Grant: 1,000 - 200,000 USD
Contact: Ken Sternad, President; (404) 828-6374; fax (404) 828-7435
Internet: http://responsibility.ups.com/UPS+Foundation/Focus+On+Giving/Nonprofit+Effectiveness
Sponsor: United Parcel Service (UPS) Foundation
55 Glenlake Parkway NE
Atlanta, GA 30328

Utah Arts Council General Support Grants 1838

These grants offer general, nonproject-oriented support to Utah's arts organizations that have already developed a full range of programming and staffs appropriate to their discipline. Support will permit organizations whose primary purpose and activities are the production and/or coordination of programs in the performing, visual, or literary arts to continue, strengthen, and expand current programs. Applicants are limited to requests of no more than 20 percent of their preceding year's actual income. Applicants for general support should not assume that this grants program will be ongoing or that funding is renewable if awarded one time.
Requirements: Established Utah arts organizations are eligible. Applicants must have a paid staff for administrative, technical, and artistic duties. Grants must be matched with at least an equal amount of cash. Applicants must submit a copy of an audit by an independent accounting firm for the preceding fiscal year.
Geographic Focus: Utah
Date(s) Application is Due: Oct 1
Contact: Sherry Waddingham, Grants Officer; (801) 236-7550 or (801) 236-7555; fax (801) 236-7556; swaddingham@utah.gov
Internet: http://www.arts.utah.org/grants
Sponsor: Utah Arts Council
617 E South Temple
Salt Lake City, UT 84102-1177

V.V. Cooke Foundation Grants 1839

The foundation awards grants to nonprofits in Kentucky, with an emphasis on support of the Baptist Church and religious organizations, schools and higher education institutions, and medical education. Children and youth organizations also receive support. Types of funding include: general operating support; continuing support; annual campaigns; capital campaigns; building construction and renovation; equipment acquisition; program development; and professorships. Application deadlines are January 15, April 15, July 15, and October 15.
Requirements: Grants are awarded to nonprofit organizations in Kentucky.
Restrictions: Grants are not awarded to individuals or for general endowment funds, scholarships, fellowships, or loans.
Geographic Focus: Kentucky

Date(s) Application is Due: Jan 15; Apr 15; Jul 15; Oct 15
Amount of Grant: 100 - 50,000 USD
Samples: Campbellsville U (Campbellsville, KY), Cumberland College (Williamsburg, KY), and Georgetown College (Georgetown, KY)—to raise funds for student financial aid and for capital projects, $90,000 jointly.
Contact: Theodore L. Merhoff, Executive Director; (502) 241-0303; merhoff@bellsouth.net or cookefdn@bellsouth.net
Sponsor: V.V. Cooke Foundation
P.O. Box 202
Pewee Valley, KY 40056-0202

Valentine Foundation Grants 1840

The foundation supports organizations and programs that empower women and girls to recognize and develop their full potential or that are making efforts to change established attitudes that discourage women and girls from realizing their potential. Grants are made to support effective fundamental change, including efforts to change attitudes, policies, and social patterns. Funding is generally split to offer equal support to programs for girls and programs for women. Programs for women must include advocacy for social change. A two-page descriptive letter must meet the listed application deadline date; if interested, the foundation will invite a full proposal.
Requirements: The foundation primarily funds nonprofits serving the greater Philadelphia area or that have a national focus.
Restrictions: The foundation will not fund scholarships, endowments, or capital.
Geographic Focus: All States
Date(s) Application is Due: Jun 30
Amount of Grant: 5,000 - 15,000 USD
Samples: Women's Campaign Internatational, Philadelphia, PA, $10,000—Global Awareness and Girl's Leadership Initiative pilot program; Women Thrive, Washington, DC, $5,000—general operating; Women's Way, Philadelphia, PA, $39,000—Education and Advocacy Initiative.
Contact: Alexandra Frazier, Director; (610) 642-4887; fax (610) 642-4887; info@valentinefoundation.org
Internet: http://www.valentinefoundation.org/guidelines.html
Sponsor: Valentine Foundation
300 Quarry Lane
Haverford, PA 19041

Valley Foundation Grants 1841

The foundation makes grants to nonprofit Santa Clara County, CA, organizations for programs and projects in the areas of medical services and health care for lower income households, the arts, seniors, and education. Types of support include research, general operating budgets, endowment, and matching funds. Applicants are required to submit a one- or two-page letter of intent describing the organization, need to be addressed, goals of the project, and total project budget. A full proposal will be requested if the project falls within the foundation's areas of interest. The board meets four times each year to consider requests. Letters of intent must be submitted electronically by the listed application deadlines.
Requirements: Nonprofits in Santa Clara County, California, may submit applications.
Restrictions: The foundation avoids grants that provide more than one-fourth of an organization's total budget in a 12-month period, usually expecting community and applicant commitment to a project through cost sharing. Applications cannot be accepted for the benefit of individuals, political purposes, or religious purposes.
Geographic Focus: California
Date(s) Application is Due: Feb 1; May 1; Jul 1; Nov 1
Amount of Grant: 10,000 - 100,000 USD
Contact: Contact; (408) 358-4545; fax (408) 358-4548; admin@valley.org
Internet: http://www.valley.org
Sponsor: Valley Foundation
16450 Los Gatos Boulevard, Suite 210
Los Gatos, CA 95032-5594

van Beuren Charitable Foundation Grants 1842

The foundation awards grants to eligible Rhode Island nonprofit organizations in its areas of interest, including environment, land resources, history/archeology, and human services. Types of support include building construction/renovation, capital campaigns, general operating grants, land acquisition, and program development. Proposal requirements and application are available on the Web site.

Requirements: Rhode Island nonprofit organizations serving Newport County are eligible.
Geographic Focus: Rhode Island
Date(s) Application is Due: Jun 15
Amount of Grant: 2,000 - 250,000 USD
Contact: John van Beuren; (401) 846-8167; fax (401) 849-6859; vbcfnd@aol.com
Internet: http://www.vbcf.net
Sponsor: Van Beuren Charitable Foundation
P.O. Box 4098
Middletown, RI 02842

Vancouver Foundation Disability Supports for Employment Grants   1843
The purpose of the Disability Supports for Employment Fund (DSEF) is to support new approaches to employment for people with disabilities that may complement or augment existing programs in the community. The intent of the program is to support initiatives by non-profit, charitable organizations that will promote the social and economic independence of individuals with disabilities.
Requirements: Grants are available to assist eligible organizations throughout B.C. who are working to increase employment opportunities and ultimately the rate of employment for persons with disabilities in their communities. Projects must demonstrate that they do not duplicate or replicate existing government-funded programs, supports and services for persons with disabilities. There is a two-stage application process. The first stage, submit a Letter of Inquiry, consisting of an informal proposal to determine basic suitability and eligibility. The second stage is a full application. If your Letter of Inquiry fits within the funding guidelines you will be sent a grant application form with specific instructions for completion. The deadline dates are June 18 for the Letter of Inquiry and August 13 for the grant application. Applicant will receives final decision approximately 12 weeks after deadline.
Geographic Focus: All States, Canada
Date(s) Application is Due: Jun 18
Contact: Andria Teather, Director; (604) 688-2204; fax (604) 688-4170; info@vancouverfoundation.ca
Internet: http://www.vancouverfoundation.ca/grants/specialprograms.htm
Sponsor: Vancouver Foundation
555 West Hastings Street, Suite 1200
Vancouver, BC V6B 4N6 Canada

Vanguard Public Foundation Grant Funds   1844
Vanguard provides funding to groups in northern California under four categories; the Social Justice Fund, the Community Institution Building Program, the Technical Assistance and Capacity Building Program, and the Social Justice Sabbatical Fund. Types of support include seed money, technical assistance, and operating expenses. Priority is given to projects without access to traditional funding sources because they may be thought to be risky, controversial, or of low priority. Vanguard strongly encourages coalitions that emphasize joint strategies and projects. Visit the web site for application guidelines. The next deadline to submit a proposal for the Social Justice Fund is October 14 and for a Social Justice Sabbatical is December 15. Annual deadline dates may vary; contact program staff for exact dates.
Requirements: Vanguard funds new or existing organizations involved in direct organizing or advocacy that are based in northern California (i.e., all counties north of Monterey). At the time a grant is made, an organization must either be tax-exempt or have a fiscal sponsor.
Restrictions: Vanguard does not fund capital campaigns or equipment purchase; organizations involved in direct services, research, or education, unless the proposed project clearly has an organizing component and cannot be supported within the general program budget; production costs for film; out-of-state travel; one-time conferences or events not integrally related to ongoing organizing; organizations with access to traditional funding sources and budgets of over $200,000 (unless the project for which funds are requested is unlikely to attract support because of its risky or controversial character); and costs already incurred.
Geographic Focus: California
Date(s) Application is Due: Oct 14; Dec 15
Contact: Grants Director; (415) 487-2111; fax (415) 487-2124; danielle@vanguardsf.org or vpf@vanguardsf.org
Internet: http://www.vanguardsf.org
Sponsor: Vanguard Public Foundation
383 Rhode Island Street, Suite 301
San Francisco, CA 94103

VDH Rescue Squad Assistance Fund Grants   1845
The Financial Assistance for Emergency Medical Services Grants Program, known as the Rescue Squad Assistance Fund (RSAF) Grant Program is a multi-million dollar matching grant program for Virginia governmental, non-profit EMS agencies and organizations to provide financial assistance based on a demonstrated need. Items eligible for funding include EMS equipment and vehicles, computers, EMS management programs, courses/classes and projects benefiting the recruitment and retention of EMS members. RSAF is primarily a reimbursement grant that requires the grantee to make the purchase for the awarded item(s) and then submit an invoice for reimbursement.
Requirements: Applicant must be a Virginia non-profit agency/organization or governmental organization involved in emergency medical service (ems); applicant must submit verification of its FIN. Verification can be provided in the following formats: copy of the original letter from the IRS issuing FIN, copy of the latest tax returns (1st page only), statement from the County Administrator or City Manager of the municipality stating that the application is non-profit or a government agency and verifies their FIN; applicant must submit a copy (1st page only) of the most recent Federal Tax Return from the IRS (Form 990); applicant must submit the Virginia Office of EMS Affirmation Page in its entirety including the original signature of the Authorized Agent, the Fiscal Officer (Treasurer) and the Operational Medical Director (OMD). All Grant Applications must be submitted via the Internet. The Affirmation page is due by September 15 with original signatures. Faxed Applications will not be accepted. Submit all grant information to: Office of Emergency Medical Services, Attn: Amanda Davis - Grant Manager, 109 Governor Street, Suite UB-55, Richmond, VA 23219.
Restrictions: Applications submitted with line items less then $500.00 will be disqualified.
Geographic Focus: Virginia
Date(s) Application is Due: Sep 15
Contact: Amanda Davis; (804) 864-7600; fax (804) 864-7580
Internet: http://www.vdh.virginia.gov/OEMS/Grants/index.htm
Sponsor: Virginia Department of Health
P.O. Box 2448
Richmond, VA 23218

Vernon K. Krieble Foundation Grants   1846
The Foundation was established in 1984 by the family of Professor Vernon K. Krieble, scientist, educator, inventor, and entrepreneur. Recognizing that the Foundation's assets are the product of a free and democratic society, the founders considered it fitting that those assets be used "to further democratic capitalism and the preserve and promote a society of free, educated, healthy and creative individuals." The Foundation offers support to non-profit charitable and educational organizations that demonstrate leadership in furthering the original objectives, so that future generations can aspire to and achieve their full potential in a free society. Awards range from $2,500 to $50,000. There are no deadlines.
Requirements: Nonprofit 501(c)3 organizations are eligible. Funding is provided only for those organizations and projects which involve public policy research and education on issues supporting the preservation, and in some cases the restoration, or freedom and democracy in the United States, according to the principles of the Founding Fathers. Written proposals should include a summary of the project, the project budget, the amount requested, the qualifications of individuals involved, and a copy of the organization's Internal Revenue Service determination letter.
Geographic Focus: All States
Samples: Foundation for West Hartford Schools, West Hartford, Connecticut, $2,500 - general support; Leadership Program of the Rockies, Denver, Colorado, $50,000 - general support; and Atlas Economic Research Foundation, Arlington, Virginia, $25,000 - general support.
Contact: Helen E. Krieble, President; (303) 758-3956; fax (303) 488-0068
Internet: http://www.krieble.org/grants
Sponsor: Vernon K. Krieble Foundation
1777 S Harrison Street, Suite 807
Denver, CO 80210

Viacom Foundation Grants (Formerly CBS Foundation)   1847
The purpose of the foundation is to strengthen the communities in which Viacom employees and audiences live and work. Grants are awarded to nonprofit organizations in the areas of arts & culture, children/youth/family, diversity, education, environment, health/medical, industry, social/civic/human services. Types of support include general operating grants, matching gifts, continuing support, annual campaigns, capital campaigns, curriculum development, program grants, and scholarships to children of Viacom employees only. Grants

are made through corporate contributions and employee matching gifts to selected nonprofit organizations on a one-to-one basis.

Requirements: To submit an application send a proposal outlining project and expected benefit(s), copy of IRS 501(c)3 determination letter, financial plan, list of board of directors and officers, and a copy of latest audited financial statements.

Restrictions: The program does not make loans or grants for advertising, endowments, or for capital costs including construction and renovation. Individuals are not eligible.

Geographic Focus: All States

Contact: Karen Zatorski, Vice President, Public Affairs; (212) 975-8552

Internet: http://www.viacom.com/fundingoverview.jhtml

Sponsor: Viacom Foundation

51 West 52nd Street

New York, NY 10019

Victor E. Speas Foundation Grants 1848

The Victor E. Speas Foundation was established to provide medical care for the needy, to further medical research, and to support and promote quality educational, cultural, human-services, and health-care programming. In the area of arts, culture, and humanities, the foundation supports programming that: fosters the enjoyment and appreciation of the visual and performing arts; strengthens humanities and arts-related education programs; provides affordable access; enhances artistic elements in communities; and nurtures a new generation of artists. In the area of education, the foundation supports programming that: promotes effective teaching; improves the academic achievement of, or expands educational opportunities for, disadvantaged students; improves governance and management; strengthens nonprofit organizations, school leadership, and teaching; and bolsters strategic initiatives of area colleges and universities. In the area of health, the foundation supports programming that improves the delivery of health care to the indigent, uninsured, and other vulnerable populations and addresses health and health-care problems that intersect with social factors. In the area of human services, the foundation funds programming that: strengthens agencies that deliver critical human services and maintains the community's safety net and helps agencies respond to federal, state, and local public policy changes. In the area of community improvement, the foundation funds capacity-building and infrastructure-development projects including: assessments, planning, and implementation of technology for management and programmatic functions within an organization; technical assistance on wide-ranging topics, including grant writing, strategic planning, financial management services, business development, board and volunteer management, and marketing; and mergers, affiliations, or other restructuring efforts. Grant requests for general operating support and program support will be considered. Grants from the foundation are one year in duration. Application materials are available for download at the grant website. There are no application deadlines for the Victor E. Speas Foundation. Proposals are reviewed on an ongoing basis.

Requirements: Applicants must have 501(c)3 tax-exempt status and serve the residents of Kansas City, Missouri. Two copies of the completed application must be mailed.

Restrictions: Grant requests for capital support will not be considered. The trust does not support requests from individuals, organizations attempting to influence policy through direct lobbying, or any political campaigns.

Geographic Focus: Missouri

Samples: Childrens Mercy Hospital Foundation, Kansas City, Missouri, $100,000, to fund research and clinical trials of reformulated adult drugs to benefit pediatric patients with rare and neglected blood and other cancers; Open Options, Kansas City, Missouri, $25,000, United Cerebral Palsy of Greater Kansas City technology upgrade; Metropolitan Community Colleges Foundation, Kansas City, Missouri, $50,000, for medical equipment for the Health Science Institute training facility.

Contact: Spence Heddens; (816) 292-4301; Spence.heddens@baml.com

Internet: https://www.bankofamerica.com/philanthropic/fn_search.action

Sponsor: Victor E. Speas Foundation

1200 Main Street, 14th Floor, P.O. Box 219119

Kansas City, MO 64121-9119

Victoria Foundation Grants 1849

The foundation concentrates on addressing the educational and socioeconomic challenges within the city of Newark and pressing environmental concerns throughout New Jersey. Five major goals of the foundation are to foster community and professional leadership, support capacity-building efforts of nonprofits, enhance the effectiveness of community institutions, encourage community collaborations, and achieve racial and ethnic equity. Victoria's

grantmaking activities are concentrated in the areas of education, environment, neighborhood development and urban revitalization, and youth and families. Types of support include general operating support, continuing support, seed money grants, building and renovations, matching funds, scholarship funds, projects/programs, research, consulting services, and technical assistance. Grants generally are for one year, with possible renewal. The foundation's trustees meet in June and November to review grant applications. Elementary and secondary schools are asked to submit proposals by March 1 for funding for the next school year. Specific guidelines for elementary and secondary schools are available upon request. Receipt of proposals will be acknowledged within two weeks.

Requirements: The foundation funds 501(c)3 tax-exempt organizations in New Jersey.

Geographic Focus: New Jersey

Date(s) Application is Due: Feb 1; Mar 1; Aug 1

Amount of Grant: 5,000 - 200,000 USD

Samples: Bank Street College of Education (New York, NY)—to develop two New Beginnings demonstration schools and at least six demonstration classrooms in two primary schools in Newark, NJ, $350,000.

Contact: Catherine McFarland, Executive Officer; (973) 748-5300; fax (973) 748-0016; CatherineMcFarland@victoriafoundation.org

Internet: http://www.victoriafoundation.org/how_guidelines.html

Sponsor: Victoria Foundation

946 Bloomfield Avenue, 2nd Floor

Glen Ridge, NJ 07028

Vigneron Memorial Fund Grants 1850

The Vigneron Memorial Fund was established in 1959 to support charitable organizations that work to improve the lives of physically disabled children and adults. Preference is given to charitable organizations that serve the people of the city of Providence or the town of Narragansett, Rhode Island. Capital requests that fund handicapped assistive devices (wheelchairs, walkers, etc.) or adaptive equipment (lift installation, ramp installation, etc.) are strongly encouraged. Grant requests for general operating or program support will also be considered. The majority of grants from the Vigneron Memorial Fund are one year in duration. Applicants must apply online at the grant website. Applicants are strongly encouraged to do the following before applying: review the downloadable state application procedures for additional helpful information and clarifications; review the downloadable online-application guidelines at the grant website; review the foundation's funding history (link is available from the grant website); review the online application questions in advance; and review the list of required attachments. These will generally include: a list of board members, financial statements (audited, reviewed, or compiled by independent auditor); an organization summary; a list of other funding sources; an IRS Determination letter; and other required documents. All attachments must be uploaded in the online application as PDF, Word, or Excel files. The Vigneron Memorial Fund shares a mission and grantmaking focus with the John D. & Katherine A. Johnston Foundation. Both foundations have the same proposal deadline date of 11:59 p.m. on April 1. Applicants will be notified of grant decisions before May 31.

Requirements: Applicants must have 501(c)3 tax-exempt status.

Restrictions: The fund does not support requests from individuals, organizations attempting to influence policy through direct lobbying, or any political campaigns.

Geographic Focus: Rhode Island

Date(s) Application is Due: Apr 1

Contact: Emma Greene; (617) 434-0329; emma.m.greene@baml.com

Internet: https://www.bankofamerica.com/philanthropic/fn_search.action

Sponsor: Vigneron Memorial Fund

225 Franklin Street, 4th Floor, MA1-225-04-02

Boston, MA 02110

Virginia Commission for the Arts General Operating Grants 1851

The commission awards grants for general operating support to assist organizations of artistic merit in fulfilling their missions by providing funds to maintain their stability and encourage their advancement. Funds may be awarded to cover general operating expenses, special projects, construction or renovation costs, and reserve funds. Most general operating support grants are awarded for a two-year period. Organizations may apply for 10 percent of their previous year's cash income for each year of the grant period. Application materials are available on the Web site.

Requirements: Virginia organizations whose primary purpose is the arts (excluding units of government and educational institutions and their private companion foundations), that have an independent governing board, and that are exempt from federal income tax under Section 501(c)3 of the Internal Revenue Code are eligible to apply. Organizations must be incorporated for at least a year before applying for General Operating Support and must have completed a season of programs.

Geographic Focus: Virginia
Date(s) Application is Due: Mar 1
Amount of Grant: 500 - 150,000 USD
Contact: Cathy Welborn, Program Coordinator; (804) 225-3132; fax (804) 225-4327; catherine.welborn@arts.virginia.gov
Internet: http://www.arts.virginia.gov/grants/infrastructure/support_artorg.html
Sponsor: Virginia Commission for the Arts
223 Governor Street, 2nd Floor
Richmond, VA 23219-2010

Virginia Commission for the Arts Project Grants   1852

The primary purposes of Virginia Commission for the Arts Project Grants are: to increase access to high quality arts for all Virginians; to increase opportunities for artists to create and present their work; and to expand arts education opportunities for young people. This grant program supports a wide variety of arts activities and is open to any not-for-profit organization presenting the arts. It is one of the Commission's most competitive grant programs. Generally, the Commission will not support the same project for more than three years. The Commission will favor applications for the creation and/or production of new works by Virginia artists. Eligible activities include: commissions of new works of art; performances, exhibitions, film or video screenings, readings, and publication of literature; operating support for new and emerging arts organizations (organizations whose primary purpose is the arts, that are three years old or less, and that had a previous year's income of less than $50,000); artist residencies; workshops, seminars, classes; guest artists; educational programs of arts organizations; classes or other training in all disciplines of the arts; summer arts camps; scholarships for young people for arts instruction; arts festivals; architectural feasibility studies; surveys and planning; conferences; information and advisory services to artists and arts organizations; space and equipment for artists; touring events from out of state; and transportation for school children, older adults, and other special groups to attend arts events.
Requirements: Virginia not-for-profit organizations, units of government, or educational institutions that meet the basic eligibility criteria are eligible. Each department of a college or university is considered to be a separate applicant. Organizations receiving general operating support grants will not be eligible for Project Grants.
Geographic Focus: Virginia
Date(s) Application is Due: Mar 1
Contact: Cathy Welborn, Program Coordinator; (804) 225-3132; fax (804) 225-4327; catherine.welborn@arts.virginia.gov
Internet: http://www.arts.virginia.gov/grants/accessible/project_grants.html
Sponsor: Virginia Commission for the Arts
223 Governor Street, 2nd Floor
Richmond, VA 23219-2010

**Virginia Environmental Endowment Kanawha and Ohio River   1853
Valleys Program**

Currently limited to the Kanawha and Ohio River Valleys of Kentucky and West Virginia, this program supports research, education, and community action on water quality and the effects of water pollution on public health and the environment. Emphasis is given to collaboration by citizens, government, and industry to develop effective public policies and to increasing public participation in water quality monitoring and watershed management.
Requirements: Constructive, result-oriented projects that are conducted by existing nonprofit organizations are funded. Activities that unite business, government, and civic interests for environmental improvement are encouraged, as are projects that serve as models for other communities. Organizations must be in Kentucky or West Virginia.
Geographic Focus: Kentucky, West Virginia
Date(s) Application is Due: Jun 15
Samples: Kentucky Waterways Alliance (Munfordville, KY)—for a statewide citizens' group that works to monitor and protect water quality and to raise public awareness about related issues, $40,000 over two years; West Virginia Rivers Coalition (Elkins, WV)—to develop scientifically sound criteria for determining the level of nutrients in West Virginia rivers, $17,200.
Contact: Gerald McCarthy, Executive Director; (804) 644-5000; fax (804) 644-0603; info@vee.org
Internet: http://www.vee.org/programs.cfm
Sponsor: Virginia Environmental Endowment
1051 E Cary Street, 3 James Center, Suite 1400, P.O. Box 790
Richmond, VA 23218-0790

Virginia Environmental Endowment Mini Grants   1854

Mini grants are awarded in the areas of environmental education, and water protection quality. The focus of environmental education grants is to increase training in environmental education for educators and school administrators and to expand the use of existing educational resources (curricula, multi-media programs, publications, field studies) in schools and community programs. Projects must focus on water quality, land use, and/or sustainable communities; and must include training for teachers/project leaders and service learning activities that engage students and community members in research to solve environmental problems. Water quality protection grants are awarded to increase public involvement in the restoration and protection of Virginia's water resources through water quality testing and monitoring, pollution prevention, and public education. Matching funds from other sources are usually required. Mini grants may include support for training, research, data collection and analysis, monitoring equipment, supplies, curriculum materials, publications, printing, and promotion. Requests for computer and multi-media equipment and instructional software must be accompanied by specific plans for related teacher training, curriculum integration, and long-term maintenance. Guidelines are available online.
Requirements: Primary, intermediate, and secondary schools (public and private), as well as nongovernmental, nonprofit community organizations in Virginia, are eligible to apply.
Restrictions: Local, state, and federal government agencies and programs are not eligible. Grants will not be provided for salaries or benefits of school personnel or for field trips outside Virginia. Grants will not be awarded for political action programs, capital drives and building funds, boats, scholarships, endowments, lawsuits and litigation, or overhead costs.
Geographic Focus: Virginia
Date(s) Application is Due: Jun 15; Dec 1
Amount of Grant: 1,000 - 5,000 USD
Samples: Fishburn Park Elementary School (Roanoke, VA)—for curriculum programs, teacher training, and habitat design in wetlands and water protection, $4425 matched by $3955; Turner Ashby High School (Bridgewater, VA)—for water quality education programs, $3483 matched by $4347.
Contact: Gerald McCarthy, Executive Director; (804) 644-5000; fax (804) 644-0603; info@vee.org
Internet: http://www.vee.org/programs.cfm
Sponsor: Virginia Environmental Endowment
1051 E Cary Street, 3 James Center, Suite 1400, P.O. Box 790
Richmond, VA 23218-0790

Virginia Environmental Endowment Virginia Program Grants   1855

The program focuses specifically on improving the quality of the environment for the direct benefit of the citizens of the Commonwealth of Virginia. Emphasis is given to the following programs: pollution prevention, natural resources conservation, sustainable communities, and environmental education; to enable citizens to identify local environmental problems, develop creative solutions, and share results with other communities; and to support legal research and education on other policies and laws that affect Virginia's environment. Types of support include operating budgets, continuing support, seed grants, matching funds, scholarship funds, project development, research, conferences and seminars, and publications. Applicants must submit four copies of full proposals for consideration. A copy of the annual report may be requested, wherein explicit application instructions are listed.
Requirements: Eligible for funding are constructive, result-oriented projects that are conducted by existing Virginia nonprofit organizations. Activities that unite business, government, and civic interests for environmental improvement are encouraged, as are projects that serve as models for other communities.
Geographic Focus: Virginia
Date(s) Application is Due: Jun 15; Dec 1
Samples: Nature Conservancy-Virginia Program Office (Charlottesville, VA)—for its campaign to increase financing for Virginia's natural resources, $90,000; Shenandoah Valley Pure Water Forum (Harrisonburg, VA)—to help implement a user-friendly resource on technical and scientific data related to water quality and quantity in the Shenandoah Valley, $24,344; Rivanna Conservation Society (Palmyra, VA)—to protect Virginia's Rivanna River and its tributaries and to increase the society's membership and member participation, $15,000 over two years.
Contact: Gerald McCarthy; (804) 644-5000; fax (804) 644-0603; info@vee.org
Internet: http://www.vee.org/programs.cfm
Sponsor: Virginia Environmental Endowment
1051 E Cary Street, 3 James Center, Suite 1400, P.O. Box 790
Richmond, VA 23218-0790

Visiting Nurse Foundation Grants 1856

The foundation awards grants in support of home- and community-based health care for the medically underserved in Cook and the collar counties of Lake, McHenry, DuPage, Kane and Will, with a focus on Chicago. Priority areas are home health care services; prevention and health promotion; and early intervention. Preference is given to programs using nurses to provide the care. Types of support include program, capital, and general operating grants. Letters of intent should be submitted by deadline dates listed, and full proposals will be by invitation only.
Requirements: Nonprofit organizations in Cook, Lake, McHenry, DuPage, Kane, and Will counties of Illinois are eligible.
Restrictions: No grants are made to individuals.
Geographic Focus: Illinois
Date(s) Application is Due: Jan 19; Apr 19; Oct 20
Amount of Grant: 15,000 - 80,000 USD
Contact: Robert N. DiLeonardi, Executive Director; (312) 214-1521; fax (312) 214-1529; info@vnafoundation.net
Internet: http://www.vnafoundation.net
Sponsor: Visiting Nurse Association Foundation
20 N Wacker Drive, Suite 3118
Chicago, IL 60606

Vulcan Materials Company Foundation Grants 1857

The company foundation supports nonprofit organizations in company-operating areas. Grants support a broad array of programs and projects in the areas of health and welfare, community and economic development, education (including an employee matching grants program), the environment, law and justice, women and children, arts and humanities, minorities, and literacy. Requests will be considered for support of general operating expenses, capital and annual campaigns, scholarship funds, research, continuing support, and seed money. There are no application deadlines.
Requirements: The foundation awards grants only to public charities and units of government, such as public schools and parks. A public charity is any Section 501(c)3 charitable organization that is not a private foundation because it meets one of the three internal Revenue Code definitions: 509(a)1, 509(a)2 or 509(a)3.
Restrictions: The foundation does not fund individuals; organizations outside the United States; telephone or mass-mail appeals, political organizations; testimonial dinners; sectarian religious activities; organizations which have discriminatory practices; or athletic, labor, fraternal and veterans associations. The Foundation generally will not consider requests from organizations located in communities where Vulcan has no operations, offices or employees.
Geographic Focus: Alabama, Arizona, Arkansas, California, Florida, Georgia, Illinois, Indiana, Iowa, Kansas, Kentucky, Louisiana, Maryland, Mississippi, Missouri, New Mexico, North Carolina, Pennsylvania, South Carolina, Tennessee, Texas, Virginia, Wisconsin
Amount of Grant: Up to 28,000,000 USD
Samples: Auburn U Foundation (Auburn U, AL)—for scholarships and fellowships, $45,000; Family and Child Services (Birmingham, AL)—for youth programs, $20,000; Metropolitan Arts Council (Birmingham, AL)—for general support, $79,233.
Contact: Program Contact; (205) 298-3222; giving@vmcmail.com
Internet: http://www.vulcanmaterials.com/social.asp?content=guidelines
Sponsor: Vulcan Materials Company Foundation
P.O. Box 385014
Birmingham, AL 35238-5014

W.P. and H.B. White Foundation Grants 1858

The foundation awards grants to nonprofits in the metropolitan area of Chicago, IL, for social services; early-childhood, elementary, higher, and adult education; and health. Types of support include general operating budgets, continuing support, annual campaigns, building funds, capital campaigns, and special projects. The board meets in March, June, September, and December to consider requests.
Requirements: Only Illinois organizations are eligible to apply.
Geographic Focus: Illinois
Date(s) Application is Due: Feb 1; May 1; Aug 1; Nov 1
Amount of Grant: 10,000 - 30,000 USD
Samples: Austin Career Education Ctr (Chicago, IL)—for operating support, $12,000; Greater Chicago Food Depository (Chicago, IL)—for operating support, $20,000; Roosevelt U (Chicago, IL)—for program support, $10,000.
Contact: M. Margaret Blandford, Executive Director; (847) 446-1441
Sponsor: W.P. and H.B. White Foundation
540 Frontage Road, Suite 3240
Northfield, IL 60093

W.W. Smith Charitable Trust Grants 1859

The trust awards grants regionally in its areas of interest, including basic medical research dealing with cancer, AIDS, and heart disease; scholarship programs for undergraduate students at four-year universities and colleges; and proposals that address specifically food, clothing, and shelter for children and the aged. Resources are concentrated in areas where the most need can be discerned and where government or private assistance has not been available. Types of support include capital projects, challenge/matching grants, general operating grants, program grants, and research grants. Requests for grants for food, clothing, and shelter for children and the aged are considered throughout the year. Application deadlines are June 15 for cancer and AIDS research; and September 15 for heart research. Grants may be for more than one year but not for more than three years.
Requirements: Grant recipients are limited to organizations within the five-county area of Pennsylvania including Buck, Chester, Delaware, Montgomery, and Philadelphia Counties. Organizations must be tax-exempt and not classified as private foundations or private operating foundations.
Restrictions: After three consecutive years of funding, at least two years must elapse before further applications from the organization may be considered.
Geographic Focus: Pennsylvania
Date(s) Application is Due: Jun 15; Sep 15
Amount of Grant: 15,000 - 84,000 USD
Samples: La Salle U (Philadelphia, PA)—for financial aid for students, $98,000; Philadelphia College of Bible (Langhorne, PA)—for financial aid for students, $58,000.
Contact: Frances Pemberton; (610) 397-1844; fax (610) 397-1680
Internet: http://www.wwsmithcharitabletrust.org
Sponsor: W.W. Smith Charitable Trust
200 Four Falls Corporate Center, Suite 300
West Conshohocken, PA 19428

W. Waldo and Jenny Lynn M. Bradley Foundation Grants 1860

Established in Georgia in 1997 by W. Waldo and Jenny Lynn Bradley, the Foundation's primary fields of interest include higher education, hospitals, the arts, and Protestant agencies and churches. With a geographic focus in Georgia and North Carolina, the major type of funding is general operating support. There are no specific application forms or deadlines, and applicants should forward a two- to three-page letter outlining the need and overall annual operating budget of the organization. A copy of the organization's 501(c)3 letter or church status proof should be included.
Geographic Focus: Georgia, North Carolina
Amount of Grant: 500 - 10,000 USD
Samples: Bascom-Louise Gallery Corporation, Highlands, North Carolina, $5,000 - general operating support; Community Foundation of Western North Carolina, Highlands, North Carolina, $1,000 - general operating support; Wesley Monumental United Methodist Church, Savannah, Georgia, $10,000 - general operating support.
Contact: W. Waldo Bradley, President; (912) 447-7000
Sponsor: W. Waldo and Jenny Lynn M. Bradley Foundation
204 Old West Lathrop Avenue, P.O. Box 1408
Savannah, GA 31402-1408

Wallace Global Fund Grants 1861

The Wallace Global Fund is guided by the vision of the late Henry A. Wallace, former Secretary of Agriculture and Vice-President under Franklin D. Roosevelt. Committed to serving the general welfare, his life exemplified farsightedness, global vision, and receptivity to new ideas. The Fund supports activities at the global and national level, and will consider significant local or regional initiatives offering the potential to leverage broader national or global impact. It will consider proposals for either core or project-specific support. It does not fund purchase of land, capital construction, profit-making businesses, debt reduction, endowment campaigns, fundraising drives/events, or scholarships, tuition assistance or other forms of personal financial aid. Grants are being reviewed on a quarterly basis in March, June, September and December.
Requirements: Applicants based in the United States must be registered 501(c)3 non-profit educational organizations. Applicants based outside the United States must show 501(c)3 equivalency under U.S. law and, if invited to submit a proposal, will be asked to sign an affidavit stating this equivalency. Potential grantees without 501(c)3 status will be asked for further documentation regarding the charitable purpose of the activity.
Restrictions: Grants are not made to: individuals; universities; for-profit organizations; endowments; capital fund projects; scholarships; conferences; books or magazines; building construction; or travel (not including project-

related travel). The fund does not support film or video projects, the acquisition of land, or grants intended to support candidates for political office.
Geographic Focus: All States
Amount of Grant: 2,000 - 400,000 USD
Samples: Inter-American Association for Environmental Defense, Oakland, California, $45,000 - project support to combat violations of environmental and human rights law associated with Brazil's Belo Monte hydroelectric dam as well as other large dams in Mexico and Panama; As You Sow, San Francisco, California, $150,000 - project support to launch a major progressive shareholder advocacy campaign focused on coal divestment.
Contact: Ellen Dorsey, Executive Director; (202) 452-1530; fax (202) 452-0922; contact@wgf.org
Internet: http://www.wgf.org/grants
Sponsor: Wallace Global Fund
1990 M Street NW, Suite 250
Washington, D.C. 20036

Walt Disney Company Foundation Grants   1862
The foundation funds medical and health services, health and welfare of children, youth activities, higher education, community funds, music, and cultural arts in Los Angeles and Orange Counties in California and Orange and Osceola Counties in Florida. Types of support include general operating support, continuing support, annual campaigns, capital campaigns, program development, scholarship funds, fellowships, and employee-related scholarships. Previous grants have supported downtown revitalization in both New York City, where Disney redeveloped an old Times Square theater, and Los Angeles, where support has been given for a new music hall that will be home to the Los Angeles Philharmonic Orchestra.
Requirements: 501(c)3 organizations in California and Florida may apply.
Restrictions: Disney will not make grants for scholarships, religious organizations, building campaigns, start-up campaigns, seed purposes, research, loans, conferences, general fund drives, annual charitable appeals, and political purposes.
Geographic Focus: California, Florida, New York
Amount of Grant: 1,000 USD
Samples: Boys and Girls Clubs of America (Atlanta, GA)—for the group's 2006 Centennial Celebration and to support clubs in Southern California and central Florida, $3 million.
Contact: Tillie Baptie; (818) 560-1006; fax (818) 563-5271
Internet: http://disney.go.com/disneyhand/contributions/wdcfoundation.html
Sponsor: Walt Disney Company Foundation
500 S Buena Vista Street
Burbank, CA 91521-0987

Walter and Elise Haas Fund Grants   1863
The mission of the fund is to help build a healthy, just, and vibrant society in which people feel connected to and responsible for their community. The fund supports nonprofit organizations in its areas of interest, including the arts—arts education, preservation of cultural heritage, cultural commons, and the Creative Fund; economic security—incomes, assets, and economic development; Jewish life—promoting diversity, creative expression, building partnerships, and new leadership; education—youth leadership, parent organizing, community partnerships, and school partnerships with the community; and other grantmaking interests. Types of support include operating budgets, technical assistance, continuing support, seed money, land acquisition, emergency funds, capital campaigns, building funds, special projects, equipment, matching funds, and endowment funds. There are no application deadlines. Submit an application cover sheet with the proposal.
Requirements: 501(c)3 tax-exempt organizations that are not classified as 509(a) private foundations, fiscal sponsors meeting these classifications, and governmental entities are eligible. Applicant organization must be based in or managing significant activities in San Francisco or Alameda County. Within Alameda County, the fund places the highest priority on projects in Oakland and Berkeley. The Jewish Life program area's geographic focus extends to the broader Bay Area. At present, the Creative Work Fund considers applications from Alameda, Contra Costa, San Francisco, and Solano counties.
Restrictions: As a general rule, the fund does not provide grants to individuals or to for-profit entities; for general fundraising benefits and events; for endowment campaigns (Rare exceptions may be made for organizations that have a long-standing relationship to the fund's legacy or when endowment goals are incorporated into a larger capital campaign.); for the creation of a film or video, or of original creative art work, except through the Creative Work Fund; or for scholarships or fellowships.

Geographic Focus: California
Contact: Pamela David, Executive Director; (415) 398-4474
Internet: http://www.haassr.org/html/current_programs/index.cfm
Sponsor: Walter and Elise Haas Fund
1 Lombard Street, Suite 305
San Francisco, CA 94111-1130

Walter L. Gross III Family Foundation Grants   1864
The foundation awards grants to eligible Ohio and Kentucky nonprofit organizations in its areas of interest, including animals and wildlife, Christian churches and organizations, community outreach programs, education, environment, health care and medical, and social services. Grants are considered on a case-by-case basis and have been awarded to support building construction/renovation and general operating support. There are no application forms or deadlines with which to adhere, and applicants should begin by contacting the office directly.
Requirements: Ohio and Kentucky 501(c)3 nonprofits are eligible to apply.
Geographic Focus: Kentucky, Ohio
Amount of Grant: 1,000 - 20,000 USD
Samples: Habitat for Humanity, Cincinnati, Ohio—for general support, $10,000; Miami Uuniversity Foundation, Oxford, Ohio—for general support, $300,000; Our Daily Bread, Cincinnati, Ohio—for general support, $2,000.
Contact: Walter L. Gross III, President; (513) 785-6060 or (513) 785-6072; fax (513) 683-9467
Sponsor: Walter L. Gross III Family Foundation
9435 Waterstone Boulevard, Suite 390
Cincinnati, OH 45249-8227

Walter S. Johnson Foundation Grants   1865
The foundation invests in programs to help children and youth throughout northern California, with particular interest in the San Francisco Bay area and in Washoe County, Nevada. The foundation's grants reflect one or more of three goals: ensure the well-being of children and youth, strengthen public education, and assist young people in the transition to adulthood. To strengthen public education, grants are made for the professional development of educators—especially recruitment, preparation, and support of new teachers. It also helps reform how schools prepare students for college. In supporting youth in their transition to adulthood, grants are made for school-to-career training, teaching, and support activities. The foundation helps nonprofits focusing on positive youth attributes and explores opportunities to work with adjudicated youth. Additional funding interests include improving support services in low-income neighborhoods and helping families in crises, such as homelessness, divorce, or domestic violence situations. From time to time, the foundation makes grants that are outside the regular guidelines. Some reflect special board interests, others may respond to major natural disasters, and still others provide an opportunity to explore potential new areas for future grant making. Types of support include general operating grants, research grants, and special projects. Potential applicants are encouraged to call before submitting an application.
Requirements: Proposals are accepted from non-profit organizations throughout Northern California and Washoe County, Nevada.
Restrictions: The foundation does not consider proposals for grants to individuals or to religious organizations for sectarian purposes. Funds are not provided for capital projects, organizational deficits, or general operating support.
Geographic Focus: California, Nevada
Amount of Grant: 3,000 - 50,000 USD
Samples: Forum for Youth Investment Impact Strategies (Washington, DC)—to provide technical assistance to 11 district-community partnerships of a high school reform initiative, $100,000; Markkula Center/Character Based Literacy Project, Santa Clara University (Santa Clara, CA)—to continue implementing the Character Based Literacy curriculum, document student gains, and develop and implement a business plan, $200,000; Berkeley Biotechnology Education (CA)— for continuing support of its school-to-career program, $60,000; Catholic Charities of the East Bay (Oakland, CA)—to create a coordinated continuum of services for youth who are leaving the foster care system, $75,000; YouthBuild USA (Somerville, MA)—to strengthen its youth-development programs in California, $200,000.
Contact: Donna Takasuka, Grants Administrator; (650) 326-0485; fax (650) 326-4320; dtakasuka@wsjf.org
Internet: http://www.wsjf.org
Sponsor: Walter S. Johnson Foundation
525 Middlefield Road, Suite 160
Menlo Park, CA 94025

Warsh-Mott Legacy Grants 1866

The foundation awards grants in its areas of interest, including biotechnology, economic globalization— balancing short-term efforts that oppose the NAFTA/WTO/FTAA trade regimes with long-term efforts to develop alternative economic models; and food sovereignty—seed saving, soil building, protecting pollinators, and preserving traditional knowledge of how food is grown. Types of support include continuing support, equipment acquisition, matching grants, general operating grants, publications, research, special projects, and technical assistance. Submit a letter of inquiry; full proposals are by invitation.

Requirements: Applicant organizations must be classified as a 501(c)3 by the U.S. Internal Revenue Service. Foreign applicants should note that the foundations make a very limited number of grants abroad.

Restrictions: Grants do not support endowments, capital funds, or film/video projects.

Geographic Focus: All States

Amount of Grant: 15,000 - 30,000 USD

Samples: U of Texas, School of Public Health (Houston, TX)—for study of dioxins and effects on public health, $20,000. Council for Responsible Genetic (Boston, MA)—for general support, $30,000. Nevada Outdoor Recreation Assoc (Carson City, NV)—to purchase equipment), $20,000.

Contact: Contact; (707) 874-2942; fax (707) 874-1734; inquiries@csfund.org

Internet: http://www.csfund.org/procedures.html

Sponsor: Warsh-Mott Legacy Foundation

469 Bohemian Highway

Freestone, CA 95472

Wayne and Gladys Valley Foundation Grants 1867

The foundation awards grants to California nonprofits in its primary areas of interest, including education at all levels, health care and medical research, youth and families, human services, sciences and engineering, and religion. Types of support include general operating support, building construction/renovation, program development, professorships, research, and matching funds. There are no application forms or deadlines. The board meets in February, May, September, and November to consider requests.

Requirements: California nonprofits in Alameda, Contra Costa, and Santa Clara Counties are eligible.

Geographic Focus: California

Samples: U of the Pacific (Stockton, CA)—for its new biological-sciences center, $2.5 million; Santa Clara U (CA)—to construct a new library, $15 million; Dominican U of California (San Rafael, CA)—for a new science and technology center, $2.25 million.

Contact: Michael Desler; (510) 466-6060; fax (510) 466-6067; info@wgvalley.org

Sponsor: Wayne and Gladys Valley Foundation

1939 Harrison Street, Suite 510

Oakland, CA 94612-3532

Wayne County Foundation - Vigran Family Foundation Grants 1868

Lifelong Richmond, Indiana, resident Stanley Vigran considered forming a private foundation as a way to support causes that were important to him and his family including education, religion, and the arts. The Vigran family remains actively involved through a separate board which oversees the operations of the organization. Vigran's family continues his legacy of giving in the Whitewater Valley and remain involved in the causes that were so much a part of their father's work. Contact the Foundation for the application and further guidelines.

Requirements: Interested applicants should submit a one-page letter of inquiry.

Geographic Focus: Indiana

Date(s) Application is Due: Sep 1

Contact: Stephen C. Borchers, Executive Director; (765) 962-1638; fax (765) 966-0882; steve@waynecountyfoundation.org

Internet: http://www.waynecountyfoundation.org/grant_center/vigran.html

Sponsor: Vigran Family Foundation / Wayne County Foundation

33 South 7th Street, Suite 1

Richmond, IN 47374

Weatherwax Foundation Grants 1869

The foundation awards grants in Michigan to projects that promote and support education, civic and social programs, culture, science, and the arts, primarily in the greater Jackson area and, to a lesser extent, in the adjacent counties. Types of support include building construction and renovation; matching and challenge grants; general operating grants; program development; scholarships; annual and capital campaigns; and emergency funds. The initial approach is a two-page grant proposal that may be submitted at any time. Granting decisions are made in January, May, and August.

Requirements: Giving primarily in Hillsdale, Lenawee, and Jackson counties, MI.

Restrictions: No grants to individuals; or for computer purchases.

Geographic Focus: Michigan

Amount of Grant: 1,000 - 200,000 USD

Samples: Albion College (MI)—for music facility renovation, $125,000; Michigan Theatre (MI)—for restoration, strategic planning, and executive search, $27,500; Family Service and Children's Aid (MI)—for general operating support and neighborhood outreach activities, $45,491.

Contact: Program Contact; (517) 787-2117; fax (517) 787-2118

Internet: http://www.lib.msu.edu/harris23/grants/wfbrochu.htm

Sponsor: Weatherwax Foundation

P.O. Box 1111

Jackson, MI 49204

Weaver Foundation Grants 1870

The mission of the foundation is to help the Greater Greensboro community enhance and improve the quality of life and the economic environment for its citizens while developing a sense of philanthropy, civic education, and commitment in current and future generations of the founders' families. The focus areas include support for education; programs for children and youth; protection of the environment; efforts to reduce poverty and improve the lives of the disadvantaged and the needy; advancement of human and civil rights, racial tolerance, and diversity; enhancement of parks, recreation, and the quality of life; and economic development. Inquiries are welcomed via letter, telephone, or email; full proposals are by invitation. Grants are generally made quarterly.

Requirements: 501(c)3 nonprofits serving the greater Greensboro, North Carolina, community are eligible.

Restrictions: The foundation does not support political programs or voter registration efforts, conferences, travel, video production, fraternal groups, individuals, or religious organizations.

Geographic Focus: North Carolina

Amount of Grant: 5,000 - 50,000 USD

Contact: Tara Sandercock, Vice President for Programs; (336) 379-9100 or (336) 378-7910; fax (336) 275-9602; rlm@weaverfoundation.com

Internet: http://www.weaverfoundation.com/guidelines/index.php

Sponsor: Weaver Foundation

324 W. Wendover Avenue, Suite 300, P.O. Box 26040

Greensboro, NC 27408-8440

webMethods Foundation Grants 1871

The foundation awards grants to nonprofit organizations in the greater District of Columbia area focused on low-income and affordable housing and on issues surrounding homeless families, single mothers, and youth. Types of support include grants for new initiatives, general operations, and capacity building. Guidelines are available online.

Requirements: 501(c)3 charitable organizations within a 100-mile radius of Washington, DC, are eligible.

Geographic Focus: District of Columbia

Contact: Grants Administrator; (703) 460-6080; fax (703) 460-2599; foundation@webMethods.org

Internet: http://www.webMethods.org

Sponsor: WebMethods Foundation

3930 Pender Drive

Fairfax, VA 22030

Weeden Foundation Grants 1872

The purpose of the foundation is to address the adverse impact of the growing human population and overuse of natural resources on the biological fabric of the planet. The main priority of the foundation is biodiversity. Population growth and overconsumption have also evolved into major program interests. Proposed projects should protect ecosystems and wildlife or raise the status of women and increase awareness about family planning. The foundation awards general operating, seed money, and project/program grants. Applicants may submit a letter of inquiry. If interested, the foundation will request a full proposal. Send requests six weeks prior to the board meetings in March, June, and October.

Requirements: 501(c)3 nonprofit organizations are eligible.

Restrictions: The foundation does not: award grants for endowment or capital fund projects; support large organizations with well-established funding sources, except to assist them in launching promising, new projects for which funding is not readily available; allow any portion of a grant to be used for university overhead or indirect costs; award general support grants, except to small organizations with entire missions that coincide with an area of interest to the foundation; or award grants to individuals, but does provide support for

an individual's project if it is sponsored by a domestic or foreign educational, scientific, or charitable organization.
Geographic Focus: All States
Amount of Grant: 10,000 - 30,000 USD
Samples: Alaska Conservation Foundation (AK)—$15,000; Alternatives to Growth Oregon (OR)—$50,000; Population Coalition—$25,000.
Contact: Contact; (212) 888-1672; weedenfdn@weedenfdn.org
Internet: http://www.weedenfdn.org
Sponsor: Weeden Foundation
747 3rd Avenue, 34th Floor
New York, NY 10017

Westar Energy Foundation Grants   **1873**
The foundation awards grants to nonprofit organizations in company operating areas in Kansas. Areas of interest include children and youth, particularly educational programs related to enhancing employment opportunities; health programs related to the general well-being of the community; seniors, particularly with energy assistance programs; and environmental programs, particularly programs cooperating with federal, state, and local government units in nonpartisan efforts to improve the environment or educate the public about environmental issues. Types of support include building funds, capital campaigns, continuing support, emergency funds, equipment, fellowships, in-kind gifts, general operating budgets, renovation projects, research, scholarship funds, and seed money. There are no application deadlines; the board meets quarterly to consider requests.
Requirements: Nonprofit organizations in company-operating areas of Kansas are eligible to apply.
Geographic Focus: Kansas
Amount of Grant: 300 - 10,000 USD
Samples: Exploration Place (Wichita, KS)—for its capital campaign, and for the Season of Creativity exhibit, $100,000 and $40,000, respectively.
Contact: Cynthia McCarvel, President; (785) 575-1544; fax (785) 785-6399
Internet: http://www.wstnres.com/corp_com/contentmgt.nsf/publishedpages/foundation?opendocument&menu=5
Sponsor: Westar Energy Foundation
P.O. Box 889
Topeka, KS 66601-0089

West Virginia Commission on the Arts Major Institutions Support   **1874**
   Grants
The purpose of the West Virginia Commission on the Arts Major Institutions Support Grants is to support and stabilize organizations by providing financial assistance toward their overall budgets for arts programming. Selection criteria include artistic excellence, effective management, community impact and year-round programming and accessibility to audiences and artists. Funding awarded is between 2% and 6% of the organization's operating budget. Match is achieved through the organization's operating budget.
Requirements: Applicant organizations must: have a minimum operating budget of at least $1,000,000 or more; have been in existence for five years as a West Virginia nonprofit during which time a permanent, paid, professional staff, including a business manager and artistic director, have administered the organization's programming on an annual basis; have received Grants for at least three previous grant cycles; serve a large audience that represents a broad cross section of citizens, including people who are disabled or institutionalized, senior citizens, lower income groups, and culturally diverse audiences; demonstrate compliance with Section 504 of the Rehabilitation Act and the Americans with Disabilities Act; and provide longstanding local arts service and welcome and outreach to state and regional audiences.
Restrictions: The following institutions are ineligible: organizations whose primary thrust is education and which award academic credits; organizations receiving operating funds from other state agencies; organizations whose main purpose is not the arts; divisions or departments of larger institutions; and national service organizations.
Geographic Focus: West Virginia
Date(s) Application is Due: Mar 1
Contact: Barbara Anderson, Grants Coordinator; (304) 558-0240; fax (304) 558-2779; Barbie.J.Anderson@wv.gov
Internet: http://www.wvculture.org/arts/grantbook/generalcats.htm#major
Sponsor: West Virginia Commission on the Arts
1900 Kanawha Boulevard E
Charleston, WV 25305-0300

West Virginia Commission on the Arts Mid-Size Institutions   **1875**
   Support Grants
The purpose of the West Virginia Commission on the Arts Mid-Size Institutions Support Grants is to support and stabilize organizations by providing financial assistance toward their overall budgets for arts programming. Mid-size institutions are eligible for one operating support grant. The selection criteria include artistic excellence, effective management, community impact and year-round programming and accessibility to audiences and artists. Funding is between 2% and 15% of the organization's operating budget. Match is achieved through the organization's operating budget. New applicants must submit a letter of intent by December 1.
Requirements: Eligible applicant organizations must: have an operating budget of $150,000 to $1,000,000; have been incorporated as a non-profit for five years and have been a successful applicant to the West Virginia Commission on the Arts for three grant cycles; serve a broad cross-section of citizens, including but not be limited to citizens of varying ages, ethnicities, abilities, gender, income and educational level, with reasonable outreach to be inclusive; demonstrate compliance with Section 504 of the Rehabilitation Act and the Americans with Disabilities Act; and provide longstanding arts service, welcome and outreach to state and regional audiences.
Restrictions: Ineligible applicants include the following: organizations whose primary thrust is education and which award academic credits, i.e., colleges, universities and other degree-granting institutions; organizations receiving operating funds from other state agencies; organizations whose main purpose is not the arts; divisions or departments of larger institutions; and national service organizations.
Geographic Focus: West Virginia
Date(s) Application is Due: Mar 1
Contact: Barbara Anderson, Grants Coordinator; (304) 558-0240; fax (304) 558-2779; Barbie.J.Anderson@wv.gov
Internet: http://www.wvculture.org/arts/grantbook/generalcats.htm#mid
Sponsor: West Virginia Commission on the Arts
1900 Kanawha Boulevard E
Charleston, WV 25305-0300

WestWind Foundation Reproductive Health and Rights Grants   **1876**
Concerned with an exploding population in the Latin American and Caribbean region caused by inadequate access to reproductive health services, the Trustees of the WestWind Foundation decided to create a program that would support NGOs that work to provide services and improve access both in the region and in other parts of the globe. The program operates with the understanding of the international agreement made in Cairo in 1994 at the International Conference on Population and Development (ICPD), when the global community affirmed its commitment to address population growth by working to ensure individual rights and freedoms rather than demographic targets. In lieu of these trends, the goals of the Reproductive Health and Rights program are to support NGOs that seek to: improve access to reproductive health services, particularly in the LAC region; promote reproductive health and rights, both domestically and abroad; and promote adolescent sexual and reproductive health, both domestically and in the LAC region. he foundation supports organizations that seek to advance a range of reproductive health issues, including, but not limited to: supporting emergency contraception; promoting adolescent sexuality education and empowerment; preventing maternal mortality; and providing post-abortion care. Applicants should submit an online Letter of Inquiry (LOI) prior to the annual deadline. Typically, WestWind will respond to LOIs between 4 to 6 weeks after the letter has been received.
Requirements: The RHR Program currently supports non-governmental organizations (NGOs) that work both domestically and abroad to improve women's access to reproductive health services. Grants in the RHRP area are made primarily to U.S. based organizations for: international projects in the Latin America and Caribbean region; and projects that have national significance. There is also a small portion of funds that are available for global, opportunistic projects.
Geographic Focus: All States
Date(s) Application is Due: Mar 1
Amount of Grant: 5,000 - 225,000 USD
Contact: Kristen Miller, Program Consultant; (434) 977-5762, ext. 24; fax (434) 977-3176; bonnell@westwindfoundation.org or info@westwindfoundation.org
Internet: http://www.westwindfoundation.org/program-areas/reproductive-health-rights/
Sponsor: WestWind Foundation
204 East High Street
Charlottesville, VA 22902

Weyerhaeuser Company Foundation Grants   1877

The foundation's mission is to improve the quality of life in communities where Weyerhaeuser has a major presence and to provide leadership that increases public understanding of issues where society's needs intersect with the interests of the forest products industry. Community service grants include awards in the fields of education and youth, health and welfare, civic and community improvement, and culture and the arts. In addition to community grants, industry-related awards are made to educational institutions, environmental groups, and professional organizations that promote further understanding of how the forest products industry responds to a changing society. Types of support include seed money, building construction/renovation, equipment acquisition, employee-related scholarships, publication, conferences and seminars, fellowships, lectureships, operating budgets, research, program development, employee matching gifts, and technical assistance. Applicants should send a short letter that introduces the project and sponsoring organization and provide tax-exempt status evidence. If further consideration is warranted, the foundation may ask for additional information or a formal proposal. Proposals may be submitted at any time.

Requirements: Applying organizations must have nonprofit, tax-exempt status. To be considered for funding, an organization must: serve a community within a 50-mile radius of a major Weyerhaeuser facility; support a state-wide issue of interest to the Foundation and Weyerhaeuser in the key states of Alabama, Arkansas, Louisiana, Mississippi, North Carolina, Oklahoma, Oregon or Washington; or support a selected, high-priority national or international initiative directly related to the sustainability and importance of working forests. A limited number of smaller awards are also made to other locales where fewer employees are based.

Restrictions: Grants are not awarded to individuals or for political campaigns, activities that influence legislation, religious organizations seeking funds for theological purposes, or funds to purchase tickets or tables at fundraising benefits.

Geographic Focus: Alabama, Arizona, Arkansas, California, Colorado, District of Columbia, Georgia, Idaho, Illinois, Kentucky, Louisiana, Maryland, Michigan, Minnesota, Mississippi, Missouri, New Hampshire, New Jersey, New Mexico, North Carolina, Ohio, Oklahoma, Oregon, Pennsylvania, South Carolina, Texas, Utah, Virginia, Washington, West Virginia, Wisconsin

Date(s) Application is Due: Aug 31

Contact: Anne Levya, Team Coordinator; (253) 924-3159; fax (253) 924-3658; foundation@weyerhaeuser.com or anne.leyva@weyerhaeuser.com

Internet: http://www.weyerhaeuser.com/Sustainability/Foundation

Sponsor: Weyerhaeuser Company Foundation

P.O. Box 9777

Federal Way, WA 98063-9777

Whirlpool Foundation Grants   1878

Building on its history of concern for the communities in which Whirlpool operates, the foundation gives priority to projects addressing three strategic issues: lifelong learning, comprising programs addressing basic education, job training or retraining, and continuing education; cultural diversity, which includes support of programs that enable communities to appreciate diversity and promote better understanding among people through the study of language, customs, and traditions, and innovative cultural exchanges; and quality family life, which supports innovative community-based responses designed to strengthen families, improve parenting capabilities, and address the balance between parenting and job performance. Foundation resources are allocated across three programs—foundation grants; employee-directed programs, such as matching gifts and Dollars for Doers programs; and scholarships for employees' dependents. Additional types of support include matching funds, operating budgets, annual campaigns, emergency funds, building funds, equipment, and research. Applications are reviewed four times annually. Applicants are encouraged to contact the office for company operating areas and for additional information including where to submit applications.

Requirements: Tax-exempt organizations worldwide in Whirlpool communities are eligible.

Restrictions: Grants will not be made to individuals; for-profit organizations; political causes; religious-related organizations; social, labor, veterans, or fraternal organizations; athletic associations and events; fund-raising benefits; United Way agencies seeking general operating support; or national groups whose local chapters have already received support.

Geographic Focus: All States

Amount of Grant: 1,000 - 5,000 USD

Samples: Lake Michigan College (MI)—for the center for technical training, $1 million over four years; Gilda's Club (New York, NY)—to educate families about the value of social and emotional support when family members are living with cancer, $200,000 over two years.

Contact: Pamela Silcox, Operations Manager; (269) 923-5584; fax (269) 925-0154; pamela_j_silcox@whirlpool.com

Internet: http://www.whirlpoolcorp.com/responsibility/building_communities/whirlpool_foundation.aspx

Sponsor: Whirlpool Foundation

2000 North M-63

Benton Harbor, MI 49022-2692

Whitehall Foundation Neurobiology Research Grants   1879

Through its program of grants and grants in aid, the foundation assists scholarly research in the life sciences. The foundation is currently interested in basic research in invertebrate and vertebrate (excluding clinical) neurobiology, specifically investigations of neural mechanisms involved in sensory, motor, and other complex functions of the whole organism as these relate to behavior. Research grants are available to established scientists of all ages working at accredited institutions and will be awarded for up to three years, with possible renewal on a competitive basis for a maximum of two years. Grants in aid are designed for researchers at the assistant professor level who experience difficulty in competing for research funds because they have not yet become firmly established. Grants in aid will also be made to senior scientists. The foundation's policy is to assist those dynamic areas of basic biological research that are not heavily supported by federal agencies or other foundations with specialized missions. Types of support include personnel (salary support for students and technicians); permanent equipment, materials, and supplies needed to complete the project; travel for research; publication costs; and overhead (no more than 25 percent or supplies). Applicant should initiate the proposal process by submitting a one-page letter written in technical language identifying the nature of the research proposal and indicating whether the request is for a grant or grant in aid. Grant application forms will be sent to those applicants whose proposed project matches the foundation's current funding interests. Deadlines listed are for letters of intent.

Requirements: Accredited U.S. institutions are eligible. The foundation prefers to support scientists at the beginning of their career and those senior scientists who have maintained productivity. The principal investigator must hold no less than the position of assistant professor or the equivalent.

Geographic Focus: All States

Date(s) Application is Due: Jan 15; Apr 15; Oct 1

Amount of Grant: Up to 30,000 USD

Samples: Daniel Pollen, U of Massachusetts (MA)—for research on the cerebral integration in the primate visual system, $40,000 of three-year grant; Richard Ivry, U of California (CA)—for research on the role of the cerebellum in temporal processing, $24,000 final payment on three-year grant; Paul Black, Boston U (Boston, MA)—to support research on brain-immune system interactions, $130,020 final payment on three-year grant.

Contact: Director; (561) 655-4474; fax (561) 655-4978; email@whitehall.org

Internet: http://www.whitehall.org

Sponsor: Whitehall Foundation

P.O. Box 3423

Palm Beach, FL 33480

Whitehorse Foundation Grants   1880

The Whitehorse Foundation was established in 1990 as a supporting organization of The Seattle Foundation. The mission of The Whitehorse Foundation is to fund organizations working to improve the quality of life for residents of Snohomish County, Washington. Each grant application to the Foundation is thoughtfully considered by the Foundation's Board of Trustees. There is a two-step application process. The first step in seeking support is to submit a concise two-page letter of inquiry describing your project and request. The second step is a formal application process for those requests that are determined to meet the Foundation's funding criteria. Letters of inquiry can be submitted at any time and the board meets twice a year to consider funding requests. Grants are made to nonprofit organizations for project support or ongoing operating support. The Foundation is interested in programs in the early stages of development, which convey an achievable funding plan (demonstrating strong community commitment) or a compelling impact. The Foundation is interested in programs that: focus on prevention and root causes of problems rather than intervention; address many problems at once, rather than one problem at a time; strengthen families' capacity to support, nurture and guide their children; promote responsible parenthood to improve children's emotional, economic and social well-being; enable families to acquire the knowledge and skills needed for self-sufficiency; involve families and community residents in program design, development and management; will have a significant and ongoing impact; and offer opportunities for leveraging resources by forming partnerships with other grantmakers, other nonprofits, the government and the private sector.

Requirements: The Whitehorse Foundation supports nonprofit organizations in Snohomish County that work to improve the lives of children, youth and families. All applicant organizations must qualify as tax-exempt under section 501(c)3 of the IRS code.

Geographic Focus: Washington

Amount of Grant: Up to 250,000 USD

Samples: Cocoon House, Everett, Washington, $45,000 - to support the home visiting component of Project S.A.F.E.; Deaconess Children's Services, Everett, Washington, $40,000 - to support the Teen Parent Advocacy Program; Lutheran Community Services Northwest, Sea Tac, Washington, $230,000 - to support the Family Support Centers in Snohomish County.

Contact: Ceil Erickson, Grantmaking Director; (206) 515-2131 or (206) 515-2109; fax (206) 622-7673; c.erickson@seattlefoundation.org or grantmaking@seattlefoundation.org

Internet: http://www.seattlefoundation.org/nonprofits/whitehorse/Pages/WhitehorseFoundation.aspx

Sponsor: Whitehorse Foundation

1200 Fifth Avenue, Suite 1300

Seattle, WA 98101-3151

Widgeon Point Charitable Foundation Grants   1881

The foundation supports nonprofits in New York and Connecticut in its areas of interest, including secondary, higher, legal, and medical education; youth; zoos; museums; arts and culture; conservation and environment; historic preservation; family planning; libraries; and religion. Types of support include general operating budgets, capital campaigns, building funds, endowment funds, equipment acquisition, conferences and seminars, publications, and renovation projects. There are no application deadlines. Applicants should submit a two-page letter of application.

Requirements: Nonprofits in New York and Connecticut are eligible. The foundation does not accept unsolicited proposals. Interested and qualified organizations should submit a letter of inquiry prior to preparing a formal proposal. There are no specific deadlines.

Restrictions: Grants are not awarded to individuals or for endowments, capital costs, renovation, equipment, conferences, publications, and media projects.

Geographic Focus: Connecticut, New York

Amount of Grant: 1,000 - 25,000 USD

Contact: Jeffrey Coopersmith, (516) 483-5800 or (516) 483-5815; jcoopersmith@csvpc.com

Sponsor: Widgeon Point Charitable Foundation

50 Charles Lindbergh Boulevard, Suite 605

Uniondale, NY 11553-3650

Wieboldt Foundation Grants   1882

The Wieboldt Foundation limits its grant making to the Chicago metropolitan area. The foundation supports multi-issue community organizing groups that work in low-income neighborhoods, that are accountable to neighborhood residents, and through which people are empowered to have a major voice in shaping decisions that affect their lives.

Requirements: The Wieboldt Foundation supports organizations that: organize by enlisting and nurturing participation of a large number of neighborhood residents, organizations and institutions; recruit, develop, and formally train local leadership; enable local residents to develop an agenda, to devise strategies, and to carry out action effectively to address issues; demonstrate innovative strategies or create new local institutions that strengthen local community capacity; broaden their impact by working with other groups, whenever possible; are led by a board of directors that is representative of and accountable to community residents; show evidence of significant local fundraising. To be considered for financial support, send us a Letter of Inquiry to awards@wieboldt.org outlining the nature of your organization and rationale for funding from the Wieboldt Foundation. Letters of Inquiry will be reviewed by staff and a committee of the board who will make a determination on whether to invite your organization to submit a full proposal.

Restrictions: The Wieboldt Foundation generally does not fund individuals, studies and research, conferences, capital development, or direct or social service programs.

Geographic Focus: Illinois

Date(s) Application is Due: Jun 1; Aug 3; Oct 5; Nov 30

Amount of Grant: 3,000 - 40,000 USD

Samples: Woods Fund of Chicago, Chicago, IL, $5,000 - for support of Saul Alinsky Centennial Symposium; Midwest Academy, Chicago, IL, $15,000

- Summer Internship Program; Women & Girls Collective Action Network, Chicago, IL, $10,000 - for general operating support;

Contact: Regina McGraw, Executive Director; (312) 786-9377, ext. 1; fax (312) 786-9232; reginam@wieboldt.org

Internet: http://wieboldt.org/grant-guidelines/

Sponsor: Wieboldt Foundation

53 West Jackson Boulivard, Suite 838

Chicago, IL 60604

Wilbur and Patsy Bradley Family Foundation Grants   1883

Established in Missouri in 2000, the Wilbur and Patsy Bradley Family Foundation offers support to the arts, higher education programs, and Protestant agencies and churches throughout the State of Missouri. Since there are no application forms, applicants should forward a letter on their organization's letterhead outlining the project and budgetary needs. There are no annual deadlines, and grants range from $500 to $1,500.

Requirements: Applicants must serve the residents of Missouri. The Foundation pays particular attention to those that serve the communities of Lebanon or Springfield.

Geographic Focus: All States, Missouri

Amount of Grant: 500 - 1,500 USD

Samples: Lebanon High School Band, Lebanon, Missouri, $1,000 - for band equipment; Missouri State University Foundation, Springfield, Missouri, $1,300 - for general operations; Juanita K. Hammons Performance Society, Springfield, Missouri, $1,000 - for general operations.

Contact: Wilbur H. Bradley, (417) 532-7784 or (417) 588-2281

Sponsor: Wilbur and Patsy Bradley Family Foundation

401 Blue Bird Lane

Lebanon, MO 65536-2079

Wilbur Foundation Grants   1884

The Wilbur Foundation concentrates its funding in the field of humanities, especially history, literature, religion and philosophy. It seeks to support institutions and projects that are calculated to uphold or carry on the traditions of society. Applications are accepted between September 1 and December 31.

Requirements: Tax-exempt nonprofit organizations that reflect a concern for historical continuity and studies of a traditional nature may apply.

Restrictions: Except for resident fellowships, no grants are made to individuals, and the foundation does not consider grants for general building purposes.

Geographic Focus: All States

Date(s) Application is Due: Dec 31

Contact: Gary Ricks; (805) 563-1082; grants@wilburfoundation.org

Internet: http://www.wilburfoundation.org/grant.htm

Sponsor: Wilbur Foundation

P.O. Box 3370

Santa Barbara, CA 93130-3370

WILD Foundation Grants   1885

Founded in 1974, WILD is the only international organization dedicated entirely and explicitly to wilderness protection around the world. WILD works to protect the planet's last wild places and the wildlife and people who depend upon them, because wilderness areas provide essential social, spiritual, biological and economic benefits. The WILD Foundation focuses on four main program areas: World Wilderness Congress, wilderness policy and research, communications and field projects. Refer to the Foundations website for more detailed information on each program of interest. There are no specific deadlines with which to adhere. Contact the Foundation for further application information and guidelines.

Geographic Focus: All States

Contact: Charlotte Baron; (303) 442-8811; fax (303) 442-8877; info@wild.org

Internet: http://www.wild.org/main/about/

Sponsor: WILD Foundation

717 Poplar Avenue

Boulder, CO 80304

Willard and Pat Walker Charitable Foundation Grants   1886

The Willard and Pat Walker Charitable Foundation awards grants to Arkansas nonprofit organizations in its areas of interest, including: the arts; children and youth services; health organizations; higher education; residential and custodial hospice care; and social services. Types of support include: building construction and renovation; capital campaigns; continuing support; endowments; equipment; general operating grants; matching grants; program development; and scholarship endowment funds. There are no application forms, so applicants should provide a detailed description of their project and

the amount of funding requested. There are two annual deadlines of March 1 and October 1. The Board meets twice per year, in April and November
Requirements: Arkansas nonprofit organizations are eligible to apply.
Restrictions: Individuals are not eligible.
Geographic Focus: Arkansas
Date(s) Application is Due: Mar 1; Oct 1
Amount of Grant: Up to 1,000,000 USD
Samples: Crystal Bridges Museum of American Art, Bentonville, Arkansas, $1,000,000 - endowment contribution; New School, Fayetteville, Arkansas, $1,000,000 - challenge grant; Razorback Foundation, Fayetteville, Arkansas, $625,000 - capital campaign.
Contact: John M. Walker, President; (479) 582-2310; fax (479) 582-2292; walkerfamily1@sbcglobal.net
Sponsor: Willard and Pat Walker Charitable Foundation
P.O. Box 10500
Fayetteville, AR 72703-2857

William A. Badger Foundation Grants   1887

The Nabors to Neighbors Foundation was created in 2007 to assist charitable organizations focusing on need based projects for direct programming, capital and operating initiatives. This is a family foundation dedicated to organizations that deliver measurable results, seek partnerships and collaborations, utilize their resources within their respective communities while working to increase equity for those most in need. The Foundation encourages nonprofit organizations to apply who specialize in, though not limited to, improving the lives of children, education and medical initiatives. The Foundation makes no geographic restrictions on distributions. However, it has been the practice of the Trustees to make grants within Whitfield County, specifically Dalton, located in north Georgia. Requests must be postmarked by February 1, July 9 or October 1 in order to be considered.
Requirements: The Nabors to Neighbors Foundation makes grants to qualified 501(c)3 organizations. All requests must include: background information on the organization, including a brief history, the organization's current address and phone number and the name and title or the primary contact; the goals, objectives, and budget for the one project or program for which funds are being requested; the amount of the grant requested; summary of how the funds will be used; supporting financial information on the organization, to include current financial status and listing of Board of Trustees; copy of organization's tax exemption letter from the Internal Revenue Service. Application form is available online and all requests must be postmarked by February 1, July 9 or October 1 in order to be considered.
Restrictions: Grants are not made to: individuals; an organization to be used as pass-through funds for an ineligible organization Faith-based organizations without a 501(c)3 exemption; organizations with political purposes, nor to organizations which discriminate on the basis of race, ethnic origin, sexual or religious preference, age or gender.
Geographic Focus: All States
Date(s) Application is Due: Feb 1; Jul 9; Oct 1
Contact: Trustee, c/o Wachovia Bank; grantinquiries8@wachovia.com
Internet: https://www.wachovia.com/foundation/v/index.jsp?vgnextoid=108bf296ac212210VgnVCM100000617d6fa2RCRD&vgnextfmt=default
Sponsor: Nabors to Neighbors Foundation
3280 Peachtree Road NE, Suite 400, MC G0141-041
Atlanta, GA 30305

William and Charlotte Parks Foundation for Animal Welfare Grants   1888

The foundation awards grants to support animal protection to both animal protection organizations and to individual scholars who are pursuing a course of study that might advance the goals of the trust founders. Organizations may receive funds for capital projects, for general operating expenses, or for specific projects. Doctoral or post-doctoral candidates may receive funds to support a specific research project. These funds must be distributed through an organization with 501(c)3 status. Deadlines are May 1 for project, operating, and capital grants; and December 1 for PhD/veterinary fellowships. Application and guidelines are available online.
Requirements: 501(c)3 tax-exempt organizations are eligible. A non-U.S. applicant must be registered as a charitable organization in the home country.
Restrictions: Grants will not normally be awarded to improve animal health, for local spay/neuter assistance, to save endangered species, to rehabilitate wildlife, or to support political candidates. Grants focused on the conservation or protection of wild animal populations will not be funded. Grants will not ordinarily be made to organizations with an annual income of more than $1 million or a large asset base, with the exception of institutions of higher learning.
Geographic Focus: All States

Date(s) Application is Due: May 1; Dec 1
Amount of Grant: 10,000 - 30,000 USD
Contact: Donna Pease, (301) 548-7726; info@parksfoundation.org
Internet: http://www.parksfoundation.org
Sponsor: William and Charlotte Parks Foundation
700 Professional Drive
Gaithersburg, MD 20879

William B. Dietrich Foundation Grants   1889

The Foundation awards funding to nonprofits preferably for local needs. There are no submission deadlines. Areas of interest include children, the elderly, AIDS, museums, and libraries.
Requirements: Applicants may apply in writing, outlining the nature of the organization, the intended use of funds requested. A copy of the Internal Revenue Service determination letter should be submitted.
Restrictions: No grants are provided for individuals.
Geographic Focus: All States
Contact: Frank G. Cooper, President; (215) 979-1919
Sponsor: William B. Dietrich Foundation
P.O. Box 58177
Philadelphia, PA 19102-8177

William Blair and Company Foundation Grants   1890

Contributing to the community is an important part of the culture of William Blair and Company. The Foundation was officially established in Illinois in 1980, with giving primarily centered around metropolitan Chicago. All partners of the firm contribute part of their individual share of profits to the Foundation. Donation requests are made to the Foundation by partners and employees. The Foundation supports a broad range of causes including: civic affairs; public safety; arts and culture; higher education; youth-oriented activities; healthcare research; cultural affairs; and civic charities. Types of support include: annual campaigns; building and renovation; capital campaigns; general operating support; endowments; fellowships; internship programs; and scholarship funding. There are no specific deadlines or applications forms required. Funding typically ranges from $500 to $25,000.
Requirements: Requests can be made by sending a letter with a general description of the organization and its special purpose. Activities should have a significant impact on the Chicago metropolitan area.
Geographic Focus: Illinois
Samples: Doctors without Borders, Chicago, Illinois, $20,500 - general operating support; Department of Prints & Drawing at the Art Institute of Chicago, Illinois, $5,000 - general operating support; Greater Chicago Food Depository, Chicago, Illinois, $10,000 - general operating support.
Contact: E. David Coolidge III, Vice President; (312) 236-1600
Sponsor: William Blair and Company Foundation
222 W Adams Street, 28th Floor
Chicago, IL 60606

William Boss Foundation Grants   1891

The Foundation supports the arts, higher education, human service programs, libraries/library science, museums, performing arts, and youth programs. Types of support include general operating and program specific.
Requirements: Applicants should submit the following: copy of IRS determination letter, detailed description of project and amount of funding requested, and additional materials and supporting documentation.
Restrictions: Giving is primarily restricted to Minnesota. No grants for individuals.
Geographic Focus: Minnesota
Date(s) Application is Due: Jun 15
Contact: Dan McKeown, Treasurer; (651) 653-0599
Sponsor: William Boss Foundation
5858 Centerville Road
St. Paul, MN 55127-6804

William C. Kenney Watershed Protection Foundation Ecosystem   1892 Grants

Established in California in 1994, the William C. Kenney Watershed Protection Foundation supports small, local environmental groups working to protect key threatened wild rivers in the Western United States and larger campaigns for ecosystems that contain significant wild rivers (i.e., the Arctic Refuge, southern Utah, Oregon, and California). Grants also support regional and national organizations that disseminate information and training on national policy issues that directly impact the work of local groups and projects that provide training and information in communication skills and strategies. Types of support include general operating support, technical assistance, capacity building, advocacy, and special projects. Previous grant recipients are eligible for opportunity grants.

Requirements: 501(c)3 nonprofit organizations in British Columbia or the Western United States, including Alaska, Arizona, California, Colorado, Idaho, Montana, Nevada, New Mexico, Oregon, Utah, Washington, and Wyoming, are eligible. Organizations must have annual operating budgets under $740,000, collaborate with other groups, be innovative, and produce measurable results.

Restrictions: Grants do not support watershed restoration, land acquisition, endowments, research, or legal work. The foundation does not accept unsolicited applications for its Leadership Grants.

Geographic Focus: Alaska, Arizona, California, Colorado, Idaho, Montana, Nevada, New Mexico, Oregon, Utah, Washington, Wyoming, Canada

Amount of Grant: Up to 30,000 USD

Contact: Jay P. Kenney, Grants Administrator; (303) 722-0722; fax (415) 369-9180; jay@kenneyfdn.org

Sponsor: William C. Kenney Watershed Protection Foundation
910 Gaylord Street
Denver, CO 80206-3754

William C. Woolf Foundation Grants   1893

The foundation exists to enhance the quality of life for citizens of Shreveport, LA, and awards one-year grants to eligible Louisiana nonprofit organizations for a variety of programs and activities. Proposals must meet the listed application deadline and include a copy of the IRS tax-determination letter.

Requirements: 501(c)3 tax-exempt organizations located in northwestern Louisiana are eligible.

Restrictions: Grants are not made to individuals.

Geographic Focus: Louisiana

Amount of Grant: 300 - 50,000 USD

Contact: Barbara York, Chair

Sponsor: William C. Woolf Foundation
333 Texas Street, SH 2069
Shreveport, LA 71101

William D. Laurie, Jr. Charitable Foundation Grants   1894

The William D. Laurie, Jr. Charitable Foundation, named after the Vice President and Detroit Manager of J. Walter Thompson Company, was established in Rhode Island in 2002. The Foundation's primary fields of interest include the support of: animal and wildlife programs; education; and health organizations. There are no formal application requirements, and interested parties should begin by forwarding a proposal letter to the Foundation office. No annual deadlines have been identified. Typical awards have recently ranged from $250 to $2,000.

Requirements: Any 501(c)3 organization located in, or supporting residents of, Rhode Island are welcome to apply.

Geographic Focus: Rhode Island

Amount of Grant: 250 - 2,000 USD

Samples: Leukemia and Lymphoma Society, Cranston, Rhode Island, $250 - general operating support; Naval War College Foundation, Newport, Rhode Island, $2,000 - general operating support; Potter League for Animals, Newport, Rhode Island, $1,000 - general operating support.

Contact: David H. Laurie, Trustee; (401) 423-1811 or (401) 423-0403

Sponsor: William D. Laurie, Jr. Charitable Foundation
15 Dumplings Drive
Jamestown, RI 02835-2904

William E. and Bertha E. Schrafft Charitable Trust Grants   1895

The trust makes grants to charitable institutions in the greater Boston, MA, metropolitan area that are involved with education of indigent or otherwise disadvantaged youth. Grants are awarded for programs or projects, continuing support, annual campaigns, general operating support, and scholarship funds. The trustees meet approximately six times each year to consider requests; there are no application deadlines.

Requirements: Grants are awarded to nonprofit organizations in Massachusetts, with emphasis on the Boston area.

Restrictions: Grants are not awarded to individuals or for matching gifts, seed money, emergency funds, or deficit financing.

Geographic Focus: Massachusetts

Amount of Grant: 5,000 - 25,000 USD

Samples: Mother Caroline Academy and Education Ctr (MA)—for general operating support, $15,000; Institute of Contemporary Art (MA)—for a teen education program, $10,000; Gordon College (MA)—for scholarship support, $45,000; Catholic Schools Foundation (MA)—for the inner-city scholarship fund, $15,000.

Contact: Karen Faulkner, Executive Director; (617) 457-7327; funding@ schrafftcharitable.org

Internet: http://www.schrafftcharitable.org

Sponsor: William E. and Bertha E. Schrafft Charitable Trust
One Boston Place, 34th Floor
Boston, MA 0002108-4408

William G. and Helen C. Hoffman Foundation Grants   1896

Helen C. Hoffman resided in the Village of South Orange, New Jersey. Her foundation was established in 1998 in memory of herself and her husband after the death of their daughter Corinne Blair. Her testamentary wish was to establish this foundation for charitable, religious, scientific, literary, and educational purposes. Her preference was to support blindness and its cure. Approximately 90% of the grants will provide support to the blind and, to medical research for the prevention of blindness. The remaining 10% will fund annual grants in the following areas of interest: education, the arts, environment and, social/civic causes. Requests must be received by January 15 for the March meeting and, August 22 for the October meeting. Application forms are available online. Applicants will receive notice acknowledging receipt of the grant request, and subsequently be notified of the grant declination or approval.

Requirements: Any U.S. 501(c)3 non-profit organizations may apply. Proposals should be submitted in the following format: completed Common Grant Application Form; an original Proposal Statement; an audited financial report and a current year operating budget; a copy of your official IRS Letter with your tax determination; a listing of your Board of Directors. Proposal Statements (second item in the above Format) should answer these questions: what are the objectives and expected outcomes of this program/project/request; what strategies will be used to accomplish your objective; what is the timeline for completion; if this is part of an on-going program, how long has it been in operation; what criteria will you use to measure success; if the request is not fully funded, what other sources can you engage; an Itemized budget should be included; please describe any collaborative ventures. Prior to the distribution of funds, all approved grantees must sign and return a Grant Agreement Form, stating that the funds will be used for the purpose intended. Progress reports and Completion reports must also be filed as required for your specific grant. All current grantees must be in good standing with required documentation prior to submitting new proposals to any foundation.

Restrictions: Grants are not made for political purposes, nor to organizations which discriminate on the basis of race, ethnic origin, sexual or religious preference, age or gender.

Geographic Focus: All States

Date(s) Application is Due: Jan 15; Aug 22

Amount of Grant: 5,000 - 15,000 USD

Samples: Tri-County Scholarship Fund, $5,000—scholarships for economically disadvantaged students to receive a private elementary/secondary education; New Eyes for the Needy, Inc., $20,000— eyeglasses for poor Kentuckians; Christian Health Care Center Foundation, $10,000— support senior subsidies for adult day services.

Contact: Wachovia Bank, N.A., Trustee; grantinquiries2@wachovia.com

Internet: https://www.wachovia.com/foundation/v/index.jsp?vgnextoid=5228 52199c0aa110VgnVCM1000004b0d1872RCRD&vgnextfmt=default

Sponsor: William G. and Helen C. Hoffman Foundation
190 River Road, NJ3132
Summit, NJ 07901

William G. Baker, Jr. Memorial Fund Grants   1897

The William G. Baker, Jr. Memorial Fund was established in 1964 by Mary S. Baker in memory of her husband. The fund continues the Baker's civic-minded philanthropic tradition, offering grants that range from $1,000 to $40,000. Its grant making program primarily benefits the residents of the greater Baltimore area. The Fund commits its resources to enhance the region's economy and quality of life through investments in a broadly defined cultural sector in which all residents may participate and thrive. Its grants will support artistic and cultural organizations and their partners that enhance an individual's sense of self and pleasure and make Baltimore a more attractive place to live, work and play.

Requirements: Organizations (or their fiscal agents) serving the Baltimore area that qualify as public charities under section 501(c)3 of the Internal Revenue Code and do not discriminate on the basis of race, creed, national origin, color, physical handicap, gender or sexual orientation are eligible to apply.

Restrictions: No grants will be made to individuals, or for religious/sectarian purposes or deficit financing.

Geographic Focus: Maryland
Date(s) Application is Due: Jan 1; Mar 3; Jul 7; Sep 26
Amount of Grant: 1,000 - 40,000 USD
Contact: Odessa Hampton; (410) 332-4171; ohampton@bcf.org
Internet: http://www.bcf.org/ourgrants/ourgrantsdetail.aspx?grid=1
Sponsor: William G. Baker, Jr. Memorial Fund
2 East Read Street, 9th Floor
Baltimore, MD 21202

William G. Gilmore Foundation Grants   1898

The foundation supports nonprofits primarily in the San Francisco Bay Area, CA; some funding also in Pueblo, CO and Portland, OR. Giving primarily for the arts, health, and children, youth, and social services.
Requirements: California, Colorado, and Oregon nonprofits are eligible to apply. Contact the Foundation for additional application information.
Restrictions: No grants to individuals.
Geographic Focus: California, Colorado, Oregon
Amount of Grant: 1,000 - 50,000 USD
Samples: YMCA of Pueblo, Pueblo, CO, $50,000; Queen of the Valley Hospital Foundation, Napa, CA, $50,000; Pueblo Child Advocacy Center, Pueblo, CO, $5,000;
Contact: Faye Wilson; (415) 546-1400; fax (415) 391-8732
Sponsor: William G. Gilmore Foundation
120 Montgomery Street, Suite 1880
San Francisco, CA 94104-4317

William G. McGowan Charitable Fund Grants   1899

The fund awards grants to eligible nonprofit organizations that are devoted to three specific philanthropic goals: developing the talents and gifts of the very young, especially those who have been disenfranchised by virtue of low income status, inner-city conditions or family situations; funding for selected areas of medical research directed toward finding cures for, or relieving the pain and suffering of, those afflicted with debilitating conditions or diseases; and the McGowan Scholars program, which provides financial assistance to selected college and university students interested in pursuing an undergraduate or graduate degree at a college or university business school accredited by the International Association for Management Education or Association of Collegiate Business Schools and Programs.
Requirements: Nonprofit organizations in the following states and cities are eligible: Chicago, IL; District of Columbia and its Virginia suburbs; metropolitan Kansas City, western New York; and northeast Pennsylvania.
Restrictions: The fund does not support multiyear grants; accept requests online; or fund art or theatrical activities, building funds, church renovation campaigns, or endowments.
Geographic Focus: California, District of Columbia, Illinois, Missouri, New York, Pennsylvania, Virginia
Date(s) Application is Due: Jan 2; May 1; Sep 1
Amount of Grant: 10,000 - 100,000 USD
Samples: Rochester Institute of Technology, College of Applied Science (NY)—to construct the Center for Telecommunications, $2 million; U of the Pacific (Stockton, CA)—for a scholarship for a business student, $18,000; Foundation for the National Archives (Washington, DC)—for the National Archives Experience, which will make important American documents accessible to the public and teach visitors about the value of archives, $5 million.
Contact: Bernard Goodrich, Executive Director; (301) 320-8570; fax (301) 320-8627; goodric@aol.com or info@mcgowanfund.org
Internet: http://www.mcgowanfund.org/guidelines.html
Sponsor: William G. McGowan Charitable Fund
P.O. Box 40515
Washington, D.C. 20016-0515

William G. Selby & Marie Selby Foundation Innovative Partnership   1900
Grants

The goal of this Program is to encourage human services and arts organizations to work in collaboration. Innovative Partnerships will continue to be based on joint efforts of arts and human service providers to develop programs and deliver services together which could not be accomplished separately. A collaborative planning process should identify needs, clarify objectives of both partners and identify the resources and strengths each partner can bring to the project. The results of engaging in such a process will be sustained benefits for both organizations, as well as meaningful outcomes for the program participants. Peripheral benefits will evolve for both organizations as a true partnerships takes hold and develops overtime. The Foundation will accept joint applications from

arts and human services organizations for grants up to $10,000. Applications must be in the Foundation office by 5:00 p.m. on December 1st.
Requirements: Nonprofit organizations from Sarasota and Manatee counties, Florida, are eligible.
Restrictions: Schools and/or day care facilities Pre-K through 12 are not eligible.
Geographic Focus: Florida
Date(s) Application is Due: Dec 1
Amount of Grant: Up to 10,000 USD
Samples: Circus Sarasota, $10,000 (each)—to build a sustaining partnership with Laughter Unlimited; Sarasota Coalition on Substance Abuse, $6,620 (each)—to build a sustaining partnership with Poetry in Motion.
Contact: Janet D. Noah, Grants Manager; (941) 957-0442; fax (941) 957-3135; jnoah@selbyfdn.org
Internet: http://www.selbyfdn.org/applyInnovative.html
Sponsor: William G. Selby and Marie Selby Foundation
1800 Second Street, Suite 750
Sarasota, FL 34236

William J. and Dorothy K. O'Neill Foundation Grants   1901

Foundation grantmaking activities include family, health, arts and culture, community, animals, education, environment, employment, fatherhood, recreation, religion, law enforcement/crime, human services, and housing. Types of support include general operating support, program development, seed grants, and matching funds. The foundation has no formal application form; requests should be made in writing. Grants are awarded for capacity building activities that develop or improve the effectiveness, impact and strength of: the organization's Board of Trustees and/or its Board leadership; the organization's strategic plan; the organization's staff; and the organization's programs. Grant requests should include the amount requested; specific project including goals, objectives, approach, and methods; project budget and timeline; other sources of funding; evaluation plan; qualifications and experience of key personnel; description of organization; most recent annual report; and copy of IRS classification letter. Requests may be submitted at any time but will be considered four times each year when the grantmaking committee meets. Annual deadline dates may vary; contact program staff for exact dates.
Requirements: 501(c)3 organizations in metropolitan areas where O'Neill family members currently live are eligible, including Washington, DC; Naples, FL, area; Big Island, HI; Baltimore/Annapolis, MD; New York, NY area; Cincinnati/Cleveland, OH; Columbus and Licking County, OH; Richmond/Virginia Beach, VA; and Houston, TX.
Restrictions: The foundation does not make grants to individuals, to organizations that are wholly outside the United States, or in response to form letters for annual appeals.
Geographic Focus: District of Columbia, Florida, Hawaii, Maryland, New York, Ohio, Texas, Virginia
Date(s) Application is Due: Jan 24; Apr 25; Jul 18; Oct 10
Amount of Grant: 35,000 - 620,000 USD
Samples: Children's Museum of Manhattan (New York, NY)—for new program development, $20,000; Virginia Supportive Housing (Richmond, VA)—for administrative structure changes, $20,000; Highbridge Community Life Ctr (Bronx, NY)—for CFO position, $20,000; North Union Farmers Market (Cleveland, OH)—for field worker consultant, $20,912.
Contact: Contact; (216) 831-4134; fax (216) 831-3779; oneillfdn@aol.com
Internet: http://www.oneillfdn.org/application.htm
Sponsor: William J. and Dorothy K. O'Neill Foundation
30195 Chagrin Boulevard, Suite 250
Cleveland, OH 44124

William J. Brace Charitable Trust   1902

The William J. Brace Charitable Trust was established in 1958 to support and promote quality educational, cultural, human-services, and health-care programming, with a preference for the following three areas: the education and health of children; the health and care of older adults; and hospitals in Kansas City, Missouri. Grant requests for general operating support and program support will be considered. Grants from the Trust are one year in duration. There are no application deadlines for the Brace Charitable Trust. Proposals are reviewed on an ongoing basis. Applicants may download the application and Missouri state guidelines at the grant website. Applicants are strongly encouraged to review the state guidelines for additional helpful information and clarifications on the three areas of interest. Most recent awards have ranged from $35,000 to as high as $100,000.

Restrictions: The Trust generally supports organizations that serve the residents of Kansas City, Missouri. Grant requests for capital support will not be considered.
Geographic Focus: Missouri
Amount of Grant: 35,000 - 100,000 USD
Samples: Mid-America Regional Council Community Services Corporation, Kansas City, Missouri, $50,000 - program development (2014); Saint Lukes Hospital Foundation, Kansas City, Missouri, $50,000 - program development (2014); Children's Center for the Visually Impaired, Kansas City, Missouri, $46,200 - program development.
Contact: Scott Berghaus, Senior Vice President; (816) 292-4300 or (816) 292-4301; scott.berghaus@ustrust.com
Internet: https://www.bankofamerica.com/philanthropic/grantmaking.action
Sponsor: William J. Brace Charitable Trust
1200 Main Street, 14th Floor, P.O. Box 219119
Kansas City, MO 64121-9119

William K. Warren Foundation Grants   1903
The foundation awards grants to eligible nonprofit organizations in its areas of interest, including Catholic healthcare facilities, Catholic social services, education, and medical research. Types of support include building construction/renovation, endowment campaigns, general operating support, program development, and research grants. Grants are awarded primarily in Oklahoma. There are no application forms or deadlines. The board meets semiannually.
Geographic Focus: Oklahoma
Amount of Grant: 1,000 - 50,000 USD
Samples: Salvation Army of Tulsa (OK)—for general operating support, $135,000; Saint Anthony Hospital Foundation (Oklahoma City, OK)—for general support, $100,000.
Contact: Grants Administrator; (918) 492-8100
Sponsor: William K. Warren Foundation
P.O. Box 470372
Tulsa, OK 74147-0372

William L. and Victorine Q. Adams Foundation Grants   1904
Incorporated in 1984, The William L. and Victorine Q. Adams Foundation is a private, charitable organization dedicated to improving the lives of young people through consideration of funding requests from organizations whose mission is to improve education, strengthen neighborhoods and support institutions that will enhance the quality of life and general welfare of Baltimore's citizens. Primary fields of interest include: community and economic development; education; and human services. Funding comes in the form of general operating support. The annual application deadline is May 1. Recent awards have ranged from $500 to $16,000.
Requirements: Applicants must be 501(c)3 agencies serving the residents of Baltimore, Maryland, and its surrounding suburbs.
Geographic Focus: Maryland
Date(s) Application is Due: May 1
Amount of Grant: 500 - 16,000 USD
Samples: Baltimore Symphony Orchestra, Baltimore, Maryland, $12,000 - general operating support; Baltimore School of the Arts, Baltimore, Maryland, $13,500 - general operating support; Baltimore Freedom Academy, Baltimore, Maryland, $10,000 - general operating support for education.
Contact: Blanche Rodgers, Program Officer; (410) 783-3216 or (410) 783-3208; brodgers@ar-companies.com
Internet: http://www.adamsfound.org/about/index.html
Sponsor: William L. and Victorine Q. Adams Foundation
1040 Park Avenue, Suite 300
Baltimore, MD 21201-5635

William M. Weaver Foundation Grants   1905
Established in Texas in 2003 by the William M. Weaver Charitable Trust, the Foundation offers funding support primarily in Dawson County, Texas. Its major fields of interest include: community development; economic development; and Protestant agencies and churches. Financial support typically comes in the form of general operating costs. There are no specified application forms required, so interested parties should formulate a proposal in letter form. This two- or three-page approach should include a detailed program overview, budgetary needs, and any goals that the organization has established. There are no annual deadlines listed. Most recent grants have ranged from $5,000 to just over $100,000.
Requirements: Any 501(c)3 or Protestant agency/church serving the residents of Dawson County, Texas, are welcome to apply.
Geographic Focus: Texas

Amount of Grant: 5,000 - 100,000 USD
Samples: Lamesa Community Players, Lamesa, Texas, $71,884 - theater renovation; Medical Arts Hospital, Bryan, Texas, $52,112 - landscaping; First Presbyterian Church, Lamesa, Texas, $102,578 - operating support.
Contact: Elwood Freeman, (806) 872-5457
Sponsor: William M. Weaver Foundation
2651 JBS Parkway, Building 4, Suite E
Odessa, TX 79762

William N. and Myriam Pennington Foundation Grants   1906
The foundation supports education, health, and medical research in Nevada. Funding priority is given to organizations serving children and youth, the elderly, and the economically disadvantaged. Types of support include general operating support, building construction/renovation, equipment acquisition, and scholarships to individuals.
Requirements: Nevada nonprofits may apply for grant support.
Geographic Focus: Nevada
Amount of Grant: 2,500 - 200,000 USD
Samples: Assistance League of Reno-Sparks (Reno, NV)—for general support, $15,000; U of Nevada, Department of Speech Pathology (Reno, NV)—for equipment, $17,500.
Contact: Kent Green, Foundation Manager; (775) 333-9100
Sponsor: William N. and Myriam Pennington Foundation
441 W Plumb Lane
Reno, NV 89509

William Penn Foundation Grants   1907
The principal mission of the foundation is to help improve the quality of life in the Delaware Valley. Grants are made in the categories of children, youth, and families; arts and culture; and environment and communities. Under the category of children, youth, and families, grants are made to promote the full development of children and youth to become capable adults and productive citizens, with special emphasis on key transitions in their lives. Preference is given to programs that promote healthy birth outcomes and early childhood health; school readiness—facilitating a successful transition to school, and K-12 arts education; youth development—making an effective transition to higher education or work; and violence reduction—concern for vulnerable youth. In the area of environment and communities, grants are awarded to promote vital communities within a healthy regional ecosystem. Funding priorities include watersheds and ecosystems—protecting lands, enhancing stewardship; revitalize communities—strengthening of core urban centers; and smart growth—enhancing prosperity and livability of the region. In the area of arts and culture, preference will be given to projects that enable the creation and presentation of high-quality artistic work; provide support for artists in advancing their careers; encourage active participation in the cultural life of the region; preserve and promote the region's cultural assets; create new cultural opportunities in and for a particular neighborhood or community; and strengthen arts and cultural organizations in their core programs and administration. Written requests are accepted throughout the year; there are no formal deadlines.
Requirements: Grants are awarded to IRS 501(c)3 tax-exempt organizations in the Pennsylvania counties of Montgomery, Chester, Bucks, and Delaware; and Camden County, NJ. Environmental grants are made in a larger region, approximately a 100-mile radius from Philadelphia. In some instances, government agencies may be eligible if no nonprofit organization can conduct the equivalent activity.
Restrictions: Grants do not support individuals, nonpublic or charter schools, rehabilitation treatments, debt reduction, religious or political activities, hospital capital projects, housing construction, projects for the elderly, medical research, or replacement of government support.
Geographic Focus: New Jersey, Pennsylvania
Amount of Grant: 100,000,000 USD
Samples: Committee of Seventy (Philadelphia, PA)—for its strategic plan to advance good government in the metropolitan Philadelphia region, including through ethics legislation, an enforceable code of conduct for city employees, campaign-finance requirements for local candidates, oversight of the state's new gaming industry, and more transparent government contracts, $500,000 over two years.
Contact: Janet Haas; (215) 988-1830; moreinfo@williampennfdn.org
Internet: http://www.williampennfoundation.org/info-url3564/info-url.htm
Sponsor: William Penn Foundation
100 N 18th Street, 11th Floor
Philadelphia, PA 19103

William Robert Baird Charitable Trust Grants 1908

The trust awards grants to Louisiana and Mississippi nonprofits in its areas of interest, including food banks, social services, children and youth services, and economically disadvantaged. Types of support include general operating support, program development, emergency fund, capital campaigns, endowment funds, and matching funds. There are no application forms or deadlines.

Requirements: Louisiana and Mississippi nonprofits may apply.

Restrictions: Individuals are ineligible.

Geographic Focus: Louisiana, Mississippi

Amount of Grant: 2,000 - 40,000 USD

Samples: Care Lodge Domestic Violence Shelter, Meridian, MS, $14,800; Wesley House Community Center, Meridian, MS, $39,500; Special Olympics Mississippi, Meridian, MS, $5,400.

Contact: John David Barr, Trust Administrator c/o Citizens National Bank; (601) 484-5887; jdbarr@ecitizensnationalbank.com

Sponsor: William Robert Baird Charitable Trust

512 22nd Avenue, P.O. Box 911

Meridian, MS 39302-5853

William T. Grant Foundation Youth Service Improvement Grants 1909

The program supports activities conducted by community-based organizations in the New York metropolitan area to improve the quality of services for young people (8-25 years of age). The program is designed to help good programs get better. Organizations should identify aspects of their current services that require improvement and propose a project with two main elements: (1) a plan of activities to improve the program services, and (2) an assessment plan to track the implementation of the improvement plan and its short-term results. Applications are accepted in the spring and the fall.

Requirements: To be eligible for consideration, organizations must have 501(c)3 tax-exemption; provide services to youth located in the New York metropolitan area, defined as the following counties: (in New York) Bronx, Kings, Nassau, New York, Putnam, Queens, Richmond, Rockland, Suffolk, and Westchester counties; (in New Jersey) Bergen, Essex, Hudson, Hunterdon, Mercer, Middlesex, Monmouth, Morris, Ocean, Passaic, Somerset, Sussex, and Union counties; and (in Connecticut) Fairfield, New Haven, and Litchfield counties; serve youth aged 8-25 years; and have an operating budget between $250,000 and $5.0 million. In the case of organizations that serve youth only, this is the total organizational budget. In the case of multipurpose organizations (i.e., those not exclusively focused on youth), the organizational operating budget must be less than $20 million, and the budget for services to youth (direct and indirect costs) must be between $250,000 and $5.0 million.

Restrictions: The program program does not award grants to organizations that do not serve youth directly; staff from applicant organizations must have direct contact with youth at the point-of-service. The program does not support ongoing service delivery, general operating support, organizational development activities not directly related to improving the quality of youth services, service expansion or program growth, building campaigns, scholarships, endowments, lobbying, or awards to individuals.

Geographic Focus: Connecticut, New Jersey, New York

Amount of Grant: Up to 25,000 USD

Samples: Mental Health Association of New York - ($25,000) Adolescent Skills Center Internship-to-Work Program; Opportunities for a Better Tomorrow - ($25,000) Curriculum Development and Outcomes-Based Lesson Planning; Youth Communication New York - ($25,000) Improving Youth Services Through Enhanced Staff Training; Family ReEntry - ($25,000) Transitions Mentoring Program for Incarcerated Youth: Post-Release Improvement Project.

Contact: Sharon Brewster, ODF Grants Coordinator; (212) 752-0071; fax (212) 752-1398; sbrewster@wtgrantfdn.org

Internet: http://www.wtgrantfoundation.org/funding_opportunities/service-improvement-grants/youth_service_improvement/youth_service_improvement_grants

Sponsor: William T. Grant Foundation

570 Lexington Avenue, 18th Floor

New York, NY 10022-6837

Wilson-Wood Foundation Grants 1910

The Wilson-Wood Foundation established in 1983, supports organizations involved with: adult education; aging, centers/services; children/youth, services; education; health care; housing/shelter, development; human services; nutrition; women, centers/services. Giving is limited to the Manatee-Sarasota, Florida area, for for the underprivileged and the less fortunate in the community.

Requirements: Non-profits in the Manatee-Sarasota, Florida area are eligible to apply. Initial approach should be a phone call to the Foundation prior to submitting a the letter of inquiry (must be received by June 1). There is no application form required. Applicants must submit two copies of the proposal. Application must include the following information: timetable for implementation and evaluation of project; qualifications of key personnel; name, address and phone number of organization; copy of IRS Determination Letter, must be dated within the past 10 years; brief history of organization and description of its mission; copy of most recent annual report/audited financial statement/990; descriptive literature about organization; listing of board of directors, trustees, officers and other key people and their affiliations; detailed description of project and amount of funding requested; copy of current year's organizational budget and/or project budget; listing of additional sources and amount of support.

Restrictions: No support for foreign organizations, supporting organizations, or private foundations. No grants to individuals, or for endowment funds, deficit financing, travel projects, research, fundraising costs, multi-year projects, conferences, emergency funding or start up costs.

Geographic Focus: Florida

Date(s) Application is Due: Jun 1

Amount of Grant: 8,000 - 30,000 USD

Samples: Childrens Academy of Southwest Florida, Bradenton, FL, $30,000; Meals on Wheels Plus of Manatee, Bradenton, FL, $20,000; Habitat for Humanity, Venice Area, Venice, FL, $25,000;

Contact: Susan Wood, Executive Director; (941) 966-3635

Sponsor: Wilson-Wood Foundation

930 Scherer Way

Osprey, FL 34229-6867

Windward Youth Leadership Fund Grants 1911

The Windward Youth Leadership Fund (WYLF) is a way for youth to apply for and "earn" up to $5,000 for their club or group activities by doing something positive for Windward Oahu. In addition to engaging youth in community service, one of the primary goals of this small grants program is to help youth build their leadership skills. Although parents, coaches and teachers may provide guidance, the projects must be youth-driven.

Requirements: Groups with at least three participants up to age 18 may apply including, but not limited to: school classes, teams, clubs, etc; youth activity groups, hula halau, music groups, scouts, etc; programs that serve youth; church youth groups; youth sports teams. Applicant groups must have a base in Windward Oahu, a majority of youth participants must be Windward Oahu residents and service projects should serve communities along the Windward coast from Kahuku to Waimanalo. Applicants must be a public school or a nonprofit 501(c)3 organization or have a sponsoring agency that is a 501(c)3 organization that can receive the funds. Youth groups can not use the Windward Youth Leadership Fund to raise funds for their own group by doing a service project that also benefits their own group. Youth groups are also encouraged to undertake projects that broaden their horizons beyond the scope of their everyday activities.

Restrictions: Applications that do not clearly demonstrate participation of youth in the project planning and writing of the proposal will most likely be denied.

Geographic Focus: Hawaii

Amount of Grant: 500 - 5,000 USD

Contact: Elizabeth Murph, (808) 263-7073; bmurph@castlefoundation.org

Internet: http://castlefoundation.org/windward-youth.htm

Sponsor: Harold K. L. Castle Foundation

1197 Auloa Road

Kailua, HI 96734

Wisconsin Arts Board Artistic Program I Support Grants 1912

Artistic Program Support I (APS I) provides artistic, program, and operational support to established nonprofit arts institutions of the highest artistic level, whose primary mission is to create and produce arts programming of significant statewide impact on the cultural life of Wisconsin. The goals of the program are to sustain organizational and financial stability and high-quality arts programming; ensure long-range planning as an approach to increasing the effectiveness of arts organizations; and increase local, statewide, and regional leadership in the arts among arts organizations in Wisconsin. Types of activities funded include general operating expenses; artistic and technical/production personnel expenses; outside artistic fees and services; artistic space rental/expenditures; production/exhibition expenses; and acquisition of artwork. Applicants are required to use the electronic application process in addition to mailing paper copies and originals to the Arts Board. Guidelines are available online.

Requirements: 501(c)3 tax-exempt arts organizations that qualify as a charitable organization under 170(c) of the Internal Revenue Code of 1954 as amended are eligible. Applicants must have a minimum annual operating budget of $698,000 in their most recently completed fiscal year to be eligible.

Restrictions: Arts Board policy does not allow applicants to apply for APS I if they receive funding through other Wisconsin Arts Board programs, excluding the Arts Challenge Initiative.

Geographic Focus: Wisconsin

Date(s) Application is Due: Nov 15

Contact: Manager; (608) 266-0190; artsboard@arts.state.wi.us

Internet: http://arts.state.wi.us/static/aps1.htm

Sponsor: Wisconsin Arts Board

101 E Wilson Street, 1st Floor

Madison, WI 53702

Wisconsin Arts Board Arts Challenge Initiative Grants   1913

The Arts Challenge Initiative helps Wisconsin nonprofit arts organizations leverage income from private sources. The program is intended to spur the fund-raising efforts of arts organizations by providing state funds to organizations whose fund-raising efforts meet or exceed the total amount of eligible income raised in the previous year. The program includes three categories: minority organizations, organizations with budgets over $100,000, and organizations with budgets under $100,000. Guidelines and applications are available on the Web site.

Requirements: Only nonprofit arts organizations in Wisconsin are eligible to apply.

Geographic Focus: Wisconsin

Date(s) Application is Due: Aug 1

Contact: Mark Fraire, Grant Programs and Services Specialist; (608) 264-8191; fax (608) 267-0380; mark.fraire@arts.state.wi.us

Internet: http://arts.state.wi.us/static/aci.htm

Sponsor: Wisconsin Arts Board

101 E Wilson Street, 1st Floor

Madison, WI 53702

Women's Foundation of Minnesota Grants   1914

The fund supports women and girls organizing for economic, political, and social change. Foundation grants are made in the following areas: social change/systems change—projects by and for women and/or girls that are designed to have a significant impact on societal attitudes and behaviors, or result in needed systemic change benefiting women and girls; grassroots empowerment—projects that bring together previously unorganized, traditionally underserved groups of women and/or girls as an initial organizing step in the process of social/systems change; and women, money, and social change—funding for new and innovative efforts that will stimulate giving and increase support for organizations, projects, and efforts benefiting women and/or girls. Types of support include start-up costs, program support, general operating support, technical assistance, and one- to two-year grants.

Requirements: Minnesota grassroots and established organizations operated by and for women and/or girls are eligible.

Restrictions: Grants do not support individuals, capital or endowment campaigns, political campaigns, or religious programs or activities.

Geographic Focus: Minnesota

Date(s) Application is Due: Jul 1

Contact: Pamela Moore, Program Officer; (888) 337-5010 or (612) 337-5010, ext. 23; fax (612) 337-0404; Pamela@wfmn.org

Internet: http://www.wfmn.org

Sponsor: Women's Foundation of Minnesota

155 Fifth Avenue S, Suite 900

Minneapolis, MN 55401

Women's Foundation of Southern Arizona Go Girls! Sports Grants   1915

The foundation is a social change organization committed to helping women and girls overcome economic, political, gender, and social barriers. Grant categories include health, safety, and well-being for women and girls; economic justice for women and girls; and innovative programs that improve the status of women and girls. Types of support include project specific support, general operating support, and planning or start-up support. Applicants must submit an electronic letter of intent by the listed application deadline. Guidelines are available online.

Requirements: Southern Arizona nonprofit organizations are eligible.

Restrictions: The foundation does not provide funds for individuals; campaigns to elect candidates to public office; capital fund drives; debt reduction; endowments; fundraising events or one-time conferences; scholarships, fellowships, and tuition reimbursement; programs inconsistent with federal, state, and local non-discrimination statutes regarding equal employment opportunity; programs that promote religious activities; programs outside of Pima, Cochise, and Santa Cruz counties in southern Arizona; or individual classrooms or schools.

Geographic Focus: Arizona

Date(s) Application is Due: Oct 1

Amount of Grant: Up to 10,000 USD

Contact: Laura Penny, Program Officer; (520) 622-8886; fax (520) 770-1500; lpenny@womengiving.org

Internet: http://www.womengiving.org/programs/gogirl.php

Sponsor: Women's Foundation of Southern Arizona

2250 E Broadway Boulevard

Tucson, AZ 85719

Women's Foundation of Southern Arizona Grants   1916

Grants support projects that focus on the underlying root causes of problems faced by women and girls and create fundamental, long-term change; are community based and involve the target population in the design, development, and evaluation of the program; and foster collaboration among groups sharing similar interest areas. Preference will be given to issues such as health insurance coverage for nonelderly women, suicide among women, and the number of women living in poverty. Grants are awarded for project-specific support, general operating support, and planning or start-up support.

Requirements: Nonprofit organizations with 501(c)3 status, or emerging grassroots organizations or informal groups who have come together for a program that is consistent with the fund's mission may apply. Groups without tax-exempt status must consist of more than five women and have some type of governing body.

Restrictions: The fund does not provide funds for individuals, capital fund drives, endowments, campaigns to elect candidates to public office, programs that promote religious activities, programs outside the southern Arizona area, programs that are inconsistent with nondiscrimination ordinances regarding equal employment opportunity, and agencies that have been funded by SAWF for the last three consecutive years.

Geographic Focus: Arizona

Date(s) Application is Due: Oct 1

Amount of Grant: 600 - 10,000 USD

Samples: Boys and Girls Club of Tucson (AZ)—for the SMART Girls program, a health, fitness, prevention/education, and self-esteem enhancement program for girls ages 10 to 15, $3000; Planned Parenthood (AZ)—for TAG, an active group of young women providing peer-to-peer outreach, education, and traning and support to young women in southern Arizona as it relates to holistic sexuality and prevention, $4000.

Contact: Laura Penny, Program Officer; (520) 622-8886; fax (520) 770-1500; lpenny@womengiving.org

Internet: http://www.womengiving.org/grantmaking

Sponsor: Women's Foundation of Southern Arizona

2250 E Broadway Boulevard

Tucson, AZ 85719

Women's Funding Alliance Grants   1917

The alliance supports nonprofits in Washington for programs and projects supporting women and children in its areas of interest, including poverty, sexual assault, discrimination, domestic violence, education, and reproductive rights. Preference will be given to organizations that have women in leadership positions and who incorporate diversity in their projects and agencies. Grants are awarded once a year in the following areas: general operating support, capacity building, project specific and population specific. Nonprofits interested in being included on the request-for-proposal list can email the alliance. All Letters of Inquiry are due on May 31st. Applicants invited to submit a full proposal will be notified the third week of June. Full proposals are due in the Women's Funding Alliance office by 5:00 PM on July 23rd.

Requirements: Washington nonprofits are eligible.

Geographic Focus: Washington

Amount of Grant: 1,000 - 15,000 USD

Samples: Parents Organizing for Welfare and Economic Rights (P.O.WER), Olympia, WA, $15,000—P.O.WER will lead civic engagement efforts to educate and register new women voters and develop low-income, politically involved female leaders within WA State; Statewide Poverty Action Network, Seattle, WA, $10,000— to fund their Vote for a Change campaign in order to increase voter turnout and participation among low-income citizens in Washington State, nearly 60% of which are women; Equal Rights Washington, Seattle, WA, $25,000—funding to build leadership and civic engagement skills in lesbian, bisexual, transgender and queer (LBTQ) women in order to create social change and eliminate heterosexism and homophobia throughout health care and public health systems.

Contact: Sara Reyerson, (206) 467-6733; fax (206) 467-7537; sara@wfalliance.org or wfa@wfalliance.org

Internet: http://www.wfalliance.org/apply_for_funding.htm
Sponsor: Women's Funding Alliance
603 Stewart Street, Suite 207
Seattle, WA 98101-1229

Women's Fund of Rhode Island Grants   **1918**
The fund awards grants to eligible Rhode Island nonprofit organizations for projects designed to help level the playing field for women and girls. The fund is particularly interested in the following issues: leadership—including political participation and leadership, professional development opportunities, developing leadership in girls and women, and preteen prevention strategies to address self-esteem and self-advocacy issues; health, education, and well-being—including poverty, violence, teen pregnancy, self-esteem, health education and disease prevention, and K-16 education and adult literacy; economic autonomy—including women-owned enterprise, employment readiness and opportunity, and equal and livable wage; rights—including self-determination, public policy, and government action that assures the well-being of women and girls including immigrants. Types of support include project specific support, general operating support, planning, and start-up support. The fund considers funding on a year-to-year basis and does not make multiyear commitments. Application guidelines and forms are available online. The application deadline is for letters of intent.
Requirements: 501(c)3 nonprofits that serve women and girls who reside in Rhode Island and organizations applying through 501(c)3 fiscal agents that serve the target populations and area are eligible. The fund prefers to support organizations that have limited access to other donors.
Restrictions: The fund will not support projects that discriminate on the basis of ethnicity, race, color, creed, religion, gender, national origin, age, disability, marital status, sexual orientation, gender identity, or any veteran's status; or projects that present or incorporate religion in any manner. Grants do not support individuals or scholarships, capital or endowment, biomedical research or debt reduction, fundraising events or campaigns to elect candidates to public office.
Geographic Focus: Rhode Island
Date(s) Application is Due: Feb 18
Amount of Grant: 2,500 - 25,000 USD
Contact: Marcia Conee-Tighe, (401) 274-4564; fax (401) 331-8085
Internet: http://www.rifoundation.org/wfri/html/index.htm
Sponsor: Rhode Island Foundation
1 Union Station
Providence, RI 02903

Wood-Claeyssens Foundation Grants   **1919**
The Foundation awards grants to eligible California nonprofit organizations. Types of support include annual campaigns, capital campaigns, continuing support, and general operating support. An application is available on the website.
Requirements: California 501(c)3 organizations serving Santa Barbara and Ventura Counties are eligible.
Restrictions: Funding is not available to individuals or to organizations that discriminate on the basis of age, gender, race, ethnicity, sexual orientation, disability, national origin, political affiliation or religious belief.
Geographic Focus: California
Date(s) Application is Due: Jun 30
Samples: Senior Concerns, Thousand Oaks, California, $15,000; Many Mansions, Thousand Oaks, California, $30,000; and Dream Foundation, Santa Barbara, California, $30,000.
Contact: Noelle Claeyssens Burkey, President; (805) 966-0543; fax (805) 966-1415; wcf0543@gmail.com
Internet: http://www.woodclaeyssensfoundation.com/Funding.htm
Sponsor: Wood-Claeyssens Foundation
P.O. Box 30586
Santa Barbara, CA 93130-0586

Woods Charitable Fund Grants   **1920**
This program seeks to strengthen the community by improving opportunities and life outcomes for all people in Lincoln, Nebraska. Areas of interest include human services; education; civic and community; and arts and culture. The Fund gives considerations to programs and initiatives related to the following: support to organizations that haven't traditionally served refugees and immigrants but are trying to integrate them into their client bases and work forces; expanding English language education for New Americans; helping develop community acceptance and appreciation for New Americans; and extending research and planning concerning immigrants and refugees in Lincoln. Interested applicants are asked to contact the Fund by telephone or by sending a two page letter

of intent, including budget information, by mail, facsimile or email. After reviewing the letter of intent, the Fund may request a complete application. Grants range from $1,000 to $100,000 with the average size being $21,500.
Requirements: Generally applicants should be 501(c)3 organizations serving Lincoln, Nebraska. Funding is provided in four principle ares of interest: human services; education; civic and community life; and arts and culture.
Restrictions: The following are ineligible: capital projects for health care institutions; environmental programs; funding of endowments; fundraising benefits or program advertising; individual needs; medical and scientific research; programs for individual schools; religious programs; residential care and medical clinics; scholarships and fellowships; and sponsorships. College and university proposals are reviewed only if they directly involve faculty and/or students in applied projects of benefit and concern to the community. Ineligible organizations are those that have had proposals approved or declined in the preceding twelve months or that are recipients of active, multiyear grants. This does not apply when organizations are involved in collaborative proposals.
Geographic Focus: Nebraska
Samples: Planned Parenthood of the Heartland, Inc., Lincoln, Nebraska, $50,000, human services funding; Community Development Resources, Lincoln, Nebraska, $20,000, general operating; and Lincoln and Lancaster County Child Guidance Center, Lincoln, Nebraska, $50,000, human services funding.
Contact: Pam Baker, Executive Director; (402) 436-5971; fax 402) 742-0123; pbaker@woodscharitable.org
Internet: http://www.woodscharitable.org/about/index.html
Sponsor: Woods Charitable Fund
P.O. Box 81309
Lincoln, NE 68501

Woods Fund of Chicago Grants   **1921**
The goal of Woods Fund of Chicago is to increase opportunities for less advantaged people and communities in the metropolitan area, including the opportunity to shape decisions affecting them. The Foundation supports nonprofits in engaging people in civic life, addressing the causes of poverty and other challenges facing the region, promoting more effective public policies, reducing racism and other barriers to equal opportunity, and building a sense of community and common ground. The Foundation is particularly interested in supporting those organizations and initiatives that focus on enabling work and reducing poverty within Chicago's less-advantaged communities. Grants are concentrated in three program areas: community organizing; public policy; and the intersection of community organizing and public policy. In addition, a limited number of grants are awarded in the arts and culture program area. Applicants must submit an inquiry form. If the Foundation responds favorably, applicants will be asked to submit a full application. Inquiry forms are accepted January 1 through the last business day in January and July 1 through the last business day in July.
Requirements: Applicants must be 501(c)3 organizations in the metropolitan Chicago area.
Restrictions: Areas not eligible include: business or economic development projects; capital campaigns, capital projects, and capital acquisitions; endowments; fundraising benefits or program advertising; health care organizations; housing construction or rehabilitation; individual needs; medical or scientific research; programs in and for individual public and private schools; religious or ecumenical programs; residential care, rehabilitation, counseling, clinics and recreational programs; scholarships and fellowships; and social and welfare services, except special projects with a clear public policy strategy.
Geographic Focus: Illinois
Samples: Albany Park Neighborhood Council, Chicago, Illinois, $35,000 - operating support for a multi-issue grassroots organization in a diverse, immigrant neighborhood; Brighton Park Neighborhood Council, Chicago, Illinois, $35,000 - operating support for a multi-issue grassroots organization in a working class Latino neighborhood; Center for Tax and Budget Accountability, Chicago, Illinois, $60,000 - operating support of a bipartisan fiscal think tank focused on ensuring fair tax and economic policies for less-advantaged residents of Illinois; and Action Now, Chicago, Illinois, $35,000 - operating support for a multi-issue grassroots organization organizing on issues such as foreclosure prevention, living wage jobs, and quality schools.
Contact: Deborah D. Clark, Grants and Operations Manager; (312) 782-2698; fax (312) 782-4155; dclark@woodsfund.org
Internet: http://www.woodsfund.org/site/epage/61436_735.htm
Sponsor: Woods Fund of Chicago
35 East Wacker Drive, Suite 1760
Chicago, IL 60601

Woodward Governor Company Charitable Trust Grants   **1922**

The company-sponsored trust supports nonprofits in areas of company operations, including Rockford, IL; Fort Collins, CO; and Stevens Point, WI. Areas of interest include vocational education, adult basic education, and literacy programs; health care, health organizations, and hospices; delinquency prevention programs and services; services for minorities and immigrants; human services for the homeless, community and economic development; and arts/culture, including museums. Types of support include general operations, annual campaigns, capital campaigns, continuing support, equipment acquisition, seed funding, and emergency funding. There are no application deadline dates; receipt of proposals is preferred in March and July. Applications forms are not required.

Requirements: Only Colorado, Illinois, and Wisconsin organizations are eligible to apply.

Restrictions: Grants are not awarded to individuals or for endowment funds, research, scholarships, fellowships, special projects, publications, conferences, loans, or matching gifts.

Geographic Focus: Colorado, Illinois, Wisconsin

Amount of Grant: 500 - 200,000 USD

Contact: Pam Johnson, Chair, Contributions Committee

Sponsor: Woodward Governor Company Charitable Trust

5001 N Second Street

Rockford, IL 61125-7001

Wortham Foundation Grants   **1923**

The foundation awards grants to nonprofits in Harris County, TX, in its areas of interest, including arts, performing arts, museums, community improvement, and civic beautification projects. Types of support include general operating support, continuing support, annual campaigns, capital campaigns, endowment funds, emergency funds, seed money, and matching funds. Proposals should be submitted preferably by the second week of January, April, July, and October for board meetings in February, May, August, and November. Obtain application forms from the office.

Requirements: Houston nonprofits in Harris County, TX, are eligible.

Restrictions: Grants are generally not awarded to colleges, universities, hospitals, or individuals.

Geographic Focus: Texas

Amount of Grant: 10,000 - 100,000 USD

Contact: Barbara Snyder; (713) 526-8849; bsnyder@wortham.org

Sponsor: Wortham Foundation

2727 Allen Parkway, Suite 1570

Houston, TX 77019

Wyoming Arts Council Community Services Grants   **1924**

Two grant categories exist within this program: Project and Multiple Project. Project grants are for a specific, one-time arts project or event. Multiple Project grants are for two or more projects or events in the performing, visual, literary, media, folk, or multidisciplinary arts. Annual deadline dates may vary; contact program staff for exact dates.

Requirements: Wyoming nonprofit organizations are eligible to apply.

Geographic Focus: Wyoming

Date(s) Application is Due: Mar 15

Amount of Grant: Up to 5,000 USD

Contact: Rita Basom, Community Services Program Manager; (307) 777-7109; fax (307) 777-5499; rbasom@state.wy.us

Internet: http://wyoarts.state.wy.us/gto.html

Sponsor: Wyoming Arts Council

2320 Capitol Avenue

Cheyenne, WY 82002

Xerox Foundation Grants   **1925**

Xerox Foundation Grants assist a variety of social, civic and cultural organizations that provide broad-based programs and services in cities where our employees work and live. The Foundation also remains committed to a program of grants to colleges and universities to prepare qualified men and women for careers in business, science, government, and general education. The Foundation seeks to further advance knowledge in science and technology, and to enhance learning opportunities for minorities and the disadvantaged. Worldwide, Xerox philanthropy tries to engage national leadership in addressing major social problems and to support programs in education, employability and cultural affairs. Other areas of particular focus include programs responsive to the national concern for the environment and the application of information technology. Large grants may be approved for more than one year (multi-year grants). All organizations that have previously

received support on an annual basis from the Foundation, must re-submit a request each year to be evaluated for continued support.

Requirements: Grants are made only to 501(c)3 and 509(a) organizations. No specific application form is used. Requests for grants/funding should be submitted in letter form describing the project or program. This request should contain the legal name of the organization, the official contact person, its tax- exempt status, a brief description of its activities and programs, the purpose for which the grant is being requested, the benefits expected, the plans for evaluation, the projected budget, and the expected sources and amount of needed funds.

Restrictions: The foundation declines requests to support individuals; capital grants (new construction or renovation); endowments or endowed chairs; organizations supported by United Way, unless permission has been granted by United Way to a member agency to conduct a capital fund drive or a special benefit; political organizations or candidates; religious or sectarian groups; or municipal, county, state, federal, or quasi-government agencies.

Geographic Focus: All States

Amount of Grant: 500 - 50,000 USD

Contact: Joseph M. Cahalan, President; (203) 968-2453 or (203) 968-3000

Internet: http://www.xerox.com/about-xerox/citizenship/xerox-foundation/enus.html

Sponsor: Xerox Foundation

45 Glover Avenue, P.O. Box 4505

Norwalk, CT 06856-4505

Yellow Corporate Foundation Grants   **1926**

The corporate foundation supports nonprofit organizations in the Kansas City, MO, area. Categories of support include cultural programs and entertainment, education, community development, and health programs. United Way agencies in communities in which the company does business receive 80 percent of the foundation's giving. Education support goes to colleges and universities. Community development support includes economic development, urban leagues, and chambers of commerce. Health and social service support includes programs assisting the visually impaired; disabled children, including psychological disabilities; and groups that aid battered women.

Requirements: IRS 501(c)3 tax-exempt nonprofits in Missouri are eligible.

Restrictions: Grants are not made to individuals, nor to political, religious, or national health organizations.

Geographic Focus: Missouri

Contact: Daniel J. Churay, Director; (913) 696-6170

Sponsor: Yellow Corporate Foundation

10990 Roe Avenue, M.S. A515

Overland Park, KS 66211-1213

Youngstown Foundation Grants   **1927**

The foundation makes grants to nonprofit organizations in Mahoning County, OH. Organizations wishing to apply should submit a dated cover letter that includes several sentences about the organization, a paragraph or two explaining the proposed project or program (including goals, objectives, and strategies for implementation as applicable), amount requested, and IRS tax-exemption determination letter. Submit the original and nine copies of the proposal. Applications are accepted at any time.

Requirements: Nonprofits in Mahoning County, OH, may submit applications for grant support.

Restrictions: Grants are not made to individuals.

Geographic Focus: Ohio

Contact: G.M. Walsh; (216) 744-0320; fax (330) 744-0344

Sponsor: Youngstown Foundation

P.O. Box 1162

Youngstown, OH 44501

Youth Philanthropy Project   **1928**

The program encourages young people from across the region to participate in community service and to develop leadership skills, and especially encourages student volunteerism and philanthropy by engaging young people in decision-making about the distribution of grant dollars.

Requirements: Any youth-run organization that impacts the City of Richmond, Henrico, Hanover and Chesterfield Counties that is in need of funding for programs that benefit the community. Applicants may include, but are not limited to, church youth groups, school clubs or volunteer organizations that involve youth in the planning, implementation and evaluation of the proposed program. Consideration is given to youth-driven organizations that provide programs or services relating to one or more of the following focus areas - [1] Creating Safe Neighborhoods: Supporting a community where

neighbors share an interest in protecting their communities and providing residents with the tools to identify and address their assets and needs; [2] Strengthening Families: Encouraging families to build stronger, healthier, and more productive environments for themselves, their community and their children; and [3] Achieving Academic Success: Supporting programs that promote literacy, improve test scores, increase school attendance, and encourage parental involvement.
Restrictions: Applications sent by facsimile or email will not be accepted.
Geographic Focus: Virginia
Date(s) Application is Due: Apr 12; Oct 12
Amount of Grant: 500 - 10,000 USD
Contact: Susan Hallett, Program Officer; (804) 330-7400, ext. 124; fax (804) 330-5992; shallett@tcfrichmond.org
Internet: http://www.tcfrichmond.org/page2479.cfm
Sponsor: Community Foundation Serving Richmond and Central Virginia
7501 Boulders View Drive, Suite 110
Richmond, VA 23225

YSA Global Youth Service Day Lead Agency Grants   1929

Youth Service America and State Farm will support up to 100 Global Youth Service Day (GYSD) and Semester of Service Lead Agencies for Global Youth Service Day (mid-April). Lead Agencies are local, regional, or statewide organizations across the United States, and the Canadian provinces of Alberta, Ontario, or New Brunswick that increase the scale, visibility, and impact of Global Youth Service Day by taking a lead role in their city, region, or state. These Lead Agencies convene a planning coalition of at least 10 partner organizations that collectively engage at least 600 youth volunteers in service on GYSD, engage local media and elected officials, and plan a high profile signature project or celebration of service. The Agencies receive a $2,000 GYSD planning grant sponsored by State Farm, travel support to attend the Youth Service Institute, and ongoing training and technical assistance from Youth Service America to ensure a successful Global Youth Service Day or Semester of Service. Past Lead Agencies have leveraged their position as a GYSD Lead Agency to strengthen their programs, form new partnerships, expand their volunteer base, garner media attention, gain support from local public officials, and secure additional funding.
Requirements: Lead agencies must be located in one of the 50 states, the District of Columbia, or the Canadian provinces of Alberta, Ontario, or New Brunswick; demonstrate the organizational capacity to fulfill the responsibilities of a lead agency; have the ability to engage a variety of community groups; have the ability to plan to mobilize a citywide, regional, or statewide National Youth Service Day celebration involving more than 500 youth volunteers in service over the weekend of the event; and respond to quick deadline press opportunities.
Geographic Focus: All States, Canada
Date(s) Application is Due: Jul 17
Amount of Grant: 2,000 USD
Contact: Chris Wagner, Manager of Outreach; (202) 296-2992; fax (202) 296-4030; outreach@ysa.org
Internet: http://www.ysa.org/grants/leadagency
Sponsor: Youth Service America
1101 15th Street NW, Suite 200
Washington, D.C. 20005

Z. Smith Reynolds Foundation Community Economic Development 1930 Grants

The Foundation seeks to foster economic well-being for all families and to build economic vitality and sustainability for all communities. The Foundation invests in organizations and projects that achieve the following: protects and increases the incomes and assets of low-income families and individuals; and increases community control of economic assets and economic independence for the benefit of rural or low-income residents. New programs, rather than those that are well-established and well-funded, receive priority consideration. Types of support include operating budgets, continuing support, annual campaigns, seed grants, matching funds, projects/programs, conferences and seminars, and technical assistance.
Requirements: The foundation makes grants only to nonprofit, tax-exempt, charitable organizations and institutions in North Carolina.
Restrictions: The foundation does not give priority to: the arts; capital campaigns; computer hardware or software purchases; conferences, seminars, or symposiums; crisis intervention programs; fund raising events; historic preservation; local food banks; or substance abuse treatment programs.
Geographic Focus: North Carolina
Date(s) Application is Due: Feb 1; Aug 1

Amount of Grant: 5,000 - 14,000,000 USD
Contact: Mary Fant Donnan, (800) 443-8319, ext. 101 or (336) 725-7541, ext. 101; fax (336) 725-6069; maryd@zsr.org or info@zsr.org
Internet: http://www.zsr.org/community.htm
Sponsor: Z. Smith Reynolds Foundation
147 South Cherry Street, Suite 200
Winston-Salem, NC 27101-5287

Z. Smith Reynolds Foundation Democracy and Civic Engagement   1931 Grants

The Foundation seeks to foster a government that is accountable to the needs of the people; a media that provides fair and substantial information on issues facing the state and its people; a citizenry that is engaged, well-informed and participates in the life of the state; and sound public policy that is built upon comprehensive and balanced research. New programs, rather than those that are well-established and well-funded, receive priority consideration. Types of support include operating budgets, continuing support, annual campaigns, seed grants, matching funds, projects/programs, conferences and seminars, and technical assistance.
Requirements: The foundation makes grants only to nonprofit, tax-exempt, charitable organizations and institutions in North Carolina.
Restrictions: The foundation does not give priority to: the arts; capital campaigns; computer hardware or software purchases; conferences, seminars, or symposiums; crisis intervention programs; fund raising events; historic preservation; local food banks; or substance abuse treatment programs.
Geographic Focus: North Carolina
Date(s) Application is Due: Feb 1; Aug 1
Amount of Grant: 5,000 - 14,000,000 USD
Contact: Joy Vermillion Heinsohn, (800) 443-8319, ext. 106 or (336) 725-7541, ext. 106; fax (336) 725-6069; joyv@zsr.org or info@zsr.org
Internet: http://www.zsr.org/democracy.htm
Sponsor: Z. Smith Reynolds Foundation
147 South Cherry Street, Suite 200
Winston-Salem, NC 27101-5287

Z. Smith Reynolds Foundation Environment Grants   1932

The Foundation seeks to conserve, protect, improve and restore the state's natural areas; to ensure clean air and water for all North Carolinians; and to minimize the burden of the state's environmental hazards, particularly on marginalized communities. The Foundation invests in organizations and projects that: prevent poor communities and communities of color from bearing a disproportionately high or adverse burden of environmental hazards; guarantee clean water for all; guarantee clean air for all; conserve green space; and guarantee a healthy coastal ecosystem. New programs, rather than those that are well-established and well-funded, receive priority consideration. Types of support include operating budgets, continuing support, annual campaigns, seed grants, matching funds, projects/programs, conferences and seminars, and technical assistance.
Requirements: The foundation makes grants only to nonprofit, tax-exempt, charitable organizations and institutions in North Carolina.
Restrictions: The foundation does not give priority to: the arts; capital campaigns; computer hardware or software purchases; conferences, seminars, or symposiums; crisis intervention programs; fund raising events; historic preservation; local food banks; or substance abuse treatment programs.
Geographic Focus: North Carolina
Date(s) Application is Due: Feb 1; Aug 1
Amount of Grant: 5,000 - 14,000,000 USD
Contact: Hawley Truax, (800) 443-8319, ext. 120 or (336) 725-7541, ext. 120; fax (336) 725-6069; hawleyt@zsr.org or info@zsr.org
Internet: http://www.zsr.org/environment.htm
Sponsor: Z. Smith Reynolds Foundation
147 South Cherry Street, Suite 200
Winston-Salem, NC 27101-5287

Z. Smith Reynolds Foundation Pre-Collegiate Education Grants   1933

The Foundation seeks to foster an educational system that provides each student in North Carolina the constitutionally guaranteed right of a sound, basic education regardless of race, socio-economic status, gender, geography or other discriminating factors. The Foundation invests in organizations and projects that: train, place and retain highly-qualified teachers for every child and skilled administrators for every school, with particular emphasis on increasing the number of people of color in those positions; and improve educational achievement through equity in education. New programs, rather than those that are well-established and well-funded, receive priority consideration. Types of support include operating budgets, continuing support, annual campaigns, seed grants, matching funds, projects/programs, conferences and seminars, and technical assistance.

Requirements: The foundation makes grants only to nonprofit, tax-exempt, charitable organizations and institutions in North Carolina.

Restrictions: The foundation does not give priority to: the arts; capital campaigns; computer hardware or software purchases; conferences, seminars, or symposiums; crisis intervention programs; fund raising events; historic preservation; local food banks; or substance abuse treatment programs.

Geographic Focus: North Carolina

Date(s) Application is Due: Feb 1; Aug 1

Amount of Grant: 5,000 - 14,000,000 USD

Contact: Leslie Winner, Executive Director; (800) 443-8319, ext. 105 or (336) 725-7541, ext. 105; fax (336) 725-6069; lwinner@zsr.org or info@zsr.org

Internet: http://www.zsr.org/precollegiate_edu.htm

Sponsor: Z. Smith Reynolds Foundation

147 South Cherry Street, Suite 200

Winston-Salem, NC 27101-5287

Z. Smith Reynolds Foundation Small Grants   1934

The Z. Smith Reynolds Foundation now offers a Small Grants Process for grant requests of up to $35,000 per year for up to two years. Small grants are made in the areas of community building and economic development, the environment, governance, public policy and civic engagement, pre-collegiate education, and social justice or equity. In addition to funding projects that achieve the goals of each focus area, the foundation has an interest in building the capacity of organizations and in promoting organizational development. New programs, rather than those that are well-established and well-funded, receive priority consideration. Types of support include operating budgets, continuing support, annual campaigns, seed grants, matching funds, projects/programs, conferences and seminars, and technical assistance.

Requirements: The foundation makes grants only to nonprofit, tax-exempt, charitable organizations and institutions in North Carolina.

Restrictions: The foundation does not give priority to: the arts; capital campaigns; computer hardware or software purchases; conferences, seminars, or symposiums; crisis intervention programs; fund raising events; historic preservation; local food banks; or substance abuse treatment programs.

Geographic Focus: North Carolina

Date(s) Application is Due: Aug 3

Contact: Leslie Winner, Executive Director; (800) 443-8319, ext. 105 or (336) 725-7541, ext. 105; fax (336) 725-6069; lwinner@zsr.org or info@zsr.org

Internet: http://www.zsr.org/small_grants.htm

Sponsor: Z. Smith Reynolds Foundation

147 South Cherry Street, Suite 200

Winston-Salem, NC 27101-5287

Z. Smith Reynolds Foundation Social Justice & Equity Grants   1935

The Foundation seeks to eliminate the unjust and unequal treatment of people of color, immigrants and those who are economically disadvantaged; eradicate the physical and sexual violence that threatens the lives and well-being of women; protect the rights of women to make choices about their reproductive health; and provide adolescents with information and choices that encourage them to avoid pregnancy. The Foundation invests in organizations and projects that: are non-discriminatory, just communities; and protect reproductive choice and reduce domestic violence and sexual assault. New programs, rather than those that are well-established and well-funded, receive priority consideration. Types of support include operating budgets, continuing support, annual campaigns, seed grants, matching funds, projects/programs, conferences and seminars, and technical assistance.

Requirements: The foundation makes grants only to nonprofit, tax-exempt, charitable organizations and institutions in North Carolina.

Restrictions: The foundation does not give priority to: the arts; capital campaigns; computer hardware or software purchases; conferences, seminars, or symposiums; crisis intervention programs; fund raising events; historic preservation; local food banks; or substance abuse treatment programs.

Geographic Focus: North Carolina

Date(s) Application is Due: Feb 1; Aug 1

Contact: James Gore, (800) 443-8319, ext. 124 or (336) 725-7541, ext. 124; fax (336) 725-6069; jamesg@zsr.org or info@zsr.org

Internet: http://www.zsr.org/social_justice.htm

Sponsor: Z. Smith Reynolds Foundation

147 South Cherry Street, Suite 200

Winston-Salem, NC 27101-5287

Subject Index

Community Education

Community and School Relations

Disaster Preparedness

Disaster Relief

Disasters

Disciples of Christ Church

Discrimination

Disease, Chronic

State Farm Strong Neighborhoods Grants, 1747
State Street Foundation Grants, 1749
Steelcase Foundation Grants, 1751
Steele-Reese Foundation Grants, 1752
Stella and Charles Guttman Foundation Grants, 1753
Stella B. Gross Charitable Trust Grants, 1754
Sterling and Shelli Gardner Foundation Grants, 1756
Stern Family Foundation Grants, 1757
Stewart Huston Charitable Trust Grants, 1760
Stranahan Foundation Grants, 1763
Strowd Roses Grants, 1766
Stuart Foundation Grants, 1767
Sulzberger Foundation Grants, 1768
SuperValu Foundation Grants, 1770
Susan Mott Webb Charitable Trust Grants, 1773
Susan Vaughan Foundation Grants, 1774
SVP Early Childhood Development and Parenting
    Grants, 1775
T. James Kavanagh Foundation Grants, 1778
T. Rowe Price Associates Foundation Grants, 1781
Ted Arison Family Foundation Grants, 1790
TE Foundation Grants, 1791
Telluride Foundation Community Grants, 1792
Temple Hoyne Buell Foundation Grants, 1796
Texas Commission on the Arts Arts Respond Project
    Grants, 1797
Thomas Austin Finch, Sr. Foundation Grants, 1807
Thomas B. and Elizabeth M. Sheridan Foundation
    Grants, 1808
Thomas C. Ackerman Foundation Grants, 1809
Thomas Thompson Trust Grants, 1811
Thomas W. Briggs Foundation Grants, 1813
Thompson Charitable Foundation Grants, 1814
Thompson Foundation Grants, 1815
Three Guineas Fund Grants, 1818
Topeka Community Foundation Grants, 1821
Toyota Motor North America New York Grants, 1823
TWS Foundation Grants, 1826
U.S. Bank Foundation Grants, 1827
Unilever US Grants, 1829
United Technologies Corporation Grants, 1835
V.V. Cooke Foundation Grants, 1839
Valley Foundation Grants, 1841
Vanguard Public Foundation Grant Funds, 1844
Viacom Foundation Grants (Formerly CBS
    Foundation), 1847
Victoria Foundation Grants, 1849
Virginia Environmental Endowment Kanawha and
    Ohio River Valleys Program, 1853
Vulcan Materials Company Foundation Grants, 1857
Walter and Elise Haas Fund Grants, 1863
Walter L. Gross III Family Foundation Grants, 1864
Walter S. Johnson Foundation Grants, 1865
Wayne and Gladys Valley Foundation Grants, 1867
Wayne County Foundation - Vigran Family Foundation
    Grants, 1868
Weatherwax Foundation Grants, 1869
Weaver Foundation Grants, 1870
Westar Energy Foundation Grants, 1873
Weyerhaeuser Company Foundation Grants, 1877
Wieboldt Foundation Grants, 1882
William A. Badger Foundation Grants, 1887
William Boss Foundation Grants, 1891
William D. Laurie, Jr. Charitable Found Grants, 1894
William E. and Bertha E. Schrafft Charitable Trust
    Grants, 1895
William G. & Helen C. Hoffman Found Grants, 1896
William G. McGowan Charitable Fund Grants, 1899
William J. & Dorothy K. O'Neill Found Grants, 1901
William K. Warren Foundation Grants, 1903
William L. and Victorine Q. Adams Foundation
    Grants, 1904
William N. and Myriam Pennington Foundation
    Grants, 1906
William Penn Foundation Grants, 1907
Wilson-Wood Foundation Grants, 1910
Women's Foundation of Southern Arizona Grants, 1916
Women's Funding Alliance Grants, 1917
Wood-Claeyssens Foundation Grants, 1919
Xerox Foundation Grants, 1925

Youth Philanthropy Project, 1928
Z. Smith Reynolds Foundation Pre-Collegiate
    Education Grants, 1933
Z. Smith Reynolds Foundation Small Grants, 1934

Education Reform
Achelis Foundation Grants, 39
Altria Group Education Grants, 111
American Express Foundation Historic Preservation
    Grants, 121
Anheuser-Busch Foundation Grants, 137
Bay and Paul Foundations Arts and Humanities
    Education Grants, 219
Bernard and Audre Rapoport Foundation Education
    Grants, 235
Bodman Foundation Grants, 263
Boeing Company Contributions Grants, 265
Carnegie Corporation of New York Grants, 354
Charles Stewart Mott Foundation Grants, 409
GNOF IMPACT Grants for Education, 835
Icahn Family Foundation Grants, 974
J. F. Maddox Foundation Grants, 1016
John W. Speas and Effie E. Speas Memorial Trust
    Grants, 1086
Joseph Drown Foundation Grants, 1088
Joseph H. & Florence A. Roblee Found Grants, 1089
Lewis H. Humphreys Charitable Trust Grants, 1174
Louis and Elizabeth Nave Flarsheim Charitable
    Foundation Grants, 1195
Minneapolis Foundation Community Grants, 1331
New Prospect Foundation Grants, 1383
Phil Hardin Foundation Grants, 1513
Prince Charitable Trusts Chicago Grants, 1545
Sapelo Found Environmental Protection Grants, 1681
Sprint Foundation Grants, 1740
Walter S. Johnson Foundation Grants, 1865
William J. Brace Charitable Trust, 1902

Education and Work
AEGON Transamerica Foundation Civic and
    Community Grants, 61
Brooklyn Community Foundation Green Communities
    Grants, 303
Santa Fe Community Foundation Seasonal Grants-
    Spring Cycle, 1678
Xerox Foundation Grants, 1925

Educational Administration
5 51 5 Foundation Grants, 5
Guy I. Bromley Trust Grants, 864
John W. Speas and Effie E. Speas Memorial Trust
    Grants, 1086
Lewis H. Humphreys Charitable Trust Grants, 1174
Louis and Elizabeth Nave Flarsheim Charitable
    Foundation Grants, 1195
Lumina Foundation for Education Grants, 1210
Meyer Foundation Education Grants, 1311
Nellie Mae Education Foundation District-Level
    Change Grants, 1370

Educational Evaluation/Assessment
Nellie Mae Education Foundation Research and
    Development Grants, 1371
PacifiCare Foundation Grants, 1478
Stuart Foundation Grants, 1767
William J. Brace Charitable Trust, 1902
Z. Smith Reynolds Foundation Pre-Collegiate
    Education Grants, 1933

Educational Finance
Allstate Corp Hometown Commitment Grants, 104

Educational Instruction
Bernard and Audre Rapoport Foundation Education
    Grants, 235
Head Start Replacement Grantee: Colorado, 906
Head Start Replacement Grantee: Florida, 907
Head Start Replacement Grantee: West Virginia, 908
Motorola Foundation Innovation Generation
    Collaborative Grants, 1353

Motorola Found Innovation Generation Grants, 1354
San Diego Women's Foundation Grants, 1669
SuperValu Foundation Grants, 1770
VDH Rescue Squad Assistance Fund Grants, 1845
Z. Smith Reynolds Foundation Pre-Collegiate
    Education Grants, 1933

Educational Planning/Policy
Achelis Foundation Grants, 39
Bodman Foundation Grants, 263
Charles G. Koch Charitable Foundation Grants, 401
Chicago Tribune Foundation Civic Grants, 425
GNOF IMPACT Grants for Education, 835
Guy I. Bromley Trust Grants, 864
John W. Speas and Effie E. Speas Memorial Trust
    Grants, 1086
Lewis H. Humphreys Charitable Trust Grants, 1174
Louis and Elizabeth Nave Flarsheim Charitable
    Foundation Grants, 1195
Lumina Foundation for Education Grants, 1210
Meyer Foundation Education Grants, 1311
Michael and Susan Dell Foundation Grants, 1320
Nellie Mae Education Foundation District-Level
    Change Grants, 1370
Nellie Mae Education Foundation Research and
    Development Grants, 1371
Phil Hardin Foundation Grants, 1513
Schumann Fund for New Jersey Grants, 1691
Stuart Foundation Grants, 1767
Z. Smith Reynolds Foundation Pre-Collegiate
    Education Grants, 1933

Educational Psychology
Ittleson Foundation Mental Health Grants, 1014

Educational Technology
Alcatel-Lucent Technologies Foundation Grants, 84
Corning Incorporated Foundation Educ Grants, 535
Jessie Ball Dupont Fund Grants, 1057
Leonsis Foundation Grants, 1172
Mitsubishi Electric America Foundation Grants, 1337
Motorola Found Innovation Generation Grants, 1354
Z. Smith Reynolds Foundation Pre-Collegiate
    Education Grants, 1933

Educational Theory
Guy I. Bromley Trust Grants, 864
John W. Speas and Effie E. Speas Memorial Trust
    Grants, 1086
Lewis H. Humphreys Charitable Trust Grants, 1174
Louis and Elizabeth Nave Flarsheim Charitable
    Foundation Grants, 1195
Nellie Mae Education Foundation Research and
    Development Grants, 1371

Elder Abuse
Arizona Republic Newspaper Corporate Contributions
    Grants, 167
Hearst Foundations Social Service Grants, 914
Peacock Foundation Grants, 1500
Phoenixville Community Health Found Grants, 1519

Elderly
A.V. Hunter Trust Grants, 14
Abbot and Dorothy H. Stevens Foundation Grants, 18
Aladdin Industries Foundation Grants, 74
Albert and Bessie Mae Kronkosky Charitable
    Foundation Grants, 77
Albert W. Rice Charitable Foundation Grants, 82
Alex Stern Family Foundation Grants, 91
Alfred E. Chase Charitable Foundation Grants, 95
Alfred I. DuPont Foundation Grants, 96
Amelia Sillman Rockwell and Carlos Perry Rockwell
    Charities Fund Grants, 115
Ameren Corporation Community Grants, 116
AMI Semiconductors Corporate Grants, 130
Amon G. Carter Foundation Grants, 131
Ann Peppers Foundation Grants, 145
Anschutz Family Foundation Grants, 146
Arizona Community Foundation Grants, 162

Health Care Access

Housing

Humanitarianism

Humanities

Humanities Education

Methodist Church
Danellie Foundation Grants, 564
Effie and Wofford Cain Foundation Grants, 658
Harry and Helen Sands Charitable Trust Grants, 886
MacDonald-Peterson Foundation Grants, 1224
Powell Foundation Grants, 1539
W. Waldo and Jenny Lynn M. Bradley Foundation
   Grants, 1860

Microeconomics
McCune Charitable Foundation Grants, 1275

Microenterprises
Levi Strauss Foundation Grants Programs, 1173
Sapelo Found Environmental Protection Grants, 1681
Third Wave Foundation Lela Breitbart Memorial Fund
   Grants, 1802
Third Wave Foundation Organizing and Advocacy
   Grants, 1803
Third Wave Foundation Reproductive Health and
   Justice Grants, 1804
Union Bank, N.A. Foundation Grants, 1830

Middle School
MeadWestvaco Foundation Education Grants, 1287

Middle School Education
Carnegie Corporation of New York Grants, 354
Colonel Stanley R. McNeil Foundation Grants, 477
Cooper Foundation Grants, 530
DaimlerChrysler Corporation Fund Grants, 560
Eaton Charitable Fund Grants, 642
Frank B. Hazard General Charity Fund Grants, 743
Fred & Gretel Biel Charitable Trust Grants, 752
Fred Meyer Foundation Grants, 758
George J. and Effie L. Seay Foundation Grants, 808
Helen Bader Foundation Grants, 919
Joseph S. Stackpole Charitable Trust Grants, 1091
Marjorie Moore Charitable Foundation Grants, 1247
MassMutual Foundation for Hartford Grants, 1262
McCune Charitable Foundation Grants, 1275
Medina Foundation Grants, 1291
Meyer Foundation Education Grants, 1311
Nellie Mae Education Foundation District-Level
   Change Grants, 1370
New York Life Foundation Grants, 1386
Raskob Found for Catholic Activities Grants, 1566
Reinberger Foundation Grants, 1573
Stuart Foundation Grants, 1767
William J. Brace Charitable Trust, 1902

Migrant Labor
Charles Delmar Foundation Grants, 400
Luther I. Replogle Foundation Grants, 1213
Meyer Foundation Economic Security Grants, 1310
Needmor Fund Grants, 1368
Union Bank, N.A. Foundation Grants, 1830

Migrants
AED New Voices Fellowship Program, 59
DHHS Health Centers Grants for Migratory and
   Seasonal Farmworkers, 590
Luther I. Replogle Foundation Grants, 1213
Union Bank, N.A. Foundation Grants, 1830

Migratory Animals and Birds
Alexander H. Bright Charitable Trust Grants, 90
Barbara Meyer Elsner Foundation Grants, 209
Lucy Downing Nisbet Charitable Fund Grants, 1208

Military Personnel
Anne J. Caudal Foundation Grants, 140

Military Sciences
Cord Foundation Grants, 532

Military Training
Gulf Coast Foundation of Community Operating
   Grants, 862

Mime
NYSCA Presenting: General Operating Support
   Grants, 1441

Mining
Brainerd Foundation Grants, 278
Northwest Fund for the Environment Grants, 1421

Ministry
Chapman Charitable Foundation Grants, 397

Minorities
Abbot and Dorothy H. Stevens Foundation Grants, 18
Abelard Foundation East Grants, 24
Abelard Foundation West Grants, 25
Adolph Coors Foundation Grants, 55
Akonadi Foundation Anti-Racism Grants, 69
Alberto Culver Corporate Contributions Grants, 78
Alex Stern Family Foundation Grants, 91
AmerUs Group Charitable Foundation, 127
Anheuser-Busch Foundation Grants, 137
ANLAF Int'l Fund for Sexual Minorities Grants, 139
Arlington Community Foundation Grants, 170
Avon Products Foundation Grants, 192
Ben & Jerry's Foundation Grants, 230
BMW of North America Charitable Contributions, 262
Boston Foundation Grants, 272
Boston Globe Foundation Grants, 274
Boston Women's Fund Grants, 275
Butler Manufacturing Co Foundation Grants, 320
Carnegie Corporation of New York Grants, 354
Charles Delmar Foundation Grants, 400
Chesapeake Bay Trust Outreach and Community
   Engagement Grants, 418
Chicago Board of Trade Foundation Grants, 421
Chinook Fund Grants, 430
Colgate-Palmolive Company Grants, 473
Colorado Interstate Gas Grants, 479
ConocoPhillips Foundation Grants, 521
ConocoPhillips Grants Program, 522
Cralle Foundation Grants, 541
Crossroads Fund Seed Grants, 549
Crossroads Technical Assistance Program Grants, 550
Cummins Foundation Grants, 554
Donald P. and Byrd M. Kelly Foundation Grants, 606
Dreyer's Foundation Large Grants Program, 623
Edward W. and Stella C. Van Houten Memorial Fund
   Grants, 654
Edwin S. Webster Foundation Grants, 655
Eugene M. Lang Foundation Grants, 688
Eugene McDermott Foundation Grants, 689
Florida Division of Cultural Affairs Underserved
   Cultural Community Development Grants, 727
Frederick McDonald Trust Grants, 756
GATX Corporation Grants Program, 786
George R. Wallace Foundation Grants, 812
George W. Wells Foundation Grants, 815
Georgia-Pacific Found Entrepreneurship Grants, 816
Grotto Foundation Project Grants, 859
H.J. Heinz Company Foundation Grants, 868
Health Foundation of Greater Indianapolis Grants, 910
Helen Steiner Rice Foundation Grants, 923
Jackson Foundation Grants, 1028
James Ford Bell Foundation Grants, 1035
Joseph H. & Florence A. Roblee Found Grants, 1089
Joseph S. Stackpole Charitable Trust Grants, 1091
Katharine Matthies Foundation Grants, 1112
Kroger Foundation Diversity Grants, 1147
Mary Reynolds Babcock Foundation Grants, 1260
Montana Arts Council Cultural and Aesthetic Project
   Grants, 1342
MONY Foundation Grants, 1346
Morris Stulsaft Foundation Grants, 1349
Moses Kimball Fund Grants, 1351
Motorola Foundation Innovation Generation
   Collaborative Grants, 1353
NNEDVF/Altria Doors of Hope Program, 1399
North Dakota Council on the Arts Community Access
   Grants, 1413
Norton Foundation Grants, 1422

Oppenstein Brothers Foundation Grants, 1460
PDF Community Organizing Grants, 1499
Playboy Foundation Grants, 1530
Powell Foundation Grants, 1538
Prudential Foundation Education Grants, 1554
Rayonier Foundation Grants, 1568
Rhode Island Foundation Grants, 1585
Richard & Susan Smith Family Found Grants, 1589
Robert R. Meyer Foundation Grants, 1608
Scherman Foundation Grants, 1687
Sensient Technologies Foundation Grants, 1701
Sister Fund Grants for Women's Organizations, 1712
Sony Corporation of America Corporate Philanthropy
   Grants, 1727
Sophia Romero Trust Grants, 1728
Steelcase Foundation Grants, 1751
SuperValu Foundation Grants, 1770
Textron Corporate Contributions Grants, 1799
Third Wave Foundation Lela Breitbart Memorial Fund
   Grants, 1802
Third Wave Foundation Organizing and Advocacy
   Grants, 1803
Third Wave Foundation Reproductive Health and
   Justice Grants, 1804
Union Bank, N.A. Foundation Grants, 1830
Union Carbide Foundation Grants, 1831
Victoria Foundation Grants, 1849
Vulcan Materials Company Foundation Grants, 1857
WILD Foundation Grants, 1885
Wilson-Wood Foundation Grants, 1910
Wisconsin Arts Board Arts Challenge Initiative
   Grants, 1913
Woodward Governor Company Grants, 1922
Z. Smith Reynolds Foundation Small Grants, 1934

Minorities, Ethnic
BMW of North America Charitable Contributions, 262
Margaret M. Walker Charitable Found Grants, 1236
Prudential Foundation Arts and Culture Grants, 1552
Robert R. Meyer Foundation Grants, 1608

Minority Education
Air Products and Chemicals Grants, 68
Akonadi Foundation Anti-Racism Grants, 69
Alcoa Foundation Grants, 85
Anheuser-Busch Foundation Grants, 137
ARCO Foundation Education Grants, 157
Beerman Foundation Grants, 223
BMW of North America Charitable Contributions, 262
CE and S Foundation Grants, 375
CIGNA Foundation Grants, 439
Citigroup Foundation Grants, 444
Coca-Cola Foundation Grants, 471
Colgate-Palmolive Company Grants, 473
DaimlerChrysler Corporation Fund Grants, 560
Edward W. and Stella C. Van Houten Memorial Fund
   Grants, 654
FMC Foundation Grants, 729
Head Start Replacement Grantee: Colorado, 906
Hearst Foundations Education Grants, 913
Johnson & Johnson Corp Contributions Grants, 1080
Kroger Foundation Diversity Grants, 1147
Lloyd G. Balfour Foundation Attleboro-Specific
   Charities Grants, 1189
Margoes Foundation Grants, 1238
McCune Charitable Foundation Grants, 1275
Michael and Susan Dell Foundation Grants, 1320
Miller Brewing Corporate Contributions Program
   Grants, 1327
Millipore Foundation Grants, 1328
New York Times Company Foundation Grants, 1387
Northern Trust Company Charitable Trust and
   Corporate Giving Program, 1418
NSF Partnerships in Astronomy & Astrophysics
   Research and Education (PAARE), 1428
RBC Dain Rauscher Foundation Grants, 1569
Sprint Foundation Grants, 1740
Viacom Foundation Grants, 1847
William J. Brace Charitable Trust, 1902
Xerox Foundation Grants, 1925

Ophthalmology

Oral Diseases

Oral Health and Hygiene

Oral History

Orchestras

Organ Transplants

Organic Farming

Organizational Development

Organizational Theory and Behavior

Orthopedics

Outpatient Care

Ovarian Cancer

Painting

Palliative Care

Pancreatic Cancer

Paper Industry

Parapsychology

Parent Education

Greater Worcester Community Foundation Jeppson
  Memorial Fund for Brookfield Grants, 855
Harvest Foundation Grants, 896
Helen V. Brach Foundation Grants, 924
John Deere Foundation Grants, 1066
Needmor Fund Grants, 1368
NNEDVF/Altria Doors of Hope Program, 1399
Olin Corporation Charitable Trust Grants, 1452
Pioneer Hi-Bred Community Grants, 1525
PPG Industries Foundation Grants, 1540
Robert R. Meyer Foundation Grants, 1608
Toyota Motor North America New York Grants, 1823
William G. McGowan Charitable Fund Grants, 1899
Women's Foundation of Southern Arizona Go Girls!
  Sports Grants, 1915

Safety Engineering
BMW of North America Charitable Contributions, 262

Sanitary Engineering
Bill and Melinda Gates Foundation Water, Sanitation
  and Hygiene Grants, 250
Dorr Foundation Grants, 615

Scholarship Programs, General
4-C's Foundation Grants, 3
Abell-Hanger Foundation Grants, 28
Achelis Foundation Grants, 39
Alabama State Council on the Arts Community Arts
  Operating Support Grants, 71
Aladdin Industries Foundation Grants, 74
Albuquerque Community Foundation Grants, 83
Alliant Energy Corporation Contributions, 103
American Foodservice Charitable Trust Grants, 122
Ametek Foundation Grants, 128
Andrew Family Foundation Grants, 136
Antone & Edene Vidinha Charitable Trust Grants, 148
Aratani Foundation Grants, 153
Arlington Community Foundation Grants, 170
Arthur E. and Josephine Campbell Beyer Foundation
  Grants, 174
Batts Foundation Grants, 215
Bedford Community Health Foundation Grants, 222
Bethesda Foundation Grants, 241
Bindley Family Foundation Grants, 251
Blade Foundation Grants, 252
Blue Mountain Community Foundation Grants, 259
Bodman Foundation Grants, 263
Boettcher Foundation Grants, 266
Bright Family Foundation Grants, 281
Burlington Northern Santa Fe Foundation Grants, 310
Butler Manufacturing Co Foundation Grants, 320
Campbell Soup Foundation Grants, 340
Capezio/Ballet Makers Inc Grants and Awards, 342
Carnahan-Jackson Foundation Grants, 353
Carpenter Foundation Grants, 356
Carrier Corporation Contributions Grants, 359
Catherine Manley Gaylord Foundation Grants, 364
CFFVR Appleton Education Foundation Grants, 380
CFFVR Doug & Carla Salmon Found Grants, 384
CFFVR Shawano Area Community Foundation
  Grants, 391
CFFVR Women's Fund for the Fox Valley Region
  Grants, 393
Chautauqua Region Community Found Grants, 414
Chiles Foundation Grants, 427
Clarence T.C. Ching Foundation Grants, 450
Clark-Winchcole Foundation Grants, 451
Cleveland-Cliffs Foundation Grants, 460
Coca-Cola Foundation Grants, 471
Collins Foundation Grants, 476
Community Found for Greater Buffalo Grants, 489
Community Foundation of Herkimer and Oneida
  Counties Grants, 502
Community Found of South Puget Sound Grants, 506
Community Foundation of the Verdugos Grants, 513
Constellation Energy Corporate Grants, 525
Cooper Industries Foundation Grants, 531
Cord Foundation Grants, 532
Corning Incorporated Foundation Educ Grants, 535

Crescent Porter Hale Foundation Grants, 545
Danellie Foundation Grants, 564
Dorr Foundation Grants, 615
Duke Endowment Education Grants, 630
Edward W. and Stella C. Van Houten Memorial Fund
  Grants, 654
El Paso Community Foundation Grants, 673
Elsie H. Wilcox Foundation Grants, 675
Ethyl Corporation Grants, 686
Fairfield County Community Foundation Grants, 700
Flinn Foundation Grants Programs, 720
FMC Foundation Grants, 729
Fourjay Foundation Grants, 737
Frank S. Flowers Foundation Grants, 748
Gebbie Foundation Grants, 791
General Mills Foundation Grants, 795
George and Ruth Bradford Foundation Grants, 798
George Foundation Grants, 805
Georgia-Pacific Found Entrepreneurship Grants, 816
Gil and Dody Weaver Foundation Grants, 823
Greater Saint Louis Community Found Grants, 852
Harold Simmons Foundation Grants, 881
Harry Bramhall Gilbert Charitable Trust Grants, 888
Helen V. Brach Foundation Grants, 924
High Meadow Foundation Grants, 940
Hilton Hotels Corporate Giving Program Grants, 942
Hirtzel Memorial Foundation Grants, 943
Hoglund Foundation Grants, 946
Huie-Dellmon Trust Grants, 966
Huisking Foundation Grants, 967
Idaho Power Company Corporate Contributions, 975
Iddings Foundation, 977
J. Willard & Alice S. Marriott Found Grants, 1025
J. Willard Marriott, Jr. Foundation Grants, 1026
Jacob and Charlotte Lehrman Foundation Grants, 1029
James & Abigail Campbell Family Found Grants, 1032
James R. Thorpe Foundation Grants, 1041
JELD-WEN Foundation Grants, 1052
John J. Leidy Foundation Grants, 1071
John Jewett and Helen Chandler Garland Foundation
  Grants, 1072
John M. Ross Foundation Grants, 1073
John R. Oishei Foundation Grants, 1076
Joseph Alexander Foundation Grants, 1087
Joukowsky Family Foundation Grants, 1093
Kathryne Beynon Foundation Grants, 1114
Kawabe Memorial Fund Grants, 1115
Kimberly-Clark Foundation Grants, 1133
Kopp Family Foundation Grants, 1144
Lawrence J. and Anne Rubenstein Charitable
  Foundation Grants, 1163
Leo Goodwin Foundation Grants, 1169
Lillian S. Wells Foundation Grants, 1179
Loews Foundation Grants, 1191
Louis Calder Foundation Grants, 1196
Lowell Berry Foundation Grants, 1202
Lubbock Area Foundation Grants, 1203
Lubrizol Foundation Grants, 1205
Lumpkin Family Found Healthy People Grants, 1211
Lynde and Harry Bradley Foundation Grants, 1215
M. Bastian Family Foundation Grants, 1219
Margoes Foundation Grants, 1238
Mary E. Bivins Foundation Grants, 1253
MassMutual Foundation for Hartford Grants, 1262
Mead Witter Foundation Grants, 1290
MGN Family Foundation Grants, 1318
New York Life Foundation Grants, 1386
New York Times Company Foundation Grants, 1387
NHSCA Operating Grants, 1394
Oklahoma City Community Foundation Grants, 1451
Ordean Foundation Grants, 1463
Ottinger-Sprong Charitable Found Scholarships, 1467
Owens Foundation Grants, 1472
Park Foundation Grants, 1485
Patrick and Anna M. Cudahy Fund Grants, 1492
Paul and Mary Haas Foundation Contributions and
  Student Scholarships, 1495
Percy B. Ferebee Endowment Grants, 1502
Price Family Charitable Fund Grants, 1542
Puerto Rico Community Foundation Grants, 1556

Rathmann Family Foundation Grants, 1567
Rhode Island Foundation Grants, 1585
Ruth Eleanor Bamberger and John Ernest Bamberger
  Memorial Foundation Grants, 1638
Ryder System Charitable Foundation Grants, 1642
S. Livingston Mather Charitable Trust Grants, 1649
Saint Paul Companies Foundation Grants, 1656
Samuel S. Johnson Foundation Grants, 1665
Sara Lee Foundation Grants, 1684
Simmons Foundation Grants, 1709
Square D Foundation Grants, 1741
Starr Foundation Grants, 1746
Strengthening Families - Strengthening Communities
  Grants, 1765
Strowd Roses Grants, 1766
Stuart Foundation Grants, 1767
T. James Kavanagh Foundation Grants, 1778
Temple-Inland Foundation Grants, 1795
Third Wave Foundation Lela Breitbart Memorial Fund
  Grants, 1802
Third Wave Foundation Organizing and Advocacy
  Grants, 1803
Third Wave Foundation Reproductive Health and
  Justice Grants, 1804
Thomas and Dorothy Leavey Foundation Grants, 1806
Thomas Austin Finch, Sr. Foundation Grants, 1807
Thomas B. and Elizabeth M. Sheridan Foundation
  Grants, 1808
Thompson Charitable Foundation Grants, 1814
Vulcan Materials Company Foundation Grants, 1857
W.W. Smith Charitable Trust Grants, 1859
Walt Disney Company Foundation Grants, 1862
Whirlpool Foundation Grants, 1878
William G. & Helen C. Hoffman Found Grants, 1896
William G. Gilmore Foundation Grants, 1898
William G. McGowan Charitable Fund Grants, 1899
Women's Foundation of Southern Arizona Grants, 1916
Wood-Claeyssens Foundation Grants, 1919
Xerox Foundation Grants, 1925
Z. Smith Reynolds Foundation Small Grants, 1934

School Dental Programs
Pollock Foundation Grants, 1533

School Food Programs
ConAgra Foods Foundation Community Grants, 518
ConAgra Foods Foundation Nourish Our Community
  Grants, 519

School Health Programs
Circle K Corporation Contributions Grants, 443
Colonel Stanley R. McNeil Foundation Grants, 477
DHHS Oral Health Promotion Research Across the
  Lifespan, 592
McKesson Foundation Grants, 1283
Mt. Sinai Health Care Foundation Health of the Urban
  Community Grants, 1356
Philip L. Graham Fund Health and Human Services
  Grants, 1516
Piedmont Health Foundation Grants, 1520
Seattle Foundation Health and Wellness Grants, 1697
Visiting Nurse Foundation Grants, 1856

School Libraries
MeadWestvaco Foundation Education Grants, 1287

School-to-Work Transition
Able Trust Vocational Rehabilitation Grants for
  Agencies, 36
AEGON Transamerica Foundation Civic and
  Community Grants, 61
Crail-Johnson Foundation Grants, 540
Ewing Marion Kauffman Foundation Grants and
  Initiatives, 696
Georgia-Pacific Found Entrepreneurship Grants, 816
J. Willard & Alice S. Marriott Found Grants, 1025
Meyer Foundation Economic Security Grants, 1310
Meyer Foundation Education Grants, 1311
Pentair Found Education & Community Grants, 1501
S.H. Cowell Foundation Grants, 1648

Social Services Delivery

Social Stratification/Mobility

Social Work

Soil Sciences, Soil Genesis

Solar Studies

Program Type Index

Building Construction and/or Renovation

Centers: Research/Demonstration/Service

Samuel S. Johnson Foundation Grants, 1665
TAC Arts Projects Grants, 1783
TAC Rural Arts Project Support Grants, 1787
Telluride Foundation Community Grants, 1792
Telluride Foundation Tech Assistance Grants, 1794
Texas Commission on the Arts Arts Respond Project Grants, 1797
Victoria Foundation Grants, 1849
Virginia Commission for the Arts Project Grants, 1852

Cultural Outreach

A.C. Ratshesky Foundation Grants, 13
Aaron Copland Fund Supplemental Program Grants, 17
Abbot and Dorothy H. Stevens Foundation Grants, 18
Abbott Fund Community Grants, 20
Abby's Legendary Pizza Foundation Grants, 22
Abell-Hanger Foundation Grants, 28
Abell Foundation Arts and Culture Grants, 29
Achelis Foundation Grants, 39
Ackerman Foundation Grants, 40
Adams-Mastrovich Family Foundation Grants, 42
Adams County Community Foundation of Indiana Grants, 44
Adams Foundation Grants, 51
Adolph Coors Foundation Grants, 55
AEC Trust Grants, 58
AFG Industries Grants, 63
African American Fund of New Jersey Grants, 64
A Friends' Foundation Trust Grants, 66
Agnes Gund Foundation Grants, 67
Air Products and Chemicals Grants, 68
Akonadi Foundation Anti-Racism Grants, 69
Alabama State Council on the Arts Community Arts Operating Support Grants, 71
Alabama State Council on the Arts Performing Arts Operating Support Grants, 72
Alabama State Council on the Arts Visual Arts Operating Support Grants, 73
Aladdin Industries Foundation Grants, 74
Alaska State Council on the Arts Operating Support Grants, 75
Albert and Bessie Mae Kronkosky Charitable Foundation Grants, 77
Alberto Culver Corporate Contributions Grants, 78
Albert Pick Jr. Fund Grants, 79
Albertson's Charitable Giving Grants, 80
Albuquerque Community Foundation Grants, 83
Alcatel-Lucent Technologies Foundation Grants, 84
Alexander & Baldwin Foundation Mainland Grants, 87
Alexander and Baldwin Foundation Hawaiian and Pacific Island Grants, 88
Alex Stern Family Foundation Grants, 91
Alfred P. Sloan Foundation Civic Initiatives Grants, 97
Allegheny Foundation Grants, 99
Allen Hilles Fund Grants, 101
Allstate Corp Hometown Commitment Grants, 104
Alpha Natural Resources Corporate Giving, 106
Altman Foundation Arts and Culture Grants, 108
Altria Group Arts and Culture Grants, 110
Alvin and Fanny Blaustein Thalheimer Foundation Grants, 113
Ameren Corporation Community Grants, 116
American Express Foundation Historic Preservation Grants, 121
Amerigroup Foundation Grants, 125
AmerUs Group Charitable Foundation, 127
Ametek Foundation Grants, 128
Amgen Foundation Grants, 129
Amon G. Carter Foundation Grants, 131
Anderson Foundation Grants, 134
Anheuser-Busch Foundation Grants, 137
ANLAF International Fund for Sexual Minorities Grants, 139
Anne Thorne Weaver Family Foundation Grants, 141
Ann L. and Carol Green Rhodes Charitable Trust Grants, 144
Ann Peppers Foundation Grants, 145
Anschutz Family Foundation Grants, 146
Ar-Hale Family Foundation Grants, 151
Aratani Foundation Grants, 153

Arcadia Foundation Grants, 155
Arcus Foundation Fund Grants, 158
Arie and Ida Crown Memorial Grants, 159
Arizona Commission on the Arts Community Investment Grants, 160
Arizona Community Foundation Grants, 162
Arizona Public Service Corporate Giving, 165
Arizona Republic Newspaper Corporate Contributions Grants, 167
Arthur F. and Alice E. Adams Charitable Foundation Grants, 175
Arthur F. & Arnold M. Frankel Found Grants, 176
Arts and Science Council Grants, 178
Arts Council of Winston-Salem and Forsyth County Organizational Support Grants, 179
AT&T Arts and Culture Grants, 183
Athwin Foundation Grants, 184
Atlanta Foundation Grants, 186
Auburn Foundation Grants, 189
Audrey & Sydney Irmas Foundation Grants, 190
Avon Foundation Speak Out Against Domestic Violence Grants, 191
Avon Products Foundation Grants, 192
Ayres Foundation Grants, 196
Babcock Charitable Trust Grants, 198
Back Home Again Foundation Grants, 199
Bacon Family Foundation Grants, 200
Bailey-Fischer and Porter Grants, 201
Ball Brothers Foundation General Grants, 202
Banfi Vintners Foundation Grants, 205
Bank of America Foundation Volunteer Grants, 207
Barker Welfare Foundation Grants, 211
Barrasso Usdin Kupperman Freeman and Sarver LLC Corporate Grants, 212
Barr Fund Grants, 213
Batchelor Foundation Grants, 214
Batts Foundation Grants, 215
Baxter International Corporate Giving Grants, 217
Baxter International Foundation Grants, 218
Bay and Paul Foundations Arts and Humanities Education Grants, 219
Beerman Foundation Grants, 223
Beim Foundation Grants, 224
Belk Foundation Grants, 226
Bemis Company Foundation Grants, 229
Beneficia Foundation Grants, 232
Berks County Community Foundation Grants, 234
Bernard Osher Foundation Local Arts and Educational Grants, 238
Berrien Community Foundation Grants, 239
Besser Foundation Grants, 240
Bildner Family Foundation Grants, 245
Bill and Melinda Gates Foundation Agricultural Development Grants, 246
Bill and Melinda Gates Foundation Emergency Response Grants, 247
Bill and Melinda Gates Foundation Financial Services for the Poor Grants, 248
Blade Foundation Grants, 252
Blanche and Irving Laurie Foundation Grants, 253
Blanche and Julian Robertson Family Foundation Grants, 254
Blandin Foundation Itasca County Area Vitality Grants, 256
Blue Mountain Community Foundation Grants, 259
Blum-Kovler Foundation Grants, 260
Blumenthal Foundation Grants, 261
Bodman Foundation Grants, 263
Boeing Company Contributions Grants, 265
Boettcher Foundation Grants, 266
Boise Cascade Corporation Contributions Grants, 268
Bonfils-Stanton Foundation Grants, 269
Booth Ferris Foundation Grants, 270
Boston Foundation Grants, 272
Boston Foundation Initiative to Strengthen Arts and Cultural Service Organizations, 273
Boston Globe Foundation Grants, 274
Boston Women's Fund Grants, 275
Boulder County Arts Alliance Neodata Endowment Grants, 276

Brico Fund Grants, 280
British Columbia Arts Council Arts and Cultural Service Organization Operating Assistance, 284
British Columbia Arts Council Community Councils Local Government Matching Grants, 285
British Columbia Arts Council Media Arts Organizations Operating Assistance, 287
British Columbia Arts Council Operating Assistance for Community Arts Councils, 288
British Columbia Arts Council Operating Assistance for Performing Arts Organization, 289
British Columbia Arts Council Operating Assistance for Visual Arts Organizations, 290
British Columbia Arts Council Professional Arts Festival Operating Assistance, 291
British Columbia Arts Council Professional Arts Periodicals Operating Assistance, 292
British Columbia Arts Council Professional Arts Training Organization Operating Assistance, 293
British Columbia Arts Council Project Assistance for Performing Artists, 294
British Columbia Arts Council Public Museums Operating Assistance, 295
Brooklyn Community Foundation Community Arts for All Grants, 300
Brooklyn Community Foundation Education and Youth Achievement Grants, 302
Brown Foundation Grants, 304
Bunbury Company Grants, 309
Burlington Northern Santa Fe Foundation Grants, 310
Bydale Foundation Grants, 321
Byron W. and Alice L. Lockwood Grants, 322
Caesars Foundation Grants, 328
Caleb C. and Julia W. Dula Educational and Charitable Foundation Grants, 329
California Arts Council Public Value Grants, 330
California Arts Council State-Local Partnership Grants, 331
California Arts Co Statewide Networks Grants, 332
Cambridge Community Foundation Grants, 337
Campbell Hoffman Foundation Grants, 339
Campbell Soup Foundation Grants, 340
Cape Branch Foundation Grants, 341
Carl and Eloise Pohlad Family Foundation Grants, 345
Carl C. Icahn Foundation Grants, 346
Carl Gellert and Celia Berta Gellert Foundation Grants, 347
Carl M. Freeman Foundation FACES Grants, 349
Carl M. Freeman Foundation Grants, 350
Carnegie Corporation of New York Grants, 354
Carolyn Foundation Grants, 355
Carpenter Foundation Grants, 356
Carrie Estelle Doheny Foundation Grants, 358
CCA Assistance to Artist-Run Centres Grants, 366
CCA Grants to Media Arts Organizations, 367
CCA Opera/Music Theatre Annual Grants, 368
CCA Operating Grants to Professional Theater Organizations, 369
CCA Professional Choir Program Annual Funding Grants, 370
CCA Professional Orchestra Program Annual and Multi-Year Grants, 371
CDECD Arts Catalyze Placemaking Leadership Grants, 373
CDECD Arts Catalyze Placemaking Sustaining Relevance Grants, 374
Cemala Foundation Grants, 376
CFFVR Clintonville Area Foundation Grants, 383
CFFVR Shawano Area Community Foundation Grants, 391
Chamberlain Foundation Grants, 395
Charles H. Price II Family Foundation Grants, 404
Charles M. Bair Family Trust Grants, 406
Chatlos Foundation Grants Program, 413
Chazen Foundation Grants, 415
Chesapeake Corporation Foundation Grants, 419
Chicago Board of Trade Foundation Grants, 421
Chicago CityArts Program Grants, 422
Chicago Sun Times Charity Trust Grants, 423
Chicago Title & Trust Company Found Grants, 424

William Penn Foundation Grants, 1907
Wisconsin Arts Board Artistic Program I Support Grants, 1912
Wisconsin Arts Board Arts Challenge Initiative Grants, 1913
Wood-Claeyssens Foundation Grants, 1919
Woods Charitable Fund Grants, 1920
Woods Fund of Chicago Grants, 1921
Woodward Governor Company Grants, 1922
Wortham Foundation Grants, 1923
Xerox Foundation Grants, 1925
Yellow Corporate Foundation Grants, 1926
Z. Smith Reynolds Foundation Small Grants, 1934

Curriculum Development/Teacher Training
Advance Auto Parts Corporate Giving Grants, 56
Albertson's Charitable Giving Grants, 80
Alpha Natural Resources Corporate Giving, 106
Altria Group Education Grants, 111
American Foodservice Charitable Trust Grants, 122
American Woodmark Foundation Grants, 124
Amerigroup Foundation Grants, 125
Amgen Foundation Grants, 129
Anderson Foundation Grants, 134
Ar-Hale Family Foundation Grants, 151
Aratani Foundation Grants, 153
Ayres Foundation Grants, 196
Babcock Charitable Trust Grants, 198
Ball Brothers Foundation General Grants, 202
Baxter International Corporate Giving Grants, 217
Bay and Paul Foundations Arts and Humanities Education Grants, 219
Bernard and Audre Rapoport Foundation Education Grants, 235
Bernard Osher Foundation Local Arts and Educational Grants, 238
Blanche and Julian Robertson Family Foundation Grants, 254
Boeing Company Contributions Grants, 265
Bonfils-Stanton Foundation Grants, 269
Cabot Corporation Foundation Grants, 325
California Arts Co Statewide Networks Grants, 332
Cambridge Community Foundation Grants, 337
Carl M. Freeman Foundation Grants, 350
Carnahan-Jackson Foundation Grants, 353
Carnegie Corporation of New York Grants, 354
Carolyn Foundation Grants, 355
Carrie Estelle Doheny Foundation Grants, 358
CFFVR Alcoholism and Drug Abuse Grants, 379
CFFVR Clintonville Area Foundation Grants, 383
Chapman Charitable Foundation Grants, 397
Charity Incorporated Grants, 398
Charles H. Price II Family Foundation Grants, 404
Charles Stewart Mott Foundation Grants, 409
Chestnut Hill Charitable Foundation, Inc Grants, 420
Chilkat Valley Community Foundation Grants, 428
Christensen Fund Regional Grants, 431
Circle K Corporation Contributions Grants, 443
Clarence E. Heller Charitable Foundation Grants, 449
Coca-Cola Foundation Grants, 471
Community Foundation of Greater Birmingham Grants, 498
Community Foundation of the Verdugos Educational Endowment Fund Grants, 512
Comprehensive Health Education Found Grants, 516
ConocoPhillips Foundation Grants, 521
Cooper Foundation Grants, 530
Corina Higginson Trust Grants, 533
Corning Incorporated Foundation Educ Grants, 535
Crail-Johnson Foundation Grants, 540
Dayton Power and Light Foundation Grants, 573
Delaware Division of the Arts StartUp Grants, 581
Donald C. Brace Foundation Grants, 604
Dorr Foundation Grants, 615
DTE Energy Foundation K -12 Education Grants, 627
Duke Endowment Rural Churches Grants, 631
eBay Foundation Community Grants, 643
EcoLab Foundation Youth and Educaton Grants, 644
Edward W. and Stella C. Van Houten Memorial Fund Grants, 654

Effie and Wofford Cain Foundation Grants, 658
Elizabeth Huth Coates Charitable Found Grants, 666
Ellen Abbott Gilman Trust Grants, 669
Eugene McDermott Foundation Grants, 689
Faye McBeath Foundation Grants, 706
Field Foundation of Illinois Grants, 710
Fleishhacker Foundation Education Grants, 717
Frank and Lydia Bergen Foundation Grants, 742
Frank Stanley Beveridge Foundation Grants, 749
Fremont Area Community Found General Grants, 762
Fuller Foundation Youth At Risk Grants, 771
Gibson Foundation Grants, 822
Ginger and Barry Ackerley Foundation Grants, 825
GNOF IMPACT Grants for Education, 835
Golden Heart Community Foundation Grants, 842
Goodrich Corporation Foundation Grants, 845
Greater Worcester Community Foundation Jeppson Memorial Fund for Brookfield Grants, 855
Hattie M. Strong Foundation Grants, 897
Hazel and Walter T. Bales Foundation Grants, 904
Hearst Foundations Education Grants, 913
Hilton Hotels Corporate Giving Program Grants, 942
Hoglund Foundation Grants, 946
Jack H. & William M. Light Charitable Grants, 1027
James & Abigail Campbell Family Found Grants, 1032
James R. Dougherty Jr. Foundation Grants, 1040
Jessie Ball Dupont Fund Grants, 1057
Joe W. & Dorothy Dorsett Brown Found Grants, 1062
John Jewett and Helen Chandler Garland Foundation Grants, 1072
John M. Weaver Foundation Grants, 1074
John P. McGovern Foundation Grants, 1075
John W. Speas and Effie E. Speas Memorial Trust Grants, 1086
Joseph Alexander Foundation Grants, 1087
Joseph H. & Florence A. Roblee Found Grants, 1089
Kimball International-Habig Foundation Education Grants, 1130
Kinsman Foundation Grants, 1135
LaGrange Independent Foundation for Endowments (L.I.F.E.), 1155
Laurel Foundation Grants, 1160
Lloyd A. Fry Foundation Arts Learning Grants, 1187
Lloyd G. Balfour Foundation Educational Grants, 1190
Logan Family Foundation, 1192
Lotus 88 Found for Women & Children Grants, 1193
Louis and Elizabeth Nave Flarsheim Charitable Foundation Grants, 1195
Louis Calder Foundation Grants, 1196
Lubbock Area Foundation Grants, 1203
McColl Foundation Grants, 1274
MeadWestvaco Foundation Education Grants, 1287
Merrill Lynch Philanthropic Program Grants, 1306
Meyer Foundation Education Grants, 1311
Meyer Memorial Trust Responsive Grants, 1316
Meyer Memorial Trust Special Grants, 1317
Mimi and Peter Haas Fund Grants, 1330
Mississippi Arts Commission Arts in Education Program Grants, 1334
Montgomery County Community Found Grants, 1345
Motorola Foundation Innovation Generation Collaborative Grants, 1353
Motorola Found Innovation Generation Grants, 1354
Narragansett Number One Foundation Grants, 1360
New Earth Foundation Grants, 1378
New England Biolabs Foundation Grants, 1379
New York Life Foundation Grants, 1386
Nicor Corporate Contributions, 1396
Northern Chautauqua Community Foundation Community Grants, 1417
Northrop Grumman Foundation Grants, 1419
NYSCA Arts Education: Local Capacity Building Grants (Regrants), 1434
Oppenstein Brothers Foundation Grants, 1460
PacifiCare Foundation Grants, 1478
Paul and Mary Haas Foundation Contributions and Student Scholarships, 1495
Phelps County Community Foundation Grants, 1511
Piper Trust Education Grants, 1529
Polk Bros. Foundation Grants, 1532

Procter and Gamble Fund Grants, 1549
Rathmann Family Foundation Grants, 1567
Richard & Susan Smith Family Found Grants, 1589
Richland County Bank Grants, 1598
Robbins-de Beaumont Foundation Grants, 1601
Robert Lee Blaffer Foundation Grants, 1607
Robert R. Meyer Foundation Grants, 1608
Robert W. Deutsch Foundation Grants, 1609
Rose Community Foundation Education Grants, 1623
S. D. Bechtel, Jr. Foundation / Stephen Bechtel Fund Environmental Education Grants, 1644
S. D. Bechtel, Jr. Foundation / Stephen Bechtel Fund Science, Technology, Engineering and Math (STEM) Education Grants, 1647
Saint Paul Companies Foundation Grants, 1656
Samueli Foundation Jewish Cultures and Values Grants, 1662
Samuel S. Fels Fund Grants, 1664
San Diego Women's Foundation Grants, 1669
Schlessman Family Foundation Grants, 1689
Seattle Foundation Arts and Culture Grants, 1694
Seattle Foundation Health and Wellness Grants, 1697
Sidgmore Family Foundation Grants, 1706
Sony Corporation of America Corporate Philanthropy Grants, 1727
Sorenson Legacy Foundation Grants, 1729
Sprint Foundation Grants, 1740
Strowd Roses Grants, 1766
Temple Hoyne Buell Foundation Grants, 1796
Thomas Sill Foundation Grants, 1810
Union Bank, N.A. Foundation Grants, 1830
Union Carbide Foundation Grants, 1831
Viacom Foundation Grants (Formerly CBS Foundation), 1847
Walter S. Johnson Foundation Grants, 1865
Weatherwax Foundation Grants, 1869
Weyerhaeuser Company Foundation Grants, 1877
William Penn Foundation Grants, 1907
William T. Grant Foundation Youth Service Improvement Grants (YSIG), 1909
Xerox Foundation Grants, 1925
Z. Smith Reynolds Foundation Pre-Collegiate Education Grants, 1933

Demonstration Grants
Alliant Energy Corporation Contributions, 103
American Woodmark Foundation Grants, 124
ANLAF International Fund for Sexual Minorities Grants, 139
Berks County Community Foundation Grants, 234
Bullitt Foundation Grants, 308
Burton D. Morgan Foundation Adult Entrepreneurship Grants, 311
Burton D. Morgan Foundation Collegiate Entrepreneurship Grants, 312
Caesars Foundation Grants, 328
Campbell Hoffman Foundation Grants, 339
Cause Populi Worthy Cause Grants, 365
Charles Stewart Mott Foundation Anti-Poverty Program, 408
Charles Stewart Mott Foundation Grants, 409
Circle K Corporation Contributions Grants, 443
Columbus Foundation Competitive Grants, 484
Community Foundation of Herkimer and Oneida Counties Grants, 502
Community Foundation of South Alabama Grants, 505
DHHS Oral Health Promotion Research Across the Lifespan, 592
Eastern Bank Charitable Foundation Grants, 640
Evelyn and Walter Haas, Jr. Fund Immigrant Rights Grants, 693
GNOF Metropolitan Opportunities Grants, 840
Henry J. Kaiser Family Foundation Grants, 931
Iddings Foundation, 977
IMLS Grants to State Library Administrative Agencies, 990
Ittleson Foundation AIDS Grants, 1012
Ittleson Foundation Mental Health Grants, 1014
John S. and James L. Knight Foundation Communities Grants, 1078

Emergency Programs

**Exhibitions, Collections, Performances, Video/
Film Production**

Materials/Equipment Acquisition (Computers, Books, Videos, etc.)

Religious Programs

Training Programs/Internships

Pinkerton Foundation Grants, 1523
PPG Industries Foundation Grants, 1540
Principal Financial Group Foundation Grants, 1548
Prudential Foundation Education Grants, 1554
Raskob Found for Catholic Activities Grants, 1566
Rathmann Family Foundation Grants, 1567
Robert W. Deutsch Foundation Grants, 1609
Rockefeller Brothers Democratic Practice Grants, 1614
Rockefeller Brothers Fund Sustainable Development
    Grants, 1615
Ruth Eleanor Bamberger and John Ernest Bamberger
    Memorial Foundation Grants, 1638
Samuel S. Fels Fund Grants, 1664
Santa Fe Community Foundation Seasonal Grants-
    Spring Cycle, 1678
Sidgmore Family Foundation Grants, 1706
Sioux Falls Area Community Foundation Community
    Fund Grants (Unrestricted), 1710
Sioux Falls Area Community Foundation Spot Grants
    (Unrestricted), 1711
Skaggs Foundation Grants, 1718
Sony Corporation of America Corporate Philanthropy
    Grants, 1727
Sorenson Legacy Foundation Grants, 1729
Strowd Roses Grants, 1766
Stuart Foundation Grants, 1767
Susan Mott Webb Charitable Trust Grants, 1773
TAC Arts Projects Grants, 1783
TAC Rural Arts Project Support Grants, 1787
TE Foundation Grants, 1791
Textron Corporate Contributions Grants, 1799
Union Bank, N.A. Foundation Grants, 1830
Union Carbide Foundation Grants, 1831
UPS Foundation Nonprofit Effectiveness Grants, 1837
Vancouver Foundation Disability Supports for
    Employment Grants, 1843
Xerox Foundation Grants, 1925

Travel Grants

American Chemical Society Green Chem Grants, 117
Artist Trust GAP Grants, 177
Ball Brothers Foundation Rapid Grants, 203
Carl M. Freeman Foundation Grants, 350
CJ Foundation for SIDS Program Services Grants, 446
Cystic Fibrosis Canada Transplant Center Incentive
    Grants, 555
Delaware Division of the Arts StartUp Grants, 581
Global Fund for Women Grants, 830
KFC Allied Health Research Grants, 1127
KFC Biomedical Research Grants, 1128
LaGrange Independent Foundation for Endowments
    (L.I.F.E.), 1155
McKenzie River Gathering Foundation Grants, 1282
Mississippi Arts Commission Arts-Based Community
    Development Program Grants, 1333
NCI Technologies and Software to Support Integrative
    Cancer Biology Research (SBIR) Grants, 1366
NHSCA Operating Grants, 1394
North Carolina Arts Council Support Grants, 1405
North Carolina Arts Council Outreach Program
    Grants, 1406
Pinellas County Grants, 1522
Sport Manitoba Women to Watch Grants, 1737
TSYSF Team Grants, 1824
U.S. Department of Education American Overseas
    Research Centers, 1828
Whitehall Found Neurobiology Research Grants, 1879
Youth Philanthropy Project, 1928
YSA Global Youth Service Day Agency Grants, 1929

Vocational Education

Achelis Foundation Grants, 39
Adolph Coors Foundation Grants, 55
Alpha Natural Resources Corporate Giving, 106
Bodman Foundation Grants, 263
Bush Found Health & Human Services Grants, 317
Carl M. Freeman Foundation Grants, 350
Carrier Corporation Contributions Grants, 359
Chilkat Valley Community Foundation Grants, 428
CNA Foundation Grants, 464

ConocoPhillips Foundation Grants, 521
Consumers Energy Foundation, 526
Crail-Johnson Foundation Grants, 540
Danellie Foundation Grants, 564
Duke Energy Foundation Economic Development
    Grants, 632
Elizabeth Morse Genius Charitable Trust Grants, 668
Eulalie Bloedel Schneider Foundation Grants, 690
Frank Reed and Margaret Jane Peters Memorial Fund
    II Grants, 747
Gamble Foundation Grants, 778
George W. Wells Foundation Grants, 815
GNOF Metropolitan Opportunities Grants, 840
Golden LEAF Foundation Grants, 843
Goodrich Corporation Foundation Grants, 845
Harvest Foundation Grants, 896
Hearst Foundations Social Service Grants, 914
Illinois Tool Works Foundation Grants, 989
IREX Small Grant Fund for Media Projects in Africa
    and Asia, 1007
Irvin Stern Foundation Grants, 1010
Jane Bradley Pettit Foundation Community and Social
    Development Grants, 1045
John Gogian Family Foundation Grants, 1068
JP Morgan Chase Community Devel Grants, 1100
Kessler Found Community Employment Grants, 1125
Kessler Found Signature Employment Grants, 1126
Leo Goodwin Foundation Grants, 1169
May and Stanley Smith Charitable Trust Grants, 1270
Medina Foundation Grants, 1291
Meyer Foundation Economic Security Grants, 1310
Meyer Foundation Education Grants, 1311
Oppenstein Brothers Foundation Grants, 1460
Pentair Found Education & Community Grants, 1501
Prudential Found Econ Development Grants, 1553
Reinberger Foundation Grants, 1573
Robbins-de Beaumont Foundation Grants, 1601
Robert R. Meyer Foundation Grants, 1608
Samuel S. Johnson Foundation Grants, 1665
Textron Corporate Contributions Grants, 1799
Thomas Sill Foundation Grants, 1810
TWS Foundation Grants, 1826
Union Bank, N.A. Foundation Grants, 1830
Vancouver Foundation Disability Supports for
    Employment Grants, 1843
WILD Foundation Grants, 1885
Xerox Foundation Grants, 1925

Geographic Index

Note: This index lists grants for which applicants must be residents of or located in a specific geographic area. Numbers refer to entry numbers.

IREX Small Grant Fund for Civil Society Projects in Africa and Asia, 1006
IREX Small Grant Fund for Media Projects in Africa and Asia, 1007
New England Biolabs Foundation Grants, 1379

Mali
Cargill Citizenship Corporate Giving Grants, 343
IREX Small Grant Fund for Civil Society Projects in Africa and Asia, 1006
IREX Small Grant Fund for Media Projects in Africa and Asia, 1007
New England Biolabs Foundation Grants, 1379

Malta
Cargill Citizenship Corporate Giving Grants, 343
Charles Delmar Foundation Grants, 400
Fluor Foundation Grants, 728

Mauritania
Cargill Citizenship Corporate Giving Grants, 343
IREX Small Grant Fund for Civil Society Projects in Africa and Asia, 1006
IREX Small Grant Fund for Media Projects in Africa and Asia, 1007
New England Biolabs Foundation Grants, 1379

Mauritius
Cargill Citizenship Corporate Giving Grants, 343
IREX Small Grant Fund for Civil Society Projects in Africa and Asia, 1006
IREX Small Grant Fund for Media Projects in Africa and Asia, 1007
New England Biolabs Foundation Grants, 1379

Mexico
Atkinson Foundation Community Grants, 185
Bill & Melinda Gates Found Library Grants, 249
Cummins Foundation Grants, 554
Fluor Foundation Grants, 728
Kimball International-Habig Foundation Arts and Culture Grants, 1129
Kimball International-Habig Education Grants, 1130
Kimball International-Habig Foundation Health and Human Services Grants, 1131
Kimball International-Habig Foundation Religious Institutions Grants, 1132
New Covenant Farms Grants, 1377
Patricia Price Peterson Foundation Grants, 1487
PDF Community Organizing Grants, 1499
Steelcase Foundation Grants, 1751

Moldova
Cargill Citizenship Corporate Giving Grants, 343
Charles Delmar Foundation Grants, 400
Fluor Foundation Grants, 728
John Deere Foundation Grants, 1066

Monaco
Cargill Citizenship Corporate Giving Grants, 343
Charles Delmar Foundation Grants, 400
Fluor Foundation Grants, 728

Montenegro
Cargill Citizenship Corporate Giving Grants, 343
Charles Delmar Foundation Grants, 400
Fluor Foundation Grants, 728

Morocco
Cargill Citizenship Corporate Giving Grants, 343
IREX Small Grant Fund for Civil Society Projects in Africa and Asia, 1006
IREX Small Grant Fund for Media Projects in Africa and Asia, 1007
New England Biolabs Foundation Grants, 1379

Mozambique
Cargill Citizenship Corporate Giving Grants, 343
IREX Small Grant Fund for Civil Society Projects in Africa and Asia, 1006

IREX Small Grant Fund for Media Projects in Africa and Asia, 1007
New England Biolabs Foundation Grants, 1379

Namibia
Cargill Citizenship Corporate Giving Grants, 343
IREX Small Grant Fund for Civil Society Projects in Africa and Asia, 1006
IREX Small Grant Fund for Media Projects in Africa and Asia, 1007
New England Biolabs Foundation Grants, 1379

Netherlands
Abbott Fund Community Grants, 20
Advent Software Corporate Giving Grants, 57

New Zealand
Fluor Foundation Grants, 728

Nicaragua
Atkinson Foundation Community Grants, 185
Patricia Price Peterson Foundation Grants, 1487

Niger
Cargill Citizenship Corporate Giving Grants, 343
IREX Small Grant Fund for Civil Society Projects in Africa and Asia, 1006
IREX Small Grant Fund for Media Projects in Africa and Asia, 1007
New England Biolabs Foundation Grants, 1379

Nigeria
Cargill Citizenship Corporate Giving Grants, 343
IREX Small Grant Fund for Civil Society Projects in Africa and Asia, 1006
IREX Small Grant Fund for Media Projects in Africa and Asia, 1007
New England Biolabs Foundation Grants, 1379

Norway
Advent Software Corporate Giving Grants, 57
Cargill Citizenship Corporate Giving Grants, 343
Charles Delmar Foundation Grants, 400
Fluor Foundation Grants, 728

Panama
Patricia Price Peterson Foundation Grants, 1487

Paraguay
Charles Delmar Foundation Grants, 400
New England Biolabs Foundation Grants, 1379

Peru
Charles Delmar Foundation Grants, 400
Fluor Foundation Grants, 728
New England Biolabs Foundation Grants, 1379

Philippines
Fluor Foundation Grants, 728

Poland
Bill & Melinda Gates Found Library Grants, 249
Cargill Citizenship Corporate Giving Grants, 343
Charles Delmar Foundation Grants, 400
Fluor Foundation Grants, 728
Fluor Foundation Grants, 728
Kimball International-Habig Foundation Arts and Culture Grants, 1129
Kimball International-Habig Foundation Education Grants, 1130
Kimball International-Habig Foundation Health and Human Services Grants, 1131
Kimball International-Habig Foundation Religious Institutions Grants, 1132

Portugal
Cargill Citizenship Corporate Giving Grants, 343
Charles Delmar Foundation Grants, 400
Fluor Foundation Grants, 728

Romania
Bill & Melinda Gates Found Library Grants, 249
Cargill Citizenship Corporate Giving Grants, 343
Charles Delmar Foundation Grants, 400
Fluor Foundation Grants, 728

Russia
Cargill Citizenship Corporate Giving Grants, 343
Charles Delmar Foundation Grants, 400
Fluor Foundation Grants, 728
Fluor Foundation Grants, 728
IREX Russia Civil Society Support Grants, 1005

Rwanda
Cargill Citizenship Corporate Giving Grants, 343
IREX Small Grant Fund for Civil Society Projects in Africa and Asia, 1006
IREX Small Grant Fund for Media Projects in Africa and Asia, 1007
New England Biolabs Foundation Grants, 1379

San Marino
Cargill Citizenship Corporate Giving Grants, 343
Charles Delmar Foundation Grants, 400
Fluor Foundation Grants, 728

Sao Tome & Principe
Cargill Citizenship Corporate Giving Grants, 343
IREX Small Grant Fund for Civil Society Projects in Africa and Asia, 1006
IREX Small Grant Fund for Media Projects in Africa and Asia, 1007
New England Biolabs Foundation Grants, 1379

Senegal
Cargill Citizenship Corporate Giving Grants, 343
IREX Small Grant Fund for Civil Society Projects in Africa and Asia, 1006
IREX Small Grant Fund for Media Projects in Africa and Asia, 1007
New England Biolabs Foundation Grants, 1379

Serbia
Cargill Citizenship Corporate Giving Grants, 343
Charles Delmar Foundation Grants, 400
Fluor Foundation Grants, 728

Seychelles
Cargill Citizenship Corporate Giving Grants, 343
IREX Small Grant Fund for Civil Society Projects in Africa and Asia, 1006
IREX Small Grant Fund for Media Projects in Africa and Asia, 1007
New England Biolabs Foundation Grants, 1379

Sierra Leone
Cargill Citizenship Corporate Giving Grants, 343
IREX Small Grant Fund for Civil Society Projects in Africa and Asia, 1006
IREX Small Grant Fund for Media Projects in Africa and Asia, 1007
New England Biolabs Foundation Grants, 1379

Singapore
Advent Software Corporate Giving Grants, 57
Sands Foundation Grants, 1670

Slovakia
Cargill Citizenship Corporate Giving Grants, 343
Charles Delmar Foundation Grants, 400
Fluor Foundation Grants, 728

Slovenia
Cargill Citizenship Corporate Giving Grants, 343
Charles Delmar Foundation Grants, 400
Fluor Foundation Grants, 728

Somalia
Cargill Citizenship Corporate Giving Grants, 343